Using WordPerfect® 5.1
Special Edition

Developed by Que Corporation

Using WordPerfect 5.1,® Special Edition

Copyright © 1989 by Que® Corporation

Library of Congress Catalog No. 89-64228

ISBN 0-88022-554-8

92 91 90 89   5 4 3 2 1

Interpretation of the printing code: the rightmost double-digit number is the year of the book's printing; the rightmost single-digit number is the number of the book's printing. For example, a printing code of 89-4 shows that the fourth printing of the book occurred in 1989.

Using WordPerfect 5.1, Special Edition, is based on WordPerfect 5.1.

Publishing Director	David P. Ewing
Product Development Director	Charles O. Stewart III
Acquisitions Editor	Terrie Lynn Solomon
Production Editor	Alice Martina Smith
Editors	Mary Bednarek Lisa Hunt Mike LaBonne Virginia Noble Lois Sherman
Technical Editors	Robert M. Beck Michael McCoy Anthony Rairden
Editorial Assistants	Stacey Beheler Angela Rodriguez-Rosenow
Technical Support	Timothy S. Stanley
Indexer	Joelynn Gifford
Book Production	Dan Armstrong Lori A. Lyons Sally Copenhaver Jennifer Matthews Corinne Harmon Dennis Sheehan William Hartman Bruce Steed Jodi Jensen Mary Beth Wakefield David Kline
Composed in Garamond by	William Hartman, Hartman Publishing

Elias Baumgarten, Ph.D., associate professor of philosophy at the University of Michigan at Dearborn, was a beta tester for WordPerfect 5 and 5.1. He is the recipient of a Distinguished Teaching Award and has published articles on medical ethics and other topics in philosophy.

Robert M. Beck is a former judge now practicing law in Oklahoma City. He is also a computer consultant for small-to-medium-sized law offices, a beta tester for many WordPerfect Corporation products, and a frequent participant on CompuServe's WordPerfect Support Group Forum.

Stuart Bloom is a principal of Learning Associates, Inc., a Chicago consulting group that designs training for clients in technical, financial, and assorted other fields. Bloom is also a beta tester for WordPerfect and an active member of the WordPerfect Support Group Forum on CompuServe.

Marilyn Horn Claff is Director of the Boston Computer Society's WordPerfect Special Interest Group, an assistant sysop on the WordPerfect Support Group Forum on CompuServe, and a beta tester for WordPerfect Corporation. She is also a WordPerfect Certified Instructor and an independent computer consultant.

Susan Hafer, the microcomputer specialist for Academic Computing at Wellesley College, has been using, supporting, and teaching WordPerfect on the campus since 1986. She contributed to *WordPerfect Tips, Tricks, and Traps*.

Doug Hazen, Jr., a programmer for Intellution in Norwood, MA, is a member of the Boston Computer Society's IBM PC User's Group and WordPerfect Special Interest Group.

Judy Housman, Ph.D., is a WordPerfect Certified Instructor and microcomputer consultant based in Cambridge, MA. A frequent contributor to *WordPerfect: The Magazine*, she leads the Boston Computer Society's Training and Documentation Group.

Forest Lin, Ph.D., who teaches political science at Tulsa Junior College, is the author of *WordPerfect Macro Library* and contributing author to *WordPerfect Tips, Tricks, and Traps*.

Schuyler Lininger, Jr. is an Oregon chiropractor and owner of HealthNotes Publications. He is the author of *Ventura Tips, Tricks, and Traps* and contributing author to *WordPerfect Tips, Tricks, and Traps*.

Hans A. Lustig is copy chief for an industrial advertising agency where he uses WordPerfect to write copy for industrial brochures and manuals. He contributed to *WordPerfect Tips, Tricks, and Traps*.

Michael McCoy works for WORDPRO, Inc., a computer training and consulting organization based in Rockville, MD. He has been teaching and supporting WordPerfect and other products since 1983.

James C. McKeown, Ph.D., a professor of accountancy, has worked with computers of all types for 25 years and worked with WordPerfect from version 3.0 to the present.

William J. Palm, Ph.D., professor of mechanical engineering at the University of Rhode Island, is the author of two engineering textbooks. He has been using WordPerfect to create technical documents since 1984.

Jon Pepper is president of Words Plus, a Sunderland, MA consulting firm that specializes in computer-related topics. As a well-known journalist, he has covered the computer industry for several leading publications.

Andrea Pickens is a principal of Learning Associates, Inc., a Chicago consulting group that designs training for clients in technical, financial, and assorted other fields. She is a training consultant who uses WordPerfect exclusively for newsletters, proposals, directories, leader's guides, scripts, visuals, and manuals of all kinds.

Karen Rose is the owner of Write on Target, a newsletter production and management company in Santa Rosa, CA. Rose teaches desktop publishing courses with Aldus PageMaker, on both the PC and Macintosh, at Sonoma State University and for business through Ron Person & Co. She contributed to *WordPerfect Tips, Tricks, and Traps*.

C. Brian Scott is a partner in the Portland, OR firm of Danner, Scott & Martin. In addition to his legal practice in the areas of real estate and estate planning and administration, he is the system administrator for his firm's PC network, installed in early 1986. He contributed to *WordPerfect Tips, Tricks, and Traps*.

Joel Shore is senior editor of LANWEEK for Computer Reseller News and president of Documentation Systems, a Southborough, MA, private consulting firm providing microcomputer services. He teaches a range of personal computing courses at Massachusetts Bay Community College, conducts in-house seminars, and is an active participant in several of the Boston Computer Society's Special Interest Groups. He coauthored *WordPerfect Tips, Tricks, and Traps*.

Timothy S. Stanley has worked for Que Corporation since 1985 as a technical editor. He has contributed to *Using 1-2-3 Release 3*, *Upgrading to 1-2-3 Release 3*, *Absolute Reference: The Journal for 1-2-3 and Symphony Users*, and *MS-DOS User's Guide*, Special Edition.

Anders R. Sterner is a partner of Tanner Propp Fersko & Sterner, a Manhattan firm where he practices law and does computer consulting for clients and other law firms using micro systems. He is a WordPerfect beta tester and frequent participant on the WordPerfect Support Group Forum on CompuServe.

Charles O. Stewart III is a project director and staff writer at Que Corporation. He was instrumental in determining the emphases for this book, assembled the team of contributors, and worked closely with them through manuscript development, editing, and final review. Stewart coauthored *WordPerfect Tips, Tricks, and Traps* and contributed to *Upgrading to 1-2-3 Release 3* and *Introduction to Business Software*.

TRADEMARK ACKNOWLEDGMENTS ▼

Que Corporation has made every effort to supply trademarks about company names, products, and services mentioned in this book. Trademarks indicated below were derived from various sources. Que Corporation cannot attest to the accuracy of this information.

1-2-3, Freelance Plus, Symphony, and Lotus are registered trademarks of Lotus Development Corporation.

Apple, MacPaint, LaserWriter, and LaserWriter Plus are registered trademarks of Apple Computer, Inc.

Arts & Letters is a trademark of Computer Support Corporation.

AutoCAD and AutoSketch are registered trademarks of Autodesk, Inc.

Bitstream and Fontware are registered trademarks of Bitstream Inc.

CiteRite is a trademark of JURISoft, Incorporated.

COMPAQ is a registered trademark of COMPAQ Computer Corporation.

CompuServe Information Service is a registered trademark of CompuServe Incorporated and H&R Block, Inc.

dBASE III is a registered trademark and dBASE IV is a trademark of Ashton-Tate Corporation.

DESQView is a trademark of Quarterdeck Software.

Diablo 630 is a registered trademark of Xerox Corporation.

SIGN-MASTER is a registered trademark and DIAGRAM-MASTER is a trademark of Decision Resources.

Dr. HALO is a registered trademark of Media Cybernetics, Inc.

GEM Draw, GEM Paint, and GEM Scan are trademarks of Digital Research, Inc.

Graph Plus and Windows Draw are trademarks of Micrografx, Inc.

Harvard Graphics and PFS: First Publisher are trademarks of Software Publishing Corporation.

Hercules monochrome card is a registered trademark and Hercules Graphics Card and Hercules Graphics Card Plus are trademarks of Hercules Computer Technology.

HotShot Graphics is a registered trademark of SymSoft Corporation.

HP, HP Graphics Gallery, and HP Scanning Gallery are registered trademarks and LaserJet is a trademark of Hewlett-Packard Co.

IBM and IBM PC are registered trademarks and DisplayWrite and GDDM are trademarks of International Business Machines Corporation.

InSet and HiJaak are registered trademarks of INSET Systems Inc.

ITC Bookman, ITC Zapf Dingbats, and ITC Zapf Chancery are registered trademarks of International Typeface Corporation.

Linotronic is a trademark and Helvetica, Times, and Palatino are registered trademarks of Allied Corporation.

Microsoft, MS-DOS, Microsoft Windows Paint, Microsoft Word, Microsoft Excel, Microsoft Chart, and Microsoft Mouse are registered trademarks of Microsoft Corporation.

PageMaker is a registered trademark of Aldus Corporation.

Paradox is a trademark of Ansa Corporation.

PC Paint and PC Paint + are trademarks of Mouse Systems Corporation.

PC Paintbrush is a registered trademark of ZSoft Corporation.

PlanPerfect, WordPerfect, and WordPerfect Library are registered trademarks of WordPerfect Corporation.

PostScript is a registered trademark and Adobe Illustrator is a trademark of Adobe Systems Incorporated.

Q&A is a trademark of Symantec Corporation.

Quattro is a registered trademark and Reflex is a trademark of Borland International, Inc.

R:BASE is a registered trademark of Microrim, Inc.

SuperCalc is a registered trademark of Computer Associates International, Inc.

Ventura Publisher is a registered trademark of Ventura Software Inc.

VP-Planner is a registered trademark of Paperback Software International.

WANG is a registered trademark of Wang Laboratories, Inc.

WordStar, WordStar Professional, WordStar 2000, and MultiMate are registered trademarks and MultiMate Advantage is a trademark of MicroPro International Corporation.

▼ Contents at a Glance

Introduction 1

Part I: Using WordPerfect's Basic Features

Chapter 1: Preparing To Use WordPerfect 11
Chapter 2: Creating a Document 39
Chapter 3: Editing a Document 61
Chapter 4: Working with Blocks 87
Chapter 5: Formatting and Enhancing Text 109
Chapter 6: Formatting Pages and Designing Documents 147
Chapter 7: Using the Speller and the Thesaurus 183
Chapter 8: Printing and Print Options 215
Chapter 9: Printing with Laser Printers 243
Chapter 10: Using List Files 275

Part II: Using WordPerfect's Advanced Features

Chapter 11: Creating Basic Macros 305
Chapter 12: Creating Advanced Macros 345
Chapter 13: Assembling Documents with Merge 439
Chapter 14: Sorting and Selecting Data 485
Chapter 15: Using Styles 505
Chapter 16: Using WordPerfect with Other Programs 533

Part III: Using WordPerfect's Specialized Features

Chapter 17: Working with Text Columns 559
Chapter 18: Using Math 581
Chapter 19: Creating Tables 603
Chapter 20: Customizing WordPerfect 651
Chapter 21: Working with Special Characters and Foreign Languages 691
Chapter 22: Creating Equations 711
Chapter 23: Using Footnotes and Endnotes 741
Chapter 24: Outlining, Paragraph Numbering, and Line Numbering 765
Chapter 25: Assembling Document References 793
Chapter 26: Using the Master Document Feature for Large Projects 835

Part IV: Using WordPerfect for Desktop Publishing

Chapter 27: Integrating Text and Graphics 855
Chapter 28: Producing Publications 889

Appendix A: WordPerfect 5.1 Installation and Startup 921
Appendix B: WordPerfect 5.1 for WordPerfect 5 Users 925
Index 931

TABLE OF CONTENTS

Introduction 1
Who Should Use This Book? 2
How To Use This Book 2
How This Book Is Organized 3
Where To Find More Help 7
Conventions Used in This Book 7

Part I: Using WordPerfect's Basic Features

1 Preparing To Use WordPerfect 11
What Is WordPerfect? 11
What Is WordPerfect 5.1? 12
What Hardware Do You Need To Run
    WordPerfect? 13
    Monitors and Graphics Cards 14
    Printers 14
    The Mouse 14
Starting WordPerfect on a Dual-Floppy
    System 15
Starting WordPerfect on a Hard
    Disk System 15
Troubleshooting Problems with
    Starting WordPerfect 16
Restarting WordPerfect 16
Understanding the Editing Screen 17
Using the Keyboard 19
    Using the Shift, Alt, and Control Keys 21
    Using the Function Keys 21
    Using the Alphanumeric Keyboard 24
    Using the Numeric Keypad 25
    Moving the Cursor 26
Using Pull-Down Menus 27
Using the Mouse 29
Understanding WordPerfect's Hidden
    Codes 31
Using the Help Feature 32
Taking the Tutorial 34
    Running the Tutorial on a Dual-
        Floppy System 35
    Running the Tutorial on a Hard-Disk
        System 37
Exiting from WordPerfect 38
Summary 38

2 Creating a Document 39
Writing with a Word Processor 40
Understanding WordPerfect's Built-In
    Settings 41
Entering Text 42
Inserting Blank Lines 42
Moving the Cursor with the Keyboard 43

Moving from Character to Character 43
Moving from Word to Word 44
Moving from Line to Line 44
Moving to the End of the Line or
    the Edge of the Screen 44
Moving to the Top or Bottom of
    the Screen 45
Moving to the Top of the Preceding
    Page 46
Moving to the Top of the Next Page 46
Moving the Cursor with GoTo 46
Moving to the Top or Bottom of
    a Document 47
Moving the Cursor with the Mouse 47
Inserting Text 48
Using Typeover 48
Using Both Document Windows 49
    Switching between Document
        Windows 49
    Splitting the Screen 49
Using Cancel (F1) 51
Printing an Unsaved Document 52
Saving a Document to Disk 53
Clearing the Screen and Exiting
    WordPerfect 54
Using WordPerfect To Develop Ideas 55
    Handling Writer's Block 56
    Planning Documents 57
Summary 60

3 Editing a Document 61
Retrieving a Document 62
    Using List To Retrieve a File 62
    Using Retrieve (Shift-F10) To Retrieve a
        Formatted File 65
    Combining Files by Retrieving Them 65
Revising and Editing Text 66
    Making Substantive Changes (Revision) 66
    Making Surface Changes (Editing) 67
Deleting Text 67
    Deleting a Single Character 67
    Deleting a Single Word or Portions
        of a Single Word 67
    Deleting to the End of the Line 67
    Deleting to the End of the Page 68
    Deleting Text with Esc 68
    Deleting a Sentence, Paragraph, or Page .. 68
    Deleting Text with the Mouse 69
Using the Undelete Command 70
Inserting Text 70
Overwriting Text 71
Understanding Hidden Codes 71
    Listing Hidden Codes 72
    Editing in Reveal Codes 76
Adding Simple Text Enhancements 78

Boldfacing 78
Underlining 78
Searching and Replacing 79
Searching for Text 79
Searching and Replacing Text 80
Using Search or Replace 81
Searching or Replacing Hidden Codes 82
Making Document Comments 83
Inserting Document Comments 83
Editing Document Comments 84
Converting Comments to Text 84
Converting Text to Comments 85
Hiding Document Comments 85
Using Document Comments 86
Summary 86

4 Working with Blocks 87

Understanding Block Operations and
Revision Strategies 88
How Block Works 88
Highlighting Text with Block 89
Completing the Block Operation 90
Canceling a Block 90
Rehighlighting a Block 90
Moving a Block 91
Copying a Block 91
Deleting a Block 92
Appending a Block 93
Saving a Block 93
Printing a Block 94
Enhancing Text with the Block Command .. 95
Boldfacing and Underlining
Blocked Text 95
Changing the Type Font in a Block 96
Making Blocks Uppercase or Lowercase ... 99
Centering a Block 100
Using Redline and Strikeout 100
Unenhancing Text 101
Displaying Enhanced Text On-Screen 102
Moving and Copying Text between
Documents 102
Working with Rectangular Blocks 103
Using the Block Command with Styles 106
Summary 107

5 Formatting and Enhancing Text 109

Formatting Lines and Paragraphs 110
Changing Default Settings 111
Changing the Units of Measure 111
Changing Margins 115
Setting Tab Stops 119
Using Justification 125
Centering Text 126
Making Text Flush Right 128
Using Hyphenation 128
Changing Line Height 135
Changing Line Spacing 136
Enhancing Text 137
Changing the Base Font 137
Using Proportional Spacing 139

Choosing Font Attributes 139
Using Advanced Printer Features 142
Using Document Preview 144
Summary 145

6 Formatting Pages and Designing Documents 147

Formatting Pages 148
Changing Top and Bottom Margins 149
Centering Pages Top to Bottom 150
Designing Headers and Footers 151
Numbering Pages 155
Keeping Text Together 158
Understanding Soft and Hard Page
Breaks 161
Choosing Paper and Form Sizes 162
Designing Documents 174
Changing Initial Document Settings 175
Adjusting Display Pitch 176
Using Redlining To Mark Text 176
Using Document Summaries 177
Using Other Format Options 178
Using Advance 178
Changing the Decimal Character and the
Thousands' Separator 179
Changing the Language Code 180
Using Overstrike 180
Checking Document Format with View
Document 181
Summary 182

7 Using the Speller and the Thesaurus 183

Using the Speller 184
Setting Up the Speller 185
Starting the Speller 186
Ending the Speller 194
Looking Up a Word 195
Spell-Checking a Block 197
Handling Words with Numbers 197
Working with What Is Not
Spell-Checked 197
Creating a Supplemental Dictionary 198
Viewing the Contents of a
Supplemental Dictionary 200
Using a Supplemental Dictionary 201
Using the Speller Utility 201
Adding Words to the Main Dictionary 204
Deleting Words from the Main
Dictionary 206
Compressing or Expanding a
Supplemental Dictionary 207
Using the Thesaurus 209
Starting the Thesaurus 209
Understanding the Parts of the
Thesaurus Menu 210
Viewing a Word in Context 213
Looking Up Words 214
Summary 214

8 Printing and Print Options 215

WordPerfect's Protection As You Print 216
Using Print (Shift-F7) 216
Selecting Printers 216
   When To Use the Select Printer Feature ... 217
   Using Select Printer To Define a
     New Printer 217
   Editing Printer Settings 220
Printing the Test Document 224
Considering WordPerfect Printing Methods . 224
Printing from the Screen 225
   Printing the Entire Document from
     the Screen 225
   Printing a Specific Page from the Screen .. 225
   Printing a Block from the Screen 226
Printing a Document from Disk 227
   Printing from the Print Menu 227
   Printing with the List Files Feature 228
Selecting Pages 228
Controlling the Printer 229
   Information about the Current Print Job ... 229
   Other Jobs Waiting To Be Printed 231
   The Control Printer Menu 231
Using the Print Menu 233
   Multiple Copies Generated by 233
   View Document 233
   Initialize Printer 236
   Binding Offset 236
   Number of Copies 237
   Graphics Quality 237
   Text Quality 237
Printing in Color 238
   Entering Text in Color 238
   Creating a Custom Color 239
Printing Files Created with Previous
   Versions of WordPerfect 239
   Printing from Disk 239
   Printing Version 5.1 Documents with
     Version 5 or 4.2 239
Troubleshooting Common Printer
   Problems 240
Summary 241

9 Printing with Laser Printers 243

Learning Laser Printing Vocabulary 244
Comparing LaserJet and PostScript Printers . 246
Surveying Improvements in WordPerfect
   5.1 for Laser Printers 247
Configuring WordPerfect To Work with
   Your Laser Printer 247
   Setting the Initial Font 248
   Selecting Fonts by Size 249
   Selecting Fonts by Name 250
   Changing Typeface Appearance 251
   Facilitating Printer Configuration 252
Using WordPerfect with LaserJet Printers 253
   Considering Internal Fonts 254
   Considering Cartridge Fonts 254

Considering Soft Fonts 255
Choosing between Cartridges and
   Soft Fonts 255
Developing a Font Strategy 256
Installing Fonts for LaserJet Printers 256
Setting Up Fonts for LaserJet Printers 257
Using Forms with LaserJet Printers 261
Troubleshooting Problems with
   LaserJet Printers 262
Using WordPerfect with PostScript
   Laser Printers 264
   Considering Downloadable Fonts for
     PostScript Printers 264
   Installing and Setting Up Downloadable
     Fonts for PostScript Printers 265
   Using Forms with PostScript Printers 268
   Using Specialty Typefaces with
     PostScript Printers 268
   Using Other Features with PostScript
     Printers 268
   Using Fonts with WordPerfect 5.1 That
     Were Created for WordPerfect 5 269
   Troubleshooting Problems with
     PostScript Printers 272
Troubleshooting Printing Problems 272
Summary 273

10 Using List Files 275

Discovering List Files 276
Understanding the Heading 277
Understanding the File Listing 278
Using the List Files Menu 279
   Using Retrieve 279
   Using Delete 280
   Using Move/Rename 280
   Using Print 281
   Using Short/Long Display 281
   Using Look 282
   Using Other Directory 285
   Using Copy 287
   Using Find 287
   Using Name Search 294
Marking Files 297
Copying Text from Look with the
   Clipboard Feature 299
Locking Files 301
Summary 302

**Part II: Using WordPerfect's
Advanced Features**

11 Creating Basic Macros 305

Understanding Types of Macros 307
Creating Macros 307
Running Macros 309
Stopping Macros 310

Replacing Macros 311
Controlling How Macros Run 313
  Making a Macro Visible 313
  Making a Macro Repeat 314
  Making a Macro Pause 315
  Making a Macro Call Another Macro 319
Creating Some Useful Macros 323
  A Macro That Italicizes the Preceding
    Word 324
  A Macro That Changes Directories 325
  A Macro That Changes Margins 326
  A Macro That Sets Tabs for
    Numbered Lists 327
  A Macro That Simplifies Numbered Lists ... 327
  A Macro That Reinstates Old Tab
    Settings 329
Managing Macro Files 331
  Creating Global Macros 331
  Viewing a List of Macro Files 332
  Storing Macros on Floppy Disks 333
  Manipulating and Viewing Macro Files 334
Using the Macro Editor 335
  Making a Simple Text Change 335
  Deleting WordPerfect Commands 337
  Inserting and Editing WordPerfect
    Commands 338
  Inserting Special Macro Commands 340
  Experimenting with the Macro Editor 342
  Summary 342

12 Creating Advanced Macros 345
Why Use Advanced Macro Commands? 346
Understanding Variables 348
  Understanding Variable Names 349
  Understanding Variable Types and
    Mathematical Operators 350
  Understanding Expressions 352
Understanding the Syntax of Advanced
  Macro Commands 354
Manipulating Variables 356
  {ASSIGN} 356
  {VARIABLE} 357
  {VAR n} 358
  {LEN} 359
  {MID} 360
Communicating with the User 360
  {CHAR} 360
  {TEXT} 361
  {LOOK} 361
  {INPUT} 362
  {PAUSE} 362
  {PAUSE KEY} 363
  {PROMPT} 363
  {STATUS PROMPT} 364
  {BELL} 364
Dressing Up the Display 365
  Using Control Characters 365
  Duplicating the Appearance of a
    WordPerfect Menu 368

Controlling Program Execution 369
  Understanding Program-Control
    Concepts 369
  Using Subroutines 370
  {CALL} 372
  {CASE} 374
  {ELSE} 375
  {CASE CALL} 376
  {CHAIN} 377
  {GO} 377
  {LABEL} 378
  {NEST} 379
  {RETURN}, {RETURN CANCEL}, {RETURN
    ERROR}, and {RETURN NOT FOUND} .. 379
Using Loops 381
  Using {FOR} Loops 381
  Using {FOR EACH} Loops 383
  Using {WHILE} Loops 385
  Writing Effective and Efficient Loops 387
Making Decisions 388
  {IF} Structure Logic 388
  {IF} Structure Operation 389
  {IF EXISTS} Structure Logic 390
  {IF EXISTS} Structure Operation 391
Determining System Status 391
  {KTON} 392
  {NTOK} 394
  {STATE} 394
  {SYSTEM} 396
Handling Errors 412
  {CANCEL OFF} and {CANCEL ON} 412
  {ON CANCEL} 413
  {ON ERROR} 414
  {ON NOT FOUND} 414
  {QUIT} 415
  {RESTART} 415
Controlling Macro Execution 415
  {SPEED} 416
  {WAIT} 416
  {STEP ON} and {STEP OFF} 416
Controlling the Display 420
  {DISPLAY OFF} and {DISPLAY ON} 420
  {MENU OFF} and {MENU {ON} 420
Using Miscellaneous Advanced
  Macro Commands 421
  Comment 421
  {ORIGINAL KEY} 421
  {SHELL MACRO} 422
Emulating Keystrokes 422
  {Block Append} 422
  {Block Copy} 422
  {Block Move} 422
  {Item Down} 423
  {Item Left} 423
  {Item Right} 423
  {Item Up} 423
  {Para Down} 423
  {Para Up} 423
Working with Advanced Examples 423

Converting Lowercase Letters to
Capitals (TOUPPER.WPM) 423
Handling Copy Functions (COPY.WPM) ... 427
Creating Menus (BULLETS.WPM) 428
Creating an Invoice (INVOICE.WPM): A
Complex Macro 431
Summary 438

**13 Assembling Documents with
Merge 439**
Why Use Merge? 439
Understanding a Merge 440
Providing the Fixed Information 440
Getting Variable Information into
a Merge 440
Building a Simple Merge 443
Deciding To Use Merge 443
Planning the Merge 444
Creating the Primary File 445
Creating the Secondary File 447
Merging the Files 451
Handling Special Situations 452
Using a DOS Text File as a
Secondary File 452
Skipping Empty Fields 453
Adding Fields to a Secondary File 455
Inserting the Date 455
Suppressing Unwanted Text and Codes 456
Merging Directly to the Printer 457
Including Keyboard Input in a Merge 458
Preparing Special Primary Documents
for Merges 460
Using Fill-In Forms 460
Using Mailing Labels 462
Creating Advanced Merges 466
Using {COMMENT} 466
Using Advanced Merge Commands To
Manage Fields and Records 469
Using Advanced Merge Commands To
Manipulate Variables 471
Using Advanced Merge Commands To
Communicate with the User 474
Using Advanced Merge Commands To
Control Order of Execution 475
Using Advanced Merge Commands To
Make Decisions 481
Using Advanced Merge Commands To
Determine System Status 482
Using Advanced Merge Commands To
Handle Errors 482
Using Advanced Merge Commands To
Control Merge Execution 483
Using Miscellaneous Advanced Merge
Commands 484
Summary 484

14 Sorting and Selecting Data 485
Understanding Sort Basics 486
Learning Database Terms 486

Mastering the Sort Menu 487
Building a Simple Data Set 489
Understanding the Four Kinds of Sort 489
Sorting by Line 490
Sorting by Paragraph 491
Sorting a Secondary-Merge File 493
Sorting a Table 496
Using Other Sort Features 499
Sorting a Block 499
Sorting Numerics 500
Using the Select Function 501
Using Macros To Sort 503
Summary 504

15 Using Styles 505
Deciding To Use Styles 506
Realizing the Advantages of Using Styles .. 506
Comparing Styles to Macros 507
Defining Open, Paired, and Outline Styles .. 507
Creating an Open Style 509
Creating a Paired Style 510
Creating an Outline Style 513
Selecting a Style 514
Viewing a Style with Reveal Codes 515
Applying Paired Styles to Existing Text 515
Creating a Style by Example 515
Editing a Style 516
Changing Styles 516
Deleting Selected Style Codes from
a Document 517
Saving Styles with a Document 518
Deleting a Style Definition from the
Style List 518
Creating a Style Library 519
Using Multiple Style Libraries 519
Setting the Default Style Library File 520
Saving Style Definitions in a Style Library . 521
Retrieving a Style Library 521
Updating Styles in a Document 522
Deleting a Style from the Style Library 523
Maintaining Style Libraries 524
Reviewing Sample Style Libraries 524
Using LIBRARY.STY 525
Investigating Another Style Library 525
Assessing Style Limitations 531
Summary 531

**16 Using WordPerfect with Other
Programs 533**
Understanding Basic Conversion Strategies . 534
Using Spreadsheet Information with
WordPerfect 535
Handling Wide Spreadsheets 536
Importing Spreadsheets with Text In/Out . 537
Importing a Spreadsheet as Text 537
Linking Spreadsheets and Documents 538
Updating Links 539
Using Spreadsheet Information in Merge .. 540

Using Spreadsheets Other than Lotus,
PlanPerfect, or Excel 540
Using Database Information with
WordPerfect 540
Preparing a Delimited File 541
Using a Delimited File in a Merge 541
Noting Delimited-File Considerations 542
Converting a Delimited File to
Secondary-Merge Format 542
Working with dBASE Dates 543
Using Database Reports 543
Using DOS Text Files with WordPerfect 544
Understanding the Limitations of
DOS Text Files 544
Bringing DOS Text into WordPerfect 544
Creating DOS Text with WordPerfect 546
Creating a Generic Word Processing File .. 546
Creating a DOS-Text Print File 547
Converting 5 or 4.2 Documents for
Use in 5.1 547
Converting 5.1 Documents for
Use in 5 or 4.2 547
Using WordPerfect's Convert Program 548
Converting Files for Use in WordPerfect ... 548
Translating WordPerfect into
Other Formats 552
Using Convert without Menus 555
Performing Mass Conversions 556
Summary 556

**Part III: Using WordPerfect's
Specialized Features**

17 Working with Text Columns 559
Newspaper Columns 560
Defining Newspaper Columns 560
Typing Columnar Text 563
Combining Columns with Regular Text 564
Creating Newspaper Columns from
Existing Text 565
Editing Newspaper Columns 566
Displaying One Column at a Time 567
Previewing Newspaper Columns 567
A Macro That Defines Newspaper
Columns 569
Parallel Columns 570
Defining Parallel Columns 571
Typing Text in Parallel Columns 572
Combining Parallel Columns with
Regular Text 574
Editing Parallel Columns 575
Moving Parallel Columns 575
Changing Line Spacing 576
Changing Column Leading 577
A Macro That Defines Parallel Columns 579
Summary 580

18 Using Math 581
Understanding Math Operation Basics 581
Using Numeric Columns 582
Setting Tab Stops for Math 583
Accepting the Default Definition for
Numeric Columns 583
Turning On the Math Feature 584
Entering Numbers in Numeric Columns 584
Entering Text in front of Numeric
Columns 585
Entering Math Operators in Numeric
Columns 585
Working with a Numeric-Column
Example 586
Calculating Results of Math Operations 588
Turning Off the Math Feature 588
Using More than One Math Area in a
Document 588
Specifying Text, Total, and Calculation
Columns 588
Using the Math Definition Screen 589
Changing the Default Settings 590
Changing the Decimal and Thousands-
Separator Characters 591
Using Total Columns 591
Working with a Total Column Example 593
Understanding the Guidelines for
Total Columns 593
Using Calculation Columns 594
Working with Sample Calculation
Formulas 596
Working with a Calculation-Column
Example 598
Editing a Math Definition 599
Creating a Useful Macro for Math Columns . 600
Summary 602

19 Creating Tables 603
Understanding Table Basics 603
Planning a Table Definition 605
Creating a Table 605
Understanding Table-Structure Codes 608
Moving the Cursor within a Table 610
Entering Text in a Table 613
Editing Text in a Table 615
Deleting and Creating a Table without
Using the Table Editor 617
Deleting the Table Structure 617
Restoring the Table Structure 619
Deleting an Entire Table 621
Deleting Information within a Table 621
Editing a Table with the Table Editor 624
Defining and Changing Cell, Column,
Row, and Table Formats 625
Using the Table Editor To Delete and
Undelete Columns or Rows 629
Inserting and Joining Cells, Columns,
and Rows 630

Formatting Cells 631
  Specifying Row Height 632
  Specifying Cell Characteristics 633
Creating a Table Header 633
Formatting a Block of Cells with the
  Table Editor 634
Creating Columns or Rows with Split 635
Aligning Letters or Numbers within
  Cells, Columns, or Rows 636
Changing the Graphical Line Grid 637
Copying/Moving Columns and Rows 639
Combining Formatting Codes in a Table ... 640
Adjusting the Width of Columns 641
Changing the Table's Location Relative
  to the Left Margin 642
Changing the Spacing between
  Text in Cells 644
Importing Text and Numerical Data
  into a Table 644
Using the Math Features with a Table 645
Using Combined Addition-Division
  Formulas 645
Using Averaging Formulas with Cell
  References 647
Changing the Display of Negative
  Numbers 647
Creating Newspaper Columns with Tables .. 647
Shading Cells, Columns, and Rows 648
Using Tables with Other WordPerfect
  Features 649
Summary 650

20 Customizing WordPerfect 651

Understanding the Setup Options 651
Introducing the Setup Menu 652
Customizing the Mouse 653
  Specifying the Mouse Type and Port 654
  Setting Mouse-Performance Options 656
  Designating Left-Hand Operation 657
  Choosing Assisted Mouse-Pointer
    Movement 657
Customizing the Display 658
  Setting Colors, Fonts, and Attributes 658
  Selecting Screen Types 663
  Customizing WordPerfect Menus 664
  Setting View Document Options on
    EGA and VGA Monitors 666
  Setting Edit-Screen Options 667
Customizing the Environment 670
  Setting Backup Options 671
  Customizing the Beep 672
  Setting the Cursor Speed 673
  Configuring Document-Summary
    Options 673
  Customizing List Files 674
  Specifying a Fast Save 674
  Customizing Hyphenation 675
  Setting Units of Measure 676

Customizing Initial Settings 676
  Setting DOS Text-Merge Delimiters 677
  Customizing the Date Format 677
  Customizing Equations 678
  Formatting Documents for the
    Default Printer 679
  Changing the Default Initial Codes 680
  Setting the Repeat Value 682
  Customizing the Table of Authorities 683
  Setting Print Options 683
Customizing Keyboards 685
  Selecting a Keyboard Definition 685
  Using Other Keyboard-Definition
    Options 687
  Editing a Keyboard Definition 687
Changing the Location of Auxiliary Files 688
Summary 690

21 Working with Special Characters and Foreign Languages 691

Using Special Characters 692
  Using the IBM Extended Character Set 692
  Using WordPerfect's Character Sets 695
  Displaying Special Characters On-screen .. 696
  Printing Special Characters 697
  Setting Print Quality 698
Entering WordPerfect Special Characters
  with Compose 698
  Using Ctrl-2 or Ctrl-V 698
  Using the Numeric Method 699
  Using the Mnemonic Method 700
Creating Special Characters with
  Overstrike 703
Changing Fonts 705
Working with Foreign Languages 705
  Using Foreign Language Dictionaries
    and Thesauri 705
  Entering WordPerfect Language Codes 706
  Using the Language Resource
    File (WP.LRS) 708
Summary 709

22 Creating Equations 711

Using the Equation Editor 712
  Starting the Equation Editor 712
  Examining the Editing and Display
    Windows 713
  Examining the Equation Palette 714
Using the Mouse in the Equation Editor 714
Creating an Equation in the Editing
  Window 715
Reviewing Key Terms 716
Using Commands in the Editing Window ... 717
  Understanding Precedence in the
    Equation Editor 718
  Altering the Equation Display 719
  Entering Keyboard Characters 720
  Using the Equation Keyboard 720

xiii

Using the Editing Keys 721
Using Functions in the Equation Editor 721
Using Commands To Create Equations 723
  Creating Subscripts and Superscripts 723
  Using the INT, SUM, FROM, and TO
    Commands 725
  Forming Fractions with the LEFT,
    RIGHT, and OVER Commands 726
  Creating Complex Integral Expressions 728
  Using Roots 729
  Using Diacritical Marks 730
  Using the Matrix Commands 731
  Creating Multiline Expressions with
    STACK and STACKALIGN 733
  Using Varying Symbol Sizes 734
  Using Miscellaneous Commands
    and Symbols 735
Positioning and Sizing Equations 735
  Creating a Special Equation Box 736
  Using the HORZ and VERT Commands 738
Managing Equation Files 738
  Saving an Equation as a Separate File 738
  Retrieving an Equation File 738
  Saving Equation Files in a Graphics
    Directory 739
Printing Equations 739
Summary 740

23 Using Footnotes and Endnotes 741

Using Footnotes 742
  Creating Footnotes 742
  Looking at Footnotes 745
  Adding Footnotes 749
  Deleting Footnotes 750
  Moving Footnotes 751
  Moving the Footnote and Its
    Normal Text 751
  Moving Just the Footnote 752
  Editing Footnotes 754
  Continuing Footnote Numbers in
    Several Documents 755
  Changing Footnote Options 755
Using Endnotes 759
  Working with Endnotes 760
  Changing Endnote Options 761
  Positioning Endnotes 762
Using Macros 763
Summary 764

**24 Outlining, Paragraph Numbering,
  and Line Numbering 765**

Outlining a Document 766
  Turning On Outline 766
  Creating Level Numbers 768
  Checking Line Numbering ....
  Defining Numbering Styles 770
  Investigating Numbering Styles 772

Editing an Outline 775
Deleting a Paragraph Number 776
  Adding a Paragraph Number 776
  Changing a Paragraph Number 776
  Deleting a Numbered Paragraph 777
  Moving a Numbered Paragraph 778
  Adding a Numbered Paragraph 780
  Adding a Paragraph without a Number 781
Using Outline Styles 782
Numbering a Paragraph 783
  Defining the Numbering Style 784
  Creating Numbered Paragraphs 784
  Using Fixed Paragraph Levels 785
Numbering a Line 788
  Turning On Line Numbering 788
  Checking Line Numbering 789
  Turning Off Line Numbering 789
  Changing Line Numbering Settings 790
Summary 791

25 Assembling Document References . 793

Creating Lists 795
  Marking Text for Lists 795
  Defining a List 800
  Generating Document References 801
  Considering Other Uses for Lists 803
Creating a Table of Contents 804
  Setting Up Automatic Paragraph
    Numbering 804
  Marking Text for a Table of Contents 806
  Defining the Table of Contents 811
  Generating the Table of Contents 812
  Using Multiple Tables of Contents 812
Creating a Table of Authorities 813
  Adjusting Setup for the ToA 813
  Marking Text for the ToA 813
  Defining a Table of Authorities 818
  Generating the Table of Authorities 819
Creating an Index 820
  Marking Text for the Index 821
  Defining the Index Format 823
  Generating the Index 824
  Preparing Indexes for Multiple Related
    Documents 825
Using Automatic Cross-Referencing 825
  Marking Text for Automatic
    Cross-Referencing 826
  Generating Cross-References 830
Using Automatic Document Comparison 830
  Saving an Old-Version Document for
    Comparison 831
  Comparing a New Version to an
    Old Version 831
  Purging Redlining from a Saved
    Document 833
Summary 834

26 Using the Master Document Feature for Large Projects 835

Creating Master and Subdocuments 836
Working with Subdocuments 836
Building the Master Document 838
Deleting a Subdocument 840
Expanding the Master Document 840
Creating a Table of Contents, List,
Index, or Table of Authorities 841
Marking Text for the Table of Contents 842
Defining the Table of Contents 842
Generating the Table of Contents 844
Printing the Master Document 845
Condensing the Master Document 845
Saving the Master Document 845
Using Other Features in a Master
Document 846
Inserting a New Page Number 846
Using Search and Replace 847
Spell-Checking 847
Adding Footnotes and Endnotes 848
Using Cross-References 849
Creating Subdocuments within
Subdocuments 850
Finding Other Uses for Master Documents . 850
Building Legal Contracts 850
Managing Group Writing 850
Summary 851

Part IV: Using WordPerfect for Desktop Publishing

27 Integrating Text and Graphics 855

Choosing the Type of Box 857
Choosing Box Options 860
Choosing the Border Style 861
Setting Space between Border and Text ... 862
Setting Space between Border
and Contents 863
Choosing the Caption-Numbering Style 863
Specifying Text for Caption Style 864
Setting the Position for Captions 864
Determining Offset from Paragraph 865
Determining Percent of Gray Shading....... 865
Aligning Equations within Boxes............... 865
Creating the Box 866
Entering a File Name 866
Determining the Type of Contents 867
Entering a Caption 868
Anchoring a Box to the Text 868
Aligning a Box 869
Selecting the Box Size 871
Wrapping Text around the Box 872
Entering Text in a Box 873

Editing a Box 873
Importing Graphics 874
Editing a Graphic Image 875
Moving an Image 876
Scaling an Image 877
Rotating and Mirroring an Image 877
Inverting an Image 879
Printing an Image in Black and White 881
Restoring an Image to its Original State 881
Creating Graphics Lines 881
Creating Horizontal Lines 882
Creating Vertical Lines 884
Changing the Appearance of Lines 886
Returning to the Editing Screen 886
Editing Graphics Lines 887
Using Line Draw 887
Changing the Line Style 887
Erasing the Line 888
Summary 888

28 Producing Publications 889

Realizing the Potential of Desktop
Publishing 890
Designing Publications That Work 891
Enhancing a Publication 892
Using Columns 892
Varying Paragraphs 893
Choosing Fonts 894
Adding Lines and Boxes 895
Creating Special Effects 895
Creating and Using "Two-Up" Pages 896
Including Illustrations 900
Understanding Types of Graphics 901
Vector and Bit-Mapped Images 901
TIFF Files 904
EPS Files 904
Converting Graphics Files with
GRAPHCNV.EXE 904
Using WordPerfect as a Desktop Publisher . 906
Getting the Most from WordPerfect
as a Desktop Publisher 906
Developing a Template 907
Placing Graphics 908
Adding Text 908
Creating a Newsletter 908
Creating a Two-Fold Brochure 912
Creating a Form 914
Creating an Annual Report 916
Summary 919

A WordPerfect 5.1 Installation and Start-Up 921

B WordPerfect 5.1 for WordPerfect 5 Users 925

Index 931

▼ Acknowledgments

Using WordPerfect 5.1, Special Edition, is the result of the immense efforts of many dedicated and talented people. Que Corporation thanks the following people for their contributions to the development of this book.

The many WordPerfect experts who contributed to this book, for helping ensure that it would be a worthy successor to *Using WordPerfect 5*. Each contributor brought to the new edition a measure of expertise, enthusiasm, professionalism, and commitment that was most gratifying to witness. Although group efforts are fraught with their own set of problems, this book is much stronger for having been a collaboration. Special thanks go to Stu Bloom for helping assess the scope of the revision and later making significant contributions to the book.

Bill Hartman, of Hartman Publishing, for his excellent book design and extraordinary efforts—well above and beyond the call of duty—to ensure that the book was completed on schedule.

Technical editors Bob Beck, Tony Rairden, and Michael McCoy, for subjecting the text to the kind of rigorous scrutiny that all computer books should ideally receive.

Alice Martina Smith, for her exceptional efforts, keen editorial eye, and sound judgment, which resulted in a better book. Her excellent project management skills and "can-do" attitude helped keep the book on schedule. Thanks also to editors Lisa Hunt, Mike LaBonne, Mary Bednarek, Lois Sherman, and Ginny Noble for their outstanding work on the book.

Dave Ewing, for making this project possible and providing direction, support, and guidance.

Terrie Lynn Solomon, for managing the difficult task of communicating with the many contributors and editors, and overseeing the steady stream of floppy disks and printed copy. Thanks also to Stacey Beheler and Angela Rosenow for their support to the developmental and editing staff working on this book.

Corrine Harmon, Jennifer Mathews, Dan Armstrong, Dennis Sheehan, Sally Copenhaver and Mary Beth Wakefield of Que's production staff, for their extra efforts on this project. Thanks also to Joelynn Gifford, for completing a first-rate index on a tight schedule, and for the careful proofreading done by David Kline, Lori Lyons, Jodi Jensen, and Bruce Steed.

Finally, Jeff Acerson and Paul Eddington of WordPerfect Corporation, for their assistance and cooperation throughout this book's development.

Introduction

Welcome to *Using WordPerfect 5.1*, Special Edition! This book is a worthy successor to the best-selling *Using WordPerfect 5*, which has sold over 400,000 copies since its publication in July 1988. Much of the success of *Using WordPerfect 5* can be attributed to the unprecedented collaborative approach that gave the book its distinctiveness, depth, and broad appeal.

Using WordPerfect 5.1, Special Edition, is "special" because it builds on the strengths of its predecessor by pooling the talents of a diverse collection of WordPerfect experts (many of whom contributed to the first edition), providing extensive coverage of all of WordPerfect's features, and combining tutorial steps and reference information. This new edition has been thoroughly revised, updated, and expanded to cover all the enhancements and changes with version 5.1.

Many of the authors of this book are members of a national WordPerfect support group; many participate nightly in the WordPerfect forum on the CompuServe Information Service. The authors have made this book unique among books about WordPerfect because this book is a collaboration in the best sense of that word.

Why a collaboration? Why not? Collaborative efforts are certainly not uncommon in academic, scientific, and business environments. In a study of writing on the job, Professor Paul Anderson reported that a survey of "265 professional people in 20 research and development institutions" revealed that around "19 percent of their writing [was] collaborative."[1] When you need to accomplish a complex, tough job, an excellent strategy is to pull together a team of experts, each one specializing in a particular aspect of the overall discipline.

David Macaulay, in his book *Cathedral*, uses the fictional cathedral of "Chutreaux" to detail the painstaking, difficult, *collaborative* effort that went into the making of a 13th-century Gothic cathedral. After the architect, or master builder, created the original design, he assembled a team of the best craftsmen he could find:

The craftsmen were the master quarryman, the master stone cutter, the master sculptor, the master mortar maker, the master mason, the master carpenter, the master blacksmith, the master roofer, and the master glass maker.[2]

This book on WordPerfect 5.1, a "collaboration," pools the knowledge of a range of WordPerfect experts, all masters in particular areas or applications.

As word processing software continues to evolve and becomes increasingly feature-laden, complex, and useful to a diversity of users, the need for expertise across a range of experience is clear. Only a team of experts can adequately cover a program as advanced, complex, and versatile as WordPerfect 5.1.

Who Should Use This Book?

If you're new to WordPerfect, this book's complete coverage of program features, mix of step-by-step procedures with reference information, many real-world examples, and clear instructions can help you master version 5.1 quickly. Reminder notes in the margin help cement key concepts and procedures. As you become more comfortable with WordPerfect, Cues in the margin give you hints on how to use the program more efficiently.

If you're upgrading from version 5, this book can help you make a smooth transition. A special appendix addresses compatibility issues, describes changes to existing features, and orients you to the features new with version 5.1. Helpful 5.1 icons are placed throughout the text to alert you to changes with version 5.1.

One of the more obvious changes in the user interface is the addition of pull-down menus and mouse support; a special icon (⌧) points out alternative commands for pull-down menus and mouse operation. In this book you also find complete coverage of program changes and new features. For example, the Table feature and the equation editor are totally new to version 5.1, and both receive full, chapter-length treatment. If you're an experienced WordPerfect user, you will appreciate the special tips, shortcuts, and macro ideas in this book.

How To Use This Book

Using WordPerfect 5.1, Special Edition is designed to be a complement to the manual and workbook that come with version 5.1. Beginners will find the step-by-step information in this book helpful; experienced users will appreciate the comprehensive coverage and expert advice. Once you become proficient with version 5.1, you can use this book as a desktop reference.

Each chapter in this book focuses on a particular operation or set of operations with WordPerfect 5.1. Overall, the movement of the book is from the steps typical to the creation of any document (such as entering text, spell-checking, and printing) to more specialized topics (such as macros, styles, columns, tables, equations, special characters, and integration of text with graphics). *Using WordPerfect 5.1*, Special Edition distills the "real-world" experience of many WordPerfect experts, so the book is applications oriented.

The special tips included in the body of the text either point out information often overlooked in the documentation or help you use WordPerfect more efficiently.

You will find many of these tips useful or pertinent as you become more comfortable with the software. Cautions and warnings alert you to potential loss of data or harm to your system.

Reminder margin notes provide brief synopses of basic program operation; Cue margin notes point out how to use the program more efficiently.

How This Book Is Organized

As you flip through the book, notice that it has been organized to follow the natural flow of learning and using WordPerfect 5.1. *Using WordPerfect 5.1*, Special Edition is divided into four parts:

> I: Using WordPerfect's Basic Features
>
> II: Using WordPerfect's Advanced Features
>
> III: Using WordPerfect's Specialized Features
>
> IV: Using WordPerfect for Desktop Publishing

Part I describes the steps for preparing to use WordPerfect: starting the program, running the tutorial, and completing the cycle of document preparation—planning, creating, editing, formatting, spell-checking, and printing. You also learn various block operations and how to manage your files with the List Files feature.

Part II moves into the more advanced features of the program to discuss basic macros, the macro command language and complex macros, simple merges and more complex merge operations involving the new merge language, sorting and selecting data, using styles, and using WordPerfect with other programs to convert files and import data.

Part III covers WordPerfect's specialized features, such as newspaper and parallel columns; math operations; tables; customizing program settings, including the use of alternative keyboard definitions; working with special characters and foreign languages; creating equations; footnotes and endnotes; outlining, paragraph numbering, and line numbering; creating tables of contents, lists, indexes, and tables of authority; using automatic cross-references; and creating references across files with the Master Document feature.

Part IV focuses on version 5.1's desktop publishing potential. This part of the book presents a primer on page layout, typography, design, and graphics; takes you through the mechanics of integrating text and graphics; and showcases a number of attractive documents produced with version 5.1.

Following is a chapter-by-chapter breakdown of the book's contents:

Chapter 1, "Preparing To Use WordPerfect," introduces you to WordPerfect 5.1; covers hardware and memory requirements; and shows you how to start the program on hard and floppy disk systems, run the tutorial, and exit the program. You learn about WordPerfect's editing screen, function-key commands, pull-down menus, mouse support, cursor movement (keyboard and mouse), and context-sensitive help. WordPerfect's hidden codes are introduced.

Chapter 2, "Creating a Document," gives you the opportunity to start WordPerfect and begin entering text, moving the cursor through a document with either the keyboard or the mouse, using the keyboard or the mouse to give commands, selecting menu options, canceling operations, using both document windows, printing the document, and naming and saving a file. The chapter ends with advice on how to use word processing to improve your effectiveness as a writer.

Chapter 3, "Editing a Document," looks at the next step in the composing process: revising and editing a document. After you learn the basics of retrieving a file saved to disk, you explore the various methods for deleting text. This chapter also covers how to enter simple text enhancements (bold and underline), how to use search and replace as an editing tool, and how to edit hidden codes in WordPerfect. Finally, you learn how to create document comments and use them as an aid to revision.

Chapter 4, "Working with Blocks," teaches you how to use Block to select, or highlight, text that you then can move, copy, delete, append, save, or print. You also learn to enhance a block of characters with features like bold, underlining, or italics; then you learn to enlarge or reduce the size of characters in a block.

Chapter 5, "Formatting and Enhancing Text," demonstrates how to alter the look of text on the page by changing margins, indenting text, altering line spacing and line height (leading), using various types of tabs, and centering, justifying, and hyphenating text. This chapter also explains how to change the base font to a larger size or choose a particular font appearance, such as italic or small caps.

Chapter 6, "Formatting Pages and Designing Documents," continues the topic of formatting, but goes beyond the elements of an individual page to consider overall document formatting. You learn to create headers and footers, number pages, keep certain text together, control page breaks, and define and use printer forms to create mailing labels. You also learn to establish custom settings for all your documents.

Chapter 7, "Using the Speller and the Thesaurus," teaches you to use the Speller and Thesaurus to proofread and refine your work. This chapter demonstrates how to use the Speller to check the spelling of your documents and to create custom supplemental dictionaries, if you need them. You also learn to use the Thesaurus to give your writing freshness and precision.

Chapter 8, "Printing and Print Options," the first of two chapters on printing, focuses on dot-matrix printers. In this chapter, you learn to install a printer and master the various methods of printing with WordPerfect.

Chapter 9, "Printing with Laser Printers," begins with a general discussion of laser printers and moves to the specifics of printing with the HP LaserJet Series II and with printers that support PostScript. This chapter is filled with sound advice on using built-in, cartridge, and soft fonts with a laser printer. In addition, troubleshooting tips help you solve problems you may encounter with a laser printer.

Chapter 10, "Using List Files," completes the "basics" section and explains the principles of file and hard disk management. You practice using List Files to retrieve, delete, move, rename, print, look at, copy, find, and search files on disk or in a directory. You also see how to choose the longer file-name display option offered with version 5.1.

Chapter 11, "Creating Basic Macros," provides a comprehensive introduction to 5.1 macros. This chapter teaches you how to plan, create, run, stop, replace, and edit basic macros. You can copy the macro examples provided in the chapter, or you can use the examples as a basis for your own macros. The chapter includes an introduction to the macro editor and prepares you for the macro command language, discussed in Chapter 12.

Chapter 12, "Creating Advanced Macros," presents a full treatment of WordPerfect's macro command language. This chapter teaches you the basics of macro programming, describes the advanced macro commands, supplies many tips and techniques for creating sophisticated macros, and concludes with examples of some powerful, advanced macros.

Chapter 13, "Assembling Documents with Merge," is designed for those who have never used the Merge feature before, for those who are unfamiliar with WordPerfect's Merge feature, and for WordPerfect 5 users who want to know about the many enhancements with version 5.1. You learn the basics of merge, how to perform a simple merge, how to handle special situations with merge, common uses for merge, and how to use 5.1's new macro-like merge commands. As such, this chapter is a companion piece to the preceding chapter on advanced macro programming.

Chapter 14, "Sorting and Selecting Data," teaches you about WordPerfect's sort and select features. You see how to create simple databases containing "records" that you then sort by line, paragraph, or secondary-merge file. Sorting data in 5.1's new Table feature is covered as well.

Chapter 15, "Using Styles," offers a clear, comprehensive explanation of the three types of styles (paired, open, and outline) and how to use them to format documents. You learn to create, save, select, and view styles in a style library. Shortcuts and tips for working with styles are included. In addition, this chapter provides you with a library of ready-to-use style definitions.

Chapter 16, "Using WordPerfect with Other Programs," ends the section on WordPerfect's advanced features. The chapter covers converting WordPerfect files to other file formats and importing data into WordPerfect. You learn how to import and link spreadsheets, how to import database information, how to use DOS text files, how to use earlier releases of WordPerfect, and how to use the Convert program.

Chapter 17, "Working with Text Columns," demonstrates how to create attractive text columns in newspaper ("snaking") or parallel format. You learn to use macros to make your work with columns even easier.

Chapter 18, "Using Math," is intended for those who want to include simple arithmetic calculations in their documents. This chapter shows you how to set up math columns, enter numbers, and calculate the results.

Chapter 19, "Creating Tables," provides a complete introduction to this dramatic 5.1 enhancement. You see how to create, format, edit, and enhance a table; perform math operations in a table; import text or numbers into a table; and use tables with other WordPerfect features such as macros, merge, and graphics.

Chapter 20, "Customizing WordPerfect," explains the many ways you use the Setup feature to adapt WordPerfect to your own special needs. The topics covered in this chapter include customizing WordPerfect for a mouse, customizing the screen display, setting file backup options, changing the default initial codes, and customizing keyboard layouts through the use of alternative keyboard definitions.

Chapter 21, "Working with Special Characters and Foreign Languages," examines how to access and print some of the 13 special character sets available with WordPerfect 5.1. This chapter also discusses and provides tips for working with multilingual documents in WordPerfect.

Chapter 22, "Creating Equations," takes you through the entire process of creating equations with 5.1's new equation editor, from entering text, commands, and functions, to developing complicated expressions, using miscellaneous commands and symbols, managing equation files, and printing equations.

Chapter 23, "Using Footnotes and Endnotes," explains how to incorporate footnotes and endnotes into documents. This chapter presents the steps for creating, looking at, previewing, adding, deleting, moving, customizing, and editing footnotes and endnotes.

Chapter 24, "Outlining, Paragraph Numbering, and Line Numbering," covers the steps necessary to create outlines and number paragraphs and lines. You learn to customize the defaults for footnotes and endnotes to meet the style guidelines of your particular discipline. You also learn to use 5.1's new Outline style to create custom outlines.

Chapter 25, "Assembling Document References," teaches you to mark text and generate tables of contents, lists, indexes, and tables of authorities. This chapter demonstrates how to use cross-references, styles, macros, and the Document Compare feature for lengthy, structured documents.

Chapter 26, "Using the Master Document Feature for Large Projects," builds on the preceding chapter to show you how to use the Master Document feature to create document references across any number of subdocuments. This chapter shows how the master document can simplify the task of pulling together a project comprised of many parts. You learn to create, expand, save, and condense the master document.

Chapter 27, "Integrating Text and Graphics," the first chapter in the section on desktop publishing, explores the mechanics of integrating text and graphics with WordPerfect 5.1. You see how to create a box and import graphics or enter text. You learn to position a box on the page, wrap text accordingly, and edit the images you import. Creating graphics lines and using Line Draw are also covered in this chapter.

Chapter 28, "Producing Publications," presents the principles of page layout and good design, introduces the various types of graphics, and showcases a number of attractive documents produced with WordPerfect 5.1. Each document is paired with a specification sheet explaining how the document was created.

Appendix A, "WordPerfect 5.1 Installation and Startup," covers installation and start-up of WordPerfect 5.1. The options for starting WordPerfect 5.1 are discussed also.

Appendix B, "WordPerfect 5.1 for 5 Users," helps the version 5 user make the transition to version 5.1. This appendix details the differences between the two versions and helps upgraders begin using 5.1 quickly.

At the back of the book, you will find a tear-out, color-coded, keyboard-command chart. This card includes a complete map of all the 5.1 pull-down and pop-out menus. Keep this command chart close at hand—you'll find it an invaluable aid.

Where To Find More Help

If you find yourself stymied on a particular point, WordPerfect's context-sensitive Help (F3) feature may answer your questions. Help (F3) is explained in Chapter 1. In addition, you can turn to this text or to WordPerfect's manual and workbook for help.

Should all else fail, WordPerfect Corporation provides toll-free telephone support. Call the appropriate number to receive assistance:

1-800-533-9605	Installation
1-800-321-3383	Graphics
1-800-541-5097	Printer
1-800-541-5096	Features
1-800-321-3389	Networks

One of the best sources of help is the WordPerfect Support Group (WPSG), an independent group not affiliated with WordPerfect Corporation. The group publishes an excellent monthly newsletter, *The WordPerfectionist*. You can subscribe to *The WordPerfectionist* for $36 a year by writing to the following address:

The WordPerfectionist
Newsletter of the WordPerfect Support Group
Lake Technology Park
P.O. Box 130
McHenry, MD 21541

The WordPerfectionist is intended for all levels of users and is filled with helpful hints, clever techniques, solid guidance, and objective reviews of books and software.

Conventions Used in This Book

The conventions used in this book have been established to help you learn to use the program quickly and easily.

For function-key commands, the name of the command is presented first, followed by the keystrokes used to invoke the command. For example, *Help (F3)* means that you press F3 to invoke Help. For keystrokes separated by hyphens, such as Format (Shift-F8), hold down the first key (Shift in this example) and press the second key (F8 in this example) to invoke the option. When a series of keys is separated by commas, press and release each key. To move to the top of a document, for example, press and release Home, press Home again, then press ↑ (Home, Home, ↑).

WordPerfect 5.1 lets you use both keyboard and mouse to select a menu item: you can press a letter or a menu number, or you can select an item by "clicking" it with the mouse. In this book, the name of the menu option is presented first followed by the appropriate menu-number in parentheses—for instance, **F**ootnote (**1**). The letter (the *mnemonic*) or number you press appears in bold. Pull-down or pop-out menu options are treated in a similar manner: the **S**ave option on the **F**ile pull-down menu. WordPerfect's hidden codes are also shown in bold: **[Tab]**.

Users who prefer to use the pull-down menus rather than the function keys—either with or without the mouse—should note the special ⌷ icon placed in the text. This icon flags the new alternative to the function-key commands. Following is an example of how the mouse icon appears in text:

⌷ Access the **F**ile pull-down menu and select **S**ave.

If you use a mouse with WordPerfect 5.1, you can click the right button to display the pull-down menu, and then select the desired option. You also can press Alt-= to access the pull-down menus, and then press the appropriate letter (shown in bold) of the desired option. Full instructions for using the pull-down menus and mouse appear in Chapters 1 and 2.

Special icons in the margins flag text pertinent to changes or enhancements with version 5.1. A single icon usually points to a line, sentence, or paragraph that contains information new with 5.1. Extended icons are shaded arrows that point toward each other and flag extended discussions of 5.1 features.

Uppercase letters are used to distinguish file names, DOS (disk operating system) commands, and macro commands such as {ON ERROR}. In most cases, the keys on the keyboard are represented as they appear on your keyboard (for example, G, Enter, Tab, Ctrl, Ins, and Backspace). Special words or phrases defined for the first time, the text you are asked to type, and macro variables appear in *italics*. On-screen messages appear in `digital`.

Charles O. Stewart III
Carmel, Indiana

---

[1] Paul V. Anderson, "What Survey Research Tells Us about Writing at Work," in *Writing in Nonacademic Settings*, eds. Lee Odell and Dixie Goswami (New York: The Guilford Press, 1985), p. 50.

2 David Macaulay, *Cathedral: The Story of Its Construction* (Boston: Houghton Mifflin Company, 1973), p. 9.

Part I

Using WordPerfect's Basic Features

Preparing To Use WordPerfect

Creating a Document

Editing a Document

Working with Blocks

Formatting and Enhancing Text

Formatting Pages and Designing Documents

Using the Speller and the Thesaurus

Printing and Print Options

Printing with Laser Printers

Using List Files

5.1

Preparing To Use WordPerfect

Charles O. Stewart III contributed this chapter to *Using WordPerfect 5*, on which *Using WordPerfect 5.1,* Special Edition is based. He served as project director for both books, determining content, assembling the team of contributors, and working closely with them through manuscript development, editing, and final review.

Schuyler Lininger, Jr., who recently wrote a book on Ventura Publisher for Que, revised this chapter for *Using WordPerfect 5.1,* Special Edition.

This chapter acquaints you with WordPerfect 5.1 and prepares you for Chapter 2's task of creating and printing a simple document. Beginning with a brief introduction to WordPerfect, this chapter covers the hardware you need for operating WordPerfect and shows you how to "boot," or start, WordPerfect on your computer. You also learn about WordPerfect's "clean" editing screen, the special ways WordPerfect uses the keyboard, and the context-sensitive on-line help that comes with the program. And if you're interested in taking the WordPerfect tutorial to get more comfortable with the program, this chapter provides an overview of the Tutor program and shows you how to start it.

If you need to install WordPerfect on your system, turn to Appendix A, which covers everything you need to know to get WordPerfect running on your dual-floppy or hard disk system.

Note: If you're eager to begin creating a document and are familiar with either word processing or WordPerfect, skim this chapter and then move to Chapter 2, "Creating a Document."

What Is WordPerfect?

WordPerfect is one of the world's most popular word processing software programs, currently enjoying approximately 40 to 45 percent of the word processing market. A full 27 percent of the readers of *PC Magazine* reported in early 1988 that they used WordPerfect as their word processor of choice. In the same survey, respondents noted that WordPerfect was number one where they worked.

Why is WordPerfect so popular? WordPerfect has all the basic features you would expect in a word processing package plus a full complement of advanced features. The program is suited to your needs, whether they entail short memos or complex, lengthy documents. W. E. "Pete" Peterson, Executive Vice President of WordPerfect Corporation, put it best when he said on CompuServe that "what makes WordPerfect attractive is that it gets out of your way. It's like a well-mannered houseguest who is kind enough not to disrupt your life or the way you do things." An editing screen uncluttered by menus or cryptic codes, an abundance of ever-growing features, support for a wide range of printers, and unparalleled customer assistance are just a few of the reasons why WordPerfect enjoys the preeminence it so rightly deserves.

What Is WordPerfect 5.1?

Released in the spring of 1988, WordPerfect 5 heralded a "quantum leap" forward for a product already enjoying ever-increasing popularity worldwide. Perhaps the most dramatic change in the program was its move toward desktop publishing capabilities, marking an overall trend in upper-end word processing packages in the late 1980s. Pete Peterson of WordPerfect Corporation has said that version 5 represents the biggest change in WordPerfect since the product's inception in the early 1980s.

In the fall of 1989, WordPerfect 5.1 was released. With version 5.1, WordPerfect's list of features has become even longer and includes the following:

- Context-sensitive help to allow easy access to the appropriate help menus from anywhere in the program.
- The capability to import spreadsheet files, including entire spreadsheets or ranges from Lotus 1-2-3 (up to version 2.01), MathPlan 3.0, and PlanPerfect (versions 3.0 and 5.0). WordPerfect can dynamically link and automatically update spreadsheet data.
- Automatic table creation with graphic-lines capability.
- Equation creation and editing that enable you to insert sophisticated mathematical and engineering formulas into WordPerfect documents.
- An enhanced outline feature that you can use to create outline styles and to move outline families easily.
- Pull-down menus accessible through either the keyboard or a mouse. Pull-down menus make WordPerfect easier for the novice or occasional user.
- Mouse support, which enables you to use a mouse for selecting text and making menu selections from either the new pull-down menus or the regular menus.
- Document-management features that allow for long file names for WordPerfect documents (5 and 5.1) in the List Files screen.
- Improved editing control, including enhancements to the tab and justification features.
- An extensively enhanced merge feature, in which cryptic codes have been replaced with meaningful codes and to which a full array of macro commands has been added.

- The much improved handling of labels. WordPerfect easily installs the required measurements for most popular label sizes and allows for much simpler customization of mailing labels.

- Dictionary-based hyphenation, which results in more sophisticated and accurate hyphenation of words.

- Enhanced printer drivers to provide any printer capable of printing graphics access to over 1,700 characters, even if that character is not normally available to the printer.

- Macros improved with new commands and the capability to call Shell macros from the WordPerfect Library.

- The efficient use of expanded memory.

What Hardware Do You Need To Run WordPerfect?

You can run WordPerfect on an IBM PC or completely compatible computer that has two diskette drives or a hard disk drive. WordPerfect requires DOS 2.0 or later versions and at least 404K of memory. The main program file, WP.EXE, uses approximately 217K. The rest of WordPerfect's random-access memory (RAM) requirement is used by DOS and as space for editing.

Your best bet is to have at least 512K of RAM. A computer uses RAM to store programs and data, including a portion of the disk operating system (DOS), temporarily. RAM is volatile, which means that any program or data in RAM is lost when you turn off the computer or when a power loss occurs. Run the DOS CHKDSK command, which tells you how much RAM is available on your system.

Reminder:
To run WordPerfect, your computer should have at least 512K of RAM.

WordPerfect can take advantage of expanded memory and will immediately detect it when you install the program. Expanded memory lets you load and edit very large documents because any part of the document too large for RAM goes into the expanded-memory space. WordPerfect uses overflow files to store information too large for RAM.

WordPerfect 5.1 comes on eight 5 1/4-inch diskettes or four 3 1/2-inch diskettes (not including diskettes for printer drivers). The disks contain compressed files that are useless until installed with the installation program. You can install WordPerfect 5.1 either to a hard disk or to diskettes. If you plan to run WordPerfect from diskettes, you must have either the higher-density 5 1/4-inch drives (1.2M) or 3 1/2-inch drives. Currently, WordPerfect's automatic-installation program installs only to hard disks or high-density 5 1/4-inch diskettes. To accomplish a diskette installation, you must use 10 high-density diskettes.

To run WordPerfect with fewer interruptions, you should invest in a hard disk. Although WordPerfect is already a speedy program, it runs faster and performs better on a hard disk.

Monitors and Graphics Cards

WordPerfect supports a wide range of video systems, including the Color Graphics Adapter (CGA), Enhanced Graphics Adapter (EGA), and Video Graphics Array (VGA). Other systems supported include the AT&T 6300, IBM 8514/A, Genius (full-page), and COMPAQ Portable III/386 with plasma display. If your monitor is not supported, call WordPerfect Corporation's support number for assistance; because WordPerfect is always adding support for new hardware, a new driver that will support your monitor may be available.

You can run WordPerfect on a monochrome system without a graphics card, but you won't be able to see any graphics, font changes, or font attributes (superscript, subscript, italics, small caps, and so on). With a CGA card and a color or monochrome monitor, you can see graphics in View Document mode. A color monitor with this card enables you to tinker in a limited fashion with background and foreground screen colors to differentiate font attributes. EGA and VGA systems provide better resolution in graphics mode and offer more possibilities for displaying font attributes in various color combinations.

WordPerfect also supports the Hercules Graphics Card, the Hercules Graphics Card Plus, and the Hercules InColor Card (the color version of the Hercules Graphics Card Plus). These last two cards come with the Hercules RamFont mode, which offers you true WYSIWYG (*what you see is what you get*) while in editing mode. You can thus see, on-screen in editing mode, changes in font size or appearance as they print. For example, you can see fonts in various sizes (fine, small, large, very large, extra large), italics, small caps, underline and double underline, superscript and subscript, outline, and strikeout. In short, if you want to see your document in edit mode as it appears when printed, invest in a Hercules Plus or Hercules InColor card to take advantage of the RamFont capability.

Printers

WordPerfect runs on a wide variety of printers, from dot-matrix to laser. Printer installation is covered in detail in Chapter 8. The printer drivers supplied on the Printer disks are for the most common printers. Your printer is most likely supported by WordPerfect; if not, follow the instructions in Chapter 8 for emulating a similar printer, or call WordPerfect Corporation. If you're adventurous and technically adept, you can use the Printer program (PTR.EXE) to create a custom printer driver, but this approach is not recommended for the novice. The list of supported printers is always being revised and increased, so unless you have a printer manufactured in, say, Tibet, you should be able to get a printer driver that works.

The Mouse

Reminder:

Although WordPerfect 5.1 supports a mouse, you do not have to use one.

WordPerfect 5.1 supports a mouse, but you don't need the device in order to use the program. Even if you have a mouse, you may decide you don't want to use it with WordPerfect. The mouse serves two main purposes: it is used to make selections in most menus, including the new pull-down menus, and it marks text so that you can perform a block action (such as deleting or moving) or modification (such as underlining or centering).

Virtually every type of mouse is supported, so your mouse will undoubtedly work with WordPerfect. Whether you have a two- or three-button mouse doesn't matter: WordPerfect works equally well with either type. ⌨ To modify the way WordPerfect works with the mouse (to select the appropriate driver, for example), select the **F**ile pull-down menu, choose Se**t**up, and then choose **M**ouse.

Starting WordPerfect on a Dual-Floppy System

If you haven't already formatted high-density diskettes and made working copies of the original WordPerfect diskettes, turn now to Appendix A.

You can start WordPerfect in a number of ways, as explained in Appendix A, but the simplest method is to use the WP command. This section assumes that you have installed a copy of the DOS COMMAND.COM file on your working copies of the WordPerfect 1 and WordPerfect 2 diskettes, as explained in Appendix A.

Note: If you are using an IBM PS/2, the main program files are combined on one 3 1/2-inch diskette labeled *WordPerfect 1/WordPerfect 2.*

To start WordPerfect on your computer, follow these steps:

1. Insert the working copy of the WordPerfect 1 diskette into drive A.
2. Insert a formatted data diskette into drive B.
3. Turn on the computer.
4. Respond appropriately to the operating-system prompts for the date and time. (If you have an AUTOEXEC.BAT file, this step may not be necessary.)
5. At the A> prompt, type *b:* and press Enter.

    Drive B is now the default drive, which means that any data you save to disk is saved to the data diskette in drive B.
6. Type *a:wp* and press Enter. WordPerfect is loaded into memory.

    WordPerfect prompts you to insert the WordPerfect 2 diskette. The opening screen contains WordPerfect copyright information, the version number of your copy, and an indication of the default directory that the system will use.
7. Remove the WordPerfect 1 diskette from drive A and insert the WordPerfect 2 diskette.
8. Press any key to resume loading WordPerfect.

Starting WordPerfect on a Hard Disk System

This section assumes that you have followed the directions in Appendix A for setting up your hard disk and installing WordPerfect. If you created an AUTOEXEC.BAT file (see Appendix A), WordPerfect loads automatically after you turn on the computer. (You may have to respond to the prompts for date and time, depending on how you have set up your AUTOEXEC.BAT file.)

Make certain that the drive door is open for each diskette drive on your hard disk system. Drives that use 3 1/2-inch diskettes do not have drive doors.

To start WordPerfect on your hard disk system, follow these steps:

1. Turn on the computer.

2. If necessary, respond to the prompts for date and time. The DOS prompt C> is displayed on-screen.

3. Type *cd\wp* and press Enter. The current directory is now \WP, where the main WordPerfect program files are stored on the hard disk.

   Note: For this step, it is assumed that you've created a \WP subdirectory for the main system files.

4. Type *wp* and press Enter to load WordPerfect.

You should see the opening screen for just a moment, and then the editing screen is displayed.

Troubleshooting Problems with Starting WordPerfect

If you have trouble starting WordPerfect, follow these steps:

1. Check all power cords and cables to make certain that they are connected properly.

2. Make sure that your monitor is turned on and adjusted properly.

If you're using a dual-floppy system, do the following:

1. Make certain that you formatted and copied your working and data diskettes properly (see Appendix A).

2. Make certain that your working copy of the WordPerfect 1 system diskette (or the WordPerfect 1/WordPerfect 2 3 1/2-inch diskette if you have an IBM PS/2 computer) is in drive A.

3. Check drive B to make certain that you have a formatted data diskette in the drive.

4. Make certain that the diskettes have been inserted properly and that the drive doors are closed.

If you're starting WordPerfect on a hard disk, make certain that you're starting the program from the proper directory (\WP or the directory to which you copied the main system files).

Restarting WordPerfect

What happens if you start WordPerfect and the power fails because of an electrical storm or an accidental pull of the plug? Or what happens if the program "freezes up" and no longer accepts any keyboard input, forcing you to turn off the computer or perform a "soft reboot" by pressing Ctrl-Alt-Del? In either instance, what results is an improper exit from WordPerfect. (You'll see at the end of this chapter how to exit from the program properly.)

When you restart WordPerfect, the following prompt appears on your screen:

```
Are other copies of WordPerfect currently running? Y/N
```

Select **N** in response to this prompt. If when you installed the program you chose to have WordPerfect perform a timed backup of your document, you'll eventually (depending on the intervals you've chosen for the timed backup) get the following error message:

```
Old backup file exists 1 Rename 2 Delete
```

When you choose the timed backup option through the Setup menu (see Appendix A), WordPerfect creates a temporary backup file. The temporary backup file created for the document in the Doc 1 window is WP{WP}.BK1, and the file for the document in the Doc 2 window is WP{WP}.BK2. In most cases, you should choose **D**elete (**2**) to delete the file(s). WordPerfect normally deletes such a file when you exit from the program properly.

If you choose **R**ename (**1**), the prompt New name: appears. Type a file name and press Enter. Then press any key to begin WordPerfect. To retrieve the renamed backup file, you need to know which directory you have specified in Setup for backup files (see Appendix A). The backup-files directory is where the renamed file will be located.

Caution

If you are using timed backup and a power failure causes you to lose your text on-screen (and in memory), rename and retrieve WP{WP}.BK1 or WP{WP}.BK2 immediately when you reboot. If you don't rename or retrieve the backup file before the next timed save, whatever you have on-screen is copied to WP{WP}.BK1 or WP{WP}.BK2, writing over the backup file of your other document. Although WordPerfect prompts you to rename the backup file, only the Doc 1 file is renamed. The Doc 2 backup file must be renamed as a separate operation. Remember: After a power failure or some other program abort, retrieve the timed backup file, rename it, and save it to disk as soon as possible.

Understanding the Editing Screen

The editing screen, where you will do most of your work, appears after you start WordPerfect (see fig. 1.1).

You can have the pull-down menu bar visible at all times. If you elect to have the pull-down menu bar visible, you can also choose whether you want a menu-separator line. Figure 1.2 shows the pull-down menu bar with the menu-separator line.

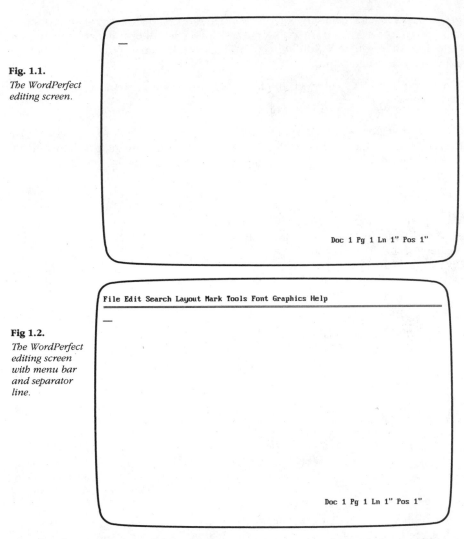

Fig. 1.1.
*The WordPerfect
editing screen.*

Doc 1 Pg 1 Ln 1" Pos 1"

File Edit Search Layout Mark Tools Font Graphics Help

Fig 1.2.
*The WordPerfect
editing screen
with menu bar
and separator
line.*

Doc 1 Pg 1 Ln 1" Pos 1"

WordPerfect's austere editing screen may seem rather intimidating at first: no menus (except possibly the pull-down menu bar) or any other "props" are visible to help you get started. Actually, the uncluttered screen comes about as close as possible to a blank piece of paper in a typewriter. WordPerfect's beauty, to recall Pete Peterson's words, is the way the program gets "out of your way," thereby freeing you to write and see on-screen as many of your words as possible. WordPerfect's editing screen provides you with the maximum area for viewing your work.

Reminder:

The information in the status line indicates the position of the cursor.

Until you name a document, which you must do before you can save it to disk, the only information on the screen is found in the bottom right corner (see fig. 1.2). This status-line information tells you the position of the *cursor*—that tiny bar of blinking light on the screen. The cursor marks the point where you begin typing characters; inserting and deleting text; retrieving documents stored on disk; and embedding special "hidden" codes for formatting and text enhancements such as bold, underline, and so forth. After you name and save a document, the document's name is displayed in the lower left corner of the screen. If you don't want WordPerfect to display the file name, you can use the Setup feature to "hide" the file name (see Chapter 20).

The first item (Doc 1) in the status line shows which document window displays the cursor. You can edit in one or two separate document windows in WordPerfect; they are referred to as Doc 1 and Doc 2. The second item is the page where the cursor is located. In figure 1.2, the cursor is on page 1. The third item indicates the cursor's vertical position, the line on which the cursor rests. The final item indicates the column in which the cursor rests—its horizontal character position.

For the default margins, WordPerfect assumes that you use 8 1/2-by-11-inch paper. (If you are using a foreign version of WordPerfect, you will have a different default paper size. In Europe, for example, the default paper size is A4, 210mm by 297mm. With 1-inch left and right margins, the printed line is 6.27 inches.) The flush-left position for the cursor is at 1 inch from the edge of the paper, and the status line reads Pos 1" or Pos 1i. The rightmost position is 7.5 inches—1 inch from the right edge of the paper—after which the cursor is repositioned at the beginning of the next line.

With WordPerfect you can have the position display in inches, centimeters, w units (1/1200's of an inch), or WordPerfect 4.2 units (see Chapters 5 and 6 for more information). You use the Setup menu to choose how you want the position values to display. (For information on how to use the Setup menu, see Chapter 20.)

When you press the Caps Lock key so that you can enter uppercase characters, Pos displays as POS. When you press the Num Lock key, the Pos indicator blinks on and off. Caps Lock and Num Lock work like toggle switches that you turn on and off. The number following the Pos indicator changes intensity or color in accordance with whatever text attribute you have chosen: bold, underline, double underline, italic, outline, shadow, small caps, redline, strikeout, superscript, subscript, fine, small, large, very large, or extra large (see Chapters 5 and 6 for an explanation of text attributes). Only a color monitor displays text attributes in various colors.

Using the Keyboard

Before you work with WordPerfect, you should know that computers come with several different types of keyboards. WordPerfect uses either the function keys or the pull-down menus to carry out many operations. Function keys are located in one of two places, depending on the type of keyboard you have.

The early Personal Computers and some PC XTs have a keyboard similar to the one shown in figure 1.3. Some Personal Computer AT keyboards are like the one shown in figure 1.4. PS/2s and other computers (including some Personal Computer ATs), which use newer processors like the 80286 and the 80386, use the Enhanced Keyboard similar to that shown in figure 1.5, although some newer Enhanced Keyboards have function keys located on the left side instead of across the top. The Enhanced Keyboard has two additional function keys that can be used by WordPerfect. The keyboards function in the same manner, but the layout of some keys is different.

Enhanced Keyboards may not work properly on older computers. Check with your dealer before replacing an XT keyboard with an Enhanced Keyboard.

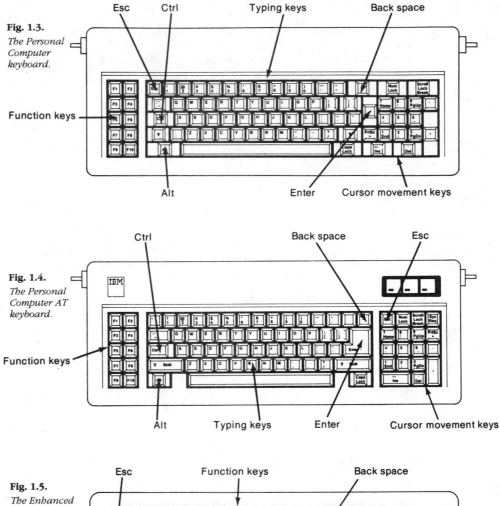

Fig. 1.3.
The Personal Computer keyboard.

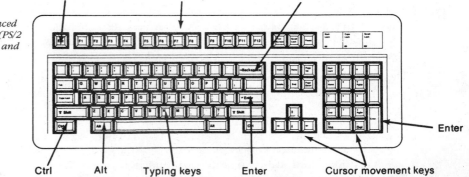

Fig. 1.4.
The Personal Computer AT keyboard.

Fig. 1.5.
The Enhanced Keyboard (PS/2 computers and others).

Keep in mind one critical but easily overlooked difference between composing with a typewriter and composing with WordPerfect: when typing normal text, you do not need to end lines at the right margin by pressing the Enter key. When you type text in WordPerfect and reach the end of a line, the text "wraps" automatically to the next line. If you're accustomed to using a typewriter, you'll find the word-wrap feature a genuine pleasure. Automatic word wrap makes it easy to create, edit, and revise your text. If you press the Enter key at the end of a line before WordPerfect has a chance to position the cursor at the beginning of the next line, you insert an unnecessary hard return (hidden code) that can wreak havoc with your text should you decide to insert or delete characters or to reformat your text in any way.

Reminder:

Because of WordPerfect's automatic word wrap, you do not have to press Enter at the end of each line.

WordPerfect uses the following three main areas of the keyboard:

- The function keys, 10 of which are at the left end of the keyboard on the IBM PC, XT, AT, and compatibles, and 12 of which are across the top of the Enhanced Keyboard shown in figure 1.5. (On the Enhanced Keyboard, WordPerfect uses all 12 function keys.)

- The alphanumeric, or "typing," keys, located in the center of the keyboard (the keys most familiar to you from your experience with typewriter keyboards).

- The numeric and cursor keys, found at the right end of the keyboard.

Using the Shift, Alt, and Control Keys

The Shift, Alt, and Control (Ctrl) keys are part of the alphanumeric keyboard. These keys are used with the function keys to carry out most of WordPerfect's commands.

The Shift key creates uppercase letters and other special characters, just as it does on a typewriter keyboard. Shift is used also with the function keys to carry out certain operations in WordPerfect.

The Alt and Ctrl keys don't do anything by themselves but work with the function keys, number keys, and letter keys to operate various commands in WordPerfect.

WordPerfect 5.1 enables you to change the built-in key assignments. Chapter 20 shows you how to use the alternative keyboard layouts supplied with version 5.1 and how to create your own personalized keyboards. For example, you might want to move the Help key from F3 to F1 or to reassign Esc as the Cancel key. If you're new to WordPerfect, become comfortable with the built-in keyboard before experimenting with the alternative keyboards or creating your own keyboard definitions.

Using the Function Keys

Central to understanding how WordPerfect operates is knowing what the function keys are used for. Each function key has four operations, depending on whether it is used alone or in combination with the Alt, Shift, and Ctrl keys. You press a function key to have WordPerfect carry out a command. The keyboard template you received with WordPerfect is color-coded in the following manner (see fig. 1.6):

Reminder:

Each function key is associated with four operations, executed through the use of the function key alone or in combination with the Alt, Shift, or Ctrl key.

- *Black* indicates what the key does alone. For example, when you press Help (F3), the opening Help screen is displayed.

- *Red* indicates that you press and hold the Ctrl key and also press one of the function keys. For example, pressing Spell (Ctrl-F2) brings up the Speller menu.

- *Green* indicates that you press and hold the Shift key and also press one of the function keys. For example, pressing Retrieve (Shift-F10) produces a status-line prompt that asks you for the name of the disk file you want to retrieve to the screen.

- *Blue* indicates that you press and hold the Alt key and also press one of the function keys. For example, pressing Block (Alt-F4 or F12) turns on the Block function.

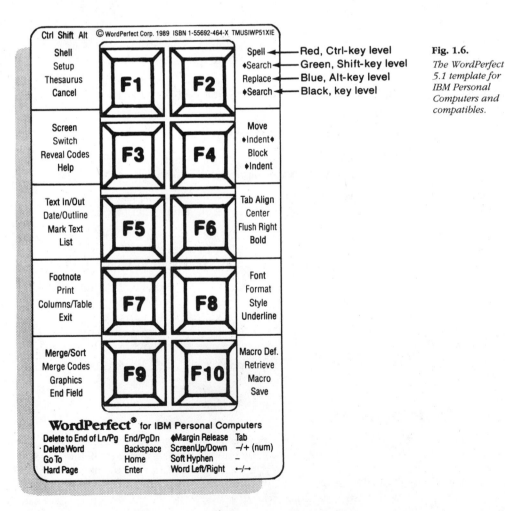

Fig. 1.6.

The WordPerfect 5.1 template for IBM Personal Computers and compatibles.

You can see an on-screen display of the function-key template if you press Help (F3) twice (see fig. 1.7).

> ## Tip
>
> If you misplace your template or the tear-out command card in the back of this book, use Shift-PrtSc to print the screen shown in figure 1.7 and then use red, green, and blue highlighters to create a temporary function-key template.

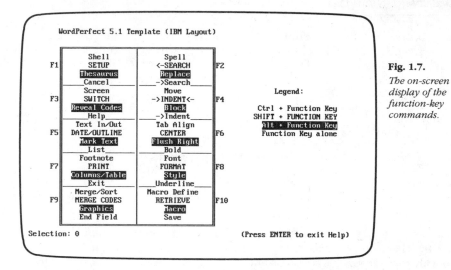

Fig. 1.7.

The on-screen display of the function-key commands.

Table 1.1 shows the function keys and what they do. If you're familiar with WordPerfect 5, you'll note that the function-key assignments have remained the same in version 5.1, except that Math/Columns (Alt-F7) has become Columns/Tables (Alt-F7), List Files (F5) has become List (F5), and Merge R (F9) has become End Field (F9).

Table 1.1
WordPerfect's Function-Key Commands

Key	Alone	Ctrl Key	Shift Key	Alt Key
F1	Cancel or Undelete	Shell (exit to DOS)	Setup	Thesaurus
F2	Forward Search	Spell	Backward Search	Replace
F3	Help	Screen	Switch	Reveal Codes
F4	Indent	Move	L/R indent	Block
F5	List	Text In/Out	Date/Outline	Mark Text
F6	Bold	Tab Align	Center	Flush Right
F7	Exit	Footnote	Print	Columns/Tables

Table 1.1 (continued)

Key	Alone	Ctrl Key	Shift Key	Alt Key
F8	Underline	Font	Format	Style
F9	End Field	Merge/Sort	Merge Codes	Graphics
F10	Save	Macro Define	Retrieve	Macro
F11*	Reveal Codes	—	—	—
F12*	Block	—	—	—

*Available only on the Enhanced Keyboard

When you press some of the function keys, such as Bold (F6) or Underline (F8), a "hidden" code for bolding or underlining text, respectively, is entered in the text. To turn off bolding or underlining, you may either press the appropriate key again or press the right-arrow key. Pressing other function keys gives you a status-line or a full-screen menu for selecting an option.

Pressing Cancel (F1) or Esc gets you out of most menus.

Using the Alphanumeric Keyboard

The alphanumeric keyboard will be most familiar to those who have used typewriters or who are just now making the transition from typewriters to word processing.

Reminder:

In WordPerfect, the keyboard works much like a typewriter keyboard. Certain keys, however, operate differently.

The keyboard works like a typewriter keyboard. For example, if you press and hold a key, the character is repeated across the screen until you release the key, as is the case with some typewriters. You use the Shift key to uppercase letters and access special characters above the number keys at the top of the keyboard, but Shift's real power in WordPerfect is that it can combine with the function keys, as described previously.

The Enter key, mentioned earlier, is used to insert a carriage return, or *hard return* (**[HRt]**), at the end of a line when automatic word wrap is not desired. In this sense, Enter works like the Return key on a typewriter, moving the cursor down one or more lines. Unlike the Return key on a typewriter, however, Enter inserts blank lines or breaks a line if you move the cursor into already typed text and press Enter. Note in figure 1.5 that the IBM PS/2 keyboard comes with two Enter keys.

You also press Enter when you want to initiate some commands in WordPerfect or when you want the system to recognize a menu option you've selected or data you've entered in a menu.

The space bar works very differently in WordPerfect. When you press the space bar, WordPerfect inserts a character space, pushing ahead any text that may follow the cursor. And if you press the Ins key on the numeric keypad (to enter Typeover mode) before pressing the space bar, the space bar wipes out any character to the left of the cursor, inserting a blank space in place of text. In WordPerfect you cannot simply press the space bar to move through a line of text, as you can with a typewriter. (To move through a line of text, you use the right- and left-arrow keys or a mouse if you have one.)

Yet another key that works differently in WordPerfect than on a typewriter is the Backspace key, sometimes represented on the keyboard by a left-pointing arrow. When you press this key, you delete text or hidden codes to the left of the cursor. Pressing the Ctrl key in combination with the Backspace key (Ctrl-Backspace) deletes a word at the cursor. Pressing the Home key and then the Backspace key deletes a word to the left of the cursor. (See Chapter 3 for an explanation of the many strategies WordPerfect provides for deleting text.)

> ### Tip
> To use Home with Backspace to delete the word immediately to the left of the cursor, you must press and release the Home key before you press the Backspace key. If you want to delete another word to the left of the cursor, you must repeat this procedure. Holding down the Home key while holding down the Backspace key or pressing it repeatedly erases the text to the left only one character at a time, which is what the Backspace key can do on its own.

Another key located in the alphanumeric section of the keyboard is the Tab key, which works in part like the Tab key on a typewriter keyboard. Each time you press Tab in WordPerfect, a hidden **[Tab]** code is inserted in the text, and the cursor moves across the screen a predefined distance that depends on how you've set the tab stops (the default is a tab stop every half-inch). But in WordPerfect, when you press the Ins key and then press Tab, you can tab through text without inserting a **[Tab]** code and bumping text ahead of the cursor.

Esc is used in the default keyboard configuration as the Repeat function, which enables you to repeat many actions, such as replaying a macro or putting a dash on the screen a specified number of times. When you press Esc, you see the following prompt on the status line:

```
Repeat Value = 8
```

You can change this value by entering a new one. The Repeat value can be permanently changed through the Setup menu (see Chapter 20). You can use the Repeat function to repeat a macro; move the cursor a specified number of characters, words, or lines; scroll the screen; or delete characters, words, or lines. The ALTRNAT keyboard definition provided with WordPerfect 5.1 assigns Help to F1, Esc to F3, and Cancel (F1) to the Esc key (see Chapter 20).

Using the Numeric Keypad

The keys in the numeric keypad at the far right of the keyboard move the cursor and scroll the text on-screen. Alternatively, you use some of these keys to enter numbers on-screen. When you press the Num Lock key, you can use the keys 0 through 9 to enter numbers; when Num Lock is off, the Home, End, PgUp, PgDn, and arrow keys move the cursor in various ways. If you are using an Enhanced Keyboard, you'll notice a second set of arrow keys. The gray minus (–) and gray plus (+) keys scroll the screen. Cursor movement is explained in detail in the following section.

Reminder:
Pressing Num Lock enables you to use the keys 0 through 9 to enter numbers.

Two additional keys on the numeric keypad are of critical importance: Ins and Del. When you want to switch to Typeover mode, which enables you to type over existing text so that you don't have to delete the old text first, you press Ins and begin typing. You'll know that Ins has been toggled "on" if you note the Typeover prompt visible on the status line.

On the Enhanced Keyboard, note that duplicate keys for Home, Page Up, Page Down, and End enable you to use the numeric keypad to enter numbers. Duplicate Insert and Delete keys are also provided on the Enhanced Keyboard.

The Del key, which you experiment and get comfortable with in Chapter 3, enables you to delete the character or hidden code on which the cursor resides. Del is also useful for deleting a highlighted block of text.

Moving the Cursor

WordPerfect comes with a number of keys or key combinations that enable you to move the cursor with precision within a file. Chief among these are the Home, PgUp, PgDn, GoTo (Ctrl-Home), and arrow keys. Precise cursor movement is especially important in positioning the cursor with respect to WordPerfect's hidden codes. (These are explained in another section.) Learning all the ways you can move the cursor through a document saves you much time in editing.

Table 1.2 summarizes the cursor-movement keys, many of which you'll explore and use in the chapters to come. (How to control the cursor with the mouse is discussed later in this chapter.) Keep in mind that you move the cursor through preexisting text or blank character spaces inserted by the space bar. Typing text or pressing Tab, Enter, or the space bar moves the cursor on a blank screen. Once you've begun a document, you can use the cursor-movement keys shown in table 1.2 to move the cursor.

Table 1.2
Cursor-Movement Keys

Key	Cursor Movement
Left (←) or right (→) arrow	One character space to the left or right
Up (↑) or down (↓) arrow	Up or down one line
Esc, *n*, ↑ or ↓ (*n* = any number)	*n* lines up or down
Ctrl← or Ctrl→	Beginning of the preceding or next word
Home, ←	Left edge of the screen or the beginning of the line
Home, →	Right edge of the screen or the end of the line
Home, Home, ←	Beginning of the line, just after any hidden codes
Home, Home, Home, ←	Beginning of the line, before any hidden codes

Table 1.2 (continued)

Key	Cursor Movement
Home, Home, → (or End)	Far right of the line
Home, ↑ (or Screen Up [gray minus key])	Top of the current screen
Home, ↓ (or Screen Down [gray plus key])	Bottom of the current screen
Ctrl-Home, ↑	Top of the current page
Ctrl-Home, ↓	Bottom of the current page
PgUp	Top of the preceding page
PgDn	Top of the next page
Esc, n, PgUp	n pages backward
Esc, n, PgDn	n pages forward
Home, Home, ↑	Top of the file
Home, Home, ↓	Bottom of the file
Ctrl-Home, n	Page number n
Ctrl-Home, x (x = any character)	Next occurrence of x (if it occurs within the next 2,000 characters)
Ctrl-Home, Ctrl-Home	Original cursor location before last major motion command was issued

Note: Ctrl-Home is known as the GoTo command.

Using Pull-Down Menus

With version 5.1, WordPerfect introduces an alternative interface: pull-down menus. Until now, users have been able to access WordPerfect menus only through the function keys. By providing pull-down menus, WordPerfect achieves several goals:

- Pull-down menus, grouped according to major categories of functions, make it easier for the occasional or new user to become familiar or productive with WordPerfect.

- Pull-down menus enable those who want to use a mouse with WordPerfect to make menu selections.

- Pull-down menus begin the process of evolution that will lead to OS/2 Presentation Manager versions of WordPerfect, which will operate in a graphical environment.

So that you can customize WordPerfect to suit yourself, the program enables you to choose to have the pull-down menu bar visible at all times or only when you want the menu bar visible. You also can choose to have a line separate the menu bar from the editing screen. You can further customize the pull-down menus by modifying the colors or attributes of the menu text or command letters.

The menu bar offers nine choices (see fig. 1.2). WordPerfect uses pull-down menus as a gateway for the regular menu system. For example, if you want to print a document, you can use the regular function-key sequence of Print (Shift-F7) to access the Print/Options screen from which you make your printing selection. With the pull-down menus, you choose **P**rint from the **F**ile menu to access the very same Print/Options screen.

Cue:

In some cases, using pull-down menus is faster than using the keyboard.

Sometimes pull-down menus contain terrific shortcuts for features that, under the function-key method, require several keystrokes. For example, to create a superscript with the function keys, you must perform three steps:

1. Press Font (Ctrl-F8).
2. Choose **S**ize (**1**).
3. Choose Su**p**rscpt (**1**).

You can accomplish the same task by accessing the **Fo**nt pull-down menu and selecting Su**p**erscript.

Because you can make so many selections with either the familiar function keys or the new pull-down menus, this book includes instructions for both methods. The book's emphasis, however, is on the function-key approach. Each time you see steps describing a procedure, the pull-down alternative, if available, is described after the function-key procedure. Even though you can access the pull-down menus without using a mouse, a mouse icon reminds you that the procedure described uses the pull-down menus.

Reminder:

To access the pull-down menus, click your mouse's right button, press Alt-=, or press and release the Alt key.

You can access the pull-down menus in three ways: If you have a mouse, you can click the right button, and the menu bar (if not already permanently visible) appears at the top of the screen (see fig. 1.2). If you don't have a mouse (or don't want to use it if you do), you can either press Alt-= or press and release the Alt key by itself. The default is Alt-=. To access the menu bar with the Alt key alone, you must select this alternative in Setup (see Chapter 20). In this book, you aren't reminded how to access the pull-down menus each time a procedure is described.

Because function keys combined with Alt can be used for many WordPerfect functions, and because many people use Alt-key macros, using the Alt key as an entree to the pull-down menus may be undesirable. Here's why: If you start to choose an Alt-key macro or an Alt-function-key command and change your mind—pressing only the Alt key—and then release the Alt key, the pull-down menu bar is at the top of the screen. Therefore, you may prefer the Alt-=default.

Once you have activated the menu bar, you can make choices with the mouse (see the next section, "Using the Mouse") or from the keyboard. To make selections from the keyboard, press the mnemonic letter for your choice. (The mnemonic letter, often the first letter of the command, is highlighted.) As an alternative to pressing a mnemonic letter, you can use the arrow keys; the right- and left-arrow keys traverse the menu bar, and the up- and down-arrow keys highlight the menu selections. Once your choice is highlighted, press Enter.

Some menus have submenus, also called *pop-out* menus. Menus that contain pop-out menus have an arrow to their right. Figure 1.8 shows the **F**ile pull-down menu and the Se**t**up pop-out menu contained within that pull-down menu.

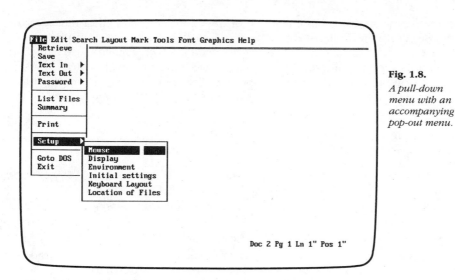

Fig. 1.8.
A pull-down menu with an accompanying pop-out menu.

If a menu item is in brackets, it is not available for selection. Usually the reason is that some other step needs to be taken first. For example, on the **E**dit pull-down menu, the **C**opy command is in brackets if text has not been previously blocked. Once text has been blocked, the **C**opy command is no longer bracketed and is available for use.

Reminder:
A menu item in brackets is unavailable for selection.

If you change your mind, you can back out of the pull-down menus one level at a time by pressing Esc, Cancel (F1), or the space bar. To back out of all the menus at once and remove the menu bar from the screen, press Exit (F7). If you are using the mouse, you can click the right button to exit; if some of the menus have been pulled down, clicking outside a menu also enables you to exit.

Using the Mouse

Accessing the pull-down menus is easier with a mouse than with the keyboard. You can easily choose items from pull-down menus by moving the mouse and *clicking* (quickly pressing and releasing) its buttons. Initially, moving the mouse makes a mouse pointer (a block cursor) appear on-screen; further movements produce corresponding on-screen movements of the mouse pointer, which enable you to make menu selections and block text. Pressing any key makes the mouse pointer disappear.

Although you can position the mouse pointer in blank areas of the screen, where there is neither text nor codes, clicking on a blank area places the mouse pointer at the last text character or code. If you are using a split screen and two windows, you can click on either one (Doc 1 or Doc 2) to move the cursor to the document in that window.

In macros, you can't position the cursor by using the mouse. If you use the mouse and pull-down menus to define macros, the commands are stored in the macro as normal keystrokes.

The mouse you are using has either two or three buttons; the kind of mouse you have doesn't matter. Buttons can be used in four basic ways: you can press and then quickly release a button (this process is called *clicking*, as mentioned earlier); you can quickly press and release the button twice (this process is called *double-clicking*); you can click and then hold a button down while moving the mouse (this process is called *dragging*); or you can click and release two (or more) buttons at the same time.

The following explains the operation of the left mouse button:

With the editing screen:
- Clicking positions the cursor.
- Clicking on a screen prompt (for example, clicking on the equal sign in `Type = to change default Dir`) is the same as pressing the specified key itself.
- Clicking or dragging in the Reveal Codes portion of the screen is impossible.
- Dragging turns on Block—as if you'd pressed Block (Alt-F4 or F12). Position the mouse pointer, press the left button, and hold it down as you drag the mouse over the text you want to block. Once you have blocked the text, you can perform such operations on it as bolding, underlining, and deleting. If you drag beyond the top or bottom edge, the text scrolls.

With pull-down menus:
- Clicking on any of the nine menu bar items makes that menu's choices visible.
- Clicking on a menu item selects that item.
- Dragging across the pull-down menu bar makes the menu for each of the nine options drop down.
- Dragging down a pull-down menu highlights each choice as you move onto it. If you highlight a menu item that has a pop-out menu, the menu will pop out. You can then drag down that menu to highlight your choice. Releasing the mouse button chooses the highlighted selection.

With other menus:
- Clicking selects menu choices. If you have turned on Assisted Mouse Pointer Movement from Setup, and if the menu list would normally place the cursor at the bottom of the screen for either typed input or a menu choice, WordPerfect will move the mouse pointer to the bottom of the screen. Otherwise, you need to reposition the mouse cursor for each prompt.
- When a prompt line for entering values appears, clicking positions the cursor on the line.

With lists:
- Double-clicking is the same as pressing Enter. For example, after choosing List **F**iles from the **F**ile pull-down menu, you can either double-click `Dir C:\WP51\*.*` or press Enter to accept the default file filter.
- Double-clicking on a file name in List **F**iles causes the file to be displayed, as if you'd highlighted the file and chosen **L**ook (**6**).

The following explains the operation of the right mouse button:

With the editing screen:

- If you have turned on Assisted Mouse Pointer Movement from Setup, and if the menu bar is not permanently visible, clicking makes it appear and places the mouse pointer on the word `File` on the menu bar.

- If you have turned on Assisted Mouse Pointer Movement from Setup, and if the menu bar is permanently visible, clicking places the mouse pointer on the word `File` on the menu bar.

- Dragging above, below, to the left of, or to the right of the visible screen scrolls the text (assuming that there is something to scroll to).

With pull-down menus and lists:
- Clicking is the same as pressing Exit (F7).

With other menus:
- Clicking is the same as pressing Exit (F7).

The following explains the effect of pressing multiple buttons and explains the operation of a three-button mouse:

- On a two-button mouse, holding down one button while clicking the other button is the same as pressing Cancel (F1).

- On a three-button mouse, clicking the middle button is the same as pressing Cancel (F1).

Understanding WordPerfect's Hidden Codes

Fundamental to understanding WordPerfect is the concept of "hidden" codes. Many times, when you press a key in WordPerfect, a hidden code is inserted into the text. Such codes can indicate tab spaces, margin settings, carriage returns (or hard returns), indents, and a host of other information that WordPerfect needs to manage your documents. Some hidden codes contain information for headers or footers, styles, footnotes or endnotes, font changes, or document comments. Other hidden codes are used to turn on and turn off a feature, such as math or columns. Many additional hidden codes come in pairs, such as the codes for bold, underline, italic, print attributes, and so forth. The first code in a pair acts as a toggle switch to turn on a feature; the second code in a pair serves to turn it off. Typical examples include the paired codes for bolding text, as shown in figure 1.9, the Reveal Codes screen for a legal document.

Reminder:
WordPerfect's hidden codes are special instructions pertaining to such matters as format and style.

Note the paired codes for bolding (**[BOLD]** and **[bold]**) the title. Also note the **[HRt]** (hard return) codes, which indicate each time the Enter key was pressed; the **[SRt]** (soft return) codes, which indicate word wrap; and the **[Tab]** code inserted when the Tab key was pressed to indent the first paragraph.

Don't worry too much about WordPerfect's hidden codes just yet. It's enough for now to know something about the concept of hidden codes, how these codes become a part of your document, and how you can see them in the Reveal Codes

(Alt-F3 or F11) screen. In Chapter 3, when you are actively involved in editing a document, you see the full range of WordPerfect's hidden codes. You learn strategies for examining, searching for, inserting, and editing codes. You learn also how to avoid problems with codes. To recall Pete Peterson's remark about WordPerfect as akin to a "well- mannered houseguest," these hidden codes stay out of your way, thereby freeing you to concentrate on your writing.

Fig. 1.9.

A screen showing Reveal Codes.

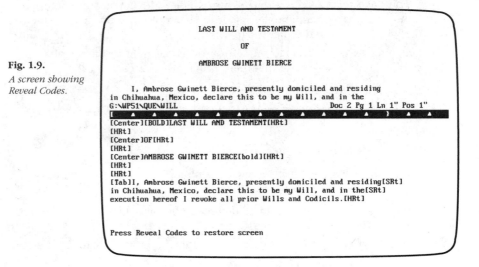

```
                          LAST WILL AND TESTAMENT

                                    OF

                          AMBROSE GWINETT BIERCE


           I, Ambrose Gwinett Bierce, presently domiciled and residing
      in Chihuahua, Mexico, declare this to be my Will, and in the
G:\WP51\QUE\WILL                              Doc 2 Pg 1 Ln 1" Pos 1"
[Center][BOLD]LAST WILL AND TESTAMENT[HRt]
[HRt]
[Center]OF[HRt]
[HRt]
[Center]AMBROSE GWINETT BIERCE[bold][HRt]
[HRt]
[HRt]
[Tab]I, Ambrose Gwinett Bierce, presently domiciled and residing[SRt]
in Chihuahua, Mexico, declare this to be my Will, and in the[SRt]
execution hereof I revoke all prior Wills and Codicils.[HRt]


Press Reveal Codes to restore screen
```

WordPerfect novices seem to experience the most trouble with WordPerfect's invisible network of codes. Once you master the concept and know how to search for hidden codes, navigate the Reveal Codes screen, and learn to edit in Reveal Codes, you'll prevent many problems that incorrect or inappropriate codes can cause.

Using the Help Feature

Reminder:

Press Help (F3) to access WordPerfect's on-line Help feature.

At almost any time, you can get information on many of WordPerfect's commands or cursor movements by pressing Help (F3) (see fig. 1.10). If you are using a diskette-based system, WordPerfect's Help file, WPHELP.FIL, is located on the WordPerfect 1 diskette. If you get an error message indicating that WordPerfect cannot find the Help files, insert the WordPerfect 1 diskette into a diskette drive, close the drive door, and type the drive letter (*a*, for example). Help can now be accessed.

With Help, you can press any letter to get a list of WordPerfect features from A to Z and the keystrokes necessary to activate those features, or you can press any function-key combination to get an explanation of that key's operation (see fig. 1.11). You must press Help (F3) first before you press any subsequent keys. Note that the Format (Shift-F8) Help screen in figure 1.11 leads to various other Help screens that provide more detail for Line, Page, Document, and Other formatting.

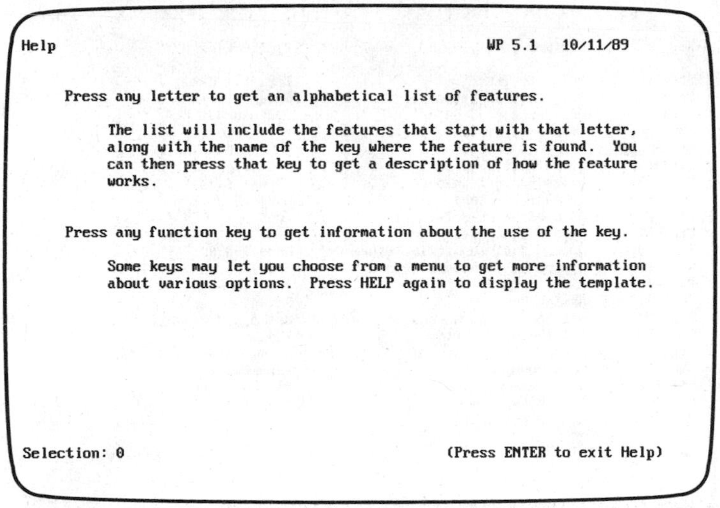

```
Help                                    WP 5.1   10/11/89


     Press any letter to get an alphabetical list of features.

          The list will include the features that start with that letter,
          along with the name of the key where the feature is found.  You
          can then press that key to get a description of how the feature
          works.


     Press any function key to get information about the use of the key.

          Some keys may let you choose from a menu to get more information
          about various options.  Press HELP again to display the template.








Selection: 0                           (Press ENTER to exit Help)
```

Fig. 1.10.
The opening Help screen.

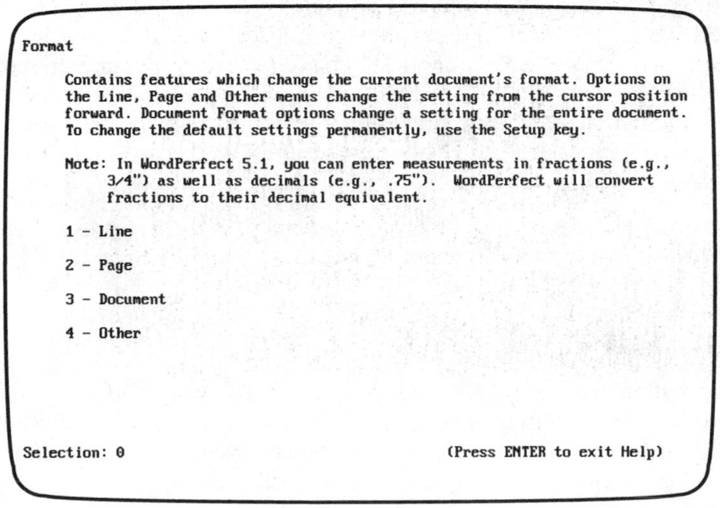

```
Format

     Contains features which change the current document's format. Options on
     the Line, Page and Other menus change the setting from the cursor position
     forward. Document Format options change a setting for the entire document.
     To change the default settings permanently, use the Setup key.

     Note: In WordPerfect 5.1, you can enter measurements in fractions (e.g.,
        3/4") as well as decimals (e.g., .75").  WordPerfect will convert
        fractions to their decimal equivalent.

     1 - Line

     2 - Page

     3 - Document

     4 - Other




Selection: 0                           (Press ENTER to exit Help)
```

Fig. 1.11.
The Format Help screen.

You can press a key such as Esc or any of the cursor-movement keys to get an explanation of what that key does in WordPerfect. If you want an alphabetical listing of WordPerfect's features, press Help (F3) and then press a letter key. For example, to view all the listings for *A*, press Help (F3) and then press the A key. You soon see the screen in figure 1.12.

To exit from any Help screen, press Enter or the space bar. Warning: Pressing Exit (F7) while in Help does not make you exit from Help; it only shows you a Help screen about Exit.

Reminder:
Press Enter or the space bar to exit from a Help screen.

Fig. 1.12.

The alphabetical Help listing for A.

```
Key              Feature [a]                      Keystrokes

Shft-F8          Absolute Tabs                    Format,1,8,t,1
Shft-F1          Acceleration Factor              Setup,1,4
Ctrl-F5          Add Password                     Text In/Out,2
Shft-F8          Advance (Printer's Platen)       Format,4,1
Ctrl-PgUp        Advanced Macros                  Macro Commands
Ctrl-F6          Align Text on Tabs               Tab Align
Shft-F8          Align/Decimal Character          Format,4,3
Ctrl-F9          Alphabetize text                 Merge/Sort,2
Ctrl-F8          Appearance of Printed Text       Font
Ctrl-F1          Append, Clipboard                Shell,3
Ctrl-F4          Append Text to a File (Block On)  Move,1-3,4
Ctrl-F1          Append to Clipboard (Block On)   Shell
Ctrl-F5          ASCII Text File                  Text In/Out,1
Shft-F1          Assign Keys                      Setup,5
Shft-F1          Attributes, On-screen            Setup,2,1
Ctrl-F8          Attributes, Printed              Font
Alt-F5           Authorities, Table of            Mark Text
Shft-F8          Auto Hyphenation                 Format,1,1
Shift-F5         Auto Paragraph Numbering         Date/Outline,5
Alt-F5           Auto Reference                   Mark Text,1
More... Type A to continue

Selection: 0                                      (Press ENTER to exit Help)
```

5.1 New with WordPerfect 5.1 is context-sensitive help. You can now summon appropriate help from anywhere in the program, not just from the main editing screen. For example, if you are in Setup and are changing mouse parameters but can't remember what "Double Click Interval" means, you can make all your other changes up to the final choice and then press Help (F3); the Help screen "Mouse - Double Click Interval" appears. Read about the feature; then press Enter or the space bar to return to where you were.

Once in Help, whether Help is regular or context-sensitive, you must press Enter or the space bar to leave; any other key simply brings up another Help screen.

Taking the Tutorial

Reminder:

WordPerfect Tutor consists of six lessons designed to acquaint you with some of the program's basic features.

WordPerfect Corporation has provided a self-paced tutorial, WordPerfect Tutor, which you can work through from beginning to end in approximately 2 1/2 hours. You don't have to complete the lessons in any particular order, nor do you have to finish a lesson to exit from the tutorial. Most of the lessons range from 12 to 20 minutes.

The tutorial begins with an introduction that explains the WordPerfect screen and the use of the keyboard. The introduction is followed by six lessons that closely parallel the first half of the "Fundamentals" section of the *WordPerfect Workbook* and use the same document examples. Because these lessons build on each other and parallel the *Workbook*, you should probably complete them in sequence.

In Lesson One, you create and print a personal note. You also learn how to clear the screen without saving the note. In Lesson Two, you type, print, and save the first draft of a letter. You also learn how to move the cursor, do some simple editing, and display a list of files in the List Files screen. In Lesson Three, you create a short memo template and learn some simple formatting and function-key commands. In Lesson Four, you retrieve and continue working on the letter you created in the second lesson. This lesson introduces you to some basic editing procedures and lets you view the letter on disk, using the **L**ook feature (**6**) in List (F5). Lesson Five resumes work on the memo created in Lesson Three. You retrieve the memo template and fill it in. In this lesson, you also learn how to underline text and edit while in the Reveal Codes screen. Lesson Six concludes the introduction to WordPerfect's fundamentals by having you complete a final draft of the letter begun in Lesson Two and then run the Speller.

After you complete the beginning lessons, you can move to the advanced lessons, which cover merge operations and the creation of a Table of Authorities. In two separate merge lessons, you learn about merge files and codes, how to run a merge, and how to deal with blank lines in merge. The first lesson concludes with a quiz on fields, records, and merge operations. If you are new to WordPerfect's merge operations, you may want to work through these two lessons. The final lesson takes you through the steps of defining, marking, and generating a Table of Authorities.

Note: The tutorial has not been extensively revised from version 5. Most new features, including pull-down menus and the mouse, are not covered in the tutorial.

You must exit from WordPerfect to run the Tutor. You cannot simply use Shell (Ctrl-F1) to exit temporarily to DOS from WordPerfect and then run the Tutor. If you do so, you are likely to get an ERROR: Insufficient memory message.

Running the Tutorial on a Dual-Floppy System

Before you can run the tutorial on a two-floppy system, make certain that the computer is on and that DOS has been loaded (the DOS prompt, A> or B>, should be displayed). To run the tutorial, follow these steps:

1. Insert the WordPerfect 1 diskette into drive A.
2. Insert the Learning diskette into drive B.
3. If the current drive is not B, change the default directory to B by typing *b:* and pressing Enter.
4. At the B> prompt, type *tutor* to load the tutorial.
5. At the prompt, type your first name and press Enter.

The sign-on screen for the Tutor is displayed (see fig. 1.13).

After you type your first name and press Enter, the Tutor's main menu is displayed (see fig. 1.14). To find out the approximate time for completing a lesson, use the up- and down-arrow keys to move the highlight bar to a lesson; then press Help (F3).

After you complete the beginning lessons, you can move to the advanced lessons by using the arrow keys to highlight Advanced Lessons on the menu and pressing Enter. The menu of advanced lessons is shown in figure 1.15.

When you finish a session, a check mark appears on the menu next to the item you have completed. You can exit from any lesson and return to the opening menu by pressing Help (F3).

To exit from the Tutor, move the highlight bar to EXIT and press Enter. You are returned to the DOS prompt.

Fig. 1.13.
The sign-on screen for the Tutor program.

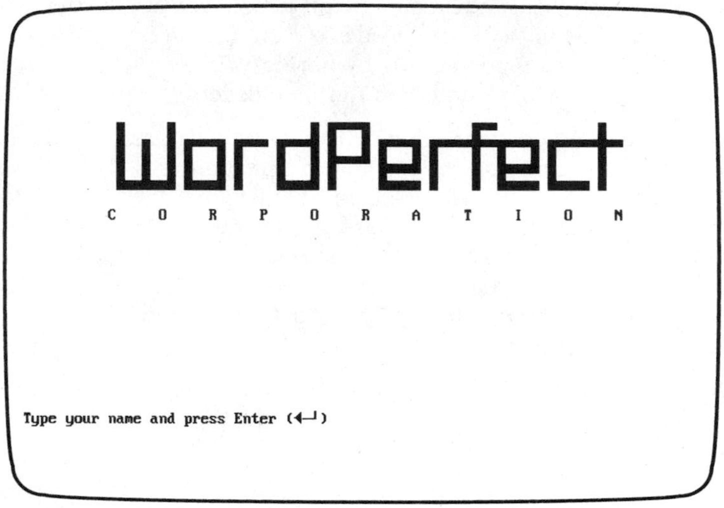

WordPerfect
CORPORATION

Type your name and press Enter (←⏎)

Fig. 1.14.
The Tutor main menu.

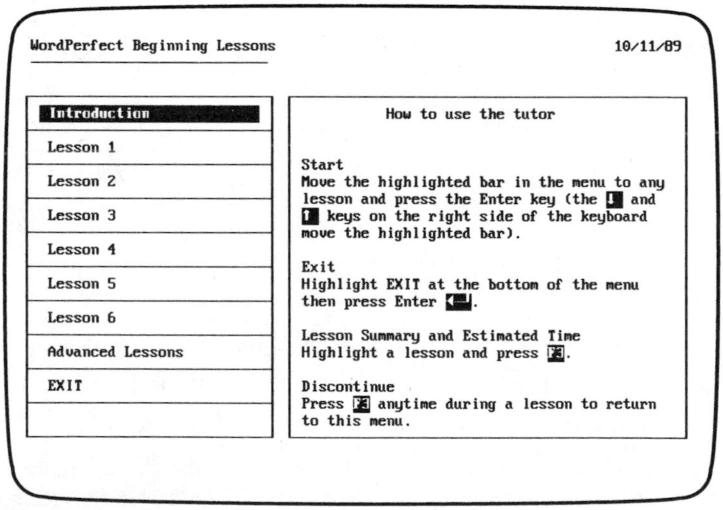

WordPerfect Beginning Lessons   10/11/89

| Introduction |
| Lesson 1 |
| Lesson 2 |
| Lesson 3 |
| Lesson 4 |
| Lesson 5 |
| Lesson 6 |
| Advanced Lessons |
| EXIT |

How to use the tutor

Start
Move the highlighted bar in the menu to any lesson and press the Enter key (the ▯ and ▯ keys on the right side of the keyboard move the highlighted bar).

Exit
Highlight EXIT at the bottom of the menu then press Enter ◁.

Lesson Summary and Estimated Time
Highlight a lesson and press ▣.

Discontinue
Press ▣ anytime during a lesson to return to this menu.

```
WordPerfect Advanced Lessons

┌─────────────────────┐  ┌──────────────────────────────────────┐
│ Mail Merge          │  │        How to use the tutor          │
│                     │  │                                      │
│ More Mail Merge     │  │ Start                                │
│                     │  │ Move the highlighted bar in the menu to any │
│ Table of Authorities│  │ lesson and press the Enter key (the ▮ and │
│                     │  │ ▮ keys on the right side of the keyboard │
│ Beginning Lessons   │  │ move the highlighted bar).           │
│                     │  │                                      │
│ EXIT                │  │ Exit                                 │
│                     │  │ Highlight EXIT at the bottom of the menu │
│                     │  │ then press Enter ⏎.                  │
│                     │  │                                      │
│                     │  │ Lesson Summary and Estimated Time    │
│                     │  │ Highlight a lesson and press ▣.      │
│                     │  │                                      │
│                     │  │ Discontinue                          │
│                     │  │ Press ▣ anytime during a lesson to return │
│                     │  │ to this menu.                        │
└─────────────────────┘  └──────────────────────────────────────┘
```

Fig. 1.15.

The Tutor menu of advanced lessons.

Running the Tutorial on a Hard Disk System

Before you can run the tutorial on a hard disk, make certain that the computer is on and that DOS has been loaded.

To run the tutorial, follow these steps:

1. If you followed the documentation's recommendation and copied the Learn files to a subdirectory you created and named \WP51\LEARN, then change directories to the \WP51\LEARN subdirectory by typing *cd \wp51\learn* and pressing Enter.

   If you didn't copy the Learn files to the hard disk, you must load those files by using the installation program. See Appendix A for information on how to install the tutorial files on your hard drive.

2. At the C:\WP51\LEARN prompt, type *tutor* to load the tutorial.

3. At the Tutor's sign-on screen, type your first name at the prompt and press Enter. The Tutor main menu is displayed (see fig. 1.14).

When you finish a session, a check mark appears on the menu next to the item you have completed. After you complete the beginning lessons, you can move to the advanced lessons by using the arrow keys to highlight Advanced Lessons on the menu and pressing Enter. You can exit from any lesson and return to the opening menu by pressing Help (F3).

To exit from the Tutor, move the highlight bar to EXIT and press Enter. You are returned to the DOS prompt.

Exiting from WordPerfect

Follow these steps to exit from WordPerfect:

1. Press Exit (F7).

   ▭▣ Access the **F**ile pull-down menu and select E**x**it.

   The status line displays the following prompt:

   ```
   Save document? No (Yes)
   ```

2. Select **N** to exit without saving. (If you have been editing a document and want to save your changes, select **Y** to save the document; then name the file, press Enter, and exit.)

   The status line displays the following prompt:

   ```
   Exit WP? No (Yes)
   ```

   Note: At this point, you can press Cancel (F1) to avoid quitting the program and keep WordPerfect running.

3. Select **Y** to exit from WordPerfect.

Summary

In this preparatory chapter, you've gotten a brief introduction to WordPerfect 5.1 and the hardware necessary to run the program. The following are among the important topics covered:

❏ The procedure for starting, or "booting," WordPerfect

❏ The function of the status line

❏ The use of the Enter key in WordPerfect

❏ The use of function keys in WordPerfect

❏ The purpose of hidden codes

❏ Different ways to move the cursor

❏ The function of the mouse

❏ WordPerfect's context-sensitive on-line Help feature

❏ The WordPerfect Tutor

In the next two chapters, you have an opportunity to put to work many of the ideas you've learned in this preparatory chapter. Chapters 2 and 3 cover creating, editing, saving, retrieving, and printing a simple document.

2

Creating a Document

Charles O. Stewart III is a product specialist and staff writer for Que Corporation. Stewart coauthored *WordPerfect Tips, Tricks, and Traps* and contributed to *Using WordPerfect 5*.

If you read Chapter 1, you already know a few WordPerfect fundamentals, such as how to start the program, what information the editing screen gives you, how to use the keyboard and mouse, how to access pull-down menus, how to take the tutorial, and how to exit the program. With that introduction to WordPerfect, you're now ready to learn more about how to create memos, short notes, letters, reports—any kind of document—with WordPerfect.

In this chapter, you learn in much more detail how to use your computer and WordPerfect to compose the documents you need. After an introduction to writing with a word processor, you look at procedures for the following:

- Entering text
- Moving the cursor through a document
- Using function keys or the mouse to give commands
- Selecting menu options by number, letter, or with the mouse
- Using Cancel (F1) or the mouse to back out of a menu or cancel a prompt
- Using both document windows
- Printing a document
- Naming and saving a document

As a bonus, this chapter provides some advice on how you can use WordPerfect to plan and draft your document. If you have trouble getting started or suffer from writer's block, you see how word processing can be of tremendous assistance. This advice is based on research into what is known about how writing habits change with word processors. If you're used to composing on a typewriter or by hand and are new to word processing, you find that many of these tips help you realize the benefits of word processing immediately! Even old hands at word processing can come away from this chapter with more than a few new ideas for getting started.

> ### Reminder
>
> If you use a mouse with WordPerfect 5.1, you can click the right button to display the pull-down menus, and then select the desired option. You also can press Alt-= to access the pull-down menus, and then press the appropriate letter of the desired option. For all instructions, assume that if a block is required to activate a pull-down menu option, the text has been blocked before the pull-down menu is accessed. Instructions for pull-down menus and the mouse are marked with the mouse icon. For more information about the mouse, see Chapter 1.

Writing with a Word Processor

Reminder:

Research reveals that word processing makes people more enthusiastic about writing.

Writing is never easy, even for experienced writers. The good fortune for those who must write is that a word processor can make writing easier. Researchers looking at what happens when people learn to write with word processors have discovered a heartening fact: people who once dreaded writing become much more positive about it after they learn to write with a word processor.

As you read in Chapter 1, composing with a word processor is different than composing in longhand or at the typewriter. Ann Berthoff writes that "composing— putting things together—is a continuum, a process that continues without any sharp breaks."[1] WordPerfect is perfectly matched to this process, allowing you to "put things together" as well as to take them apart with ease at any stage of the writing process. Rearranging, deleting, or embellishing your words on-screen is far easier than doing so at the typewriter or in longhand.

Reminder:

The "fluid" medium of word processing enables you to record your thoughts almost as fast as they occur.

With a word processor, you can get words on-screen as fast as you can type them, so you are freed from the frustration of not being able to record thoughts almost as fast as they occur. Researchers tell us that short-term memory lasts about five seconds—all the more reason to have a tool that enables you to record your ideas quickly. You can use a word processor across the full range of writing tasks—to create, format, revise, edit, save, retrieve, and print documents. As you see in Chapter 4, WordPerfect lets you save text in *blocks* (words, sentences, or paragraphs) for later retrieval and consideration.

Reminder:

Revising a document is much easier with a word processor.

Unlike a typewriter, a word processor lets you alter with great freedom what you write. With a word processor, you easily can insert new words, delete ones you don't want, or move up and down through a document to see what you have written. Because altering what you've written can be accomplished so effortlessly, you can focus on first getting words on-screen.

By freeing you from much of the drudgery of writing, WordPerfect gives you more time to be creative or to rethink your work. If poor handwriting or the tedium of recopying your work were once obstacles to writing, you find that WordPerfect gives you new enthusiasm for drafting, reworking, and polishing your text.

With WordPerfect's many formatting features, you can change the look of the text on the page, as you see in subsequent chapters. You can change margins, indent text, vary line spacing, control word spacing, put text in columns or tables, create headers and footers, center text, and so on. In this chapter, though, you focus on the built-in settings that WordPerfect assumes most users use (at least initially). Later you learn how to modify these defaults to meet your needs.

Understanding WordPerfect's Built-In Settings

Before you even put fingers to keys and begin typing, WordPerfect has been at work for you. Recall from your experience with a typewriter that you must set margins, line spacing, and tabs, for example, before you begin composing. With WordPerfect, you don't have to make any formatting decisions before you begin unless the preset values do not suit you.

Reminder:
WordPerfect comes with a number of default settings—for margins, page numbers, tabs, base font or basic character style, line spacing, and other features.

You should be familiar with the basic default settings before you begin writing. Subsequent chapters, especially those devoted to formatting, printing, and desktop publishing, explore the many ways you can alter the look of a document. For now, though, assume that the default settings are acceptable.

Table 2.1 lists just a few of WordPerfect's many built-in settings. To change any of these settings, see Chapter 20. (Don't worry if terms like *base font* and *form size* are unfamiliar to you at this time. You learn about them in later chapters.)

Table 2.1
Some of WordPerfect's Built-In Settings

Setting	Preset Value
Margins	1-inch top, bottom, left, and right
Tabs	Every 0.5 inch
Base font	Depends on printer
Line spacing	Single-spaced
Page number	None
Justification	Full (both left and right margins)
Hyphenation	Off
Form size	Letter-size paper (8 1/2-by-11 inches)
Date format	Month (word), day, year (all four digits); example: July 4, 1989
Automatic backup of files	None
File name displayed on status line	On (after you save or retrieve a document)

Entering Text

Reminder:

WordPerfect doesn't require that you give the file a name before you enter an editing screen and begin typing.

As you may remember from Chapter 1, WordPerfect's uncluttered editing screen resembles a blank sheet of paper inserted into a typewriter. Unlike some other word processors, however, WordPerfect doesn't require that you give the file a name before you enter an editing screen and begin typing. In fact, unless you want to save your work to disk, you don't ever have to give the text a file name.

If you haven't started WordPerfect and you want to follow along in this chapter, see the steps for starting WordPerfect in Chapter 1.

With the "clean" editing screen you can see as much of the text as possible. With some exceptions, what you see on-screen is what prints. In word processing jargon, WordPerfect's editing screen comes close to WYSIWYG (pronounced "wiz-ee-wig"), or What-You-See-Is-What-You-Get. The Hercules graphics cards mentioned in Chapter 1 produce an editing screen even closer to true WYSIWYG by displaying italics and different type sizes.

If you have WordPerfect running and want to get started right away, type the following paragraph. (Remember: you don't need to press Enter at the end of each line. WordPerfect "wraps" the text to the next line as your words reach the right margin.)

> *Think of a place that you can either visit or remember quite clearly, a place to which you have strong reactions. Write a personal description of it, attempting to re-create for your reader the experience of seeing or entering the place you've chosen to write about.*

Reminder:

Unlike a typewriter, WordPerfect doesn't require that you press Enter to end a line; text wraps automatically.

After you type a few words, look at the Pos indicator on the status line. This value increases as you type and as the cursor moves horizontally across the line to the right. Unlike a typewriter, WordPerfect doesn't require that you press Enter to end a line. Instead, if WordPerfect cannot fit a word on a line, it inserts a formatting code called a *soft return*. This code ends the line and "wraps" the word to the next line. This feature is often referred to as *wordwrap*.

Inserting Blank Lines

To end a paragraph or insert blank lines in the text, press the Enter key. If you're following the preceding example, when you come to the end of the last sentence, press Enter twice and type this second paragraph:

> *Details are essential in picturing whatever is described. Try to think of rich and suggestive words and phrases that will evoke emotional responses in your readers. Appeal to the senses. Use concrete nouns and active verbs.*

Your screen should look like the one in figure 2.1. When you press Enter the first time, WordPerfect inserts a hard-return code. When you press Enter the second time, WordPerfect inserts another hard-return code, creating a blank line in the text.

```
Think of a place that you can either visit or remember quite
clearly, a place to which you have strong reactions.  Write a
personal description of it, attempting to re-create for your
reader the experience of seeing or entering the place you've
chosen to write about.

Details are essential in picturing whatever is described.  Try to
think of rich and suggestive words and phrases that will evoke
emotional responses in your readers.  Appeal to the senses.  Use
concrete nouns and active verbs.
```

Fig. 2.1.

Inserting a blank line with the Enter key.

Moving the Cursor with the Keyboard

In Chapter 1 you learned that you can move the cursor through a document in one of two ways: with the keys on the numeric keypad or with the mouse. This section explains how to use the keyboard to move the cursor. To learn how to use the mouse to move the cursor, see "Moving the Cursor with the Mouse" later in this chapter.

The Enhanced Keyboard has a separate set of cursor-movement keys on the numeric keypad (you use these keys with the Num Lock key to type numbers). WordPerfect provides various ways to move the cursor through the text or to "scroll" a document. When you think of scrolling a document, imagine a continuous sheet of paper that you can roll up or down. You can, however, view only 24 lines of this text at a time, depending on your monitor (some monitors let you view more than 24 lines). The sections that follow explain the various ways to move the cursor around in the document.

Moving from Character to Character

Moving from character to character represents the smallest increment in which you can move the cursor. When you want to make small editing changes or position the cursor with respect to WordPerfect's hidden codes, this method is quite useful, but it's too slow if you want to move rapidly through large portions of text.

To move from character to character, use the following keys:

- Press the left arrow (←) to move one character left.
- Press the right arrow (→) to move one character right.

Move the cursor several characters into the last word, *verbs*, of the passage you just typed. Press and release the left arrow several times and notice the cursor's movement. If you hold down the arrow key, the cursor continues to move across the line. Notice that if you press the left arrow and reach the beginning of the line, the cursor moves to the end of the preceding line. Similarly, if you press the right arrow and reach the end of the line, the cursor moves to the beginning of the next line. You will soon find that, when it comes to cursor movement, codes are treated like characters. If you have hidden codes in the document, and you press the left or right arrow, the cursor may not appear to move. What is happening is that the cursor is moving through the hidden code.

You cannot move the cursor through "dead space" (space with no text or codes) beyond where you stop typing. Unless you press the Enter key or the space bar after the text you type, the cursor does not move through the "dead space."

Moving from Word to Word

Sometimes you want to move into a sentence quickly to edit a word, add text, enter a formatting code, or make some other sort of change. In WordPerfect, a *word* is any group of characters followed by a space, tab, indent, align, center, flush-right, or hard-return code. To move from word to word, use the following key combinations:

- Press Ctrl-right arrow (→) to move from anywhere in a word to the word to the right.
- Press Ctrl-left arrow (←) to move from the beginning of a word to the beginning of the word to the left.

Note an important difference between Ctrl-right arrow (→) and Ctrl-left arrow (←): when the cursor is anywhere other than under the first character in a word and you press Ctrl-left arrow (←), the cursor moves to the beginning of *that* word, not to the beginning of the preceding word.

Moving from Line to Line

You can move the cursor vertically from line to line, up and down the document. With this method of scrolling, you can examine a document carefully line by line and reformat as you add or delete text.

- Press the up arrow (↑) to move the cursor up a line.
- Press the down arrow (↓) to move the cursor down a line.

These keys repeat if you hold them. You can move up or down several lines at a time by pressing and holding the up or down arrow. You can move one line at a time by pressing and releasing the up or down arrow.

Moving to the End of the Line or the Edge of the Screen

Many times you want to move the cursor from some position within a line to the end of the line or the edge of the screen. With most screens, you can see 80 characters of text. If you're using the default left and right margins of one inch, and if the base font size is equivalent to 10 pitch, the lines extend from the left edge of the screen 65 characters across, making all the text visible. If you reduce the margins or change to a smaller font, the lines extend beyond the right or left edges of the screen and are not completely visible.

- Press Home then left arrow (←) to move the cursor to the beginning of the line or the left edge of the screen, whichever comes first.
- Press Home then right arrow (→) to move the cursor to the end of the line or the right edge of the screen, whichever comes first. (You also can press the End key.)

If you change margins and text "runs off" the screen, do the following:

- Press Home, Home, left arrow (←) to move the cursor to the beginning of the line, just right of any hidden codes. (Chapter 3 explains how to edit hidden codes.)
- Press Home, Home, right arrow (→) to move to the far right of the line.

The cursor's position with respect to hidden codes becomes important when you delete, enter, or examine hidden codes. To move the cursor to a position at the beginning of a line and before any hidden codes, press Home, Home, Home, left arrow (←).

Tip

You can reassign keys on the keyboard to different functions. If you're just beginning to use WordPerfect, you may be satisfied with the default or original key assignments. If you have an Enhanced Keyboard or an IBM PS/2 machine, however, you may want to select the ENHANCED keyboard definition. When you select this keyboard, you can press Home to move the cursor to the beginning of the line, just before any hidden codes. The function of Home by itself is moved to the 5 key on the numeric keypad.

The ENHANCED keyboard definition also provides keyboard shortcuts for moving the cursor up or down by sentence or paragraph. For an explanation of keyboard definitions, creating keyboard definitions, and selecting keyboard definitions, see Chapter 20.

With the sample text on-screen, use the appropriate arrow keys to move the cursor to *can* in the middle of the first line of the first paragraph. Then perform these steps:

1. Press Home and right arrow (→). The cursor moves to the end of the line or the edge of the screen.
2. Press Home and left arrow (←). The cursor moves to the beginning of the line, under the *T* of *Think*.

You also can use the End key to move the cursor to the end of a line. With the cursor anywhere in a line, press End. The cursor moves to the line's end.

Remember that if the text "runs off" the screen, you can press Home, Home, and left or right arrow to reach the beginning or the end of the line.

Reminder:
Move to the first or last character of a line that scrolls off the screen by pressing Home, Home, and left or right arrow.

Moving to the Top or Bottom of the Screen

You see how easy it is to move the cursor horizontally across a line of text. Here are a couple ways to move the cursor up and down the screen, 24 lines at a time:

- Press the Screen Up key on the numeric keypad (the gray minus sign, –) to move the cursor to the top of the screen. If your keyboard does not have a Screen Up key, press Home-up arrow (↑).

- Press the Screen Down key on the numeric keypad (the gray plus sign, +) to move the cursor to the bottom of the screen. If your keyboard does not have a Screen Down key, press Home-down arrow (↓).

Note: On some keyboards with separate cursor and numeric keypads, you must press Shift-Screen Up and Shift-Screen Down.

Notice that you cannot move the cursor to the bottom of a blank editing screen.

Moving to the Top of the Preceding Page

With the PgUp key, you can move the cursor to the first line of the preceding page. To review the flow of the text, move quickly to the first line of the preceding page and scroll the text. Press PgUp and the up arrow (↑) to check page breaks.

Moving to the Top of the Next Page

Press PgDn to move the cursor quickly to the first line of the next page as you scroll through a document. Press PgDn and the up arrow (↑) to check page breaks.

Moving the Cursor with GoTo

With WordPerfect's GoTo command (Ctrl-Home), you can move the cursor in great "leaps" through a document. For example, use GoTo to move the cursor in the following ways:

- To the top or the bottom of a page
- To a particular page number
- To the next occurrence of a particular character

You even can use GoTo to return the cursor to its starting point before you give the GoTo command, if certain conditions are met.

You can, of course, scroll laboriously through the text by holding the up-arrow or down-arrow keys, but using GoTo is much quicker.

Here is how you use GoTo to scroll a page:

- Press GoTo (Ctrl-Home) and up arrow (↑) to move the cursor to the top of a page.
- Press GoTo (Ctrl-Home) and down arrow (↓) to move the cursor to the bottom of a page.

To move the cursor quickly to a particular character, press GoTo (Ctrl-Home) and type the letter to which you want to move. You're limited in how far ahead you can move the cursor; the character you type must be found in the next 2,000 characters. This command works only *forward* in the text. You cannot use GoTo to move backward in the document.

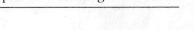
Perhaps the most common use of GoTo is to move the cursor to a specific page when you work on documents longer than one page. To move from page to page, follow these steps:

Reminder:
Use GoTo to move the cursor to a specific page when you work on documents longer than one page.

1. Press GoTo (Ctrl-Home).
2. Type the page number.
3. Press Enter.

Using GoTo to move to specific pages in a long document can be a real time-saver. The only drawback to this method of moving around a document is that you have to know the page number.

GoTo also returns the cursor to the position it occupied before the last "major motion" command. (An example of a major motion command is using Home, Home, up arrow to position the cursor at the top of a file.) In this sense, GoTo acts as a bookmark. WordPerfect remembers the cursor location and returns you to that location when you press GoTo twice.

Cue:
Press GoTo twice (Ctrl-Home, Ctrl-Home) to return the cursor quickly to its previous position.

Moving to the Top or Bottom of a Document

WordPerfect gives you a quick way to move the cursor to the top or bottom of a file. This method is most useful for documents longer than one page.

- Press Home, Home, up arrow (↑) to move the cursor to the top of a document.
- Press Home, Home, down arrow (↓) to move the cursor to the bottom of a document.

Moving the Cursor with the Mouse

You can position the cursor anywhere on the screen with the mouse by locating the mouse pointer at a specific spot and clicking the left button. *Dragging* the mouse enables you to scroll the screen up, down, left, or right to see additional text. You cannot move the cursor through "dead space" (space with no text or codes) beyond where you stop typing. If you position the mouse pointer in the dead space and click the left button, the cursor is positioned at the closest text.

To move one character left, move the mouse pointer one space left and click the left button. To move one character right, move the mouse pointer one space right and click the left button.

To move from word to word with the mouse, position the mouse pointer anywhere in the appropriate word and click the left button to relocate the cursor.

To move the cursor up or down a line, position the mouse pointer on the line you want to move to and press the left button.

To scroll up line-by-line through a document, place the mouse pointer anywhere in the top line, press and hold the right button, and drag the mouse above the visible screen. To scroll down line-by-line through a document, place the mouse pointer at the bottom of the screen, press and hold the right button, and drag the mouse below the visible screen. Scrolling stops when you reach the top or bottom of the document. If you want to block text as you scroll, press and hold the left button instead of the right button before you drag the mouse.

You can scroll left or right to see text not visible on-screen by holding the right button and dragging the mouse to either the left or right edge of the screen. Scrolling stops when you reach the beginning or end of the line.

Inserting Text

Reminder:

To add a word, phrase, or sentence to a document, position the cursor where you want to insert the text and begin typing.

One of the boons of word processing is the freedom to add text to what is already written. To add a sentence in the middle of a paragraph with a typewriter, you must retype the entire paragraph. Not so with WordPerfect. To add a word, phrase, or sentence to a document, position the cursor where you want to insert the text and then type the text. What you type is inserted to the *left* of the cursor. With WordPerfect's Block feature, explained in Chapter 4, you can cut and paste text anywhere in a document. If you store blocks of *boilerplate* (frequently used text) in a file, you can easily insert the blocks into a document.

Suppose that you want to add a sentence to an already typed paragraph. Using the example you created earlier in this chapter, move the cursor to the beginning of the second sentence in the first paragraph. Before you start, make certain that you haven't pressed the Ins key. If you pressed Ins, Typeover appears on the status line. Press Ins to switch to Insert mode (the next section explains Insert mode).

With the cursor under the *W* in *Write*, type this sentence:

> *It could be a room, a natural setting, an interesting building, the house you grew up in, King Tut's tomb--any place that interests you and that you think you can make engrossing to read about.*

Notice that as you enter new text, existing text is pushed ahead. The text is reformatted when you press down arrow (↓) once (see fig. 2.2).

Fig. 2.2.

A new sentence inserted in the middle of a paragraph.

```
Think of a place that you can either visit or remember quite
clearly, a place to which you have strong reactions.  It could be
a room, a natural setting, an interesting building, the house you
grew up in, King Tut's tomb--any place that interests you and
that you think you can make engrossing to read about.  Write a
personal description of it, attempting to re-create for your
reader the experience of seeing or entering the place you've
chosen to write about.

Details are essential in picturing whatever is described.  Try to
think of rich and suggestive words and phrases that will evoke
emotional responses in your readers.  Appeal to the senses.  Use
concrete nouns and active verbs.
```

Using Typeover

The Ins key on your keyboard works like a toggle switch, allowing you to switch from "push ahead," or Insert, mode to Typeover mode and back. When you press the Ins key, the program switches to Typeover mode, and new text *replaces* old text. Using Typeover mode is most useful when making one-for-one replacements, such as changing *adn* to *and*. (Chapter 3 explains the use of Typeover mode during editing.)

Using Both Document Windows

You may recall from Chapter 1 that WordPerfect gives you two "sheets of paper," so to speak, to work on at once if you choose to do so. WordPerfect's two document "windows" give you essentially two areas in which you can work. The status line tells you whether the Doc 1 or the Doc 2 window is the "active" work space. (The position of the cursor determines whether the window is active.)

You can type in both windows and switch back and forth between them with ease. You even can split the screen in half to look at both documents or at different parts of the same document at once. This procedure is less complicated than it sounds. Splitting the screen is useful if, for example, you're working on a long document and need to keep its beginning in mind as you work on the rest of the document.

WordPerfect's two document windows make moving text between two documents easy. Near the end of this chapter, in the section "Using WordPerfect To Develop Ideas," you learn how the window feature can help you plan and draft documents.

Switching between Document Windows

The Doc 1 window is the default window. To switch to the second document window, press Switch (Shift-F3). The status line displays Doc 2. If text is in the Doc 1 window, don't worry—it isn't lost. To switch back to the Doc 1 window, press Switch (Shift-F3) again.

In a typical situation, you may be working on a letter to a business contact and suddenly need to fire off a quick memo. No problem. Switch document windows (assuming, of course, that the second document window is empty), type the memo, print it, clear the screen, and resume working on the letter. (Before you finish this chapter, you learn how to print a document without saving it.)

Splitting the Screen

You may find it useful to see parts of two documents at once on-screen. Alternatively, you may want to use the second window to keep a list of notes to yourself (see fig. 2.3). Although you may think it needless to split the screen when you can readily switch to the other window to type notes, you may find it handy to type the notes when you can see the primary document in the other window. You may even want to have copies of the same document in both windows, but display different parts of the document in each window. This strategy is especially useful when you work on long documents.

The line across the middle of the screen is the *tab ruler line*. This is the same ruler line you see when you give the Reveal Codes command. The downward-pointing triangles represent the tab settings for the document. In figure 2.3, the tab ruler line shows default settings of tab stops every half inch. When a margin falls on a tab setting, the margin is displayed as a left brace (⁅) or a right brace (⁆). Otherwise, the margin is displayed as a left bracket ([) or a right bracket (]).

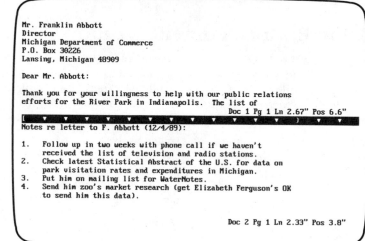

Fig. 2.3.

*The screen split
for entering notes
in the lower
window.*

```
Mr. Franklin Abbott
Director
Michigan Department of Commerce
P.O. Box 30226
Lansing, Michigan 48909

Dear Mr. Abbott:

Thank you for your willingness to help with our public relations
efforts for the River Park in Indianapolis.  The list of
                                       Doc 1 Pg 1 Ln 2.67" Pos 6.6"
[  ▼   ▼   ▼   ▼   ▼   ▼   ▼   ▼   ▼   ▼   ▼   ▼   }   ▼   ▼
Notes re letter to F. Abbott (12/4/89):

1.   Follow up in two weeks with phone call if we haven't
     received the list of television and radio stations.
2.   Check latest Statistical Abstract of the U.S. for data on
     park visitation rates and expenditures in Michigan.
3.   Put him on mailing list for WaterNotes.
4.   Send him zoo's market research (get Elizabeth Ferguson's OK
     to send him this data).

                                       Doc 2 Pg 1 Ln 2.33" Pos 3.8"
```

Before you consider the steps for splitting the screen in half, recall from Chapter 1 that one method of accessing WordPerfect menus is through the function keys: Ctrl, Alt, or Shift in combination with F1 through F10—or F1 through F12 if you have an Enhanced Keyboard. Up to now, you haven't had to use function-key commands or make menu choices. Splitting the editing screen, however, illustrates the two choices that WordPerfect gives you for making menu selections. When you press Screen (Ctrl-F3), for example, the following menu appears on the status line:

1 **W**indow; **2** **L**ine Draw; **3** **R**ewrite: **3**

To make a menu selection, do one of the following:

- Press the number next to a menu item (the default display is in **bold**).
- Press a letter, usually the first letter of the menu item (the default display is in **bold**).

To split the screen, follow these steps:

1. Press Screen (Ctrl-F3).
2. Select **W**indow (**1**). The prompt Number of lines in this window: 24 appears on the status line. (***Note:*** Some monitors may display more than 24 lines.)
3. Type *11* and press Enter.

You also can use the pull-down menu interface to split the screen by following these steps:

1. Access the **E**dit pull-down menu and select **W**indow (see fig. 2.4). The prompt Number of lines in this window: 24 appears on the status line. (***Note:*** Some monitors may display more than 24 lines.)
2. Type *11* and press Enter.

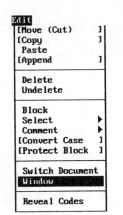

Fig. 2.4.
The Edit pull-down menu.

Your screen should be split in half, with WordPerfect's tab ruler line displayed across the middle.

To switch between windows from the keyboard, press Switch (Shift-F3). 🖰 To switch between windows with the mouse, position the mouse pointer in the appropriate window and press the left mouse button.

You may not want a 50/50 split, preferring instead to allow two-thirds of the screen for the primary document. You can type any number from 1 to 24 in response to the Number of lines in this window: prompt.

To resize the window to a full-screen display, follow the steps given to split the screen, typing *24* instead of *11* in response to the Number of lines in this window: prompt. The window then becomes a full-screen display.

Using Cancel (F1)

To cancel any function-key command or to back out of a menu, use Cancel (F1). If you press Screen (Ctrl-F3) and then decide you do not want to split the screen, for example, you can back out of the Screen menu by pressing Cancel (F1). Cancel (F1) gets you out of any screen menu or prompt.

Esc has the same function in programs such as 1-2-3 or InSet as Cancel (F1) does in WordPerfect. In fact, if you decide to try the ALTRNAT keyboard definition supplied with WordPerfect, you find that the Cancel function has been reassigned to the Esc key. (Chapter 20 explains the use of alternative keyboards.)

The Cancel (F1) key is also known as the *undelete key* because you use it to restore up to the last three text or hidden-code deletions. You learn about this use of Cancel (F1) in Chapter 3.

🖰 To cancel a command or back out of a menu with a three-button mouse, press the middle button. With a two-button mouse, press the right button to cancel a command or get out of the pull-down menu system. If you are several levels deep in the pull-down menu system and want to back up one level, press and hold the left button, press the right button, and then release both buttons.

Printing an Unsaved Document

With WordPerfect, you can be flexible about printing. If you do not want to save a document, WordPerfect still lets you print it without requiring that you save it to disk first. Printing in this manner is called *making a screen print*, because you print what has been created and stored in temporary memory.

Note: The steps that follow assume that you have installed your printer properly. For information on running the Install program, see Appendix A.

To print the document on-screen, follow these steps:

1. Press Print (Shift-F7).

    Access the **F**ile pull-down menu (see fig. 2.5) and select **P**rint.

   The Print menu appears (see fig. 2.6).

2. If the text you want to print is more than one page, select **F**ull Document (**1**). If the text you want to print is one page or less, select **P**age (**2**).

Fig. 2.5.

The **F** *ile pull-down menu.*

```
File Edit Searc]
     Retrieve
     Save
     Text In     ▶
     Text Out    ▶
     Password    ▶

     List Files
     Summary

     Print

     Setup       ▶

     Goto DOS
     Exit
```

Fig. 2.6.

The Print menu.

```
Print

     1 - Full Document
     2 - Page
     3 - Document on Disk
     4 - Control Printer
     5 - Multiple Pages
     6 - View Document
     7 - Initialize Printer


Options

     S - Select Printer              Toshiba P351/P351C
     B - Binding Offset              0"
     N - Number of Copies            1
     U - Multiple Copies Generated by  WordPerfect
     G - Graphics Quality            Medium
     T - Text Quality                High
```

WordPerfect flashes * Please Wait * on the status line as it prepares to print the text. If the printer is properly configured and connected, printing begins almost immediately.

With WordPerfect's two document windows, you can work on a document in one window, switch to the second window and print the file in that window, and return to the first window and continue working on the file as you print the other document.

Your document doesn't, however, have to be on-screen for you to print it. With WordPerfect you can print any number of documents stored on disk (floppy or hard). You even can have documents in both windows and print a document stored on disk. As you can see from the Print menu shown in figure 2.6, you can choose to print a file stored on disk. The various ways of printing and managing print jobs are explained in Chapter 8. But you know enough now to make a quick print of text on-screen.

Reminder:

The document you want to print doesn't have to be on-screen.

> **Tip**
>
> To review your writing, print frequent copies of your on-screen work. One limitation of composing on-screen is that you can't see more than 24 lines at a time. With such a narrow window for text, you can lose a sense of the whole, repeat yourself, or lose a sense of the sequence of your ideas.

Saving a Document to Disk

Usually you keep copies on disk of the documents you create. WordPerfect gives you two methods of saving a file:

- With the Save command, you save a copy of the on-screen document to disk. When you use Save, the document remains on-screen for additional work.

- With the Exit command, you save a copy of the document to disk, but the document does not have to remain on-screen. You can keep the document on-screen by pressing Cancel when the Exit WP? prompt appears.

  Use Exit to clear the screen without saving the document. This method is handy when you decide to discard what you've written.

The first time you save a document, WordPerfect prompts you for a file name. Suppose that you created the short document shown in figure 2.2 and now want to save the file. With the document on-screen, follow these steps:

1. Press Save (F10).

   ⌨ Access the **F**ile pull-down menu and select **S**ave.

   The Document to be saved: prompt appears on the status line.

2. Type a file name for the document. In this example, you can type *describe.doc* or some other unique file name. A file name consists of two parts: a *root name* (or *primary file name*) and a *suffix* (or *extension*). The root name can have one to eight characters. You can use the root name to describe the file's contents. The suffix can have one to three characters. If you use a suffix, separate it from the root name by a period (.). You can omit the optional suffix if you like. When you name a file, observe your operating-system (MS-DOS or PC DOS) guidelines for naming files.

Note: With version 5.1 you can give a file a descriptive file name of up to 40 characters. See Chapter 10 for more information on long file names.

3. Press Enter. A prompt on the status line indicates that WordPerfect is saving the file to the current drive and directory. To save the file to a different drive or directory, type the drive and directory information before you type the file name. After you name and save a file, the file name is displayed on the status line in the left corner of the screen. (You can use Setup to turn off the file-name display, as explained in Chapter 20.)

Reminder:

You can save a document under a different name.

WordPerfect responds a bit differently when you save a file that you saved before. When you issue the Save command, WordPerfect displays the file name on the status line. To save the file with the same name, press Enter. WordPerfect then prompts whether you want to replace the file on disk. If you select **Yes**, the existing version of the file is replaced with the new version. If you select **No**, you can rename the file and save it under a different name. If you want to save the document under a different name, move the cursor to the old file name and change it. You can change any of the information following the `Document to be saved:` prompt.

Clearing the Screen and Exiting WordPerfect

You can use the Exit (F7) key or the E**x**it option on the **F**ile pull-down menu for many different functions. You can use Exit to do the following:

- Save the document and clear the screen so that you can start work on a new document.
- Save the document and exit WordPerfect.
- Clear the screen without saving the document.
- Exit WordPerfect without saving the document.

To save the document and clear the screen, do the following:

1. Press Exit (F7).

    Access the **F**ile pull-down menu and select E**x**it.

2. In response to the `Save Document?` prompt, select **Yes**.

3. Type the file name under which you want to save the document and press Enter or accept the current file name by pressing Enter. In response to the `Replace?` prompt, select **Yes**.

4. In response to the `Exit WP?` prompt, select **No**.

To save the document and exit WordPerfect, do the following:

1. Use the mouse or the keyboard (F7) to select Exit.

2. In response to the `Save Document?` prompt, select **Yes**.

3. Type the file name under which you want to save the document and press Enter or accept the current file name by pressing Enter. In response to the `Replace?` prompt, select **Yes**.

4. In response to the `Exit WP?` prompt, select **Yes**.

To clear the screen without saving the document, do the following:

1. Use the mouse or the keyboard (F7) to select Exit.
2. In response to the `Save Document?` prompt, select **N**o.
3. In response to the `Exit WP?` prompt, select **N**o.

To exit WordPerfect without saving the document, do the following:

1. Use the mouse or the keyboard (F7) to select Exit.
2. In response to the `Save Document?` prompt, select **N**o.
3. In response to the `Exit WP?` prompt, select **Y**es.

Using WordPerfect To Develop Ideas

This section is an "extra" for those who want tips on writing with a word processor. If you have worked through the chapter and want some additional hands-on experience, turn to Chapter 3 and the rest of the book. If you're new to word processing, the information in this section may help you adapt your old writing habits to the "electronic scribe." Even if you've been using a word processor—any word processor—for a while, you find in this section some fresh ideas for getting the creative juices flowing.

Most writing done on the job does not require that you determine a subject or an idea for a document. Letters, memos, and reports, for example, are usually written in response to a request or a predetermined need: you respond to a customer's complaint; you write a memo recommending a certain course of action; you draw up a progress report explaining your work to date on a project.

Whether you are writing an essay at school or a memo on the job, you must plan before you write. You need to determine the scope of your message and its purpose, analyze your audience, and consider how you want to present yourself. No matter what the writing task, you may find yourself stymied or "blocked" at certain points. If you have trouble getting started, or if you're not at all sure what it is you want to say, you can use WordPerfect to generate ideas. Writing is a recursive process, one that does not proceed neatly by stages from planning to drafting to revising to final editing and polishing—and WordPerfect is a marvelous tool for assisting you through each loop of the process.

Cue:
If you're having trouble getting started, or if you're not sure what you want to say, use WordPerfect to generate ideas.

As you adapt your writing habits to the computer, keep in mind that you don't have to abandon all your old ways of doing things. If you have a penchant for jotting notes on restaurant napkins, the backs of envelopes, or in a pocket notebook, fine. You don't have to use WordPerfect for the entire composing process. But remember that WordPerfect is an ideal electronic notepad for jotting down ideas as they occur to you.

The sections that follow present tips on warming up to the writing task, discovering what you want to say, and dealing with those moments when you either can't get started or are "blocked." You also find tips on planning and drafting documents.

Handling Writer's Block

In *When a Writer Can't Write: Studies in Writer's Block and Other Composing Process Problems*, Mike Rose comments, "No one writes effortlessly. Our composing is marked by pauses, false starts, gnawing feelings of inadequacy, crumpled paper."[2]

WordPerfect can save you a mountain of "crumpled paper" but it cannot prevent those sometimes agonizing moments when the words just don't come. By removing much of the drudgery of writing, however, WordPerfect makes it easier for you to record your thoughts, even to stimulate your own creativity.

If you're a halfway decent typist, you will be amazed at how quickly you can transfer your thoughts to the screen. Researchers have found that writers talk to themselves as they compose. Many talk "out loud," rehearsing and changing phrases, clauses, sentences, and whole passages. With WordPerfect you can keep up with your running commentary and make changes and additions nearly as fast as you can speak. As an electronic scribe, WordPerfect ensures that you don't lose evanescent thoughts.

Two strategies writers find useful for combatting writer's block are brainstorming and freewriting.

Brainstorming

When you have trouble determining a sharp focus for a document—when you're not sure what you want to say—consider trying a semistructured writing exercise known as *brainstorming*.

Reminder:

When you brainstorm a writing assignment on-screen, you record ideas in list form as they occur to you.

When you brainstorm a writing assignment on-screen, you record your ideas in list form—words, phrases, even entire sentences—as they occur to you. When you brainstorm, you don't worry about typos, spelling errors, or style; you can handle those matters later. Your goal is to generate as many ideas as possible about the topic (unless you're using this method to discover a topic), the purpose, or the audience. You can create and save a file for each brainstorming session.

Brainstorming can be useful before you reach the stage where a prewriting template (described later in this chapter) may help.

Reminder:

Use one of WordPerfect's two document windows to jot notes to yourself.

WordPerfect's two document windows are useful when you want to jot notes to yourself. You can keep an *idea file* of notes that relate to a particular project. An idea file is an extension of a brainstorming file. You can save an idea file and retrieve it when you want to add more ideas to it. Chapter 4 explains how you can save a block of text to disk. You also can append a block of text to an existing file and add ideas to your idea file without retrieving the file to the screen. (You find more about file retrieval at the beginning of Chapter 3.)

Freewriting

Freewriting is less structured than brainstorming, but the two techniques are similar. Writing teacher Peter Elbow has been credited with popularizing the practice of freewriting. He defines a freewriting session as follows: "To do a freewriting exercise, simply force yourself to write without stopping for ten minutes." Peter Elbow justifies freewriting because it "separate[s] the producing process from the revising process."[3]

Begin a freewriting session with an idea or topic and, without planning or deliberation, write anything that comes into your mind about that topic. Write nonstop for at least 10 minutes. Obviously, this exercise is easier and less tiring with WordPerfect than with a typewriter or a pen or pencil. The most important point is to keep going, even if you find yourself writing nonsense or if your text begins to resemble *Finnegans Wake*. Don't make any changes or corrections. Don't worry about typos, spelling, and other errors. The most important goal in freewriting— as in brainstorming—is to stimulate your thinking and get you writing.

One variation on the freewriting technique is to examine your text after each session, extract a key idea, and use this idea as the basis for the next session of on-screen freewriting. (You may even want to split the screen, extract the key ideas from the freewriting session in one window, and copy the ideas to the second window.) This strategy, called *looping*, forces you to find the natural coherence in the text you have produced. You can create as many loops as you are inclined to. When you have a sizeable file with a number of key ideas identified, you can delete the extraneous material and keep the "good stuff," which you then can use in a prewriting template or outline.

Planning Documents

Brainstorming and freewriting at the keyboard are excellent strategies for warming up, generating ideas, and pushing your material toward a productive, critical mass. Out of chaos can come order; out of an inchoate sprawl of text on the screen—or the printout—can come the key points and direction of your message. Brainstorming and freewriting can move you closer toward a first draft, but many writers need still more preparation before formal drafting. They need interim planning.

Research into cognitive processes and the writing process suggests that experienced writers tend to have certain established mental schemas to help them in their writing tasks. That is, they have mental representations of the types of documents they need to write. They know the requirements of a particular piece of writing—whether it is a letter conveying bad news, a progress report, or a research paper—before they put fingers to keyboard. In a sense, then, they have already accomplished some planning. Experienced writers also tend to plan *more*: they make outlines, take notes, or make lists of ideas before they create a first draft. Experienced writers also try to anticipate how a reader will respond to the text. Inexperienced writers, on the other hand, often lack these internalized guidelines and have trouble meeting the demands of particular writing tasks.

Interestingly, current research suggests that writers who use computers may do less planning than they did before writing with a computer.[4] The moral: beware the inclination to begin composing immediately at the keyboard. Don't let the ease with which you can put words on-screen deceive you into assuming that planning isn't necessary. Use paper to do some prewriting, or consider some of the strategies presented in this chapter. Find the best match between your writing habits and the word processor for composing.

Reminder:
Begin a freewriting session with an idea or topic and write nonstop for 10 minutes about anything relevant to that topic.

Reminder:
Experienced writers tend to plan more: they make outlines, take notes, or make lists of ideas before they create a first draft.

Reminder:
Don't let the ease with which you can put words on the screen deceive you into assuming that planning isn't necessary.

The seductive ease with which one composes on-screen becomes particularly problematic when writers who compose on-screen are asked to revise their work and end up merely making surface changes, shuffling words around, or restating what they said without rethinking the original material.

Some researchers point out that writing on-screen makes writers unwilling to jettison poor text; in fact, the capability of making frequent printouts lends yet another premature permanency to a document.[5] On the other hand, other researchers have found that experienced writers eventually learn to use the editing tools of their word processor to revise, rearrange, and cut text extensively.

Just as experienced writers have in mind good examples for particular documents, readers have built-in expectations for the documents. Readers expect documents to follow logical patterns. When these expectations are met or surpassed, readers are usually appreciative and receptive. For example, you expect research reports to begin with a summary of findings followed by supporting data; you expect dissertations to begin with an abstract, and memos to begin with background information and a statement of the writer's purpose or recommendations.

Readers have expectations even about the sequence of elements in a paragraph or a sentence. They expect the first sentence of a paragraph to orient them to the rest of the paragraph. If you begin a sentence with new information but follow with something the reader already knows, you may force the reader to reread the sentence. The movement from new to old is unnatural and makes sentences less readable. If you don't plan your documents carefully—from sentence structure to overall design—you run the risk of violating the expectations of your readers. Frustrated readers lose confidence in the writer and may stop reading.

As part of the planning process, consider two effective tools: prewriting templates and outlines.

Using a Prewriting Template

Prewriting is everything you do up to the actual step of writing the first draft. Prewriting is very much a part of the planning stage.

Reminder:

A prewriting template is a set of prompts that forces you to answer some basic questions before you begin a document.

A *prewriting template* is a set of prompts that forces you to answer some basic questions before you begin the document. As you plan the document, you may find it helpful to use a prewriting template to refine your thinking about a particular writing task. You can ask the basic reporter's questions of *Who? What? Where? Why?* and *When?* Alternatively, you can simplify your planning to consider these questions:

- Who are you? What is your role in the organization? How do you want to present yourself, to be perceived?
- What is your subject? What do you *need* to say? What do you *want* to say?
- What is your purpose in writing? Why are you writing this document? What do you hope to achieve?

- Who is your audience? What do they already know? What do they need to know? What will your readers do with your message? What is your relationship to the audience? How will your audience react to your message? Can you anticipate this reaction and shape your message accordingly? Can you consider your message from your reader's point of view?

To create a prewriting template, begin with a fresh screen and enter the text you see in figure 2.7. Put each prompt in bold and leave several blank lines between each item. Give this document a name like TEMPLATE and save it to disk. When you need this prewriting template, you can retrieve it and use it again.

```
Speaker:

Subject:

Purpose:

Audience:
```

Fig. 2.7.
A prewriting template.

If you prefer to prewrite or plan on paper, you can add more lines between each prompt, print the template, and enter your responses by hand.

If you work on-screen, move the cursor to the right of each prompt and type notes. When you have a clear sense of how you want to present yourself, what you need to say, why you need to say it, and who your audience is—keeping in mind that the document may have multiple audiences—you are considerably closer to creating that first draft. You then can save the prewriting template to disk; be sure to use another file name so that you don't overwrite the original, blank template.

Assuming that the second document window is empty, switch windows and begin the first draft of the letter, memo, or report. If your filled-out prewriting template isn't displayed in one of the windows, you can retrieve it and refer to it as you compose your draft in the other document window. If you're writing a report that entails research, you may want to create an outline next, based in part on your template responses.

Using an Outline

An *outline* can function as a kind of template. The structure of an outline isn't easy to conceive, however, especially if the writing task promises to be lengthy. Besides, you may have been force-fed outlines in elementary and high school and balk at the idea of working from one.

Whether you use an outline depends, in part, on what type of writer you are. Some writers conceive elaborate plans and don't diverge much from those plans when they compose. Other writers do less planning or structuring and heavily revise their text. When you are in the middle of a writing task, however, even an informal or loose outline can give you some scaffolding on which to hang your ideas. Outlines

Reminder:
Even an informal outline can provide some scaffolding on which to hang your ideas.

can be useful to help you better understand the logical flow of your topics. You don't have to follow an outline rigidly; you can slot ideas here and there as they occur to you. You don't have to supply all the headings and subheadings either; you can begin with a few major categories and flesh out sections here and there. You even can use brainstorming and freewriting to generate additional ideas for sections. Later, you can go back and supply transitions and add, cut, or relocate material.

If you have trouble getting started, try the timeworn method of creating an outline first. Successful writers have learned the importance of beginning a writing task with a road map that supplies some sense of structure and outcome. WordPerfect's Outline feature can be a helpful tool as you plan your document. Even if you jot down just the major ideas as headings, you can go back later and develop each section. For detailed coverage of the Outline feature, see Chapter 24.

Summary

In this chapter, you learned a lot about using a word processor to help you write. You read about how you can do the following with WordPerfect:

❑ Type, save, and print a document

❑ Brainstorm and freewrite using WordPerfect as a composing tool

❑ Create a template to help you plan your writing tasks

❑ Use an outline to develop your ideas into a more coherent package

---

[1] Ann Berthoff, *Forming, Thinking, Writing: The Composing Imagination* (Montclair, NJ: Boynton/Cook, Publishers, Inc., 1982), p. 11.

[2] Mike Rose, *When a Writer Can't Write: Studies in Writer's Block and Other Composing Process Problems* (New York: Guilford Press, 1985), p. ix.

[3] Peter Elbow, *Writing with Power: Techniques for Mastering the Writing Process* (New York: Oxford University Press, 1981), pp. 13, 14.

[4] Gail Hawisher, "Research Update: Writing and Word Processing." eds. Cynthia Selfe and Kathleen Kiefer, *Computers and Composition*, 5, No. 2 (April 1988), p. 16.

[5] Lillian Bridwell-Bowles, Parker Johnson, and Stephen Brehe, "Composing and Computers: Case Studies of Experienced Writers," in *Writing in Real Time: Modeling Production Processes*, ed. Ann Matsuhashi (Norwood, NJ: Ablex Publishing Co., 1987), p. 90.

Editing a Document

Schuyler Lininger Jr. is an Oregon chiropractor, a vice president of sales for a major food-supplement company, a computer consultant, and a writer. Using WordPerfect and desktop publishing, he regularly produces a national newsletter for natural-food stores.

In the previous chapter, you learned how to enter text, move the cursor, make menu choices, print and save a document, and exit WordPerfect. This chapter presents the basics of editing a document.

If you are new to word processing, this chapter is fun and exciting because it introduces you to the powerful editing tools at your disposal with WordPerfect. If you are like many people, a few minutes with WordPerfect will make you wonder how you could ever again get along with only a typewriter.

In this chapter, you learn how to do the following:

- Retrieve a file
- Edit text and revise extensively
- Delete (erase) a single character, word, line, sentence, paragraph, and page
- Undelete (unerase) what you recently erased
- Overwrite text in typewriter style
- Enhance text by using **bold** typeface or underlining
- Edit in Reveal Codes (Alt-F3 or F11) for greater format control
- Use WordPerfect's powerful Search and Replace features
- Use document comments as an aid to effective writing and control over the editing process

> ### Reminder
>
> If you use a mouse with WordPerfect 5.1, you can click the right button to display the pull-down menus, and then select the desired option. You also can press Alt-= to access the pull-down menus, and then press the appropriate letter of the desired option. For all instructions, assume that if a block is required to activate a pull-down menu option, the text has been blocked before the pull-down menu is accessed. Instructions for pull-down menus and the mouse are marked with the mouse icon. For more information about the mouse, see Chapter 1. ▭▤

Retrieving a Document

In Chapter 2, you learned how to save a document. In this section, you learn how to retrieve a document into WordPerfect for editing. If you have documents created with WordPerfect 4.2 or 5, WordPerfect 5.1 automatically converts them. (Once this conversion has taken place, the document cannot be read again by WordPerfect 4.2 without saving it in WordPerfect 4.2 format. Save a document in WordPerfect 4.2 format by using Text In/Out (Ctrl-F5). WordPerfect 5 documents can be read by WordPerfect 5.1 without converting them. Commands new to 5.1 are ignored by version 5, so some formatting may be lost. If you prefer, save the file in WordPerfect 5 format by using Text In/Out (Ctrl-F5).

Documents created with other word processors, such as WordStar or MultiMate, can be converted to WordPerfect 5.1 format with a utility program supplied with WordPerfect. The conversion procedure is explained in Chapter 16.

Using List To Retrieve a File

The simplest way to retrieve a document is to use the List (F5) command. The following steps show how to use List. (A comprehensive explanation is presented in Chapter 10.)

To retrieve a document, perform the following steps:

    1. Press List (F5).

        ▭▤ Access the **F**ile pull-down menu and select List **F**iles (see fig. 3.1).

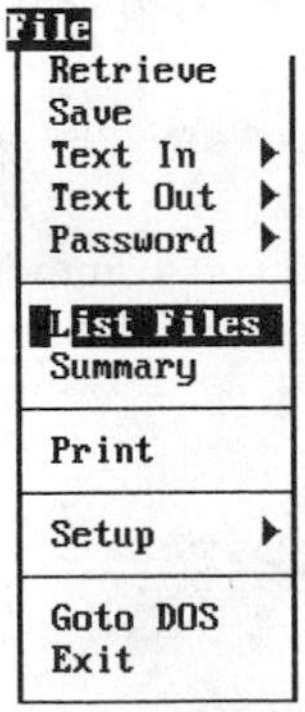

Fig. 3.1.
The File pull-down menu.

```
File
  Retrieve
  Save
  Text In    ▶
  Text Out   ▶
  Password   ▶

 List Files
  Summary

  Print

  Setup      ▶

  Goto DOS
  Exit
```

A prompt appears in the lower left corner of the screen, listing the current drive, subdirectory, and file specification. (The default file specification is *.*, which means all files.)

2. Press Enter. The editing screen is replaced by the List Files screen (see fig. 3.2).

```
10-22-89  12:14p              Directory G:\WP51\*.*
Document size:    44,340   Free:  1,261,560 Used:  1,784,926     Files:      56

    .   Current    <Dir>                 ..   Parent     <Dir>
  BETA     .       <Dir>  08-31-89 08:16p  DOC      .       <Dir>  08-30-89 07:20p
  GRAPHIC  .       <Dir>  08-30-89 04:11p  HADF     .       <Dir>  09-04-89 11:24a
  HM       .       <Dir>  09-17-89 11:43a  LEARN    .       <Dir>  08-30-89 07:19p
  LEX      .       <Dir>  08-30-89 04:11p  MACRO    .       <Dir>  08-30-89 04:11p
  MISC     .       <Dir>  09-24-89 08:57p  MK       .       <Dir>  10-19-89 02:16p
  PIX      .       <Dir>  09-21-89 12:18p  PTR      .       <Dir>  09-12-89 09:57p
  QUE      .       <Dir>  10-16-89 11:54p  STYLE    .       <Dir>  08-30-89 04:11p
  8514A    .VRS    4,797  10-05-89 01:16p  ATI     .VRS     4,937  10-05-89 01:16p
  CHARACTR .DOC   42,223  10-11-89 11:32a  CONVERT .EXE   105,201  10-11-89 11:32a
  CURSOR   .COM    1,452  10-11-89 11:32a  EGA512  .FRS     3,584  10-05-89 01:16p
  EGAITAL  .FRS    3,584  10-05-89 01:16p  EGASMC  .FRS     3,584  10-05-89 01:16p
  EGAUND   .FRS    3,584  10-05-89 01:16p  FIXBIOS .COM        50  10-11-89 11:32a
  GENIUS   .VRS   16,097  10-05-89 01:16p  GENOA   .VRS    10,972  10-05-89 01:16p
  GRAB     .COM   15,570  10-11-89 11:32a  GRAB    .DOC     2,780  10-17-89 12:08p
  GRAPHCNV .EXE  105,472  10-11-89 11:32a  HRF12   .FRS    49,152  10-05-89 01:16p
  HRF6     .FRS   49,152  10-05-89 01:16p  INSTALL .EXE    59,984  10-11-89 11:40a
  KEYS     .MRS    4,800  10-11-89 03:10p  MACROCNV .EXE   26,021  10-11-89 11:32a
  NEC      .VRS    4,682  10-05-89 01:16p ▼ WPSETUP .EXE    27,648  10-11-89 11:32a

1 Retrieve; 2 Delete; 3 Move/Rename; 4 Print; 5 Short/Long Display;
6 Look; 7 Other Directory; 8 Copy; 9 Find; N Name Search: 6
```

Fig. 3.2.

The List Files screen.

3. If you see the name of the document you want to retrieve, use the arrow keys or the mouse to highlight the file name. If you don't see the name of the document you want to retrieve, do the following:

   a. Select **N**ame Search (**N**) from the menu at the bottom of the screen.

   b. Type the first few letters of the document name. The highlight moves to the name of the document you are looking for.

   c. Press Enter to end Name Search.

      If you think you've found the document you want, but aren't sure, you can use **L**ook (**6**) to "peek" before retrieving. You can scroll through the text of the document using the arrow, Screen Up, Screen Down, and Home (in conjunction with arrow) keys.

      You also can look at the next or previous document in the list by choosing **N**ext Doc (**1**) or **P**rev Doc (**2**).

      Press Exit (F7) or Enter to return to the List Files screen.

4. When you are sure you have the right file name, choose **R**etrieve (**1**).

WordPerfect is careful about what files are retrieved. If you try to retrieve other than a WordPerfect file, the ERROR: Incompatible file format message appears.

Reminder:

To retrieve files in other than WordPerfect 4.2 or later format, or from other word processors, use the Convert utility first.

To retrieve files in other than WordPerfect 4.2 or later format, or from other word processors, use the Convert utility first. Although you can retrieve straight ASCII files using List (F5), you can exercise more format control using the Text In/Out (Ctrl- F5) feature instead.

If you have the Long Display feature on, only WordPerfect 5 and 5.1 files and directories appear on the List Files screen (see Chapter 10 for more information).

Changing Paths from the List Files Screen

If you cannot find the document you want, you may be looking on the wrong disk or in the wrong directory. To change the path, do these steps:

1. Press List (F5).

   ▭ Access the **F**ile pull-down menu and select List **F**iles.

2. Press Enter.

3. Choose **O**ther Directory (**7**) and type the name of the new directory.

4. Press Enter twice to access the directory.

Reminder:

If you're not sure which directory you want, access the List Files screen and press Enter.

If you are unsure of the name of the directory you want to change to, perform the following steps:

1. Press List (F5).

   ▭ Access the **F**ile pull-down menu and select List **F**iles.

2. Press Enter.

3. If you see a file name with <Dir> instead of the size of the file, you have found a subdirectory. Use the arrow keys or mouse to highlight the name of the directory you want. You also can use **N**ame Search to find subdirectories, but remember to include a backslash (\) before typing any letters.

4. Press Enter twice.

Changing Paths from the Document Screen

You also can change paths from the document screen. To change the directory from the document screen, perform the following steps:

1. Press List (F5).

   ▭ Access the **F**ile pull-down menu and select List **F**iles.

2. Press Enter. You see a prompt in the lower left corner of the screen similar to Dir C:\WP51*.*

3. If you want to change the default directory, press the equal sign (=) (or use the mouse to click the = in the bottom right of the screen) and type the new directory name, such as *C:\WP51\LETTERS*.

   If you want to look at a directory without changing the default path, just type the new directory name (do not press the equal sign first).

4. Press Enter.

· Using Retrieve (Shift-F10) To Retrieve a Formatted File

If you know the name of the document you want, do the following to retrieve the file:

1. Press Retrieve (Shift-F10).

    ⌨ Access the **F**ile pull-down menu and select **R**etrieve.

    The `Document to be retrieved:` prompt appears in the lower left corner of the screen.

2. Type the complete name of the document.

3. Press Enter.

If you see the message `ERROR: File not found`, verify the spelling of the file and try again. This error message also appears when you enter the incorrect disk drive, directory, or subdirectory.

If the document is in a drive or subdirectory different from the one you are currently in, you must either change drives and directories or type the complete path. Following is an example of a drive, directory, subdirectory, and document name:

C:\WP51\LETTERS\SMITH.1

Reminder:
If the document you want is in a directory different from the current directory, type the complete path.

Combining Files by Retrieving Them

You may want to combine portions of several documents to create one large document. Doctors, attorneys, and other report writers often have standard paragraphs inserted into many documents. Journalists, authors, and thesis writers often want to use previously written material. WordPerfect is a powerful editing tool that allows you to combine two or more documents into a single document.

Whenever you retrieve a document, WordPerfect adds that document to what is on-screen. If the screen is blank, you don't have to worry about combining. But if a document is already on-screen, the newly retrieved document is inserted at the cursor position. For example, if the cursor is in the middle of the current document, the new document is inserted in the middle of the current document. To combine documents, place the cursor where you want the new document inserted, and then retrieve a document with one of the methods described in the preceding sections. If you use Retrieve (Shift-F10), the new document is retrieved immediately. If you use List (F5) and a document is already on-screen, WordPerfect asks you to confirm the retrieval with the prompt:

`Retrieve into current document? No (Yes)`

Select **Y** to retrieve the document or **N** to cancel the retrieval.

Tip
Save the current document before retrieving additional text. That way, if you make a mistake, you can erase the screen and start over by retrieving the document you just saved.

Revising and Editing Text

WordPerfect serves two general groups of people. The first involves writers, journalists, doctors, lawyers, and other professionals who compose original material. The second involves typists or secretaries who must transcribe and proofread someone else's thoughts from either a recording or a manuscript.

Members of the first group may need to rewrite extensively or revise substantially their prose. The second group may verify spelling, correct punctuation and grammar, and format the final document for an appealing presentation.

In some instances, one person may do all the creating, revising, correcting, and formatting. In other instances, several people may be involved. Regardless of the circumstances, WordPerfect is a powerful tool for performing these tasks.

Making Substantive Changes (Revision)

After you create a document, you may need to revise it. Revision goes deeper than checking spelling and punctuation and formatting the document for attractive presentation. Revision requires polishing the thoughts behind the presentation.

WordPerfect makes editing so simple that users tend to polish the page and not the thought. Because the revising and editing processes use some of the same tools (for example, deleting and moving text), one function is easily confused with the other. Before word processors appeared, revision required scratching out a phrase, penciling in another, cutting a paragraph, pasting in other text, and then retyping the entire document—only to have to repeat the process. With WordPerfect, the drudgery is significantly reduced and the rewriting is easily done.

However, the same effort you devote to thinking and hard work in manual revision is also required with WordPerfect. Experienced writers use WordPerfect not only for their initial thoughts, but also as an aid to extensive rewriting.

WordPerfect 5.1 offers writers an unequaled creative environment. The following suggestions show how you can use this environment to its fullest:

- Use the *transparent nature* (the large blank screen) of WordPerfect to write thoughts quickly. (Chapter 24 shows how you can later organize the document with WordPerfect's outlining capabilities.)

- Use the editing capabilities (described later in this chapter) to eliminate unwanted text and to add new ideas or thoughts.

- Use the powerful Block feature (explained in Chapter 4) to rearrange text.

- Use WordPerfect's Thesaurus to find the "perfect" word; use the Speller to find misspellings. (Both these features are explained in Chapter 7.)

- Use the editing screen or a printed copy of the document for additional revisions.

Making Surface Changes (Editing)

WordPerfect has unparalleled editing capabilities. The editing process is comparable to polishing a gemstone. After the initial cut has been made, changes to the surface make a rock a treasure. Similarly, you can polish a document by editing in two stages. In the first, you handle rough editing, such as correcting typographical errors by deleting or adding letters and words. In this stage, WordPerfect helps you by proofreading for spelling errors and double words.

In the second, or "polishing," stage, you format the final document—how it looks when printed. Most formatting can be done using Format (Shift-F8) and Font (Ctrl-F8); formatting is discussed in detail in the next three chapters.

Deleting Text

With WordPerfect, deleting text is easy. You can delete single letters, entire words, whole sentences, complete paragraphs, or full pages with only a few keystrokes.

Deleting a Single Character

You can delete single characters three different ways in WordPerfect:

- Press the Backspace key to delete the character to the left of the cursor.
- Press the Del key to delete the character at the cursor.
- Press the space bar in Typeover mode (press Ins) to delete the character at the cursor and leave a space.

Deleting a Single Word or Portions of a Single Word

You can delete single words or portions of single words several ways in WordPerfect:

- Press Delete Word (Ctrl-Backspace) to delete a word at the cursor or to delete a word to the left of the cursor if the cursor is on a space immediately after the word.
- Press Home-Backspace to delete the word left of the cursor to the beginning of the next word.
- Press Home-Del to delete everything from the cursor to the end of the word and all intervening spaces to the beginning of the next word or character following the word.
- Press the space bar several times in Typeover mode (press Ins) to delete the characters to the right of the cursor.

Deleting to the End of the Line

To delete from the cursor position to the end of the line, press Ctrl-End. Any hard return (**[HRt]**) at the end of the line remains and is not deleted.

> **Tip**
>
> If you are familiar with WordStar, you may miss the capability of deleting a full line of text with the cursor set anywhere in the line (Ctrl-Y performs this action in WordStar). The MACRO keyboard definition (described in Chapter 20) provides the Alt-D command that duplicates the WordStar Ctrl-Y command. If you like this feature, incorporate these commands in a WordPerfect macro:
>
> {Home}{Home}{Home}{Left}{Delete to EOL}{Del}

Deleting to the End of the Page

To delete from the cursor position to the end of the page, do the following:

1. Press Delete to End of Page (Ctrl-PgDn).
2. A prompt at the bottom of the screen reads, Delete Remainder of page? No (Yes). Select **Y** to delete or **N** to change your mind.

The hard page return (**[HPg]**) at the end of the page is not deleted.

Deleting Text with Esc

You can perform the following delete operations repeatedly by using WordPerfect's repeat function:

- Delete
- Delete word
- Delete to end of line
- Delete to end of page

For example, to delete three words, do the following steps:

Reminder:

Press Esc and type the desired number to delete as many characters, words, lines, or pages as you want at one time.

1. Press Esc. The following prompt appears in the lower left corner of the screen, where the equal sign is followed by a number):

   Repeat Value =

2. Type *3* to perform the operation three times.
3. Press Delete Word (Ctrl-Backspace).

Deleting a Sentence, Paragraph, or Page

To delete separate blocks of text, do the following steps:

1. Position the cursor at the text you want to delete.
2. Press Move (Ctrl-F4) and choose **S**entence (**1**), **P**aragraph (**2**), or **P**age (**3**).

   ⌨ Access the **E**dit pull-down menu, choose **S**elect, then choose **S**entence, **P**aragraph, or **P**age from the pop-out menu.

Note: The **M**ove (Cut) command from the **E**dit menu is not the same as the Move (Ctrl-F4) keyboard command and is not available without *first* blocking the text.

The sentence, paragraph, or page to be deleted is highlighted (see fig. 3.3).

3. Choose **D**elete (**3**). The highlighted sentence, paragraph, or page is deleted.

```
October 22, 1989

Dear Chuck,

The idea for the book Using WordPerfect 5.1 is excellent. I like
your suggestion of a multi-author collaborative effort instead of
a single-author approach.

Not only will we be able to get the book out more quickly, but
also each author will be able to concentrate effort on a
specialized area. Such an approach should give us an excellent
book.

Sincerely,


Schuyler W. Lininger Jr.




1 Move; 2 Copy; 3 Delete; 4 Append: 0
```

Fig. 3.3.

A text block to be deleted.

Deleting Text with the Mouse

One great benefit of using a mouse with WordPerfect is the ability it gives you to quickly block text. You can block text more quickly with the mouse than with the Block (Alt-F4) command (for more information on using the Block command, see Chapter 4). Although you can access the **E**dit pull-down menu and use **S**elect to block a sentence, paragraph, or page, this method is cumbersome compared to using the mouse. Also, with the **S**elect command, your only options are **M**ove, **C**opy, **D**elete, or **A**ppend. If you block text with a mouse, you can perform **M**ove (Cut), **C**opy, or **A**ppend directly from the **E**dit pull-down menu; and you can perform *any other* operation that can normally be done on blocked text. Using the mouse instead of the **S**elect command is not only faster, but also more powerful.

To delete text using the mouse, do the following steps:

1. Click the left mouse button at either the upper left or lower right of the block (character, word, sentence, or paragraph) you want to delete.

2. Drag the mouse to the opposite corner of the block you are defining (the area is highlighted as you move the mouse).

3. Press the Del key.

    🖰 Access the **E**dit pull-down menu and select **D**elete.

4. Select **Y** in response to the `Delete Block?` prompt.

You also can use the **S**elect command as described in the preceding section.

Using the Undelete Command

Few things are more frustrating than accidentally deleting text. WordPerfect Corporation understands the errors users make, and so provides a way to access recent deletions. WordPerfect maintains a *buffer* (a special file) that holds the last three deletions. To undelete text, do the following:

Reminder:

To retrieve deleted text, press Cancel (F1) or access the Edit pull-down menu and select Undelete.

1. Position the cursor where you want the previously deleted text placed.

2. Press Cancel (F1).

   ⌨ Access the **E**dit pull-down menu and choose **U**ndelete.

   The following menu appears in the lower left corner of the screen:

   Undelete: 1 Restore; **2 P**revious Deletion: **0**

   A block of highlighted text appears on the editing screen—the most recently deleted text (see fig. 3.4).

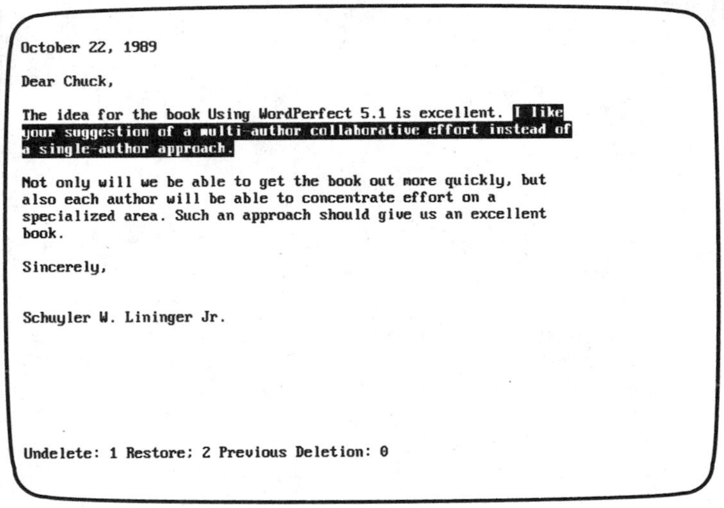

Fig. 3.4.

Using the Undelete feature.

```
October 22, 1989

Dear Chuck,

The idea for the book Using WordPerfect 5.1 is excellent. I like
your suggestion of a multi-author collaborative effort instead of
a single-author approach.

Not only will we be able to get the book out more quickly, but
also each author will be able to concentrate effort on a
specialized area. Such an approach should give us an excellent
book.

Sincerely,


Schuyler W. Lininger Jr.




Undelete: 1 Restore; 2 Previous Deletion: 0
```

3. Choose **R**estore (**1**) if the highlighted text is what you want to undelete; choose **P**revious Deletion (**2**) (or use the ↑ and ↓ keys) if you want to undelete previously deleted text. When the proper text appears on-screen, choose **R**estore (**1**).

Because deleted text is saved to a buffer file, WordPerfect may run out of memory or disk storage space if a lot of text is deleted at once. If you try to delete too much text, WordPerfect shows the warning: Delete without saving for Undelete? No (Yes). Select **Y** to delete the highlighted text, knowing you cannot restore it; select **N** to cancel the deletion.

Inserting Text

As you learned in Chapter 2, the capability to insert text is a major difference between WordPerfect and a typewriter. With a typewriter, you cannot insert a word in a previously typed sentence without retyping the sentence. With WordPerfect, you move the cursor to where you want to add the word and type away. The new word is inserted at the cursor and the old text is pushed to the right. If the text pushes off the screen to the right, press the ↓ key, and it wraps correctly to the next line.

Overwriting Text

On occasion, you may want to overwrite text instead of inserting it. You can overwrite by pressing Ins to switch to Typeover mode. In this mode, new characters you enter replace characters on-screen. Normal Insert mode pushes existing text ahead as new characters are inserted. When you press the Ins key, the word Typeover appears in the lower left corner of the screen. This message reminds you that what you type replaces what is already in the document. To return to normal Insert mode, press Ins again.

Reminder:
To replace letters in a misspelled word, place the cursor at the appropriate position, press Ins, and type the correct characters.

Understanding Hidden Codes

"Behind the scenes" of the document, WordPerfect is receiving instructions about what you want the document to look like. For instance, pressing Underline (F8) turns on underlining; pressing Underline (F8) a second time, or pressing the right-arrow key, turns off underlining.

When you press Underline (F8) (or access the **F**ont pull-down menu, select **A**ppearance, and then select **U**nderline), a *hidden code* is inserted into the document, which tells WordPerfect to begin underlining. By hiding the codes, WordPerfect keeps the document-editing screen uncluttered.

To see the hidden codes in the text, do the following steps:

1. Press Reveal Codes (Alt-F3 or F11).

   🖙 Access the **E**dit pull-down menu and select **R**eveal.

   The screen splits in half with the same text displayed in both windows. The lower part of the screen shows the hidden codes (see fig. 3.5).

2. Press Reveal Codes (Alt-F3 or F11) again to restore the normal screen.

   🖙 Access the **E**dit pull-down menu and select **R**eveal.

From figure 3.5 you can see that the hidden codes are enclosed in brackets, which make codes easily distinguishable from normal text.

WordPerfect has many codes (see table 3.1). The codes "tell" WordPerfect about everything from tab stops to point size to where to place carriage returns and page breaks. Don't memorize all the hidden codes. Some of them you may never use. If you encounter a hidden code you need to know more about, refer to the list in table 3.1. The important and common hidden codes will become familiar to you as you use them.

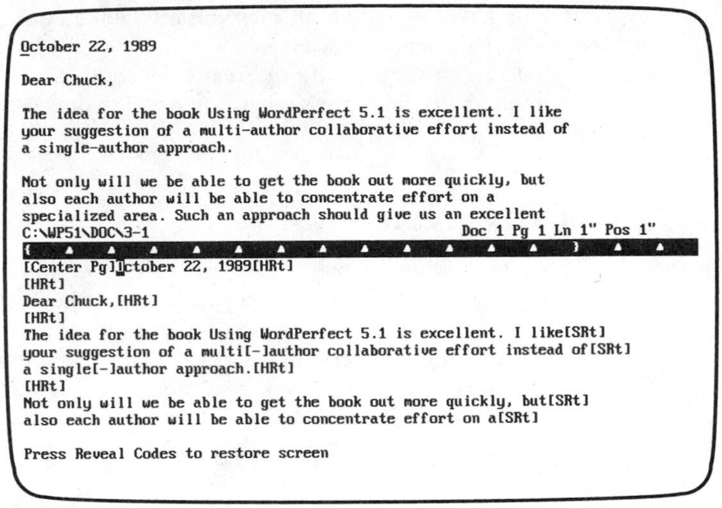

Fig. 3.5.

The Reveal Codes screen.

Listing Hidden Codes

Table 3.1 shows a complete listing of the hidden codes and what they represent.

Table 3.1
List of Hidden Codes

Hidden Code	Function
[ ]	Hard Space
[-]	Hyphen
—	Soft Hyphen
[/]	Cancel Hyphenation
[Adv]	Advance
[BLine]	Baseline Placement (new with 5.1)
[Block]	Beginning of Block
[Block Pro]	Block Protection
[BOLD] [bold]	Bold ON/off
[Box Num]	Caption in Graphics Box
[Cell]	Table Cell (new with 5.1)
[Center]	Center Text
[Center Pg]	Center Page Top to Bottom
[Cndl EOP]	Conditional End of Page
[Cntr Tab]	Center Tab
[CNTR TAB]	Hard Center Tab (new with 5.1)
[Col Def]	Column Definition
[Col Off]	End of Text Columns
[Col On]	Beginning of Text Columns
[Color]	Print Color
[Comment]	Document Comment
[Date]	Date/Time Function

Table 3.1 (continued)

Hidden Code	Function
[DBL UND] [dbl und]	Double Underlining ON/off
[Decml/Algn Char]	Decimal Character/Thousands Separator
[Dec Tab]	Decimal Tab
[DEC TAB]	Hard Decimal Tab Alignment (new with 5.1)
[Def Mark:Index]	Index Definition
[Def Mark:List]	List Definition
[Def Mark:ToA]	Table of Authorities Definition
[Def Mark:ToC]	Table of Contents Definition
[Dorm HRt]	Dormant Hard Return (new with 5.1)
[DSRt]	Deletable Soft Return
[End Def]	End of Index, List, or Table of Contents
[End Mark]	End of Marked Text
[End Opt]	Endnote Options
[Endnote Placement]	Endnote Placement
[Endnote]	Endnote
[Equ Box]	Equation Box
[Equ Opt]	Equation Box Options
[EXT LARGE] [ext large]	Extra Large Print Font ON/off
[Fig Box]	Figure Box
[Fig Opt]	Figure Box Options
[FINE] [fine]	Fine Font ON/off
[Flsh Rt]	Flush Right Text
[Font]	Base Font
[Footer]	Footer
[Footnote]	Footnote
[Force]	Force Odd/Even Page
[Ftn Opt]	Footnote Options
[Full Form]	Table of Authorities, Full Form
[Header]	Header
[HLine]	Horizontal Line
[HPg]	Hard Page
[Hrd Row]	Hard Row (new with 5.1)
[HRt]	Hard Return
[HRt-SPg]	Hard Return, Soft New Page Combination (new with 5.1)
[Hyph Off]	Hyphenation Off
[Hyph On]	Hyphenation On
[HZone]	Hyphenation Zone
[→Indent]	Indent
[→Indent←]	Left/Right Indent
[Index]	Index Entry
[Insert Pg Num]	Insert Page Number (new with 5.1)
[ISRt]	Invisible Soft Return
[ITALC] [italc]	Italic Font ON/off

Table 3.1 (continued)

Hidden Code	Function
[Just Lim]	Word/Letter Spacing/Justification Limits
[Just:Center]	Center Justification (new with 5.1)
[Just:Full]	Full Justification (new with 5.1)
[Just:Left]	Left Justification (new with 5.1)
[Just:Right]	Right Justification (new with 5.1)
[Kern]	Kerning
[L/R Mar]	Left and Right Margins
[Lang]	Language
[LARGE] [large]	Large Font ON/off
[Leading Adj]	Leading Adjustment (new with 5.1)
[Link]	Spreadsheet Link (new with 5.1)
[Link End]	End of Spreadsheet Link (new with 5.1)
[Ln Height]	Line Height
[Ln Num]	Line Numbering
[Ln Spacing]	Line Spacing
[←Mar Rel]	Left Margin Release
[Mark:List]	List Entry
[Mark:ToA]	Table of Authorities Entry
[Mark:ToC]	Table of Contents Entry
[Math Def]	Definition of Math Columns
[Math Off]	Math Off
[Math On]	Math On
!	Formula Calculation
=	Calculate Total
+	Calculate Subtotal
*	Calculate Grand Total
N	Negate Total
t	Subtotal Entry
T	Total Entry
[New End Num]	New Endnote Number
[New Equ Num]	New Equation Number
[New Fig Num]	New Figure Box Number
[New Ftn Num]	New Footnote Number
[New Tbl Num]	New Table Box Number
[New Txt Num]	New Text Box Number
[New Usr Number]	New User Box Number
[Note Num]	Footnote/Endnote Number
[Outline Lvl]	Outline Style (new with 5.1)
[Outline Off]	Outline Off
[Outline On]	Outline On
[OUTLN] [outln]	Outline Font ON/off
[Ovrstk]	Overstrike
[Paper Sz/Typ]	Paper Size and Type
[Par Num]	Paragraph Number

Table 3.1 (continued)

Hidden Code	Function
[Par Num Def]	Paragraph Numbering Definition
[Pg Num]	New Page Number
[Pg Num Style]	Page Number Style (new with 5.1)
[Pg Numbering]	Page Number Position
[Ptr Cmnd]	Printer Command
[REDLN][Redln]	Redline Font ON/off
[Ref]	Reference (Cross-Reference)
[Rgt Tab]	Right Tab
[RGT TAB]	Hard Right Tab (new with 5.1)
[Row]	Table Row (new with 5.1)
[SHADW] [shadw]	Shadow Font ON/off
[SM CAP] [sm Cap]	Small Capital Letters ON/off
[SMALL] [small]	Small Font ON/off
[SPg]	Soft New Page
[SRt]	Soft Return
[STKOUT] [stkout]	Strikeout Font ON/off
[Style Off]	Style Definition Off
[Style On]	Style Definition On
[Subdoc]	Subdocument for Master Document
[Subdoc End]	End of Subdocument
[Subdoc Start]	Beginning of Subdocument
[SUBSCPT] [subscpt]	Subscript Font ON/off
[Suppress]	Suppress Page Formatting
[SUPRSCPT] [suprscpt]	Superscript Font ON/off
[T/B Mar]	Top and Bottom Page Margins
[Tab]	Left Tab
[TAB]	Hard Left Tab (new with 5.1)
[Tab Set]	Tab Set
[Target]	Target for Cross-Reference
[Tbl Box]	Table Box
[Tbl Def]	Table Definition (new with 5.1)
[Tbl Off]	Table End (new with 5.1)
[Tbl Opt]	Table Box Options
[Text Box]	Text Box
[Txt Opt]	Text Box Options
[UND] [und]	Underlining ON/off
[Undrln][UNDRLN]	Underline Spaces/Tabs ON/off
[Usr Box]	User-Defined Box
[Usr Opt]	User-Defined Box Options
[VLine]	Vertical Line
[VRY LARGE] [vry large]	Very Large Font ON/off
[W/O Off]	Widow/Orphan Off
[W/O On]	Widow/Orphan On
[Wrd/Ltr Spacing]	Word and Letter Spacing

Some of the codes have additional information about the status of the feature contained within the brackets. For example, **[Col On]** means columns are turned on; **[L/R Mar:1",1"]** means the left and right margins are each set at one inch.

Editing in Reveal Codes

Editing in Reveal Codes (Alt-F3 or F11) (or accessing the **E**dit pull-down menu and choosing **R**eveal Codes) is different from editing normally. As you recall, you are looking at a split screen with the upper window showing the normal edit screen and the lower window showing text and hidden codes. The cursor in the upper window is normal, but the cursor in the lower window is a narrow, highlighted bar (see fig. 3.6). When the cursor in the lower window meets a hidden code, the cursor expands to cover the code, while in the upper window, the cursor remains unaltered.

Fig. 3.6.

The cursor positioned on a hidden code in Reveal Codes.

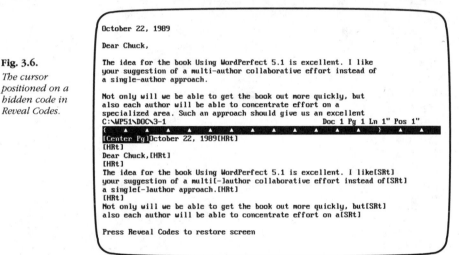

The Reveal Codes window can be distracting during the initial stages of creating a document. You use Reveal Codes most often when you edit and format a document. When the hidden codes are visible, you can see them and the effect they may have on the document. Some people like to leave the Reveal Codes window visible during editing; some people prefer to use it only when necessary. The mouse does not work in the Reveal Codes window. With that one exception, WordPerfect 5.1 allows complete editing capability in the Reveal Codes window.

Remember:

The mouse does not work in the Reveal Codes window.

You also can delete and undelete codes in Reveal Codes. The Undelete feature can recall codes you accidentally delete. If a line, paragraph, or page of text is deleted and later undeleted, all the hidden codes are restored as well as the text.

If you want to add additional boldface text within *paired codes* (codes that act as on and off switches, like **[BOLD] [bold]**), move the cursor between the **[BOLD] [bold]** codes and type the new text instead of pressing Bold (F6) again.

When you enter Reveal Codes, the upper window shows 11 lines and the lower window shows 10 lines (that leaves 3 lines in each window for the status lines and the ruler line). If you don't like the size of the Reveal Codes window, you easily can change it permanently or temporarily.

To change the number of lines in the Reveal Codes window permanently, do the following steps:

1. Press Setup (Shift-F1) and choose **D**isplay (**2**).

    ▣ Access the **F**ile pull-down menu, choose Se**t**up, and select **D**isplay.

2. Choose **E**dit-Screen Options (**6**).

3. Choose **R**eveal Codes Window Size (**6**).

4. Type the number of lines you want the Reveal Codes window to be and press Enter. The default value is 10; you can enter any value from 1 to 20. If you enter 1, only the code or the letter on which the cursor is resting shows in the Reveal Codes screen. If you enter 2 or more, the Reveal Codes screen is normal, just smaller or larger.

5. Press Exit (F7) to return to the editing screen.

To change the size of the Reveal Codes windows screen for your current session, do the following steps:

Note: If the Reveal Codes window is already visible, skip step 1.

1. Press Reveal Codes (Alt-F3 or F11).

    ▣ Access the **E**dit pull-down menu and select **R**eveal Codes.

2. Press Screen (Ctrl-F3) and choose **W**indow (**1**)

    ▣ Access the **E**dit pull-down menu and select **W**indow.

3. You see the Number of lines in this window prompt. You can either enter a new value or use the up and down arrows to interactively size the window to your specifications.

    Note: In this procedure, you size the *editing window*; in the preceding procedure, you sized the *Reveal Codes window*.

4. Press Enter (see fig. 3.7 for an example of Reveal Codes with an editing window of 17 lines instead of the default of 11).

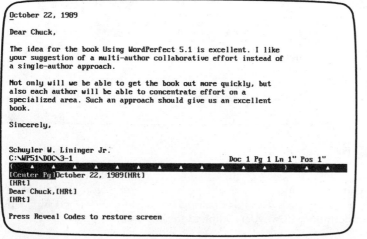

Fig. 3.7.
The Reveal Codes screen with the editing window resized.

Adding Simple Text Enhancements

The second part of the editing process is *formatting*, or preparing the document for printing. Some formatting is done as you enter the text; some is done later. The following sections focus on simple enhancements that can be done as you enter text.

Boldfacing

To create emphasis, text is **boldfaced** (made darker than regular text). Boldfacing should be used sparingly for best effect. To boldface text, complete the following steps:

1. Press Bold (F6).

   ⌨ Access the Font pull-down menu, select **A**ppearance, and select **B**old.

2. Type the text you want to boldface. As you type, depending on your monitor, you see the text you enter in boldface on-screen.

3. To turn off boldface type, press Bold (F6) again (or press the right arrow to move the cursor past the **[bold]** code).

   ⌨ Access the Font pull-down menu, select **A**ppearance, and select **B**old.

The Bold (F6) key serves as an on/off switch. Press once to turn on boldface; press again to turn off boldface (see fig. 3.8). If you press Bold (F6) twice in a row without typing any text, the text you then enter is not boldfaced.

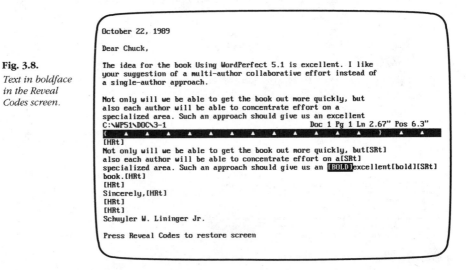

Fig. 3.8.

Text in boldface in the Reveal Codes screen.

Underlining

WordPerfect offers several styles of <u>underlining</u>. You can select either single or double underlining and choose to have spaces between words and tab spaces underlined or not underlined. These formatting options are described in Chapter 5. For simple underlining, however, complete the following steps:

1. Press Underline (F8).

    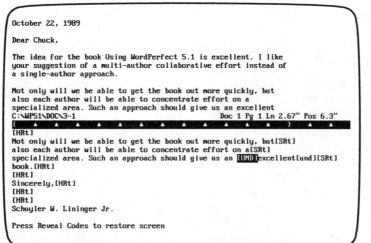 Access the **F**ont pull-down menu, select **A**ppearance, and select **U**nderline.

2. Enter the text you want underlined. Depending on your monitor, the text you type may appear underlined on-screen.

3. To turn off underlining, press Underline (F8) again (or press the right arrow to move the cursor past the **[und]** code).

    Access the **F**ont pull-down menu, select **A**ppearance, and select **U**nderline (see fig. 3.9).

Like the Bold (F6) key, the Underline (F8) key works as an on/off switch. Press once to turn on underlining, press again to turn off underlining. If you press Underline (F8) twice in a row without entering any text, the text you then enter is not underlined.

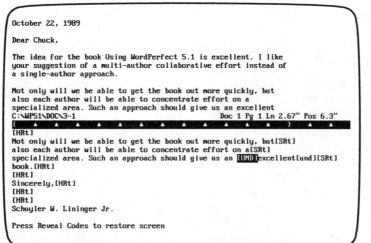

```
October 22, 1989

Dear Chuck,

The idea for the book Using WordPerfect 5.1 is excellent. I like
your suggestion of a multi-author collaborative effort instead of
a single-author approach.

Not only will we be able to get the book out more quickly, but
also each author will be able to concentrate effort on a
specialized area. Such an approach should give us an excellent
C:\WP51\DOC\3-1                              Doc 1 Pg 1 Ln 2.67" Pos 6.3"
[       ▲    ▲    ▲    ▲    ▲    ▲    ▲    ▲    ▲    ▲    }   ▲    ▲
[HRt]
Not only will we be able to get the book out more quickly, but[SRt]
also each author will be able to concentrate effort on a[SRt]
specialized area. Such an approach should give us an [UND]excellent[und][SRt]
book.[HRt]
[HRt]
Sincerely,[HRt]
[HRt]
[HRt]
Schuyler W. Lininger Jr.

Press Reveal Codes to restore screen
```

Fig. 3.9.

Text underlined in the Reveal Codes screen.

Searching and Replacing

Two of the most powerful tools offered by WordPerfect are Search and Replace. If you have faced the frustration of writing a long report and then hunting for a particular phrase or name, you can appreciate WordPerfect's search and replace capabilities.

Searching for Text

You can search for text from any point in a document, and you can search in either direction—beginning to end or end to beginning. To search for text, perform the following steps:

1. Press either Forward Search (F2) or Backward Search (Shift-F2) depending on whether you want to search to the end or to the beginning of the

document from where the cursor is in the document. (If you change your mind, press ↑ or ↓ to change the direction of the search.)

⌨ If you use a mouse, access the **S**earch pull-down menu and choose either **F**orward or **B**ackward.

A prompt appears in the lower left corner of the screen, either →Srch: or ←Srch:.

2. Enter any text, up to 60 characters, for which you want to search.

3. Press Forward Search (F2) or Esc to begin the search, regardless of the direction you are searching.

⌨ Press the right mouse button or double-click the left button to begin the search.

If one occurrence of the text matches, but you want to look for others, repeat the previous steps; however, you need not retype the text for which you are searching—WordPerfect remembers the previous search request. ⌨ If you use a mouse, repeat the search by accessing the **S**earch pull-down menu and choosing **N**ext or **P**revious.

Cue:

If you don't know how to spell a word, search for parts of a word.

You can search for parts of a word or even for words you're not sure how to spell. Look over these examples:

- If you type *and* as the word you are searching for, WordPerfect locates all words that have *and* as a part of them. For example, WordPerfect matches *and* with b*and*, R*and*y, or *And*rew.

- If you want only the specific word and not a part of a word, enter spaces before and after the search text. For example, *[space] and[space]* finds only occurrences of *And* or *and*.

- If you want to find text with a changing component, or if you are unsure of the exact spelling, use the matching character ^X (press Ctrl-V, Ctrl-X). This character matches any single character. If you type *(^X)*, the following characters match: *(1)*, *(2)*, *(3)*, and *(4)*.

- If you type in lowercase only, WordPerfect finds all occurrences of the word regardless of whether it contains uppercase or lowercase letters. For example, searching for *and* finds *And*, *AND*, or *and*. If you type in uppercase only, WordPerfect finds only uppercase matches. For example, searching for *AND* finds only *AND* but not *and* or *And*.

- If you think the text you are looking for may be in a header, footer, footnote, endnote, graphic-box caption, or text box, you must perform an extended search. An *extended search* is exactly the same as a regular search, except that you press Home before pressing the Search (F2 or Shift-F2) key. **E**xtended also can be accessed from the **S**earch pull-down menu.

Searching and Replacing Text

Sometimes you may want to replace the text you find with different text. To search for and replace text, perform the following steps:

1. Press Replace (Alt-F2).

⌨ Access the **S**earch pull-down menu and select **R**eplace.

The w/Confirm? No (Yes) prompt appears in the lower left corner of the screen.

2. If you want to be prompted for confirmation before any changes are made, select **Y**. If you want all changes made automatically, select **N** or press Enter.

   🖰 If you use a mouse, press the right mouse button to accept the default (**N**o) or double-click the left button on **Y**es to request confirmation.

3. At the →Srch: prompt, enter any text, up to 60 characters, for which you want to search.

4. If you want to change the direction of the search, press either ↑ or ↓.

5. Press Forward Search (F2) or Esc.

   🖰 Press the right mouse button or double-click the left button.

6. At the Replace with: prompt, type the replacement text. If you want the text deleted, do not enter anything and go to step 7.

7. To begin the search-and-replace operation, press Forward Search (F2) or Esc.

   🖰 Press the right mouse button or double-click the left button to begin the search.

8. If you requested confirmation in step 2, you see the Confirm? No (Yes) prompt each time the search finds a match. Select **Y** to confirm a replacement or **N** to deny a replacement. If you want to cancel the search-and-replace operation, press Cancel (F1) or Exit (F7).

   🖰 If you use a mouse, press the right button to reject the change or click the left button on either **Y**es or **N**o.

If you want to repeat the search and replace operation, repeat the previous steps; however, you need not retype the text for which you are searching and replacing— WordPerfect remembers the latest search-and-replace request. If you want, the previous search requests can be edited using the normal editing keys and functions. However, if you press an alphanumeric key before one of the arrow or editing keys, the new text is substituted for the old.

Both the Search and Replace features (but not Extended Search or Replace) can be used with Block (Alt-F4 or F12). When you define a block, the Search or Replace operation is confined to the block. Block functions are explained thoroughly in Chapter 4.

If a search fails to find a match, a message * Not found * appears in the bottom left corner of the screen. You also hear a beep if WordPerfect has been set up to beep on search failure. Chapter 20 explains how to define when WordPerfect beeps.

Using Search or Replace

You can find many uses for search or replace. Look over these ideas:

- **Check for jargon**. For example, if you write to a person unfamiliar with computers, you don't use words that only experienced users know. Also, you may want to list your own business jargon and ensure that you replace it with more common terms.

- **Check for poor writing**. For example, you may want to search your document for the pronouns *this* and *it* which often vaguely refer to something that could confuse the reader.
- **Check for cliches**. If you have a tendency to use phrases that are tired or trite, you can search and replace them with fresh images.
- **Check for matching punctuation**. You easily can forget to close a parenthesis or quotation mark. Double-check the document for proper pairing of special punctuation.
- **Check for too many spaces**. Normally, you insert two spaces after a period. If you are printing the document on a laser printer or a printer that justifies text, you probably should use only a single space after a period. You can replace all occurrences of two spaces with a single space. You can use the same technique to replace two hard returns with one hard return.
- **Expand abbreviations**. Suppose that you are writing a report about a client with the name Mrs. William Danielson III. You can type an abbreviation, such as *wd*, and later replace the abbreviation with the full name of the client. Each abbreviation saves you many keystrokes.

Cue:

Use abbreviations for long text that appears repeatedly; replace the abbreviation with the full form.

Reminder:

If you delete one of a set of paired codes, both are deleted.

Searching or Replacing Hidden Codes

WordPerfect can search or replace hidden codes. When prompted for the search text, press the function key that normally generates the code. If the code is usually generated from a second-level or third-level menu, those choices appear in a menu line at the bottom of the screen. When you select the options you want, the corresponding codes appear in the search or replace text area. Note that if you delete one of a set of paired codes (for example, **[BOLD]** or **[bold]**), both are deleted.

To search for the hidden code **[BOLD]**, do the following:

1. Press Reveal Codes (Alt-F3 or F11).

    ⌨ Access the **E**dit pull-down menu and select **R**eveal Codes.

2. Press Forward Search (F2).

    ⌨ Access the **S**earch pull-down menu and select **F**orward.

3. At the →Srch: prompt, press Bold (F6).

    Note: You cannot choose the codes for which you want to search from the pull-down menus; you **must** use the function keys.

4. Press Forward Search (F2) or Esc to begin the search.

    ⌨ Press the right mouse button or double-click the left button to begin the search.

Some codes are tricky to find. In general, you can insert codes into a Search or Replace command by pressing the correct function key and following the prompts until you find the command you're looking for. As an example, all the Merge commands are available from Merge Codes (Shift-F9) under **M**ore (**6**). To search for the second code in a paired code, press the feature key twice, use the left-arrow key to move the cursor to the first part of the pair, then delete the first code. For example, press F2, F6, left arrow, backspace, and F2 to search for the **[bold]** end code.

Making Document Comments

When you are writing, you may want to insert a note, memo, or comment as a personal reminder for later use. WordPerfect provides a way to put electronic notes in a document where you can see them on-screen, but they won't print out. Also, you can hide the comments on-screen so that they're visible only when you want them to be.

Inserting Document Comments

To insert a document comment in the document, use these steps:

1. Press Text In/Out (Ctrl-F5). The following menu appears at the bottom of the screen:

   1 DOS **T**ext; **2 P**assword; **3** Save **A**s; **4 C**omment; **5 S**preadsheet: **0**

   Choose **C**omment (**4**). From the Comment menu at the bottom of the screen choose **C**reate (**1**).

   ▭ Access the **E**dit pull-down menu, select **C**omment, and select **C**reate.

2. Type the text of the comment in the box that appears in the Document Comment screen (see fig. 3.10). You can underline or boldface text in the comment box.

3. To return to the document, press Exit (F7). The document comment appears on-screen in the middle of the text as a box surrounded by a double line (see fig. 3.11).

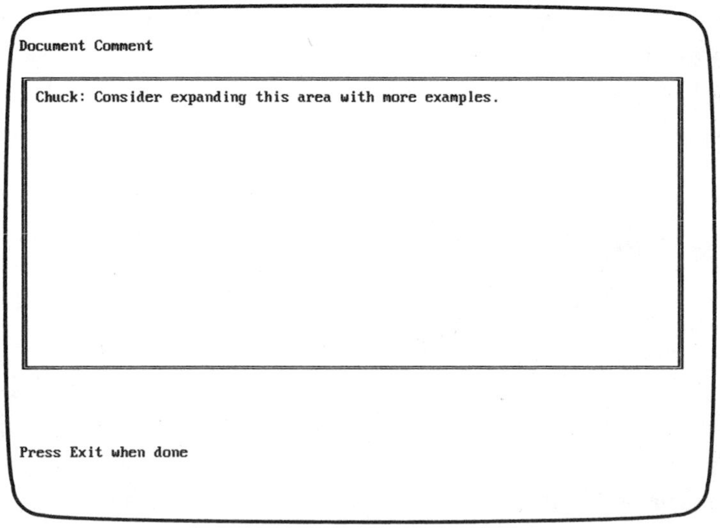

```
Document Comment

 ┌──────────────────────────────────────────────────────┐
 │ Chuck: Consider expanding this area with more examples.│
 │                                                        │
 │                                                        │
 │                                                        │
 │                                                        │
 │                                                        │
 │                                                        │
 │                                                        │
 └──────────────────────────────────────────────────────┘



 Press Exit when done
```

Fig. 3.10.
The Document Comment screen.

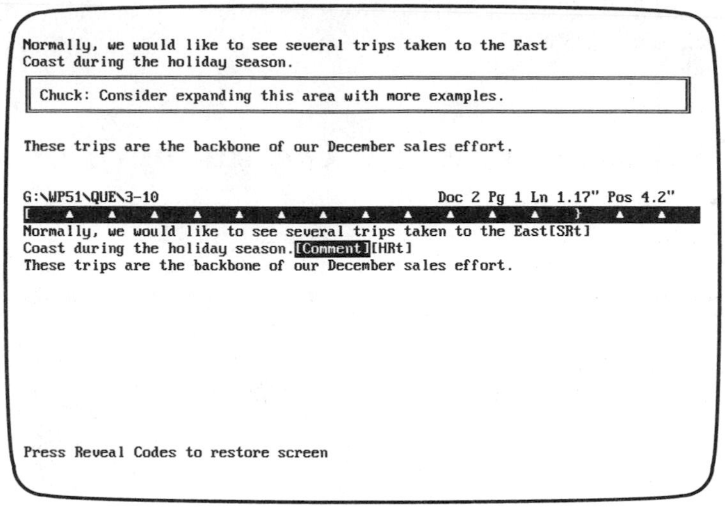

Fig. 3.11.
A document comment in text.

Editing Document Comments

If you want, you can change the comments you enter in a document. If you have more than one comment in a document, WordPerfect looks backward from the cursor for a comment to edit. If no comments precede the cursor, WordPerfect then looks forward from the cursor for a comment to edit. To edit an existing document comment, perform the following steps:

1. Move the cursor past the comment you want to edit.

2. Press Text In/Out (Ctrl-F5), choose **C**omment (**4**), and then choose **E**dit (**2**).

   ⌨ Access the **E**dit pull-down menu, choose **C**omment, and select **E**dit.

3. Change the text of the comments. All the normal editing keys operate.

4. Press Exit (F7) to return to the document.

If no comment is found, the error message * Not found * appears at the bottom of the screen.

Converting Comments to Text

Reminder:
Before you can print document comments, you must convert them to text.

If a document is a collaborative effort, numerous comments from various authors or editors may be entered during the revision or editing process. Because comments are only displayed and not printed, they must first be converted to text before they can be printed.

If you have a comment that you want to insert in the document as text to be printed, perform the following steps:

1. Move the cursor to the end of the comment you want to convert.

2. Press Text In/Out (Ctrl-F5), choose **C**omment (**4**), and choose Convert to **T**ext (**3**).

⌨ Access the **E**dit pull-down menu, select **C**omment, and choose Convert to **T**ext.

The comment is immediately converted to text, and you are returned to the editing screen. If no comment is found, the error message `* Not found *` appears at the bottom of the screen.

Caution

The Speller (Ctrl-F2) does not examine document comments for spelling errors. If you convert comments to text, check for spelling errors by running the Speller.

Converting Text to Comments

Sometimes in revising a document you find text that provides valuable information or is well written but doesn't fit with what you are writing about. Rather than delete the thought, save it for use at another time. One way to save the text is to use the Block command and save the text to another file. The technique for blocking and saving is described in Chapter 4. Another way to save the text, but keep it separate from the document you are working on, is to convert the text to a comment.

If you have text you want to keep, but not print, turn it into a comment as an alternative to deletion. To convert text into a comment, do the following steps:

1. Use the keyboard (Alt-F4 or F12) or the mouse to highlight the text you want to turn into a comment. For more information on the Block command, see Chapter 4.

2. Press Text In/Out (Ctrl-F5).

   ⌨ Access the **E**dit pull-down menu, select **C**omment, and choose **C**reate.

   The prompt `Create a comment? No (Yes)` appears at the bottom of the screen.

3. Select **Y**. The blocked text immediately appears in a comment box on the editing screen. If you select **N** or press any other key, the text is not converted.

You can convert up to 24 lines into a comment. Because comments are treated as a single word by WordPerfect, the cursor is either before the comment box or after the comment box; the entire comment box jumps when the cursor is moved.

Hiding Document Comments

You may find document comments distracting. To hide the comments from view as you work, do the following steps:

1. Press Setup (Shift-F1) and choose **D**isplay (**2**) from the Setup menu.

   ⌨ Access the **F**ile pull-down menu, select Se**t**up, and choose **D**isplay.

Cue:
Keep text separate from the current document or "hide" text you don't want printed by turning it into a comment.

2. Choose **E**dit-Screen Options (**6**).

3. Choose **C**omments Display (**2**).

4. Select **Y** or **N** to either display or not display comments.

5. Press Exit (F7) to return to the document.

Reminder:

If you want to see comments in a document other than the one you're working on, turn on the comment display.

If you hide the document comments in the document you are working on, all comments are hidden in all other documents. If you want to see comments in other documents, remember to turn on the comment display.

Using Document Comments

Besides using document comments to store simple memos and notes, you also can use it in the following ways:

- **As a writing aid**. As you write, leave brief messages about what you mean, where the text could use polish, and where you have trouble completing a thought. During the revision process, the comments should trigger your memory.

- **For collaborative writing**. If you are part of a writing team, leave messages and criticism for other team members.

- **As an editing tool**. If you are an editor, leave the author messages and comments using the Document Comment feature.

Summary

In this chapter you have learned how easily you can make changes to a document with WordPerfect. You can now do the following operations:

❏ Retrieve a previously written document

❏ Delete text by the character, word, line, sentence, paragraph, or page

❏ Recover accidental deletions by using the Undelete feature

❏ Toggle between inserting and overwriting text

❏ Make basic enhancements to text by making a word or phrase **boldfaced** or underlined

❏ Find words, names, or phrases anywhere in a document

❏ Replace any word, name, or phrase

❏ Find basic errors in punctuation and grammar

❏ Find, use, and edit hidden codes

❏ Create and edit a document comment

❏ Use document comments as a memo tool or as an aid to writing

❏ Convert comments to text and vice versa

Working with Blocks

Karen Rose, owner of Write on Target, uses desktop publishing to produce a variety of news-letters. She authored this chapter for *Using WordPerfect 5.*

Andrea Pickens is a principal of Learning Associates, Inc., which uses WordPerfect for all written materials produced for clients. She revised this chapter for *Using WordPerfect 5.1,* Special Edition.

With WordPerfect's Block command, you can select, or highlight, an area of text. Highlighting text is the first step in many timesaving WordPerfect functions, such as moving and copying text. The Block command, used in combination with other commands, gives you powerful editing capabilities.

A block of text can be as short as a single letter or as long as the entire document. Flexibility is the Block command's strength. You define the size and shape of the block, and then you specify what to do with that selected text.

In this chapter, you learn how to do the following:

- Highlight a block of text or numbers
- Move or copy a block—within and between documents
- Delete a block
- Append a block to a different document
- Save a block
- Print a block
- Enhance a block of characters with features such as boldface, underlining, and italics
- Enlarge or reduce the size of the characters in a block
- Make a block of text all uppercase or all lowercase
- Center a block
- Move or copy a rectangular block, such as a column

> **Reminder**
>
> If you use a mouse with WordPerfect 5.1, you can click the right button to display the pull-down menus, and then select the desired option. You also can press Alt-= to access the pull-down menus, and then press the appropriate letter of the desired option. For all instructions you can assume that if a block is required to activate a pull-down menu option, the text has been blocked before the pull-down menu is accessed. Both pull-down menu and mouse instructions are marked with the mouse icon. For more information about the mouse, refer to Chapter 1. 🖱

Understanding Block Operations and Revision Strategies

You can use many WordPerfect commands with or without Block. For example, you can boldface or underline text as you type. Often, however, completing the document before you add these enhancements is easier. Later, after your ideas are down, you can use the Block command to add enhancements or to reorganize your paragraphs into a more logical order. This approach lets your thoughts flow freely, without interruption, as you write.

How Block Works

On your computer screen, blocked text appears highlighted, as shown in figure 4.1. Blocked text is, in a sense, text identified as "ready." The text is ready for the second step in any of a number of operations, such as moving, copying, deleting, saving, or printing.

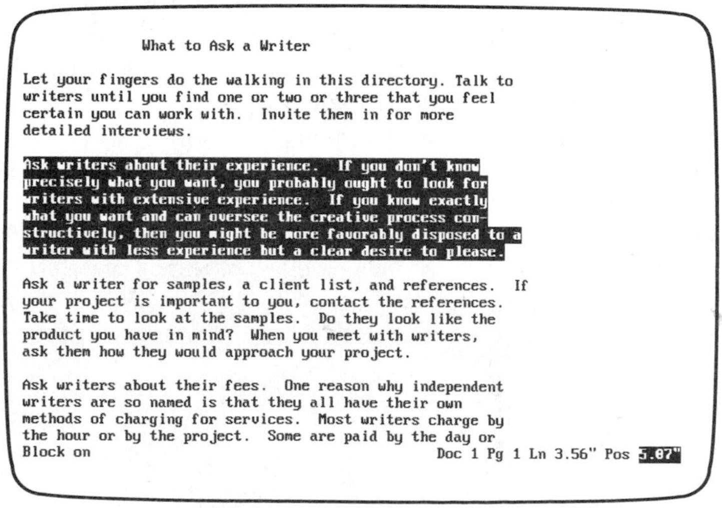

Fig. 4.1.

A highlighted block of text.

```
                    What to Ask a Writer

        Let your fingers do the walking in this directory. Talk to
        writers until you find one or two or three that you feel
        certain you can work with.  Invite them in for more
        detailed interviews.

        Ask writers about their experience.  If you don't know
        precisely what you want, you probably ought to look for
        writers with extensive experience.  If you know exactly
        what you want and can oversee the creative process con-
        structively, then you might be more favorably disposed to a
        writer with less experience but a clear desire to please.

        Ask a writer for samples, a client list, and references.  If
        your project is important to you, contact the references.
        Take time to look at the samples.  Do they look like the
        product you have in mind?  When you meet with writers,
        ask them how they would approach your project.

        Ask writers about their fees.  One reason why independent
        writers are so named is that they all have their own
        methods of charging for services.  Most writers charge by
        the hour or by the project.  Some are paid by the day or
        Block on                        Doc 1 Pg 1 Ln 3.56" Pos 5.07"
```

Highlighting Text with Block

You can highlight text by using either keyboard commands or a mouse. To highlight a block of text, you position the cursor at the beginning of the block of text you want to highlight, turn on the Block command, and move the cursor to the end of the block. That's it! The highlighted block of text is ready for the next step in your operation.

Using the Keyboard to Highlight a Block of Text

Here are the specific steps you use with the keyboard to highlight a block of text:

1. Use the cursor keys to move the cursor to the beginning of the block of text you want to highlight and press Block (Alt-F4 or F12). Notice the Block on message blinking in the bottom left of the screen.
2. Use the arrow keys to move the cursor to the end of the block of text.

Reminder:

To highlight a block with the keyboard, position the cursor at the beginning of the block, press Block, and move the cursor to the end of the block.

Using the Mouse to Highlight a Block of Text

One of the most valuable uses of the mouse interface in WordPerfect is for highlighting a block of text quickly and easily. Here are the specific steps you use with the mouse to highlight a block of text:

1. Move the mouse pointer to the beginning of the block of text you want to highlight.
2. Press and hold the left mouse button. Hold the mouse button as you move the mouse to position the mouse pointer at the end of the block of text. When you reach the end of the block you want to highlight, release the left mouse button.

Notice the Block on message blinking in the bottom left of the screen.

You can increase or decrease the amount of text highlighted after releasing the left mouse button by using the cursor-arrow keys to reposition the cursor at the end of the block.

Reminder:

To highlight a block with the mouse, position the mouse pointer at the beginning of the block, press and hold the left mouse button, and drag to the end of the block.

Tip

You can use several shortcuts to define a block, whether you use the keyboard or the mouse to turn on the Block command.

One shortcut is to use the arrow keys to define a block. For example, if you turn on Block with the cursor or mouse pointer at the *end* of the line you want to block, you can then press Home-← to move the cursor to the beginning of the line. The entire line is then highlighted.

After you turn on Block, you can use the Search command to find the text you want at the end of the block and move the cursor to that position.

Another shortcut is to turn on Block and press any character to move to the next occurrence of that character in the text. To block a sentence, for instance, turn on Block at the beginning of the sentence and type a period. The block extends to the period at the end of the sentence. To select an entire paragraph, turn on Block and press Enter. The block extends to the next occurrence of a hard return.

Completing the Block Operation

The Block on message continues to blink until you complete the Block operation by moving the block, underlining it, or performing any function that works with the Block command. The following functions work with the Block command:

Append	Mark Text	Search
Block Protect	Index	Shell
Bold	List	Append
Center	Table of Authorities	Save
Delete	Table of Contents	Sort
Flush Right	Move	Spell
Font	Block	Style
Size (All)	Tabular Column	Switch
Appearance (All)	Rectangle	Tables (version 5.1)
Format	Print	Text In/Out
Macro	Replace	Underline
	Save	

Canceling a Block

Reminder:
To cancel a block, press Cancel or Block, or click the left or center mouse button.

To cancel a block with the keyboard, press either the Cancel (F1) key or the Block (Alt-F4 or F12) key while the block is highlighted.

To cancel a block with the mouse, click the left mouse button; if you have a three-button mouse, click the center mouse button.

Rehighlighting a Block

After you highlight a block, you can perform a single editing or formatting operation. Suppose, however, that you want to make two or more changes to the same block of text. You might, for example, want to emphasize a paragraph by making it both bold and italic. After you have made one change to a block, you can use a shortcut to rehighlight the block and make the second change.

Reminder:
Rehighlight a block of text by pressing Block and pressing GoTo twice.

Start by highlighting the block of text and completing the first operation. Leave the cursor at the end of the block. Then complete the following steps to rehighlight the same block of text:

1. Press Block (Alt-F4 or F12) to turn on the Block command.
2. Press GoTo (Ctrl-Home) to activate the GoTo command.
3. Press GoTo (Ctrl-Home) again to return to the beginning of the block.

   Note: Pressing GoTo (Ctrl-Home) twice returns the cursor to the position occupied before the last operation.

If you change your mind about the amount of text you want to highlight, return to the beginning of the block and start over. To return to the beginning of a block already highlighted, press GoTo (Ctrl-Home) and then Block (Alt-F4 or F12). The block is no longer highlighted, but the Block command is still on. Now you can highlight the appropriate amount of text.

Moving a Block

You can use WordPerfect's capacity to move blocks as a powerful editing tool. With this function, you don't have to worry about preparing your report or letter perfectly the first time. Instead, you can get the ideas down and use the Block Move command to organize them later.

When you move a block of text, you delete it from one place and insert it somewhere else. You can move a block of any size to another place in the current document or to another document.

Reminder:

When you move a block of text, you delete it from its original position and place it in a new location.

Caution

The Ctrl-Ins and Ctrl-Del keys referred to in this chapter may not operate properly if you are using a keyboard definition originally created with WordPerfect 5. To overcome this problem, create dummy key definitions for Ctrl-Ins and Ctrl-Del in the keyboard definition and then delete the dummy definitions. Ctrl-Ins and Ctrl-Del then operate correctly.

To move a block of text, follow these steps:

1. Use the keyboard (Alt-F4 or F12) or the mouse to highlight the text you want to move.
2. Press Move (Ctrl-F4), select **B**lock (**1**), and select **M**ove (**1**). Alternatively, press Ctrl-Del.

   ⌨ Access the **E**dit pull-down menu and choose **M**ove.

   The highlighted block of text disappears from the screen.
3. Move the cursor where you want to move the block of text.
4. Press Enter.

The text is retrieved and displayed at the cursor's new position.

Copying a Block

The Move command removes a block of text from one position in your document and retrieves it to another position; the Copy command duplicates the block of text in another position. The original stays put, and the copy appears in the new position.

To copy a block of text, follow these steps:

1. Use the keyboard (Alt-F4 or F12) or the mouse to highlight the text you want to copy.
2. Press Move (Ctrl-F4), select **B**lock (**1**), and select **C**opy (**2**) Alternatively, press Ctrl-Ins.

   ⌨ Access the **E**dit pull-down menu and choose **C**opy.

3. Move the cursor to where you want to copy the block of text.

4. Press Enter.

You can retrieve the copied text as many times as you want. To duplicate the same block of text and retrieve it again, follow these steps:

1. Move the cursor to where you want to retrieve the block of text.

2. Press Move (Ctrl-F4), select **R**etrieve (**4**), and select **B**lock (**1**).

   ▢▤ Access the **E**dit pull-down menu, choose **P**aste, and select **B**lock (**1**).

   Alternatively, press Shift-F10; at the `Document to be retrieved:` prompt, press Enter.

   ▢▤ Access the **F**ile pull-down menu and select **R**etrieve; at the `Document to be retrieved:` prompt, press Enter.

Deleting a Block

Deleting a block of text is as simple as highlighting the text, pressing the Del or Backspace key, and confirming the deletion. To delete a block of text, follow these steps:

1. Use the keyboard (Alt-F4 or F12) or the mouse to highlight the text you want to delete.

2. Press the Del or Backspace key.

   The following message appears at the bottom left of the screen:

   `Delete Block? No (Yes)`

   WordPerfect assumes that you don't want to delete the text; if you don't, press Enter. The block remains highlighted. If you do want to delete the block, continue with the next step.

3. Select **Y**es.

Deleted text is removed. You cannot retrieve deleted text the way you retrieve text that you move or copy. You can, however, change your mind about the deletion if you catch your mistake quickly. To undelete, do the following:

1. Press the Cancel key (F1).

   ▢▤ Click the center button of a three-button mouse or hold either button of a two-button mouse and click the other button.

   The most recently deleted text reappears in the document at the cursor position.

2. Select **R**estore (**1**) to restore the deleted text.

WordPerfect lets you restore any of your last three deletions. When you press the Cancel key (F1) or use a mouse button to undelete, the following status line is displayed at the bottom left of the screen:

Undelete: 1 Restore; **2 P**revious Deletion: **0**

The screen also displays in the document the most recent deletion. If you select **R**estore (**1**), the most recent deletion is restored. If you select **P**revious Deletion (**2**), however, the second most recent deletion is shown in the text instead. To restore that deletion, select **R**estore (**1**). If you want to restore your third most recent deletion, select **P**revious Deletion (**2**) again, and then select **R**estore (**1**) to restore that deletion.

Appending a Block

Sometimes you want to add information to a WordPerfect document while you are working on a different document. While you are writing a letter to a client today, for example, you may think of an idea you want to add to a report you wrote yesterday. Rather than exiting the letter, opening the report, and adding the idea to the report, you can append the idea to the report while still working on the letter.

Follow these steps to append a block of text to another document:

1. Use the keyboard (Alt-F4 or F12) or the mouse to highlight the text you want to append to another document.

2. Press Move (Ctrl-F4), select **B**lock (**1**), and select **A**ppend (**4**).

   ⌨ Access the **E**dit pull-down menu and choose **A**ppend.

   The screen displays the Append to: message. The cursor is positioned immediately after the message so that you can enter your response.

3. Type the file name of the document to which you want to append the block.

The appended block remains in the current document and is copied to the end of the file whose name you typed in step 3. If WordPerfect cannot find a file with the name you typed, the program creates that file. The file to which you append a block of text can be either in the current directory or in another directory. To append a block of text to a file in a different directory, include the directory as part of the file name you type in step 3. To append a block to a file named IDEAS in the current directory, for example, type *IDEAS* in step 3. To append a block to a file named IDEAS in a directory called SALES, however, type \ *SALES* \ *IDEAS* in step 3. You don't see the document to which you append a block unless you exit the current document and open the appended document.

Reminder:
You can append text to a file in another directory.

Saving a Block

As you are typing a document—a legal contract is a good example—you may type a paragraph or some other block of text that you want to use again in another document. A simple way to do this is to save the block to a separate file, independent of the document in which you're currently working.

To save a block of text to a separate file, follow these steps:

1. Use the keyboard (Alt-F4 or F12) or the mouse to highlight the text you want to save to a separate file.

2. Press Save (F10).

    ▢ Access the **F**ile pull-down menu and choose **S**ave.

    The screen displays the `Block name:` message.

3. Type the name of the file to which you want to save the block and press Enter.

If the name you type is the name of an existing file, the screen displays the following message:

```
Replace <filename>? No (Yes)
```

To replace the file, select **Y**es. If you don't want to replace the file, select **N**o, type a new name, and press Enter.

The block is saved to the specified file in the current default directory. That directory may be different from the directory you're currently working in. Press List (F5) or select List **F**iles from the **F**ile pull-down menu to determine the default directory. To save the block into a different directory, include the directory as part of the file name you type in step 3.

Cue:

Use the Retrieve command to build a document out of blocks of text saved with the Block Save command.

The Block Save command works well in combination with WordPerfect's Retrieve command. You can use the two commands to build a document from previously created blocks of text. A legal office, for example, may use the same paragraphs repeatedly in many different contracts. Use the Block command to save each reusable paragraph as an individual file. Use the Retrieve command to build a contract out of the paragraphs you blocked and saved as individual files. For more about the Retrieve command, refer to Chapter 3.

Printing a Block

Sometimes you want to print only one paragraph from a letter or one page from a document. Use the Block Print command to print part of your document.

To print a block, follow these steps:

1. Use the keyboard (Alt-F4 or F12) or the mouse to highlight the text you want to print.

2. Press Print (Shift-F7).

    ▢ Access the **F**ile pull-down menu and choose **P**rint.

    The following message appears at the bottom left of the screen:

    ```
    Print block? No (Yes)
    ```

3. Press Y or click **Y**es.

The block prints on the currently selected printer. For instructions on installing a printer, refer to Appendix A. For instructions on selecting from installed printers, see Chapter 8.

Enhancing Text with the Block Command

Using the Block command, you can change the appearance of selected areas of text. You can emphasize an important paragraph by making it bold, for example, or you can call attention to a single word by underlining it. You can change the type font in a headline. You can center a title, redline edited text, or strike out text to be deleted. The Block command gives you the power to make any of these changes to a block of text that is as small as a single letter or as large as the full document.

Boldfacing and Underlining Blocked Text

You can boldface or underline text as you create your document. Often, however, you will find that typing the text normally and later using the Block command to add boldfacing or underlining is easier. WordPerfect offers you a choice of single or double underlines. The procedures for inserting the two types of underlines are similar if you use a mouse; if you use the keyboard, the procedures are different.

To boldface or single underline a block of text (or a single character), follow these steps:

1. Use the keyboard (Alt-F4 or F12) or the mouse to highlight the text you want to boldface or single underline.

2. Press Bold (F6) to make the text bold; press Underline (F8) to underline the text.

    ⌨ Access the **F**ont pull-down menu, choose **A**ppearance, and select either **B**old or **U**nderline.

To double underline a block of text, follow these steps:

1. Use the keyboard (Alt-F4 or F12) or the mouse to highlight the text you want to double underline.

2. Press Font (Ctrl-F8), select **A**ppearance (**2**), and select **D**bl Und (**3**).

    ⌨ Access the **F**ont pull-down menu, choose **A**ppearance, and select **D**ouble Underline.

Although enhanced text prints properly (assuming that your printer supports text-enhancement features such as double underlining), the text may not appear correctly on your computer screen. Double underlining, for example, probably doesn't appear as double underlining and may not be legible on monochrome monitors. Figure 4.2 shows underlined and double-underlined text as it appears on a monochrome screen (underlined text is highlighted, double-underlined text does not appear); figure 4.3 shows the same text when printed. The position number (to the right of Pos at the bottom right of the screen) reflects the enhancement of the text where the cursor is currently located.

Reminder:

Enhanced text may not appear on-screen as it is printed.

Fig. 4.2.

Underlined text as it appears on-screen.

```
                    What to Ask a Writer

Let your fingers do the walking in this directory. Talk to writers until you fin
two or three that you feel certain you can work with.  Invite them in for more d
interviews.

Ask writers about their experience.  If you don't know precisely what you want,
probably ought to look for writers with extensive experience.  If you know exact
what you want and can oversee the creative process constructively, then you migh
more favorably disposed to a writer with less experience but a clear desire to p

Ask a writer for samples, a client list, and references.  If your project is imp
you, contact the references.  Take time to look at the samples.  Do they look li
product you have in mind?  When you meet with writers, ask them how they would
approach your project.

Ask writers about their fees.  One reason why independent writers are so named i
that they all have their own methods of charging for services.  Most writers cha
the hour or by the project.  Some are paid by the day or week, some by the page,
in long-term relationships, some are paid a monthly retainer.  Some writers char
more than others.  Some are very firm about their fees, and some negotiate.  Som
writers charge different fees for different services.  You should know what you
to spend, and you should bear in mind that an hourly rate by itself is not a mea
of total cost.  Some writers work faster than others.  What expenses you will co
Block on                              Doc 1 Pg 1 Ln 4.34" Pos 1.85"
```

Fig. 4.3.

Underlined text as it appears when printed.

<u>What to Ask a Writer</u>

Let your fingers do the walking in this directory. Talk to writers until you find one or two or three that you feel certain you can work with. Invite them in for more detailed interviews.

Ask writers about their experience. If you don't know precisely what you want, you probably ought to look for writers with extensive experience. If you know exactly what you want and can oversee the creative process constructively, then you might be more favorably disposed to a writer with less experience but a clear desire to please.

Ask a writer for samples, a client list, and references. If your project is important to you, contact the references. Take time to look at the samples. Do they look like the product you have in mind? When you meet with writers, ask them how they would approach your project.

<u>Ask writers about their fees</u>. One reason why independent writers are so named is that they all have their own methods of charging for services. Most writers charge by the hour or by the project. Some are paid by the day or week, some by the page, and in long-term relationships, some are paid a monthly retainer. Some writers charge more than others. Some are very firm about their fees, and some negotiate. Some writers charge different fees for different services. You should know what you have to spend, and you should bear in mind that an hourly rate by itself is not a measure of total cost. Some writers work faster than others. What expenses you will cover should also be discussed.

Changing the Type Font in a Block

WordPerfect works well with the varieties of fonts available on many printers—particularly on laser printers, which produce high-quality print in many type sizes and styles. You can use the many type styles WordPerfect offers if your printer supports the styles.

When you change the size or appearance of a font, the starting point is what WordPerfect calls a *base font*—the normal type font. If you increase the size of a line of Courier text, for example, the result is a line of enlarged Courier. Similarly, if you outline a line of Times Roman text, the result is outlined Times Roman.

To change the base font, refer to Chapter 5. You cannot change base fonts with the Block command. You can change only the size or appearance of text using the Block command; the base font remains the same.

Note: Your printer may not support all the font sizes and appearances discussed in this section. Most impact printers (such as dot-matrix and daisy-wheel printers) support only a few type styles. Although laser printers can print an array of type sizes and styles, you generally need a font cartridge or downloadable fonts to take advantage of that capability. Check your printer manual for details.

Reminder:
You cannot change the base font with the Block command, but you can change the appearance of the base font.

Changing Font Size

You can change the text in a highlighted block to any of these font sizes:

1 Su**p**rscrpt; **2** Su**b**scrpt; **3 F**ine; **4 S**mall; **5 L**arge; **6 V**ry Large; **7 E**xt Large

Enlarged text, shown in figure 4.4, is excellent for titles and headlines; small type is ideal for the "fine print" in your documents. Superscripts and subscripts are especially useful in mathematical and scientific applications. You can use any of these font sizes in headers and footers (Chapter 6 introduces headers and footers).

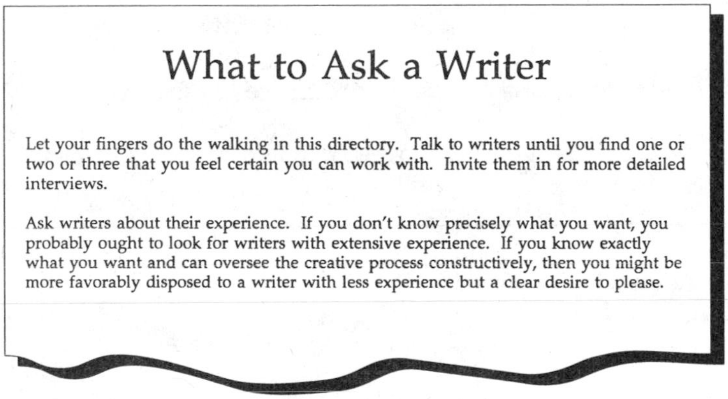

What to Ask a Writer

Let your fingers do the walking in this directory. Talk to writers until you find one or two or three that you feel certain you can work with. Invite them in for more detailed interviews.

Ask writers about their experience. If you don't know precisely what you want, you probably ought to look for writers with extensive experience. If you know exactly what you want and can oversee the creative process constructively, then you might be more favorably disposed to a writer with less experience but a clear desire to please.

Fig. 4.4.
Extra-large text used in a headline.

To change the font size of the text in a block, follow these steps:

1. Use the keyboard (Alt-F4 or F12) or the mouse to highlight the text you want to enlarge or reduce.

2. Press Font (Ctrl-F8), select **S**ize (**1**), and select the size you want.

   ▭ Access the **F**ont pull-down menu and choose the size you want.

Changing Font Appearance

You can enhance the appearance—or style—of type with bold, underline, outline, and other font attributes. Following are the choices available on the Font Appearance menu:

1 Bold **2 U**ndrln **3 D**bl Und **4 I**talic **5 O**utln **6 S**hadw **7 S**m Cap **8 R**edln **9 S**tkout

Cue:

Use outline and shadow attributes for special effects.

Boldface text is often used for emphasis; it works well with large type, for example, as a title or headline. You can use underlining or italics to identify a title or proper name. Use underlining if your printer cannot print italics. Outline and shadow generally are regarded as special effects, to be used sparingly. (Outline is available only on PostScript printers, or with some special-effects font packages.) In a graphic application, such as an advertisement for a company newsletter, outlined or shadowed words can be great attention-getters. Small caps give importance to a word or sentence and are not as overpowering as full-size caps. Redline and strikeout, discussed later in this chapter, are useful editing features. Figure 4.5 shows a number of WordPerfect's font-appearance choices.

Fig. 4.5.

Text with different font appearances (printed on a laser printer).

This is the Garamand Condensed font with no enhancements.

This text is emphasized by being boldfaced.

This text is underlined, while this is double underlined.

Titles of books and magazines should be in italics, like this.

Outline and shadow are best reserved for special effects.

SMALL CAPS GIVE EMPHASIS WITHOUT BEING AS HARD TO READ AS ALL CAPS.

Redline is useful for editing.

Strikeout is also handy for editing.

To change the appearance of a block of text, follow these steps:

1. Use the keyboard (Alt-F4 or F12) or the mouse to highlight the text you want to change.

2. Press Font (Ctrl-F8), select **A**ppearance (**2**), and select one of the font-appearance attributes.

   ⌨ Access the **Fo**nt pull-down menu, choose **A**ppearance, and select one of the font-appearance attributes.

> **Tip**
>
> The fonts your printer actually prints when you select sizes or attributes depend on several factors, including:
>
> - The fonts designated for Automatic Font Changes in the printer definition (PRS) file. Refer to the *WordPerfect Printer Definition Program* manual (available from WordPerfect Corporation) for details on how to change these fonts.
> - The font-size attribute ratios selected in the Setup: Print Options menu.
> - The fonts actually available in your printer.

Making Blocks Uppercase or Lowercase

You don't have to retype letters to change a block of text to all lowercase or all uppercase. A simple command does the typing for you! Note that when you switch from uppercase to lowercase, WordPerfect leaves certain letters capitalized— including the letter *I* when it occurs by itself and the first letters of sentences.

Reminder:

You can change the capitalization of a block of text with a single command.

To change a block of text to uppercase or lowercase, follow these steps:

1. Use the keyboard (Alt-F4 or F12) or the mouse to highlight the text you want to change to uppercase or lowercase.

2. Press Switch (Shift-F3) and select **U**ppercase (**1**) or **L**owercase (**2**).

   ⌨ Access the **E**dit pull-down menu, choose Con**v**ert Case, and select To **U**pper or To **L**ower (see fig. 4.6).

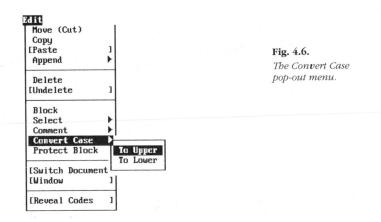

Fig. 4.6.

The Convert Case pop-out menu.

If you switch from uppercase to lowercase, be sure to review the text for accuracy. WordPerfect may not capitalize every word correctly. For example, the first letter following every period is capitalized. If you have a sentence that includes a decimal number, the result may be inappropriate capitalization.

Centering a Block

Reminder:

Each line of a centered block of text has a hard return.

You can center a block of text either as you type or after you type the text. To center a block of text as you type, center each line and end the block with a hard return. To center text after it's typed, highlight and then center the block. WordPerfect inserts a hard return at the end of each line of centered text, even if the block you center is a word-wrapped paragraph. The block appears centered both on-screen and in print. Figure 4.7 shows how Block Center can be used to center the text in a list.

Fig. 4.7.

A centered block.

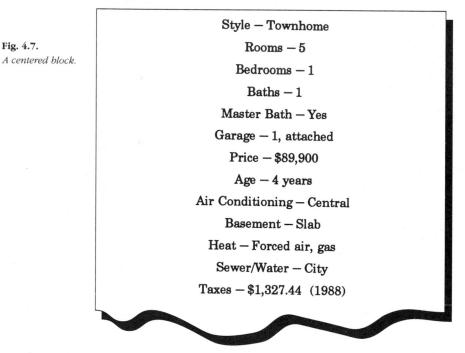

Style — Townhome

Rooms — 5

Bedrooms — 1

Baths — 1

Master Bath — Yes

Garage — 1, attached

Price — $89,900

Age — 4 years

Air Conditioning — Central

Basement — Slab

Heat — Forced air, gas

Sewer/Water — City

Taxes — $1,327.44 (1988)

To center a block of text, follow these steps:

1. Use the keyboard (Alt-F4 or F12) or the mouse to highlight the text you want to center.

2. Press Center (Shift-F6) and press Y.

   Access the **L**ayout pull-down menu, choose **A**lign, and select **C**enter.

Using Redline and Strikeout

Reminder:

Redline shows additions to text; strikeout shows text to be deleted.

You can use WordPerfect's redline and strikeout features when you want to compare revisions of a document. A writer, for example, can submit to an editor chapters on a WordPerfect disk. The editor reads the material and marks it by redlining and striking out certain passages in the document file. Redline shows text the editor added or changed; strikeout indicates text the editor wants to delete. When reviewing the edited material, the writer can see exactly what changes the editor wants to make rather than simply seeing the revised chapter.

With many printers, redline appears as a mark in the margin next to the redlined text. With other printers, such as the laser printer used to print figure 4.8, redlined text appears shaded or highlighted. If you have a color printer, redlined text can print red. Strikeout appears as characters superimposed over the text. To define the characters you want to use for redline and strikeout, refer to Chapter 3. The default characters for redline and strikeout depend on the printer and on the selections made in Setup (see Chapter 20 for more information about Setup).

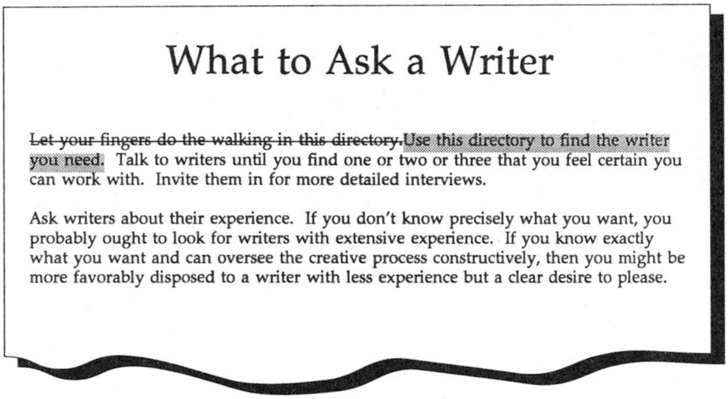

What to Ask a Writer

~~Let your fingers do the walking in this directory.~~Use this directory to find the writer you need. Talk to writers until you find one or two or three that you feel certain you can work with. Invite them in for more detailed interviews.

Ask writers about their experience. If you don't know precisely what you want, you probably ought to look for writers with extensive experience. If you know exactly what you want and can oversee the creative process constructively, then you might be more favorably disposed to a writer with less experience but a clear desire to please.

Fig. 4.8.
Redlined text highlighted; strikeout text superimposed with hyphens.

To redline or mark with strikeout a block of text, follow these steps:

1. Use the keyboard (Alt-F4 or F12) or the mouse to highlight the text you want to redline or mark with strikeout.

2. Press Font (Ctrl-F8), select **A**ppearance (**2**), and select **R**edln (**8**) or **S**tkout (**9**).

   ⌦ Access the **F**ont pull-down menu, choose **A**ppearance, and select **R**edline or **S**trikeout.

Unenhancing Text

If you use the Block command to enhance text, you generally cannot then use the Block command to return text to its normal appearance. To unenhance text, you must delete the enhancement codes.

To delete text-enhancement codes, follow these steps:

1. Move the cursor to the beginning or end of the enhanced text.

2. Press Reveal Codes (Alt-F3 or F11).

   ⌦ Access the **E**dit pull-down menu and choose **R**eveal Codes.

3. Delete either the beginning or ending text-enhancement code.

Table 4.1 lists the text-enhancement codes available in WordPerfect and explains what each code means.

Reminder:

To unenhance text, delete only one of the text-enhancement codes.

Table 4.1
Text-Enhancement Codes

Code	Enhancement	Code	Enhancement
[BOLD]	Bold	[LARGE]	Large print
[DBL UND]	Double underline	[Ovrstk]	Overstrike
[EXT LARGE]	Extra-large print	[REDLN]	Redline
[FINE]	Fine print	[SHADW]	Shadow
[Font]	Base font	[SM CAP]	Small caps
[ITALC]	Italic	[SMALL]	Small print
[Just:Center]	Center justification	[STKOUT]	Strikeout
[Just:Full]	Full justification	[SUBSCPT]	Subscript
[Just:Left]	Left justification	[SUPRSCPT]	Superscript
[Just:Right]	Right justification	[UND]	Underlining
[Kern:On]	Kerning	[VRY LARGE]	Very-large print

Displaying Enhanced Text On-Screen

Cue:

If your screen doesn't show text enhancements, reveal the codes or use the View Document command.

Many of the text enhancements you select don't display correctly on a monochrome monitor. In fact, enhanced text may not be legible at all on-screen. On color monitors, text enhancements appear in different colors and should be easy to read. If your screen text is illegible, press Reveal Codes (Alt-F3 or F11) or select **R**eveal Codes from the **E**dit pull-down menu to read the text.

To supplement the screen display, WordPerfect offers a command that shows how your document looks when printed: the View Document command. You can use this command with either the keyboard or the mouse. With the keyboard, press the Print (Shift-F7) key and select **V**iew Document (**6**). ⌨ With the mouse, choose **P**rint from the **F**ile pull-down menu and select **V**iew Document (**6**).

You can view a document in 100%, 200%, or fit-in-the-window sizes, but you must return to the document if you want to edit the text. To learn more about View Document and how to adjust the appearance of text on-screen, refer to Chapters 8 and 20.

For a true "what you see is what you get" on-screen display, add a Hercules Graphics Card to your computer. With this card, enlarged text appears larger, and italicized text appears in italics on-screen. Keep in mind that text, no matter how it looks on-screen, prints correctly if your printer supports the selected enhancements.

Reminder:

*You can switch between two documents by pressing Switch or selecting **S**witch Document from the **E**dit pull-down menu.*

Moving and Copying Text between Documents

WordPerfect's Block Move and Block Copy commands make moving and copying text between documents easy. In WordPerfect, you can open two documents at the same time. The first document is called Doc 1 and the second is called Doc 2. You can move between documents either by pressing Switch (Shift-F3) or by selecting **S**witch Document from the **E**dit pull-down menu.

The simplest way to move or copy text between documents is to begin with both documents open. Then you can highlight a block in the first document (Doc 1), switch to the second document (Doc 2), and copy or move the text.

To open a second document, follow these steps:

1. Press the Switch key (Shift-F3).

   ⌨ Access the **E**dit pull-down menu and choose **S**witch Document.

2. Retrieve or begin typing the second document.

Notice the message Doc 2 in the status line at the bottom right of the screen. Before you begin the move or copy procedure, return to the first document (Doc 1) by pressing Switch (Shift-F3) again or by choosing **S**witch Document from the **E**dit pull-down menu.

To move or copy text between documents, follow these steps:

1. Use the keyboard (Alt-F4 or F12) or the mouse to highlight the text in the first document you want to move or copy.

2. Press Move (Ctrl-F4), select **B**lock (**1**), and select **M**ove (**1**) or **C**opy (**2**). Alternatively, press Ctrl-Del (to move) or Ctrl-Ins (to copy).

   ⌨ Access the **E**dit pull-down menu and choose **M**ove (Cut) or **C**opy.

3. Press Switch (Shift-F3) to display the second document.

   ⌨ Access the **E**dit pull-down menu and choose **S**witch Document.

4. Move the cursor to the location in the second document where you want to move or copy the block; press Enter to retrieve the block.

Working with Rectangular Blocks

In WordPerfect, you can move either a grammatical block of text, such as a sentence or paragraph, or you can move any text that falls within a defined rectangular block. For example, you can move or copy a single column of text or numbers from a table with WordPerfect's Move Rectangle command (see fig. 4.9).

Day 1:	Review of 3D Concepts	3½ hours
	Basic Surfacing	4 hours
Day 2:	Basic Surfacing	7½ hours
Day 3:	Advanced Surfacing	7½ hours
Day 4:	Advanced Surfacing	7½ hours
Day 5:	Surfacing Projects	7½ hours

Fig. 4.9.

A blocked rectangle of text.

To move or copy a rectangular block, first highlight the text. Then use the Move Rectangle command to move or copy the block. You can retrieve the block into the current document or into a different document; if you retrieve into a different document, press Switch (Shift-F3) or choose **S**witch Document from the **E**dit pull-down menu.

When you retrieve a rectangle, be aware of how it will be integrated into the new text. If the page is empty, the rectangle is placed on the page with a hard return at the end of each line. If text is currently in the position where you retrieve the rectangle, the retrieved text is woven into the existing text, producing unexpected results. Figure 4.10 shows the same rectangle retrieved into a blank area of the screen and retrieved into an area where text exists.

Reminder:

Press Reveal Codes to determine whether you are including tab stops in the rectangular block.

When you move a column, you can move tab stops along with the text or numbers. If you do, the tab stops are included in the new location and are deleted from the previous location. Unexpected results may occur. To see whether you are including tab stops in the block, press Reveal Codes (Alt-F3 or F11) or choose **R**eveal Codes from the **E**dit pull-down menu during the Block operation. (See Chapter 5 for an in-depth study of tabs.)

To move or copy a rectangle, follow these steps:

1. Position the cursor at the top left corner of the text you want to move as a rectangle.

2. Press Block (Alt-F4 or F12) and move the cursor to the bottom right corner of the rectangle.

   ⌨ Hold the left mouse button and drag the mouse pointer to the bottom right corner of the rectangle.

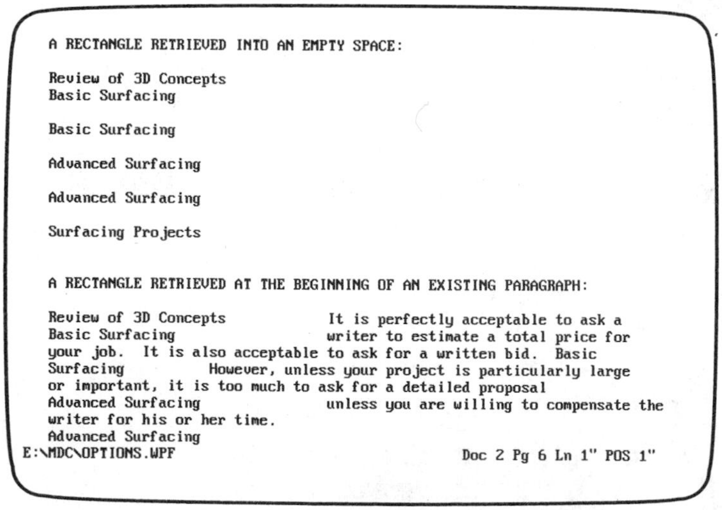

Fig. 4.10.

A rectangle retrieved into an empty area of the page and into an area where text exists.

```
A RECTANGLE RETRIEVED INTO AN EMPTY SPACE:

Review of 3D Concepts
Basic Surfacing

Basic Surfacing

Advanced Surfacing

Advanced Surfacing

Surfacing Projects


A RECTANGLE RETRIEVED AT THE BEGINNING OF AN EXISTING PARAGRAPH:

Review of 3D Concepts          It is perfectly acceptable to ask a
Basic Surfacing                writer to estimate a total price for
your job.  It is also acceptable to ask for a written bid.  Basic
Surfacing          However, unless your project is particularly large
or important, it is too much to ask for a detailed proposal
Advanced Surfacing             unless you are willing to compensate the
writer for his or her time.
Advanced Surfacing
E:\MDC\OPTIONS.WPF                        Doc 2 Pg 6 Ln 1" POS 1"
```

The text is highlighted all the way across the page, as usual. In the next step, you specify the rectangle as the only area to be highlighted. Text to the left or right of the originally selected area is excluded.

3. Press Move (Ctrl-F4) and select **R**ectangle (**3**).

   ⌨ Access the **E**dit pull-down menu, choose S**e**lect, and select **R**ectangle.

4. Select **M**ove (**1**) or **C**opy (**2**), move the cursor to where you want to retrieve the rectangle, and press Enter.

You also can delete a rectangle of text. You may, for example, want to delete a whole column of numbers from a table. To delete a rectangle, follow these steps:

1. Position the cursor at the top left corner of the text you want to move as a rectangle.

2. Press Block (Alt-F4 or F12) and move the cursor to the bottom right corner of the rectangle.

   ⌨ Hold the left mouse button and drag the mouse pointer to the bottom right corner of the rectangle.

3. Press Move (Ctrl-F4), select **R**ectangle (**3**), and select **D**elete (**3**).

   ⌨ Access the **E**dit pull-down menu, choose S**e**lect, choose **R**ectangle, and choose **D**elete (**3**).

Suppose that you want to copy a selected column of data from a table and append the data to the end of another document. Although the menu prompts suggest that you can append a rectangular block of text to a file on disk, this feature does not appear to work. If you need to transfer a rectangle to another file, you can use this workaround:

1. Press Switch (Shift-F3) to move to the other document window.

   ⌨ Access the **E**dit pull-down menu and choose **S**witch Document.

   Note: Make certain that you do not have a file in the second window.

2. Press Retrieve (Shift-F10) or List (F5).

   ⌨ Access the **F**ile pull-down menu and choose **R**etrieve to retrieve the file to which you want to add the rectangle.

3. Position the cursor where you want to insert the rectangle.

4. Press Switch (Shift-F3) to return to the original document window.

   ⌨ Access the **E**dit pull-down menu and choose **S**witch Document.

5. Highlight the text you want to copy; press Move (Ctrl-F4) and select **R**ectangle (**3**).

6. Select **C**opy (**2**). The `Move cursor; press Enter to retrieve` prompt appears on the status line.

7. Press Switch (Shift-F3) to move back to the second document window.

   ⌨ Access the **E**dit pull-down menu and choose **S**witch Document.

8. Press Enter to insert the rectangle in the second file.

9. Press Exit (F7); press Enter, type a file name, and press Enter and Y to save the second document and return to the original document.

The file you saved to disk now contains the inserted rectangle.

Using the Block Command with Styles

When you do repetitive formatting in a document or series of documents (such as the chapters of a book), using WordPerfect's styles feature can save you time. A *style* is a set of formatting instructions that defines the appearance of the text to which it's applied. A style, for example, can define the format of a chapter title as all caps, centered, bold, and extra-large text. Other styles can define the formats of subtitles, paragraphs, and figure captions within the document. The advantage of using a style is that it applies to all the text assigned to it. When you redefine a style, you change the format of all the text assigned to that style.

You can create styles in two ways. One way is to use a special Styles window. For a detailed description of this procedure, refer to Chapter 15. Perhaps an easier way to create a style, however, is by example. To create the style, you format a block of text as you want it to appear, highlight it with the Block command (making sure that you include any formatting codes in the highlighted area), and press Style (Alt-F8) or choose **S**tyles from the **L**ayout pull-down menu. Complete these steps to create a style using the Block command:

1. Use the keyboard (Alt-F4 or F12) or the mouse to highlight the text from which you want to copy a style.
2. Press Style (Alt-F8).

    ⌨ Access the **L**ayout pull-down menu and choose **S**tyles.
3. Select **C**reate (3), select **N**ame (**1**), and type the style name.
4. Press Exit (F7).

You also can choose from two ways to apply a style to text after the style is created. One way is to apply the style as you type (refer to Chapter 15 for more information about styles). Another way is to highlight the text using the Block command and then apply the style. Follow these steps to apply a style using the Block command:

1. Use the keyboard (Alt-F4 or F12) or the mouse to highlight the text to which you want to apply a style.
2. Press Style (Alt-F8).

    ⌨ Access the **L**ayout pull-down menu and choose **S**tyles.
3. Press ↓ until you highlight the style you want to apply to the selected text; select **O**n (**1**) to apply the highlighted style to the selected text. Alternatively, press N to begin a **N**ame Search, type the first few letters of the style you want, and press Enter twice to apply the style to the selected text (this method is especially useful with a long list of styles).

    ⌨ Move the mouse pointer to the style you want and double click to highlight and apply the style to the selected text.

When you use this procedure, the style applies only to the highlighted block.

Summary

The Block command is part of a process. In this chapter, you learned to use Block to highlight text on which you want to perform some operation.

Highlighting a block is the first step in all the Block operations. The basic procedures are always the same:

Using the keyboard:

1. Move the cursor to the beginning of the block of text you want to highlight and press Block (Alt-F4 or F12).

2. Use the arrow keys to move the cursor to the end of the block of text.

Using the mouse:

1. Move the mouse pointer to the beginning of the block of text you want to highlight.

2. Press and hold the left mouse button, move the mouse to drag the pointer to the end of the block, and release the left mouse button.

After you highlight a block of text, you can manipulate it in several ways. In this chapter you learned how to do the following:

❏ Move a block of text

❏ Copy a block of text

❏ Delete a block of text

❏ Append a block of text to another file

❏ Save a block of text

❏ Print a block of text

❏ Change the appearance of a block of text by making text bold, underlined, larger or smaller, uppercase or lowercase, or centered

5

Formatting and Enhancing Text

Schuyler Lininger Jr., an Oregon chiropractor and owner of HealthNotes Publications, uses desktop publishing to produce fliers, brochures, and newsletters for the health food industry.

WordPerfect offers many useful tools that delight both new and experienced users of word processors. If you have been using a typewriter, you will enjoy the way WordPerfect handles the mundane chores of setting margins and tabs; centering, justifying, underlining, and boldfacing text; indenting text; and hyphenating words. If you are an old hand with word processors but new to WordPerfect, you will be impressed with how simply and logically WordPerfect formats and enhances text. If you are an experienced user of WordPerfect 5, you will appreciate the many enhancements included in WordPerfect 5.1. These enhancements make your work even easier.

In this chapter, you will learn how to enhance text you have already entered. You will learn also how to format lines and paragraphs so that they appear as you want them when printed.

Text enhancements described in this chapter include the following:

- Using left and right margins (including margin release) and indenting text from the left and from both margins
- Using various types of tabs: left, right, center, decimal, and tabs with dot leaders
- Formatting text to make it centered, flush right, or right-justified
- Changing line spacing and adjusting the height of each line (leading)
- Manually or automatically inserting hyphens into text

109

You also will learn how to take full advantage of printer capabilities, including the following:

- Enhancing text by changing the typeface, size, and appearance of a font
- Previewing the document before printing with the graphic View Document feature

---

Reminder

If you use a mouse with WordPerfect 5.1, you can click the right button to display the pull-down menu, and then select the desired option. You also can press Alt-= to access the pull-down menus, and then press the appropriate letter of the desired option. For all instructions, assume that if a block is required to activate a pull-down menu option, the text has been blocked before the pull-down menu is accessed. Instructions for pull-down menus and the mouse are marked with the mouse icon. For more information about the mouse, see Chapter 1.

Formatting Lines and Paragraphs

Cue:

To format lines and paragraphs on the page, you most often use the Format menu (Shift-F8) or one of the first four items on the Layout pull-down menu.

This chapter focuses on formatting the elements of the page: lines and paragraphs. The next chapter guides you through designing documents and formatting the overall page. The Format menu, which is accessed with Shift-F8 (see fig. 5.1), or the Layout pull-down menu (see fig. 5.2), contain most of the functions used to format a page.

Fig. 5.1

The Format menu (Shift-F8).

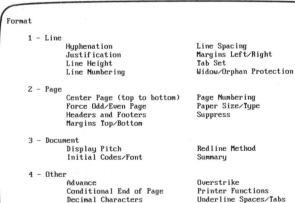

```
Format

    1 - Line
                Hyphenation                 Line Spacing
                Justification               Margins Left/Right
                Line Height                 Tab Set
                Line Numbering              Widow/Orphan Protection

    2 - Page
                Center Page (top to bottom) Page Numbering
                Force Odd/Even Page         Paper Size/Type
                Headers and Footers         Suppress
                Margins Top/Bottom

    3 - Document
                Display Pitch               Redline Method
                Initial Codes/Font          Summary

    4 - Other
                Advance                     Overstrike
                Conditional End of Page     Printer Functions
                Decimal Characters          Underline Spaces/Tabs
                Language
```

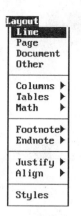

Fig. 5.2
The Layout pull-down menu.

Changing Default Settings

WordPerfect presets all global initial or default settings. *Global* settings are basic formatting options that affect the entire document. Margin, tab, and justification features are examples of global settings. If these settings do not fit your needs, you can either change the settings for the current document or use Setup (Shift-F1) to permanently change many of the settings.

Cue:
Global *settings are basic formatting options that affect the entire document.*

You can control formatting by using any of four methods: changing Setup Initial Codes; changing Document Initial Codes; inserting hidden codes; or using styles. The following sections discuss each method.

Changing Setup Initial Codes

Setup Initial Codes are WordPerfect's default formatting settings. Changes made with Setup Initial Codes are permanent and affect all new documents. If the document you are working on contains text, the changes will not take effect until you begin a new document. If you retrieve a previous document, it will retain the settings that were in place when the document was created. In other words, current and previously created documents will not reflect changes made from Setup. (Setup is discussed in more detail in Chapter 20.)

Reminder:
Changes made with Setup Initial Codes are permanent and affect all new documents.

When you begin a new document, the default formatting is modified by Setup Initial Codes. WordPerfect comes preset with a number of "factory defaults." Justification, for example, is set to Full; Left and Right Margins are set to 1 inch, and Page Numbering is set to Off.

Reminder:
Modifying Setup Initial Codes affects only new documents.

If you want all documents you create to have different defaults than those set by WordPerfect, you can modify Setup Initial Codes by performing the following steps:

1. Press Setup (Shift-F1) and select **I**nitial Settings (**4**).

   ⌨ Access the **F**ile pull-down menu, select Se**t**up, and then select **I**nitial Settings.

2. Select Initial **C**odes (**5**).

3. From the Initial **C**odes split screen, insert hidden formatting codes for margins, tabs, justification, fonts, and so on.

4. Press Exit (F7) twice.

You are then returned to the main editing screen.

Remember that modifying the Setup Initial Codes affects only new documents.

> ## Tip
>
> To "trick" an old document into accepting new Setup Initial Codes defaults, you can press the space bar once in an empty document before retrieving the file. WordPerfect is "fooled" into thinking that the retrieved file is being added to an existing document (the existing document in this case only has a single space in it), and uses the default settings of the new document.

Changing Document Initial Codes

Document Initial Codes are a series of formatting codes that override any default Setup Initial Codes that were in place when the document was created. This chapter discusses the methods of modifying a document's Initial Codes.

Reminder:

Changes made with Document Initial Codes affect the entire document you are working on regardless of where the cursor was at the time you decided to modify the Initial Codes.

To modify global formatting options for the document you are working on, you must use the Document Initial Codes feature. Changes made with Document Initial Codes affect the entire document you are working on regardless of where the cursor was at the time you decided to modify the Initial Codes.

To change the Document Initial Codes, perform the following steps:

1. Press Format (Shift-F8) and select **D**ocument (**3**).

   Access the **L**ayout pull-down menu and select **D**ocument.

2. Select Initial **C**odes (**2**).

3. From the Initial **C**odes split screen, insert hidden formatting codes for margins, tabs, justification, fonts, and so on.

4. Press Exit (F7) twice.

   You are returned to the main editing screen.

Using Hidden Formatting Codes

Hidden formatting codes can be inserted anywhere in a document to override the default Initial Codes. This chapter concentrates on this method.

Hidden codes affect text from the point at which they are inserted until another hidden code is inserted. For example, if you want a 2-inch margin instead of a 1-inch margin, you insert the code **[L/R Mar:2",2"]**. (Methods of inserting hidden codes are described in this chapter.) All text from that point forward will reflect the new margins. When you want to change the margins back, or modify the margins again, you insert another **[L/R Mar]** code.

Using Styles

Styles are one or more hidden formatting codes that are grouped and given a name before being inserted into the document. If you have assigned a particular style to a number of paragraphs, changing the style modifies all the paragraphs affected by the style. (See Chapter 15 for detailed information about the Style (Alt-F8) feature.)

Changing the Units of Measure

The on-screen dimensions of a page are often defined in terms of columns (width) and rows (height). Most monitors, for example, display 80 columns and 25 rows of text. With some word processors, including WordPerfect prior to version 5, you need to experiment in order to determine how many columns to include in the margins, how many columns to set in a line, and how many rows to leave for the top and bottom page margins. If you change fonts, calculations are often thrown off, and the printed document doesn't always turn out as expected. This process results in much wasted time.

WordPerfect 5.1 eliminates all this guesswork. Now, regardless of the font you select, you can set absolute margins. You do not have to calculate how many columns and rows fit on a page. In addition, you do not need to be concerned with the size of the font in order to produce a printed page with perfect margins.

Examine the status line in the lower right corner of the WordPerfect screen. The screen should display something like the following (the numbers vary depending on the cursor's position in the document):

```
Doc 1 Pg 1 Ln 1" Pos 1"
```

With WordPerfect 5.1, you can select among the following options for units of measurement:

" or **i** = inches	Inches, the default setting in WordPerfect 5.1, are the best units for measuring margins and tabs.
c = centimeters	One centimeter equals 0.39 inch; 1 inch equals 2.54 centimeters.
p = points	One point equals 0.01384 inch or 1/72 inch; 72 points equal 1 inch. Because fonts often are measured in point sizes, you may want to use these units for measuring font height (especially with laser printers).
w = 1200ths of an inch	One **w** unit equals 1/1200ths of an inch. You may want to use **w** units when you need precise page or line positioning, such as when you use WordPerfect to fill in forms.
u = WordPerfect 4.2 units (lines and columns)	Most word processors and versions of WordPerfect before 5 use these units of measurement. You may want to use this setting if your main printer is dot-matrix or letter quality; these printers measure by lines and columns. If you have a laser printer, however, use either inches or points; these units provide control over character placement.

To change the units of measure to centimeters, follow these steps:

1. Press Setup (Shift-F1) and select **E**nvironment (**3**).

    ⌨ Access the **F**ile pull-down menu, select Se**t**up, and then select **E**nvironment.

2. Select **U**nits of Measure (**8**).

3. From the Setup: Units of Measure menu (see fig. 5.3), select **D**isplay and Entry of Numbers for Margins, Tabs, etc. (**1**), and then press C to select centimeters.

Fig. 5.3

The Setup: Units of Measure menu.

```
Setup: Units of Measure

    1 - Display and Entry of Numbers            "
            for Margins, Tabs, etc.

    2 - Status Line Display                     "

Legend:

    " = inches
    i = inches
    c = centimeters
    p = points
    w = 1200ths of an inch
    u = WordPerfect 4.2 Units (Lines/Columns)
```

4. Select **S**tatus Line Display (**2**), and then press C to select centimeters.

5. Press Exit (F7) to return to the document. The status line, which now displays the cursor position in terms of centimeters, should read as follows:

    `Doc 1 Pg 1 Ln 2.54c Pos 2.54c`

Reminder:

If you change units of measurement, all unit displays, including those contained in hidden codes, automatically change to reflect the new choice.

The unit of measure you select for **D**isplay and Entry of Numbers for Margins, Tabs, etc. (**1**) determines the units used in menu choices for hyphenation zone, margins (top, bottom, left, and right), tab settings, paper size, and display pitch. The unit of measure you select for **S**tatus Line Display (**2**) determines which units are displayed in the status line at the lower right corner of the screen. If you change units of measurement, all unit displays, including those contained in hidden codes, immediately and automatically change to reflect the new choice.

In any menu that requires a measurement, such as changing left and right margins (see the next section, "Changing Margins), you can force WordPerfect to use a non-default measurement. If, for example, you have set the Units of Measure to centimeters, but want to enter left and right margins in inches, simply include *"* or *i* after the number; WordPerfect will override the default setting of Units of Measure. In such menus, WordPerfect will also convert fractions to decimals. For example, WordPerfect will convert *6/7"* to *0.857"*.

⬦ 5.1 ⬦

Tip
Always include the unit type in any measurements used in macro commands. The macros will then work correctly even if the Units of Measure are changed.

Changing Margins

WordPerfect 5.1 calculates margins as being a certain distance from the edges of the paper. You can set one-inch left and right margins, for example, without being concerned about the number of characters in the line of text. WordPerfect tracks the size of both the page and the font and automatically determines how many characters can fit on a line or page.

You can change the margin settings at any time. When you enter a margin change, that change affects only text from that point forward. Text entered before the change retains the previous margins. If you want to change the margins for an entire document, either go to the beginning of the document and set the margins, or change the Initial Codes. (To move the cursor to the beginning of the document, press Home, Home, ↑.)

Reminder:

To move the cursor to the beginning of the document, press Home, Home, ↑.

Changing Left and Right Margins

To change the left and right margins, follow these steps:

1. Press Format (Shift-F8) and select **Line** (**1**).

   ⌨ Access the **L**ayout pull-down menu and select **L**ine.

2. From the Format: Line menu (see fig. 5.4), select **M**argins Left/Right (**7**). The cursor moves to the right of the **M**argins Left/Right menu item. (Notice that in this case the left and right margins are calculated in inches.)

```
Format: Line

    1 - Hyphenation                    No

    2 - Hyphenation Zone - Left        10%
                          Right        4%

    3 - Justification                  Full

    4 - Line Height                    Auto

    5 - Line Numbering                 No

    6 - Line Spacing                   1

    7 - Margins - Left                 1"
                  Right                1"

    8 - Tab Set                        Rel: -1", every 0.5"

    9 - Widow/Orphan Protection        No
```

Fig. 5.4

The Format: Line menu.

3. Type a new value for the left margin and press Enter.

4. Type a new value for the right margin and press Enter.

5. Press Exit (F7) to return to the document.

Caution

If a Margins Left/Right code is placed after text on a line, WordPerfect 5.1 automatically inserts a hard-return code **[HRt]**, and the Margins Left/Right code is placed at the beginning of the next line.

Changing Margins in Headers and Footers

You can set the left and right margins for footers and headers independently from the overall page margins. To change footer and header margins, complete the steps in the preceding section while you are entering or editing a header or footer. Footers and headers are discussed in detail in Chapter 6.

Using Margin Release

Margin Release (Shift-Tab) releases the left margin and causes that margin to shift temporarily one tab stop to the left. This feature is particularly useful for creating lists. The number appears to the left of the margin, but the notation stays within the normal margins (see fig. 5.5).

Fig. 5.5

A list created with the Margin Release feature.

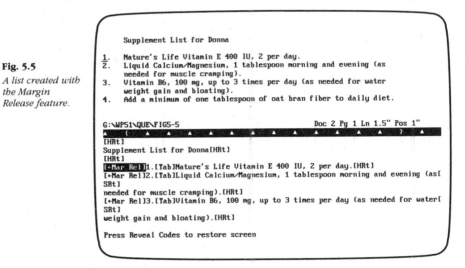

To enter text to the left of the left margin, follow these steps:

1. Move the cursor to the left margin by pressing Enter or Home, ←.

2. Press Margin Release (Shift-Tab) to move the cursor one tab stop to the left.

   ⌨ Access the **L**ayout pull-down menu, select **A**lign, and then select **M**argin Rel ←.

   Repeat step 2 if you want to move an additional tab stop to the left.

3. Type the text.

4. Press Tab to return to the normal left margin.

Caution

Don't press Margin Release (Shift-Tab) when the cursor is in the middle of a line of text. If you do, text to the right of the Margin Release code may overwrite text to the left of the Margin Release code. If there is no tab stop to the left of the cursor, the line will begin at the left edge of the page.

Indenting Text

An indent temporarily resets either the left or both the left and right margins. You can emphasize one or more paragraphs by offsetting them.

- *To indent only the left margin*, press Indent (F4).

  ▣ Access the **L**ayout pull-down menu, select **A**lign, and then select Indent →.

- *To indent both the left and right margins*, press Left-Right Indent (Shift-F4).

  ▣ Access the **L**ayout pull-down menu, select **A**lign, and then select Indent →←.

Note: The Indent feature is available by selecting **A**lign from the **L**ayout menu and then choosing **I**ndent → or In**d**ent →←. However, for this feature, the function-key approach requires fewer steps than the pull-down menu approach.

Caution
Never use the space bar for indenting or tabbing. If your printer uses proportional typefaces, text will not align properly at the left indent or tab stop. Instead, use the Tab key or the appropriate Indent keys.

Indenting from the Left Margin

To indent only the left margin, press Indent (F4). Indent moves an entire paragraph one tab stop from the left margin. When you press Indent (F4), the cursor moves to the right one tab stop and then temporarily resets the left margin. Everything you type until you press Enter is indented one tab stop. To indent more than one tab stop, press Indent (F4) more than once.

The Indent (F4) feature is useful when you are creating a list. You can, for example, indent and align a series of numbered blocks of text. If you use only the Tab key to indent the text next to a number, the second and consecutive lines of text are not indented. Instead, they wrap to the next line and align with the number. Figure 5.6 illustrates various types of indents.

Cue:
Use Indent (F4) when you are creating a list.

Complete the following steps to create a list by using the Indent (F4) feature:

1. Move the cursor to the left margin.
2. Press the item number (for example, **1**), and then press Tab.
3. Press Indent (F4) and then type the text of the item.

   ▣ Access the **L**ayout pull-down menu, select **A**lign, and then select Indent →.

4. Press Enter to stop indenting and return to the normal margins.

Fig. 5.6

A variety of indents created with the Indent (F4) and Left-Right Indent (Shift-F4) features.

Schuyler W. Lininger, Jr., D.C.   Fall Quarter
PRACTICAL NUTRITION OBJECTIVES

1.   Provide a foundation for the practice of nutritional
     therapeutics.
2.   Provide a rationale for the nutritional approach.
3.   Provide standards against which the efficacy of a
     therapeutic approach can be assessed and monitored.
4.   Offer a basis for the appreciation of the underlying
     relationship between biocmechanical and biochemical
     functioning.

EVALUATION PROCESS

     The evaluation process will be based on the investigation of
     an assigned nutritional problem utilizing the scientific
     literature and a final examination. Grading will be on a
     straight percentage basis: 90-100 = A; 80-90 = B; etc.

     All papers must be typed on non-erasable paper. Papers
     are expected to be properly punctuated, to use proper
     grammar, and to be proofed for spelling errors.

G:\WP51\QUE\FIG5-6   Doc 2 Pg 1 Ln 1" Pos 1"

Indenting from Both Margins

Use Left-Right Indent (Shift-F4) to indent a paragraph from both the right and left margins. When you press Left-Right Indent (Shift-F4), the cursor moves to the right one tab stop and temporarily resets both the left and right margins. Everything you type until you press Enter is indented one tab stop from the left margin and the same distance from the right margin. To indent from both margins more than one tab stop, press Left-Right Indent (Shift-F4) more than once (see fig. 5.6).

To indent a paragraph you already have typed, complete the following steps:

1. Place the cursor at the left margin and press Left-Right Indent (Shift-F4).

    Access the **L**ayout pull-down menu, select **A**lign, and then select **In**dent →←.

2. Press ↓. The paragraph appears indented from both margins.

Creating a Hanging Paragraph

Cue:

Use hanging paragraphs to simplify indenting in various reports, such as bibliographies.

You can create a hanging paragraph by using a combination of Margin Release (Shift-Tab) and Indent (F4). In a hanging paragraph, the first line is flush with the left margin and the rest of the paragraph is indented to the first tab stop (see fig. 5.7). Hanging paragraphs are useful in various reports, such as bibliographies.

To create a hanging paragraph, press Indent (F4) and then Margin Release (Shift-Tab) before you begin to type. Only the first line of the paragraph is outdented to the normal margins, and the rest of the paragraph is indented to the first tab stop. Pressing Enter restores the margins to their normal settings. Subsequent paragraphs are normal in appearance.

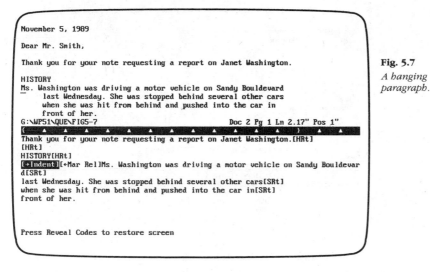

Fig. 5.7

A hanging paragraph.

Complete the following steps to create a hanging paragraph:

1. Move the cursor to the left margin.
2. Press Indent (F4).

    Access the **L**ayout pull-down menu, select **A**lign, and then select In**d**ent →.

3. Press Margin Release (Shift-Tab).

    Access the **L**ayout pull-down menu, select **A**lign, and then select In**d**ent →←.

4. Type the text and press Enter.

Setting Tab Stops

WordPerfect comes with tab stops predefined at intervals of one-half inch for 14 inches (relative to the margin from −1" to +13"). Four basic types of tabs are available in WordPerfect: left, center, right, and decimal. Each type of tab can have a *dot leader*—a series of periods before the tab. Figure 5.8 illustrates the various tab types.

WordPerfect 5.1 now offers two ways tabs are measured in relation to the margin or physical page: **A**bsolute and **R**elative to Margin (the default).

Absolute tabs, which are the same as in WordPerfect 5, are set in relation to the left edge of the physical page. The hidden code for Absolute tabs looks similar to the following:

[Tab Set:Abs: 0", every 0.5"]

Relative to Margin tabs, new with WordPerfect 5.1, are set in relation to the left margin setting. If the left margin changes, the tabs adjust to the new margin setting. The hidden code for Relative to Margin tabs looks similar to the following:

[Tab Set:Rel: +1", +2", +3", +3.5"]

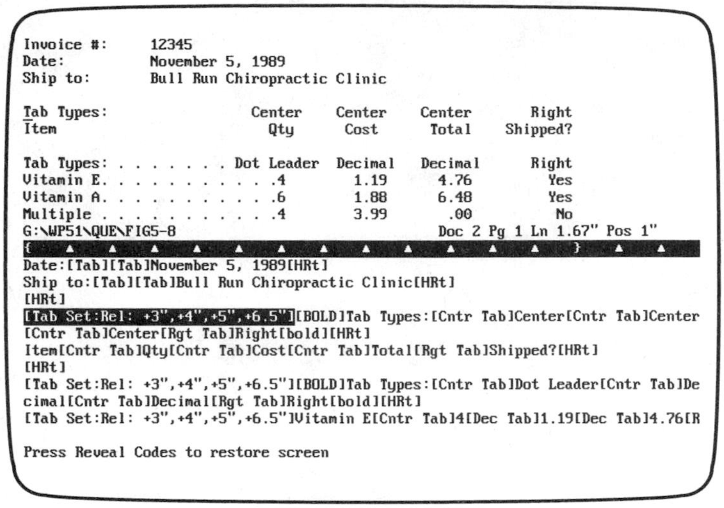

Fig. 5.8

Examples of tab types.

```
┌─────────────────────────────────────────────────────────────────┐
│ Invoice #:      12345                                             │
│ Date:           November 5, 1989                                 │
│ Ship to:        Bull Run Chiropractic Clinic                     │
│                                                                   │
│ Tab Types:                Center    Center   Center     Right    │
│ Item                      Qty       Cost     Total      Shipped? │
│                                                                   │
│ Tab Types: . . . . . . . Dot Leader  Decimal  Decimal    Right   │
│ Vitamin E. . . . . . . . . . .4        1.19     4.76      Yes     │
│ Vitamin A. . . . . . . . . . .6        1.88     6.48      Yes     │
│ Multiple . . . . . . . . . . .4        3.99      .00      No      │
│ G:\WP51\QUE\FIG5-8                           Doc 2 Pg 1 Ln 1.67" Pos 1" │
│ {   ▲    ▲    ▲    ▲    ▲    ▲    ▲    ▲    ▲    ▲   }   ▲    ▲    │
│ Date:[Tab][Tab]November 5, 1989[HRt]                             │
│ Ship to:[Tab][Tab]Bull Run Chiropractic Clinic[HRt]             │
│ [HRt]                                                             │
│ [Tab Set:Rel: +3",+4",+5",+6.5"][BOLD]Tab Types:[Cntr Tab]Center[Cntr Tab]Center │
│ [Cntr Tab]Center[Rgt Tab]Right[bold][HRt]                        │
│ Item[Cntr Tab]Qty[Cntr Tab]Cost[Cntr Tab]Total[Rgt Tab]Shipped?[HRt] │
│ [HRt]                                                             │
│ [Tab Set:Rel: +3",+4",+5",+6.5"][BOLD]Tab Types:[Cntr Tab]Dot Leader[Cntr Tab]De │
│ cimal[Cntr Tab]Decimal[Rgt Tab]Right[bold][HRt]                  │
│ [Tab Set:Rel: +3",+4",+5",+6.5"]Vitamin E[Cntr Tab]4[Dec Tab]1.19[Dec Tab]4.76[R │
│                                                                   │
│ Press Reveal Codes to restore screen                             │
└─────────────────────────────────────────────────────────────────┘
```

With Relative to Margin tabs, if you want a tab stop to be one inch from the left margin, the tab will always be one inch in from the margin even if you later change the margin settings.

The following describes WordPerfect's tab types:

Left tabs	The first line is indented to the tab stop, and text continues to the right. Subsequent lines return to the normal left margin. Left tab is the most common tab type.
Center tabs	Text is centered at the tab stop. A center tab works similar to the Center (Shift-F6) feature. A center tab, however, can force centering anywhere in the line—not just in the center of the margins. Use center tabs to create column headings.
Right tabs	After a right tab stop, text continues to the left. A right tab stop works similar to the Flush Right (Alt-F6) feature. A right tab, however, can be anywhere in the line—not just at the right margin. Use right tabs to create headings over columns of numbers or dates.
Decimal tabs	After a decimal tab stop, text continues to the left until you type the alignment character; then text continues to the right. A decimal tab works similar to the Tab Align (Ctrl-F6) feature. With decimal tabs, however, you preset the alignment point as a tab stop. The default alignment character is a period; you can change the default to any character you want. Use decimal tabs to line up columns of numbers.
Tabs with dot leaders	Any of the four tab types can be preceded by dots (periods) as a leader. Use dot leaders for long lists, such as phone lists, that require visual scanning from left to right.

Cue:

Use dot leaders for long lists, such as phone lists, that require visual scanning from left to right.

Changing Tab Settings

When you change the tab settings, the settings affect only the text from the point where you make the change. To change the entire document, go to the beginning of the document and reset the tab stops, or change the Initial Codes. (To move the cursor to the beginning of the document, press Home, Home, ↑.)

If you change the tabs after text has been entered, all tabs will reformat automatically. When you use left tabs, a **[Tab]** code that reflects the tab settings is inserted. Center tabs insert a **[Cntr Tab]** code; right tabs insert a **[Rgt Tab]** code; and decimal tabs insert **[Dec Tab]** code.

A number of options are available for setting the tab stops. You can set tab stops one at a time, or you can specify the increment and set multiple tab stops for the first 7.5 inches. If you want to set extended tabs (from 8 inches to 54.5 inches), you must set them individually. You can set a maximum of 40 tabs. Similarly, you can delete a single tab stop, all the tab stops, or only the tabs to the right of the cursor.

Reminder:
You can set a maximum of 40 tabs.

To change tab stops, follow these steps:

1. Press Format (Shift-F8) and select **L**ine (**1**).

   ⌨ Access the **L**ayout pull-down menu and select **L**ine.

2. From the Format: Line menu, select **T**ab Set (**8**). The bottom of the screen displays a graphic representation of the current tab stops, called the *tab ruler* (see fig. 5.9).

```
L...L...L...L...L...L...L...L...L...L...L...L...L...L...
!   ^   !   ^   !   ^   !   ^   !   ^   !   ^   !   ^   !
-1"      0"      +1"     +2"     +3"     +4"     +5"     +6"
Delete EOL (clear tabs); Enter Number (set tab); Del (clear tab);
Type; Left; Center; Right; Decimal; .= Dot Leader; Press Exit when done.
```

Fig. 5.9
The tab ruler.

3. *To delete a single tab stop*, use the cursor keys or mouse to move to the tab you want to delete; or type the number that represents the number of units from the left margin the tab stop you want to delete is, and then press Enter to position the cursor at that tab stop. (The units can be inches, centimeters, points, 1200ths of an inch, or WordPerfect 4.2 units.) Press Del or Backspace to delete the tab.

   To delete all the tab stops, move the cursor to the left margin (press Home, Home, ←), and press Delete to End of Line (Ctrl-End).

   To delete the tab stops to the right of the cursor, type the number of units (inches, centimeters, points, 1200ths of an inch, or WordPerfect 4.2 units) from the point you want to delete tabs to the right, and then press Enter. Then press Delete to End of Line (Ctrl-End).

4. *To add a single tab stop*, use the cursor keys or mouse to move the cursor to the position at which you want a tab stop; or type the number that represents how many units from the left margin the tab stop you want to add is, and then press Enter to position the cursor on that tab stop. Select **L**eft to add a left tab, **C**enter to add a center tab, **R**ight to add a right tab, or **D**ecimal to add a decimal tab. To add a dot leader, press the period (**.**) before exiting.

To add multiple left tab stops, type the unit at which you want the tabs to begin, press the comma (,), and then type the increment you want the tabs spaced. For example, to space tabs one-half inch apart beginning at one inch, type *1,.5* and press Enter.

To add multiple center, right, or decimal tab stops and dot leaders, use the cursor keys to move the cursor to the position at which you want the tab stops to begin, or type the unit where you want the tabs to begin and press Enter. Then select **C**enter, **R**ight, or **D**ecimal. If you want a dot leader, also press the period (.). Type the unit where you want the tab stops to begin, press the comma (,), and then type the increment you want the tabs spaced. For example, to space right-aligned tabs one-half inch apart beginning at one inch, position the cursor at one inch and press **R**ight; then type *1,.5* and press Enter.

5. *To change the tab type*, select **T**ype and then select either **A**bsolute (**1**) or **R**elative to Margin (**2**).

6. Press Exit (F7) twice to return to the document.

Setting Hard Tabs

With WordPerfect 5.1, you can add *hard tabs*. A hard tab enables you to insert any of the four tab types regardless of the tab settings. For example, suppose that you want a particular tab to be centered, but that the tab settings are for all left tabs. In previous versions of WordPerfect, you had to change tab settings to make one of the tab stops a center tab.

Cue:

Use hard tabs so that you can insert any of the four tab types regardless of the tab settings.

With WordPerfect 5.1, you can make any tab stop any type of tab whether the tab stop has been defined as a **L**eft, **C**enter, **R**ight, or **D**ecimal tab. You accomplish this by entering a hard left, hard center, hard right or hard decimal tab. To enter a hard tab, use the keystrokes listed in table 5.1.

In hidden codes, both regular and hard tabs look the same, except that the code for a hard tab appears in all uppercase letters. Once a tab has been made a hard tab, it retains that type of hard tab's identity regardless of any later changes to the tab settings.

Table 5.1
Types of Hard Tabs

Tab Type	Tab Code	Hard Tab Code	Keystrokes for Hard Tab
Left Tab	**[Tab]**	**[TAB]**	Home, Tab
Center Tab	**[Cntr Tab]**	**[CNTR TAB]**	Home, Center (Shift-F6)
Right Tab	**[Rgt Tab]**	**[RGT TAB]**	Home, Flush Right (Alt-F6)
Decimal Tab	**[Dec Tab]**	**[DEC TAB]**	Home, Tab Align (Ctrl-F6)

Comparing Tab to Indent

WordPerfect's Tab and Indent features are similar in some ways, but each has specific uses. Table 5.2 lists the differences between these features.

Table 5.2
Tab and Indent Uses

Feature	Function
Tab	Indent only the first line of a paragraph from the left margin.
Indent (F4)	Indent the entire paragraph from the left margin.
Left-Right Indent (Shift-F4)	Indent the entire paragraph equally from both margins.

Pressing Tab When Outline Is On

If you have turned on the Outline function, the Tab key causes changes in the hierarchy of an outline. A Roman numeral I, for example, might change to an A. If you encounter this unexpected result, be sure to turn off the Outline feature.

To turn the Outline feature off or on, follow these steps:

1. Press Date/Outline (Shift-F5) and select **O**utline (**4**).
2. Select **O**n (**1**) or O**ff** (**2**) to turn Outline on or off.

   ⌨ Access the **T**ools pull-down menu, select **O**utline, and then select either **O**n or O**ff**.

When the Outline feature is on, the word `Outline` appears in the lower left corner of the screen. Chapter 24 discusses the Outline feature in detail.

Displaying the Tab Ruler

To view the current tab settings, you can use the Window feature to display a tab ruler at the bottom of the screen.

Complete the following steps to display an on-screen tab ruler:

1. Press Screen (Ctrl-F3) and select **W**indow (**1**).

   ⌨ Access the **E**dit pull-down menu and select **W**indow.

   The program displays the following prompt along with a number after the colon:

   `Number of lines in this window:`

   The number after the colon varies depending on the capabilities of your monitor or what number you entered for the /SS start-up option when you loaded WordPerfect. (For a complete discussion of start-up options, see Appendix A.)

2. Enter a number that is one less than the number in the prompt. For example, if the prompt displays *24*, type *23* or press ↑ once.

3. Press Enter. A tab ruler appears at the bottom of the screen (see fig. 5.10). The curly braces, { and }, mark the left and right margins. The triangles mark the tab stops. Instead of braces, the program may display flat brackets, such as **[** and **]**. The brackets indicate that the tab stops have been changed from their default values.

Fig. 5.10

The tab ruler displayed at the bottom of the screen.

```
G:\WP51\QUE\FIG5-10                          Doc 2 Pg 1 Ln 1" Pos 1"
[   ▲    ▲    ▲    ▲    ▲    ▲    ▲    ▲    ▲   ]  ▲    ▲
```

To eliminate the tab ruler, repeat the previous steps, but for step 3, type one more than the number displayed by the prompt, or press ↓ once.

Using Tab Align

Tab Align (Ctrl-F6) jumps the cursor to the right one tab stop. All text you type moves to the left of the tab stop until you type the alignment character (the default is a period). After you type the alignment character, the text begins moving to the right of the tab stop. Figure 5.11 illustrates how information can be aligned at the right with a colon using the Tab Align feature.

Fig. 5.11

Examples of uses for Tab and Tab Align.

```
(Information aligned at the left with Tab.)

        Name:     John Doe
        Address:  1212 Main Street
        City:     Sandy
        State:    Oregon

(Information aligned with Tab align and a colon as the alignment
character.)

           Name:  John Doe
        Address:  1212 Main Street
           City:  Sandy
          State:  Oregon
```

Complete the following steps to create text aligned at the right on a specific character:

1. Press Tab Align (Ctrl-F6).

    ▭ Access the **L**ayout pull-down menu, select **A**lign, and then select **T**ab Align.

    The cursor moves right one tab stop, and the `Align char = .` message appears in the lower left corner of the screen.

2. Type the text.

3. Type the alignment character (in this case, a period).

If you want to align text at the right without displaying the alignment character, you can repeat step 1, type the text, and then press Enter before pressing the alignment character. The typed text is right-justified at the tab stop.

The alignment character can be any character you want. In the example in figure 5.11, the alignment character is a colon (:). To align names and addresses, use a colon. To align numbers, an equal sign (=) is best.

Cue:

To align names and addresses, use a colon with Tab Align (Ctrl-F6). To align numbers, use an equal sign (=) or decimal.

To change the alignment character, follow these steps:

1. Press Format (Shift-F8) and select **O**ther (**4**).

    ▭ Access the **L**ayout pull-down menu and select **O**ther.

2. From the Format: Other menu, select **D**ecimal/Align Character (**3**). The cursor moves to the right of the **D**ecimal/Align Character menu item.

3. Type a new alignment character and press Enter twice.

   Note: Do not change the character for the thousands separator. (See Chapter 18 for more information about the thousands separator.)

4. Press Exit (F7) to return to the document.

Using Justification

WordPerfect 5.1 expands on the concept of justified type. In WordPerfect 5, the term *justification* refers to whether text is aligned flush along the right margin or is ragged. WordPerfect 5.1 offers the following four types of justification:

Full Justification	**F**ull Justification aligns the text on the printed page along both the right and left margins. **F**ull Justification is WordPerfect 5.1's default setting.
Left Justification	**L**eft Justification leaves a ragged right margin.
Center Justification	**C**enter Justification centers all text. If you block and center text using Center (Shift-F6), WordPerfect 5.1 inserts a **[Just:Center]** code at the beginning of the block and inserts at the end of the block a justification code for whatever type of justification was previously active.
Right Justification	**R**ight Justification aligns all text on the right margin, leaving the left margin ragged. If you block and right-align text using Flush Right (Alt-F6), WordPerfect 5.1 inserts a **[Just:Right]** code at the beginning of the block and inserts at the end of the block a justification code for whatever type of justification was previously active.

5.1

Caution

If you use the Block feature on multiple lines of text to either center or right-align text, WordPerfect resets the justification at the end of the block to the previously active justification setting. If you later attempt to change the default Initial Codes, insert a Justification code at the beginning of the document, add justification codes elsewhere in the document, or delete one of the center or right-align codes in an attempt to change the document's default justification, the reset codes previously inserted by WordPerfect will not change.

Use **F**ull Justification when you have a printer capable of proportional spacing and you want a formal look. Hyphenation improves the appearance of fully justified text. If the printer is not capable of proportional spacing or if you want the document to be less formal, change the setting to **L**eft Justification.

Figure 5.12 is a printout that illustrates text with a ragged right margin and text that is fully justified.

Cue:
*Use F*ull Justification *when you have a printer capable of proportional spacing and you want a formal look.*

Fig. 5.12

Justified versus unjustified text, with and without hyphenation.

```
The next two paragraphs are set to Justification Left.

This line has so many characters that the very next
extraordinarily long word wraps to the next line, creating a gap
at the right margin.

Turn on hyphenation to improve the look of the text. The extraor-
dinarily long word is hyphenated, creating a visual appearance
that is much more attractive.

The next two paragraphs are set to Justification Full.

This   line  has   so   many   characters   that  the   very  next
extraordinarily long word wraps to  the next line, creating a gap
at the right margin.

Turn on hyphenation to improve the look of the text. The extraor-
dinarily  long word is  hyphenated, creating a  visual appearance
that is much more attractive.
```

Because **F**ull Justification is not visible on-screen, you must use **V**iew Document (see the section "Using Document Preview") or print the page to see the full effect of **F**ull Justification. Because text is justified by adding spaces between words and letters, the attractiveness of justified text depends on the capabilities of your printer.

You can change the justification setting by using the Format menu. If the cursor is within the body of the document, the new setting affects only the portion of the document that follows the cursor position. To change the justification setting for the entire document, either go to the top of the document first or change the Initial Codes. (To move the cursor to the beginning of the document, press Home, Home, ↑.)

To change the justification setting, follow these steps:

1. Press Format (Shift-F8) and select **L**ine (**1**).

   ⌨ Access the **L**ayout pull-down menu and select **L**ine.

2. From the Format: Line menu, select **J**ustification (**3**).

3. Select either **L**eft (**1**), **C**enter (**2**), **R**ight (**3**), or **F**ull (**4**).

4. Press Exit (F7) to return to the document.

If you are not sure whether justification is on or off, complete steps 1 and 2 to check the setting. Then press Exit (F7) to return to the document.

Centering Text

Centering text with a typewriter can be a tedious task. With WordPerfect, you can perform this job easily. You can center a line of text either as you type it or after the text is entered.

To center a line of text that you are about to type, follow these steps:

1. Move the cursor to the left margin of a blank line and press Center (Shift-F6).

Access the **L**ayout pull-down menu, select **A**lign, and then select **C**enter.

The cursor jumps to the point midway between the two margins.

2. Type the text.

3. Press Enter.

If you type more characters than the margins can hold, the rest of the text wraps to a second line. Only the first line, however, is centered. To center several lines, use the Block function described in Chapter 4 or temporarily change justification to **C**enter.

If you want to center text around a specific point on-screen, press the space bar until the cursor is at the point on which you want the text centered. Press Center (Shift-F6). Notice that the cursor does not move. Then begin typing.

If you want to center text within defined text columns, place the cursor in the left margin of the column in which you want the text centered. Then follow the preceding three steps for centering. Refer to figure 5.13 for examples of various types of text alignments.

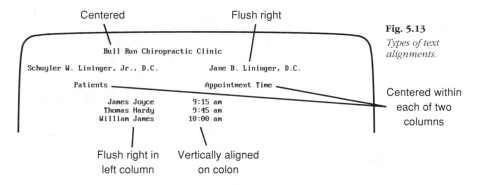

Cue:

To center several lines, use the Block function or temporarily change justification to Center.

Fig. 5.13
Types of text alignments.

Complete the following steps to center the text in a previously typed line:

1. Place the cursor at the left margin of the line of text you want to center; or press the space bar until you are positioned at the point you want the text centered.

2. Press Center (Shift-F6)

    Access the **L**ayout pull-down menu, select **A**lign, and then select **C**enter.

   The text jumps to the center of the screen.

3. Press ↓. The text appears centered on-screen.

Caution

If you use the space bar to move the cursor before activating the centering feature, the text line may start to the left of the left-margin setting unless the number of spaces you have typed are equal to at least half the number of characters in the line of text.

Making Text Flush Right

In certain documents, you may want the text to be flush right for the far right heading of a series of columns, dates, or other business headings. You can make text flush right either as you type it or after the text is entered.

Use the following steps to line up along the right margin the text you are about to type:

1. Move the cursor to the left margin.
2. Press Flush Right (Alt-F6).

    ⌨ Access the **L**ayout pull-down menu, select **A**lign, and then select **F**lush Right.

    The cursor jumps to the right margin.
3. Type the text. The text you type travels from right to left.
4. Press Enter to stop typing text flush right.

Caution

If you type more characters than the margins can hold, the extra text wraps to the next line. Only the first line of text is flush right. If you want several lines of text to be right-aligned, use Block (described in Chapter 4) or temporarily change the Justification to Right.

Complete the following steps to make the text in a previously typed line flush right:

1. Position the cursor at the left margin, or move the cursor to the point that you want text to the right of the cursor to be flush right.
2. Press Flush Right (Alt-F6).

    ⌨ Select **A**lign from the **L**ayout menu, and then select **F**lush Right.

    The line of text jumps to the right.
3. Press ↓. The line appears flush right on-screen.

Using Hyphenation

When a line of text becomes too long to fit within the margins, the last word in the line wraps to the next line. With short words, wrapping does not present a problem. With long words, however, the following problems can occur:

- If **J**ustification is set to **L**eft, a large gap can appear at the right margin, making the margin appear too ragged.
- If **J**ustification is set to **F**ull, large spaces between words become visually distracting.

Hyphenating a long word at the end of a line solves the problem and creates a visually attractive printed document. When you use WordPerfect's hyphenation feature, the program fits as much of the word as possible on one line before hyphenating and wraps the balance of the word to the next line (notice the hyphenation of the word *extraordinarily* in fig. 5.12).

Turning hyphenation on or off inserts a hidden code into the document that affects only the portion of the document after the cursor position. To hyphenate the entire document, either turn on the Hyphenation feature at the top of the document or change the Initial Codes. (To move the cursor to the beginning of the document, press Home, Home, ↑.)

Cue:

To hyphenate the entire document, turn on Hyphenation at the top of the document or change the Initial Codes.

To turn the hyphenation feature on or off, perform the following steps:

1. Press Format (Shift-F8) and select **L**ine (**1**).

    ▭ Access the **L**ayout pull-down menu and select **L**ine.

2. Select **H**yphenation (**1**).

3. Select **Y** or **N**.

4. Press Exit (F7) to return to the document. A **[Hyph On]** or **[Hyph Off]** code is inserted into the document.

Changing the Default Hyphenation Settings

Your preferences for hyphenation are controlled from the Setup menu. To change the default hyphenation settings, perform the following steps:

1. Press Setup (Shift-F1) and select **E**nvironment (**3**).

    ▭ Access the **F**ile pull-down menu, select Se**t**up, and then select **E**nvironment.

2. Select **H**yphenation (**6**), and then select either **E**xternal Dictionary/Rules (**1**) or **I**nternal Rules (**2**).

3. Select **P**rompt for Hyphenation (**7**), and then select **N**ever (**1**), **W**hen Required (**2**), or **A**lways (**3**).

4. Press Exit (F7) to return to the document.

External Dictionary/Rules or **I**nternal Rules refers to the set of rules WordPerfect uses to determine hyphenation points. In WordPerfect 5, to get adequate hyphenation, you needed to purchase a separate hyphenation module. With WordPerfect 5.1, hyphenation points are built in to the U.S. spelling dictionary.

Reminder:

WordPerfect uses External Dictionary/ Rules or Internal Rules to determine hyphenation points.

Tip

If you are using a foreign language or United Kingdom spelling dictionary, check with WordPerfect for the availability of a hyphenation module or dictionary. Also, if you are adding words to the WordPerfect dictionary (such as Stedman's Medical Dictionary of 68,000 medical terms from Reference Software), check with the vendor to see if hyphenation points are included in the word list.

External Dictionary/Rules (consisting of WP{WP}US.LEX and WP{WP}US.HYC) contains more words and is more complete (but requires more disk space) than

Internal Rules. If you add words to the spelling dictionary or want to add or change any hyphenation points, you can use the SPELL.EXE utility. (See Chapter 7 for more information about the SPELL.EXE program).

Prompt for Hyphenation instructs WordPerfect how to respond to words requiring hyphenation when you have turned the hyphenation feature on. If you select **N**ever, WordPerfect will hyphenate automatically; if WordPerfect comes across a word it doesn't know how to hyphenate, the word will be skipped. If you select **W**hen Required, WordPerfect stops on words that it doesn't know or cannot determine how to hyphenate. If you select **A**lways, WordPerfect will stop on every word that falls within the hyphenation zone (see the section "Changing the Hyphenation Zone").

When the **P**rompt for Hyphenation option is set to **W**hen Required or **A**lways, WordPerfect may prompt you to position the hyphen in any long word that needs to be broken. The following prompt appears at the bottom of the screen:

```
Position hyphen; Press ESC
```

A word that requires hyphenation follows the prompt, with the suggested hyphenation point marked by a hyphen (see fig. 5.14). You can respond to the prompt in any of three ways:

- To accept the suggested hyphenation point, *press the Esc key.* The word is hyphenated at that point.

- If the suggested hyphenation point is not acceptable, *reposition the hyphenation point* by moving the cursor left or right using the arrow keys. (The arrow keys move only a certain number of characters left or right.) When you have positioned the cursor to your satisfaction, press the Esc key.

- If the word cannot be hyphenated satisfactorily, *press Cancel (F1).* Pressing Cancel (F1) permanently rejects hyphenation for that word. WordPerfect inserts the hidden code [/] before the word. You must manually delete this code before WordPerfect can hyphenate the word.

Fig. 5.14

The prompt for manual hyphenation.

```
Position hyphen; Press ESC hyphen-ation.
```

5.1

Reminder:

When working with the Hyphenation feature, keep a dictionary handy to verify syllable breaks.

WordPerfect continues to prompt you for hyphenation points throughout the entire document. Prompted hyphenation, therefore, can be tedious. In addition, because the hyphenation points suggested by WordPerfect are often incorrect, you can easily make mistakes in hyphenation. Keep a dictionary handy to verify syllable breaks.

If you set **P**rompt for Hyphenation to **N**ever, WordPerfect will not ask you for hyphenation points.

Interrupting Hyphenation

If you set **P**rompt for Hyphenation to either **W**hen Required or **A**lways, you may be interrupted to hyphenate words while you type or edit. If you are being interrupted too much, use the steps in the preceding section to turn off hyphenation. Then wait until you complete the document before turning on hyphenation again. At that point, you can determine the proper syllable breaks for all the words in question.

If you want to interrupt the hyphenation process only briefly, press Exit (F7). Hyphenation is temporarily halted until the immediate command (such as scrolling or spell-checking) is completed. Use this feature when you turn on hyphenation and then begin spell-checking or scrolling. By pressing Exit (F7), you can complete the scroll or spell-check before resuming hyphenation.

Reminder:
Press Exit (F7) to temporarily halt the hyphenation process.

Changing the Hyphenation Zone

WordPerfect comes with a preset hyphenation zone. When hyphenation is on, this zone determines whether a word should be hyphenated or wrapped to the next line. The hyphenation zone is preset in percentages of line length: the left hyphenation zone is preset at 10%; the right hyphenation zone is preset at 4%.

Reminder:
The hyphenation zone is preset in WordPerfect.

On a standard document page, 8.5 inches wide with a 1-inch left margin and a 1-inch right margin, a line of text can be 6.5 inches in length. The left hyphenation zone is 0.65" (10% of 6.5 inches), and the right zone is 0.26" (4% of 6.5 inches). If the line length becomes longer, the zones become larger but retain the same proportions.

The following examples illustrate how WordPerfect uses these zones in a standard document:

- *If the word begins at or before the left zone* (0.65 inches from the right margin) and continues past the right zone (0.26 inches from the right margin), the word requires hyphenation. The word is too long to wrap without leaving a large gap.

- *If the word begins at or after the left zone* (0.65 inches from the right margin) and continues past the right zone (0.26 inches from the right margin), the word wraps to the next line. The word is either too short to hyphenate or short enough so that it won't leave a large gap.

You can customize the zones with the following effects:

- *If you make the zone smaller,* either by making the left zone a smaller percentage (for instance 9%) or the right zone a larger percentage (for instance 5%), more hyphenation is required. (The right zone should not exceed the left zone.) With justification off, a more even right margin is produced with a smaller hyphenation zone.

- *If you make the zone larger,* either by making the left zone a larger percentage (for instance 11%) or the right zone a smaller percentage (for instance 3%), less hyphenation is required. (The numbers should not exceed the margins.) With justification on, too large a hyphenation zone causes gaps in the line.

Refer to figure 5.15 for a better understanding of hyphenation zones.

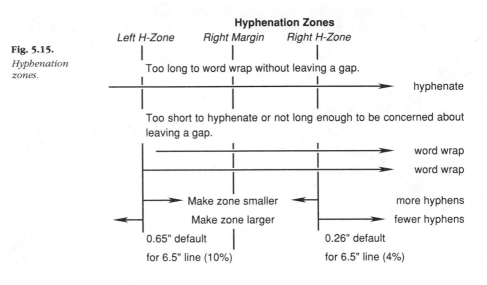

Fig. 5.15.
Hyphenation zones.

To change the hyphenation-zone setting for the entire document, go to the top of the document first or change the Initial Codes. (To move the cursor to the beginning of the document, press Home, Home, ↑.) If the cursor is positioned within the document, the new setting affects only the portion of the document following the cursor.

To change the hyphenation zone, follow these steps:

1. Press Format (Shift-F8) and select **L**ine (**1**).

   ⌨ Access the **L**ayout pull-down menu and select **L**ine.

2. Select Hyphenation **Z**one Left/Right (**2**). The cursor moves to the right of the Hyphenation **Z**one Left/Right menu item.

3. Type a new value for the left zone and press Enter.

4. Type a new value for the right zone and press Enter.

5. Press Exit (F7).

Understanding the Types of Hyphens and Soft Returns

WordPerfect enables you to create several types of hyphens and dashes. Although hyphens and dashes may appear the same on-screen, WordPerfect interprets them differently. So that you can determine which kind of hyphen or dash has been entered, you should edit text with Reveal Codes (Alt-F3 or F11) turned on.

Table 5.3 shows the differences between the various types of hyphens and soft returns.

Table 5.3
Types of Hyphens and Soft Returns

Type	Keystroke	Purpose	Hidden Code
Hard hyphen	Hyphen key	Inserts a regular hyphen	[–]
Hyphen	Home, hyphen	Causes WordPerfect to treat a hyphenated word as a single word	–
Soft hyphen	Ctrl-hyphen	Inserts a hyphen that appears when a word breaks at the end of a line	Highlighted –
Dash	Home, hyphen, hyphen	Keeps two hyphens together	–[–]
Hard space	Home, space	Keeps two words together	[]
Invisible soft return	Home, Enter	Inserts a line break without hyphenating	**[ISRt]**
Deletable soft return	(no keystroke)	Forces a line break without hyphenating	**[DSRt]**
Dormant hard return	(no keystroke)	Hard return at the top of a new page becomes dormant to eliminate unnecessary white space; changes back to hard return when not at page top	**[Dorm HRt]**

When you press the hyphen key, a hard hyphen is inserted into the document. That hyphen appears as [–] in Reveal Codes (Alt-F3 or F11). Hard hyphens always are visible on-screen and appear when the document is printed. If a hard hyphen appears in a word that needs to be hyphenated at the end of a line, WordPerfect uses the hard hyphen as the breaking point instead of prompting you.

When you press Home, hyphen, a hyphen character is inserted into the document. This character appears as an unhighlighted – in Reveal Codes (Alt-F3 or F11). Hyphen characters always are visible on-screen and appear when the document is printed. The program treats a hyphen character as part of the word, as though the hyphen were another character. If a hyphen character appears in a word being hyphenated by WordPerfect, you may be prompted for a hyphen breaking point.

Reminder:

If a hyphen character appears in a word being hyphenated by WordPerfect, you may be prompted for a hyphen breaking point.

Pressing Ctrl-hyphen inserts a soft hyphen into the document. That hyphen appears as a highlighted – in Reveal Codes (Alt-F3 or F11). Soft hyphens are inserted between syllables during hyphenation. You can insert your own soft hyphen at points you want hyphenation to occur. Soft hyphens are visible and print only when appearing as the last character in a line; otherwise, soft hyphens are hidden.

> ### Tip
>
> You cannot produce a soft hyphen by using the numeric keypad's minus sign in combination with the Ctrl key. You must instead use the hyphen key at the top of the keyboard. Pressing the numeric keypad's minus sign by itself moves the cursor to the top of the screen. If you turn on Num Lock, you can produce a hard hyphen by pressing the numeric keypad's minus sign.

Cue:

Press Home, hyphen, hyphen to type a dash so that the two hyphens stay together.

When you need to type a dash, use a combination of two types of hyphens. For the first hyphen, use the hyphen character (Home, hyphen). For the second hyphen, use a hard hyphen (press the hyphen key alone). This technique ensures that regardless of where the line breaks, the two hyphens stay together.

When you need to keep two or more words together, insert a hard space between the words. You can create a hard space by pressing Home, space. Words separated by hard spaces are not wrapped to the next line unless all the words joined by hard spaces are wrapped.

Suppose, for example, that you always want the name of your business, Jones' Retail Hardware Supply, to appear on one line. You would type *Jones'*; press Home, space; type *Retail*; press Home, space; type *Hardware*; press Home, space; and then type *Supply*. A hard space appears as **[ ]** in Reveal Codes.

You can insert manually an invisible soft return when you want to control a line break. You may, for example, not want certain words to be broken by a hyphen or space, such as words that have a slash (and/or, either/or) or words connected with an ellipsis ("a great...fantastic film"). An invisible soft return breaks the line where you specify. Create the invisible soft return by pressing and releasing the Home key and then pressing Enter. An invisible soft return appears as **[ISRt]** in Reveal Codes. If editing changes the line ending, the paragraph reformats; you do not have to remove the return.

WordPerfect inserts a deletable soft return if hyphenation is off and a line doesn't fit between margins.

All hard returns **[HRt]** become dormant hard returns **[Dorm HRt]** at the top of a new page to avoid unnecessary white space. WordPerfect automatically changes from **[HRt]** to **[Dorm HRt]** and back again.

Removing Soft Hyphens

Reminder:

Simply turning off hyphenation does not remove the hyphens already in place.

When a word is hyphenated, WordPerfect inserts a soft hyphen at each point where a word can be hyphenated. Soft hyphens are displayed on-screen or printed by the printer if they appear at the end of a line of text; otherwise, they are hidden. If you later decide that you would like to have an unhyphenated document, you must remove these soft hyphens. Simply turning off hyphenation does not remove the hyphens already in place.

After turning off hyphenation, complete the following steps to remove the soft hyphens from a document:

1. Press Home, Home, ↑ to move the cursor to the beginning of the document.

2. Press Replace (Alt-F2).

   ⌨ Access the **S**earch pull-down menu and select **R**eplace.

   The w/Confirm? No (Yes) prompt appears.

3. Press Enter to select **N**o.

   ⌨ Press the right mouse button.

   The → Srch: prompt appears.

4. Press Ctrl-hyphen. Pressing this key combination creates a soft hyphen.

5. Press Search (F2).

   ⌨ Press the right mouse button.

   The Replace with: prompt appears.

6. Press Search (F2).

   ⌨ Press the right mouse button.

All the soft hyphens in the document are removed.

Changing Line Height

The vertical distance between the base of a line of text and the base of the line of text above or below is called *line height*. Printers call line height *leading* because in the days of manual typesetting, the amount of space between lines was controlled by placing thin strips of lead between the lines. WordPerfect 5.1 automatically controls line height.

Reminder:
Leading *is the vertical distance between the base of a line of text and the base of the line of text above or below.*

If you change point sizes, WordPerfect adjusts the line height. If you change the point size from 10 to 18, for example, the line height is also increased.

Because WordPerfect handles line height automatically, you usually do not need to adjust it manually. If, however, you want to fit on a single page all the text of a document that contains one full page plus two extra lines, you can pick up the extra lines of text by reducing the line height.

Reminder:
WordPerfect handles line height automatically, but you can change it.

Because line-height changes are not visible on-screen, you must either display the page with **V**iew Document (see the section "Using Document Preview") or print the page to see the effect of any changes. Figure 5.16, displayed with **V**iew Document, shows how line height changes are created automatically by WordPerfect when different fonts sizes are mixed on the same page.

You can use the Format (Shift-F8) menu to change the line height. Keep in mind that to change the line height for the entire document, you must either first go to the top of the document or change the Initial Codes. (To move the cursor to the beginning of the document, press Home, Home, ↑.) If the cursor is within the document, the new setting affects only the portion of the document following the cursor.

Reminder:
To change the line height for the entire document, you must either first go to the top of the document or change the Initial Codes.

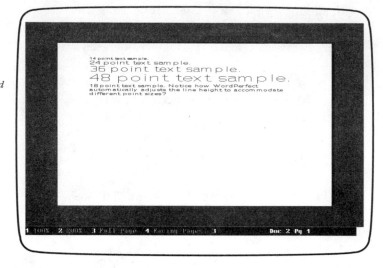

Fig. 5.16
Line-height changes displayed with View Document.

To change the line height, complete these steps:

1. Press Format (Shift-F8) and select **L**ine (**1**).

   ⌨ Access the **L**ayout pull-down menu and select **L**ine.

2. Select Line **H**eight (**4**).

   The following prompt appears at the bottom of the screen:

      1 Auto; **2 F**ixed: **0**

3. Select **A**uto (**1**) to have WordPerfect calculate the line height automatically, or select **F**ixed (**2**) to enter a fixed line height.

   When prompted for a number, type a number with up to three decimal places, and then press Enter. Depending on what units of measurement you have selected, the number should be entered in inches, centimeters, points, 1200ths of an inch (w units), or WordPerfect 4.2 units.

4. Press Exit (F7) to return to the document.

> **Caution**
>
> The line-height feature does not work on printers that can print only 6 lines per inch.

Changing Line Spacing

Reminder:

Single spacing is WordPerfect's default line spacing.

Single spacing is WordPerfect's default line spacing. To double- or triple-space a document, you do not have to manually place two hard returns after each line. Instead, you can use the Format (Shift-F8) menu to change the line spacing. Remember that to change the line spacing for the entire document, you must either first go to the top of the document, or change the Initial Codes. (To move the cursor to the beginning of the document, press Home, Home, ↑.) If the cursor is within the document, the new setting affects only the portion of the document following the cursor.

You do not see changes in line spacing on-screen except when the setting is a whole number (such as 1, 2, or 3), or a decimal number equal to or greater than 0.5 (such as 1.6, which would look the same as 2 on-screen). To see the effect of any changes, you must either display the page with **V**iew Document (see this chapter's "Using Document Preview" section) or print the page.

To change the line spacing, complete these steps:

1. Press Format (Shift-F8) and select **L**ine (**1**).

   ⌨ Access the **L**ayout pull-down menu and select **L**ine.

2. Select Line **S**pacing (**6**). The cursor moves to the right of the Line **S**pacing menu item.

3. Type any number with up to two decimal places, and then press Enter.

   To double-space, type *2*. For one-and-a-half spaces between lines, type *1.5*. You can increase line spacing by small amounts by typing a number such as *1.02*. Likewise, you can decrease line spacing by a small amount by entering a number that is less than 1, such as *0.95*.

   Note: If the number you type reduces the line spacing too much, the lines of text may print partially one on top of another.

4. Press Exit (F7) to return to the document.

> ### Tip
>
> WordPerfect 5.1 automatically converts fractional numbers into their decimal equivalents. For example, if you enter *1 5/8* and press Enter, WordPerfect will convert the number to 1.62.

Enhancing Text

One of WordPerfect's exceptional features is the program's capability to get the most out of whatever printer you use. Although some text enhancements are evident on-screen (depending on your monitor), most are realized on the printed page. The Font feature controls the size and appearance of characters when they are printed.

Changing the Base Font

When you installed your printer, you selected an initial base font. You chose the initial base font from a list of fonts available on your printer. The *base font* is the font the document will use for printing. Depending on the capabilities of your printer and its selection of fonts, you can select additional fonts or change a font's size and appearance.

Reminder:

The base font *is the font the document will use for printing.*

To change the base font for the entire document, you must first go to the top of the document or change the Initial Codes. (To move the cursor to the beginning of the document, press Home, Home, ↑.) If the cursor is within the document, the new setting affects only the portion of the document that follows the cursor.

To change the base font, follow these steps:

1. Press Font (Ctrl-F8) and select Base **F**ont (**4**).

   ▭ Access the F**o**nt pull-down menu and select Base F**o**nt.

   The Base **F**ont menu appears, listing all the fonts that the selected printer can use (see fig. 5.17).

Tip

If you have a printer that can print using both portrait and landscape fonts, and you have defined a form with one of these orientations, WordPerfect will display a list of fonts for the orientation defined on the form—either all portrait or all landscape fonts. Certain printers, including PostScript, can print in either portrait or landscape with all their fonts. (For more information on printing, see Chapters 8 and 9.)

Depending on the printer, the program may offer several screens of font choices. To access successive screens, scroll with the arrow keys, the PgDn or PgUp keys, or the Screen Up or Screen Down keys. The highlighted font with an asterisk to its left is the current base font.

2. Press **N**ame Search and type the first letters of the font you want. Press Enter when the cursor bar highlights the name of the font you want to use in the document. Press Enter to change the base font and return to the document.

   ▭ Use the mouse pointer to highlight the font you want. Double-click the font to select it.

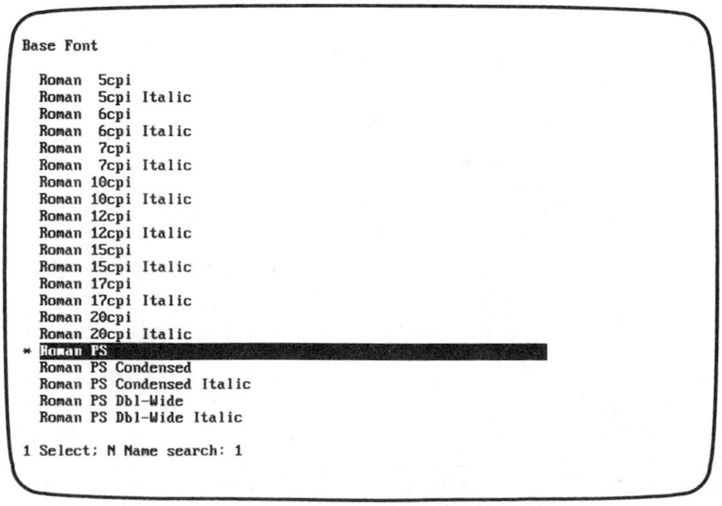

Fig. 5.17
The Base Font menu.

```
Base Font

     Roman  5cpi
     Roman  5cpi Italic
     Roman  6cpi
     Roman  6cpi Italic
     Roman  7cpi
     Roman  7cpi Italic
     Roman  10cpi
     Roman  10cpi Italic
     Roman  12cpi
     Roman  12cpi Italic
     Roman  15cpi
     Roman  15cpi Italic
     Roman  17cpi
     Roman  17cpi Italic
     Roman  20cpi
     Roman  20cpi Italic
  *  Roman  PS
     Roman  PS Condensed
     Roman  PS Condensed Italic
     Roman  PS Dbl-Wide
     Roman  PS Dbl-Wide Italic

  1 Select; N Name search: 1
```

Using Proportional Spacing

Some printers allow *proportional spacing*—a feature that gives a printed page a more pleasing appearance by allowing for different widths of characters. The letter *w*, for example, is wider than the letter *i*. Normally, when these letters are printed, both are given the same amount of space; the result can be gaps that are visually distracting. With proportional printing, the letter *w* is given more space than the letter *i*, creating a more aesthetic and professional-looking line of text.

When you examine the list of fonts available with your printer, notice any that have proportional spacing; these are designated by the initials `PS` or the word `proportional`. The list in figure 5.17 shows several available proportional fonts, including `Roman PS` and `Roman PS Condensed`. If no fonts have the `PS` designation, either the printer does not allow proportional printing, or WordPerfect does not support proportional printing for that particular printer.

> **Tip**
>
> With dot-matrix printers, proportional spacing often slows down the job of printing. Use a nonproportional font for drafts of the document and reserve the proportionally spaced font for the final printing. Examine figure 5.18 and compare the examples of draft and proportional printing.

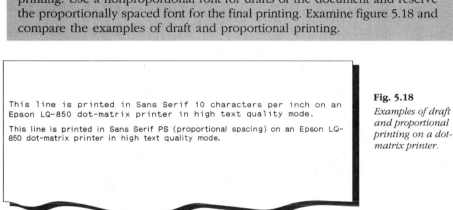

```
This line is printed in Sans Serif 10 characters per inch on an
Epson LQ-850 dot-matrix printer in high text quality mode.

This line is printed in Sans Serif PS (proportional spacing) on an Epson LQ-
850 dot-matrix printer in high text quality mode.
```

Fig. 5.18

Examples of draft and proportional printing on a dot-matrix printer.

Choosing Font Attributes

WordPerfect divides font attributes into two categories: *size* and *appearance*. When you alter the size or appearance, the `Pos` indicator in the lower right portion of the screen takes on the characteristics of your choice. How the `Pos` indicator and the text look on-screen depends on what kind of monitor and display card you have. Both the `Pos` indicator and the text on-screen look the same.

Changing the Font Size

You can make the font size smaller or larger. You may want to make a font smaller for a footnote number or a mathematical formula, for example. Make a font larger to emphasize a heading, column head, title, or letterhead.

To change the size of the base font, follow these steps:

1. Press Font (Ctrl-F8) and select **S**ize (**1**). Another menu, one with seven size attributes appears:

   1 Su**p**rscpt; **2** Su**b**scpt ; **3 F**ine; **4 S**mall; **5 L**arge; **6 V**ry Large; **7 E**xt Large; **0**

2. Select any one of the attributes to change the size of the base font.

   ▭ Access the F**o**nt pull-down menu and select one of the seven sizes listed.

Keep in mind that WordPerfect automatically tracks the vertical height of the larger or smaller letters and adjusts the margins and the number of lines per page. Larger fonts use more vertical space and allow fewer letters per line; smaller fonts use less vertical space and allow more letters per line.

Depending on your printer's capabilities, changing *size* has the following effects on a font:

- *Superscript* reduces the size of the base font and places text slightly above the line of printed text. Use this option for footnote numbers and mathematical formulas.

- *Subscript* reduces the size of the base font and places text slightly below the line of printed text. Use this option for mathematical formulas.

- *Fine* and *Small* decrease incrementally the size of the base font.

- *Large*, *Very Large*, and *Extra Large* increase incrementally the size of the base font.

Figure 5.19 illustrates several of these font size options.

Fig. 5.19
Mixed font sizes and appearances.

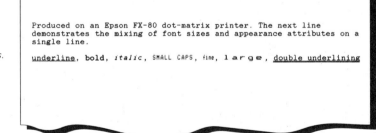

```
Produced on an Epson FX-80 dot-matrix printer. The next line
demonstrates the mixing of font sizes and appearance attributes on a
single line.

underline, bold, italic, SMALL CAPS, fine, l a r g e , double underlining
```

Changing the Font Appearance

To emphasize certain text, you can change a font's appearance. Appearance changes such as outline, shadow, small capital letters, bold, italic, and underline are appropriate for headings, titles, letterheads, book and magazine titles, foreign words, and captions. Appearance changes such as strikeout and redline emphasize document changes and revisions.

To change the appearance of any font, follow these steps:

1. Press Font (Ctrl-F8) and select **A**ppearance (**2**). Another menu, one with nine appearance attributes, is displayed at the bottom of the screen:

   1 Bold; **2** Undln; **3 D**bl Und; **4** Italc; **5** Outln; **6** Shadw; **7** Sm Cap; **8** Redln; **9** Stkout; **0**

2. Select any one of the appearance attributes to change a font's appearance.

   Access the **Fo**nt pull-down menu, select **A**ppearance, and then select one of the nine appearance attributes from the pop-out menu.

In general, changing *appearance* has the following effects on a font:

- *Bold* darkens the font just as the Bold key (F6) does. Using the Bold key (F6) to turn the bold appearance attribute on and off takes fewer keystrokes than using the Font key (Ctrl-F8) or pull-down menu.

- *Underline* turns underlining on just as the Underline key (F8) does. Using the Underline key (F8) to turn underlining on and off takes fewer keystrokes than using the Font key (Ctrl-F8) or pull-down menu.

- *Double Underline* underlines text twice.

  Note: WordPerfect's default settings underline spaces—but not tabs. If you want to change these settings, see the section, "Changing the Defaults for Underlining."

- Text marked as *Italic* is printed in italics.

- *Outline* and *Shadow* create special effects that depend on the printer.

- When you select *Small Capitals*, all text is printed in small capital letters.

- *Redline* and *Strikeout* mark over text in certain ways that depend on the printer.

Placing Different Attributes or Font Sizes on the Same Line

You can mix more than one appearance attribute or font size with various font-size attributes. Your printer determines whether or not these combinations work. Test your printer's capabilities by printing the file called PRINTER.TST included with the WordPerfect program. For instructions on how to print this file, see Chapter 8.

Changing the Defaults for Underlining

WordPerfect automatically underlines spaces between words but does not underline tab spaces unless you change the default settings. You can use the Format menu to change these default settings. Remember that to change the default underlining settings for the entire document, you either must first go to the top of the document or change the Initial Codes. (To move the cursor to the beginning of the document, press Home, Home, ↑.) If the cursor is within the document, the new settings affect only the portion of the document following the cursor.

Reminder:

To underline tab spaces, you must change WordPerfect's default underline settings.

To change underlining, follow these steps:

1. Press Format (Shift-F8) and select **O**ther (**4**).

   Access the **La**yout pull-down menu and select **O**ther.

2. Select **U**nderline Spaces/Tabs (**7**). The cursor moves to the right of the **U**nderline Spaces/Tabs menu item.

3. Select **Y** or **N** for each item.

4. Press Exit (F7) to return to the document.

Restoring Font Size and Appearance to Normal

You can end a change in font size and appearance in two ways. The best method for ending the attributes depends on how many attributes you have used. After you remove the attributes, text is restored to the font size and appearance in effect before the attributes were changed.

When you have made a combination of attribute changes, use the following method for restoring font size and appearance to normal:

Press Font (Ctrl-F8) and select **N**ormal (**3**).

⌨ Access the **Fo**nt pull-down menu and select **N**ormal.

This selection pushes the cursor beyond all size- and appearance-attribute codes.

When only one attribute is on, use the following method:

Press Reveal Codes (Alt-F3 or F11) to display the attributes that are turned on.

Note that each size or appearance attribute has a paired code. The capitalized code turns the attribute on; the lowercase code turns the attribute off. Press → to move the cursor past the attribute off code.

If you have several attributes on at the same time, press → enough times to move the cursor past all the codes. In other words, if you have attributes in effect, either choose the **N**ormal font or press the right-arrow key. Both methods move the cursor past the attribute codes.

Using Advanced Printer Features

You can use any of six advanced printer features to modify the way the text appears when printed. For the most part, you do not need to change WordPerfect's default settings. Once you become comfortable with these features, you can experiment with the settings on the Format: Printer Functions menu (see fig. 5.20) and observe how your document changes.

Reminder:

Kerning *is the subtle altering of spaces between letters to achieve a better visual appearance.*

The first option on the Format: Printer Functions menu is **K**erning (**1**). You can turn the kerning feature on or off by specifying **Y**es or **N**o. *Kerning* is the subtle altering of spaces between letters to achieve a better visual appearance. Kerned letters are unequally spaced according to a mathematical model.

Some letters take up more space than others, and normally this inequity does not present a problem. With larger point sizes, however, certain letter combinations are visually distracting when you use the default letter spacing. For instance, the letters *T* and *i* together can create a visual distraction. The letter *T* has a horizontal bar that acts as a roof. The letter *i* looks better tucked under that roof rather than spaced in the normal way. This tucking of specific letter pairs is called kerning.

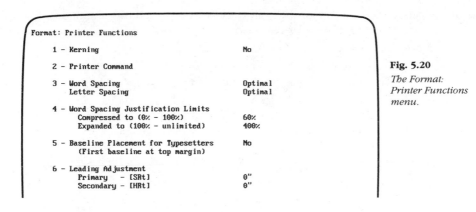

```
Format: Printer Functions

    1 - Kerning                          No

    2 - Printer Command

    3 - Word Spacing                     Optimal
        Letter Spacing                   Optimal

    4 - Word Spacing Justification Limits
        Compressed to (0% - 100%)        60%
        Expanded to (100% - unlimited)   400%

    5 - Baseline Placement for Typesetters   No
        (First baseline at top margin)

    6 - Leading Adjustment
        Primary   - [SRt]                0"
        Secondary - [HRt]                0"
```

Fig. 5.20

*The Format:
Printer Functions
menu.*

Kerning does not occur for all letter pairs—only for those defined by the font supplier. Note that monospaced typefaces (such as Courier) allow the same amount of space for each character and cannot be kerned.

The **P**rinter Command (**2**) option, which is discussed in detail in Chapter 9, enables you to send instructions directly to the printer either as a command or as a file. Any instructions you send are embedded as **[Ptr Cmnd:]** codes and remain in the document. When the program encounters a **[Ptr Cmnd:]** code, the instructions you entered are sent to the printer. The capabilities of your printer determine whether such instructions are necessary and whether advanced features are available.

When you select **W**ord Spacing/Letter Spacing (**3**), a **W**ord Spacing menu appears at the bottom of the screen. That menu offers you four choices:

- **N**ormal (**1**) sets the letter spacing to the width considered optimal by the manufacturer of the printer.

- **O**ptimal (**2**) resets the letter spacing to the default width considered optimal by WordPerfect Corporation.

- **P**ercent of Optimal (**3**) enables you to modify spacing according to your taste or needs.

  At the prompt, enter a negative number to reduce the amount of space between letters and words or enter a positive number to increase the space. Entering *0* is the same as the optimal (default) setting. Your printer may not work with the setting you select. If you select a setting that won't work, WordPerfect adjusts the setting.

- **S**et Pitch (**4**) changes the pitch (the number of characters per inch).

- Selecting Word Spacing **J**ustification Limits (**4**) turns on this feature and embeds in the text the following hidden code:

  [Just Lim:nn,nnn]

  This code affects the document from the point of insertion. With the **W**ord Spacing Justification feature, you can expand or compress spacing between words and letters to justify a line of text. Once selected, enter figures for

Compressed to (0%–100%) and Expanded to (100%–unlimited). For unlimited compression or expansion, type *999%*.

Note: Right-justification must be on for this feature to have an effect.

- **B**aseline Placement for Typesetters (**5**) works when Line Height is set to **F**ixed. This feature forces baseline positioning to the top margin.

- **L**eading Adjustment (**6**) enables you to specify additional leading to the line height. You can select extra leading for lines separated by either soft or hard returns. Figure 5.21 displays an example of 3 points of extra leading following hard returns.

Fig. 5.21

An example of the Leading Adjustment feature.

```
This sentence wraps to the next line using a soft return [SRt],
no additional leading has been added to the line height.

These two paragraphs are separated by a hard return [HRt]. The
Leading Adjustment feature adds 3 points of leading after a hard
return.
```

To make changes on the Format: Printer Functions menu, follow these steps:

1. Press Format (Shift-F8) and select **O**ther (**4**).

   ⌨ Access the **L**ayout pull-down menu and select **O**ther.

2. Select **P**rinter Functions (**6**).

3. Select any of the six options and make changes accordingly.

4. Press Exit (F7) to return to the editing screen.

Using Document Preview

WordPerfect displays text on-screen in standard-size characters. Depending on your monitor, you may see specific attributes such as bold or italic; you may not see other attributes. WordPerfect does not, for example, display 32-point text on-screen.

To see how each attribute is displayed on your monitor and to make any desired changes, complete the following steps:

1. Press Setup (Shift-F1) and select **D**isplay (**2**).

   ⌨ Access the **F**ile pull-down menu, select Se**t**up, and then select **D**isplay.

2. Select **C**olors/Fonts/Attributes (**1**). The Setup: Fonts/Attributes screen shows how each attribute looks on your monitor. Depending on your monitor, different options are available so that you can customize each attribute display.

3. Select **S**creen Attributes (**1**).

4. Use the cursor keys to move to any attribute you want to change and press the appropriate key or keys until the attribute is as you want it. You have different menu names and choices for colors and attributes depending on your monitor's capabilities and whether you have a monochrome or color monitor.

5. When you have finished examining or changing attributes, press Exit (F7) twice to return to the document screen.

Accurate judging of what the page will look like when printed cannot be done merely by looking at the regular WordPerfect screen. With a graphics monitor, however, you can use the View Document option on the Print menu to display on-screen a picture of the final page. You cannot edit the page, but you can view it, edit it, and then view it again. Chapter 8 explains how to use View Document.

Cue:

If you have a graphics monitor, you can use View Document to display on-screen a picture of the final page.

Summary

In this chapter, you learned about the powerful and easily accessible features that WordPerfect 5.1 offers for formatting and enhancing documents. You now should be able to perform the following tasks in order to control how text appears on the printed page:

❏ Alter the units of measurement from inches to WordPerfect 4.2 units, points, 1200ths of an inch, or centimeters

❏ Change the left and right margins, use margin release, and indent text

❏ Change tab settings and tab types (left, right, center, decimal, and dot leader)

❏ Center text, make text flush right, change justification settings, and change line spacing and leading

❏ Use the hyphenation feature and change the hyphenation zone

You also should be able to take advantage of your printer's capabilities by using the following procedures:

❏ Enhance text using font attributes such as size and appearance

❏ Use advanced printer functions such as letter spacing

❏ Verify formatting with the document preview function

Formatting Pages and Designing Documents

Karen Rose is the owner of Write on Target, a newsletter production and management company in Santa Rosa, CA. She wrote this chapter for *Using WordPerfect 5*.

Jon Pepper is president of Words Plus, a consulting firm based in Sunderland, Massachusetts, that specializes in computer-related topics. Mr. Pepper has also been a journalist covering the computer industry for several leading publications.

Robert M. Beck is a former judge practicing law in Oklahoma City. Mr. Beck is a beta tester for WordPerfect products.

Mr. Pepper and Mr. Beck revised this chapter for *Using WordPerfect 5.1, Special Edition*.

First impressions count. Whether you're a boss looking at a memo, a client looking at a report, or an employer looking at a resume, you form a first impression of the page in your hands. And your decision whether to read the page or put it down may depend on how that page looks—that is, whether it appears friendly, inviting, and easy to read.

"Ease of reading" refers to clarity. When you look at a page, is it clear what type of information the page contains? Is it clear what page you're reading? Is it clear where you must turn for more information? Is it clear where sections begin and end? In this chapter, you learn to use WordPerfect formatting features to design documents that are clear, interesting, and—above all—readable.

Reminder

If you use a mouse with WordPerfect 5.1, you can click the right button to display the pull-down menus, and then select the desired option. You also can press Alt-= to access the pull-down menus, and then press the appropriate letter of the desired option. For all the instructions, you can assume that if a block is required to activate a pull-down menu option, the text has been blocked before the pull-down menu is accessed. Instructions for pull-down menus and the mouse are marked with the mouse icon. See Chapter 1 for details on using the mouse.

Formatting Pages

Designing a document means making formatting choices at several levels. At the most global level, you make formatting choices for the entire document. At the next level, you make formatting choices for pages or groups of pages.

Page formatting includes decisions about how the pages in your document look. What are top and bottom margins? Is text centered, top to bottom, on the page? Are there headers and footers, and if so, on which pages? Are there automatic page numbers, and if so, where on the page do they appear? Is there text or a chart that must be kept together on a page? Must pages start at a certain point in the text? WordPerfect conveniently includes most formatting choices in the Format menu, shown in figure 6.1. The Format menu is displayed when you press Format (Shift-F8). A different type of format menu is displayed if you access the **L**ayout pull-down menu from the menu bar (see fig. 6.2).

Fig. 6.1.

The Format menu.

```
Format

   1 - Line
              Hyphenation              Line Spacing
              Justification           Margins Left/Right
              Line Height             Tab Set
              Line Numbering          Widow/Orphan Protection

   2 - Page
              Center Page (top to bottom)   Page Numbering
              Force Odd/Even Page            Paper Size/Type
              Headers and Footers           Suppress
              Margins Top/Bottom

   3 - Document
              Display Pitch           Redline Method
              Initial Codes/Font      Summary

   4 - Other
              Advance                 Overstrike
              Conditional End of Page Printer Functions
              Decimal Characters      Underline Spaces/Tabs
              Language

Selection: 0
```

Fig. 6.2.

*The **L**ayout pull-down menu.*

```
Layout
  Line
  Page
  Document
  Other

  Columns  ▶
  Tables   ▶
  Math     ▶

  Footnote ▶
  Endnote  ▶

  Justify  ▶
  Align    ▶

  Styles
```

Notice that four categories appear on the Format menu shown in figure 6.1: Line, Page, Document, and Other. These categories correspond to four levels of formatting. Line-formatting commands control the appearance of individual lines; page-formatting commands control the appearance of entire pages; document-formatting commands control the appearance of the document as a whole; and other formatting commands control additional formatting features.

Changing Top and Bottom Margins

The top margin is the distance between the top edge of the paper and the first line of text. Likewise, the bottom margin is the distance between the bottom edge of the paper and the bottom line of text. Until a different setting changes the margin, a margin setting applies to all text falling after it in a document. You set top and bottom margins by using the Format: Page menu (see fig. 6.3), which is listed in the Format menu, or by accessing the **L**ayout pull-down menu and selecting **P**age.

```
Format: Page

    1 - Center Page (top to bottom)      No

    2 - Force Odd/Even Page

    3 - Headers

    4 - Footers

    5 - Margins - Top                     1"
                  Bottom                  1"

    6 - Page Numbering

    7 - Paper Size                        8.5" x 11"
              Type                        Standard

    8 - Suppress (this page only)
```

Fig. 6.3.
The Format: Page menu.

WordPerfect's default margins are measured in decimal inches. If, for example, you want a top margin of 1 1/2 inches, type *1.5* in the Format Page menu or access the **L**ayout pull-down menu, select **P**age, and type *1.5*.

To set top and bottom margins in a document, move the cursor to where you want margin settings to begin—ordinarily, at the beginning of the document—and do the following:

1. Press Format (Shift-F8) and select **P**age (**2**).

    Access the **L**ayout pull-down menu and select **P**age.

2. Select **M**argins (**5**) to set top and bottom margins.

3. Type the new top margin, in decimal inches, and press Enter (to accept the current measurement, just press Enter). Then type the new bottom margin, in decimal inches, and press Enter (to accept the current measurement, just press Enter).

4. Press Exit (F7) to return to the document.

Allowing for Headers, Footers, and Page Numbers

Reminder:
Headers, footers, and page numbers are printed on the margin, not within the margin.

To include headers, footers, or page numbers in a document, plan margins accordingly. WordPerfect never prints these special text features inside a margin. Headers, footers, and page numbers are printed on the margin, and additional space (about one line) is left between the text and any header, footer, or page number.

If, for example, you want text to begin printing one inch from the top of the page but you want a header to print one-half inch from the top of the page, the top margin should be one-half inch.

Hand-Feeding Pages into a Platen Printer

If you hand-feed pages into a printer that has a platen, WordPerfect assumes that you roll the paper in one inch. (A platen printer rolls paper through like a typewriter. Most daisywheel and dot-matrix printers are platen printers.) If the top margin is set for one inch or less, printing begins at the print head. But if the top margin is set for more than one inch, the printer advances the paper by the margin amount minus one inch before printing begins. For example, if the top margin is one-half inch, the paper won't advance at all before printing begins, but if the margin is one-and-one-half inches, the paper advances one-half inch before printing begins.

If the top margin of a document is less than one inch, hand-feed paper into a platen printer by the amount of the margin. If the top margin is more than one inch, roll the paper in one inch.

Centering Pages Top to Bottom

At times, you may want to override the margins on a page and simply center all text on the page from top to bottom. You may, for example, want to center the title page of a report, as shown in figure 6.4.

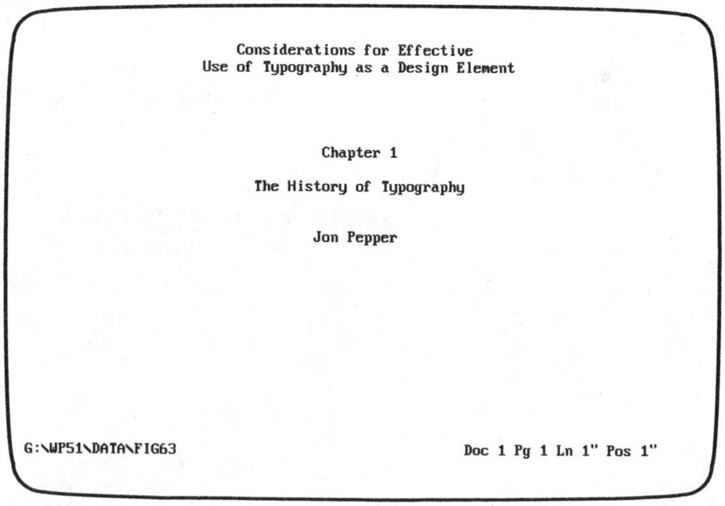
Considerations for Effective
Use of Typography as a Design Element
Chapter 1
The History of Typography
Jon Pepper
G:\WP51\DATA\FIG63
Doc 1 Pg 1 Ln 1" Pos 1"

Fig. 6.4.
A centered title page.

Centering top to bottom works a bit differently from setting margins. When you set margins, the settings apply to all following pages until WordPerfect encounters a new margin setting. But when you center a page top to bottom, the setting applies to just one page—the page where you make the setting.

The end of a centered page can be defined either by WordPerfect, with a soft page break (calculated from margin settings), or by you, with a hard page break (press Ctrl-Enter). Usually, a page centered from top to bottom is a separate page, shorter than the other pages in a document. Ending the centered page with a hard page break ensures that the page never merges accidentally with the next page.

When you choose the **C**enter Page (top to bottom) (**1**) command, be sure that the cursor is at the very beginning of the page, before any other formatting codes. Use Reveal Codes (Alt-F3 or F11) to verify this position.

To center a page top to bottom, move the cursor to the beginning of the page (before other formatting codes) and follow these steps:

1. Press Format (Shift-F8) and select **P**age (**2**).

   ⌨ Access the **L**ayout pull-down menu and select **P**age.

2. Select **C**enter Page (top to bottom) (**1**) and then press Exit (F7) to return to the document.

The only way to remove page centering is to delete the code. To determine the position of the code, use Reveal Codes (Alt-F3 or F11) or access the **E**dit pull-down menu and select **R**eveal Codes.

Designing Headers and Footers

A *header* is a block of text (or numbers or graphics) that appears at the top of a page. A *footer* is, similarly, a block that appears at the bottom of a page. Headers and footers can appear on all pages, on even pages only, on odd pages only, or on all pages except pages on which they are suppressed.

You can include one or two headers or footers on a page. Because you can designate them to appear on even-only or odd-only pages, you can set them up so that one header or footer appears on even pages and another appears on odd pages. If two headers appear on one page, be sure that they don't overlap. One header may be flush left; the other may be flush right—or they may appear on different lines.

Reminder:
One page can have as many as two headers and two footers.

Headers and footers can be up to a page long (but that won't leave much room for text!). Headers and footers also can employ most WordPerfect formatting functions, such as bold, underline, and centering. You can include automatic page numbering by inserting a special code, ^B (Ctrl-B), in either a header or a footer. Once created, a header or footer can be edited or deleted easily.

Headers and footers print at the top and bottom margins of pages, and WordPerfect leaves a space of about one line between the header or footer and the text of the document. (To leave more space between the text and the header or footer, include extra lines as part of the header or footer.) Headers and footers don't print inside the margins. If you have a one-inch top margin and a one-line header, for example,

Reminder:
Headers and footers do not print in the margin area.

WordPerfect prints the header at one inch, skips a line, and begins printing text on the next line.

You can't see headers or footers on the main editing screen. To see them, press Print (Shift-F7) and select **V**iew Document (**6**), or access the **F**ile pull-down menu, select **P**rint, and then select **V**iew Document (**6**). You can read the first 50 characters of a header or footer by choosing Reveal Codes (Alt-F3 or F11) or, alternatively, accessing the **E**dit pull-down menu and selecting **R**eveal Codes.

You can remove or edit headers and footers after you create them. You also can suppress them so that they don't appear on certain pages.

Creating New Headers and Footers

Create headers and footers at the beginning of a document. If you create them elsewhere, they may move when you insert or delete text.

To create a new header or footer, follow these steps:

1. Press Format (Shift-F8) and select **P**age (**2**).

   ▢▤ Access the **L**ayout pull-down menu and select **P**age.

2. To create a header, select **H**eaders (**3**); to create a footer, select **F**ooters (**4**). You can create two headers (A and B) and two footers (A and B).

3. Select Header **A** (**1**) or Header **B** (**2**), or select Footer **A** (**1**) or Footer **B** (**2**).

4. Select Every **P**age (**2**) if you want the header or footer to appear on every page in the document, **O**dd pages (**3**) if you want the header or footer to appear on odd pages only, or E**v**en pages (**4**) if you want the header or footer to appear on even pages only.

5. Type the text of the header or footer.

   Use any WordPerfect formatting command as you type the text of a header or footer. You can, for example, create a bold header or an underlined footer.

6. Press Exit (F7) to save the header or footer and return to the Format: Page menu. Press Exit (F7) again to return to the document.

Including Automatic Page Numbering in a Header or Footer

To include automatic page numbering in a header or footer, simply press Ctrl-B as part of the header or footer text. If, for example, you want the header to read *Page 1* on the first page and to continue numbering pages consecutively, type *Page*, press the space bar once, and then hold the Ctrl key while you press B. Although previous versions of WordPerfect enable you to type Ctrl-N to insert a number, version 5.1 does not recognize that key combination.

To include automatic page numbering in a header or footer, follow these steps:

1. Start a new header or footer or edit an existing one, typing any text that is to precede the page number.

2. Press Ctrl-B and then press Exit (F7) twice.

Editing Headers and Footers

After you create a header or footer, you can change it. You can edit its text so that it reads differently, or you can change its formatting so that it looks different.

To edit a header or footer, follow these steps:

1. Press Format (Shift-F8) and select **P**age (**2**).

    ⌨ Access the **L**ayout pull-down menu and select **P**age.

2. To edit a header, select **H**eaders (**3**); to edit a footer, select **F**ooters (**4**). Then select Header **A** (**1**) or Header **B** (**2**), or Footer **A** (**1**) or Footer **B** (**2**).

3. Select **E**dit (**5**) and edit the header or footer. Then press Exit (F7) to return to the Format: Page menu. Press Exit again to return to the document.

To discontinue a header or footer, follow these steps:

1. Press Format (Shift-F8) and select **P**age (**2**).

    ⌨ Access the **L**ayout pull-down menu and select **P**age.

2. To remove a header, select **H**eaders (**3**); to remove a footer, select **F**ooters (**4**). Then select Header **A** (**1**) or Header **B** (**2**), or select Footer **A** (**1**) or Footer **B** (**2**).

3. Select **D**iscontinue (**1**).

Suppressing Headers and Footers

You can suppress any or all headers and footers so that they don't appear on a specified page. You don't want on a report's title page, for example, a header consisting of the title of the report.

To suppress a header or footer, move the cursor to the beginning of the page where you want to suppress the header or footer and follow these steps:

1. Press Format (Shift-F8) and select **P**age (**2**).

    ⌨ Access the **L**ayout pull-down menu and select **P**age.

2. Select S**u**ppress (this page only) (**8**) and select the header or footer to suppress:

    Suppress **A**ll Page Numbering, Headers, and Footers (**1**)
    Suppress Headers and Footers (**2**)
    Suppress **H**eader A (**5**)
    Suppress H**e**ader B (**6**)
    Suppress **F**ooter A (**7**)
    Suppress F**o**oter B (**8**)

3. Select **Y** to suppress the header or footer.

4. Press Exit (F7) to return to the Format: Page menu. Press Exit again to return to the document.

Searching and Replacing in Headers and Footers

Searching for and replacing text in a header is only one step different from searching for and replacing text in a document. Simply press the Home key before you press Forward Search (F2) or Replace (Alt-F2), and continue the search or replace as usual. Search and replace is a quick way to change the title or date in all headers and footers in a report.

To search for text in a header or footer, follow these steps:

1. Press the Home key and then press Forward Search (F2).

   ▭ Access the **S**earch pull-down menu and select **F**orward.

2. Type the text to search for and press Forward Search (F2) or Esc.

   WordPerfect searches through headers, footers, endnotes, and footnotes to find the text. When the text is found, you can edit it as usual.

3. Press Exit (F7) to return to the document.

To replace text in a header or footer, follow these steps:

1. Press the Home key and then press Replace (Alt-F2).

   ▭ Access the **S**earch pull-down menu and select **R**eplace.

2. Select **Y** if you want to confirm each replacement; select **N** if you want to replace without confirming. Press the up-arrow key to search backward through headers and footers. If you change your mind, press the down-arrow key to search forward.

3. Type the text to be replaced. Press Forward Search (F2) or Esc, and then type the new text.

4. Press Forward Search (F2) or Esc to start the search.

   Headers and footers are usually embedded in a document before text begins. To find the text, press the Home key three times and then the right-arrow key before you begin the replace procedure. Or press the up-arrow key (as in step 2) to search backward. When the text to be replaced is found, confirm or deny the replacement.

5. If you chose to confirm each replacement, select **Y** to make the replacement; select **N** to leave the text as it is. Then press Exit (F7) to return to the document.

Including Graphics in Headers and Footers

You can include graphics as part of a header or footer in two ways: by drawing boxes or by retrieving a graphic created in a graphics program. Use a box around a footer, for example, to call attention to a page number. Or include a previously drawn logo in a header to create stationery for your business. Follow the general steps below to add a graphic element—such as a horizontal line appearing across the tops and bottoms of all pages—to your document.

1. Press Format (Shift-F8) and select **P**age (**2**).

   ▭ Access the **L**ayout pull-down menu and select **P**age.

2. To create a header, select **H**eaders (**3**); to create a footer, select **F**ooters (**4**). Then select Header **A** (**1**) or Header **B** (**2**), or Footer **A** (**1**) or Footer **B** (**2**). For this example, choose Every **P**age (**2**).

   This series of commands displays the header/footer creation screen, where you can type and format text or create graphics. Or you can create a combination of text and graphics. To continue creating a graphic, perform the following steps.

3. Press Graphics (Alt-F9) and create the box or line.

   ⌨ Access the **G**raphics pull-down menu and create the box or line.

   Feel free to use the Reveal Codes feature when you create a graphic. For example, to delete an incorrect line, it's easiest to press Reveal Codes (Alt-F3 or F11), find the line code, delete the line code, and re-create the line.

4. Press Exit (F7) to return to the Format: Page menu. Press Exit (F7) again to return to the document.

Numbering Pages

Automatically numbering pages in a document is as easy as telling WordPerfect how and where you want the numbers to appear on the page. Page numbering begins with whatever number you specify. If you write a book, you will probably print Chapter 1 beginning with page 1. But you may print Chapter 6 beginning with page 147.

Page numbers print on the margin. You won't see them on the page until you print a document, but you can preview them if you press Print (Shift-F7) and select **V**iew Document (**6**) or if you access the **L**ayout pull-down menu, select **P**age, and then select **V**iew Document (**6**).

New with version 5.1 is an additional menu level for page numbering (see fig. 6.5) that offers four options: starting a new page number, determining the page-number style, inserting a page-number style in a document as text, and positioning a page number.

Format: Page Numbering

   1 - New Page Number   9

   2 - Page Number Style   ^B

   3 - Insert Page Number

   4 - Page Number Position   No page numbering

Fig. 6.5.
The Format: Page Numbering menu.

Positioning the Page Number

The page number can appear in any of six positions on the page or in either of two positions on alternating pages. You choose the position from the Format: Page Numbering screen, shown in figure 6.6.

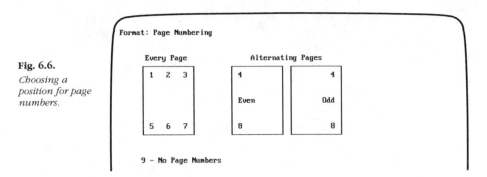

Fig. 6.6.

Choosing a position for page numbers.

Page numbers can appear at the top of the page—on the left, center, or right. They also can appear at the bottom of the page—on the left, center, or right. For facing pages, such as in a book or newsletter, page numbers can appear on the left side of even pages (left-facing pages) and on the right side of odd pages (right-facing pages). The currently selected page-number position is listed on the Format: Page menu.

To position page numbers, follow these steps:

1. Press Format (Shift-F8) and select **P**age (**2**).

    Access the **L**ayout pull-down menu and select **P**age.

2. Select Page **N**umbering (**6**) and then Page Number **P**osition (**4**).

3. Type the number corresponding to the position where you want page numbers to appear on the page:

    1 top left
    2 top center
    3 top right
    5 bottom left
    6 bottom center
    7 bottom right
    4 top outside, facing pages
    8 bottom outside, facing pages
    9 No page numbers

4. Press Exit (F7) to return to the document.

Page numbering begins where you select page numbering. Be sure that you're at the beginning of the document if you want page numbering to begin on page 1.

Starting a New Page Number

Page numbering, which can begin with any number, can be in Arabic numerals (1, 2, 3) or lowercase Roman numerals (i, ii, iii). You can change page numbering at any point in your document, and the change takes effect from that point forward.

To change the starting page number, move the cursor to where you want new page numbering to begin and follow these steps:

1. Press Format (Shift-F8) and select **P**age (**2**).

    Access the **L**ayout pull-down menu and select **P**age.

2. Select Page **N**umbering (**6**) and then **N**ew Page Number (**1**). Type the starting page number and then press Exit (F7) to return to the document.

To number with Roman numerals, use this procedure to change the starting page number, even if you plan to start at Roman numeral i.

Suppressing Page Numbering

You can suppress page numbering for a single page so that no page numbers appear on that page. Numbering continues uninterrupted on the following pages.

To suppress page numbering for one page, move the cursor to the beginning of the page and follow these steps:

1. Press Format (Shift-F8) and select **P**age (**2**).

   ⌨ Access the **L**ayout pull-down menu and select **P**age.

2. Select S**u**ppress (this page only) (**8**) and then select Suppress **P**age Numbering (**4**). Select **Y** at the prompt.

In long documents you may occasionally want to force a page to be even-numbered or odd-numbered. For example, the first page of a chapter in a book or a subsection in a report usually begins on an odd-numbered page. On a double-sided document, the odd-numbered page is the page on the right. Look at the status line at the bottom right of the screen to see the number of the page you're currently on.

To force a page to be even-numbered or odd-numbered, move the cursor to the top of the page and follow these steps:

1. Press Format (Shift-F8) and select **P**age (**2**).

   ⌨ Access the **L**ayout pull-down menu and select **P**age.

2. Select F**o**rce Odd/Even Page (**2**). Choose **O**dd (**1**) if you want the current page to be odd-numbered; choose **E**ven (**2**) if you want the current page to be even-numbered.

3. Press Exit (F7) to return to the document.

If you force an even page number for a page that's already even-numbered, no change is made. Page 4, for example, remains page 4. But if you force an even page number on an odd-numbered page, the page number changes to the next higher number. Page 3, for example, becomes page 4. The same principle applies when you force an odd page number on a currently even-numbered page.

Inserting Page Numbers and Page-Number Styles

Version 5.1 has two new page-number options: Page Number Style and Insert Page Number. The former lets you insert a text string without going to the header or footer menu; the latter lets you insert a page-number style at the current cursor location in a document as text. To specify the page-number style, complete the following steps:

1. Press Format (Shift-F8), select **P**age (**2**), and then select Page **N**umbering (**6**).

   ⌨ Access the **L**ayout pull-down menu, select **P**age, and then select Page **N**umbering (**6**).

2. Choose Page Number **S**tyle (**2**) and type your text—for example, *Jim's Report, Page* or simply *Page*. Press Enter; WordPerfect puts the code for page numbering (^B) at the end of the text string. Then press Exit (F7) to return to the document.

When the document prints, the text you entered precedes each page number.

To insert a page number into your text, complete the following steps:

1. Press Format (Shift-F8), select **P**age (**2**), and then select Page **N**umbering (**6**).

   ▭ Access the **L**ayout pull-down menu, select **P**age, and then select Page **N**umbering (**6**).

2. Choose **I**nsert Page Number (**3**); the current page number is inserted into the document as text at the cursor location.

Keeping Text Together

WordPerfect calculates the length of each page in a document, depending on the margins. When one page is full, a new page begins. In many cases, though, you want to prevent a block of text from breaking between two pages. A chart, for example, should be kept on a single page.

With WordPerfect you have three ways to prevent unwanted page breaks (discussed in detail in the following sections). The Conditional End of Page command groups a given number of lines so that they don't break across two pages. The Block Protect command protects a given block of text from breaking. Avoid widows and orphans with the Widow/Orphan Protection command so that the first or last line isn't separated from a paragraph.

When WordPerfect encounters a protected block of text, it calculates whether enough room exists to print the whole block on the page. If there is not enough room, the page ends, and the block shifts to the top of the following page. The page before the protected block may thus be shorter than other pages.

WordPerfect's automatic page breaks are called *soft page breaks*. Another way to prevent unwanted page breaks is to insert hard page breaks by pressing Ctrl-Enter. A hard page break forces the page to break, but this type of break may be the least desirable because it must be removed manually (just as it is inserted manually). A soft page break, on the other hand, is automatically recalculated when you make adjustments affecting page length. (See "Understanding Soft and Hard Page Breaks," later in this chapter.)

A soft page break appears as a single dashed line across the page. A hard page break appears as a double dashed line.

Using the Conditional End of Page Command

Use the Conditional End of Page command to keep a specified number of lines together on a page. You may, for example, want to make sure that all titles or subheads in a document are followed by at least three lines of text.

To ensure that a particular type of title or subhead is always followed by the correct number of lines, you can include a Conditional End of Page command in style sheets.

Cue:

Include Conditional End of Page commands in style sheets.

To apply the Conditional End of Page command, move the cursor to the line *above* the lines you want to keep together and follow these steps:

1. Press Format (Shift-F8) and select **O**ther (**4**).

   ⌨ Access the **L**ayout pull-down menu and select **O**ther.

2. Select **C**onditional End of Page (**2**) and, in response to the prompt, type the number of lines you want to keep together.

3. Press Exit (F7) to return to the document. Press the down-arrow key enough times so that you can see the new page break.

Using the Block Protect Command

With Block Protect you can protect any block of text from being broken by a soft page break. Use Block Protect, for example, to prevent a chart from breaking across two pages (see figs. 6.7 and 6.8).

To protect a block of text, move the cursor to the beginning of the block and follow these steps:

1. Press Block (Alt-F4 or F12).

   ⌨ Access the **E**dit pull-down menu and select **B**lock.

2. Move the cursor to the end of the block (but don't include the final return at the end of a paragraph).

   ⌨ Drag the mouse to highlight the block.

3. Press Format (Shift-F8) and then select **Y** to protect the block.

   ⌨ Access the **E**dit pull-down menu and select Pro**t**ect Block.

```
friends about the successes that are available to them by turning to our
fine garments, and those dogs are telling their friends.

If ever there was a true fashion revolution, it is certainly measured in the
outcry of support for Fido's Fine Fashions. Is this just a dog story? No
way, in fact, check out the excellent sales figures so far.

                        Sales Figures
                     Fido's Fine Fashions
                        January, 1990

                  Region 1      Region 2      Region 3
Shepards          45,999        34,000        22,000
Poodles           21,000        15,000        10,000
------------------------------------------------------------------
Small dogs        17,850        18,000        21,000
Setters           34,000        31,000        21,000

As you can see, things are going extremely well so far, and we are excited
about the future of dog wear. We will be starting a new ad campaign that
is sure to make our dog creations the envy of every canine lover and
canine the world over. This is a big day in dogdom, and we are happy to
be even a small part of it.
                              Doc 2 Pg 2 Ln 2.36" Pos 2.99"
```

Fig. 6.7.

A page break in a chart.

Fig. 6.8.

*Using Block
Protect to prevent
a page break in a
chart.*

```
fine garments, and those dogs are telling their friends.

If ever there was a true fashion revolution, it is certainly measured in the
outcry of support for Fido's Fine Fashions. Is this just a dog story? No
way, in fact, check out the excellent sales figures so far.

_____
                            Sales Figures
                         Fido's Fine Fashions
                           January, 1990

                        Region 1      Region 2      Region 3
        Shepards        45,999        34,000        22,000
        Poodles         21,000        15,000        10,000
        Small dogs      17,850        18,000        21,000
        Setters         34,000        31,000        21,000

As you can see, things are going extremely well so far, and we are excited
about the future of dog wear. We will be starting a new ad campaign that
is sure to make our dog creations the envy of every canine lover and
canine the world over. This is a big day in dogdom, and we are happy to
be even a small part of it.
                                      Doc 2 Pg 2 Ln 3.72" Pos 1"
```

Choose the Block Protect command to protect blocks that may vary in size. If you protect a chart (see fig. 6.8), for example, you can add lines of data later, and the protection remains in effect. If the size of the block within the block-protect codes exceeds the length of the page, however, WordPerfect automatically adjusts the codes to protect only the maximum number of lines that will fit on a single page.

Preventing Widows and Orphans

An *orphan* is the first line of a paragraph that appears by itself at the end of a page. A *widow* is the last line of a paragraph that appears by itself at the top of a page. Most page designers prefer to avoid widows and orphans. Activating the Widow/ Orphan Protection command at the beginning of a document prevents their occurrence throughout an entire document.

Figure 6.9 shows how a page may look before Widow/Orphan Protection is activated. Before Widow/Orphan Protection is activated, only the last line of a paragraph appears after a soft page break (a widow); after Widow/Orphan Protection, two lines appear after the page break (see fig. 6.10).

To prevent widows and orphans, follow these steps:

1. Move the cursor to the beginning of the document (or to wherever you want protection to begin), press Format (Shift-F8), and select **L**ine (**1**).

   Move the cursor to the beginning of the document (or to wherever you want protection to begin), access the **L**ayout pull-down menu, and select **L**ine.

2. Select **W**idow/Orphan Protection (**9**) and select **Y** to turn on protection. Press Exit (F7) to return to the document.

```
has its main application as an archival medium. A Pioneer WORM drive that
can write 327MB on each side of the media will run around $3,000, though
connectors and interface cards will bump that up to about $3,700.

WORM is still somewhat of a leading edge technology, though more reliable,
second generation products are now on the market. These newer drives afford
the ability to use write once technology at no performance penalty over hard
disks. That is, you can access them at the same speed and more or less for the
────────────────────────────────────────────────────────────────────
same price as a good hard disk drive.

Though still a bit more expensive that a Winchester hard disk that offers
similar storage capacity, there is at least one very good reason to look to
WORM technology for archival purposes. If your WORM drive crashes, you
haven't lost any data. The laser-readable media will still be intact. If your
720MB hard disk full of critical business data crashes, it's probably time to
look for a new job. The only bright spot might be if your resume wasn't
among the lost data.

The third optical technology, and the one that has garnered the most media
noise of late is Magneto-optical. This hybrid technology uses a laser beam to
read and write data to a magnetic/optical, removable hard disk media. Much
of the focus on MO technology came about because of the Canon MO drive
that is supposed to be standard equipment on the NeXT computer. While the
D:\WORD50\DATA\SEYBOLD1.TXT              Doc 2 Pg 1 Ln 9.82" Pos 1.7"
```

Fig. 6.9.

A "widow," separated from the rest of the paragraph by a page break.

```
has its main application as an archival medium. A Pioneer WORM drive that
can write 327MB on each side of the media will run around $3,000, though
connectors and interface cards will bump that up to about $3,700.

WORM is still somewhat of a leading edge technology, though more reliable,
second generation products are now on the market. These newer drives afford
the ability to use write once technology at no performance penalty over hard
────────────────────────────────────────────────────────────────────
disks. That is, you can access them at the same speed and more or less for the
same price as a good hard disk drive.

Though still a bit more expensive that a Winchester hard disk that offers
similar storage capacity, there is at least one very good reason to look to
WORM technology for archival purposes. If your WORM drive crashes, you
haven't lost any data. The laser-readable media will still be intact. If your
720MB hard disk full of critical business data crashes, it's probably time to
look for a new job. The only bright spot might be if your resume wasn't
among the lost data.

The third optical technology, and the one that has garnered the most media
noise of late is Magneto-optical. This hybrid technology uses a laser beam to
read and write data to a magnetic/optical, removable hard disk media. Much
of the focus on MO technology came about because of the Canon MO drive
that is supposed to be standard equipment on the NeXT computer. While the
D:\WORD50\DATA\SEYBOLD1.TXT              Doc 2 Pg 2 Ln 3.34" Pos 1.79"
```

Fig. 6.10.

The same document after Widow/Orphan Protection is turned on.

Widow and orphan protection takes effect where you activate it and remains in effect until you turn it off. To turn it off, repeat the process, selecting **N** (for no) in step 2. Alternatively, you may delete the code by pressing Reveal Codes (Alt-F3 or F11) or by accessing the **E**dit pull-down menu and selecting **R**eveal Codes.

Note: Unlike earlier versions, WordPerfect 5.1 protects paragraphs consisting of only two lines by moving the orphan line to the top of the next page.

Understanding Soft and Hard Page Breaks

WordPerfect uses two types of page breaks. Soft page breaks, calculated automatically, depend on margin settings. Hard page breaks are inserted manually.

Using Soft Page Breaks

Reminder:
A soft page break is automatically recalculated when text is added to the document.

WordPerfect inserts a soft page break when it gets to the end of a page of text (or when it encounters a protected block of text that won't fit on the current page). Text then continues on the following page. When text is added to a document or deleted from it, soft page breaks are automatically recalculated so that pages always break correctly.

On-screen, a soft page break appears as a single dashed line. When you press Reveal Codes (Alt-F3 or F11) or access the **E**dit pull-down menu and select **R**eveal Codes, the code for a soft page break appears: **[SPg]**.

Note: A soft page break is represented by the code **[SPg]** *unless* the page break was originally a hard return, in which case the code is **[HRt-SPg]**.

In previous versions of WordPerfect, a hard return code **[HRt]** immediately following a **[SPg]** would print a blank line at the top of the page. WordPerfect 5.1 converts the **[HRt]** into a dormant hard return **[DORM HRt]** to prevent the extra line at the top of the page.

Using Hard Page Breaks

Reminder:
A hard page break forces the page to break at a particular point.

To force a page to break at a certain spot—for example, at the beginning of a new section in a report—enter a hard page break. The page always breaks there, no matter what happens.

On-screen, a hard page break appears as a double dashed line. When you press Reveal Codes (Alt-F3 or F11) or access the **E**dit pull-down menu and select **R**eveal Codes, the code for a hard page break appears: **[HPg]**.

To insert a hard page break, move the cursor to the beginning of the text that should appear on a new page and press Ctrl-Enter. The only way to override a hard page break is to delete it.

To delete a hard page break, move the cursor to the beginning of the line just below the double dashed line on-screen and press the Backspace key, or move the cursor to the last space before the double dashed line and press the Del key.

You also can delete a hard page break by pressing Reveal Codes (Alt-F3 or F11) and deleting the code, or by accessing the **E**dit pull-down menu, selecting **R**eveal Codes, and deleting the code.

Choosing Paper and Form Sizes

In WordPerfect, you must specify the size, type, orientation, and location (in the printer) of the paper on which you want to print a document. Your paper may be letterhead—a sheet of standard-size paper on which you print in normal "portrait" (vertical) orientation. Or your paper may be a business envelope—a horizontal piece of paper measuring only 4 by 9 1/2 inches—that you print in "landscape" (horizontal) orientation.

In version 5, you could specify these options in one of two places: the Format menu and the Print menu. In version 5.1, however, only the Format menu is used to specify forms and paper.

Defining and Using Printer Forms

In order to turn your on-screen or on-disk document into a printed document, WordPerfect must know the make and model of your printer and the characteristics of the paper on which you want your document printed. The make and model of your printer are defined in a PRS file selected through the WordPerfect installation program. If the correct PRS file has not been installed on your system, then before proceeding with this section, follow the instructions in Appendix A for selecting and installing a printer definition.

After you select the printer definition, you must define a form (sometimes called *template*) for each type of sheet (page, envelope, or label) on which you want to print a document. In WordPerfect 5, you can define printer forms under either the Page Format feature or the Select Printer feature. In WordPerfect 5.1, the defining of printer forms has been consolidated under the Page Format feature and made easier. If you press Cancel (F1) one or more times at any menu during the forms-definition process, WordPerfect backs out through the various menus but does not create the new form.

Note: The menus shown as figures in the following exercise may differ from the menus displayed on your screen. The differences, if any, are limited to optional variables, which may be changed by the user. All fixed menu options should match those shown in the figures. For the purposes of this exercise, assume that you are using a laser printer. Also, some of these instructions may not apply to defining a form for a nonlaser (dot-matrix, daisywheel, and so on) printer. Instructions applicable only to laser printers are identified as such and can be omitted if your printer is not a laser printer.

To define a permanent new form, do the following:

1. Press Format (Shift-F8) and select **P**age (**2**).

   ⌨ Access the **L**ayout pull-down menu and select **P**age.

2. Select Paper **S**ize (**7**); WordPerfect displays the Format: Paper Size/Type menu shown in figure 6.11. See table 6.1 at the end of this series of steps for an explanation of each category listed in the menu.

```
Format: Paper Size/Type
                                               Font  Double
Paper type and Orientation   Paper Size    Prompt Loc   Type  Sided  Labels

Standard                     8.22" x 12"     No   Contin Port  No
Standard                     8.27" x 11.69"  No   Contin Port  No
Standard                     8.5" x 11"      No   Contin Port  No
[ALL OTHERS]                 Width ≤ 13.2"   Yes  Manual       No


1 Select; 2 Add; 3 Copy; 4 Delete; 5 Edit; N Name Search: 1
```

Fig. 6.11.

The Format: Paper Size/Type menu.

3. Select **A**dd (**2**); WordPerfect displays the Format: Paper Type menu shown in figure 6.12.

Choosing any of the first seven options from the Format: Paper Type menu selects that option's name as the paper type on the Format: Edit Paper Definition menu (see step 4). Selecting the **A**ll Others (**8**) option stops the form-definition process and returns you to the Format: Paper Size/Type menu. Selecting the **O**ther (**9**) option causes WordPerfect to prompt you to enter a name for the other form type. The name you type becomes the form's name, as described earlier.

Fig. 6.12.

The Format: Paper Type menu.

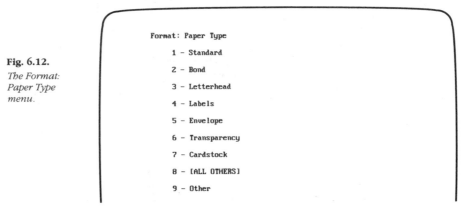

```
Format: Paper Type

    1 - Standard

    2 - Bond

    3 - Letterhead

    4 - Labels

    5 - Envelope

    6 - Transparency

    7 - Cardstock

    8 - [ALL OTHERS]

    9 - Other
```

Tip

If you have an existing form similar to the new form you want to define, you can shorten the definition process by using the existing form as a template for the new form. Use **N**ame Search or the arrow keys to move the cursor to the existing form, and select **C**opy (**3**). WordPerfect creates a duplicate of the existing form, which you can modify by selecting **E**dit (**5**). If you want to modify an existing form, move the cursor to the form name and select **E**dit (**5**). Selecting this option causes WordPerfect to display the Format: Edit Paper Definition menu shown in figure 6.13 instead of the Format: Paper Type menu shown in figure 6.12.

4. Select **S**tandard (**1**); WordPerfect displays the Format: Edit Paper Definition menu shown in figure 6.13. On your screen, the [FILENAME] portion of [FILENAME].PRS is the name of WordPerfect's definition for your printer.

5. Select **P**aper Size (**1**) from the Format: Edit Paper Definition menu; WordPerfect displays the Format: Paper Size menu shown in figure 6.14. Choose any of the first nine options, and WordPerfect uses the predefined dimensions listed for the option you select. If you select **O**ther, WordPerfect prompts you to define the width and height for the form.

```
Format: Edit Paper Definition

        Filename                 [FILENAME].PRS

    1 - Paper Size               8.5" x 11"

    2 - Paper Type               Standard

    3 - Font Type                Portrait

    4 - Prompt to Load           No

    5 - Location                 Continuous

    6 - Double Sided Printing    No

    7 - Binding Edge             Left

    8 - Labels                   No

    9 - Text Adjustment - Top    0"
                        Side     0"
```

Fig. 6.13.
*The Format: Edit
Paper Definition
menu.*

```
Format: Paper Size              Width  Height

    1 - Standard                (8.5" x 11")

    2 - Standard Landscape      (11" x 8.5")

    3 - Legal                   (8.5" x 14")

    4 - Legal Landscape         (14" x 8.5")

    5 - Envelope                (9.5" x 4")

    6 - Half Sheet              (5.5" x 8.5")

    7 - US Government           (8" x 11")

    8 - A4                      (210mm x 297mm)

    9 - A4 Landscape            (297mm x 210mm)

    o - Other
```

Fig. 6.14.
*The Format:
Paper Size menu.*

6. For the purposes of this exercise, select Standard Landscape (**2**) to select a form 11 inches wide and 8 1/2 inches high. WordPerfect displays the Format: Edit Paper Definition menu, as shown in figure 6.15. The paper size has changed to 11" × 8.5". The paper type has changed to Standard - Wide.

7. Select Paper **T**ype (**2**); WordPerfect displays the Format: Paper Type menu shown in figure 6.12.

Choosing any of the first seven options selects that option as the paper type on the Format: Edit Paper Definition menu. Selecting **A**ll Others (**8**) returns you to the Format: Edit Paper Definition menu. If you select **O**ther (**9**), WordPerfect prompts you to enter a name for the other form type. The name you type becomes the form's name, as described earlier.

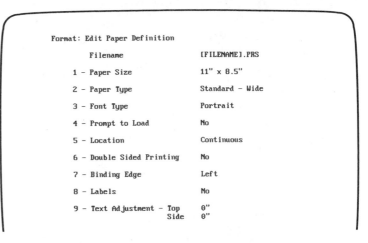

Fig. 6.15.

The Format: Edit Paper Definition menu, reflecting a new paper size and type.

```
Format: Edit Paper Definition

          Filename                    [FILENAME].PRS

     1 - Paper Size                   11" x 8.5"

     2 - Paper Type                   Standard - Wide

     3 - Font Type                    Portrait

     4 - Prompt to Load               No

     5 - Location                     Continuous

     6 - Double Sided Printing        No

     7 - Binding Edge                 Left

     8 - Labels                       No

     9 - Text Adjustment - Top        0"
                           Side       0"
```

Tip

If you have more than three forms, or if more than one person works with the forms you define, use the **O**ther (**9**) option to give each form a distinctive, descriptive name. For example, assume that the user has a printer with a dual-bin sheet feeder. Bin 1 contains the letterhead sheet; bin 2 contains the blank second sheet. Define one form that selects its sheets from bin 1 and call it LETTERHEAD. Define another form that selects its sheets from bin 2 and call it SECOND SHEET. Anyone using WordPerfect can immediately tell which forms to select for the first sheet and second sheet.

If the SECOND SHEET form is placed in the first page after the LETTERHEAD form, WordPerfect automatically uses the sheets in bin 2 for all pages after page 1.

8. For the purposes of this exercise, select **O**ther (**9**). WordPerfect displays the prompt Other form type:, which lets you choose your own unique name for the form.

9. For the purposes of this exercise, type *TEST* (in all capital letters). WordPerfect displays the Format: Edit Paper Definition menu shown in figure 6.16. The paper type has changed to TEST - Wide.

10. Select **F**ont Type (**3**); WordPerfect displays the prompt **Orientation: 1 P**ortrait; **2 L**andscape: **0**. See table 6.1 for an explanation of portrait and landscape orientations, options available under Font Type. If you do not use a laser printer, you can omit this option when you define the form.

11. Regardless of whether you use a laser printer, choose **L**andscape (**2**). WordPerfect displays the Format: Edit Paper Definition menu shown in figure 6.17. The font type has changed to Landscape.

12. Select P**r**ompt to Load (**4**); WordPerfect displays the prompt No (Yes). Select **Y** (for yes) only if you want to hand-feed sheets into your printer. For the purposes of this exercise, the assumption is that you do not hand-feed sheets into the printer.

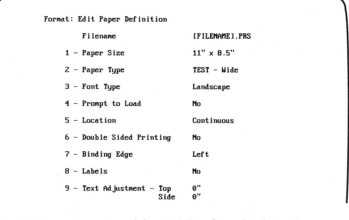

Fig. 6.16.
The Format: Edit Paper Definition menu, reflecting a new paper type.

Fig. 6.17.
The Format: Edit Paper Definition menu, reflecting a new font type.

13. Press **L**ocation (**5**); WordPerfect displays the prompt **Location: 1** **C**ontinuous; **2 B**in Number; **3 M**anual: **0**. The default setting is **C**ontinuous (**1**). Choose **C**ontinuous (**1**) if the printer uses continuous paper inserted by a tractor feed. Choose **M**anual (**3**) if the sheets are inserted by hand. Choose **B**in Number (**2**) if the sheets are inserted individually by a feeder from one or more cassettes. WordPerfect displays a Bin number: prompt. For the purposes of this exercise, the assumption is that you have a sheet feeder and that the paper is being drawn from bin (cassette) number 1.

14. Press 1. WordPerfect displays the Format: Edit Paper Definition menu shown in figure 6.18. The location has changed to Bin 1.

15. Select **D**ouble Sided Printing (**6**); WordPerfect displays the prompt No (Yes). Select **Y** (for yes) if you have a laser printer capable of printing on both sides of the sheet (a process called *duplex printing*). If you do not use a duplex laser printer, you can omit this option when you define the form. For the purposes of this exercise, the assumption is that your printer does not print on both sides of the sheet. Select **N** or Cancel (F1).

```
Format: Edit Paper Definition

              Filename                [FILENAME].PRS

        1 - Paper Size                11" x 8.5"

        2 - Paper Type                TEST - Wide

        3 - Font Type                 Landscape

        4 - Prompt to Load            No

        5 - Location                  Bin 1

        6 - Double Sided Printing     No

        7 - Binding Edge              Left

        8 - Labels                    No

        9 - Text Adjustment - Top     0"
                             Side     0"
```

Fig. 6.18.

The Format: Edit Paper Definition menu, reflecting a new location.

16. Select **B**inding Edge (**7**); WordPerfect displays the prompt **Binding Edge: 1 T**op; **2 L**eft: **0**. The default selection is **L**eft (**2**). If you have a laser printer capable of duplex printing (printing on both sides of the sheet), this option controls the way the document prints on each side of the sheet.

    Select **T**op (**1**) to print the document with the second side upside-down so that the document can be bound on the top. Select **L**eft (**2**) to print the document in the same manner on both sides of the sheet so that the document can be bound on the side. If you do not use a duplex laser printer, you can omit this option when you define the form. For the purposes of this exercise, the assumption is that your printer does not print on both sides of the sheet. Select **N** or Cancel (F1).

17. Press **L**abels (**8**); a No (Yes) prompt appears. Select **Y** (for yes); WordPerfect displays the Format: Labels menu shown in figure 6.19. See table 6.2 at the end of this series of steps for an explanation of each category listed on the menu.

```
Format: Labels

        1 - Label Size
                        Width           11"
                        Height          8.5"

        2 - Number of Labels
                        Columns         1
                        Rows            1

        3 - Top Left Corner
                        Top             0"
                        Left            0"

        4 - Distance Between Labels
                        Column          0"
                        Row             0"

        5 - Label Margins
                        Left            0"
                        Right           0"
                        Top             0"
                        Bottom          0"
```

Fig. 6.19.

The Format: Labels menu.

⟨5.1⟩

Tip

WordPerfect 5.1 comes with a macro named LABELS.WPM, which through an on-screen menu automates the definition of label forms. Press Macro (Alt-F10) and type *labels*. WordPerfect displays the Label Page/Size Definitions menu shown in figure 6.20. The menu options cover the 19 most common types of labels. Use this macro to define your label form(s). If none of the 19 options fits your particular need, the quickest way to define a new form is to invoke the LABELS macro and select the definition that most closely resembles the form you require, and then use the procedures outlined earlier to edit the form's settings.

```
               Label Page/Size Definitions

Mnu Label Sizes        # of labels per..
ltr   H x W           Sheet Row Column   Examples
  A   1" x 2 5/8"       30    3    10    Avery 5160/5260
  B   1" x 4"           20    2    10    Avery 5161/5261
  C   1 1/3" x 4"       14    2     7    Avery 5162/5262
  D   2" x 4"           10    2     5    Avery 5163
  E   3 1/3" x 4"        6    2     3    Avery 5164
  F   2/3" x 3 7/16"    30    2    15    Avery 5266
  G   1/2" x 1 3/4"     80    4    20    Avery 5267
  H   2 3/4" x 2 3/4"    9    3     3    Avery 5196
  I   1 1/2" x 4"       12    2     6    Avery 5197
  J   8 1/2" x 11"       1    0     0    Avery 5165
  K   1" x 2 5/8"       30    3    10    3M 7730
  L   1 1/2" x 2 5/6"   21    3     7    3M 7721
  M   1" x 2 5/6"       33    3    11    3M 7733
  N   2 1/2" x 2 5/6"   12    3     4    3M 7712
  O   3 1/3" x 2 5/6"    9    3     3    3M 7709
  P   11" x 8 7/16"      1    0     0    3M 7701

  (↑↓), (Mnu Ltr), or (*), then Press Enter; More=PgDn

Selection: A
```

Fig. 6.20.

The Label Page/Size Definitions menu.

Tip

On the main editing screen, a label form displays each label as an individual page separated from other labels by a **[HRt-SPg]** code, designating a soft page break. To see how the labels will look when printed, use the **V**iew Document (**6**) feature.

Enter the settings appropriate for the label form you want to create. For the purposes of this exercise, the assumption is that you are not defining a label form. Press Cancel (F1) to return to the Format: Edit Paper Definition menu, and change the **L**abels option to "No."

18. When you use a form, the printed image may need to be moved horizontally or vertically on the sheet. Make major changes (a quarter-inch or more) by adjusting the printer's hardware settings. If minor changes (less than a quarter-inch) are required, or if the printer's hardware cannot make the major changes, WordPerfect offers a way to fine-tune the placement of the printed image on the sheet.

Select Text Adjustment (**9**); WordPerfect displays the prompt **Adjust Text: 1 Up**; **2 D**own; **3 L**eft; **4 R**ight: **0**. Choose any of these options, and WordPerfect displays the prompt Text Adjustment Distance: 0". Enter the amount of adjustment that you want to make. A whole number such as 1 moves the image an equivalent amount of inches. A decimal number such as 0.1 moves the image an equivalent decimal amount of an inch.

5.1

Tip

WordPerfect 5.1 automatically converts fractional numbers such as 1/4" into their decimal equivalents—0.25" in this example.

If you need to move the printed image one inch down the sheet and a half-inch to the left, select Text Adjustment (**9**), select **D**own (**2**), type *1*, and press Enter; then select Text Adjustment (**9**), select **L**eft (**3**), type *0.5*, and press Enter. For the purposes of this exercise, the assumption is that you have made the changes described in this paragraph. The Format: Edit Paper Definition menu should appear as shown in figure 6.21.

Fig. 6.21.

The Format: Edit Paper Definition menu, reflecting new text-adjustment specifications.

```
Format: Edit Paper Definition

        Filename                    [FILENAME].PRS

   1 - Paper Size                   11" x 8.5"

   2 - Paper Type                   TEST - Wide

   3 - Font Type                    Landscape

   4 - Prompt to Load               No

   5 - Location                     Bin 1

   6 - Double Sided Printing        No

   7 - Binding Edge                 Left

   8 - Labels                       No

   9 - Text Adjustment - Top        1"      Down
                         Side       0.5"    Left
```

19. Press Exit (F7), Enter, or the space bar; WordPerfect displays the Format: Paper Size/Type menu, as shown in figure 6.22. WordPerfect automatically adds the form to its permanent forms list.

Caution

Do *not* press either Cancel (F1) or Esc before pressing one of the three keys listed in step 19. Pressing either Cancel (F1) or Esc cancels all the settings you have entered.

```
Format: Paper Size/Type
                                                    Font   Double
Paper type and Orientation   Paper Size   Prompt Loc  Type  Sided  Labels

   Standard                  8.22" x 12"     No  Contin  Port  No
   Standard                  8.27" x 11.69"  No  Contin  Port  No
   Standard                  8.5" x 11"      No  Contin  Port  No
   TEST - Wide               11" x 8.5"      No  Bin 1   Port  no
   [ALL OTHERS]              Width ≤ 13.2"   Yes Manual        No


 1 Select; 2 Add; 3 Copy; 4 Delete; 5 Edit; N Name Search: 1
```

Fig. 6.22.

The Format: Paper Size/Type menu showing a new form.

Table 6.1
Headings in the Format: Paper Size/Type Menu

Heading	Explanation
Paper Type	The name you choose for the form.
Orientation	The physical dimensions of the sheet and the relationship of its height to its width. If you select a sheet size whose width exceeds its height, WordPerfect automatically adds the descriptive term *Wide* after the name you choose for the form. If you select a sheet size whose height exceeds its width, WordPerfect leaves this section blank.
Paper Size	The actual dimensions of the sheet on which WordPerfect will print the document. These dimensions can be a standard size, such as 8 1/2 by 11 inches, or a unique size, such as 4 by 9 inches.
Prompt	An indication of whether WordPerfect is to request a specific instruction from you before it prints. The most common prompt is for the printer Go command to print each sheet of a document on a printer that requires the user to insert each sheet of paper manually.
Location (Loc)	An indication of how the paper comes into the printer. *Manual* means that the user will insert each sheet. *Continuous* means that the paper is on a roll and fed by a tractor feeder. *Bin* means that the paper is in one or more cassettes inserted in a feeder attached to the printer. With multiple-bin sheet feeders, WordPerfect automatically selects the paper from the bin designated for the form.
Font Type	An indication of whether WordPerfect is to print with characters in Portrait (parallel) or Landscape (perpendicular) orientation, relative to the paper's insertion edge. This setting has meaning only when you use a laser printer. If you use a nonlaser printer, Font Type means nothing to WordPerfect and is disregarded.

Table 6.1 (continued)

Heading	Explanation
Font Type (continued)	Most laser printers are constructed to accept paper sizes of only 8 1/2 inches or fewer as the insertion edge. Font Type tells WordPerfect whether to print the text lines parallel or perpendicular to the insertion edge of the paper. After the form is defined and you select it for a document, WordPerfect automatically limits your Base Font choices to those fonts in the orientation designated under Font Type.
	For example, if the sheet is 8 1/2 by 11 inches, its insertion edge is the 8 1/2-inch edge. Set the font type for Portrait (parallel) orientation, and the document prints with the 11-inch side as its right edge. Set the font type for Landscape (perpendicular) orientation, and the document prints with the 8 1/2-inch side as its right edge.
Double Sided	An indication of whether you have a laser printer with the capability for duplex printing—automatically printing on both sides of the paper. Other options selected in conjunction with this setting enable you to designate the binding edge and orientation of each sheet with respect to the other.
Labels	An indication of whether to print the document in a label format. Other options selected in conjunction with this setting enable you to designate the label format. WordPerfect uses this information to simplify the creation and printing of labels.

Table 6.2
Headings in the Format: Labels Menu

Heading	Explanation
Label Size	The size—the width and height—of each label. The measurements should reflect the actual size of the label, not counting any space between labels or the desired label margins.
Number of Labels	The maximum number of labels to be printed on a sheet. The printing grid is described as the number of columns (labels) across the top of the page and number of rows (labels) down the page.

Table 6.2 (continued)

Heading	Explanation
Top Left Corner	The position within the Label Size form at which the printing of each label is to start. *Top* refers to the distance from the form's top edge; *Left* refers to the distance from the form's left edge.
Distance Between Labels	The amount of space to leave between label forms. *Column* refers to the distance between the bottom of one label and the top of the next label; *Row* refers to the distance between labels from side to side.
Label Margins	The amount of space to leave for the top/bottom and left/right margins of each label form.

In addition to enabling you to define a permanent print form, WordPerfect enables you to define a temporary form, which you use only during the current editing session. To define a temporary form, do the following:

Reminder:

You can define temporary as well as permanent print forms.

1. Press Format (Shift-F8) and select **P**age (**2**).

   ⌨ Access the **L**ayout pull-down menu and select **P**age.

2. Select Paper **S**ize (**7**); WordPerfect displays the Format: Paper Size/Type menu.

3. Move the cursor to the [ALL OTHERS] form and press **E**dit (**5**); WordPerfect displays the Format: Edit Paper Definition menu shown in figure 6.23.

```
Format: Edit Paper Definition

      Filename              [FILENAME].PRS

      Paper Type            [ALL OTHERS]

   1 - Maximum Width        13.2"

   2 - Prompt to Load       Yes

   3 - Location             Manual

   4 - Text Adjustment - Top    0.11"  Up
                      Side    0"
```

Fig. 6.23.

The Format: Edit Paper Definition menu.

4. Using the techniques outlined in the preceding set of steps, edit the form to meet your needs for the current session.

To use the printer definitions, do the following:

1. Press Format (Shift-F8) and select **P**age (**2**).

   ⌨ Access the **L**ayout pull-down menu and select **P**age.

2. Select Paper **S**ize (**7**); WordPerfect displays the Format: Paper Size/Type menu shown in figure 6.22.

3. Use the arrow keys to move the cursor bar to the form you want to use.

Tip

You may use **N**ame Search and begin typing the name of the form until the cursor bar highlights the form. You also may use the PgDn, PgUp, gray minus (–), and gray plus (+) keys to scroll through the list. These keys are especially useful when the available-forms list has more entries than can be displayed on the screen.

---

4. Choose **S**elect (**1**) and press Exit (F7) to choose the form definition and return to the main editing screen.

Note: To take effect with the page on which it is located, the print-definition code must come before any other code or any text in the document. If any other code or any text is placed before the print-definition code, it does not take effect until the next page of the document.

Tip

Press the Cancel (F1) or Esc key to exit from the Format: Paper Size/Type menu and return to the main editing screen without selecting a form definition.

Also, if you have one or more forms that you frequently use, record steps 1 through 4 in an Alt-key macro. For example, if you have a form for legal paper, you can record the steps as the Alt-L macro (*L* for *legal form*).

Designing Documents

Line-formatting commands affect the appearance of lines of text in a document; page-formatting commands affect the appearance of pages; and document-formatting commands affect the overall design of a document. To see the options available for document formatting, press Format (Shift-F8) and choose **D**ocument (**3**), or access the **L**ayout pull-down menu and choose **D**ocument.

The Format: Document menu lists five document-formatting functions (see fig. 6.24). With the first option, **D**isplay Pitch (**1**), you can set the space between letters for the document. Initial **C**odes (**2**) lets you modify WordPerfect's default settings for the document. With **R**edline Method (**4**), you define how redlining appears on printed pages. And with **S**ummary (**5**), you can fully describe a document for future reference. For a discussion of Initial Base **F**ont (**3**), see Chapters 8 and 9.

Many line-formatting commands are explained in Chapter 5. Page-formatting commands are explained earlier in this chapter.

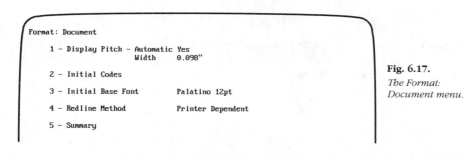

```
Format: Document

    1 - Display Pitch - Automatic  Yes
                        Width      0.098"

    2 - Initial Codes

    3 - Initial Base Font          Palatino 12pt

    4 - Redline Method             Printer Dependent

    5 - Summary
```

Fig. 6.17.
*The Format:
Document menu.*

Changing Initial Document Settings

WordPerfect comes equipped with a set of default format settings—margins, tab settings, paper size, and others. If you make no format changes, these settings govern the appearance of the document. You can, however, override these default settings individually by using Format commands.

As an alternative to using the individual Format commands, you can use the Initial Codes menu to change format settings for an entire document before you begin working.

The changes you make apply to the current document and are saved with the document. They override WordPerfect's default settings, and they override Initial Settings made through the Setup (Shift-F1) command.

To make formatting choices for all WordPerfect documents, use the Setup (Shift-F1) command. Select Initial Settings (**5**) and then Initial Codes (**4**). WordPerfect displays a ruler. At this point, press Format (Shift-F8) and make formatting choices. These choices apply to the current document and all WordPerfect documents, but they have lowest priority in your document. Formatting choices made directly through the Format command have first priority in a document, and formatting choices made through the Initial Settings menu within the Format menu have second priority. Format settings made with the Setup command have third priority.

Reminder:
Formatting specified through the Format command overrules formatting specified through the Initial Settings menu in Setup.

To change the initial settings for a document, follow these steps:

1. Press Format (Shift-F8) and select Document (**3**).

   ▭ Access the Layout pull-down menu and select Document.

2. Select Initial Codes (**2**) and press Format (Shift-F8) again to redisplay the Format menu. Make any format changes you want and then press Exit (F7) three times to return to the document.

   You also can use Initial Codes to create templates—formatted but text-empty model documents. Templates are extremely useful when you do the same type of project over and over. A template is like a blank document; it contains the settings and the basic information you need to start. Before you make any changes to the template, save it under a unique name so that it is preserved for the next time.

Adjusting Display Pitch

Pitch—the number of characters per inch—is familiar to typists as *pica* or *elite*. Just as on a typewriter, WordPerfect's display pitch refers to the fractional value of an inch occupied by each character in a document.

With the Display Pitch feature, you can control the amount of space between characters. But this capability to tighten or loosen text is used by WordPerfect only when needed. If, for example, you create a chart including centered columns of numbers and overlapping columns, WordPerfect adjusts the display pitch to prevent overlapping characters, as shown in figure 6.25.

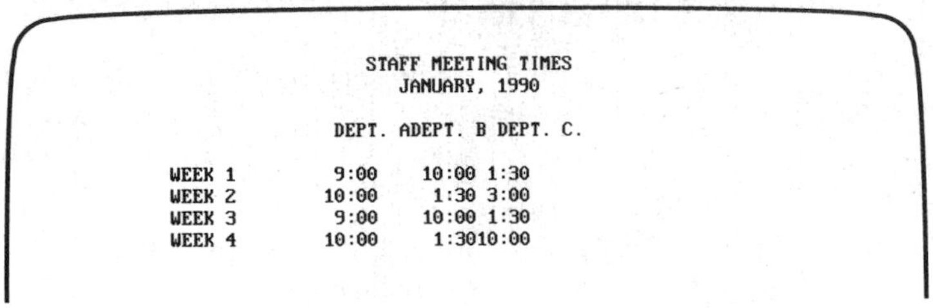

Fig. 6.25.

Condensed overlapping columns.

```
                        STAFF MEETING TIMES
                          JANUARY, 1990

                        DEPT. ADEPT. B DEPT. C.

          WEEK 1         9:00    10:00 1:30
          WEEK 2        10:00     1:30 3:00
          WEEK 3         9:00    10:00 1:30
          WEEK 4        10:00     1:3010:00
```

You either can let WordPerfect adjust the display pitch automatically, or you can set the display pitch yourself.

To set the display pitch, follow these steps:

1. Press Format (Shift-F8) and select **D**ocument (**3**).

   ▭ Access the **L**ayout pull-down menu and select **D**ocument.

2. Select **D**isplay Pitch (**1**) and select **N** to set your own display pitch. Then type a display-pitch width (in inches, from 0.03 to 0.5) and press Enter.

3. Press Exit (F7) to return to the document. To let WordPerfect adjust the display pitch automatically, follow the these same steps, but select **Y** rather than **N** in step 2.

The display pitch setting is saved with the document. The setting regulates the entire document.

Using Redlining To Mark Text

Redlining is a method of marking text that has been edited, added to, or deleted from a document. When several people have input in the final appearance of a document, redlining is a useful way to let everyone know what changes are proposed or made.

The term *redlining* originated when people used red pens to edit draft copies of documents before passing them on to the next editor. Today, people share disks instead, and redlining is a word processing function. In WordPerfect, you can choose how redlining appears on a printed page.

To set WordPerfect's redlining method, follow these steps:

1. Press Format (Shift-F8) and select **D**ocument (**3**).

    ▭ Access the **L**ayout pull-down menu and select **D**ocument.

2. Select **R**edline Method (**4**) and choose one of three redlining methods:

    Printer Dependent (**1**)—marks redlined text according to your printer's definition of redlining

    Left (**2**)—prints a redline character in the margin to the left of the redlined text

    Alternating (**3**)—prints a redline character in the outside margins of alternating pages

3. If you choose **L**eft (**2**) or **A**lternating (**3**) in the preceding step, you can now type a redline character; if you choose **P**rinter Dependent (**1**), press Exit (F7) to return to the document.

To learn how to use (and remove) redlining in a document, refer to Chapter 3.

Using Document Summaries

Sometimes it helps to keep track of information about your documents. With the Document Summary command, you can keep a record of a file's name, the date it was originally created, its subject, its author, and its typist. You can also write a several-line comment about the document.

Reminder:
A document summary contains basic information about the document, such as its subject and date of creation.

Document-summary information is stored in a special window. Every file has a document summary, which automatically includes certain information such as the file name, the date the file was created, and the first several lines of the document. (You can replace the text in the comment box with your comments.) Under some conditions, the summary includes a subject or account.

Besides the information automatically included in the document summary, you can add or change a descriptive file name (a handy feature when the eight-character file name isn't long enough to describe your file well), the author's name, the typist's name, and comments.

Follow these steps to create a document summary:

1. Press Format (Shift-F8) and select Document (**3**).

    ▭ Access the **L**ayout pull-down menu and select **D**ocument.

2. Select **S**ummary (**5**) and choose any of the changeable items listed in the Document Summary window:

    Creation Date (**1**)
    Document **N**ame/Document Type (**2**)
    Author/**T**ypist (**3**)
    Subject (**4**)
    Ac**c**ount (**5**)
    Keywords (**6**)
    Abstract (**7**)

3. Type the information you need for your summary, press Enter, and then press Exit (F7) to return to the document.

5.1

In WordPerfect 5.1, you can edit the creation date if you like, although WordPerfect fills in the original date automatically. WordPerfect also automatically fills in the subject if the subject-search text is on the first page. You can change the default subject-search text through Initial Settings, accessed through Setup (Shift-F1). The Abstract feature, which is also new, displays the first part of the document (you can edit the first part of the document if you like) to help you see what the document is about.

You may not always remember to create a document summary, so WordPerfect has a way to remind you. Using the Setup menu, you can activate a reminder; then when you save or quit, the Document Summary window pops up on-screen. See Chapter 20 for more information on the document-summary prompt.

Using Other Format Options

Among the four categories of commands listed in the Format menu, the Other category, shown in figure 6.26, is the miscellaneous category. It includes commands that don't specifically apply to lines, pages, or a document as a whole.

Fig. 6.26.
The Format: Other menu.

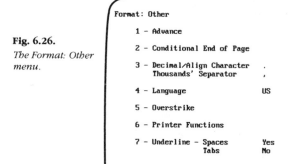

```
Format: Other

     1 - Advance

     2 - Conditional End of Page

     3 - Decimal/Align Character        .
         Thousands' Separator           ,

     4 - Language                       US

     5 - Overstrike

     6 - Printer Functions

     7 - Underline - Spaces             Yes
                     Tabs               No
```

Four commands that let you modify WordPerfect's conventions are listed under Other: **A**dvance (**1**), **D**ecimal/Align Character Thousands' Separator (**3**), **L**anguage (**4**), and **O**verstrike (**5**).

Using Advance

The Advance feature can make your printer move a specified distance up, down, right, or left from the current printing position. The option is most often used to help fill in preprinted forms. To use the Advance printer functions, perform the following steps:

1. Press Format (Shift-F8), select **O**ther (**4**), and then select **A**dvance (**1**).

   ▭ Access the **L**ayout pull-down menu, select **O**ther, and then select **A**dvance (**1**).

2. Choose one of the following: **U**p (**1**), **D**own (**2**), **L**ine (**3**), **L**eft (**4**), **R**ight (**5**), or **P**osition (**6**). You are prompted for a numerical entry; enter a number to indicate the decimal inches you want to advance in the selected direction.

3. Press Exit (F7) to return to the editing screen.

Changing the Decimal Character and the Thousands' Separator

Using the Decimal Character feature, you can change the appearance of numbers in two ways. First, you can redefine the decimal character, which is usually a period. Second, you can redefine the thousands' separator, which is usually a comma. Decimal characters and thousands' separators are changed in a single operation.

WordPerfect's tabbing options include decimal tabs. When you use a decimal tab, numbers line up under a decimal character embedded in the number, rather than from the right or left edge of the number. This feature is quite useful when you create tables that include columns of dollar amounts or fractional numbers.

With the Decimal Character command, you can change the decimal character used for tab alignment. If you change the decimal character from a period to a colon (:), for example, the column of numbers lines up by the colon in each number. Figure 6.27 shows a list of meeting times in which a colon is used as the decimal character.

```
                    STAFF MEETING TIMES
                      JANUARY, 1990

                  DEPT. A      DEPT. B      DEPT. C.

         WEEK 1    9:00        10:00         1:30
         WEEK 2   10:00         1:30         3:00
         WEEK 3    9:00        10:00         1:30
         WEEK 4   10:00         1:30        10:00
```

Fig. 6.27.

Columns of meeting times that use a colon (:) as the decimal character.

As a default, WordPerfect includes left-aligned tabs set at every half-inch. When you want different tabs for a project such as a table that lists prices, you can set decimal tabs at the spacing you need. Refer to Chapter 5 for more information about setting tabs.

WordPerfect also can perform math calculations for you (see Chapter 18). The results may include a number in the thousands, with the thousands separated by a comma. If you want the thousands separated by a character other than a comma, use the Thousands' Separator feature. In Swedish, for example, thousands are separated by a period, and decimals are indicated by a comma—just the opposite of how they appear in English.

To change the decimal character and the thousands' separator, follow these steps:

1. Press Format (Shift-F8) and select **O**ther (**4**).

   ▭ Access the **L**ayout pull-down menu and select **O**ther.

2. Select **D**ecimal/Align Character Thousands' Separator (**3**); type the new decimal character and then type the new thousands' separator.

3. Press Exit (F7) to return to the document.

Changing the Language Code

If you write in a language other than English, or if your documents include sections written in another language, you can check your work with spelling files and thesaurus files specific to the language.

WordPerfect's default language is English. When you check spelling in a document, WordPerfect refers to its English dictionary. But if a document includes a section in Spanish, you can instruct WordPerfect to refer to a Spanish dictionary instead. To cause WordPerfect to refer to a spelling or thesaurus dictionary in another language, insert a language code at the beginning of the section written in the other language.

The language code remains in effect until WordPerfect encounters a different language code. So if only a section of a document is in another language, be sure to insert US, the code for English, where English resumes.

To change the language code, follow these steps:

1. Press Format (Shift-F8) and select **O**ther (**4**).

   ▭ Access the **L**ayout pull-down menu and select **O**ther.

2. Select Language (**4**) and type the language code.

   Be sure to type the correct code. WordPerfect does not prompt you if the code is incorrect. If you press Help (F3) while the cursor is on the language code, WordPerfect displays a list of available codes.

3. Press Exit (F7) twice to accept the change and return to the document.

WordPerfect comes equipped with only English dictionaries. Order other dictionaries (for a price) from WordPerfect Corporation.

Using Overstrike

Usually only one character per space appears in a WordPerfect document. Sometimes, though, you want two (or more) characters to appear in the same space. For example, you may want to create foreign characters, such as û, é, or ñ.

Use Overstrike to create foreign and scientific characters that your printer doesn't support. If your printer does support these characters, use the printer's characters instead. To use the printer's characters, insert a printer escape code where you want the character to appear (see Chapter 21).

To create an overstrike, move the cursor to the point where you want two (or more) characters to print in the same place and then follow these steps:

1. Press Format (Shift-F8) and then choose **O**ther (**4**).

   ⌨ Access the **L**ayout pull-down menu and select **O**ther.

2. Choose **O**verstrike (**5**) and then **C**reate (**1**); type each character that is to appear in the same space. Then press Enter and press Exit (F7) to return to the document.

Overstrike characters do not appear on-screen, but they appear on the document when you print or in View Document mode. On-screen, only the last character of the overstrike appears. Use Reveal Codes (Alt-F3 or F11) to check the accuracy of overstrikes before you print.

Note that you can't create an overstrike character and use it again in a document. You must create the character anew each time it is to appear.

Reminder:
You must re-create an overstrike character each time you want to use it.

You also can edit an overstrike character once it's been created. To do so, follow these steps:

1. Move the cursor to the point just after the overstrike.

2. Press Format (Shift-F8) and choose **O**ther (**4**).

   ⌨ Access the **L**ayout pull-down menu and select **O**ther.

3. Choose **O**verstrike (**5**).

4. Select **E**dit (**2**) and type the new overstrike characters.

5. Press Enter and then Exit (F7) to return to the document.

When you select **E**dit (**2**), WordPerfect searches backward through the text and displays the first overstrike character the program finds. If none is found, WordPerfect then searches forward through the text.

Checking Document Format with View Document

One of WordPerfect's handiest features is the View Document command. View Document shows you as closely as possible what a document will look like when you print it.

Use View Document to preview page breaks, headers and footers, page numbers, columns, lines, illustrations, and graphics. Use it frequently to check your progress when you create a complex document; the feature can often save you time by identifying mistakes before you print them, and it can alert you early to problem areas. Figure 6.28 shows a full-page view of a document. See Chapter 8 for more information on using the View Document feature.

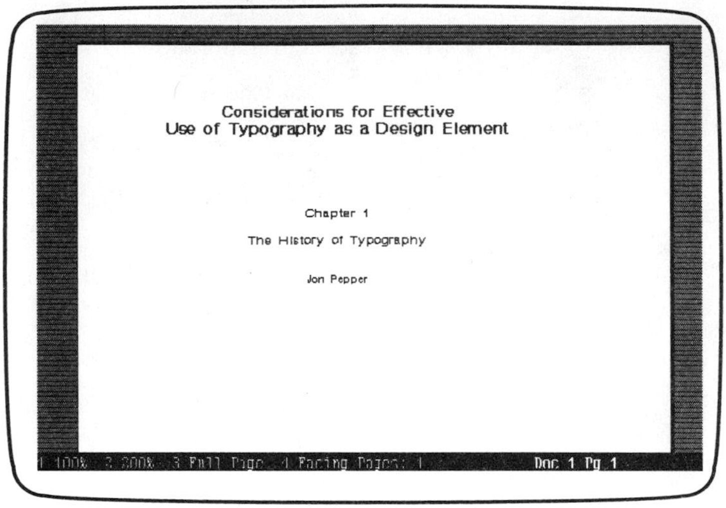

Fig. 6.28.

A full-page view of a document.

Summary

In this chapter, you learned the following techniques for formatting pages and designing documents:

❏ How to center a title

❏ How to add and edit headers and footers

❏ How to number pages

❏ How to protect blocks of text and prevent widows and orphans

❏ How to choose and edit paper and form sizes

❏ How to use other aspects of the Format menu

Using the Speller
and the Thesaurus

Susan Hafer has been using, supporting, and teaching WordPerfect at Wellesley College since 1986 and brings her knowledge of version 5.1 to this chapter.

WordPerfect's Speller and Thesaurus provide you with two valuable tools for increasing your efficiency and accuracy as a writer. The Speller contains a dictionary with more than 100,000 words and helps you proofread your work by searching for spelling mistakes and common typing errors such as transposed, missing, extra, or wrong letters, some capitalization errors, and double words like *the the*. You can use the Speller also when you know what a word sounds like but aren't sure of its spelling.

You can look up words in the Speller, add words to the built-in dictionary, or create your own dictionaries of terms specific to your profession. The Speller contains only the correct spelling of words; it does not contain definitions. If you need to look up a word's meaning, use a conventional dictionary. The Speller dictionary also contains correct hyphenation locations for every word WordPerfect includes in the dictionary, making automatic hyphenation with 5.1 work more efficiently (Chapter 5 explains more about hyphenation).

Although the mouse interface new with version 5.1 enables you to invoke the Speller or Thesaurus from the **T**ools pull-down menu and select menu options, you cannot select replacement words using the mouse.

If you write in a language other than English, spell-checking a document is a tedious chore. You can use language codes from the Format: Other menu to skip sections of text in other languages (see Chapter 21 for more information). If you don't use language codes, the Speller stops at almost every word. Fortunately, WordPerfect dictionaries in other languages are available. If you need a foreign-language dictionary, call WordPerfect Corporation to find out which languages are available. Most dictionaries are word-list based, which you can modify using the Speller Utility program. Some dictionaries are algorithmic and can find more words correctly, but you cannot modify such dictionaries.

The on-line Thesaurus, with more than 10,000 *headwords* (words that serve as primary references), saves you time. You quickly can find *synonyms* (words with similar meanings) and *antonyms* (words with opposite meanings) as you type or edit a document. You no longer have to thumb through a printed thesaurus.

The Speller and the Thesaurus work essentially the same way in version 5.1 as they did in version 4.2. To convert a dictionary from 4.2, see "Using the Speller Utility" later in this chapter. A version 5 dictionary can be used by version 5.1 for normal spell-checking, but because the word list was not hyphenated in version 5, hyphenation does not work if you use the version 5 dictionary. Because letters are used as a Reference menu to select individual words within the Speller or Thesaurus, *you select menu options by numbers, not by mnemonic letters.*

This chapter shows you how to use the Speller and the Thesaurus as part of the cycle of drafting, revising, editing, and proofreading. In this chapter, you learn to do the following tasks:

- Access the Speller or Thesaurus on a floppy or a hard disk system
- Spell-check a word, page, document, or block of text
- Create and use your own customized dictionaries
- Add or delete words to the built-in dictionary
- Use the Thesaurus as an aid to composition: replacing words, viewing words in context, and looking up additional words

Reminder

If you use a mouse with WordPerfect 5.1, you can click the right button to display the pull-down menus, and then select the desired option. You also can press Alt-= to access the pull-down menus, and then press the appropriate letter of the desired option. For all instructions, assume that if a block is required to activate a pull-down menu option, the text has been blocked before the pull-down menu is accessed. Instructions for pull-down menus and the mouse are marked with the mouse icon. For more information about the mouse, see Chapter 1.

Using the Speller

WordPerfect's Speller compares each word in a document against the words in its dictionary. The main dictionary is made up of a list of common words (words most frequently used) and a list of main words (words generally found in dictionaries). Both lists are combined in the main dictionary file WP{WP}US.LEX. The Speller checks every word against its list of common words; if the program does not find the word there, WordPerfect looks in its list of main words. If you have your own supplemental dictionary, WordPerfect looks there as well. Words found in any of the dictionaries are considered correct by the program.

For words that the program does not find, you can use the Speller to replace the misspelled words with an alternative spelling that the program suggests, or you can edit words by typing the correct spelling. You also can add words to a supplemental dictionary. You can create several supplemental dictionaries of specialized terms—for instance, terms used for law, engineering, medicine, literary criticism, or entomology—and use these special dictionaries during a spell-check.

The Speller does not find all typos, so although using the Speller does help, the Speller doesn't completely replace a human proofreader. If you type *them* when you meant to type *then*, for example, or *their* instead of *there*, your mistake is not noted by the Speller. Because these words are actual words in the dictionary, the Speller considers them correct, even though they are incorrect in the context of the sentence. For these reasons, proofread your document after using the Speller.

The Speller's built-in dictionary contains some variant spellings. For example, the Speller includes *fetish* and *fetich*, *doughnut* and *donut*, *etiology* and *aetiology*, *flutist* and *flautist*, *numbskull* and *numskull*, *soubriquet* and *sobriquet*, and *yogurt* and *yoghurt*.

Setting Up the Speller

If your computer uses 3 1/2-inch diskettes, the Speller and Thesaurus files are found on the single Speller/Thesaurus diskette. If your computer uses 5 1/4-inch diskettes, the Speller and Thesaurus files are on two diskettes.

The main dictionary file, WP{WP}US.LEX, contains both the main and common word lists. The file WP{WP}US.SPW is also used by the Speller and must be installed in the same directory as WP{WP}US.LEX. When you run the Speller for the first time and add words to the dictionary, a supplemental dictionary file, WP{WP}US.SUP, is created. Use the Speller Utility, SPELL.EXE, to make changes to the main dictionary and to create or make changes to a supplemental dictionary (see "Using the Speller Utility" later in this chapter).

To install WordPerfect's Speller and Thesaurus files, see Appendix A of this book.

If you have a floppy disk system, be sure that you specify the locations of your supplemental dictionaries from Setup. If you omit this step, the program cannot find the dictionaries. Chapter 20 explains the operation of Setup.

If you have a hard disk drive, the standard installation puts the Speller and Thesaurus files in the C:\WP51 directory. If you chose to customize the installation, you may have created a separate subdirectory for the Speller and Thesaurus files. (You don't have to store these files in a separate subdirectory, but doing so keeps the main program directory from becoming cluttered with too many files.) The Install program automatically changes the Setup Location of Files option to reflect the new subdirectory, so you do not need to do so unless you move the files after you complete the installation procedure.

If you want to see where WordPerfect looks for the Speller, Thesaurus, and Hyphenation files, do the following:

1. Press Setup (Shift-F1) and select **L**ocation of Files (**6**).

   ⌨ Access the **F**ile pull-down menu, choose Se**t**up, and select **L**ocation of Files.

2. If the location is incorrect, select **T**hesaurus/Spell/Hyphenation (**3**), type the directory where these files are located, and press Enter. Then type the directory for the supplemental files (the files containing customized additions) and press Enter.

Figure 7.1 shows the file locations for the main dictionary, supplemental dictionaries, and the Thesaurus. If you have a special supplemental dictionary—such as a special file of medical, legal, or discipline-specific terms—and do not specify its directory here, WordPerfect looks for it in the directory specified in the Documents line or, if no Documents directory is specified, in the directory current when you run the Speller. For example, figure 7.1 shows the Speller, Thesaurus, and Hyphenation files in the directory C:\WP51\LEX; because no directory is specified for a supplemental dictionary, WordPerfect looks for a supplemental dictionary file in the directory specified on the Documents line (C:\QUE\CHAPTERS).

Fig. 7.1.

The location of the Speller and Thesaurus files in the Setup: Location of Files menu.

```
Setup: Location of Files

    1 - Backup Files                          C:\

    2 - Keyboard/Macro Files                  C:\WP51

    3 - Thesaurus/Spell/Hyphenation
                           Main               C:\WP51\LEX
                           Supplementary

    4 - Printer Files                         C:\WP51

    5 - Style Files                           C:\WP51
              Library Filename                LIBRARY.STY

    6 - Graphic Files                         C:\WP51\GRAPHICS

    7 - Documents                             C:\QUE\CHAPTERS
```

Tip

If your computer does not have a hard disk but does have expanded or extended memory, you can copy the Speller and Thesaurus files into a RAM or virtual disk to make these WordPerfect features easier and faster to use. Refer to your DOS manual for instructions on creating a RAM disk.

Starting the Speller

You can use the Speller on dual floppy disk systems as well as on hard disk systems. A disadvantage to using the Speller on a dual floppy system is that you must first retrieve the document from the data diskette in drive B, remove the data diskette, and insert the Speller diskette in drive B before you can spell-check a document. When you want to save the spell-checked document, you must remember to remove the Speller diskette from drive B and reinsert the data diskette. Moreover, floppy disk storage space limits the size of the dictionaries you can use. With a hard disk system, you don't have to swap diskettes or worry about dictionary size.

To practice spell-checking a document, type the text in italics that follows, including the spelling errors. Use this text to complete the steps for using the Speller.

> *A haard disk can be purchased from mail order firms or from computer stores in the area: BOston, Newton, Wellesley, Framingham, Needham, and so forth. The change you experience in going from a floppy disk system to one with a harddisk is both frustrating and exciting. It is something new to to learn and you are busy, and if you do not keep your files organised they become harder to locate in the maze of subdirectories. Or, worse yet, you didn't take the tiem to figure out subdirectories, so all your files are lumped together--rather like throwing papers in a fileing cabinet with n folders.*

To start the Speller, follow these steps:

1. *Save the document* to disk by pressing Save (F10) and responding to any prompts that appear.

   ⌑ Access the **F**ile pull-down menu, choose **S**ave, and answer the questions.

2. If you want to check just a word or a page, place the cursor anywhere within the word or page you want to check. If you want to check the entire document, you do not need to position the cursor in any particular location.

3. If you have a floppy disk system, remove the data diskette from drive B and insert the Speller diskette. If you have installed the Speller on the hard disk, you do not need to change diskettes.

Reminder:

Save the document before you run the Speller.

Caution

Before you remove the diskette, make sure that WordPerfect isn't doing a backup of your work. * Please wait * appears at the bottom of the screen during backup. You can lose the document if the computer is writing to the diskette when you take it out.

---

4. Press Spell (Ctrl-F2).

   ⌑ Access the **T**ools pull-down menu and choose **S**pell.

   The following menu appears at the bottom of the screen:

Check: 1 Word; **2** Page; **3** Document; **4** New Sup. Dictionary; **5** Look Up; **6** Count: **0**

5. Select the desired menu choice.

Because you want to spell-check the entire document for this example, select Document (**3**).

> **Tip**
>
> Because supplemental dictionaries are just regular WordPerfect document files, you can protect the dictionaries with a password (see Chapter 10 for more information on locking files with a password). If the dictionary you use is protected, a `Password:` prompt appears at the bottom of the screen when you start the Speller or select a protected New Sup. Dictionary (**4**) from the Check menu. If you mistype the password or press Enter or Cancel (F1) in response to the `Password:` prompt, the following message appears:
>
> **1** Re-enter Password; **2** Continue Without Supplemental Dictionary
>
> Select Re-enter Password (**1**) if you know the password and mistyped it; select Continue Without Supplemental Dictionary (**2**) if you do not know the password.

To look up the word where the cursor is located, select Word (**1**). If WordPerfect finds the word in its dictionary, the cursor moves to the next word in the document, and the Check menu remains at the bottom of the screen. You can continue checking words or choose another option from the Check menu. If the word isn't found, alternative spellings may be offered. You can press Cancel (F1) to cancel the check and exit the Speller.

If you select Page (**2**), WordPerfect displays the `* Please Wait *` message as it looks up every word on the page where the cursor is located. After checking the page, the message `Word Count: xxx Press any key to continue` appears, where *xxx* is replaced by a number. Press any key to return to the Check menu; the cursor has moved to the first word of the next page. You can continue checking words or choose another option.

You can use a new or different supplemental dictionary to spell-check the document if you select New Sup. Dictionary (**4**) (see "Using a Supplemental Dictionary" later in this chapter). The next time you start the Speller, however, the default WP{WP}US.SUP dictionary is used.

To enter a new word to spell-check, select Look Up (**5**) (see "Looking Up a Word" later in this chapter). To count all the words in the document, select Count (**6**) (see "Ending the Speller" later in this chapter). Numbers alone, without adjoining text, are not counted; apostrophes and soft hyphens (Ctrl-hyphen) are included as part of a single word. Other punctuation characters are word separators and do not cause numbers to be counted as words. *$55.20* and *(617)* are not counted, for example, although *x2120* is counted. Hard hyphens (Home, hyphen) in version 5.1 are counted as word separators as well, contrary to the WordPerfect manual.

If you forgot to insert the Speller diskette and do not have the Speller files on a hard disk, or if you forgot to specify the location of the Speller files in the Setup: Location of Files menu, you see the following message:

WP{WP}US.LEX not found: 1 Enter Path; **2** Skip Language; **3** Exit Spell: **3**

If you forgot to insert the Speller diskette, insert the diskette in drive B and select Enter Path (**1**). At the `Temporary dictionary path:` prompt, type *B:* and press Enter. If you forgot to specify the location on the hard disk, select Enter Path (**1**). At the `Temporary dictionary path:` prompt, type the path *C:\wp51\lex* and press Enter.

Use Skip Language (**2**) if you have marked passages in a foreign language with language codes (Chapter 21 explains language codes) and have not purchased the Speller for that language. This option prevents the Speller from stopping at most foreign words in those passages.

As soon as the Speller finds a word not in its dictionary, the Speller stops, highlights the word, and provides a list of alternative spellings (see fig. 7.2).

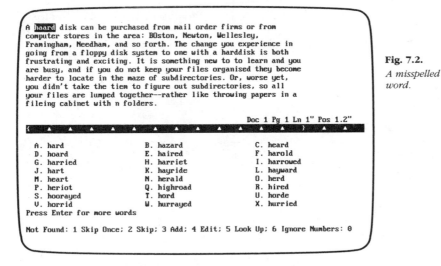

Fig. 7.2.
A misspelled word.

At the bottom of the screen is the Not Found menu:

Not Found: 1 Skip Once; **2** Skip; **3** Add; **4** Edit; **5** Look Up; **6** Ignore Numbers: **0**

You have several options: you can select a correct spelling from the replacements, skip the word (if it is spelled correctly, for instance), add the word to the supplemental dictionary, or edit the word (type the correct spelling). Each of these options is described in the following sections.

Selecting a Correct Spelling

When the Speller encounters a word not found, it highlights the word, displays a list of alternative spellings, and displays the Not Found menu.

To select a word from the replacement list, complete the following steps:

1. Find the correct spelling in the list of alternative spellings. If you do not see the correct spelling and WordPerfect displays `Press Enter for more words` (as it does in fig. 7.2), press Enter or the space bar to display more alternatives. Otherwise, refer to the subsequent sections of this chapter.

Reminder:
The Speller provides a list of suggested alternatives to a word it cannot find in its dictionary.

> **Tip**
>
> After you press Enter or space bar and WordPerfect displays another list of words, you can display a word on a previous screen by pressing Enter or space bar until the list with the desired word appears.

For this example, you see many alternative spellings for the typo *haard* (see fig. 7.2). The correct spelling is, of course, *hard*.

2. Press the letter next to the replacement spelling you want to select. For instance, press A for *hard*.

   The new word automatically replaces the misspelled word in the text. If the misspelled word is capitalized, the Speller leaves the word capitalized after replacing it.

Once you correct the word, the Speller continues checking the rest of the text.

> **Tip**
>
> You do not need to wait for all the spelling alternatives to be displayed on-screen. As soon as you see the correct spelling, press its letter and the Speller immediately replaces the word.

Correcting Irregular Case

Reminder:

The Speller finds irregularities in the capitalization of words.

The Speller also checks for some common errors in the appearance of words in uppercase or lowercase letters. A special menu appears (see fig. 7.3). You can replace the word containing the irregular capitalization with the Speller's guess about the correct case. For example, *cAse* is changed to *Case*, *CAse* to *Case*, *cASE* to *CASE* (common when Caps Lock is on and you forget), and *caSE* or *caSe* to *case*.

Fig. 7.3.

The Irregular Case menu.

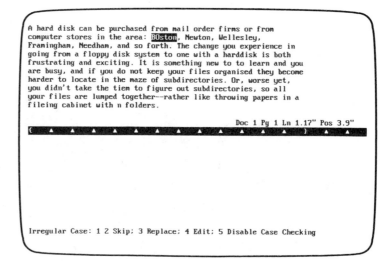

If the unusual capitalization is actually correct for the word, select Skip (**1** or **2**) from the menu to have the Speller continue without making any change to the word. Both Skip **1** and **2** function the same: both skip the word this time. If you have many such words with odd case selections, however, it may be better to select Disable Case Checking (**5**) so that the Speller does not stop at the rest of these words as well.

You can select Replace (**3**) to have the case for this word corrected. As you can see in figure 7.3, however, the Speller does not show you how it will correct the case. Look at the *case* examples at the beginning of this section to determine how the Speller probably will correct the word; if you are still unsure how the word will be corrected, select Edit (**4**) to fix the word yourself.

To fix a word with irregular case, complete the following steps:

1. Read the text and determine whether the irregular case is a mistake.

2. Select the action you want to perform from the menu at the bottom of the screen. For instance, select Replace (**3**) to replace *BOston* with *Boston.*

Skipping Words Spelled Correctly

Many correctly spelled words are not included in the WordPerfect dictionary. Remember that the dictionary contains only a limited number of words. In the sample text, for example, the next word not found is *Wellesley,* a town name. *Wellesley* is spelled correctly but is not found in the dictionary. Notice that the preceding city name, *Newton,* passes with no problem. The dictionary contains many common American proper names, including personal names like *Catherine;* other less common names, like *Kathryn,* are not included.

When the Speller notes a word as incorrect, the Not Found menu appears at the bottom of the screen. When a word on which the Speller stops is spelled correctly, you can skip the word or add it to your supplemental dictionary.

If a word appears only once or twice in a document, and you have no plans to use it in other documents, skip the word by selecting Skip (**2**) and continue with the rest of the spell-check. Choosing this Skip option ignores the word now and for the rest of the document. If you want to skip the word this time only, select Skip Once (**1**) instead. If the Speller encounters the word in the document again, the Speller stops and prompts you once more. Skip Once (**1**) is the better choice if the word is spelled correctly but may be a misspelling of another word in your document. (For example, you may abbreviate *thesaurus* in your text as *thes;* however, you may later mistype *these* as *thes.* You want the Speller to catch that typo for you.)

Adding Words Spelled Correctly

If you frequently use a word not in the Speller's dictionary, select Add (**3**) from the Not Found menu. The Speller then stores the word in memory and skips any future occurrences of the word in the document. At the end of the spell-check, all words you added to the dictionary are saved to the current supplemental dictionary. (The default supplemental dictionary is named WP{WP}US.SUP; you can change the default by selecting New Sup. Dictionary (**4**) from the Check menu.)

Reminder:
If a word you use frequently is not in the Speller's dictionary, you can add the word to the supplemental dictionary.

If you skip and add many words during a spell-check session, the computer may run out of memory. If this happens, WordPerfect removes skipped words from memory to make room for added words. If no skipped words can be removed, the message `Dictionary Full` appears; Exit (F7) from the spell-check so that the added words can be written to the supplemental dictionary. To finish spell-checking the document, refer to "Spell-Checking a Block" later in this chapter.

Words in an *uncompressed* supplemental dictionary are not offered as alternative spellings (compressed dictionaries are explained later in this chapter). If you misspell in the text one of the words you added to the dictionary (for example, you type *Wellesly* instead of *Wellesley*), the correct spelling is not one of the alternatives presented in the Not Found menu. You have to correct the word yourself. However, if you add the word to the main dictionary or compress the supplemental dictionary by using the Speller Utility, the word *is* offered as an alternative.

For the example used in this chapter, select Add (**3**) from the Not Found menu to add *Wellesley* to the supplemental dictionary (you should add at least one word to the supplemental dictionary so that you can see what the file looks like later). WordPerfect stores *Wellesley* in memory and creates a supplemental dictionary at the end of the spell-check session.

You may want to add *Framingham* and *Needham* (names of towns) to the supplemental dictionary also when the Speller stops at those words.

Editing a Word

When the correct alternative spelling is not offered for an incorrectly spelled word, you must enter the correct spelling yourself. Consider the incorrectly spelled word *harddisk* shown in figure 7.4.

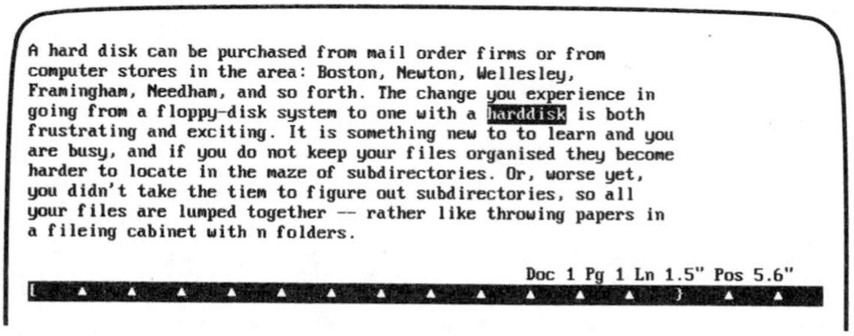

Fig. 7.4.

Editing a misspelled word.

```
A hard disk can be purchased from mail order firms or from
computer stores in the area: Boston, Newton, Wellesley,
Framingham, Needham, and so forth. The change you experience in
going from a floppy-disk system to one with a harddisk is both
frustrating and exciting. It is something new to to learn and you
are busy, and if you do not keep your files organised they become
harder to locate in the maze of subdirectories. Or, worse yet,
you didn't take the tiem to figure out subdirectories, so all
your files are lumped together -- rather like throwing papers in
a fileing cabinet with n folders.

                                        Doc 1 Pg 1 Ln 1.5" Pos 5.6"
```

To enter a correct spelling, complete the following steps:

1. Select Edit (**4**) from the Not Found menu at the bottom of the screen or press → or ←. The prompt `Spell Edit: Press Exit when done` appears and the cursor moves to the highlighted word in the text.

> **Tip**
>
> If WordPerfect displays a list of word options, and you select Edit (**4**) but change your mind, press Cancel (F1). WordPerfect redisplays the list of word options.

2. Press → or ← to move right or left and make the corrections to the word. For instance, move the cursor between *hard* and *disk* and type a space.

3. Press Exit (F7) when you have finished the correction.

The Speller rechecks the corrected word and stops at the same place again if the corrected version is not in its dictionary.

Eliminating Double Words

In addition to finding misspelled words, the Speller stops at double words. In the example, the next problem the Speller finds is the double word *to to* (see fig. 7.5).

Reminder:
The Speller finds double words.

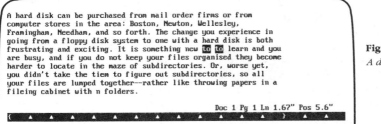

A hard disk can be purchased from mail order firms or from computer stores in the area: Boston, Newton, Wellesley, Framingham, Needham, and so forth. The change you experience in going from a floppy disk system to one with a hard disk is both frustrating and exciting. It is something new to to learn and you are busy, and if you do not keep your files organised they become harder to locate in the maze of subdirectories. Or, worse yet, you didn't take the tiem to figure out subdirectories, so all your files are lumped together--rather like throwing papers in a fileing cabinet with n folders.

Doc 1 Pg 1 Ln 1.67" Pos 5.6"

Fig. 7.5.
A double word.

When WordPerfect encounters a double word, the program does not show alternative spellings. The Speller displays the following Double Word menu, which differs slightly from the normal Not Found menu:

Double Word: 1 2 Skip; **3** Delete 2nd; **4** Edit; **5** Disable Double Word Checking

If you accidentally typed two words instead of one, select Delete 2nd (**3**). The program deletes one word and leaves the other.

Select Skip (**1** or **2**) if the double word is legitimate. Both Skip options on the Double Word menu do the equivalent of Skip Once (**1**) on the normal Not Found menu. You cannot "skip this word now and for the rest of this document" for double words. For example, the double word in the following sentence is correct; you can select either Skip (**1** or **2**) to skip the double word:

She had explained that that job would be difficult for him.

If one of the words is a typo, select Edit (**4**) and enter the correct spelling (for instance, if you typed *that that* when you meant *than that*).

If a document contains many legitimate double words, select Disable Double Word Checking (**5**). If you use this option, carefully proofread the text yourself for double words you do not want in the document.

To fix a double word, complete the following steps:

1. Read the text and determine whether the double word is a mistake.
2. Select the action you want to perform. For instance, select Delete 2nd (**3**). The Speller continues checking the rest of your text.

In the example used in this chapter, The Speller stops at three more words: *organised*, which you should replace with *organized*; *tiem*, which you should replace with *time*; and *fileing*, which you should replace with *filing*.

Notice that the *n*, which should have been *no* in the last line of the text, was not caught by the Speller; all single-letter words are accepted as valid.

Ending the Speller

Reminder:
If you made one word into two words during the spell-check, the word count at the end of the procedure is inaccurate.

When the Speller finishes, it displays the number of words checked. Because you spell-checked the entire document for this example, the word count shows the number of words in the entire document (see fig. 7.6). If you edited one word during the spell-check and made it into two words (as was the case with ***harddisk***), the count is inaccurate. Because the count is a count of words *checked*, ***harddisk*** was counted as one word, and the corrected ***hard disk*** was counted as another two words (for a total of three words). If you want an accurate count of the words in a document, select Count (**6**) from the Check menu. All words are counted, even articles and conjunctions, but stand-alone numbers are not counted.

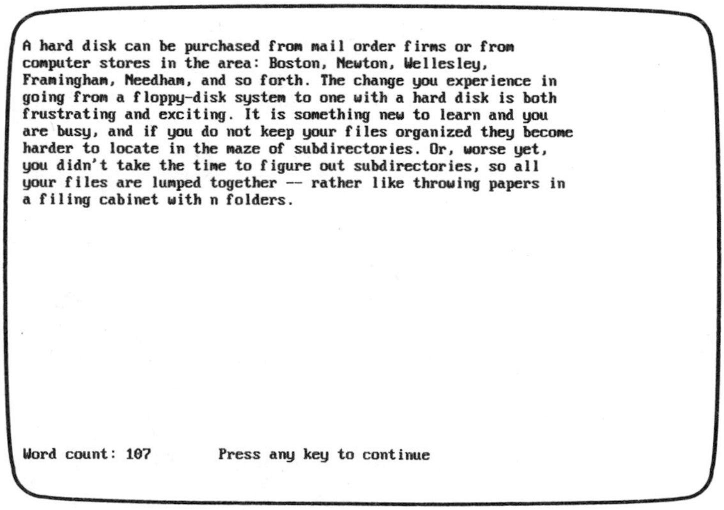
A hard disk can be purchased from mail order firms or from
computer stores in the area: Boston, Newton, Wellesley,
Framingham, Needham, and so forth. The change you experience in
going from a floppy-disk system to one with a hard disk is both
frustrating and exciting. It is something new to learn and you
are busy, and if you do not keep your files organized they become
harder to locate in the maze of subdirectories. Or, worse yet,
you didn't take the time to figure out subdirectories, so all
your files are lumped together -- rather like throwing papers in
a filing cabinet with n folders.
Word count: 107
Press any key to continue

Fig. 7.6.
The word count at the end of a spell-check.

Reminder:
Press Cancel (F1) to discontinue a spell-check.

If you have to interrupt the Speller to do something else with the computer, press Cancel (F1) instead of selecting a menu option. A count of the words checked appears with the message `Press any key to continue`. Press any key to return to the editing screen.

After you exit the Speller, save the document by pressing Save (F10). Floppy disk users should keep in mind that spelling corrections made to the document are in the computer's temporary memory. To save the changes to a diskette, exit the Speller, remove the Speller diskette from drive B, and reinsert the appropriate data diskette before saving the spell-checked document.

Looking Up a Word

As you type, you can look up words you don't know how to spell. The word *aggrieve*, for example, is one of those pesky "ie vs. ei" words you probably use very rarely and forget how to spell.

When you look up a word, you can type either a word or a word pattern. A *word pattern* is a rough guess at a word's spelling. In a word pattern, you type an asterisk (*) to replace several unknown letters or a question mark (?) to replace one unknown letter. After you press Enter, the Speller displays all the words that match the word pattern.

Reminder:

Speed up a word look-up by placing wild card(s) in the middle of the word rather than at the beginning or end.

> **Caution**
>
> Placing a *?* wild card at the beginning of a word can give incorrect results in the original release of 5.1. If you look up *?rctic*, for example, you see a list of words including *arctic*. In addition, however, you also see words beginning with *az*, such as *azaleas* and *azaserine*. Use the * wild card at the beginning of the word to avoid the problem.

To look up a word with the Speller, complete the following steps:

1. If you have a floppy disk system, put the Speller diskette in drive B.
2. Press Spell (Ctrl-F2).

    ⌨ Access the **T**ools pull-down menu and choose **S**pell.
3. Select Look Up (**5**). The Word or word pattern: prompt appears.
4. Type the word or word pattern you want to look up and press Enter.

    For example, type *aggr*ve* and press Enter. The Speller displays all words in its dictionary that begin with the letters *aggr*, are followed by some number of letters, and end with *ve* (see fig. 7.7).
5. Press Exit (F7) twice to return to the document. Alternatively, you can type another word or word pattern to look up.

    For this exercise, type *aggr??ve* and press Enter. The screen shown in figure 7.8 appears. Notice the difference between using asterisks and question marks. Fewer words appear when you use question marks because each question mark represents a single letter; an asterisk can represent any number of letters.

When you look up a word, you cannot automatically insert one of the displayed words into your document, so be sure to write down the correct spelling.

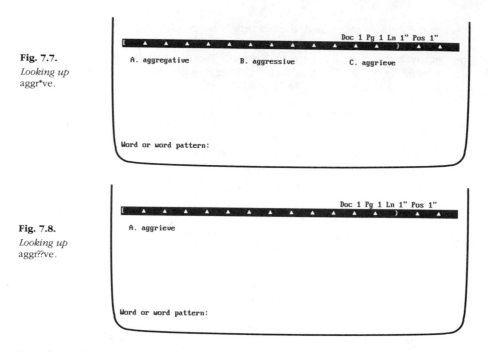

Fig. 7.7.
Looking up
aggr*ve.

```
                                                    Doc 1 Pg 1 Ln 1" Pos 1"
[  ▲    ▲    ▲    ▲    ▲    ▲    ▲    ▲    ▲    ▲    ▲    }   ▲    ▲

     A. aggregative          B. aggressive          C. aggrieve




Word or word pattern:
```

Fig. 7.8.
Looking up
aggr??ve.

```
                                                    Doc 1 Pg 1 Ln 1" Pos 1"
[  ▲    ▲    ▲    ▲    ▲    ▲    ▲    ▲    ▲    ▲    ▲    }   ▲    ▲

     A. aggrieve




Word or word pattern:
```

You do not have to enter question marks and asterisks in every word you look up. Any word you enter without wild-card characters is treated as a *phonetic* spelling (spelling of a word the way it sounds or the way it is pronounced). For instance, you can type *sik* at the Word or word pattern: prompt and press Enter. Figure 7.9 shows the alternatives to this word; press any key to see the rest of the list.

Fig. 7.9.
A phonetic look up of sik.

```
                                                    Doc 1 Pg 1 Ln 1" Pos 1"
{  ▲    ▲    ▲    ▲    ▲    ▲    ▲    ▲    ▲    ▲    ▲    }

     A. psych          B. psyche          C. sac
     D. sack           E. sacs            F. sake
     G. salk           H. sauce           I. sax
     J. sec            K. seek            L. seeks
     M. seiche         N. seq             O. sex
     P. sexe           Q. sic             R. sick
     S. sikh           T. silk            U. sioux
     V. six            W. soak            X. soaks

Press any key to continue
```

You can see that in addition to checking for similar spellings, the Speller selects words that are phonetically close (those with similar pronunciations) to the spelling (see fig. 7.9). Using this feature, you should be able to find the spelling of any word you know how to pronounce but not spell.

Reminder:

You can look up other words as you run the Speller.

You can look up a word from the Not Found menu in exactly the same way. For example, if the Speller stops at a word and you want to look up some possibilities that don't appear in the list of alternatives, select Look Up (**5**), type a word pattern, and then select Edit (**4**) to replace the word in your text with the word you looked up.

> **Tip**
>
> If you use an automatic spell-check program or a shorthand word expander such as PRDt from Productivity Software Inc. as a terminate-and-stay-resident (TSR) program, disable the TSR or remove it from memory before using the Speller or Thesaurus. If the TSR is active, you may find the Speller features difficult to use and you may get inaccurate results.

Spell-Checking a Block

In addition to being able to spell-check a word, a page, or an entire document, you can pick out a particular block of text to spell-check.

To spell-check a block, complete the following steps:

1. Use the keyboard (Alt-F4 or F12) or the mouse to block the text you want to spell-check.
2. If you have a floppy disk system, replace the data diskette in drive B with the Speller diskette.
3. Press Spell (Ctrl-F2).

    ⌨ Access the **T**ools pull-down menu and choose **S**pell.

The Check menu does not appear because the Speller "knows" you want to check only the block and automatically begins the spell-check. Otherwise the Speller runs no differently.

Use the Block method of spell-checking if you have to Cancel (F1) in the middle of a spell-check, leaving the first part of a document corrected but the last part untouched.

Handling Words with Numbers

During a spell-check, words containing numbers (for instance, *x1234* or *F1-F10*) can be treated as normal words (you can skip, add, and edit them). The Ignore Numbers (**6**) option in the Not Found menu tells the Speller to ignore all words that contain numbers. If a document includes many legitimate words containing numbers, speed up the spell-check by adding the list of words containing numbers to a supplemental dictionary or by blocking the words in a temporary comment (see the following section).

Working with What Is Not Spell-Checked

Even if you request a spell-check of an entire document, some parts are *not* checked. Text in tables, text boxes, equation captions, headers, footers, footnotes, and endnotes are checked, but the *body* of an equation whose contents are marked as an equation (as opposed to text or graphics), text in the codes section of the Styles feature, and document comments are not checked. Although misspellings in the codes section of the Styles feature are not caught, they *are included in the word count for the document.*

Reminder:

Even if you spell-check the entire document, the body of an equation and document comments are not checked.

Document comments are blocked-off sections of text displayed on-screen but not printed (document comments are explained in Chapter 3). If your document contains one or more sections of abnormal text (tables containing abbreviations or many words containing numbers), you can block each section (up to 1010 characters, or about 12 lines) and turn it into a comment. You may have to break up the abnormal text into smaller sections if it is too long to fit into a comment. After the spell-check, convert the comments back into normal text.

Creating a Supplemental Dictionary

You can create a supplemental dictionary as a normal WordPerfect document; you also can create a supplemental dictionary one word at a time by selecting Add (**3**) from the Not Found menu during a spell-check or by using the Speller Utility. If you create a supplemental dictionary before you begin typing your document, the spell-check process runs faster because you prevent the Speller from asking you about the words in the supplemental dictionary.

> **Caution**
>
> Do not include document comments (described in Chapter 3) in a supplemental dictionary. If you compress the dictionary, the comments are added to the word list. If you add words to the supplemental dictionary during a spell-check, the comments are simply discarded.

Cue:

Create supplemental dictionaries for each of many topics.

Create a dictionary specific to one document or project by keeping a list of words in Doc 2 as you type a document in Doc 1. Save the list and select it as a dictionary from the Check menu when you spell-check the associated document or any other document on a related topic.

To create a supplemental dictionary as a WordPerfect document, complete the following steps:

1. If you have a floppy disk system, insert a blank formatted diskette in drive B.

2. Begin a new document. If you just accessed WordPerfect, you have already begun a new document. If you have a document on-screen, press Exit (F7), save the text, and select **N**o at the `Exit WP?` prompt.

Cue:

Sort the word list to make the dictionary work faster.

3. Type the list of words that appear in your document but are not in the Speller's main dictionary, pressing Enter after each word.

   You do not have to alphabetize the list or type it in lowercase letters. If you sort the list alphabetically, however, the dictionary works faster.

   If you want to compress the supplemental dictionary, consider hyphenating the words as you enter them so that the words in the text can be automatically hyphenated when you turn on hyphenation. Use hard hyphens (Home, hyphen) rather than the regular hyphen key.

4. Press Save (F10) to save the list.

   ▭ Access the **F**ile pull-down menu and select **S**ave.

Note: With WordPerfect 5, you could lock up your computer if you did not use Fast Save to save a supplemental dictionary file. WordPerfect 5.1 does not have this problem, but you should continue to save supplemental dictionary files unformatted.

5. When prompted for a file name, type the directory name and the file name. Although WordPerfect does not require that you use the extension SUP, using this extension enables you to identify the supplemental dictionary files.

For example, hard disk users who want to name the file MEDICAL.SUP and store the file with the Speller files in the C:\WP51\LEX directory should type the following:

C:\WP51\LEX\MEDICAL.SUP

Floppy disk users should type *B:* and the file name when saving the supplemental dictionary. To use the supplemental dictionary, however, you must copy it to either the Speller diskette or the data diskette so that the file is available (is in your computer) when you run the Speller.

Figure 7.10 shows MEDICAL.SUP, a supplemental dictionary of medical terms.

```
File: C:\QUE\CHAPTERS\MEDICAL.SUP          WP5.0      Revised: 11-04-89 09:25a

amytal
BSP
CNS
CPK
CSF
DAP
eos
FBS
FTA
FTI
Gardnerella
glabellar
GYN
HEENT
hematest
hemoccult
hpf
IgG
LDH
lytes

Look: 1 Next Doc; 2 Prev Doc: 0
```

Fig. 7.10.

The MEDICAL.SUP supplemental dictionary.

Tip

WordPerfect's main dictionary contains many medical and legal terms (for instance, *folate*, *lymphadenopathy*, and *Rorschach*). To avoid duplications and save memory space and disk space, run a spell-check on your list of words before saving the list as a supplemental dictionary. Delete any entries that WordPerfect passes (finds in its main dictionary).

Cue:

You can use only one supplemental dictionary per spell-check, but you can combine several supplemental dictionaries into one.

You can set up several supplemental dictionaries for different projects. Although you are limited to one supplemental dictionary per spell-check, you can merge two or more dictionaries together and save them under a new name. (To retrieve two files together, first retrieve one from List Files, leave the cursor at the end of the first file, and retrieve the second file from List Files. Select **Y**es at the Retrieve into current document? prompt.) Then start the Speller and select New Sup. Dictionary (**4**) from the Check menu. Type the name of the merged file.

Viewing the Contents of a Supplemental Dictionary

If you added any words to a dictionary during a spell-check or if you created another supplemental dictionary, you can review the words that the supplemental dictionary contains. (If you haven't used either of these options, a supplemental dictionary has not been created yet and cannot be reviewed.)

To review an uncompressed supplemental dictionary, complete the following steps:

1. Press List (F5).

   ⌨ Access the Files menu and select **L**ist Files.

2. Type the name of the directory where the supplemental dictionaries are located and press Enter.

   If you store supplemental dictionary files in a directory called C:\WP51\LEX, for example, type C:WP51\LEX and press Enter. Floppy disk users should type *B:* or *A:*, depending on which drive contains the supplemental dictionary files, and press Enter.

3. Move the cursor to the desired supplemental dictionary file name. Unless you gave the file another name, select WP{WP}US.SUP. (This name is automatically given to a supplemental dictionary.)

   If you don't see the file you want to view, check the location of your files in the Setup menu to be sure that you specified the correct directory (see "Setting Up the Speller" earlier in this chapter).

4. Select **L**ook (**6**) from the List Files screen.

   Figure 7.11 displays the supplemental dictionary created earlier in this chapter. Notice that only one word appears per line. The words are in alphabetical order and are all lowercase.

5. Press Exit (F7) twice to return to the document.

From the List Files screen, you can select **R**etrieve (**1**) to edit the selected dictionary file like a regular document. Be sure to save it if you make any changes to it.

```
File: C:\QUE\CHAPTERS\WP{WP}US.SUP          WP5.1      Revised: 11-04-89 05:27p

framingham
needham
wellesley
```

Fig. 7.11.
*Viewing a
supplemental
dictionary.*

Using a Supplemental Dictionary

The Speller automatically uses a supplemental dictionary if the supplemental dictionary you want to use is called WP{WP}US.SUP and is stored in the location specified on the Setup: Location of Files menu (see "Setting Up the Speller" earlier in this chapter). You can direct the Speller to use other supplemental dictionaries, however.

Reminder:
The supplemental dictionary WP{WP}US.SUP is automatically used during a spell-check.

To use another supplemental dictionary, do the following:

1. If you have a floppy disk system, insert the Speller diskette in drive B.

2. Press Spell (Ctrl-F2) and select **N**ew Sup. Dictionary (**4**) from the Check menu.

   Access the **T**ools menu, select **S**pell, and select **N**ew Sup. Dictionary (**4**) from the Check menu.

3. At the `Supplemental dictionary name:` prompt, type the name of the supplemental dictionary and press Enter.

   Be sure to specify the drive and directory if they do not match the location of the files you specified with Setup.

   For example, type *C:\WP51\LEX\MEDICAL.SUP* and press Enter if the supplemental dictionary MEDICAL.SUP is located in the directory \WP51\LEX on the hard disk (C:).

4. Continue the spell-check as normal, requesting a check of a word, page, or entire document.

If the dictionary you specify does not exist, the Speller does not notify you; the file you specify is used as the new supplemental dictionary to which you can add words during the spell-check. If you notice that the Speller stops at words you know are contained in your supplemental dictionary, verify the name and location of the supplemental dictionary and try again.

If you used hard hyphens (Home, hyphen) to hyphenate words in the list, you must compress the supplemental dictionary file before using it. See "Compressing or Expanding a Supplemental Dictionary" later in this chapter.

Using the Speller Utility

In addition to using the Speller from within a document in WordPerfect, you can use the Speller Utility (the SPELL.EXE program) to manipulate the contents of a dictionary. Uncompressed supplemental dictionaries are just alphabetical lists of words in normal WordPerfect document format; you can add or delete words in

Reminder:
Use the Speller Utility to manipulate the contents of dictionaries.

these dictionaries by using WordPerfect itself or the Speller Utility. Main dictionaries and compressed supplementals, however, are more than just lists of words, so you can't retrieve them into WordPerfect. Instead, you use the Speller Utility program to manipulate the contents of these more complex dictionaries. You can add words to or delete words from dictionaries, including the common and main word lists of the main dictionary. You can optimize new dictionaries you have created, display the common word list, check the location of a word, or compress a supplemental dictionary.

To use the Speller Utility options, complete the following steps:

1. Use WordPerfect's GoTo DOS feature by pressing Ctrl-F1.

    ⌨ Access the **F**ile pull-down menu and select **G**oTo DOS.

    Note: If you do not have enough conventional memory to run the Speller Utility while WordPerfect is still in memory, Exit (F7) from WordPerfect and begin at the operating system level.

2. If you have a hard disk, change to the directory containing the Speller files (for instance, C:\WP51\LEX).

    If you have a floppy disk system, do the following:

    a. Insert the Speller diskette in drive A and the diskette containing the supplemental dictionary in drive B.

    b. If you are not at the B> prompt, type *B:* and press Enter.

3. If you have a hard disk, type *spell* and press Enter. If you have a floppy disk system, type *A:spell* and press Enter.

    The Speller Utility menu appears; the name of the dictionary you can modify appears in the upper right corner (see fig. 7.12). (The original WordPerfect 5.1 manual shows this menu incorrectly.)

Fig. 7.12.
The Speller Utility menu.

```
 Spell -- WordPerfect Speller Utility                      WP{WP}US.LEX
    0 - Exit
    1 - Change/Create Dictionary
    2 - Add Words to Dictionary
    3 - Delete Words from Dictionary
    4 - Optimize Dictionary
    5 - Display Common Word List
    6 - Check Location of a Word
    7 - Look Up
    8 - Phonetic Look Up
    9 - Convert 4.2 Dictionary to 5.1
    A - Combine Other 5.0 or 5.1 Dictionary
    B - Compress/Expand Supplemental Dictionary
    C - Extract Added Words from Wordlist-based Dictionary
```

The Speller Utility menu provides several options. If you want to change the dictionary being edited, select Change/Create Dictionary (**1**), enter a dictionary name, and perform any of the available options for the specified dictionary. The dictionary you select may be compressed or uncompressed.

Add Words to Dictionary (**2**) and Delete Words from Dictionary (**3**) are explained in the next sections.

After you create a new dictionary, select Optimize Dictionary (**4**) to help WordPerfect access the words in the list more quickly and efficiently. After optimizing, the compressed portion of the dictionary takes less room on disk; its contents are accessed faster also.

To review the words contained in the common word list, select Display Common Word List (**5**). After reviewing the list, press Exit (F7) to return to the Speller Utility menu.

You can check in which word list (main or common) a word is located by choosing Check Location of Word (**6**). Type the word you want to locate and press Enter. The location appears on-screen. Press Exit (F7) to return to the Speller Utility menu.

Look up words just as you do during a spell-check with options Look Up (**7**) and Phonetic Look Up (**8**). If you have selected a supplemental dictionary, only those words that are compressed are found.

WordPerfect 4.2 users can convert dictionaries to WordPerfect 5.1 format by choosing Convert 4.2 Dictionary to 5.1 (**9**). WordPerfect 5 dictionaries should work with 5.1 for spell-checking documents. The version 5 dictionary is not hyphenated, however, so the automatic hyphenation feature of 5.1 does not work as well as with version 5.1 dictionary files.

Combine two main dictionaries into one large one with Combine Other 5.0 or 5.1 Dictionary (**A**). Perhaps you often use more than one language within a single document and find that using the language code to automatically switch between dictionaries is tedious. If so, you can combine the main U.S. English dictionary (WP{WP}US.LEX) with the separately purchased French dictionary (WP{WP}FR.LEX), for example.

Tip

If you did not add words to the dictionary you used with version 5, use the standard 5.1 dictionary instead of converting the old file. If you did add words to the version 5 dictionary, you can use Combine Other 5.0 or 5.1 Dictionary (**A**) to "fool" 5.1 into "converting" a version 5 dictionary into a 5.1 dictionary, keeping all the words you added to the version 5 dictionary and ending up with a 5.1 list that includes hyphenation for the words in the 5.1 dictionary. To do this, select Change/Create Dictionary (**1**) and specify the version 5 dictionary you want to convert. Then select Combine Other 5.0 or 5.1 Dictionary (**A**) and enter the name and path of the 5.1 dictionary. Where version 5 and 5.1 words match, 5.1 words overwrite version 5 words, leaving a hyphenated word.

You can compress or expand a supplemental dictionary by using Compress/ Expand Supplemental Dictionary (**B**), as described later in this chapter.

If you have added words to a wordlist-based dictionary that you use, and then purchase an algorithmic dictionary from WordPerfect Corporation, you can select

Extract Added Words from a Wordlist-based Dictionary (**C**) to add those words to the algorithmic dictionary. If you save lists of words added to supplemental dictionaries, you do not have to use this option. After you select this option, you are prompted to enter the path name (if the file is not in the current directory) and file name of the wordlist-based dictionary. Then you enter the path name (if necessary) and the file name of the algorithmic dictionary. Then you enter the name of a supplemental dictionary where words not recognized by the algorithmic dictionary are to be copied.

Adding Words to the Main Dictionary

Reminder:

Add commonly used words to the main dictionary instead of a supplemental dictionary to improve the effectiveness of the Speller.

If you use certain words in many documents, you can add these words to the main dictionary rather than include them in a supplemental dictionary. (If you have a floppy disk system, the limited space on a diskette may limit the number of words you can add to the main dictionary.) One advantage of adding words to the main dictionary is to improve the effectiveness of spell-checking. Remember that words in the main dictionary (or a compressed supplemental dictionary) are offered as alternative spellings on the Not Found menu screen; words in an uncompressed supplemental dictionary are not.

You can create a supplemental dictionary—a list of words with one word per line—and then add all the words in that list to the main dictionary, or you can add individual words to the main or the supplemental dictionary. Although version 5.1 appears to do so faster than previous versions, be aware that updating the dictionary takes some time. As an example, this section adds to the main dictionary the list of words in the WP{WP}US.SUP supplemental dictionary, which was created earlier in this chapter.

If you plan to use the automatic hyphenation feature of 5.1, insert dashes at appropriate hyphenation points in the words being added. You can do this in the supplemental dictionary by editing it as a normal document. If you are adding individual words to the main dictionary, simply insert the hyphen as you type. Use the standard dash (-) key for the hyphen.

To add words to the main or the supplemental dictionary, do the following:

1. Start the Speller Utility from the operating system prompt.

2. If the dictionary you want to change is different than the one named in the upper right corner of the screen, select the desired file by using the Create/Change Dictionary (**1**) option.

3. Select Add Words to Dictionary (**2**). The Add Words menu appears (see fig. 7.13).

Fig. 7.13.
The Add Words menu.

```
Spell -- Add Words                                    WP{WP}US.LEX

0 - Cancel - do not add words
1 - Add to common word list (from keyboard)
2 - Add to common word list (from a file)
3 - Add to main word list (from keyboard)
4 - Add to main word list (from a file)
5 - Exit
```

You can add words to the main or common word list from the keyboard (typing one word at a time) or from an existing list stored in a file on disk.

4. Select the action you want to perform.

For this example, you want to add the words from WP{WP}US.SUP (the supplemental dictionary) to the main word list. Select Add to main word list (from a file) (**4**).

Note: Adding words to the common word list automatically adds the words to the main word list as well.

Caution

Do not add a *compressed* supplemental dictionary to a main dictionary; this action may cause the computer to lock up. Expand the supplemental dictionary before you add it to the main dictionary using the Speller Utility.

Tip

If you created a supplemental dictionary using the normal editing screen, sort the list alphabetically to make the Speller run faster.

---

5. At the Enter file name: prompt, type the file name of the supplemental dictionary and press Enter. For instance, type *WP{WP}US.SUP* and press Enter.

6. The words are not added immediately, so you can add more words (menu options **1** through **4**) or cancel the additions (menu option **0**).

When you are done adding words, select Exit (**5**) to add the words to the word list and exit from the menu. If you added at least one word and select Exit (**5**), you see the following message:

```
Updating dictionary
* Please Wait *
```

WordPerfect writes the words to the dictionary, starting with the words beginning with *A* (the message Writing a's appears) and proceeding through the entire alphabet. Gradually all the words are written to the dictionary, but the process takes a while to complete.

Reminder:
Updating the dictionary may take some time.

Caution

Do not continue with the process if you see the following message:

```
Insufficient room on drive A: for temporary files.
Do not remove diskette in drive A:
Enter drive letter for temporary files:
```

If this message appears, press Cancel (F1).

---

7. When the additions are complete and you return to the Speller Utility menu, select Exit (**0**) to exit back to the operating system.

> **Tip**
>
> Rename and save the supplemental dictionary file after its words have been added to the main dictionary file. If the main dictionary file becomes corrupted or is otherwise lost, you can use the original supplemental dictionary file to rebuild the main dictionary file quickly and easily. Whenever you add words to the main dictionary file, add the words to the file containing the words previously added. If disk space is a problem, move the supplemental dictionary file to its own diskette and keep it in a safe place.

During a spell-check, the Speller no longer stops at the words you have added; the words you added may even appear as alternative spellings for other words.

Deleting Words from the Main Dictionary

Reminder:

Delete words from the main dictionary to make room for other words or to "clean up" the dictionary.

Besides adding words, you also can delete words from the main or supplemental dictionary to make room for other words or just to clean up the dictionary. For example, you may want to get rid of single-letter words like *n* or obscure terms you never use.

In this exercise, you delete the words you added to the main dictionary in the previous section.

To delete words from the main dictionary, complete the following steps:

1. Start the Speller Utility from the operating system prompt.

2. If the dictionary you want to change is different than the one named in the upper right corner of the screen, select the desired file by using the Create/Change Dictionary (**1**) option.

3. Select Delete Words from Dictionary (**3**). The Delete Words menu appears (see fig. 7.14). This menu is similar to the Add Words menu shown in figure 7.13.

   You can delete words from the main or common word list from the keyboard (typing one word at a time) or from an existing list stored in a file on disk.

   Because supplemental dictionaries contain only one list, and not both a common and a main word list, options **1** and **2** (deleting from the common word list) are disabled. If you are working on a supplemental dictionary and select one of these options, the message `Not functional with supplemental dictionary` appears. Select option **3** or **4** instead.

4. Select the action you want to perform. For this example, select Delete from main word list (from a file) (**4**).

   Note: Deleting words from the main word list automatically deletes the words from the common word list as well, if the words were in both lists.

```
Spell -- Delete Words                            WP{WP}US.LEX
0 - Cancel - do not delete words
1 - Delete from common word list (from keyboard)
2 - Delete from common word list (from a file)
3 - Delete from main word list (from keyboard)
4 - Delete from main word list (from a file)
5 - Exit
```

Fig. 7.14.
The Delete Words menu.

5. At the Enter file name: prompt, type the file name containing the list of words you want to delete from the main word list and press Enter. For instance, type *WP{WP}US.SUP* and press Enter.

6. The words are not deleted immediately, so you can delete more words (menu options **1** through **4**) or cancel the deletions (menu option **0**).

   When you are done deleting words, select Exit (**5**) to delete the words from the word list and exit the menu. If you have deleted at least one word and select Exit (**5**), you see the following message:

   ```
   Updating dictionary
   * Please Wait *
   ```

   WordPerfect writes the newly revised list of words to the dictionary, starting with the words beginning with *A* (the message Writing a's appears) and proceeding through the entire alphabet. Gradually all the words are written to the dictionary, but the process takes a while to complete.

Caution

Do not continue with the process if you see the following message:

```
Insufficient room on drive A: for temporary files.
Do not remove diskette in drive A:
Enter drive letter for temporary files:
```

If this message appears, press Cancel (F1).

---

7. When the deletions are complete and you return to the Speller Utility menu, select Exit (**0**) to exit back to the operating system.

Compressing or Expanding a Supplemental Dictionary

If your reason for adding words to the main dictionary is to have them appear as alternative spellings on the Not Found screen, consider compressing a supplemental dictionary instead. Compressing a supplemental dictionary is preferable when, for example, you have several distinct supplemental lists that you don't want jumbled together in the main dictionary.

Compressing makes the file smaller and speeds up the spell-check process. If you compress a file, you can no longer edit it as a normal WordPerfect document. To

Reminder:
Compress a supplemental dictionary to have its words appear as alternative spellings on the Not Found screen.

add or delete words from the list after compressing it, you must use the Speller Utility, select the supplemental dictionary, and then use the add and delete options from the Speller Utility menu. Alternatively, you can expand the compressed file and edit the file as a normal document again.

You must compress a supplemental dictionary if you hyphenated the word list.

Caution

If you compress a supplemental dictionary that was hyphenated using dashes instead of hard hyphens (Home, hyphen), dashes are replaced with hard returns, resulting in a jumbled list of nonsense words.

To compress a supplemental dictionary, complete the following steps:

1. Start the Speller Utility and select Change/Create Dictionary (**1**) from the main menu. The Change Dictionary menu appears (see fig. 7.15).

Fig. 7.15.
The Change Dictionary menu.

```
Spell -- Change Dictionary                              WP{WP}US.LEX

0 - Cancel - do not change dictionary
1 - Change/Create main dictionary
2 - Change/Create supplemental dictionary
```

2. Select Change/Create supplemental dictionary (**2**) from the menu and type the name of the supplemental dictionary you want to use. Press Enter.

   If the dictionary you want to use is not in the same directory as the Speller Utility, you must include the path.

3. When the Speller Utility menu reappears, select Compress/Expand Supplemental Dictionary (**B**). The Compact/Uncompact Supplemental Dictionary menu appears (see fig. 7.16).

   If you did not select a supplemental dictionary, WordPerfect displays the message `Not functional with main dictionary`.

Caution

If you use the original release of WordPerfect 5.1 (11/6/89) and include a long path name as part of the file name in step 2, you may encounter a problem: the monitor may flash as it attempts to write the menu on-screen. In a few minutes, the menu appears, although it is distorted. Because the menu title is quite long, the title *and* the long path name cannot fit. Avoid this problem by copying the supplemental dictionary into the directory containing the SPELL.EXE program.

---

4. Select the action you want to perform.

   If you want to compress a supplemental dictionary, select option **1**; if you want to expand a compressed supplemental dictionary, select option **2**. For this example, select option **1**.

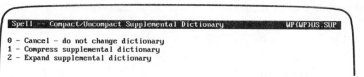

Fig. 7.16.

The Compact/ Uncompact Supplemental Dictionary menu.

5. When the compressing is complete and you return to the Speller Utility menu, select Exit (**0**) to exit back to the operating system.

Using the Thesaurus

The Thesaurus can add freshness and variety to your writing by suggesting alternative words for your use. The Thesaurus also helps you to be more precise in your writing—when you can't find quite the word you need, use the Thesaurus. Consider, for example, the sample text in figure 7.6; you may decide that the word *exciting* isn't quite right.

The Thesaurus offers antonyms and synonyms. *Synonyms* have meanings similar to but not exactly the same as the original word. Some words are more or less formal than others or have positive or negative connotations. The Thesaurus only lists these words; you must decide which one most closely fits your meaning. Don't abuse the Thesaurus by using inappropriate words.

Reminder:
The Thesaurus offers both synonyms and antonyms.

To use the Thesaurus, you must know how to spell the word you want to look up. If you are not sure how to spell a word, first look up the spelling by using the wild cards * and ? with the Speller.

In the past, WordPerfect Corporation received complaints about the sexist nature of the Thesaurus. These complaints were addressed in the summer 1989 version of WordPerfect 5. If you have been using an older version of the Thesaurus, you may be startled when you compare it with the 5.1 Thesaurus, especially for such words as *man* and *woman*.

Starting the Thesaurus

To practice using the Thesaurus, display or type the corrected paragraph used to practice the Speller (see fig. 7.6).

To start the Thesaurus, complete the following steps:

1. If you have a floppy disk system, remove the data diskette from drive B and insert the Thesaurus diskette.

Caution
Before you remove the diskette, make sure that WordPerfect isn't doing a backup of your work. * Please wait * appears at the bottom of the screen during backup. You can lose the document if the computer is writing to the diskette when you take it out.

2. Place the cursor anywhere between the first character and the space following the word you want to look up. For instance, place the cursor under the period (.) following the word *exciting*.

3. Press Thesaurus (Alt-F1).

   🖱 Access the **T**ools pull-down menu and select **T**hesaurus.

The screen splits; the normal text (if any) appears in the top half of the screen, and the Thesaurus menu and word list appear in columns in the bottom half (see fig. 7.17).

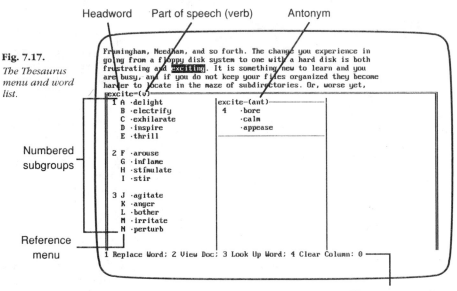

Headword   Part of speech (verb)   Antonym

Fig. 7.17.
The Thesaurus menu and word list.

Numbered subgroups

Reference menu

Thesaurus menu

If the menu is empty and `Word:` appears at the bottom of the screen, your cursor may not have been within a word boundary when you activated the Thesaurus. Alternatively, the Thesaurus could not find the word you requested. In either case, type the word you want to look up at the `Word:` prompt and press Enter.

Understanding the Parts of the Thesaurus Menu

Several items that help you use the Thesaurus appear in the Thesaurus menu screen. The word you looked up, called a *headword* because it has a body of similar words attached to it, appears at the top of the first column. Some synonyms and antonyms for a headword are headwords themselves and are noted with a small bullet. In figure 7.17, all words shown are headwords.

The words are divided into parts of speech (see table 7.1) and numbered subgroups. The column of letters to the left of the words is called the Reference menu; you refer to the words by these letters.

Table 7.1
Parts of Speech from the Thesaurus Menu

Part of Speech	Abbreviation	Part of Speech	Abbreviation
Adjective	(a)	Verb	(v)
Noun	(n)	Antonym	(ant)

Replacing a Word

If you see a word with which you want to replace the one in your text, select the replacement. For this example, you can select *delight* from the list to replace *exciting*, and then add *ful* to make the word *delightful*.

To replace a word in text with one from the Thesaurus menu, do the following:

1. Select Replace Word (**1**) from the Thesaurus menu. The prompt `Press letter for word` appears.

2. From the Reference menu, press the letter that corresponds to the replacement word. For example, press A to select the word *delight*.

   The Thesaurus menu disappears, and the program inserts in the text the word you selected (see fig. 7.18). (Remember to add *ful* to *delight*!)

```
Framingham, Needham, and so forth. The change you experience in
going from a floppy disk system to one with a hard disk is both
frustrating and delightful. It is something new to learn and you
are busy, and if you do not keep your files organized they become
harder to locate in the maze of subdirectories. Or, worse yet,
you didn't take the time to figure out subdirectories, so all
your files are lumped together--rather like throwing papers in a
filing cabinet with no folders.
```

Fig. 7.18.

The word exciting *replaced with* delightful.

3. If you use a floppy disk system, remember to remove the Thesaurus diskette, replace it with the data diskette, and save the document.

Selecting More Words

If you don't see the right word on the Thesaurus menu screen, or you want to try other words, you can expand the word list.

For example, suppose that you think the meaning of *delightful* is close to the word you're looking for but not exactly right. You could replace *exciting* with *delightful* and then use the Thesaurus for *delightful*, but that process is tedious. Instead, request more words from the Thesaurus menu before choosing the replacement.

Reminder:

Display more words on the Thesaurus menu screen by selecting new headwords from the existing alternatives.

For this example, start over again. Replace the word *exciting* in the text: press Undelete (F1), or retype the word *exciting* and delete the word *delightful*. Place the cursor in the word *exciting* and start the Thesaurus. If you have a floppy disk system, remember to replace diskettes.

Take another look at the Thesaurus menu in figure 7.17. Remember that words marked with a bullet also are headwords, as are all the words in figure 7.17. You can look up any of these words for more ideas.

Words without bullets are not headwords. If you look up a word without a bullet, the message `Word not found` appears, or WordPerfect looks up a similar word instead (rather than looking up *exciting*, for example, WordPerfect looked up *excite*).

To see additional words from the Thesaurus menu, complete the following steps:

1. From the words listed by the Thesaurus, choose one close to the meaning you want.

2. Press the letter beside the word. For example, press A to select *delight* so that you can see some synonyms for that word.

   Words associated with the new headword appear in the next column to the right of the previous headword (see fig. 7.19). Notice that the Reference menu (the column of letters) moves to the second column.

Fig. 7.19.

A second headword selected.

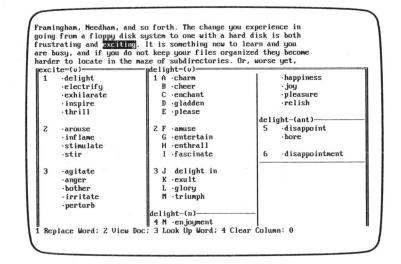

3. Select a replacement word or select another headword to see additional words. For example, press I to select *fascinate* as the next headword (see fig. 7.20).

Maneuvering inside the Thesaurus

Reminder:

Move the Reference menu from column to column with the right and left arrows.

When you select a new headword, the Reference menu (the column of letters) moves to the new column of words. Each column contains only one headword and its associated words. Use ← and → to move the Reference menu between columns.

You can select up to three headwords to view at one time, as shown in figure 7.20. When you select a fourth headword, the third column is replaced with the new selection. Alternatively, you can select Clear Column (4) from the Thesaurus menu to clear the current column (the one containing the Reference menu) and select another word.

```
Framingham, Needham, and so forth. The change you experience in
going from a floppy disk system to one with a hard disk is both
frustrating and  exciting . It is something new to learn and you
are busy, and if you do not keep your files organized they become
harder to locate in the maze of subdirectories. Or, worse yet,
┌excite=(v)════════════╦delight=(v)════════════╦fascinate=(v)════════════
│1   ·delight          ║1   ·charm             ║1 A ·bewitch
│    ·electrify         ║    ·cheer             ║  B ·captivate
│    ·exhilarate        ║    ·enchant           ║  C ·charm
│    ·inspire           ║    ·gladden           ║  D ·enchant
│    ·thrill            ║    ·please            ║
│                       ║                       ║2 E ·absorb
│2   ·arouse            ║2   ·amuse             ║  F ·engross
│    ·inflame           ║    ·entertain         ║  G ·enthrall
│    ·stimulate         ║    ·enthrall          ║  H ·grip
│    ·stir              ║    ·fascinate         ║
│                       ║                       ║3 I ·appeal to
│3   ·agitate           ║3    delight in        ║  J ·interest
│    ·anger             ║    ·exult             ║  K ·intrigue
│    ·bother            ║    ·glory             ║
│    ·irritate          ║    ·triumph           ║fascinate-(ant)──────────
│    ·perturb           ║                       ║4 L ·bore
│                       ║delight-(n)────────────║  M ·weary
│                       ║4   ·enjoyment         ║
│1 Replace Word; 2 View Doc; 3 Look Up Word; 4 Clear Column: 0
```

Fig. 7.20.
*A third headword
selected.*

The headword choices in a column automatically wrap to the adjacent column to
the left unless that column has its own headword. If the columns are full, the
remaining words in the headword list continue down the column past the bottom
of the screen. Use ↑ and ↓ to move from one numbered group to the next within
the columns. You can go directly to a particular subgroup by pressing GoTo (Ctrl-
Home), typing the desired subgroup number, and then pressing Enter. Use PgUp,
PgDn, Screen Up (the gray – key), and Screen Down (the gray + key) to move to
the top or bottom of the column. The unbroken lines below the groups of words
in a column indicate the end of a headword's groupings of alternative words. For
instance, note the line below *triumph* in the second column and *intrigue* in the
third column of figure 7.20.

To move the Reference menu and select a replacement word, follow these steps:

1. Press ← or → until the Reference menu is in the column containing the
   desired replacement. For example, press ← twice to move to the first
   column containing the word *exhilarate.*

2. Replace the word in the text with the desired alternative. For example, if
   you decide that *exhilarate* is the best replacement for *exciting,* select
   Replace Word (**1**) and press the letter C. (Remember to delete the *e* and
   add *ing.*) The final text should look like the that shown in figure 7.21.

```
Framingham, Needham, and so forth. The change you experience in
going from a floppy disk system to one with a hard disk is both
frustrating and exhilarating. It is something new to learn and
you are busy, and if you do not keep your files organized they
become harder to locate in the maze of subdirectories. Or, worse
yet, you didn't take the time to figure out subdirectories, so
all your files are lumped together--rather like throwing papers
in a filing cabinet with no folders.
```

Fig. 7.21.
The word exciting
replaced with
exhilarating.

Viewing a Word in Context

If you are unsure of a word's exact meaning in the context of your writing, you can
see more of the text surrounding the word in the document. To see more of the

Reminder:

Display more of the text surrounding the word you want to replace by selecting View Doc from the Thesaurus menu.

text, you can Exit (F7) from the Thesaurus, scroll through the text, and then reselect Thesaurus (Alt-F1). Alternatively, you can opt to view the document from the Thesaurus menu.

To see more of the document without exiting the Thesaurus, complete the following steps:

1. Select View Doc (**2**) from the Thesaurus menu. The cursor moves within the text to the word you are looking up.

2. Use the cursor keys to see the rest of your document.

3. Press Exit (F7) to return to the Thesaurus. As an alternative, you can place the cursor on another word and press Thesaurus (Alt-F1) to look up a new word.

Looking Up Words

While in the Thesaurus, you can look up other words that come to mind by doing the following:

1. Select Look Up Word (**3**).

2. At the Word: prompt, type the new word you want to look up and press Enter.

If the word is a headword, the Thesaurus displays the word with all its subgroups of synonyms and antonyms. If the word is not a headword, WordPerfect either looks up another similar word or displays the message Word Not Found. You can choose to look up another word, or you can press Cancel (F1).

Summary

Although you may still need a conventional dictionary to look up the meanings of words, WordPerfect's Speller and Thesaurus are handy tools that can help you improve your writing. In this chapter, you have learned how to use the Speller to complete the following tasks:

❏ Replace misspelled words with suggested alternatives

❏ Correct a word yourself

❏ Leave out parts of a document from a spell-check

❏ Create and use supplemental dictionaries

❏ Count the number of words in a document

❏ Add and delete words from the main or common word list

❏ Compress a supplemental dictionary

You also have learned how to use the Thesaurus to complete the following tasks:

❏ Look up synonyms and antonyms

❏ Review additional words for your selection

❏ Replace one word with another that is more fitting

Printing and
Print Options

Joel Shore originally wrote this chapter for *Using WordPerfect 5*. He is president of Documentation Systems, a private consulting firm that provides microcomputer services. Mr. Shore is also senior editor of LANWEEK for *Computer Reseller News*, and he teaches personal computing courses at Massachusetts Bay Community College.

Jon Pepper revised this chapter for *Using WordPerfect 5.1, Special Edition*. He is president of Words Plus, a firm that provides computer consulting services. Mr. Pepper also works as a journalist, covering the computer industry for many leading publications.

With all of WordPerfect's sophisticated tools to aid in the composition and formatting of a document, you can lose sight of the program's primary function: committing your words to paper. Because printing is what word processing is all about, WordPerfect 5.1 has paid special attention to this function. In fact, much of WordPerfect 5 has been redesigned and rewritten to take advantage of the latest advances in printer technology.

In this chapter, you examine all aspects of printing. First, you tell WordPerfect what kind of printer you have; this process is called *defining and selecting*. You indicate the styles of type that you have available and which one you expect to use most of the time. Next, you list the sizes and kinds of material on which you plan to print, from continuous forms to letterheads, envelopes, transparencies, or labels. You learn how to print an entire document or just a portion. Perhaps most important, you learn techniques to help you manage your printing activities efficiently. No matter what kind of printer you have, this chapter will be of help to you. For a discussion of laser printing, refer to the next chapter.

The designers of WordPerfect have gone to great lengths to make printing as easy and flexible as possible. You can edit a document while it is being printed, or you can edit two documents simultaneously (using the split screen feature) while printing a third document directly from a disk file!

> **Reminder**
>
> If you use a mouse with WordPerfect 5.1, you can click the right button to display the pull-down menus, and then select the desired option. You also can press Alt-= to access the pull-down menus, and then press the appropriate letter of the desired option. For all instructions, assume that if a block is required to activate a pull-down menu option, the text has been blocked before the pull-down menu is accessed. Instructions for pull-down menus and the mouse are marked with the mouse icon. See Chapter 1 for more information about the mouse. ▭▤

WordPerfect's Protection As You Print

WordPerfect is smart enough to place a protective barrier between you and your printer. It is virtually impossible for printing problems to cause a document to be lost or scrambled.

How does WordPerfect protect you? When you print, WordPerfect creates a temporary file on your hard disk and stores in that file a copy of the document to be printed (up to the last page you want to print). The actual printing is done from this file. While WordPerfect prints the document from the newly created file, you can continue to edit the text being displayed on-screen. Any changes that you make are *not* reflected in the file being printed. When the print job has finished, WordPerfect automatically erases the temporary print file from disk.

By using this complex procedure, WordPerfect can store many of these temporary print files and use them to build a *job list*. Fortunately, all of this activity takes place behind the scenes.

Using Print (Shift-F7)

Reminder:

The main Print menu provides access to all WordPerfect 5.1 print functions.

Most of WordPerfect's printing features are available through the Print (Shift-F7) command. When you press Print (Shift-F7) or select **P**rint from the **F**ile pull-down menu, the Print screen is displayed. This screen contains the main Print menu (see fig. 8.1), which uses the entire screen to show various printing options.

If you are in the process of installing WordPerfect, you need to do some work before you can print. You first must *select* a printer, thus tailoring WordPerfect to your specific printer make and model.

Selecting Printers

Printers are like people from around the world; they don't speak the same language. Printer manufacturers, in an effort to differentiate themselves and provide unique features, have developed proprietary printer command languages. Even different models made by the same manufacturer may use incompatible commands. Sending the same command from your computer to two different

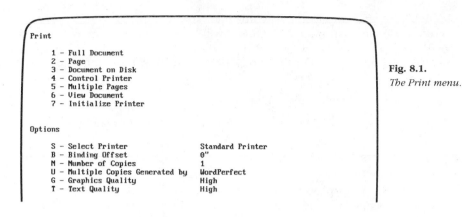

```
Print

    1 - Full Document
    2 - Page
    3 - Document on Disk
    4 - Control Printer
    5 - Multiple Pages
    6 - View Document
    7 - Initialize Printer


Options

    S - Select Printer            Standard Printer
    B - Binding Offset            0"
    N - Number of Copies          1
    U - Multiple Copies Generated by   WordPerfect
    G - Graphics Quality          High
    T - Text Quality              High
```

Fig. 8.1.
The Print menu.

printers may, for example, produce a margin change in one printer and turn on underlining in the other. If WordPerfect had a huge chart that listed every printer make and model across the top and every possible printing feature along the left margin, all the resulting boxes could be filled in with the appropriate printer command. Fortunately, WordPerfect Corporation has done this exhaustive research by working with printers on loan from the manufacturers. The results have been saved in the files found on the Printer disks shipped with WordPerfect.

Literally hundreds of printers are supported by WordPerfect. To make sure that you achieve the results you expect, you must tell WordPerfect which printer make and model you are using. You use the Select Printer feature to do this.

When To Use the Select Printer Feature

The Select Printer feature actually combines two important tasks: (1) *defining* a printer or printers, in which you tell WordPerfect the kind of equipment you have, and (2) *selecting* one of the defined printers for your current needs. You use the Select Printer feature to define printers when you initially install WordPerfect and, thereafter, only when you change or add printers, or when you change information about the printer(s) you have selected. You can select a printer from the list of those you have defined as often as you like. For a quick draft of a long document, you may want to use a dot-matrix printer and then switch to another printer for the final, letter-quality copy.

Reminder:
Use the Select Printer feature to define and select a printer.

Using Select Printer To Define a New Printer

WordPerfect must know many things about your printer before the program can take full advantage of the printer's features. What is the make and model? What printing styles (fonts) are built-in? Which one do you intend to use for "normal" printing? What computer port is the printer connected to? Is the printer a parallel or serial type? Are you using a sheet feeder? If so, how many bins does it have? Does your printer generate both draft- and letter-quality output? If so, which will you use most often?

In the following example, you tell WordPerfect that you plan to use a Hewlett-Packard LaserJet Series II printer and that it will be connected to the computer's standard parallel printer port, called LPT1. If you are using a different printer, you may not need to make some of the choices indicated here. Follow the steps that are appropriate for your printer.

To select a printer, complete the following steps:

1. Press Print (Shift-F7) to display the main Print menu and choose **S**elect Printer (**S**).

   ▭ Access the **F**ile pull-down menu, select **P**rint, and choose **S**elect Printer (**S**).

   WordPerfect displays the Select Printer screen (see fig. 8.2). At the top of the screen, you can see a list of all currently identified printers. If you have previously defined any printers, they are listed here also. Because WordPerfect can speak only one printer language at a time, an asterisk (*) indicates the active printer.

Fig. 8.2.
The Select Printer screen.

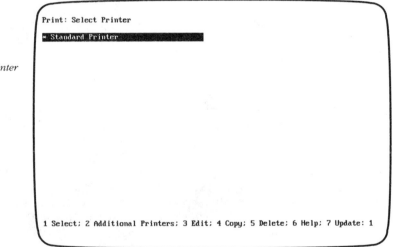

2. Select **A**dditional Printers (**2**).

   If you did not copy the printer files to your hard disk during installation, or if you are using a floppy disk system, WordPerfect displays the `Printer files not found` error message.

   If this message appears, you must go back and run the Install program to install additional printer files.

Tip

Installing all the printer files on your hard disk needlessly wastes a substantial amount of valuable space. Because you use these files only when selecting printers, you can be more efficient by installing only the printers you will be using. You can always add new printers later if needed.

3. Move the highlight bar to the desired printer brand and model (see fig. 8.3).

   Use the up (↑) and down (↓) arrows and Screen Up (the gray – key) and Screen Down (the gray + key) to move through the list of printers.

```
Select Printer: Additional Printers

  Apple LaserWriter
  Apple LaserWriter IINT
  Apple LaserWriter IINTX
  Apple LaserWriter Plus
  AST TurboLaser
  Brother HL-8e
  Dataproducts LZR-1260
  Destiny PageStyler
  Digital LN03R (ScriptPrinter)
  Digital PrintServer 40
  DOS Text Printer
  EiconScript
  Fortis DP600S
  Fujitsu RX7100PS
  HP LaserJet
  HP LaserJet 2000
  HP LaserJet IID
  HP LaserJet IIP
  HP LaserJet Series II
  HP LaserJet Series II (Basic)
  HP LaserJet+, 500+

1 Select; 2 Other Disk; 3 Help; 4 List Printer Files; N Name Search: 1
```

Fig. 8.3.

The Select Printer: Additional Printers screen.

If the printer you want is not listed, select **O**ther Disk (**2**) to specify another directory where your printer files may be located. If you have used the Install program and still cannot find the printer you want, call the WordPerfect customer support line to see whether a driver for your printer is available.

Tip

In a pinch, you may be able to substitute printer definitions. If your dot-matrix printer is not listed, try using the Epson-FX definition. It is as close to a universal dot-matrix printer as any definition can be. If you have a print-wheel or thimble-type letter-quality printer that is not listed, try using the Diablo 630 printer definition.

4. To select the highlighted printer, choose **S**elect (**1**).

   The file name displayed on-screen is WordPerfect's suggested name for the printer-definition file that WordPerfect is about to create. If you like, you can edit this name, but it is better, and easier, to accept the suggested name. Printer-definition files should always have a file extension of PRS.

5. Press Enter to accept the name for the printer-definition file.

   A progress report at the bottom of the screen shows the number of fonts remaining to be created.

   While the PRS file is being created, WordPerfect displays some helpful information and hints about the selected printer (see fig. 8.4). Reading this information carefully now may save you time later.

Fig. 8.4.

The Select Printer:
Help screen.

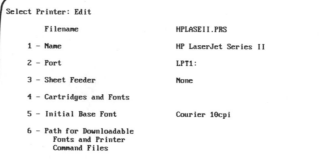

```
Printer Helps and Hints:  HP LaserJet Series II
9/21/89
Initializing the printer will delete all soft fonts in printer memory and
those fonts marked with an asterisk (*) will be downloaded.

Line draw is not supported with proportionally spaced fonts.
```

6. Press Exit (F7). The Select Printer: Edit screen, shown in figure 8.5, displays the current settings for the selected printer.

Fig. 8.5.

The Select Printer:
Edit screen.

```
Select Printer: Edit

          Filename                HPLASEII.PRS

    1 - Name                      HP LaserJet Series II

    2 - Port                      LPT1:

    3 - Sheet Feeder              None

    4 - Cartridges and Fonts

    5 - Initial Base Font         Courier 10cpi

    6 - Path for Downloadable
        Fonts and Printer
        Command Files
```

7. Press Enter to accept the current settings or press a menu number (or highlighted letter) to change that item. (See the following section, "Editing Printer Settings.")

   WordPerfect returns you to the Select Printer screen, which has been fully updated and now lists the printer you have just defined.

You have finished defining your printer. Next, you need to *select* it to tell WordPerfect that you intend to print on the printer.

1. Move the highlight bar to the name of the printer you have defined and press Enter, or choose **S**elect Printer (**1**) to make this the active printer.

   WordPerfect returns you to the main Print menu. Notice that the Print menu has been updated and now shows that the printer you have just defined is the active printer. Any print operation from now on uses this printer until you select a different one.

2. Press Enter to return to the document.

Remember that you can define as many printers as you like, but only one can be active at a time.

Cue:

To save disk space, do not create more printer definitions than you need, and delete from disk the PRS files you no longer need.

Editing Printer Settings

Reminder:

You can change printer settings easily and as often as you like.

Now that WordPerfect knows what kind of printer you are using, you need to indicate your specific configuration. The printer settings initially displayed are WordPerfect's "best guess." You can change these settings at any time: when you first create a printer definition or later.

To change a printer setting, complete the following steps:

1. Press Print (Shift-F7) and choose **S**elect Printer (**S**) to display the Select Printer menu.

    Access the **F**ile pull-down menu, select **P**rint, and choose **S**elect Printer (**S**).

2. Using the up and down arrows, move the highlight bar to the printer setting you want to edit, and select **E**dit (**3**).

Now you can select any of the features described in the following sections. Refer to figure 8.5 as you continue reading.

Name

The full name (up to 36 characters) is the one that WordPerfect uses when referring to this printer. You can see the full name displayed when you press Print (Shift-F7). Most likely, you will never need to change this description.

Port

The *port* is the socket on the back of the computer to which the printer is connected. Ports are of two types: *parallel* and *serial*. If your printer is of the parallel variety (as most are), it is connected to a port named LPT. The first parallel port is LPT1, and the second, if you have one, is LPT2. Serial printers are connected to ports named COM1 and COM2. If you select a COM port, WordPerfect automatically asks you to enter additional information, including the speed at which the computer sends data to the printer (baud rate), and information about how the data is organized (parity, stop bits, and start bits). Now is not the time to make an educated guess. Refer to your printer's technical reference manual (or, in some cases, to the WordPerfect Printer Help screen) for the appropriate values.

Sheet Feeder

The Sheet Feeder setting enables you to indicate whether your printer is equipped with a cut-sheet feeder. The procedure for selecting a sheet feeder is the same as that for selecting a printer. WordPerfect displays a list of compatible sheet feeders; you simply move the highlight bar to the appropriate choice and choose **S**elect (**1**) or press Enter.

Caution

The **F**orms (**4**) option, for defining forms, was part of the Select Printer menu in WordPerfect 5. This option has been moved to the Format menu in WordPerfect 5.1. To reach the Format: Page menu, you press Format (Shift-F8), choose **P**age (**2**), and select Paper Size/Type (**7**). Or you can access the **L**ayout pull-down menu, select **P**age, and choose Paper Size/Type (**7**). See Chapter 6 for more on defining forms.

5.1

Cartridges and Fonts

With this option, you can tell WordPerfect which typefaces (fonts) you have available for use by your printer. Depending on your printer's capabilities, these optional fonts may be plug-in cartridges, special font files stored on your hard disk and downloaded from the computer to the printer as needed, or both. If your printer is not able to use optional fonts, WordPerfect displays the message This printer has no other cartridges or fonts on the status line at the bottom of the screen.

Depending on your printer, when you select **C**artridges and Fonts (**4**), WordPerfect displays the number of slots available for plug-in font cartridges, the amount of memory in the printer for storing downloaded font files, or both (see fig. 8.6). Version 5.1 also adds a category for built-in fonts. Now you can treat built-in fonts in the same manner as cartridges or soft fonts.

To indicate where you want to specify fonts, complete these steps:

1. Move the highlight bar to the location where you want to specify fonts and choose **C**artridges and Fonts (**4**) from the Select Printer: Edit screen.

   WordPerfect displays a list of optional predefined fonts or the built-in fonts, depending on which category you choose.

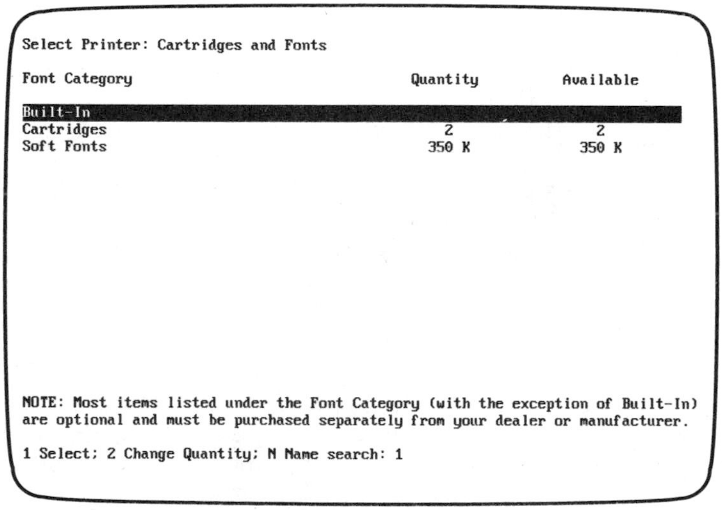

Fig. 8.6.

The Select Printer: Cartridges and Fonts screen.

```
Select Printer: Cartridges and Fonts

Font Category                          Quantity        Available

Built-In
Cartridges                                 2               2
Soft Fonts                               350 K           350 K
```

```
NOTE: Most items listed under the Font Category (with the exception of Built-In)
are optional and must be purchased separately from your dealer or manufacturer.

1 Select; 2 Change Quantity; N Name search: 1
```

2. Move the highlight bar to the fonts you are selecting and (depending on your printer) indicate whether the fonts must be loaded before the print job or whether they can be loaded during the print job.

If you are choosing downloadable fonts, WordPerfect subtracts the memory required for the fonts from the total memory available. Both figures are displayed at the top right of the screen.

Initial Base Font

Initial base font is the typeface (Times, for example), style (Roman), and size (10 points in height, where 1 point is 1/72") in which WordPerfect prints standard text and by which other fonts (such as large or small) are defined. For example, if you specify 10-point Times Roman to be the initial font, then—using Font (Ctrl-F8) and selecting **S**ize (**1**)—Large type is 12 point. If, however, you choose 12 point to be the initial font, then Large type is 14 point.

All defined fonts, including those built-in by the manufacturer and optional fonts you choose under **C**artridges and Fonts (**4**), are listed on the Select Printer: Initial Font screen (see fig. 8.7). If you chose additional fonts with **C**artridges and Fonts (**4**), you will probably want to use one of those for the initial font.

Tip

When working with a document, you can temporarily change the initial font by pressing Font (Ctrl-F8) and selecting Base **F**ont (**4**), or accessing the **F**ont pull-dow menu and selecting Base Font.

```
Select Printer: Initial Font

▸ Courier 10cpi
  Courier 10cpi Bold
  Helv  6pt (AC)
  Helv  6pt Bold (AC)
  Helv  6pt Italic (AC)
  Helv  8pt (AC)
  Helv  8pt (Z1A)
  Helv  8pt Bold (AC)
  Helv  8pt Italic (AC)
  Helv 10pt (AC)
  Helv 10pt (Z1A)
  Helv 10pt Bold (Z1A)
  Helv 10pt Italic (Z1A)
  Helv 12pt (Z1A)
  Helv 12pt Bold (Z1A)
  Helv 12pt Italic (Z1A)
  Helv 14pt Bold (Z1A)
  Line Draw 10cpi (Full)
  Line Printer 16.67cpi
  Line Printer 16.67cpi (Z1A)
  TmsRmn 8pt (Z1A)

1 Select; N Name search: 1
```

Fig. 8.7.

The Select Printer: Initial Font screen.

Path for Downloadable Fonts and Printer Command Files

If you store font files on your hard disk drive, you enter for this option the full path and directory in which the fonts are stored. Note that you are limited to one directory. WordPerfect 5.1 introduces the concept of *font libraries*. When you choose the category of Soft Fonts from the Select Printer: Cartridges and Fonts menu, you first see a submenu of each font family (see fig. 8.8). From these menus, you can easily select soft fonts.

Cue:

Store your font files in a separate directory; house-keeping is easier if they are not intermixed with your WordPerfect files.

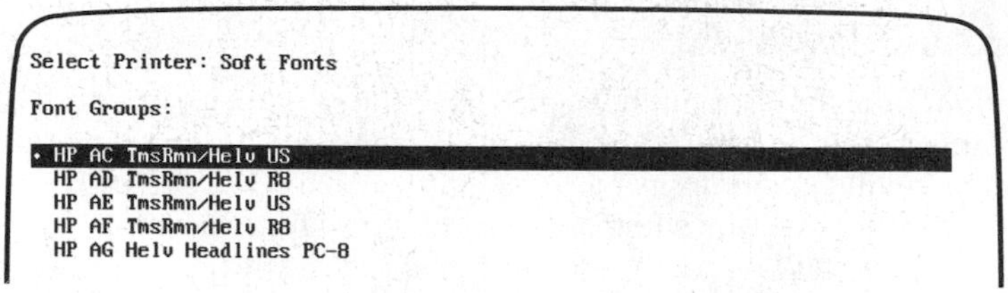

Fig. 8.8.

The Select Printer:
Soft Fonts screen.

```
Select Printer: Soft Fonts

Font Groups:

• HP AC TmsRmn/Helv US
  HP AD TmsRmn/Helv R8
  HP AE TmsRmn/Helv US
  HP AF TmsRmn/Helv R8
  HP AG Helv Headlines PC-8
```

Printing the Test Document

Reminder:

Use WordPerfect's PRINTER.TST file to test your printer definition before you print documents.

Before you begin to print documents, you may want to test the printer definition you have just created and selected. For this purpose, WordPerfect includes a file named PRINTER.TST.

To print the test document, complete the following steps:

1. Retrieve the file PRINTER.TST to the screen either by pressing Retrieve (Shift-F10) and typing the file name, or by pressing List (F5), moving the highlight bar to the file name, and selecting **R**etrieve (**1**).

    ▭ If you use a mouse, access the **F**ile pull-down menu, select **R**etrieve, and type the file name.

2. Press Print (Shift-F7) to display the Print menu, and select **F**ull Document (**1**).

    ▭ Access the **F**ile pull-down menu, choose **P**rint, and select **F**ull Document (**1**).

    Features that do not print properly may not be supported by your printer.

> **Caution**
>
> Make sure that any mechanical settings, such as DIP (dual in-line package) switches, are set according to the manufacturer's instructions provided in your printer's manual.

Now that WordPerfect knows about your printer and you have tested a document, you can begin printing your documents.

Considering WordPerfect Printing Methods

Reminder:

WordPerfect enables you to print from the screen as well as from disk.

One of WordPerfect's great flexibilities is its alternative options for printing documents. The most common method, printing the document you are currently editing, is called *printing from the screen*. This method gives you the option of printing the entire document, a specific page, or a block of any size. WordPerfect enables you to use most of its other features while printing from the screen.

The second method of printing is called *printing from disk*. With this method, you can print a file directly from disk without having to retrieve the document to the screen, and you can specify which pages to print.

> ### Tip
>
> Unlike WordPerfect 5, WordPerfect 5.1 enables you to print a document saved with the Fast Save feature.

With WordPerfect, you never need to wait until one print job is finished before submitting the next. You can submit as many print jobs as you want and as often as you like. WordPerfect keeps track of all the jobs by creating a job list.

To manage the job list, WordPerfect provides one of its most important and powerful features: Control Printer. With the Control Printer feature, you can display a progress report on the current print job, cancel or suspend print jobs, move any print job to the top of the job list, and display the entire list of jobs waiting to be printed. Control Printer is examined in detail later in this chapter.

Printing from the Screen

You can print all or part of the document you are currently editing. Printing the entire document or just the current page requires only three keystrokes. If you want to print just part of a page, such as a sentence or a paragraph, WordPerfect can do that almost as easily through the Block feature.

Printing the Entire Document from the Screen

To print the entire document from the screen, complete the following steps:

1. Press Print (Shift-F7) to display the Print menu.

   ▭▤ Access the **F**ile pull-down menu and choose **P**rint.

2. Select **F**ull Document (**1**) to print the entire document. WordPerfect returns you to the document screen.

WordPerfect automatically creates and formats a print job for the active printer.

To see a progress report about this print job or other pending jobs, you must return to the Print menu and select **C**ontrol Printer (**4**) to display the Control Printer screen.

When the document has finished printing, WordPerfect automatically begins printing the next print job if there is one.

Printing a Specific Page from the Screen

Before WordPerfect can print a page from the screen, the program needs to know which page or pages you want to print. Simply move the cursor to any location on the desired page. You do not need to enter a page number.

To print one page of the document shown on-screen, perform these steps:

1. Position the cursor anywhere on the page you want to print and press Print (Shift-F7).

   ▭ Access the **F**ile pull-down menu and select **P**rint.

2. Select **P**age (**2**) to print the current page. WordPerfect returns you to the document screen.

If the selected page is not near the beginning of the document, you may notice a pause before printing actually begins. The reason is that WordPerfect scans the document from the beginning to find the proper format settings (tabs, margins, fonts, and so on) to use for printing the page.

To see a progress report about this print job, you must return to the Print menu and select **C**ontrol Printer (**4**) to display the Control Printer screen.

When the document has finished printing, WordPerfect automatically begins printing the next print job if there is one.

To print specific pages from the screen, select **M**ultiple Pages (**5**) from the Print menu and then specify the pages at the prompt that appears at the bottom of the screen (see the section "Selecting Pages" later in the chapter).

Printing a Block from the Screen

Sometimes printing an entire document or an entire page just won't do. If you need to print a single sentence, a paragraph, a page and a half, or five pages from a larger document, you should use WordPerfect's Block feature.

As you have seen, printing the entire document or a full page from the screen is easy because WordPerfect knows where the document begins and ends and where page breaks occur. That is not the case with the kinds of structures listed in the preceding paragraph. You need to tell WordPerfect where a block begins and ends.

To print a block, complete these steps:

1. Move the cursor to the beginning of the block you want to print and press Block (Alt-F4 or F12).

   ▭ Access the **E**dit pull-down menu and select **B**lock.

   The message Block on flashes at the lower left corner of the screen.

2. Move the cursor to the end of the block you want to print.

   ▭ Drag the mouse across the section of text you want to block.

Tip

Use good cursor-movement technique to save time. Remember that the block automatically advances to the next occurrence of any character you type. You can advance the block to the end of the current paragraph by simply inserting a hard return (pressing Enter). Press PgDn to advance the block to the next page. Press the period (.) key to advance to the end of the current sentence.

3. Press Print (Shift-F7).

⌨ Access the **F**ile pull-down menu and select **P**rint.

Something different happens when you press Print while Block is on. Instead of displaying the full-screen Print menu, WordPerfect displays a prompt on the status line at the bottom of the screen: Print Block? No (Yes). To be on the safe side, WordPerfect has already suggested No as its choice.

4. If you choose not to print the block, press Enter or select **N** to confirm the choice, or select **Y** to print the block.

You must select **Y** to print the block. Pressing any other key confirms the choice of No and cancels the print operation.

Highlighting disappears from the block once you have chosen to print it. If you choose not to print, the block stays highlighted because WordPerfect assumes that you intend to perform a block operation other than printing.

Printing a Document from Disk

You can print a document directly from disk without the need to display the document on the screen. You can print directly from disk with Print (Shift-F7) or List (F5). As indicated previously, a document saved in WordPerfect 5.1 with the Fast Save feature can be printed.

Caution
If the file you are printing is on a diskette, never remove it from the drive until the print job is complete.

Printing from the Print Menu

If you know the name of the file you want to print from disk, you can use the main Print menu. Just type the file name and specify the pages you want to print from disk.

Caution
You must know the complete file name before starting to print from disk. No provision is made for looking at the List Files screen once you have pressed Print (Shift-F7).

To print from disk using the Print menu, perform these steps:

1. Press Print (Shift-F7) to display the Print menu, select **D**ocument on Disk (**3**), and type the file name for the document.

⬛ Access the **F**ile pull-down menu, select **P**rint to display the Print menu, select **D**ocument on Disk (**3**), and type the file name for the document.

The prompt Pages: (All) is displayed on the status line.

2. Press Enter to print the entire document, or enter the pages you want printed (see the section "Selecting Pages" later in the chapter).

WordPerfect reads the file from disk and creates a print job that is added to the job list.

Printing with the List Files Feature

If you are not sure of the name of the file you want to print, you can use the List Files feature to display a list of available files.

To print from disk using the List Files feature, complete the following steps:

1. Press List (F5) and then Enter to display the file list.

⬛ Access the **F**ile pull-down menu and choose List **F**iles.

2. If the file is not on the disk drive (or directory) shown, enter the appropriate path and file name before pressing Enter.

3. Move the highlight bar to the file you want to print and select **P**rint (**4**). The prompt Pages: (All) appears on the status line.

4. Press Enter to print the entire document, or enter the pages you want printed (see the next section "Selecting Pages").

WordPerfect reads the file from disk and creates a print job that is added to the job list.

Selecting Pages

Reminder:

Pages to be printed from a document do not need to be specified consecutively.

When printing from a disk file, you can specify which pages to print. Pages specified do not need to be consecutive. For example, you can specify pages 3 through 6, 11, 21 and 22, and 30 to the end of the document.

Imagine that you are working with a document containing the New Page Number feature (Shift-F8, 2, 6) several times to mix Roman and Arabic numerals or to restart the page numbering for a new chapter. The document looks like this:

Front matter	pages i–vii
Chapter 1	pages 1–10
Chapter 2	pages 1–17
Chapter 3	pages 1–28

Table 8.1 lists several scenarios for printing selected pages from the example and shows what you must enter. WordPerfect defines a new section as any point at which a code for New Page Number is inserted. (When referring to a section, you must type the code for that section and then a colon.)

Table 8.1
Specifying Pages To Print from Disk

What You Want To Print	*What You Must Enter*
The entire document	i–
All front matter	i–vii
All front matter and all of Chapter 1	i–10
All of Chapter 1	1–10 or 1:1–10
Chapter 1, page 1 only	1 or 1:1
Chapter 1, pages 4 and 5	4,5 or 1:4,5
All of Chapter 2 only	2:1–17
Chapter 2, pages 5–7	2:5–7
Chapter 3, pages 1, 4, 7–9, and 13	3:1,4,7–9,13

Controlling the Printer

WordPerfect's Control Printer feature is a powerful tool for managing your printing activities. You can cancel individual print jobs or all jobs. You can display a list of all jobs waiting to be printed. You can move any print job to the top of the list. You can even suspend printing temporarily and then resume printing if the printer has jammed or needs a new ribbon. All these control activities are located on the Control Printer screen.

Reminder:
You use the Control Printer feature to manage your most important printing activities.

To display the Control Printer screen, perform the following steps:

1. Press Print (Shift-F7) to display the Print menu.

   ⌨ Access the **F**ile pull-down menu and choose **P**rint.

2. Select **C**ontrol Printer (**4**).

WordPerfect displays the Control Printer screen (see fig. 8.9). The screen is divided into three sections: Current Job, Job List, and a printer control menu. For purposes of illustration, the example shows several print jobs.

Information about the Current Print Job

The most important print job is the one currently printing. WordPerfect maintains constant watch over the status of the print job and continually updates the Control Printer screen. The following sections explain each line of the Control Printer screen.

Job Number

Every time you attempt to print, WordPerfect creates a print job. A print job can be an entire document, a page, or a block of any size. WordPerfect keeps track of each print job by assigning a job number. Whenever you start WordPerfect, the first job you print is assigned job number 1. The job number is incremented by 1 for each subsequent print job during the same editing session.

Fig. 8.9.

*The Control
Printer screen.*

```
Print: Control Printer

Current Job

Job Number: 4                               Page Number:  3
Status:      Printing                       Current Copy: 1 of 1
Message:     None
Paper:       Standard 8.5" x 11"
Location:    Continuous feed
Action:      None


Job List

Job  Document              Destination      Print Options
 4   (Screen)              LPT 1            Graphics=High
 5   (Screen)              LPT 1            Graphics=High


Additional Jobs Not Shown: 0



1 Cancel Job(s); 2 Rush Job; 3 Display Jobs; 4 Go (start printer); 5 Stop: 0
```

Status

The status line tells you what WordPerfect is trying to do. If the job is printing normally, the message displayed is Printing. If you forgot to turn on the printer and WordPerfect cannot communicate with it, the message displayed is Trying to Print.

Paper

The paper line indicates the form and size of the paper being used for the document currently printing. If you are using standard continuous-form 8 1/2-by-11-inch paper, this setting displays Standard 8.5" × 11".

Location

The location setting indicates the location from which the paper is being fed into the printer. For standard continuous-form paper, this setting shows Continuous feed. For printers with sheet feeders, the setting may show Bin 1, Bin 2, and so on.

Message

If everything is printing normally, WordPerfect displays None on the message line. If WordPerfect is unable to communicate with the printer, the message Printer not accepting characters is displayed. As intuitive as WordPerfect is, it needs your help to solve the problem.

Page Number

WordPerfect shows the page number currently being sent to the printer. The displayed number may not be the page actually being printed. Your printer may have internal memory that can accept and store pages faster than the printer can print an individual page. WordPerfect sends the pages as fast as the printer can accept them. Thus, if the printer can store five pages, WordPerfect sends that much and indicates that the current page number is 5 even though the printer may still be printing page 1.

Current Copy

The current copy line tells you two things: the number of copies requested and which copy is currently printing.

Other Jobs Waiting To Be Printed

The center of the Control Printer screen, labeled Job List, displays information about the next three print jobs (see fig. 8.9). If more than three print jobs are pending, WordPerfect indicates the number in the message Additional Jobs Not Shown. The following sections describe each column in the Job List section of the screen.

Job

This setting is the job number assigned by WordPerfect when you submitted the print job.

Document

This item indicates the source of the document. When you print from the screen, the name (Screen) displays. If you are printing directly from a disk file, the path (either full or abbreviated) and file name are shown.

Destination

The printer port for the currently selected printer appears here. For standard parallel printers, this setting is LPT1.

Print Options

Special options selected for a print job, such as Rush, are displayed here.

The Control Printer Menu

The bottom line of the screen presents five printer control options: **C**ancel Job(s), **R**ush Job, **D**isplay Jobs, **G**o (start printer), and **S**top.

Cancel Job(s)

Select **C**ancel Job(s) (**1**) to cancel any print job. WordPerfect asks whether you want to cancel all jobs or just the current one. To cancel the current print job, simply press Enter. To cancel all print jobs, type an asterisk (*). Select **Y**es at the Cancel all print jobs? No (Yes) prompt. If the printer does not respond immediately, you may see the message Press Enter if printer doesn't respond.

Rush Job

With **R**ush Job (**2**), you can print any job immediately, no matter how far down it is in the list of jobs waiting to be printed. You can either interrupt the current print job or wait until it is finished.

If you choose to interrupt the current job, it will automatically resume printing when the rush job is done. If necessary, WordPerfect prompts you to change forms in the printer for the rush job and then to reinsert the original forms for the resumed job.

Display Jobs

Select **D**isplay Jobs (**3**) to display any additional print jobs not displayed on the Control Printer screen. That screen displays information for a maximum of three print jobs. The information displayed is the same as that for the Control Printer job list. Press any key to continue.

Go (Start Printer)

Select **G**o (start printer) (**4**) to resume printing after a form change or after suspending printing with **S**top (**5**). You also may need to send a **G**o command after canceling a print job.

Printing resumes on page 1 if the document consists of a single page, or if the print job stopped on the first page of a multipage document. Otherwise, WordPerfect asks for the page number on which you want printing to resume.

Stop

Select **S**top (**5**) to stop or suspend printing without canceling the print job. Use this option if the printer runs out of paper or jams, or if you need to replace the ribbon or otherwise intervene in the printing operation. When you have corrected the problem, select **G**o (**4**) and enter the page number where you want printing to resume.

Using the Print Menu

You have used the main Print menu (accessed by pressing Shift-F7) to select printers; print an entire document or just a page from the screen; print a document from disk; and, most important, control the printer. Some additional options located on the Print menu are also important tools in your overall management of printing activities. The options include M**u**ltiple Copies Generated by, **V**iew Document, **I**nitialize Printer, **B**inding Offset, **N**umber of Copies, **G**raphics Quality, and **T**ext Quality. You can use these additional options to manage your printing efficiently.

Multiple Copies Generated By

Some printers are capable of reprinting a job a number of times after receiving the printer information only once. If your printer has that capability, specify it here to increase print speed. If your printer does not have the capability, the setting returns to the default of WordPerfect.

To use the M**u**ltiple Copies Generated by (**U**) option, complete the following steps:

1. Press Print (Shift-F7) to display the Print menu.

    ▭ Access the **F**ile pull-down menu and select **P**rint.

2. Select M**u**ltiple Copies Generated by (**U**) and choose **P**rinter (**2**).

View Document

View Document (**6**) enables you to preview the appearance of a page before you print it. Everything that can appear on a page—including text, headers, footers, graphics, page numbers, and footnotes—is displayed exactly as it will be printed on the page within any limitations imposed by your display hardware. If, for example, your computer cannot display graphics, the View Document feature displays text only. The actual printed page, therefore, is not portrayed accurately.

Reminder:
With View Document (6), you can preview a page before you print it.

After viewing a document, press Cancel (F1) to return to the Print menu, or Exit (F7) to return to the document screen.

To view a document, complete these steps:

1. Position the cursor anywhere on the page you want to view.

2. Press Print (Shift-F7) to display the Print menu and select **V**iew Document (**6**).

    ▭ Access the **F**ile pull-down menu, select **P**rint, and choose **V**iew Document (**6**).

WordPerfect shifts your computer into graphics mode and displays on the status line the current page and the page number. To show the "bigger picture," WordPerfect offers several options to help you move in for a closer look or take a step back. These options are described in the following sections.

100% Page

Choose the 100% (**1**) option to view the page at full size (see fig. 8.10). Because most monitors cannot show an entire page at full size, you will probably see only a portion of the page. Use the cursor-movement keys to shift the image up, down, right, or left until the desired portion of the page comes into view. You should be able to read text at this size.

Fig. 8.10.

View Document at 100%.

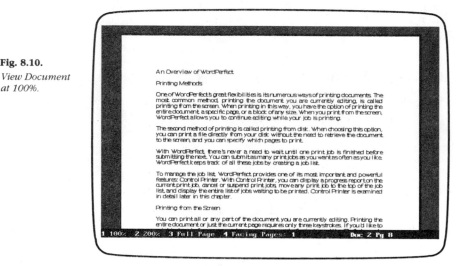

200% Page

The 200% (**2**) option displays the page at twice the normal height and width (see fig. 8.11). At this magnification, you can see only a small portion of the page, but text is clearly legible. If you are using a proportional font, WordPerfect reproduces it as faithfully as possible within the limitations of your particular hardware configuration. Use the cursor-movement keys to shift the image up, down, right, or left until the desired portion of the page comes into view.

Tip

If you press the End key, the image is shifted to the right edge of the document, on the current line. Pressing Ctrl-Home, ↑ moves the displayed image to the top of the document page. Pressing Ctrl-Home followed by ↓, →, or ← moves the image to the bottom, right, or left edge, respectively, of the document page.

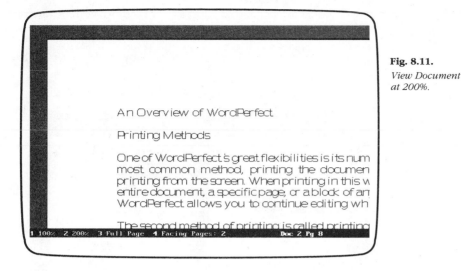

Fig. 8.11.
*View Document
at 200%.*

Full Page

Choose the Full Page (**3**) option to view the entire current page (see fig. 8.12). Text may not be readable at this size, but the layout of the page is clearly visible. Use the PgUp and PgDn keys to view the preceding or succeeding page, or use GoTo (Ctrl-Home) with a specific page number to view that page.

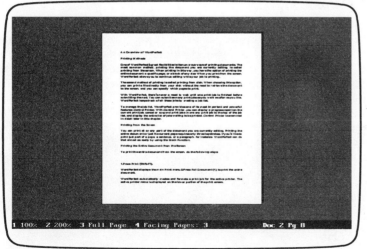

Fig. 8.12.
*View Document
with Full Page (**3**).*

Facing Pages

Select the Facing Pages (**4**) option to display the full-page images of two consecutive pages as they would appear in a book (see fig. 8.13). Note several guidelines when using this option. First, in a book, page 1 is always a right-hand page and, therefore, has no facing page. If you choose this option with the cursor on page 1, WordPerfect does not display a facing page. Second, an even-numbered page is always displayed on the left; its facing page is the next page number. For example, facing pages would be 20 and 21; they could never be 19 and 20.

Fig. 8.13.

View Document with Facing Pages (4).

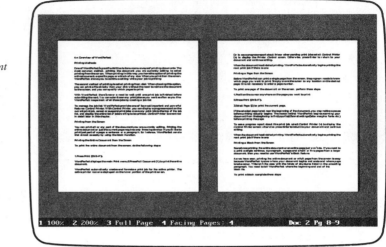

Initialize Printer

The **I**nitialize Printer (**7**) option on the Print menu *downloads* (sends) to the printer any font files you designate as `Present when print job begins` with the **C**artridges and Fonts (**4**) option on the Select Printer: Edit screen. WordPerfect looks for these files in the disk directory you specified in the Path for **D**ownloadable Fonts and Printer Command Files (**6**) option on the Select Printer: Edit screen.

> **Caution**
>
> When you select the Initialize Printer (**7**) option from the Print menu, any fonts previously downloaded to the printer are erased.

Binding Offset

Reminder:

Binding Offset provides an extra margin for binding the final copy of a document.

Select **B**inding Offset (**B**) from the Print menu to make two-sided xerographic copies of a printed document. Setting a binding width shifts odd-numbered pages to the right and even-numbered pages to the left by the indicated amount. **B**inding Offset provides an extra margin along the inside edge of the paper for binding the final copy.

To set a binding width, complete these steps:

1. Press Print (Shift-F7) to display the Print menu; select **B**inding Offset (**B**).

   ⌨ Access the **F**ile pull-down menu, select **P**rint, and select **B**inding Offset.

2. Type a binding-width value and press Enter.

The binding-width setting stays in effect until you change it again or exit WordPerfect. Once you set a binding width, every print job you create is shifted. WordPerfect does not insert a binding-width code in your document. Note that you can change this default setting through the Setup: Initial Settings menu. For more information about the Setup menu, refer to Chapter 20.

Number of Copies

If you need more than one copy of a print job, select **N**umber of Copies (**N**) from the Print menu and enter the number of copies here *before* creating the print job. WordPerfect uses the same print job over and over to print the requested number of copies. The number of copies requested remains set at the new value until you change it back to 1.

Graphics Quality

Use the **G**raphics Quality (**G**) option on the Print menu to control the degree of resolution (sharpness) that the printer uses to print graphics images. Higher-resolution images take longer to print than lower-resolution images. If the printer has trouble printing text and graphics simultaneously, select the Do **N**ot Print (**1**) option from the Graphics Quality menu to print the text first. You can then reload the paper and choose the degree of graphics quality you need for printing the graphics images.

Text Quality

The **T**ext Quality (**T**) option is identical to the **G**raphics Quality (**G**) option except that the former controls text only. If you must print text and graphics as two separate print jobs, remember to set **T**ext Quality (**T**) to Do **N**ot Print (**1**) when you want to print the graphics images.

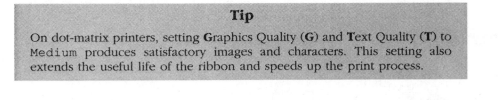

Tip

On dot-matrix printers, setting **G**raphics Quality (**G**) and **T**ext Quality (**T**) to Medium produces satisfactory images and characters. This setting also extends the useful life of the ribbon and speeds up the print process.

Printing in Color

If your printer supports color printing, use the Print Color feature to specify the color in which you want the text to print. You can change colors as often as you like.

The Print Color feature also enables you to create a color mix of your own design by adjusting the mix of component colors (red, green, and blue) that make up the color you select.

Reminder:

With the Print Color feature, you can create your own color mix for the text you want to print.

Entering Text in Color

You can specify a color for text as you type. To specify a color, complete these steps:

1. Press Font (Ctrl-F8) and select Print **C**olor (**5**).

   ⌨ Access the F**o**nt pull-down menu and select Print **C**olor.

   WordPerfect displays the Print Color screen (see fig. 8.14).

Fig. 8.14.

The Print Color screen.

```
Print Color


                             Primary Color Mixture
                            Red      Green     Blue

             1 - Black       0%       0%       0%
             2 - White      100%     100%     100%
             3 - Red        67%       0%       0%
             4 - Green       0%      67%       0%
             5 - Blue        0%       0%      67%
             6 - Yellow     67%      67%       0%
             7 - Magenta    67%       0%      67%
             8 - Cyan        0%      67%      67%
             9 - Orange     67%      25%       0%
             A - Gray       50%      50%      50%
             N - Brown      67%      33%       0%
             0 - Other

             Current Color   0%       0%       0%
```

2. Press the highlighted number or letter to select the color for the text, and press Enter to return to the text.

   WordPerfect inserts a code into the document, specifying the color name.

All text entered from this point on is printed in the color you specified. To return to normal black text, access the Font menu, choose Print **C**olor (**5**), and select Blac**k** (**1**).

You cannot use the Block feature to assign a color to a block of existing text. Instead, you must first move the cursor to where you want the color change to take place, insert a color code, move the cursor to where you want to change the color again, and insert another color code.

Creating a Custom Color

If none of the predefined colors suits your needs, you can create a custom color. To create a custom color, complete these steps:

1. Press Font (Ctrl-F8), select Print **C**olor (**5**), and choose **O**ther (**O**).

   Access the **Fo**nt pull-down menu, select Print **C**olor, and select **O**ther (**O**).

2. Enter a percentage for the red, green, and blue components.

   The percentages can (and probably will, in many cases) add up to more than 100%. Cyan, for example, is a mixture of 0% red, 67% green, and 67% blue. The percentages total more than 100% because green is contributing 67% of the total green available, and blue is doing the same.

3. Press Enter to return to the text.

   WordPerfect inserts a code into the document, specifying the red, green, and blue percentages entered.

All text that you enter from this point on is printed in your custom color. To return to normal black text, access the Font menu, choose Print **C**olor (**5**) again, and select Blac**k** (**1**).

Printing Files Created with Previous Versions of WordPerfect

Moving from version 5 and especially from version 4.2 (or any other previous version) to version 5.1 is bound to create problems, even for the most experienced user. Some common problems are discussed in the following sections.

Printing from Disk

You cannot print directly from disk any files created with previous versions of WordPerfect. If you try, WordPerfect displays the message ERROR: Incompatible file format. You must retrieve the file into WordPerfect 5.1 with Retrieve (Shift-F10) before you attempt to print. WordPerfect automatically converts the file to version 5.1 format when the file is retrieved.

Printing Version 5.1 Documents with Version 5 or 4.2

Never use an earlier version of WordPerfect to perform any operation on a file created with version 5.1. Although it is theoretically possible in some cases to use WordPerfect 5 to print a document created with WordPerfect 5.1, you may cause your computer to freeze up. You also may damage your file beyond repair. Files saved in version 5.1 contain hundreds of internal codes (for example, for new features) that previous versions cannot recognize.

If you must print a version 5.1 file in a version 5 or 4.2 environment (usually when you give the file to someone who has not yet upgraded), you *must* save the document in the appropriate format by pressing Text In/Text Out (Ctrl-F5) and then choosing **S**ave As (**3**). ▭ Or you can access the **F**ile pull-down menu and select Text **O**ut. No matter which method you use, WordPerfect presents a menu containing the options to save the document in **G**eneric (**1**), **W**ordPerfect 5.0 (**2**), or Word**P**erfect 4.2 (**3**) format.

Troubleshooting Common Printer Problems

There are so many links in the chain from creating to printing a document that it's a marvel things don't go wrong more often. WordPerfect Corporation has tried to anticipate most of the difficulties that can occur and to provide you with immediate feedback through the Control Printer screen. Unfortunately, sometimes things just seem to go wrong for no reason at all. This section presents some common printing problems and suggests possible solutions.

Be sure that you display the Control Printer screen either by pressing Print (Shift-F7) and selecting **C**ontrol Printer (**4**) or by accessing the **F**ile pull-down menu, selecting **P**rint, and selecting **C**ontrol Printer (**4**). Act on any displayed messages before attempting any of these suggestions.

Printer Does Not Print

- Make sure that the printer is plugged in and turned on.
- Make sure that the printer is on-line.
- Make sure that WordPerfect is not waiting for a **G**o (start printer) (**5**) command from the Control Printer screen.
- Make sure that the current print job (if any) has not been stopped with the **S**top (**5**) option. Check the Control Printer screen.
- Check the printer. Is it out of paper? Has the paper jammed? Is the ribbon out?
- Check all plugs and connections, including the keyboard and both ends of the printer cable.
- Make sure that you have selected the correct printer definition.
- Make sure that the printer has been defined correctly. If the printer is of the serial variety, be sure that the baud rate, parity, and start/stop bits have been entered accurately.
- Shut off the printer, wait several seconds, and then turn it back on. This clears any commands (and downloaded fonts) previously sent to the printer.
- As a last resort, save your documents, exit WordPerfect, and shut off the printer. Start everything again and try printing.

Printer Is Printing Nonsense

- Check all plugs and connections, including the keyboard and both ends of the printer cable.

- Make sure that the printer has been defined correctly. If the printer is of the serial variety, be sure that the baud rate, parity, and start/stop bits have been entered accurately.

- If the nonsense occurs at every other character, chances are that you have a serial printer and you may have entered incorrect values for the baud rate, parity, or start/stop bits. Check the printer's technical reference manual.

- Big chunks of good text followed by big chunks of nonsense characters usually indicate problems in defining a serial printer.

Summary

In this chapter, you saw that WordPerfect is equipped with a broad range of powerful tools enabling you to get the most out of your printer. To use these tools, you must first define your printer properly and then select it. Although not difficult, many steps along the way deserve careful consideration.

You also learned how to perform the following tasks:

- ❏ Print an entire document, a single page, or a block of text from the screen
- ❏ Print a document from disk
- ❏ Specify information about the current print job and about other jobs waiting to be printed
- ❏ Enter text in color and create a custom color

In addition, you worked with the Control Printer screen—WordPerfect's nerve center for managing all your printing activities—and with the main Print screen from which other printing options are accessed.

Printing with Laser Printers

Joel Shore originally cowrote this chapter for *Using WordPerfect 5*. He is president of Documentation Systems, a private consulting firm that provides micro-computer services.

Schuyler Lininger, Jr., who cowrote this chapter for *Using WordPerfect 5*, is an Oregon chiropractor and the owner of HealthNotes Publications. He uses desktop publishing to produce fliers, brochures, and newsletters for the health food industry.

Jon Pepper revised this chapter for *Using WordPerfect 5.1*, Special Edition. He is president of Words Plus, a firm that provides computer consulting services. Mr. Pepper also works as a journalist, covering the computer industry for many leading publications.

In the preceding chapter, you learned how to use WordPerfect to manage printing activities. This basic knowledge is important, whether you use a dot-matrix, daisywheel, or laser printer.

Because laser printing is different from other printing technologies however, this chapter examines additional techniques essential to using a laser printer. You learn the basic vocabulary of laser printing, examine WordPerfect's use of fonts, and investigate some problems that commonly occur when you use a laser printer. Regardless of the laser printer you own, this chapter can help you produce better documents more efficiently.

The chapter is arranged so that you can easily find the information for your particular printer. Begin, however, by reading the introductory sections through the section "Facilitating Printer Configuration." If you have a LaserJet, the next section features information specific to the LaserJet family of printers, followed by a section for PostScript users.

Reminder

If you use a mouse with WordPerfect 5.1, you can click the right button to display the pull-down menus, and then select the desired option. You also can press Alt-= to access the pull-down menus, and then press the appropriate letter of the desired option. For all the instructions, you can assume that if a block is required to activate a pull-down menu option, the text has been blocked before the pull-down menu is accessed. Instructions for pull-down menus and the mouse are marked with the mouse icon. 🖱

Learning Laser Printing Vocabulary

Because laser printers have more features than other printers, new words are needed to describe these features. To understand how the features work, you must first understand the vocabulary of laser printing.

Reminder:
Printing text with a laser printer means working with fonts.

At the heart of laser printing are fonts. Printing text with a laser printer means working with fonts. A *font* is a complete set of all characters of a single typeface in the same size, style, and weight. Consider these terms carefully, referring to the three typefaces in figure 9.1.

Fig. 9.1.
Three categories of typeface.

This is Helvetica, a sans-serif typeface. Note the straight strokes. Helvetica looks good at larger point sizes.

This is Times, a serif typeface. Note the tails on each letter. Good for body text and long stretches of smaller point sizes since it is easy to read.

This is Cloister Black. A decorative typeface and not easy to read. It should be used only for impact.

- *Typeface* refers to the overall artistic design of the character set or to a style of type. In figure 9.1, the typefaces are Helvetica, Times, and Cloister Black. The three basic typeface categories are *serif*, which has fine lines that finish off the main strokes (Times); *sans-serif*, which has only straight strokes (Helvetica); and *decorative* type, which has a special look (Cloister Black).
- *Font* refers to a set of characters with a specific typeface, point size, and weight. For example, *10-point Times* constitutes a font. Using Font (Ctrl-F8), you can change the **S**ize (**1**) and **A**ppearance (**2**) of a font. In WordPerfect documentation, "font" is used inexactly—sometimes when "typeface" is more accurate. WordPerfect relies heavily on the use and management of fonts to vary the appearance of text on a laser printer. After you learn to work with fonts, you will find that printing with a laser printer is no more difficult than printing with a dot-matrix or daisywheel printer.
- *Style* tells you whether the font is upright (Roman) or slanted (italic).
- *Size*, measured in points, determines the nominal character height. There are 72 points to an inch; therefore, 10 points equal approximately 0.14 inches.

Most text in books is set in 10-point type. In WordPerfect, seven different point sizes are predefined through the Size menu, which you access by pressing Font (Ctrl-F8) and selecting **S**ize (**1**). The sizes available are superscript, subscript, fine, small, large, very large, and extra large. (These options are available also through the F**o**nt pull-down menu.) How these sizes correlate to specific point sizes is discussed later. Examples of different point sizes are shown in figure 9.2. Note that the point sizes shown are slightly smaller than the actual sizes.

Reminder:
Seven point sizes are available through the Font menu.

This is 8 point type. It is hard to read.

This is 10 point type. Good for body text.

This is 12 point type. Good for body text.

This is 14 point type. Good for subheads.

This is 18 point type. Good for subheads and some heads.

This is 24 point type. Good for headlines.

This is 36 point type. Good for mastheads.

This is 72 pts.

Fig. 9.2.
Helvetica typeface at different point sizes.

- *Weight* refers to thickness of characters, such as light, normal, or bold. In WordPerfect, you choose weights by pressing Font (Ctrl-F8) and selecting **A**ppearance (**2**). In addition to bold and italic, you can select underline, double underline, outline, shadow, small capitals, redline, and strikeout. Chapter 5 contains more about these features.

Rember:
Single-key commands, such as F6 for Bold and F8 for Underline, still work in WordPerfect 5.1.

- *Spacing,* either fixed or proportional, indicates whether all characters in the font are of equal width. Typewriter-like fonts such as Courier or Prestige use *fixed spacing,* where every character is exactly the same width. *Proportional* fonts, however, vary the width of every character; an *i* or *l* requires much less space than a *W* or *M.* See examples of fixed and proportional spacing in figure 9.3.

Fig. 9.3.

Examples of character spacing.

> This is a fixed-space typeface (Courier).
>
> This is a proportionally spaced typeface (Times).

- *Pitch* specifies the number of characters that can fit in one horizontal inch. Courier is normally printed at 10 pitch, and Prestige Elite is normally printed at 12 pitch. Pitch is never specified with proportional fonts.

- *Portrait* and *landscape* describe the orientation of the paper. Normal text is printed in portrait mode, where an 8 1/2-by-11-inch paper prints vertically. In landscape mode, the paper prints horizontally, like an artist's rendering of a landscape. Portrait mode is the most common orientation, but landscape mode is often used for printing lengthy, multiple-column charts and spreadsheets.

- *Symbol set* describes the collection of characters in a font. The Roman-8 symbol set includes many characters used in foreign languages, such as the following:

    ç, ü, é, â, and ñ

    The IBM-US symbol set includes all characters that can be displayed on an IBM Personal Computer.

Comparing LaserJet and PostScript Printers

Two general kinds of laser printers are available: the Hewlett-Packard LaserJet family and its compatibles, and PostScript printers. These two kinds of printers differ chiefly in the way they regard a page. The LaserJet printers handle a page as an assortment of characters, whether the page contains text, graphics, or a combination of text and graphics. The PostScript printers, however, operate with a *page description language* (PDL) that treats a page as a picture or a graphic, rather than as a collection of characters.

Reminder:

Two kinds of laser printers are available: the Hewlett-Packard LaserJet family and compatibles, and PostScript printers.

What are the implications of these differences? With a character-based printer like the LaserJet, all fonts must be available at the time of printing. In addition to using the LaserJet's built-in type fonts, you can add additional typefaces either with a *cartridge* (which fits into a slot on the printer) or with *soft fonts* (which are downloaded by WordPerfect to the printer at the time of printing). A PostScript printer can use a mathematical model or outline of a typeface to create type in any point size. Instead of storing each point size in a cartridge or on disk, PostScript printers require only a single outline for each typeface and weight.

You will find information about each kind of laser printer in this chapter. But before examining each specific kind of printer, you need to know generally how to use WordPerfect with laser printers.

Note: In the procedures in this chapter, the Hewlett-Packard LaserJet Series II has been used in demonstrating WordPerfect's laser printing capabilities. These references to the LaserJet (as a standard non-PostScript laser printer) do not imply a recommendation or an endorsement; they merely reflect the popularity of the LaserJet family of printers.

Surveying Improvements in WordPerfect 5.1 for Laser Printers

WordPerfect 5.1 adds two significant laser printing improvements. First, fonts are grouped in *libraries*, or collections of fonts. Second, multiple copies of documents can be generated by either WordPerfect (as was the case with version 5) or the printer.

Cue:
You will see font libraries only if they are supported by your printer. For example, daisywheel printers do not support font libraries.

A font library, such as the AC HELV/TMS Roman soft font set, makes it easier for you to select and sort the fonts you want to use. In version 5.1, built-in fonts are shown as a category, along with cartridges and soft fonts, on the Cartridges and Fonts menu. You can access that menu by pressing Print (Shift-F7), choosing **S**elect Printer (**S**), selecting **E**dit (**3**), and selecting **C**artridges and Fonts (**4**). ⌨ An alternative method of displaying the Print menu is to access the **F**ile pull-down menu and select **P**rint.

With WordPerfect 5.1, generating multiple copies by printer is much faster than having WordPerfect redownload fonts and plot graphics for each copy. Because the pages are stacked rather than collated through the M**u**ltiple Copies Generated by option (on the Print menu), the option is best used for single-page or relatively short documents that you don't mind collating by hand.

Advanced printer features are available through Format (Shift-F8). These features include kerning, sending commands to the printer (either from a command line or a file), word and letter spacing, baseline placement for typesetters, and leading adjustment. For more information about the advanced printer features, see Chapter 5.

Configuring WordPerfect To Work with Your Laser Printer

The WordPerfect configuration procedure is identical for both kinds of laser printers. You must first define your printer, which is explained in the preceding chapter. You must then select the fonts you want to use in normal printing. After this initial setup is completed, you can invoke many options during normal editing. Font selection is covered next.

Note: If you have a Hewlett-Packard LaserJet printer, you must also select either a font cartridge or specific soft fonts before you can select printer fonts. (This is not necessary for PostScript printers.) Refer to the later section "Using WordPerfect with LaserJet Printers" for instructions concerning hard and soft fonts on a LaserJet.

> **Tip**
>
> Each typeface has its own personality. The personalities of typefaces can interact on the page—with certain consequences for the reader. An error that beginners often make is to use too many fonts on one page. Experienced typesetters agree that many different fonts, point sizes, and weights on a single page obscure rather than facilitate communication.

Setting the Initial Font

Once your printer has been installed, and—on the LaserJet—you have selected the appropriate soft or hard fonts, you must assign the initial font for the printer. This process is identical for both LaserJet and PostScript printers.

The initial font, also called the *base font* on the Font (Ctrl-F8) menu, is the font in which ordinary text is printed and by which font sizes and attributes are defined. If, for example, you specify Times Roman 10-point as the initial font, selecting **L**arge (**5**) from the Font menu automatically prints in the next largest Times font available. Choosing **V**ry Large (**6**) prints in the second largest size, and so on.

Any font from either the Initial Font or Base Font list can serve as the base font (the default font). Remember that if you change the base font in the middle of a document, you see font changes displayed in the text only after the point of change. If you intend to change the base font for an entire document, first press Home, Home, ↑ to move the cursor to the beginning of the document.

> **Tip**
>
> After you move the cursor to the top of the document, if you want to return the cursor to its previous location, press GoTo (Ctrl-Home) twice.

To change the initial font permanently, follow these steps:

1. Press Print (Shift-F7) to display the Print menu, and choose **S**elect Printer (**S**).

   ▢ Access the **F**ile pull-down menu, select **P**rint, and choose **S**elect Printer (**S**).

2. From the Select Printer menu, choose **E**dit (**3**) and select **I**nitial Base Font (**5**).

3. Using the arrow keys, move the highlight bar to your choice of initial font and choose **S**elect (**1**) to select the initial font. (If you have a PostScript printer, you see the `Point size:` prompt. Type a number and press Enter.)

4. Press Exit (F7) three times to return to the document.

A base font of either 10 or 12 points is easiest on the eyes. Fonts smaller than 10 points are hard to read; fonts larger than 12 points are useful for headings but not ordinary business text.

Choosing a serif typeface (like Times) or a sans-serif typeface (like Helvetica) is a matter of personal taste. Because serif fonts are easier to read for long stretches, serif is usually a good choice for body text. Notice that most newspapers and magazines use serif type. (Times type was developed for the London *Times* itself.) Sans-serif looks best in larger point sizes (notice street and traffic signs).

You can change the initial font for a document without making a permanent change. To make an initial font change for the document you are currently editing, follow these steps:

1. Press Format (Shift-F8) to display the Format menu, and choose **D**ocument (**3**).

    ⌨ Access the **L**ayout pull-down menu and select **D**ocument.

2. Choose Initial **F**ont (**3**).

3. Using the arrow keys, move the highlight bar to your choice of initial font and choose **S**elect (**1**) to select the initial font. (If you have a PostScript printer, you see the `Point size:` prompt. Type a number and press Enter.)

4. Press Exit (F7) to return to the document.

Selecting Fonts by Size

WordPerfect provides two ways to change fonts: by size and by name. When you select fonts by size, WordPerfect's printer intelligence enables someone else to print your document even without the same fonts or printer. Because fonts are specified by size (such as large) or appearance (such as italic), WordPerfect can formulate a best guess, no matter what kind of printer you use.

Reminder:
With WordPerfect, you can change fonts either by size or by name.

Font attributes like *large* and *italic* may or may not appear on-screen. Depending on your monitor type, different attributes are visible in either edit mode or View Document mode. Refer to Chapter 5 for more information.

Complete the following steps to select typeface size:

1. Press Font (Ctrl-F8) and select **S**ize (**1**) from the menu at the bottom of the screen.

    ⌨ Access the **F**ont pull-down menu.

2. Select the typeface size you want from the choices presented: Su**p**erscript (**1**), Su**b**script (**2**), **F**ine (**3**), **S**mall (**4**), **L**arge (**5**), **V**ery Large (**6**), and **E**xtra Large (**7**).

When you alter the size, the `Pos` (Position) indicator in the lower right portion of the screen shows your choice. (What the `Pos` indicator and text size look like on-screen depends on what kind of monitor and display card you have. Both the `Pos` indicator and the text look the same.) WordPerfect automatically tracks the vertical height of the larger or smaller letters and adjusts margins and number of lines per page.

With PostScript printers, the base font is scaled larger or smaller by a certain percentage (see fig. 9.4). For example, you must experiment to determine just how much bigger "extra large" makes a 14-point base font. You can maintain more control by changing the base font and entering an exact point size instead of relying on relative scaling from the Size menu. Although WordPerfect has certain default percentages, you can alter them through the Setup: Initial Settings menu. For more information about the Setup menu, refer to Chapter 20.

Fig. 9.4.
Changing point size.

fine-6 pts small-8 pts no change-12 pts large-14 pts

very large-22 pts

extra large-30 pts

Selecting Fonts by Name

Changing fonts by name gives you more control over fonts. To change fonts by name, follow these steps:

1. Press Font (Ctrl-F8) and select Base **F**ont (**4**).

   ⌨ Access the F**o**nt pull-down menu and select Base F**o**nt.

   WordPerfect displays the Base Font screen (see fig. 9.5), listing all fonts defined for the printer.

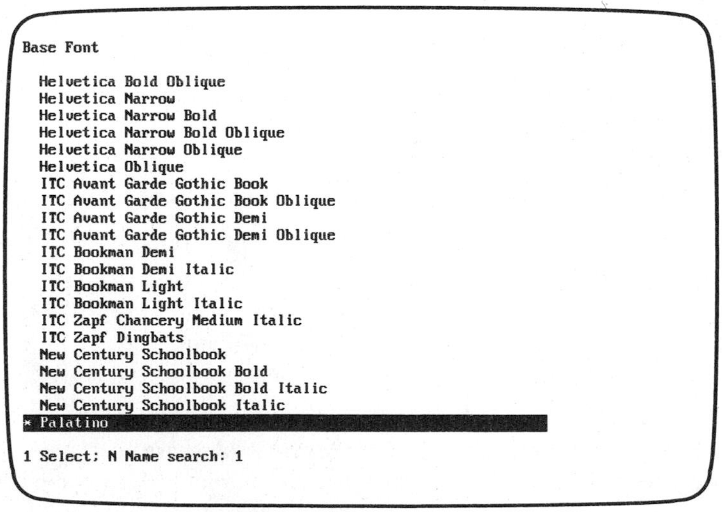

Fig. 9.5.
The Base Font screen.

```
Base Font

    Helvetica Bold Oblique
    Helvetica Narrow
    Helvetica Narrow Bold
    Helvetica Narrow Bold Oblique
    Helvetica Narrow Oblique
    Helvetica Oblique
    ITC Avant Garde Gothic Book
    ITC Avant Garde Gothic Book Oblique
    ITC Avant Garde Gothic Demi
    ITC Avant Garde Gothic Demi Oblique
    ITC Bookman Demi
    ITC Bookman Demi Italic
    ITC Bookman Light
    ITC Bookman Light Italic
    ITC Zapf Chancery Medium Italic
    ITC Zapf Dingbats
    New Century Schoolbook
    New Century Schoolbook Bold
    New Century Schoolbook Bold Italic
    New Century Schoolbook Italic
  * Palatino

1 Select; N Name search: 1
```

2. Move the highlight bar to the font you want. Press Enter to select the font and return to the document.

   Note: With PostScript printers, you see the Point size: prompt. You must then enter any point size from 0.1 to as large a point size as the page can hold. Point sizes can be entered with up to two decimal places.

3. If you press Reveal Codes (Alt-F3 or F11), you can see that WordPerfect inserts a font-change code that identifies the new font by name (see fig. 9.6).

```
than printing with your dot-matrix or daisywheel printer.

Style tells you whether the font is upright (Roman) or slanted (italic).

Size, measured in points, determines the nominal character height. There are 72
to an inch; therefore, 10 points equal approximately 0.14 inches.

Most text in books is set in 10-point type. In WordPerfect, seven different
point sizes are predefined in the Size (1) submenu of Font (Ctrl-F8). These
sizes are superscript, subscript, fine, small, large, very large, and extra larg
How these sizes correlate to specific point sizes is discussed later. You can
D:\WORD50\DATA\9.TXT                          Doc 2 Pg 2 Ln 3.77" Pos 1"
[        ▲   ▲    ▲   ▲     ▲     ▲    ▲     ▲    ▲    ▲     }    ▲     ▲
[HRt]
[Font:Palatino 14pt]Most text in books is set in 10-point type. In WordPerfect,
seven different[SRt]
point sizes are predefined in the Size (1) submenu of Font (Ctrl-F8). These[SRt]

■izes are superscript, subscript, fine, small, large, very large, and extra larg
e.[SRt]
How these sizes correlate to specific point sizes is discussed later. You can[SR
t]
see examples of different point size in[SRt]

Press Reveal Codes to restore screen
```

Fig. 9.6.
Reveal Codes showing the font change by name.

All text following this code prints in the new font. To return to the original base font, perform this process again. You cannot choose the **N**ormal (**3**) option through Font (Ctrl-F8) to return to the original font, because you have explicitly changed the base font. This method works well as long as the specified font exists and is available when the document is printed. If, however, another printer is used or some fonts are unavailable, WordPerfect substitutes available fonts. These substitutions may make your final document printout look different from the one you planned.

Changing Typeface Appearance

Change the appearance of a typeface by following these steps:

1. Press Font (Ctrl-F8) and select **A**ppearance (**2**) from the menu bar that appears at the bottom of the screen.

   ⌨ Access the **Fo**nt pull-down menu and select **A**ppearance.

2. Select the typeface modification you want from the choices presented: **B**old (**1**), **U**nderline (**2**), **D**ouble Underline (**3**), **I**talic (**4**), **O**utline (**5**), S**h**adow (**6**), Small **C**ap (**7**), **R**edline (**8**), and **S**trikeout (**9**).

To see how each appearance affects output, print out the PRINTER.TST file, located in your WordPerfect directory. Figure 9.7 shows various appearances.

When you select an attribute, depending on your monitor, the text and the Pos indicator in the lower right portion of the screen show your choice.

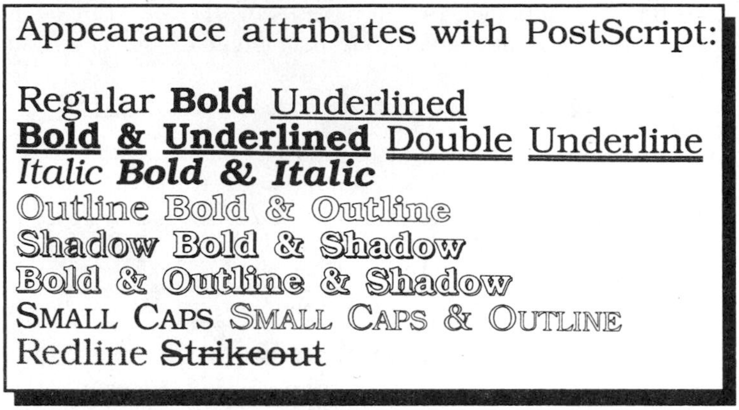

Fig. 9.7.

Appearance attributes (with a PostScript printer).

Appearance attributes with PostScript:

Regular **Bold** Underlined
Bold & Underlined Double Underline
Italic ***Bold & Italic***
Outline Bold & Outline
Shadow Bold & Shadow
Bold & Outline & Shadow
Small Caps Small Caps & Outline
Redline ~~Strikeout~~

Facilitating Printer Configuration

To help you use different base fonts for different documents or change the printer port easily, you may want to have the same printer configured several different ways. Rather than change the configurations each time, you can copy the definition, make changes, and save them under a new name. To reconfigure your printer, follow these steps:

1. Press Print (Shift-F7) to display the Print menu, and choose **S**elect Printer (**S**) to display the Select Printer screen.

   ▭ Access the **F**ile pull-down menu, select **P**rint, and choose **S**elect Printer (**S**).

2. Highlight the printer for which you want an alternative configuration and select **C**opy (**4**) from the menu at the bottom of the screen. After the Printer Helps and Hints screen appears, press Exit (F7).

3. Select **N**ame (**1**) and type a new name for the printer; use a name that describes the new default font or printer port (for example, type *Palatino 10-pt* or *LaserWriter COM 2*).

Reminder:

You can maintain several printer definitions and select the one you want with a simple command.

Now you can select a different printer configuration with a simple command. You no longer need to reconfigure your printer for different uses. If you configure your printer for more than one use, you can, for example, easily print the two reports in figures 9.8 and 9.9, each of which has a different typeface.

Tip

PostScript files are *device-independent*. This means that a document can be printed to disk and that the file can be output on any PostScript device including a Linotronic, which will print the document in typeset quality. Many service bureaus around the country offer this service for a nominal per-page charge.

1. HISTORY AND EXAMINATION
On June 19, 1987 at approximately 3 pm, Mr. Williams was involved in a vehicular accident at Highway 26 and 362nd in Sandy, Oregon. As reported by Mr. Williams:

Stopping to let vehicle #3 turn left, I was immediately struck by a 2 ton truck, vehicle #2. The impact pushed my vehicle #1 into vehicle #3 causing extensive damage to latter vehicle. My head lurched forward, then whipped back. The glass in the cab of vehicle #1 shattered.

Mr. Williams reported neck and sore throat pain immediately after the accident. This pain made work difficult. He denies any pain prior to the accident and has not been in previous accidents of this sort since he had a resolved whiplash injury in 1978.

Mr. Williams is a pleasant and cooperative 39 year old man weighing 190 pounds and standing 6'1". He was examined in my office on January 10, 1988. Cervical range of motion was reduced to 60 from 70 degrees in both left and right rotation. Left lateral flexion was reduced from 40 to 30 degrees and right lateral flexion was only 25 degrees. Flexion and extension were normal. All restricted ranges were painful.

Fig. 9.8.

A report in Helvetica typeface printed with a PostScript printer.

1. HISTORY AND EXAMINATION
On June 19, 1987 at approximately 3 pm, Mr. Williams was involved in a vehicular accident at Highway 26 and 362nd in Sandy, Oregon. As reported by Mr. Williams:

Stopping to let vehicle #3 turn left, I was immediately struck by a 2 ton truck, vehicle #2. The impact pushed my vehicle #1 into vehicle #3 causing extensive damage to latter vehicle. My head lurched forward, then whipped back. The glass in the cab of vehicle #1 shattered.

Mr. Williams reported neck and sore throat pain immediately after the accident. This pain made work difficult. He denies any pain prior to the accident and has not been in previous accidents of this sort since he had a resolved whiplash injury in 1978.

Mr. Williams is a pleasant and cooperative 39 year old man weighing 190 pounds and standing 6'1". He was examined in my office on January 10, 1988. Cervical range of motion was reduced to 60 from 70 degrees in both left and right rotation. Left lateral flexion was reduced from 40 to 30 degrees and right lateral flexion was only 25 degrees. Flexion and extension were normal. All restricted ranges were painful.

Fig. 9.9.

A report in Times typeface printed with a PostScript printer.

If your system is capable (a Hercules, CGA, EGA, or VGA video adapter and compatible monitor are required), WordPerfect enables you to preview a document before printing. You use the **V**iew Document (**6**) option on the Print menu. To preview a document, follow these steps:

Reminder:

Use the View Document feature to preview a document before printing.

1. Press Print (Shift-F7) to display the Print menu, and choose **V**iew Document (**6**).

   ⌨ Access the **F**ile pull-down menu, select **P**rint, and choose **V**iew Document (**6**).

   You see a graphics representation of the page. Use PgUp, PgDn, and GoTo (Ctrl-Home) to view different pages.

2. Press Exit (F7) to return to the editing screen; press the space bar to return to the Print menu.

Using WordPerfect with LaserJet Printers

Hewlett-Packard LaserJet printers differ from some other laser printers in that the fonts used in printing can come from up to three sources: internal fonts, cartridge fonts, and soft fonts. Built-in fonts appear in the Cartridges and Fonts menu and

Reminder:

With LaserJet printers, you can use internal fonts, cartridge fonts, and soft fonts.

may be deselected there. WordPerfect must be made aware of any cartridge fonts or soft fonts you may be using. This section discusses the three types of LaserJet fonts and shows you how to set up WordPerfect for LaserJet use.

Considering Internal Fonts

Internal fonts are easiest to work with. Built into the printer by the manufacturer, they are always available. Table 9.1 lists the internal fonts in the LaserJet Series II. If, for some reason, you do not want built-in fonts to be available to WordPerfect, you can deselect them through the Cartridges and Fonts menu. Follow these steps:

1. Press Print (Shift-F7) and choose **S**elect Printer (**S**).

   ▭ Access the **F**ile pull-down menu, select **P**rint, and choose **S**elect Printer (**S**).

2. Select **E**dit (**3**), select **C**artridges and Fonts (**4**), and choose **S**elect (**1**) to select built-in fonts.

3. For built-in fonts that you do not want to be available, press the asterisk (*) key to deselect them.

4. Press Exit (F7) five times to return to the editing screen.

Table 9.1
LaserJet Series II Internal Fonts

Typeface	Weight	Spacing	Pitch	Point Size	Style	Symbol Set	Orientation
Courier	Medium	Fixed	10	12	Upright	Roman-8	Portrait
Courier	Medium	Fixed	10	12	Upright	Roman-8	Landscape
Courier	Medium	Fixed	10	12	Upright	IBM-US	Portrait
Courier	Medium	Fixed	10	12	Upright	IBM-US	Landscape
Courier	Bold	Fixed	10	12	Upright	Roman-8	Portrait
Courier	Bold	Fixed	10	12	Upright	Roman-8	Landscape
Courier	Bold	Fixed	10	12	Upright	IBM-US	Portrait
Courier	Bold	Fixed	10	12	Upright	IBM-US	Landscape
LPC*	Medium	Fixed	16.66	8.5	Upright	Roman-8	Portrait
LPC	Medium	Fixed	16.66	8.5	Upright	Roman-8	Landscape
LPC	Medium	Fixed	16.66	8.5	Upright	IBM-US	Portrait
LPC	Medium	Fixed	16.66	8.5	Upright	IBM-US	Landscape

*Line Printer Compressed

Considering Cartridge Fonts

Cartridge fonts (sometimes called *hard fonts*) are available from Hewlett-Packard and third-party manufacturers. From three to over a hundred fonts are contained in a cartridge that fits a slot in the printer, normally in the front. An important advantage of cartridge fonts is that they do not use any LaserJet internal memory.

The cartridges currently available from Hewlett-Packard include special fonts to print Internal Revenue Service tax forms, supermarket-style UPC (universal product code) bar codes, and machine-readable OCR (optical character recognition) text.

Considering Soft Fonts

Soft fonts are files stored on disk and *downloaded* (sent), as needed, from the computer to the laser printer's internal memory. Because these fonts are stored in the printer's internal memory, they reduce the memory available for graphics and for storing pages to print.

Reminder:
Soft font are stored on disk and downloaded to the laser printer's internal memory.

Thousands of soft fonts are available from a wide variety of manufacturers. Because soft fonts are inexpensive to manufacture, their prices are relatively low. If you cannot find a font to fit your needs, you can buy software to design your own. If the graphic artist in you is yearning for expression, creating your own soft font is the answer.

Choosing between Cartridges and Soft Fonts

Choosing between cartridges and soft fonts for a LaserJet is not an easy task. Fortunately, with many laser printers, you can use both types simultaneously. The LaserJet Series II, for example, is equipped with two slots for cartridge fonts and has internal memory for storing soft fonts. Still, you should understand the differences between the two LaserJet printing strategies.

Cartridge fonts offer the following advantages:

- Available as soon as you plug them in—without downloading. You must, however, reset the printer either with the front panel buttons or by powering down and backing up when changing or loading cartridges.

- Completely self-contained and do not use internal memory.

- Easily and quickly installed. Selection, however, is more limited than for soft fonts, and prices can be higher, depending on the cartridge you are considering.

Soft fonts offer these advantages:

- Less expensive than hardware-based cartridges.

- Widely available. You can find a large selection of typefaces from many manufacturers.

- Versatile. You can mix and match soft fonts, downloading only those you need and designing your own fonts with available software. (Keep in mind that soft fonts use valuable internal memory and must be stored on a hard disk for maximum efficiency.)

Developing a Font Strategy

Many people combine cartridge and soft fonts. This technique balances the cost of fonts against memory use, and ease of use against the need to download. Table 9.2 summarizes a mix of fonts commonly used in a business environment.

Table 9.2
Sample Font Strategies

Typefaces	Type	Remarks
Courier	Internal	Always available, good for typewriter-like output.
Line Printer	Internal	Always available, good for spreadsheets.
Prestige Elite	Cartridge G	Saves memory, good for executive correspondence, includes line-drawing characters.
Times and Helvetica	Cartridge Z1A	Saves memory; normal point sizes and styles are adequate for most standard office work.
Times and Helvetica	Soft AD Set	Excellent supplement to Z cartridge; includes a broad range of larger and smaller sizes; download only what you need for a given job.

You do not need to limit your library of soft fonts to the AD set. Hewlett-Packard distributes several handsome text-font families, including ITC Garamond, Century Schoolbook, and Zapf Humanist 601; and headline typefaces, including Broadway, Coronet Bold, Cooper Black, University Roman, Bauer, Bodoni, and Black Condensed. Furthermore, over a hundred independent manufacturers market thousands of different fonts licensed from type foundries worldwide. Whatever your needs, you should be able to find a font to satisfy them.

Installing Fonts for LaserJet Printers

To install fonts on the LaserJet II printer, you use different techniques, depending on the font installed. These same procedures can be used for the older Hewlett-Packard LaserJet and LaserJet+, except that soft fonts cannot be used with the original LaserJet. (They can be used with the LaserJet+, however.)

Installing Cartridge Fonts

Few things in life are easier than installing a cartridge font. Follow these steps:

1. Take the printer off-line by pressing the On-Line button on the printer's control panel. Make sure that the On-Line light goes off after you press the button.

2. Insert the cartridge all the way. Make sure that the label is facing up and double-check that the cartridge is inserted all the way.

3. Press the Continue/Reset button until *Reset* shows in the window. (The printer will return to on-line and ready status when you release the button.) Or turn the printer off and then back on.

You learn how to tell WordPerfect to use the font cartridge later in this chapter.

Installing Soft Fonts

Because so many companies make soft fonts for the LaserJet, this chapter cannot cover all the different installation procedures. The process is usually quite simple, however. To install the fonts, just follow the directions that come with the soft fonts you purchase. Then read the section "Setting Up Soft Fonts" to let WordPerfect know that you have soft fonts available for your LaserJet or compatible printer.

Installing Bitstream

The WordPerfect package contains information about ordering a Bitstream Installation Kit for use with WordPerfect. Included with the kit are four Swiss typefaces (Bitstream's version of Helvetica); four Dutch typefaces (Bitstream's version of Times Roman); and the Upright, Medium weight of Bitstream Charter (other styles and weights of Bitstream Charter are for sale). Bitstream Fontware works with PostScript-compatible printers or Hewlett-Packard LaserJet-compatible printers. You can purchase the kit from WordPerfect.

Note: Bitstream Fontware does not work with dot-matrix printers, non-LaserJet-compatible printers, or non-PostScript-compatible printers. The one exception is the HP DeskJet, an inkjet printer that *is* supported.

Setting Up Fonts for LaserJet Printers

Once you have installed the fonts, you need to tell WordPerfect which fonts you will be using. The procedure varies, depending on whether you are using cartridge fonts or soft fonts.

Setting Up Cartridge Fonts

To indicate to your LaserJet which cartridges you will be using, follow these steps:

1. Press Print (Shift-F7) to display the Print menu (see fig. 9.10), and choose **S**elect Printer (**S**) to display the Print: Select Printer screen (see fig. 9.11).

    ▭ Access the **F**ile pull-down menu, select **P**rint, and choose **S**elect Printer (**S**).

2. Move the highlight bar to the appropriate printer and select **E**dit (**3**) to display the Select Printer: Edit screen (see fig. 9.12).

```
Print

     1 - Full Document
     2 - Page
     3 - Document on Disk
     4 - Control Printer
     5 - Multiple Pages
     6 - View Document
     7 - Initialize Printer

Options

     S - Select Printer            HP LaserJet Series II
     B - Binding Offset            0"
     N - Number of Copies          1
     U - Multiple Copies Generated by  WordPerfect
     G - Graphics Quality          High
     T - Text Quality              High
```

Fig. 9.10.
The Print menu.

```
Print: Select Printer

     Apple LaserWriter Plus
   ▶ HP LaserJet Series II
     NEC Silentwriter LC-890




















   1 Select; 2 Additional Printers; 3 Edit; 4 Copy; 5 Delete; 6 Help; 7 Update: 1
```

Fig. 9.11.
The Print: Select Printer screen.

```
Select Printer: Edit

            Filename              HPLASEII.PRS

     1 - Name                     HP LaserJet Series II

     2 - Port                     LPT1:

     3 - Sheet Feeder             None

     4 - Cartridges and Fonts

     5 - Initial Base Font        TmsRmn 12pt (Z1A)

     6 - Path for Downloadable
         Fonts and Printer
         Command Files
```

Fig. 9.12.
The Select Printer: Edit screen.

Reminder:

For a LaserJet Series II printer, you can specify two cartridges simultaneously—one for each cartridge slot.

3. Select **C**artridges and Fonts (**4**) to display the Select Printer: Cartridges and Fonts screen (see fig. 9.13).

For a LaserJet Series II printer, WordPerfect lets you specify two cartridges simultaneously because the printer is equipped with two cartridge slots.

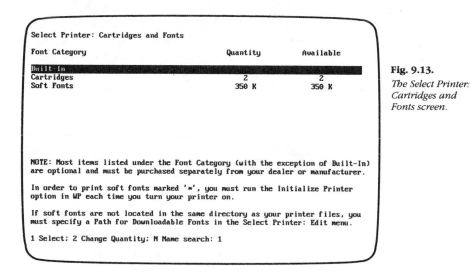

Fig. 9.13.

The Select Printer: Cartridges and Fonts screen.

4. Highlight `Cartridges` and choose **S**elect (**1**). WordPerfect displays a list of the font cartridges currently available from Hewlett-Packard and other manufacturers, depending on the printer version installed (see fig. 9.14).

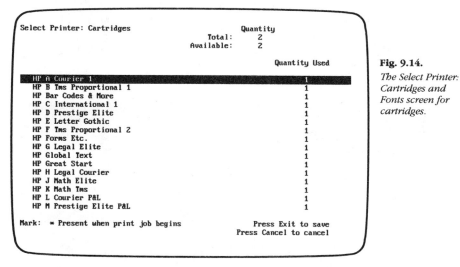

Fig. 9.14.

The Select Printer: Cartridges and Fonts screen for cartridges.

5. Move the highlight bar to the cartridge(s) you want, press the asterisk (*) key to select the cartridge, and press Exit (F7) to complete the selection process.

Because you cannot change cartridges during a print job, your only choice is * Present when print job begins.

The top right corner of the screen tells you how many slots the printer has and how many you used.

Setting Up Soft Fonts

As with cartridge fonts, you must inform WordPerfect about the various soft fonts you intend to use with your LaserJet. To select soft fonts, follow these steps:

1. Press Print (Shift-F7) to display the Print menu, and choose **S**elect Printer (**S**) to display the Select Printer screen.

    ⌨ Access the **F**ile pull-down menu, select **P**rint, and choose **S**elect Printer (**S**).

2. Move the highlight bar to the appropriate printer, select **E**dit (**3**) to display the Select Printer: Edit screen, and choose **C**artridges and Fonts (**4**) to display the Select Printer: Cartridges and Fonts screen.

Reminder:

If you have added memory to your LaserJet, you can increase the amount of printer memory available for storing soft fonts.

3. WordPerfect says that for the LaserJet Series II, 350K of printer memory is available for storing soft fonts. If you added memory to your LaserJet, you can change this amount by pressing Change **Q**uantity (**2**) and entering the new amount. Any soft fonts currently marked as with an * (Present when print job begins) will reduce the available memory.

4. Highlight Soft Fonts and choose **S**elect (**1**).

    WordPerfect displays a list of the font libraries that are installed or currently available from Hewlett-Packard. Note that this is a new feature with version 5.1. Instead of showing all the soft fonts, WordPerfect groups them by families to make it easier for you to select fonts (see fig. 9.15). For this example, highlight the AC TmsRmn/Helv US family and choose **S**elect (**1**).

Fig. 9.15.

The Select Printer: Cartridges and Fonts screen for font groups.

```
Select Printer: Soft Fonts

Font Groups:

 HP AC TmsRmn/Helv US
 HP AD TmsRmn/Helv R8
 HP AE TmsRmn/Helv US
 HP AF TmsRmn/Helv R8
 HP AG Helv Headlines PC-8










 1 Select; N Name search: 1
```

5. You will now see a list of all the fonts in that font family (see fig. 9.16). Move the highlight bar to the soft fonts you want, and press either * (Present when print job begins) or + (Can be loaded/ unloaded during job) to select. Then press Exit (F7) to complete the selection process.

```
 Select Printer: Soft Fonts                    Quantity    * Fonts
                                       Total:    350 K        32
                                   Available:    350 K        32

 HP AC TmsRmn/Helv US                                Quantity Used

   (AC) Helv  6pt                                         8 K
   (AC) Helv  6pt (Land)                                  8 K
   (AC) Helv  6pt Bold                                    8 K
   (AC) Helv  6pt Bold (Land)                             8 K
   (AC) Helv  6pt Italic                                  8 K
   (AC) Helv  6pt Italic (Land)                           8 K
   (AC) Helv  8pt                                         9 K
   (AC) Helv  8pt (Land)                                  9 K
   (AC) Helv  8pt Bold                                   11 K
   (AC) Helv  8pt Bold (Land)                            11 K
   (AC) Helv  8pt Italic                                 10 K
   (AC) Helv  8pt Italic (Land)                          10 K
   (AC) Helv 10pt                                        13 K
   (AC) Helv 10pt (Land)                                 13 K
   (AC) Helv 10pt Bold                                   13 K
   (AC) Helv 10pt Bold (Land)                            13 K

 Mark:  * Present when print job begins         Press Exit to save
        + Can be loaded/unloaded during job     Press Cancel to cancel
```

Fig. 9.16.

The Select Printer: Cartridges and Fonts screen for soft fonts.

Soft fonts are downloaded to the LaserJet either before or during the print job, depending on how you have marked them.

Select * Present when print job begins for fonts you use frequently. WordPerfect assumes that fonts marked with an asterisk (*) are present in the printer when the print job begins. This means that you must select **I**nitialize Printer (**7**) from the Print menu to instruct WordPerfect to download them to your printer before starting the first print job of a WordPerfect session.

The top right corner of the screen tells you how much total printer memory is designated as available for soft fonts, and how much of that memory remains available after downloading the soft fonts currently marked with an *.

Select + Can be loaded/unloaded during job for fonts you use less frequently. WordPerfect downloads these fonts "on the fly" when they are called for in a document you are printing.

Reminder:

Fonts you use only occasionally should be marked with a plus sign (+).

After you have marked all the fonts with either * or +, you must tell WordPerfect where to find the soft fonts. If you press Exit (F7) three times, you return to the Select Printer: Edit screen (refer to fig. 9.12). Then complete the following steps:

1. Select Path for **D**ownloadable Fonts and Printer Command Files (**6**).
2. Type the full path name and press Enter.
3. Press Enter or Exit (F7) three more times to return to the main editing screen.

You can now select soft fonts just as you select any other internal or cartridge font.

Using Forms with LaserJet Printers

The LaserJet Series II family of printers can handle many different sizes of paper and envelopes. For automatic feeding (marked Contin in the Format: Paper Size/ Type menu), each size requires its own paper tray. Table 9.3 lists the names, sizes,

Reminder:

For automatic feeding with a LaserJet Series II printer, each size of paper requires its own paper tray.

and various Hewlett-Packard part numbers for the Hewlett-Packard trays available. This information is useful when you are defining new forms with WordPerfect (as discussed in Chapter 6). Sizes for which no specific tray is available must be fed manually, through the manual-feed guides on the top of a tray.

To change between portrait- and landscape-mode printing, you do not have to change paper trays; you select a landscape form, and then select the appropriate landscape font(s). If you do not select a specific landscape font, WordPerfect selects from the fonts available the landscape font(s) nearest those defined for the default or the specific fonts in the document. On the LaserJet IID and IIP, all portrait fonts are also available in landscape, because these printers have the capability of rotating the fonts. Thus, you do not have to select a landscape font. (Note that printing rotated fonts is considerably slower than printing them in their normal orientation.)

Table 9.3
Hewlett-Packard Series II Paper Sizes and Trays

Form Type	Paper Tray Size	Hewlett-Packard Part Number
Letter size	8 1/2 x 11 inches	92295B
Legal size	8 1/2 x 14 inches	92295C
A4	210mm x 297mm	92295D
Executive size	182mm x 257mm	92295E
Envelope tray	—	92295F

The envelope tray is special; it can handle four different envelope sizes, which are listed in table 9.4.

Table 9.4
Envelope Sizes Supported by the Envelope Tray

Envelope	Type Size
Com-10	4 1/8 x 9 1/2 inches
Monarch	3 7/8 x 7 1/2 inches
C5	229mm x 162mm (9 x 6.4 inches)
DL	110mm x 220mm (4.3 x 8.6 inches)

Troubleshooting Problems with LaserJet Printers

All troubleshooting problems listed in the preceding chapter on printing apply generally to laser printers. The problems listed in this section, however, apply specifically to LaserJet printers.

Handling Problems with Cartridge Fonts

If you have trouble with cartridge fonts, any of the following problems may be the cause:

- The cartridges have been installed, but their installation has not been indicated to WordPerfect. You must use the **C**artridges and Fonts (**4**) option on the Select Printer: Edit screen to tell WordPerfect which cartridges are installed.

- You may be using the wrong font for regular printing. Use the **I**nitial Base Font (**5**) option on the Select Printer: Edit screen to tell WordPerfect which font to use for normal printing.

- The cartridge may no longer work. Hewlett-Packard specifies the life expectancy of a font cartridge in *number of insertions*. If you frequently swap font cartridges, you may need to replace them.

- If you receive an FE Cartridge error message on the control panel, you removed a font cartridge without first taking the printer off-line. You must shut the printer off and then turn it back on. You must also redownload any soft fonts with the **I**nitialize Printer (**7**) option on the Print menu.

Handling Problems with Soft Fonts

If you have problems with soft fonts, here are some possible causes and solutions:

- The soft fonts may not be downloaded. Make sure that WordPerfect knows where the fonts are. Do this through the Path for **D**ownloadable Fonts and Printer Command Files option (**6**) on the Select Printer: Edit screen. Make sure also that you have initialized your printer by selecting **I**nitialize Printer (**7**) from the Print menu.

- The desired fonts may not be selected. Use the **C**artridges and Fonts (**4**) option on the Select Printer: Edit screen to tell WordPerfect which fonts you have. Do not select fonts you don't have.

- The fonts may be erased from the LaserJet's memory. If you turn off the printer, its memory is cleared. Use the **I**nitialize Printer (**7**) option on the Print menu to reload each font that you marked with an asterisk (Present when print job begins).

- The computer may be unable to download soft fonts. You probably have the original LaserJet. To use soft fonts, you must have a LaserJet+, LaserJet 500+, or a LaserJet Series II.

- You may be using the wrong font for normal printing. Use the **I**nitial Base Font (**5**) option on the Select Printer: Edit screen to tell WordPerfect which font should be used for normal printing.

- If you have trouble printing soft fonts or printing complete graphics images, you may need to install more memory in your LaserJet. Soft fonts and graphics images consume large amounts of memory. Fortunately, Hewlett-Packard and other manufacturers offer several add-on memory boards for the LaserJet. Consult your dealer for more details.

- If a page is incomplete, the printer may be out of memory. Everything printed on a single page must fit into the printer's memory simultaneously. The LaserJet should display 20 ERROR on its control panel when it has insufficient memory. For a quick remedy, redo the page so that it contains fewer graphics, downloads fewer soft fonts, or both. For a permanent remedy, add a memory expansion board. Many third-party memory and enhancement boards are available in addition to those listed in table 9.5.

Table 9.5
Hewlett-Packard LaserJet Series II Memory Boards

Amount of Memory	Part Number	Remarks
1 megabyte	33443A	Recommended for the single-user environment
2 megabytes	33444A	Recommended for multiuser (network) environments or single-user environments in which many soft fonts are downloaded simultaneously
4 megabytes	33445A	Recommended for special memory-intensive applications like CAD (computer-assisted drafting); certainly not needed for word processing

Using WordPerfect with PostScript Laser Printers

If you have a PostScript laser printer, you will learn in this part of the chapter how to use your printer to best advantage with WordPerfect. If something doesn't happen in the sequence described, double-check your work and begin again.

Considering Downloadable Fonts for PostScript Printers

Reminder:

A variety of downloadable fonts (fonts that are not built-in) are now available for PostScript printers.

Even though an excellent selection of fonts comes with a PostScript printer, an even more incredible selection is available. New font choices become available every day. Several companies offer downloadable fonts (fonts that are not built-in) for use with PostScript printers. Two of these companies are Bitstream and Adobe. Downloadable font outlines are stored on disk and downloaded, as needed, from your computer to the laser printer's internal memory.

Check your documentation or call the toll-free, printer-support line at WordPerfect for the latest information about the PostScript fonts supported by your printer. Note that all Bitstream fonts are supported, as well as a growing number of fonts from the Adobe library.

Installing and Setting Up Downloadable Fonts for PostScript Printers

If you use a PostScript printer, you will want access to as many fonts as you can for flexibility in designing all your documents. This section shows you how to get the most from downloadable fonts.

Installing Downloadable Fonts from Adobe

If you purchase fonts from Adobe, complete, easy-to-follow instructions are provided for installing the fonts, including an auto-install program. Follow the directions to install your Adobe fonts for WordPerfect. You can then download them to your printer by following the directions provided here.

Installing Bitstream Fonts

The WordPerfect package contains information about ordering a Bitstream Installation Kit for use with WordPerfect. Included with the kit are four Swiss typefaces (Bitstream's version of Helvetica); four Dutch typefaces (Bitstream's version of Times Roman); and the Upright, Medium weight of Bitstream Charter (other styles and weights of Bitstream Charter are for sale). Bitstream Fontware works with PostScript-compatible printers or Hewlett-Packard LaserJet-compatible printers. You can purchase the kit from WordPerfect.

The documentation accompanying the Bitstream Installation Kit for WordPerfect is clear, and installing the fonts is a straightforward process. The entire process is menu-driven, with concise help messages. If you run into a problem, help is available from WordPerfect (through the toll-free line) or Bitstream (through a toll call).

Tip

Most PostScript printers come with Helvetica and Times already built-in. If you have these two typefaces, don't add the Swiss and Dutch Fontware typefaces because they duplicate fonts you already have under a different name. Bitstream Charter is not a typeface you will have in your printer. Bitstream offers a variety of different fonts for different purposes. With the installation kit, you can take advantage of them all.

Setting Up WordPerfect for PostScript Downloadable Fonts

You must inform WordPerfect about the various downloadable fonts you intend to use with your PostScript printer. To select downloadable fonts, complete these steps:

1. Press Print (Shift-F7) to display the Print menu (see fig. 9.17), and choose **S**elect Printer (**S**) to display the Print: Select Printer screen (see fig. 9.18).

   ▭ Access the **F**ile pull-down menu, select **P**rint, and choose **S**elect Printer (**S**).

```
Print

    1 - Full Document
    2 - Page
    3 - Document on Disk
    4 - Control Printer
    5 - Multiple Pages
    6 - View Document
    7 - Initialize Printer


Options

    S - Select Printer            Apple LaserWriter Plus
    B - Binding Offset            0"
    N - Number of Copies          1
    U - Multiple Copies Generated by  WordPerfect
    G - Graphics Quality          High
    T - Text Quality              High
```

Fig. 9.17.

The Print menu.

```
Print: Select Printer

  * Apple LaserWriter Plus
    HP LaserJet Series II
    NEC Silentwriter LC-890














1 Select; 2 Additional Printers; 3 Edit; 4 Copy; 5 Delete; 6 Help; 7 Update: 1
```

Fig. 9.18.

The Print: Select Printer menu.

2. Move the highlight bar to the appropriate printer and select **E**dit (**3**) to display the Select Printer: Edit screen (see fig. 9.19).

```
Select Printer: Edit

        Filename              APLASPLU.PRS

    1 - Name                  Apple LaserWriter Plus

    2 - Port                  LPT1:

    3 - Sheet Feeder          None

    4 - Cartridges and Fonts

    5 - Initial Base Font     Courier 12pt

    6 - Path for Downloadable  C:\WP51\FONTS
        Fonts and Printer
        Command Files
```

Fig. 9.19.

The Select Printer: Edit menu.

3. Select **C**artridges and Fonts (**4**) to display the Select Printer: Cartridges and Fonts screen.

   Note: If the printer files were not installed on your hard disk or are not on your current disk, WordPerfect will ask for the directory for the printer files. Either specify a directory or insert the correct Printer disk into the drive, type the appropriate drive letter, and press Enter.

4. WordPerfect says that for the Apple LaserWriter Plus, 120K of printer memory is available for storing downloadable fonts. If you have more memory, you can change this amount by pressing Change **Q**uantity (**2**) and entering the new amount.

5. Choose **S**elect (**1**) and move the highlight bar to the cartridge(s) you want; press either * or + to select. WordPerfect displays a list of downloadable fonts currently available.

Soft fonts are downloaded to the LaserJet either before or during the print job, depending on how you have marked them.

Select `* Present when print job begins` for fonts you use frequently. WordPerfect assumes that fonts marked with an asterisk (*) are present in the printer when the print job begins. This means that you must select **I**nitialize Printer (**7**) from the Print menu to instruct WordPerfect to download them to your printer before starting the first print job of a WordPerfect session.

The top right corner of the screen tells you how much total printer memory is designated as available for soft fonts, and how much of that memory remains available after downloading the soft fonts currently marked with an *.

Select `+ Can be loaded/unloaded during job` for fonts you use less frequently. WordPerfect downloads these fonts "on the fly" when they are called for in a document you are printing.

After you have marked all the fonts with either * or +, you must tell WordPerfect where to find the soft fonts. If you press Exit (F7) three times, you return to the Select Printer: Edit screen (refer to fig. 9.12). Then complete the following steps:

1. Select Path for **D**ownloadable Fonts and Printer Command Files (**6**).

2. Type the full path name and press Enter.

3. Press Enter or Exit (F7) three more times to return to the main editing screen.

You can now select soft fonts just as you select any other internal or cartridge font.

Using Forms with PostScript Printers

PostScript printers can handle several different sizes of media. This information is useful when you are defining new forms with WordPerfect (see Chapter 6 for more information on defining and using forms).

Using Specialty Typefaces with PostScript Printers

Most typefaces built into PostScript or other laser printers are useful for business correspondence and reports. The typeface you choose can add or detract from the communication. Enjoy experimenting; find out what appeals to you and what your correspondents find pleasing.

Considering Typeface Suggestions

A variety of available typefaces can be more confusing than limited choices. Here are some suggestions to help you decide which font to use for certain occasions:

- For legibility and ease of reading long stretches of text, try a serif typeface like Times, ITC Bookman, Palatino, or New Century Schoolbook.

- For a modern look, try Avant Garde.

- For lists or tabular material, try Courier (monospaced type, like that of a typewriter—not proportional), Helvetica, or Helvetica Narrow.

- For headlines or text with a larger point size, try a sans-serif typeface like Helvetica or Avant Garde.

- For a calligraphic look or for invitations, try Zapf Chancery.

- For mathematical or Greek letters, use Symbol.

- For emphasis and for fun, try Zapf Dingbats (a collection of nonalphabet characters, including check marks, pointing hands, stars, boxes, playing card symbols, circled numbers, and arrows). These fonts are not available for the HP LaserJet.

Because Symbol and Zapf Dingbats typefaces have nonalphabet characters and no counterparts in the IBM character set, these typefaces do not show up on-screen except as letters or numbers. They do, however, print correctly as the Dingbat or Symbol character chosen. Used sparingly, these special characters can greatly enhance a document's appeal.

Using Display Fonts

Certain fonts are not appropriate for everyday use but, if carefully selected, can create great impact in flyers or brochures. Bitstream has several sets of Headline typefaces. One set includes Cooper Black, Broadway, Cloister Black, and University Roman. Another set includes Brush Script, Blippo Black, Hobo, and Windsor. See figure 9.20 for an example of these eight typefaces.

Using Other Features with PostScript Printers

Reminder:
You can purchase a "speed up" program to help make your PostScript printer run faster.

Most PostScript laser printers are serial printers, and serial printers are notoriously slow. In reality, this slowness is due to the speed at which your computer transmits data through the serial printer port. If the slowness of your computer becomes a problem, you can purchase a "speed up" program to make your laser printer run faster.

Bitstream Cooper Black

University Roman

Broadway

Cloister Black

Brush Script

Blippo Black

Hobo

Windsor

Fig. 9.20.
*Bitstream
Headline series
display fonts.*

Using Fonts with WordPerfect 5.1 That Were Created for WordPerfect 5

Because the printer drivers for version 5.1 are new, you should reinstall your printer and use the most up-to-date printer drivers and soft font programs you can obtain. If, however, you have a large font library already installed for version 5, you can convert that library for use with version 5.1 by using the PTR (printer) program supplied with version 5.1. To convert a third-party font set (like the Bitstream fonts) from version 5 to version 5.1, complete the following steps:

1. At the DOS prompt, type *PTR* to start the printer program. Then press Retrieve Document (Shift-F10) and type the appropriate file name to retrieve the version 5 ALL file that contains the fonts you want to convert. Select **Y** when asked whether you want to convert the file. A list of printers appears.

2. Highlight the printer definition you want to edit and then press Enter. From the menu that appears (see fig. 9.21), highlight `Fonts` and press Enter again.

Reminder:
You can use the PTR (printer) program supplied with WordPerfect 5.1 to convert a font library already installed for version 5.

Cue:
Make sure that you back up your version 5 ALL file before converting a third-party font set.

```
File: G:\WP51\WPRINT2.ALL

              Printer: Apple LaserWriter Plus/IINT/IINTX

   Fonts
   Forms
   Graphics Resolutions
   Helps and Hints about Printer
   Miscellaneous Numbers
   Miscellaneous Questions
   Printer Commands
   Resources
   Soft Font Format Type




   Press Enter to Look or Edit; A - Z Name Search;
   Do all that apply
```

Fig. 9.21.
*The PTR program
menu.*

3. From the menu that appears (see fig. 9.22), select **A**dd (**1**) and press Ctrl-Enter to use the default pattern. When you are prompted for a name, type *Bitstream* (for this example) as the name of the font library you want to create (see fig. 9.23).

Fig. 9.22.

The Font menu.

```
File: G:\WP51\WPRINT2.ALL

              Printer: Apple LaserWriter Plus/IINT/IINTX
                         Font Libraries
  ┌─────────────────────────────────────────────────────────────┐
  │ Built-In                                                      │
  │   *Apple LaserWriter Plus/IINT/IINTX                          │
  │ Soft Fonts (Kb)                                               │
  │   *Apple LaserWriter Plus/IINT/IINTX                          │
  │                                                               │
  │                                                               │
  │                                                               │
  │                                                               │
  │                                                               │
  │                                                               │
  │                                                               │
  │                                                               │
  │                                                               │
  │                                                               │
  ├─────────────────────────────────────────────────────────────┤
  │ 1 Add; 2 Delete; 3 Rename; 4 Copy; 5 Update Flag;            │
  │ * Select; Backspace Unmark; Enter Look or Edit; A - Z Name Search; │
  └─────────────────────────────────────────────────────────────┘
```

Fig. 9.23.

Entering the name of the font library you want to create.

```
File: G:\WP51\WPRINT2.ALL

              Printer: Apple LaserWriter Plus/IINT/IINTX
                         Font Libraries
  ┌─────────────────────────────────────────────────────────────┐
  │ Built-In                                                      │
  │   *Apple LaserWriter Plus/IINT/IINTX                          │
  │ Soft Fonts (Kb)                                               │
  │   *Apple LaserWriter Plus/IINT/IINTX                          │
  │                                                               │
  │                                                               │
  │                                                               │
  │                                                               │
  │                                                               │
  │                                                               │
  │                                                               │
  │                                                               │
  │                                                               │
  │                                                               │
  ├─────────────────────────────────────────────────────────────┤
  │ Name:  Bitstream                                              │
  └─────────────────────────────────────────────────────────────┘
```

4. Select Soft Fonts (Kb), and the library you just named appears in the Font Libraries list. Highlight the printer you are working with and press Enter. A list of soft fonts now appears (see fig. 9.24).

5. Use the asterisk (*) key to mark each font that you want copied to the new font library. Then select **C**opy (**4**). Highlight the font library you just created and press Enter. The fonts are copied, and you are returned to the list of fonts. Press Exit (F7) to return to the list of font libraries (see fig. 9.25).

5.1

```
File: G:\WP51\WPRINT2.ALL

                 Printer: Apple LaserWriter Plus/IINT/IINTX
            (Soft Fonts [Kb]): Apple LaserWriter Plus/IINT/IINTX

   (FW) Activa Bold (WP PostScript)
   (FW) Activa Bold Italic (WP PostScript)
   (FW) Activa Italic (WP PostScript)
   (FW) Activa Roman (WP PostScript)
   (FW) Bernhard Modern Bold (WP PostScript)
   (FW) Bernhard Modern Bold Italic (WP PostScript)
   (FW) Bernhard Modern Italic (WP PostScript)
   (FW) Bernhard Modern Roman (WP PostScript)
   (FW) Bits Charter Black (WP PostScript)
   (FW) Bits Charter Black Italic (WP PostScript)
   (FW) Bits Charter Italic (WP PostScript)
   (FW) Bits Charter Roman (WP PostScript)
   (FW) Bitstream Cooper Black (WP PostScript)
   (FW) Bitstrm Amerigo Bold (WP PostScript)
   (FW) Bitstrm Amerigo Bold Italic (WP PostScript)
   (FW) Bitstrm Amerigo Italic (WP PostScript)
 ▼ (FW) Bitstrm Amerigo Roman (WP PostScript)

1 Add; 2 Delete; 3 Rename; 4 Copy;
Press Enter to Look or Edit; A - Z Name Search;
```

Fig. 9.24.

A list of soft fonts.

```
File: G:\WP51\WPPS1.ALL

            (Shared) Printer: Apple LaserWriter IINTX
                       Font Libraries

Built-In
    AST TurboLaser
    Digital Internal Plus
    IBM 4216-30 Plus Internal
   *PostScript 13 Internal
   *PostScript 35 Internal
Soft Fonts (Kb)
    AST TurboLaser
   *bitstream

1 Add; 2 Delete; 3 Rename; 4 Copy; 5 Update Flag;
* Select; Backspace Unmark; Enter Look or Edit; A - Z Name Search;
```

Fig. 9.25.

The Font Libraries screen showing the Bitstream addition.

6. Highlight the font library you just created and select **C**opy (**4**). Enter the name of the 5.1 ALL file to which you want the new font library copied. Exit the ALL file you are editing and retrieve the ALL file into which you copied the font library. If you are not sure, you can press List (F5) for a list of printer files.

7. Highlight the name of your printer and press Enter. Then highlight Fonts and press Enter; highlight the font library you copied and press *.

8. Press Exit (F7) to save the ALL file. Press Exit again to exit the PTR program.

Your fonts are now available in version 5.1.

Troubleshooting Problems with PostScript Printers

If your printer will not print, start with this list to see whether you can isolate and correct the problem:

- Check the power. Are both the printer and the computer plugged in?
- Check the printer status lights. Is the printer on-line? Is paper in the paper tray? Is the toner cartridge installed properly?
- Check the cable. Do you have the correct cable? If there is more than one place to plug the cable into the computer, have you plugged it into the correct place?
- Check the printer-emulation switch. Some PostScript printers have switches or dials that offer choices between PostScript and Diablo or Epson emulation. If there is a switch or dial, is it set correctly?
- Check your selection on the Print menu. Have you selected the correct printer? Is it installed? Is the correct port selected? If it is a serial port (COM), have you chosen the correct baud, parity, and so on?
- If you are using soft fonts, make sure that you have initialized your printer by selecting Initialize Printer (7) from the Print menu.
- Contact WordPerfect customer support, through which a whole group of support people can help you with your problem. If you buy a printer and cannot find it on the printer choices or cannot find an emulation listed in the manual, call WordPerfect. You can get help selecting the correct printer definition, or you may even have a new printer definition sent to you.

If none of these suggestions corrects the problem, try reinstalling WordPerfect and reselecting the printer. This sometimes works.

Troubleshooting Printing Problems

If your print quality is inferior, consider the following solutions:

- The toner cartridge may need replacing. Replace the toner cartridge when print output is too light or uneven. Lines running the length of the paper indicate a scratched photoconductor drum inside the toner cartridge.
- The paper path or corona wires may need cleaning. Turn off the printer and use a cotton swab moistened with isopropyl alcohol to clean the interior as the owner's manual instructs.
- The fuser roller pad may need cleaning or replacing. A new pad is included with every replacement toner cartridge.
- You may be using an improper paper type. For general work, use photocopy paper. For cotton bond letterheads, use paper that does not create paper dust. Textured or woven papers may not work well.

If the printer seems to take a long time to print pages, perhaps the text contains graphics. Pages containing graphics always take longer to print than text-only pages. Waiting time varies with the number of graphics on the page and the amount of memory your printer has.

Summary

This chapter showed you how to coexist peacefully with your Hewlett-Packard LaserJet printer or compatible, or your PostScript laser printer. You saw that it takes patience and work to get the most out of either type of laser printer. In the chapter, you learned the following:

- ❏ How to work with internal, cartridge, and soft fonts
- ❏ How fonts can be powerful tools in your everyday work
- ❏ What a PostScript printer is and how it is different from other laser printers
- ❏ How new features in WordPerfect 5.1 can help you get the most out of your PostScript printer

Now that your laser printer is operational, you can quickly print letters, reports, and other documents that look the way you want them to look.

10

Using List
Files

Doug Hazen, Jr., a computer programmer who lives in the Boston area, originally wrote this chapter for *Using WordPerfect 5*. He is a member of the Boston Computer Society WordPerfect Special Interest Group and works for Intellution, Inc., in Norwood, Massachusetts.

C. Brian Scott, a partner in the Portland, Oregon, law firm Danner, Scott & Martin, specializes in real estate and estate planning and administration and serves as the system administrator for his firm's PC network. He has been heavily involved with WordPerfect since 1986. He revised this chapter to reflect the changes and enhancements with version 5.1

This chapter shows you how WordPerfect's List Files feature can help you deal with DOS and manage your files and directories. Over the course of the chapter, you will do the following:

- Review the parts of the List Files screen: the heading, the two kinds of file listings, and the menu

- Use List Files to help you with common DOS and WordPerfect operations, such as displaying a list of files, deleting, moving, copying, and renaming files; making, changing, and deleting directories; and viewing, retrieving, and printing documents

- Perform List Files operations on multiple files by using a feature called *file marking*

- Search several files at once for a word or phrase by using the Find option

- By using Block when running WordPerfect 5.1 under the WordPerfect Office's shell, copy text from a file without first retrieving that file

To get the most from this chapter, you need some elementary understanding of DOS features such as files, directories, wild cards, and basic DOS commands. If you aren't familiar with this information, you may want to read one of Que's best-selling books on DOS: *Using DOS* or *MS-DOS User's Guide*, Special Edition. For an easy-to-use quick reference, see also *DOS QueCards*.

Reminder

If you use a mouse with WordPerfect 5.1, you can click the right button to display the pull-down menus, and then select the desired option. You also can press Alt-= to access the pull-down menus, and then press the appropriate letter of the desired option. For all the instructions, you can assume that if a block is required to activate a pull-down menu option, the text has been blocked before the pull-down menu is accessed. Instructions for pull-down menus and the mouse are marked with the mouse icon. See Chapter 1 for details on using the mouse. 🖱

Take special notice, however, that the pull-down menus cannot be accessed from within the List Files screen. The mouse will work normally to select menu choices from the regular List Files menus. But certain features that are not on these menus, such as Search, Mark Text, Block, and Text In/Out, can be accessed only with the function keys when you work within the List Files screen.

Discovering List Files

Reminder:

Pressing List (F5) once or choosing List Files from the File pull-down menu when you are at the main editing screen shows you the current default directory.

List Files is one of WordPerfect's nicer features. You can use it to accomplish within WordPerfect much of the file and directory management you ordinarily do in DOS. To get to the List Files screen, press List (F5); 🖱 alternatively, you can access the File pull-down menu (see fig. 10.1) and select List **F**iles. In the lower left corner of the screen, WordPerfect displays the word Dir followed by a file specification for all files in the current directory, such as C:\WP51\TEXT*.*. Pressing List (F5) once or choosing List **F**iles from the **F**ile pull-down menu when you are at the main editing screen always shows you the current default directory.

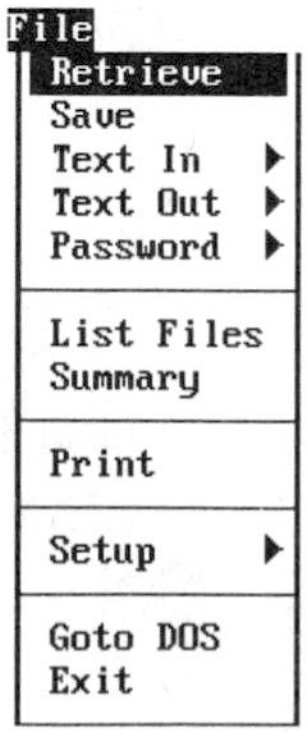

Fig. 10.1.

The F ile pull-down menu, which contains the option List F iles.

```
File
  Retrieve
  Save
  Text In    ▶
  Text Out   ▶
  Password   ▶

  List Files
  Summary

  Print

  Setup      ▶

  Goto DOS
  Exit
```

The file-specification message appearing in the lower left corner of the screen indicates that WordPerfect is ready to give you a file listing of all files in the current directory. If this file listing is the one you want, simply press Enter. If it is not the one you want, you can type a new file specification; the original one disappears and is replaced by the new one. You can edit the file specification, just as you edit regular text, by using the WordPerfect key combinations listed in table 10.1.

Table 10.1
WordPerfect Key Combinations for Editing the File Specification

Key Combination	Effect
End	Moves cursor to end of file specification
Home ←	Moves cursor to beginning of file specification
Del	Deletes character at cursor
Backspace	Deletes character to left of cursor
Ctrl-End	Deletes to end of file specification

If you use these editing commands, the old file specification stays on-screen for you to edit. Change the file specification to what you want; then press Enter.

For now, press Enter to accept the default file specification (that is, to list all files in the current directory). The default List Files display appears (see fig. 10.2). The three sections of this screen are the heading, the file listing, and the menu.

```
11-16-89  12:24a            Directory G:\WP51\TEXT\*.*
Document size:    56,502   Free:  4,694,016 Used:     350,491      Files:      27

.      Current    <Dir>          ..     Parent    <Dir>
1017WPRS.HL     1,348  10-12-89 12:37p   1017WPRS.MIL    3,963  10-12-89 12:37p
1200WOT .BSD   11,821  10-12-89 11:52a   1201WOT .NOT    9,554  10-12-89 11:30a
1202WOT .D      9,874  06-08-89 10:56a   1203WOT .AGR    1,665  06-07-89 03:55p
1204WOT .AGR   11,092  09-28-89 02:34p   1205WOT .WAI    5,845  06-12-89 12:11p
1291AWOT.AGR   45,337  11-08-89 11:26a   1291DOC .CMP   48,596  11-07-89 05:56p
1291WOT .AGR   45,379  11-08-89 11:59a   322LPRP .AFF    7,058  10-12-89 12:39p
387LPRP .ADD      381  10-12-89 12:38p   53LREM  .NOT   12,270  10-12-89 02:36p
64AOFF  .BRO   53,327  10-16-89 07:01p   COMPL   .TST   14,631  11-14-89 05:02p
LTRCBS  .       5,194  10-25-89 10:10a   SUMM    .LST    1,425  11-03-89 08:52p
SUMMARIE.       1,139  10-29-89 12:01a   TEMPMRG .IVY      533  10-18-89 03:23p
TEMPMRG .PSK      512  11-02-89 02:04p   TEST1   .AFF    7,364  10-12-89 12:59p
TEST1   .L     10,310  10-18-89 04:25p   TEST2   .TBL    7,526  10-12-89 03:29p
TEST3   .TBL    7,570  10-12-89 03:36p   TEST4   .TBL   12,857  10-12-89 03:37p
WAP42   .RB    13,920  03-26-86 11:59a

1 Retrieve; 2 Delete; 3 Move/Rename; 4 Print; 5 Short/Long Display;
6 Look; 7 Other Directory; 8 Copy; 9 Find; N Name Search: 6
```

Fig. 10.2.

The default (short) display of the List Files screen.

In addition to the default display, WordPerfect offers a long display of the List Files screen. See the section "Using Short/Long Display."

5.1

Understanding the Heading

At the top of the default List Files display, you see a two-line heading that contains useful information. On the top line, from left to right, are the date, the time, and the directory being listed. On the second line, from left to right, are the size of the document currently being edited, the amount of free space left on the disk, the amount of disk space taken by files in the current file listing, and the number of files shown in the listing.

Understanding the File Listing

Reminder:

Press Print (Shift-F7) to print the file listing.

The second section is a two-column file listing arranged in alphabetical order across the screen (files whose names start with numbers are listed first). This listing shows the complete file name, the file size, and the date and time the file was created or last modified. You can print this listing, along with most of the information in the heading, on your currently selected printer by pressing Print (Shift-F7) (see fig. 10.3).

Fig. 10.3.

A List Files screen printed with Print (Shift-F7).

```
11-16-89  12:26a                 Directory G:\WP51\TEXT\*.*
Free:  4,751,360

.      Current    <Dir>            ..     Parent     <Dir>
1017WPRS.HL      1,348  10-12-89 12:37p | 1017WPRS.MIL      3,963  10-12-89 2:37p
1200WOT .BSD    11,821  10-12-89 11:52a | 1201WOT .NOT      9,554  10-12-89 1:30a
1202WOT .D       9,874  06-08-89 10:56a | 1203WOT .AGR      1,665  06-07-89 3:55p
1204WOT .AGR    11,092  09-28-89 02:34p | 1205WOT .WAI      5,845  06-12-89 2:11p
1291AWOT.AGR    45,337  11-08-89 11:26a | 1291DOC .CMP     48,596  11-07-89 5:56p
1291WOT .AGR    45,379  11-08-89 11:59a | 322LPRP .AFF      7,058  10-12-89 2:39p
387LPRP .ADD       381  10-12-89 12:38p | 53LREM  .NOT     12,270  10-12-89 2:36p
64AOFF  .BRO    53,327  10-16-89 07:01p | COMPL   .TST     14,631  11-14-89 5:02p
LTRCBS  .        5,194  10-25-89 10:10a | SUMM    .LST      1,425  11-03-89 8:52p
SUMMARIE.        1,139  10-29-89 12:01a | TEMPMRG .IVY        533  10-18-89 3:23p
TEMPMRG .PSK       512  11-02-89 02:04p | TEST1   .AFF      7,364  10-12-89 2:59p
TEST1   .L      10,310  10-18-89 04:25p | TEST2   .TBL      7,526  10-12-89 3:29p
TEST3   .TBL     7,570  10-12-89 03:36p | TEST4   .TBL     12,857  10-12-89 3:37p
WAP42   .RB     13,920  03-26-86 11:59a |
```

> **Tip**
>
> The date and time display in List Files is controlled by a Language Resource file called WP.LRS, located in the same directory as WP.EXE. You can edit this file with WordPerfect 5.1 to change the display. On pages 363 through 369 of the WordPerfect 5.1 manual are excellent instructions for doing so.

Notice the top line of the file listing:

```
.  Current   <Dir>              ..  Parent   <Dir>
```

`<Dir>` indicates that the items are directories. If other directories were to appear in the listing, they would be similarly labeled. The entry labeled `Current` refers to the currently listed directory. The other entry, labeled `Parent`, refers to the parent directory of the listed directory.

On-screen, a highlight bar appears on the `Current` directory name. You can move this bar with the cursor keys or with the mouse to highlight any name in the listing. You also can move the bar with the usual WordPerfect cursor-movement key combinations, listed in table 10.2.

Table 10.2
WordPerfect Cursor-Movement Key Combinations

Key Combination	Location the Cursor Is Moved To
Home ↓	Last file on-screen
keypad +	Last file on-screen
Home ↑	First file on-screen
keypad –	First file on-screen
Home, Home, ↓	Last file in listing
Home, Home, ↑	Current directory in listing

Using the List Files Menu

The List Files menu at the bottom of the screen in figure 10.2 presents 10 command choices. You can select any command by pressing either the appropriate number or the highlighted letter or by double-clicking the mouse button after placing the mouse pointer on the menu option. Each choice acts on the highlighted file or directory.

When you pick one of the menu commands, WordPerfect often asks for confirmation, initially presenting a No choice. For example, if you select **D**elete (**2**) to delete the file TEST3.TBL, WordPerfect asks

```
Delete C:\BOOK\TEST3.TBL? No (Yes)
```

You can, of course, select either **Y** (to delete the file) or **N** (to cancel the command).

Using Retrieve

Retrieve (**1**) works like Retrieve (Shift-F10) from the editing screen and like **R**etrieve from the **F**ile pull-down menu: the option brings a file into WordPerfect for editing, inserting the file at the cursor position. If you already have a file on-screen, WordPerfect asks

```
Retrieve into current document? No (Yes)
```

Select **Y** if you want to combine the new file with the file you already have on-screen. Select **N** if you don't want to combine the files.

WordPerfect tries to protect you from retrieving improper files. It does not retrieve program files, nor does it retrieve any temporary or permanent WordPerfect system files or macro files.

Reminder:
*Using **R**etrieve (1), you can retrieve and convert to WordPerfect 5.1 a DOS text file or a file created with an earlier version of WordPerfect.*

The **R**etrieve (**1**) option *will* retrieve and automatically convert to WordPerfect 5.1 format any DOS text file or any file created with an earlier version of WordPerfect. The conversion occurs automatically, without any prompt to the user except the question about retrieving into the current document. WordPerfect does display the message DOS Text Conversion in Progress while the conversion takes place.

You may also retrieve a DOS text file by pressing Text In/Out (Ctrl-F5) when the file name of a DOS text file is highlighted. (You cannot access the **F**ile pull-down menu while in the List Files display.) The only visible difference between using these two methods is evident when you already have a file open in the main editing screen. In that case, pressing Text In/Out (Ctrl-F5) causes the message (DOS) Retrieve *d:\path\filename?* No (Yes) to be displayed. Whichever method you use, the DOS text conversion is the same as that achieved through the selection of Text In/Out (Ctrl-F5), DOS **T**ext (**1**), and **R**etrieve (**3**), which turns hard returns in the hyphenation zone into soft returns. This selection is equivalent to accessing the **F**ile pull-down menu, choosing Text **In**, and then choosing DOS Text (CR/LF to **S**rt).

Note: A new safety feature prevents the accidental changing of the retrieved document's format. If a retrieved document was originally in WordPerfect format, WordPerfect will offer the present file name as the default when you press Save (F10). If you press Text In/Out (Ctrl-F5), select DOS **T**ext (**1**), and select **S**ave (**1**), WordPerfect does not offer any file name as a default. Similarly, if the retrieved file was originally a DOS text file, WordPerfect will offer no default name when you press Save (F10) but will offer the present file name as a default if you select Text In/Out (Ctrl-F5), DOS **T**ext (**1**), and **S**ave (**1**).

Although you cannot activate the pull-down menu bar while using the List Files feature, you can use the mouse to move the cursor and thus select any choice on the menu display.

Using Delete

Selecting **D**elete (**2**) or pressing the Del key deletes either files or directories. If the highlight bar is on a file, that file is deleted. If the bar is on a directory, that directory is deleted as long it contains no files; WordPerfect gives you an error message if you try to delete a directory that contains files. Whether you're deleting files or directories, WordPerfect asks Delete *name*? No (Yes). Select **Y** to confirm the deletion; select **N** or any other key to cancel the deletion.

Using Move/Rename

To rename a file, highlight the name of the file you want to change; select **M**ove/Rename (**3**). WordPerfect displays the prompt

New name: *drive:\path\filename.ext*

in which the term *drive:\path\filename.ext* represents the default file name. You can either edit the default file name or type a new one (in which case the default file name disappears). If you accidentally enter the name of an existing file, WordPerfect displays the prompt

Replace *drive:\path\filename.ext*? No (Yes)

in which the term *drive:\path\filename.ext* represents the name of the existing file. Selecting **Y** deletes the file that has the same name and replaces it with the file that has the name being changed.

Moving a file means transferring it to a different directory or disk drive. To move a single file, highlight the name of the file you want to change and select **M**ove/Rename (**3**). WordPerfect displays the message New name: followed by the full path name of the current file. Edit the path name to display the drive and directory to which you want the file to be moved; then press Enter. In a single operation, you can both move a file and change its name.

> **Tip**
>
> If you want to change only the drive letter, first move the cursor to the character after the drive letter and press Backspace to delete the old drive letter; then type the new letter. Doing so prevents the entire path from being deleted when you type the first letter of the new path name.

Using Print

Selecting **P**rint (**4**) prints the highlighted file on the currently selected printer. If a different printer was defined when the file was saved, the message Document not formatted for current printer. Continue? No (Yes) appears. Selecting **Y** causes the file to be printed on the current printer, although the formatting may be altered.

With version 5.1, you can print files that were saved through the Fast Save option without first retrieving them into the editing screen. The printing speed for these files may be substantially slower than that for regularly saved files, however, because WordPerfect must construct and format a temporary file on your disk before sending the job to the printer.

For more information on printing, see Chapters 8 and 9.

Using Short/Long Display

Short/Long Display (**5**) enables you to toggle between the default (short) List Files display and a long display. When you select this option, WordPerfect offers this menu line:

      (**1**) **S**hort Display; (**2**) **L**ong Display: **2**

To choose the long display, select **L**ong Display (**2**) and press Enter, or simply press Enter twice to accept the default choice of 2 (see fig. 10.4). The default number changes from 2 to 1 when the current display is long.

Unlike the short display, the long display lists each file on a separate row. Each row's right half shows the same information found in the short display. The left half of each row, however, includes from the document summary the first 30 characters of the descriptive name as well as the file type, provided that the file has a document summary containing either of the two items. The files are listed in alphabetical order, except that the descriptive file name, if available, is used as the sort file name.

Reminder:
The long display includes from the document summary the first 30 characters of a file's descriptive name and the file type, provided that a summary exists for the file and includes those items.

Fig. 10.4.

A long List Files display.

```
11-05-89  04:41p              Directory G:\WP51\TEXT\*.*
Document size:    42,492   Free:  7,413,760 Used:     196,548    Files:      22
Descriptive Name                     Type    Filename     Size    Revision Date

Current Directory                            .          <Dir>
Parent Directory                             ..         <Dir>
                                             1203WOT .AGR    1,665  06-07-89 03:55p
                                             1204WOT .AGR   11,092  09-28-89 02:34p
                                             1205WOT .WAI    5,845  06-12-89 12:11p
                                             322LPRP .AFF    7,058  10-12-89 12:39p
                                             387LPRP .ADD      381  10-12-89 12:38p
                                             53LREM  .NOT   12,270  10-12-89 02:36p
                                             64AOFF  .BRO   53,327  10-16-89 07:01p
Bargain and Sale Deed                        1200WOT .BSD   11,821  10-12-89 11:52a
Bargain and Sale Deed                        1202WOT .D      9,874  06-08-89 10:56a
Estate MIL (secondary merge)                 1017WPRS.MIL    3,963  10-12-89 12:37p
Letter form                                  LTRCBS  .       5,194  10-25-89 10:10a
Letter form                                  TEST1   .L     10,310  10-18-89 04:25p
Promissory Note - Moskovitz/Da               1201WOT .NOT    9,554  10-12-89 11:30a
                                             SUMM    .LST    1,425  11-03-89 08:52p
                                             SUMMARIE.       1,139  10-29-89 12:01a
Template for Heir/Devisee addr               1017WPRS.HL     1,348  10-12-89 12:37p

1 Retrieve; 2 Delete; 3 Move/Rename; 4 Print; 5 Short/Long Display;
6 Look; 7 Other Directory; 8 Copy; 9 Find; N Name Search: 6
```

Reminder:

Use the long display to extract WordPerfect document files from a directory that contains a mixture of files.

When deciding whether to use the long display, keep in mind that it—unlike the short display—shows only WordPerfect 5 and 5.1 files. You can thus use the long display as a quick way to extract WordPerfect document files from a directory containing a mixture of files. In addition, because the extra information provided by the long display is extracted from a file's document summary, each file must be opened and read by WordPerfect before the display can be created. A long display for a large directory can therefore take several minutes to create.

Using Look

Reminder:

Use Look to examine files quickly.

The Look feature enables you to examine files quickly. When the highlight bar is on a file, selecting **L**ook (**6**) displays the highlighted file without retrieving it into WordPerfect (see fig. 10.5). You cannot edit the file.

Fig. 10.5.

Using Look to examine a file that doesn't have a document summary.

```
File: G:\LIB\WILLS\40ALWIM.POA          WP5.1     Revised: 11-04-89 11:38p

                        Power of Attorney for Health Care

        I appoint Name of agent~, whose address is Agent's address~, and whose te
number is phone # of agent~, as my attorney-in-fact for health care decisions.
of agent~,  whose address is Agent's address~, and whose telephone number is ph
agent~, as my alternative attorney-in-fact for health care decisions.  I author
fact appointed by this document to make health care decisions for me when I am
making my own health care decisions.  I have read the warning below and underst
consequences of appointing a power of attorney for health care.

        I direct that my attorney-in-fact comply with the following instructions o
the attached supplementary instructions).

        In addition, I direct that my attorney-in-fact have authority to make deci
following:

                Withholding or withdrawal of life-sustaining procedures with the unde
                death may result.


Look: 1 Next Doc; 2 Prev Doc: 0
```

Because 6 is the default menu choice, you don't have to press 6 to look at a file; you can simply press Enter. (Or you can click the mouse button twice to activate the Look feature.) When a file, as in figure 10.5, does not have a document summary, the following are displayed at the top of the screen: the full DOS path name, the WordPerfect version (for 5 and 5.1 files only) in which the file is saved, and the most recent revision date and time. (As explained shortly, if the file has a document summary, additional information appears at the top of the screen, and the summary—not the text of the file—is displayed.)

Although you can move the cursor through the file by using many of the usual WordPerfect cursor-movement commands, several cursor commands change their actions in Look. PgDn and PgUp operate the same as **N**ext Doc (**1**) and **P**rev Doc (**2**) (which are discussed shortly). If the text lines extend past the screen's right edge, the right-arrow key moves the displayed text to the left five characters at a time until only the text that was originally to the right of the screen edge is displayed. After the text is moved to the left, pressing the left-arrow key moves the displayed text to the right five characters at a time. Pressing the Home and right-arrow keys together moves the displayed text off the screen to the left, leaving displayed only the text that was originally off the screen. Pressing the Home and left-arrow keys together restores the text lines to the original display.

◆ 5.1

If you press S, the Look option continuously scrolls each succeeding line of the document. Pressing S again (or the space bar) stops the scrolling. Press Exit (F7) or Enter to leave Look.

When you select **L**ook (**6**) for a file that doesn't have a document summary, you see at the bottom of the screen the following menu:

◆ 5.1

Look: 1 **N**ext Doc; **2** **P**rev Doc: **0**

Selecting **N**ext Doc (**1**) or PgDn moves the cursor to the first page of the next file in the file list; selecting **P**rev Doc (**2**) or PgUp moves the cursor to the first page of the preceding file in the list. You can thus quickly scan the document summaries and first pages of a list of files. To limit the number of files to be scanned, use a file specification (such as *.LTR) when going into List Files.

You can search for text with Forward Search (F2) and Reverse Search (Shift-F2). When a match is found, the matching characters will be highlighted. You cannot, however, search for text in headers, footers, or footnotes with the Look option. If the word found by a search operation is past the right edge of the regular display screen, the cursor will stop at the left edge of the line in which the word is located, but the word will not be highlighted.

Tip

The Look feature initially places the cursor at the bottom of the screen, not at the top of the screen. A Forward Search operation does not check for the character string above the cursor's location. Move the cursor to the top of the screen before beginning the search operation.

As mentioned earlier, files containing a document summary are shown differently in Look from those without a document summary. If you select **L**ook (**6**) for a file that contains a document summary, the summary is displayed (see fig. 10.6). The heading contains a second line displaying the file's long document name, the document type, and the file's creation date. The long name and document type are extracted from user entries into the document summary. If there are no entries for Name: and Type:, blanks are shown. The creation date shows the date and time when the document summary was created. That date will remain the same, regardless of revisions to the file, until the summary is deleted.

Fig. 10.6.

Looking at a file containing a document summary.

```
File: G:\LIB\WILLS\25LWIM.POA                    WP5.0      Revised: 12-07-88 05:10p
Name: POA to fund Living Trust                               Created: May 26, 1988

Subject    Wills Library

Author     cbs
Typist     cbs
Abstract
   This is a limited Power of Attorney that allows the Trustee of an existing
   living trust to move assets into the trust in the event of the incapacity of
   the grantor of the trust.  Most often used with a Standby Trust.  Needed
   whenever the Grantor is also initial Trustee of a Living Trust.




Look Doc Summ: 1 Next; 2 Prev; 3 Look at text; 4 Print Summ; 5 Save to File: 0
```

At the bottom of the screen in figure 10.6, note the menu, which differs from that shown in figure 10.5. Selecting **L**ook at text (**3**) enables you to view the file in the usual fashion. Selecting **P**rint Summ (**4**) sends the document summary to the printer. If you select **S**ave to file (**5**), you are prompted for the name of a file to which the document-summary information will be saved. If the file you designate already exists, you are given the choice of replacing the file or appending the current document summary to the end of the file.

In addition to using Look to examine files, you can use the feature to skim other directories. With the highlight bar on the `Current` directory, press Enter once, edit the displayed file specification or type a new one, and press Enter again. You have *not* changed directories; you are simply seeing a file listing of the other directory. You can also accomplish this result by pressing List (F5) and editing the displayed file specification whenever the file list is being displayed—regardless of the location of the highlight bar.

You can use the Look command to inspect directories another way. Place the highlight bar on a directory entry (other than `Current`) in the file listing, as in figure 10.7. Press Enter; WordPerfect displays a `Dir` message followed by the file specification. Press Enter again; WordPerfect displays the file listing of this highlighted directory. You can look at any directories in this new listing the same way.

```
11-05-89  06:08p            Directory G:\WP51\*.*
Document size:    44,689   Free:  7,397,376  Used:  1,977,169    Files:    50

.     Current    <Dir>                    ..    Parent    <Dir>
BACK          .   <Dir>   10-11-89 01:54p  GRAPH         <Dir>   10-11-89 01:04p
LEARN         .   <Dir>   10-11-89 01:04p  LEX-TH    .   <Dir>   10-11-89 01:03p
MACROS        .   <Dir>   10-11-89 01:03p  PRINT         <Dir>   10-11-89 01:04p
SETUP         .   <Dir>   10-11-89 01:46p  STYLES    .   <Dir>   10-11-89 01:04p
TEXT          .   <Dir>   10-11-89 02:16p  8514A   .URS    4,797  09-22-89 10:48a
ATI    .URS    4,937  09-22-89 10:48a  CONVERT .EXE 104,689  09-22-89 10:35a
CURSOR .COM    1,452  09-22-89 10:35a  EGA512  .FRS   3,584  09-22-89 10:48a
EGAITAL .FRS   3,584  09-22-89 10:48a  EGASMC  .FRS   3,584  09-22-89 10:48a
EGAUND  .FRS   3,584  09-22-89 10:48a  FIXBIOS .COM      50  09-22-89 10:35a
GENIUS  .URS  15,473  09-22-89 10:48a  GENOA   .URS  10,972  09-22-89 10:48a
GRAB    .COM  15,602  09-22-89 10:35a  HRF12   .FRS  49,152  09-22-89 10:48a
HRF6    .FRS  49,152  09-22-89 10:48a  INSTALL .EXE  58,720  09-22-89 11:03a
KEYS    .MRS   4,800  09-22-89 10:09a  NEC     .URS   4,682  09-22-89 10:48a
PARADISE.URS  14,492  09-22-89 10:48a  STANDARD.CRS   2,557  09-22-89 10:35a
STANDARD.IRS   4,373  09-22-89 10:09a  STANDARD.PRS   1,942  09-22-89 10:09a
STANDARD.URS  28,426  09-22-89 10:09a  VERTICOM.URS   4,945  09-22-89 10:48a
VGA512  .FRS   4,096  09-22-89 10:48a  VGAITAL .FRS   4,096  09-22-89 10:48a
VGASMC  .FRS   4,096  09-22-89 10:48a ▼ VGAUND  .FRS   4,096  09-22-89 10:48a

Dir G:\WP51\TEXT\*.*
```

Fig. 10.7.

Preparing to look at a new directory.

Note current directory and highlighted directory

In this way, you can travel up or down the directory tree, examining each directory in turn. Remember, though, that you have not changed your current directory. You are simply listing files in other directories.

Tip

You can use the Look option to discover the purpose of macros you may have forgotten about. If you look at a macro file, you can see the description you entered when you created the macro (you do put in macro descriptions, don't you?).

Using Other Directory

Select Other Directory (7) to change the current default directory. The result of making this choice depends on where the highlight bar is. When the highlight bar is on the name of a subdirectory and you select Other Directory (7), WordPerfect displays in the lower left corner of the screen the message New directory = followed by the name of the highlighted directory, as in figure 10.8.

Press Enter; WordPerfect displays the message Dir followed by the file specification for all the files in the highlighted directory. After changing the file specification, press Enter again; WordPerfect changes to the new directory and displays its listing. If you decide you don't want to change directories after all, just press Cancel (F1) before pressing Enter the second time.

If the bar is on the upper left directory name (Current) or on a file name when you issue the Other Directory command, WordPerfect displays the same prompt: New directory = followed by the path to the current directory. You can change to any other directory at this point by editing the directory path to show the desired directory and by then pressing Enter.

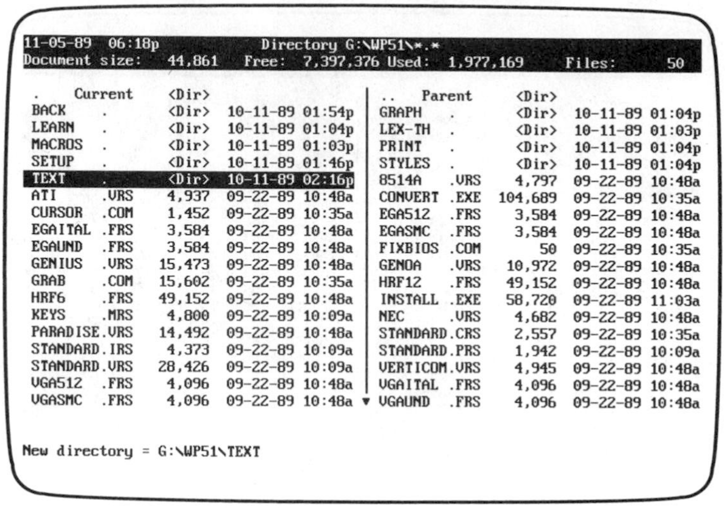

Fig. 10.8.

Preparing to change directories in List Files.

```
11-05-89  06:18p              Directory G:\WP51\*.*
Document size:   44,861  Free:  7,397,376 Used:  1,977,169    Files:      50

.    Current    <Dir>                  ..    Parent     <Dir>
BACK       .     <Dir>  10-11-89 01:54p  GRAPH      .     <Dir>  10-11-89 01:04p
LEARN      .     <Dir>  10-11-89 01:04p  LEX-TH     .     <Dir>  10-11-89 01:03p
MACROS     .     <Dir>  10-11-89 01:03p  PRINT      .     <Dir>  10-11-89 01:04p
SETUP      .     <Dir>  10-11-89 01:46p  STYLES     .     <Dir>  10-11-89 01:04p
TEXT       .     <Dir>  10-11-89 02:16p  8514A    .URS     4,797  09-22-89 10:48a
ATI      .URS    4,937  09-22-89 10:48a  CONVERT  .EXE   104,689  09-22-89 10:35a
CURSOR   .COM    1,452  09-22-89 10:48a  EGA512   .FRS     3,584  09-22-89 10:48a
EGAITAL  .FRS    3,584  09-22-89 10:48a  EGASMC   .FRS     3,584  09-22-89 10:48a
EGAUND   .FRS    3,584  09-22-89 10:48a  FIXBIOS  .COM        50  09-22-89 10:35a
GENIUS   .URS   15,473  09-22-89 10:48a  GENOA    .URS    10,972  09-22-89 10:48a
GRAB     .COM   15,602  09-22-89 10:35a  HRF12    .FRS    49,152  09-22-89 10:48a
HRF6     .FRS   49,152  09-22-89 10:48a  INSTALL  .EXE    58,720  09-22-89 11:03a
KEYS     .MRS    4,800  09-22-89 10:09a  NEC      .URS     4,682  09-22-89 10:48a
PARADISE.URS    14,492  09-22-89 10:48a  STANDARD.CRS     2,557  09-22-89 10:35a
STANDARD.IRS     4,373  09-22-89 10:09a  STANDARD.PRS     1,942  09-22-89 10:09a
STANDARD.URS    28,426  09-22-89 10:09a  VERTICOM.URS     4,945  09-22-89 10:48a
VGA512   .FRS    4,096  09-22-89 10:48a  VGAITAL  .FRS     4,096  09-22-89 10:48a
UGASMC   .FRS    4,096  09-22-89 10:48a ▼ VGAUND   .FRS     4,096  09-22-89 10:48a

New directory = G:\WP51\TEXT
```

Reminder:

Using the Other Directory feature, you can directly access any directory on your hard disk.

You can edit both the New directory = and Dir messages (see fig. 10.9), just as you could edit the original message you got when you first pressed List (F5) from the editing screen or accessed the **F**ile pull-down menu and chose List **F**iles. Thus you can directly change to any directory on your hard disk.

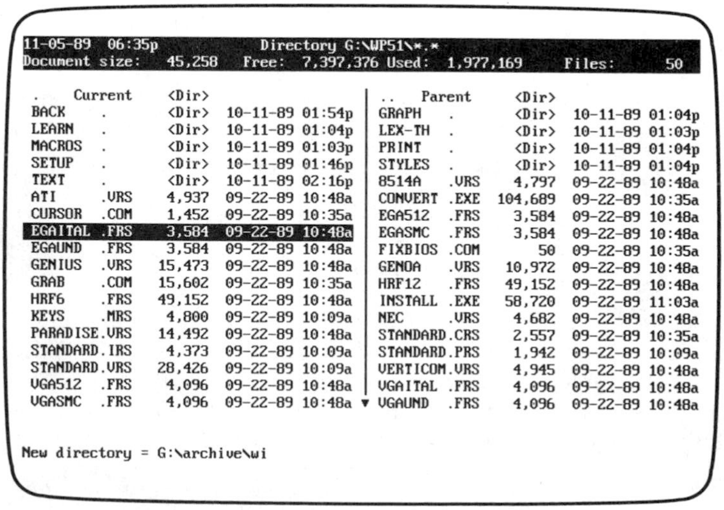

Fig. 10.9.

Preparing to change directories without first highlighting a subdirectory name.

```
11-05-89  06:35p              Directory G:\WP51\*.*
Document size:   45,258  Free:  7,397,376 Used:  1,977,169    Files:      50

.    Current    <Dir>                  ..    Parent     <Dir>
BACK       .     <Dir>  10-11-89 01:54p  GRAPH      .     <Dir>  10-11-89 01:04p
LEARN      .     <Dir>  10-11-89 01:04p  LEX-TH     .     <Dir>  10-11-89 01:03p
MACROS     .     <Dir>  10-11-89 01:03p  PRINT      .     <Dir>  10-11-89 01:04p
SETUP      .     <Dir>  10-11-89 01:46p  STYLES     .     <Dir>  10-11-89 01:04p
TEXT       .     <Dir>  10-11-89 02:16p  8514A    .URS     4,797  09-22-89 10:48a
ATI      .URS    4,937  09-22-89 10:48a  CONVERT  .EXE   104,689  09-22-89 10:35a
CURSOR   .COM    1,452  09-22-89 10:35a  EGA512   .FRS     3,584  09-22-89 10:48a
EGAITAL  .FRS    3,584  09-22-89 10:48a  EGASMC   .FRS     3,584  09-22-89 10:48a
EGAUND   .FRS    3,584  09-22-89 10:48a  FIXBIOS  .COM        50  09-22-89 10:35a
GENIUS   .URS   15,473  09-22-89 10:48a  GENOA    .URS    10,972  09-22-89 10:48a
GRAB     .COM   15,602  09-22-89 10:35a  HRF12    .FRS    49,152  09-22-89 10:48a
HRF6     .FRS   49,152  09-22-89 10:48a  INSTALL  .EXE    58,720  09-22-89 11:03a
KEYS     .MRS    4,800  09-22-89 10:09a  NEC      .URS     4,682  09-22-89 10:48a
PARADISE.URS    14,492  09-22-89 10:48a  STANDARD.CRS     2,557  09-22-89 10:35a
STANDARD.IRS     4,373  09-22-89 10:09a  STANDARD.PRS     1,942  09-22-89 10:09a
STANDARD.URS    28,426  09-22-89 10:09a  VERTICOM.URS     4,945  09-22-89 10:48a
VGA512   .FRS    4,096  09-22-89 10:48a  VGAITAL  .FRS     4,096  09-22-89 10:48a
UGASMC   .FRS    4,096  09-22-89 10:48a ▼ VGAUND   .FRS     4,096  09-22-89 10:48a

New directory = G:\archive\wi
```

You can create a new directory by entering a previously nonexistent name at the prompt that appears after you select **O**ther Directory (**7**). If you enter *frog*, WordPerfect asks Create frog? No (Yes). If you select **Y**, WordPerfect creates a new directory called FROG as a subdirectory of the currently listed directory. Select **N** if this result isn't what you want.

You also can change or create directories right from the WordPerfect editing screen. Press List (F5) or access the **F**ile pull-down menu and select List **F**iles; then press =. WordPerfect responds the same way as in the List Files screen.

Using Copy

Like the DOS COPY command, the Copy option copies the highlighted file. If you select **C**opy (**8**), WordPerfect displays the message Copy this file to:. You can copy the file to another disk or directory, or you can copy the file to the current directory by entering a new file name instead of a drive or directory.

Using Find

The first option on the Find menu, **N**ame (**1**), enables you to locate a file or group of files in the list by searching for letter patterns that are part of the file name. This process is similar to the way Search—either Forward (F2) or Reverse (Shift-F2)— operates, except that Name will search through the entire displayed file list, regardless of the current location of the highlight bar. If you know that the file you are searching for contains the letters *et*, you can quickly locate only those files in the list that have *et* in the name. Specifying *et* as the search string would find files named JOHN.LET, MEETING.NOT, LETTER.TOM, GETSTR.EXE, and so on.

All the remaining options (except Undo) enable you to search through one or more files in the file listing for a word or phrase, without retrieving the files into WordPerfect. You, for example, determine which documents are about a certain subject by searching for a word or phrase related to that subject.

Reminder:
Use the Find feature to search through files for a particular word or phrase.

To start a search, select **F**ind (**9**). You will see a screen like that in figure 10.10.

```
11-05-89  10:00p              Directory G:\LIB\REALTY\*.*
Document size:    50,804  Free:  7,380,992 Used:  1,080,546   Files:     126

     Current   <Dir>                  ..    Parent    <Dir>
  10LRE    .1       3,271  11-03-88 04:04p   10LRE    .2         709  11-03-88 04:04p
  10LRE    .3       1,091  11-03-88 04:04p   10LRE    .4       1,308  11-03-88 04:04p
  10LRE    .5       4,472  11-03-88 04:04p   10LRE    .6       3,722  11-03-88 04:04p
  10LRE    .7       5,530  11-03-88 04:05p   10LRE    .8       9,736  11-03-88 04:05p
  10LREM   .EMA    30,118  10-17-89 06:00p   11LREM   .EMA    25,347  10-17-89 06:00p
  12ALREM  .LSK    33,238  05-17-89 04:02p   12LRE    .2       1,139  11-03-88 04:05p
  12LRE    .3       1,040  11-03-88 04:05p   12LRE    .4       1,344  11-03-88 04:05p
  12LRE    .5       1,680  11-03-88 04:05p   12LRE    .6       1,936  11-03-88 04:06p
  12LRE    .7       2,543  07-24-89 06:44p   12LREM   .LSK    38,051  05-30-89 10:11a
  13LRE    .10      1,808  11-03-88 04:06p   13LRE    .11      1,424  11-03-88 04:06p
  13LRE    .12      1,296  11-03-88 04:06p   13LRE    .13      1,168  11-03-88 04:06p
  13LRE    .14      1,040  11-03-88 04:06p   13LRE    .15        912  11-03-88 04:06p
  13LRE    .16        912  11-03-88 04:06p   13LRE    .17      1,040  11-03-88 04:06p
  13LRE    .18      1,040  11-03-88 04:06p   13LRE    .19        912  11-03-88 04:06p
  13LRE    .2       1,552  11-03-88 04:06p   13LRE    .3       1,168  11-03-88 04:06p
  13LRE    .4       1,168  11-03-88 04:07p   13LRE    .7       1,251  11-03-88 04:07p
  13LRE    .9       1,168  11-03-88 04:07p   13LREM   .LSK    37,561  05-16-89 01:35p
  14LRE    .MOK     2,969  11-03-88 04:07p ▼ 14LREM   .MOK     3,998  11-03-88 04:07p

Find: 1 Name; 2 Doc Summary; 3 First Pg; 4 Entire Doc; 5 Conditions; 6 Undo: 0
```

Fig. 10.10.

Preparing to begin a Find operation.

You can restrict your search to just the document summaries (see Chapter 6) or to just the first page of each file, or you can search entire files. The **C**onditions option (**5**), discussed in detail later, provides additional tools to limit the scope of a search and to specify multiple search criteria. Search patterns (also discussed in detail later) can include words, phrases, or logical expressions.

To find files by using a search pattern, complete the following steps:

1. Select **F**ind (**9**).

2. Select one of the following: **D**oc Summary (**2**), to search only the document summary in each file; First **P**g (**3**), to search only the first page (or first 4,000 characters, whichever comes first) of each document; or **E**ntire Doc (**4**), to search an entire file.

3. When WordPerfect displays the `Word pattern:` message, type the word or search pattern you're looking for—*trustdeed*, for example—and press Enter.

WordPerfect displays the total number of files to be searched and a running tally of the number of files it has searched.

When the search is finished, WordPerfect displays a new file list showing only the files that contain the target word or phrase. The upper right corner of the List Files screen shows the number of files found (see fig. 10.11). Notice that the number of files in figure 10.11 has been reduced to 40 from the 126 files in figure 10.10.

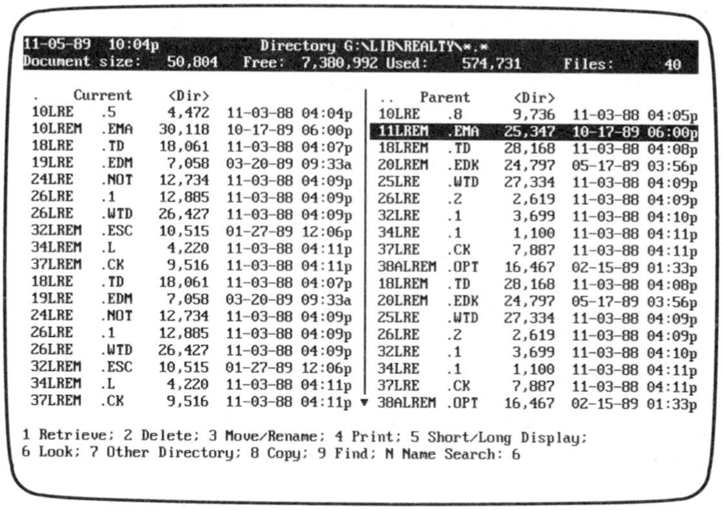

Fig. 10.11.

The file list after a Find operation.

```
┌─────────────────────────────────────────────────────────────────────┐
│ 11-05-89  10:04p           Directory G:\LIB\REALTY\*.*               │
│ Document size:    50,804   Free:  7,380,992 Used:   574,731   Files:    40 │
│                                                                     │
│        .   Current  <Dir>              ..   Parent   <Dir>          │
│     10LRE   .5        4,472  11-03-88 04:04p  10LRE    .8      9,736  11-03-88 04:05p │
│     10LREM  .EMA     30,118  10-17-89 06:00p  11LREM   .EMA   25,347  10-17-89 06:00p │
│     18LRE   .TD      18,061  11-03-88 04:07p  18LREM   .TD    28,168  11-03-88 04:08p │
│     19LRE   .EDM      7,058  03-20-89 09:33a  20LREM   .EDK   24,797  05-17-89 03:56p │
│     24LRE   .NOT     12,734  11-03-88 04:09p  25LRE    .WTD   27,334  11-03-88 04:09p │
│     26LRE   .1       12,885  11-03-88 04:09p  26LRE    .2      2,619  11-03-88 04:09p │
│     26LRE   .WTD     26,427  11-03-88 04:09p  32LRE    .1      3,699  11-03-88 04:10p │
│     32LREM  .ESC     10,515  01-27-89 12:06p  34LRE    .1      1,100  11-03-88 04:11p │
│     34LREM  .L        4,220  11-03-88 04:11p  37LRE    .CK     7,887  11-03-88 04:11p │
│     37LREM  .CK       9,516  11-03-88 04:11p  38ALREM  .OPT   16,467  02-15-89 01:33p │
│     18LRE   .TD      18,061  11-03-88 04:07p  18LREM   .TD    28,168  11-03-88 04:08p │
│     19LRE   .EDM      7,058  03-20-89 09:33a  20LREM   .EDK   24,797  05-17-89 03:56p │
│     24LRE   .NOT     12,734  11-03-88 04:09p  25LRE    .WTD   27,334  11-03-88 04:09p │
│     26LRE   .1       12,885  11-03-88 04:09p  26LRE    .2      2,619  11-03-88 04:09p │
│     26LRE   .WTD     26,427  11-03-88 04:09p  32LRE    .1      3,699  11-03-88 04:10p │
│     32LREM  .ESC     10,515  01-27-89 12:06p  34LRE    .1      1,100  11-03-88 04:11p │
│     34LREM  .L        4,220  11-03-88 04:11p  37LRE    .CK     7,887  11-03-88 04:11p │
│     37LREM  .CK       9,516  11-03-88 04:11p ▼ 38ALREM .OPT   16,467  02-15-89 01:33p │
│                                                                     │
│ 1 Retrieve; 2 Delete; 3 Move/Rename; 4 Print; 5 Short/Long Display; │
│ 6 Look; 7 Other Directory; 8 Copy; 9 Find; N Name Search: 6        │
└─────────────────────────────────────────────────────────────────────┘
```

You can then use Look to examine each file in turn by pressing Enter (or by selecting **L**ook [**6**]). Or you can retrieve each file individually into WordPerfect by pressing **R**etrieve (**1**). If you retrieve a file, however, remember that to retain the same file listing, you must go back to the List Files screen by pressing List (F5) twice (rather than F5 followed by Enter).

Caution

Find is a memory-intensive activity. If WordPerfect does not have enough RAM available to process the Find operation, the search will fail *without warning.* You will receive no error messages, only the same `Not Found` message displayed when a search fails normally. Make a special effort to maximize RAM whenever you perform a Find operation on more than a few

Caution (continued)

files. You can get increased RAM by having no files open for editing; changing your keyboard in Setup to the original keyboard; and, if necessary, temporarily changing your default printer selection to a printer, such as the standard printer, that has a small PRS file. You can also ease memory problems by using the techniques discussed in the next section that limit the number of files searched.

Reducing the Number of Files To Search

The fewer files you have to search, the faster the search goes. You can use a couple of methods to reduce the number of files to be searched by Find. The first method is to call up the List Files screen with a file specification other than the default *.*. Remember that this file specification includes all files in the current directory. If possible, reduce the number of files in the listing by specifying some subgroup of files.

Reminder:

If you can, specify a subgroup of files to be searched.

For example, your \WIP\OTHER directory may contain several contracts that you have drafted, along with contracts and other documents drafted by other people in your office. You know that somewhere in the 117 files in that directory is the contract for Smith that you drafted last week and now need to modify. If you have followed a consistent file-naming pattern, such as ending the file names of all contracts with the extension AGR, you can quickly obtain a restricted list to search through with Find.

To obtain this restricted file list, follow these steps:

1. Press List (F5).

   ⌨ Access the **F**ile pull-down menu and select List **F**iles.

2. After the file specification appears, move the cursor to the end of it and replace the *.* with *.agr. Then press Enter. The List Files screen appears, with only the 24 contract files listed. Select **F**ind (**9**) to access the search menu.

3. Select **E**ntire Doc (**4**).

4. Type the word that you want to find: *Smith*

5. Press Enter to start the search.

The other method of restricting the number of files you need to search is to mark only the files you want to search (see the section "Marking Files"). Use this method if you cannot specify with a wild card the files you want to search. Suppose that because you haven't used a consistent file-naming pattern, you have this group of files to search through for the Smith contract:

    1214WOT.EMA
    1220WOT.K
    1247WOT.COA
    1285WOT.CON
    1291WOT.AGR

Limiting your search to only these files is less convenient to arrange than selecting files that are consistently named (and thus you learn a lesson in efficient file-naming), but setting the search limits is still not difficult:

1. Press List (F5) and then Enter.

   ▭ Access the **F**ile pull-down menu, select List **F**iles, and press Enter.

2. Move the highlight bar to each of the files you want to include in the search and press the asterisk key.

3. Select **F**ind (**9**) to display the Find menu.

4. Select **E**ntire Doc (**4**).

5. Type the word you're searching for: *Smith* (see fig 10.12). Press Enter to start the search.

Fig. 10.12.

Preparing to search on marked files.

```
11-05-89  11:51p              Directory G:\WIP\OTHER\*.*
Document size:    53,634  Free:  7,323,648 Used:     187,508    Marked:         5

     . Current    <Dir>                 ..    Parent    <Dir>
   1200WOT .BSD   17,718  05-31-89 04:34p   1201WOT .NOT    7,748  06-12-89 03:37p
   1202WOT .D      9,874  06-08-89 10:56a   1203WOT .AGR    1,665  06-07-89 03:55p
   1204WOT .AGR   11,092  09-28-89 02:34p   1205WOT .WAI    5,845  06-12-89 12:11p
   1206WOT .AME    5,674  06-12-89 12:08p   1207WOT .EA     1,555  06-12-89 10:45a
   1208WOT .REM    3,415  06-14-89 11:54a   1209WOT .NOT    9,367  06-15-89 11:48a
   1210AWOT.ADD   22,783  07-11-89 01:44p   1210WOT .ADD   20,844  06-15-89 03:54p
   1211WOT .EMA   36,809  06-15-89 05:51p   1212WOT .AGR   12,715  06-30-89 01:10p
   1213WOT .BSD    8,456  06-16-89 12:08p  *1214WOT .EMA   31,368  06-19-89 06:06p
   1215WOT .ADD    5,691  06-21-89 04:01p   1216WOT .AOK   25,826  06-27-89 10:31a
   1217WOT .MEM    4,467  06-28-89 12:32p   1218WOT .MEM    5,482  06-28-89 12:52p
   1219WOT .MIN    6,328  07-31-89 04:05p   1220AWOT.K     29,375  07-31-89 03:37p
   1220AWOT.LST    2,663  07-06-89 04:36p  *1220WOT .K     29,086  07-06-89 05:07p
   1221WOT .AGR    6,761  07-06-89 05:13p   1222WOT .MEM    6,394  07-12-89 10:02a
   1223WOT .AGR    6,974  07-06-89 05:02p   1223WOT .ART    5,944  07-14-89 04:56p
   1223WOT .EMA   49,621  07-18-89 10:53a   1224WOT .ASM    8,145  07-14-89 04:57p
   1224WOT .LST    4,993  07-18-89 04:48p   1225WOT .ADD    4,887  07-18-89 04:07p
   1227WOT .LSK   37,726  08-01-89 04:31p   1228WOT .RPT   37,444  07-24-89 11:49a
   1229WOT .EMA   42,696  07-24-89 10:19a ▼ 1230WOT .ADD   12,326  07-21-89 06:18p


Word pattern: Smith
```

After finishing the search, WordPerfect lists only those files that match the search criterion (see figure 10.13).

Fig. 10.13.

The file list after a successful search.

```
11-05-89  11:57p              Directory G:\WIP\OTHER\*.AGR
Document size:    53,634  Free:  7,368,704 Used:      52,288    Files:          1

     . Current    <Dir>                 |   ..    Parent    <Dir>
   1291WOT .AGR   52,288  11-02-89 09:52a










1 Retrieve; 2 Delete; 3 Move/Rename; 4 Print; 5 Short/Long Display;
6 Look; 7 Other Directory; 8 Copy; 9 Find; N Name Search: 6
```

Using the Find Conditions Option

The fifth menu choice in Find provides even more flexible search options than the basic Find options. To use the Find Conditions option, follow these steps:

1. Select **F**ind (**9**) from the List Files screen.

2. Select **C**onditions (**5**); the Find: Conditions screen appears (see fig. 10.14).

```
Find: Conditions                    Files Selected:    117

    1 - Perform Search
    2 - Reset Conditions

    3 - Revision Date - From
                         To

    4 - Text - Document Summary
               First Page
               Entire Document

    5 - Document Summary
        Creation Date - From
                         To

        Document Name
        Document Type
        Author
        Typist
        Subject
        Account
        Keywords
        Abstract

Selection: 1
```

Fig. 10.14.

The Find: Conditions screen.

In the upper right corner of the screen is the number of files selected. This number signifies all the files in the directory, unless you have marked files with an asterisk or have obtained a limited list by using a file specification, in which case the number reflects the number of marked files or the number of files matching the file specification.

The first choice on the menu, **P**erform Search (**1**), starts a search. When the search is finished, WordPerfect displays a file list containing only those files matching the search criteria.

The second choice, **R**eset Conditions (**2**), eliminates any search criteria you've previously entered and returns all Find Conditions options to their pristine state.

You can use the Revision **D**ate (**3**) choice to restrict the search to files that were last revised within the range of specified dates. The revision date is the DOS file date that is displayed for a file in the short file listing. To specify dates as search criteria, follow these steps:

1. Select Revision **D**ate (**3**).

2. Type a date in mm/dd/yy format.

3. Press Enter to move the cursor to the To date field.

4. Type the date.

5. Press Enter once more.

Once you have specified a date range as a search criterion, the range will remain in effect until you change or delete the range, reset the search conditions (thereby clearing *all* search criteria), or look at or change to another directory.

Reminder:

By selecting Text (4) from the Find Conditions menu, you can incorporate three different searches into a single pass.

Text (4) provides you with an extremely flexible tool to use for designing searches. You can enter a separate search pattern for each of the options provided: Document Summary, First Page, and Entire Document. Doing so enables you to combine up to three different searches into a single pass through the selected files. Compare this feature to the regular Find menu, which enables you to specify only a single search pattern restricted to only one of these choices.

Be aware that if you specify more than one condition, all conditions must be true for a file before it will be selected. To enter a search condition for Text (4), follow these steps:

1. Select Text (4).
2. Use ↑ or ↓ to position the cursor on the portion of the documents in which you want to search.
3. Type the desired search string (see "Specifying Search Patterns") and press Enter.
4. Select Perform Search (1) to begin the search.

The Document Summary (5) option adds increased flexibility to your searches. Whereas you can search only an entire summary with a search pattern entered from the regular Find menu, with Document Summary (5) you can search either the whole summary or any one or more of its individual fields: Creation Date, Document Name (the long document name), Document Type, Author, Typist, Subject, Account, Keywords, or Abstract. You may enter a separate search pattern for each field searched. To enter search criteria for a document-summary field, follow these steps:

1. From the Find: Conditions screen, select Document Summary (5).
2. To search one or more individual fields of the summary, press ↓ or ↑ to move to the field(s) you want. Type a search pattern for each field you want to search; press Enter.
3. Select Perform Search (1) to start the search.

Specifying Search Patterns

Reminder:

Use logical operators and wild cards to refine your search.

A search pattern may consist of a single word or several words. Both exact phrases and "hazy" phrases can by used as search criteria. In addition, logical operators and wild cards can be used to refine the search further. Case distinctions are ignored.

Although you are given extremely wide latitude in defining the search patterns, you are limited to 39 characters for any single pattern. A question mark (?) may be used to stand for any single character; an asterisk (*) may be used to represent 0 or more characters.

To designate phrases of more than one word, surround the words in the phrase with quotation marks. Leave a space between the last letter of the phrase and the closing quotation mark to force WordPerfect to search for an exact match. The following are examples of phrase patterns:

Pattern	Result
Smith	Locates all files containing the word *Smith*
d?sk	Locates all files containing the pattern, which includes the words *disk*, *desk*, and *dusk*
"my car"	Locates files containing patterns such as *my car*, *my carpet*, and *my carnation*
"my car "	Locates files containing the exact phrase *my car*
"my*car"	Locates files containing patterns such as *my dingy old Persian carpet*, *my mother gave me a beautiful red carnation*, and *myocarditis*

You can combine words with logical operators to refine the search further. WordPerfect recognizes the following logical operators in Find:

Operator	Effect
semicolon (;)	Logical AND; locates files containing *both* words joined by the semicolon
space ( )	Logical AND; locates files containing *both* words joined by the space
comma (,)	Logical OR; locates files containing either word joined by the comma
dash (-)	Logical NOT; locates files that *do not* contain the word or phrase

The following list shows some examples of the use of logical operators in a search string:

Pattern	Result
Smith Jones Smith;Jones	Finds only files containing both *Smith* and or *Jones*
Smith,Jones	Finds files containing either *Smith* or *Jones*
Jones,Smith;John	Finds files containing either *John* and *Smith* or *John* and *Jones*
John-Jones-Smith	Finds files containing *John* but neither *Jones* nor *Smith*
John "my car "	Finds files containing *John* and the exact phrase *my car*
four-way	Finds files containing *four* but not *way*
"four-way"	Finds files containing the phrase *four-way*

Undo (**6**), the last option on the Find menu, reverses the results of the last search. Suppose that a search of all files in the directory ends with eight files marked. A second search of those eight files ends with two files marked. If you decide that the second search was a mistake, select **Undo** (**6**); the file list returns to a listing of the eight previously found files. Now you can search them with different criteria. You can undo up to three levels this way.

Maximizing the Use of Find

As you can see from the foregoing examples, Find searches for character patterns rather than words. If you search for an exact phrase match by putting a space before the closing quotation mark, you will not locate words followed by punctuation marks. Moreover, the logical operators do not provide a good way to combine several criteria into a single search string. Logical operations are performed in order from left to right, and there is no simple way to cause an operator to affect more than one word or phrase.

Another complicating factor to remember about Find searches is that Find locates words anywhere in a document, including in headers, footers, and footnotes. A search in Look, however, does not find words in these places. So if Find locates some files in which only a header, footer, or footnote contains the word you're searching for, you won't be able to locate the word in those files by using Search (F2) from **Look** (**6**).

You can maximize your results with Find by using the following strategies:

1. Keep your files organized. Take advantage of subdirectories to group similar files together.

2. Keep directories small. If a working directory contains over 150 files, consider whether some files could be removed to an archive directory.

3. Use a consistent naming pattern that will enable you to shorten your first search list by using a file specification (such as *.LTR) or **N**ame (**1**).

4. Try to search for important words or phrases that will appear in the document summary or on the first page of the files.

5. If you must search a large number of files, use a series of searches that successively narrow your list of files to scan; take advantage of **U**ndo (**6**) to back out of any search operation that misses your target file.

6. When you have narrowed your search list to a manageable number of files and want to locate a file for retrieval, quickly scan the list by using **L**ook (**6**) combined with Forward Search (F2), **N**ext Doc (**1**), and **P**rev Doc (**2**).

Using Name Search

Using **N**ame Search (**N**), you can quickly move the highlight bar to a file name in the listing as you type the name. To start, press N and then type the first letter of the file name for which you want to search—for example, CONTRACT. If you type *c*, the highlight bar jumps to the first file name starting with that letter (see fig. 10.15).

If you type *o* as the second letter of the name, the highlight bar jumps to the first file name that starts with these two letters (see fig. 10.16). If no file name starts with those letters, the highlight bar moves to the file name that is as close (alphabetically) to that combination as possible.

```
11-18-89  09:08p              Directory G:\WP\MACROS\DOCS\*.*
Document size:    66,982  Free:  7,008,256 Used:     430,078     Files:      88

     Current      <Dir>                ..   Parent     <Dir>
A-BASE  .WP5     17,168  11-03-88 03:33p │ ACK     .     1,189  11-03-88 03:25p
ACKCORP .         1,299  11-03-88 03:25p │ ADDEND  .     2,275  11-17-89 03:25p
AFF     .         3,960  06-08-89 03:24p │ ANSWER  .     5,159  11-03-88 03:26p
CAPCIRC .         5,083  05-24-89 09:17a │ CAPCOL  .     2,371  05-18-89 10:28a
CAPCOL  .1       10,032  10-19-89 11:33a │ CAPCOL  .2    9,427  05-24-89 09:10a
CAPCOL  .3        9,502  05-24-89 09:16a │ CAPCOL  .4    9,489  05-24-89 09:16a
CAPCOL  .5        9,612  05-24-89 09:16a │ CAPCOL  .6    9,463  05-24-89 09:16a
CAPCOL  .7        9,419  05-24-89 09:16a │ CAPCOL  .8    9,834  05-24-89 09:16a
CAPDIST .         4,868  05-24-89 09:17a │ CAPDOM  .     4,959  05-24-89 09:17a
CAPPROB .         4,585  05-24-89 09:17a │ CAPUS   .     5,042  05-24-89 09:17a
CERTACC .         1,438  11-03-88 03:27p │ CERTMAIL.     1,847  05-13-89 06:13p
CERTOFF .         1,887  05-13-89 06:17p │ CERTPERS.     1,748  05-13-89 06:17p
CITES   .         1,354  11-03-88 03:27p │ COMMENT .SRT    796  11-03-88 03:27p
COMPLT  .         7,644  10-06-89 04:22p │ COMPROM .     1,233  02-23-89 04:25p
CONTRACT.         8,773  10-30-89 04:54p │ COPY    .     1,111  11-03-88 03:27p
COPY    .TXT      1,221  08-01-89 05:10p │ COURT   .     9,080  10-06-89 04:20p
COURTLAS.         1,488  11-03-88 03:27p │ COVER   .     7,571  03-06-89 12:23p
COVER   .BOX      3,829  03-06-89 11:58a ▼ COVER1  .     1,552  11-03-88 03:34p

c                      (Name Search; Enter or arrows to Exit)
```

Fig. 10.15.

The effect, on a name search, of typing the first letter.

```
11-18-89  09:08p              Directory G:\WP\MACROS\DOCS\*.*
Document size:    66,982  Free:  7,008,256 Used:     430,078     Files:      88

     Current      <Dir>                ..   Parent     <Dir>
A-BASE  .WP5     17,168  11-03-88 03:33p │ ACK     .     1,189  11-03-88 03:25p
ACKCORP .         1,299  11-03-88 03:25p │ ADDEND  .     2,275  11-17-89 03:25p
AFF     .         3,960  06-08-89 03:24p │ ANSWER  .     5,159  11-03-88 03:26p
CAPCIRC .         5,083  05-24-89 09:17a │ CAPCOL  .     2,371  05-18-89 10:28a
CAPCOL  .1       10,032  10-19-89 11:33a │ CAPCOL  .2    9,427  05-24-89 09:10a
CAPCOL  .3        9,502  05-24-89 09:16a │ CAPCOL  .4    9,489  05-24-89 09:16a
CAPCOL  .5        9,612  05-24-89 09:16a │ CAPCOL  .6    9,463  05-24-89 09:16a
CAPCOL  .7        9,419  05-24-89 09:16a │ CAPCOL  .8    9,834  05-24-89 09:16a
CAPDIST .         4,868  05-24-89 09:17a │ CAPDOM  .     4,959  05-24-89 09:17a
CAPPROB .         4,585  05-24-89 09:17a │ CAPUS   .     5,042  05-24-89 09:17a
CERTACC .         1,438  11-03-88 03:27p │ CERTMAIL.     1,847  05-13-89 06:13p
CERTOFF .         1,887  05-13-89 06:17p │ CERTPERS.     1,748  05-13-89 06:17p
CITES   .         1,354  11-03-88 03:27p │ COMMENT .SRT    796  11-03-88 03:27p
COMPLT  .         7,644  10-06-89 04:22p │ COMPROM .     1,233  02-23-89 04:25p
CONTRACT.         8,773  10-30-89 04:54p │ COPY    .     1,111  11-03-88 03:27p
COPY    .TXT      1,221  08-01-89 05:10p │ COURT   .     9,080  10-06-89 04:20p
COURTLAS.         1,488  11-03-88 03:27p │ COVER   .     7,571  03-06-89 12:23p
COVER   .BOX      3,829  03-06-89 11:58a ▼ COVER1  .     1,552  11-03-88 03:34p

co                     (Name Search; Enter or arrows to Exit)
```

Fig. 10.16.

The effect, on a name search, of typing a second letter.

If you still don't find the file, type the third letter—*n* in this example. The highlight bar jumps to the first file name starting with these three letters (see fig. 10.17).

If you make a mistake or change your mind, press Backspace; the highlight bar jumps to the previous position. Once the file name you want is highlighted, turn off Name Search by pressing Cancel (F1), Enter, or one of the arrow keys. Then you can do any of the operations described in this chapter—for example, Retrieve, Delete, or Print.

Fig. 10.17.

The effect, on a name search, of typing a third letter.

```
 11-18-89  09:08p              Directory G:\WP\MACROS\DOCS\*.*
 Document size:    66,982   Free:  7,008,256 Used:      430,078    Files:      88

      .    Current   <Dir>                     ..    Parent    <Dir>
 A-BASE  .WP5    17,168  11-03-88 03:33p │  ACK     .        1,189  11-03-88 03:25p
 ACKCORP .        1,299  11-03-88 03:25p │  ADDEND  .        2,275  11-17-89 03:25p
 AFF     .        3,960  06-08-89 03:24p │  ANSWER  .        5,159  11-03-88 03:26p
 CAPCIRC .        5,083  05-24-89 09:17a │  CAPCOL  .        2,371  05-18-89 10:28a
 CAPCOL  .1      10,032  10-19-89 11:33a │  CAPCOL  .2       9,427  05-24-89 09:10a
 CAPCOL  .3       9,502  05-24-89 09:16a │  CAPCOL  .4       9,489  05-24-89 09:16a
 CAPCOL  .5       9,612  05-24-89 09:16a │  CAPCOL  .6       9,463  05-24-89 09:16a
 CAPCOL  .7       9,419  05-24-89 09:16a │  CAPCOL  .8       9,834  05-24-89 09:16a
 CAPDIST .        4,868  05-24-89 09:17a │  CAPDOM  .        4,959  05-24-89 09:17a
 CAPPROB .        4,585  05-24-89 09:17a │  CAPUS   .        5,042  05-24-89 09:17a
 CERTACC .        1,438  11-03-88 03:27p │  CERTMAIL.        1,847  05-13-89 06:13p
 CERTOFF .        1,887  05-13-89 06:17p │  CERTPERS.        1,748  05-13-89 06:17p
 CITES   .        1,354  11-03-88 03:27p │  COMMENT .SRT       796  11-03-88 03:27p
 COMPLT  .        7,644  10-06-89 04:22p │  COMPROM .        1,233  02-23-89 04:25p
 CONTRACT.        8,773  10-30-89 04:54p │  COPY    .        1,111  11-03-88 03:27p
 COPY    .TXT     1,221  08-01-89 05:10p │  COURT   .        9,080  10-06-89 04:20p
 COURTLAS.        1,488  11-03-88 03:27p │  COVER   .        7,571  03-06-89 12:23p
 COVER   .BOX     3,829  03-06-89 11:58a ▼ COVER1  .        1,552  11-03-88 03:34p


 con                               (Name Search; Enter or arrows to Exit)
```

5.1

Reminder:

You can use the Name Search feature with directory names as well as file names.

WordPerfect 5.1 enables you to use Name Search to search for directory names as well as file names. To use this feature, just type a backslash (\) before the first character of the directory name you are searching for (see figure 10.18).

Fig. 10.18.

A name search for a directory.

```
 11-18-89  09:28p              Directory G:\LIB\*.*
 Document size:    68,622   Free:  7,008,256 Used:          0    Files:       0

      .    Current   <Dir>                     ..    Parent    <Dir>
 ADOPT   .       <Dir>  09-14-88 12:18p │  APPEAL  .       <Dir>  09-14-88 12:18p
 ARBIT   .       <Dir>  09-14-88 12:18p │  BANKRUPT.       <Dir>  09-14-88 12:18p
 BUSINESS.       <Dir>  09-14-88 12:18p │  CONSUMER.       <Dir>  09-14-88 12:19p
 CONTRACT.       <Dir>  09-14-88 12:19p │  CRIM    .       <Dir>  09-14-88 12:19p
 DIVORCE .       <Dir>  09-14-88 12:19p │  GUARD   .       <Dir>  09-14-88 12:19p
 JUVE    .       <Dir>  09-14-88 01:36p │  LIENS   .       <Dir>  09-14-88 01:37p
 LITIG   .       <Dir>  09-14-88 12:19p │  OFCFORM .       <Dir>  09-14-88 01:38p
 PROBATE .       <Dir>  09-14-88 12:19p │  REALTY  .       <Dir>  09-14-88 12:19p
 TAX     .       <Dir>  09-14-88 01:38p │  WILLS   .       <Dir>  09-14-88 12:19p
 WORKCOMP.       <Dir>  09-20-88 06:52p │




 \r                                (Name Search; Enter or arrows to Exit)
```

In addition to providing the Name Search method of locating files and directories, WordPerfect has now made both Forward Search (F2) and Reverse Search (Shift-F2) fully available within the List Files display. You can thus search for any character or sequence of characters located anywhere within a file name or directory name. This feature is particularly useful in the long display (see "Using Short/Long Display") because a search operation will look for the defined search string in the long-name and document-type fields as well as in the DOS-name field. For example, specifying the search string *Cont*, as in figure 10.19, will find a file having *Contract* specified as a document type (see fig. 10.20).

5.1

```
11-18-89  09:57p          Directory G:\WP51\TEXT\*.*
Document size:    69,935   Free:  7,008,256 Used:       364,464      Files:       37
Descriptive Name                  Type      Filename     Size      Revision Date

Current Directory                              .        <Dir>
Parent Directory                               ..       <Dir>
                                            1203WOT .AGR   1,665   06-07-89 03:55p
                                            1204WOT .AGR  11,092   09-28-89 02:34p
                                            1205WOT .WAI   5,845   06-12-89 12:11p
                                            322LPRP .AFF   7,058   10-12-89 12:39p
                                            387LPRP .ADD     381   10-12-89 12:38p
                                            53LREM  .NOT  12,270   10-12-89 02:36p
                                            64AOFF  .BRO  53,327   10-16-89 07:01p
Bargain and Sale Deed                       1200WOT .BSD  16,917   11-16-89 11:56p
Bargain and Sale Deed                       1202WOT .D     9,874   06-08-89 10:56a
Circuit Court caption - genera              COMPL   .TST  14,631   11-14-89 05:02p
                                            CODES   .TST   5,298   11-18-89 04:17p
Estate MIL (secondary merge)                1017WPRS.MIL   3,963   10-12-89 12:37p
Letter form                                 LTRCBS  .      5,194   10-25-89 10:10a
Letter form                                 TEST1   .L    10,310   10-18-89 04:25p
Promissory Note - Moskovitz/Da              1201WOT .NOT   9,554   10-12-89 11:30a
Roadway Maintenance Agreement   Contract    1291AWOT.AGR  45,337   11-08-89 11:26a


-> Srch: Cont
```

Fig. 10.19.

Preparing to use Forward Search (F2) in the long-file-list display.

```
11-18-89  09:57p          Directory G:\WP51\TEXT\*.*
Document size:    69,935   Free:  7,008,256 Used:       364,464      Files:       37
Descriptive Name                  Type      Filename     Size      Revision Date

Current Directory                              .        <Dir>
Parent Directory                               ..       <Dir>
                                            1203WOT .AGR   1,665   06-07-89 03:55p
                                            1204WOT .AGR  11,092   09-28-89 02:34p
                                            1205WOT .WAI   5,845   06-12-89 12:11p
                                            322LPRP .AFF   7,058   10-12-89 12:39p
                                            387LPRP .ADD     381   10-12-89 12:38p
                                            53LREM  .NOT  12,270   10-12-89 02:36p
                                            64AOFF  .BRO  53,327   10-16-89 07:01p
Bargain and Sale Deed                       1200WOT .BSD  16,917   11-16-89 11:56p
Bargain and Sale Deed                       1202WOT .D     9,874   06-08-89 10:56a
Circuit Court caption - genera              COMPL   .TST  14,631   11-14-89 05:02p
                                            CODES   .TST   5,298   11-18-89 04:17p
Estate MIL (secondary merge)                1017WPRS.MIL   3,963   10-12-89 12:37p
Letter form                                 LTRCBS  .      5,194   10-25-89 10:10a
Letter form                                 TEST1   .L    10,310   10-18-89 04:25p
Promissory Note - Moskovitz/Da              1201WOT .NOT   9,554   10-12-89 11:30a
Roadway Maintenance Agreement   Contract    1291AWOT.AGR  45,337   11-08-89 11:26a

1 Retrieve; 2 Delete; 3 Move/Rename; 4 Print; 5 Short/Long Display;
6 Look; 7 Other Directory; 8 Copy; 9 Find; N Name Search: 6
```

Fig. 10.20.

The result of using Forward Search (F2) in long-file-list display.

Marking Files

To perform certain List Files functions simultaneously on more than one file, use file marking.

You can perform many of the List Files operations on a number of files simultaneously by using *file marking*—that is, by first marking those files. To mark files, follow these steps:

1. Press List (F5) and then Enter to get to the List Files screen.

    ⌨ Access the **F**ile pull-down menu, select List **F**iles, and press Enter.

2. Move the highlight bar to the first file you want to mark.

3. Press the asterisk key.

WordPerfect puts a bold asterisk to the left of the highlighted file name, then moves the highlight bar automatically to the next file name in the listing.

4. Move the highlight bar to each file you want to include, and mark those files (see fig. 10.21).

Fig. 10.21.

Marked files in the default display.

```
11-18-89  10:13p               Directory C:\BOOK\CHAP10\*.*
Document size:   70,577  Free:  1,183,744 Used:      3,019      Marked:      8

  10-16    .PIX   2,387  11-18-89 09:14p | 10-17    .PIX   2,389  11-18-89 09:17p
  10-18    .PIX   2,070  11-18-89 09:30p | 10-19    .PIX   2,409  11-18-89 09:58p
  10-2     .FST  86,569  11-06-89 12:22a | 10-2     .PIX   2,405  11-16-89 12:29a
  10-20    .PIX   2,612  11-18-89 09:59p | 10-3     .FST  46,209  11-04-89 10:03p
  10-3     .PIX   2,411  11-04-89 11:31p | 10-4     .FST  81,899  11-06-89 12:24a
  10-4     .PIX   2,416  11-05-89 04:44p | 10-5     .FST  69,589  11-06-89 12:26a
  10-5     .PIX   2,764  11-05-89 06:00p | 10-6     .FST  42,997  11-06-89 08:26p
  10-6     .PIX   2,142  11-06-89 08:24p | 10-7     .FST 111,524  11-06-89 12:29a
  10-7     .PIX   2,389  11-05-89 06:09p | 10-8     .FST 112,013  11-06-89 12:31a
  10-8     .PIX   2,403  11-05-89 06:19p | 10-9     .FST 111,783  11-06-89 12:32a
  10-9     .PIX   2,405  11-05-89 06:37p | 25LWIM   .POA  10,555  11-18-89 03:29p
  40LWIM   .POA  32,029  11-04-89 03:28p | CHAP10   .50   32,667  10-27-89 06:32p
  CHAP10   .51   35,128  10-28-89 10:54p | CHAP10   .REV  70,224  11-18-89 10:05p
  CODES    .TST   4,995  11-18-89 03:23p | LOCK     .TST     361  11-05-89 07:07p
  TEST     .        481  11-04-89 05:19p |*TEST     .1       341  11-18-89 04:53p
 *TEST     .2       341  11-18-89 04:53p |*TEST     .3       336  11-18-89 04:54p
 *TEST     .4       336  11-18-89 04:54p |*TEST     .5       343  11-18-89 04:55p
 *TEST     .6       342  11-18-89 04:55p |*TEST     .7       639  11-18-89 08:06p
 *TEST     .8       341  11-18-89 05:00p | TEST     .9       342  11-18-89 05:00p

1 Retrieve; 2 Delete; 3 Move/Rename; 4 Print; 5 Short/Long Display;
6 Look; 7 Other Directory; 8 Copy; 9 Find; N Name Search: 6
```

If you want to mark all the files in the listing, press Home and then the asterisk key, or press Mark Files (Alt-F5). Pressing those same keys when files are already marked will unmark all marked files.

With marked files, the last two fields of the screen heading change. The `Used:` field shows the combined size of the marked files. The `Files:` field changes to `Marked:` and shows the number of marked files.

Pressing Print (Shift-F7) to print a directory listing containing marked files prints the marks as well. Printing the marks is useful, for example, for saving a record of which files were printed or deleted.

Not all menu operations work on marked files. You cannot, for instance, retrieve all marked files at once. You can, however, use the following options with marked files:

Delete (**2**)

Move (**3**) (but not Rename)

Print (**4**) (on the currently selected printer)

Copy (**8**) (to a different drive or directory)

Find (**9**) (This feature works as usual, except that the Find Conditions screen shows the number of marked files rather than the total number of files in the listing.)

WordPerfect keeps in RAM a "picture" of the last file list displayed. Pressing List (F5) twice recalls the last file list displayed during the current editing session, exactly as the list appeared when it was on-screen. Any files added to the directory after you return to the main document-editing screen *will not be displayed* unless you update the list of files by moving the cursor bar to the .Current <Dir> entry and pressing Enter twice.

If you have marked files and then gone to the editing screen, you can redisplay the same file list, complete with the same marked files, by pressing List (F5) twice. This technique works as long as the list containing the marked files was the last file list you displayed.

The following steps demonstrate how to move a group of files (the assumption is that you have already marked the files you want to move):

1. Select **M**ove/Rename (**3**).

2. Select **Y** in response to the prompt Move marked files? No (Yes).

   If you select **N** (or any other key except **Y**) in response to the prompt, WordPerfect displays the New name message, which enables you to rename the file indicated by the highlight bar, as described in the section "Using Move/Rename."

3. When you see the prompt Move marked files to:, type the directory or drive where you want to move the files; press Enter.

When you use any of the commands that work with marked files, WordPerfect asks you to confirm the requested operation on the marked files. If you select **Y**, WordPerfect continues with the operation. If you select **N**, WordPerfect asks whether you want to perform the operation on the file the highlight bar is on. (If you select **N** after requesting a Move operation, WordPerfect asks whether you want to rename.)

Copying Text from Look with the Clipboard Feature

WordPerfect has added a powerful new feature for users who run WordPerfect under WordPerfect Office's Shell program. When you select **L**ook (**6**) in this situation, you can copy to the clipboard—for retrieval into another WordPerfect file or any other application that can use the clipboard—a block from a file that you are viewing. To use this feature, take the following steps:

1. Start WordPerfect from the Office Shell menu.

2. Press List (F5).

   ⌨ Access the **F**ile pull-down menu and select List **F**iles.

3. To accept the proposed directory, press Enter. If you don't want the proposed directory, edit the file specification to show another directory; then press Enter.

4. Move the highlight bar to a file from which you want to extract information.

Reminder:
If you run WordPerfect under WordPerfect Office or WordPerfect Library, you can use Look to copy a file block to the clipboard.

5. Select **L**ook (**6**).

6. Move the cursor to the beginning of the section you want to copy. If the file has a document summary, select **L**ook at text (**3**) and then move the cursor.

7. Press Block (Alt-F4 or F12) and move the cursor to highlight the block you want to copy (see fig. 10.22).

   Mouse users must activate Block with the function keys and use the arrow keys and/or Forward Search (F2) to move the cursor. Dragging the mouse will not activate Block, nor will the mouse move the cursor to highlight the text.

Fig. 10.22.

A highlighted block in Look.

```
┌─────────────────────────────────────────────────────────────────┐
│ File: C:\BOOK\CHAP10\40LWIM.POA          WP5.1     Revised: 11-04-89 03:28p │
│                                                                   │
│                   Power of Attorney for Health Care               │
│                                                                   │
│     I appoint Name of agent˜, whose address is Agent's address˜, and whose te │
│ number is phone # of agent˜, as my attorney-in-fact for health care decisions. │
│ of agent˜, whose address is Agent's address˜, and whose telephone number is ph │
│ agent˜, as my alternative attorney-in-fact for health care decisions. I author │
│ fact appointed by this document to make health care decisions for me when I am │
│ making my own health care decisions. I have read the warning below and underst │
│ consequences of appointing a power of attorney for health care.   │
│                                                                   │
│     I direct that my attorney-in-fact comply with the following instructions o │
│ the attached supplementary instructions).                         │
│                                                                   │
│     In addition, I direct that my attorney-in-fact have authority to make deci │
│ the following:                                                    │
│                                                                   │
│          Withholding or withdrawal of life-sustaining procedures with the unde │
│          that death may result.                                   │
│                                                                   │
│ Clipboard: 1 Save; 2 Append: 0                                    │
└─────────────────────────────────────────────────────────────────┘
```

8. Press Shell (Ctrl-F1). You will be presented with the options **S**ave (**1**) and **A**ppend (**2**).

9. To copy to the clipboard and replace any existing clipboard text, select **S**ave (**1**). To copy to the clipboard and append to the end of any existing clipboard text, select **A**ppend (**2**).

10. Once the material has been saved to the clipboard, press either Exit (F7) or Cancel (F1) twice to return to the main editing screen.

11. From a WordPerfect editing screen, select Shell (Ctrl-F1).

   Access the **F**ile pull-down menu and select **G**o to Shell.

   You will see the following menu:

   1 Go to Shell; **Clipboard: 2 S**ave; **3 A**ppend; **4 R**etrieve; **5** DOS **C**ommand: **0**

12. Select **R**etrieve (**4**). All clipboard text and formatting codes will be inserted at the cursor position. Figure 10.23 shows the text marked in figure 10.22, after it has been retrieved from the clipboard.

All text in the highlighted block is saved to the clipboard, including text that is to the right of the visible screen border. All formatting codes contained within the boundaries of the copied text in the source file are copied with the block. Formatting codes contained in styles present within the block are copied, but the style code itself is not copied. Merge codes are also copied. The formatting of the

```
┌─────────────────────────────────────────────────────────────┐
│  ▐████████ Power of Attorney for Health Care ████████▌        │
│                                                               │
│       I appoint {PROMPT}Name of agent~{KEYBOARD}, whose address is {PROMPT}Agent │
│ number is {PROMPT}phone # of agent~{KEYBOARD}, as my attorney-in-fact for health │
│ of agent~{KEYBOARD}, whose address is {PROMPT}Agent's address~{KEYBOARD}, and w │
│ agent~{KEYBOARD}, as my alternative attorney-in-fact for health care decisions. │
│                                                               │
│                                                               │
│                                                               │
│                                    Doc 2 Pg 1 Ln 1" Pos 1"    │
│ (   ▲   ▲   ▲   ▲   ▲   ▲   ▲   ▲   ▲   ▲   }   ▲   ▲          │
│ [Font:*Bits Charter Roman 11pt (ASCII Business) (FW, Port)][T/B Mar:0.75",0.22"] │
│ [Just:Full][Hyph On][Par Num Def:][Suppress:HA][Header A:Every page;[Open Style: │
│ PoaHead] ... ][Footer A:Every page;[Style On:PoaFoot] ... ][VRY LARGE][SM CAP][C │
│ enter][BOLD]Power of Attorney for Health Care[bold][sm cap][vry large][HRt]     │
│ [HRt]                                                         │
│ [HRt]                                                         │
│ [TAB]I appoint [Mrg:PROMPT]Name of agent~[Mrg:KEYBOARD], whose address is [Mrg: │
│ PROMPT]Agent's address~[Mrg:KEYBOARD], and whose telephone[SRt]                 │
│ number is [Mrg:PROMPT]phone # of agent~[Mrg:KEYBOARD], as my attorney[-]in[-]fac │
│                                                               │
│ Press Reveal Codes to restore screen                         │
└─────────────────────────────────────────────────────────────┘
```

Fig. 10.23.

A Reveal Codes view of a block retrieved through the clipboard.

copied text in the source file will not be copied with the retrieved text unless the formatting codes are located within the boundaries of the copied block.

If you use this new feature with the other List Files tools that enable you to locate and scan through files quickly without retrieving them, you will be able to assemble a file quickly by using pieces from many different source files. You can also have two active files open for editing and still locate and retrieve into one of the open files an important segment of text from a third file—nearly the equivalent of having additional document-editing windows.

Locking Files

You can assign a password to files so that no one but you can retrieve them, examine them with the **L**ook option (**6**) in List Files, or print them. If you decide that you want to guard your files with password protection, keep one important caution in mind: if you forget the password, the file will be inaccessible to you. *Don't forget your password!*

Reminder:

If you forget a file's password, you cannot access the file.

Assume that you have a file on-screen and want to save and "lock" it with a password. Do the following:

1. Press Text In/Out (Ctrl-F5), select **P**assword (**2**), and then select **A**dd/Change (**1**).

    Access the **F**ile pull-down menu, select Pass**w**ord, and then select **A**dd/Change.

2. At the Enter Password: prompt, type up to 24 characters for your password; press Enter.

3. WordPerfect prompts you to reenter the password. Type the password again and press Enter. If you make a typing error or don't enter the correct password, you get an error message and are prompted to go through the process again for identifying a password for your file.

4. To complete the process of password protection, press Save (F10) or Exit (F7).

    ⌨ Access the **F**ile pull-down menu and select **S**ave or E**x**it.

Your password can include any character in the WordPerfect character sets. Press Compose (Ctrl-2), or ⌨ access the **F**ont pull-down menu and select **Ch**aracters, to enter any character that you cannot directly type from the keyboard.

Before you retrieve a locked file, make certain that you have a clear editing screen. When you attempt to retrieve a file by pressing either Retrieve (Shift-F10) or List (F5), or ⌨ by accessing the **F**ile pull-down menu and choosing **R**etrieve or List Files, WordPerfect prompts you to enter the password. Unless you enter the correct password, WordPerfect will not retrieve the document to the screen.

When you want to "unprotect" a file, you begin by retrieving the file as you would retrieve any password-protected file. With the document on-screen, press Text In/Out (Ctrl-F5), select **P**assword (**2**), and choose **R**emove (**2**). ⌨ If you are using the pull-down menus, access the **F**ile pull-down menu, select Pass**w**ord, and select **R**emove. To verify that your document is now unlocked, save the file and then retrieve it again. WordPerfect no longer prompts you to enter a password.

Summary

In this chapter, you learned about WordPerfect's List Files feature. Remember that with List Files, you can perform many file and directory operations that you ordinarily have to do from DOS. For example, you can do the following tasks:

❏ Delete files and directories (with **D**elete [**2**])

❏ Rename and move files (with **M**ove/Rename [**3**])

❏ Look at a file's contents (with **L**ook [**6**])

❏ Change the current directory (with **O**ther Directory [**7**])

❏ Create new directories (with **O**ther Directory [**7**])

❏ Copy files (with **C**opy [**8**])

In addition, with List Files you can perform many WordPerfect functions more conveniently:

❏ Retrieve WordPerfect or DOS files (with **R**etrieve [**1**])

❏ Print WordPerfect or DOS files (with **P**rint [**4**])

❏ Search for words or phrases in files on the disk (with **F**ind [**9**])

❏ Copy text from a file on disk through the Office Clipboard without first retrieving the file

List Files can make your WordPerfect sessions more convenient, efficient, and effective—and the feature is easier to learn and use than the corresponding DOS commands.

Part II

Using WordPerfect's Advanced Features

Creating Basic Macros

Creating Advanced Macros

Assembling Documents with Merge

Sorting and Selecting Data

Using Styles

Using WordPerfect with Other Programs

Creating Basic Macros

Elias Baumgarten, associate professor of philosophy at the University of Michigan at Dearborn, was a beta tester for WordPerfect 5 and 5.1. He has developed hundreds of macros for himself and others.

Macros are one of the most useful and exciting features of WordPerfect 5.1. In its simplest form, a *macro* is a file you create to represent a series of keystrokes. After you create a macro, you can just type the name of the macro instead of typing all the keystrokes.

Using even a few macros can help to "complete" WordPerfect for you by tailoring it to your personal needs. Every word processing program has features that you can use in easy, one- or two-key procedures. In WordPerfect you can, for example, delete a word in one step (by pressing Ctrl-Backspace), but you need more keystrokes to delete a sentence or a paragraph. If you are someone who often deletes whole sentences or paragraphs, you can create macros to make those tasks—or any others—just as easy as deleting a word.

You can create a macro to perform nearly any task that you can accomplish with a series of keystrokes. Suppose, for instance, that you occasionally need to do something intricate, such as set up a format for columns. You can create a macro that collects and saves all the required keystrokes under one name. Then, whenever you want to set up columns, you won't need to search your desk drawer for your notes. You simply invoke the macro, which tells WordPerfect, "Do all that again."

Macros are like tiny programs within the larger WordPerfect program. Just as you invoke WordPerfect (WP.EXE) by typing *wp*, you run each of your macros by pressing the keys for its name. You have more control, though, over the macros you create than you have over commercial programs like WordPerfect. You decide what to name your macros. You decide also what your macros do when they run.

Reminder:
When you invoke a macro, WordPerfect executes the keystrokes in the macro automatically.

305

Aside from their obvious advantages, macros are fun to create and use. In this chapter, you first learn these basic macro skills:

- Understanding types of macros
- Creating macros
- Running macros
- Stopping macros
- Replacing macros
- Controlling how your macros run

You then learn how to create a number of useful macros and how to manage your macro files. Finally, you learn how to use the macro editor, which enables you to alter a macro without having to create it from scratch.

To help you become familiar with WordPerfect macros, this chapter also includes the following features:

- Samples of useful macros
- Techniques to apply when you create your own macros
- Tips on using macros

You will best learn macro techniques if you practice creating the sample macros in this chapter. Because macros draw on other WordPerfect procedures, you may learn some new tricks for using WordPerfect as you work through this chapter. Be sure, in particular, to create the AD macro. That macro is used in many of the examples throughout the chapter.

You should know some bad news and some good news about WordPerfect 5.1. The bad news is that WordPerfect 5.1 cannot run macros created in versions of WordPerfect before version 5. The good news is that you can run most of the macros you created in WordPerfect 5 without modification in version 5.1. You should be aware, however, that some commands have changed in WordPerfect 5.1, and if any of these commands are included in your macros, you will need to change those macros.

WordPerfect 5.1 includes a macro editor that is built into the program. This chapter introduces you to the macro editor and shows you how to modify macros, including those you created with WordPerfect 5. The macro editor enables you not only to change macros after you create them, but also to create extremely flexible and powerful macros. The most complex functions of the macro editor require use of a command language, which is discussed separately in Chapter 12, "Creating Advanced Macros."

Reminder:

If you created macros in WordPerfect 5, you may need to change some of them before they will work properly in WordPerfect 5.1.

> **Reminder**
>
> If you use a mouse with WordPerfect 5.1, you can click the right button to display the pull-down menus, and then select the desired option. You also can press Alt-= to access the pull-down menus, and then press the appropriate letter of the desired option. For all the instructions, you can assume that if a block is required to activate a pull-down menu option, the text has been blocked before the pull-down menu is accessed. Instructions for pull-down menus and the mouse are marked with the mouse icon. 🖰

Understanding Types of Macros

You can create and run four kinds of macros: Alt-*letter* macros, descriptive macros, unnamed macros, and keyboard macros. An Alt-*letter* macro has a name that consists of the Alt key plus a letter from A to Z—for example, Alt-K or Alt-X. A descriptive macro has a name of one to eight characters, such as TABS or MARGIN5. An unnamed macro is, from a user's point of view, named with the Enter key. (WordPerfect names this macro WP{WP}.WPM, but for most purposes, you do not need to be concerned about this.) A keyboard macro is one you create by redefining any key in WordPerfect. For instance, you can redefine the F8 function key (Underline) to turn on italics instead of underline. For more information about creating macros from key definitions, refer to Chapter 20.

The macros that are simplest to create and use are Alt-*letter* macros. Choose Alt-*letter* names, therefore, for the macros you will use most often. Be sure to use macro names that will remind you of what the macros do. For instance, you might use the name Alt-C for a macro that centers text.

> **Reminder:**
> *The simplest macros to create and use are Alt-letter macros.*

All macros have file names that include the three-letter extension WPM. The full file name of a descriptive macro called TABS, for example, is TABS.WPM. You do not need to be concerned about the WPM extension except when you manipulate macros as files, either in DOS or through the List (F5) feature. You will learn more about handling macros as files later in this chapter.

Creating Macros

Before you can use a macro, you need to create it. In this section, you learn the five steps required to create macros. You then create your first macro—something short but useful.

Before practicing with macros, store your current document by either pressing Save (F10) or selecting **S**ave from the **F**ile pull-down menu. That way, you won't need to worry about affecting any of your permanent files. You can safely practice making macros with the document that remains on-screen right after you save it. (Just be sure not to save the document again with the same name!) Or you can start with a blank screen and type a few lines of text whenever you need something for a macro to act on.

You create a macro in five steps:

1. To begin macro recording, press Macro Define (Ctrl-F10).

   ▭ Access the **T**ools pull-down menu, select **M**acro, and choose **D**efine (see fig. 11-1).

   At the bottom of the screen, the prompt `Define macro:` is displayed. In plainer English, this prompt is asking, "What is the *name* of your macro?"

2. Type the name of the macro. For an Alt-*letter* macro, hold down the Alt key and press a letter from A to Z. For a descriptive macro, type one to eight characters (letters or numbers) and press Enter. For an unnamed macro, just press Enter.

   The prompt `Description:` appears on-screen.

> **Reminder:**
> *When creating a macro, you don't need to provide the WPM extension when you give the macro's name.*

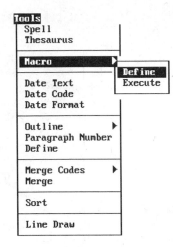

Fig. 11.1.

The pop-out menu for defining and executing macros.

3. Type a short description of what the macro does. Use any description, containing up to 39 characters, that will help remind you of the macro's purpose. Then press Enter.

   Macro Def blinks at the bottom of the screen. Think of this blinking message as a reminder that the program is recording and remembering all your keystrokes.

4. Give the commands that you want recorded for the macro. Give them in the exact order in which you want them played back when you run the macro.

5. To end macro recording, press Macro Define (Ctrl-F10) again.

   ⌨ Access the **T**ools pull-down menu, select **M**acro, and choose **D**efine.

Note: All the commands you use to define a macro also affect the current document. When you create a macro, for example, to change tab settings, you also change the tab settings at the cursor position in the document. You can use Reveal Codes to verify the tab setting changes in the current document.

Reminder:

To create a macro, either press Macro Define (Ctrl-F10) or access the Tools pull-down menu, select Macro, and choose Define.

Now practice these five steps by creating a useful macro, one that inserts your return address. For this macro, assume that you want to make each line of your address flush with the right margin. Later in the chapter, you will create an address macro that uses a different format.

Complete the following steps to create a macro that provides your return address:

1. To begin macro recording, press Macro Define (Ctrl-F10).

   ⌨ Access the **T**ools pull-down menu, select **M**acro, and choose **D**efine.

   The prompt Define macro: appears, asking for the name of the macro.

2. Type *ad* and press Enter. The prompt Description: is displayed.

3. Type *Return address, flush right* and press Enter. The blinking Macro Def message appears.

4. Press Flush Right (Alt-F6).

    ⌨ Access the **L**ayout pull-down menu, choose **A**lign, and select **F**lush Right.

5. Type *Mount of Olives Hotel* (or the first line of your actual address) and press Enter.

6. Press Flush Right (Alt-F6).

    ⌨ Access the **L**ayout pull-down menu, choose **A**lign, and select **F**lush Right.

7. Type *Daoud, MI 48104* (or your actual city, state, and ZIP code) and press Enter to position the cursor one line below the return address (see fig. 11.2).

8. To end macro recording, press Macro Define (Ctrl-F10).

    ⌨ Access the **T**ools pull-down menu, select **M**acro, and choose **D**efine.

Tip

When you want to use a formatting code (such as Enter in step 7) or certain punctuation together with the text in a macro, include the formatting or punctuation as part of the macro.

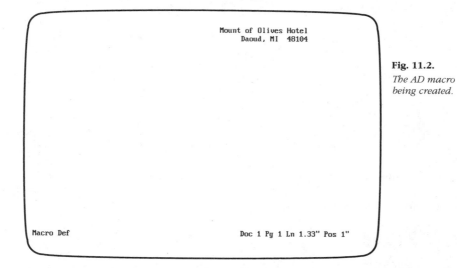

```
                              Mount of Olives Hotel
                                Daoud, MI  48104
```

```
Macro Def                      Doc 1 Pg 1 Ln 1.33" Pos 1"
```

Fig. 11.2.
The AD macro being created.

Running Macros

How you run a macro depends on what kind it is. Of course, before you run any type of macro, you must first have created it.

To run an Alt-*letter* macro, simply press the Alt-*letter* combination. If, for example, you have created an Alt-C macro to center a line of text, you invoke the macro by holding down the Alt key and pressing the letter C.

Reminder:

*To run an Alt-*letter* macro, just press the Alt-*letter* combination.*

To run a descriptive macro, either press Macro (Alt-F10) or access the **T**ools pull-down menu, select **M**acro, and choose E**x**ecute. Next, type the name of the macro (one to eight characters) and press Enter.

To run an unnamed macro, either press Macro (Alt-F10) or access the **T**ools pull-down menu, choose **M**acro, and select E**x**ecute. Then press Enter.

Notice that the command to *run* descriptive and unnamed macros is different from the one you use to *define* those macros. If, when you want to run a macro, you press Macro Define (Ctrl-F10) by mistake, simply press Cancel (F1). You can press Cancel (F1) also to back out of defining a macro.

Now try using the return-address macro. Because the macro you created is a descriptive one (named AD), use the following procedure:

1. Press Exit (F7) and respond to the prompts to save any needed files and clear the screen.

    ⌨ Access the **F**ile pull-down menu, choose E**x**it, and select **N** twice.

2. Press Macro (Alt-F10).

    ⌨ Access the **T**ools pull-down menu, select **M**acro, and choose E**x**ecute.

3. Type *ad* and press Enter.

Stopping Macros

Reminder:

Press Cancel (F1) to back out of defining a macro or to stop a macro in progress.

You use Cancel (F1) in many instances to "back out" of a process you started. You can use this command also to back out of defining a macro, or to stop a macro in progress. If, for example, the macro is not doing what you expected, just press Cancel (F1).

You can stop a macro definition before or after you name the macro. If you start to create a macro but have not yet named the macro, pressing Cancel (F1) cancels the macro definition and returns you to the document. If you have already named the macro, you cannot cancel it, but you can end macro definition by either pressing Macro Define (Ctrl-F10) or accessing the **T**ools pull-down menu, selecting **M**acro, and choosing **D**efine. Although the macro is created with the name you assigned it, you can then delete, rename, replace, or edit the macro. These are common procedures you learn as you work with macros in this chapter.

Caution

Be aware that even an incomplete macro can create unwanted codes in a document. After you cancel a macro, use Reveal Codes and then delete the unwanted codes.

Replacing Macros

Fortunately, imperfect macros are easily replaced. You may want to replace a macro because it does not do what you want, or because you change your mind about exactly what you want the macro to do.

Suppose, for example, that the return-address macro does not do everything you want. Because you will be using your return address in letters, you decide that you usually will want to include a third line containing the current date. You must then decide which way you want the macro to run:

- If you want to add the date manually when you need it, keep the macro the way it is.
- If you want the macro sometimes to insert only your return address and other times to insert both the return address and the date, create a second macro that includes both the return address and the date.
- If you need only one macro that inserts both the return address and the date, keep the AD macro name and change what it does.

You can change what the AD macro does in one of two ways:

- Replace the macro.
- Edit the macro by using the macro editor.

Replacing a macro is often simpler than editing it. To replace a macro with another one of the same name, use the following steps:

1. To begin macro recording, press Macro Define (Ctrl-F10).

   ⌨ Access the **T**ools pull-down menu, select **M**acro, and choose **D**efine.

2. Enter the name of the macro you want to replace. WordPerfect asks whether you want to **R**eplace (**1**) the macro, **E**dit (**2**) the macro, or simply change its **D**escription (**3**).

3. Choose **R**eplace (**1**). As a protection, WordPerfect asks you to confirm that you want to replace the macro. Select **Y**, and WordPerfect then asks for a description of the new macro.

4. Enter a description of the macro.

5. Type the keystrokes you want the macro to record.

6. To end macro recording, press Macro Define (Ctrl-F10).

   ⌨ Access the **T**ools pull-down menu, select **M**acro, and choose **D**efine.

This procedure is exactly like creating a macro for the first time except that you are prompted to replace or edit the macro and then asked to confirm your intention.

Before you replace the AD macro, be sure to save any file you need. Then complete the following steps to replace the AD macro with one that inserts both your return address and the current date:

1. Press Macro Define (Ctrl-F10).

   ⌨ Access the **T**ools pull-down menu, select **M**acro, and choose **D**efine.

   The prompt `Define macro:` appears on-screen.

2. Type *ad* and press Enter. WordPerfect does not let you change an existing macro without warning. The program displays this prompt:

   AD.WPM Already Exists: 1 Replace; **2 E**dit; **3 D**escription: **0**

3. Choose **R**eplace (**1**). WordPerfect asks for confirmation.

4. Select **Y**. The `Description:` prompt then appears, as if you were creating the macro for the first time.

5. Type *Return address and date, flush right* and press Enter. The blinking `Macro Def` message appears.

6. Press Flush Right (Alt-F6).

   ⌨ Access the **L**ayout pull-down menu, choose **A**lign, and select **F**lush Right.

7. Type *Mount of Olives Hotel* (or the first line of your actual address) and press Enter.

8. Press Flush Right (Alt-F6).

   ⌨ Access the **L**ayout pull-down menu, choose **A**lign, and select **F**lush Right.

9. Type *Daoud, MI 48104* (or your actual city, state, and ZIP code) and press Enter.

10. Press Flush Right (Alt-F6).

    ⌨ Access the **L**ayout pull-down menu, choose **A**lign, and select **F**lush Right.

11. Press Date/Outline (Shift-F5) and select Date **F**ormat (**3**).

    ⌨ Access the **T**ools pull-down menu and select Date **F**ormat.

12. Regardless of the date format already shown, type *3 1, 4* and press Enter.

Tip

When creating a macro, you should supply information for items such as date format (or search) even if the desired response is already displayed. This technique ensures that the macro will run correctly in the future.

---

13. Select Date **T**ext (**1**) from the choices at the bottom of the screen. The current date appears on-screen below the return address. The date is correct if your computer has a built-in clock that remembers the date or if you answered a prompt for the date when you started the computer. Even if the date is wrong now, the macro will work properly after you have corrected the date.

14. Press Enter twice. Because you usually will want two blank lines after the return address, you include them here as part of the macro.

15. To end macro recording, press Macro Define (Ctrl-F10).

    ⌨ Access the **T**ools pull-down menu, select **M**acro, and choose **D**efine.

Now you can test the new AD macro. First, either press Macro (Alt-F10) or access the **T**ools pull-down menu, choose **M**acro, and select E**x**ecute. Then type *ad* and press Enter. Your return address and the current date appear on-screen, flush right.

You probably will replace macros often while you are learning to create them. Later in this chapter, you learn how to change what a macro does without creating it again from scratch. You will see how to "get inside" a macro and edit it; that procedure is especially useful for modifying complex macros.

Controlling How Macros Run

WordPerfect macros offer you a great deal of flexibility. When you create a macro, you can control not only *what* you want each macro to do but *how* you want the macro to do it. You can run a macro visibly or invisibly, one time or repeatedly, silently or with bells and whistles. (Well, at least bells.)

Reminder:
You control what *you want a macro to do and* how *you want the macro to do it.*

You use Macro Commands (Ctrl-PgUp) to access many of these "how to run" options. When you press Macro Commands (Ctrl-PgUp) while recording a macro, the blinking `Macro Def` message is replaced temporarily with the following menu:

>   **1 P**ause; **2 D**isplay; **3 A**ssign; **4 C**omment: **0**

Your next keystroke selects one of these options and is therefore not included as something for the macro to record and play back. You learn about Macro Commands (Ctrl-PgUp) and some of the other "how to run" options in the following sections.

Making a Macro Visible

From the options for controlling the way a macro runs, you can choose whether you want the macro to run invisibly or whether you want to see each command in the macro carried out, just as if it were being typed quickly. If you do not instruct WordPerfect otherwise, it runs macros invisibly. The macros you have created so far in this chapter have run invisibly.

Reminder:
When the display feature is turned on, you can watch a macro execute.

You may want to run a macro with the display feature turned on so that you can watch the macro execute. The Display option may be especially useful when you are learning to create your own macros. Because you can easily turn the display feature off and on (using the macro editor), even after you have created a macro, don't hesitate to experiment.

> **Tip**
>
> If you want a macro to pause after it executes each step, use the {STEP} command in the macro editor. Refer to the discussion of the macro editor in this chapter, and see also the discussion of the {STEP} command in the next chapter. {STEP} is often useful for determining why a macro is not executing as expected.

To see how WordPerfect's Display option works, you can create a macro that deletes a sentence. WordPerfect requires several steps to erase a sentence, but you can create a macro that executes the steps instantly. Because this procedure is one that you probably will use often, you should assign the macro an Alt-*letter* name.

To create a macro named Alt-E that erases a sentence while WordPerfect's display feature is turned on, follow these steps:

1. Press Macro Define (Ctrl-F10).

    ▭ Access the **T**ools pull-down menu, select **M**acro, and choose **D**efine.

2. At the `Define macro:` prompt, press Alt-E. At the `Description:` prompt, type *Erase a sentence or a block* and press Enter.

   `Macro Def` blinks at the bottom of the screen.

   This time, you do not want the macro to start recording keystrokes right away. You first want to tell WordPerfect how to run the macro.

3. Press Macro Commands (Ctrl-PgUp) and select **D**isplay (**2**). The screen displays the following prompt:

   `Display execution? No (Yes)`

4. Select **Y**. The blinking `Macro Def` message reappears; enter the keystrokes that define the macro.

5. Press Move (Ctrl-F4) and select **S**entence (**1**) from the menu that appears.

   ▣ Access the **E**dit pull-down menu, choose Se**l**ect, and select **S**entence.

   Another menu appears at the bottom of the screen:

   1 Move; **2 C**opy; **3 D**elete; **4 A**ppend: **0**

6. Select **D**elete (**3**).

7. To end macro recording, press Macro Define (Ctrl-F10).

   ▣ Access the **T**ools pull-down menu, select **M**acro, and choose **D**efine.

Now try the "erase a sentence" macro by placing the cursor anywhere in a sentence and pressing Alt-E. Although the macro performs quickly, the "display on" feature enables you to verify that the sentence you want deleted is indeed the one that is blocked and erased.

Making a Macro Repeat

Occasionally, you may want to make a macro run more than one time. Perhaps you want to delete three consecutive sentences with the Alt-E macro. Although you could, of course, press Alt-E three times, there is an easier way.

Pressing the Esc key repeats any WordPerfect command. If you press Esc and then the letter *e*, the screen displays eight *e*s. You also can change the default of eight to some other number. For example, if you press Esc, type *4*, and then press the up arrow, the cursor moves up four lines.

Reminder:
You can use the Esc key to repeat a macro.

You can repeat a macro the same way. You press Esc, indicate the number of times you want the macro to run, and invoke the macro. You invoke the macro by pressing Alt and the appropriate letter; or you can press Macro (Alt-F10) to run the macro, type the name of the descriptive macro, and press Enter. Be sure that you invoke the macro *immediately* after indicating the number of repetitions.

Practice making a macro repeat itself by using the Alt-E macro that erases a sentence. Begin by typing four short sentences and positioning the cursor anywhere in the first sentence. Then follow these steps to erase the first three sentences:

1. Press Esc.

2. Type *3*.

3. Press Alt-E.

Making a Macro Pause

One of the most useful options for controlling how a macro runs is the Pause option. You can make a macro pause while it is running so that you can enter a command or some text. Then the macro can continue running.

You access the Pause option in the same way you accessed the Display option for making the Alt-E macro visible. When you are creating a macro, you press Macro Commands (Ctrl-PgUp) to display the options for controlling the way the macro runs.

To practice using the Pause option, you create two macros: one to create headings and another to format letters.

Reminder:

The Pause option causes a macro to pause so that you can enter a command or some text.

A Macro That Creates Headings

A useful macro that includes a pause is one that sets up the format for a heading. Suppose that you want most of your headings to be centered, in boldface type, and in uppercase letters. Instead of giving each of those formatting commands, you can have a macro perform them for you.

Place the cursor at the beginning of the line where you want the heading. Then complete the following steps to create a macro that displays a heading:

1. Press Macro Define (Ctrl-F10).

    ⌨ Access the **T**ools pull-down menu, select **M**acro, and choose **D**efine.

2. At the `Define macro:` prompt, press Alt-H (for heading). At the `Description:` prompt, type *Centered, bold, uppercase heading* and press Enter. `Macro Def` blinks on-screen.

3. Press Center (Shift-F6) and then Bold (F6).

    ⌨ Access the **L**ayout pull-down menu, select **A**lign, choose **C**enter, and press Bold (F6).

    Now that the format is set up, you can have the macro pause so that you can enter a particular heading.

4. Press Macro Commands (Ctrl-PgUp). The following menu is displayed:

    1 Pause; **2 D**isplay; **3 A**ssign; **4 C**omment: **0**

5. Select **P**ause (**1**).

    Nothing noticeable happens at this point. `Macro Def` keeps blinking, but the macro does not record actual keystrokes until you press Enter. Before pressing Enter, you should type some kind of "stand in" heading so that the rest of the macro is easier to create. This heading, however, does not become part of the macro.

6. Type *the jacqueline lawson teaching award* and press Enter. Notice that you don't need to capitalize anything in the heading. The next steps of the macro take care of that.

7. Block the text by pressing Block (Alt-F4 or F12) and then pressing Home, Home, ←.

☐ Access the **E**dit pull-down menu, select **B**lock, and press Home, Home, ←.

Note that you cannot block text by dragging the mouse during macro definition.

8. To change to uppercase, press Switch (Shift-F3) and select **U**ppercase (**1**).

☐ Access the **E**dit pull-down menu, select Con**v**ert Case, and choose To **U**pper.

The entire heading you typed changes to uppercase letters.

The macro could stop right here. But because you usually want at least two blank lines after the heading, include the next two steps.

9. Press End to position the cursor at the end of the heading and press Enter twice to insert two blank lines after the heading.

10. Press Macro Define (Ctrl-F10).

☐ Access the **T**ools pull-down menu, select **M**acro, and choose **D**efine.

Now clear the screen (press F7 and select **N** twice) and test the new macro by completing these steps:

1. Press Alt-H. The cursor moves to the center of the line, the Bold feature is turned on, and the macro pauses for your input.

You need to type some kind of heading in order to see the macro work. Because the macro will change the heading to uppercase, you can type the entire heading in lowercase letters.

2. Type *a two-state solution* and press Enter. The heading changes to uppercase, and the cursor is positioned two lines beneath the heading.

If you want WordPerfect to display a prompt when the macro pauses, you can use the {PROMPT} command, accessed through the macro editor. The special macro commands are discussed briefly toward the end of this chapter and in more detail in Chapter 12.

A Macro That Formats Letters

Earlier in this chapter, you created a macro that inserts your return address and the current date. Using the additional features you have learned, you now can create a more powerful macro that combines text with formatting commands. The next macro you create formats a letter in the following ways:

- Formats the page for a two-inch top margin
- Includes your return address, using tab settings (instead of Flush Right)
- Pauses three times so that you can enter three lines of a recipient's address
- Enters the salutation

To create the letter-formatting macro, first save any needed files and clear the screen. Then follow these steps:

1. Press Macro Define (Ctrl-F10).

   ▣ Access the **T**ools pull-down menu, select **M**acro, and choose **D**efine.

2. At the `Define macro:` prompt, type *let* (for letter) and press Enter. At the `Description:` prompt, type *Format for letter* and press Enter. `Macro Def` blinks on-screen.

3. Press Format (Shift-F8) to display the Format menu, select **P**age (**2**) from the Format: Page menu, and choose **M**argins (**5**).

   ▣ Access the **L**ayout pull-down menu, choose **P**age, and select **M**argins (**5**).

4. Type *2"* and press Enter twice.

Tip

If you have used the Setup menu to display units in something other than inches, WordPerfect automatically converts inches to the other unit of measure. If you have not changed units of measure through the Setup menu, you can omit the references to inches.

---

5. Press Enter again to return to the Format menu.

6. Select **L**ine (**1**) and choose **T**ab Set (**8**).

7. Press Home, Home, ← to move to the beginning of the line.

8. Press Ctrl-End to clear the current tab settings.

9. Type *4.7"* and press Enter.

   Note: If this tab setting is not the best one for your address, you can change the setting later. For this setting, assume that the tab stops are relative, which is the WordPerfect default. See Chapter 5 for a discussion of relative and absolute tabs.

10. Press Exit (F7) twice to return to the editing screen.

11. Press Tab, type *8826 Mast Road* (or your own street address), and press Enter.

12. Press Tab, type *Mulvihill, CA 90505* (or your own city, state, and ZIP code), and press Enter.

13. Press Tab.

14. To select the format you want for the date, press Date/Outline (Shift-F5) and select Date **F**ormat (**3**).

    ▣ Access the **T**ools pull-down menu and select Date **F**ormat.

15. Regardless of the date format already shown, type *3 1, 4* and press Enter.

16. Select Date **T**ext (**1**) from the menu at the bottom of the screen.

    The current date appears on-screen below the return address. The date is correct if your computer has a built-in clock that remembers the date, or if you answered a prompt for the date when you started the computer.

17. Press Enter four times.

Reminder:
What you type during a pause (until you press Enter) does not become part of the macro.

18. Press Macro Commands (Ctrl-PgUp). The following menu appears:

    1 Pause; **2 D**isplay; **3 A**ssign; **4 C**omment: **0**

19. Select **P**ause (**1**). Keep in mind that what you type during a pause (until you next press Enter) does not become part of the macro.
20. Type any name, such as *Ms. Holly Arida*, and press Enter twice. The first Enter ends the pause; the second Enter is recorded in the macro.
21. Press Macro Commands (Ctrl-PgUp) and select **P**ause (**1**) again.
22. Type any street address, such as *418 Ramallah Avenue*, and press Enter twice.
23. Press Macro Commands (Ctrl-PgUp) again.
24. Select **P**ause (**1**) again.
25. Type any city, state, and ZIP code—for example, *Haifa, NY 10110*—and press Enter to end the pause.
26. Press Enter twice to insert a blank line below the address.
27. Type *Dear* and press the space bar once.
28. To end macro recording, press Macro Define (Ctrl-F10).

    Access the **T**ools pull-down menu, select M**a**cro, and choose **D**efine.

Now clear the screen and try the new macro by completing these steps:

1. To run the macro, press Macro (Alt-F10).

   Access the **T**ools pull-down menu, select M**a**cro, and choose E**x**ecute.

2. At the `Macro:` prompt, type *let* and press Enter. The macro pauses four lines below the return address and waits for you to enter the recipient's name and address.
3. Type the recipient's name and title—for example, *Ms. May Berry, President.* Then press Enter.

   The macro pauses again for your input.

4. Type the first line of the recipient's address, such as *Arab-Jewish Peace Committee,* and press Enter.

   The macro pauses for the last line of the address.

5. Type the recipient's city, state, and ZIP code, such as *Dearborn, MI 48126.* Then press Enter.

   `Dear` appears with the cursor in the appropriate place, ready for you to type a name and begin the letter.

Figure 11.3 shows the screen after you run the macro.

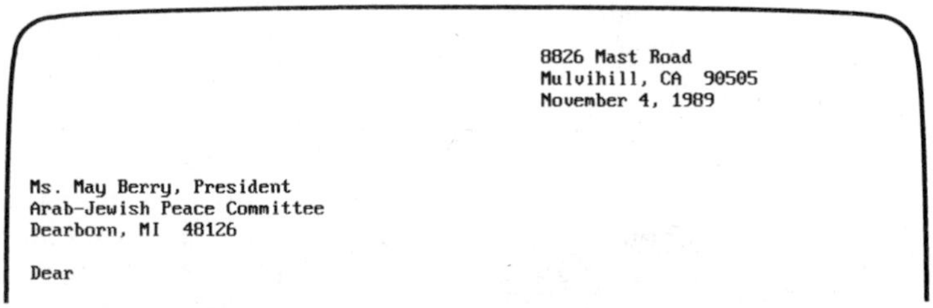
8826 Mast Road
Mulvihill, CA 90505
November 4, 1989
Ms. May Berry, President
Arab-Jewish Peace Committee
Dearborn, MI 48126
Dear

Fig. 11.3.
The results of the LET macro.

You now have created a fairly complicated macro that combines formatting commands, text, and pauses. Although intricate macros like this one can save you much time, you may want several smaller macros that you can piece together in different ways to make up a longer macro, as described in the next section.

Making a Macro Call Another Macro

You can connect macros to one another in two ways. The first method is to *chain* one macro to another. If, for example, macro B is chained to macro A, macro B will run when macro A is completed. The second method is to *nest* one macro within another. Suppose that macro B is nested within macro A. Macro A starts to run and then calls macro B. After macro B runs to completion, the rest of macro A runs to completion (or until another nested macro is called).

Reminder:
If you want a macro to run a second macro through chaining or nesting, you must define each macro separately.

The basic technique in both cases is the same. You create one macro in the usual way—by either pressing Macro Define (Ctrl-F10) or accessing the **T**ools pull-down menu, selecting M**a**cro, and choosing **D**efine. While you are creating the first macro, you call the second macro, which you must create separately. The difference between chaining and nesting is in the way you call the second macro.

If the second macro will be chained to the first, you define the first macro completely. Instead of immediately ending macro recording, however, you first press Macro (Alt-F10) to give the command to execute the second macro (or you can access the **T**ools pull-down menu, select M**a**cro, and choose E**x**ecute). You then provide the name of the second macro. If you are calling an Alt-*letter* macro, you can press Alt and the appropriate letter instead of typing the macro's name, but be sure to give the command to execute the second macro *before* you provide its name. You then end macro recording for the first macro by either pressing Macro Define (Ctrl-F10) or accessing the **T**ools pull-down menu, selecting M**a**cro, and choosing **D**efine.

Use the following sequence to chain a macro:

1. Give the command to begin defining the first macro.
2. Provide the actual keystrokes to define the first macro.
3. Give the command to execute the second macro.
4. Give the command to end defining the first macro.

The first macro then "knows" that before it finishes running, it will execute a second macro.

If you want to nest a second macro within the first macro, you also call the second macro while creating the first, but in a different way. The second macro must be an Alt-*letter* macro, not a descriptive macro (unless you use the macro editor). You call the second macro by pressing the Alt key and the appropriate letter; you do *not* first use the command to execute the macro—as you do when you chain the second macro to the first. Pressing Alt-*letter* tells WordPerfect to run the second macro immediately and then return to running the first one. You press Alt-*letter* at the exact point where you want the second macro to run within the first macro. You then continue defining the first macro.

Reminder:
When nesting a macro, press Alt-letter at the exact point where you want the second macro to run within the first macro.

> **Tip**
>
> To avoid error messages when creating nested macros, you should first create the "inside" macro (the nested Alt-*letter* macro) and then create the "host" macro.

To nest a macro, use the following sequence:

1. Give the command to begin defining the first macro.
2. Provide the keystrokes to begin defining the first macro.
3. Press Alt-*letter* (the name of the second macro) at the exact point where you want the second macro to run.
4. Provide the keystrokes for defining the rest of the first macro.
5. Give the command to end defining the first macro.

> **Tip**
>
> When you call a macro, WordPerfect looks for it in the current drive and directory, in the drive or directory where WordPerfect's program files are stored, and in the location you specified in the Setup menu. If the macro is not in any of these places, you must call it by its full path name (excluding the WPM extension). For more about path names, see the section "Managing Macro Files."

Creating a Simple Chained Macro

Reminder:

When chaining a macro, you end one macro with a command to call another macro.

Chaining macros is an easy way to simplify the task of creating a complex macro. If the macro you want to create ends with a series of commands that you already have stored in a different macro, you can make that other macro the last command of the new macro.

Suppose, for example, that you are a teacher and you want to create a macro for the different handouts you distribute to students. You want all the handouts to include the name of the university, the semester, and your name. In addition, you want the macro to pause so that you can insert the name of the course. Then you want the macro to do what the Alt-H macro does: specify the format for a boldfaced, centered, uppercase heading and pause for you to insert the contents.

You do not need to re-create in the new macro all the commands in the Alt-H macro. You can create the beginning of a macro, which will consist of new commands, and then end with a command to run the Alt-H macro. That macro will then be chained to the new macro.

Because the new macro will "set up" handouts, you can name it SU. Notice that the last command in the macro definition links the Alt-H macro to the new SU macro. Follow these steps to chain the two macros that will set up handouts:

1. Press Macro Define (Ctrl-F10).

    ⌨ Access the **T**ools pull-down menu, select **M**acro, and choose **D**efine.

2. At the `Define macro:` prompt, type *su* and press Enter. At the `Description:` prompt, type *Setup for course handouts* and press Enter. `Macro Def` blinks on-screen.

3. Type *Bir Zeit University* and press Flush Right (Alt-F6).

   ⌨ Access the **L**ayout pull-down menu, select **A**lign, and choose **F**lush Right.

4. Type *Professor Kimberly Gasaway* (or a name of your choice) and press Enter.

5. Type *Fall 1995* and press Flush Right (Alt-F6) again.

   ⌨ Access the **L**ayout pull-down menu, select **A**lign, and choose **F**lush Right.

   Later in the chapter, you learn how to modify a small part of a macro, such as the date.

6. Press Macro Commands (Ctrl-PgUp). The following menu appears:

   1 Pause; **2 D**isplay; **3 A**ssign; **4 C**omment: **0**

7. Select **P**ause (**1**).

8. For stand-in text, type *Business Ethics* and press Enter three times (once to end the pause and twice to insert two hard returns).

   You are now ready to chain this macro to the Alt-H macro.

9. Press Macro (Alt-F10).

   ⌨ Access the **T**ools pull-down menu, select **M**acro, and choose E**x**ecute.

10. Press Alt-H. The Alt-H macro is now chained to the SU macro.

11. To end macro recording, press Macro Define (Ctrl-F10).

    ⌨ Access the **T**ools pull-down menu, select **M**acro, and choose **D**efine.

Because you already have created the Alt-H macro, the SU macro should work right away. Follow these steps to run the SU macro:

1. Press Macro (Alt-F10).

   ⌨ Access the **T**ools pull-down menu, select **M**acro, and choose E**x**ecute.

2. Type *su* and press Enter. `Bir Zeit University, Professor Kimberly Gasaway`, and `Fall 1995` appear on-screen. The cursor is positioned at the right, ready for you to insert the name of the course.

3. Type a course name, such as *Liberation Movements*, and press Enter. The Alt-H macro begins to run. The cursor is centered, waiting for you to enter a heading.

4. Type a heading, such as *women and liberation*. You do not need to capitalize any of the letters.

5. Press Enter to indicate that your input is completed.

The macro does the rest of its work. Figure 11.4 shows the results.

Fig. 11.4.

*The results of the
SU macro.*

```
Bir Zeit University                    Professor Kimberly Gasaway
Fall 1995                                       Liberation Movements
                        WOMEN AND LIBERATION
```

> ## Tip
>
> You can use this method of chaining to establish other formats that end also
> with the Alt-H macro. You may, for example, use certain margins and tab
> settings for special documents. You can create a macro that formats the
> margins and tabs in a particular way and then runs the Alt-H macro.

A chain of macros is not limited to two. You can have a second macro call a third
macro, and a third call a fourth. Obviously, the more intricate the chain you want
to create, the more planning you must do.

Chaining a Macro to Itself

Another way to repeat a macro, aside from using the Esc key, is to chain the macro
to itself. The problem with this method, however, is that you create an endless
loop. The first macro calls itself, and calls itself again, and again—theoretically, for
eternity. The problem is not as awesome as it seems because, in practice, you can
stop the macro by pressing Cancel (F1).

Reminder:

*Simple macros may
stop automatically
when a search fails.*

This odd repetition has a practical use. Because simple WordPerfect macros may
stop automatically when a search fails, you can include a search within a macro and
then chain the macro to itself. The macro performs the search, does whatever you
created the macro to do, and then searches again. The macro performs the
specified action on each item that the macro finds, and then stops when the search
fails. You will discover more uses for this looping technique after you have learned
some of WordPerfect's advanced features.

Creating a Nested Macro

Reminder:

*When nesting
macros, you include
one or more macros
in the middle of
another macro.*

When you nest macros, you can include one or more macros in the middle of
another macro. The host macro (the one in which macros are nested) runs the
nested macros at the places it finds them in its list of commands. The host macro
then takes back control and completes the rest of its own commands. Notice how
nesting differs from chaining: a nested macro can be located anywhere in the
original macro, whereas a chained macro must be the last command of the original
macro.

The procedure for creating a nested macro is similar to that for a chained macro.
With nested macros, however, you should first create all the inside macros that will
be nested. You then create the host macro, which refers to—and instantly
executes—the nested macros. When you chain macros, you must also create each
macro separately, but you can create the macros in any order. Another requirement

for creating nested macros is that the inside macros—the ones referred to by the host macro—must be Alt-*letter* macros if you are creating the host macro in the usual way, through Macro Define (Ctrl-F10). If you use the macro editor, you can nest descriptive macros as well as Alt-*letter* macros.

To practice creating a nested macro, first create a simple macro, named Alt-Z, that includes text. Then create a host macro and nest the Alt-Z macro within it. Start with the following steps to create the Alt-Z macro:

1. To begin macro recording, press Macro Define (Ctrl-F10).

    ▣ Access the **T**ools pull-down menu, select **M**acro, and choose **D**efine.

2. At the `Define macro:` prompt, press Alt-Z. Then press Enter to bypass the `Description:` prompt.

3. Type some text, such as *Peace with Justice.*

4. To end macro recording, press Macro Define (Ctrl-F10).

    ▣ Access the **T**ools pull-down menu, select **M**acro, and choose **D**efine.

Now you are ready to create the host macro with the Alt-Z macro nested within it:

1. To begin macro recording, press Macro Define (Ctrl-F10).

    ▣ Access the **T**ools pull-down menu, select **M**acro, and choose **D**efine.

2. At the `Define macro:` prompt, type *host* and press Enter. To bypass the `Description:` prompt, press Enter.

3. Type *This is a host macro that will call Alt-Z* and press Enter.

4. Press Alt-Z. The nested Alt-Z macro (unlike a chained macro) is executed immediately.

5. Press Enter and type some text, such as *This text follows the execution of a nested macro.*

6. Press Macro Define (Ctrl-F10).

    ▣ Access the **T**ools pull-down menu, select **M**acro, and choose **D**efine.

Reminder:

To call a nested macro, just press the appropriate Alt-letter combination instead of invoking the command to execute a macro.

Now run the new macros by either pressing Macro (Alt-F10) or accessing the **T**ools pull-down menu, selecting **M**acro, and choosing E**x**ecute. Next, type *host* and press Enter to run the host macro. Notice that the Alt-Z macro runs as part of the host macro, and control then returns to the host macro.

After you have worked with the practice macros ALTZ.WPM and HOST.WPM, you may want to delete them. Deleting macros is discussed in the section "Manipulating and Viewing Macro Files" later in this chapter. You can delete macro files also from DOS.

Creating Some Useful Macros

You do not have to be a macro expert to create macros that will help you with your everyday work. In this section, you learn to create some useful macros. As you create them, think about how you can use the following techniques, which you learned earlier, to create other macros on your own:

- Use Macro Commands (Ctrl-PgUp) to insert a pause or turn the display feature on or off at any point in the macro.
- Use the Esc key to repeat a descriptive or Alt-*letter* macro, first indicating the number of times you want the macro to repeat and then giving the command to execute the macro.
- Connect macros by chaining or nesting them.

A Macro That Italicizes the Preceding Word

Italicizing a word in WordPerfect requires several steps, as you learned in Chapter 5. When you need to italicize just one word, however, you can use an easier method. You can type the word and then use a macro to italicize the last word you typed.

Suppose that you were asked to type the following sentence:

Corporations should focus *only* on profits.

(Of course, *you* would never create such a sentence yourself.) Complete the following steps to create a macro named Alt-I that italicizes the word *only* after you type it:

1. Type *Corporations should focus only*

   The cursor is positioned immediately after the last character you want to italicize.

2. Press Macro Define (Ctrl-F10).

   ⌨ Access the **T**ools pull-down menu, select **M**acro, and choose **D**efine.

3. At the `Define macro:` prompt, press Alt-I and type *Italicize preceding word.* Press Enter.

   `Macro Def` blinks on-screen.

4. To block the text, press Block (Alt-F4 or F12) and then Ctrl-←.

   ⌨ Access the **E**dit pull-down menu, select **B**lock, and press Ctrl-←.

   During macro definition, you cannot block text by dragging the mouse.

5. To italicize the block, press Font (Ctrl-F8), choose **A**ppearance (**2**), and select **I**talc (**4**).

   ⌨ Access the **F**ont pull-down menu, select **A**ppearance, and choose **I**talics.

   The word *only* is italicized.

6. Press GoTo (Ctrl-Home) twice.

7. Press the right arrow twice. The cursor returns to its original position— after the code that turns off italics.

8. To end macro recording, press Macro Define (Ctrl-F10).

   ⌨ Access the **T**ools pull-down menu, select **M**acro, and choose **D**efine.

You can use this macro to italicize either the last word you typed or any word typed previously. In both cases, you position the cursor immediately after the word you want to italicize and press Alt-I. Using a macro is simpler than blocking a word and giving the appropriate commands each time you want to italicize the word.

After the word is italicized, you can press the space bar and continue typing. Note that you could have included the space as part of the macro, but you would then need to use Backspace whenever you wanted the word to be followed by punctuation instead.

A Macro That Changes Directories

If you have a hard disk, you often need to change from one directory to another. You can create a macro for each directory you want to change to, and you can use an abbreviated form of each directory's name for the names of the macros. You can make the macro end so that you remain at the editing screen, or you can have the macro take you to the List Files screen for your new directory. Of course, you can use macros that change directories only if you have first created the directories to which you want to change.

Suppose that you have a directory called \BUSINESS\ACCOUNTS. The following macro, named ACC, changes the current directory to C:\BUSINESS\ACCOUNTS while you remain at the editing screen. For this macro, an assumption is that you are already in drive C. Complete these steps to create the macro:

1. To begin macro recording, press Macro Define (Ctrl-F10).

   ⌨ Access the **T**ools pull-down menu, select **M**acro, and choose **D**efine.

2. At the `Define macro:` prompt, type *acc* and press Enter. At the `Description:` prompt, type *Change to "\business\accounts" directory* and press Enter.

   `Macro Def` blinks on-screen.

3. Press List (F5).

   ⌨ Access the **F**ile pull-down menu and select List **F**iles.

4. Type an equal sign (=). Typing = informs WordPerfect that you want to change directories, not just look at the files in a directory.

5. Type *\business\accounts* and press Enter. The current directory is now C:\BUSINESS\ACCOUNTS.

6. Press Cancel (F1) to return to the editing screen.

7. To end macro recording, press Macro Define (Ctrl-F10).

   ⌨ Access the **T**ools pull-down menu, select **M**acro, and choose **D**efine.

If you want a macro to take you to the List Files screen instead of ending at the editing screen, the process is only slightly different. The next macro, named ODF, changes directories to C:\BUSINESS\ACCOUNTS\OVERDUE and ends at the List Files screen for that new directory. As for the preceding macro, an assumption for this macro is that you are already in drive C. Complete these steps to create the macro:

1. To begin macro recording, press Macro Define (Ctrl-F10).

   ⌨ Access the **T**ools pull-down menu, select **M**acro, and choose **D**efine.

2. At the `Define macro:` prompt, type *odf* and press Enter. The *od* stands for the subdirectory OVERDUE; the *f* stands for files.

3. At the `Description:` prompt, type *Change to Overdue subdirectory, List* and press Enter.

   Notice that the full path name of \BUSINESS\ACCOUNTS\OVERDUE is too long to include in the macro description.

   `Macro Def` blinks on-screen.

4. Press List (F5).

   ▭ Access the **F**ile pull-down menu and select List **F**iles.

5. Type an equal sign (=). Typing = informs WordPerfect that you want to change to another drive or directory, not just look at the files in that drive or directory while you remain in the current directory.

6. Type *business\accounts\overdue* and press Enter. The current directory is now \BUSINESS\ACCOUNTS\OVERDUE.

Cue:

You can press the space bar instead of Enter to see a list of your files.

7. Press Enter to display the List Files screen. The screen displays the list of files for the directory \BUSINESS\ACCOUNTS\OVERDUE.

8. To end macro recording, press Macro Define (Ctrl-F10).

   ▭ Access the **T**ools pull-down menu, select M**a**cro, and choose **D**efine.

A Macro That Changes Margins

You can create a macro to make any formatting command easier. Suppose, for example, that the default right and left margins are each 1 inch. Because you often need to change each margin to 1.5 inches, however, you want to create a macro that makes the changes quickly. Complete the following steps to create that macro:

1. To begin macro recording, press Macro Define (Ctrl-F10).

   ▭ Access the **T**ools pull-down menu, select M**a**cro, and choose **D**efine.

Reminder:

You cannot use a period in a macro name.

2. At the `Define macro:` prompt, type *mar15* and press Enter. You cannot use a period as part of a macro name, but you can use a hyphen to name the macro MAR-15 or MAR1-5 if you prefer.

3. At the `Description:` prompt, type *Change right and left margins to 1.5"* and press Enter.

   `Macro Def` blinks on-screen.

4. To go to the menu to edit margins, press Format (Shift-F8) and select **L**ine (**1**).

   ▭ Access the **L**ayout pull-down menu and choose **L**ine.

5. Select **M**argins (**7**) from the full-screen menu that appears.

6. Type *1.5"* and press Enter. Then type *1.5"* and press Enter again.

7. Press Exit (F7) to return to the editing screen.

8. To end macro recording, press Macro Define (Ctrl-F10).

   ▭ Access the **T**ools pull-down menu, select M**a**cro, and choose **D**efine.

After you run this macro, you can verify the margin change with Reveal Codes.

A Macro That Sets Tabs for Numbered Lists

You can use macros to shorten any WordPerfect commands you use often. Suppose, for instance, that you often change tab settings when you create numbered lists. The setting you find most useful for numbered lists is +0.4.

> ### Tip
>
> The exact tab setting you want depends on the font you are using. The +0.4 tab setting works well with a nonproportional 10-pitch font. For this setting, an assumption is that that you have not changed WordPerfect's default of using tabs that are relative to margins.

To create a macro that changes tab settings, follow these steps:

1. To begin macro recording, press Macro Define (Ctrl-F10).

   Access the **T**ools pull-down menu, select **M**acro, and choose **D**efine.

2. At the `Define macro:` prompt, type *tablist* and press Enter. At the `Description:` prompt, type *Format tabs for lists* and press Enter. `Macro Def` blinks on-screen.

3. To go to the menu to edit tabs, press Format (Shift-F8) and select **L**ine (**1**).

   Access the **L**ayout pull-down menu and choose **L**ine.

4. Select **T**ab Set (**8**) from the full-screen menu that appears.

5. To remove present tab settings, press Home, Home, ←. Then press Ctrl-End to delete to the end of the line.

6. Type *0.4″* and press Enter. (You could also type *+0.4″*.) If you have set up WordPerfect to use another unit of measure, WordPerfect converts inches to the unit of measure you selected.

7. Press Exit (F7) twice.

8. To end macro recording, press Macro Define (Ctrl-F10).

   Access the **T**ools pull-down menu, select **M**acro, and choose **D**efine.

The tab settings have now been changed. Retain the new tab settings as you work through the next few macros. You will first use these tab settings in a macro that simplifies numbered lists.

A Macro That Simplifies Numbered Lists

With tabs set for numbered lists, you can create another macro to help you enter the numbered items. This macro, named Alt-N, indents each item in the list and saves you the trouble of continually pressing Indent (F4). Follow these steps to create the macro:

1. To begin macro recording, press Macro Define (Ctrl-F10).

   Access the **T**ools pull-down menu, select **M**acro, and choose **D**efine.

2. At the `Define macro:` prompt, press Alt-N (for number). At the `Description:` prompt, type *Numbered lists* and press Enter.

   `Macro Def` blinks on-screen.

3. Press End to move the cursor to the end of the current line. Then press Enter twice to move the cursor to the left margin and to insert a blank line.

4. Press Macro Commands (Ctrl-PgUp) to give a "how to run" command.

5. Select **P**ause (**1**) and press Enter to end the pause.

   Note that in this case, you can create the macro easily without typing a "stand in" for the item number.

6. Type a period (.) and press Indent (F4).

7. To end macro recording, press Macro Define (Ctrl-F10).

   ⌨ Access the **T**ools pull-down menu, select **M**acro, and choose **D**efine.

   Only a period (.) is now visible on-screen.

Try running the new Alt-N macro. Because you want to keep the tabs set by the TABLIST macro, do not clear the screen. Complete these steps to test the Alt-N macro:

1. Press Alt-N. The cursor moves down two lines, and the macro pauses for your input.

2. Type *1* and press Enter. A period is inserted, and the cursor moves one tab stop to the right. Either press Reveal Codes (Alt-F3 or F11) or select **R**eveal Codes from the **E**dit pull-down menu; notice that an **[→Indent]** code has been inserted. Keep Reveal Codes on.

3. Type *Human and political rights should be granted to all peoples of the world.*

   The text is indented and forms an even column 0.4" from the left margin.

4. Press Word Left (Ctrl-←).

   You will now see that the macro works even if the cursor is not at the end of the line when you press Alt-N. (The End command in step 3 of the preceding sequence takes care of cursor positioning.)

5. Press Alt-N again. Each time you press Alt-N, the macro inserts a blank line and pauses for you to type a number.

6. Type *2* and press Enter.

   Figure 11.5 shows what the screen looks like at this point if you are in Document 1 and have Reveal Codes turned on.

Tip

You may want to enhance the Alt-N macro. You can, for example, add a tab-align feature so that the periods after each number line up evenly. Later, when you learn about WordPerfect's automatic-numbering feature, you may want to create a macro that inserts automatic paragraph numbers instead of pausing for you to type the numbers manually (see Chapter 25).

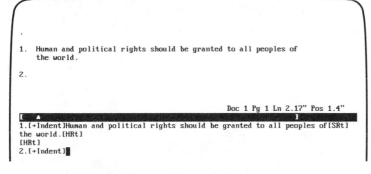

Fig. 11.5.
A numbered list being created with the Alt-N macro.

A Macro That Reinstates Old Tab Settings

With a little imagination, you can develop a macro that reinstates the tab settings before you last changed them. Such a macro enables you to change tabs for certain tasks, like numbering a list or inserting a return address, and then to restore the earlier tab settings.

Because you used the TABLIST macro to change tab settings in previous examples, now is a good time to create a macro that restores the original tab settings. Press Reveal Codes (Alt-F3 or F11) or select **R**eveal Codes from the **E**dit pull-down menu and watch what this macro does as you create it. You may learn some tricks that you can apply elsewhere as well.

This macro works only if you have typed some text since the most recent change in tab settings. (Changing tabs twice in succession would be pointless anyway.) Complete the following steps to create a macro that reinstates the original tab settings:

1. To begin macro recording, press Macro Define (Ctrl-F10).

    Access the **T**ools pull-down menu, select M**a**cro, and choose **D**efine.

2. At the `Define macro:` prompt, type the name *oldtabs* and press Enter. At the `Description:` prompt, type *Restore previous tab settings* and press Enter.

   `Macro Def` blinks on-screen.

3. Press Backward Search (Shift-F2).

    Access the **S**earch pull-down menu and select **B**ackward.

> **Tip**
>
> When creating a macro, you should supply information for items in a search (or date format) even if the correct response is already displayed. Otherwise, you cannot be sure that the macro will always execute properly.

4. To indicate that the search is for the tab setting code, press Format (Shift-F8) and select **L**ine (**1**).

   ▭▤ Access the **L**ayout pull-down menu and choose **L**ine.

5. Select **T**ab Set (**8**).

6. Press Search (F2). The cursor in Reveal Codes is positioned immediately after the code for the most recent tab setting.

7. Press the left arrow. The cursor in Reveal Codes now appears to be on the tab setting code. This position actually is *before* the place where the tab change takes effect.

   Now you need to go to the Format: Line screen to record in the document the code for the old tab settings.

8. Press Format (Shift-F8), select **L**ine (**1**), and choose **T**ab Set (**8**).

   ▭▤ Access the **L**ayout pull-down menu, select **L**ine, and choose **T**ab Set (**8**).

   You see the tab settings currently in effect. These are the old settings because the cursor is positioned before the tab setting code.

9. Press Exit (F7) twice to insert into the document the code for the *old* tab settings. This insertion will be temporary.

10. Press Backspace. The old tab setting code is deleted. Like all deletions in WordPerfect, that code is held in memory in case you later decide to undelete it.

11. Press GoTo (Ctrl-Home) twice. The cursor returns to its original position.

12. Press Cancel (F1). The last deletion (the old tab setting) appears. Figure 11.6 shows the screen at this point.

13. Select **R**estore (**1**) from the Undelete menu. The old tab settings are restored.

14. To end macro recording, press Macro Define (Ctrl-F10).

    ▭▤ Access the **T**ools pull-down menu, select **M**acro, and choose **D**efine.

You probably will want to turn off Reveal Codes after you define the macro. Either press Reveal Codes (Alt-F3 or F11) or select **R**eveal Codes from the **E**dit pull-down menu.

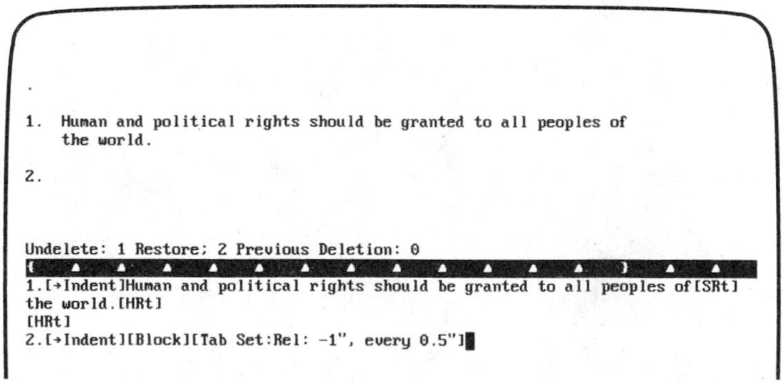

Fig. 11.6.

The previous tab setting ready to be restored.

```
.
1.  Human and political rights should be granted to all peoples of
    the world.
2.



Undelete: 1 Restore; 2 Previous Deletion: 0
{    ▲    ▲    ▲    ▲    ▲    ▲    ▲    ▲    ▲    ▲    ▲    }    ▲    ▲
1.[→Indent]Human and political rights should be granted to all peoples of[SRt]
the world.[HRt]
[HRt]
2.[→Indent][Block][Tab Set:Rel: -1", every 0.5"]█
```

Managing Macro Files

Before learning to use the macro editor, you will benefit by knowing about macros as files. In Chapter 10, you learned how to manipulate document files with WordPerfect's List Files feature. Some of the techniques you learned also apply to macro files.

All macros are stored as files on disk, just as document and program files are stored. Macro files are similar to document files in that you create both kinds of files, but macro files are also like program files (such as WP.EXE or SPELL.EXE) because macros can instruct your computer to perform a series of operations.

Reminder:
Like document files and program files, macro files are stored on disk.

Just as a program file has a unique file name extension (typically EXE), a macro file has the three-letter extension WPM, which identifies the file as a WordPerfect macro. A descriptive macro has the full file name you would expect: the name of the macro, a period, and the WPM extension. The AD macro, for example, is saved in a file called AD.WPM. An Alt-*letter* macro has a full file name consisting of ALT and one additional letter—with no hyphen between ALT and the letter. The WPM extension is added just as it is for a descriptive macro. An Alt-L macro, for instance, is saved in a file called ALTL.WPM, and both WordPerfect and DOS treat it as a file with a regular file name. WordPerfect gives an unnamed macro (created with the Enter key) the name WP{WP}.WPM.

For any macro command in which you press the Alt key and a letter, you can instead type each letter of the file name—for example, *a*, *l*, *t*, and *l*. In a few instances, you *must* type the full file names of macros in this way. These instances are discussed later in the chapter.

Keep in mind that a macro file, like all other files, has a full path name that identifies the drive and directory where the macro file is stored. The file name of the AD macro is AD.WPM, but its full path name might be something like C:\MACROS\AD.WPM or B:AD.WPM. The full path name of an Alt-K macro in the COURSES directory in drive C would be C:\COURSES\ALTK.WPM. Occasionally, you will need to refer to macros by their full path names.

Creating Global Macros

If you do not tell WordPerfect where to store a macro, the program stores it in whatever drive and directory you are in when you create the macro. And if you do not instruct WordPerfect otherwise, the program looks in the current directory (the one in which you are working) for a macro that you want to run. WordPerfect looks also in the drive or directory where your WordPerfect program files are stored. Therefore, if you are working in the LETTERS directory in drive C and you press Alt-L to run a macro stored in the ACCOUNTS directory, WordPerfect cannot find it. The screen displays the following message:

```
ERROR: File Not Found - ALTL.WPM
```

Reminder:
To run a macro located in a different drive or directory, use the macro's full path name.

One way to run a macro located in a different drive or directory is to use the macro's full path name. If the Alt-L macro is in C:\ACCOUNTS and you are not, either press Macro (Alt-F10) or access the **T**ools pull-down menu, select **M**acro, and choose

Execute. Then, instead of pressing just Alt-L, type *c:\letters\altl.* (If you are already in drive C, typing *\letters\altl* is sufficient.) Now WordPerfect knows where to look. Because you are using a macro command, the WPM extension is assumed even if you don't provide it. However, when you manipulate macro files by pressing List (F5) or selecting List **F**iles from the **F**ile pull-down menu, you must type the WPM extension.

An easier way to run macros is to make all of them *global.* Global macros run no matter which directory is current. You make the macros global through the Setup menu. Then, when you create a macro, it is stored in the location you specified through Setup, rather than in the current drive or directory. Even more important, when you call a macro, WordPerfect always looks for that macro in the place where the macros have been stored, regardless of where you are when you call the macro.

With Setup, you easily can make all future macros global. Perhaps you have already done this, or someone may have done it for you. To check the location of your macro files, follow these steps:

1. Press Setup (Shift-F1) and select **L**ocation of Files (**6**).

    ⌨ Access the **F**ile pull-down menu, select Se**t**up, and choose **L**ocation of Files.

2. Check **K**eyboard/Macro Files (**2**) to see whether a drive or directory is indicated on the right side of the screen.

    Make a note of where your macro files are being stored; you will use this information later. If no drive or directory is indicated, each macro is being stored in whatever drive and directory you are working in when you created the macro.

3. Press Exit (F7) to exit from the Setup menu.

After you have used Setup to specify a place to store your macro files, all macros you create from that point on are global macros. Those macros work whenever you use WordPerfect (as long as the macros are on disk in your computer). For more information on making global changes through the Setup menu, see Chapter 20.

Viewing a List of Macro Files

To display the names of your macro files, you can either press List (F5) or select List **F**iles from the **F**ile pull-down menu. At this point, you should have at least one macro—the AD macro that you created earlier. Before you can see that macro on the List Files screen, you must determine where the macro is stored. If no drive or directory was indicated when you went to the Setup screen and checked **L**ocation of Files (**6**), the AD macro is in the current directory. If a particular drive or directory was listed, the AD macro is stored in that location.

Reminder:

To display the names of your macro files, either press List (F5) or select List Files from the File pull-down menu.

Keep in mind that the drive or directory indicated on the Setup screen affects only the macros you create after you change the entry for **L**ocation of Files (**6**). If the AD macro is not in the directory indicated on the Setup screen, you can move the macro to that directory. You learn how to move macros later in the chapter.

Use the List Files feature to display the names of any macros you have stored:

1. Press List (F5).

    ⌨ Access the **F**ile pull-down menu and select List **F**iles.

2. If your macros are in the current drive or directory, type *.wpm* and press Enter (or the space bar). A list of all files with a WPM extension appears.

    If your macros are in a different drive or directory, type its name followed by *.wpm* and press Enter (or the space bar). For example, if the macros are stored in C:\MACROS, type *c:\macros*.wpm*. If the macros are stored on a floppy disk in drive B, type *b:*.wpm* (or simply *b:*.wpm*).

    If the directory you want to look at is on your current drive, you don't need to include the letter of the drive. For example, if you are working in C:\LETTERS and want to see files in C:\MACROS, you can just press List (F5), type *macros*, and press Enter.

3. To find AD.WPM among the files, select **N**ame Search (**N**), type *ad*, and press Enter. AD.WPM is highlighted.

WordPerfect lists the files with a WPM extension in the drive or directory you selected. On the screen this file may be the only one you see; or, if you have other macros, AD.WPM will be one of several files.

Storing Macros on Floppy Disks

If you are using a floppy disk system, you can have global macros by storing them on the WordPerfect working program disk #2. This is the program disk that must remain in drive A while you are running WordPerfect. You can instruct WordPerfect to store your macros and run them automatically from drive A. Complete the following steps:

1. Press Setup (Shift-F1) and select **L**ocation of Files (**6**).

    ⌨ Access the **F**ile pull-down menu, select Se**t**up, and choose **L**ocation of Files.

2. Select **K**eyboard/Macro Files (**2**).

3. Type *a:* and press Enter.

4. Press Exit (F7).

Your macros will be stored on whatever disk is in drive A. If you later use a different working program disk #2, you will need to copy the macro files to the new disk before you can access them.

You can store only as many macros in drive A as the free space on the floppy disk allows. The amount of free space is indicated on the second line of the List Files screen. A macro may vary in size from a few bytes to more than 20,000 bytes. The more printer files or other files you keep in drive A, the less free disk space you will have for macros. If you run out of space for macros in drive A, you can store them in drive B along with your documents.

Manipulating and Viewing Macro Files

You already know how to use List Files to manipulate regular documents. Although macro files (like program files) cannot be retrieved or printed by WordPerfect 5.1, they can be deleted, moved or renamed, and copied. You also can view descriptions of your macros from the List Files screen with **L**ook (**6**). When you first start creating macros, you may rarely need to manipulate your macro files. As you develop more macros, however, you probably will find that performing a few simple file-management tasks can be useful.

Keep in mind that the List Files feature performs actions on an *entire* file—deleting the file, moving or renaming it, or creating a copy of the whole file in another directory or drive. If you want to manipulate the contents of a file, such as a portion of a document, you must go inside the file itself and make changes, instead of using List Files. You use List Files when you want to delete, move or rename, or copy a whole macro *as a file*, rather than change the contents of a macro.

When you manipulate macros with List Files, you must always include the WPM extension as part of the file name. Otherwise, WordPerfect does not recognize the file as a macro.

The List Files options work the same way for macro files as for regular document files. For a full explanation of these options, see Chapter 10. You can use any of the following List Files options to manipulate macro files:

- **D**elete (**2**) a macro file (or group of macro files). You delete a macro file when you don't want any macro with that name. (You also can use the Del key.)

- **M**ove/Rename (**3**) a macro file when you want to move a macro (or group of macro files) to another directory or disk, or when you want to rename a macro. Be sure to include the WPM extension in the new name.

- **C**opy (**8**) a macro file (or group of macro files) to another directory or disk while leaving the original file in place.

- **L**ook (**6**) at a macro to check the macro description.

In Chapter 10, you learned how to manipulate a group of files by marking them first. You can use the same technique to delete, move, or copy macro files. You mark the files with asterisks and respond to the prompts just as you would if you were acting on any other group of files.

Just as you can use **L**ook (**6**) to see a document file without actually retrieving the file, you can look at a macro file. The only part of the display that will mean anything to you is the macro description. If you wrote a clear description when you created the macro, you will now reap your reward.

Imagine that a year from now, after having created hundreds of useful macros for yourself and your friends, you come across an odd-looking file, called AD.WPM, in your \MACROS directory. You wonder what in the world this macro does. With the cursor on the macro name in the List Files screen, you press **L**ook (**6**) or just press Enter, and you see the description you wrote when you first created the macro. Below the description, you see some other items that don't make any sense.

Computer people call these symbols "garbage" because they are not readily intelligible as ordinary language. Figure 11.7 shows how AD.WPM appears after you use **L**ook (**6**) from the List Files screen.

```
File: C:\MACROS\AD.WPM                          Revised: 11-04-89 09:06p

Return address and date, flush right
================================================================================
"=CM
ç
ç
ç
ç
ç
```

Fig. 11.7.

A look at the AD.WPM macro from the List Files screen.

Using the Macro Editor

You now have learned to create a variety of macros. You also know how to replace a macro with an entirely new one. Sometimes, however, you will want to make just a small change in a macro. If the macro is an intricate one, you won't want to create it from scratch. Fortunately, you don't have to: WordPerfect includes a macro editor.

The macro editor enables you to modify a macro by using some of the same editing commands you use in the normal editing screen. The macro editor also makes available many powerful programming commands that you can include in your macros only through the macro editor. In this section, you learn how to modify a macro, and you become acquainted with a few of the programming commands. A complete discussion of these commands is provided in the next chapter.

Reminder:

Many powerful programming commands are available through the macro editor.

Making a Simple Text Change

Suppose that you have a macro which includes your return address and the date, such as the AD macro you created earlier in the chapter. What do you do if you want to change some part of the address but keep everything else in the macro the same? This task is a prime candidate for the macro editor.

To edit a macro, you begin as if you were going to create the macro from scratch, using the same name. Complete the following steps to modify the address in the AD macro:

1. To begin macro recording, press Macro Define (Ctrl-F10).

   ⌨ Access the **T**ools pull-down menu, select **M**acro, and choose **D**efine.

2. At the `Define macro:` prompt, type *ad* and press Enter.

   Keep in mind that WordPerfect will not let you change an existing macro without warning. The program displays the following prompt:

   AD.WPM Already Exists: 1 Replace; **2 E**dit: **3 D**escription: **0**

3. Select **E**dit (**2**).

If you wanted to change only the description of the macro without modifying what it does, you would choose **D**escription (**3**) instead. After changing the description, you press Exit (F7) twice to avoid changing any codes in the macro.

The macro editing screen appears (see fig. 11.8).

The cursor is placed so that you can begin editing the macro. Each macro element is shown in the rectangular box that fills most of the screen. Text is shown as regular text, WordPerfect commands are enclosed in curly braces, and spaces are shown as small dots. Text is the easiest element of a macro to edit.

Tip

You can use the Enter key to change the appearance of the commands in the macro editor. An {Enter} code will not be added to the macro unless you give a special command first (see the section "Inserting and Editing WordPerfect Commands" later in the chapter).

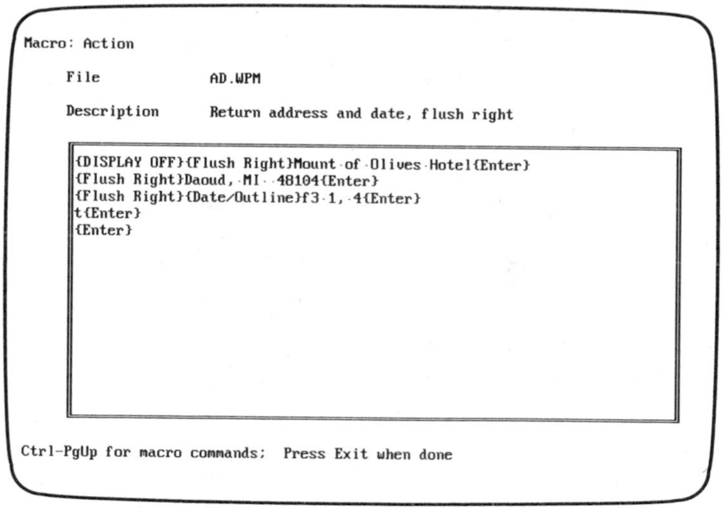

Fig. 11.8.

The macro editing screen.

```
Macro: Action

    File            AD.WPM

    Description     Return address and date, flush right

    {DISPLAY OFF}{Flush Right}Mount·of·Olives·Hotel{Enter}
    {Flush Right}Daoud,·MI··48104{Enter}
    {Flush Right}{Date/Outline}f3·1,·4{Enter}
    t{Enter}
    {Enter}




Ctrl-PgUp for macro commands;  Press Exit when done
```

4. Use the arrow keys to move the cursor to the M in Mount of Olives Hotel.

5. Delete Mount of Olives Hotel with the Del key (letter by letter). If you use Ctrl-Backspace, you may accidentally delete the {Enter} code following Hotel.

6. Position the cursor after the {Flush Right} code and type *Benna Kessler* (see fig. 11.9).

7. To exit the macro editor and save your changes, press Exit (F7) once.

```
Macro: Action

    File            AD.WPM

    Description     Return address and date, flush right

   ┌─────────────────────────────────────────────────────┐
   │ {DISPLAY OFF}{Flush Right}Benna Kessler{Enter}        │
   │ {Flush Right}Daoud, MI  48104{Enter}                  │
   │ {Flush Right}{Date/Outline}f3 1, 4{Enter}             │
   │ t{Enter}                                              │
   │ {Enter}                                               │
   │                                                       │
   │                                                       │
   │                                                       │
   │                                                       │
   │                                                       │
   │                                                       │
   │                                                       │
   │                                                       │
   └─────────────────────────────────────────────────────┘

  Ctrl-PgUp for macro commands;  Press Exit when done
```

Fig. 11.9.
The macro editing screen after a text change.

Deleting WordPerfect Commands

You can change more than just text with the macro editor. You might decide, for example, that you want a return-address macro that does not include the Flush Right commands. Although you could edit the macro to delete those commands, you might instead want to have two macros: one with the Flush Right commands and one without them.

You cannot use WordPerfect's built-in macro editor to save a second copy of the macro under a different name, but that doesn't mean that you have to create the second macro from scratch. You can first use List (F5) to make a copy of the AD.WPM macro, and call it AD2.WPM. You can then use the macro editor to edit the AD2 macro.

Complete these steps to make a copy of the AD.WPM macro:

1. Press List (F5).

   ⌨ Access the **F**ile pull-down menu and select List **F**iles.

   The name of the current directory appears. You want to work with the files in your macro directory without changing the current directory.

2. Type the name of the directory where the macros are located and press Enter. For example, type *macros* and press Enter (or the space bar).

3. To find the AD macro, select **N**ame Search (**N**), type *ad.wpm*, and press Enter. The AD.WPM macro is highlighted.

4. Select **C**opy (**8**) from the List Files menu. The screen displays the following prompt:

   ```
   Copy this file to:
   ```

5. Type *ad2.wpm* and press Enter.

6. To exit the List Files screen, press Exit (F7) or the space bar.

You now have an AD2 macro identical to the AD macro. Next, you learn how to modify the AD2 macro without affecting the original AD macro. You learn also how to change a macro description.

Complete the following steps to change the description of the AD2 macro and to eliminate the Flush Right commands from the macro:

1. To begin macro recording, press Macro Define (Ctrl-F10).

   ⌨ Access the **T**ools pull-down menu, select **M**acro, and choose **D**efine.

2. At the `Define macro:` prompt, type *ad2* and press Enter. The screen displays the following prompt:

   AD.WPM Already Exists: 1 Replace; **2** Edit: **3** Description: **0**

3. Because you want to change the description of the macro, as well as edit the macro itself, select **D**escription (**3**).

   The `Description:` prompt appears at the bottom of the regular editing screen. You can use many of the same editing commands you used before.

4. Press End.

Reminder:
You cannot use Block to edit macro descriptions.

5. Use the Backspace key to delete the comma (,) and `flush right` from the description. Note that you cannot use Block to edit the description.

6. Press Enter or Exit (F7) once to begin editing the macro itself. The macro editing screen appears with the cursor positioned for you to make changes in the macro. You can use the Del key to erase all three {Flush Right} codes.

7. Use the arrow keys to position the cursor on the opening brace of the first {Flush Right} code. Then press Del.

   The {Flush Right} code is deleted.

8. To remove the second and third {Flush Right} codes, repeat step 7 for each of those codes.

9. To exit the macro editor, press Exit (F7) once.

Inserting and Editing WordPerfect Commands

Reminder:
*To go to the macro editor, press Macro Define (Ctrl-F10), give the name of the macro you want to edit, and choose **E**dit (**2**) from the menu.*

You can do much more with the macro editor than just edit text or delete commands. You can add new commands or edit old ones. To add most commands, go to the macro editor, position the cursor at the appropriate place within the window of macro commands, and press the same keys you would press if you were in the regular editing screen. You cannot use WordPerfect menus within the macro editor, but you can use the mouse to position the cursor.

To add commands to a macro, you need to remember or write down in advance exactly what commands you want to include. Suppose, for example, that you want to change the date format in the AD2 macro so that the day of the week is included before the date. To find out what commands are required, you probably will need to exit the macro editor and write down the commands you will need. If you do this, you will see that you need the following formatting commands to enter the day of the week and the date:

Date/Outline (Shift-F5)

Date Format (3)

6, 3 1, 4

Now, using the macro editor, you must determine where the old codes for the date are located. Notice in figure 11.9 the following portion of the macro:

{Date/Outline}f3 1, 4

(Remember that the macro editor inserts dots to indicate spaces.)

To change the command to include the day of the week, you need to change the original commands to these:

{Date/Outline}f6, 3 1, 4

Just position the cursor on the 3, type 6, type a comma, and insert a space.

You can use the Enter key to change the appearance of the codes in the macro editor. Within the macro editor, pressing the Enter key (when used in the usual way) only rearranges the appearance of the commands; pressing Enter does not insert an {Enter} command in the macro.

The Enter key is one of several exceptions to the general rule that any text or commands which you type in the macro editor become inserted as part of the macro itself. If, for example, you press Underline (F8), you insert an {Underline} code into the macro editing screen, and that Underline command becomes part of the macro. To edit or change the appearance of commands in the macro editor, however, you can use keys such as Del, Backspace, and Enter without adding codes to the macro itself. In addition, you can use Exit (F7 or the right mouse button) to leave the macro editor without adding an {Exit} code, and you can use Cancel (F1) to back out of changes you have made.

Sometimes you *will* want to add to the macro itself the codes of {Backspace}, {Del}, {Enter}, {Exit}, and {Cancel}. You can add those codes in one of two ways: you can add one code at a time, or you can add a series of codes.

To add only one code, press Ctrl-V and then press the key for the code you want to add. Ctrl-V tells the macro editor that the next command is a code to insert in the macro itself. For instance, if you press Ctrl-V and then press Enter, an {Enter} code is inserted in the macro.

Reminder:
Pressing Ctrl-V tells the macro editor that the next command is a code to be inserted in a macro.

To add a series of codes, press Macro Define (Ctrl-F10), add the codes you need, and then press Macro Define (Ctrl-F10) again. Any commands you enter after first pressing Macro Define (Ctrl-F10) become part of the macro itself. Figure 11.10 shows how the macro editing screen looks after you press Macro Define (Ctrl-F10) the first time. WordPerfect displays the following message at the bottom of the screen:

```
Press Macro Define to enable editing
```

In plainer English, this message says, "Press Macro Define (Ctrl-F10) again when you want to stop inserting codes in the macro." Pressing Macro Define (Ctrl-F10) at this point will put you back in regular editing, where pressing certain keys, such as Enter and Exit (F7), does *not* insert codes in the macro but instead simply changes the appearance of the codes in the macro editor.

If you don't make the mistake of inserting a few unwanted codes after pressing Macro Define (Ctrl-F10) in the macro editor, you may be the first WordPerfect user not to do so. Suppose, for example, that you press Exit (F7) to stop editing and then find that you mistakenly inserted an {Exit} code into the macro. Or you may try to erase a code you just entered by mistake and then make the further mistake of pressing Backspace, only to insert the {Backspace} code. These errors are easily corrected. You first press Macro Define (Ctrl-F10) to "enable editing," and then use the Backspace key to delete any unwanted codes. You then can press Exit (F7) to leave the macro editor, saving any changes you have made.

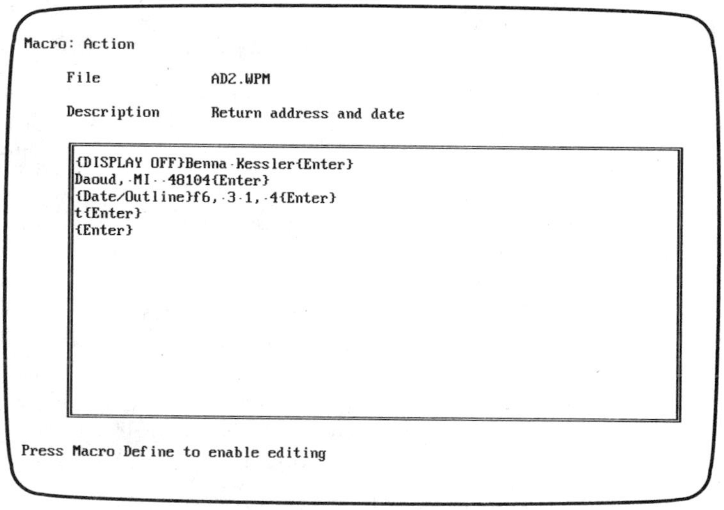

Fig. 11.10.
The macro editing screen while codes are being inserted.

```
Macro: Action

        File            AD2.WPM

        Description     Return address and date


    {DISPLAY OFF}Benna Kessler{Enter}
    Daoud, MI  48104{Enter}
    {Date/Outline}f6, 3 1, 4{Enter}
    t{Enter}
    {Enter}




    Press Macro Define to enable editing
```

You have another option for correcting your mistakes in the macro editor. You can press Cancel (F1) to back out of changes you have made to a macro. The program displays the following prompt:

    Cancel changes? No (Yes)

Select **Y** to exit the macro editor without saving any changes.

Inserting Special Macro Commands

With the macro editor, you can add or modify regular WordPerfect commands, and you can also insert special macro commands at any point in the macro. You are familiar with some of these special macro commands—for example, "display on" and "pause." These and other commands enable you to create intricate programs. To gain access to the special commands, you press Macro Commands (Ctrl-PgUp) while inside the macro editor.

Complete the following steps to access the macro editor and to add the {DISPLAY ON} command to the AD2 macro:

Reminder:

To access the special macro commands, press Macro Commands (Ctrl-PgUp) while inside the macro editor.

1. To begin macro editing, press Macro Define (Ctrl-F10).

   ▭ Access the **T**ools pull-down menu, select **M**acro, and choose **D**efine.

2. At the prompt Define macro:, type *ad2* and press Enter.

3. Select **E**dit (**2**). The cursor is positioned at the beginning of the macro.

4. Press Del to delete the {DISPLAY OFF} code.

5. Press Macro Commands (Ctrl-PgUp). A window that lists the special commands opens in the upper right corner of the screen. A block cursor is on the first command: {;}comment~. To move the block cursor to other commands, either use the cursor keys or type the first letter (or in some cases, letters) of the command.

6. To move the block cursor to the {DISPLAY OFF} command, type *d*.

7. Press the down arrow once to position the block cursor on {DISPLAY ON}, as shown in figure 11.11.

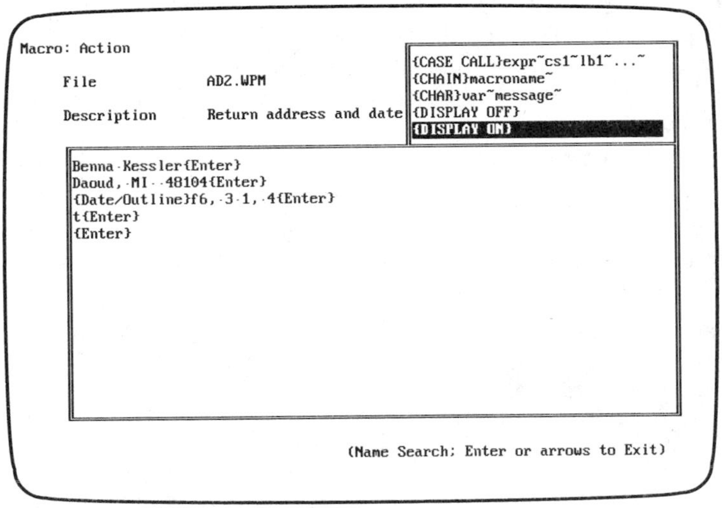

```
Macro: Action

     File          AD2.WPM          {CASE CALL}expr~cs1~lb1~...~
                                     {CHAIN}macroname~
     Description    Return address and date {CHAR}var~message~
                                     {DISPLAY OFF}
                                     {DISPLAY ON}

   Benna·Kessler{Enter}
   Daoud,·MI··48104{Enter}
   {Date/Outline}f6,·3·1,·4{Enter}
   t{Enter}
   {Enter}




               (Name Search; Enter or arrows to Exit)
```

Fig. 11.11.
Macro commands in the macro editor.

8. To insert the highlighted command, press Enter. The command is inserted at the point in the macro where you invoked Macro Commands (Ctrl-PgUp).

A {DISPLAY ON} code is inserted in the macro. You can delete this code by pressing Backspace.

Tip

You can use the Backspace and Del keys to delete any changes in the macro editor, and you can press Cancel (F1) to back out of all the changes you have made. To save your changes and return to the editing screen, press Exit (F7).

Experimenting with the Macro Editor

As you experiment further with the macro editor, keep these guidelines in mind:

Reminder:

To insert a special command in a macro, place the cursor on the command and press Enter.

- To display in the macro editor the list of special macro commands, press Macro Commands (Ctrl-PgUp).

- To insert a special command in the macro, position the cursor on the command and press Enter.

- To move from the window of special commands back to the regular macro editor without inserting a command, press Cancel (F1) or Exit (F7).

- To move to the top of the list of special macro commands when the cursor is already within the special commands window, press the space bar.

You may find several of the special macro commands useful in your own macros. Here are some ideas:

- You can add {BELL} to a macro so that you are reminded when the macro pauses for your input.

- You can add {PROMPT}*message~* to a macro so that it asks you a question or reminds you of something while running.

- You can use {;}*comment~* to add comments to a macro without affecting the way it runs. This feature can be helpful when you want to go back and edit a complicated macro.

- You can use {DISPLAY ON} and {DISPLAY OFF} if you change your mind about how you want a macro to run.

- You can use {NEST}*macroname~* to nest a descriptive macro or an Alt-*letter* macro. Recall that outside the macro editor, nested macros must be Alt-*letter* macros.

Each of the special macro commands has a required *syntax*—an exact way that you must insert the command in the macro editor. For example, if you nest a macro called TABS, you must insert the {NEST} code, type the name of the macro (*tabs*), and type a tilde (~) to indicate the end of the macro name.

These commands enable you to create complicated routines. Like all programming, programming with WordPerfect macros requires careful planning and organization. The next chapter introduces you to macro programming.

Summary

In this chapter, you saw how a macro can save you time by storing a group of keystrokes. When you want to insert those keystrokes in a document, you just run the macro.

You learned to perform the following macro techniques:

❏ Create Alt-*letter*, descriptive, and unnamed macros

❏ Run different types of macros

❏ Manage your macros files with the List Files feature

❏ Change the Setup screen so that you can run any macro regardless of the current drive or directory

❏ Control the way your macros run

Specifically, you learned how to set up a macro so that you can see each step it performs, how to make a macro pause so that you can insert a command or some text, and how to include in a macro a command to run a different macro.

❏ Create some macros for everyday use

❏ Use the macro editor to modify macros after you have created them

Don't expect to create perfect macros every time you try. You can improve your odds of success by working through the steps of a macro before you begin creating it. If the steps work when you perform them one by one, they are likely to work in a macro. Before you create a complicated macro, you may want to write down each of the steps. Don't be afraid to experiment.

12

Creating Advanced Macros

For 15 years **Stuart Bloom** has been teaching people how to program computers; he has been working with WordPerfect macros since 1985.

Sophisticated macro capability has always been one of WordPerfect's strengths. Version 5 added a macro programming language to the keystroke-macro capability of earlier versions. With version 5.1, WordPerfect introduces significant enhancements to that programming language.

In Chapter 11, you learned how to define keystroke macros. You also learned how to use WordPerfect's internal macro editor. In this chapter, the assumption is that you know how to enter keystrokes into macros both interactively and in the macro editor.

The WordPerfect macro language is a programming language, albeit a highly specialized one. If you've never programmed before, don't worry: this chapter leads you step by step through the few basic principles of programming that you'll need to master in order to use WordPerfect's advanced macro commands effectively. You may well be surprised at how soon you will be writing macros that fully exploit the advanced capabilities of WordPerfect.

This chapter also describes the WordPerfect macro language and provides some examples that you can use as points of departure for your own macro-development efforts. You can skip or skim through the basic material, which discusses some fundamental programming concepts. The idiosyncrasies of the WordPerfect macro language are identified in marginal reminders and boxed tips and cautions; you should read these as you come to them.

The chapter begins with a discussion of why you may want to use the advanced macro commands. You will learn some of the advanced capabilities you gain by using macros, discover how variables are used in macros, and learn syntax (or format) rules

345

that apply to all the advanced macro commands. Each of the advanced macro commands is described in detail. For each command, you'll learn its purpose and the specific syntax that governs its use, as well as get tips on how to use the command effectively. Each command is illustrated by one or more simple examples. For many commands, there is also a reference to one or more advanced "usage examples."

These advanced examples, which make up the final section of the chapter, are four moderately complex macros. These macros illustrate practical uses of most of the advanced macro commands. A detailed explanation accompanies each usage example.

Why Use Advanced Macro Commands?

To use advanced macro commands effectively, you need to develop an understanding of a few basic concepts that many people think of as "programming." This chapter guides you through the concepts and principles you need to know, and when you've finished reading it, you'll probably agree that advanced macro commands aren't that hard. Yet you may be wondering whether investing the time needed to understand these commands is worth your while.

Learning how to use advanced macro commands is probably a worthwhile task if you've felt a need to add control and flexibility to WordPerfect, if you'd like to automate common tasks beyond what you can do with simple keystroke macros, or if you're responsible for automating complex tasks for other users. The following are some examples of what you can do with advanced macro commands.

Create menus. One reason WordPerfect has done so well in the personal-computer market is its ease of use. Another reason is its rich set of complex features. But not all the complex features are easy to use. You can make complex features *easier* to use by creating menus.

The WordPerfect character sets include more than 1,500 characters. To use a character that's not on your keyboard, however, you must either memorize the code for the character or look the code up every time you want to use it. But if you use some characters all the time, you can create a menu of those characters.

Figure 12.1 shows an example of such a menu. With this menu, you can easily enter any of a number of bullet characters. If you assign this macro to Alt-B, you can create a paragraph symbol simply by pressing Alt-B and then pressing the letter I. The macro that creates this menu uses a number of advanced macro commands. See the description of BULLETS.WPM in the section "Working with Advanced Examples" for a listing of this macro.

Figure 12.2 is a simpler menu, also created with advanced macro commands. This menu offers an alternative to WordPerfect's multikeystroke copy function. See the description of COPY.WPM in the section "Working with Advanced Examples" for a listing of this macro.

```
1    Small round black bullet
2    Medium round black bullet
3    Large round black bullet
4    Small hollow black bullet
5    Medium hollow black bullet
6    Large hollow black bullet
7    Small square black box
8    Medium square black box
9    Large square black box
A    Small square hollow box
B    Medium square hollow box
C    Large square hollow box
D    Pointing finger
E    Check mark
F    Arrow
G    Arrowhead
H    Box with X
I    Paragraph symbol
J    Section symbol

0    Cancel



Type the number or letter of the bullet character: 0
```

Fig. 12.1.

A custom full-screen menu.

```
Copy: 1 Sentence; 2 Paragraph; 3 Page: 0
```

Fig. 12.2.

A custom status-line menu.

Automate repetitive tasks. If you work for an organization, you may be required to insert documents' file names somewhere within the documents. Before version 5.1, you could not do this task automatically with WordPerfect. Now, however, using advanced macro commands, you can create a macro that includes in any document not only the file name but also (if you like) the DOS path to the file. See this chapter's description of the {SYSTEM} command for details.

Integrate WordPerfect's advanced features. WordPerfect 5.1 has a huge number of advanced features. Although most features are in themselves not difficult to use, the sheer number of options can overwhelm less experienced users. If your organization needs people who can use WordPerfect in a sophisticated way, you can help meet that need with macros. You can build custom step-by-step procedures that hide some of the complexity from the average user. The INVOICE.WPM macro in the section "Working with Advanced Examples" is one example of a custom-built macro that automates a moderately complex task.

Create complete applications systems. Creating a complete applications system—a multimodular set of macros that completely automates an office function—may be your ultimate goal. Developing such an applications system is beyond the scope of this book. But if you learn how to use the capabilities that WordPerfect macros provide, you'll be able to put macros together to develop large, complex systems. All the tools needed to accomplish that ambitious goal are discussed in this chapter.

Unlike keystroke macros, advanced macro commands do more than simply replicate WordPerfect keystrokes. But advanced macro commands have two important characteristics in common with simpler commands—they tell the computer what to do, and they perform their functions in a sequence of defined steps. Each WordPerfect function key has a specific purpose; each advanced macro command also has a specific purpose. And just as each keystroke function has a set of rules governing its use, so does each advanced macro command.

Advanced macros consist of several elements. In most advanced macros, you will find a combination of the following:

- WordPerfect commands, which consist of keystrokes, like {Enter} or {Search}; menu choices, like the choices on formatting menus or "Yes" and "No" responses to questions; and responses to prompts, such as file names

- Portions of the text that will be typed into your document

- The advanced macro commands themselves

- Variables, which are described in the following section

Understanding Variables

Variables are one of the key tools available to you, the macro developer, for controlling the operation of the macro. WordPerfect uses variables to store information. One well-known programmer, quoting Winnie-the-Pooh, described a variable as "a useful pot to put things in."[1] It's hard to think of a simpler, more accurate definition. To follow the programmer's analogy, think of WordPerfect variables as resembling a series of pots, such as those shown in figure 12.3.

Fig. 12.3.
"Pots" (variables) used to store information.

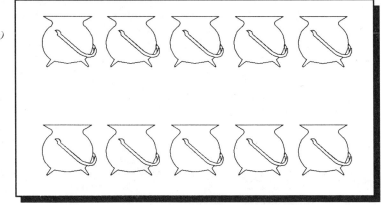

Each pot represents a specific place in the computer's memory where WordPerfect can store something. "Something" may be a user's name, a file name, or a keystroke—anything that can be represented as data by WordPerfect. If, for example, you tell WordPerfect to store the current page number, WordPerfect stores it in a variable—or, in terms of the analogy, WordPerfect "puts it in a pot."

The reason to have WordPerfect store something is that you want to use the stored data later in the macro. You might store a page number in a variable because you want to go to that page number later.

Understanding Variable Names

When you tell WordPerfect to store data in a variable, you know that the program stores the data in one of its "pots"—but unless you know which pot you've told WordPerfect to put the data in, you won't be able to tell WordPerfect to retrieve it.

You can keep track of WordPerfect's pots by giving each one a number, as shown in figure 12.4. You can now tell WordPerfect to store the page number in, for example, pot 3; when you're ready to take the page number back out and use it, you can tell WordPerfect to give you the contents of pot 3.

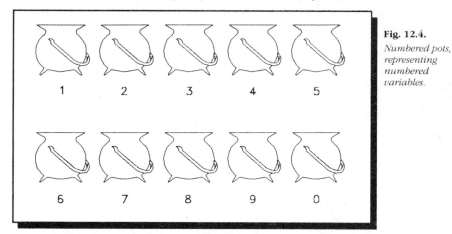

Fig. 12.4.

Numbered pots, representing numbered variables.

The foregoing example illustrates WordPerfect's *numbered variables*. Although WordPerfect 5's numbered variables were useful tools for the macro developer, they had limitations. First, there were only 10 of them; a complicated macro may require many variables. Second, keeping track of which number has been used for which data can be difficult.

WordPerfect 5.1 has addressed this problem by providing, in addition to the 10 numbered variables (0 through 9), *named variables*. Continuing the pot analogy, figure 12.5 shows examples of named variables.

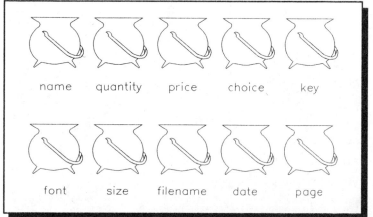

Fig. 12.5.

Named pots, representing named variables.

Reminder:
WordPerfect 5.1 offers named variables as well as 10 numbered variables.

A WordPerfect variable name must follow these rules:

- The characters allowed are any characters you can type from the keyboard, including characters in WordPerfect's extended character set. The following are all legal variable names: *filename*, *file_name*, and *file2*.

- No distinction is made between lowercase and capital letters. The names *Filename*, *filename*, and *FILENAME* all refer to the same variable.

Reminder:

Only the first seven characters are significant in a WordPerfect variable name.

Although a variable name can be of any reasonable length—more than 50 characters are allowed—WordPerfect actually uses only the first seven characters.

The terms *filename1* and *filename2* look different to you, but to WordPerfect they are the same variable because their first seven characters—*filenam*—are the same. If you tell WordPerfect to put the text LETTER.WP into the variable named *filename1* and later tell WordPerfect to put the text MEMO.WP into the variable named *filename2*, WordPerfect will put both bits of text into the same variable, which it calls *filenam*. Because a variable can hold only one thing at a time, when WordPerfect puts MEMO.WP into *filenam*, MEMO.WP replaces LETTER.WP. At any given time, a variable contains the last thing you've put into it.

WordPerfect recognizes *file1* and *file2* as two different variables because there is a difference within the first seven characters.

If you want to save the current page number, you can name a variable *page*. To save the file name, you can name a variable *filename*. You can create up to 256 variables, giving each a name of your choosing. Numbered variables are really just a special class of named variables. Assigning a value to a variable named 1 is same operation as assigning a value to a variable numbered 1.

Understanding Variable Types and Mathematical Operators

So far, you've learned that a variable is a place to put "things" and that those "things" can include various kinds of data. One of the limitations of WordPerfect variables is the form of data you can put into variables.

Reminder:

What you put into a variable determines whether it is an integer variable or a string variable.

WordPerfect has two types of variables: *integer variables* and *string variables*. The variable type is determined by what you put into the variable. You should understand the difference between these types, because the type of variable determines how you can use the variable.

With either a string or an integer variable, you can do the following:

- Assign the variable a value
- Display the variable's value on-screen
- Assign the variable's value to a different variable
- Check whether the variable is identical to another variable or to text

Reminder:

Only integer variables can be used in mathematical calculations.

With an integer variable, you also can do the following:

- Use the variable's value in a mathematical calculation
- Check whether the variable is equal to, greater than, or less than another variable or a number

In WordPerfect 5.1, an integer variable is a whole number that lies in the range –2,147,483,648 to +2,147,483,647. (In version 5, integers were limited to the range 0 to +65,535.)

For clarity's sake, the preceding paragraph shows commas within numbers; when you actually enter integers into a WordPerfect variable, however, you enter them without commas. In version 5.1, the only characters you can enter into an integer variable are the digits 0 through 9 and the following mathematical operators:

$$+ - * / \%$$

(Mathematical operators are explained later in this section.) In version 5, only digits were accepted in integer variables.

Note that WordPerfect variables—and the WordPerfect macro language in general—can handle only whole numbers. Decimal values are not available in macros, although you can work with decimals if you create macros that interact with WordPerfect's math feature. You also can simulate decimal arithmetic. See INVOICE.WPM in the section "Working with Advanced Examples" for an example of simulating decimal arithmetic in WordPerfect macros.

Reminder:
Only whole numbers can be used in WordPerfect macro-language calculations.

The following are integer variables:

        0
       13
      –13
  4555423
 –4555423

The following are *not* integer variables:

    1,265   (not an integer variable because of the comma)
    45817.3   (not an integer variable because of the decimal)

Caution

If you put a positive number larger than 2,147,483,647 or a negative number smaller than –2,147,483,648 into an integer variable, WordPerfect will accept the number and treat it like an integer, but the answers you get when you use the variable in mathematical computations will be incorrect.

The mathematical operators in WordPerfect macros are shown in table 12.1. The addition (+) and subtraction (–) operators should be familiar to you. The multiplication operator is an asterisk (*).

Caution

If a division, subtraction, or multiplication results in an answer outside the range of WordPerfect integer variables, the result will not be correct.

Table 12.1
Mathematical Operators

Operator	Meaning	Example	Result
+	Addition	9+4	13
−	Subtraction	9−4	5
*	Multiplication	9*4	36
/	Integer division	9/4	2
%	Remainder	9%4	1

Division is less straightforward. You will recall that WordPerfect macros can deal only with integers—whole numbers. If a division operation, signified by a slash (/), results in a remainder, the remainder is ignored. Therefore, as shown in table 12.1, the division operation 9/4 results in the answer 2, not 2.25.

Use the remainder operator (%) to obtain the remainder of a division. When 9 is divided by 4, the answer is 2 with a remainder of 1. You can obtain this remainder with the expression 9%4, as shown in table 12.1. To obtain the complete results of dividing 9 by 4, you must use two expressions: 9/4 and 9%4.

If in an integer variable you insert an expression containing a mathematical operator, WordPerfect *evaluates* (computes) the expression that you entered into the variable and stores the result of the evaluation in the variable.

A *string variable* is a variable that does not meet the definition of an integer; a string can consist of up to 120 characters. The following are string variables:

WordPerfect

1,265   (not an integer variable because of the comma)

45817.3   (not an integer variable because of the decimal)

Understanding Expressions

Many of the advanced macro commands discussed in this chapter compare two items and then perform different actions based on the results of the comparison. Typically, the comparison determines whether the items are equal or not equal, or whether one is greater than or less than the other. The result of the comparison is always a number representing either true or false. WordPerfect represents a true result with −1 and a false result with 0.

The terms of the comparison are often referred to as the *expression*. The process of performing the comparison is referred to as *evaluating* the expression; the results of the evaluation are *returned*. In other words, if *var1* equals 1 and *var2* equals 2, then

    var1=var2

is an expression, and the evaluation of the expression returns a 0 (false). See table 12.2 for examples of expressions and results; the table is based on the assumption that *var1* equals 1 and that *var2* equals 2. The symbol = means "equals"; the symbol != means "is not equal to"; the symbol > means "greater than"; and the symbol < means "less than" (see also table 12.8 in the section "Using {WHILE} Loops").

Table 12.2
Expressions and Results

Expression	Result	Explanation
var1=var2	0 (false)	Does *var1* equal *var2*? No, so the result is false (0).
var2=2	–1 (true)	Does *var2* equal the number 2? Yes, so the result is true (–1).
var1!=var2	–1	Is *var1* not equal to *var2*? The numbers are not equal, so the result is true (–1).
var1!=1	0	Is *var1* not equal to the number 1? The numbers are equal, so the result is false (0).
var1>45	0	Is *var1* greater than the number 45? No, so the result is false (0).
var2<3	–1	Is *var2* less than the number 3? Yes, so the result is true (–1).
var2>2	0	Is *var2* greater than the number 2? No, the numbers are equal, so the result is false (0).

Note that table 12.2 does not contain a direct "greater than or equal to" comparison. To make such a comparison, you must combine comparisons within one expression. To do this, you must use either the AND or the OR *logical operator* (see table 12.3). The AND operator is expressed as an ampersand (&); the OR operator is expressed as a vertical bar (|). You place the operator between two comparisons.

Table 12.3
Logical Operators

Operator	Meaning	Description
&	AND	If *both* expressions are true, then the complete statement is true. If *either* expression is false, then the complete statement is false.
		OR	If *either* expression is true, then the complete statement is true. If *both* expressions are false, then the complete statement is false.
!	NOT	If the expression would be true without the !, then the statement is false. If the expression would be false without the !, then the statement is true.

As table 12.3 indicates, when you use the AND (&) operator between two comparisons, both comparisons must return a true (–1) result before the entire expression can return a true result. If either comparison returns a false (0) result, the entire operation returns a false result.

When you use the OR (|) operator, and either comparison returns a true result, the entire expression returns a true result. The entire expression returns a false result only if both comparisons return a false result. (The NOT operator is not discussed in this chapter; it is included in the table for completeness.)

See table 12.4 for examples of multiple comparisons; the table is based on the assumption that *var1* equals 1 and that *var2* equals 2.

Table 12.4
Multiple Comparisons and Results

Expression	Result	Explanation
var1=1&var1=2	0 (false)	Is *var1* equal to the number 1 *and* is *var1* equal to the number 2? Because only one of the comparisons is true, the result is false (0).
var2=var1|var2>var1	–1 (true)	Is *var2* equal to *var1* or is *var2* greater than *var1*? Because one of the comparisons is true, the result is true.
var1>–100&var1<100	–1	Is *var1* greater than –100 *and* is *var1* less than 100? Both conditions are true, so the entire expression is true.

Often you will want to compare strings of text. To do so, you must enclose both parts of the comparison within quotation marks. See the discussion of the {VARIABLE} command for more information on this point.

Understanding the Syntax of Advanced Macro Commands

When you enter advanced macro commands in the macro editor (by pressing Ctrl-PgUp and selecting from the list, as described in Chapter 11), the commands are shown enclosed in curly braces; the command to sound a bell, for example, is shown as {BELL}.

Many advanced macro commands require *arguments*. An argument is an element of data that the macro command needs in order to do its work. For example, the {PROMPT} command tells WordPerfect to display a message on the status line. To do its work, the {PROMPT} command needs to know the message to be displayed. Therefore, the syntax of the {PROMPT} command requires a message as an argument:

{PROMPT}*message~*

This syntax indicates that when you use the {PROMPT} command, you must follow it with a message. The message is an argument for the {PROMPT} command.

WordPerfect also needs to know where an argument ends. The device WordPerfect uses to find the end of an argument is the tilde (~). Every argument must end with a tilde.

Reminder:
Every argument must end with a tilde.

Assume that you want to use the {PROMPT} command to display a message that reads *Type the date; then press Enter.* You would enter it like this:

{PROMPT}Type the date; then press Enter.~

Some advanced macro commands require more than one argument. In such a command, you separate the arguments with tildes. For example, the {CHAR} command has two arguments; the first is the name of a variable, and the second is a message to be displayed. The syntax of the command is as follows:

{CHAR}*variable~message~*

When you use the {CHAR} command, you need both of the arguments and both of the tildes. To prompt the user to enter a character that will be assigned to the variable *number,* you would put the following command in your macro:

{CHAR}number~Enter a number between 1 and 4~

When one advanced macro command is used as the argument of another advanced macro command, and when each of the commands requires arguments, the situation may call for more than one tilde in succession. For example, the {ON CANCEL} command requires an argument (and thus a tilde); its syntax is the following:

{ON CANCEL}*action~*

The argument *action* indicates the action the macro is to take if the user presses the Cancel (F1) key. Assume that the action is to go to a place in the macro definition that is identified by the label *exit.* To tell a macro to go somewhere, use the {GO} command, which has an argument of its own. The syntax of the {GO} command is as follows:

{GO}*label~*

So to tell the macro, "If the user presses the Cancel (F1) key, go to the place named *exit,*" you use the {ON CANCEL} command and, as its argument, the {GO} command, with its argument. The complete command is this:

{ON CANCEL}{GO}exit~~

Note the two tildes. The first tilde marks the end of {GO}'s argument. WordPerfect knows, then, that the argument to {GO} is *exit.* The second tilde marks the end of {ON CANCEL}'s argument, which is *{GO}exit~.*

Reminder:
If your macro does not work properly, check whether you omitted or misplaced tildes.

The most common mistakes made by macro developers are the omission of tildes and the misplacement of tildes. If your macro does not operate correctly, check the tildes first.

Manipulating Variables

Two uses for advanced macro commands in macro development are to tell WordPerfect to "put this piece of data into a variable with that name" and to "retrieve the data stored under that name." In this section, you'll learn about some of the commands that perform these two jobs. (Other macro commands that manipulate variables are discussed in the sections "Communicating with the User" and "Using Loops.")

The commands discussed in this section are {ASSIGN}, which puts data into a variable; and {VARIABLE}, {VAR *n*}, {LEN}, and {MID}, which get data out of a variable.

{ASSIGN}

The {ASSIGN} command puts a value into a variable. The syntax is the following:

{ASSIGN}*variable~value~*

The argument *variable* is the variable name. The argument *value* can be a number, a text string, or an expression. An expression can consist of an arithmetic equation or another variable.

{ASSIGN} enables you as the macro developer to get data into a macro without user intervention. Other methods—all of which require the user to supply data—are discussed in the section "Communicating with the User."

Consider the following examples. This line assigns the value 1,000 to the variable *number*.

{ASSIGN}number~1000~

In this next line, the text string YES is assigned to the variable *1*:

{ASSIGN}1~YES~

The line that follows assigns the sum of the expression 12+53 to the variable *sum*:

{ASSIGN}sum~12+53~

The following macro assigns 12 to the variable *1* and 53 to the variable *2*; it then adds the two variables and displays the result, as shown in figure 12.6:

{ASSIGN}1~12~
{ASSIGN}2~53~
{ASSIGN}sum~{VAR 1}+{VAR 2}~
The sum of {VAR 1} and {VAR 2} is {VARIABLE}sum~

For more examples of the {ASSIGN} command, see the listings for the macros BULLETS.WPM, COPY.WPM, INVOICE.WPM, and TOUPPER.WPM in the section "Working with Advanced Examples."

```
The sum of 12 and 53 is 65.




                                          Doc 1 Pg 1 Ln 1" Pos 3.7"
```

Fig. 12.6.
*The result of using
{ASSIGN} to add.*

{VARIABLE}

The {VARIABLE} command lets you access the contents of a variable. You use this command either to put the variable contents in a document or to use the contents in another macro command. The syntax is as follows:

{VARIABLE}*name~*

The term *name* represents any combination of WordPerfect characters.

As mentioned earlier, although you can have a long variable—over 50 characters—WordPerfect uses only the first 7 characters to identify the variable. If, for example, you use the terms *expensesmarch* and *expensesapril* to represent two variables, WordPerfect treats them as the same variable, because the first 7 letters—*expense*—are identical.

When you compare the value of a string variable to another value, you must surround in quotation marks both the variable name and the value to which the variable is being compared. For example, assume that you have assigned a letter to a variable named *userinput.* You want to test whether that letter is an *A.* Use this format:

{IF}"{VARIABLE}userinput~"="A"~

Reminder:
*You must surround
the name and value
of a string variable
with quotation marks
when using the
variable in a
comparison.*

Note that quotation marks surround the complete variable name—including the {VARIABLE} command itself and the tilde that marks the end of the name. (The last tilde is part of the {IF} command syntax and is not included within the quotation marks.)

If you are comparing two string variables, you must surround both with quotation marks. Assume that you have two variables, *entry1* and *entry2*, and that you have assigned strings to both; now you want to test them to see whether they are equal. Enter the following:

{IF}"{VARIABLE}entry1~"="{VARIABLE}entry2~"~

This discussion applies only to comparison operations, not to assignment operations. You do *not* use quotation marks in any WordPerfect commands except {IF} and {WHILE}.

The following macro assigns the text string *Welcome to WordPerfect Macros* to a variable named *message* and then prints the text string on the screen, as shown in figure 12.7.

    {ASSIGN}message~Welcome to WordPerfect Macros~
    {VARIABLE}message~

```
Welcome to WordPerfect Macros.




                                                    Doc 1 Pg 1 Ln 1" Pos 4"
```

Fig. 12.7.
The result of using {VARIABLE} to display a message.

Reminder:

Do not include the {VARIABLE} command where a variable is required.

Notice that the first line of the macro does not include the {VARIABLE} command. The {ASSIGN} command *requires* the name of a variable as its first argument. Including the {VARIABLE} command anywhere in a WordPerfect macro that requires a variable is wrong. In addition to {ASSIGN}, other commands that require variable arguments are {CHAR}, {FOR}, {FOR EACH}, {IF EXISTS}, {LEN}, {LOOK}, {MID}, and {TEXT}.

The following lines (which are part of a larger macro) print the message *The size is too large* if the value of the variable named *size* is greater than 13:

    {IF}{VARIABLE}size~>13~
        The size is too large.
    {END IF}

For more examples of the {VARIABLE} command, see the listings for the macros BULLETS.WPM, INVOICE.WPM, TESTCAP.WPM, and TOUPPER.WPM in the section "Working with Advanced Examples."

{VAR *n*}

The {VAR *n*} command performs the same functions as the {VARIABLE} command. The difference is that {VAR *n*} lets you more easily access the values stored in the numbered variables. The syntax of the command is the following:

    {VAR *n*}

The *n* is replaced by a single digit from 0 through 9 (for example, {VAR 3}). {VAR *n*} is an alternative way to assign a value to a numbered variable. The following commands are equivalent:

{VAR 7}
{VARIABLE}7~

To enter the command {VAR *n*} in the macro editor, do the following:

1. Press Ctrl-V.

2. Press Alt-*n*, where *n* is the number of the variable. To insert {VAR 4}, for example, press Alt-4.

The following example assigns the value 2,456 to variable number 3 and then prints the value on the screen, as shown in figure 12.8:

{ASSIGN}3~2456~
{VAR 3}

2456

Doc 1 Pg 1 Ln 1" Pos 1.4"

Fig. 12.8.
The result of using {VAR n} to display text.

Note that the {ASSIGN} command does not take the form {VAR *n*}; only the number of the variable being assigned is required. For a full explanation, see the examples for the {VARIABLE} command. For more examples of the {VAR *n*} command, see the listings for the macro COPY.WPM in the section "Working with Advanced Examples."

{LEN}

5.1

{LEN} returns the length of a string variable. The syntax is the following:

{LEN}*var*~

The term *var* represents the name or number of the string variable. The following commands exemplify the use of {LEN} to display the number 38 on the screen:

{ASSIGN}string~Using WordPerfect 5.1, Special Edition~
{LEN}string~

5.1

For another example of the {LEN} command, see the listing for the macro INVOICE.WPM in the section "Working with Advanced Examples."

{MID}

{MID} is used to "take apart" a string variable; the command returns a substring (part of the string). The syntax is the following:

{MID}*var~offset~count~*

The term *var* is the name (or number) of a variable; *offset* is the number of the first character of the substring you want to use (counting the first character as 0); *count* is the number of characters to include in the substring.

The following commands display *WordPerfect* on-screen:

{ASSIGN}string~Using WordPerfect 5.1, Special Edition~
{MID}string~6~11~

For another example of the {MID} command, see the listing for the macro INVOICE.WPM in the section "Working with Advanced Examples."

Communicating with the User

In the preceding section, you learned about macro commands that primarily manipulate variables. In this section, you'll learn about advanced macro commands that communicate with the user: {CHAR}, {TEXT}, and {LOOK}, which get data from the user and put the data into a variable; {INPUT}, {PAUSE}, and {PAUSE KEY}, which pause the action of the macro to let the user take some action; and {PROMPT}, {STATUS PROMPT}, and {BELL}, which give information to the user.

{CHAR}

The {CHAR} command accepts a single character (or any other single keystroke) and assigns the character (or key) to a variable. A message can be displayed on the status line to prompt the user. The syntax of the command is the following:

{CHAR}*variable~message~*

If you type a digit, the variable is an integer variable. If you type anything else, the variable is a string variable (see "Understanding Variables" earlier in this chapter).

In the example

{CHAR}reply~Do you want to continue? Yes (No)

the macro displays the question Do you want to continue? Yes (No) on the status line and waits for you to press a single key. When you press the key, the macro assigns the value of the key to the variable *reply*, and the message disappears.

If you want the macro to wait for a keystroke without displaying a message, you can omit the message text:

{CHAR}1~~

Note that the syntax of the {CHAR} command requires two tildes, whether or not you include a message.

For more examples of the {CHAR} command, see the listings for the macros BULLETS.WPM, COPY.WPM, and TESTCAP.WPM in the section "Working with Advanced Examples."

{TEXT}

{TEXT} is similar to {CHAR} except that {TEXT} accepts up to 120 characters and assigns the input to a variable. A message can be displayed on the status line to prompt the user. The syntax of the command is the following:

{TEXT}*variable~message~*

The following macro prompts for the user's name, assigns the name to the variable *user*, and then prints a welcome message:

{TEXT}user~Type your full name and press Enter.~
Hello {VARIABLE}user~ and welcome to this macro!

{LOOK}

{LOOK} checks to see whether you have typed a character; if you have, the macro assigns the character to the variable named. If no character has been typed, {LOOK} deletes the contents of the variable. The syntax of the command is the following:

{LOOK}*variable~*

If you have a complex keyboard defined with several key definitions—particularly if you have redefined some of the keys that WordPerfect uses for special purposes—you may find that sometimes you want to use the original meaning of the key rather than the redefined meaning. You can, of course, deactivate the entire keyboard by pressing Ctrl-6, but then you must reactivate it to use your specialized keys, and that process requires going through the Setup menu.

By assigning the key definition shown in the following example to one of the keys (or key combinations) on your keyboard—for example, Ctrl-I—you can instruct WordPerfect to ignore, for the next keypress only, any key redefinitions and use the original, unaltered meaning of the key.

{CANCEL OFF}	{;} so Cancel can be redefined~
{ASSIGN}key~~	{;} key must be empty to enter the loop~
{WHILE}"{VARIABLE}key~"=""~	{;} as long as key is empty, loop~
{LOOK}key~	{;} pressing any key puts a value into key~
{END WHILE}	{;} when key has a value, exit from the loop~
{ORIGINAL KEY}	{;} use original value of the last key pressed~

Assume, for example, that you rarely use the Tab Align (Ctrl-F6) feature and so have redefined Ctrl-F6 to display all the files in the current directory that have the extension WP. Now, however, you need to use the original function of Tab Align. Press Ctrl-I and then Tab Align (Ctrl-F6); you will enter a **[Dec Tab]** code into your document.

The first command in the macro turns the Cancel (F1) key off; if it failed to do this, the macro would not work for the Cancel (F1) key if you had redefined that key. Then you remove any value that may be in the variable *key*. The {WHILE} loop and the {LOOK} command are what make this operation work. {LOOK} will return nothing until the user presses a key. As long as {LOOK} returns nothing, *key* will be empty. As long as *key* is empty, the {WHILE} loop will continue to loop. As soon as the user presses a key, however, {LOOK} assigns the value of that key to *key*. Because *key* is no longer empty—it now has a value—the macro exits from the {WHILE} loop. The next command, {ORIGINAL KEY}, instructs WordPerfect to take the last key pressed; ignore any keyboard redefinition; and execute the key's normal, unaltered function.

{INPUT}

{INPUT} displays a message on the status line and then pauses to let the user take any desired action. When the user presses Enter, the message is erased, and the next command in the macro is executed. The syntax for {INPUT} is the following:

> {INPUT}*message~*

Reminder:

When {INPUT} is used in a macro, Enter terminates the pause; when {INPUT} is used in a merge, End Field (F9) terminates the pause.

The following macro automates the process of marking a figure box. The macro prompts the user for a target name and assigns the name to a variable. The macro then executes the {Mark Text} keystrokes necessary to mark the reference and target. At the appropriate place in this sequence, the macro pauses to let the user position the cursor on the target figure, displaying an appropriate message to tell the user what to do. Finally, the macro names the target with the name stored in the variable.

> {TEXT}target~Enter the target name: ~
> {DISPLAY OFF}
> {Mark Text}rbgf
> {INPUT}Position the cursor after the figure to mark, then press {Enter}.~
> {Enter}
> {VARIABLE}target~{Enter}

{PAUSE}

{PAUSE} is similar to {INPUT} except that {PAUSE} does not display a message. {PAUSE} stops the macro and lets the user edit, type new text, or press function keys. When the Enter key is pressed, the macro resumes execution with the next command. The syntax for {PAUSE} is the following:

> {PAUSE}

The following commands direct the user to position the cursor on the text box. They then stop the macro and let the user move the cursor. When the user presses Enter, the macro resumes execution.

{PROMPT}Position the cursor on the Text Box and press Enter.~
{PAUSE}

{PAUSE KEY}

{PAUSE KEY} is identical to {PAUSE} except that the macro designer can specify which key will end the pause. This feature is useful when you want to let the user press the Enter key without ending the pause. The syntax for {PAUSE KEY} is the following:

{PAUSE KEY}*key*~

The *key* is the key that terminates the pause; the argument can be any WordPerfect key. You enter the key into the macro definition by pressing the key (after first pressing Ctrl-V, if necessary; see "Inserting and Editing WordPerfect Commands" in Chapter 11).

{PAUSE KEY} enables the user to take action that may require the use of the Enter key. You may, for example, want a macro to pause so that the user can enter some descriptive information, which might run several paragraphs. Paragraphs are ended when the user presses the Enter key. If you use {PAUSE}, then as soon as the user presses Enter to end the first paragraph, the {PAUSE} terminates. Using {PAUSE KEY} enables you to define a different key as the terminating key.

The following commands display a message and pause to let the user type a description. The use of {PAUSE KEY} lets the user type several paragraphs of information. When the user presses the End Field (F9) key, the macro continues.

{PROMPT}Enter a description; press F9 when done.~
{PAUSE KEY}{End Field}~

{PROMPT}

{PROMPT} displays a message on the status line. As soon as the user presses a key, or as soon as the macro encounters any other key command, the message disappears. The syntax of the command is as follows:

{PROMPT}*message*~

The following commands display a message and initiate a pause for user action. As soon as the user presses the first key, the message disappears. When the user presses the End Field (F9) key, the macro continues.

{PROMPT}Enter a description; press F9 when done.~
{PAUSE KEY}{End Field}~

{STATUS PROMPT}

{STATUS PROMPT} is similar to {PROMPT} except that the message remains on the status line until the macro executes an {INPUT} command or another {STATUS PROMPT} command. The message does not disappear when the macro terminates and will prevent some normal WordPerfect messages from being displayed.

> ### Caution
>
> Your macro must take some action to remove the message displayed with a {STATUS PROMPT}. If you use {STATUS PROMPT} and the user presses Cancel (F1) before the macro reaches the command that removes the message, the message remains displayed until the user exits from WordPerfect (or runs another macro that contains a {STATUS PROMPT} or {INPUT} command).

The syntax for {STATUS PROMPT} is the following:

{STATUS PROMPT}*message*~

Use {PROMPT} when you want the message to disappear as soon as the user takes some action. Use {STATUS PROMPT} when you want the message to be displayed until the macro removes it.

Using {STATUS PROMPT} with a blank message, as shown in the following example, removes the message from the screen. The commands display a message and initiate a pause for user action. The message remains displayed while the user enters the description. When the user presses the End Field (F9) key, the message disappears, and the macro continues.

    {STATUS PROMPT}Enter a description; press F9 when done.~
    {PAUSE KEY}{End Field}~
    {STATUS PROMPT}~

{BELL}

{BELL} sounds a beep, which is a useful means of gaining the user's attention. The syntax is as follows:

    {BELL}

Consider the following macro, which performs a merge. At the end of the merge, the macro sounds two beeps to alert the user that the merge has been completed.

    {Merge/Sort}m   {;} start a merge~
    {PAUSE}{Enter}   {;} let user name the primary document~
    {PAUSE}{Enter}   {;} let user name the secondary document~
                       {;} WP performs the merge here~
    {BELL}   {;} sound a tone~
    {WAIT}2~   {;} wait 2/10ths of a second~
    {BELL}   {;} sound another tone

Dressing Up the Display

This section discusses control characters that, in conjunction with {CHAR}, {TEXT}, {INPUT}, {PAUSE}, or {PAUSE KEY}, create fancy menus, pop-up dialog boxes, and other display enhancements.

The material covered is slightly advanced. You can create many useful macros without using the methods described here. These methods, however, allow you a great deal of control over how your screen looks while your macros are executing.

Using the procedures discussed in this section, you can do the following:

- Create handsome full-screen menus, like the one shown in figure 12.1
- Create "pop-up" messages and menus
- Create menus that look and operate like native WordPerfect menus, such as the one in figure 12.2
- Call the user's attention to important information by enhancing the way it is displayed

Using Control Characters

The display is enhanced in WordPerfect macros through the use of *control characters*. There are two types of control characters: attribute characters and cursor-positioning characters. *Attribute characters* control the color (and other display attributes) of your messages and menus. *Cursor-positioning characters* control where your macros place messages and menus on the screen.

Control characters can be used in any WordPerfect advanced macro command that displays a message: {CHAR}, {TEXT}, {INPUT}, {PROMPT}, and {STATUS PROMPT}.

Reminder:
Attribute characters control the color, and cursor-positioning characters control the location of your message and menus.

Using Attribute Characters

Attribute characters affect the way characters appear in your messages and menus. In WordPerfect 5.1, all messages in macro commands initially display in bold. Table 12.5 lists the attribute characters used to display specific attributes. The *Enter as...* column shows the keystrokes needed to turn the attribute on and off. The *Shown as...* column shows the characters as they actually appear in the macro editor.

Table 12.5
Attribute Characters To Turn Specific Attributes On or Off

Attribute	ON or OFF?	Enter as...	Shown as...
Blink	ON	Ctrl-N Ctrl-P	{^N}{^P}
	OFF	Ctrl-O Ctrl-P	{^O}{^P}
Bold	ON	Ctrl-]	{^]}
	OFF	Ctrl-\	{^\}
Bold	ON	Ctrl-N Ctrl-L	{^N}{Del to EOP}
	OFF	Ctrl-O Ctrl-L	{^N}{Del to EOP}

Table 12.5 (continued)

Attribute	ON or OFF?	Enter as...	Shown as...
Fine	ON	Ctrl-N Ctrl-D	{^N}{^D}
	OFF	Ctrl-O Ctrl-D	{^O}{^D}
Italics	ON	Ctrl-N Ctrl-H	{^N}{Home}
	OFF	Ctrl-O Ctrl-H	{^O}{Home}
Double	ON	Ctrl-N Ctrl-K	{^N}{Del to EOL}
Underline	OFF	Ctrl-O Ctrl-K	{^N}{Del to EOL}
Large	ON	Ctrl-N Ctrl-B	{^N}{^B}
	OFF	Ctrl-O Ctrl-B	{^O}{^B}
Outline	ON	Ctrl-N Ctrl-G	{^N}{^G}
	OFF	Ctrl-O Ctrl-G	{^O}{^G}
Redline	ON	Ctrl-N Ctrl-H	{^N}{Enter}
	OFF	Ctrl-O Ctrl-H	{^O}{Enter}
Reverse	ON	Ctrl-R	{^R}
Video	OFF	Ctrl-S	{^S}
Reverse	ON	Ctrl-N Ctrl-Q	{^N}{^Q}
Video	OFF	Ctrl-O Ctrl-Q	{^O}{^Q}
Shadow	ON	Ctrl-N Ctrl-I	{^N}{Tab}
	OFF	Ctrl-O Ctrl-I	{^O}{Tab}
Small	ON	Ctrl-N Ctrl-C	{^N}{^C}
	OFF	Ctrl-O Ctrl-C	{^O}{^C}
Small	ON	Ctrl-N Ctrl-O	{^N}{^O}
Caps	OFF	Ctrl-O Ctrl-O	{^O}{^O}
Strikeout	ON	Ctrl-N Ctrl-M	{^N}{^M}
	OFF	Ctrl-O Ctrl-M	{^O}{^M}
Subscript	ON	Ctrl-N Ctrl-F	{^N}{^F}
	OFF	Ctrl-O Ctrl-F	{^O}{^F}
Superscript	ON	Ctrl-N Ctrl-E	{^N}{^E}
	OFF	Ctrl-O Ctrl-E	{^O}{^E}
Underline	ON	Ctrl-T	{^T}
	OFF	Ctrl-U	{^U}
Underline	ON	Ctrl-N Ctrl-N	{^N}{^N}
	OFF	Ctrl-O Ctrl-N	{^O}{^N}
Very	ON	Ctrl-N Ctrl-A	{^N}{^}
Large	OFF	Ctrl-O Ctrl-A	{^O}{^}

Notice that most of the attributes require two characters to turn them on and two characters to turn them off. When WordPerfect sees the character {^N}, it knows that the next character will identify an attribute to turn on. When WordPerfect sees the character {^O}, it knows that the next character identifies an attribute to turn off. The combination {^N}{Home} (entered as ^N^H) means "turn on italics." The combination {^O}{Home} means "turn off italics." In the following example, the word *very* is italicized when the macro is executed:

{PROMPT}Be {^N}{Home}very{^O}{Home} careful not to erase the file.~

Notice in table 12.5 that three attributes—Bold, Reverse Video, and Underline—have alternative single-character forms. In the following example, the *Y* in *Yes* and the *N* in *No* are boldfaced:

{CHAR}~save~Do you want to save the file? {^]}Y{^\}es ({^]}N{^\}o)~

Table 12.6 shows two special characters: {^V} and {^Q}. Together they let you duplicate, on any computer, the way a WordPerfect menu looks.

Table 12.6
Attribute Characters Used To Turn Mnemonic Attributes On and Off

ON or OFF?	Enter as...	Shown as...	Notes
ON	Ctrl-V Ctrl-V	{^V}	—
OFF	Ctrl-Q	{^Q}	{^Q} turns off *all* display attributes.

The {^Q} character turns off any display attributes that are on. It can be used in place of any of the OFF codes listed in table 12.5. If you are not combining attributes in a message, you can use {^Q} as a simple way to turn any attribute off.

Reminder:
Use {^V} to duplicate the mnemonics used in WordPerfect menus.

By default, WordPerfect menus use bold to highlight the mnemonic character. Using WordPerfect's Setup function, you can specify a different attribute for WordPerfect menus. If you use the {^V} control character in your macros, WordPerfect will use it as the currently selected menu attribute. If, for example, you have chosen Very Large as the menu-letter attribute, the following command will cause the *C* in *Copy* and the *M* in *Move* to display in the Very Large attribute:

{CHAR}select~Action: 1 {^V}C{^Q}opy; 2 {^V}M{^Q}ove: ~

Using Cursor-Positioning Characters

You can use the cursor-positioning control characters to build full-screen menus and enhance smaller menus. These characters are shown in table 12.7. Most require no explanation because they duplicate WordPerfect's regular cursor-movement keys.

The {Del to EOP} command requires some discussion. This command clears the screen and positions the cursor in the top left corner of the screen. Although a portion of the document may appear to have been erased, this is not the case; the menu screen produced during the execution of message-writing advanced macro commands is completely independent of the document screen. You should, however, restore the document screen after you have finished your menu.

Table 12.7
Cursor-Positioning Control Characters

Enter as...	Shown as...	Action
Ctrl-V Home	{Home}	Positions the cursor in the upper left corner of the screen
Ctrl-V Enter	{Enter}	Positions the cursor at the beginning of the next line
Ctrl-V Ctrl-End	{Del to EOL}	Deletes everything from the cursor position to the end of the line
Ctrl-PgDn	{Del to EOP}	Positions the cursor in the upper left corner of the screen and clears the screen
Ctrl-M	{^M}	Positions the cursor at the beginning of the current line
Ctrl-V Up	{Up}	Moves the cursor up one line
Ctrl-V Down	{Down}	Moves the cursor down one line
Ctrl-V Left	{Left}	Moves the cursor left one character
Ctrl-V Right	{Right}	Moves the cursor right one character
Ctrl-P	{^P}	Positions the cursor by using screen coordinates

To restore the document screen, do the following in the macro editor:

1. Press Screen (Ctrl-F3).
2. Press R.

You can use the {^P} character to position the cursor anywhere on the screen (except for the first row or first column) by entering screen coordinates. Using this character is a shortcut for the other methods listed in table 12.7. A full discussion of the {^P} method is beyond the scope of this book; refer to the discussion in the WordPerfect manual for details.

Duplicating the Appearance of a WordPerfect Menu

You now have all the tools you need to duplicate the appearance of a WordPerfect status-line menu. The Move menu, which follows, is typical of a WordPerfect status line on a computer whose user has changed the mnemonic attribute to Underline:

Move: 1 Sentence; **2** Paragraph; **3** Page; **4** Retrieve: **0**

Most WordPerfect status-line menus consist of the following:

- The menu name in bold (such as **Move**), followed by a colon.
- Each numeric choice, also in bold.
- Each mnemonic-letter choice in the chosen attribute, such as Underline (the default is Bold).

- The text of the menu choices, in normal (unenhanced) text. A semicolon follows each choice except the last one, which is followed by a colon.
- The default numeric response, in bold, at the end of the menu. The cursor rests under the default response.

To reproduce the Move menu using WordPerfect attribute characters, issue the following commands in the macro editor:

{CHAR}choice~{^]}Move: 1{^Q} {^V}S{^Q}entence; {^]}2{^Q} {^V}P{^Q}aragraph;
{^]}3{^Q} P{^V}a{^Q}ge; {^]}4{^Q} {^V}R{^Q}etrieve: {^]}0{^Q}{Left}~

Notice the {Left} command immediately before the ending tilde. This command positions the cursor under the default menu choice.

For more examples of control-character use, see the listings for the macros BULLETS.WPM and COPY.WPM in the section "Working with Advanced Examples."

Controlling Program Execution

This section covers some of the commands that change the order of program execution. These commands are the essence of "programming." If you have never programmed before, you may find the concepts and commands discussed in this section challenging. But by reading the material carefully and studying the examples closely—particularly the more complex examples in the section "Working with Advanced Examples"—you will learn how to use the commands to make WordPerfect macros do your bidding.

Understanding Program-Control Concepts

If a macro encounters no program-control commands, it starts at the first command and continues executing until the last command, at which point it terminates. This arrangement is satisfactory for very simple macros, and indeed, most macros you define interactively from the keyboard fall into this category. But to do more complex and useful operations, you need the ability to change the order in which WordPerfect macros execute commands.

To change the order of command execution, you use a group of commands that has the capability to transfer program control to different places within the macro (or, in some cases, to entirely different macros). The command that has program control is the command that is currently executing. *Transferring program control* means directing the macro to *branch* to another place for its next command.

Reminder:
Use branching commands to transfer program control.

Branching commands—or transfer-of-control commands—can be divided into three broad categories:

- Branching commands that call *subroutines*. These 11 advanced macro commands are concerned with subroutines: {CALL}, {CASE}, {CASE CALL}, {CHAIN}, {GO}, {LABEL}, {NEST}, {RETURN}, {RETURN CANCEL}, {RETURN ERROR}, and {RETURN NOT FOUND}.

- Branching commands that *repeat* a series of commands until a specified condition is satisfied. These are discussed in the section "Using Loops." Three kinds of loops are available in WordPerfect macros: {FOR} {END FOR} loops, {FOR EACH} {END FOR} loops, and {WHILE} {END WHILE} loops. Each of these loops may also use the {NEXT} or {BREAK} command.

- Branching commands that fall into the category of "general-purpose conditional commands." WordPerfect's {IF} and {IF EXISTS} commands and their related commands are in this category. Because these commands are more general in nature—they are used for other purposes, in addition to branching—they are discussed in the section "Making Decisions."

Using Subroutines

The term *subroutine* describes a separate set of macro commands, designated by a name, that performs part of the macro's task. If you're familiar with programming languages, you have probably worked with subroutines, functions, or procedures; the term *subroutine* encompasses all those concepts.

Reminder:

Subroutines make complex macros easier to create.

Because long, complex macros can be difficult to write, troubleshoot, and revise, anything you can do to reduce complexity will help. Using subroutines breaks long macros into smaller, more manageable pieces—and so makes them easier to write, debug, and maintain. Programmers call this practice *modularizing* a program.

Another reason to use subroutines is that WordPerfect macros have some limitations that more general-purpose programming does not. Some operations that can be done without subroutines in languages like BASIC, C, Fortran, or Pascal require you to use subroutines in WordPerfect.

Selecting Subroutine Types

You can choose one of six types of subroutines. Each is implemented by a specific advanced macro command that transfers control to a subprogram and (in all but one case) by certain commands that must be present in the called subroutine. The subroutine method you choose depends on three major factors:

- The location of the subroutine
- Whether the transfer to a specific subroutine is conditional or unconditional
- Whether control is to return to the calling routine after the subroutine has completed executing its commands

Table 12.8 lists these factors, along with the commands necessary to implement each of the six methods. The table is discussed in the material that follows.

Where Is the Subroutine Located?

You can use WordPerfect macro subroutines stored in the same macro file, or you can use as a subroutine a macro stored in a separate file.

The {CHAIN} and {NEST} commands are used to call subroutines stored in a separate macro file. In order to call a program stored in a separate macro file, the

Table 12.8
Subroutine Choices

Calling Command	Subroutine Location	Transfer of control is...	Control returns to caller?	Required Commands in Subroutine
{CALL} {RETURN}*	Same file	Unconditional	Yes	{LABEL}
{CASE}	Same file	Conditional	No	{LABEL}
{CASE CALL} {RETURN}*	Same file	Conditional	Yes	{LABEL}
{CHAIN}	Another file	Unconditional	No	—
{GO}	Same file	Unconditional	No	{LABEL}
{NEST}	Another file	Unconditional	Yes	{RETURN}**

* One of these commands is required: {RETURN}, {RETURN CANCEL}, {RETURN ERROR}, or {RETURN NOT FOUND}.

** Technically, after the last command in the called macro file has executed, control will return even if there is no {RETURN} type of command in the subprogram. Good programming practice suggests including a specific {RETURN}-type command, however.

calling command must receive as an argument the file name of the called macro (including the path if the macro is not in the designated macro directory).

The {CALL}, {CASE}, {CASE CALL}, and {GO} commands transfer control to subroutines within the same macro file. If you want the macro to branch to a subroutine in the same file, the calling command must receive as an argument the name of the subroutine. Subroutines are named with the {LABEL} statement.

Is Transfer of Control Conditional?

The {CASE} and {CASE CALL} commands are conditional-transfer mechanisms. *Conditional transfer*, in this context, means that the commands transfer control to one of several subroutines, based on the answer to a question. The answer to the question can come from the user, result from a calculation, or be based on the current state of the system.

{CALL}, {CHAIN}, {NEST}, and {GO} transfer control unconditionally; that is, they always transfer control to the same subroutine every time the macro runs. You can use these commands to implement conditional control, but to do so you must use the {IF} statement (discussed in the section "Making Decisions").

Does Control Return to the Caller?

When control is transferred to a subroutine, one of two situations can occur after all the commands in the subroutine have executed: the subroutine can officially "end," with control transferred back to the calling routine; or control can be returned to WordPerfect. If control is returned to the calling routine at the end of the subroutine, macro execution resumes with the command that immediately follows the command that called the subroutine.

If the subroutine is called by a {CALL}, {CASE CALL}, or {NEST} command, control should be transferred back to the caller by one of the four {RETURN} statements ({RETURN}, {RETURN CANCEL}, {RETURN ERROR}, or {RETURN NOT FOUND}). The failure to return control after using one of these commands is poor macro-development practice, because macros that fail to return control when they are expected to do so are almost guaranteed to be difficult to understand, debug, and revise.

Passing Variables

Variables in WordPerfect are *global* (except for certain variables in merges that are explicitly created with the {LOCAL} command). A global variable retains its value even when the macro that created it terminates or calls another macro as a subroutine. The only time a variable loses its value is when the variable is specifically "erased" by a blank assignment statement (such as {ASSIGN}var~~) or when you exit from WordPerfect. For an applied example of passing values in variables, see the macros TOUPPER.WPM and TESTCAP.WPM in the section "Working with Advanced Examples."

Nesting Subroutines

You can *nest* subroutines; that is, you can have one subroutine transfer control to another subroutine, which can in turn call another subroutine, which can call another, and so on. WordPerfect limits subroutine nesting to 20 levels. Each time you use a {NEST} command, you use 2 levels. Each time you use a {CALL} or {CASE CALL} command, you use 1 level.

The limit of 20 levels is ample for all but the most complex macros. If you are writing a major applications system in WordPerfect macros, you need to be aware of the limit; for most purposes, however, you can ignore it.

Following are discussions of the commands used to control program execution, including a discussion of the {ELSE} command when used with {CASE}.

{CALL}

{CALL} transfers control to a subroutine within the same file. When the subroutine is terminated by a {RETURN}, {RETURN CANCEL}, {RETURN ERROR}, or {RETURN NOT FOUND} command, the macro resumes execution with the command following the {CALL} command. The syntax for {CALL} is the following:

{CALL}*label*~

The term *label* represents the name of the subroutine. The subroutine must be named with a {LABEL} statement. {CALL} is most useful when you want to use the same set of commands several times in a macro.

```
{CHAR}reply~{^]}Do you want to delete the blocked text?{^\} {^V}N{Q}o
    ({^V}Y{^Q}es)~
{IF}"{VARIABLE}reply~"="y" | "{VARIABLE}reply~"="Y"~
    {Del}
    {IF}{STATE}&1024~{;} if WP asks "Do you want to delete?"~
        y
    {END IF}
{ELSE}
    {Block}
{END IF}
```

If you need to perform this action four or five times in your macro, entering all that code would be a lot of work, would make your macro unnecessarily large, and would make the macro harder to debug (because you have more chances to make a typing error or miss a tilde, and because it is harder to see the logical structure of the program at a glance).

If you create the foregoing set of commands just once and give it a name (thus making it a subroutine), you can use the {CALL} statement to go to those commands, execute them, and then return to the point in the program that called the subroutine.

The following macro lines are the same lines, now in subroutine form, along with one example of how a {CALL} command would call them. Assume that the commands immediately preceding the {CALL} have blocked some text that the user may want to delete. The {CALL} transfers control to the *confirm* subroutine (identified by {LABEL}confirm~). The subroutine commands execute, just as they did before. After the second {END IF} command, the {RETURN} transfers control back to the line immediately following the {CALL}—to the line containing the commands {Home}{Home}{Up}, which move the cursor to the top of the document.

```
{;}commands to position the cursor and turn block on~
{CALL}confirm~
{Home}{Home}{Up}

.

.

{LABEL}confirm~
    {CHAR}reply~{^]}Do you want to delete the blocked text?{^\} {^V}N{Q}o
        ({^V}Y{^Q}es)~
    {IF}"{VARIABLE}reply~"="y" | "{VARIABLE}reply~"="Y"~
        {Del}
        {IF}{STATE}&1024~ {;}if WP asks "Do you want to delete?"~
            y
        {END IF}
    {ELSE}
        {Block}
    {END IF}
{RETURN}
```

For more examples of the {CALL} command, see the listing for the macro INVOICE.WPM in the section "Working with Advanced Examples."

Reminder:
Using subroutines for often-repeated operations reduces typing, makes errors less likely, and makes macros easier to debug.

{CASE}

{CASE} examines the result of an expression and branches to one of a number of subroutines, based on the result of the expression. After the subroutine completes executing, control does *not* return to the calling routine. The syntax is as follows:

{CASE}*expression~case1~label1~case2~label2~...caseN~labelN~~*

Note that two tildes must follow the last label. The last tilde tells WordPerfect where the {CASE} command ends. For more examples of the {CASE} command, see the listing for the macro COPY.WPM in the section "Working with Advanced Examples."

The following macro prompts the user to enter a number between 1 and 5. The macro then displays either a message indicating whether the number entered was odd or even, or (if the user entered anything other than a number between 1 and 5) an error message.

```
{CHAR}number~Enter a number between 1 and 5: ~
{CASE}{VARIABLE}number~
     1~odd~
     2~even~
     3~odd~
     4~even~
     5~odd~
~
You did not enter a number between 1 and 5.
{QUIT}

{LABEL}odd~
     You entered an odd number.
{QUIT}

{LABEL}even~
     You entered an even number.
{QUIT}
```

If the user enters, for example, the number 2, the macro will assign that value to *number* and, when it looks at the {CASE} statement, will assign the expression a value of 2. The macro then looks at the cases, in order. The first case is 1. Because there is not a match between the case (1) and the expression (2), the macro goes to the next case. The next case is 2. The expression is equal to this case, so control is transferred to the subroutine named in the label associated with case 2—the *even* subroutine. The *even* subroutine (identified by the line {LABEL}even~) displays the message *You entered an even number*. The {QUIT} command terminates the macro and returns control back to the main WordPerfect program.

Had the user entered 3, there would not have been a match until case 3. Then control would have transferred to the label associated with case 3, the *odd* subroutine, which would have printed the message *You entered an odd number*.

If the user had entered 7, none of the cases would have matched. Control would have passed to the line immediately following the {CASE} command, and

WordPerfect would have displayed the message *You did not enter a number between 1 and 5.*

Note: The foregoing macro shows one way of formatting a {CASE} command. All the cases are indented; on each line, there is only one case and its corresponding label, and the final tilde is on a line by itself, aligned with the word {CASE}. There are other acceptable ways to format a {CASE} statement. The key is to be able to associate each label with its corresponding case accurately and consistently. Select one method and use it consistently.

The following example shows a {CASE} command that uses a logical comparison. Before studying the macro, however, you need to understand how WordPerfect macros represent values of true and false. In a logical comparison, WordPerfect considers the value –1 true and any other value false.

Reminder:
In logical comparisons, -1 is "true"; any other value is "false."

In the following macro, the user is prompted to enter two numbers. The macro compares them by using the {CASE} command and prints out a message indicating whether the two numbers are equal. Notice that 0 is used to represent a false result. This is a convention; any number other than –1 could have been used.

```
{CHAR}num1~Enter a digit: ~
{CHAR}num2~Enter a digit: ~
{CASE}num1=num2~
    –1~equal~
    0~unequal~
~

{LABEL}equal~
    The numbers you entered are equal.
{QUIT}

{LABEL}unequal~
    The numbers you entered are not equal.
{QUIT}
```

For more examples of the {CASE} command, see the listing for the macro COPY.WPM in the section "Working with Usage Examples."

{ELSE}

The {ELSE} command, when used in a {CASE} statement, handles all conditions of the expression not explicitly provided for.

For example, the following lines branch to *{LABEL}yes~* if the user enters *y* or *Y*; to *{LABEL}no~* if the user enters *n* or *N*; and to *{LABEL}maybe~* if the user enters anything else.

```
{CHAR}0~Input: ~
{CASE}{VAR 0}~
    y~yes~Y~yes~
    n~no~N~no~
    {ELSE}~maybe~
~
```

{CASE CALL}

The {CASE CALL} command examines the result of an expression and branches to one of a number of subroutines, based on the result of the expression. After the subroutine completes executing, control returns to the calling routine. The syntax for {CASE CALL} is the following:

{CASE CALL}*expression~case1~label1~case2~label2~...caseN~labelN~~*

Note that there must be two tildes following the last label. The last tilde tells WordPerfect where the {CASE CALL} command ends.

Reminder:

{CASE CALL} is exactly like {CASE} except that in the former, control returns after the subroutine executes.

The {CASE CALL} command is identical to the {CASE} command, with one exception. With the {CASE} command, control does not return after the subroutine executes. With {CASE CALL} command, control returns.

The following macro segment prompts the user to enter a number corresponding to a prize. The macro prints a line of boilerplate, then evaluates a {CASE CALL} expression. Next the macro branches to a subroutine, according to the value of the variable *prize*, and prints the message corresponding to the specific prize. Control then returns to the command that follows the {CASE CALL} command, and the macro prints the rest of the message.

```
{CHAR}prize~Prize: 1 Flea collar; 2 Dog food; 3 Clipping: ~
We are happy to announce that your pet has won
{CASE CALL}prize~
      1~collar~
      2~food~
      3~clipping~

   ~
{Enter}
{Enter}
   Please call at our store at your earliest convenience to claim your prize.
   Thank you for participating in our contest.
{RETURN}

{LABEL}collar~
   a Fleaze Away flea collar, guaranteed to keep your dog clean and
   comfortable for six months or more.
{RETURN}

{LABEL}food~
   50 pounds of Hugo's Dog Grub, specially formulated to provide your dog
   with every nutrient he needs.

{LABEL}clipping~
   a certificate for 50% off on a custom clipping, good for six months from the
   date of this letter.
{RETURN}
```

For more examples of the {CASE CALL} command, see the listing for the macro BULLETS.WPM in the section "Working with Advanced Examples."

{CHAIN}

The {CHAIN} command transfers control to a macro stored in another file. Control is not transferred until the currently executing macro terminates. Control does not return to the original macro. The syntax for {CHAIN} is the following:

{CHAIN}*filename~*

The file name does not have to include the WPM extension.

The {CHAIN} command will be executed—that is, control will be transferred to the named macro—only if all three of the following conditions are met:

- The calling macro must terminate either with a {RETURN} statement or by simply reaching the last command in the macro file. If the macro is terminated by a {QUIT}, {RETURN CANCEL}, {RETURN ERROR}, {RETURN NOT FOUND}, or {RESTART} command, the chaining will not occur. The calling macro cannot terminate in an unsuccessful search. (An unsuccessful search ends macro execution.) If the user terminates the calling macro by pressing Cancel (F1), the chained macro is not executed.

- The {CHAIN} command must be the last {CHAIN} command to be executed in the executing macro. If a second {CHAIN} command is encountered, the first {CHAIN} command is canceled; provided that the other necessary conditions are satisfied, the macro file named by the second {CHAIN} command is executed.

- The macro named as the argument to the {CHAIN} command must be in the currently active macro directory, or the path must be specified.

Consider the following two sets of commands. The statement *{CHAIN}macro2* in MACRO1.WPM causes the macro MACRO2.WPM to execute after all the commands in MACRO1.WPM have executed. The result is shown in figure 12.9.

The file MACRO1.WPM contains these commands:

{CHAIN}macro2~
This line was printed by MACRO1.WPM.{Enter}
{RETURN}

The file MACRO2.WPM contains these commands:

This line was printed by MACRO2.WPM.
{RETURN}

{GO}

{GO} transfers control to a named subroutine within the same macro file. Control does *not* return to the calling routine. The syntax of the command is the following:

{GO}*label~*

{GO} is a very simple command. It transfers control, unconditionally, to the named subroutine.

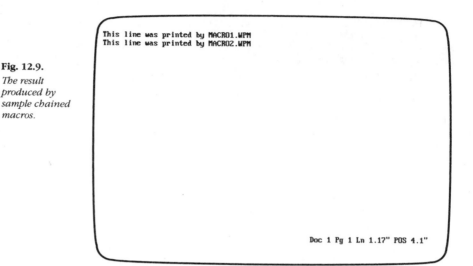

Fig. 12.9.
The result produced by sample chained macros.

In WordPerfect 5, you had to use {GO} to implement loops because there was no other way to make a loop. WordPerfect 5.1 provides three sophisticated loop mechanisms (discussed in the section "Using Loops"). There is no reason to use {GO} for looping; you should avoid using the command for that purpose.

It is also easy to overuse {GO} in simple transfer-of-control situations. To the extent possible, you should use {CALL} and (where conditional capabilities are required) {CASE} and {CASE CALL}. Ideally, the use of {GO} should be restricted to error-handling routines.

For examples of appropriate uses of {GO}, see the examples for the commands {ON ERROR} and {ON NOT FOUND} in the section "Handling Errors." See also the listings for the macros BULLETS.WPM, COPY.WPM, and TESTCAP.WPM in the section "Working with Advanced Examples."

{LABEL}

The {LABEL} command identifies a subroutine by name. Macro execution can be directed to a {LABEL} by a {CALL}, {CASE}, {CASE CALL}, or {GO} command. The syntax is the following:

{LABEL}*label~*

There are no restrictions on the length of a label. Each label in a macro must have a unique name. If a label name is repeated, the first one that appears is the one to which control is transferred when the label is named in a transferring command.

See the examples for the {CALL}, {CASE}, and {CASE CALL} commands in this section for examples of the {LABEL} command. See also the listings for the macros BULLETS.WPM, COPY.WPM, INVOICE.WPM, and TESTCAP.WPM in the section "Working with Advanced Examples."

{NEST}

{NEST} executes as a subroutine a macro stored in another macro file. When the second macro has finished executing, the first macro takes control again and resumes execution at the first command following {NEST}. The syntax for {NEST} is the following:

{NEST}*macroname~*

The term *macroname* represents the file name of the macro to which control is to be transferred. Control is transferred as soon as the {NEST} command is encountered. You do not need to include the WPM extension, but you must include the path if the file is not in the currently active macro directory.

Control will not return to the calling macro if the nested macro terminates with a {QUIT} or {RESTART} command. If the nested macro returns a cancel condition (which can be caused by a {RETURN CANCEL} command or by the user's pressing the Cancel [F1] key), an error condition (through a {RETURN ERROR}), or a "not found" condition (through a {RETURN NOT FOUND}), control will return to the calling macro, but the calling macro will then immediately terminate unless there is an {ON CANCEL}, {ON ERROR}, or {ON NOT FOUND} command in effect in the calling macro. See the section "Handling Errors" for more details.

You can nest macros several levels deep, subject to the limitations discussed earlier in this chapter.

In the following example, NEST1.WPM prints a message and transfers control to NEST2.WPM, which prints another message. NEST2.WPM then transfers control back to NEST1.WPM, which prints a third message.

These commands are in NEST1.WPM:

This is message 1, printed by NEST1.WPM{Enter}

{NEST}nest2

This is message 3, printed by NEST1.WPM{Enter}

These are the commands in NEST2.WPM:

This is message 2, printed by NEST2.WPM{Enter}

The result of running NEST1 is shown in figure 12.10.

For more examples of the {NEST} command, see the listings for the macros TESTCAP.WPM and TOUPPER.WPM in the section "Working with Advanced Examples."

{RETURN}, {RETURN CANCEL}, {RETURN ERROR}, and {RETURN NOT FOUND}

All four {RETURN} statements cause subroutine execution to cease and cause control to be returned to the calling routine. If there is no calling routine—that is, if the currently executing statements have not been called as a subroutine—then a {RETURN}-type statement terminates the macro and returns control to the main WordPerfect program.

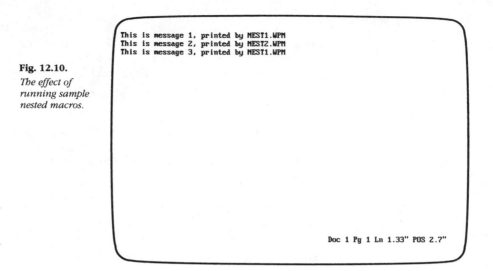

Fig. 12.10.

The effect of running sample nested macros.

Note: If the statement is {RETURN} (not {RETURN CANCEL}, {RETURN ERROR}, or {RETURN NOT FOUND}), and if a {CHAIN} command has been executed by the macro, control is transferred to the chained macro rather than to WordPerfect.

{RETURN CANCEL} indicates a cancel condition to the calling routine. The condition is the same as if the subroutine had been terminated with the Cancel (F1) key. If the calling routine has an {ON CANCEL} command, the action specified by that command is carried out.

{RETURN ERROR} indicates an error to the calling routine. If the calling routine has an {ON ERROR} command, the action specified by that command is carried out.

{RETURN NOT FOUND} indicates a "search not found" condition to the calling routine. If the calling routine has an {ON NOT FOUND} command, the action specified by that command is carried out.

The syntax for the {RETURN} commands is as follows:

{RETURN}
{RETURN CANCEL}
{RETURN ERROR}
{RETURN NOT FOUND}

See the examples for the {CALL}, {CASE CALL}, and {NEST} commands in this section for examples of the {RETURN} command. See also, in the section "Working with Advanced Examples," the listings for the macros BULLETS.WPM, COPY.WPM, and INVOICE.WPM for examples of the {RETURN} command; COPY.WPM for an example of the {RETURN CANCEL} command; and TOUPPER.WPM for an example of the {RETURN ERROR} command.

Using Loops

In WordPerfect 5, looping was possible only through the combination of the {GO} and {LABEL} commands. This combination worked but was neither elegant nor easy to achieve.

WordPerfect 5.1 provides three much more sophisticated looping facilities. Each has a specific set of situations for which it is well suited. Each loop type is implemented by several discrete commands. In this section, the commands that implement each loop are discussed together; that is, all the {FOR} loop commands are discussed together, all the {FOR EACH} loop commands are discussed together, and all the {WHILE} loop commands are discussed together.

A *loop* instructs WordPerfect to perform a particular set of commands until an exit condition is satisfied. At the beginning of the loop is a command that makes a test. This command tests the current state of some system condition—usually the value of a variable—against a defined exit condition. If the exit condition is not satisfied, the commands within the loop execute. If the exit condition is satisfied, the loop terminates, and program control passes to the first command after the loop. Thus each loop must have at least three components:

- A command that tests the exit condition. In all three types of WordPerfect macro loops, the first command in the loop tests the exit condition.

- Something that changes the result of the exit test from "not satisfied" to "satisfied." If the exit-test result never changed to "satisfied," the loop would never terminate; the macro would loop forever.

- A command to mark the end of the loop so that WordPerfect knows where to transfer control when the exit condition is satisfied.

Using {FOR} Loops

A {FOR} loop is based on the {FOR} command, which checks to see whether a counter variable has reached a predetermined value. When the counter variable has reached the value, the exit test is satisfied, and control passes to the first command following the loop.

You should use a {FOR} loop when you want a loop to execute a certain number of times and when you can determine how many times the loop should execute at the time you create the macro. If you cannot determine how many times the loop should execute, you should not use a {FOR} loop; you should use a {WHILE} loop instead.

Reminder:
Use a {FOR} loop when you know how many times the loop should execute.

The syntax for {FOR} loops is as follows:

{FOR}*var~startval~stopval~step~*
{END FOR}
{BREAK}
{NEXT}

Every {FOR} loop must have one, and only one, {FOR} command and one, and only one, {END FOR} command. The {BREAK} and {NEXT} commands are optional. For examples of {FOR} loops, see the section "{NEXT}" in the "Using {FOR} Loops" discussion.

{FOR}

The {FOR} command is the first command in the loop. It has four arguments:

- *var* is the name of a variable that is used as a counter. Each time the {FOR} command executes, it examines the value of *var*.
- *startval* is the value to which *var* is initialized at the beginning of the loop.
- *stopval* is the value against which the {FOR} command tests the value of *var* each time the loop executes.
- *step* is the amount by which *var* is changed each time the {FOR} command is executed. If *step* is positive, the value of *step* is added to *var* on every loop; if *step* is negative, the value of *step* is subtracted from *var*.

If the {FOR} loop is counting up (*step* is positive), the exit test is this: "Is the value of *var* greater than *stopval*?" If the exit test fails (the value of *var* is not greater than *stopval*), WordPerfect executes the statements in the loop. If the exit test is satisfied (the value of *var* is greater than *stopval*), the loop terminates, and WordPerfect transfers control to the first command following the loop.

If the {FOR} loop is counting down (*step* is negative), the exit test is this: "Is the value of *var* less than *stopval*?" If the exit test fails (the value of *var* is not less than *stopval*), WordPerfect executes the statements in the loop. If the exit test is satisfied (the value of *var* is less than *stopval*), the loop terminates, and WordPerfect transfers control to the first command following the loop.

{END FOR}

{END FOR} marks the end of the {FOR} loop. All commands between {FOR} and {END FOR} are "in the loop." When the macro reaches the {END FOR} command, it branches back to the {FOR} command for another test of the exit condition.

{BREAK}

The {BREAK} command aborts the operation of the {FOR} loop. If the macro encounters {BREAK} while executing a {FOR} loop, program control immediately shifts to the first command after the {END FOR} command.

{NEXT}

The {NEXT} command, like {BREAK}, interrupts the normal flow through the loop, instructing WordPerfect to skip all the commands between the {NEXT} command and the {END FOR} statement. Control transfers immediately to the {END FOR} statement, which means that control transfers back to the {FOR} statement; another exit test is made, and *var* is increased (or decreased) by the *stepval*. See the section

"Writing Effective and Efficient Loops" for recommendations on the use of {BREAK} and {NEXT}.

The following macro prints the message "This is loop #*n*" 10 times, replacing *n* with the value of *counter* each time. The loop counts from 1 to 10.

```
{FOR}counter~1~10~1~
     This is loop #{VARIABLE}counter~
{END FOR}
```

This macro does the same, but counts from 10 down to 1.

```
{FOR}counter~10~1~-1~
     This is loop #{VARIABLE}counter~
{END FOR}
```

This macro counts by twos from 2 to 20.

```
{FOR}counter~2~20~2~
     This is loop #{VARIABLE}counter~
{END FOR}
```

For more examples of the {FOR} loop commands, see the listing for the macro INVOICE.WPM in the section "Working with Advanced Examples."

Using {FOR EACH} Loops

A {FOR EACH} loop executes the commands in the loop once for each of a predefined set of values. On each loop, one of the set of values is assigned to a specified variable.

You should use a {FOR EACH} loop when you need to execute a loop a predefined number of times, changing the value of one variable each time. When the change to the variable is simply an addition or subtraction of a constant number, a {FOR} loop is usually simpler to write and easier to understand.

Reminder:
Use a {FOR EACH} loop to execute a loop a specific number of times, changing a variable each time.

The syntax for {FOR EACH} loops is as follows:

```
{FOR EACH}var~expr1~...exprN~~
{END FOR}
{BREAK}
{NEXT}
```

Every {FOR EACH} loop must have one, and only one, {FOR EACH} command and one, and only one, {END FOR} command. The {BREAK} and {NEXT} commands are optional. For an example of a {FOR EACH} loop, see the section "{NEXT}" in the "Using {FOR EACH} Loops" discussion.

{FOR EACH}

The {FOR EACH} command has one variable argument, *var*, and a set of expression arguments, *expr1* through *exprN*. Note that an extra tilde is required after the last

5.1

expression argument to tell WordPerfect that the {FOR EACH} command has ended. On the first loop, *expr1* is evaluated, and its value is assigned to *var*. On the next loop, *expr2* is evaluated, and so on.

On each loop, the {FOR EACH} command not only changes the value of *var* but also applies this exit test: "Have all the expressions in the list been used?" If they have not (the test fails), the loop executes again. If they have (the test succeeds), the loop terminates, and program control passes to the first command following the loop.

{END FOR}

{END FOR} marks the end of the {FOR EACH} loop. All commands between the {FOR EACH} statement and the {END FOR} are "in the loop." When the macro reaches the {END FOR} command, it branches back to the {FOR EACH} command for another test of the exit condition.

{BREAK}

The {BREAK} command aborts the operation of the {FOR EACH} loop. If the macro encounters a {BREAK} command while executing a {FOR EACH} loop, program control immediately shifts to the first command after the {END FOR} command.

{NEXT}

The {NEXT} command, like {BREAK}, interrupts the normal flow through the loop, instructing WordPerfect to skip all the commands between {NEXT} and {END FOR}. Control transfers immediately to the {END FOR} statement, which means that control transfers back to the {FOR EACH} statement; another exit test is made. See the section "Writing Effective and Efficient Loops" for recommendations on the use of {BREAK} and {NEXT}.

The following macro is used to record the number of hours an employee has worked each day of the week. A separate file is maintained for each day. The files are named MON.WP, TUE.WP, WED.WP, and so on.

```
{FOR  EACH}day~MON~TUE~WED~THU~FRI~SAT~SUN~~
    {Retrieve}{VARIABLE}day~.WP{Enter}
    {Home}{Home}{Down}
    {TEXT}hours~Enter number of hours worked~
    {Date/Outline}t{Tab}{VARIABLE}hours~  Hours
    {Exit}y{Enter}yn
{END FOR}
```

The arguments to the {FOR EACH} statement are the variable *day* and seven expressions, each a three-letter abbreviation for a day of the week. The macro first assigns MON to the variable *day*, then combines the variable with the file extension WP to form the complete file name MON.WP. Next the macro retrieves the file, goes to the end of the file, and prompts the user to enter the number of hours worked. It then inserts the current date (to indicate when the information was entered) and the number of hours, saves the file, and clears the screen. The {END FOR} command transfers control back to the {FOR EACH} command, which makes the exit test (the test fails because you are not yet at the end of the expression list) and assigns TUE to *day*. The action is repeated for each expression through the end of the list.

Using {WHILE} Loops

A {WHILE} loop is used when a predefinable number of loops is not required—that is, when the number of times the loop is executed is likely to vary, based on the user's input, the state of the system at the time the loop executes, or a number of other possible factors. This flexibility makes {WHILE} the most useful looping construction. You will probably use more {WHILE} loops than any other type.

Reminder:
Use {WHILE} loops when you don't know how many times the loop will execute.

The syntax for {WHILE} loops is as follows:

{WHILE}*expr~*
{END WHILE}
{BREAK}
{NEXT}

Every {WHILE} loop must have one, and only one, {WHILE} command; some change occurring within the loop or caused by the commands within the loop that will, at some point, cause the exit test to succeed; and one, and only one, {END WHILE} command. For examples of {WHILE} loops, see the section "{NEXT}" in the "Using {WHILE} Loops" discussion.

{WHILE}

The argument of the {WHILE} command, *expr* is an expression that evaluates to true or false. If the expression is true, the exit test fails, and the commands in the loop are executed. If the expression is false, the exit test succeeds, and control is transferred to the first statement after {END WHILE}.

In most cases, you use a *relational operator* with the {WHILE} command. Table 12.9 lists the relational operators and their meanings, along with examples of their use with {WHILE} and {IF} commands.

WordPerfect also provides the three logical operators listed in table 12.3.

{END WHILE}

{END WHILE} marks the end of the {WHILE} loop. When macro execution reaches the {END WHILE} statement, control is transferred back to the corresponding {WHILE} statement for an exit test.

{BREAK}

The {BREAK} command aborts the operation of the {WHILE} loop. If the macro encounters a {BREAK} command while executing a {WHILE} loop, program control immediately shifts to the first command after the {END WHILE} command.

Table 12.9
Relational Operators

Operator	Meaning	Examples	
=	Equal to	{WHILE}{VARIABLE}x~=0~	while *x* is equal to 0
		{IF}{VARIABLE}x~=0~	if *x* is equal to 0
!=	Not equal to	{WHILE}{VARIABLE}x~!=0~	while *x* is not equal to 0
		{IF}{VARIABLE}x~!=0~	if *x* is not equal to 0
>	Greater than	{WHILE}{VARIABLE}x~>0~	while *x* is greater than 0
		{IF}{VARIABLE}x~>0~	if *x* is greater than 0
<	Less than	{WHILE}{VARIABLE}x~<0~	while *x* is less than 0
		{IF}{VARIABLE}x~<0~	if *x* is less than 0

{NEXT}

The {NEXT} command, like {BREAK}, interrupts normal flow through the loop, instructing WordPerfect to skip all the commands between {NEXT} and {END WHILE}. Control transfers immediately to the {END WHILE} statement, which means that control transfers back to the {WHILE} statement so that another exit test can be made. See the section "Writing Effective and Efficient Loops" for recommendations on the use of {BREAK} and {NEXT}.

The following commands implement a simple form of a common entry-checking routine. A {CHAR} statement, which prompts the user for input and assigns the input to a variable named *entry*, is included in a {WHILE} loop.

```
{ASSIGN}entry~9~
{WHILE}{VARIABLE}entry~>4~
    {ASSIGN}entry~0~
    {CHAR}entry~Action: 1 Exit and Save; 2 Exit No Save; 3 Save 4; New File: 0~
{END WHILE}
```

The exit test compares *entry* to the highest number on the menu: 4. If *entry* is greater than 4, the user typed an illegal number, so the loop executes again to give the user another chance to make a legitimate entry.

Reminder:

You usually initialize the variable before starting a {WHILE} loop.

You must initialize *entry* to a value greater than 4; otherwise, the commands within the loop would never execute. In the example, a value of 9 is assigned to *entry*. The need to initialize a variable is common when you work with {WHILE} loops.

The commands that follow improve on the loop used in the discussion of {FOR EACH}, and they illustrate the idea of *nested loops*—one loop inside another loop. The outer loop—the {WHILE} loop—executes once for each employee. The inner {FOR EACH} loop executes seven times for each employee, one time for each day of the week. A {WHILE} loop was chosen for the outer loop because at the time the macro was written, its developer didn't know how many employees there would be.

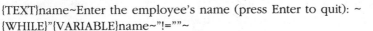

```
{TEXT}name~Enter the employee's name (press Enter to quit): ~
{WHILE}"{VARIABLE}name~"!=""~
    {FOR EACH}day~MON~TUE~WED~THU~FRI~SAT~SUN~~
        {Retrieve}{VARIABLE}day~.WP{Enter}
        {Home}{Home}{Down}
        {TEXT}hours~Enter number of hours worked~
        {Date/Outline}t{Tab}{VARIABLE}name~{Tab}{VARIABLE}hours~  Hours
        {Exit}y{Enter}yn
    {END FOR}
    {TEXT}name~Enter the employee's name (press Enter to quit): ~
{END WHILE}
```

Note the {WHILE} statement:

```
{WHILE}"{VARIABLE}name~"!=""~
```

WordPerfect requires quotation marks around both elements when you compare nonnumeric (string) variables. This statement means "Execute the statements in the loop while the variable *name* is not equal to an empty string." By pressing Enter, the user signifies that all employee names have been entered. Pressing Enter results in the assignment of an "empty" value to the variable *name*. An empty string variable is represented by a pair of quotation marks with nothing between them. As long as the user enters a name, therefore, the {WHILE} loop executes; when the user just presses Enter, the {WHILE} loop terminates.

For more examples of the {WHILE} and {END WHILE} commands, see the listing for the macro INVOICE.WPM in the section "Working with Advanced Examples." See also an application of {WHILE} loops in the examples for the {LOOK} command.

Writing Effective and Efficient Loops

Several recommended practices that, although not strictly *rules*, are considered good programming practice by most professional programmers. Incorporating these practices into your loops increases the likelihood that the loops will work right with a minimum of debugging time and effort; work consistently for all forseeable conditions; and be easy to interpret and decipher six months or a year from now, when you or someone else needs to go back into the macro and change something.

Most loops can be written without a {BREAK} or {NEXT} command. Reserve {BREAK} and {NEXT} for unusual situations, such as errors. {BREAK} and {NEXT} are often the easy way out, but they are usually not the best way when you consider the difficulties of debugging and revising a macro that contains a number of {BREAK} and {NEXT} statements. If you cannot figure out a way to write your loop without using {BREAK} and {NEXT}, consider using a different type of loop.

Reminder:
Use {BREAK} or {NEXT} only after you have tried to find an alternative.

From a debugging standpoint, even worse than the use of {BREAK} and {NEXT} is the use of {GO} or {CASE} within a loop to transfer control outside the loop. It should *never* be necessary to use {GO} or {CASE} within a loop (unless the point to which they transfer control is also within the loop). This recommendation does not apply to the use of {CALL}, {CASE CALL}, and {NEST}, which is acceptable practice because although these commands transfer control out of the loop, control returns to the exact point from which it was transferred.

Looping with {GO} and {LABEL} is possible but not recommended. The practice makes macros difficult to read and leads to abuses. Furthermore, {FOR}, {FOR EACH}, and {WHILE} loops are easier to write than {GO}/{LABEL} loops.

Making Decisions

When writing advanced macros, you frequently need to take action based on the answer to a question. You may need to transfer program control when a variable is a certain value, or you may need to assign a value to a variable according to an entry a user has made to another variable.

Decision-making logic in WordPerfect macros is implemented through four basic commands. Two of these—{CASE CALL} and {CASE}—are discussed in the section "Controlling Program Execution." The commands discussed in this section are {IF} and {IF EXISTS}. Three other commands are used with the {IF} and {IF EXISTS} commands and are discussed in this section: {BREAK}, {ELSE}, and {END IF}.

{IF} Structure Logic

The {IF} command and its associated commands form the basic, general-purpose decision-making mechanism in WordPerfect macros. If the {IF} statement evaluates to true, a designated set of commands is executed. If the {IF} statement evaluates to false, the commands are not executed. An alternative set of commands, to be executed if the the {IF} statement is false, may be included.

The syntax for an {IF} logic structure is as follows:

```
{IF}expr~
{ELSE}
{END IF}
{BREAK}
```

Every {IF} logic structure must have one, and only one, {IF} command and one, and only one, {END IF} command. The {BREAK} and {ELSE} commands are optional.

{IF}

{IF} causes a set of commands to be executed or not executed, depending on the value of a variable or the result of a comparison.

The term *expr* represents an expression, usually a conditional statement that uses a relational operator (see table 12.9 for a list of WordPerfect's relational operators).

If the expression evaluates to true, WordPerfect executes all the commands between the {IF} command and the first {ELSE}, {BREAK}, or {END IF} command. *expr* can also include the logical operators shown in table 12.3.

{ELSE}

{ELSE} provides an alternative set of commands. The commands following {ELSE} are executed only if the {IF} statement evaluates to false. If the {IF} command evaluates to true, the commands following the {ELSE} command have no effect.

{END IF}

{END IF} marks the end of the {IF} structure.

{BREAK}

If a {BREAK} command occurs within an {IF} structure, program control branches immediately to the first command following {END IF}. If possible, avoid using {BREAK} within {IF} structures.

{IF} Structure Operation

The following conditions apply if there is no {ELSE} statement within the {IF} and {END IF} statements:

- If the {IF} statement is true, the commands between {IF} and {END IF} are executed. After the commands have executed, program execution continues with the commands following the {END IF}.
- If the {IF} statement is false, the commands between {IF} and {END IF} are not executed. Program control branches immediately to the command following the {END IF}.

The following conditions apply if there is an {ELSE} statement:

- If the {IF} statement is true, the commands between {IF} and {ELSE} are executed. After the commands have executed, program execution branches to the command following {END IF}.
- If the {IF} statement is false, the commands between {IF} and {ELSE} are not executed. Program control branches immediately to the command following {ELSE}. The commands between {ELSE} and {END IF} are executed; then macro execution continues with the commands following {END IF}.

The following commands assign the value 50 to the variable *number* if the value of the variable *response* is Y. Remember that WordPerfect requires quotation marks around both elements when you compare nonnumeric (string) variables.

```
{IF}"{VARIABLE}response~"="Y"~
    {ASSIGN}number~50~
{END IF}
```

The following commands do exactly the same thing, except that if the value of *response* is not Y, they assign the value 25 to *number*.

```
{IF}"{VARIABLE}response~"="Y"~
    {ASSIGN}number~50~
{ELSE}
    {ASSIGN}number~25~
{END IF}
```

For more examples of the {IF}, {ELSE}, and {END IF} commands, see the listings for the macros COPY.WPM and TOUPPER.WPM in the section "Working with Advanced Examples."

{IF EXISTS} Structure Logic

Reminder:

{IF EXISTS} checks to see whether a variable contains a value.

An {IF EXISTS} structure checks to see whether a variable contains a value. If there is a value, a designated set of commands is executed. If the variable is empty—there is no value—the commands are not executed. An alternative set of commands, to be executed if the variable is empty, may be provided.

The syntax for an {IF EXISTS} logic structure is as follows:

```
{IF EXISTS}var~
{ELSE}
{END IF}
{BREAK}
```

Every {IF EXISTS} logic structure must have one, and only one, {IF EXISTS} command and one, and only one, {END IF} command. The {BREAK} and {ELSE} commands are optional.

{IF EXISTS}

{IF EXISTS} causes a set of commands to be executed or not executed, depending on whether a variable has a value. *var* is the variable to be tested.

{ELSE}

{ELSE} provides an alternative set of commands. The commands following the {ELSE} command are executed only if the variable in the {IF EXISTS} statement is empty. If the variable has a value, the commands following the {ELSE} command have no effect.

{END IF}

{END IF} marks the end of the {IF EXISTS} structure.

{BREAK}

If a {BREAK} command occurs within an {IF EXISTS} structure, program control branches immediately to the first command following {END IF}. If possible, avoid using {BREAK} within {IF EXISTS} structures.

{IF EXISTS} Structure Operation

The operation of an {IF EXISTS} structure is very similar to that of an {IF} structure. Refer to the section "{IF} Structure Operation" for an explanation.

The following excerpt from a subroutine asks the user to supply an employee name. If the user types a name, the subroutine prints the name. If the employee simply presses Enter, the subroutine returns an error condition to the calling routine.

```
{TEXT}name~Enter the employee's name: ~
{IF EXISTS}name~
    Employee name: {VARIABLE}name~
{ELSE}
    {RETURN ERROR}
{END IF}
```

Determining System Status

As you create advanced macros, you will often find that you need to know key facts about the current status of the system. The action you want your program to take often depends on answers to questions like these:

- Is Reveal Codes on or off?
- Is a menu displayed? If so, which one?
- Is Block on?
- Is Typeover on?
- Is the character at the current cursor position a character or a code? If a character, which character? If a code, which code?
- Has the document been modified since the last time it was saved? Since the last time it was generated?
- What is the name of the document?
- What is the current position of the cursor relative to the top of the paper? Relative to the left edge of the paper?

In WordPerfect 5, one of the most serious limitations of the macro command language was the inability to determine certain critical information about the status of the system. WordPerfect 5.1 has significantly improved your ability to find out key system information.

The commands discussed in this section are {KTON}, {NTOK}, {STATE}, and {SYSTEM}.

{KTON}

{KTON} takes a WordPerfect key and returns a code number corresponding to that key. Table 12.10 shows the codes corresponding to WordPerfect's keys. The syntax for {KTON} is the following:

{KTON}

Table 12.10
WordPerfect Key Codes

Key	Code	Key	Code	Key	Code
!	33	E	69	j	106
"	34	F	70	k	107
#	35	G	71	l	108
$	36	H	72	m	109
%	37	I	73	n	110
&	38	J	74	o	111
'	39	K	75	p	112
(	40	L	76	q	113
)	41	M	77	r	114
*	42	N	78	s	115
PrintScrn	42	O	79	t	116
+	43	P	80	u	117
,	44	Q	81	v	118
−	45	R	82	w	119
.	46	S	83	x	120
/	47	T	84	y	121
0	48	U	85	z	122
1	49	V	86	{	123
2	50	W	87	|	124
3	51	X	88	}	125
4	52	Y	89	Ctrl-A	32769
5	53	Z	90	Ctrl-B	32770
6	54	[	91	Ctrl-C	32771
7	55	\	92	Ctrl-D	32772
8	56	]	93	Ctrl-E	32773
9	57	^	94	Ctrl-F	32774
:	58	_	95	Ctrl-G	32775
;	59	`	96	Home	32776
<	60	a	97	Ctrl-H	32776
=	61	b	98	Tab	32777
>	62	c	99	Ctrl-I	32777
?	63	d	100	Enter	32778
@	64	e	101	Ctrl-J	32778
A	65	f	102	Ctrl-End	32779
B	66	g	103	Ctrl-K	32779
C	67	h	104	Ctrl-PgDn	32780
D	68	i	105	Ctrl-L	32780

Table 12.10 (continued)

Key	Code	Key	Code	Key	Code
Ctrl-M	32781	F9	32808	Ctrl-F3	32838
Ctrl-N	32782	F10	32809	Ctrl-F4	32839
Ctrl-O	32783	Shift-F1	32812	Ctrl-F6	32841
Ctrl-P	32784	Shift-F2	32813	Ctrl-F5	32841
Ctrl-Q	32785	Shift-F3	32814	Ctrl-F7	32842
Ctrl-R	32786	Shift-F4	32815	Ctrl-F8	32843
Ctrl-S	32787	Shift-F5	32816	Ctrl-F9	32844
Ctrl-T	32788	Shift-F6	32817	Ctrl-F10	32845
Ctrl-U	32789	Ctrl-PrintScrn	32818	Backspace	32848
Ctrl-V	32790	Shift-F7	32818	Delete	32849
Up	32791	Shift-F8	32819	Ctrl-Backspace	32850
Ctrl-W	32791	Shift-F10	32820	Ctrl-Right	32851
Ctrl-X	32792	Shift-F9	32820	Ctrl-Left	32852
Right	32792	Alt-F1	32824	End	32853
Left	32793	Alt-F2	32825	Ctrl-Home	32856
Ctrl-Y	32793	F11	32826	PgUp	32857
Down	32794	Alt-F3	32826	PgDn	32858
Ctrl-Z	32794	F12	32827	Insert	32861
Esc	32795	Alt-F4	32827	Shift-Tab	32862
F1	32800	Alt-F5	32829	Ctrl-Enter	32863
F2	32801	Alt-F6	32829	Alt-Left	32869
F3	32802	Alt-F7	32830	Alt-Right	32870
F4	32803	Alt-F8	32831	Alt-Up	32871
F5	32804	Alt-F9	32832	Alt-Down	32872
F6	32805	Alt-F10	32833	Ctrl-Delete	32877
F7	32806	Ctrl-F1	32836	Ctrl-PgUp	64556
F8	32807	Ctrl-F2	32837	~	64570

The following command shows the use of the {KTON} command to display on-screen the number for WordPerfect's Help key:

{KTON}{Help}~

The following commands implement a rudimentary help system that the user can activate by pressing WordPerfect's normal Help (F3) key. The commands prompt the user for an account code; a user who does not know the account code can press Help (F3). Instead of seeing WordPerfect's normal help function, the user will see a help message at the bottom of the screen.

```
{ASSIGN}code~0~
{WHILE}{VARIABLE}code~=0~
    {CHAR}code~Enter the account code (Press F3 for help) ~
    {IF}{KTON}{VARIABLE}code~~=32802~
        {CALL}help~
```

```
{ELSE}
    {VARIABLE}code~
{END IF}
{END WHILE}
{QUIT}
{LABEL}help~
    {PROMPT}Cash 1; Receivables 2; Payables 3 - Press Enter to continue~
    {PAUSE}
    {ASSIGN}code~0~
{RETURN}
```

For another example of the {KTON} command, see the listing for the macro TOUPPER.WPM in the section "Working with Advanced Examples."

{NTOK}

{NTOK} takes a number and returns a value corresponding to a WordPerfect key. If the number corresponds to one of the characters in WordPerfect's character sets, {NTOK} returns the character. If the number corresponds to a WordPerfect function key, the function for that key is executed. The keys and the corresponding codes are shown in table 12.10.

The syntax for {NTOK} is the following:

{NTOK}*number~*

The following commands prompt the user to press a key. When the user presses a key, the key is converted to the corresponding number by {KTON} and then converted immediately back to the key by {NTOK}. The result is exactly the action that the key would have produced in the first place. (The commands do absolutely nothing useful, but they do demonstrate how {KTON} and {NTOK} work.)

```
{CHAR}key~Press a key ~
{NTOK}{KTON}{VARIABLE}key~~~
```

For another example of the {KTON} command, see the listing for the macro TOUPPER.WPM in the section "Working with Advanced Examples."

{STATE}

Using {STATE}, you can find information about the current status of WordPerfect. Table 12.11 lists the states for which you can test with the {STATE} command. The syntax for {STATE} is the following:

{STATE}&*code~*

The term *code* represents the value shown in the *Code* column in table 12.11. The AND operator (&) is required in the command.

Table 12.11
{STATE} Command Codes

Code	State
3	Document
4	Main editing screen
8	Editing structure other than main menu
16	Macro definition active
32	Macro execution (always set)
64	Merge active
128	Block active
256	Typeover active
512	Reveal Codes active
1024	Yes/No question active
2048	In a list

The {STATE} command can be used as an argument with the {ASSIGN}, {CASE}, {CASE CALL}, {IF}, and {WHILE} commands, as in the examples that follow.

This command puts the number of the current document into *docnum*:

    {ASSIGN}docnum~{STATE}&3~

The following commands perform an {Exit} operation that returns you to the main editing screen if WordPerfect is not already at the main editing screen. Note that there are no commands between the {IF} and {ELSE} statements; if the condition is true (WordPerfect is at the main editing screen), nothing is done. Action is required only if WordPerfect is *not* currently at the main editing screen.

    {IF}{STATE}&4~
    {ELSE}
        {Exit}
    {END IF}

These commands turn Block off if it is on:

    {IF}{STATE}&128~
        {Block}
    {END IF}

If WordPerfect asks a question requiring a yes or no answer, these commands supply a Y to answer the question:

    {IF}{STATE}&1024~
        Y
    {END IF}

For another example of the {STATE} command, see the listing for the macro COPY.WPM in the section "Working with Advanced Examples."

{SYSTEM}

The {SYSTEM} command lets you determine information about the current status of the system. The items that {SYSTEM} can report on are shown in tables 12.12, 12.13, and 12.14. The syntax of the command is the following:

{SYSTEM}*sysvar~*

The term *sysvar* represents the name of the variable, as shown in the *System Variable* column of table 12.12. You may also use a numeric value for the variable; numeric values are shown in parentheses following the variable name in table 12.12.

Table 12.12
System Variables Returned by the {SYSTEM} Command

System Variable	Description of Information Returned	Values Returned
Attrib (1)	Current font attribute	1　Extra Large 2　Very Large 4　Large 8　Small 16　Fine 32　Superscript 64　Subscript 128　Outline 256　Italics 512　Shadow 1024　Redline 2048　Double Underline 4096　Bold 8192　Strikeout 16384　Underline 32768　Small Caps
Cell (2)	Current cell position in a table	—
CellAttr (3)	Font attribute of the current cell	See the list for *Attrib*.
CellState (24)	State of a cell. The value returned must be processed to obtain useful information.	To obtain the justification in effect in the cell, divide by 256 the value returned ({SYSTEM}24~/256). The result of the division is interpreted as follows:

Table 12.12 (continued)

System Variable	Description of Information Returned	Values Returned
CellState (24) (continued)		0 Left justified 1 Full justified 2 Center justified 3 Right justified 4 Decimal justified To obtain other information about the cell, mod the value returned by 256 ({SYSTEM}24~%256). The result is interpreted as follows: 1 Justify is cell-specific 2 Attribute is cell-specific 4 Cell is bottom-aligned 8 Cell is center-aligned 16 Contents type is "text" 32 Contents is a formula 64 Cell is locked If the cursor is not in a cell, the result returned is meaningless.
Column (3)	Current column number in a table or in text columns	0 if the cursor is not within a column or table; otherwise, the column number counting from the left.
Document (4)	Status of the current document. If the value is anything other than those shown in the right-hand column, the document has not been modified since the last save or generate.	1 Document has been modified since last save. 4 Document has been modified since last generate. 5 Document has been modified since last save, and document has been modified since last generate. 256 Document is blank (you have just started WordPerfect or have just exited to a clear screen). 512 Cursor is in a table.

5.1

Table 12.12 (continued)

System Variable	Description of Information Returned	Values Returned
Document (4) (continued)		1024 Cursor is between **[Math On]** and **[Math Off]** codes (or between **[Math On]** and the end of the file). 2048 Cursor is between **[Outline On]** and **[Outline Off]** codes (or between **[Outline On]** and the end of the file).
Endnote (5)	Number of the current endnote	—
Equation (6)	Equation number. To obtain the first-level number, divide the result by 32 ({SYSTEM}6~/32). To obtain the second-level number, mod the value returned by 32 ({SYSTEM}6~%32).	—
Figure (7)	Number of the current figure; derived in the same manner described under *Equation*	—
Footnote (8)	Number of the current footnote	—
Left (9)	Item immediately to the left of the cursor	If a character, returns the character; if a code, returns an integer (see table 12.13)
Line (10)	Vertical position of the cursor from the top of the page in 1/1200ths of an inch	—

5.1

Table 12.12 (continued)

System Variable	Description of Information Returned	Values Returned
List (11)	Current list status. A list is any list in WordPerfect where you can perform a name search.	65535 The cursor is not in a list. 0 The list is empty. Other The number of items in the list. "Current" and "Parent" each count as an item. If List Files is active, {SYSTEM}List~ returns 2 plus the number of files in the list.
Menu (13)	The menu currently active	See table 12.14.
Name (12)	File name of the current document, including the extension (if any)	—
Page (14)	Current page number	—
Path (15)	DOS path to the current document	Terminated with a backslash, as in C:\WP51\
Pos (16)	Horizontal position of the cursor from the left edge of the page in 1/1200ths of an inch	—
Print (17)	Current print status	1 No characters sent to printer yet 2 Attempt has been made to send characters to printer 8 Printer waiting for a Go 16 Trying to rush job 32 Trying to cancel job 64 Network down 128 Printing in progress 256 Downloading a file 2048 Last print job ended abnormally

Table 12.12 (continued)

System Variable	Description of Information Returned	Values Returned
Right (18)	Item on which the cursor is resting	If a character, returns the character; if a code, returns an integer (see table 12.13). In a merge, returns 0 if the cursor is on a **[SRt]** or **[SPg]** code.
Row (22)	Current row number	0 if the cursor is not in a table.
ShellVer (25)	Current Shell version number. To obtain the major version number, divide the result by 256 ({SYSTEM}25~/256). To obtain the minor version number, mod the value returned by 256 ({SYSTEM}25~%256).	If Shell is not running, returns 0.
TableBox (19)	Number of the current table box; derived in the same manner described under *Equation*	—
TextBox (20)	Number of the current text box; derived in the same manner described under *Equation*	—
UserBox (21)	Number of the current user box; derived in the same manner described under *Equation*	—

Table 12.13
Codes Returned by {SYSTEM}Left~ and {SYSTEM}Right~

Code	Meaning	Code	Meaning
56864	{ASSIGN} merge code	56869	{CANCEL ON} merge code
56865	{BELL} merge code	56870	{CASE} merge code
56866	{BREAK} merge code	56871	{CASE CALL} merge code
56867	{CALL} merge code	56872	{CHAIN MACRO} merge code
56868	{CANCEL OFF} merge code		

Table 12.13 (continued)

Code	Meaning	Code	Meaning
56873	{CHAIN PRIMARY} merge code	56910	{PAGE ON} merge code
		56911	{PRINT} merge code
56874	{CHAIN SECONDARY} merge code	56906	{PROCESS} merge code
		56912	{PROMPT} merge code
56875	{CHAR} merge code	56913	{QUIT} merge code
56876	{COMMENT} merge code	56914	{RETURN} merge code
56877	{CTON} merge code	56915	{RETURN CANCEL} merge code
56878	{DATE} merge code		
56879	{DOCUMENT} merge code	56916	{RETURN ERROR} merge code
56880	{ELSE} merge code		
56881	{END FIELD} merge code	56917	{REWRITE} merge code
56882	{END FOR} merge code	56927	{STATUS PROMPT} merge code
56883	{END IF} merge code		
56884	{END RECORD} merge code	56918	{STEP OFF} merge code
56885	{END WHILE} merge code	56919	{STEP ON} merge code
56886	{FIELD} merge code	56931	{STOP} merge code
56930	{FIELD NAMES} merge code	56920	{SUBST PRIMARY} merge code
56887	{FOR} merge code		
56889	{GO} merge code	56921	{SUBST SECONDARY} merge code
56890	{IF} merge code		
56891	{IF BLANK} merge code	56922	{SYSTEM} merge code
56892	{IF EXISTS} merge code	56923	{TEXT} merge code
56893	{IF NOT BLANK} merge code	56924	{VARIABLE} merge code
		56925	{WAIT} merge code
56928	{INPUT} merge code	56926	{WHILE} merge code
56894	{KEYBOARD} merge code	54022	Advance
56895	{LABEL} merge code	55047	Auto Reference
56929	{LEN} merge code	53505	Base Font Change
56896	{LOCAL} merge code	54024	Baseline Placement
56897	{LOOK} merge code	50188	Bold Off
56898	{MID} merge code	49932	Bold On
56899	{MRG CMND} merge code	39424	Cancel Hyphenation ([/])
56900	{NEST MACRO} merge code	56320	Cell
56901	{NEST PRIMARY} merge code	49632	Center
		34304	Center Page
56902	{NEST SECONDARY} merge code	49610	Center Tab
		49648	Center with Dot Leaders
56903	{NEXT} merge code	53761	Column Definition
56904	{NEXT RECORD} merge code	44800	Columns Off
		34560	Columns On
56905	{NTOC} merge code	55554	Comment
56907	{ON CANCEL} merge code	55553	Conditional EOP
56908	{ON ERROR} merge code	55296	Date Code
56909	{PAGE OFF} merge code	55296	Date Format Options*

5.1

Table 12.13 (continued)

Code	Meaning	Code	Meaning
54016	Dec Align	53251	Hyphenation Zone
54016	Decimal/Alignment Character	49664	Indent
		49665	Indent Left/Right
49472	Decimal Tab	55043	Index
49472	Decimal Tab (with Tab Align key)	55299	Insert Page Number
		37632	Insertable Soft Return
49474	Decimal Tab (with Tab key)	50184	Italic Off
55042	Definition (Table of Contents, List, Index, Table of Authorities)	49928	Italic On
		53254	Justification
		55555	Kern
36864	Deletable Soft Return	54033	Language
39168	Dormant Hard Return	50178	Large Off
50187	Double Underline Off	49922	Large On
49931	Double Underline On	55557	Leading Adjustment
55041	EndMark (Table of Contents, List)	53249	Left/Right Margin Set
		53248	Line Height
54785	Endnote	54021	Line Numbering
53764	Endnote Options	53250	Line Spacing
55045	Endnote Placement	49536	Margin Release
55812	Equation Box	55040	Mark (Table of Contents, List)
53769	Equation Options		
50176	Extra Large Off	53760	Math
49920	Extra Large On	53760	Math Define
55808	Figure Box	43008	Math Off
53765	Figure Box Options	42752	Math On
50180	Fine Off	54019	New Endnote Number
49924	Fine On	54032	New Equation Box Number
49504	Flush Right	54028	New Figure Box Number
49520	Flush Right with Dot Leaders	54018	New Footnote Number
		54020	New Page Number
54530	Footer A	54029	New Table Box Number
54531	Footer B	54030	New Text Box Number
54784	Footnote	54031	New User Box Number
53763	Footnote Options	36096	Note Number (within a footnote or endnote)
54023	Force Odd/Even		
40960	Hard Space	56067	Open Style
54528	Header A	45568	Outline Off
54529	Header B	50183	Outline Off (font)
55813	Horizontal Line	55556	Outline On
43264	Hyphen (-)	49927	Outline On (font)
44288	Hyphen (inserted during hyphenation)	56066	Outline Style
		55298	Overstrike
40448	Hyphenation Off	53256	Page Number Position
40704	Hyphenation On	54034	Page Number Style

Table 12.13 (continued)

Code	Meaning	Code	Meaning
53259	Paper Size/Type	49926	Subscript On
55297	Paragraph Number	50181	Superscript Off
53762	Paragraph Number	49925	Superscript On
	Definition	53255	Suppress
53504	Print Color	49410	Tab
55552	Printer Command	49408	Tab ("sticky")
50186	Redline Off	53252	Tab Set
49930	Redline On	54017	Tab/Space Underline
49480	Right Tab	55809	Table Box
49498	Right Tab with Dot Leader	53766	Table Box Options
56321	Row	53771	Table Definition
50185	Shadow Off	55044	Table of Authorities
49929	Shadow On	56322	Table Off
50191	Small Caps Off	55048	Target
49935	Small Caps On	55810	Text Box
50179	Small Off	53767	Text Options
49923	Small On	53253	Top/Bottom Margin Set
44032	Soft Hyphen (Ctrl-hyphen)	50190	Underline Off
35840	Soft Page/Hard Return	49934	Underline On
53773	Spreadsheet Link	55811	User Box
53774	Spreadsheet Link End	53768	User Box Options
50189	Strikeout Off	55814	Vertical Line
49933	Strikeout On	50177	Very Large Off
56065	Style Off	49921	Very Large On
56064	Style On	35584	Widow/Orphan Off
56067	Style On or Style Off	35328	Widow/Orphan On
55049	Subdocument	54026	Word/Letter Spacing
55051	Subdocument End	54027	Word Spacing Justification
55050	Subdocument Start		Limit
50182	Subscript Off		

In general, menus that offer you a choice among alternatives are assigned unique WordPerfect menu numbers. Prompts that require you to enter free-form information, as well as most yes/no prompts, are not assigned unique numbers; when such prompts are displayed, WordPerfect returns the number of the master menu or of the editing screen.

Table 12.14 expands on the list in the WordPerfect manual, which is incomplete and has a number of errors. Menus not documented in the manual are marked with an asterisk. Menus that return values other than those shown in the manual are referenced to numbered table notes, which appear at the end of the table.

Table 12.14
Menu Numbers Returned by {SYSTEM}menu~

Number	Menu or Screen
65535	Editing screens (includes all editing screens, such as the main editing screen; screens for footnotes, endnotes, styles codes, document initial codes, footers, and headers; and the graphics-box text-editing screen)
65535	Help screens*
32856	GoTo*
49	Undo (F1)
177	Setup (Shift-F1)
346	Mouse
165	Type
363	Port*
221	Display
187	Colors/Fonts/Attributes
190	Fonts/Attributes (Hercules Plus)*
165	Graphics Screen Type
165	Text Screen Type
341	Menu Options
342	View Document Options
343	Edit Screen Options
347	Environment
68	Backup Options
44	Beep Options
181	Cursor Speed
348	Document Summary
349	Hyphenation*
101	Prompt for Hyphenation*
55	Units of Measure
45	Initial Settings
344	Merge
345	Equations
400	Graphical Font Size*
379	Horizontal Alignment*
380	Vertical Alignment*
208	Keyboard for Editing*
220	Table of Authorities
105	Print Options
252	Multiple Copies Generated By*
202	Graphics Quality*
199	Text Quality*
11	Redline Method*
208	Keyboard Layout
209	Edit
235	Key: Edit*
303	Map*
56	Location of Files

Table 12.14 (continued)

Number	Menu or Screen
110	Thesaurus (Alt-F1)*
32824	(word not found)*
102	Shell (Ctrl-F1)
32801	Search (F2)*[1]
26	Mark Text (Alt-F5) Search*
162	Defs and Refs Search*
175	Subdocs Search*
197	Date/Outline (Shift-F5) Search*
386	Text In/Out (Ctrl-F5) Search*
3	Footnote (Ctrl-F7) Search*
13	Footnote or Endnote Search*
353	Columns/Tables (Alt-F7) Search*
16	Columns Search*
27	Math Search*
167	Styles (Alt-F8) Search*
22	Format (Shift-F8) Search*
51	Format Line Search*
73	Hyphen*
100	Line*
193	Format Page Search*
6	Header*
117	Footer*
228	Page Number*
195	Format Other Search*
196	Printer Functions*
147	Font (Ctrl-F8) Search*
148	Size Search*
149	Appearance Search*
340	Merge Codes (Shift-F9) Search*
136	Graphics (Alt-F9) Search*
198	Figure Search*
203	Table Box Search*
204	Text Box Search*
205	User Box Search*
336	Line Search*
37	Equation Search*
32813	Reverse Search (Shift-F2)*[1]
32825	Replace (Alt-F2)*[1]
17	Spell (Ctrl-F2)
38	Screen (Ctrl-F3)
38	Line Draw*
30	Move (Ctrl-F4, block off)
23	(block on)*
32	Move Copy Delete Append*
112	Retrieve

Table 12.14 (continued)

Number	Menu or Screen
32804	List (F5)*[2]
305	List Files screen[2]
401	Short/Long Display*
334	Look (document summary display)*
335	Look (file text display)*
114	Look (documents saved without document summary)*
232	Find*
241	Conditions*
4	Date/Outline (Shift-F5)[3]
57	Date Format*
350	Outline[3]
24	Paragraph Number Level*
79	Define
256	Outline Styles*
263	Edit*
339	Type*
201	Enter*
370	Delete*
78	Mark Text (Alt-F5)
159	Cross Reference*[4]
154	Tie Reference To[4]
244	Graphics Box Type*
121	Define*
88	Table of Contents*
85	List*
85	Index*
36	Table of Authorities*
176	Generate*
60	Text In/Out (Ctrl-F5)
70	DOS Text
249	Password
388	Save As
250	Comment
250	Comment Editing Screen*
259	Spreadsheet
260	Import*
261	Type*
260	Create Link*
261	Type*
260	Edit Link*
261	Type*
314	Link Options*
32806	Exit (F7)
74	Print (Shift-F7)
217	Control Printer[5]
217	Job List*

Table 12.14 (continued)

Number	Menu or Screen
153	View Document
133	Select Printer
76	Additional Printers
76	Help[6]
47	List Printer Files
134	Edit
46	Port*
75	Sheet Feeder
42	Cartridges/Fonts
132	Initial Base Font
133	Help
252	Multiple Copies Generated By*
202	Graphics Quality*
199	Text Quality
353	Columns/Tables (Alt-F7)
16	Columns
33	Define
255	Type*
296	Tables
296	Create
298	Edit
301	Insert*
309	Delete*
318	Move*
324	Move Copy Delete*
319	Retrieve*
325	Size
311	Format
306	Cell
323	Type
351	Attributes
148	Size
149	Appearance
352	Justify
308	Vertical Alignment
367	Lock
307	Column
307	Width
231	Attributes
148	Size
149	Appearance*
317	Justify[7]
312	Row Height
299	Lines
145	Line Types (all)*
300	Shading*

5.1

Table 12.14 (continued)

Number	Menu or Screen
298	Header[8]
297	Math
313	Options
333	Table Position*
298	Join
302	Split
28	Math
28	Define*
3	Footnote (Ctrl-F7)
137	Footnote
67	Options
92	Numbering Method*
223	Line Separating*
392	Endnote[9]
135	Options
92	Numbering Method*
3	Endnote Placement
155	Format (Shift-F8)
5	Line
331	Justification*
20	Line Height*
12	Tab Set*
1	Page
156	Force Odd/Even*
6	Headers
240	Header A
240	Header B
117	Footers
240	Footer A
240	Footer B
368	Page Numbering
9	Page Number Positioning
328	Paper Size/Type
327	Edit Paper Definition
230	Paper Size
229	Paper Type
330	Font Type
234	Location
356	Labels*
359	Binding Edge*
10	Suppress
169	Document
132	Initial Base Font
11	Redline Method
125	Summary
25	Other
150	Advance
164	Overstrike

5.1

Table 12.14 (continued)

Number	Menu or Screen
7	Printer Functions
84	Printer Command*
93	Word Spacing*
151	Letter Spacing*
59	Styles (Alt-F8)
387	Edit[10]
174	Type*
201	Enter*
370	Delete*
147	Font (Ctrl-F8)
148	Size
149	Appearance[11]
132	Base Font[11]
146	Color
340	Merge Codes (Shift-F9)
340	More[12]
136	Graphics (Alt-F9)
393	Figure[13]
138	Create or Edit
257	Contents*
139	Anchor Type*
140	Vertical Position (Page)*
152	Vertical Position (Character)*
142	Horizontal Position (Paragraph)*
141	Horizontal Position (Page)*
142	Margin*
210	Size*
402	Edit (Graphic)*
374	Edit (Equation, bottom window)*
375	(top window)*
381	Options*
399	List*
144	Options
145	Border Style*
239	First Level Numbering*
239	Second Level Numbering*
143	Position of Caption (all except Equation)*
183	Position of Caption (Equation only)
115	Position of Caption (sublevel)*
394	Table Box[13]
395	Text Box[13]
396	User Box[13]
227	Lines
224	Horizontal
243	Horizontal Position*
361	Vertical Position*

5.1

Table 12.14 (continued)

Number	Menu or Screen
226	Vertical
242	Horizontal Position*
140	Vertical Position
397	Equation[13]
62	Merge/Sort (Ctrl-F9)
52	Sort
61	Keys*
109	Action*
108	Order*
107	Type*
32809	Save (F10)[14]
32833	Macro (Alt-F10)*
32821	Retrieve (Shift-F10)*
237	Macro Define (Ctrl-F10)
222	Macro Already Exists*
32845	Description (when defining a new macro)*
222	Description (when revising an existing description)*
236	Macro Edit screen*
236	Macro Commands*
264	Pull-Down Menu Bar
265	File
273	Text In
321	Spreadsheet*
272	Text Out
293	Password
377	Setup
266	Edit
274	Select
322	Comment
275	Convert Case*
287	Search
277	Replace
268	Layout
276	Columns
378	Tables
286	Math
279	Footnotes
280	Endnotes
283	Justify
290	Align
376	Mark
288	Cross-Reference
289	Table of Authorities
285	Define
295	Master Documents
294	Document Compare

5.1

Table 12.14 (continued)

Number	Menu or Screen
271	Tools
281	Macro
284	Outline
282	Merge Codes
269	Font
278	Appearance
267	Graphics
279	Figure
279	Table Box
279	Text Box
279	User Box
279	Equation
291	Line
292	Help

[1] Submenus for the Search, Reverse Search, and Replace functions return identical numbers.

[2] 32804 is the (undocumented) menu number when F5 is pressed and WordPerfect prompts for the list specification. 305, the documented List (F5) value, is the menu number once the List Files screen has been displayed.

[3] Date/Outline (Shift-F5) is documented as menu 350 in the WordPerfect manual. The actual menu number returned in the 11/6/89 release of WordPerfect is 24. Menu 350 is the Outline submenu.

[4] Cross-Reference is documented as 154 in the WordPerfect manual; in the 11/6/89 release of WordPerfect, the value returned is 159. 154 is the value returned for the Tie Reference To submenu.

[5] In the WordPerfect manual, the Control Printer menu is shown as returning a value of 0. In the 11/6/89 release, the actual value returned is 217.

[6] In the WordPerfect manual, Select Printer Help is documented as 133. In the 11/6/89 release of WordPerfect, the Help screen returns a value of 76.

[7] In the WordPerfect manual, the Column Justify menu is listed as returning a value of 298. In the 11/6/89 release of WordPerfect, it returns a value of 317.

[8] In the WordPerfect manual, the Header menu is listed as returning a value of 338. In the 11/6/89 release of WordPerfect, the menu actually returns 298.

[9] In the WordPerfect manual, the value given for the Endnote menu is 137. In the 11/6/89 release of WordPerfect, the actual value returned is 392.

[10] In the WordPerfect manual, the Styles Edit menu is shown returning a value of 59. In the 11/6/89 release of WordPerfect, the menu actually returns a value of 387.

[11] In the WordPerfect manual, the Font Appearance menu is shown returning a value of 132, and the Base Font menu a value of 146. In the 11/6/89 release of WordPerfect, the Font Appearance menu actually returns a value of 149, and the Base Font menu a value of 132.

[12] In the WordPerfect manual, the Merge Codes More menu is shown returning a value of 346. In the 11/6/89 release of WordPerfect, the menu actually returns a value of 340.

[13] Create, Edit, and Options menu numbers are the same for Figure, Table Box, Text Box, User Box, and Equation.

[14] If you have Create Document Summary on Save/Exit set to Yes in Setup (see Chapter 20), WordPerfect will return a value of 125 at the Save prompt until you have assigned a file name.

The following macro checks to see whether columns are off (in which case the value of {SYSTEM}column~ is 0) or on. If columns are off, the macro turns them on; if they are on, it turns them off.

```
{DISPLAY OFF}                 {;} turn display off to eliminate flashing~
{Columns/Tables}c             {;} activate the columns function~
{IF}{SYSTEM}Column~=0~        {;} if we're not in a column~
    o                         {;} turn columns on (this is the letter "o")~
{ELSE}                        {;} otherwise, we're in a column~
    f                         {;} so turn columns off~
{END IF}
```

The following macro creates a header that includes the file name of the current document. The macro tells WordPerfect to create a header for every page; in the header the macro puts the file name at the left margin, the page number in the center, and the date at the right margin.

```
{DISPLAY OFF}                        {;} turn display off to eliminate flashing~
{Format}phap                         {;} create Header A for every page~
{SYSTEM}Name~                        {;} insert filename of the document;
{Center}{^B}                         {;} add a centered page number~
{Flush Right}{Date/Outline}c         {;} add the date, flush right~
{Exit}                               {;} exit from the header definition screen~
{Exit}                               {;} return to the main editing screen~
```

See the example for the {ORIGINAL KEY} command later in this chapter.

Handling Errors

No matter how carefully you craft your macros, the people who use them will find ways to make errors. A well-designed macro anticipates errors and incorporates ways to handle errors gracefully.

WordPerfect's native error-handling capabilities are quite sophisticated. But the authors of WordPerfect cannot predict everything you will want to do with your macros. The commands in this section provide you with the ability to handle errors in a way that *you* determine. You can use them, within limits, to bypass and supersede WordPerfect's default error-handling activities.

The advanced macro commands discussed in this section are {CANCEL OFF}, {CANCEL ON}, {ON CANCEL}, {ON ERROR}, {ON NOT FOUND}, {QUIT}, and {RESTART}.

{CANCEL OFF} and {CANCEL ON}

{CANCEL OFF} deactivates the Cancel (F1) key until the macro terminates or until a {CANCEL ON} command is reached. The syntax of the commands is as follows:

```
{CANCEL OFF}
{CANCEL ON}
```

{CANCEL OFF} is useful if you want to use the Cancel (F1) key as an input key, because pressing Cancel (F1) usually terminates the execution of your macro. {CANCEL OFF} is also useful if you want to prevent the user from interrupting a particular part of a macro.

The Cancel (F1) key can be reprogrammed with the {ON CANCEL} command. However, using {CANCEL OFF} is the only way to prevent the Cancel (F1) key from terminating a macro during an {INPUT}, {PAUSE}, or {PAUSE KEY} operation, because {ON CANCEL} is not operative during those commands.

If a {CANCEL OFF} command is in effect, you can press Ctrl-Break to terminate macro execution. Refer the example for the {LOOK} command to see the {CANCEL OFF} command in action.

{ON CANCEL}

The {ON CANCEL} command tells WordPerfect what to do when the user presses the Cancel (F1) key during a macro. {ON CANCEL} reprograms the Cancel (F1) key temporarily by directing the macro to take a specified action if the user presses Cancel (F1) (or if a subroutine terminates with {RETURN CANCEL}). The syntax of the command is the following:

> {ON CANCEL}*action*~

The *action* is limited to these commands: {BREAK}, {CALL}, {GO}, {QUIT}, {RESTART}, {RETURN}, {RETURN CANCEL}, {RETURN NOT FOUND}, and {RETURN ERROR}. {RETURN CANCEL} is the default; if there is no {ON CANCEL} currently active, pressing Cancel (F1) causes the macro to return to the calling routine or to WordPerfect, showing a cancel condition. Don't forget to put two tildes at the end of an {ON CANCEL} command if the *action* is {CALL} or {GO}.

Reminder:
If the action is {CALL} or {GO}, put two tildes at the end of the {ON CANCEL} command.

The {ON CANCEL} command does not work when the macro has been paused by a {PAUSE}, {PAUSE KEY}, or {INPUT} command. Unless the Cancel (F1) key has been deactivated through a {CANCEL OFF} command, the macro terminates if the user presses Cancel (F1) during a pause caused by one of these commands.

The {ON CANCEL} command is specific to the level of execution in which it is called; that is, if you call a subroutine, and you want your {ON CANCEL} command to be in effect for that subroutine, you must issue the {ON CANCEL} command within that subroutine.

Reminder:
You must use an {ON CANCEL} command in every subroutine in which you want the command to be in effect.

The following example calls the routine named *confirm* and gives you an opportunity to confirm that you want to cancel. If you confirm the cancellation, the routine returns to WordPerfect by means of the {QUIT} command (which always terminates all macro execution). If you say that you do not want to cancel, the {RETURN} command returns you the point in the macro where you pressed Cancel (F1).

> {ON CANCEL}{CALL}confirm~~
>
> {;} main body of the macro here~

```
{LABEL}confirm~
    {CHAR}conf~Do you really want to Cancel? No (Yes)~
    {IF}"{VARIABLE}conf~"="Y"|"{VARIABLE}conf~"="y"~
        {QUIT}
    {END IF}
{RETURN}
```

For more examples of the {ON CANCEL} command, see the listings for the macros BULLETS.WPM, INVOICE.WPM, and COPY.WPM in the section "Working with Advanced Examples."

{ON ERROR}

{ON ERROR} tells WordPerfect what to do if an error occurs during the execution of a macro. Errors include those that occur during macro execution, during normal WordPerfect operations, or while you are in DOS (accessed through the Shell [Ctrl-F1] key combination). The syntax of the command is the following:

{ON ERROR}*action~*

Reminder:

If the action is {CALL} or {GO}, put two tildes at the end of the {ON ERROR} command.

The *action* is limited to these commands: {BREAK}, {CALL}, {GO}, {QUIT}, {RESTART}, {RETURN}, {RETURN CANCEL}, {RETURN NOT FOUND}, and {RETURN ERROR}. {RETURN ERROR} is the default; if there is no {ON ERROR} currently active, an error condition causes the macro to return to the calling routine or to WordPerfect, showing an error condition. Don't forget to put two tildes at the end of an {ON ERROR} command if the *action* is {CALL} or {GO}.

The following example causes WordPerfect to go to a subroutine called *error* when an error is encountered. The *error* subroutine sounds a tone, prints an error message, and—when the user presses a key—returns to WordPerfect.

{ON ERROR}{GO}error~~

{;} main body of the macro here.

```
{LABEL}error~
    {BELL}
    {CHAR}0~An error has occurred. Press any key to return to WordPerfect.~
{RETURN ERROR}
```

For another example of the {ON ERROR} command, see the listing for the macro TESTCAP.WPM in the section "Working with Advanced Examples."

{ON NOT FOUND}

{ON NOT FOUND} tells WordPerfect what to do if a search fails during the execution of a macro. The search can be a {Search} function search, a name search in a list, or a word search in List Files. {ON NOT FOUND} is also used if a subroutine called by the macro returns with a "not found" condition. The syntax of the command is the following:

{ON NOT FOUND}*action~*

The *action* is limited to these commands: {BREAK}, {CALL}, {GO}, {QUIT}, {RESTART}, {RETURN}, {RETURN CANCEL}, {RETURN NOT FOUND}, and {RETURN ERROR}. {RETURN NOT FOUND} is the default; if there is no {ON NOT FOUND} currently active, a failed search causes the macro to return to WordPerfect or to the calling subroutine, showing a "not found" condition. Don't forget to put two tildes at the end of an {ON NOT FOUND} command if the *action* is {CALL} or {GO}. See INVOICE.WPM in the section "Working with Advanced Examples" for an example of {ON NOT FOUND}.

Reminder:
If the action is {CALL} or {GO}, put two tildes at the end of the {ON NOT FOUND} command.

{QUIT}

{QUIT} terminates the macro immediately and returns control directly to WordPerfect. If the currently executing macro has been called as a subroutine from another macro through the {NEST} command, or if the macro has previously executed a {CHAIN} command, the {NEST} or {CHAIN} is ignored. The syntax for {QUIT} is the following:

    {QUIT}

For an example of the {QUIT} command, see the example for the {ON CANCEL} command.

{RESTART}

The {RESTART} command terminates macro execution at the end of the currently executing macro and returns control to WordPerfect. If the currently executing macro has been called as a subroutine from another macro through the {NEST} command, or if the macro has previously executed a {CHAIN} command, the {NEST} or {CHAIN} is ignored. The syntax for {RESTART} is the following:

    {RESTART}

The difference between the {QUIT} command and the {RESTART} command is that {QUIT} stops macro execution immediately, whereas {RESTART} enables the currently executing macro file to finish executing. Both return control directly to WordPerfect, regardless of any {CHAIN} or {NEXT} commands that may have been executed.

Executing a {CHAIN} command after the {RESTART} cancels the effect of the {RESTART} command. The newly chained macro is executed as it normally would be; if the macro containing the {RESTART} was nested, that macro will return to the macro that called it rather than return to WordPerfect.

Controlling Macro Execution

The commands covered in this section enable you to control certain aspects of the way your completed macros execute. These commands are useful when you debug macros and may be useful when you need to control macro speed. The commands discussed in this section are {SPEED}, {WAIT}, {STEP ON}, and {STEP OFF}.

{SPEED}

The {SPEED} command slows macro execution. The syntax is the following:

{SPEED}*100ths_second~*

The argument *100ths_second* is the number of hundredth-second intervals that WordPerfect will wait between each command (a value of 100 equals 1 second). The default value is 0; that is, WordPerfect executes macro commands as fast as your computer is capable of executing them.

This command is principally useful in debugging macros; it enables you to slow down the action enough to observe what is happening.

The following command inserts a half-second (50 × 0.01 second) interval between the execution of each WP macro command:

{SPEED}50~

{WAIT}

The {WAIT} command inserts a timed wait into a macro. The syntax is the following:

{WAIT}*10ths_second~*

The argument *10ths_second* is a number that will be multiplied by 0.1 to determine the length of time that the macro will wait.

The difference between the {WAIT} and {SPEED} commands is that {SPEED} inserts an interval between all commands from the time the {SPEED} command is executed. {WAIT} inserts a single pause at the place in the macro where the {WAIT} command occurs.

The following commands sound the bell, initiate a half-second wait, and sound the bell again:

{BELL}
{WAIT}5~
{BELL}

{STEP ON} and {STEP OFF}

The {STEP ON} command causes the macro to display execution information at the bottom of the screen as it executes. The user must press a key between the display of each item. {STEP OFF} causes the macro to execute normally again. The syntax of the commands is as follows:

{STEP ON}
{STEP OFF}

The {STEP ON} command, which is used to debug macros, enables you to see what is happening as the macro executes. {STEP ON} displays several types of information:

- Advanced macro commands. Each advanced macro command is represented by a code; the commands display in the format *MACRO CMD n*, where *n* is the code. A list of macro-command codes appears in table 12.15.

- Keystroke commands. Each keystroke command is displayed in the format *Key Cmd n*, where *n* is a code. This category includes cursor-control and display-control characters. A list of key-command codes appears in table 12.16.

- Numbered variables. The variable identifier displays as *VAR n*, where *n* is a digit from 1 to 9.

- All text, exactly as it appears in the macro editor.

- The current value of each variable, each time that variable is referenced. For example, in the following sequence, after the characters *var~* are displayed (one at a time) on the screen, the value of *var*—whatever the user typed in at the {CHAR} statement—is displayed.

      {CHAR}var~3~
      {IF}{VARIABLE}var~=3~

      . . .
      {END IF}

- Keystroke macro numbers. If an alternative keyboard is in use and a macro contains a key defined as a macro on that keyboard, the message KEY MACRO n displays, where *n* is the key macro number. To determine which key the key macro number references, you must display the edit screen for the keyboard. See information on alternative keyboards in Chapter 20.

- Alt-*letter* keystrokes, which appear as **ALT x**, where *x* is the letter.

Table 12.15
Macro-Command Codes

Code	Macro Command	Code	Macro Command
1	{ASSIGN}	15	{END FOR}
2	{BELL}	16	{END IF}
3	{BREAK}	17	{END WHILE}
4	{CALL}	18	{FOR}
5	{CANCEL OFF}	19	{FOR EACH}
6	{CANCEL ON}	20	{GO}
7	{CASE}	21	{IF}
8	{CASE CALL}	22	{LABEL}
9	{CHAIN}	23	{LOOK}
10	{CHAR}	24	{NEST}
11	{;}	25	{NEXT}
12	{DISPLAY OFF}	26	{SHELL MACRO}
13	{DISPLAY ON}	27	{ON CANCEL}
14	{ELSE}	28	{ON ERROR}

Table 12.15 (continued)

Code	Macro Command	Code	Macro Command
29	{ON NOT FOUND}	45	{STEP OFF}
30	{PAUSE}	46	{ORIGINAL KEY}
31	{PROMPT}	47	{IF EXISTS}
32	{QUIT}	48	{MENU OFF}
33	{RESTART}	49	{MENU ON}
34	{RETURN}	50	{STATUS PROMPT}
35	{RETURN CANCEL}	51	{INPUT}
36	{RETURN ERROR}	52	{VARIABLE}
37	{RETURN NOT FOUND}	53	{SYSTEM}
38	{SPEED}	54	{MID}
39	{STEP ON}	55	{NTOK}
40	{TEXT}	56	{KTON}
41	{STATE}	57	{LEN}
42	{WAIT}	58	{~}
43	{WHILE}	59	{PAUSE KEY}
44	{Macro Commands}		

Table 12.16
Key-Command Codes

Code	Key Command	Code	Key Command
1	{^A}	19	{^S}
2	{^B}	20	{^T}
3	{^C}	21	{^U}
4	{^D}	22	{^V}
5	{^E}	23	{^W}
6	{^F}	24	{^X}
7	{^G}	25	{^Y}
8	{^H}	26	{^Z}
9	{^I}	27	{^[}
10	{^J}	28	{^\}
11	{^K}	29	{^]}
12	{^L}	32	{Cancel}
13	{^M}	33	{Forward Search}
14	{^N}	34	{Help}
15	{^O}	35	{Indent}
16	{^P}	36	{List Files}
17	{^Q}	37	{Bold}
18	{^R}	38	{Exit}

Table 12.16 (continued)

Code	Key Command	Code	Key Command
39	{Underline}	77	{Define Macro}
40	{Merge Return}	80	{Backspace}
41	{Save}	81	{Delete Right}
44	{Setup}	82	{Delete Word}
45	{Backwards Search}	83	{Word Right}
46	{Switch}	84	{Word Left}
47	{Left/Right Indent}	85	{End}
48	{Date/Outline}	86	{Home}{Home}{Left}
49	{Center}	88	{GoTo}
50	{Print}	89	{PgUp}
51	{Format}	90	{PgDn}
52	{Merge Commands}	91	{Screen Down}
53	{Retrieve}	92	{Screen Up}
56	{Thesaurus}	93	{Typeover}
57	{Search/Replace}	94	{Left Margin Release}
58	{Reveal Codes}	95	{HPg}
59	{Block}	96	{Soft Hyphen}
60	{Mark Text}	97	{Hard Hyphen}
61	{Flush Right}	98	{Hard Space}
62	{Math/Columns}	99	{Para Up}
63	{Style}	100	{Para Down}
64	{Graphics}	101	{Item Left}
65	{Macro}	102	{Item Right}
68	{Shell}	103	{Item Up}
69	{Spell}	104	{Item Down}
70	{Screen}	105	{Alt-Home}
71	{Move}	106	{Delete Row}
72	{Text In/Out}	107	{Menu Bar}
73	{Tab Align}	108	{Block Append}
74	{Footnote}	109	{Block Move}
75	{Font}	110	{Block Copy}
76	{Merge/Sort}		

The macro that follows contains a {STEP ON} command, whose purpose is to determine whether the macro (which is not running correctly) is executing the {WHILE} loop. (The macro will never execute the {WHILE} loop because a tilde is missing at the end of the {VARIABLE} command.)

```
{ASSIGN}myvar~1~
{STEP ON}
{WHILE}{VARIABLE}myvar>0~
    {NEST}macro2~
{END WHILE}
```

Controlling the Display

The commands in this section provide you with tools to turn off the on-screen display of information during macro execution (and to turn the display back on, when appropriate). The commands covered are {DISPLAY OFF}, {DISPLAY ON}, {MENU OFF}, and {MENU ON}.

{DISPLAY OFF} and {DISPLAY ON}

{DISPLAY OFF} disables the display of menus and prevents the screen from being updated by the action of the macro. The syntax is the following:

    {DISPLAY OFF}
    {DISPLAY ON}

In general, you want to disable the display of information while a macro is executing. If you do not, the result of each macro command is displayed on the screen as the command executes. This display not only distracts the user but also slows the speed of macro execution, because WordPerfect must take the time to update the screen.

If you want the user to interact with a WordPerfect menu, and the display is off, you will need to execute a {DISPLAY ON} command. WordPerfect automatically restores the display when a macro terminates.

The following commands retrieve a file and move the cursor to the end of the file. Text is not displayed during these operations, because the display is off.

    {DISPLAY OFF}
    {Retrieve}MYFILE.WP{Enter}
    {Home}{Home}{Down}

Note: When the display is off, a {PROMPT} command will display its message, and then the message will immediately disappear. You should thus turn the display on before using the {PROMPT} command.

{MENU OFF} and {MENU ON}

{MENU OFF} turns WordPerfect menus off during macro execution. Text written to the screen by the macro displays normally. {MENU ON} restores the normal operation of the menus. The syntax of the commands is as follows:

    {MENU OFF}
    {MENU ON}

{MENU OFF} works the same as {DISPLAY OFF}, with one exception: {MENU OFF} enables the display of text written to the screen by your macro, whereas {DISPLAY OFF} disables both the menu display and text display. {MENU OFF} does not disable prompts that ask for information such as file names. It disables menus, both full-screen menus and status-line menus.

{MENU ON} turns menu display back on. WordPerfect automatically turns the menu display on when a macro terminates.

The following commands retrieve a file, move the cursor to the bottom of the file, and create a figure box. Because the display is on but menus are off, the text is shown on the screen when it is retrieved, and the last page of text appears when the bottom of the file is reached. The Figure Definition menu is not displayed because menus are off. When the figure has been created, the screen is updated to show the box.

```
{DISPLAY ON}
{MENU OFF}
{Retrieve}28-02.wpf{Enter}
{Home}{Home}{Down}
{Graphics}fc
{Exit}
```

Using Miscellaneous Advanced Macro Commands

This section covers the Comment, {ORIGINAL KEY}, and {SHELL MACRO} commands.

Comment

With the Comment command, you can embed your own remarks into a macro. Everything you type between {;} and ~ is ignored during the execution of the macro. The syntax of the command is the following:

{;}*comment*~

Use comments to document your macro. You can place comments on the same line as macro commands or on lines by themselves. There are no limits to the length and to the number of comments you can use in a macro, provided that the total length of the macro does not exceed the capacity of the macro editor.

{ORIGINAL KEY}

The {ORIGINAL KEY} command is used in keyboard definitions to instruct WordPerfect to ignore the redefinition for a particular key and use the original, unaltered definition. The syntax of the command is the following:

{ORIGINAL KEY}

{ORIGINAL KEY} returns the "unredefined" value of the last key pressed. That key may have been pressed before the macro started, or it may have been pressed in response to a {CHAR}, {LOOK}, {TEXT}, {INPUT}, {PAUSE}, or {PAUSE KEY} command.

Assume that most times when you select the **Filename** (**1**) option from the Graphics Edit screen, you immediately list the WPG files in the Graphics directory. This operation requires many keystrokes; each time you do it, you must select **Filename**

(**1**), press List (F5), type *.wpg*, and press Enter. Making this process a one-keystroke operation could save you much work.

Suppose that you decide to program the F key to do all the work. However, you want the F key to act in this way only when you're working with the Graphics Edit screen. Through a combination of the {SYSTEM}Menu~ function and the {ORIGINAL KEY} command, you can achieve exactly this result.

From the Keyboard Edit screen, you enter the commands listed below as a definition for the F key (see Chapter 20 for a discussion of the Keyboard Edit screen).

{IF}{SYSTEM}menu~=138~	{;} if the Graphics Definition menu is active when F is pressed~
F	{;} type an F~
{List}	{;} call List Files~
*.wpg	{;} enter the file specification for List Files~
{Enter}	{;} display the List Files screen~
{ELSE}	{;} if the Graphics Definition screen is not active~
{ORIGINAL KEY}	{;} just use the original meaning of the key~
{END IF}	

See the discussion of the {LOOK} command for another example of {ORIGINAL KEY}.

{SHELL MACRO}

This command has been provided in WordPerfect 5.1 for compatibility with future releases of WordPerfect Library, beginning with version 2.1 of Library. You will be able to use this command to invoke Shell macros from WordPerfect 5.1 macros. At the time WordPerfect 5.1 was released, this command had no useful function.

Emulating Keystrokes

The commands in this section do nothing more than the equivalent keystrokes entered from the screen. Their main application is to provide for more readable macros. Each is described very briefly.

{Block Append}

The {Block Append} command duplicates the keystrokes Move (Ctrl-F4) **B**lock **A**ppend.

{Block Copy}

The {Block Copy} command duplicates the keystrokes Move (Ctrl-F4) **B**lock **C**opy.

{Block Move}

The {Block Move} command duplicates the keystrokes Move (Ctrl-F4) **B**lock **M**ove.

{Item Down}

The {Item Down} command moves the cursor down one cell in a table. In an outline, the command moves the cursor down to the next major level.

{Item Left}

The {Item Left} command moves the cursor left one column or left one cell.

{Item Right}

The {Item Right} command moves the cursor right one column or right one cell.

{Item Up}

The {Item Up} command moves the cursor up one cell in a table. In an outline, the command moves the cursor up to the next major level.

{Para Down}

The {Para Down} command moves the cursor to the beginning of the next paragraph.

{Para Up}

The {Para Up} command moves the cursor to the beginning of the current paragraph. If the cursor is already at the beginning of a paragraph, {Para Up} moves the cursor to the beginning of the previous paragraph.

Working with Advanced Examples

This section provides the macros TOUPPER.WPM, COPY.WPM, BULLETS.WPM, and INVOICE.WPM as advanced "usage" examples and explains how they operate. The macro TESTCAP.WPM is included in connection with TOUPPER.WPM. Refer to Chapter 11 for information on how to use the macro editor to create and modify macros.

Converting Lowercase Letters to Capitals (TOUPPER.WPM)

In macro development, you will often find it handy to convert a lowercase letter to a capital letter, or vice versa. This capability is useful when you want to have the macro accept a response of Y or N (for "Yes" or "No") and then test that response with an {IF} command. But the user may type either a lowercase letter or a capital. Although you can write the macro so that it tests for either capital or lowercase letters (see the macro INVOICE.WPM for an example), a simpler and more elegant solution is to convert whatever the user types to a capital letter and then use the capital letter in the programming statement.

Most programming languages provide a built-in facility for performing this task; the WordPerfect macro language does not. The macro TOUPPER.WPM, discussed in this section, provides this capability. The macro TESTCAP.WPM is included in the discussion as a mechanism to test TOUPPER.WPM.

TOUPPER.WPM starts with a character it calls *response*. The macro uses WordPerfect character numbers to test *response*. The character may be a lowercase letter, an uppercase letter, or "something else"—that is, a nonalphabetic character. If the character is a lowercase letter, the macro converts the letter to uppercase. If the character is an uppercase letter, the macro does nothing with it. If the character is not a letter, the macro returns an error to the calling macro.

The macro TOUPPER.WPM is as follows:

> {;} TOUPPER.WPM~
>
> {;} Converts a lowercase letter passed in the variable "response" to a capital letter. Returns an error condition if the variable passed is not a letter.~

```
{ASSIGN}charnum~{KTON}{VARIABLE}response~~~
                              {;} find the character number and assign the
                                  number to the variable "charnum"~
{IF}{VARIABLE}charnum~>96&{VARIABLE}charnum~<123~
                              {;} if character is lowercase letter~
    {ASSIGN}charnum~{VARIABLE}charnum~–32~
                              {;} convert its character number to the
                                  character number of the corresponding
                                  uppercase letter~
    {ASSIGN}response~{NTOK}{VARIABLE}charnum~~~
                              {;} convert that character number back to a
                                  character~
{ELSE}                        {;} character is not a lowercase letter~
    {IF}{VARIABLE}charnum~<65|{VARIABLE}charnum~>90~
                              {;} if it is not an uppercase letter~
        {RETURN ERROR}        {;} it's not a letter at all, so return an error
                                  code to the calling macro~
    {END IF}
{END IF}
{RETURN}
```

The first macro line assigns to the variable *charnum* the WordPerfect number for the character represented by *response*. After this statement executes, the same character is represented by two different variables, but in two different ways. Assume that the character represented by *response* is a lowercase *k*. If you display the values of both *response* and *charnum* immediately after this statement executes, *response* would display *k*, but *charnum* would display 108 (the WordPerfect character number that represents lowercase *k*). The {KTON} command in the macro line is the mechanism that actually converts the variable *response* to its WordPerfect character number.

Note that there are three tildes at the end of the line. The reason is that all three advanced macro commands in the line require an ending tilde. The first tilde ends the {VARIABLE} command, the second ends the {KTON} command, and the last ends the {ASSIGN} command.

If the WordPerfect number contained in the variable *charnum* is between 97 (the number for lowercase *a*) and 122 (the number for lowercase *z*), the character is a lowercase letter. The first {IF} statement checks for this condition by asking the following:

Is the value of *charnum* both greater than 96 *and* less than 123?

If the answer to that question is "true," the character is a lowercase letter. The AND operator (&) is used to implement the dual nature of the question. The conditions on both sides of the & must be true for the {IF} statement to be true.

The WordPerfect character numbers for the lowercase alphabet extend from 97 to 122. The character numbers for the uppercase alphabet extend from 65 to 90. If you subtract 32 from the character number for any lowercase number, you have the character number for its uppercase equivalent. For example, if you subtract 32 from 107 (the character number for *k*), you have 75, which is the character number for *K*.

If the first {IF} statement is true, the next {ASSIGN} macro line subtracts 32 from the value of the *charnum* variable and then assigns the result back to *charnum*. If the value of *charnum* is 107 (*k*), for example, the value will be 75 (*K*) after this statement executes.

A mirror image of the first line in the macro, the fourth macro statement takes the value of *charnum* (which has just been modified by the preceding statement), converts it to the corresponding character value, and then assigns that value to *response*. The {NTOK} command performs the actual conversion. The result of the {NTOK} command is then assigned to *response* by the assignment statement. If the value of *charnum* is 75, for example, then after this line executes, *response* will have the value *K*.

The rest of the lines in the macro, until the last {ENDIF}, are all executed if the {IF} statement is false; therefore, this {ASSIGN} command is the last line that will execute before the final {ENDIF}.

If the first {IF} statement is false—that is, if the character represented by *response* is not a lowercase letter—then the lines following the {ELSE} command (line 5) will execute.

The macro already knows, if it reaches the sixth macro line, that the character is not a lowercase letter. This macro line checks whether the character is an uppercase letter.

An uppercase letter has a character number between 65 (*A*) and 90 (*Z*). The OR operator (|) means that if *either* statement within the parentheses is true, then the whole expression is true. In other words, if the value of *charnum* is less than 65 (in which case the character is not an uppercase letter) *or* the value of *charnum* is greater then 90 (in which case the character is not an uppercase letter), then the net result of the two commands linked by | is "true." And if either statement is true, the character is not a letter; an error should be returned.

Assume that the value of *charnum* is 82 (uppercase *R*). The number 82 is neither less than 65 nor greater than 90, so the expression linked by | is false. On the other hand, assume that the value of *charnum* is 53 (the digit *5*). The first statement (is *charnum* less than 65?) is true, so the statement evaluates to true.

If the character is not a letter—that is, if the preceding {IF} statement is true—the {RETURN} command—the last command in the macro—is executed; this macro returns to the calling macro, showing an error condition.

The macro TESTCAP.WPM is included in this discussion as a mechanism to test TOUPPER.WPM. TESTCAP asks the user to type a letter, which it assigns to the variable *response*. TESTCAP then calls TOUPPER, which converts *response* to a capital letter if *response* was a lowercase letter and which returns an error condition if *response* was neither a capital nor a lowercase letter. The macro TESTCAP.WPM is as follows:

> {;} TESTCAP.WPM~
>
> {;} Tests TOUPPER.WPM by passing it a character and printing the returned character. Prints an error message if TOUPPER returns an error condition.

{ON ERROR}{GO}error~~	{;} if there's an error returned by a subprogram, go to {LABEL}error~
{CHAR}response~Type a letter: ~	{;} get a character from the user~
{NEST}toupper~	{;} call the subprogram to change a lowercase letter to a capital letter~
{VARIABLE}response~	{;} display the letter on the screen~
{QUIT}	{;} terminate the macro~
{LABEL}error~	{;} these commands execute if TOUPPER returns an error~
Error! {VARIABLE}response~ is not a letter.{Enter}	
	{;} print an error message~
{QUIT}	{;} terminate the macro~

Note that nesting is possible in this macro because WordPerfect variables are global. (Global variables retain their value even when a macro terminates or calls another macro.) The variable *response* is initially created and assigned a value (a character) in TESTCAP. The variable retains this value when it is used by TOUPPER. If *response* is a lowercase letter, TOUPPER changes its value to an uppercase letter. The change in value is retained when TESTCAP takes control again, so the command *{VARIABLE}response~* will display an uppercase letter.

To change TOUPPER.WPM so that it converts capital letters to lowercase letters, make these changes:

> 1. Copy the file TOUPPER.WPM to a file called TOLOWER.WPM. (Be sure that you add the WPM extension to the TOLOWER file name.)

2. In TOLOWER.WPM, change the line

{IF}{VARIABLE}charnum~>96&{VARIABLE}charnum~<123~

to

{IF}{VARIABLE}charnum~>64&{VARIABLE}charnum~<91~

3. In TOLOWER.WPM, change the line

{ASSIGN}charnum~{VARIABLE}charnum~–32~

to

{ASSIGN}charnum~{VARIABLE}charnum~+32~

4. In TOLOWER.WPM, change the line

{IF}{VARIABLE}charnum~<65 I {VARIABLE}charnum~>90~

to

{IF}!({VARIABLE}charnum~>96&{VARIABLE}charnum~<123)~

To make TESTCAP test TOLOWER, simply change the line *{NEST}toupper~* to read *{NEST}tolower~*.

Handling Copy Functions (COPY.WPM)

The macro COPY.WPM implements a reduced-keystroke copy. If Block is on, the macro operates on the assumption that you want to copy a block (and that assumption is based on one that copying a block is a much more common function than copying a rectangle or tabular column). If Block is not on, the macro displays a custom menu, and you choose whether to copy the sentence, paragraph, or page. The macro then uses the facilities of WordPerfect's normal Move function to execute the user's request. In doing so, the macro "hides" the normal two-level Move function menus.

If you press Cancel (F1) while the custom menu is displayed, however, WordPerfect terminates the macro but not the Move function. Because the macro is "hiding" the Move menu, the normal Move menu is left on-screen when you terminate the macro; you must press Cancel (F1) (or Enter) a second time. You thus need some way to get rid of the Move menu.

The Exit (F7) function will get rid of the Move menu. The solution to the problem, then, is to make the Cancel (F1) key perform the normal Exit (F7) function *before* the macro terminates. The first line in the COPY macro reprograms the Cancel (F1) key with the *{ON CANCEL}{GO}out~~* command, which tells WordPerfect, "If the Cancel key is pressed, then instead of canceling the macro, do whatever the commands in the *{LABEL}out~* subprogram require." The *{LABEL}out~* subprogram uses an {Exit}, which terminates the Move function, and a {RETURN CANCEL} command, which terminates the macro.

Note: The {^]}, {^V}, and {^Q} characters in the {CHAR} command are used to make the custom menu look like WordPerfect's normal menus. See the section "Using Control Characters" in this chapter for information on how to use these characters.

The COPY.WPM macro is as follows:

```
{;} COPY.WPM~
{ON CANCEL}{GO}out~~              {;} reprogram the Cancel (F1) key~

{Move}                           {;} start WP's Move function~

{IF}{STATE}&128~                 {;} Block is on~
    {ASSIGN}1~1~                 {;} {VAR 1} assigned to "Block"~
{ELSE}                           {;} Block is not on~
    {CHAR}1~                     {;} display menu for user to choose~
    {^]}Copy: 1{^Q} {^V}S{^Q}entence; {^]}2{^Q} {^V}P{^Q}aragraph;
    {^]}3{^Q} P{^V}a{^Q}ge: {^]}0{^Q}{Left}~
{END IF}
{CASE}{VAR 1}~                    {;} process menu selection or default Block
                                     choice~

    1~proc~S~proc~s~proc~        {;} sentence or block~
    2~proc~P~proc~p~proc~        {;} paragraph~
    3~proc~A~proc~a~proc~~       {;} page~
{Cancel}                         {;} something else picked~
{RETURN}                         {;} return to the editing screen~

{LABEL}proc~                     {;} process the menu selection~
    {VAR 1}                      {;} {VAR 1} has the menu selection~
    2                            {;} copy~
{RETURN}                         {;} return to the editing screen~

{LABEL}out~
    {Exit}                       {;} terminate the macro and the Move
                                     function~

{RETURN}                         {;} return to the editing screen~
```

The COPY.WPM macro can easily be changed to implement Move functions. Simply change the word in the {CHAR} statement from *Copy* to *Move* and change the third line in the *{LABEL}proc* subroutine to *1*.

Creating Menus (BULLETS.WPM)

BULLETS.WPM is a straightforward example of building menus with WordPerfect advanced macro commands.

As a means of creating the menu, some of the cursor-positioning commands are inserted in the *message* portion of the {CHAR} command. The cursor-positioning commands used are these:

- {Del to EOP}, which clears the screen and positions the cursor in the upper left corner. Insert this command in the macro editor by pressing Ctrl-V, then Ctrl-PgDn.
- {^M}, which moves the cursor to the leftmost column.

- {Down}, which moves the cursor down one line. Note that you can accomplish the same thing you accomplish with {^M} and {Down} by placing an {Enter} at the end of each line.

The {CASE CALL} statement processes the user's input. If the user types one of the menu choices, the subroutine corresponding to that menu choice is executed. Control then returns to the first statement following the {CASE CALL} statement, which rewrites the screen (to remove the menu from the screen and restore the document) and returns control to the main WordPerfect program. If the user fails to select one of the menu choices, the {Rewrite} and {QUIT} routines are also executed.

The other subroutines all do essentially the same job: they insert the user-specified character into the document, using the Compose (Ctrl-V) feature.

The BULLETS.WPM macro is as follows:

{ON CANCEL}{GO}exit~~{;}to ensure a graceful exit~

{ASSIGN}bullet~0~
{CHAR}bullet~
{Del to EOP}
{^M}1   Small round black bullet
{^M}{Down}2   Medium round black bullet
{^M}{Down}3   Large round black bullet
{^M}{Down}4   Small hollow black bullet
{^M}{Down}5   Medium hollow black bullet
{^M}{Down}6   Large hollow black bullet
{^M}{Down}7   Small square black box
{^M}{Down}8   Medium square black box
{^M}{Down}9   Large square black box
{^M}{Down}A   Small square hollow box
{^M}{Down}B   Medium square hollow box
{^M}{Down}C   Large square hollow box
{^M}{Down}D   Pointing finger
{^M}{Down}E   Check mark
{^M}{Down}F   Arrow
{^M}{Down}G   Arrowhead
{^M}{Down}H   Box with X
{^M}{Down}I   Paragraph symbol
{^M}{Down}J   Section symbol
{^M}{Down}
{Down}0   Cancel
{^M}{Down}{Down}{Down}{Down}
{^]}Type the number or letter of the bullet character: 0{^\}{Left}~

{CASE CALL}{VARIABLE}bullet~~
    1~srb~
    2~mrb~

```
            3~lrb~
            4~srh~
            5~mrh~
            6~lrh~
            7~ssb~
            8~msb~
            9~lsb~
            A~ssh~a~ssh~
            B~msh~b~msh~
            C~lsh~c~lsh~
            D~finger~d~finger~
            E~check~e~check~
            F~arrow~f~arrow~
            G~arrowhead~g~arrowhead~
            H~Xbox~h~Xbox~
            I~paragraph~i~paragraph~
            J~section~j~section~

        ~
    {Screen}r
    {QUIT}
    {LABEL}srb~
            {^V}4,3{Enter}
    {RETURN}

    {LABEL}mrb~
            {^V}4,0{Enter}
    {RETURN}

    {LABEL}lrb~
            {^V}4,44{Enter}
    {RETURN}

    {LABEL}srh~
            {^V}4,45{Enter}
    {RETURN}

    {LABEL}mrh~
            {^V}4,1{Enter}
    {RETURN}

    {LABEL}lrh~
            {^V}4,37{Enter}
    {RETURN}

    {LABEL}ssb~
            {^V}4,47{Enter}
    {RETURN}
```

```
    {LABEL}msb~
            {^V}4,2{Enter}
    {RETURN}

    {LABEL}lsb~
            {^V}4,46{Enter}
    {RETURN}

    {LABEL}ssh~
            {^V}4,49{Enter}
    {RETURN}

    {LABEL}msh~
            {^V}4,48{Enter}
    {RETURN}

    {LABEL}lsh~
            {^V}4,38{Enter}
    {RETURN}

    {LABEL}finger~
            {^V}5,21{Enter}
    {RETURN}

    {LABEL}check~
            {^V}5,23{Enter}
    {RETURN}

    {LABEL}arrow~
            {^V}6,21{Enter}
    {RETURN}

    {LABEL}arrowhead~
            {^V}6,27{Enter}
    {RETURN}

    {LABEL}Xbox~
            {^V}5,25{Enter}
    {RETURN}

    {LABEL}paragraph~
            {^V}4,5{Enter}
    {RETURN}

    {LABEL}section~
            {^V}4,6{Enter}
    {RETURN}

    {LABEL}exit~
            {Screen}
    {RETURN}
```

Creating an Invoice (INVOICE.WPM): A Complex Macro

The INVOICE.WPM macro prompts the user for the information necessary to complete an invoice. As the user responds, the macro creates the invoice. When the user has finished, the macro is saved under a user-specified file name.

Because the macro is heavily commented, this discussion does not include a line-by-line commentary but instead highlights several features of the macro. You will find it helpful to study this macro, and its comments, closely; several useful advanced techniques are employed in the macro.

Structure

The macro is structured into a main body and a set of subroutines. Execution runs through the main body, from top to bottom, passing through several loops on the way. {CALL} statements are used to execute labeled subroutines (and some of the subroutines call other subroutines). Incorporating some of the called subroutines into the main body of the macro is possible, but in a complex macro such as this one, you will find the macro much easier to read, troubleshoot, and revise if you break as much out into subroutines as you can.

Loops

In the main body of the macro, you will see a {FOR} loop nested inside a {WHILE} loop. The purpose of the {FOR} loop is to ensure that no more than 40 invoice items are listed on one page. The purpose of the {WHILE} loop is to keep repeating the item-entry instructions until the user signals (by entering the code 999) that all items have been entered.

If the count reaches 40 items, the {FOR}-loop exit condition is satisfied, and the {FOR} loop is exited. However, because the item code is not 999, the macro knows that the user has not finished entering items. Therefore, the outer {WHILE} loop continues to execute. The subroutine *{LABEL}newpage*, which begins a new page, is executed; the {FOR} loop is reinitialized to 1; and the process starts over again.

Note the {BREAK} statement inside the {FOR} loop. This statement permits the user to terminate item entry by entering 999 before the count of 40 has been reached. If you are using a {FOR} loop that you may need to terminate before the exit condition in the {FOR} statement has been satisfied—as is the case here—the use of the {BREAK} statement is the best way to accomplish such a termination. You will often find, however, that it is simpler and more elegant to replace the {FOR} loop with a {WHILE} loop and thus eliminate the {BREAK}.

{DISPLAY OFF} and {DISPLAY ON}

A number of {DISPLAY OFF} and {DISPLAY ON} codes are scattered throughout the macro. {DISPLAY OFF} codes are used to turn the display off in order to prevent prompts and menus from flashing on the screen and distracting the user. Although these {DISPLAY OFF}s are not strictly necessary—the macro will work just fine without them—including {DISPLAY OFF} (and {MENU OFF}) codes in your macros makes them more professional and polished.

If you simply turn the display off and leave it off, however, WordPerfect will not update the screen as information is entered. In this macro, you *want* the information to be shown on the screen as the user enters it so that the user can keep track of what is going on. Therefore, the macro uses {DISPLAY ON} codes to let the screen be updated with information.

"Decimal" Arithmetic

WordPerfect macros are limited to integer arithmetic. Unlike all practical general-purpose programming languages, the WordPerfect Programming Language provides no way to handle decimal numbers. You can simulate decimal arithmetic, however, if you know in advance how many decimal places are involved and whether the user can be trained to enter numbers without typing a decimal point.

The basic strategy, as implemented in this macro, is this:

- Enter all data as integers. For example, to enter a value of 1.98, the user would type *198*.

- Do all arithmetic with the data in integer format. For example, to multiply 1.98 by 7, the user should specify the arithmetic expression as *198*7*.

- Convert integers to the predetermined number of decimals when you are ready to insert the information into the document. You can accomplish this conversion through the {MID} and {LEN} commands.

Obviously, there are restrictions. If you are assuming two decimal places, you cannot, for example, multiply 1.98 by 7.39, because the answer would have four decimal places. But within limits, the technique demonstrated in INVOICE.WPM is useful, particularly when you need to handle data as dollars and cents.

In INVOICE.WPM, the user enters the data in integer format within the main body of the macro. The main body performs multiplication (quantity times price each) and addition (to accumulate the total of all items on the invoice). When the macro needs to display the data, the main body uses the {CALL} statement to have the *{LABEL}convert* subroutine convert the integer data into dollars and cents.

The INVOICE.WPM macro is as follows:

```
{;} -------------------------------------------------------------------------------
                         main body of the macro starts here~

{DISPLAY OFF}                         {;} to prevent confusing displays~
{ON CANCEL}{CALL}confirm~~            {;} if user presses Cancel~
{ON ERROR}{GO}notfound~~              {;} if INVFORM.WP is not found~
{Retrieve}invform.wp{Enter}           {;} get the INVFORM.WP template~
{;} create invoice header~
     {;} title the first page and insert the date~
     {Center}Invoice{Enter}
```

```
{Enter}
{Enter}
{Flush Right}{Date/Outline}t{Enter}
{Enter}
{Enter}
{;} enter "sold to" information~
SOLD TO:{Enter}
{DISPLAY ON}                   {;} so user can see what's happening~
{TEXT}name~Enter the customer's name: ~
{Tab}{VARIABLE}name~{Enter}{;} insert the name, go to next line~
{TEXT}addr~Enter the customer's street address: ~
{Tab}{VARIABLE}addr~{Enter} {;} insert the street address, go to next line~
{TEXT}city~Enter the customer's city: ~
{Tab}{VARIABLE}city~          {;} insert the city~
{ASSIGN}state~~
{WHILE}{LEN}state~!=2~        {;} only allow the user to enter a 2-character
                                  state abbrev~
    {TEXT}state~Enter 2-letter abbreviation for customer's state: ~
{END WHILE}
,  {VARIABLE}state~           {;} insert comma and space~
{TEXT}zip~Enter the customer's zip code: ~
     {VARIABLE}zip~{Enter}    {;} insert space and zip code~
{Enter}{Enter}               {;} insert two blank lines~
{;} insert style ItemTabs, which sets correct tabs for displaying individual
    items on the invoice and displays a title line~
    {DISPLAY OFF}             {;} user doesn't need to see this~
    {Style}{Search}ItemTabs{Enter} {;} search for a style by name~
    {Enter}                   {;} turn style on~
    {DISPLAY ON}              {;} let user see what's happening~
{;} get invoice items from user via keyboard input and insert each item into
    document~
    {ASSIGN}code~0~           {;} initialize item code~
    {ASSIGN}grtotal~0~        {;} variable to accumulate grand total~
    {WHILE}{VARIABLE}code~!=999~
                             {;} until user says all items entered~
      {FOR}items~1~40~1~      {;} maximum of 40 items per page~
        {TEXT}code~Enter the item code (999 to quit): ~
        {IF}{VARIABLE}code~!=999~
                             {;} if the user doesn't want to quit~
        {VARIABLE}code~
                             {;} insert item code into document~
        {TEXT}descrip~Enter a description: ~
        {Tab}{MID}descrip~0~30~
                             {;} insert first 30 characters of description
                                 into document~
        {TEXT}quan~Enter the quantity: ~
```

```
        {Tab}{VARIABLE}quan~
                        {;} insert quantity into document~
        {TEXT}eaprice~Enter the price each in cents (no decimals): ~
        {ASSIGN}integer~{VARIABLE}eaprice~~
                        {;} prepare to convert price each to dollars-
                            and-cents~
        {CALL}convert~   {;} call conversion routine~
        {Tab}{VARIABLE}decimal~
                        {;} insert price each in dollars-and-cents
                            into document~
        {ASSIGN}totprice~{VARIABLE}quan~*{VARIABLE}eaprice~~
                        {;} compute total price for this item~
        {ASSIGN}integer~{VARIABLE}totprice~~
                        {;} prepare to convert total price to dollars-
                            and-cents~
        {CALL}convert~   {;} call conversion routine~
        {Tab}{VARIABLE}decimal~
                        {;} insert total price in dollars-and-cents into
                            document~
        {ASSIGN}grtotal~{VARIABLE}grtotal~+{VARIABLE}totprice~~
                        {;} increase grand total by total price for this
                            item~
            {Enter}      {;} move to next line~
        {ELSE}           {;} user entered 999, wants to quit~
            {BREAK}      {;} go to statement after {END FOR}~
        {END IF}
      {END FOR}
      {IF}{VARIABLE}code~!=999~
                        {;} reached the end of the page, but user
                            has more items to enter~
            {CALL}newpage~   {;} prepare a new page~
        {END IF}
      {END WHILE}
  {;} format and display grand total, save invoice under user-specified
      filename~
        {ASSIGN}integer~{VARIABLE}grtotal~~
                        {;} prepare to convert grand total~
        {CALL}convert~       {;} call conversion routine~
        {Enter}              {;} insert a blank line~
        Total Amount Due
        {Flush Right}{Flush Right}   {;} dot leaders~
        $ {VARIABLE}decimal~         {;} insert $ sign and grand total~
        {CALL}filename~              {;} get a filename from user~
        {ON ERROR}{CALL}filename~~
                        {;} if the user enters an illegal name~
        {Save}{VARIABLE}fname~{Enter}
                        {;} save file under user-specified name~
```

```
    {RETURN}
{;} end of main body of the macro, start subroutines~
{;} -------------------------------------------------------------------------------- ~
{;} --------------------------------------------------------------------------------
    these subroutines implement the decimal display of quantitative information
    that has been entered as integers and arithmetically manipulated as
    integers~

{LABEL}convert~
{;} this subroutine converts an integer variable (named integer) into a
    decimal-formatted string variable (named decimal)~
    {IF}{VARIABLE}integer~<0&{LEN}integer~<4~
                                    {;} if neg. number less than 99~
        {IF}{LEN}integer~=2~        {;} if neg. number less than 9~
            {ASSIGN}decimal~–0.0{MID}integer~1~1~~   {;}  format it~
        {ELSE}                      {;} neg. number between 10 and 99~
            {ASSIGN}decimal~–0.{MID}integer~1~2~~    {;}  format it~
        {END IF}
    {ELSE}                          {;} all integers except neg. numbers less
                                        than 99~
        {IF}{LEN}integer~>1~        {;} not a single digit~
            {ASSIGN}dsize~{LEN}integer~–2~
                                    {;} length of "dollars" portion~
            {ASSIGN}cents~.{MID}integer~{VARIABLE}dsize~~2~~
                                    {;} last two digits are "cents"~
        {ELSE}                      {;} a single digit~
            {ASSIGN}dsize~0~        {;} length of "dollars" is 0~
            {ASSIGN}cents~.0{VARIABLE}integer~~
                                    {;} "cents" is .0 + last digit~
        {END IF}
        {IF}{VARIABLE}dsize~>6~     {;} 1,000,000 or more~
            {CALL}million~          {;} handles million-dollar variables~
        {ELSE}                      {;} 999,999 or less~
            {IF}{VARIABLE}dsize~>3~ {;} but 1,000 or more~
                {CALL}thousand~     {;} handles thousand-dollar variables~
            {ELSE}                  {;} 999 or less~
                {IF}{VARIABLE}dsize~~ {;} 1 or more~
                    {CALL}hundred~  {;} handles variables 1–999~
                {ELSE}              {;} must be 0~
                    {ASSIGN}dollars~0~ {;} so assign it a value of 0~
                {END IF}
            {END IF}
        {END IF}
    {ASSIGN}decimal~{VARIABLE}dollars~{VARIABLE}cents~~
                                    {;} put dollars with cents~
```

```
        {END IF}
{RETURN}

{LABEL}hundred~
        {;} this subroutine formats dollar values 1 through 999~
        {ASSIGN}dollars~{MID}integer~0~{VARIABLE}dsize~~~
                                {;} get dsize digits from front of integer~
{RETURN}

{LABEL}thousand~
        {;} this subroutine formats dollar values 1,000 through 999,999~
        {ASSIGN}i~{VARIABLE}dsize~–3~
                                {;} number of digits to precede comma~
        {ASSIGN}dollars~{MID}integer~0~{VARIABLE}i~~,~
                                {;} insert digits and comma~
        {ASSIGN}dollars~{VARIABLE}dollars~{MID}integer~{VARIABLE}i~~3~~
                                {;} insert remaining digits~
{RETURN}

{LABEL}million~
        {;} this subroutine formats dollar values 1,000,000 and up~
        {ASSIGN}i~{VARIABLE}dsize~–6~
                                {;} number of digits to precede 1st comma~
        {ASSIGN}dollars~{MID}integer~0~{VARIABLE}i~~,~
                                {;} insert digits and comma~
        {ASSIGN}dollars~{VARIABLE}dollars~{MID}integer~{VARIABLE}i~~3~,~
                                {;} 3 more digits and another comma~
        {ASSIGN}i~{VARIABLE}i~+3~  {;} position of first digit in hundreds~
        {ASSIGN}dollars~{VARIABLE}dollars~{MID}integer~{VARIABLE}i~~3~~
                                {;} last 3 digits~
{RETURN}
{;} -------------------------------------------------------------------------------------
        the next two subroutines implement the file-saving features~

{LABEL}filename~
{;} this subroutine gets a filename and calls the chkfile subroutine to make
        sure that the filename is not already in use~
        {ASSIGN}goodname~0~       {;} to enter the {WHILE} loop~
        {WHILE}{VARIABLE}goodname~=0~  {;} until we have a good name~
            {TEXT}fname~Filename for saving invoice: ~
                                {;} get name from user~
                {DISPLAY OFF}        {;} to prevent confusion~
                {CALL}chkfile~       {;} call routine to check filename~
        {END WHILE}
{RETURN}
```

```
{LABEL}chkfile~
{;} this subroutine makes sure that the filename in {VARIABLE}fname does not
    already exist~
        {List}                              {;} list files~
        {VARIABLE}fname~{Enter}             {;} list only files matching the variable
                                                name~
        {IF}{SYSTEM}list~=2~               {;} if number of items = 2, filename doesn't
                                                exist yet~
            {ASSIGN}goodname~–1~  {;} so it's a usable name~
        {END IF}
        {Exit}                              {;} exit from list files~
{RETURN}
{;} ---------------------------------------------------------------------------------------
    these are some miscellaneous subroutines~

{LABEL}confirm~
  {;} this subroutine finds out whether user meant to press Cancel~
    {CHAR}cancel~Do you want to cancel? No (Yes)~
                                    {;} get user to confirm Cancel~
    {IF}"{VARIABLE}cancel~"="Y" | "{VARIABLE}cancel~"="y"~
                                    {;} if user wants to cancel~
        {Exit}nn                    {;} user wants to cancel, so clear
                                        document~
        {QUIT}                      {;} end macro, return control to
                                        WordPerfect~
    {END IF}
{RETURN}                            {;} otherwise, simply continue with
                                        statement following where user pressed
                                        Cancel~

{LABEL}notfound~
  {;} this subroutine informs the user of the error and terminates operation~
    {ON CANCEL}
        {Cancel}
    {BELL}
    {PROMPT}Error: INVFORM.WP must be in the current directory~
    {WAIT}20~                       {;} leave message displayed 2 seconds~
{RETURN ERROR}

{LABEL}newpage~
  {;} this subroutine inserts a hard page and advances the cursor down
    12 lines~
    {HPg}                           {;} insert hard page~
    {Enter}{Enter}{Enter}{Enter}{Enter}{Enter}{Enter}{Enter}{Enter}
    {Enter}{Enter}{Enter}           {;} go down 12 lines~
    {Style}{Search}ItemTabs{Enter} {;} insert header line and set tabs~
    {Enter}                         {;} insert a blank line~
{RETURN}
```

Summary

In this chapter, you learned how to use the advanced macro commands, with which you can create menus, automate repetitive tasks, integrate WordPerfect's advanced features, and create complete applications systems. In learning the function and syntax of the various commands, you also were introduced to the following:

❑ Variables and the ways in which macros use them

❑ Mathematical operators

❑ Expressions and logical operators

❑ Control characters

❑ Subroutines

❑ {FOR}, {FOR EACH}, and {WHILE} loops

❑ Four advanced macros that demonstrate how advanced macro commands are used

---

[1] Holub, Allen I. *The C Companion*. Englewood Cliffs, N.J.: Prentice-Hall, 1987.

Assembling Documents with Merge

Stuart Bloom has been teaching people to program computers for 15 years; he extends his expertise in working with macros to this chapter on using merge commands.

Merge capabilities are expected in all but the most basic word processor. WordPerfect has had a rich set of merge capabilities from the program's beginning. But version 5.1 significantly increases these capabilities.

If you are an experienced WordPerfect user, you have some relearning to do. Although the old merge codes and techniques work in version 5.1, you will miss out on some useful capabilities if you don't learn the new way. The new way isn't harder—in some ways it's easier—and the principles are the same, but all the codes have changed. WordPerfect simplifies the transition by providing a method for automatically converting old merge files.

Cue:

You still can use the old merge codes in WordPerfect 5.1, but the new codes are easier to use and more powerful.

Reminder

If you use a mouse with WordPerfect 5.1, you can click the right button to display the pull-down menus, and then select the desired option. You also can press Alt-= to access the pull-down menus, and then press the appropriate letter of the desired option. For all the instructions, assume that if a block is required to activate a pull-down menu option, the text has been blocked before the pull-down menu is accessed. Instructions for pull-down menus and the mouse are marked with the mouse icon. Refer to Chapter 1 for more information about the mouse. ▭

Why Use Merge?

Merge is appropriate for almost any kind of document with *standard formatting* that needs to be used with *varying text*. Examples include form letters, fill-in forms, and mailing labels.

Merge is also useful when you have *boilerplate text* that needs to be combined with varying text. Examples include standard documents, such as legal contracts, and catalogs and lists.

You can maintain your list data in any database manager that can output in delimited text files. You can put your catalog formatting in WordPerfect files.

Understanding a Merge

A *merge* is a method of combining information that changes with information that does not. The result is a finished document. The basic process, shown in figure 13.1, can increase productivity because you need to enter only *once* any information that does not change.

Variable information can include a variety of text. Suppose that you decide to turn your address book into a WordPerfect merge application. The variable information includes names, addresses, and telephone numbers.

Fig. 13.1.
A merge that combines fixed information with variable information to produce a finished document.

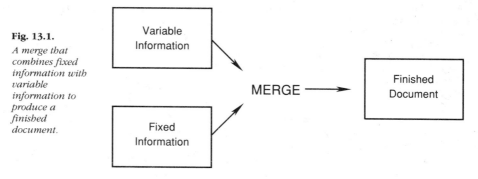

The *fixed information*, which is the same for each document, includes formatting codes and fixed text.

Providing the Fixed Information

You place the fixed information for a WordPerfect merge into a *primary merge file*, or *primary file*. Included are the formatting codes and any fixed text that go into each document. Included also in the primary file are codes that show where each item of variable information is to be placed.

When you tell WordPerfect to perform a merge, the program reads the information in the primary file. WordPerfect gets the variable information from the sources designated by the primary file and places that material in the indicated locations. The information in the primary file thus "controls" the merge.

Getting Variable Information into a Merge

WordPerfect provides several ways to get variable information into a merge. The most common—and most generally useful—method is to place the variable information in a *secondary-merge file*, or *secondary file*. A second method is to enter variable information directly from the keyboard at the time the merge is performed. A third method is to put variable information into regular WordPerfect text files.

Most of the discussion in this chapter pertains to the use of a secondary file. For details on entering variable information from the keyboard, see "Including Keyboard Input in a Merge" later in this chapter. For information on the use of WordPerfect text files, see the discussion of the {DOCUMENT} command in "Using Advanced Merge Commands To Control Order of Execution" later in this chapter.

Designing a Secondary File

Remember that a secondary file is one containing variable information to be inserted in a primary document during a merge. You must organize the secondary file so that WordPerfect can determine what information is to be used at each point in the primary file. You accomplish this by dividing a secondary file into *records* and *fields*.

Understanding Records

A *record* is one complete set of variable information. If, for example, you are using merge to create a set of mailing labels, a record is all the variable information to be included on one label. If you are using merge to produce a form letter, a record is all the variable information to be included in one letter. If you are using merge to assemble legal documents, a record is all the variable information to be included in one contract.

Understanding Fields

A *field* is one item of information in a record. If you are creating mailing labels, you can divide each record into the following fields:

- Recipient's name
- Street address
- City
- State
- ZIP code

Reminder:
Put variable information into records and fields in the secondary file.

If you are creating a form letter, each place where you want to insert an item of variable information defines a field. If you are assembling legal documents, you can define each paragraph as a field.

Using Different Kinds of Secondary Files

A secondary file can be a standard WordPerfect file that contains special codes marking the end of each record and the end of each field. You can include in the secondary file a number of other codes to handle special situations, but only two codes are required: a code to mark the end of a record, and a code to mark the end of each field within each record. You learn what the codes look like and how to enter them in "Building a Simple Merge" later in the chapter.

You can use secondary files maintained by Notebook, one of several useful programs marketed by WordPerfect Corporation in its WordPerfect Library package. A Notebook file is a standard WordPerfect merge file with some additional codes used strictly by Notebook. WordPerfect ignores these codes and treats the Notebook file exactly like a standard WordPerfect secondary file.

WordPerfect 5.1 can use changeable information stored in delimited DOS text files. *Delimited* simply means that within a DOS text file are formatting codes marking the end of each record and each field. You tell WordPerfect what these codes are through Setup (Shift-F1). More details about such files are provided later in "Using a DOS Text File as a Secondary File."

Reminder:

Delimited DOS text files can be used as secondary files.

Converting Old Merge Codes

This section is of interest only if you have used the merge capabilities of WordPerfect 5 or earlier versions, or if you need to understand the merge codes in a document prepared with earlier versions of the program.

The merge codes that existed in versions 4.2 and 5 are listed in table 13.1. Also shown are the new merge commands that are equivalent to the old codes. In some cases, the syntax of the command has changed slightly; for details about a particular command's use or its syntax, consult the appropriate section in the last half of the chapter. If you have a *primary* file created with version 4.2 (or earlier), you *must* use the technique described here to convert the codes.

Table 13.1
New Merge Commands with Equivalent Old-Style Merge Codes

New Command	Old Code	Meaning
{KEYBOARD}	^C	Pause for user input
{DATE}	^D	Insert the current date
{END RECORD}	^E	End of data for this secondary file record
{FIELD}*fieldname~*	^F*name*^	Field identifier in primary file
{CHAIN MACRO}*macro~*	^G*macro*^G	Execute macro after merge has finished
{NEXT RECORD}	^N	Move to next secondary-file record
{PROMPT}*message~*	^O*message*^O	Display message on-screen
{NEST PRIMARY}*file~*	^P*file*^P	Change primary file and then return to original when new file exits
{QUIT}	^Q	Terminate the merge
{END FIELD}	^R	End of data for this field
{SUBST SECONDARY}*file~*	^S*file*^S	Switch secondary files immediately
{PRINT}	^P	Send merged document to printer and clear from memory
{REWRITE}	^U	Rewrite the screen
{MRD CMND}*codes* {MRG CMND}	^V*codes*^V	Insert these codes in merged document

You can automatically convert to the new format a document containing old merge codes. To convert such a document, follow these steps:

1. Press Home, Home, Home, ↑ to move to the top of the document.
2. Press Merge/Sort (Ctrl-F9). The following menu appears:

   1 **M**erge; **2** **S**ort; **3** **C**onvert Old Merge Codes: **0**

3. Select **C**onvert Old Merge Codes (**3**). WordPerfect converts the codes for you.

Reminder:
WordPerfect 5.1 provides a quick and automatic way to convert old merge codes to the new format.

Tip

To convert codes back to the old format, save the document as a version 4.2 or version 5 document (see Chapter 16).

Building a Simple Merge

In this section, you learn the importance of planning a merge, and you see how to create the primary and secondary files necessary to perform a simple merge. You learn also how to tell WordPerfect to combine the files in a merge operation.

Deciding To Use Merge

Assume that you are an elementary school teacher and you need to schedule an appointment with the parents of each student to review the child's progress. You want to write a letter to the parents of each child, suggesting a date and time for the conference. The year before, you mimeographed a form letter and inserted by hand each child's name and the suggested date and time for the conference. This year, you want to make your letters look more professional. You decide to write a standard business letter. Would this be a good time to use a merge?

To answer that question, you must analyze the requirements. You want to say the same thing to each child's parents—you would like to tell them something about the purpose of the conference, to encourage them to attend, and to ask them to start thinking about questions they might want to ask. You have a fair amount of *fixed information* that is the same in each letter.

To make the communication more personal, however, you want to include in each letter the name and address of the addressees and the date and time of the meeting. It would also be nice to include the child's name in the letter. And it would be nice to include a personal salutation—for example, *Dear Mr. and Mrs. Richards*—instead of using *Dear Parent.* From these requirements, you can readily see that you have some *variable information* to include.

With both fixed and variable information to handle, you decide to use a merge to create the letters.

Planning the Merge

A few minutes spent planning a merge often saves you much time in entering data later. The planning process involves deciding what information is fixed and what information is variable, and then assigning names to each item of variable data.

Determining the Variable Data

The first step in planning a merge is to decide what the variable data is. In other words, you must decide what to put in the primary file (fixed data) and what to put in the secondary file (variable data).

Begin by looking at the information that will change from letter to letter. Figure 13.2 shows a list of students, the name and address of each child's parents, and the date and time of each proposed conference.

Fig. 13.2.
The variable data.

As you examine your list, notice a couple of patterns. First, all the parents live in the same city and state, but their ZIP codes vary. If you include the city and state in the variable data, you have to type *Chicago, Illinois* in each record in the secondary file. But if you include the city and state as fixed data, you have to type *Chicago, Illinois* only once—in the primary file. Because the ZIP code varies from letter to letter, you must include the ZIP code as variable data in the secondary file.

Notice also that all the appointments are in October. You therefore can include the name of the month (fixed data) in the primary file, and the day of the month (variable data) in the secondary file. The list of secondary data fields is shown in figure 13.3.

Fig. 13.3.
*The secondary
(variable) data
for the sample
merge.*

Parent's Name

Child's Name

Street Address

Zip

Salutation

Date

Time

Assigning Field Names

After you have decided on your variable data, you are ready to think about field names. Each item of variable data that is used independently should be designated as a field. Assign a *field name* to each item of variable data. Each field name should be short but descriptive, indicating what data is contained in the field. You can use one-word or multiple-word names; for example, you can use the name *Child* for the field that holds the name of the child, or you can call this field *Child Name*.

After giving the matter some thought, you decide on field names for the variable data. Your choices are shown in figure 13.4.

Parent
Child
StreetAddress
Zip
Salutation
Date
Time

Fig. 13.4.
Field names for the sample merge.

Creating the Primary File

Once you have decided on field names, you are ready to create the primary file. You create this file by typing the fixed information you want to appear in the finished document, including all necessary formatting. In each place where you want an item of variable data to appear, you insert a {FIELD} code and the name of each field. To include a field name, follow these steps:

1. Position the cursor at the exact place in the primary file where you want the variable data to appear in the finished document.

2. Press Merge Codes (Shift-F9) to display a menu bar at the bottom of the screen.

   Access the **T**ools pull-down menu and select Me**r**ge Codes to display the Merge Codes pop-out menu (see fig. 13.5).

3. Choose **F**ield (**1**).

4. At the Enter Field: prompt, type the name of the field exactly as you have defined it. For example, to enter the name of the Parent field, type *Parent.*

5. Press Enter.

WordPerfect inserts a {FIELD} code, followed by the name of the field and a tilde (~). The tilde tells WordPerfect where the field name ends. Figure 13.6 shows how the primary file (the primary document), appears on-screen with the {FIELD} code inserted. In earlier versions of WordPerfect, a field in a primary document was indicated by the ^F code.

Reminder:
The tilde following each field name tells WordPerfect where the field name ends. Do not delete the tilde.

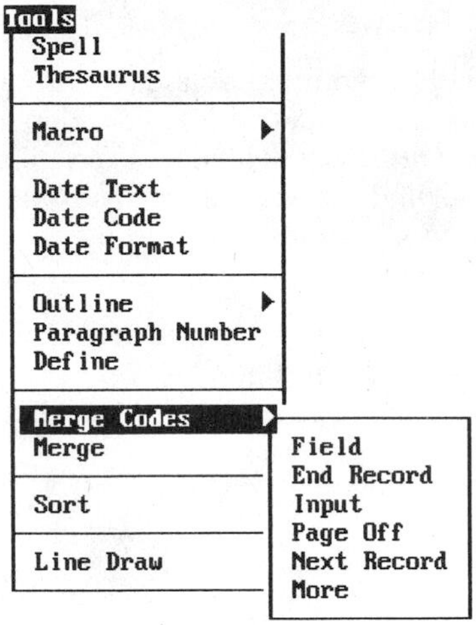

Fig. 13.5.

The Tools pull-down menu with the Merge Codes pop-out menu.

```
Tools
  Spell
  Thesaurus

  Macro              ▶

  Date Text
  Date Code
  Date Format

  Outline            ▶
  Paragraph Number
  Define

  Merge Codes        ▶    Field
  Merge                   End Record
                          Input
  Sort                    Page Off
                          Next Record
  Line Draw               More
```

Fig. 13.6.

The primary document with one {FIELD} code.

```
                        Jean Thomas
                  Buena Park Public School
                    1214 W. Buena Avenue
                   Chicago, Illinois 60613
                      (312) 404-1212


September 23, 1989



{FIELD}Parent~
```

Continue typing the primary document, inserting {FIELD} codes where they are needed. For this example, figure 13.7 shows the on-screen appearance of the document after you have finished typing it. Note that the Child field is used twice in the primary file; you can use an item of secondary data in the primary file as many times as you like by simply including a {FIELD} code and the field name.

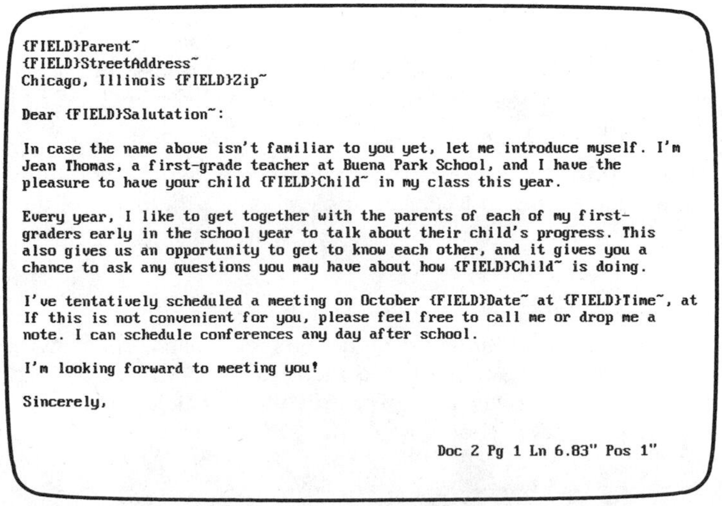

Fig. 13.7.

The primary document with all {FIELD} codes displayed.

```
{FIELD}Parent~
{FIELD}StreetAddress~
Chicago, Illinois {FIELD}Zip~

Dear {FIELD}Salutation~:

In case the name above isn't familiar to you yet, let me introduce myself. I'm
Jean Thomas, a first-grade teacher at Buena Park School, and I have the
pleasure to have your child {FIELD}Child~ in my class this year.

Every year, I like to get together with the parents of each of my first-
graders early in the school year to talk about their child's progress. This
also gives us an opportunity to get to know each other, and it gives you a
chance to ask any questions you may have about how {FIELD}Child~ is doing.

I've tentatively scheduled a meeting on October {FIELD}Date~ at {FIELD}Time~, at
If this is not convenient for you, please feel free to call me or drop me a
note. I can schedule conferences any day after school.

I'm looking forward to meeting you!

Sincerely,


                                      Doc 2 Pg 1 Ln 6.83" Pos 1"
```

After you have created the primary document, you will want to print it. The printed version, shown in figure 13.8, includes each field name followed by a tilde. The {FIELD} codes do not appear in the printed version of the document.

```
                        Jean Thomas
                  Buena Park Public School
                    1214 W. Buena Avenue
                   Chicago, Illinois 60613
                      (312) 404-1212


    September 23, 1989


    Parent~
    StreetAddress~
    Chicago, Illinois Zip~

    Dear Salutation~:

    In case the name above isn't familiar to you yet, let me introduce myself. I'm
    Jean Thomas, a first-grade teacher at Buena Park School, and I have the
    pleasure to have your child Child~ in my class this year.

    Every year, I like to get together with the parents of each of my first-
    graders early in the school year to talk about their child's progress. This
    also gives us an opportunity to get to know each other, and it gives you a
    chance to ask any questions you may have about how Child~ is doing.

    I've tentatively scheduled a meeting on October Date~ at Time~, at the school.
    If this is not convenient for you, please feel free to call me or drop me a
    note. I can schedule conferences any day after school.

    I'm looking forward to meeting you!

    Sincerely,


    Jean Thomas
```

Fig. 13.8.
A printed copy of the primary document, showing field names.

Creating the Secondary File

The secondary file includes the variable data for the merge. This data is arranged into fields and records. To create the secondary file (the secondary document), you need to take the following actions:

- Place at the beginning of the secondary file a special record that tells WordPerfect the name of each field.

- Enter the data for each record, field by field.

Inserting Field Names into a Secondary Document

In WordPerfect 5 and earlier versions, using named fields in a merge document was difficult (unless you were using the Notebook program in the WordPerfect Library). Therefore, most people didn't use named fields; they used numbered fields. The first field in a secondary-file record was Field 1, the second field was Field 2, and so on.

For records with just a few fields, this approach was satisfactory. If, for example, a record consisted of three fields—such as name, address, and telephone number— you could easily remember that *name* was Field 1, *address* was Field 2, and *telephone number* was Field 3. However, if you had more than, say, 10 fields for each record, you might not remember which field number was assigned to each item of variable data. Furthermore, you could easily lose track of the field number as you entered data. If you accidentally skipped a field, the results of the entire merge usually turned to gibberish.

In WordPerfect 5.1, using named fields is much easier—so much easier, in fact, that you will want to take the extra step necessary to use this capability. That step is to insert a special record at the beginning of the secondary file to tell WordPerfect what field names you have assigned. To insert the special record and the field names into your secondary document, complete these steps:

1. Begin a new document (the secondary file).

2. Press Merge Codes (Shift-F9) to display a menu bar at the bottom of the screen.

    ⌨ Access the **T**ools pull-down menu and select Me**r**ge Codes to display the Merge Codes pop-out menu.

3. Select **M**ore (**6**). The Merge Codes selection box appears (see fig. 13.9).

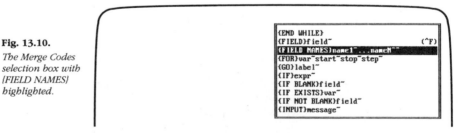

Fig. 13.9.
The Merge Codes selection box.

```
{ASSIGN}var~expr~
{BELL}
{BREAK}
{CALL}label~
{CANCEL OFF}
{CANCEL ON}
{CASE}expr~cs1~lb1~...csN~lbN~~
{CASE CALL}expr~cs1~lb1~...csN~lbN~~
{CHAIN MACRO}macroname~              (^G)
{CHAIN PRIMARY}filename~
```

4. Highlight the {FIELD NAMES} line in the Merge Codes selection box (see fig. 13.10). Either use the cursor keys to move the highlight bar to {FIELD NAMES}, or start typing the words *field names*.

    ⌨ Move the mouse pointer to the Merge Codes selection box. Press and hold the left mouse button. Drag the mouse to move the highlight bar to the bottom of the Merge Codes selection box; the list in the box scrolls. Drag the mouse to move the highlight bar to the {FIELD NAMES} line (see fig. 13.10).

Fig. 13.10.
The Merge Codes selection box with {FIELD NAMES} highlighted.

```
{END WHILE}
{FIELD}field~                          (^F)
{FIELD NAMES}name1~...nameN~~
{FOR}var~start~stop~step~
{GO}label~
{IF}expr~
{IF BLANK}field~
{IF EXISTS}var~
{IF NOT BLANK}field~
{INPUT}message~
```

5. With the highlight bar on {FIELD NAMES}, press Enter.

    ⌨ Double-click the {FIELD NAMES} line.

6. At the `Enter Field 1:` prompt, type the name of the first field. In this example, type *Parent*. Then press Enter.

> ## Caution
>
> In the secondary file, make sure that you type each field name *exactly* as you typed it in the primary file. If the field names in the two files are not the same, the merge *does not* work. If, for instance, you use *parent* in the primary file and *parents* in the secondary file, the merge fails.

7. WordPerfect responds with the prompt `Enter Field 2:`. Type the name of the second field. In this example, type *Child*. Then press Enter.

8. If you have more fields, continue to enter their names at the prompts. In this example, type *StreetAddress* for Field 3, type *Zip* for Field 4, type *Salutation* for Field 5, type *Date* for Field 6, and type *Time* for Field 7.

9. After you type the last field name, simply press Enter at the next prompt for a field name. The "empty" response tells WordPerfect that you are finished.

Reminder:
Pressing Enter in response to a prompt for a field name tells WordPerfect that you are finished entering field names.

After you finish entering all the field names, WordPerfect inserts a {FIELD NAMES} record at the top of the document, as shown in figure 13.11.

```
{FIELD NAMES}Parent~Child~StreetAddress~Zip~Salutation~Date~Time~~{END RECORD}
================================================================================
```

Field: Parent   Doc 1 Pg 2 Ln 1" Pos 1"

Fig. 13.11.
The secondary document after the {FIELD NAMES} record has been completed.

Notice that the {FIELD NAMES} record contains the following:

- The {FIELD NAMES} merge code at the beginning of the record. This tells WordPerfect that the record is special.

- The name of each field, just as you typed it.

- A tilde (~) at the end of each field name. The tilde tells WordPerfect where one name ends and the next one begins.

- An extra tilde and an {END RECORD} code after the last field name. These items tell WordPerfect where the record ends.

> **Tip**
>
> If you mistakenly press Enter before you type all the field names, you can still add field names to the list. See "Adding Fields to a Secondary File" later in this chapter.

Entering Fields and Records

Once you have the {FIELD NAMES} record in the secondary file, you are ready to begin entering the variable data.

Notice in figure 13.11 that the name of the first field is displayed in the lower left corner of the screen. WordPerfect knows, from the {FIELD NAMES} record, that you are in a secondary file. It also knows that the first field in each record is named *parent*.

To enter the record for the first student, Amy Bolcom, follow these steps:

1. Make sure that the cursor is at the top of page 2, immediately following the page break.

2. Type the names of the first child's parents exactly as you want the names to appear in the address block. In this example, type *Mr. and Mrs. George Bolcom*. Do *not* press Enter.

Cue:

In earlier versions of WordPerfect, the end of a field was indicated by the ˆR code.

3. Press End Field (F9). WordPerfect inserts an {END FIELD} code and a hard return after the name you have typed. The screen appears as shown in figure 13.12.

Fig. 13.12.
The secondary file with one field entered.

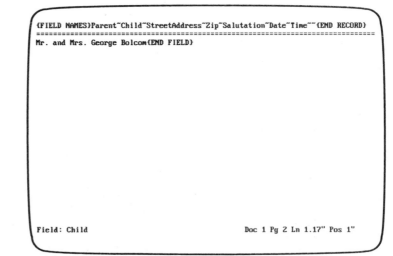

```
{FIELD NAMES}Parent~Child~StreetAddress~Zip~Salutation~Date~Time~~{END RECORD}
==============================================================================
Mr. and Mrs. George Bolcom{END FIELD}




Field: Child                                      Doc 1 Pg 2 Ln 1.17" Pos 1"
```

4. Notice that the field name indicator in the lower left corner has changed to Child. Type the name of the child. In this example, type *Amy*.

5. Press End Field (F9).

6. Type the rest of the information for the first record. Make sure that you press End Field (F9) at the end of each field, including the last one.

7. When you have entered all the fields for the Bolcoms, press Merge Codes (Shift-F9).

   ⌨ Access the **T**ools pull-down menu and select Me**r**ge Codes to display the Merge Codes pop-out menu.

8. Select **E**nd Record (**2**). An {END RECORD} code appears, followed by a hard page break (see fig. 13.13).

Cue:

In earlier versions of WordPerfect, the end of a record was indicated by the ^E code.

```
{FIELD NAMES}Parent~Child~StreetAddress~Zip~Salutation~Date~Time~~{END RECORD}
================================================================================
Mr. and Mrs. George Bolcom{END FIELD}
Amy{END FIELD}
4319 N. Racine{END FIELD}
60613{END FIELD}
Mr. and Mrs. Bolcom{END FIELD}
October 13{END FIELD}
3:30{END FIELD}
{END RECORD}
================================================================================




Field: Parent                          Doc 1 Pg 3 Ln 1" Pos 1"
```

Fig. 13.13.

The secondary file with a complete record entered.

9. Repeat steps 2 through 8 for each record. Make sure that you start each record on a separate page.

10. When you finish entering records, save the file. Choose a descriptive file name, such as NAMES.

Merging the Files

Performing a merge—no matter how complicated your primary and secondary files may become—is always the same, simple procedure. To perform a merge, follow these steps:

1. Start with an empty document.

2. Press Merge/Sort (Ctrl-F9). From the menu that appears, select **Merge** (**1**).

   ⌨ Access the **T**ools pull-down menu and select **M**erge.

3. At the `Primary file:` prompt, type the name of the primary file and press Enter. Make sure that you include the file extension and the path name, if necessary. If you have forgotten the name of the document, press List (F5) to see a list of files.

4. At the `Secondary file:` prompt, type the name of the secondary file (including the extension and path name, if necessary) and press Enter. Again, you can press List (F5) to see a list of files.

WordPerfect merges the primary file with the secondary file. While this is happening, WordPerfect displays the message `* Merging *` in the lower right corner of the screen; the rest of the screen is blank. When the merge is finished, WordPerfect displays the merged document on-screen. You can treat the document as you would any other WordPerfect document.

Caution

A merge operation creates the merged file in memory only. You must save the merged file if you want to reuse it.

Each record in the secondary file is represented by one letter in the merged document. WordPerfect inserts a hard page break between these letters. To prevent a page break, see "Suppressing Unwanted Text and Codes" later in this chapter.

Note: If you use the Document Summary feature (see Chapter 6), you may want to change the document summary for the merged file before you save it. Otherwise, the document summary information from the primary file is used for the merged file.

Handling Special Situations

The simple merge techniques described in the preceding section are adequate for many situations requiring merges. But WordPerfect has even more powerful merge capabilities. You can pick and choose from these capabilities for your particular merge needs. In this section, you learn to use some additional merge capabilities.

Using a DOS Text File as a Secondary File

WordPerfect 5.1 enables you to use a DOS text file as a secondary file. Virtually all database management programs can produce reports in a delimited format. Remember that *delimited* simply means that records and fields are separated by defined characters. In concept, then, a delimited DOS text file is equivalent to a WordPerfect secondary file—both have defined ways of separating records and separating fields.

Because different database programs use different characters as delimiters, WordPerfect lets you designate characters or codes as delimiters during a merge. The default delimiter that separates fields is the comma, and the default delimiter that separates records is the hard return.

You perform a merge with a DOS text file in the same way that you perform a merge with a WordPerfect secondary file. When the merge operation starts, WordPerfect recognizes that the secondary file is a DOS text file and displays the Merge: DOS Text File menu (see fig. 13.14). You use this menu to designate the delimiters present in your text file. You can designate a single character or multiple characters to mark the beginning and end of each field or record. (In many cases, you do not have to designate a beginning delimiter.) After you have defined the delimiters, proceed with the merge as normal.

If the default delimiters shown on the Merge: DOS Text File menu are correct for your file, simply press Enter to proceed with the merge. If, however, you need to change the delimiters, follow these steps:

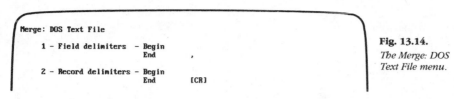

```
Merge: DOS Text File

    1 - Field delimiters  - Begin
                            End         ,

    2 - Record delimiters - Begin
                            End        [CR]
```

Fig. 13.14.
*The Merge: DOS
Text File menu.*

1. From the Merge: DOS Text File menu, select **F**ield delimiters (**1**) or **R**ecord delimiters (**2**). The procedure you follow is identical for either option.

2. To designate a Begin delimiter, type the character or characters present in the DOS text file to mark the beginning of the field or record. If, for example, you are defining field delimiters and the beginning of a field is designated by a double quotation mark, type ". If you need to enter special characters, use the following guidelines:

   - To insert a **[TAB]** character, press Tab.
   - To insert a line-feed character, press Enter. Line feeds are displayed by the symbol **[LF]**.
   - To insert a carriage return, press Ctrl-M. Carriage returns are displayed by the symbol **[CR]**.

3. Press ↓ to move to the End delimiter.

4. Repeat step 2 for the End delimiter.

5. Press ↓ to conclude the operation.

After you establish the field and record delimiters, press Enter to proceed with the merge.

If you ordinarily use DOS text files with a particular delimiter format, you can change the defaults for the DOS text-file option through Merge on the Setup: Initial Settings menu. Refer to Chapter 20 for instructions on using Setup.

Skipping Empty Fields

WordPerfect 5.1 offers a new method of skipping empty fields; this method replaces the ^Fn?^ code used in versions 4.2 and 5. The ^Fn?^ code enabled you to skip information at the end of a line. Like all the old merge codes, ^Fn?^ is still available in WordPerfect 5.1, but the method described in this section is more flexible. You can omit selected information no matter where that information appears in the primary file.

With merges, you often need to incorporate information that may, for some records, be blank. Suppose that you are creating a set of mailing labels for potential customers. You have defined the following fields in the primary file:

{FIELD}Name~, {FIELD}Position~
{FIELD}Department~
{FIELD}Company~
{FIELD}StreetAddress~
{FIELD}City~, {FIELD}State~ {FIELD}ZipCode~

This approach works fine, as long as the secondary file has all the information for each recipient. But suppose that you don't know the position for someone on the mailing list. The Position field in the secondary file is therefore blank. When you perform the merge, the label for that person looks like this:

Mr. Chester Riley,
Production Department
Forbes Aircraft Company
1313 Bluebird Terrace
Pasadena, CA 91107

Note the unwanted comma following the recipient's name.

Or suppose that you don't know the department for another recipient. That record in the secondary file therefore has a blank Department field. The merge produces this result:

Mr. Gilbert Kujala, Administrative Manager

Nichols Copper Works
7456 Old Fairburn Road
Atlanta, GA 30349

Neither of these results is satisfactory. Fortunately, WordPerfect provides a way to handle missing fields gracefully.

Reminder:

Enclose text or formatting codes within {IF NOT BLANK} and {END IF} commands to tell WordPerfect to omit the text or codes when a field is blank.

The key is to enclose the potentially missing data within a *conditional statement*. This statement consists of the merge commands {IF NOT BLANK} and {END IF}. You put an {IF NOT BLANK} command, followed by a field name and a tilde, immediately before any fixed information or formatting codes that you want omitted from the merged document if the field is blank. You put an {END IF} code after the text or codes to be omitted. Be sure to provide a tilde after the field name.

In the first example, if the Position field is blank, you want to skip the comma and the blank space. You therefore insert *{IF NOT BLANK}Position~* before the comma. After the blank space, you insert *{END IF}*. You are, in effect, telling WordPerfect to include these characters only if the Position field is not blank.

In the second example—a blank Department field—you want to eliminate the blank line if the Department field is blank. Accomplish this by enclosing the hard return at the end of the Department field line within the commands *{IF NOT BLANK}Department~* and *{END IF}*—to tell WordPerfect to include this hard return only if the Department field is not blank. Consider the following lines:

```
{FIELD}Name~{IF NOT BLANK}Position~, {END IF}{FIELD}Position~{END IF}
{FIELD}Department~{IF NOT BLANK}Department~
{END IF}{FIELD}Company~
{FIELD}StreetAddress~
{FIELD}City~, {FIELD}State~ {FIELD}ZipCode~
```

Note that it is not necessary to include the omitted field itself within the {IF NOT BLANK} and {END IF} commands. If the field is blank, WordPerfect simply ignores it. Including the field, however, does not constitute an error.

For more applications of conditional logic, see "Using Advanced Merge Commands To Make Decisions" later in this chapter.

Adding Fields to a Secondary File

Sometimes, no matter how carefully you plan a merge, you discover after you begin to create the secondary file that you need to add a field or two.

Before you enter any data, you can add a field anywhere within the field list simply by including the field name and a tilde. Assume, for example, that the existing field list looks like this:

{FIELD NAMES}Name~Position~Company~StreetAddress~City~State~ZipCode~~{END RECORD}

To add a Department field after the Position field, just insert the added field:

{FIELD NAMES}Name~Position~Department~Company~StreetAddress~City~State~ZipCode~~{END RECORD}

Note: You must save and retrieve the modified secondary file before WordPerfect recognizes the added field.

If you have already entered some data, adding a field is considerably trickier. Not only do you need to add the name to the field list, but you also must insert the field into *every existing record*. Because inserting a field into the wrong place in a record is easy to do—and if that happens, your merged file will probably become gibberish—you should add fields at the *end* of a record in the secondary file. Because you can use secondary-file fields in any order within the primary file, the fields don't need to be in any particular order in the secondary file—as long as every record in the secondary file has the same fields in the same order.

Reminder:

Always add fields at the end of a record in the secondary file.

If, for example, you added the Department field to the end of each record in the secondary file, the {FIELD NAMES} record would look like this:

{FIELD NAMES}Name~Position~Company~StreetAddress~City~State~ZipCode~Department~~{END RECORD}

You do not need to delete an unwanted field from the secondary file. Simply remove from the primary file the command (code) to use the unnecessary field. WordPerfect then ignores the field during the merge.

Inserting the Date

You may want WordPerfect to insert the current date into the merged document each time you perform a particular merge. You can accomplish this task by placing a {DATE} code in the primary file.

Note: The {DATE} merge code causes WordPerfect to insert the date on which the document is *merged*. If you want the date on which the document is *printed* to appear in the finished document, insert a date code using the Date Code feature of Date/Outline (Shift-F5). See Chapter 24 for more information.

To insert the date into the primary file, complete these steps:

1. Position the cursor at the point in the document where the date is to appear.
2. Press Merge Codes (Shift-F9) and select **M**ore (**6**).

    ⌨ Access the **T**ools pull-down menu, select Me**r**ge Codes, and choose **M**ore.

3. Highlight the {DATE} line in the Merge Codes selection box that appears. Either use the cursor keys to move the highlight bar to {DATE}, or start typing the word *date*.

⌨ Move the mouse pointer to the Merge Codes selection box. Drag the mouse to move the highlight bar to the {DATE} line.

4. With the highlight bar on the {DATE} line, press Enter.

⌨ Double-click the {DATE} line.

A {DATE} code appears in the document (see fig. 13.15).

Cue:

In earlier versions of WordPerfect, the date code was indicated by ^D.

```
                              Jean Thomas
                         Buena Park Public School
                          1214 W. Buena Avenue
                          Chicago, Illinois 60613
                             (312) 404-1212



        {DATE}



        {FIELD}Parent~
        {FIELD}StreetAddress~
        Chicago, Illinois {FIELD}Zip~

        Dear {FIELD}Salutation~:
```

Fig. 13.15.
The {DATE} code in the sample conference letter.

When you merge the primary file with the secondary file, the current date is inserted in the merged document.

Suppressing Unwanted Text and Codes

By default, WordPerfect inserts a hard page break in the merged document after the program finishes processing the data for each record in the secondary file. For many applications, such as creating a letter, this insertion is exactly what you want.

In some merge applications, however, you may want multiple records to appear on the same page in the finished document. To accomplish this, insert in the primary file a code that tells WordPerfect not to insert a hard page break after processing each record in the secondary file.

Suppose that you are using a merge file to produce a catalog for an office supply distributor (see fig. 13.16).

You want each catalog item to be recognized as a record. Yet you want more than one item to appear on a page. You can accomplish this by placing a {PAGE OFF} command at the end of each record in the primary file.

Reminder:

A {PAGE OFF} code inserted in the primary file tells WordPerfect to suppress a hard page break.

To suppress hard page breaks between records, complete the following steps, using the conference-letter example developed earlier in the chapter:

1. Position the cursor anywhere within the primary file.

2. Press Merge Codes (Shift-F9) and select **P**age Off (**4**).

⌨ Access the **T**ools pull-down menu, select Me**r**ge Codes, and choose **P**age Off.

A {PAGE OFF} code appears in the document (see fig. 13.17).

Magnifique-8 Laser Printer

8 page-per-minute laser printer. Create complete publications, presentation-quality graphics materials, much more on this state-of-the art laser printer. Two paper trays for ease of use. Advanced solid-state electronics. Price includes 1 MB memory, standard letter-size and legal-size paper trays, one toner cartridge.

Price Schedule:

1	2-5	6+
1,800.00	1,760.00	1,715.00

Magnifique-12 Laser Printer

12 page-per-minute laser printer. This printer has features similar to the Magnifique-8, but is for the truly high-volume operation. Can handle 11x17 sheets with optional 11x17 paper tray, *sold below*. This rugged, modern unit will handle the toughest jobs in any office. Price includes 2 MB memory, standard letter-size and legal-size paper trays, one toner cartridge.

Price Schedule:

1	2-5	6+
2,800.00	2,650.00	2,515.00

Letter-Sized Paper Tray

Standard letter-sized paper tray for the Magnifique-8 or Magnifique-12 printers. Capacity 225 sheets. Made of high-impact polystyrene.

Price Schedule:

1	2-6	7-12	12-20	21+
18.00	17.40	17.05	16.90	16.75

Legal-Sized Paper Tray

Legal-sized paper tray for the Magnifique-8 or Magnifique-12 printers. Capacity 225 sheets. Made of high-impact polystyrene.

Price Schedule:

1	2-6	7-12	12-20	21+
21.00	20.40	20.10	19.95	19.90

Fig. 13.16.
A sample catalog page.

```
{PAGE OFF}
                    Jean Thomas
              Buena Park Public School
                 1214 W. Buena Avenue
                Chicago, Illinois 60613
                   (312) 404-1212



September 23, 1989
```

Fig. 13.17.
The {PAGE OFF} code used to suppress hard page breaks between records.

Note: In earlier versions of WordPerfect, you had to insert three commands to achieve the result of the {PAGE OFF} command in version 5.1. The three commands were represented by ^N^P^P.

Merging Directly to the Printer

If you have a complex document or many records in the secondary file, the merged file can be quite large. A file in WordPerfect is limited only by the amount of disk space available. But even if your disk is large enough to handle the merged file, large files are cumbersome.

You can instead send the merged document directly to a printer, record by record. In other words, as soon as WordPerfect finishes merging the data from one secondary record, the merged result is sent to the printer. Because the merged document itself is cleared out by WordPerfect, the merge for each record begins with a new document. This approach prevents the creation of a large document.

The approach has some limitations, however. If you need to save the document for later reuse, you cannot do so. You also lose the ability to do any editing to the merged document before printing it. In addition, merges to the printer tend to be somewhat slower than regular merges; therefore, your computer is tied up for a longer period of time.

You create a merge to the printer by inserting a {PRINT} code into a document, instructing WordPerfect to send the document to the printer. Somewhere in the primary or secondary document, you must also include a {PAGE OFF} code. If you do not include this code, the printer ejects a blank sheet between records.

To merge to the printer, complete these steps:

1. Move the cursor to the top of the primary file.

2. Insert a {PAGE OFF} code. See "Suppressing Unwanted Text and Codes" earlier in this chapter for detailed instructions.

3. Move the cursor to the bottom of the primary file.

4. Press Merge Codes (Shift-F9) and select **M**ore (**6**).

   ▷ Access the **T**ools pull-down menu, select Me**r**ge Codes, and choose **M**ore.

5. Highlight the {PRINT} line in the Merge Codes selection box that appears. Either use the cursor keys to move the highlight bar to {PRINT}, or start typing the word *print*.

   ▷ Move the mouse pointer to the Merge Codes selection box. Drag the mouse to move the highlight bar to the {PRINT} line.

6. With the highlight bar on the {PRINT} line, press Enter.

   ▷ Double-click the {PRINT} line.

   A {PRINT} code appears in the document (see fig. 13.18).

Fig. 13.18.

The primary document showing the {PRINT} code for merging directly to the printer.

```
I've tentatively scheduled a meeting on {FIELD}Date~ at {FIELD}Time~, at the sch
this is not convenient for you, please feel free to call me or drop me a note.
I can schedule conferences any day after school.

I'm looking forward to meeting you!

Sincerely,



Jean Thomas{PRINT}

                                                        Doc 1 Pg 1 Ln 7.17" Pos 1.92"
```

Including Keyboard Input in a Merge

At the time you perform a merge, you may want to enter from the keyboard all or part of the information that is usually in the secondary file. When you choose this strategy, WordPerfect stops as it processes each record in the secondary file and waits for you to enter the data. This strategy is useful when some of the secondary-file information changes each time you do the merge.

Recall the previous example of scheduling conferences with parents. Suppose that you want to use the same secondary file to schedule spring appointments. You therefore decide not to include the date and time of each parent's conference in the secondary file, but to enter that data from the keyboard when you perform the merge.

Using this strategy, you place in the primary file an {INPUT} code, indicating where WordPerfect is to pause for keyboard input. You insert the keyboard input code *instead of* a field code.

When WordPerfect reaches the {INPUT} code for each copy of the merged document, the program pauses and displays on-screen the document, as merged to that point. In addition, WordPerfect displays a prompt, which you specify, on the status line. This prompt reminds you of the data to be entered at this point. You type the required data and, to signify that you have finished, press End Field (F9).

To indicate that WordPerfect should pause for keyboard input and then display a message indicating what the user is to do, follow these steps:

1. Place the cursor in the primary document at the place where the data entered from the keyboard is to be inserted.

2. Press Merge Codes (Shift-F9) and select **I**nput (**3**).

    ⌨ Access the **T**ools pull-down menu, select Me**r**ge Codes, and choose **I**nput.

    The Merge Codes selection box appears.

3. Highlight the {INPUT} line in the Merge Codes selection box. Either use the cursor keys to move the highlight bar to {INPUT}, or start typing the word *input.*

    ⌨ Move the mouse pointer to the Merge Codes selection box. Drag the mouse to move the highlight bar to the {INPUT} line.

4. With the highlight bar on the {INPUT} line, press Enter.

    ⌨ Double-click the {INPUT} line.

5. At the Enter Message: prompt, type the message you want to appear when WordPerfect pauses for input. For example, you can type *Type the conference date, then press F9.*

6. When you have typed the message, press Enter.

    An {INPUT} code, followed by the message, appears in the primary document. WordPerfect inserts a tilde after the message to indicate where it ends. The code and message appear as shown in figure 13.19.

Note: In earlier versions of WordPerfect, a prompt, enclosed by a pair of ^O codes, was shown in the primary document. A ^C code, which told WordPerfect to pause for keyboard input, appeared after the second ^O code.

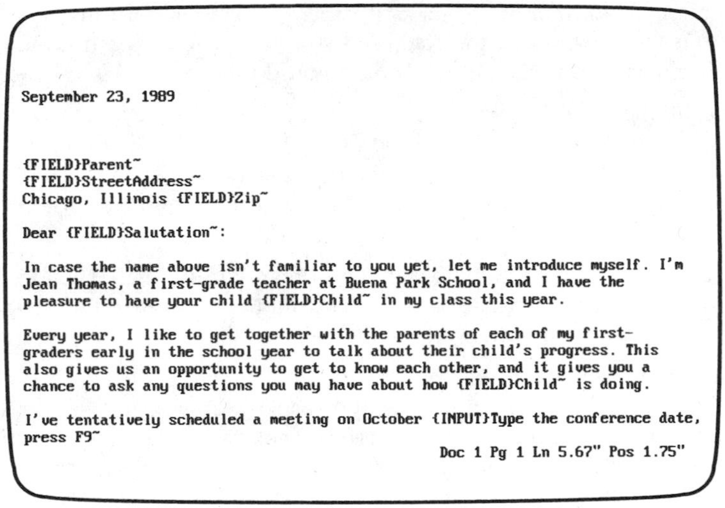

Fig. 13.19.

The {INPUT} code and message in the primary document.

```
September 23, 1989


{FIELD}Parent~
{FIELD}StreetAddress~
Chicago, Illinois {FIELD}Zip~

Dear {FIELD}Salutation~:

In case the name above isn't familiar to you yet, let me introduce myself. I'm
Jean Thomas, a first-grade teacher at Buena Park School, and I have the
pleasure to have your child {FIELD}Child~ in my class this year.

Every year, I like to get together with the parents of each of my first-
graders early in the school year to talk about their child's progress. This
also gives us an opportunity to get to know each other, and it gives you a
chance to ask any questions you may have about how {FIELD}Child~ is doing.

I've tentatively scheduled a meeting on October {INPUT}Type the conference date,
press F9~
                                                  Doc 1 Pg 1 Ln 5.67" Pos 1.75"
```

Preparing Special Primary Documents for Merges

In this section, two special types of primary documents are discussed: fill-in forms and mailing labels. You learn how to use WordPerfect's capabilities to create merges with these special kinds of documents.

Using Fill-In Forms

Suppose that you have a form like the one shown in figure 13.20 and you want to use the printer to fill in the blanks. You can use the Merge feature to speed up the process. Again, the merge process requires some preparation, but once you set up the procedure, it is easy to use.

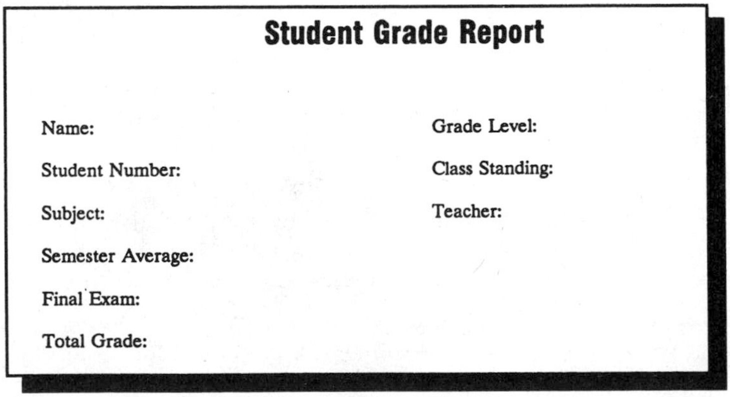

Fig. 13.20.

A sample preprinted form.

Student Grade Report

Name:	Grade Level:
Student Number:	Class Standing:
Subject:	Teacher:
Semester Average:	
Final Exam:	
Total Grade:	

You need to determine where merge codes are to be entered so that each field in the secondary file prints in the intended place on the form. The best approach is to take a copy of the form and, starting from the upper left corner, measure the exact distance to the beginning location of each entry to be made on the form. Mark the coordinates of each entry right on the form, as shown in figure 13.21. Also measure and mark the top, bottom, left, and right margins. If you have a constant distance height between lines on the form, measure the line height and note it on the form.

Student Grade Report

Name: *Line 2.1", Pos 2.3"*

Student Number: *Line 2.5", Pos 2.3"*

Subject: *Line 2.4", Pos 2.3"*

Semester Average: *Line 3.3", Pos 2.3"*

Final Exam: *Line 3.7", Pos 2.3"*

Total Grade: *Line 4.1", Pos 2.3"*

Grade Level: *Line 2.1", Pos 5.8"*

Class Standing: *Line 2.1", Pos 5.8"*

Teacher: *Line 2.1", Pos 5.8"*

Fig. 13.21.
A preprinted form with locations marked.

After you mark all the locations on the form and before you create the primary file, check that you have a paper definition with the appropriate size, location, and other characteristics. (See Chapter 6 for more information on defining paper sizes.) Select the appropriate paper size by following these steps:

1. Press Format (Shift-F8) and select **P**age (**2**).

   ⌨ Access the **L**ayout pull-down menu and select **P**age.

2. Select Paper **S**ize (**7**). The Format: Paper Size/Type menu appears (see fig. 13.22).

Format: Paper Size/Type

Paper type and Orientation	Paper Size	Prompt	Loc	Font Type	Double Sided	Labels
Envelope - Wide	9.5" x 4"	No	Manual	Land	No	
Standard	8.5" x 11"	No	Contin	Port	No	
Standard	8.5" x 14"	No	Contin	Port	No	
Standard - Wide	11" x 8.5"	No	Contin	Land	No	
Standard - Wide	14" x 8.5"	No	Contin	Land	No	
[ALL OTHERS]	Width ≤ 8.5"	Yes	Manual		No	

Fig. 13.22.
The Format: Paper Size/Type menu.

3. Highlight the appropriate paper size and choose **S**elect (**1**).

4. Press Exit (F7) to return to the document.

Now you are ready to create the primary file. Follow these steps:

1. Check the top, bottom, left, and right default margin settings for the form. Make sure that the margins are no larger than those you have measured and noted on the form. Refer to Chapter 6 for information on setting margins.

2. If the form has a constant line height, you can save a few operations by setting WordPerfect's line height to that of the form. To set the line height, refer to the instructions in Chapter 5.

3. Use the Advance feature (see Chapter 6) to position the cursor at the first field on the top line of the form. You probably will have to insert two advance codes: an advance-to-line code, which places the cursor at the correct vertical location; and an advance-to-position code, which places the cursor at the correct horizontal location.

4. Enter the appropriate merge code. If you are merging from a secondary file, enter a {FIELD} code. If you are merging from the keyboard, enter an {INPUT} code and a message. Refer to "Creating a Primary File" earlier in this chapter for instructions on entering {FIELD} codes. Refer to "Including Keyboard Input in a Merge" earlier in this chapter for instructions on {INPUT} codes and messages.

   Note: If you want to insert the current date, WordPerfect can do this automatically. For instructions, refer to "Inserting the Date" earlier in this chapter.

5. If additional fields are on the first line of the form, use the advance-to-position code to locate the cursor at each field. Insert the appropriate merge code at each position.

6. When you finish defining fields on the first line of the form, press Enter.

7. If you have set WordPerfect's line height to that of the form, you should be at the correct vertical position for the fields on the second line of the form. Otherwise, enter an advance-to-line code to position the cursor vertically. Enter an advance-to-position code to position the cursor horizontally.

8. Repeat steps 5 through 8 until you have finished all the fields on the form. Your on-screen form should look like the one shown in figure 13.23.

Fig. 13.23.
The primary file with merge codes only.

	Student Grade Report		
Name:	{FIELD}Name~	Grade Level:	{FIELD}Level~
Student Number:	{FIELD}Number~	Class Standing:	{FIELD}Stand~
Subject:	{FIELD}Subj~	Teacher:	{FIELD}Teacher~
Semester Average:	{FIELD}Semester~		
Final Exam:	{FIELD}Final~		
Total Grade:	{FIELD}TotalGrade~		

You are now ready to perform the merge operation. For instructions, refer to the earlier section "Merging the Files."

Using Mailing Labels

Mailing labels are one of the classic applications of merge capabilities. WordPerfect has always had the capability to create mailing labels. In WordPerfect 5.1, a new approach has been taken to positioning information correctly on label stock. In this section, you learn how to use the new Labels feature.

Creating a Label Definition

The first step is to create a *label definition*. You do this by defining a paper size and type showing the number of labels, the dimensions of each label, the arrangement of labels on the paper, and the margins you want to maintain on each label.

You need a ruler and a sample label sheet to help you create this definition. Once you have obtained these items, complete the following steps to create a label definition:

1. Press Format (Shift-F8) and choose **P**age (**2**).

   ⌨ Access the **L**ayout pull-down menu and select **P**age.

2. Select Paper **S**ize (**7**). The Format: Paper Size/Type menu appears (refer to fig. 13.22).

3. Select **A**dd (**2**). The Format: Paper Type menu appears.

4. Select **L**abels (**4**). The Format: Edit Paper Definition menu appears (see fig. 13.24).

```
Format: Edit Paper Definition

        Filename              HPLASEII.PRS

    1 - Paper Size            8.5" x 11"

    2 - Paper Type            Labels

    3 - Font Type             Portrait

    4 - Prompt to Load        No

    5 - Location              Continuous

    6 - Double Sided Printing No

    7 - Binding Edge          Left

    8 - Labels                No

    9 - Text Adjustment - Top  0"
                        Side   0"
```

Fig. 13.24.

The Format: Edit Paper Definition menu.

5. Choose **L**abels (**8**). At the No (Yes) prompt, select **Y**. The Format: Labels menu appears (see fig. 13.25). The defaults on this menu vary, depending on your printer.

Tip

If you want to enter dimensions in units of measure other than those in effect as your system defaults, enter the appropriate unit-of-measure code after each dimension. See Chapter 5 for details on units of measure.

---

6. Measure the size of one label on the sheet. Do not include the space between the labels. If the label is not the same size as that shown under Label Size on the Format: Labels menu, choose Label **S**ize (**1**). Type the actual width (the horizontal dimension) and length (the vertical dimension) of the label. Press Enter after you type each dimension.

Cue:

If the default for any dimension is correct for your labels, you don't need to reenter the information on the Format: Labels menu.

5.1

Fig. 13.25.

The Format: Labels menu.

```
Format: Labels

     1 - Label Size
                    Width              2.63"
                    Height             1"

     2 - Number of Labels
                    Columns            3
                    Rows               10

     3 - Top Left Corner
                    Top                0.5"
                    Left               0.188"

     4 - Distance Between Labels
                    Column             0.125"
                    Row                0"

     5 - Label Margins
                    Left               0.013"
                    Right              0.123"
                    Top                0"
                    Bottom             0"
```

7. If the number of labels on one sheet is different from the number shown under `Number of Labels` on the menu, choose **N**umber of Labels (**2**). Then type the number of columns (the side-to-side count) and the number of rows (the up-and-down count) of labels on the label sheet. Press Enter after you type each dimension.

8. Measure the distance from the top of the label sheet to the point where you want printing to start on the top left label. Also measure the distance from the left edge of the paper to the point where you want printing to start on the top left label. If either of these dimensions is different from the defaults shown under `Top Left Corner` on the menu, choose Top Left **C**orner (**3**). Type the dimensions you have measured for the top distance and the left distance. Press Enter after you type each dimension.

9. Measure the distance (the gap) between labels. If the Column distance shown under `Distance Between Labels` on the menu is different from the distance between adjacent labels (side to side), or if the Row distance shown on the menu is different from the distance between the bottom of one label and the top of the next label, select **D**istance Between Labels (**4**). Type the correct values for the Column and Row distances. Press Enter after you type each distance.

10. If any of the margins you want to maintain *on individual labels* is different from those shown under `Label Margins` on the menu, select Label **M**argins (**5**). Type the correct values for left, right, top, and bottom margins. Press Enter after you type each margin.

11. When you finish defining the labels, press Exit (F7).

    The Format: Edit Paper Definition menu reappears. The new definition is shown. You can identify this definition by the word `Labels` in the far left column and by the label arrangement in the far right column.

    If the paper you intend to use for labels is something other than standard continuous-form paper (or paper kept in the paper tray if you use a laser printer), or if you want WordPerfect to prompt you to load the paper, you may want to change other settings on this menu. See Chapter 6 for full information about using these options.

12. When you have completed work with the Format: Edit Paper Definition menu, press Exit (F7) three times to return to the document.

WordPerfect provides a macro, LABELS.WPM, that automatically creates label definitions for a variety of popular label sheets. You can run this macro and, if your labels are listed on the menu that appears, create the label definition you need. Refer to Chapter 11, "Creating Basic Macros," for information on how to run macros.

Using the Label Definition

To use the new label definition in a merge operation, you must first select the definition and then enter the merge commands needed to create the primary file. To select the definition, follow these steps:

1. Begin a new document. This document will become the primary file.
2. Press Format (Shift-F8) and select **P**age (**2**).

    🖱 Access the **L**ayout pull-down menu and select **P**age.

3. Select Paper **S**ize (**7**). The Format: Paper Size/Type menu appears.
4. Use the cursor keys to highlight the new definition.
5. Choose **S**elect (**1**).
6. Press Exit (F7) to return to the document.

You now can enter the {FIELD} commands (and other merge commands as well) to create the primary file for your mailing-label merge.

Dealing with Idiosyncrasies of Labels

WordPerfect creates each label as a *logical page*. If, for example, you have a paper size/type definition specifying 3 columns of labels and 10 rows, WordPerfect interprets the definition as 30 logical pages. All these logical pages are printed on the same sheet of paper, or—put another way—on a single *physical* page. This concept is new: it provides some significant capabilities but also introduces a few limitations. Some label properties you should know about are discussed in the following chart.

Page Size	Each label is a logical page. If you have defined the labels as being 1" high and 2.63" wide, WordPerfect sees a page of those exact dimensions. If you try to type more text than can fit on a page of that size, WordPerfect inserts a soft page break.
Headers, Footers, and Page Numbers	If you define a header for every page, that header appears on every *logical* page. If you define such a header for a 3-by-10 sheet of labels, you get 30 headers—one on each label. The same is true for footers or page numbers. If you want to number each *page* of labels, no straightforward method of numbering is available.
Printing Individual Pages	Because WordPerfect sees each label as a logical page, giving WordPerfect a command to print a single page causes

WordPerfect to do just that—print a single *logical* page (in other words, one label). This is *not* evident when you use the Print View feature, which shows a complete page of printed labels. But when you press Print (Shift-F7) and select **P**age (**2**), or when you designate anything other than All as a print-page range, you probably will not get what you expect. If you need to print less than the full document, the only reliable way to do so is to block the labels you want to print, and then print the block. Refer to Chapter 4 for more information about printing blocks.

Creating Advanced Merges

Most of the merge commands covered so far in this chapter have been available to WordPerfect users for many years. With version 5.1, you now have available a rich set of advanced merge commands that extend WordPerfect merge capabilities into the realm of programming. These merge capabilities nicely complement the advanced macro commands introduced in WordPerfect 5 and enhanced in version 5.1.

By using advanced merge commands, you can accomplish the following tasks:

- *Create conditional merges.* In a conditional merge, the primary file reads information located in the secondary file (or entered at the keyboard) and, based on that information, decides which of several actions to take.

- *Manipulate variables.* You can assign values to variables, perform mathematical calculations on variables, and format variables. (Variables are discussed in Chapter 12; for information about the special characteristics of WordPerfect variables, refer to "Understanding Variables" in Chapter 12.)

You also can use advanced merge commands to manage fields and records, to communicate with the user, to control the order of execution, to determine system status, to handle errors, and to control merge execution.

Using {COMMENT}

Reminder:

The {COMMENT} command causes WordPerfect to ignore a block of text, commands, or codes during a merge.

The {COMMENT} command causes WordPerfect to ignore a block of text, commands, or codes during a merge operation. Use the following syntax for {COMMENT}:

{COMMENT}*something*~

The argument *something* can be any text, characters, or codes you want. WordPerfect ignores the argument during a merge. In other words, the text does not appear in the merged document, the commands are not executed, and the codes have no effect.

Using {COMMENT} To Format Complex Statements

To make your merge files more readable, break up complex merge commands by placing each command on a separate line. If you need to change the files—or if you are looking for the cause of a problem—you will find that files with commands assigned to individual lines are much easier to read.

For the same reason, it's a good practice to indent any text and commands enclosed by a pair of merge commands that go together. Assume, for example, that you are creating mailing labels; you are using an {IF NOT BLANK} statement, which is always paired with an {END IF} statement. You could indent the lines this way:

    {IF NOT BLANK}Address~
      {FIELD}Address~
    {ENDIF}**[HRt]**

If you indent the text and codes affected by the {IF NOT BLANK} and {END IF} commands, you can look at the merge file and quickly see what commands are to be executed if the Address field is not blank. Although the advantage of indenting may not be fully evident in this simple example, when commands get more complex, you will find that logical and consistent indenting can save you much time by reducing confusion.

Cue:
Indent text and codes affected by a pair of commands.

These formatting practices are recommended for merge files and macros. When you write macros in the macro editor (see Chapter 11), you can accomplish this formatting by simply pressing Enter at the end of each line and using Tab to indent lines. When WordPerfect is executing a macro, the program knows to ignore the formatting within the macro file itself.

In merge files, however, things work differently. A merge file is a WordPerfect document file. WordPerfect interprets any hard returns or tabs in the primary file as hard returns or tabs, and therefore inserts the hard returns or tabs into every record in the merged file.

The same lines would look like this in Reveal Codes:

    {IF NOT BLANK}Address~**[HRt]**
    [Tab]{FIELD}Address~**[HRt]**
    {ENDIF}**[HRt]**

If the Address field is not blank, what is actually inserted into each mailing label is the following: a hard return, a tab, the contents of the address field, and two more hard returns. If the Address field contained *1313 Bluebird Terrace*, the mailing label would look like this:

> Mr. Chester Riley
>
>   1313 Bluebird Terrace
>
> Pasadena CA 94131

This is probably not how you want your mailing labels to look. You can solve the problem by putting the statement on one line:

    {IF NOT BLANK}Address~{FIELD}Address~{ENDIF}**[HRt]**

This solution works for simple statements like this one. But more complex statements are nearly impossible to write, read, and debug when they are written this way.

5.1

Consider an example used later for the {MID} and {LEN} commands. You would have to put that statement all on one line. Although this statement cannot be shown on one line in this book, WordPerfect keeps it on one line on-screen, and you would have to scroll the screen horizontally to see the entire statement:

{PAGE OFF}{FIELD}Item~**[Rgt Tab]**{FIELD}Quantity~**[Rgt Tab]**{MID}{FIELD}PriceEach~~0~{LEN}
{FIELD}PriceEach~~**[–]**2~.{MID}{FIELD}PriceEach~~{LEN}{FIELD}PriceEach~~**[–]**2~2~**[Rgt Tab]**{ASSIGN}
TotPrice~{FIELD}Quantity~*{FIELD}PriceEach~~{MID}{VARIABLE}TotPrice~~0~{LEN}{VARIABLE}
TotPrice~~**[–]**2~.{MID}{VARIABLE}TotPrice~~{LEN}{VARIABLE}TotPrice~~**[–]**2~2~**[HRt]**

WordPerfect *can* fit all this on one line (because the program knows that the merge commands themselves do not consume any space in the merged document). Still, you will find such a line extremely difficult to read.

Fortunately, there's a solution—using the {COMMENT} command. {COMMENT} tells WordPerfect, "Ignore my argument." In other words, the {COMMENT} command instructs WordPerfect to ignore anything between the {COMMENT} code and the tilde. You can use this command to insert hard returns, tabs, and other formatting commands that you don't want to appear in the merged document.

To use {COMMENT} with the {IF NOT BLANK} example, rewrite the expression this way:

{IF NOT BLANK}address~{COMMENT}**[HRt]**
[Tab]~{FIELD}address~{COMMENT}**[HRt]**
~{ENDIF}**[HRt]**

WordPerfect ignores the **[HRt]** code at the end of the first line and the **[Tab]** code at the beginning of the second line because these codes occur between the first {COMMENT} and its tilde. The **[HRt]** code at the end of the second line is ignored also, because that code occurs between the second {COMMENT} and *its* matching tilde. (You want to retain the **[HRt]** code after the {ENDIF} because that code moves you to the next line in the mailing label.)

With Reveal Codes turned off, the expression actually looks like the following:

{IF NOT BLANK}address~{COMMENT}
  ~{FIELD}address~{COMMENT}
~{ENDIF}

You can rewrite the second, more complex example this way:

{PAGE OFF}{COMMENT}**[HRt]**
~{FIELD}Item~**[Rgt Tab]**{COMMENT}**[HRt]**
~{FIELD}Quantity~**[Rgt Tab]**{COMMENT}**[HRt]**
~{MID}{FIELD}PriceEach~~0~{LEN}{FIELD}PriceEach~~**[–]**2~.{COMMENT}**[HRt]**
~{MID}{FIELD}PriceEach~~{LEN}{FIELD}PriceEach~~**[–]**2~2~**[Rgt Tab]**{COMMENT}**[HRt]**
~{ASSIGN}TotPrice~{FIELD}Quantity~*{FIELD}PriceEach~~{COMMENT}**[HRt]**
~{MID}{VARIABLE}TotPrice~~0~{LEN}{VARIABLE}TotPrice~~**[–]**2~.{COMMENT}**[HRt]**
~{MID}{VARIABLE}TotPrice~~{LEN}{VARIABLE}TotPrice~~**[–]**2~2~**[HRt]**

Reminder:
Using {COMMENT} to document merge files makes reading and troubleshooting them much easier.

Using {COMMENT} To Document Merge Files

You can include text between the {COMMENT} command and its tilde to explain what your commands mean. Documenting your merge files, particularly when the logic is complex, makes it easier to read and troubleshoot your files later.

You may want, for example, to include a comment explaining the meaning of the {MID} command:

>   {MID}{FIELD}PriceEach~~0~{LEN}{FIELD}PriceEach~~[–]2~.{COMMENT}
>   Insert all but the last two characters in the PriceEach
>   field into the merged document.~

Note the tilde at the end of the comment.

Using Advanced Merge Commands
To Manage Fields and Records

You can use a group of advanced merge commands to define fields in secondary files and to insert values from those fields into primary files.

The following commands are generally used in secondary files:

>   {FIELD NAMES}
>   {END FIELD}
>   {END RECORD}

These commands are used mainly in primary files:

>   {FIELD}
>   {NEXT RECORD}

{FIELD NAMES}

The {FIELD NAMES} command assigns names to fields in secondary files. Use the following syntax for {FIELD NAMES}:

>   {FIELD NAMES}*field1~field2~...fieldN~~*

The *field1* through *fieldN* arguments are names you assign to fields. The first field that appears in a record in the secondary file is designated with the first name assigned as an argument to the {FIELD NAMES} command, the second field is designated with the second argument, and so on.

You can define up to 100 field names. If you have more than 100 fields, you must use numbered fields for the 101st field and all additional fields.

Reminder:
For all fields over 100, you must use numbered fields instead of named fields.

Refer to "Assigning Field Names" earlier in this chapter for a discussion and an example of the {FIELD NAMES} command.

{END FIELD}

You use the {END FIELD} command in a secondary file to mark the end of a field. The syntax of this command is simple:

>   {END FIELD}

Refer to "Entering Fields and Records" earlier in this chapter for a discussion and an example of {END FIELD}.

{END RECORD}

You use {END RECORD} in a secondary file to mark the end of a record. Use the following syntax:

{END RECORD}

Again, see "Entering Fields and Records" earlier in this chapter for a discussion of this command and an example of its use.

{FIELD}

The {FIELD} command in a primary file indicates where the value of a secondary-file field should be used. {FIELD} requires the following syntax:

{FIELD}*fieldname~*

The argument *fieldname* is the name of the field, as defined in the {FIELD NAMES} statement in the secondary file. If you are using unnamed fields, this argument must be a number, referring to the location of the field in the secondary file. For example, the first field is {FIELD}1~, the second field is {FIELD}2~, and so on.

Reminder:
You can refer to a named field by its name or number.

You can refer to a field to which you have assigned a name by its name or number. If you have more fields than you have assigned names, you can refer to the unnamed fields by number. If, for instance, you have named five fields but your records have seven fields, you can refer to the first five fields by their assigned names or numbers. You can refer to the sixth and seventh fields by number only—{FIELD}6~ and {FIELD}7~—unless you add names for those fields to the {FIELD NAMES} record, as discussed earlier.

See "Creating a Primary File" earlier in this chapter for more information on the {FIELD} command and an example of its use.

{NEXT RECORD}

The {NEXT RECORD} command causes a merge to skip a record in the secondary file. Use the following syntax for {NEXT RECORD}:

{NEXT RECORD}

Typically, a merge uses the records in a secondary file in order. {NEXT RECORD} is used—often with conditional logic—to skip records.

The following command causes the merge to move to the next record if the value of the Quantity field is less than 10:

{IF}{FIELD}Quantity~<10~
  {NEXT RECORD}
{END IF}

If the value of the Quantity field is 10 or more, the current record is used.

Using Advanced Merge Commands
To Manipulate Variables

The advanced merge commands that you use most often with variables are {ASSIGN}, {LOCAL}, {VARIABLE}, {LEN}, and {MID}. If you are generally unfamiliar with variables or the special characteristics of WordPerfect variables, refer to "Understanding Variables" in Chapter 12.

{ASSIGN}

The {ASSIGN} command puts a value into a variable. {ASSIGN} requires the following syntax:

> {ASSIGN}*variable~value~*

Reminder:
The {ASSIGN} command puts a value into a variable.

The argument *variable* is the variable name. The argument *value* can be a field value, number, text string, or expression. An expression can consist of an arithmetic equation or another variable.

Suppose that you are performing a merge that combines, for a number of inventory items, the quantity of the item in stock with the value of one item (in cents) to produce a report that shows the total value of the inventory for the item. Assume that the secondary file contains the following data:

> {FIELD NAMES}Item~Quantity~PriceEach~~{END RECORD}
> ===
>
> Pencils{END FIELD}
> 307{END FIELD}
> 198{END FIELD}
> {END RECORD}
> ===
>
> Erasers{END FIELD}
> 98{END FIELD}
> 149{END FIELD}
> {END RECORD}
> ===

The primary file contains the following:

> {FIELD}Item~**[Rgt Tab]**{COMMENT}**[HRt]**
> {FIELD}Quantity~**[Rgt Tab]**{COMMENT}**[HRt]**
> {FIELD}PriceEach~**[Rgt Tab]**{COMMENT}**[HRt]**
> {ASSIGN}TotPrice~{FIELD}Quantity~*{FIELD}Price~~{COMMENT}**[HRt]**
> {VARIABLE}TotPrice~{PAGE OFF}**[HRt]**

The primary file inserts the three fields, separated by right tabs. The {ASSIGN} command then assigns the product of the Quantity and PriceEach fields to the variable TotPrice. The {VARIABLE} command displays the resulting TotPrice—the total retail value of the item in cents.

Here is the resulting output from the sample data:

Pencils	307	198	60786
Erasers	98	149	14602

See this chapter's discussion of the {MID} command to learn how to format the output in dollars and cents. For other examples, see the discussion of the {ASSIGN} command in Chapter 12.

{LOCAL}

Reminder:
When a merge ends, a variable created by the {LOCAL} command ceases to exist.

The {LOCAL} command is equivalent to the {ASSIGN} command, with one exception. Unlike all other variables in WordPerfect, variables created by the {LOCAL} command are local to the file and to the merge; when the merge ends, or when the merge accesses a different file, the variable ceases to exist. Use the following syntax for {LOCAL}:

{LOCAL}*variable~value~*

The argument *variable* is the variable name. The argument *value* can be a field value, number, text string, or expression. An expression can consist of an arithmetic equation or another variable.

Reminder:
When a global variable and a {LOCAL} variable have the same name, the {LOCAL} variable takes precedence.

If you give to a global variable (created with any other variable-creating commands, with a macro, or interactively from the keyboard) the same name as a {LOCAL} variable, the global variable is masked by the {LOCAL} variable. In other words, any commands using that name affect the {LOCAL} variable but not the global variable during the merge or in the file where the {LOCAL} variable was created. When WordPerfect exits from the file or the merge in which the {LOCAL} variable is in effect, the global variable has the value it had at the time the {LOCAL} variable was created.

You cannot give the same name to a {LABEL} variable and a {LOCAL} variable in the same file.

For an example of the {LOCAL} command, refer to the discussions of {ASSIGN} in this chapter and in Chapter 12. The output is exactly the same if {LOCAL} were used in place of {ASSIGN}.

{VARIABLE}

The {VARIABLE} command lets you access the contents of a variable. You use this command either to put the variable contents in a document or to use the contents in another command. Use the following syntax:

{VARIABLE}*name~*

The *name* is the name of existing variable. {VARIABLE} is used the same way in macros and merges. For a detailed discussion of the {VARIABLE} command, refer to Chapter 12. Refer also to the example presented for the {ASSIGN} command in this chapter.

{LEN}

The {LEN} command returns the length of an expression. Use the following syntax for {LEN}:

{LEN}*expression~*

The *expression* can be a variable, a field, or text. If the value of {FIELD}Item~ is *Deluxe Pencils*, for example, the following statement returns a value of 14:

{LEN}{FIELD}Item~~

For more examples of the use of {LEN}, see the next section on the {MID} command.

{MID}

The {MID} command is used to "take apart" an expression. {MID} returns a substring (that is, a part of the expression). Even if the expression is an integer, the value returned from the {MID} command is nonetheless a string value. {MID} requires the following syntax:

{MID}*expression~ offset~ count~*

The *expression* can be a variable or a field; *offset* is the number of the first character in *expression* that is to be included in the substring (counting the first character as 0). The *count* is the number of characters to include in the substring.

If the value of {FIELD}Item~ is *Deluxe Pencils*, the following statement returns the substring *Deluxe*:

{MID}{FIELD}Item~~0~6~

The first six characters form the value of the field, starting with the 0th (first) character.

WordPerfect macros and merges do mathematics only with integers (whole numbers). You can use the {MID} command to create a "decimal" answer if you know in advance the number of decimal places. For example, assume that the value of {VARIABLE}TotPrice~ is 652423. You know that this represents 652423 cents, or, expressed another way, $6524.23. You can use {MID} and {LEN} to place the decimal in the correct location. Use the following complete expression:

{MID}{VARIABLE}TotPrice~~0~{LEN}{VARIABLE}TotPrice~~−2~.{COMMENT}**[HRt]**
{MID}{VARIABLE}TotPrice~~{LEN}{VARIABLE}TotPrice~~−2~2~

This expression can be considered in two parts, each governed by a {MID} command. Here is the first part:

{MID}{VARIABLE}TotPrice~~0~{LEN}{VARIABLE}TotPrice~~−2~.

This part tells WordPerfect, "When you reach this command during the merge, take the variable TotPrice. Starting at character 0, return a substring. Calculate the substring by subtracting 2 (the number of decimal places) from the total length of the value of the variable. Then insert a decimal point." The first part of the statement, therefore, places *6524*. in the merged document.

The second part of the expression is the following:

{MID}{VARIABLE}TotPrice~~{LEN}{VARIABLE}TotPrice~~−2~2~

This part tells WordPerfect, "When you reach this command during the merge, take the variable TotPrice. Starting at a character determined by subtracting 2 from the total length of the value of the variable, take the next two characters." This second

Reminder:
When using {MID}, make sure that you start counting characters with zero (0).

part of the statement places *23* in the document. Because the second part immediately follows the first part, with no intervening spaces or returns, the result is the value *6524.23* in the merged document.

If you apply this technique to the earlier {ASSIGN} example, you have this complete statement:

{PAGE OFF}{COMMENT}**[HRt]**
{FIELD}Item~**[Rgt Tab]**{COMMENT}**[HRt]**
{FIELD}Quantity~**[Rgt Tab]**{COMMENT}**[HRt]**
{MID}{FIELD}PriceEach~~0~{LEN}{FIELD}PriceEach~~[–]2~.{COMMENT}**[HRt]**
{MID}{FIELD}PriceEach~~{LEN}{FIELD}PriceEach~~[–]2~2~**[Rgt Tab]**{COMMENT}**[HRt]**
{ASSIGN}TotPrice~{FIELD}Quantity~*{FIELD}PriceEach~~{COMMENT}**[HRt]**
{MID}{VARIABLE}TotPrice~~0~{LEN}{VARIABLE}TotPrice~~[–]2~.{COMMENT}**[HRt]**
{MID}{VARIABLE}TotPrice~~{LEN}{VARIABLE}TotPrice~~[–]2~2~**[HRt]**

When the primary file containing this statement is merged with the secondary data, you get this result:

Pencils	307	1.98	607.86
Erasers	98	1.49	146.02

Using Advanced Merge Commands To Communicate with the User

When you prepare merges, you may want to communicate with the user of the merge. You can use the {CHAR}, {TEXT}, and {LOOK} commands to get data from the user and put the data into a variable. You can use {INPUT} and {KEYBOARD} to pause the action of the merge to let the user take some action. You can use {PROMPT}, {STATUS PROMPT}, and {BELL} to give information to the user.

The following chart lists the commands used to communicate with the user. Refer to Chapter 12 for more information about these commands.

Command	Syntax	Description
{BELL}	{BELL}	Sounds a beep.
{CHAR}	{CHAR}*variable~ message~*	Accepts a single character (or any other single keystroke) and stores it in the specified variable. You can specify a message prompt to appear on the status line.
{LOOK}	{LOOK}*variable~*	Checks to see whether a character has been typed. If not, the contents of the specified variable are deleted.
{PROMPT}	{PROMPT}*message~*	Displays the specified message on the status line. When a key is pressed or another key command is encountered, the message disappears.

Command	Syntax	Description
{STATUS PROMPT}	{STATUS PROMPT} *message~*	Same as {PROMPT} except message remains until the merge executes an {INPUT} or another {STATUS PROMPT} command.
{TEXT}	{TEXT}*variable~ message~*	Similar to {CHAR} except {TEXT} accepts up to 120 characters.
{INPUT}	{INPUT}*message~*	Displays the specified message on the status line and pauses to let user take desired action. {INPUT} rewrites the screen. User must press End Field (F9) when finished (not Enter as in macros).
{KEYBOARD}	{KEYBOARD}	Rewrites the screen and pauses to let user enter information. User presses End Field (F9) when finished. {KEYBOARD} is the same as {INPUT} with a blank message prompt.

Using Advanced Merge Commands To Control Order of Execution

This section covers some of the commands that change the order of merge execution. These commands add tremendous power to what you can do with merges. If you have developed advanced WordPerfect macros or if you have experience in a programming language, you may be familiar with the concepts and commands discussed in this section.

Changing the Order of Execution

If no commands to change the order of execution are encountered, the primary file starts with the first record in the secondary file, creates a record in the merged file containing the information in that secondary record, and then does the same for the second record and for each remaining record in the secondary file. When the primary file has processed all the records, the merge terminates.

This approach is satisfactory for many merges. But to do more complex merge operations, you will want to change the order in which merges execute commands. Changing the order of execution is known as *branching*.

Reminder:
To change the order of merge execution, use advanced merge commands that implement branching.

You branch in merges by using commands that perform one of the following operations:

- Change the primary or secondary files and designate the time and conditions under which they are activated.
- Change the order in which commands within the primary file are executed.
- Change the order in which records within the secondary file are processed.

The commands that accomplish these operations can be divided into the following categories:

- Branching commands that call *subroutines*. The following advanced merge commands relate to subroutines:

{CALL}	{NEST MACRO}
{CASE}	{PROCESS}
{CASE CALL}	{RETURN}
{CHAIN MACRO}	{RETURN CANCEL}
{GO}	{RETURN ERROR}
{LABEL}	

- Branching commands that *repeat* a series of operations until a specified condition is satisfied. The following two kinds of loops are available for use with the merge commands:

{FOR} loops	{FOR} loops also use the commands {NEXT}, {BREAK}, and {END FOR}
{WHILE} loops	{WHILE} loops also use the commands {BREAK} and {END WHILE}

- Branching commands that *change* the primary or secondary file being used in the merge operation, or that *insert* information from separate files. The following advanced merge commands implement this type of branching:

{CHAIN PRIMARY}	{NEST SECONDARY}
{CHAIN SECONDARY}	{SUBST PRIMARY}
{DOCUMENT}	{SUBST SECONDARY}
{NEST PRIMARY}	

Other branching commands can be considered "general-purpose conditional commands." In WordPerfect, {IF} and its related commands are examples. Such commands are used for other purposes besides branching. For a discussion of the general-purpose commands, see "Using Advanced Merge Commands To Make Decisions" later in this chapter.

Using Subroutines

A *subroutine* is a set of merge commands and text that performs part of what needs to be done to accomplish the goal of the merge. Each subroutine is designated by a name.

The following chart lists the advanced merge commands that define subroutines and transfer control to subroutines. Refer to Chapter 12 for more information about these commands.

Command	Syntax	Description
{CALL}	{CALL}*label~*	Transfers control to the specified subroutine. When the subroutine is terminated by a {RETURN}, {RETURN CANCEL}, or {RETURN ERROR} command, the merge resumes execution with the command following the {CALL} command.

Command	Syntax	Description
{CASE}	{CASE}*expression~ case1~label1~case2~ label2~...caseN~ labelN~~*	Examines the result of an expression and branches to one of a number of subroutines, based on the result of the expression. After the subroutine finishes, control does *not* return to the calling routine.
{CASE CALL}	{CASE CALL}*expression~ case1~label1~case2~ label2~...caseN~ labelN~~*	Similar to {CASE} except that control *does* return to the calling routine.
{CHAIN MACRO}	{CHAIN MACRO}*filename~*	See following section.
{GO}	{GO}*label~*	Transfers control to the specified subroutine in the same file. Control *does not* return to the calling routine.
{LABEL}	{LABEL}*label~*	Identifies a subroutine by name.
{NEST MACRO}	{NEST MACRO}*filename~*	See following section.
{PROCESS}	{PROCESS}*code*{PROCESS}	Immediately executes the text, codes, or commands between the {PROCESS} codes.
{RETURN}	{RETURN}	Causes subroutine execution to cease and returns control to the calling routine.
{RETURN CANCEL}	{RETURN CANCEL}	Same as {RETURN}.
{RETURN ERROR}	{RETURN ERROR}	Same as {RETURN}.

{CHAIN MACRO}

{CHAIN MACRO} starts a macro executing *at the end* of the merge. Place {CHAIN MACRO} in the secondary file with the following syntax:

   {CHAIN MACRO}*filename~*

The argument *filename* is the file name of the macro to be chained. The file name does not have to include the WPM extension, but it may include a path name. The named macro must be in the currently active macro directory, or you must include the path to the macro in the *filename* argument.

The {CHAIN MACRO} command must be the last (or the only) {CHAIN MACRO} command to be executed during the merge. If a second {CHAIN MACRO} command is encountered, the first {CHAIN MACRO} command is canceled. Provided that the other necessary conditions are satisfied, the macro file named by the second {CHAIN MACRO} command is executed.

{NEST MACRO}

{NEST MACRO} causes a macro to be executed immediately. After the macro executes, the merge resumes at the point following the {NEST MACRO} command. Use the following syntax for {NEST MACRO}:

{NEST MACRO}*filename~*

The argument *filename* is the file name of the macro to be nested. The file name does not have to include the WPM extension but may include a path name. The named macro must be in the currently active macro directory, or you must include the path to the macro in the *filename* argument.

Putting the {NEST MACRO} command into a primary file causes the named macro to be executed once for each record. Putting {NEST MACRO} into a secondary file causes the macro to be executed once.

Using Loops

The basic principles of loops are discussed in "Using Loops" in Chapter 12. You should read that material if you are unfamiliar with the concept of looping. You use the advanced merge commands {FOR} and {WHILE} to create loops in the same way you use {FOR} and {WHILE} in macros.

Incorporating Other Files

In most cases, your merge will use a single primary file and a single secondary file. For more complex merges, you may need to use more than one primary file or one secondary file. The commands described in this section are used to accomplish such merges.

{CHAIN PRIMARY}

In a primary file, the {CHAIN PRIMARY} command executes the merge with the named primary file as soon as the current primary file finishes processing the current record in the secondary file. The new primary file begins with the first record of the current secondary file.

Use the following syntax for {CHAIN PRIMARY}:

{CHAIN PRIMARY}*filename~*

The argument *filename* is the name of the primary file to which control is to be chained. If the file is not in the current directory, you must include a path name.

The {CHAIN PRIMARY} command must be the last {CHAIN PRIMARY} command to be encountered during the merge. If a second {CHAIN PRIMARY} command is encountered, the first {CHAIN PRIMARY} command is canceled. Provided that other necessary conditions are satisfied, the primary file named by the second {CHAIN PRIMARY} command takes over when the current primary file finishes.

In the following example, the {CHAIN PRIMARY} command placed in a primary file starts the merge again, using the new primary file REPEAT.PRI:

{CHAIN PRIMARY}REPEAT.PRI~

REPEAT.PRI starts with the first record in the current secondary file. REPEAT.PRI starts as soon as the current primary file finishes with the current record in the secondary file.

{CHAIN SECONDARY}

In a secondary file, {CHAIN SECONDARY} continues the current merge operation but shifts to the named secondary file when the end of the current secondary file has been reached. This command requires the following syntax:

{CHAIN SECONDARY}*filename~*

The argument *filename* is the name of the secondary file, which is to be used when the end of the current secondary file is reached. If the file is not in the current directory, you must include a path name.

The {CHAIN SECONDARY} command must be the last {CHAIN SECONDARY} command to be encountered during the merge. If a second {CHAIN SECONDARY} command is encountered, the first {CHAIN SECONDARY} command is canceled; records in the file named by the new {CHAIN SECONDARY} command are then used to continue the merge.

{CHAIN SECONDARY} is useful when you have a large data base. You can break the secondary files into more manageable sizes and put a {CHAIN SECONDARY} command in each.

Assume, for example, that you have the secondary files listed in the left column of table 13.2. All the secondary files listed include several hundred records, and each file has the same named fields. Each secondary file includes also the command shown in the right column.

Table 13.2
Examples of the {CHAIN SECONDARY} Command

File Name	The {CHAIN SECONDARY} Command
DATA1.SEC	{CHAIN SECONDARY}DATA2.SEC~
DATA2.SEC	{CHAIN SECONDARY}DATA3.SEC~
DATA3.SEC	{CHAIN SECONDARY}DATA4.SEC~
DATA4.SEC	None

Suppose that you start a merge with the primary file PROCESS.PRI and the secondary file DATA1.SEC. PROCESS.PRI processes all the records in DATA1.SEC. Then, because of the {CHAIN SECONDARY}DATA2.SEC~ command in DATA1.SEC, PROCESS.PRI processes all the records in DATA2.SEC. PROCESS.PRI next processes all the records in DATA3.SEC and then all the records in DATA4.SEC. Because no {CHAIN SECONDARY} command is included in DATA4.SEC, the merge terminates when the last record in DATA4.SEC has been processed.

5.1

{DOCUMENT}

Reminder:
*{DOCUMENT}
inserts a named
document into a
merged file.*

The {DOCUMENT} command inserts a named document into the merged file. None of the codes in the document are processed; the document is inserted exactly as it exists on disk. Use the following syntax for {DOCUMENT}:

{DOCUMENT}*filename~*

The argument *filename* is the name of the file to be inserted. If the file is not in the current directory, you must include a path name.

{NEST PRIMARY}

In a primary file, {NEST PRIMARY} transfers control of the merge to a named primary file. When the nested primary file has finished processing the current record in the secondary file, control returns to the original primary file. Use the following syntax for {NEST PRIMARY}:

{NEST PRIMARY}*filename~*

The argument *filename* is the name of the primary file to which control is to be transferred. If the file is not in the current directory, you must include a path name.

{NEST SECONDARY}

{NEST SECONDARY} causes the currently executing primary file to process all the records in the named secondary file. After all the records in the nested file have been processed, the primary file returns to the original secondary file and resumes processing with the first record following the {NEST SECONDARY} command. Use the following syntax:

{NEST SECONDARY}*filename~*

The argument *filename* is the name of the secondary file to be processed. If the file is not in the current directory, you must include a path name.

{SUBST PRIMARY}

The {SUBST PRIMARY} command is equivalent to the {CHAIN PRIMARY} command, with one exception. Control is transferred to the named file immediately, rather than at the end of the current primary file's normal processing cycle. As with {CHAIN PRIMARY}, control with {SUBST PRIMARY} does not return to the original primary file when the new primary file has finished processing. {SUBST PRIMARY} requires the following syntax:

{SUBST PRIMARY}*filename~*

The argument *filename* is the name of the primary file to which control is to be transferred. If the file is not in the current directory, you must include a path name.

{SUBST SECONDARY}

{SUBST SECONDARY} is equivalent to {CHAIN SECONDARY}, with one exception. The new secondary file is substituted for the current secondary file immediately, rather than after all records in the current secondary file have been processed. As

5.1

with {CHAIN SECONDARY}, with {SUBST SECONDARY} the primary file does not return to the original secondary file after finishing with the new secondary file.

Using Advanced Merge Commands To Make Decisions

When creating advanced merges, you frequently need to take action based on the answer to a question. You may need to execute a series of commands based on the value of a variable. Or you may need to assign to a variable a value based on that of a field in a secondary-file record.

Decision-making logic in WordPerfect merges is implemented with a few basic commands. Two of these—{CASE} and {CASE CALL}—are included in "Using Advanced Merge Commands To Control Order of Execution" earlier in this chapter.

Reminder:

Decision-making logic is implemented in merges with {IF}, {IF EXISTS}, {IF BLANK}, and {IF NOT BLANK}.

{IF}

{IF} is used the same way in macros and merges. Use the following syntax for {IF}:

> {IF}*expression*~

If *expression* evaluates to true, a designated set of commands is executed. If *expression* evaluates to false, the commands are not executed, or the set of commands preceded by {ELSE} are executed. For a discussion of {IF} structures and their logic, refer to Chapter 12.

{IF EXISTS}

The {IF EXISTS} command is used the same way in macros and merges. {IF EXISTS} requires the following syntax:

> {IF EXISTS}*variable*~

{IF EXISTS} checks the specified variable to see whether the variable contains a value. If there is a value, a designated set of commands is executed. If there is no value, the commands are not executed, or the set of commands preceded by {ELSE} are executed. Refer to Chapter 12 for a discussion of {IF EXISTS} structures and their logic.

{IF BLANK} and {IF NOT BLANK}

{IF BLANK} executes a set of commands conditionally, depending on whether a field has a value. If the field does not have a value, the {IF BLANK} statement evaluates to true, and a designated set of commands is executed. If the {IF BLANK} statement evaluates to false, the commands are not executed, or the set of commands preceded by {ELSE} are executed.

{IF NOT BLANK} works the same way, except that it evaluates to true if the field is *not* blank—that is, if the field has a value. The {IF NOT BLANK} command is the equivalent of the {IF EXISTS} command; {IF NOT BLANK} applies the same test to fields that {IF EXISTS} applies to variables. Use the following syntax for {IF BLANK} and {IF NOT BLANK}:

{IF BLANK}*field~*
{IF NOT BLANK}*field~*

For an example of the {IF BLANK} command, see "Suppressing Unwanted Text and Codes" earlier in this chapter.

Using Advanced Merge Commands To Determine System Status

As you create merges, you often find that you need to know key facts about the current status of the system. Refer to "Determining System Status" in Chapter 12 for some examples of the kinds of system information you can obtain. You use the advanced merge commands {CTON}, {NTOC}, and {SYSTEM} to determine system status.

The following chart lists the advanced merge commands used to determine system status. Refer to Chapter 12 for detailed descriptions of the functional equivalents of these commands: {KTON}, {NTOK}, and {SYSTEM}.

Command	Syntax	Description
{CTON}	{CTON}	Takes a WordPerfect key and returns a code number corresponding to that key.
{NTOC}	{NTOC}	Takes a code and returns the value corresponding to a WordPerfect key.
{SYSTEM}	{SYSTEM}*sysvar~*	Determines the current status of the specified system variable. Table 12.12 lists the variables you can substitute for *sysvar*.

Using Advanced Merge Commands To Handle Errors

WordPerfect's native error-handling capabilities are quite sophisticated. But the authors of WordPerfect could not have predicted everything you want to do with your merges. The commands in this section enable you to handle errors in a way that *you* determine they should be handled. You can use these commands, within limits, to bypass or supersede WordPerfect's default error-handling activities.

The following chart lists the advanced merge commands used to handle errors. Refer to Chapter 12 for more information about these commands.

Command	Syntax	Description
{CANCEL OFF}	{CANCEL OFF}	Deactivates the Cancel (F1) key until the merge terminates or {CANCEL ON} is encountered.

Command	Syntax	Description
{CANCEL ON}	{CANCEL ON}	Activates the Cancel (F1) key.
{ON CANCEL}	{ON CANCEL}*action*~	Temporarily reprograms the Cancel (F1) key; also takes control when a subroutine returns a {RETURN CANCEL} command.
{ON ERROR}	{ON ERROR}*action*~	Tells WordPerfect what to do if an error occurs during the merge.
{QUIT}	{QUIT}	Immediately terminates the merge and returns control to WordPerfect.

Using Advanced Merge Commands To Control Merge Execution

This group of commands enables you to control certain aspects of the execution of a merge. These commands are useful for debugging merges and may be useful when you need to control how fast a merge executes.

{STEP ON} and {STEP OFF}

The {STEP ON} command causes the merge to display information at the bottom of the screen as the merge executes. The user must press a key after the display of each item. {STEP OFF} causes the merge to execute normally again. Use the following syntaxes for these commands:

    {STEP ON}
    {STEP OFF}

{STEP ON} is useful in debugging merges. With {STEP ON}, you can see what is happening as the merge executes. If the next step in the merge is a character, the character is displayed. If the next step is a keystroke, the keystroke is displayed. If the next step is a merge command, the merge command is displayed. The current value of a variable is displayed immediately after the tilde following the variable name.

Reminder:
Controlling the execution of a merge with {STEP ON} is helpful in debugging merges.

{STOP}

The {STOP} command terminates execution of the merge operation immediately. Control returns to the main WordPerfect program. If the primary file has been nested, the {STOP} command overrides the nesting; control does not return to the calling file. Any chain commands are also ignored. {STOP} has the following syntax:

    {STOP}

In the following example, if the value of the Count field is zero, the merge ends and control returns to WordPerfect:

    {IF}{FIELD}Count~=0~
      {STOP}
    {END IF}

{WAIT}

The {WAIT} command inserts a timed pause, specified in tenths of a second, into the merge. {WAIT} is used the same way in macros and merges. {WAIT} requires the following syntax:

{WAIT}*10ths_second~*

See the discussion of {WAIT} in Chapter 12.

Using Miscellaneous Advanced Merge Commands

The merge commands in this section fall into no easily definable category. They accomplish a variety of tasks.

The following chart lists the miscellaneous advanced merge commands.

Command	Syntax	Description
{DATE}	{DATE}	Inserts the current date (the date of the merge). For an example, see "Inserting the Date" earlier in this chapter.
{MRG CMND}	{MRG CMND} *something* {MRG CMND}	Enables you to place text, commands, and codes into a secondary file and have these elements inserted directly into the merged document. The elements are not processed by the primary file.
{PAGE OFF}	{PAGE OFF}	Suspends automatic generation of a hard page break between records in the merged document.
{PAGE ON}	{PAGE ON}	Resumes automatic generation of hard page breaks.
{PRINT}	{PRINT}	Sends everything currently in memory to the default printer and clears the document from memory. For an example, see "Merging Directly to the Printer" earlier in this chapter.
{REWRITE}	{REWRITE}	Rewrites the screen.

Summary

In this chapter, you learned how to use WordPerfect's merge capabilities. Specifically, you learned the following tasks:

- ❏ How to build and perform simple merges
- ❏ How to improve merges by incorporating advanced merge commands
- ❏ How to develop sophisticated conditional merges based on secondary-file contents or keyboard input

Sorting and Selecting Data

Forest Lin, Ph.D., an expert on WordPerfect products, wrote this chapter for *Using WordPerfect 5*.

Stuart Bloom has used WordPerfect's data management features in his work of developing and maintaining catalog listings for professional organizations. He revised this chapter for *Using WordPerfect 5.1*, Special Edition.

Robert M. Beck wrote the section in this chapter about sorting tables, a new feature with WordPerfect 5.1. Mr. Beck is a computer consultant for small to medium-size law offices.

The Sort feature provides some important functions you can use to manage data. Sort can manipulate data in several ways; for example, it can sort items by line, paragraph, or table. Sort also can select (extract) items that meet specific criteria.

Although WordPerfect's Sort feature cannot match specialized database management programs in power or features, it has enough versatility to handle relatively simple data management problems. When Sort is combined with other WordPerfect features—such as Search, Replace, Merge, Math, Table, and Macros—it becomes a useful management tool.

You can improve WordPerfect's built-in data management functions by using the Notebook program included in WordPerfect Office (a product marketed separately by WordPerfect Corporation and formerly called WordPerfect Library). Notebook works directly with WordPerfect merge files to make easier editing, sorting, selecting, and browsing through merge files.

Reminder

If you use a mouse with WordPerfect 5.1, you can click the right button to display the pull-down menus, and then select the desired option. You also can press Alt-= to access the pull-down menus, and then press the appropriate letter of the desired option. For all instructions, assume that if a block is required to activate a pull-down menu option, the text has been blocked before the pull-down menu is accessed. Instructions for pull-down menus and the mouse are marked with the mouse icon. For more information about the mouse, see Chapter 1. ⌨

Understanding Sort Basics

This section introduces basic terms, the options you use in the Sort menu, and the techniques you need to create a simple database, which you use in the next section.

Learning Database Terms

A *database* is a collection of data. A database consists of *records*, which in turn consists of *fields*, which in turn contain *words*, the smallest units. A record is a collection of related pieces of information; each piece of information in a record is stored in a field; a word is a combination of letters or numbers in a field. A *table* used as a database consists of records, cells, lines, and words. See "Sorting a Table" later in this chapter for more information.

To use a concrete example, an address list is a simple database. All the pieces of information relating to one person constitute a record. Each piece of information—such as name, street number, city, state, and ZIP code—is placed in a separate field. The pieces of information must be entered in the correct fields: names in the first field, streets in the second, and so on. If the information is not arranged properly, WordPerfect cannot manipulate it properly.

A database is saved as a file with a unique name to distinguish the database file from other files. Like any WordPerfect file, a database can be as large as disk space permits.

WordPerfect can manipulate four types of records: a line, a paragraph, a secondary-merge file record, or a table. A *line record* ends with a hard or soft return; a *paragraph record* ends with two hard returns. You must distinguish between line sort and paragraph sort because using an improper sort can distort a database. As explained in Chapter 13, a *secondary-merge file* contains records, each of which has fields. A field in a secondary-merge file ends with an {END FIELD} code, and a record ends with {END RECORD} (these codes are new in version 5.1). Tables are sorted in a completely different manner, as explained in "Sorting a Table" later in this chapter.

When you create a line or paragraph database, fields are separated by tab codes. Suppose that you want to create a database containing the names, home phone numbers, and office phone numbers of your sales contacts. In each line, you enter a name and press Tab; enter the home phone number and press Tab; and finally enter the office phone number and press Enter to end the line (record). When data is arranged in this manner, WordPerfect understands that names are in the first field, home phone numbers are in the second field, and office phone numbers are in the third field.

A field can hold one or more words. A word can contain any printable character or number and is separated from other words with a space. In the address-list example, the first field can have a name with two or more words, each separated with a space. When you want to sort the names, you tell WordPerfect which word in that field it is to use to do the sort.

When you sort a database other than a table, WordPerfect asks you for an input and an output file. An *input file* is the database, saved on disk, that you want to sort;

an *output file* is the sorted (or selected) file, which you can send to the screen or save on disk. You also can sort data that appears on the screen and send the sorted data to the screen.

WordPerfect can sort numeric or alphanumeric records in *ascending* (from low to high) or *descending* (from high to low) order. Numerics are sorted according to their arithmetic values; alphanumerics are sorted according to ASCII values, except that uppercase and lowercase letters are placed next to each other. (In true ASCII order, the lowercase alphabet as a group appears *after* the uppercase alphabet.) For example, the second line of the following example is an ascending alphanumeric sort of the items in the first line:

A B C D a b c d 1 2 3 4 ! @ # – + ( )

– ! ( ) + # @ 1 2 3 4 A a B b C c D d

Mastering the Sort Menu

At the beginning of each sorting operation, after you specify input and output files, WordPerfect displays the Sort menu (see fig. 14.1). You must understand the menu thoroughly before you can use Sort effectively, particularly if you intend to do complex maneuvers. (The Sort menu that appears when you sort a table is different from the menu shown in fig. 14.1; refer to "Sorting a Table" later in this chapter.)

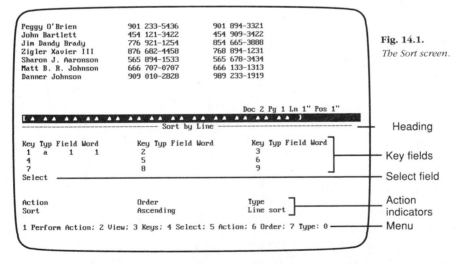

Fig. 14.1.
The Sort screen.

The Sort screen is divided into five areas. The first area, the heading, shows the preset default `Sort by Line`. The second area shows nine keys, each of which has three fields where you can enter the criteria to sort your data. The third area is the Select field where you enter the formulas to select (extract) specific records from a database. The fourth area indicates the Action, Order, and Type (which coincides with the heading) of the sort. The fifth area, at the bottom of the screen, shows the menu with seven options, which are explained in the next few paragraphs.

The first menu option, **P**erform Action (**1**), instructs WordPerfect to begin sorting using the key or keys, selected criteria, action, order, and type shown on the rest of the Sort screen. Before you select this option, make sure that the type and order of the sort specify the kind of sort you want to do.

When you select the **V**iew (**2**) option, the cursor jumps to the data to be sorted. You can move the cursor around to view the data, but you cannot edit. Press Exit (F7) to return to the Sort menu.

The **K**eys (**3**) option enables you to define and change the *keys* (criteria) used to sort. Because nine keys are represented on the display, you can establish nine sets of criteria by which to sort the file. When you select **K**eys (**3**), the bottom of the screen displays the following instructions:

Type: a = **A**lphanumeric; **n** = **N**umeric; Use arrows; Press **Exit** when done

The cursor jumps to the first item in the first key. You now can move the cursor to make changes—to add or delete, for example. Press Ctrl-End to delete all the entries in all the key fields except Key 1.

The default values in Key 1 are preset at a 1 1. These values mean that the Sort type is alphanumeric and that the first word in the first field is to be used as the basis for sorting.

Negative values can be entered in each key. For example, if you want to use the third word from the end of the field as the basis for the sort, enter *−3* under the Word category.

If sorting by Key 1 results in ties (equal values, such as same names or numbers), you can use Key 2, Key 3, and so on, to break the ties. If the database has many records with *Smith* as the last name, for example, you may want to specify Key 1 as the last names (type *−1* under Word), Key 2 as the first names (type *1* under Word), and Key 3 as middle names (type *2* under Word).

Note: The key choices are slightly different if you are sorting a table; refer to "Sorting a Table" later in this chapter for more information.

The **S**elect (**4**) option on the Sort menu lets you enter a formula so that you can direct WordPerfect to select certain records. This option is explained in greater detail in "Using the Select Function" later in this chapter.

Action (**5**) is activated after you choose **S**elect (**4**). **A**ction (**5**) provides two options: **S**elect and Sort (**1**) and Select **O**nly (**2**). Choose the first option to sort selected records; choose the second option only to select the records.

The **O**rder (**6**) option enables you to choose an **A**scending (**1**) or **D**escending (**2**) order for your sort.

The **T**ype (**7**) option produces the following choices for the type of sort you want to perform:

Type: 1 Merge; **2 L**ine; **3 P**aragraph: **0**

These options are explained in "Understanding the Four Kinds of Sort" later in this chapter.

Building a Simple Data Set

Figure 14.2 shows a sample set of data that this chapter uses to explain how to use the Sort function. If you want to follow the examples in this chapter, you should enter this data into your computer. Each name is one field, home phone is one field, and office phone is one field. Each person is one record. This database has, therefore, three fields and seven records.

```
                    SALES CONTACTS 1

Name                Home Phone        Office Phone

Peggy O'Brien       901 233-5436      901 894-3321
John Bartlett       454 121-3422      454 909-3422
Jim Dandy Brady     776 921-1254      854 665-3888
Zigler Xavier III   876 682-4458      768 894-1231
Sharon J. Aaronson  565 894-1533      565 678-3434
Matt B. R. Johnson  666 707-0707      666 133-1313
Danner Johnson      909 010-2828      989 233-1919
```

Fig. 14.2.

A sample database.

If you intend to experiment with this data, don't type the heading lines for now. If you do add the heading lines (the headings at the tops of the three columns), you must block the database (excluding the headings) before sorting or selecting (see "Sorting a Block" later in this chapter).

Before entering the records (lines), change the tab stops. Relative tab stops at +2.5" and +4.5" work well with this database. To change the tab stops, press Format (Shift-F8), select **L**ine (**1**), and select **T**ab **S**et (**8**) to go to the Tab Set screen. Select relative tabs by pressing T and R. Erase the existing tab stops by pressing Home, Home, ←, and Ctrl-End. Enter tabs at +2.5" and +4.5" by typing *2.5* and pressing Enter, and then typing *4.5* and pressing Enter. Exit from the Tab Set screen by pressing Exit (F7) twice.

Start typing the information shown in figure 14.2. Press Tab after you enter each field. The three fields must be separated by **[Tab]** codes. If you press the space bar to move the cursor to the next field, WordPerfect cannot sort the records correctly. When you come to the end of a record (line), press Enter. Following these instructions satisfies the sort requirement that each record is separated by a **[HRt]** (hard return) code and each field by a **[Tab]** code.

If you want to keep a database you have created, always save it before sorting it or selecting records from it. After a sorting operation, the database on-screen may be distorted; having a backup file is convenient. Save a database just as you do a standard document file.

Cue:
Save the database before you perform a sort or select operation.

Understanding the Four Kinds of Sort

Sort can manipulate four kinds of databases: a line, a paragraph, a secondary-merge file, and a table. You use a different type of sort for each kind of database. Use a line sort when records are lines, a paragraph sort when records are paragraphs, and a merge sort when sorting a secondary-merge file.

Sorting by Line

You can use the address database shown earlier in this chapter to learn the simple technique of sorting by line. The detailed procedures for this operation are given later in this section. Before you begin, however, you should understand the general procedure you follow for any type of sort.

Regardless of the type of sort you do, you start with these five steps:

1. Press Merge/Sort (Ctrl-F9) and select **S**ort (**2**) from the following menu:

   1 Merge; **2 S**ort; **3 C**onvert Old Merge Codes: **0**

   ⌨ Access the **T**ools pull-down menu and select **S**ort.

2. When the prompt Input file to sort: (Screen) appears, type the file name of the desired database and press Enter. If you want to sort the database displayed on-screen, just press Enter.

Reminder:

If you specify the same file name for the input file and the output file, the sorted output file overwrites the original input file.

3. When the prompt Output file for sort: (Screen) appears, type the file name where you want the output data to be placed and press Enter. If you use the input file name, the new (sorted) file overwrites the original database. If you give a different name, the sorted file is saved as a separate file.

   If you are not familiar with Sort, direct the output (sorted) file to the screen. If a sorting operation is not satisfactory, you can try again. When the Sort works as you want, you can save the file over the original or as a new file.

   After you specify an output file name and press Enter, the Sort menu appears (see fig. 14.1).

4. Select **T**ype (**7**) to change the type of sort you want to perform. Select **M**erge (**1**), **L**ine (**2**), or **P**aragraph (**3**).

5. Select **P**erform Action (**1**).

After you have performed the preliminary steps for a sort (but not yet selected **P**erform Action), the screen is divided into two halves. The top half displays the first lines of the file you want to sort; the bottom half shows the Sort screen (refer to fig. 14.1).

If you select **P**erform Action (1) without changing any of the options on the sort menu, the result appears as shown in figure 14.3. WordPerfect has sorted the lines by first names—that is, by the first word in the first field of each record.

Fig. 14.3.

Records sorted by first name.

```
                          SALES CONTACTS 1

Name                      Home Phone         Office Phone

Danner Johnson            909 010-2828       989 233-1919
Jim Dandy Brady           776 921-1254       854 665-3888
John Bartlett             454 121-3422       454 909-3422
Matt B. R. Johnson        666 707-0707       666 133-1313
Peggy O'Brien             901 233-5436       901 894-3321
Sharon J. Aaronson        565 894-1533       565 678-3434
Zigler Xavier III         876 682-4458       768 894-1231
```

Reexamine the Sort menu in figure 14.1; you can see that this menu requested a sort by these criteria (the first word in the first field). If you want to sort by last name, you must change some items in the menu.

Display the Sort menu and select **K**eys (**3**). The cursor jumps to Key 1, resting at the a under the Type category. The a indicates that the sort is based on alphanumeric items—anything containing characters and numbers. For this example, you do not have to change this setting. Press → to move the cursor to the 1 under the Field category. Because you want to sort based on the first field, this category needs no change. Press → again to move the cursor to the 1 under the Word category. Because you do *not* want to sort by the first word (first name), change this number. Type *–1* to replace the default value of 1. Typing *–1* directs WordPerfect to sort by the last word (the first word from the end) in the field.

Because the database contains two records with the same last name, you should set up the sort to use first names to break such a tie. Press → three more times to move the cursor to the Word category in Key 2; Key 2 now shows the default values a 1 1. Press Exit (F7) to return the cursor to the bottom of the screen. Select **P**erform Action (**1**); the results of this new sort are shown in figure 14.4.

Reminder:

Enter values in the Key 2 fields to break potential ties that result from Key-1 criteria.

SALES CONTACTS 1

Name	Home Phone	Office Phone
Sharon J. Aaronson	565 894-1533	565 678-3434
John Bartlett	454 121-3422	454 909-3422
Jim Dandy Brady	776 921-1254	854 665-3888
Zigler Xavier III	876 682-4458	768 894-1231
Matt B. R. Johnson	666 707-0707	666 133-1313
Danner Johnson	909 010-2828	989 233-1919
Peggy O'Brien	901 233-5436	901 894-3321

Fig. 14.4.
Records sorted by last name.

Notice that Zigler Xavier III is misplaced in this sort. During the sort, WordPerfect used the last word in the field (in this case, III). To remedy this odd situation, replace the space between *Xavier* and *III* with a hard space: delete the space, press Home, and then press the space bar. Press Reveal Codes (Alt-F3 or F11) to see the **[ ]** code connecting the two words. From now on, the two words are treated as one and are sorted correctly (see fig. 14.5).

SALES CONTACTS 1

Name	Home Phone	Office Phone
Sharon J. Aaronson	565 894-1533	565 678-3434
John Bartlett	454 121-3422	454 909-3422
Jim Dandy Brady	776 921-1254	854 665-3888
Matt B. R. Johnson	666 707-0707	666 133-1313
Danner Johnson	909 010-2828	989 233-1919
Peggy O'Brien	901 233-5436	901 894-3321
Zigler Xavier III	876 682-4458	768 894-1231

Fig. 14.5.
The final sort of records by last name.

Sorting by Paragraph

Reminder:

A paragraph database (called a free-form database*) separates records with two hard returns.*

A database can contain records made up of paragraphs, where the records are separated by two consecutive hard returns. Such a database gives you considerable freedom to organize your data. The records no longer have to adhere to the rigid structure of lines and fields. A record can be one line or a full page, as long as one record is separated from the next record with two hard returns. A database made up of paragraphs is often referred to as a *free-form database*, or simply a *text base*.

As the freedom to organize data increases, the room to manipulate data decreases—the price you pay for not adhering to rigid structure. If you enter data without adhering to a structure, you limit your ability to manipulate data. In a paragraph database, for example, you no longer can sort by line, field, or word. Even if you could find a way to sort under certain circumstances, the sorting would be relatively meaningless.

To make a paragraph database more manageable, however, you can add *some* structure. For example, you can designate the first one or two lines of each record for certain uniform items, each entered into a fixed field. After designating the fixed fields, the rest of the entry can be free-form. Figure 14.6 is an example of this compromise arrangement.

Fig. 14.6.

A paragraph database with fixed fields in the first row.

```
                        SALES CONTACTS 2

       Name                   Home Phone        Office Phone

       Sharon J. Aaronson      565 094-1533      565 670-3434
       Met in Chicago computer show. Info manager for IMB Co., a large
       retail chain of soft goods. Her company is in the market for a
       large number of new PC's within a year. Good prospect of selling
       out products.

       John Bartlett           454 121-3422      454 909-3422
       VP for finance of ABC Finance C. The company has a large fund to
       finance startup high-tech ventures. Could be tapped if future
       clients need financing to purchase our products.

       Jim Dandy Brady         776 921-1254      854 665-3088
       A slick salesman, dynamic, has an impressive record. Met him a
       few times in different computer shows. Could hire him if we need
       more salespeople.

       Zigler Xavier III       876 602-4458      876 094-1231
       Dynamic positive-thinking, fast-talking, sometimes mouth-foaming
       professional speaker. Heard him speak to enthusiastic audiences.
       Could invite him to talk to our salespeople. Fee is $5,000 plus
       expenses.

       Danner Johnson          989 010-2828      989 223-1919
       Sales manager for Chip Tech. Company makes high-quality add-on
       boards for PC. A potential supplier for us.

       Matt R. B. Johnson      666 707-0707      666 133-1313
       Met in IBM seminar in New York. Runs a chain of retail stores
       selling IBM products. While he competes with us for similar
       clientele, there could be some way we could cooperate someday.

       Peggy O'Brien           901 233-5436      901-894-3321
       Personnel director for IBM. Could approach her to employ our
       laid-off workers.
```

Figure 14.6 keeps the first line of each record from the original address database but also includes variable information. The first line of each record (paragraph) is rigidly structured. The lines following the fixed fields can be anything, as long as each record is together. Remember to separate the records by inserting two consecutive hard returns (separate the first line from the free-form text with a hard return).

The database in figure 14.6 can be manipulated like the original database in figure 14.2. However, you must make sure that the heading in the Sort menu shows `Sort by Paragraph` instead of `Sort by Line`.

To select a Paragraph sort, display the Sort menu, select **T**ype (**7**), and then select **P**aragraph (**3**). The Type column in the menu now shows `Paragraph sort`, and the heading shows `Sort by Paragraph`. Now you can choose other options, specify the input and output files, and select **P**erform Action (**1**).

If you use a line sort to sort paragraphs, the outcome is predictable. Each line is treated as a separate unit (remember that line sorts assume that a record ends with a hard or soft return). After sorting, data is completely jumbled and the neatly arranged paragraphs are gone forever—unless you saved a copy of the original file on disk.

When you select paragraph sort, the Sort menu is slightly different. Each key has four fields instead of the three displayed for line sort. Because a paragraph can contain multiple lines, you need the new Line field to specify which line to base the sort on. The paragraph sort-key display looks like the following:

Reminder:

Because a paragraph can have several lines, the Sort menu offers a fourth category, Line, by which you can sort.

```
Key     Typ     Line     Field     Word
 1       a        1         1        1
```

To sort the modified paragraph database on-screen, follow these steps:

1. Press Merge/Sort (Ctrl-F9) and select **S**ort (**2**).

   ⌨ Access the **T**ools pull-down menu and select **S**ort.

2. When the `Input file to sort: (Screen)` prompt appears, type a file name and press Enter.

3. When the `Output file for sort: (Screen)` prompt appears, press Enter to output to the screen.

4. Select **T**ype (**7**) and select **P**aragraph (**3**).

5. Select **K**eys (**3**), move cursor to the Word category in Key 1, and type *−1*.

6. Press → twice to display the default values a 1 1 1 in Key 2.

7. Press Exit (F7) and select **P**erform Action (**1**).

Some of these steps may not be necessary. For example, step 4 is not needed if you have previously selected paragraph sort.

The database is now sorted based on the last name in the first line of each record (see fig. 14.7).

Sorting a Secondary-Merge File

A *secondary-merge file* is nothing more than a database with implanted merge codes, which WordPerfect uses to do a merge. Once a database exists, you can convert it to a secondary-merge file by using the Replace feature to convert some codes. In this section, you build a database, convert it to a secondary-merge file, and sort the merge file.

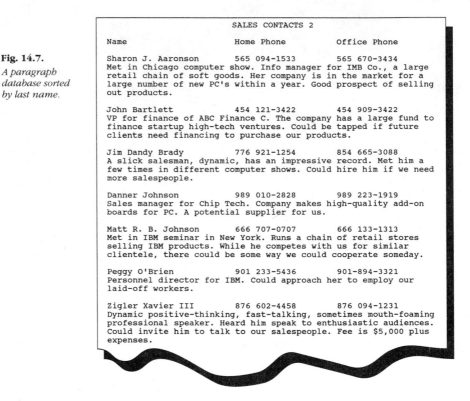

Fig. 14.7.

*A paragraph
database sorted
by last name.*

```
                        SALES CONTACTS 2

Name                    Home Phone          Office Phone

Sharon J. Aaronson       565 094-1533        565 670-3434
Met in Chicago computer show. Info manager for IMB Co., a large
retail chain of soft goods. Her company is in the market for a
large number of new PC's within a year. Good prospect of selling
out products.

John Bartlett            454 121-3422        454 909-3422
VP for finance of ABC Finance C. The company has a large fund to
finance startup high-tech ventures. Could be tapped if future
clients need financing to purchase our products.

Jim Dandy Brady          776 921-1254        854 665-3088
A slick salesman, dynamic, has an impressive record. Met him a
few times in different computer shows. Could hire him if we need
more salespeople.

Danner Johnson           989 010-2828        989 223-1919
Sales manager for Chip Tech. Company makes high-quality add-on
boards for PC. A potential supplier for us.

Matt R. B. Johnson       666 707-0707        666 133-1313
Met in IBM seminar in New York. Runs a chain of retail stores
selling IBM products. While he competes with us for similar
clientele, there could be some way we could cooperate someday.

Peggy O'Brien            901 233-5436        901-894-3321
Personnel director for IBM. Could approach her to employ our
laid-off workers.

Zigler Xavier III        876 602-4458        876 094-1231
Dynamic positive-thinking, fast-talking, sometimes mouth-foaming
professional speaker. Heard him speak to enthusiastic audiences.
Could invite him to talk to our salespeople. Fee is $5,000 plus
expenses.
```

Suppose that you are the current president of the Okie Bird Watchers Society. You could use a database like the one in figure 14.8 to keep track of your flock. Building such a database is simple. Just set proper tab stops and enter each line (just as you did to create fig. 14.2).

Fig. 14.8.

*The Okie Bird
Watchers Society
database.*

```
                  Okie Bird Watchers Society

LName   FName   Address          City          Phone      $$$

Wing    Red     1234 5th St.     Oakdale       299-4533   100
Foxxe   Fanny   999 Broad St.    Cedar City    990-5544   250
Jay     Blu     222 Main St.     Ridge City    858-3322   300
Byrd    Ima     298 Center Rd.   Jinx          922-2166   50
Byrd    Ura     298 Center Rd.   Jinx          922-2166   220
Fish    Ham     3030 Circle Dr.  Spring        484-4949   120
Fish    Golda   3030 Circle Dr.  Spring        484-4949   110
Salmon  Whitey  844 Gill St.     Crease City   888-4040   60
Salmon  Smokey  844 Gill St.     Crease City   888-4040   70
```

When you want to notify members of certain upcoming events, you can convert the database to a secondary-merge file, which you can use to merge with your letter.

To convert a database to a secondary-merge file, enter an {END FIELD} code at the end of each field and an {END RECORD} code at the end of each record. Refer to Chapter 13 for instructions on entering these codes. Remember that the {END FIELD} and {END RECORD} codes in version 5.1 replace the merge codes used in version 5.

When you finish entering {END FIELD} and {END RECORD} codes, the database is converted to a secondary-merge file like the one that follows. What you see on-screen is a long list of fields, one per line, with a page break between records.

Reminder:

To convert a database into a secondary-merge file, replace the tabs between fields with {END FIELD} and the hard returns at the ends of the records with {END RECORD}.

Wing{END FIELD}
Red{END FIELD}
1234 5th St.{END FIELD}
Oakdale{END FIELD}
299-4533{END FIELD}
100{END RECORD}
Foxxe{END FIELD}
Fanny{END FIELD}2
999 Broad St.{END FIELD}
Cedar City{END FIELD}
990-5544{END FIELD}
250{END RECORD}
Jay{END FIELD}
Blu{END FIELD}
222 Main St.{END FIELD}
Ridge City{END FIELD}
58-3322{END FIELD}
300{END RECORD}
Byrd{END FIELD}
Ima{END FIELD}
290 Center Rd.{END FIELD}
Jinx{END FIELD}
922-2166{END FIELD}
50{END RECORD}
Byrd{END FIELD}
Ura{END FIELD}
290 Center Rd.{END FIELD}

Jinx{END FIELD}
922-2166{END FIELD}
220{END RECORD}
Fish{END FIELD}
Ham{END FIELD}
3030 Circle Dr.{END FIELD}
Spring{END FIELD}
484-4949{END FIELD}
120{END RECORD}
Fish{END FIELD}
Golda{END FIELD}
3030 Circle Dr.{END FIELD}
Spring{END FIELD}
484-4949{END FIELD}
110{END RECORD}
Salmon{END FIELD}
Whitey{END FIELD}
844 Gill St.{END FIELD}
Crease City{END FIELD}
888-4040{END FIELD}
60{END RECORD}
Salmon{END FIELD}
Smokey{END FIELD}
844 Gill St.{END FIELD}
Crease City{END FIELD}
888-4040{END FIELD}
70{END RECORD}

This secondary-merge file now can be sorted (refer to "Sorting by Line" earlier in this chapter for the basic procedures used to sort). From the Sort menu, select **T**ype (**7**) and then select **M**erge (**1**). The heading on the Sort menu should read Sort Secondary Merge File. Set the values of Key 1 to a 1 1 1 (to sort by last names); set Key 2 to a 2 1 1 (to sort by first names). Select **P**erform Action (**1**) to get the following result:

Byrd{E D FIELD}
Ima{END FIELD}
290 Center Rd.{END FIELD}
Jinx{END FIELD}
922-2166{END FIELD}
50{END RECORD}
Byrd{END FIELD}
Ura{END FIELD}
290 Center Rd.{END FIELD}
Jinx{END FIELD}
922-2166{END FIELD}
220{END RECORD}
Fish{END FIELD}
Golda{END FIELD}
3030 Circle Dr.{END FIELD}
Spring{END FIELD}
484-4949{END FIELD}
110{END RECORD}
Fish{END FIELD}
Ham{END FIELD}
3030 Circle Dr.{END FIELD}
Spring{END FIELD}
484-4949{END FIELD}
120{END RECORD}
Foxxe{END FIELD}
Fanny{END FIELD}
999 Broad St.{END FIELD}

Cedar City{END FIELD}
990-5544{END FIELD}
250{END RECORD}
Jay{END FIELD}
Blu{END FIELD}
222 Main St.{END FIELD}
Ridge City{END FIELD}
858-3322{END FIELD}
300{END RECORD}
Salmon{END FIELD}
Smokey{END FIELD}
844 Gill St.{END FIELD}
Crease City{END FIELD}
888-4040{END FIELD}
70{END RECORD}
Salmon{END FIELD}
Whitey{END FIELD}
844 Gill St.{END FIELD}
Crease City{END FIELD}
888-4040{END FIELD}
60{END RECORD}
Wing{END FIELD}
Red{END FIELD}
1234 5th St.{END FIELD}
Oakdale{END FIELD}
299-4533{END FIELD}
100{END RECORD}

You can use this file to merge with a primary file as explained in Chapter 13. If you want to select only certain records to merge, refer to "Using the Select Function" later in this chapter. You also can save this file for future use.

Sorting a Table

The Sort feature works in a slightly modified way with a table. For a table sort, each row in the table is considered a record. Each cell in a table is treated as a field. A table can have a maximum of 32,765 records (rows), each containing a maximum of 32 fields (cells). The maximum number of fields (cells) in a table is 1,048,480. The Sort feature works only with tables located in the main document. Sort does not work on tables located in headers, footers, footnotes, endnotes, style codes, or graphics boxes.

Reminder:

Always save the table to disk before sorting it.

The complex nature of a table may make sorting tabular data not worth the effort. Small, simple tables (tables with single-row cells) are easier to sort. *Always* save the table to disk before performing any sort action. After you sort the table, if the results are not what you expect or need, you can retrieve the original version of the table from disk.

Even with a small, simple table, defining more than one key for a sorting operation may produce inaccurate results. Define only one key per sort to yield the most accurate results.

The information in the records (rows) of a table is sorted by the following means:

- Field (cell) within the row
- Line within the field (cell)
- Word within the line

The terminology used with a table also changes slightly during a sort. For sorting purposes, *rows* are horizontal records assigned consecutive numbers from top to bottom beginning with *1*. *Cells* are vertical stacks of fields assigned consecutive numbers from left to right beginning with *1*; cells take their names from the intersection of the field and record.

As an example, cell C2 in a table becomes cell 32 for purposes of planning the sort. The *3* is the field (column) number. The *2* is the record (row) number. Figure 14.9 shows a table with real-estate sales information created by using the instructions in Chapter 19.

Fig. 14.9.
A table with real-estate sales information.

1989 SALES FIGURES				
Parcel	Sales Price	No. of Acres	Price per Acre	Seller
Black Acre	$50,000.00	50.0	$1,000.00	Smith, T.
White Acre	$20,000.00	10.0	$2,000.00	Jones, J.
Red Acre	$35,000.00	28.0	$1,250.00	Hermanson
Green Acre	$60,000.00	12.0	$5,000.00	Haney
Blue Acre	$50,000.00	17.0	$2,941.18	Smith, B.
Yellow Acre	$25,000.00	22.0	$1,136.36	Jones, S.
Brown Acre	$15,000.00	5.5	$2,727.27	Hermanson
Orange Acre	$2,000.00	5.0	$400.00	Smith, B.
Purple Acre	$11,500.00	4.3	$2,674.42	Jones, J.
Gray Acre	$22,380.20	80.0	$279.75	Haney
Average:	$29,088.02	23.38	$1,244.14	Top Seller Gross Amt: Haney
TOTALS:	$240,880.20	183.80	N/A	

To sort the table shown in figure 14.9 alphabetically by parcel name, follow these steps:

1. Move the cursor to the cell A3, where the text *Black Acre* is located.

2. Use the keyboard (Alt-F4 or F12) or the mouse to block cell 1 in row 3 through cell 5 in row 12 (see fig. 14.10).

   Note: Make sure that the starting and ending points of the block are inside the table. If the block's starting and ending points are both outside the table-definition codes, the Sort feature ignores the table and performs a Sort by Line operation.

Fig. 14.10.
*Blocking a table
for sorting.*

Black Acre	$50,000.00	50.0	$1,000.00	Smith, T.
White Acre	$20,000.00	10.0	$2,000.00	Jones, J.
Red Acre	$35,000.00	28.0	$1,250.00	Hermanson
Green Acre	$60,000.00	12.0	$5,000.00	Haney
Blue Acre	$50,000.00	17.0	$2,941.18	Smith, H.
Yellow Acre	$25,000.00	22.0	$1,136.36	Jones, S.
Brown Acre	$15,000.00	5.5	$2,727.27	Hermanson
Orange Acre	$2,000.00	5.0	$400.00	Smith, H.
Purple Acre	$11,500.00	4.3	$2,674.42	Jones, J.
Gray Acre	$22,380.20	30.0	$279.75	Haney
Average:	$29,088.02	$23.38	$1,244.14	Top Seller Gross Amt:
TOTALS:	$240,880.20	$183.80	N/A	Haney

Block on   Cell E12 Doc 1 Pg 1 Ln 5.23" Pos 5.5"

3. Press Merge/Sort (Ctrl-F9). Select **S**ort (**2**) from the following menu:

   1 Merge; **2 S**ort; **3 C**onvert Old Merge Codes: **0**

   ⌨ Access the **T**ools pull-down menu and select **S**ort.

4. WordPerfect skips the input file and output file prompts displayed for other types of sorts and displays the Sort Table menu (see fig. 14.11) instead of the usual Sort menu.

   In the Sort Table menu, `Cell` and `Line` replace `Field` in the key-field area of the screen. For sorting purposes, use the Cell column as you do the Field column in other types of sort. Because a cell can contain multiple lines, you can use the Line column to designate the line in the cell on which you want to base the sort within the cell. The default is line 1.

Fig. 14.11.
*The Sort Table
menu.*

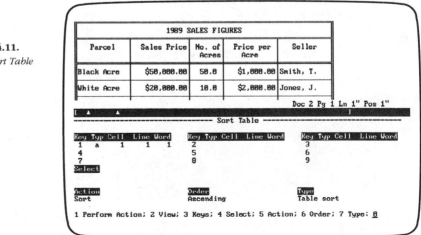

1989 SALES FIGURES				
Parcel	Sales Price	No. of Acres	Price per Acre	Seller
Black Acre	$50,000.00	50.0	$1,000.00	Smith, T.
White Acre	$20,000.00	10.0	$2,000.00	Jones, J.

Doc 2 Pg 1 Ln 1" Pos 1"

```
[ ▲      ▲                                              ]
------------------------------ Sort Table ------------------------------
Key Typ Cell  Line Word    Key Typ Cell  Line Word    Key Typ Cell  Line Word
 1  a    1     1    1       2                            3
 4                          5                            6
 7                          8                            9
Select

Action                     Order                        Type
Sort                       Ascending                    Table sort

1 Perform Action; 2 View; 3 Keys; 4 Select; 5 Action; 6 Order; 7 Type; 0
```

Note: Although designating the line can speed the sorting process, you must be sure that the information on which you want to base the sort is on the same line in each cell. If the information is located on different lines in the cells, the sort may produce inaccurate results.

5. Define the key and order options you want to use in the sort operation (refer to the instructions earlier in this chapter).

On the Sort Table menu, you cannot change the defaults for **A**ction (**5**) and **T**ype (**7**); the defaults are Sort and Table sort.

6. Select **P**erform Action (**1**). If you accept the default settings shown in figure 14.11, the sort produces a table organized alphabetically by parcel name (see fig. 14.12).

Reminder:
If you sort a table with multiple-line cells, make sure that the information on which you want to base the sort is on the same line in each cell.

Parcel	Sales Price	No. of Acres	Price per Acre	Seller
Black Acre	$50,000.00	50.0	$1,000.00	Smith, T.
Blue Acre	$50,000.00	17.0	$2,941.18	Smith, H.
Brown Acre	$15,000.00	5.5	$2,727.27	Hermanson
Gray Acre	$22,380.20	80.0	$279.75	Haney
Green Acre	$60,000.00	12.0	$5,000.00	Haney
Orange Acre	$2,000.00	5.0	$400.00	Smith, H.
Purple Acre	$11,500.00	4.3	$2,674.42	Jones, J.
Red Acre	$35,000.00	28.0	$1,250.00	Hermanson
White Acre	$20,000.00	10.0	$2,000.00	Jones, J.
Yellow Acre	$25,000.00	22.0	$1,136.36	Jones, S.
Average:	$29,088.02	23.38	$1,244.14	Top Seller

C:\WP51\TABLE.TST   Cell A13 Doc 1 Pg 1 Ln 5.55" Pos 1.39"

Fig. 14.12.
A table after sorting.

The sort moves each cell's associated attributes and lines. After sorting the table, you may have to edit the table's structure to restore the original format. Refer to Chapter 19 for information on creating, editing, and formatting a table.

Using Other Sort Features

You can use the Sort feature to manipulate all kinds of records. This section explains how you can apply Sort to two practical situations: sorting a block and sorting numbers.

Sorting a Block

Occasionally, you may not want to sort an entire database. To sort only a portion of a database, use the Block function to highlight the necessary portion and then sort. The database shown in figure 14.2 has two heading lines. If you sort the whole database file, these lines are included among the items to be sorted. To sort correctly—without the two heading lines—block the database, minus the heading lines.

Using the database in figure 14.2 as an example, this section explains how to sort a block. If you typed the telephone-number database earlier in this chapter, type the two heading lines now, if you have not already done so. To sort a block, do the following:

1. Move the cursor to the beginning of the first record or the empty line just above it. Use the keyboard (Alt-F4 or F12) or the mouse to highlight all the records; the highlight should end on the line just below the last record.

2. Press Merge/Sort (Ctrl-F9).

   ⌧ Access the **T**ools pull-down menu and select **S**ort. The Sort menu appears.

Reminder:

When text is highlighted, pressing Merge/Sort displays the Sort menu.

When text is highlighted, pressing Merge/Sort (Ctrl-F9) displays the Sort menu immediately. Because a defined block is already in memory, WordPerfect does not prompt you to enter input and output files. Sorting a block affects the current file; you cannot select a block and sort it to a separate output file. Once the Sort menu appears, select options and set values as usual.

The bottom of the screen displays the Sort menu as usual, and the top of the screen shows the beginning of the block. If you want to view the file being sorted, you can scroll only in the highlighted area; other parts of the file are off-limits.

When you sort blocked text, only the highlighted part of the file is affected; the rest of the file remains unaltered.

Sorting Numerics

Cue:

Sort numbers of equal lengths as numerics or alphanumerics; sort numbers of unequal lengths as numerics.

Numbers can be sorted as alphanumerics or numerics. Numbers of equal lengths, such as phone numbers or social security numbers, can be sorted correctly as numerics or alphanumerics. If you have numbers of unequal lengths, however, you must do a numeric sort to arrange the numbers correctly according to their arithmetic values.

This section uses the Okie Bird Watchers Society database (fig. 14.8) as an example of a numeric sort. To sort this database on the $$$ column, you change several values on the Sort menu. From the Sort menu, select **T**ype (**7**) and select **L**ine (**2**). Then change the values of Key 1 to n 6 1; select **O**rder (**6**) and choose **D**escending (**2**). Select **P**erform Action (**1**) to display the results shown in figure 14.13.

Fig. 14.13.

The database after a numeric sort.

```
                    Okie Bird Watchers Society

     LName   FName   Address          City         Phone     $$$

     Jay     Blu     222 Main St.     Ridge City   858-3322  300
     Foxxe   Fanny   999 Broad St.    Cedar City   990-5544  250
     Byrd    Ura     298 Center Rd.   Jinx         922-2166  220
     Fish    Ham     3030 Circle Dr.  Spring       484-4949  120
     Fish    Golda   3030 Circle Dr.  Spring       484-4949  110
     Wing    Red     1234 5th St.     Oakdale      299-4533  100
     Salmon  Smokey  844 Gill St.     Crease City  888-4040   70
     Salmon  Whitey  844 Gill St.     Crease City  888-4040   60
     Byrd    Ima     298 Center Rd.   Jinx         922-2166   50
```

Columns of numbers also can be totaled, averaged, and manipulated in other ways as explained in Chapter 18. If you want, you can type the dollar sign ($) in front of each number without interfering with the sorting or selection of records (true only in a numeric, not alphanumeric, sort).

Using the Select Function

If you have a large database, you can make good use of the Select function. Select extracts records that meet criteria you specify. Only the selected records—a smaller and more manageable number—appear on-screen so that you can do whatever you want with them.

When you choose **S**elect (**4**) from the Sort menu, the cursor moves to the middle of the menu, just under the Select field (see fig. 14.1). At the same time, the bottom of the menu displays the following:

=(OR), *(AND), =, <>, >, <, >=, <=; Press **Exit** when done

Use the operators displayed at the bottom of the screen to enter a selection formula. To select successfully, combine an accurate formula with correct values in pertinent key fields. As an alternative, you can do a *global select* (to select the records satisfying the selection formula, regardless of the values in the key fields), as explained in the following paragraphs.

Reminder:
Type a formula in the Select field and specify criteria in the key fields to select specific items.

Using the database in figure 14.2 as an example, the following steps explain how to select the two "Johnsons." Display the database on-screen, access the Sort menu, and follow these steps:

1. Select **T**ype (**7**) and choose **L**ine (**2**).
2. Select **K**eys (**3**). The cursor moves to Key 1.
3. Press → twice, type *–1*, and press Exit (F7). The values of Key 1 change to a 1 -1.
4. Choose **S**elect (**4**). The cursor moves to the Select field.
5. Type *key1=johnson* and press Enter.
6. Select **P**erform Action (**1**). All the records disappear except the two "Johnson" records.

If you do a global select, you do not have to specify values for key fields; the global select disregards values in the key fields. All you need to do is enter a formula like the following:

keyg=johnson

The *g* (for *global*) after *key* directs WordPerfect to select any record where *johnson* appears anywhere in the record.

Reminder:
To do a global select, enter a formula that begins with keyg= and disregard the key fields.

Consider the paragraph database in figure 14.6; suppose that you want to use the versatile global select function to select all the records that contain references to IBM. With the database on-screen, access the Sort menu and follow these steps:

1. Select **T**ype (**7**) and choose **P**aragraph (**3**). If you specify **L**ine (**2**) for this example, WordPerfect selects lines and not paragraphs.

2. Choose **S**elect (**4**), type the formula *keyg=IBM*, and press Enter.

3. Select **P**erform Action (**1**).

Theoretically two records should be selected: the Matt Johnson and the Peggy O'Brien records. However, only Matt Johnson's record appears. Peggy O'Brien's record contains a reference to IBM, but the reference ends with a period, and *IBM.* (with a period) does not equal IBM (without a period). You can remedy this discrepancy by change the formula to the following:

keyg=IBM + keyg=IBM.

With the additional selection criterion, both records are selected from the database. Although punctuation affects the selection of records, capitalization does not. *IBM* and *ibm* are both selected by the *keyg=IBM* formula.

You can enter a long formula in the Select field. Entered text moves to the left to make room for more text. You also can use the cursor keys to move left or right and do limited editing within the typed formula. Press Enter or Exit to return to the menu bar at the bottom of the screen.

Refer to the Okie Bird Watchers Society database (fig.14.8) for another example of a complex formula used to select records. Assume that you want to select the records of people who live in a particular town and who contribute a particular sum of money.

With the database on-screen, access the Sort menu and make sure that **L**ine (**2**) is the type of sort being performed. Follow these steps:

1. Select **K**eys (**3**) and change the values of Key 1 to a 4 1 and Key 2 to n 6 1. These values specify a selection based on fields 4 (City) and 6 ($$$).

2. Press Exit (F7), choose **S**elect (**4**), type the formula *key1=spring * key2>100*, and press Enter or Exit (F7).

   This formula instructs WordPerfect to select anyone who lives in the city of Spring (field 4) AND who contributes more than 100 dollars (field 6).

3. Select **P**erform Action (**1**); two records that meet this criteria appear: Ham Fish and Golda Fish.

Reminder:

*Insert spaces before and after the + and * operators and use parentheses to separate elements of the formula.*

If you use a complex formula, you must observe some rigid rules. You must insert a space *before and after* the operators + (OR) and * (AND). In addition, you must use parentheses to separate some variables. Because parentheses can alter the meaning of a formula, you must place them correctly. For example, the following complex formula refers to figure 14.8 and has the first two formulas inside a pair of parentheses:

*(key1=jinx + key1=spring) * key2>=100*

This formula instructs WordPerfect to select any record with the city of Jinx OR Spring, AND with a dollar amount greater than or equal to 100. With this formula, WordPerfect selects the records for Ura Byrd, Ham Fish, and Golda Fish.

If you alter the placement of parentheses in the formula, you get different results. Consider the following formula:

*key1=jinx + (key1=spring * key2>=100)*

This formula instructs WordPerfect to select any record from the city of Jinx OR any record that has a dollar amount greater than or equal to 100 from the city of Spring. With this formula, four records are selected: Ima Byrd, Ura Byrd, Ham Fish, and Golda Fish.

When a formula is in the Select field, you cannot do an ordinary sort. To do a sort again, you must first erase the formula. To erase a formula, use the following steps:

1. Access the Sort menu and choose **S**elect (**4**).
2. When the cursor moves to the Select field, press Ctrl-End to erase the formula.
3. Press Enter and continue with other Sort steps.

By default, WordPerfect sorts the selected records. If you have a very large file, the sort process can take some time. If you do not need sorted records, you can bypass the sorting operation. To select records without sorting them, follow these steps:

Reminder:
Sorting selected records can take some time; turn off sorting of selected records.

1. After you have specified the keys, choose **A**ction (**5**).
2. Choose Select **O**nly (**2**).

Using Macros To Sort

You can put the Macro feature to good use if you use Sort often. Repetitive sort keystrokes can be stored in a macro and quickly replayed, saving you time and trouble.

Cue:
Because sorts use repetitive keystrokes, macros are ideal time savers.

To create a macro to store the beginning keystrokes for a screen sort, do the following:

1. Press Macro Define (Ctrl-F10).
   ▭ Access the **T**ools pull-down menu and select **M**acro **D**efine.
2. Press Alt-S to indicate the name of the macro.
3. Type the description *To sort from screen to screen* and press Enter.
4. Press Merge/Sort (Ctrl-F9), select **S**ort (**2**), and press Enter twice.
   ▭ Access the **T**ools pull-down menu and select **S**ort.
5. Press Macro Define (Ctrl-F10), or access the **T**ools pull-down menu and select **M**acro **D**efine again.
6. Press Cancel (F1).

Although the macro definition is complete after step 5, the `Macro Def` message remains on the status line, and the Sort menu is still on-screen. Pressing Cancel (F1) in step 6 returns the screen to the regular document.

To sort a database with this macro, retrieve the file you want to sort and activate the macro by pressing Alt-S. In a short time, the Sort menu appears. Use the menu to examine messages and select options for the current sort operation. When you have made your choices, select **P**erform Action (**1**). If you want to sort with the same criteria a second time in the same session, just activate the macro and type *1*; everything is done for you. WordPerfect retains the last sort settings until you exit the program.

Reminder:
To rerun a sort macro using the same criteria, activate the macro and type 1.

If your needs are specific and fixed, enter all the keystrokes into a macro. Suppose that you built a large file based on the paragraph database in figure 14.6, and that you often need to select records that contain the word *sales*. Use the following steps to create a macro to help in this specific instance:

1. Press Macro Define (Ctrl-F10).

   ⌨ Access the **T**ools pull-down menu and select **M**acro **D**efine.

2. Type *sales* as the macro name and press Enter.

3. Type the description *To select sales-related records* and press Enter.

4. Press Merge/Sort (Ctrl-F9) and select **S**ort (**2**).

   ⌨ Access the **T**ools pull-down menu and select **M**acro **D**efine.

5. Type the name of the file from which you want to select records and press Enter twice.

6. Select **T**ype (**7**) and choose **P**aragraph (**3**).

7. Choose **S**elect (**4**), press Ctrl-End to clear any existing formula, type the formula *keyg=sales*, and press Exit (F7).

8. Select **P**erform Action (**1**).

9. Press Macro Define (Ctrl-F10), or access the **T**ools pull-down menu and select **M**acro **D**efine again.

To use this macro, Press Macro Define (Ctrl-F10) or access the **T**ools pull-down menu and select **M**acro **D**efine. Type *sales* and press Enter. The macro retrieves the file specified in step 5 and selects only the records containing the word *sales*; all the other records do not appear on-screen.

You can edit the existing macro so that it selects records containing the word *personnel* rather than *sales*; refer to Chapter 11 for information about editing macros.

Summary

This chapter has explained the following techniques:

❏ How to build databases

❏ How to sort and select records from the databases

❏ How to sort data in a table

❏ How to use macros to save time in sorting operations

When you build a database, keep the following points in mind:

❏ Records in a line database are separated by hard returns.

❏ Records in a paragraph database are separated by two hard returns.

❏ Fields inside a record are separated by a tab code.

15

Using Styles

As a beta tester for WordPerfect Corporation, **Marilyn Horn Claff** offers expert advice and suggestions for the development of WordPerfect. She is Director of the Boston Computer Society's WordPerfect Special Interest Group, an Assistant Sysop on the WordPerfect Support Group Forum on CompuServe, and a WordPerfect Certified Instructor.

S tyle (Alt-F8) is a powerful tool you can use to control the format of a single document or a group of documents. Each of the three categories of styles you learn in this chapter consists of regular WordPerfect codes you can turn on or off in the document. Style can include almost any formatting code you use manually, as well as graphics and text. Using Style is easy: you define and name a style, and when you want to use that style, you select it from a list.

Style definitions are saved in the current document. You also may save them to a master style library file to use with other documents.

This chapter teaches you how to accomplish the following tasks:

- Create open, paired, and outline styles
- Use a style in a document; apply a style to a block
- Edit, save, and delete style definitions
- Save style definitions to a style library to use with other documents
- Retrieve styles from the library, update the documents with styles from the library, and maintain the style library
- Review sample style libraries

> **Reminder**
>
> If you use a mouse with WordPerfect 5.1, you can click the button on the right to display the pull-down menus, and then select the desired option. You also can press Alt-= to access the pull-down menus, and then press the appropriate letter of the desired option. For all instructions, assume that if a block is required to activate a pull-down menu option, the text has been blocked before the pull-down menu is accessed. Instructions for pull-down menus and the mouse are marked with the mouse icon. For more information about the mouse, see Chapter 1. ☐▤

Deciding To Use Styles

If you are a new WordPerfect user, you may be tempted to skip this chapter and return to it later. Don't! If you understand how to use WordPerfect formatting codes in a document, you can define and use styles.

Unless you examine a document in Reveal Codes, a document formatted with styles looks the same as a document formatted manually. If the results look the same whether you use styles or codes, why do you need styles?

Suppose that you write a 40-page proposal with three sets of margins and four levels of section headings. The boss approves the proposal, but she does not like the margin settings for the tables. She also wants you to use a different font for the third-level headings.

If you inserted the formatting codes manually, you must find each wrong code, delete it, and insert a new code. Changing the format codes is no easy task because you cannot easily search for and replace specific code settings. You can search for generic formatting codes, such as margin change or font change; however, you cannot use Replace (Alt-F2) to replace a code that sets the left margin to 1.25 inches with a code for a 1.5-inch margin, nor can you replace an 11-point Helvetica font code with a 12-point Chancellor font code.

Using Styles provides a simple solution to this problem. If you use Styles to format the proposal, you can make the changes effortlessly, just by changing two of the style definitions in the style list. Even better, you can save the new styles to a master style list so that the next time you write a proposal, you can use the same format.

Realizing the Advantages of Using Styles

Using Styles offers many advantages over manual formatting. With Styles you can do the following:

- Save formatting time and keystrokes
- Make easier revisions
- Encourage formatting consistency within a single document
- Share formatting specifications easily with other users

- Reduce "code clutter" in Reveal Codes and choose formats by name and description
- Treat a group of codes as a single object so that codes that belong together stay together
- Gain time to think about writing

Comparing Styles to Macros

Both the Style and Macro features are used to streamline repetitive formatting tasks in WordPerfect. Style, however, has an advantage over macros. When you use a macro to insert formatting codes in the document, you save keystrokes, but the file is identical to a file formatted manually. Once you have entered the codes in the document, you still cannot change them easily. If you need to change the font used for all the embedded citations, you must change each font code individually.

Instead, you can create a style called Citation and assign the style to each quotation. Then, if necessary, you can change the format of all the quotations by redefining the Citation style. To speed the application of a style, you can create a macro to apply it.

Reminder:

When you format a document, use Styles to save keystrokes and make reformatting easier.

Defining Open, Paired, and Outline Styles

WordPerfect styles fall into three categories: *open, paired,* and *outline.*

Open styles remain in effect until you override the style codes, either by using another style or by inserting other formatting codes manually. You do not turn off open styles.

Use open styles for formatting that affects an entire document. For example, you can use an open style to select a paper size and type; set the document margins, tabs, line spacing, and base font; choose the hyphenation type and zone; turn on or off justification; and turn on widow/orphan protection.

If you want an open style to affect an entire document, move the cursor to the beginning of the document before turning on the style.

Paired styles are turned on and off throughout the document. For example, you can create a paired style called Heading that makes a section heading bold and italic. When you use this style, WordPerfect inserts a **[Style On: Heading]** code in the document before the cursor position, and a **[Style Off: Heading]** code after the cursor position. After you type the heading text, turn off the style. If you need to change the text of the heading, just position the cursor between the **[Style On: Heading]** and the **[Style Off: Heading]** codes and make the change.

Use paired styles for titles, section headings, tables, embedded quotations, or even entire chapters. Paired styles are appropriate for any element of the document that has a beginning and an end.

Paired styles are broken into three subgroups, according to the method you select to turn off the style when you create it:

Enter = [HRt]	Keep the style on until you turn it off by returning to the Styles menu and choosing Off (**2**). Use this method for styles that extend over multiple paragraphs or that must contain hard returns. Pressing Enter inserts a new line.
Enter = Off	Turn off the style when you press Enter. Use this method for styles that affect only a single paragraph, such as a section heading.
Enter = Off/On	Turn off and immediately turn on the style when you press Enter. Off/On styles are ideal for formatting a series of similar paragraphs. For example, you can use an Off/On style to create consecutive hanging paragraphs or bulleted lists.

Outline styles organize and format hierarchical material. An outline style is a family of up to eight open or paired styles assigned to a specific outline or paragraph-numbering level.

Outline styles are a hybrid of the Outline and Styles features. You can define an outline-style family either in the Styles menu or in the Outline menu, but you can apply outline styles only through the Outline or Paragraph Numbering features. You cannot apply outline styles by turning them on at the Styles menu. In every other way, outline styles function like regular paired or open styles.

Despite their name, outline styles need not contain paragraph-numbering codes or resemble conventional outlines. The word *outline* refers solely to the method with which the outline-style codes are inserted into the document. When you insert a paragraph-number code, WordPerfect invokes the outline-style level that corresponds to that paragraph-number level. For example, when an outline-style family is in effect and you use Paragraph Number Level 2, WordPerfect turns on the level 2 style for that outline-style family.

Outline styles are appropriate for any material that needs to be organized hierarchically. You can use outline styles to insert customized paragraph-numbering and outline-numbering levels, and to format different levels of subject headings.

Cue:

Use outline styles to insert paragraph numbers and outline-numbering levels, and to format subject headings.

Although outline styles may appear to be more complex than regular open or paired styles, they are well worth the effort to learn. Outline styles offer the following advantages over regular styles:

- Outline styles are easier to use. Just choose the numbering outline style from the Paragraph Numbering menu and turn on Outline (Shift-F5, 4) or insert paragraph-number codes.

- Outline styles allow you to use Outline features such as **M**ove, **C**opy, and **D**elete Family. (An outline *family* is the current level and all levels beneath it.) You also can adjust the style levels of a family by using the arrow keys.

- Outline styles are adjusted easily by pressing Tab or Shift-Tab to lower or raise the style to the next level. This method is more convenient than deleting a style code, blocking the text, and turning on a different style.

> ### Tip
>
> If you have many styles for different level headings, combine them into a single outline style. You can convert regular open or paired style definitions to outline definitions. Just edit the style, change the Style Type to outline, and tell WordPerfect the name of the outline style and the style level.

Creating an Open Style

An envelope is a typical application for an open style. With an envelope style, you can print one envelope or a batch of envelopes (just separate each address with a hard page break). To set up an envelope style, you have to select the envelope form size, and set the top, bottom, left, and right margins. You also may want to choose a particular font for the text to be printed on the envelope. To create an open style, complete the following steps:

1. Press Style (Alt-F8).

   ⌨ Access the **L**ayout pull-down menu and select **S**tyles.

   The Styles List appears with the following menu at the bottom of the screen:

   1 On; **2 O**ff; **3 C**reate; **4 E**dit; **5 D**elete; **6 S**ave; **7 R**etrieve; **8 U**pdate: **1**

2. Press **C**reate (**3**). The Styles: Edit menu appears (see fig. 15.1). Notice that two items on the menu are already filled in with the default values.

```
Styles: Edit

    1 - Name

    2 - Type          Paired

    3 - Description

    4 - Codes

    5 - Enter         HRt
```

Fig. 15.1.

The Styles: Edit menu.

3. Select **N**ame (**1**), type the name of the style, and press Enter. For example, type *Envelope* and press Enter.

   Assign a name whose meaning will be clear to you when you see the style name six months from now. (Remember that although you can read the style description in the Styles menu, you see the name of the style, not the description, when you look at the document in Reveal Codes).

   The style name is not a file name, so you may use any characters you want. You can enter up to 12 characters including spaces. Style names are not case-sensitive; WordPerfect considers *header*, *HEADER*, and *Header* to be the same style name.

4. Select **T**ype (**2**). The following menu appears:

   Type: 1 Paired; **2 O**pen; **3 O**utline: **O**

5. Select **O**pen (**2**).

6. Select **D**escription (**3**), type a short description of what the style does, and press Enter. For example, type *Standard Envelope w/Preprinted Return Address* and press Enter.

The description may contain up to 54 characters. Make the description precise. (You can edit the description later if you change the definition of the style).

Tip

To keep track of revised styles, include the date in the style description whenever you create or revise a style definition.

---

7. Select **C**odes (**4**). A screen that resembles a document-editing screen with active Reveal Codes appears. As a reminder that you are in the style window, WordPerfect displays the message `Style: Press Exit when done.` You can see the codes you are inserting as you create the style in the lower half of the screen. If you include text in the style definition, the text is visible in both halves of the screen.

8. Insert the formatting codes and text that you want in the style, as though you are editing a WordPerfect document. To insert the Envelope Paper Size/Type code, press Format (Shift-F8), select **P**age, Paper **S**ize/Type, and then select the 9.5 x 4 Envelope form (**S**). Change the top margin to 2 inches and the bottom margin to 0.5 inch by using the Format Page: Margins menu (press Shift-F8, P, M, 2", 0.5"). Change the left margin to 4.5 inches and the right margin to 0.5 inch by using the Format: Line Margins menu (press Shift-F8, L, M, 4.5", 0.5"). Insert a code for the base font by pressing Font (Ctrl-F8, 4) and selecting the font you want (for this example, select Dutch Roman 11pt).

9. Press Exit (F7) three times to return to the document.

Notice that the Reveal Codes section of the style window shows the codes you have entered (see fig. 15.2).

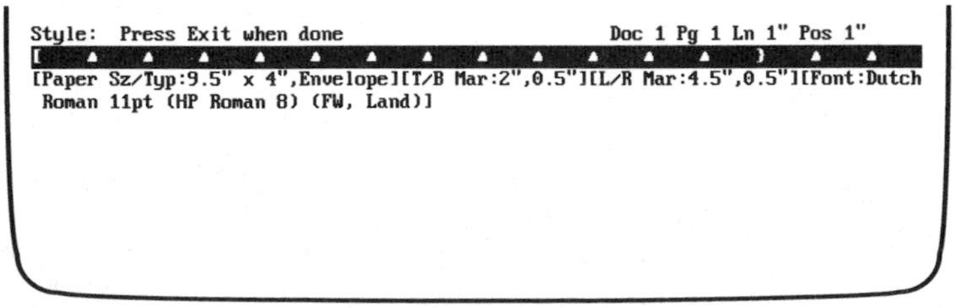

Fig. 15.2.
The Reveal Codes screen for Envelope style.

```
Style:  Press Exit when done                        Doc 1 Pg 1 Ln 1" Pos 1"
[▲  ▲   ▲   ▲   ▲   ▲   ▲   ▲   ▲   ▲   ▲   ▲  ]   ▲   ▲
[Paper Sz/Typ:9.5" x 4",Envelope][T/B Mar:2",0.5"][L/R Mar:4.5",0.5"][Font:Dutch
Roman 11pt (HP Roman 8) (FW, Land)]
```

Creating a Paired Style

Creating a paired style is more involved than creating an open style. A paired style gives you two additional capabilities: you can control the position of the formatting codes relative to the text; and you can choose a method for turning off the style.

Many of WordPerfect's formatting codes consist of two codes: one to turn on the feature, and another to turn off the feature. For example, when you underline a word, you press Underline (F8), type the word, and press Underline (F8) again. In Reveal Codes, you see the formatting codes **[UND]**word**[und]**. As with several other pairs of WordPerfect codes, capital letters indicate the beginning of a formatting feature, and lowercase letters indicate the end of the feature.

Instead of manually inserting formatting codes, you can use a style to format the text. For example, if you want a heading in the document to be both bold and italic, you can create a paired style to turn on and off bold and italic attributes.

To create a paired style, complete the following steps:

1. Press Style (Alt-F8).

    ⌨ Access the **L**ayout menu and select **S**tyles.

2. Select **C**reate (**3**). The Styles: Edit menu appears.

3. Select **N**ame (**1**), type the name of the style, and press Enter. For example, type *Emphasized* and press Enter.

    Because paired style is the default setting, you do not have to specify the **T**ype (**2**) setting.

4. Select **D**escription (**3**), type a description of the style, and press Enter. For example, type *Bold and Italic* and press Enter.

5. Select **C**odes (**4**). The Paired Codes screen appears (see fig. 15.3). Notice that the cursor is before the comment box. The comment box represents the text you type when you use this paired style. You can insert formatting codes and text before the comment, after the comment, or both before and after the comment. Certain codes, however, have no effect if they are placed after the comment *and* there is a corresponding code of the same type before the comment. For example, a font or margin code placed *after* the comment has no effect if there is a font or margin code *before* the comment. The behavior of formatting codes after the comment in a paired style is governed by a complicated set of rules. To determine the effect of formatting codes in the Off section of a paired style, position the cursor on the **[Style Off]** code and examine it in Reveal Codes. No matter what codes are included in the style definition, Reveal Codes displays the actual interpretation of the style definition.

6. Enter the formatting codes that should appear before the text. For example, press Bold (F6) and Italic (Ctrl-F8, A, I). You need not turn off codes in a paired style; WordPerfect turns off all codes automatically when you turn off the style.

    Notice that the codes you use appear in the Reveal Codes half of the screen.

7. Press Exit (F7) to return to the Styles: Edit menu.

8. Select **E**nter (**5**). The following menu appears:

    Enter: 1 HRt; 2 Off; 3 Off/On: 0

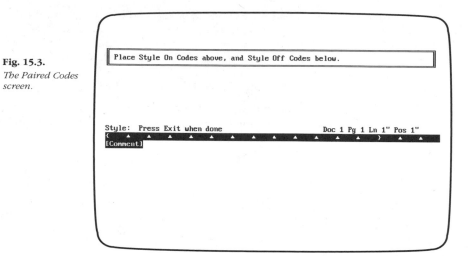

Fig. 15.3.
The Paired Codes screen.

9. Select the effect that pressing Enter has with a paired style. This selection controls how you turn off the style. For example, select **Off** (**2**); when you press Enter, you turn off the style.

10. Press Exit (F7) twice to return to the document.

Turning Off a Paired Style

Steps 8 and 9 in the preceding procedure specify the effect pressing Enter has when you use a paired style, and how you turn off a paired style. Because you mainly use the newly created Emphasized style on short passages that do not contain hard-return codes, Enter is a convenient way to turn off the style. Use this style for chapter titles and section headings. Notice that if you select **Off** (**2**), pressing Enter does not insert a hard return; pressing Enter turns off the style and leaves the cursor in place. If you want a blank line after the heading, insert a hard return in the style itself, after the comment box.

Reminder:

If you do not select Off (2) for the action the Enter key has with a paired style, you must turn off the style manually.

For other types of formatting, you can make other selections. For example, to format longer sections of text, do not turn off the style when you press Enter. Instead, select **HRt** (**1**) from the Enter menu. Pressing Enter inserts new lines, and the style remains in effect until you turn it off. To turn off the style, press Style (Alt-F8) or ⌨ select **S**tyles from the **L**ayout pull-down menu, and select **Off** (**2**). Use this method for styles that span multiple paragraphs.

If you want to format a series of paragraphs, select Off/**O**n (**3**) from the Enter menu. Pressing Enter turns off and then immediately turns on the style. Use this option to format a series of similar paragraphs or single lines, such as bulleted items or hanging paragraphs. To turn off this style for good, press Alt-F8 to return to the Style menu and select **Off** (**2**).

> ### Tip
> To turn off a paired style (or any other paired code), press the right-arrow key. This trick works because it moves the cursor past the hidden **[Style Off]** code.

Inserting Paired Codes in a Style Definition with Block

Not all WordPerfect's paired codes can be entered directly into a style definition. Several codes, such as Block Protect, Table of Contents, and Lists, require that the Block command be on. In the Styles Codes screen, you must press Block (Alt-F4 or F12), move the cursor to the other side of the comment, and press the key that corresponds to the code you need.

> ### Tip
> Using Table of Contents codes in paired styles is a trick that saves you a great deal of work. In the following example, all the formatting codes are included within the Table of Contents codes so that the same formatting is picked up in the table of contents. If you want to mark only the text for the table of contents, block only the **[Comment]** code.

If you want to mark a heading for the first level of the table of contents, you must use Block. To insert paired codes with Block, complete the following steps:

1. Move to the Styles Codes screen (press Style [Alt-F8] or ⌨ select **S**tyles from the **L**ayout menu, and select **C**reate [**3**] to create a new style or **E**dit [**4**] to edit an existing style; then select **C**odes [**4**]).
2. Press Block (Alt-F4 or F12).
3. Press Home, Home, ↓ to block the entire style. You cannot use the mouse to block the comment in a paired style unless you also block text. Because most styles lack text, using a mouse to edit styles is not recommended.
4. Press Mark Text (Alt-F5) and select To**C** (**1**).
5. When prompted for the `ToC level`, type the level number and press Enter.
6. Press Exit (F7) three times to return to the document.

Reminder:
You cannot use the mouse to block the comment in a paired style unless you also block text.

Note: Because WordPerfect lets you define a Block in either direction, you can block text with the cursor on either side of the comment.

Creating an Outline Style

Creating an outline style is similar to creating a series of paired or open styles:

1. Press Style (Alt-F8).
   ⌨ Access the **L**ayout menu and select **S**tyles.
2. Select **C**reate (**3**), select **T**ype (**2**), and choose Ou**t**line (**3**). WordPerfect prompts you for the name of the outline style and the number level. Enter the name of the outline style. For example, enter *Num Scheme*. At the `Level Number (1-8):` prompt, type a number from 1 to 8.

Selecting a Style

Once you define a style, you select that style from the Styles list to use in the document. For example, to format a heading, select the Emphasized style.

To select a style, complete the following steps:

1. Press Style (Alt-F8).

   🖱 Access the **L**ayout menu and select **S**tyles.

   The styles you defined are listed alphabetically by name (see fig. 15.4).

Fig. 15.4.

The Styles list.

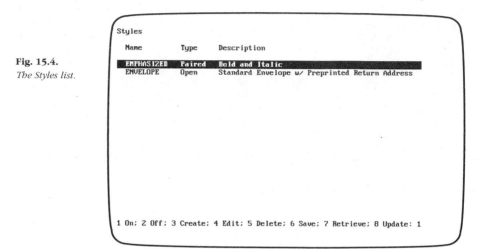

```
Styles

Name          Type      Description

EMPHASIZED    Paired    Bold and Italic
ENVELOPE      Open      Standard Envelope w/ Preprinted Return Address










1 On; 2 Off; 3 Create; 4 Edit; 5 Delete; 6 Save; 7 Retrieve; 8 Update: 1
```

2. Highlight the style you want. For example, highlight Emphasized. Use PgUp or the gray minus key to move the cursor bar to the first style on the screen. Use PgDn or the gray plus key to move the cursor bar to the last style on the screen. Press Home, Home, ↑ to move to the beginning of the list; press Home, Home, ↓ to move to the end of the list.

   If the list contains many styles, you can use Name Search (F2 or N) to move quickly to the style you want. Press Forward Search (F2) and start typing the name of the style. When the cursor is on the name, press Enter.

Tip

If you create a macro to turn on a style, use Name Search to select the style. The macro then works correctly even if you add or delete other style definitions.

---

3. Select **O**n (**1**). You return to the document. Remember that the style you select affects only the text *after* the cursor.

4. Type the heading and press Enter. For example, type *Chapter 1* and press Enter. Notice that the text is both bold and italic. This style turns off automatically when you press Enter. If the style does not turn off automatically, press Style (Alt-F8) and select Off (**2**) to turn off the style.

Viewing a Style with Reveal Codes

To confirm that you inserted the style code, press Reveal Codes (Alt-F3 or F11). You should see a **[Style On:]** code with the style name after the colon. Move the cursor to the **[Style On:]** code; the code expands to display all the formatting codes that the style contains. If you forget what a style does, use Reveal Codes (Alt-F3 or F11) to view the style instead of returning to the Style menu to read the style description or examine the codes.

Applying Paired Styles to Existing Text

Frequently, you do not make the final decision about how a document is formatted until you have already typed a draft. You therefore must be able to apply styles to text you have already typed. Use Block to apply styles to existing text.

Reminder:
You can apply styles to text you have already typed.

To apply a paired style to a block of text, complete the following steps:

1. Place the cursor at one end of the block you want to define.
2. Press Block (Alt-F4 or F12).
3. Press Style (Alt-F8).

    🖰 Access the **L**ayout pull-down menu and select **S**tyles.

4. Use the cursor or mouse to highlight the paired style you want.
5. Select **O**n (**1**) or move the mouse to **O**n (**1**) and click to apply the style to the block.

When you return to the document, the block is formatted with the style you selected.

Creating a Style by Example

WordPerfect does not have a true style-by-example feature, but you can use Block to create a new style from existing codes in the document by following these steps:

Reminder:
Use Block to copy formatting codes into a style.

1. Press Reveal Codes (Alt-F3 or F11).
2. Move the cursor to the formatting codes in the document you want to copy.
3. Press Block (Alt-F4 or F12).
4. Highlight the codes you want to copy.

    Note: You cannot use the mouse to create a style by example.

5. Press Style (Alt-F8).
6. Select **C**reate (**3**).

The codes become part of a style. Name the style, enter a style definition, and decide how the style should be turned off.

> **Tip**
>
> The preceding method places only codes in the style; it eliminates any text in the block from the new style. If you want to include the text, block the area as described, press Copy (Ctrl-Ins), Style (Alt-F8), Create (**3**), Codes (**4**), and Enter. Name the style, select the type, enter the description, and (if the type is Paired) select the effect of the Enter key.

Editing a Style

One of the best features of Style is the way it can easily change the formatting codes in a document. Remember, you cannot search for specific styles, so you cannot search for one style and replace that style with another. Instead, you redefine the current style. For example, if you decide headings should be only bold, not bold and italic, you can delete the italic code from the style definition. All the headings reflect the change immediately.

To edit a style definition, complete the following steps:

1. Press Style (Alt-F8).

   ⌨ Access the **L**ayout menu and select **S**tyles.

   The Styles list appears.

2. Use the cursor to highlight the style you want to change. For example, highlight Emphasized.

3. Select **E**dit (**4**). The Styles: Edit screen appears.

4. Select the item you want to change and make changes. For example, select **C**odes (**4**) and delete the italic codes.

5. Press Exit (F7) twice (or three times if you edited codes) to return to the document.

> **Caution**
>
> WordPerfect allows you to edit a style definition name and description at any time. If you rename a style, WordPerfect lets you rename the styles in the document at the same time. In most cases, you should select **Y** in response to the Rename Styles in Document? prompt. If you select **N**, you cannot reformat the text to which the style is assigned because the link between the style name and the text is broken.

Changing Styles

Reminder:
You can search for three generic style codes: [Style On], [Style Off], and [Open Style].

Sometimes you may have to use a different style in place of the style you originally chose. Although you cannot search for exact style codes, you can search for three generic style codes: **[Style On]**, **[Style Off]**, and **[Open Style]**. You can search for these codes to find the styles you want to change.

For example, suppose that you use three style definitions for section headings called First, Second, and Third. You decide to simplify the appearance of the document by eliminating the second-level headings. Some of the second-level headings then become first-level headings; the rest become third-level headings. You can search for the generic style code and delete the codes for second-level headings, block the text, and reassign it to another style.

> ### Tip
>
> If you use outline styles for the first-, second-, and third-level headings, these steps are not necessary. Just press Tab or Shift-Tab to adjust the level of the style, or use Move Family (Shift-F5, O, M, ← or →) to move all the styles in a family to a higher or lower style level. *Always* use outline styles for hierarchical text.

To change a style code, complete the following steps:

1. Press Forward Search (F2).
2. Press Style (Alt-F8). The following menu appears:

   1 Style **O**n; **2** Style O**ff**; **3** Open Style: **0**

3. Press the style code for which you want to search. For example, select Style **O**n (**1**).
4. Press Forward Search (F2).
5. When you locate the text you want to change, delete the style code. For example, delete the **[Style On:Second]** code.
6. Press (Alt-F4 or F12) or use the mouse to highlight the block of text to which you want to assign a new style.
7. Press Style (Alt-F8).
8. Use the cursor or the mouse to highlight the new style definition.
9. Select **O**n (**1**).

Deleting Selected Style Codes from a Document

In addition to changing the style for a section of text, you may want to delete a style code from a document. To delete an open style, delete the **[Open Style]** code. To delete a paired style, delete either the **[Style On]** or the **[Style Off]** code.

A quick way to delete selected style codes is to use Replace with Confirm (Alt-F2) to replace the style codes with nothing.

If you want to delete all occurrences of a style code—along with the corresponding style definition—from a document, press Style (Alt-F8), highlight the style definition you want to delete, select **D**elete (**5**), and choose Including Codes (**2**) as described in "Deleting a Style Definition from the Style List" later in this chapter.

Cue:

Use Replace with Confirm (Alt-F2) to replace the style codes with nothing.

Saving Styles with a Document

When you create a style, the style definition becomes part of the document you are editing. If you exit from the document without saving, or if the power goes off and you lose the document, the style definition also is lost. If you are working in Doc 1, switch to Doc 2, and call up the style list, you may not see the same style list that you saw in Doc 1.

When you save a document, the styles you defined on the Styles list are saved as part of the document prefix whether or not you used the styles to format the text. Each time you use a style, the information in the style definition is repeated. Although this design may seem wasteful, it has two advantages: WordPerfect formats the document quickly on-screen without having to seek the information in a table; and, if you inadvertently delete a style definition active in the document, the text still formats correctly.

Deleting a Style Definition from the Style List

Because all the styles are saved with a document regardless of whether you used them, you should delete unused style definitions from the list. Your original formatting intentions are more clear to someone else (or to you six months later) if extra style definitions are removed.

To delete a style definition from the list, complete the following steps:

1. Press Style (Alt-F8).

   ⌨ Access the **L**ayout menu and select **S**tyles.

   The Styles list appears.

2. Use the cursor or the mouse to highlight the style you want to delete.

3. Select **D**elete (**5**). The following menu appears:

   Delete Styles: 1 Leaving Codes; **2 I**ncluding Codes; **3 D**efinition Only: **0**

4. Choose **1** to delete the style definition and convert the corresponding style codes to regular WordPerfect codes. Choose **2** to delete both the style definition and all corresponding style codes in the document. Choose **3** to delete the definition without affecting the style codes in the document.

Caution

Selecting **D**efinition Only (**3**) from the Delete Styles menu is generally not a good idea. The style definition is the key to controlling and changing document formats. If you delete the definition without deleting the style codes, you no longer control the text governed by the style codes. For example, if you use a heading style throughout the document and later delete the heading style definition, you can no longer manipulate the headings as a group.

> **Caution** (continued)
>
> Another danger is that you may reformat the document unwittingly by retrieving a style library containing a style definition with the same name as the style definition you deleted. Normally, if a style is already defined, WordPerfect warns you when you retrieve a style library with a style definition by the same name and gives you the option of retrieving only the styles not defined in the current document.

Creating a Style Library

WordPerfect's Style feature lets you use styles not only in the document in which you create them, but also in other WordPerfect documents.

To use styles in more than one document, you must save the style to a *style library file*—a WordPerfect document that consists solely of style definitions. You can create as many style libraries as you want, with each library containing as many styles as you want. Each style must have a unique name within the style library, but you can give styles the same name if they are part of different libraries.

Reminder:

You can save styles in a library file and use the same styles in different documents.

You may find that keeping all style definitions in one library file is easier; you can specify a default style library whose definitions appear when you press Style (Alt-F8). Or, you may prefer to create several style libraries; with several libraries, you simply retrieve the appropriate library from the Style menu and select the desired style.

> **Caution**
>
> If you have multiple style libraries, designating a default style library may be more hindrance than help because you cannot easily clear the default style definitions from the screen. Each time you retrieve a style library file, new style definitions are added to the ones already saved with the document. Unless individual style definitions are deleted from the Style list, they are saved with the document whether you use them or not.

Using Multiple Style Libraries

Multiple style libraries are a powerful tool for writers who use different formats for the same material. If every style library contains a set of style definitions whose names and functions correspond to the style definitions of other style libraries, you can use these definitions to reformat documents instantaneously.

For example, suppose that you have three different style libraries for three different magazine formats. Each library uses identical names for each of the style definitions in the library. You can format the first version of an article using the default style library file. If the article is rejected by the first-choice magazine, you can retrieve the document, use the Styles menu to retrieve the style library for the second-choice magazine, and print the second version. If that version is rejected, you can format it with the style library for the third-choice magazine.

Setting the Default Style Library File

> **Tip**
>
> Define a style directory in Setup. If you use a single collection of styles, make that collection the default style library file. If you switch among several style library files, leave the library file name blank in Setup.

To manage the styles, designate a style library directory and a default style library file in Setup. Both these settings are optional, but you can manage the styles more easily if you use these options.

Specify the default style by pressing Setup (Shift-F1) and selecting **L**ocation of Files (**6**). (Chapter 20 provides information about using the Setup: Location of Files screen).

Select **S**tyle Files (**5**) and enter the name of the directory where you want to keep the style library files. If you leave this line blank, WordPerfect looks for and saves style library files in the current directory, unless you type a full path name when you retrieve or save the style library files. Specifying a default style directory in Setup allows you easy access to all the style library files from any directory, and allows you to use List Files to see a list of the style library files.

Reminder:

You must provide the names of existing directories on the Setup: Location of Files screen.

Note: WordPerfect allows you to enter only the names of *existing* directories. If you have not created the directory you plan to use for the style files, exit this menu, create the directory, and then return to this menu.

Choose a file name that you won't confuse with other documents and files. If you enter the name of a nonexistent file, the error message ERROR: File not found—C:\STYLES\MASTER.LST appears when you press Style (Alt-F8). The message disappears once you save the styles to a file.

If a default style directory is not defined, WordPerfect looks for the style library file name in the current directory, unless you have specified a path for the file name. WordPerfect saves a style library in the default styles directory if such a directory is defined in Setup, or in the current directory if a style directory is not defined and you do not type a full path name.

> **Tip**
>
> To manage the style library files easily, keep them in a separate directory defined in Setup.

Saving Style Definitions in a Style Library

If you create styles that you plan to use in other documents, you must save the styles to the style library. Then you can use the styles to format other documents.

To save style definitions to a style library, complete the following steps:

1. Create the styles as described earlier in this chapter.

2. From the Styles list screen, select **S**ave (**6**). The Filename: prompt appears.

3. Type the file name and press Enter. You can use any valid file name you want. If the file already exists, WordPerfect displays the Replace C:\WP51\STYLES\LIBRARY.STY? No (Yes) prompt.

   Select **Y** if you want to replace the old style library with the styles on-screen. If you select **N**, WordPerfect asks you to enter another file name for the new file.

4. Press Exit (F7) to return to the document.

Tip

You also can save the style definitions by pressing Save (F10) at the Styles menu and entering the name of the file.

Caution

Pay attention to the word *replace* in the prompt WordPerfect displays. As with regular WordPerfect documents, *replace* means "overwrite the old file with the new file." Styles in the old style library not on the Styles list are lost if you agree to the replacement. If you think that the old library contains styles not displayed on the Styles list, use the Retrieve option to bring in styles whose names are different *before* you save the style library file. (Retrieve is described in the next section).

Retrieving a Style Library

Once you create and save a style library file, you can use the styles from that file in other documents. The default style library appears when you press Style (Alt-F8); if you do not have a default style library, the style list is blank (unless the current document already contains styles). You can select a style from this list or retrieve another style library file. For example, although the default library style file is C:\STYLES\LIBRARY.STY, you may want to use another library style file called C:\STYLES\REPORT.STY.

To retrieve another style library file, complete the following steps:

1. Press Style (Alt-F8).

   ⌨ Access the **L**ayout menu and select **S**tyles.

   The style list from the default library appears.

2. Select **R**etrieve (**7**).

3. Type the name of the style library file you want to use and press Enter, or press List (F5) and Enter to view the style directory. (If you did not define a style directory in Setup, List [F5] displays the files in the current directory.) From the List Files screen, you can retrieve the style library just like a regular document.

   If styles in the current document have the same names as styles in the style library you are retrieving, the `Style(s) already exist. Replace? No (Yes)` prompt appears.

4. Select **Y** to read in all the style definitions in the new library, overwriting the styles already in the document. Select **N** to read in only the style definitions with names different from those in the document.

5. Press Exit (F7) to return to the document.

Reminder:
When you retrieve a new style library file, you can overwrite styles in the current document.

Remember that only the style definitions on-screen (and in the current document, if you are in one) are affected by the choice of the new library file. If you have not used any styles in a document, you can safely overwrite the default styles.

Also, note that you retrieve only a *copy* of the style library file. If you modify any of the styles and want to save the new version, you must save the style definitions to the style library again, specifying the name of the library file when prompted. (The styles are not saved to the default style library if you just press Enter at the `Filename:` prompt.)

Updating Styles in a Document

You can use a style library to update styles in documents. For example, suppose that you create a report using the library file REPORT.STY. When you work on another report, you can change the headings and save the style. Use **U**pdate (**8**) from the Styles list screen to format the first document with the new style from the library file.

The **U**pdate option copies the styles from the default library to the document on-screen. Update works in one direction only: from the default style library to the document on-screen. Use **U**pdate to reformat the current document if you changed the default style master library.

The **U**pdate option is similar to Retrieve, but with three differences:

- When you use Retrieve, you must designate the name of the style library file you want to use. Update always uses the default library file.

- Retrieve warns you if the retrieved file will overwrite style definitions in the current file and gives you the option of retrieving only the styles with different names. Update assumes that you want to overwrite the current styles with the styles in the default style library, and does not warn you about overwriting duplicate style names.

- Update is faster and easier to use than Retrieve and requires fewer keystrokes.

To update the document with the current style in the library file, complete the following steps:

1. Retrieve the document.
2. Press Style (Alt-F8).

    ⌨ Access the **L**ayout menu and select **S**tyles.
3. Select **U**pdate (**8**).
4. Press Exit (F7) to return to the document.
5. Save the document.

Tip

To determine what styles the default style library file contains, switch to Doc 2, clear the screen (if you have a document loaded), and press Style (Alt-F8).

Tip

Always save the document before using either the Retrieve or Update option. Then examine the document; you may want to print a few pages. If the document is not formatted the way you want, exit the document without saving it and retrieve the document again.

Deleting a Style from the Style Library

To delete a style definition from the current document, press Style (Alt-F8) or ⌨ access the **L**ayout menu and select **S**tyles, highlight the name of the style, and select **D**elete (**5**). WordPerfect displays this menu:

Delete Styles: 1 Leaving Codes; **2** Including Codes; **3** Definition Only: **0**

If you choose **L**eaving Codes (**1**), the definition is deleted from the styles list, but the corresponding codes in the document are converted to regular WordPerfect codes.

If you choose **I**ncluding Codes (**2**), both the style definition and the corresponding codes are deleted from the document.

If you choose **D**efinition Only (**3**), the style definition is deleted from the style list, but the corresponding style codes in the document are not affected. When WordPerfect encounters the style codes for the deleted definition in the document, it resurrects the deleted style definition (minus the description, which cannot be determined from the document). By deleting all the styles on the style list with Definition Only and moving the cursor through the document, you can discover which styles are actually used in the document. By deleting unused style definitions, you can decrease the size of the document and make the formatting easier to understand.

When you delete a style from the Style list saved with the document, only the current document, not the style library file, is affected.

> **Tip**
>
> When you use the **U**pdate option, current versions of *all* the styles in the style library become part of the document. You may want to delete unused styles from the document again after updating.

To delete a style from the master style library, you must select **S**ave (**6**) from the Styles list screen after deleting the style and specify the same master style file name.

Maintaining Style Libraries

To manage the library file, consider the following tips:

- Choose a file name extension such as STY or WPS for style library files and use the extension consistently. Do not use that extension with other files. By using a unique extension, you are unlikely to lose the library files or to overwrite them with regular WordPerfect documents.

- Keep all style library files in the same directory and make a backup of that directory whenever you update the style libraries.

- Keep track of the styles in each library file. One easy way to keep the style lists current is to do a print screen of the style list in each library whenever you edit the style; keep the printouts together in a notebook.

- Make the style descriptions as detailed as possible so that you do not have to study the codes to figure out what the style does.

- Include the date so that you can tell at a glance when the style was last revised.

- Purge outdated style definitions from the library files, especially from the master library file. The master library file need not contain a copy of every style you have used in a document. The master library file should include only styles you may use for future documents.

- Delete unused style definitions from the document, but be careful not to delete active styles from the document. The option to delete the Style Definition Only makes this task easy.

Reviewing Sample Style Libraries

WordPerfect comes with the LIBRARY.STY library file. You can use the sample libraries defined in the following sections, or you can create a personalized style library.

Using LIBRARY.STY

WordPerfect's sample style library, LIBRARY.STY, is installed from the Install/Learn/Utilities 1 master disk to the styles directory you defined in Setup. If you did not define a styles directory (or you did a basic installation rather than a customized installation), the style library is copied to the WordPerfect directory. Even if you do not plan on using LIBRARY.STY, look at it; you may get some style ideas. LIBRARY.STY includes the following predefined styles:

Reminder:
LIBRARY.STY is a style library that comes with WordPerfect 5.1.

Style Name	Type	Description
Bibliogrphy	Paired	Bibliography
Doc Init	Paired	Initialize document style
Document	Outline	Document style
Pleading	Open	Header for numbered pleading paper
Right Par	Outline	Right-aligned paragraph numbers
Tech Init	Open	Initialize technical style
Technical	Outline	Technical document style

Bibliogrphy is a paired style for outdented, or hanging, paragraphs. The Enter key is defined as Off/On so that you can easily create a series of hanging paragraphs.

Doc Init is a paired style that sets the document outline style. Doc Init contains a Table of Contents definition code in the On section and a new page number in the Off section. When you generate a Table of Contents, the ToC is placed between the On and Off style codes.

Note: You cannot enter a Table of Contents definition code directly into a style; you must enter the code in a document and use **M**ove or **U**ndelete to insert the code in the style definition.

Document is an example of an outline style. The eight outline levels contain Paragraph Numbering and Table of Contents codes.

Pleading style formats pages with fixed-line spacing and vertical lines and line numbers in the left margins. The formatting codes are placed in a header so that they affect every page.

Right Par is an outline style that creates eight levels of hanging paragraphs with right-aligned paragraph numbers. Two hard returns separate paragraphs with a blank line. The Enter key for this group is defined as Off/On.

Tech Init sets the technical outline style and turns the outline on.

Technical is an outline style used to format technical papers.

Investigating Another Style Library

The following sections describe style libraries you can use as models when designing your own style library. You can change any of the attributes in the styles to match your needs.

Creating Dissertation and Dissert-Chpt Styles

If you must write a dissertation, check with your academic department for precise requirements, then use or alter this style to format the dissertation.

Many formatting requirements for dissertations are intended to make the papers easier to read in media such as microfilm and microfiche. For this reason, footnotes (printed at the bottom of each page) are preferable to endnotes (printed at the end of the chapter or at the end of the dissertation). Margins must be generous and uniform to ensure that nothing is lost when the dissertation is copied.

> **Tip**
>
> If you plan to use a different printer for the final copy of the dissertation, include all the formatting codes that may affect the document, even if they duplicate the current default settings. Although you can include these codes as Document Initial Codes, include them in the style definition so that you can change the format of all the chapters at once if necessary.

The *Dissertation* style sets up the document format; turns on Left Justification **[Just:Left]** and widow/orphan protection **[W/O On]**; designates Courier 10 pitch (PC-8) as the base font; selects the custom paragraph numbering style **[Par Num Def:DISSERT-CHPT]**; and sets line spacing to double spacing **[Ln Spacing:2]**. The underline style code **[Undrln]** ensures that tabs and spaces are not underlined.

Top, bottom, and right margins are set at 1"; the left margin is 1.5" to allow for binding. Page numbers print in the upper right corner **[Page Numbering:Top Right]**, except for the first page of each chapter. The **[Suppress:PG BC]** code causes the page number to print at the bottom center on the first page of every chapter.

The Dissertation style depends on two tricks. First, a Footnote Options code is inserted *after* the base font code **[Courier 10cp1]**. The placement of the Footnote Options code after the base font code guarantees that the footnote prints in Courier. (WordPerfect's footnotes print in whatever font is in effect when the Footnote Options code is used; if there is no Footnote Options code, footnotes print in the documents initial font.)

The second trick is that the Paragraph Number Definition code is inserted in the regular editing screen and copied into the style definition. This step is necessary because you cannot directly create a Paragraph Number Definition in a style definition.

Figure 15.5 shows the Styles Edit Codes screen for the Dissertation style.

The *Dissert-Chpt* style shown in figure 15.6 is an outline style consisting of eight levels. All the chapter and section titles and headings in the dissertation are assigned to a different outline style. By using an outline style, you can change the style level assigned to an individual title or to a family of outline levels. (See the beginning of this chapter for advantages of using an outline style.)

```
Style:  Press Exit when done                   Doc 1 Pg 1 Ln 1" Pos 1"
[    ▲     ▲     ▲     ▲     ▲     ▲  .  ▲     ▲     ▲     ▲     ▲  ]  ▲     ▲
[Font:Courier 10cpi][Ftn Opt][Par Num Def:DISSERT-CHPT][T/B Mar:1",1"][L/R Mar:1
.5",1"][Ln Spacing:2][Pg Numbering:Top Right][Suppress:Pg BC][Undrln:][Just:Left
]
```

Fig. 15.5.

The Styles Edit Codes screen for the Dissertation style.

```
Outline Styles: Edit

  Name:              DISSERT-CHPT

  Description:       Chapters, Sections, Headers


  Level  Type      Enter

    1    Paired    HRt
    2    Paired    HRt
    3    Paired    HRt
    4    Paired    HRt
    5    Paired    HRt
    6    Paired    HRt
    7    Paired    HRt
    8    Paired    HRt
```

Fig. 15.6.

The Dissert-Chpt outline style.

Figure 15.7 shows the Styles Edit Codes screen for the Dissert-Chpt style. The comment indicates where the chapter title is positioned. Note that the word *Chapter* and the comment are both contained within the **[Mark:TOC,1]** and **[End Mark:TOC,1]** codes. Because the **[BOLD]** and **[Just:Center]** codes precede the **[Mark:TOC,1]** code, they are not picked up when the Table of Contents is generated. Since codes in the On section of a paired style automatically revert to their previous settings when the style is turned off, there is no need to use a **[bold]** or **[Just:Left]** code in the Off portion of the style. The Advance Down code causes the printer to advance 3/4 inch before the text begins.

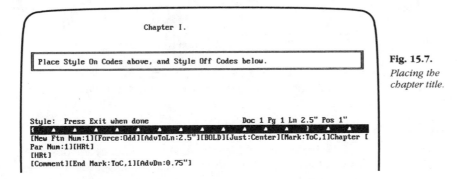

```
                        Chapter I.

  ┌──────────────────────────────────────────────────────────────┐
  │ Place Style On Codes above, and Style Off Codes below.        │
  └──────────────────────────────────────────────────────────────┘




Style:  Press Exit when done                   Doc 1 Pg 1 Ln 2.5" Pos 1"
[    ▲     ▲     ▲     ▲     ▲     ▲     ▲     ▲     ▲     ▲     ▲     ▲     ▲
[New Ftn Num:1][Force:Odd][AdvToLn:2.5"][BOLD][Just:Center][Mark:ToC,1]Chapter [
Par Num:1][HRt]
[HRt]
[Comment][End Mark:ToC,1][AdvDn:0.75"]
```

Fig. 15.7.

Placing the chapter title.

After turning on the Dissertation and Dissert-Chpt styles, the document should look like the one shown in figure 15.8.

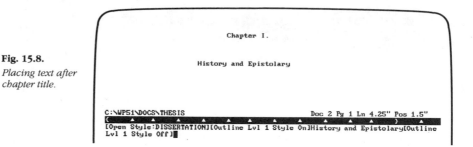

Fig. 15.8.
Placing text after chapter title.

Cue:

Use the Master Document feature to obtain consecutive page and chapter numbering and to create a Table of Contents for the dissertation or other long documents.

So far, the document contains two style codes and the text *History and Epistolary*. Each subsequent chapter should begin with the Dissert-Chpt style, Level 1. When you combine the chapters into one document or use the Master Document feature, the chapters are numbered consecutively.

The second-level outline style, shown in figure 15.9, numbers and marks a heading for the second level of the Table of Contents. The paragraph number carries over into the table of contents because the paragraph number code is placed between the Table of Contents mark codes.

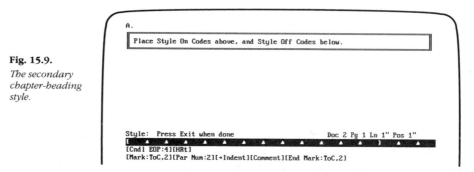

Fig. 15.9.
The secondary chapter-heading style.

A Conditional End of Page code is set to keep the next four lines together on a page. The style begins with a hard return because a Conditional End of Page code must be on the line preceding the text the code affects. When this style follows a soft page break, the hard return becomes a Dormant Hard Return and does not print.

Creating Letterhead Style

A letterhead is a typical application for an open style. The letterhead style described in this section prints a graphics logo and return address at the top of the first page.

With WordPerfect 5.1, you can use graphic images in style definitions.

> **Tip**
>
> When graphics are used in style definitions, the graphics are not stored in the document itself. When WordPerfect needs to display or print a graphics image that is part of a style definition, it looks for the graphic image on disk.

You may be tempted to include the date as part of the Letterhead style. Unfortunately, neither Date Text nor Date **[Date:3 1, 4]** is very useful in a style definition. If you use the Date Text code, every letter is date-stamped with the date on which you created the Letterhead style. If you use the Date code, whenever you retrieve a file created with the style the date changes to the current date. If you need to print a copy of a letter with the original date a week later, the date is no longer correct.

Rather than include the date as part of the Letterhead style, use a macro to turn on the style and insert the date text. The macro can insert the date of the day you invoke the macro, not the date on which the style was created.

Figure 15.10 shows the Letterhead style in Print View. Figure 15.11 shows how the style looks in View Document.

```
┌FIG 1─────────────┐              Wheeling and Dealing
│                  │           1001 West Wainwright Circle
└                  ┘            Wheeling, West Virginia  26003
                             Where There's a Wheel There's a Deal




Style:  Press Exit when done                  Doc 1 Pg 1 Ln 1" Pos 1"
[Paper Sz/Typ:8.5" x 11",Standard][L/R Mar:1",1"][T/B Mar:0.3",1"][Fig Opt][Fig
Box:1;BICYCLE.WPG;][Font:Zapf Humanist Roman 12pt (HP Roman 8) (FW, Port)][AdvDn
:0.5"][Just:Right][Kern:On][Font:Zapf Humanist Bold 11pt (HP Roman 8) (FW, Port)
][EXT LARGE]Wheeling and Dealing[ext large][HRt]
[VRY LARGE]1001 West Wainwright Circle[HRt]
Wheeling, West Virginia  26003[vry large][HRt]
[Font:*Zapf Humanist Bold Italic 12pt (HP Roman 8) (FW, Port)]Where There's a Wh
eel There's a Deal[DSRt]
[Just:Left][Kern:Off][HRt]
[AdvToLn:2.75"][T/B Mar:1",1"][Font:Zapf Humanist Roman 12pt (HP Roman 8) (FW, P
ort)]
```

Fig. 15.10.

The Letterhead style in Print View.

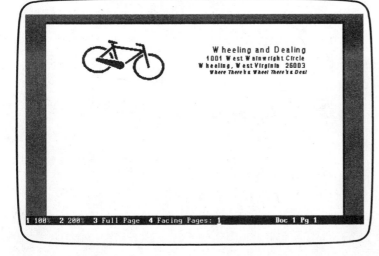

Fig. 15.11.

The Letterhead style in View Document.

Creating Citation Style

Use the Citation style shown in figure 15.12 to set off quoted material from the body of the text. This style is simple: single-spacing **[Ln Spacing:1]**, italics **[ITALC]**, and Left-Right indent **[Indent]** are included in the On section of the style (before the comment); no codes are included in the Off section (after the comment). The single-spacing and italics in the On section of the style are automatically turned off in the Off section.

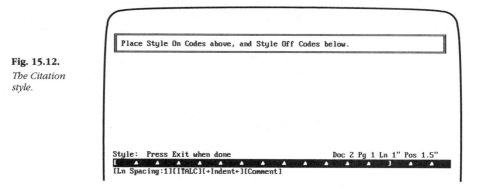

Fig. 15.12.
The Citation style.

Creating French Style

When a writing assignment requires you to mix languages in the same document, use language codes to tell WordPerfect which date format, dictionary, thesaurus, and hyphenation modules to use for each section of the document. You can create a paired style for each language that includes the language code in the On section of the style. No code is required in the Off section; when you turn the style off, WordPerfect reverts to the language code in effect before you turned the style on. Figure 15.13 shows the style for the French language.

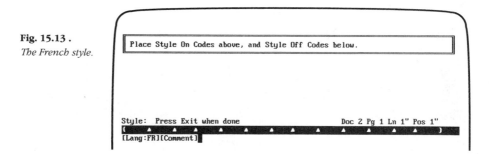

Fig. 15.13 .
The French style.

In this example of a paired style, Enter is treated as a **[HRt]**. If you write entire documents in a foreign language, you can define the style to be an Open style.

Assessing Style Limitations

Although using styles can simplify formatting, you should note a few limitations:

- You cannot control all formatting through styles.
- You cannot clear the Styles screen easily; you must delete unwanted style definitions one by one.
- You cannot search for specific style codes in the document.
- You cannot use an existing style as a model for another style.

Summary

WordPerfect's Style feature is worth the effort to learn. With styles you can accomplish tasks impossible to do in earlier versions of WordPerfect, including the following:

- ❑ Create an open style to format an entire document
- ❑ Create a paired style to format sections of text
- ❑ Create outline styles to manipulate hierarchical material
- ❑ Make formatting revisions by redefining the style
- ❑ Create a library of styles to use with multiple documents
- ❑ Use style libraries to simplify formatting and revision, to maintain consistent formatting of a set of documents, and to share styles with other users

16

Using WordPerfect with Other Programs

Judy Housman is a microcomputer-software consultant and trainer in such programs as WordPerfect, 1-2-3, dBASE, Reflex, and Quattro. She wrote this chapter for *Using WordPerfect 5*.

Michael McCoy is a microcomputer trainer and consultant in the Washington, D.C., area and has been teaching and supporting WordPerfect and other software packages since 1983.

Jon Pepper is president of Words Plus, a consulting firm based in Sunderland, Massachusetts, that specializes in computer-related topics.

Mr. McCoy and Mr. Pepper revised this chapter for *Using WordPerfect 5.1*, Special Edition.

As you've learned from earlier chapters, WordPerfect is a superb word processor. In most offices, however, tasks are so varied that even the most sophisticated word processor must be supplemented with other programs. For this reason, an office is likely to choose several programs, in addition to WordPerfect, that meet special needs—perhaps a spreadsheet to handle budgets and a database to track customers and their orders.

Specialized software packages make the transferring of information necessary. WordPerfect is designed to read the information created within different programs and convert that information to a workable WordPerfect file. This chapter explains how to make file conversions between WordPerfect and spreadsheets, databases, and other word processors, including how to use the following:

- spreadsheet files
- database files
- DOS text files (ASCII files)
- WordPerfect's Convert program
- conversion facilities in other programs

The chapter concentrates on the most common translation problems, but it also offers techniques for solving more specialized problems. Many users won't perform every conversion discussed here, so you may prefer to concentrate on techniques that apply to your own situation. If you use WordPerfect exclusively, you can skip this chapter. By reading it, however, you may learn ways to perform more efficiently by using WordPerfect with another program.

Perhaps you haven't yet realized how using another program with WordPerfect can be useful. Let's look at some common situations that require file conversion. Assume that you create a spreadsheet in Lotus 1-2-3 or PlanPerfect and now need to include that information in a long budget report—a cumbersome or impossible task with most spreadsheets. The ideal way to perform this task is to create the spreadsheets and then incorporate the budget within a WordPerfect document. This method lets you take advantage of the spreadsheet's sophisticated calculation capabilities and WordPerfect 5.1's superb print formatting.

Because WordPerfect offers limited database capabilities, you probably keep customer and order information in a dedicated database (a software package, such as dBASE or R:BASE, designed to handle information organized in tables). To send personalized letters to clients without retyping information already in the computer, you can use WordPerfect's merge capabilities. Simply transfer information from your database into a file that WordPerfect can use as a secondary-merge file.

Finally, if you switch from another word processor to WordPerfect or if you work with a document created in a different word processor, you must convert documents to WordPerfect format. WordPerfect offers several methods for conversion; the one you choose determines how much additional work is required to reestablish the format of the original documents.

Reminder

If you use a mouse with WordPerfect 5.1, you can click the right button to display the pull-down menus, and then select the desired option. You also can press Alt-= to access the pull-down menus, and then press the appropriate letter of the desired option. For all the instructions, you can assume that if a block is required to activate a pull-down menu option, the text has been blocked before the pull-down menu is accessed. Instructions for pull-down menus and the mouse are marked with the mouse icon. See Chapter 1 for details on using the mouse. ▭▤

Understanding Basic Conversion Strategies

The goal of a conversion is to convert from one format to another while retaining as much of the original format as possible or while making the resulting file as useful as possible. To achieve this goal, you should try the following conversion strategies:

Use another format directly with WordPerfect. Whenever you can use a file in another format directly with WordPerfect, do so. This approach makes conversion as easy as possible while retaining most formatting.

Convert with WordPerfect's Convert program. Using the Convert program lets you retain as much of the original formatting as possible.

Convert with intermediate formats. If the Convert program does not convert a format directly into WordPerfect, you may be able to convert to an intermediate format and then convert to WordPerfect. If you are going from WordPerfect to a format not supported by Convert, see whether the destination program can use one of the formats Convert does support.

Use DOS text. This conversion technique is the least desirable one because it loses most of the original formatting in a file. Use this option only when you have no other way to convert your information.

Using Spreadsheet Information with WordPerfect

WordPerfect 5.1 can now directly retrieve spreadsheets from Lotus 1-2-3 (except Release 3), PlanPerfect, and Excel. In addition, you can now create links between your spreadsheet files and WordPerfect document so that when you update the spreadsheet, the same information in WordPerfect can be easily updated as well.

Retrieving a Spreadsheet with 5.1

To use a spreadsheet in version 5.1, all you need to do is retrieve it by using either List (F5) or Retrieve (Shift-F10). WordPerfect automatically recognizes the file as a spreadsheet and retrieves it into a WordPerfect table.

To retrieve a spreadsheet, perform the following steps:

1. Press List (F5).

   ▢ Access the **F**ile pull-down menu and select List **F**iles.

   If you remember the file's path and name, you can instead use Retrieve (Shift-F10) to retrieve the file.

2. Type the name of the directory that contains your spreadsheet files and press Enter.

3. Highlight the name of the spreadsheet you want to retrieve and press **R**etrieve (**1**).

You will see the message `* Importing Spreadsheet *` at the bottom left of the screen. When the spreadsheet is retrieved, you will see that it has been brought into a WordPerfect table, as shown in figure 16.1.

The table format lets you more easily adjust the width and format of columns, draw lines around different parts of your spreadsheet, or even use some basic math functions. For detailed information about working with WordPerfect tables, see Chapter 19, "Creating Tables."

Reminder:

WordPerfect can retrieve 1-2-3 spreadsheet files (except Release 3 files), PlanPerfect 3.0 and 5.0 files, and Excel files.

Fig. 16.1.

A spreadsheet retrieved as a table.

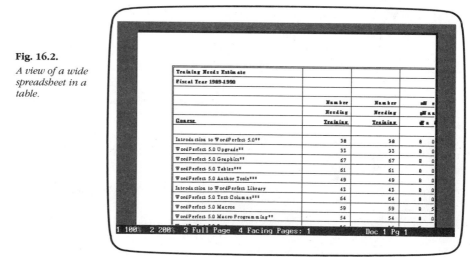

```
┌─────────────────────────────────────────────────────────────┐
│ The Secret Guide to Computers, Purchases                    │
│ For May 1989                                                 │
│                                                              │
│ Date  Paid to              For                   Amount     │
│ ────  ──────────────────── ──────────────────── ─────────── │
│   7   Air France           Mbabane trip          $699.00    │
│   2   Food for Thought     lunch with Anders      $44.57    │
│   6   Brickskellar         lunch with Anne E.     $15.00    │
│                                                  ─────────── │
│       Total                                      $758.57    │
└─────────────────────────────────────────────────────────────┘

                                    Doc 2 Pg 1 Ln 1" Pos 1"
```

Handling Wide Spreadsheets

If you try to retrieve a very wide spreadsheet, you will see the message WARNING Table extends beyond right margin. The spreadsheet will be retrieved, but if you examine it by pressing Print (Shift-F7) and selecting **V**iew Document (**6**), you will see that the table prints off the right edge of the paper and that the columns at the right edge print on top of each other, as in figure 16.2.

Fig. 16.2.

A view of a wide spreadsheet in a table.

To correct this problem, try the following:

- Change your paper size to a wide size.
- Change to a smaller font.
- Use Text In/Out to retrieve only part of the spreadsheet (see the next section for more information about this feature).

Importing Spreadsheets with Text In/Out

Most of the time, the direct retrieval of a spreadsheet is satisfactory. At times, however, you may want more control over how your spreadsheet is formatted when it is retrieved. In such cases, you can import the spreadsheet through WordPerfect's Text In/Out feature. Using this feature, you can import a part of the spreadsheet. You can also import the spreadsheet as WordPerfect text, as opposed to table format.

To import part of a spreadsheet with Text In/Out, do the following:

1. Press Text In/Out (Ctrl-F5), select **S**preadsheet (**5**), and select **I**mport (**1**).

   ⌨ Access the **F**ile pull-down menu, select Text **I**n, select **S**preadsheet, and then select **I**mport.

   As you can see in figure 16.3, from this screen you can designate the file name, the range you want to import, and the type of import.

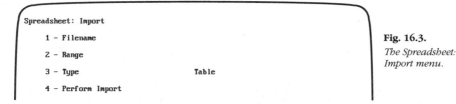

```
Spreadsheet: Import

    1 - Filename

    2 - Range

    3 - Type                    Table

    4 - Perform Import
```

Fig. 16.3.

The Spreadsheet: Import menu.

2. Select **F**ilename (**1**); type the name of your spreadsheet, including the appropriate path and directory name, and press Enter. Notice that WordPerfect automatically fills in the **R**ange (**2**) option to include the entire spreadsheet.

3. Choose **R**ange (**2**) and enter the range you want. You can use a named range or type the range coordinates.

4. To finish the import, select **P**erform Import (**4**).

Importing a Spreadsheet as Text

Usually when you retrieve or import a spreadsheet, WordPerfect puts it in a WordPerfect table. You can, however, import the spreadsheet as normal WordPerfect text. When you import as text, WordPerfect calculates and sets tabs for the spreadsheet and then puts each column at the appropriate tab setting.

If you import as text you lose the table features: the easy formatting of columns and column widths and the ability to perform simple calculations easily. In addition, if you import a wide spreadsheet as text, WordPerfect wraps all lines that extend beyond the right margin.

Reminder:

When you import a spreadsheet as text, you lose table features.

To import a spreadsheet as text, do the following:

1. Press Text In/Out (Ctrl-F5), select **S**preadsheet (**5**), and select **I**mport (**1**).

    ▱ Access the **F**ile pull-down menu, select Text **I**n, select **S**preadsheet, and then select **I**mport.

2. Select **F**ilename (**1**); type the name of your spreadsheet, including the appropriate path and directory name, and press Enter.

3. Choose **T**ype (**3**) and select T**e**xt (**2**).

4. To finish the import, select **P**erform Import (**4**).

Linking Spreadsheets and Documents

In addition to providing for the easy retrieval of spreadsheets, WordPerfect 5.1 lets you link your original spreadsheet file with the document (or documents) that it has been imported into. By linking a spreadsheet and a document, you can update information in the spreadsheet, recalculate all formulas, and then easily update the same information in your WordPerfect document.

Reminder:

A spreadsheet that is already retrieved into WordPerfect cannot be linked.

Note that you must create the link at the same time that you first import the spreadsheet. You cannot link a spreadsheet that has already been retrieved into WordPerfect.

To import and link a spreadsheet, do the following:

1. Move the cursor to the place where you want to import the linked spreadsheet.

2. Press Text In/Out (Ctrl-F5), select **S**preadsheet (**5**), and select **C**reate Link (**2**).

    ▱ Access the **F**ile pull-down menu, select Text **I**n, select **S**preadsheet, and then select **C**reate Link.

    The Create Link menu offers the same options as the Spreadsheet Import menu shown in figure 16.3.

3. Select **F**ilename (**1**) and type the name of the spreadsheet file you want to import and link to. Remember to enter the full path name of the spreadsheet file.

    You can import and link all or part of the spreadsheet, and you can import the linked spreadsheet as a table or as text.

4. Choose **P**erform Link (**4**) to create the link.

Figure 16.4 shows a linked spreadsheet imported as a text file. Note the on-screen box that shows the beginning and end of the link, including the name of the file that you are linked to.

If you want, you can turn off the display of the link codes. To turn off the code display, do the following:

1. Press Text In/Out (Ctrl-F5), select **S**preadsheet (**5**), and select **L**ink Options (**4**).

👈 Access the **F**ile pull-down menu, select Text **In**, select **S**preadsheet, and then select **L**ink Options.

You will see the menu shown in figure 16.5. The Update Link options are discussed in the next section.

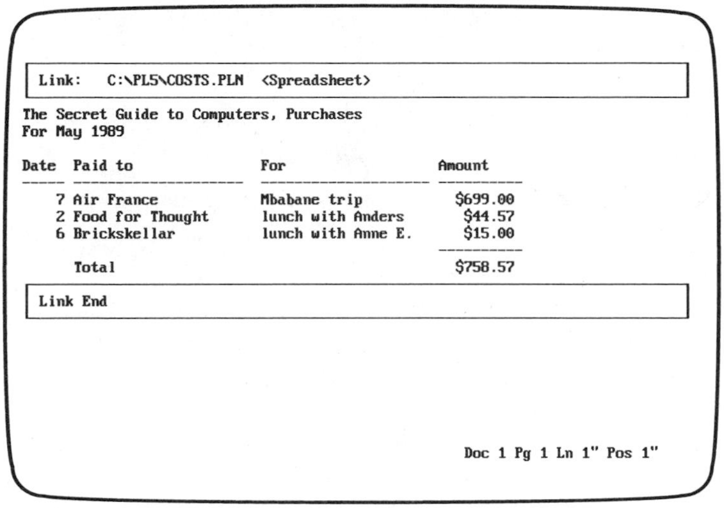

```
Link:   C:\PL5\COSTS.PLN  <Spreadsheet>

The Secret Guide to Computers, Purchases
For May 1989

Date  Paid to              For                Amount
____  _____  _____   _____
   7 Air France            Mbabane trip        $699.00
   2 Food for Thought      lunch with Anders    $44.57
   6 Brickskellar          lunch with Anne E.   $15.00
                                               _____
     Total                                     $758.57

Link End




                                    Doc 1 Pg 1 Ln 1" Pos 1"
```

Fig. 16.4.

A spreadsheet retrieved as text and linked.

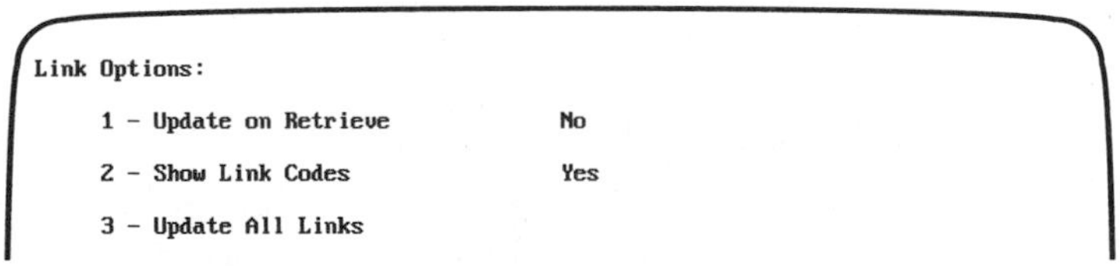

```
Link Options:

    1 - Update on Retrieve        No

    2 - Show Link Codes           Yes

    3 - Update All Links
```

Fig. 16.5.

The Link Options menu.

2. Select **S**how Link Codes (**2**) and **N**o to turn off the display of the codes.

If you decide to change the range of cells linked to, or if you want to change the format from table to text (or vice versa), you must edit the link. To edit the link, do the following:

1. Position your cursor between the link codes.

2. Press Text In/Out (Ctrl-F5), select **S**preadsheet (**5**), and select **E**dit Link (**3**).

    👈 Access the **F**ile pull-down menus, select Text **In**, select **S**preadsheet, and then select **E**dit Link.

Updating Links

When you update information in your linked worksheet, you will want to update the same information in your document. You can update your document in two ways:

- Manually, at any time you choose once you have retrieved the file
- Automatically, whenever you retrieve the file

Reminder:

You can update documents either manually or automatically.

To update the link manually, follow these steps:

1. Retrieve the document containing the link.
2. Press Text In/Out (Ctrl-F5), select **S**preadsheet (**5**), and select **L**ink Options (**4**).

    ⌨ Access the **F**ile pull-down menu, select Text **I**n, select **S**preadsheet, and then select **L**ink Options.

    The menu shown in figure 16.5 appears.
3. Select **U**pdate All Links (**3**); all links in your current document will be updated.

To have WordPerfect automatically update all links in your document any time you retrieve the document, follow these steps:

1. Retrieve the document containing the link.
2. Press Text In/Out (Ctrl-F5), select **S**preadsheet (**5**), and select **L**ink Options (**4**).

    ⌨ Access the **F**ile pull-down menu, select Text **I**n, select **S**preadsheet, and then select **L**ink Options.
3. Select Update on **R**etrieve (**1**) and then select **Y**es.
4. Save the document. If you do not save the document after changing Update on **R**etrieve to **Y**es, the links will not be updated when you retrieve the document.

Using Spreadsheet Information in Merge

By using conversion programs, you can prepare from a spreadsheet a file that can be used as a WordPerfect secondary-merge file. See the later section "Using WordPerfect's Convert Program" for more information.

Using Spreadsheets Other than Lotus, PlanPerfect, or Excel

If you are using a spreadsheet other than Lotus 1-2-3, PlanPerfect, or Excel, you cannot bring your spreadsheet information directly into WordPerfect. Instead, you must first convert your information into one of the formats that WordPerfect recognizes. Most spreadsheets now have the capability to translate their information into Lotus 1-2-3 format, which can then be used within WordPerfect.

Using Database Information with WordPerfect

You have several ways to bring information from databases into WordPerfect. Unfortunately, none is as easy as bringing spreadsheet information into WordPerfect. To use database information in WordPerfect, you must first do one of two things:

- Prepare a delimited file that can be used directly in a WordPerfect merge or converted into WordPerfect secondary-merge format
- Print a report to disk as a DOS text file, which can be retrieved into WordPerfect

Preparing a Delimited File

Most databases enable you to prepare a copy of the database in DOS text format (see the section "Using DOS Text Files with WordPerfect" for a complete description of DOS text files). This copy of the database uses particular characters to separate (or "delimit") one field from another and one record from another. Typically, a comma (,) is used to delimit fields; a carriage return (CR), line feed (LF), or both are used to delimit records.

Each database program has different ways of creating delimited files. The following instructions demonstrate how to create a delimited file from within dBASE III:

1. Start dBASE.
2. To translate a dBASE file called CUSTOMER into delimited form, type *use CUSTOMER* at the dot prompt.
3. Type *copy to CUSTOMER delimited* to create the delimited file CUSTOMER.TXT.

   If you want only certain fields from the original file to appear, list the field names after the word *copy*. Suppose that you type the following command:

   copy NAME STREET CITY STATE to CUSTOMER delimited

   Only the NAME, STREET, CITY, and STATE fields would be copied to the delimited file.
4. Leave dBASE by typing *quit* at the dot prompt.

> ### Tip
> You can give the resulting delimited file an extension; for example, the file can be called CUSTOMER.MRG. If you don't supply an extension, dBASE adds the extension TXT to the file name you use.

Once you have the delimited file, you can use it as is in a WordPerfect merge or convert it to a WordPerfect secondary-merge file.

Using a Delimited File in a Merge

To use the delimited file in a merge, you must set up a primary-merge document that uses the appropriate fields. See Chapter 13, "Assembling Documents with Merge," for specific instructions on creating a primary-merge file.

After preparing the primary-merge file, you are ready to begin the merge:

1. Press Merge/Sort (Ctrl-F9) and select **M**erge (**1**).

   ⌨ Access the **T**ools pull-down menu and select **M**erge.

2. Type the name of the primary file and press Enter.

3. Type the name of the delimited file and press Enter. You will see the screen shown in figure 16.6.

Fig. 16.6.
The Merge: DOS Text File menu.

4. If necessary, enter the delimiters for your delimited file. You should not need to enter a beginning delimiter. If you need to enter a **[CR]** code as a delimiter, press Ctrl-M.

5. Press Enter to begin the merge.

Noting Delimited-File Considerations

When dBASE III creates a delimited file, the program automatically uses the comma as the field delimiter. This custom can create problems if a field contains a comma. In such a case, the comma within the field could be mistaken as a field delimiter. To avoid such problems, dBASE automatically surrounds all character fields with quotation marks (") when it creates a delimited field.

As a result, when you use the delimited file in a WordPerfect merge, you may find that you need to remove the quotation marks. You can do so easily by using the Replace (Alt-F2) feature.

Other databases enable you to specify what characters you want to use as delimiters. If you have such an opportunity, you should use a character that is not commonly used; the vertical bar (|) and tilde (~) are good choices.

Converting a Delimited File to Secondary-Merge Format

As an alternative to using a delimited file directly in a merge, you can convert the file to WordPerfect secondary-merge format by using WordPerfect's Convert program. When you convert the delimited file, the Convert program automatically replaces the field delimiters with {END FIELD} codes and the record delimiters with {END RECORD} codes. In addition, the program removes all the quotation marks dBASE adds to the file.

For detailed instructions on converting delimited files to secondary-merge format, see the section "Using WordPerfect's Convert Program."

Working with dBASE Dates

When you prepare a delimited file in dBASE, all dates are changed to an eight-digit number. The date 12/31/89, for example, is changed to the number 19891231—a rather difficult number to read. To prevent this problem, you may want to change each dBASE date field (which contains the entire month, day, and year information) to individual month, day, and year fields. At the same time, you can change the number representing the month to the actual name of the month. To do so, you must modify the structure of your database to add the new fields; then you must convert the information in the existing date field into the information for the individual month, day, and year fields.

Cue:

Change dBASE date fields to individual month, day, and year fields.

Suppose that one of the fields in your database is a date field called BIRTHDAY. You can modify the structure of the database to include new fields named BIRMONTH, BIRDAY, and BIRYEAR.

To modify the structure, do the following, pressing Enter after each step:

1. Type *use filename*

   Note: In this step and in step 2, replace *filename* with the name of your file.

2. Type *copy filename to temp*

3. Type *use temp*

4. Type *modify structure*

5. Add the following fields:

   BIRMONTH (a character field with a width of nine)

   BIRDAY (a numerical field with a width of two and no decimal places)

   BIRYEAR (a numerical field with a width of four and no decimal places)

6. Press Ctrl-End when you are finished modifying the structure.

Now you are ready to convert the date field BIRTHDAY to the three individual fields. At the dot prompt, do the following, pressing Enter after each step:

1. Type *replace all birmonth with cmonth (birthday)*

2. Type *replace all birday with day (birthday)*

3. Type *replace all biryear with year (birthday)*

4. Type *copy to newfile delimited*

   Note: Replace *newfile* with the name you want to use for your delimited file.

Thus if a certain record contains the birthday 12/15/60, BIRMONTH is December, BIRDAY is 15, and BIRYEAR is 1960.

Using Database Reports

Most databases can prepare printed data reports. Most also enable you to "print" these reports to a file as a DOS text file. Once you have the file containing the report, you can easily retrieve the file into WordPerfect. See the following section for more information about DOS text files and the use of those files within WordPerfect. As mentioned earlier, using DOS text to transfer information is the least desirable conversion method. Use the method only as a last resort.

Using DOS Text Files with WordPerfect

DOS text is the DOS-based world's closest approximation of a common language. More realistically, DOS text files are the "least common denominator" for most programs. As a result, the DOS text file is a common means of transferring information between programs.

Reminder:
DOS text is also called ASCII text.

DOS text is also known as ASCII, which stands for American Standard Code for Information Interchange. ASCII is a standardized system for translating ones and zeros to numbers, punctuation marks, symbols, and special computer characters. A DOS text file consists of letters, numbers, punctuation marks, math symbols, and a few special codes, such as tabs and carriage returns, that have the same meaning across programs.

Understanding the Limitations of DOS Text Files

When you use DOS text files to transfer information, you can encounter major problems with such formatting options as tabs, indents, and centering. Because DOS text does not include formatting codes for these features, all formatting is converted into spaces. This conversion creates problems when you try to edit a DOS text file. For example, if you add text, indented paragraphs wrap to the margin, and spaces used to align the paragraph are moved into the middle of the lines.

Reminder:
If possible, use some means other than DOS text to transfer information.

You also lose all the special codes from any program that supports advanced features. For example, word processors lose all formatting such as bold, underline, and so on, whereas in spreadsheets, all formulas are converted into numbers. Thus whenever you can, find some way other than DOS text to transfer information from program to program. If you have no alternative, however, or if your main goal is to transfer text with little or no special formatting, DOS text files provide a convenient universal language.

Bringing DOS Text into WordPerfect

Two codes are always at the end of every line in a DOS text file: a carriage return (CR) and a line feed (LF). These terms come from an older generation when computers could output only information to a printer. The CR code told the printer to return the carriage to the beginning of the line; the LF code told the printer to feed the paper up one line.

WordPerfect has two ways to use DOS text: through the Retrieve and Text/In Out features. The Retrieve feature converts all CR/LF codes in the DOS text file to WordPerfect **[HRt]** codes. Text/In Out provides the same option but also lets you convert CR/LF codes (with a few exceptions) into WordPerfect **[SRt]** codes.

The method you choose depends on the information you want to retrieve. Retrieve (CR/LF to **[HRt]**) is generally more effective for information organized by lines, as in:

- Database reports, which usually collect related information on one line
- Database delimited files that mark the end of each record with a CR/LF
- Tables of numeric or statistical information

Text In/Out (CR/LF to **[SRt]**) is generally more effective for text that flows from line to line. This kind of information can typically be found in word processors and electronic mail systems.

Converting CR/LF Codes to [SRt] Codes

If WordPerfect converted all CR/LF codes to **[SRt]** codes, your text would contain no breaks at all, and you would not be able to tell where paragraphs, new section, and titles begin and end. Therefore, when WordPerfect uses the CR/LF to SRt option in converting a DOS text file, the following guidelines are followed:

- A CR/LF that is not in the hyphenation zone is converted to a **[HRt]**. WordPerfect assumes that short lines, such as those used for headings and those that end paragraphs, should end with a **[HRt]**.

  Note: The hyphenation zone is the area at the end of the line that WordPerfect uses to determine whether a word needs to be hyphenated.

- If the CR/LF code is immediately followed by another CR/LF code, both codes are converted to **[HRt]** codes. This is true even if the first CR/LF code is in the hyphenation zone. In such a case, WordPerfect assumes that two CR/LF codes in succession indicate the beginning of a new paragraph.

- All other CR/LF codes in the hyphenation zone are converted to **[HRt]** codes.

Retrieving a DOS Text File (CR/LF to [HRt])

The easiest way to bring a DOS text file into WordPerfect is to retrieve it as you would a regular WordPerfect file. Perform the following steps:

1. Press List (F5).

   ▢ Access the **F**ile pull-down menu and select List **F**iles.

   If you remember the name of the file, it may be faster to use Retrieve (Shift-F10).

2. Type the name of the DOS text file you want to retrieve, including the drive and extension, if necessary, and press Enter. At the bottom left of the screen you will see the message DOS Text Conversion in Progress, and then your document will appear on the screen.

Using Text In/Out (CR/LF to [SRt])

To bring in a DOS text file and have WordPerfect convert the CR/LF codes to **[SRt]** codes, do the following:

1. Press Text In/Out (Ctrl-F5), select DOS **T**ext (**1**), and select **R**etrieve (CR/LF to [SRt] in HZone) (**3**).

    ⌨ Access the **F**ile pull-down menu, select Text **I**n, and select DOS Text (CR/LF to **S**Rt).

2. Type the name of the DOS text file you want to convert and press Enter.

Creating DOS Text with WordPerfect

WordPerfect also can create DOS text files from a WordPerfect document. Remember, however, that these files will lose all special WordPerfect formatting such as tabs, indents, bold, underline, headers and footers, and footnotes.

To save a WordPerfect document as a DOS text file, do the following:

1. Have the document on-screen.

2. Press Text In/Out (Ctrl-F5), select DOS **T**ext (**1**), and select **S**ave (**1**).

    ⌨ Access the **F**ile pull-down menu, select Text **O**ut, and select DOS **T**ext.

Reminder:
Do not give the DOS text file the same name as your WordPerfect document.

3. Type the name for the DOS text file, including the disk and path name if you like, and press Enter. Be careful, however: give the DOS text file a name different from the name of the WordPerfect document.

Creating a Generic Word Processing File

WordPerfect provides another way to save files in DOS text: the generic word processing format. The differences between a DOS text file and a generic word processing file are these:

- **[SRt]** codes are converted to CR/LF codes in DOS text but are converted to spaces in generic word processing format.

- **[Tab]** codes are converted to spaces in DOS text but are retained as **[Tab]** codes in generic word processing format.

To save a file in generic word processing format, do the following:

1. Have the document on-screen.

2. Press Text In/Out (Ctrl-F5), select Save **A**s (**3**), and select **G**eneric (**1**).

    ⌨ Access the **F**ile pull-down menu, select Text **O**ut, and select **G**eneric.

3. Type the name for the generic text file, including the disk and path name if you like, and press Enter. Be careful, however: give the generic file a name different from the name of the WordPerfect document.

Creating a DOS-Text Print File

When you save a WordPerfect document as DOS text or in generic word processing format, all special codes—including headers, footers, page numbers, and footnotes—are stripped from the document. However, by "printing" your file to a DOS text file, you can create a DOS text file that includes these features.

To print a document to a DOS text file, you must change your selected printer's settings so that the document prints to a file instead of to a parallel or serial port. To change the printer's settings, do the following:

1. Press Print (Shift-F7).

   ⌐⊟ Access the **F**ile pull-down menu and select **P**rint.

2. Choose **S**elect Printer (**S**).

3. Highlight the printer you want to use; choose **E**dit (**3**).

4. Select **P**ort (**3**) and then select **O**ther (**8**).

5. Type the name of the file you want to create, including the disk and path name if you like, and press Enter. Be sure that you do not use the name of your WordPerfect document.

6. Now print the document the way you normally would. Doing so creates a DOS text file with headers, footers, page numbers, and footnotes in place as they would be when printed.

Converting 5 or 4.2 Documents for Use in 5.1

To use a document created in WordPerfect 5 or 4.2 with version 5.1, you simply need to retrieve the document. WordPerfect automatically converts the file from the older version. You may notice, especially when converting from 4.2, that some codes cannot be converted directly.

Appendix B discusses how to change—or not to change—formats during a conversion. Such a change might be the move from a 4.2 font to a 5.1 font or the automatic change from underlining to italics.

Converting 5.1 Documents for Use in 5 or 4.2

When you first use WordPerfect 5.1, you will doubtless need to send a file to someone still using version 5 or even 4.2. To convert a 5.1 file into either 5 or 4.2 format, do the following:

1. Have the document on-screen.

2. Press Text In/Out (Ctrl-F5), select Save **A**s (**3**), and select either **W**ordPerfect 5 (**2**) or Word**P**erfect 4.2 (**3**).

⌨ Access the **F**ile pull-down menu, select Text **O**ut, and select either **W**P5.0 or W**P**4.2.

3. Type the name of the file you want to create, including the disk and path name if you like, and press Enter. Be sure that you do not use the name of your WordPerfect 5.1 document.

Using WordPerfect's Convert Program

WordPerfect Corporation provides a separate program, Convert, to translate files from other formats to WordPerfect 5.1 or from WordPerfect 5.1 to other formats. The program is an important tool for data transfer.

If you are familiar with WordPerfect 5, you will find that the Convert program has not changed significantly with version 5.1. To run Convert, you must exit from WordPerfect to the DOS prompt. Convert is not available from within WordPerfect.

To use the Convert program from the DOS prompt, do the following:

1. Change to the directory where the file you want to convert is located.

2. Type *\wp51\convert* and press Enter.

   Note: Replace *\wp51* with the name of the directory where your copy of the Convert program is stored.

3. Type the name of the file you want to convert (the input file) and press Enter.

   Note: If you get the message `Error—Invalid Input File Name` or `File does not exist`, try specifying the directory in which the file is kept, or check the spelling of the file name.

4. Type the name you want to give to the converted file (the output file) and press Enter. If a file is already using the file name you select, the message `Confirm Overwrite of <filename> (Y/[N])` appears. If you want to replace the old file, press Y. Otherwise, press N and enter a new name.

The menu in figure 16.7 appears. From this menu, you can convert WordPerfect files to and from various formats. The following sections explain your options.

Converting Files for Use in WordPerfect

All the entries shown in figure 16.7, except selections 0 and 1, convert files for use in WordPerfect. Selections 2, 3, 4, 5, 6, 8, and B convert files from other word processors. Selection A converts spreadsheet files. Selection 9 converts database delimited files. Selection 7 converts files formatted in a special, and rarely used, telecommunications format.

```
Name of Input File? \dp\dbreport.txt
Name of Output File? \51docs\dbreport.txt

0 EXIT
1 WordPerfect to another format
2 Revisable-Form-Text (IBM DCA Format) to WordPerfect
3 Final-Form-Text (IBM DCA Format) to WordPerfect
4 Navy DIF Standard to WordPerfect
5 WordStar 3.3 to WordPerfect
6 MultiMate Advantage II to WordPerfect
7 Seven-Bit Transfer Format to WordPerfect
8 WordPerfect 4.2 to WordPerfect 5.1
9 Mail Merge to WordPerfect Secondary Merge
A Spreadsheet DIF to WordPerfect Secondary Merge
B Word 4.0 to WordPerfect

Enter number of Conversion desired
```

Fig. 16.7.
*The Convert
menu.*

Intermediate Formats

If you do not see your program on the menu, you may still be able to convert your document without having to use DOS text. To do so, you must use one of the formats shown as an *intermediate* format. Examine the program's documentation for instructions on how to convert the program to other formats. If you find instructions for conversion to one of the formats supported by WordPerfect, you can do the following:

1. Use your program to convert to the intermediate format.
2. Use the Convert program to convert from the intermediate format to WordPerfect.

For example, WordPerfect's Convert program does not convert files directly from the Palantir word processor. However, Palantir lets you convert from Palantir to WordStar. Therefore, you can first convert a Palantir document to WordStar by using Palantir's conversion procedures, then convert the WordStar document to WordPerfect by using WordPerfect's Convert program.

Because many word processors can convert to WordStar format, WordStar is a good candidate as an intermediate format. If you have access to Document Content Architecture (DCA), however, you may find that it is even better as an intermediate format. DCA is a standard established by IBM for the transfer of word processing programs across IBM systems—from microcomputers to mainframe computers. DCA is designed to preserve features during the translation between different word processors.

Word Processing Conversions

The Convert program will convert from Revisable- and Final-Form-Text, Navy DIF, MultiMate Advantage II, seven-bit transfer, WordStar 3.3, Microsoft Word 4.0, and WordPerfect 4.2 formats.

Translating from Revisable-Form-Text (DCA)

Revisable-Form-Text (RFT) is text formatted according to IBM's Document Content Architecture (DCA). Many programs, particularly the DisplayWrite series of word processors, can convert to DCA/RFT. Those files can, in turn, be converted to WordPerfect format. To translate from Revisable-Form-Text, choose Revisable-Form-Text (IBM DCA Format) to WordPerfect (**3**).

Translating from Final-Form-Text (DCA)

Final-Form-Text is like the preceding selection but is used primarily on some IBM mainframe computers. To translate from Final-Form-Text, choose Final-Form-Text (IBM DCA Format) to WordPerfect (**4**).

Translating from Navy DIF

Navy DIF (Data Interchange Format) is a format developed by the Navy to ease the transfer of word processing information from various types of computers. To translate from Navy DIF, choose Navy DIF Standard to WordPerfect (**4**).

Translating from WordStar

To translate from WordStar to WordPerfect, choose WordStar 3.3 to WordPerfect (**5**). The Convert program completes the translation of the original WordStar document into WordPerfect format.

If you have WordStar 2000, you must first translate from WordStar 2000 to WordStar Professional Format. You then can convert the resulting document into WordPerfect format by using the WordStar 3.3 to WordPerfect (**5**) selection.

Translating from MultiMate Advantage II

To translate from MultiMate to WordPerfect, choose MultiMate Advantage II to WordPerfect (**6**). The conversion also works with MultiMate 3.3 and MultiMate Advantage.

Translating from WordPerfect 4.2

Retrieving a WordPerfect 4.2 file into 5.1 automatically converts the file to 5.1 format. However, if you want to convert many files at once, you can use the Convert program. To convert several 4.2 files, do the following:

1. Copy the 4.2 files into the same directory.
2. Start the Convert program.
3. When prompted for the name of the input file, type *42docs**.* and press Enter. Replace *42docs*\ with the name of the directory you are using.
4. When prompted for the name of the output file, type *51docs**.* and press Enter. Replace *51docs*\ with the name of the directory you are using for 5.1 documents.
5. Select WordPerfect 4.2 to WordPerfect 5.1 (**8**).

Translating from Microsoft Word

To translate from Microsoft Word 4.0 to WordPerfect 5.1, choose Word 4.0 to WordPerfect (**B**).

Spreadsheet Conversions

In most cases, you will now want to retrieve the information in the spreadsheet directly into WordPerfect. See the earlier section "Using Spreadsheet Information with WordPerfect" for more information.

At times, however, you may want to use spreadsheet information in a merge (as with information set up as a database within a spreadsheet). To do so, you must first use the spreadsheet's translate feature to convert the spreadsheet into the spreadsheet DIF format. Then use the Convert program and select Spreadsheet DIF to WordPerfect Secondary Merge (**A**).

Database Delimited-File Conversions

In the section "Using Database Information with WordPerfect," you learned how to prepare a database file for use in a WordPerfect merge. You also can use the Convert program to prepare a WordPerfect secondary-merge document from a delimited file. The advantage to using Convert is that the program can automatically strip characters used to identify character fields.

To convert a delimited file (also called a "mail merge" file), do the following:

1. Choose Mail Merge to WordPerfect Secondary Merge (**9**). The Convert program then prompts `Enter Field delimiter characters or decimal ASCII values enclosed in {}` (see figure 16.8).

```
Name of Input File? \dp\dbreport.txt
Name of Output File? \51docs\dbreport.txt

0 EXIT
1 WordPerfect to another format
2 Revisable-Form-Text (IBM DCA Format) to WordPerfect
3 Final-Form-Text (IBM DCA Format) to WordPerfect
4 Navy DIF Standard to WordPerfect
5 WordStar 3.3 to WordPerfect
6 MultiMate Advantage II to WordPerfect
7 Seven-Bit Transfer Format to WordPerfect
8 WordPerfect 4.2 to WordPerfect 5.1
9 Mail Merge to WordPerfect Secondary Merge
A Spreadsheet DIF to WordPerfect Secondary Merge
B Word 4.0 to WordPerfect

Enter number of Conversion desired 9

Enter Field delimiter characters or decimal ASCII values enclosed in {}
```

Fig. 16.8.

*The prompt that appears after you select Mail Merge to WordPerfect Secondary (**9**).*

2. Type the character used as the field delimiter and press Enter. If you are using dBASE, the delimiter is a comma (,). The prompt `Enter Record delimiter characters or decimal ASCII values enclosed in {}` appears.

Records in delimited files are usually separated by a CR/LF combination. This combination is typed as {13}{10}.

3. Type the character used as the record delimiter and press Enter. Remember that ASCII codes for nontext characters must be surrounded by curly brackets. The prompt Enter character to be stripped from file or press Enter if none appears.

4. If your database uses a character to indicate character fields, type that character and press Enter. Otherwise, just press Enter.

Seven-Bit Format Conversion

Some older telecommunications systems read information in the form of seven-bit data words. In other words, these systems require seven bits as one character of information. The seven-bit format conversion makes it possible to take information from such a system and convert that information to the more usual eight-bit format. To convert from a seven-bit format, choose Seven-Bit Transfer Format to WordPerfect (**7**).

Translating WordPerfect into Other Formats

Convert lets you convert files from WordPerfect 5.1 to other formats. After starting Convert, you will see the menu in figure 16.7. To convert from WordPerfect to another format, select the option WordPerfect to another format (**1**). The menu in figure 16.9 appears.

Fig. 16.9.
The Convert To menu.

```
Name of Input File? \51docs\report.mmc
Name of Output File? \51docs\report.doc

0 EXIT
1 Revisable-Form-Text (IBM DCA Format)
2 Final-Form-Text (IBM DCA Format)
3 Navy DIF Standard
4 WordStar 3.3
5 MultiMate Advantage II
6 Seven-Bit Transfer Format
7 ASCII Text File
8 WordPerfect Secondary Merge to Spreadsheet DIF

Enter number of output file format desired
```

You can see that many of the choices are the same as for converting to WordPerfect. Notice that you can convert to ASCII text and that no selection for converting to WordPerfect 4.2 is available.

Word Processing Conversions

The WordPerfect Convert program will convert to Revisable- and Final-Form-Text, Navy DIF, MultiMate Advantage II, WordStar 3.3, seven-bit transfer, and ASCII text formats. As mentioned earlier, if you need to convert to a format not shown, try to find an intermediate format that you can convert into the format you need.

Translating to Revisable-Form-Text (DCA)

Many programs, particularly the DisplayWrite series of word processors, can use files in DCA/RFT. To use WordPerfect with those programs, convert from WordPerfect to DCA/RFT and then convert to the program you want to use.

To translate to Revisable-Form-Text, choose Revisable-Form-Text (IBM DCA Format) (**1**).

Translating to Final-Form-Text (DCA)

Final-Form-Text is like the preceding selection but is used primarily on some IBM mainframe computers. To translate to Final-Form-Text, choose Final-Form-Text (IBM DCA Format) (**2**).

Translating to Navy DIF

Navy DIF (Data Interchange Format) is a format developed by the Navy to ease the transfer of word processing information from various types of computers. To translate to Navy DIF, choose Navy DIF Standard (**3**).

Translating to WordStar

To translate from WordPerfect to WordStar, choose WordStar 3.3 (**4**). If you have WordStar 2000, you must first translate to WordStar 3.3 and then use WordStar 2000's conversion procedure and convert from WordStar Professional Format.

Translating to MultiMate Advantage II

To translate to MultiMate, choose MultiMate Advantage II to WordPerfect (**5**). The conversion also works with MultiMate 3.3 and MultiMate Advantage.

Remember that MultiMate recognizes a file as a word processing document only if the file has a DOC extension, so give your output files a DOC extension.

Translating to ASCII Text (DOS Text)

Although you can convert individual WordPerfect 5.1 files to DOS text, you must use the Convert program if you want to convert several files at once. To convert several files, do the following:

1. Copy the 5.1 files into the same directory.
2. Start the Convert program.
3. When prompted for the name of the input file, type *51con**.* and press Enter. Replace *51con*\\ with the name of the directory you are using.
4. When prompted for the name of the output file, type *51con**.txt* and press Enter. Replace *51con*\\ with the name of the directory you are using.
5. Select ASCII Text File (**7**).

Spreadsheet Conversions

If you want to convert WordPerfect information for use in a spreadsheet, that information must be in the form of a WordPerfect secondary-merge document. (For information on creating a secondary-merge document, see Chapter 13, "Assembling Documents with Merge.") You can then use the Convert program to convert this file to a spreadsheet DIF file. Then, from within your spreadsheet, you can translate the DIF file to a spreadsheet. You will probably need to adjust the spreadsheet's column widths after the last conversion.

To convert the secondary-merge file into spreadsheet DIF, do the following:

1. Start the Convert program.
2. Type the name of the input file and press Enter. Remember to type the drive and directory, if necessary.
3. Type the name of the output file and press Enter.
4. Select the option WordPerfect to another format (**1**).
5. Select WordPerfect Secondary Merge to Spreadsheet DIF (**8**).

To translate DIF into 1-2-3, complete these steps:

1. Enter the Lotus Translate facility, either through the Lotus Access Menu or by typing *trans*. The Translate menu walks you through translating a DIF file into a 1-2-3 or Symphony worksheet. Make selections by moving the cursor to the appropriate choice and pressing Enter.
2. Select the choice Translate a DIF file column by column.

If the DIF file you want to translate is in a directory other than the current one, the file will not appear in the list of available files. When the Translate utility lists available files, press the Esc key twice to find your file. The cursor is then positioned at a blank space entitled Source. Type the name of the drive and directory where the file you want to translate is located. Follow that information with the file template: *.dif* (that is, c:\data*.dif)

The Translate utility produces a file with the same file name as the translated DIF file—and an appropriate extension such as WK1 or WKS. You can retrieve this file into 1-2-3, although you will probably have to change column-width settings.

Database Conversions

You cannot easily convert a WordPerfect document into a format usable in a database. To make such a conversion you must do the following:

1. Use the Convert program to convert a secondary-merge document to spreadsheet DIF format.
2. Use a spreadsheet translate procedure to convert the DIF file to a spreadsheet.
3. Adjust the format of the spreadsheet so that the data is displayed properly.
4. Use the spreadsheet translate procedure to convert the spreadsheet to a DBF database file, which can then be used by the database.

Seven-Bit Format Conversion

As discussed in the section on converting to WordPerfect, some older telecommunications systems read information in the form of seven-bit data words. To translate from WordPerfect to documents using such systems, you must convert the normal eight-bit format to seven-bit. To convert to seven-bit format, choose Seven-Bit Transfer Format (**6**).

Using Convert without Menus

If you perform a particular conversion often, WordPerfect's prompts and your responses become second nature. The Convert program menus become unnecessary, and you may even come to regard them as a nuisance. Fortunately, you can bypass the menus: at the DOS prompt in the subdirectory where the Convert program is located, simply type *convert* and then type each response in turn, separating them with spaces. If you remember only the first few steps, just type *convert* and those responses (separated by spaces) that you do remember. The program bypasses the steps you remember.

Reminder:
You can bypass Convert's menus if you like.

The syntax for conversion into WordPerfect is as follows:

> *convert input output n (field delimiter) (record delimiter) (characters to be stripped)*

where *input* is the input file's name, with drive and directory if necessary; *output* is the output file's name; and *n* is the number of the conversion type. The last three entries are necessary only if you select Mail Merge to WordPerfect Secondary Merge (**9**).

The syntax for conversion from WordPerfect is as follows:

> *convert input output 1 n*

where *input* is the input file's name, with drive and directory if necessary; *output* is the output file's name; and *n* is the number of the conversion type. You must type the 1 to select the WordPerfect to another format (**1**) option.

Consider the following examples. The command

> convert \mm\letter.doc \51docs\letter.wp 6

converts a MultiMate file to a WordPerfect document. Remember that the MultiMate file must be in the current directory, or the Convert program responds with `Error—Invalid Input File Name` or `File does not exist`. The LETTER.WP file is placed in the current subdirectory.

The command

> convert c:\data\clients.txt \51docs\clients.sf 9 , {13}{10}

converts a mail-merge file named CLIENTS.TXT, located in the C:\DATA directory, to the WordPerfect secondary-merge file CLIENTS.SF, in the \51DOCS directory.

Performing Mass Conversions

With WordPerfect, you can use the DOS wild card *. Thus the command

    convert *.doc *.wp 5

converts all MultiMate files in the current directory to WordPerfect files with the extension WP. Be careful, however, that all files in the directory with the DOC extension are, in fact, MultiMate files.

Summary

In this chapter, you learned that WordPerfect can exchange information with other software. This exchange feature enables you to accomplish any task with the best tool. For example, you can now do the following tasks:

- ❏ Incorporate budgets from 1-2-3 by simply retrieving the spreadsheet or by using the new Spreadsheet option from the Text In/Out (Ctrl-F5) menu.
- ❏ Translate other word processors to and from WordPerfect by using the Convert program.
- ❏ Merge information from a dBASE file into a WordPerfect letter either directly or with the help of Convert.
- ❏ Use intermediate formats for data transfer.
- ❏ Decide between performing a necessary manipulation in the original program or in the program to which data is transferred.

Transferring data in and out of WordPerfect sometimes takes many steps, but with a little practice the process becomes routine. Because most business presentations involve both numbers and text, which must be combined to create a useful report, data transfer has assumed increasing importance. Data transfer is an important method of combining powerful numerical and data analysis with WordPerfect's superior text-handling capabilities.

5.1

Part III

Using WordPerfect's Specialized Features

Working with Text Columns

Using Math

Creating Tables

Customizing WordPerfect

Working with Special Characters
and Foreign Languages

Creating Equations

Using Footnotes and Endnotes

Outlining, Paragraph Numbering,
and Line Numbering

Assembling Document References

Using the Master Document Feature
for Large Projects

17

Working with Text Columns

Hans Lustig, a copy chief for an industrial advertising agency, uses WordPerfect to write copy for industrial brochures and manuals. Through his work, he has developed expertise in working with text columns in WordPerfect.

WordPerfect offers you a powerful feature that lets you put your text in one of two types of columns: newspaper columns, also called *snaking* columns, and parallel columns. *Newspaper columns* provide flowing text that wraps from the bottom of one column to the top of the next column and then wraps back to the first column on the left on the next page. *Parallel columns* are read from left to right across the page, unlike newspaper columns, which are read from top to bottom.

In this chapter, you explore WordPerfect's columns feature. The basic procedure for invoking the columns feature is the same for both newspaper-style columns and parallel columns. You learn how to set up both kinds of columns, how to work with them, and how to edit them, as well as how to mix columns with regular text and preview your masterpiece. You learn also how to use macros, the keyboard-mapping capability of WordPerfect, to speed up the process. You start with newspaper columns and walk through the various procedures step by step; then you do the same with parallel columns.

Reminder
If you use a mouse with WordPerfect 5.1, you can click the right button to display the pull-down menus, and then select the desired option. You also can press Alt-= to access the pull-down menus, and then press the appropriate letter of the desired option. For all the instructions, you can assume that if a block is required to activate a pull-down menu option, the text has been blocked before the pull-down menu is accessed. Instructions for pull-down menus and the mouse are marked with the mouse icon. See Chapter 1 for details on using the mouse.

Newspaper Columns

If you're a newspaper reporter, a copywriter for an advertising agency, or simply a club member who has been roped into doing the monthly newsletter, you probably want your text in column format. Even simple newsletter copy, such as you see in figure 17.1, looks better and is easier to read if the copy is in newspaper-column format. Compared to text in page-wide printing, text in columns is easier for the eye to follow, particularly if the text is spaced correctly (neither too close together nor too far apart).

Fig. 17.1.

An example of newspaper columns.

New Drivers School Location

There's been a change in the location for this year's drivers school for the Windy City Chapter, and I know you'll love this one! Instead of going to Blackhawk Farms, we'll be going up to Road America in beautiful Elkhart Lake, Wisconsin.

This way, all you hotshoes will have about 4.5 miles instead of 2.5 miles to thrash your Bimmers around the track. It'll also be easier on your brakes than Blackhawk, due to the longer straights that'll give them a chance to cool off between turns.

The dates will remain the same, May 21 and 22. Lodging, as always, will be available at Siebkens and Barefoot Bay in Elkhart Lake, or at Motels in Sheboygan or Fond du Lac. Remember, you must make your own reservations. Remember also that Siebkens is basically a summertime resort, which means NO HEAT

in the rooms. Also no phones and no credit cards. But LOTS of ATMOSPHERE.

The rates at both Siebkens and Barefoot Bay are quite reasonable, $24 and $48 (single/double) at Siebkens and $59.95 at Barefoot Bay for either single or double. Driving directions to Elkhart Lake will be included with your registration package, along with a map of the area.

SATURDAY DINNER

There'll be dinner at Siebkens Saturday night, with a choice of fish, duck or prime rib. The cost will be $15 plus tip. We'll have a cash bar also, but remember you'll want a clear head the next morning or your Bimmer will start playing tricks on you. So go easy on the liquid stuff.

If you want to join us for dinner, let Registration know Saturday morning what your

choice of entree is, otherwise there'll be no food waiting for you.

PRETECH AT LEO'S

Pretech will as always be at Leo Franchi's Midwest Motor Sports. The date is April 23. This will give you a chance to get anything fixed before the drivers school. A tech sheet is enclosed with the registration package. Be sure to fill it out and bring it along. There is no charge for the tech inspection. We're planning to start at 9 a.m. and go until everybody is done.

If you miss the tech at Leo's, you'll have to go to your favorite mechanic and bring proof of the inspection and any repairs that were made. Remember, NO TECH - NO TRACK.

We look forward to seeing you all at Elkhart Lake.

Enjoy!

Note: For those of you who have never been to Road America, here's a little tip: At this time of year, the weather up there in dairy country is rather unpredictable. Be prepared to either fry or freeze.

That's all there is for now. Oh - bring brake pads! They may come in handy. A couple

of cans of oil will be useful also, particularly for the older cars which are wont to use a

bit more. And, of course, you'll want to have your tools handy just in case.

One more thing, watch out for the Wisconsin constabulary, they always find a great chance to balance their budget when we come up there. So take it easy on Highway 57. That's their favorite moneymaker.

Defining Newspaper Columns

Putting your information into columns is much easier than using Tab and Indent (F4) to produce columns. Once you begin with Tab and Indent, you must continue to use them for every paragraph, because a hard return takes you back to the left margin. In addition, depending on how wide you want each column, you must reset your margins before you start and reset them back to the original when you finish.

With WordPerfect you can have as many as 24 columns across a page, and you have many choices for setting them up. You use the columns feature by pressing Columns/Tables (Alt-F7) or by accessing the **L**ayout pull-down menu and selecting **C**olumns (see fig. 17.2).

Reminder:

*To access the columns feature, press Columns/ Tables (Alt-F7) or access the **L**ayout pull-down menu and select **C**olumns.*

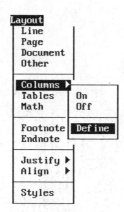

Fig. 17.2.

*The **L**ayout pull-down menu with **C**olumns selected.*

When you select **C**olumns and **D**efine from either the regular or the pull-down menu, the Column Definition screen appears (see fig. 17.3) and displays the default settings. If you want the default settings for your document, simply press Exit (F7). Then at the position where you want to start your columnar text, select **O**n (**1**) from the next menu. For a different format, follow the steps in this section.

```
Text Column Definition

    1 - Type                        Newspaper

    2 - Number of Columns           2

    3 - Distance Between Columns

    4 - Margins

    Column    Left     Right    Column    Left     Right
     1:       1"       4"        13:
     2:       4.5"     7.5"      14:
     3:                          15:
     4:                          16:
     5:                          17:
     6:                          18:
     7:                          19:
     8:                          20:
     9:                          21:
    10:                          22:
    11:                          23:
    12:                          24:

Selection: 0
```

Fig. 17.3.

The Column Definition screen.

To define newspaper-style columns, do the following:

1. Move the cursor to the position where you want to start the columns.

2. Press Columns/Tables (Alt-F7) and select **C**olumns (**1**).

3. Select **D**efine (**3**) to display the Column Definition menu (see fig. 17.3).

   ⌨ Access the **L**ayout pull-down menu, select **C**olumns, and then select **D**efine.

4. Select **N**umber of Columns (**2**) if you want to have more than two columns of text; type the number of columns you want and press Enter.

   (To define newspaper columns, you do not need to select **T**ype (**1**), because Newspaper is the default setting in WordPerfect.)

5. Select **D**istance Between Columns (**3**) if you want a different amount of space between your columns than the default 0.5" (half-inch). Type the amount and press Enter.

6. Now select **M**argins (**4**).

   In most cases, you can accept the default margins offered by WordPerfect, which automatically calculates the column margins according to the margins you set for your document.

   You can change both the left and the right outside margins if you want your columns to be wider or narrower than the basic document. Set the remaining margins according to the spacing you want between columns.

   The columns that the default margins give you are of equal width and are spaced evenly across the page. If you want columns of a different width, you must type in the margins for the columns you want and press Enter after each number.

7. Press Enter when you're finished defining the columns and select **O**n (**1**) to turn on columns.

You're ready to start typing your newsletter or document.

Reminder:

Adjust the hyphenation zone or hyphenate manually to reduce the raggedness of columns.

WordPerfect inserts into your document a column-definition code, **[Col Def: {column margins}]**, which you can check in Reveal Codes (Alt-F3 or F11). As figure 17.4 shows, all your formatting codes are there, from hyphenation to justification to column definition. For columns, you may want to reset the hyphenation zone to reduce the raggedness of the right side of the column. (The defaults are 10% left and 4% right.) The type of video you use (monochrome, CGA, EGA, VGA), along with the monitor you use, affect how much you see on-screen. Your screen, therefore, may not look exactly like the screen shown here.

Because hyphenation zones in columns are quite narrow, you may want to hyphenate some words manually to eliminate some of the raggedness.

If your text will be printed in a newsletter or brochure, keep the following rule of thumb in mind when defining column width for readability: for 9-point type, the text should not be wider than 18 picas (3 inches); for 10-point type, the text should not be wider than 20 picas (about 3.3 inches); and so on in the same relationship (based on 6 picas per inch).

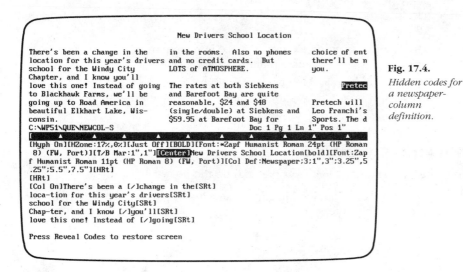

Fig. 17.4.
Hidden codes for a newspaper-column definition.

WordPerfect's default for spacing between columns is 0.5" (a half-inch), which is generous. When you print your newsletter with the default spacing, you get lots of white space between columns, so you might want to change the spacing to 0.25" or 0.35", which gives you a more attractive printed page.

Reminder:
WordPerfect offers a default of 0.5" for spacing between columns.

Typing Columnar Text

Typing columnar text is the same as typing a regular document. The text wraps automatically within the column and wraps to the top of the next column when you reach the bottom of the page. WordPerfect inserts the code **[SPg]**, indicating a soft page-break, at the bottom of each column because each is treated as a separate page by the program.

Moving the Cursor

Cursor movement in columns is the same as in a regular document—with some exceptions. The GoTo combination (Ctrl-Home) works with the arrow keys in the following ways:

- GoTo (Ctrl-Home), → moves the cursor to the next column.
- GoTo (Ctrl-Home), Home, → moves the cursor to the last column on the right.
- GoTo (Ctrl-Home), ← moves the cursor to the previous column.
- GoTo (Ctrl-Home), Home, ← moves the cursor to the first column on the left.
- Home, ↓ moves the cursor to the bottom of the column on the current screen (if the column fills the entire screen).
- Home, ↑ moves the cursor to the top of the column on the current screen (if the column fills the entire screen).

- The ↑ and ↓ keys by themselves work as in any document and scroll through all columns consecutively.
- The → and ← keys work within the column and move the cursor to the top or bottom of the adjacent column, depending on direction.
- The gray plus (+) and minus (–) keys move the cursor to the bottom or the top of the on-screen column, respectively (if the column fills the entire screen).

Centering Column Headings

To center a column heading over the text, do the following:

Move the cursor to the left margin of the column, press Center (Shift-F6), type the heading, and press Enter

or

▭ Access the **L**ayout pull-down menu, select **A**lign, and then select **C**enter.

If the heading already exists, do the following:

Move the cursor to the beginning of the heading, block the heading by pressing Block (Alt-F4 or F12), move the cursor to the end of the heading, press Center (Shift-F6), and select **Y** at the prompt.

▭ Move the mouse cursor to the beginning of the heading, hold the left mouse button, drag the cursor to the end of the heading to block it, and release the button. Next, access the **L**ayout pull-down menu, select **A**lign, and then select **C**enter. Select **Y** at the prompt.

Combining Columns with Regular Text

You can switch back and forth between columns and regular text as many times as you like (see fig. 17.5). The original column definitions stay in effect for your document until you insert new definitions.

At the point in your columnar document where you want to change to regular text, do the following:

1. Press Columns/Tables (Alt-F7), select **C**olumns (**1**), and then select Off (**2**).

   ▭ Access the **L**ayout pull-down menu, select **C**olumns, and then select **O**ff.

2. Type the regular text and press Enter at the end.

3. To return to columnar text, press Columns/Tables (Alt-F7), select **C**olumns (**1**), and press **O**n (**1**).

   ▭ Access the **L**ayout pull-down menu, select **C**olumns, and then select **O**n.

```
The dates will remain the    cost will be $15 plus tip. We'll    If you miss t
same, May 21 and 22. Lodg-   have a cash bar also, but          you'll have t
ing, as always, will be avail- remember you'll want a clear     rite mechanic
able at Siebkens and Barefoot head the next morning or your     of the inspec
Bay in Elkhart Lake, or at    Bimmer will start playing tricks  repairs that
Motels in Sheboygan or Fond   on you. So go easy on the         member, NO TE
du Lac. Remember, you must    liquid stuff.                     TRACK.
make your own reservations.
Remember also that Siebkens   If you want to join us for        We look forwa
is basically a summertime re- dinner, let Registration know     you all at El
sort, which means NO HEAT     Saturday morning what your
                                                                Enjoy!

     Note:   For those of you who have never been to Road America, here's a li
             At this time of year, the weather up there in dairy country is ra
             table. Be prepared to either fry or freeze.

That's all there is for now.  of cans of oil will be useful       bit more. And
Oh - bring brake pads! They   also, particularly for the older   you'll want a
may come in handy. A couple   cars which are wont to use a        handy just in

     One more thing, watch out for the Wisconsin constabulary, they always fin
     chance to balance their budget when we come up there. So take it easy on
     Highway 57. That's their favorite moneymaker.
C:\WP51\QUE\NEWCOL-S                          Doc 1 Pg 1 Ln 9.28" Pos 1.5"
```

Fig. 17.5.

Combining newspaper columns with regular text.

If you mix text with this technique and want to keep the columns an even length, figure out in advance how many lines deep the columns will be before the start of the regular text. Then type your columnar text that many lines and press Ctrl-Enter, which inserts a **[HPg]** code into the document and takes you to the top of the next column. If you don't go through this procedure, you will probably end up with lots of white space in the printed text. If the last column is shorter than the ones on the left, then after you turn off the columns feature, the cursor jumps to the bottom of the columns when you press Enter.

Creating Newspaper Columns from Existing Text

If you have an existing document that you want to convert to columns, do the following to change the text to a newspaper-column format:

1. Position the cursor at the beginning of the document. If your document has an overall heading, position the cursor on the line below the heading, unless you want to include the heading in the first column.

2. Press Columns/Tables (Alt-F7), define your columns, press Enter, and turn on the columns feature by choosing **O**n (**1**).

   Access the **L**ayout pull-down menu, select **C**olumns, select **D**efine, define your columns, and select **O**n.

3. Press the down-arrow key.

WordPerfect automatically reformats the text into columns.

If you have hyphenation turned on, WordPerfect either hyphenates the text automatically or continually asks you to confirm hyphenation. Depending on the length of your text, this operation can be fairly lengthy.

Editing Newspaper Columns

Editing newspaper columns is not much different from editing standard text. You can delete text, insert text, and change attributes (bolding, underlining, and so on) just as you do in regular text, and cursor movement in columns is similar to cursor movement in regular text. Because the basic editing is the same as the procedures you learned in Chapter 3, this section concentrates on the procedures for manipulating columns.

When you're using the columns feature, the editing keys work within the column as illustrated in table 17.1.

Table 17.1
Editing Keys in Columns

Editing Keys	Function
Ctrl-End	Erases to the end of the line in the column you are editing
Ctrl-PgDn	Erases to the end of the column, starting at the cursor position
→	Moves the cursor to the right within the column
←	Moves the cursor to the left within the column
↑	Scrolls up all columns together
↓	Scrolls down all columns together

Reminder:
To move, copy, delete, or append an entire column, first block the column.

You can use Move (Ctrl-F4) to cut or copy a sentence or paragraph within the column, but if you want to manipulate a whole column, you must block the column first.

To cut or move text within the column, do the following:

1. Press Move (Ctrl-F4).
2. Select either **S**entence (**1**), **P**aragraph (**2**), or **P**age (**3**).

   ▭ Access the **E**dit pull-down menu, choose S**e**lect, and then choose **S**entence, **P**aragraph, or P**a**ge.

   Even though WordPerfect considers each column a page, the program moves, copies, or deletes the full page of text, not just one column, when you select P**a**ge (**3**).
3. Select either **M**ove (**1**), **C**opy (**2**), **D**elete (**3**), or **A**ppend (**4**).

If you want to move or copy information within a column, WordPerfect asks you to put the cursor at the new location and press Enter. To move or copy the whole page, you should have a hard page-break just before the place to which you want to move or copy. If you don't, WordPerfect inserts a **[SPg]** code for you.

Tip

When you are in the middle of a move operation and the message `Move cursor, press Enter to retrieve` appears on the status line, you can insert a hard page-break without terminating the move operation. Just move the cursor to the place where you want to retrieve the text and press Ctrl-Enter. Wordperfect inserts a **[HPg]** code and resumes prompting you to press Enter to retrieve the text.

To manipulate (move, copy, delete, or append) a complete column, do the following:

1. Go to the top of the column and press Block (Alt-F4 or F12).

   ▢ Access the **E**dit pull-down menu and select **B**lock.

2. Press PgDn, use the up arrow to get back to the last line in the column, and press End to include that line.

3. Press Move (Ctrl-F4); select **B**lock (**1**); and press **M**ove (**1**), **C**opy (**2**), **D**elete (**3**), or **A**ppend (**4**).

   ▢ From the **E**dit pull-down menu, select **M**ove, **C**opy, **D**elete, or **A**ppend.

To retrieve the block, move the cursor to the new location and press Enter.

Displaying One Column at a Time

If the on-screen display of your columns looks too crowded, you can eliminate the multiple-column display and have WordPerfect show one column at a time on-screen.

To display one column at a time on-screen, do the following:

1. Press Setup (Shift-F1) and select **D**isplay (**2**).

   ▢ Access the **F**ile menu, select Se**t**up, and then select **D**isplay.

2. Select **E**dit-Screen Options (**6**) and **S**ide-by-Side Columns display (**7**).

3. Select **N** if you don't want the side-by-side display; select **Y** if you want to have all columns displayed on-screen.

4. Press Exit (F7).

If you scroll through a single-column display, the columns are displayed as separate pages, but in their respective positions. In other words, the first column is on the left side on page 1 (see fig. 17.6); the second column is in its proper margins on page 2, and so forth. (This technique does not work the same way with parallel columns; each parallel-column segment is separated by rules designating hard page-breaks, but the columns all show on-screen at the same time.)

If you are in the List Files screen and press Enter when the cursor is on a columnar document, the display also appears as a single column, as if you had specified it that way.

Previewing Newspaper Columns

You can preview your columns with the **V**iew Document (**6**) feature. Choose 100% (**1**) to see the document at approximately the size it will be on the printout (see fig. 17.7). If you want to see what the full page looks like (see fig. 17.8), press Full Page (**3**).

Reminder:

To see what your printed columns will look like, use the View Document feature.

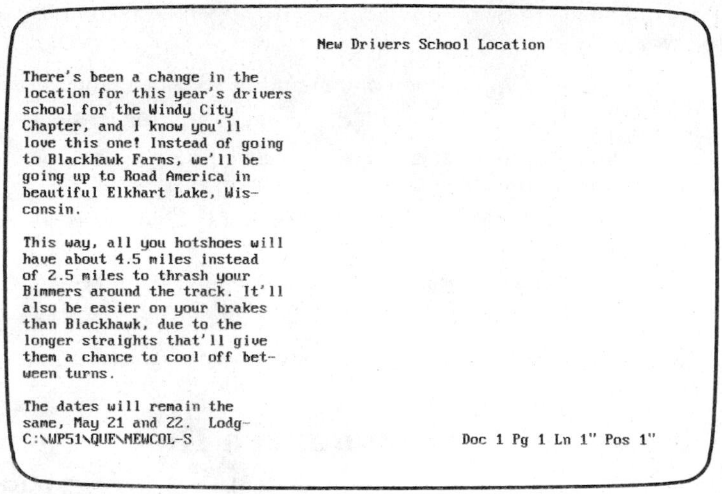

Fig. 17.6.

A single-column display.

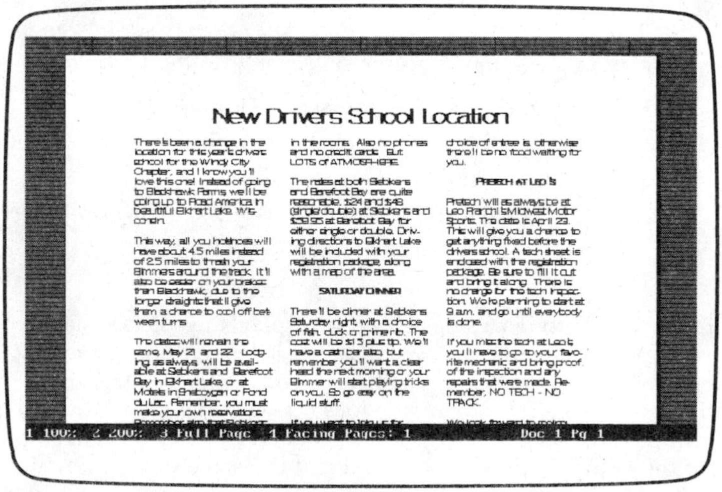

New Drivers School Location

There's been a change in the location for this year's drivers school for the Windy City Chapter, and I know you'll love this one! Instead of going to Blackhawk Farms, we'll be going up to Road America in beautiful Elkhart Lake, Wisconsin.

This way, all you hotshoes will have about 4.5 miles instead of 2.5 miles to thrash your Bimmers around the track. It'll also be easier on your brakes than Blackhawk, due to the longer straights that'll give them a chance to cool off between turns.

The dates will remain the same, May 21 and 22. Lodg-
C:\WP51\QUE\NEWCOL-S

Doc 1 Pg 1 Ln 1" Pos 1"

Fig. 17.7.

View Document at 100%.

To preview your document, do the following:

1. Press Print (Shift-F7) to bring up the Print menu.

   ⌨ Access the **F**ile pull-down menu and select **P**rint.

2. Press **V**iew Document (**6**) to see what the document will look like on the printed page.

3. Press Exit (F7) to return to the document.

If the number of lines in each column is unequal and you don't like the way the columns look on the page, you can even things out with a little mathematics. Simply add the number of lines and divide the total by the number of columns.

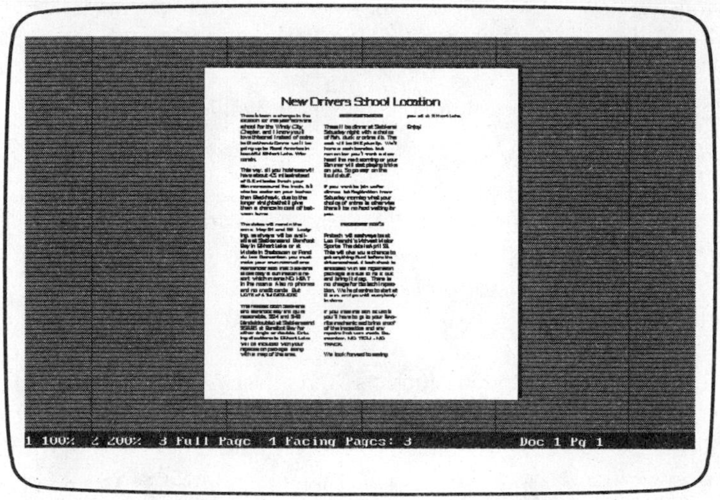

Fig. 17.8.
View Document at Full Page.

If you're working with 3 columns, for example, you may end up with 2 long columns and 1 short column (see figure 17.8). Adding the lines (54 + 54 + 20 = 128, for example) and dividing by 3 columns produces 42.666, close enough to 43 lines. Next, go to the first column and insert a **[HPg]** code (Ctrl-Enter) at the end of line 43. Insert another **[HPg]** code at line 43 in the second column. You then have 3 columns of approximately equal length (see fig. 17.9).

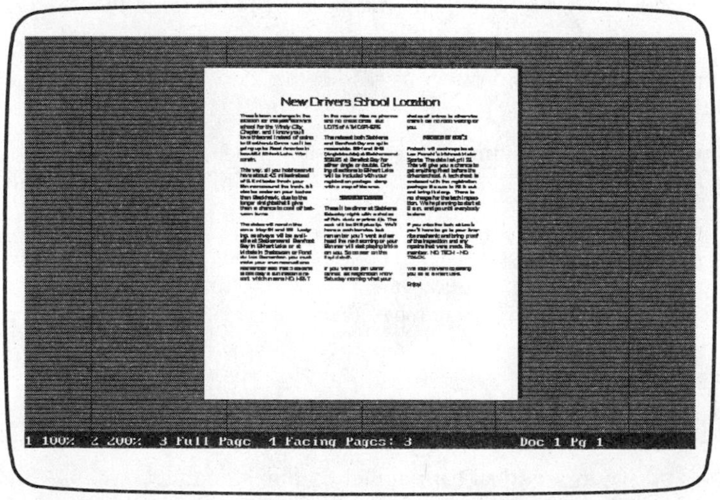

Fig. 17.9.
Newspaper columns with even column length.

A Macro That Defines Newspaper Columns

If you expect to use the same column definition frequently, save yourself time by writing a macro that lets you call up the predefined columns with just a few keystrokes. (For a more detailed explanation of WordPerfect macros, see Chapters 11 and 12.)

Cue:
A macro can save you time if you use a particular column definition often.

Macros from previous versions of WordPerfect may not work with version 5.1. You can use WordPerfect 5.1's internal macro editor to edit them for the new version, or you can rewrite them.

To define a macro that speeds up creating newspaper or parallel columns, do the following:

1. Press Macro Define (Ctrl-F10).

   🖰 Access the **T**ools pull-down menu, select **M**acro, and then select **D**efine.

2. Name your macro Alt-C for *columns*. (You can use any Alt-key combination and call the macro whatever helps you to remember its function.)

3. Type a short macro description, such as *Newsletter Columns*, and press Enter.

   The words Macro Def start flashing in the lower left corner of the screen.

4. Press Columns/Tables (Alt-F7), select **C**olumns (**1**), and select **D**efine (**1**).

   🖰 Access the **L**ayout pull-down menu, select **C**olumns, and then select **D**efine.

5. Define the columns as outlined in the section "Defining Newspaper Columns."

6. After turning the columns feature on, press Macro Define (Ctrl-F10) again to finish the macro.

   🖰 Access the **T**ools pull-down menu, select **M**acro, and then select **D**efine.

The macro will appear in your macro directory under the name you have given it (ALTC.WPM, for example).

The next time you want to use columns, simply position the cursor at the point where you want them to begin, press Alt-C, and start typing the text in your columns.

If you later decide to edit the macro, perhaps to change the margins of the columns, only the codes appear in the edit box. Therefore, you have to know in advance the keystrokes to enter. You may find it easier to erase the old macro and write a new one.

Parallel Columns

Listings, schedules, and so on are ideal for parallel columns. Parallel columns are handy if you're setting up a tour itinerary, for instance. The first column might contain the date; the next, the location; the third, the hotel or dinner location; the next, any special attractions to visit; and another, comments regarding that particular point in the tour. Once the columns are set up, you easily can go from one column to the next. And if you save your column setup as a macro or a style, the setup is always available with only a few keystrokes.

Defining Parallel Columns

Unlike newspaper columns, parallel columns are designed to be read across the page from left to right. Setting up parallel columns follows the same basic steps as setting up newspaper columns; however, parallel columns require some preplanning because most columns are not the same width. First figure out how many columns you need and then decide how wide each column should be. Finally, consider the hyphenation zone for the columns.

Reminder:
Parallel columns are read across the page.

If you normally work with hyphenation on, be aware that the hyphenation zone in columns, particularly narrow ones such as you might use with parallel columns, is small. WordPerfect figures the hyphenation in percentages, the default being 10% left and 4% right. For a 2-inch column, for instance, the default settings mean that the left hyphenation zone is 0.2 inches and the right hyphenation zone 0.08 inches. With a 10-character-per-inch font, the zone allows you only 2 characters on the left and less than 1 character on the right. Because of this narrow zone, you may have to insert hyphens manually to straighten out the column lines. The same, of course, applies to newspaper columns, but the hyphenation problems are less noticeable there because the columns are generally wider.

Suppose that you need to set up parallel columns for a tour itinerary (see fig. 17.10).

```
┌──────────────────────────────────────────────────────────────────┐
│                      Windy City Tour Schedule                      │
│                                                                    │
│        Date         Location      Hotel        Sightseeing    Rem  │
│                                                                    │
│   Oct 24      Luxembourg     Aerogolf-     Tour of the   The Kasemat│
│                              excellent     Kasematten    are an anci│
│                              restaurant    and if time   fortificati│
│                              serving       permits, a    the Luxembo│
│                              French and    short visit   Swiss area │
│                              Luxembourg    to the Lux-   of the most│
│                              cuisine -     embourg       turesque ar│
│                              the frog      Swiss area    the country│
│                              legs and                              │
│                              Chateau-                              │
│                              briand are                            │
│                              highly                                │
│                              recom-                                │
│                              mended                                │
│                                                                    │
│   Oct 25      Trier          Dorint        Porta Nigra; Supposedly │
│                                            Cathedral     ed in 2000 │
│                                            and Imperial  this small │
│                                            Baths         became the │
│   C:\WP51\QUE\TOUR.ITI          Col 1 Doc 1 Pg 1 Ln 1.86" Pos 1.1" │
└──────────────────────────────────────────────────────────────────┘
```

Fig. 17.10.

An example of parallel columns.

To define parallel columns, do the following:

1. Press Center (Shift-F6).

   ▣ Access the **L**ayout pull-down menu, select **A**lign, and then select **C**enter.

2. Type *Windy City Tour Schedule* as the overall heading for the document.

3. Press Enter twice to space down.

4. Press Columns/Tables (Alt-F7), select **C**olumns (**1**), and select **D**efine (**3**).

   ▣ Access the **L**ayout pull-down menu, select **C**olumns, and then select **D**efine.

5. Select **T**ype (**1**) and choose either **P**arallel (**2**) or Parallel with **B**lock Protect (**3**).

   If you choose Parallel with **B**lock Protect (**3**) to set up a tour itinerary, for instance, each section of columns in the listing begins with a **[BlockPro: On]** code, ends with a **[BlockPro:Off]** code, and automatically is kept together by WordPerfect.

6. Next, select **N**umber of Columns (**2**), press 5, and press Enter.

7. Select **D**istance Between Columns (**3**), type *0.25*, and press Enter.

8. Finally, select **M**argins (**4**) and type the margin definitions that appear in figure 17.11, pressing Enter after each one.

   Remember, you can set the margins wider or narrower than the regular document to suit your specific requirements.

9. Press Enter when you are completely finished, and select **O**n (**1**) to turn on the columns feature.

Fig. 17.11.

The Parallel Column Definition screen.

```
Text Column Definition

   1 - Type                              Parallel

   2 - Number of Columns                 5

   3 - Distance Between Columns          0.25"

   4 - Margins

   Column   Left     Right    Column   Left     Right
     1:     0.5"     1.5"       13:
     2:     1.75"    2.75"      14:
     3:     3"       4"         15:
     4:     4.25"    5.5"       16:
     5:     5.75"    7.5"       17:
     6:                         18:
     7:                         19:
     8:                         20:
     9:                         21:
    10:                         22:
    11:                         23:
    12:                         24:

Selection: 0
```

Figure 17.12 shows how column 3 breaks across the page. Notice that the line indicating a soft page-break extends only through column 3 because no text appears in either column 4 or 5.

Typing Text in Parallel Columns

Typing text in parallel columns is different from typing text in newspaper columns, because the former requires that you move from column to column to set up the list. In the tour itinerary, for instance, after you type the text for the first column (Date), you enter a **[HPg]** code (Ctrl-Enter) to position the cursor at the next column, where you type the location. Again enter a **[HPg]** code to get to the third column, and so on across the page. When you enter a **[HPg]** code at the end of the text in the right column, the program returns the cursor to the left column, and you can start a new entry.

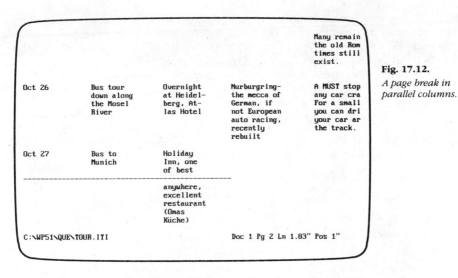

Fig. 17.12.

A page break in parallel columns.

WordPerfect inserts hidden codes for each column, depending on the type of column. Regular parallel columns start with **[Col On]**, have the code **[HPg]** between columns, and end with **[Col Off]** at the end of the text in the right column.

Parallel columns with Block Protect start with **[Block Pro:On][Col On]**, have a **[HPg]** code between columns, and end with **[Block Pro:Off][Col Off]**. The Block Protect column is useful when you do not want to split a column across a page break but want to keep all the text together on one page. If the right column, for instance, is too long to fit on the same page, WordPerfect inserts the code **[SPg]** at the beginning of the left column and moves the columns as a block to the next page.

Reminder:

Use the Block Protect feature to prevent a column from breaking across two pages.

To see how typing in parallel columns works, suppose that you have established the format for the columns, and you're ready to start the text. First, put in the individual column headings, center them, and put them in bold (refer to fig. 17.10).

To enter the columns headings, do the following:

1. Press Center (Shift-F6).

    ⌨ Access the **L**ayout pull-down menu, select **A**lign, and then select **C**enter.

2. Press Bold (F6), type *Date*, and press Bold (F6).

3. Press Ctrl-Enter to go to the next column; press Center (Shift-F6).

4. Press Bold (F6), type *Location*, and press Bold (F6).

5. Press Ctrl-Enter to go to column 3; press Center (Shift-F6).

6. Press Bold (F6), type *Hotel*, and press Bold (F6).

7. Press Ctrl-Enter to go to column 4; press Center (Shift-F6).

8. Press Bold (F6), type *Sightseeing*, and press Bold (F6).

9. Press Ctrl-Enter to go to the last column; press Center (Shift-F6).

10. Press Bold (F6), type *Remarks*, and press Bold (F6).

Note: If you use center justification, you do not have to center each heading separately; any text you type in a column is automatically centered in each column until you select a different type of justification. To activate center justification, press Format (Shift-F8), **L**ine (**1**), **J**ustification (**3**), and **C**enter (**2**); ▢⊟ alternatively, access the **L**ayout pull-down menu, select **L**ine, and then select **J**ustification (**3**) and **C**enter (**2**). When you need to change the type of justification, repeat this step and select a different justification option.

Now that you have set up the headings, you are ready to start typing the body of the document. Be sure that hyphenation is on. Insert hyphens manually if you must so that your tour schedule looks like the one in figure 17.10.

To type text in your columns, do the following:

1. Press Ctrl-Enter to go back to the left column and type *Oct 24.*
2. Press Ctrl-Enter to go to the next column and type *Luxembourg.*
3. Press Ctrl-Enter to go to column 3 and type the following text:

   Aerogolf – excellent restaurant serving French and Luxembourg cuisine – the frog legs and Chateaubriand are highly recommended.
4. Press Ctrl-Enter to go to column 4 and type the following text:

   Tour of the Kasematten and if time permits, a short visit to the Luxembourg Swiss area.
5. Press Ctrl-Enter to go to the last column and type the following text:

   The Kasematten are an ancient fortification; the Luxembourg Swiss area is one of the most picturesque areas of the country.

Combining Parallel Columns with Regular Text

As with newspaper columns, you can mix parallel columns with regular text (see fig. 17.13). You must, however, be at the end of the text in the right column in order to combine the two properly. If you turn off the columns feature while the cursor is in a middle column, the columns get out of alignment.

Fig. 17.13.

Combining parallel columns with regular text.

```
Oct 24       Luxembourg    Aerogolf-      Tour of the    The Kasemat
                           excellent      Kasematten     are an anci
                           restaurant     and if time    fortificati
                           serving        permits, a     the Luxembo
                           French and     short visit    Swiss area
                           Luxembourg     to the Lux-    of the most
                           cuisine -      embourg        turesque ar
                           the frog       Swiss area     the country
                           legs and
                           Chateau-
                           briand are
                           highly
                           recom-
                           mended

        Note:              It's advisable to bring some raingear on this tour.
                           Fall in Europe can be rather moist at times. We disc-
                           laim any responsibility for the weather, although we'll
                           be happy to take credit for it if it's sunny.

Oct 25       Trier         Dorint         Porta Nigra;   Supposedly
                           Hotel          Cathedral      ed in 2000
                                          and Imperial   this small
                                          Baths          became the

C:\WP51\QUE\TOUR.ITI                      Col 2 Doc 1 Pg 1 Ln 3.3" Pos 1.75"
```

To combine parallel columns with regular text, do the following:

1. Move the cursor to the end of the text in the right column.
2. Press Columns/Tables (Alt-F7), select **C**olumns (**1**), and then select **O**ff (**2**).

    ⌨ Access the **L**ayout pull-down menu, select **C**olumns, and then select **O**ff.
3. Type the regular text.
4. When you have finished typing, press Columns/Tables (Alt-F7), select **C**olumns (**1**), and select **O**n (**1**) to return to the columns.

    ⌨ Access the **L**ayout pull-down menu, select **C**olumns, and then select **O**n.

Editing Parallel Columns

You edit in parallel columns just as you do in newspaper columns, but you must remember to create new column sections by entering a **[HPg]** code (Ctrl-Enter). Be careful when you use the Del key as you edit; do not accidentally erase one of the hidden column codes.

If you do erase a code, leave the cursor in the position where you accidentally erased the code and go into Reveal Codes (Alt- F3 or F11). Then reinsert the code in its proper place by pressing Columns/Tables (Alt-F7), selecting **C**olumns (**1**), and **O**n (**1**). To see how this procedure works, press Reveal Codes (Alt-F3 or F11), move the cursor to a **[Col Off]** code, and press the Del key. Then press Columns/Tables (Alt-F7), select **C**olumns, (**1**), select **O**n (**1**), and watch the code reappear.

You can do your editing in Reveal Codes if you like, although you will have a cluttered screen.

Unlike the cursor movement in newspaper columns, the cursor movement in parallel columns is the same as in regular text. The cursor-movement keys function in the following manner:

Reminder:
In parallel columns, the cursor moves as it does in regular text.

- GoTo (Ctrl-Home), → moves the cursor to the column on the right.
- GoTo (Ctrl-Home), Home, → moves the cursor to the last column on the right edge of the document.
- GoTo (Ctrl-Home), ← moves the cursor to the column on the left.
- GoTo (Ctrl-Home), Home, ← moves the cursor to the first column on the left edge of the document.
- Home, ↓ moves the cursor to the bottom of the screen.
- Home, ↑ moves the cursor to the top of the screen.
- The gray + and – keys move the cursor to the bottom or the top of the screen, respectively.

Moving Parallel Columns

If you decide to move one section of parallel-column text to another location in the document, you can move the section—carefully—but this maneuver is tricky and perhaps best done in Reveal Codes. You *must* include the **[Column On]** and **[Column Off]** codes in the move.

To move a section of a parallel column to another location in the document, do the following:

1. Move the cursor to the first column of the section you want to move.

2. Press Home, Home, ← to get to the left margin, making sure that the cursor is in front of the **[Col On]** code, and press Block (Alt-F4 or F12).

   ▭ Select **B**lock from the **E**dit pull-down menu.

3. Press the sequence GoTo (Ctrl-Home), → four times.

4. Move the cursor down to include the last line of the right column in the block. Be sure to include the **[Col Off]** code by looking in Reveal Codes.

5. Press Move (Ctrl-F4), select **B**lock (**1**), and select **M**ove (**1**).

   ▭ Access the **E**dit pull-down menu and select **M**ove.

6. Move the cursor to the spot where you want to insert the block and press Enter.

If the margins of the columns are wider than those of the regular document, you have to press Margin Release (Shift-Tab) before pressing Enter.

Changing Line Spacing

Reminder:

WordPerfect enables you to change the line spacing of a column.

The capability to change the line spacing within columns is a handy feature of WordPerfect. If you want to double-space the Sightseeing column, for example, WordPerfect enables you to do so (see fig. 17.14).

Fig. 17.14.

Line spacing changed in one parallel column.

```
                             Windy City Tour Schedule

           Date         Location        Hotel         Sightseeing            Rem

      Oct 24        Luxembourg      Aerogolf-      Tour of the        The Kasemat
                                    excellent                         are an anci
                                    restaurant     Kasematten         fortificati
                                    serving                           the Luxembo
                                    French and     and if time        Swiss area
                                    Luxembourg                        of the most
                                    cuisine -      permits, a         turesque ar
                                    the frog                          the country
                                    legs and       short visit
                                    Chateau-
                                    briand are     to the Lux-
                                    highly
                                    recom-         embourg
                                    mended
                                                   Swiss area

      Oct 25        Trier           Dorint         Porta Nigra;       Supposedly
                                    Hotel          Cathedral          ed in 2000
                                                   and Imperial       this small
                                                   Baths              became the
      C:\WP51\QUE\TOUR.ITI                    Col 4 Doc 1 Pg 1 Ln 1.86" Pos 4.25"
```

To change the line spacing in a parallel column, do the following:

1. Move the cursor to the beginning of the column where you want to start the spacing change. For this example, position your cursor on the *T* of the word *Tour*.

2. Press Format (Shift-F8) and select **L**ine (**1**).

   ⌨ Access the **L**ayout pull-down menu and select **L**ine.

3. Select Line **S**pacing (**6**), press 2 for double-spacing, and press Enter.

4. Press Exit (F7) twice to accept the spacing and return to the document.

The text is now double-spaced from the position where you inserted the double-spacing code. If you don't also want the Remarks column double-spaced, simply move the cursor to the first letter of the first word in that column (the *T* in *The*) and repeat steps 2 through 4, pressing 1 for single-spacing. You can repeat this procedure as often as you like, changing spacing from one column to the next. If you have one or two columns that you always want double-spaced, set up a couple of macros or use a style code to change the spacing.

If you know in advance that you want the first two columns of your schedule to be single-spaced and the remainder of the columns double-spaced, you can change the line spacing as you type. When you get to the end of the last single-spaced column, just press Ctrl-Enter to go to the next column and continue with the steps for changing line spacing. The remainder of the text is double-spaced until you enter another code for a different line spacing. Again, using a macro or style code would be faster and easier.

Changing Column Leading

You can change the space between the lines of text in a column in finer increments than single-spacing or double-spacing the lines. *Leading* (pronounced led´ding) is the spacing between individual lines; by default, WordPerfect uses two points of leading. Leading adjustments should be very small—a fraction of a point—to avoid notice.

> **Tip**
>
> Use paired styles for leading changes that you want to affect only certain parts of the text. Enclose the text to be respaced between Style On and Style Off codes. The Style Off code restores the original spacing automatically. See Chapter 15 for more information on defining and using Styles.

To change WordPerfect's default leading, follow these steps:

1. Place the cursor at the point in the document where you want the leading change to begin.

2. Press Format (Shift-F8) and choose **O**ther (**4**).

   ⌨ Access the **L**ayout pull-down menu and select **O**ther.

   The Format: Other menu appear´s (see fig. 17.15).

3. Select **P**rinter Functions (**6**). The Format: Printer Functions menu appears (see fig. 17.16).

<5.1>

Fig. 17.15.

The Format: Other menu

```
Format: Other

    1 - Advance

    2 - Conditional End of Page

    3 - Decimal/Align Character        .
        Thousands' Separator          ,

    4 - Language                      US

    5 - Overstrike

    6 - Printer Functions

    7 - Underline - Spaces            Yes
                    Tabs              No
```

Fig. 17.16.

The Format: Printer Functions menu.

```
Format: Printer Functions

    1 - Kerning                              No

    2 - Printer Command

    3 - Word Spacing                         Optimal
        Letter Spacing                       Optimal

    4 - Word Spacing Justification Limits
        Compressed to (0% - 100%)            60%
        Expanded to (100% - unlimited)       400%

    5 - Baseline Placement for Typesetters   No
        (First baseline at top margin)

    6 - Leading Adjustment
        Primary   - [SRt]                    0"
        Secondary - [HRt]                    0"
```

4. Select **L**eading Adjustment (**6**).

5. Type a value for the primary leading adjustment and press Enter. The primary leading adjustment is the amount WordPerfect is to vary from the default two-point leading between lines ending in soft return **[SRt]** codes (lines that WordPerfect has word-wrapped). To move lines closer together, type a negative number; to move lines farther apart, type a positive number. You may find it convenient to enter leading adjustment in fractional point sizes.

   For example, to reduce the spacing between lines by about 10%, type −.*2p* (2/10 of a point is 10% of the default 2 points). To increase the spacing by about 25%, type .*5p.*

6. Type a value for the secondary leading adjustment and press Enter. The secondary leading adjustment is the amount WordPerfect is to vary from the default two-point leading between lines ending in hard return **[HRt]** codes (lines that you end by pressing Enter). Enter values in the same way as in step 5. You can use the secondary leading adjustment as an alternative way to change interparagraph spacing; in some situations, secondary leading may be more convenient to use than Advance codes.

<5.1>

7. Press Enter to return to the document.

A Macro That Defines Parallel Columns

In parallel columns, as in newspaper columns, you can speed up the process of defining columns by using either macros or styles, particularly if you use the same setups on a regular basis. In this section, you learn how to create macros to set up parallel columns. (For information on how you can use styles to automate this process, see Chapter 15.)

This example uses the setup for the tour itinerary to create a macro. To create a macro that speeds up the definition of parallel columns, do the following:

1. Press Macro Define (Ctrl-F10).

   ⌨ Access the **T**ools pull-down menu, select **Ma**cro, and then select **D**efine.

2. Name the macro Alt-T for *tour.*

3. Type *Tour itinerary* for th description and press Enter.

   The words Macro Def start flashing in the lower left corner of the screen.

4. Press Columns/Tables (Alt-F7) to start the column definition.

   ⌨ Access the **L**ayout pull-down menu, select **C**olumns, and then select **D**efine.

5. Follow steps 1 through 9 outlined previously in the section "Defining Parallel Columns." Pressing **O**n (**1**) to turn the column on should be the last step in your macro definition.

6. Press Macro Define (Ctrl-F10) to end the macro definition.

   ⌨ Access the **T**ools pull-down menu, select **Ma**cro, and then select **D**efine.

If you frequently change the spacing within parallel columns, you can write a macro to change the spacing for you.

To create a macro to change the spacing within parallel columns, do the following:

1. Press Macro Define (Ctrl-F10) and name the macro Alt-D.

   ⌨ Access the **T**ools pull-down menu, select **Ma**cro, select **D**efine, and name the macro Alt-D.

2. Type *Change to double-spacing* for the description and press Enter.

3. Press Format (Shift-F8) and select **L**ine (**1**).

   ⌨ Access the **L**ayout pull-down menu and select **L**ine.

4. Select Line **S**pacing (**6**), press 2, press Enter, and then press Exit (F7).

5. Press Macro Define (Ctrl-F10) to end the macro definition.

   ⌨ Access the **T**ools pull-down menu, select **Ma**cro, and then select **D**efine.

Do the same for single-spacing, giving the macro the appropriate name and changing the 2 in step 4 to a 1.

Summary

You do not need the column format for everything you write, but when you do want to use columns, WordPerfect provides you with a powerful feature. The columns feature is not the easiest concept to learn, but if you have worked your way through this chapter, you should have a good idea of the feature's capabilities.

In this chapter, you have learned to do the following:

❏ Define newspaper columns

❏ Define parallel columns

❏ Type in columns

❏ Edit in columns

❏ Mix columns with regular text

❏ Create macros for newspaper columns and parallel columns

WordPerfect columns are designed to help you write more simply and efficiently. With experience, columns become just as easy for you to use as any other feature. And if you combine columns with WordPerfect's graphics capability, you have the makings of a good desktop publishing system. The quality of the printed piece, of course, depends also on the printer you are using, but even with a good dot-matrix printer, you can achieve excellent results.

18

Using
Math

James McKeown, Ph.D., has worked with computers for 25 years and with WordPerfect from version 3 to the present. He is the author of this chapter for *Using WordPerfect 5*.

Andrea Pickens, a Chicago-area training consultant, has developed training to assist clients with hardware and software conversions. She revised this chapter for *Using WordPerfect 5.1*, Special Edition.

By the time you reach this point in the book, you probably have decided that WordPerfect can do just about anything with words and letters, but you may be wondering what WordPerfect can do with numbers.

WordPerfect supports two basic types of math operations. The simpler operation adds numbers in vertical columns and displays the sum at the bottom of each column. The more complex type of operation can add, subtract, multiply, or divide numbers horizontally. You can use either of these two kinds of operations to handle numbers within a document.

This chapter explains the basic steps for all math operations. First you learn how to use the simple column-addition operation and some useful options, such as the subtotal, grand total, and negate (reverse the sign) features. Then you learn how to change default settings of the Math feature to adjust the way a math operation appears in your document—for example, changing the number of places shown to the right of the decimal point in your math results. You also learn how to perform horizontal calculations using addition, subtraction, multiplication, and division; and how to set up formulas for complex calculations.

Understanding Math Operation Basics

To use WordPerfect math operations, you must arrange numbers in columns, using tabs. You may want text, such as item descriptions, in columns next to the number columns, as shown in figure 18.1.

581

Reminder

If you use a mouse with WordPerfect 5.1, you can click the right button to display the pull-down menus, and then select the desired option. You also can press Alt-= to access the pull-down menus, and then press the appropriate letter of the desired option. For all instructions, assume that if a block is required to activate a pull-down menu option, the text has been blocked before the pull-down menu is accessed. Instructions for pull-down menus and the mouse are marked with the mouse icon. For more information about the mouse, see Chapter 1.

Dear Susan:

Here is a summary of the books we added to our business library in September and October:

9/11	The Business Writer's Handbook	Brusaw	$19.95
9/11	Management	Drucker	11.95
9/25	You Can Negotiate Anything	Cohen	4.50
	September Total		$36.40+
10/9	Getting New Clients	Connor	22.50
10/16	Saying What You Mean	Claiborne	18.95
10/16	Legal Writing	Brand	17.95
	October Total		$59.40+
	TOTAL		$95.80=

Fig. 18.1.
A letter using the WordPerfect Math feature.

Reminder:
To use the Math feature, numbers must be in formatted columns; if you only want to add numbers in a column, WordPerfect's default formatting is sufficient.

All math operations are performed on numbers in columns, whether the operation is performed vertically down a column or horizontally across columns. To use any math operation, perform the following steps:

1. Set tabs for the columns.
2. Define the type and format of each column. This step specifies what is to appear in each column, such as text or numbers, and how the results of the operations are to appear. If you are simply using *numeric columns*—adding numbers vertically down a column—you can skip this step because WordPerfect defaults to the appropriate settings for numeric columns.
3. Turn on the Math feature.
4. In the established columns, enter text for captions, numbers for the operation, and math operators (such as a + sign) to tell WordPerfect what to do with the numbers.
5. Calculate the results of the operation you have set up.
6. Turn off the Math feature.

These steps are general; more specific steps are provided in this chapter, depending on the type of math operation you want to perform.

Using Numeric Columns

Using numeric columns to add numbers is the simplest math operation in WordPerfect. *Numeric columns* are simply that: columns of numbers WordPerfect sums when given the appropriate command. The first step in using numeric columns, as with any WordPerfect math operation, is to set tab stops for the columns in which the numbers are entered. The following sections detail the procedures for using numeric columns.

Setting Tab Stops for Math

You set tabs for math columns in exactly the same way you set tabs for text. (The basic procedure for setting tab stops is described in Chapter 5.) If you want column headings, type the headings before setting the tab stops so that you can place the tab stops where you want them, directly below the column headings. In a column of numbers, the tab stop determines where the decimal is aligned. To set tab stops for math columns, follow these steps:

1. Position the cursor after any column headings.
2. Press Format (Shift-F8), select **L**ine (**1**), and select **T**ab Set (**8**).

   ▭ Access the **L**ayout pull-down menu, choose **L**ine, and select **T**ab Set (**8**).
3. Move the cursor to the left end of the tab bar and press Ctrl-End to remove the existing tab stops.
4. Move the cursor to the position where you want the first column to appear; select **L**eft to set the tab stop for the first column.

   Note: The first math column cannot start at the left margin; it must begin at a tab stop to the right of the left margin.
5. Repeat step 4 for the second and subsequent columns.
6. Press Exit (F7) twice to return to the editing screen.

Because all numbers you enter with the Math feature are aligned on the tab stop, the type of tab you set (left, right, center, or decimal) makes no difference. (When you incorporate text columns into a math operation, however, the type of tab stop you set *does* determine how the text is aligned.)

As you set tabs, make the columns wide enough to contain the largest numbers you plan to put into them. If numbers extend outside the columns, the math operations give incorrect results.

Reminder:
Numbers in math columns are aligned with the decimal at the tab stop, so be sure that you leave room to the left of the first tab stop for the largest number you expect in the column.

Accepting the Default Definition for Numeric Columns

Once you set the tabs for the math columns, the next step is to define the type and format of the columns. When you work with numeric columns, however, this step is not necessary because the default settings appropriately define the columns for numeric operations. Defining the type and format of math columns is discussed later in this chapter. Following are the default math-column definitions:

- Every column is a numeric column; that is, every column consists of numbers to be totaled vertically.
- Results are displayed with two digits after the decimal point.
- Negative results are displayed in parentheses, for example *(42.25)*.

Turning On the Math Feature

After setting the tab stops and defining the columns (or accepting the default definitions), turn on the Math feature. To turn on the Math feature, follow these steps:

1. Position the cursor *after* the tab settings for the math columns but *before* the part of the document that is to contain the math operations. Use Reveal Codes (Alt-F3 or F11) to check the placement of the cursor.
2. Press Columns/Table (Alt-F7), select **M**ath (**3**), and select **O**n (**1**).

   ⌨ Access the **L**ayout pull-down menu, choose **M**ath, and select **O**n.

The word Math appears in the lower left corner of the screen. This indicator shows that the cursor is in a math area of the document. Everything from this point forward in the document is included in the math area until you indicate the end of the math area by turning off the Math feature. Use Reveal Codes (Alt-F3 or F11) to see the position of the **[Math On]** code that indicates the beginning of the math area. Make sure that the Math indicator appears on-screen whenever you intend to enter numbers or operators to be used by the Math feature.

Reminder:

When you turn on the Math feature, everything in the document below that point is included in the math operations; turn off the Math feature where you want the math area to end.

Entering Numbers in Numeric Columns

With the Math feature turned on, you can enter numbers in the columns you defined. Use the following procedure to enter numbers into a numeric column:

1. Press Tab or Tab Align (Control-F6) to position the cursor at the appropriate column.

   ⌨ Access the **L**ayout pull-down menu, choose **A**lign, and select **T**ab Align to position the cursor at the appropriate column.
2. Type the desired number; press Tab to proceed to the next column or press Enter to go to the next line.
3. Type additional numbers in the columns.

As you enter each number, be sure that the decimal point is in the appropriate position. (If you enter a whole number, you don't need to enter the decimal point.) Negative numbers can be entered either with a preceding minus sign or enclosed in parentheses.

The number appears as you type it (with the number of decimal places and the negative-number format that you enter); WordPerfect formats the totals according to the math-column definition, but does not alter the format of the numbers you type.

Consider the following column of numbers:

```
12
 7.00
(18.3)
 1.6
-2.14+
```

The column looks sloppy because the numbers are typed inconsistently—using two different decimal places and showing negative numbers in two ways (with a minus sign and parentheses). Although the appearance of the column is poor, the inconsistent format doesn't confuse WordPerfect; the calculation still produces the correct result. The result is displayed according to the definition for the math column. In this case, the default definition has been used, so the result is displayed to two decimal places (rounded as necessary) and with a negative number shown by parentheses.

To change the format of the *result*, change the definition of the column (see "Using the Math Definition Screen" later in this chapter). To make the appearance of the column consistent, you must type the numbers consistently, using the same number of decimal places and the same indicator for negative numbers, as shown in this column of numbers:

```
    12.00
     7.00
  (18.30)
     1.60
   (2.14)+
```

Entering Text in front of Numeric Columns

Because the first math column cannot start at the left margin but must begin at a tab to the right of the left margin, you can leave space between the left margin and the first tab stop for text such as labels, captions, or descriptions of the numbers appearing in the math columns (see fig. 18.2).

```
Rent                    850.00
Utilities               110.00
Phone                    35.00
Car payment             225.00
Gas, maint.             100.00
Car insurance            95.00
Home insurance           50.00
Parking                  60.00
Groceries               200.00
Clothing                225.00
Entertainment           250.00
```

Fig. 18.2.

A numeric column with captions.

Entering text in the space between the left margin and the first tab stop does not affect math calculations. You enter text in this location just as you would anywhere in the document: position the cursor where you want the text to begin and type the text.

Entering Math Operators in Numeric Columns

Math operators are the symbols you use to specify what calculation should be performed and where the result should be displayed. For example, the + symbol is a math operator meaning *subtotal the numbers above and display the result here*. In figure 18.3, the + operator has been entered at the bottom of the numeric column. When the column is calculated, the sum of the numbers in the column are displayed at the location of the + sign.

Reminder:

Math operators specify what operation is to be performed and where the result is to be displayed.

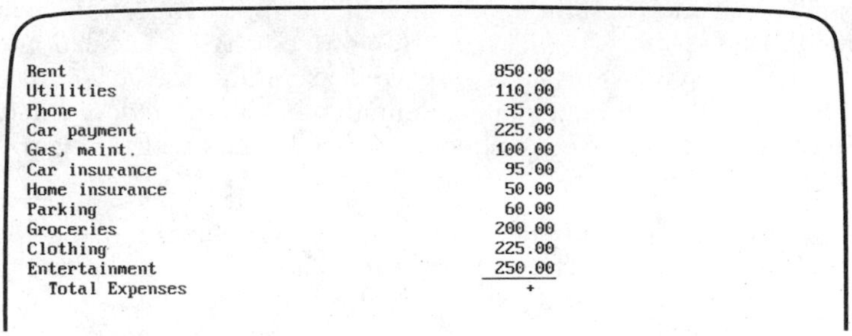

Fig. 18.3.

A numeric column with a + operator.

```
Rent                    850.00
Utilities               110.00
Phone                    35.00
Car payment             225.00
Gas, maint.             100.00
Car insurance            95.00
Home insurance           50.00
Parking                  60.00
Groceries               200.00
Clothing                225.00
Entertainment           250.00
    Total Expenses          +
```

You can use six math operators in a numeric column (see table 18.1). You enter a math operator by using the Tab key to position the cursor where you want to display the result and typing the appropriate operator.

Table 18.1
Functions of Math Operators

Symbol	Function	Description
+	Subtotal	Add all numbers in the column above the + since the last total or subtotal was taken (or from the beginning of the column).
t	Extra subtotal	Treat the number immediately following this operator as a subtotal.
=	Total	Add all subtotals (+) and extra subtotals (numbers preceded by t operators) since the last total.
T	Extra total	Treat the number immediately after this operator as a total.
*	Grand total	Add all totals (=) and extra totals (numbers preceded by T operators) since the last grand total.
N	Negate	Reverse the sign of the result or number immediately following this operator for use in further calculations.

Although WordPerfect usually accepts instructions without distinguishing between uppercase and lowercase letters, you must make that distinction when you use the math operators T and t. The uppercase T means something quite different to the program than the lowercase t. If you use the wrong case for the operator, the results are not correct.

Working with a Numeric-Column Example

To see how you can use some of the math operators in a document, look at the sample letter in figure 18.4. The first three amounts are entered as normal numbers with no operators. The + sign in the total expenses line is an operator telling WordPerfect to subtotal the numbers above it.

```
Dear Bob:

I enclose a copy of the receipts for my travel expenses last month.  These
included:

Airfare                          $746.55
Hotels                            843.18
Meals                             218.42
   Total expenses                 $+

Less:  Travel advance           Nt1500.00

Reimbursement requested           $=
```

Fig. 18.4.

A sample letter using math before calculation.

After WordPerfect computes the total expenses subtotal, you want to subtract the travel advance from the subtotal. You can subtract this number in several ways. You can precede the number with a minus sign or enclose the number in parenthesis to show that it is a negative number. Figure 18.4, however, uses the N operator to tell WordPerfect to *negate* (change the sign of) the number. The N operator causes the 1500.00 value to be subtracted from (or added as a negative number to) the preceding subtotal to compute the total reimbursement requested.

Keeping the Numbers Straight

The preceding section explains how the N operator negates, or changes the sign of, the travel advance amount. Notice that another operator is used with the 1500.00 value in figure 18.4: the t operator. The ·t operator tells WordPerfect to consider –1500.00 a subtotal, so that the value can be added to the existing subtotal. Without this operator, WordPerfect would not add –1500.00 to the subtotal.

Reminder:

Use the t operator to mark a value as a subtotal to be included in the numeric-column calculations.

In a document that has numbers, subtotals, totals, and grand totals, WordPerfect keeps the math straight for you by only adding together numbers at the same level. In other words:

- Numbers without operators can only be added to other numbers without operators.

- Subtotals (+) can only be added to other subtotals, or to numbers designated as "extra subtotals" with the lowercase t operator.

- Totals (=) can only be added to other totals, or to numbers designated as "extra totals" with the uppercase T operator.

Enhancing Math Documents with Symbols

Figure 18.4 also shows two ways you can enhance the appearance of math documents: using dollar signs and underlines. You can insert dollar signs in the places where they should appear in the finished document. You also can use the standard Underline (F8) key to tell WordPerfect to underline the results of the calculations. These symbols do not affect the math operations.

Calculating Results of Math Operations

Although figure 18.4 displays the math operators, it does not show any math results. To display the results of the operations you have set up, you must tell WordPerfect to do the calculation.

To do the calculation, press Columns/Table (Alt-F7), select **M**ath (**3**), and then select **C**alculate (**4**). ⬚ If you use a mouse or the pull-down menus, access the **L**ayout pull-down menu, choose **M**ath, and select **C**alculate.

The calculations appear on-screen (see fig. 18.5). Although the operators still appear on-screen, they do not appear when you print the document. (You can check the document by viewing it as described in Chapter 8.)

Fig. 18.5.

A sample letter using math after calculation.

```
Dear Bob:

I enclose a copy of the receipts for my travel expenses last month.  These
included:

Airfare                              $746.55
Hotels                                843.18
Meals                                 218.42
    Total expenses                 $1,808.15+

Less:  Travel advance               Mt1500.00

Reimbursement requested              $308.15=
```

If you change the numbers or operators in a math area, you must recalculate. Be sure that the cursor is in the math area (between the **[Math On]** and **[Math Off]** codes) when you perform the calculation.

Turning Off the Math Feature

When you are satisfied that the math computations are complete, place the cursor at then end of the math area and turn off the Math feature.

Turn off the Math feature by pressing Columns/Table (Alt-F7), selecting **M**ath (**3**), and selecting O**ff** (**2**). ⬚ If you use a mouse, access the **L**ayout pull-down menu, choose **M**ath, and select O**ff**.

Using More than One Math Area in a Document

Reminder:

You can have as many math areas in a document as you choose.

You can turn on the Math feature as needed for other math areas of the document. A document can have any number of math areas. You can tell whether the cursor is in a math area by observing the Math indicator in the lower left of the screen.

Specifying Text, Total, and Calculation Columns

The first part of this chapter uses numeric columns to perform the simplest WordPerfect math operation—adding columns of numbers. WordPerfect's default settings define all math columns as numeric columns. However, you can use additional options to redefine columns in a math area as text columns, total columns, or calculation columns.

Text columns are used to enter captions. You can enter either numbers or text in text columns, but anything entered in text columns is interpreted as text and is not used in calculations. (You can enter text in nontext columns, but the text may cause incorrect results in calculations. Within a math area of a document, text should be entered only at the left margin—which is not a math column—and in columns defined as text columns.)

Total columns are used with numeric columns to show totals to the right of numeric columns rather than within them.

Calculation columns are used to calculate horizontally across columns of numbers.

Using the Math Definition Screen

You define math columns in a document as text, total, or calculation columns by using the Math Definition screen. You also use the Math Definition screen to tell WordPerfect what calculations you want performed and how you want the results displayed. To use the Math Definition screen to define the math columns, set up the columns as follows:

1. Set the tabs for your columns.

2. Position the cursor after the **[Tab]** codes (use Reveal Codes to help position the cursor).

3. Press Columns/Table (Alt-F7), select **M**ath, and select **D**efine.

    ⌨ Access the **L**ayout pull-down menu, choose **M**ath, and select **D**efine.

The Math Definition screen appears (see fig. 18.6).

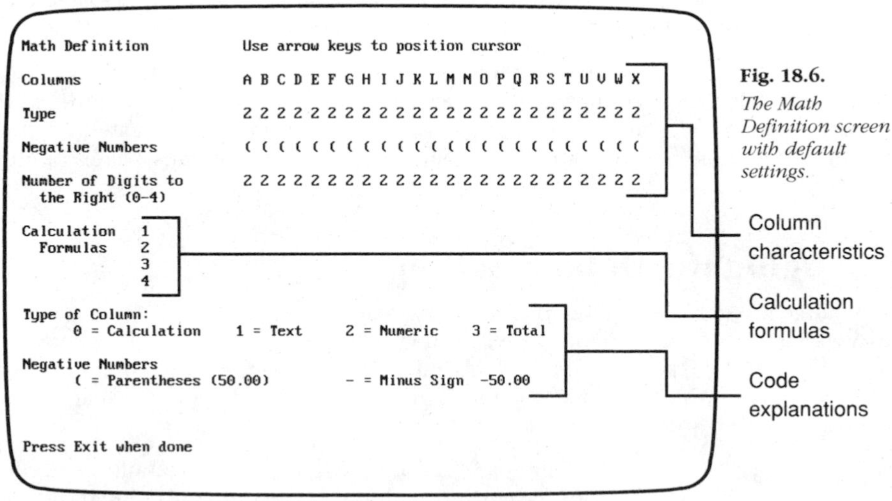

Fig. 18.6.

The Math Definition screen with default settings.

Column characteristics

Calculation formulas

Code explanations

The Math Definition screen is divided into three areas. The top area enables you to specify certain characteristics about the columns. In the middle area, you can enter calculation formulas for up to four columns. The bottom area explains the codes used in the top area; you do not input or change information in the bottom area.

WordPerfect uses the letters *A* through *X* to identify the math columns in a document. The letter *A* represents the column aligned on the first tab stop, *B* represents the second tab stop from the left margin, and so on. You use column letters to define a calculation formula for a calculation column (as described later in this chapter). You can use up to 24 columns (represented by the first 24 letters of the alphabet)—far more than you need for most documents.

The Type, Negative Numbers, and Number of Digits to the Right lines on the Math Definition screen display the settings for each column. The Type line specifies the type of column. Set this option to 0 for calculation columns, 1 for text columns, 2 for numeric columns, or 3 for total columns. The default setting for all columns is 2 (numeric columns).

The Negative Numbers line specifies the format used to display negative numbers that are the results of calculations. Set this option to – to display negative numbers with a preceding minus sign; for example, *–42.25*. Set this option to (to display negative numbers in parentheses; for example, *(42.25)*. The default setting for all columns is ((parentheses). The setting you specify on the Math Definition screen affects only the display of numbers that result from calculations. Any number you enter into a column appears as you type it, regardless of the negative-number format setting for that column.

The Number of Digits to the Right line indicates the number of digits displayed to the right of the decimal point in calculated numbers. You can specify a number from 0 to 4; the default is 2 decimal places. WordPerfect rounds the calculated numbers to the number of decimal places you specify in this setting. As with the negative-number format, this setting affects only the number of digits displayed for numbers that result from calculations.

The middle area of the Math Calculation screen allows you to create formulas for up to four calculation columns. When you calculate the math area, WordPerfect displays in each calculation column the result of the formula you created for that column. For more information, see "Using Calculation Columns" later in this chapter.

Changing the Default Settings

To change the column characteristics for any math column in a document, use the arrow keys to move the cursor to the column you want to change and type the new code. For example, if you want to change the type characteristic of column A to a total column, move the cursor to the 2 under the A and type *3*. Change the negative-number and decimal-places characteristics for a column in the same way.

You do not have to set all 24 columns (A through X) on the Math Definition screen. If you intend to use only one calculation column, for example, the settings for column A are the only ones that matter. If you intend to use two calculation columns, set columns A and B. Just make sure that the settings are correct for the number of columns you intend to use.

When you have the codes set the way you want them, press Exit (F7) to leave the Math Definition screen and return to the Math/Columns menu.

Changing the Decimal and Thousands-Separator Characters

In WordPerfect, the period (.) is the default setting for the decimal character; the comma (,) is the default setting for the thousands separator. With these default settings in place, WordPerfect displays one million (with two digits to the right of the decimal) as 1,000,000.00—with alignment based on the period.

If the default settings are unsatisfactory, you can change them. Press Format (Shift-F8) and choose **O**ther (**4**). ⌨ If you use a mouse, access the **L**ayout pull-down menu and choose **O**ther. The Format: Other menu appears (see fig. 18.7). Select **D**ecimal/Align Character (**3**) and type the desired decimal character and thousands-separator character. Press Exit (F7) to return to the editing screen. If you change the setting so that the comma is the decimal character and the period is the thousands separator, WordPerfect displays one million as 1.000.000,00—with alignment based on the comma.

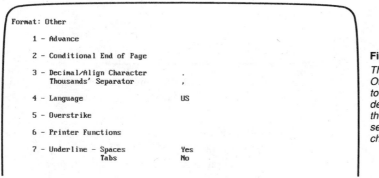

Fig. 18.7.

The Format: Other menu used to change decimal and thousands-separator characters.

Using Total Columns

The difference between a numeric column and a total column is that the subtotal operators (+) in a total column add items in the column immediately to the left of the total column. Subtotal operators in numeric columns add items in the same column.

To understand how subtotal operators work in total columns, assume that the Math Definition screen shown in figure 18.8 defines the current math area. Column A is a numeric column (indicated by type 2); column B is a total column (indicated by type 3). Type numbers in the math columns according to the following chart:

Column A	Column B
15.00	
(22.00)	
27.00	t25.00
80.00	
(18.00)	
40.00	+

Fig. 18.8.

The Math Definition screen for a total column.

```
Math Definition          Use arrow keys to position cursor

Columns                  A B C D E F G H I J K L M N O P Q R S T U V W X

Type                     2 3 2 2 2 2 2 2 2 2 2 2 2 2 2 2 2 2 2 2 2 2 2 2

Negative Numbers         ( ( ( ( ( ( ( ( ( ( ( ( ( ( ( ( ( ( ( ( ( ( ( (

Number of Digits to      2 2 2 2 2 2 2 2 2 2 2 2 2 2 2 2 2 2 2 2 2 2 2 2
   the Right (0-4)

Calculation      1
   Formulas      2
                 3
                 4

Type of Column:
      0 = Calculation    1 = Text      2 = Numeric    3 = Total

Negative Numbers
      ( = Parentheses (50.00)          - = Minus Sign  -50.00


Press Exit when done
```

Consider the subtotal operator at the bottom of column B. After performing the math calculation, the + changes to 62.00+. How does WordPerfect arrive at this figure?

Remember that the subtotal in column B, a total column, is the subtotal of the items from the column to the left (column A in the example). Addition starts in column A with the line preceding the subtotal operator in column B and continues upward until it reaches, but does not include, a line that contains another subtotal, total, or grand total in column B.

In the example, the subtotal operation does not include 40.00 because it is on the same line as the subtotal operator (+). The operation also excludes 27.00 and all numbers above it because those numbers are on the same line or above the line containing the extra subtotal (t25.00). The only numbers in column A above the subtotal line and below the extra subtotal number are 80 and (18.00); the subtotal is calculated and displayed as 62.00+.

Reminder:

Do not put an item in a total column on the same line as an item in the column to the left.

The values 40.00 and 27.00 in column A are not included in any calculation specified by the total column (column B). Unless you have a particular reason to do so, do not put an item in a total column on the same line as an item in the column to the left of the total column. If you violate this rule, the item in the column to the left is ignored by all calculations specified in the total column.

Working with a Total-Column Example

Total columns are particularly useful for such applications as entering simple accounting statements. Consider the simple income statement shown in figure 18.9. The Math Definition for this document is positioned above the Service Revenue line. Assume that the definition used for this figure is the same as the definition shown in figure 18.8. The first math column is a numeric column, and the second math column is a total column (the space to the left of the first column holds text labels).

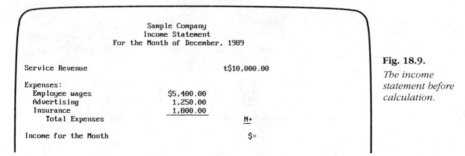

Fig. 18.9.

The income statement before calculation.

Individual expense amounts are entered in the numeric column. The subtotal operator (+) in the total column instructs WordPerfect to add the expense amounts in the numeric column. The *N* preceding the + indicates that the Total Expenses value is to be subtracted from the Service Revenue amount when the total is calculated. The $10,000 Service Revenue amount is preceded by the t operator so that the $10,000 is included in the total calculation (indicated by the = in the Income for the Month line). After the calculation has been performed, the document appears as shown in figure 18.10.

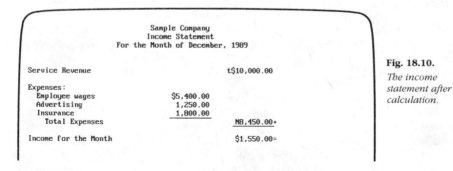

Fig. 18.10.

The income statement after calculation.

Understanding the Guidelines for Total Columns

Using total columns can improve the appearance of the document and can allow you to use a set of columns to compute several levels of totals. Consider the following guidelines when working with total columns:

- The column to the left of the leftmost total column can be either a calculation or a numeric column.

  Do not use any items in the numeric or calculation column other than simple numbers or calculation results shown with an exclamation point (!). (WordPerfect uses ! to show that the calculation should be performed at that position.)

- In a total column, use only subtotal operators (+) when you want to add numbers from the column to the left.

  (Although subtotal operators do not add subtotals in numeric columns, when subtotal operators appear in total columns they *do* add subtotals from the column to the left.) When placing the subtotal operators, remember that an item immediately to the left of a subtotal operator is not included in any subtotal.

- You can include a number with the t operator in a total column so that the number is added to the subtotals in the same column.

  Because the t operator is a subtotal designator, place the t so that it does not interfere with the operation of any subtotals in the same column below the t. (Don't do what was done in the example in the preceding section. Placing t25.00 in the third line of column B prevented the subtotal operator from including the numbers in the top three lines of column A.)

- In addition to the subtotal operator (+), you can include the total (=), extra total (T), and grand total (*) operators in the rightmost total column.

  In a total column, the total (=) and grand total (*) items operate in a vertical fashion, as if they were in a simple numeric column.

Using Calculation Columns

Reminder:

Use calculation columns to perform math operations on horizontal lines of numbers.

Numeric and total columns add vertical columns of numbers. Calculation columns calculate numbers on a single line of a document and are sometimes called *horizontal calculations*. Although using calculation columns can be more complex than using numeric and total columns, the WordPerfect Math feature is still limited to simple calculations.

A *calculation column* stores results of calculations performed horizontally. The calculation formula applies to the entire calculation column; the results in that column depend on the values in the horizontal rows in the math area. For example, if you have four columns (A, B, C, and D), and you designate column D as the calculation column, you can have the calculation formula add columns A, B, and C and store the results in column D. The formula is evaluated for each row in the math area. Columns A, B, and C are added for row 1 and the result is stored in column D of row 1; columns A, B, and C are added for row 2 and the result is stored in column D of row 2; and so on.

WordPerfect allows up to four calculation columns per math area. You use the Math Definition screen to specify a column as a calculation column by inserting the 0 code in the Type line as shown for column D of figure 18.11.

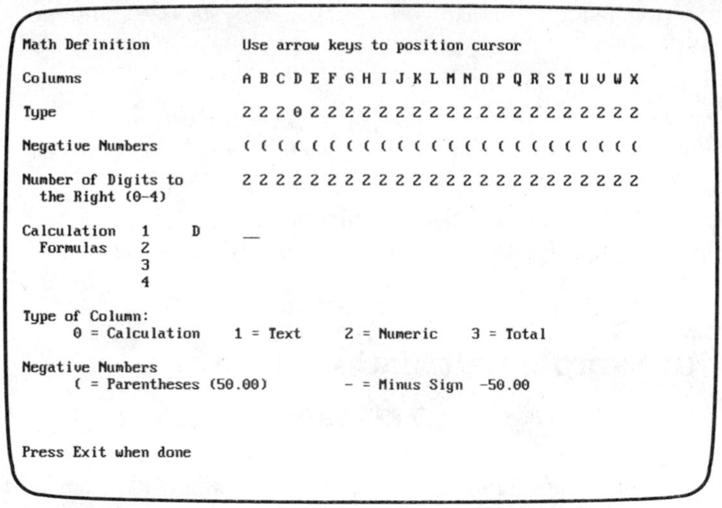

```
Math Definition          Use arrow keys to position cursor

Columns                  A B C D E F G H I J K L M N O P Q R S T U V W X

Type                     2 2 2 0 2 2 2 2 2 2 2 2 2 2 2 2 2 2 2 2 2 2 2 2

Negative Numbers         ( ( ( ( ( ( ( ( ( ( ( ( ( ( ( ( ( ( ( ( ( ( ( (

Number of Digits to      2 2 2 2 2 2 2 2 2 2 2 2 2 2 2 2 2 2 2 2 2 2 2 2
  the Right (0-4)

Calculation    1    D    __
  Formulas     2
               3
               4

Type of Column:
     0 = Calculation    1 = Text     2 = Numeric    3 = Total

Negative Numbers
     ( = Parentheses (50.00)       - = Minus Sign  -50.00


Press Exit when done
```

Fig. 18.11.

The Math Definition screen for a calculation column.

When you insert a 0 for the Type code, WordPerfect automatically moves the cursor to the middle of the screen so that you can enter the calculation formula for the calculation column. In figure 18.11, the cursor is positioned at Calculation Formula 1. WordPerfect automatically places the D to the left of the cursor to indicate that this calculation formula gives instructions to calculate results stored in column D.

The calculation formula can include the following numbers:

- Numbers in other columns (either to the left or right of the calculation column) in the same line of the document
- The number on the preceding line in the calculation column
- Numbers you type explicitly into the formula

The calculation formula can include also the following four standard arithmetic operators:

+   Add

−   Subtract

*   Multiply

/   Divide

WordPerfect also has four special functions that can be used by themselves as calculation formulas. They include the following:

+   Add numbers across numeric columns

+/   Average numbers across numeric columns

=   Add numbers across totals columns

=/   Average numbers across totals columns

These special functions are limited to use as complete formulas in themselves; they cannot be used within calculation formulas that contain other operators, numbers, or column indicators.

When you enter a calculation formula, you can use the standard arithmetic operators, you can use letters to refer to columns (other columns on the same line or the same column in the preceding line), and you can type numeric constants explicitly.

Do not use spaces in calculation formulas. A space has the same effect as pressing the Enter key: the space signals that you have completed entering the formula.

WordPerfect calculates the formula from left to right, but you can modify this order by using parentheses. You cannot, however, put a set of parentheses inside another set of parentheses.

Working with Sample Calculation Formulas

Assume that you have a document with the following four numeric columns (A, B, D, and E):

Column A	Column B	Column C	Column D	Column E
1.00	2.00		4.00	5.00
18.30	0.05		0.00	3.00

The letters above the columns are to help you identify the columns. The letters are not required for the Math feature and have no effect on it.

Suppose that you want to enter a calculation formula for column C. First consider some possible calculation formulas as they relate to the figures in columns A, B, D, and E. In the following charts, the first group of numbers or letters represents the calculation formula. The second group of numbers represents the results of the calculation formula displayed in the two lines of column C. The explanation of the formulas follow the numbers themselves.

Formula	Results
3*2	6.00
	6.00

Reminder:
Using only numbers in a calculation formula always gives the same results.

If you use only numbers in a formula (with no letters to reference other columns), each line displays the same result.

3–1/2	1.00
	1.00

Be careful when you use fractions; the result may not be what you anticipated. The formula 3–1/2 does not mean 3 minus one-half; it means 3 minus 1 divided by 2. Because WordPerfect performs each operation in sequence from left to right, the program first performs the subtraction (3–1), giving a result of 2. This result is divided by 2 to give the final result of 1.00 (equal to 2/2). If you want the division performed first, use parentheses. For example, the formula 3–(1/2) produces the result 2.50.

A+B/D	0.75
	??

This result also may be different from what you expected. Remember that WordPerfect calculates from left to right; in this example, WordPerfect calculates the addition first and then the division. The calculation for the first line is 1.00 + 2.00 = 3.00 divided by 4.00 = 0.75. If you want to divide column B by column D before adding column A, use the formula A+(B/D), which results in 1.50 (2.00 divided by 4.00 = 0.50; 1.00 + 0.50 = 1.50).

If you have a formula for which the result cannot be calculated, WordPerfect displays the result as question marks. The question marks in the second line of this example reflect WordPerfect's inability to divide the number 18.35 (the sum of columns A and B) by 0.

    A*B   2.00

                  0.92

In the Math Definition for these examples, the default setting of two decimal places is in effect. When a formula produces a number with more than two digits to the right of the decimal point, WordPerfect rounds the number to two decimal places (or to the number of decimal places specified on the Math Definition screen). In the second line of this example, 18.30 multiplied by 0.05 results in 0.915. WordPerfect rounds this number to 0.92.

    A*B+C   2.00

                  2.92

This formula references the calculation column itself (column C). The C in this formula instructs WordPerfect to use the number in the preceding line of column C. That number in the preceding column is normally the result of the same calculation for the preceding line, but can also be a number inserted manually (as described later).

In this example, the formula is intended to compute a cumulative sum, or running total, of the product of column A multiplied by column B. Although the formula is A*B+C, the result for the first line of column C really reflects the result of the formula A*B, because column C of the preceding line does not have a number or a result. A running total normally starts in this way. The result for the second line is A*B for the second line plus the result from the preceding line (0.92 + 2.00 = 2.92). If you added a third line to the math area, the program would add A*B for the third line to the 2.92 result in column C of the second line.

An important point to remember when you devise a calculation formula for running totals is to put at the end of the equation the calculation for adding the previous line. Putting the calculation for the previous line at the beginning of the equation (C+A*B, for example) doesn't work because the addition is performed first. Performing the addition first means that the previous total (from column C of the previous line) is added to column A of the current line, and this sum is multiplied by B. The formula C+A*B gives a result quite different from the desired running total. C+A*B results in 2.00 on the first line, but 1.02 on the second line (2.00 + 18.30 = 20.30; 20.30 * 0.05 = 1.015; 1.015 rounded up to two decimal places is 1.02).

Reminder:
In a running-total formula, place the equation that adds the previous subtotal at the end of the formula.

Working with a Calculation-Column Example

To give a more complete example of the use of calculation columns, assume that you want to prepare an invoice similar to the one shown in figure 18.12, where the amount billed for each product is calculated by WordPerfect. The headings are typed before the Math Definition is inserted. (The capital letters above the headings are to help you identify the columns and have no effect on the calculations.) The Math Definition for this example is the one shown in figure 18.11 with Calculation Formula 1 entered as A*B*(−C/100+1).

Fig. 18.12.

The invoice before calculation.

Product	(A) Number of units	(B) Unit Price	(C) Discount	(D) Amount Billed
1 inch springs	1000	5.305	15%	$!
5 inch springs	32	8.001	35%	!
Leaf springs	27	14.010	15%	!
Total amount billed				$+

After you enter the calculation formula, the middle of the Math Definition screen looks like the following:

```
Calculation   1      D      A*B*(-C/100+1)
Formulas      2
              3
              4
```

The formula looks strange but must be entered this way to describe the correct calculation without inserting parentheses within another set of parentheses—a shortcut WordPerfect does not allow.

Using this formula, WordPerfect first takes the number entered in column C of the current line, changes the number's sign (because of the minus sign), and divides the number by 100 to convert the number to a decimal fraction equal to the discount percentage ($-15/100 = -0.15$). Although the percent symbol appears in column C, WordPerfect uses only the number portion of the value. The result is then added to 1 ($-0.15 + 1.00 = 0.85$).

WordPerfect first calculates the value within parentheses (0.85 in this case) before doing anything with columns A and B. After the expression within the parentheses is calculated, WordPerfect calculates the formula from left to right as if the formula had been entered as A*B*result. A*B is calculated (1000 * 5.305 = 5305); this product is multiplied by the result of the calculation in parentheses (5305 * 0.85 = 4509.25). Figure 18.13 shows the result of this calculation.

Fig. 18.13.

The invoice after calculation.

Product	(A) Number of units	(B) Unit Price	(C) Discount	(D) Amount Billed
1 inch springs	1000	5.305	15%	$4,509.25!
5 inch springs	32	8.001	35%	166.42!
Leaf springs	27	14.010	25%	283.70!
Total amount billed				$4,959.37+

After you enter the Math Definition, turn on Math, and enter the numbers, the display should look like figure 18.12. An exclamation point appears in column D for each product line. WordPerfect uses the ! to indicate that the defined calculation is to be performed for that line, and the result displayed in column D.

WordPerfect inserts the ! only if you have tabbed over to the calculation column. The program does not insert the ! and does not perform the calculation for that line if you just enter information up through the Discount column and press Enter. To obtain calculation results for that line, you must press the Tab key to move to the column containing the calculation formula before pressing Enter.

If you do not want the calculation formula to be calculated and displayed for a given line, simply delete the ! for that line. The last line (Total amount billed) of column D should contain the sum of the values in the Amount Billed column rather than the result of a column-C calculation. To achieve the proper calculation, replace the ! for the last line with a + operator, which indicates that the program should calculate and insert a subtotal for that column (refer to fig. 18.12).

After making the change, perform the calculations by pressing Columns/Table (Alt-F7) and selecting **C**alculate (**2**). ⌨ If you use a mouse, access the **L**ayout pull-down menu, choose **M**ath, and select **C**alculate. The display looks like the one in figure 18.13. The operators ! and + appear on-screen, but do not appear on the printed document. (You can verify that the operators do not appear on the printed document by using View Document.)

Editing a Math Definition

On occasion, you may have to modify a Math Definition. For example, if you alter the layout of the document, you may have to change the Math Definition. Also, if your Math Definition does not give you the desired results, you must alter it.

To change a Math Definition, do the following:

1. Place the cursor immediately after the Math Definition (**[Math Def]**) code you want to edit. Press Reveal Codes (Alt-F3 or F11) to locate the codes; position the cursor to highlight the character or code following **[Math Def]**.

2. Press Columns/Table (Alt-F7), select **M**ath (**3**), and select **D**efine (**3**).

   ⌨ Access the **L**ayout pull-down menu, choose **M**ath, and select **D**efine.

3. Edit the Math Definition by moving the cursor to the specification(s) you want to change and typing the new specification(s).

4. Press Exit (F7) to return to the Math/Columns menu.

5. Press 0 (or the space bar) to leave the Math/Columns menu.

6. Press ← to move past the edited Math Definition.

7. Press the Backspace key to delete the old Math Definition.

   Note: Unless you have a good reason to save the old Math Definition, delete it. (If you keep old, unused definitions in a document, you may find them confusing as you continue to edit the document.)

Reminder:

The ! marks the location in a calculated column where the results of the formula are to be displayed.

You can change a calculation formula by reentering the 0 code for the appropriate column in the Math Definition screen. The cursor is placed in a position to edit the previously defined calculation formula for that column. The formula is edited in the same way that file names are edited: if your first keystroke is a character, WordPerfect erases the previous formula because the program assumes that you want to replace the formula. If you want to edit the existing formula, either press Insert/Typeover (Ins) to go to Typeover mode, or use the cursor-control keys to move the cursor before editing the formula. If you want to insert something at the beginning of the existing formula, press Insert/Typeover twice to access Insert mode at the beginning of the formula.

Reminder:

You can delete a formula by pressing Enter without editing the formula or by changing the Type code for a calculation column.

Remember that pressing Enter without doing any editing of the formula erases the formula. A calculation formula for a column is erased also if you enter a type code other than 0 for that column. If you inadvertently enter an incorrect Type code in a calculation column, revert to the previous Math Definition by pressing Cancel (F1). Then restart the Math Definition edit by selecting **M**ath Def (**2**).

If you want to adjust the position of one or more columns, position the cursor *in front of* the Math Definition code and change the tabs by pressing Format (Shift-F8), selecting **L**ine (**1**), and selecting **T**ab Set (**8**). 🖰 If you use a mouse, access the **L**ayout pull-down menu, select **L**ine, and select **T**ab Set (**8**).

Remember that numeric columns are aligned with the decimal character at the specified tab stop. Insert new codes for the columns you want to move. Before leaving the Tab Set screen, be sure that you delete the tab-stop codes from the original locations for the columns you have moved.

Creating a Useful Macro for Math Columns

Most WordPerfect macros used with the Math feature are specific to an application, but one general-purpose macro exists that you may find useful.

To understand the macro's usefulness, recall that WordPerfect does not perform calculations automatically. You must tell WordPerfect to do the calculation after you enter the numbers in a math area. If you change any numbers in a math area or change the settings in a Math Definition, you must tell WordPerfect to perform the calculation again to update the math area based on the new information. If you have more than one math area in a document, you have to update each math area separately. (When you tell WordPerfect to calculate one math area, no other math area is affected.)

The best way to ensure that all math areas are calculated properly before printing is to tell WordPerfect to perform the calculation in each math area just before you print—a tedious task if you have several math areas in the document. The macro presented in this section performs this function for you.

The macro is actually two macros. Because you do not want to start from the top of the document after each calculation, the first macro sets up and calls the second macro, which then repeats itself.

Begin by creating the first macro in the following manner:

1. Press Macro Define (Ctrl-F10) to begin the macro definition.

    ⌨ Access the **T**ools pull-down menu, choose **M**acro, and select **D**efine.

2. Type *recalc* and press Enter to name the macro.

3. Type *To recalculate all math areas in a doc* and press Enter to give the macro a description.

4. Press Home, Home, Home, ↑ to go to the top of the document, in front of all format codes.

5. Press Macro (Alt-F10).

    ⌨ Access the **T**ools pull-down menu and choose **M**acro.

6. Type *recalc2* and press Enter to invoke the macro RECALC2.

7. Press Macro Define (Ctrl-F10) to end the definition of the first macro.

    ⌨ Access the **T**ools pull-down menu, choose **M**acro, and select **D**efine.

Follow these steps to create the second macro:

1. Press Macro Define (Ctrl-F10) to begin the second macro definition.

    ⌨ Access the **T**ools pull-down menu, choose **M**acro, and select **D**efine.

2. Type *recalc2* and press Enter to name the macro.

3. Type *To recalculate a math area and loop* and press Enter to give the macro a description.

4. Press Forward Search (F2), press Columns/Table (Alt-F7), select **M**ath (**3**), and select **O**n (**1**) to search for **[Math On]** codes.

    ⌨ Access the **S**earch pull-down menu, choose **F**orward, press Columns/Table (Alt-F7), select **M**ath (**3**), and select **O**n (**1**) to search for **[Math On]** codes.

5. Press Forward Search (F2) to indicate the end of the search string.

6. Press → to move across the **[Math On]** code.

7. Press Columns/Table (Alt-F7), select **M**ath (**3**), and select **C**alculate (**4**).

    ⌨ Access the **L**ayout pull-down menu, select **M**ath, and select **C**alculate.

8. Press Macro (Alt-F10).

    Access the **T**ools pull-down menu, choose **M**acro, and select **E**xecute.

9. Type *recalc2* and press Enter.

    This step causes WordPerfect to invoke the macro RECALC2 again until the search is unsuccessful (because all **[Math On]** codes have been processed).

10. Press Macro Define (Ctrl-F10) to end the definition of the second macro.

    ⌨ Access the **T**ools pull-down menu, choose **M**acro, and select **D**efine.

To invoke these macros, do the following:

1. Press Macro (Alt-F10).

    ⌨ Access the **T**ools pull-down menu, choose **M**acro, and select **E**xecute.

2. Type *recalc* and press Enter.

When you invoke RECALC, the macro moves the cursor to the top of the document in front of all codes and calls RECALC2. RECALC2 finds each math area, tells WordPerfect to perform the calculation for that math area, and calls itself again. RECALC2 stops calling itself when no further math areas are found.

Summary

WordPerfect's Math feature provides the limited facility for performing simple arithmetic calculations in a document. The Math feature works well for documents where columns of numbers must be added or where simple calculations involving different columns in the same line are needed.

WordPerfect's Math feature is not a substitute for a spreadsheet. To do anything other than very simple calculations, you should use a standard spreadsheet program such as 1-2-3 or SuperCalc to perform the computations. You then can print the results to a disk file in text format and retrieve that file into WordPerfect using the techniques described in Chapter 16.

Another option for more complicated calculations is to use PlanPerfect, a spreadsheet with the capability to transfer material directly into WordPerfect.

Remember the following points when using the Math feature:

❑ Be sure to set the Math Definition before turning on the Math feature (unless you want to use the default settings).

❑ If your calculations do not appear to be working correctly (results appear incorrectly or no results appear), edit the Math Definition to be sure that it is defined correctly.

❑ When you want to edit or examine the Math Definition, be sure that you position the cursor immediately *after* the **[Math Def]** code for the existing Math Definition.

❑ Calculate each math area before printing the document, or create a macro to perform this function for you.

❑ If you have any difficulty changing numbers or operators in a math area, delete the numbers and start over.

Creating Tables

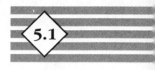

Robert M. Beck is a former judge practicing law in Oklahoma City. He also is a computer consultant for small to medium-size law offices. His experience with the new Table feature began during beta testing of WordPerfect 5.1.

*T*able is a powerful new WordPerfect feature that combines the best aspects of columns, math functions, and spreadsheets. If you use **[Tab]** codes to put text in column format or the Columns feature of earlier versions of WordPerfect, you will find the Table feature easy to learn and easier to use. Although **[Tab]** codes and the Columns feature remain options in WordPerfect 5.1, just about anything that can be done with those features can be done quicker and easier with the Table feature. If you use a spreadsheet program—especially PlanPerfect 5.0—you already know approximately 90 percent of how the Table feature works.

Reminder

If you use a mouse with WordPerfect 5.1, you can click the right button to display the pull-down menus, and then select the desired option. You also can press Alt-= to access the pull-down menus, and then press the appropriate letter of the desired option. For all instructions, assume that if a block is required to activate a pull-down menu option, the text has been blocked before the pull-down menu is accessed. Instructions for pull-down menus and the mouse are marked with the mouse icon. For more information about the mouse, see Chapter 1.

Understanding Table Basics

When you create a table, a group of connected empty boxes (called *cells*) forms a grid on-screen. The grid is composed of columns and rows of cells. *Columns* are vertical stacks of cells named from left to right with letters of the alphabet beginning with *A*. *Rows* are horizontal lines of cells named from top to bottom with numbers beginning with *1*. A cell is the intersection of a column and a row. The cell takes its name from the column and row. For example, the cell formed by the intersection of column A and row 1 is called cell A1. Figure 19.1 depicts the table format and terminology.

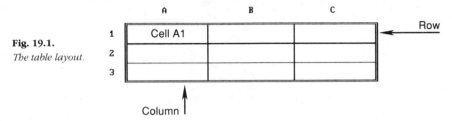

Fig. 19.1.
The table layout.

Reminder:

A cell can be as small as a single character or as large as a single page of the document.

WordPerfect enables you to create a table as small as a single cell or as large as 32 columns wide by 32,765 rows high, and containing 1,048,480 cells. An individual cell can be as small as a single letter or as large as a single page of the document.

Consider each cell as a minidocument within the main document. Within a cell you can use all of WordPerfect's size and attribute format options to create and edit text. With a few exceptions, text editing and cursor-movement keys function as they do in the main document.

You can use most of the document features and codes in a table, including macros, styles to format the table, style codes that include a table, column headers that automatically print at the top of each sheet in a multipage table, automatic references, and footnotes and endnotes. In addition, you can mark text for an Index, Table of Contents, Table of Authorities, or List and wrap text around the table by putting the table into a graphic box.

Tables can be created side by side or one on top of the other. Columns, rows, and cells can be split or joined. The lines that make up the table grid can be printed or omitted without affecting the information within the table. If the table is larger than the sheet on which it is to be printed, WordPerfect automatically splits the table vertically at columns and horizontally (where possible) at rows.

Using the Table feature, you can create parallel and newspaper columns, create merge templates that function as fill-in forms, create mathematical formulas and perform math functions, sort data, import spreadsheet information into the table, and place a table into a graphic box and a graphic box into a table.

You can retrieve a spreadsheet into a document as a table. You also can use the Retrieve and Text In/Out features to bring text and numerical data into a table.

As you enter text into a cell, the cell expands downward as necessary. As you delete text, the cell contracts to the smallest height required by the largest cell in the row. You can move or copy text between table cells, and between cells and the main document.

This chapter shows you how to create, format, and edit a table; enter, format, and edit text in a table; perform mathematical operations in a table; and import data into a table. The chapter concludes with some suggestions on how to use the Table feature with other features to simplify document creation.

Note: Depending on the printer form definition and font type you use, the table, text, status line, and other variable information displayed on your screen may differ slightly from that shown in the figures in this chapter. All fixed WordPerfect menu options on your screen should match those shown in the figures in this chapter.

Planning a Table Definition

The primary function of a table is to organize many separate pieces of related information into a grid structure that shows the relationship of each piece to the others. An ideal table organizes data in a manner that makes it easy to understand and evaluate. The specific table structure depends on the nature of the information and what the author intends to convey with it. At minimum, however, a table contains text, columns, rows, and cells. If the data includes numbers, the table also may require mathematical operations and formulas.

Reminder:
Define the table in a way that makes data easy to understand.

Using the Table feature is like shopping in a grocery store. Without any preplanning you can walk in and spend hours roaming the aisles looking at each item to decide if you want or need it. If you plan, however, you can make a list of the items you want and need before you leave home. When you use a list, you do not look at individual items but only select those items you previously decided to buy. Define the table structure to present your data in a logical manner before you invoke the Table feature; that way you can quickly select only the features you need.

Defining a table begins by determining the type of facts to be organized, how each fact relates to the whole, and where to place the facts in the table. Frequently, the type of facts dictate the table's *structure*, but the table's *format* (column width, row height, font size and appearance, and the like) is almost always a matter of individual preference.

WordPerfect permits tables larger than a single sheet. However, a table larger than a page of a document may be difficult to read and lessen the impact the information has on the reader. If the table is wider than a single page, consider breaking it into two or more tables.

Although you can organize information in a table in many ways, most business applications present tables in spreadsheet format. In a spreadsheet, each column contains similar information for each of the rows. Each cell in the first row usually contains a title describing the category of information below it. Each column should be formatted for the type of information it contains. For example, a column containing numerical information with 10 characters or less should be formatted as numeric with a width of at least 10 characters.

Creating a Table

Although one of WordPerfect's most powerful features, tables are easy to create even for a first-time user. A table can be created on a blank screen or in an existing document. You can use any size sheet to create a table, which can be located anywhere within the document. In this chapter, you create a table, in spreadsheet format, which contains the following information: the name of real-estate acreages, selling prices, number of acres, prices per acre, and agents selling the property.

5.1

For the purpose of this chapter, start with a blank screen and define a printer form as follows:

1. Press Format (Shift-F8). Select **P**age (**2**). Select Page **S**ize (**7**). From the Format: Paper Size/Type menu, select the form defined as `Standard 8.5" × 11" Portrait`. Exit back to the main document.

2. Press Font (Ctrl-F8). Select Base **F**ont (**4**). Select a nonproportional 10-point font, such as Courier 10.

3. Press Format (Shift-F8). Select **L**ine (**1**) and select Tab **S**et (**8**).

4. Press Home, ←. Press Ctrl-End. Select **T**ype. WordPerfect displays this menu:

    Tab Type: 1 Absolute; **2 R**elative to Margin: **0**

    Select **R**elative to Margin (**2**). Type *2.3,1.3* and press Enter. Exit to the main document.

5. Press Enter twice.

The Initial Codes for the document should be as shown in figure 19.2.

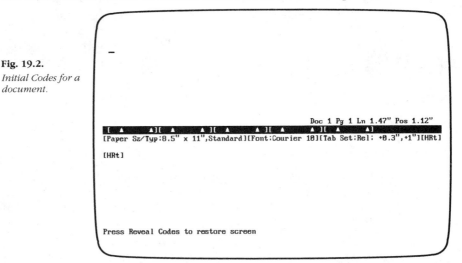

Fig. 19.2.
Initial Codes for a document.

The table editor lets you define and change the table's structure and format. The table's *structure* is the physical layout of the rows and columns, and the size and type of the graphical grid lines. The table's *format* is the appearance of the text in the cells. Text cannot be entered or edited while the table editor is active.

Note: A table structure is created automatically when a spreadsheet is imported as a table. The Import feature is discussed later in this chapter.

Before creating a table, position the cursor at the left margin. If the cursor is located anywhere else in a line of text, WordPerfect inserts a **[HRt]** code at the cursor location and moves the cursor to the left margin on the next line.

To create a table, move the cursor to the left margin and follow these steps:

1. Press Columns/Table (Alt-F7). WordPerfect displays a menu at the bottom of the screen:

    1 Columns; **2 T**ables; **3 M**ath: **0**

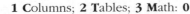 **5.1**

2. Select **T**ables (**2**); WordPerfect displays a new menu:

Table: 1 Create; **2 E**dit: **0**

3. Select **C**reate (**1**).

⌨ Access the **L**ayout pull-down menu, select **T**ables, and then select **C**reate (see fig. 19.3).

Note: Once the table editor is active, you cannot access the pull-down menu bar. You *can* use the mouse to select options on the table-editor menus.

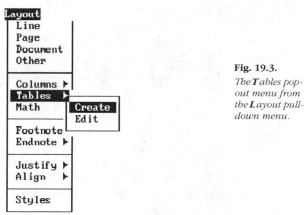

Fig. 19.3.
*The **T**ables pop-out menu from the **L**ayout pull-down menu.*

4. WordPerfect displays the `Number of Columns: 3` prompt, showing a default of 3.

Enter a value from 1 to 32. WordPerfect automatically calculates the space between the document's left and right margins and formats the column widths to fill all available space. For this example, type *5* and press Enter to create a table with five columns.

5. WordPerfect displays the `Number of Rows: 1` prompt, showing a default of 1.

Enter a value from 1 to 32,765. By default, WordPerfect creates a single row that is one text-line high. Type *9* and press Enter to create a table with nine rows. WordPerfect creates a blank table and displays the table-editor menu (see fig. 19.4). The status line at the bottom of the screen adds the cell location.

Caution

You cannot stop the table-creation process unless you reboot the computer. If you mistakenly enter a large value for the number of rows (such as 5,000 when you meant 50 or 500), you get a table requiring a large amount of RAM and disk space and taking several minutes to create. For example: a 1-column, 32,000-row table without text requires more than one megabyte of memory, uses 1,000 8.5" × 11" pages, and takes more than three minutes to create on a 386 25MHz system.

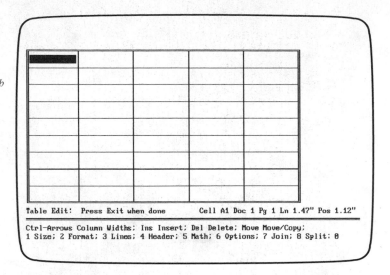

Fig. 19.4.
*A blank table with
the table-editor
menu.*

While in the table editor, WordPerfect expands the cursor to highlight the cell in which the cursor is located. When you create a table, WordPerfect places the cursor in cell A1 (the upper left corner of the table).

At this point, you can use one or more of the table-editor options to define the table's format, or you can exit from the editor and return to the main document.

Reminder:

Use F7 to leave the table editor.

For this exercise, press Exit (F7) to leave the table editor. Although you can use Cancel (F1) or Esc to back out of most menu options when editing a table, Exit (F7) is the only method you can use to leave the table editor. The cursor returns to its normal size and remains in the cell in which it was located when you pressed Exit (F7).

6. Press Save (F10) to save the table.

   ▢ Access the **F**ile pull-down menu and select **S**ave.

   Type *table.tst* as the name of the file and press Enter.

Understanding Table-Structure Codes

Reminder:

To see the table-definition codes, exit the table editor and use Reveal Codes.

Once you create a table, you may want to see the hidden codes that define the table. With the file TABLE.TST on-screen, press Reveal Codes (Alt-F3 or F11). ▢ If you use a mouse, access the **E**dit pull-down menu and select **R**eveal Codes. WordPerfect displays the table above the division bar; the codes defining the table appear below the bar, as shown in figure 19.5.

Note: The Reveal Codes feature is one of the few WordPerfect editing features that does not work, or have an equivalent function, from within the table editor. You can use the feature only when the table editor is not active.

5.1

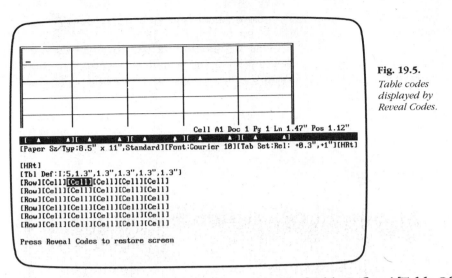

Fig. 19.5.

Table codes displayed by Reveal Codes.

WordPerfect uses paired codes to define a table. The **[Table Def]** and **[Table Off]** codes mark the boundary of a table. The table-definition code contains several useful pieces of information. Consider the code **[Tbl Def:I;5,1.3",1.3",1.3", 1.3",1.3"]**; the *I* is the Roman numeral of the table (subsequent tables are numbered II, III, and so on). WordPerfect keeps track of the number and status of each table in a document, even if the table is located in a graphics box, endnote, or footnote. If you delete or insert a table, WordPerfect renumbers the subsequent tables.

The *5* following the table number in the definition code specifies the number of columns in the table. The next five numbers define the widths of the columns. In this example, the five **1.3"** numbers mean that columns A, B, C, D, and E are each 1.3 inches wide. The **[Row]** and **[Cell]** codes in figure 19.5 define the table's structure. The **[Tbl Off]** code marks the end of the table definition. The lines that make up the table grid do not display in Reveal Codes because they are graphical lines, not ASCII characters.

Note: If your printer does not print graphical characters, the table's grid lines do not print.

Tip

When you use the Look feature—press List (F5), press Enter, and select Look (**6**) or ▢▤ access the **F**ile pull-down menu, select List **F**iles, and select Look (**6**)—only the first line for each cell is displayed. Use View Document to see the table with its grid lines.

WordPerfect offers other information regarding the width of the columns. In the information bar separating the document from the Reveal-Codes screen, each pair of [and] characters shows the actual location of the left and right margins for each column. Each ▲ shows the location of a tab stop in the column.

5.1

5.1

Reminder:

You cannot delete individual [Row], [Cell], or [Tbl Off] codes.

To prevent the accidental destruction of a table while editing the main document, WordPerfect does not permit deletion of individual **[Row]**, **[Cell]**, or **[Tbl Off]** codes. The only way to alter the table structure outside the table editor is to delete the beginning table-definition code. Deleting the beginning code removes all other table-definition codes but preserves the data. Blocking and deleting the entire table destroys the table *and* all the data.

Note: When you delete only the beginning table-definition code, WordPerfect separates the data in each column with a hard tab code (**[TAB]**); data in each row is separated with a hard return code (**[HRt]**). You cannot use the Undelete (F1) feature to restore the table's structure. The method for re-creating a table is explained later in this chapter.

Moving the Cursor within a Table

Reminder:

You can move the cursor in a table by using the Tab key and the arrow keys.

Moving the cursor in a table is as easy as moving it in the main WordPerfect document. The Tab and arrow keys (individually and in conjunction with the Ctrl, Shift, Alt, and Home keys) move the cursor among the cells in a table. Outside the table editor, most of the cursor-movement keys function in the same manner that they do in the main WordPerfect document. See Chapters 1 and 2 for information on cursor-movement keys. The cursor-movement keys that function differently in a table outside the table editor are listed in table 19.1.

The mouse moves the cursor within a table in the same way it does in a regular document. Move the mouse pointer to the cell in which you want the cursor and click the left button.

In table 19.1, a hyphen between keys means to press both keys simultaneously. A comma between keys means to release one key before pressing the next key.

Table 19.1
Keys for Moving in Tables Outside the Table Editor

Press	To Move to this Position
↑	Same relative position on the bottom line of the cell above; out of the table if the cursor is in the top row of the table.*
↓	Same relative position on the top line of the cell below; out of the table if the cursor is in the bottom row of the table.*
→	First character of the first line in the next cell in forward sequence (from cell A1 to cell B1, for example, or from cell C1 to A2, if C is the last column in the table); out of the table if the cursor is on the last character of the last cell in the table.*
←	Last character of the last line in the next cell in reverse sequence (from cell B1 to cell A1, for example, or from cell A2 to cell C1, if C is the last column of the table); out of the table if the cursor is on the first character of cell A1.*

 5.1

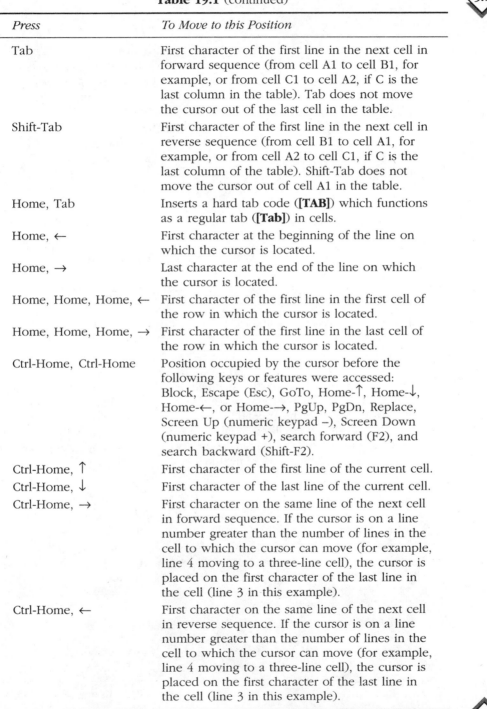

Table 19.1 (continued)

Press	To Move to this Position
Tab	First character of the first line in the next cell in forward sequence (from cell A1 to cell B1, for example, or from cell C1 to cell A2, if C is the last column in the table). Tab does not move the cursor out of the last cell in the table.
Shift-Tab	First character of the first line in the next cell in reverse sequence (from cell B1 to cell A1, for example, or from cell A2 to cell C1, if C is the last column of the table). Shift-Tab does not move the cursor out of cell A1 in the table.
Home, Tab	Inserts a hard tab code (**[TAB]**) which functions as a regular tab (**[Tab]**) in cells.
Home, ←	First character at the beginning of the line on which the cursor is located.
Home, →	Last character at the end of the line on which the cursor is located.
Home, Home, Home, ←	First character of the first line in the first cell of the row in which the cursor is located.
Home, Home, Home, →	First character of the first line in the last cell of the row in which the cursor is located.
Ctrl-Home, Ctrl-Home	Position occupied by the cursor before the following keys or features were accessed: Block, Escape (Esc), GoTo, Home-↑, Home-↓, Home-←, or Home-→, PgUp, PgDn, Replace, Screen Up (numeric keypad –), Screen Down (numeric keypad +), search forward (F2), and search backward (Shift-F2).
Ctrl-Home, ↑	First character of the first line of the current cell.
Ctrl-Home, ↓	First character of the last line of the current cell.
Ctrl-Home, →	First character on the same line of the next cell in forward sequence. If the cursor is on a line number greater than the number of lines in the cell to which the cursor can move (for example, line 4 moving to a three-line cell), the cursor is placed on the first character of the last line in the cell (line 3 in this example).
Ctrl-Home, ←	First character on the same line of the next cell in reverse sequence. If the cursor is on a line number greater than the number of lines in the cell to which the cursor can move (for example, line 4 moving to a three-line cell), the cursor is placed on the first character of the last line in the cell (line 3 in this example).

Table 19.1 (continued)

Press	To Move to this Position
Ctrl-Home, Home, →	First character of the first line of the last cell in the row in which the cursor is located.
Ctrl-Home, Home, ←	First character of the first line of the first cell in the row in which the cursor is located.
Ctrl-Home, Home, ↑	First character of the first line of the top cell in the column in which the cursor is located.
Ctrl-Home, Home, ↓	First character of the first line of the bottom cell in the column in which the cursor is located.
Ctrl-Home, Home, Home, ↑	First character of the first line in cell A1.
Ctrl-Home, Home, Home, ↓	First character of the first line of the last cell in the table.

* If a cell has two or more lines of text, the cursor must be on the top or bottom line to move vertically between cells. If a cell has text, the cursor must be on the first character of the top line or the last character of the bottom line to move horizontally between cells. If a cell has no text, the cursor moves to the cell in the direction indicated by the arrow.

Reminder:

You can use the Alt key with the enhanced arrow keys on an Enhanced Keyboard to move the cursor between cells.

The Enhanced Keyboard has a second set of arrow keys located between the alphabet keys and the numeric keypad. If you have an Enhanced Keyboard (101 or more keys) and an enhanced ROM BIOS, you can use the Alt key with the enhanced arrow keys to move the cursor among cells. This feature does not work with the arrow keys on the numeric keypad. The enhanced arrow keys that function with the Alt key are listed in table 19.2. In table 19.2 a hyphen between keys means to press both keys simultaneously. A comma between keys means to release one key before pressing the next key.

Caution

The keys listed in table 19.2, and some other Alt-key combinations, may not work as described if you use a keyboard definition originally created using WordPerfect 5, even if the keyboard definition has been edited using WordPerfect 5.1. If the enhanced arrow keys do not function properly on an enhanced keyboard, create a new keyboard definition using WordPerfect 5.1 to correct the problem.

Tip

Use a keyboard definition to reassign cursor-movement keys to the keys convenient for you. If you have an Enhanced Keyboard, you can create a keyboard definition called TABLES; redefine the enhanced arrow keys that work with the Alt key to work without the Alt key. See Chapter 20 for information about creating keyboard definitions.

Table 19.2
Alt-Arrow Keys for Moving in Tables

Press	To Move to this Position
Alt-Enhanced ↑	First character in the cell immediately above the current cell; does not move the cursor out of the table.
Alt-Enhanced ↓	First character in the cell immediately below the current cell; does not move the cursor out of the table.
Alt-Enhanced →	First character on the same line of the next cell in forward sequence. If the cursor is on a line number greater than the number of lines in the cell to which the cursor can move (for example, line 4 moving to a three-line cell), the cursor is placed on the first character of the last line in the cell (line 3 in this example).
Alt-Enhanced ←	First character on the same line of the next cell in reverse sequence. If the cursor is on a line number greater than the number of lines in the cell to which the cursor can move (for example, line 4 moving to a three-line cell), the cursor is placed on the first character of the last line in the cell (line 3 in this example).
Alt-Home, Enhanced ↑	First character in the cell at the top of the current column.
Alt-Home, Enhanced ↓	First character in the cell at the bottom of the current column.
Alt-Home, Enhanced →	First character in the last cell of the current row.
Alt-Home, Enhanced ←	First character in the first cell of the current row.
Alt-Home, Home, Enhanced ↑	First character in cell A1.
Alt-Home, Home, Enhanced ↓	First character in the last cell of the table.

Entering Text in a Table

The beginning of this chapter advised you to consider each cell in a table as a minidocument. The reason is that when you enter or edit text, the four edges of the cell are treated as the edges of a page. You enter, format, and edit text in a cell in the same way as you do the main document. However, editing text in multiple cells using Block differs slightly from editing text in the main document.

Text and data also can be brought into a table using the Import and Retrieve features discussed later in this chapter. WordPerfect's Move and Copy features

Reminder:
You can enter, format, and edit text in a cell in the same way you do the main document.

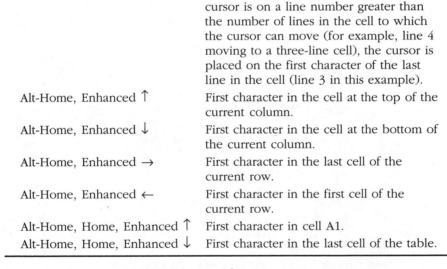

theoretically can shift many pages of text in a single operation. When either of these features is used to shift text into a table, the amount of text that is actually transferred is limited by the cell's maximum size. Remember that a cell can be as small as a single character or as large as a single page.

The instructions in the following sections assume that you have edited the table as directed in the section preceding.

The term *text* as used in the following exercises encompasses all alphabetical characters, ASCII characters, and numbers entered for use by the Math feature. The following chart lists sample directions and meanings used in the exercises in this chapter.

Example	*Meaning*
Enter *text*	Type the characters in italic and press the Enter key.
Type *text*	Type all characters in italic but do *not* press the Enter key.

Follow these steps to retrieve the file TABLE.TST and add text to the table:

1. Press Retrieve (Shift-F10).

    ▭ Access the **F**ile pull-down menu and select **R**etrieve.

    Enter *table.tst*.

2. Move the cursor to cell A1. Enter *Black Acre (Oklahoma County)*. WordPerfect expands row 1 to accommodate the text.

3. Move to cell B1 by pressing Tab. Enter *$50,000.00*.

4. Move to cell C1 by pressing Ctrl-Home, →. Enter *50*.

5. Move to cell E1 by pressing Ctrl-Home, Home, →. Enter *Smith, T.* (include the period after the *T*).

6. Move to cell A2 by pressing →. Enter *White Acre*.

7. Move to cell A3 by pressing ↓. Enter *Red Acre*.

8. Move down through the remaining cells in column A (cells A4 through A9) and enter the following names:

Cell	*What You Type*
A4	Gren Acres (include misspelling)
A5	Blue Acre
A6	Yellow Acre
A7	Brown Acre
A8	Orange or Yellow-Green Acre
A9	Purple Acre

9. Move to cell B9 by pressing →. Enter *$11,500.00*.

10. Move to cell B8 by pressing ↑. Enter *$2,000.00*.

11. Move up through the remaining cells in column B (cells B7 through B2) and enter the following numbers:

Cell	*What You Type*
B7	$15,000.00
B6	$25,000.00
B5	$50,000.00
B4	$60,000.00
B3	$35,000.00
B2	$20,000.00

12. Move through the remaining cells in column C (C2 through C9) and enter the following numbers:

Cell	What You Type
C2	10
C3	28
C4	12
C5	17
C6	22
C7	5.5
C8	5.0
C9	4.3

13. Move to cell E9 by pressing Ctrl-Home, Home, Home, ↓. Enter *Jones, J.* (include the period after the *J*).

14. Move through the remaining cells in column E (E8 through E2) and enter the following names:

Cell	What You Type
E8	Smith, H.
E7	Hermanson
E6	Jones, S.
E5	Smith, H.
E4	Haney
E3	Hermanson
E2	Jones, J.

15. Save the table as TABLE.TST.

Editing Text in a Table

A rule by which most writers live is *good writing is rewriting*. Rewriting involves the editing of text. Text in a table requires editing just as much as text in the main document. With the Table feature, editing text in a table is just as easy as editing text in the main WordPerfect document.

Reminder:
You can edit text in a table in the same way that you edit text in the regular document.

Do the following steps to practice editing text in a table:

1. If it is not on-screen, retrieve TABLE.TST. Move the cursor above the table by pressing PgUp.

   Note: If a table does not fill the entire screen, press one of the following keys to move the cursor above the table (depending on the table's location on-screen and the cursor's location in the table): PgUp, Screen Up (numeric keypad –), or Home-↑. Press one of the following keys to move the cursor *below* the table: PgDn, Screen Down (numeric keypad +), or Home-↓.

2. Press Search (F2) to use the Search feature to find the left parenthesis in cell A1.

   ⌨ Access the **S**earch pull-down menu and select **F**orward.

   Type *(* (the left parenthesis). Press Search (F2) or Esc to begin the search. The cursor moves to cell A1.

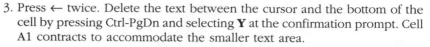

3. Press ← twice. Delete the text between the cursor and the bottom of the cell by pressing Ctrl-PgDn and selecting **Y** at the confirmation prompt. Cell A1 contracts to accommodate the smaller text area.

4. Move the cursor to the letter *G* in the word *Gren* in cell A4. Press Ctrl-End to delete the line. Enter *Green Acre*.

5. Move the cursor below the table. Press Replace (Alt-F2).

   ▭ Access the **S**earch pull-down menu and select **R**eplace.

   Select **N** to have WordPerfect perform the replace operation without confirmation. Press ↑ to search backwards through the text.

   Press Del to remove the default search string. Type *or Yellow-Green Acre* as the text for which to search.

   Press either Search (F2) or Esc. Type *Acre* as the replacement text.

   Press either Search (F2) or Esc to begin the replace operation. Cell A8 automatically contracts as its contents change to *Orange Acre*.

Tip

When using the Search or Replace features, type the search-string characters or codes before using ↑ or ↓ to change the direction of the search. If you use the arrow keys to change the search direction before entering the new search string, you must manually delete the old search string before entering the new search string.

---

6. Save the file as TABLE.TST using Save (F10).

   ▭ Access the **F**ile pull-down menu and select **S**ave.

   The table appears as shown in figure 19.6.

Fig. 19.6.

A table after editing and spell-checking.

Black Acre	$50,000.00	50		Smith, T.
White Acre	$20,000.00	10		Jones, J.
Red Acre	$35,000.00	28		Hermanson
Green Acre	$60,000.00	12		Haney
Blue Acre	$50,000.00	17		Smith, H.
Yellow Acre	$25,000.00	22		Jones, S.
Brown Acre	$15,000.00	5.5		Hermanson
Orange Acre	$2,000.00	5.0		Smith, H.
Purple Acre	$11,500.00	4.3		Jones, J.

C:\WP51\TABLE.TST   Cell E3 Doc 1 Pg 1 Ln 2.83" Pos 7"

Deleting and Creating a Table without Using the Table Editor

You can change the structure and format of a table without using the table editor. On older systems without an Enhanced Keyboard and ROM BIOS, you are limited to deleting and creating the basic table structure. On systems with an Enhanced keyboard and ROM BIOS, you also can use Insert Row (Ctrl-Ins) and Delete Row (Ctrl-Del) to change the table structure outside of the table editor.

Reminder:
You can change the structure or format of the table at any time, whether or not the table contains text.

> **Tip**
> Always save the table as a file on disk before editing the table's structure.

Deleting the Table Structure

To delete an existing table structure from the document, follow these steps:

1. Press Retrieve (Shift-F10) and enter *table.tst* as the file to retrieve.

   📖 Access the **F**ile pull-down menu, select **R**etrieve, and enter *table.tst* as the file to retrieve.

2. Press **Reveal** Codes (Alt-F3 or F11).

   📖 Access the **E**dit pull-down menu and select **R**eveal Codes.

3. Move the cursor to highlight the table-definition code (see fig. 19.7).

4. Press Del to delete the code. The table grid disappears and the text reformats (see fig. 19.8).

```
┌─────────────┬─────────────┬────┬──────┬──────────────┐
│Black Acre   │$50,000.00   │50  │      │Smith, T.     │
├─────────────┼─────────────┼────┼──────┼──────────────┤
│White Acre   │$20,000.00   │10  │      │Jones, J.     │
├─────────────┼─────────────┼────┼──────┼──────────────┤
│Red Acre     │$35,000.00   │20  │      │Hermanson     │
├─────────────┼─────────────┼────┼──────┼──────────────┤
│Green Acre   │$60,000.00   │12  │      │Haney         │
└─────────────┴─────────────┴────┴──────┴──────────────┘
C:\WP51\TABLE.TST                        Doc 1 Pg 1 Ln 1.33" Pos 1"
[       ▲        ▲                              ]
[Paper Sz/Typ:8.5" x 11",Standard][Font:Courier 10][Tab Set:Rel; +0.3",+1"][HRt]

[HRt]
[Tbl Def:I;5,1.3",1.3",1.3",1.3",1.3"]
[Row][Cell]Black Acre[Cell]$50,000.00[Cell]50[Cell][Cell]Smith, T.
[Row][Cell]White Acre[Cell]$20,000.00[Cell]10[Cell][Cell]Jones, J.
[Row][Cell]Red Acre[Cell]$35,000.00[Cell]20[Cell][Cell]Hermanson
[Row][Cell]Green Acre[Cell]$60,000.00[Cell]12[Cell][Cell]Haney
[Row][Cell]Blue Acre[Cell]$50,000.00[Cell]17[Cell][Cell]Smith, H.
[Row][Cell]Yellow[SRt]

Press Reveal Codes to restore screen
```

Fig. 19.7.
Highlighting the table-definition code.

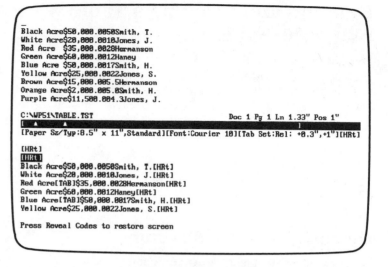

Fig. 19.8.

Text after deleting the table-definition code.

Tip

To delete the table-definition code without using Reveal Codes, move the cursor to the first character or space in cell A1 and press either Backspace or Del. In either case, WordPerfect displays the `Delete [Tbl Def:I]? No (Yes)` prompt. Select **Y** to delete the code.

Note: You occasionally may see phantom **[Row]**, **[Cell]**, or **[Tab Off]** codes after deleting the table-definition code. Moving the cursor through the document causes these codes to vanish.

When the table grid disappears, the table's contents reformat as follows:

- A **[HRt]** code replaces the table-definition code

- A **[TAB]** code is placed between the last character of one cell and the first character of the cell to the right *if* the tab settings in the main document equal or exceed the number of columns that were in the table

- A **[HRt]** follows the last character in the last cell of the row (see fig. 19.8)

Reminder:

You cannot delete individual [Row], [Cell], or [Tbl Off] formatting codes; you can delete the [Hrd Row] code only.

To prevent the accidental destruction of a table while editing, WordPerfect does not permit deletion of individual **[Row]**, **[Cell]**, or **[Tbl Off]** codes. A hard-row (**[Hrd Row]**) code, created by pressing Ctrl-Enter to break a table across two pages, is the only table-formatting code you can delete.

If you do not have an Enhanced Keyboard and ROM BIOS, the only way to alter the table structure outside of the table editor is to delete the beginning table-definition code.

Restoring the Table Structure

When you delete a table-definition code, you cannot re-create the table by using the Undelete feature. If you delete the table-definition code and you have no copy of the table saved on disk (either as a file you created or as a file created by timed backup), you can re-create the table only by one of these methods:

- Blocking the text of the table and using the Columns/Table feature to re-create the table. You can do this only if the contents of the cells are separated by a **[Tab]**, **[TAB]**, or **[HRT]** code. Then you may have to edit the table structure and format.

- Redefining the table structure and retyping the text; alternatively, you can reorganize the data into groups and use either Move or Copy to place the text into the cells.

When you delete the table-definition code, WordPerfect uses the current tab settings and margins when placing a **[TAB]** or **[HRt]** code between cell contents. If you have fewer tab settings in the document than cells in a row, the contents of several cells may run together (see fig. 19.8). Because of this limitation, using Block to re-create the table may be more difficult and take longer than redefining the table structure, reformatting the table, and reentering the text from the keyboard.

Reminder:
If you delete a table-definition code, WordPerfect uses the current tab settings and margins to try to separate cell contents.

To re-create the table structure of the TABLE.TST file, which was deleted in the preceding section, follow these steps:

1. Move the cursor to the first character you want in cell A1. Press Format (Shift-F8) and select **L**ine (**1**).

   ⌨ Access the **L**ayout pull-down menu and select **L**ine.

2. Select **T**ab Set (**8**); press Home, →; and press Ctrl-End.

3. Select **T**ype (**T**). WordPerfect displays the following menu:

   Tab Type: 1 Absolute; **2 R**elative to Margin: **0**

4. Select **A**bsolute (**1**). Enter *2.3,1.3* to specify the new tab settings. WordPerfect automatically enters tab settings every 1.3 inches, beginning at location 2.3"—the original location of column B. Press Exit (F7) to return to the main editing screen.

5. Press Home, Tab to insert hard tab (**[TAB]**) codes between the fields as shown in figure 19.9.

6. Use the keyboard (Alt-F4 or F12) or the mouse to highlight all the text to be included in the new table. (see fig. 19.10).

7. Press Columns/Table (Alt-F7). The following menu appears:

   1 Columns; **2 T**ables; **3 M**ath: **0**

8. Select **T**ables (**2**). The following menu appears:

   Table: 1 Create; **2 E**dit: **0**

9. Select **C**reate (**1**). The following menu appears:

   Create Table from: 1 Tabular Column; **2 P**arallel Column: **0**

10. Select **T**abular Column (**1**). WordPerfect creates a table structure similar to that shown in figure 19.11.

    ***Note:* P**arallel Columns (**2**) operates only if the highlighted block of text was formatted as parallel columns.

11. Delete the Absolute-Tab code (see fig. 19.9) created in step 4.

Fig. 19.9.

Table text with formatting codes.

```
Black Acre    $50,000.00    50              Smith, T.
White Acre    $20,000.00    10              Jones, J.
Red Acre      $35,000.00    28              Hermanson
Green Acre    $60,000.00    12              Haney
Blue Acre     $50,000.00    17              Smith, H.
Yellow Acre   $25,000.00    22              Jones, S.
Brown Acre    $15,000.00    5.5             Hermanson
Orange Acre   $2,000.00     5.0             Smith, H.
C:\WP51\TABLE.TST                           Doc 1 Pg 1 Ln 1.5" Pos 1"
```
```
[Paper Sz/Typ:8.5" x 11",Standard][Font:Courier 10][Tab Set:Rel: +0.3",+1"][HRt]

[HRt]
[Tab Set:Abs: 2.3", every 1.3"][HRt]
[B]lack Acre[TAB]$50,000.00[TAB]50[TAB][TAB]Smith, T.[HRt]
White Acre[TAB]$20,000.00[TAB]10[TAB][TAB]Jones, J.[HRt]
Red Acre[TAB]$35,000.00[TAB]28[TAB][TAB]Hermanson[HRt]
Green Acre[TAB]$60,000.00[TAB]12[TAB][TAB]Haney[HRt]
Blue Acre[TAB]$50,000.00[TAB]17[TAB][TAB]Smith, H.[HRt]
Yellow Acre[TAB]$25,000.00[TAB]22[TAB][TAB]Jones, S.[HRt]

Press Reveal Codes to restore screen
```

Fig. 19.10.

Text blocked for table recreation.

```
Black Acre    $50,000.00    50              Smith, T.
White Acre    $20,000.00    10              Jones, J.
Red Acre      $35,000.00    28              Hermanson
Green Acre    $60,000.00    12              Haney
Blue Acre     $50,000.00    17              Smith, H.
Yellow Acre   $25,000.00    22              Jones, S.
Brown Acre    $15,000.00    5.5             Hermanson
Orange Acre   $2,000.00     5.0             Smith, H.
Purple Acre   $11,500.00    4.3             Jones, J.

Block on                                    Doc 1 Pg 1 Ln 2.83" Pos 7.1"
```
```
Yellow Acre[TAB]$25,000.00[TAB]22[TAB][TAB]Jones, S.[HRt]
Brown Acre[TAB]$15,000.00[TAB]5.5[TAB][TAB]Hermanson[HRt]
Orange Acre[TAB]$2,000.00[TAB]5.0[TAB][TAB]Smith, H.[HRt]
Purple Acre[TAB]$11,500.00[TAB]4.3[TAB][TAB]Jones, J.[HRt]
```

Fig. 19.11.

A re-created table structure.

Black Acre	$50,000.00	50		Smith, T.
White Acre	$20,000.00	10		Jones, J.
Red Acre	$35,000.00	28		Hermanson
Green Acre	$60,000.00	12		Haney
Blue Acre	$50,000.00	17		Smith, H.
Yellow Acre	$25,000.00	22		Jones, S.
Brown Acre	$15,000.00	5.5		Hermanson
Orange Acre	$2,000.00	5.0		Smith, H.

```
Table Edit:    Press Exit when done        Cell A1 Doc 1 Pg 1 Ln 1.64" Pos 1.12"

Ctrl-Arrows Column Widths; Ins Insert; Del Delete; Move Move/Copy;
1 Size; 2 Format; 3 Lines; 4 Header; 5 Math; 6 Options; 7 Join; 8 Split; 0
```

In this exercise, the table was re-created in the identical format of the original table; re-creation of a more complex table is not as simple. The re-creation process frequently requires additional editing and reformatting to make the new table a duplicate of the original table. You learn how to edit the structure later in this chapter. For the purposes of this exercise, clear the screen.

The second way to re-create a table involves defining a new table structure using the same steps required to create the original table. After the table structure is created, insert the text by retyping it or blocking and moving it into the cells.

Reminder:

Delete the entire table—definition codes as well as text—by highlighting the table and pressing Del.

Deleting an Entire Table

Earlier in this chapter you learned how to delete the table-definition code to remove the table structure from the document. When you delete the table-definition code, the text of the table still remains. You can delete the entire table—table-definition code as well as text—by following these instructions:

1. Press Retrieve (Shift-F10) and enter *table.tst* as the file name to retrieve.

    ▭ Access the **F**ile pull-down menu, select **R**etrieve, and enter *table.tst*.

2. Use the keyboard (Alt-F4 or F12) or the mouse to highlight the entire table. WordPerfect highlights only the text; the graphical grid lines are not ASCII characters and are not highlighted.

3. Press Del or Backspace and select **Y** at the prompt to confirm the deletion.

    The entire table, including text, is deleted from the file. If you want, you can undelete a table you accidentally deleted. To undelete a table, follow the remaining steps.

4. Press Undelete (F1).

    ▭ Access the **E**dit pull-down menu and select **U**ndelete.

5. Select **R**estore (**1**) from the menu displayed at the bottom left of the screen. WordPerfect places the original table back into the document at the cursor location.

6. Clear the screen by pressing Exit (F7).

    ▭ Access the **F**ile pull-down menu, select E**x**it, and press N twice.

Deleting Information within a Table

Table 19.3 list the keys that delete text and rows in a table. In the table, a hyphen between keys means to press and hold down the first key and press the second key.

To practice deleting various units of text from the TABLE.TST file, follow these instructions:

1. Press Retrieve (Shift-F10) and enter *table.tst*.

    ▭ Access the **F**ile pull-down menu, select **R**etrieve, and enter *table.tst*.

2. Move the cursor to the first character in cell A2.

3. Use the keyboard (Alt-F4 or F12) or the mouse to block the table from cell A2 to the last character in cell E2. WordPerfect highlights only the text; the graphical grid lines are not highlighted.

Table 19.3
Keys to Delete Text from a Table

Press	To Delete these Characters
Del	The character at the cursor's location. If you hold down this key, all text to the right of the cursor within the cell is deleted; eventually, all text from the cursor to the end of the table is deleted. If you highlight a block of text and press Del, the block is deleted.
Ctrl-Del	The text and the row in which the cursor is located. Ctrl-Del works only if you have an Enhanced Keyboard (a keyboard with 101 or more keys) and a ROM BIOS which supports the extra keys. You can use the keyboard-definition feature described in Chapter 20 to assign this function to a key on a standard keyboard. You cannot restore the row by using Undelete (F1).
Backspace	The character to the left of the cursor. If you hold down this key, all text to the left of the cursor within the cell is deleted; eventually, all text from the cursor to the beginning of the table is deleted. If you highlight a block of text and press Backspace, the block is deleted.
Ctrl-F4	A sentence or paragraph within a cell, or all text between the cursor and the last cell on the current page, depending on the submenu you select.
Ctrl-End	All text from the cursor to the end of the line.
Ctrl-PgDn	All text from the cursor to the end of the cell.

Reminder:

You can use Ctrl-Del to delete the current row of a table only if you have an Enhanced Keyboard; you cannot restore the deleted row with Undelete.

4. Press Del or Backspace. Select **Y** at the prompt to confirm the deletion. The information in cells A2 through E2 is deleted and the row contracts to a height of one character (see fig. 19.12).

Fig. 19.12.

The table after deleting a row.

Black Acre	$50,000.00	50		Smith, T.
Red Acre	$35,000.00	28		Hermanson
Green Acre	$60,000.00	12		Haney
Blue Acre	$50,000.00	17		Smith, H.
Yellow Acre	$25,000.00	22		Jones, S.
Brown Acre	$15,000.00	5.5		Hermanson
Orange Acre	$2,000.00	5.0		Smith, H.
Purple Acre	$11,500.00	4.3		Jones, J.

C:\WP51\TABLE.TST   Cell A3 Doc 2 Pg 1 Ln 2.03" Pos 1.12"

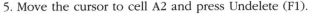

Note: The Delete feature only removes information *within cells.* To delete an entire row or column of cells, you use the table editor, explained in the next section. If you have an Enhanced Keyboard and enhanced ROM BIOS, you can use Ctrl-Del to delete a row without using the table editor.

5. Move the cursor to cell A2 and press Undelete (F1).

   ⌨ Access the **E**dit pull-down menu and select **U**ndelete.

6. Select **R**estore (**1**) from the option menu displayed at the bottom of the screen. WordPerfect does not preserve the deleted material in separate cell structures; the contents of cells A2 through E2 are placed into cell A2 (see fig. 19.13).

Reminder:

When you delete multiple cells and then undelete them, all the cell contents are placed in the current cell.

Black Acre	$50,000.00	50		Smith, T.
White Acre$20,00 0.0010Jone s, J._				
Red Acre	$35,000.00	28		Hermanson
Green Acre	$60,000.00	12		Haney
Blue Acre	$50,000.00	17		Smith, H.
Yellow Acre	$25,000.00	22		Jones, S.
Brown Acre	$15,000.00	5.5		Hermanson
Orange Acre	$2,000.00	5.0		Smith, H.
Purple Acre	$11,500.00	4.3		Jones, J.

C:\WP51\TABLE.TST   Cell A2 Doc 1 Pg 1 Ln 2.25" Pos 1.62"

Fig. 19.13.
A table with undeleted text all in cell A2.

You can use the following key combinations with a table in the same way you use them with a document: Del, Backspace, Ctrl-Backspace (delete a word), Home-Backspace (delete word to the left), Ctrl-End (delete to end of line), and Ctrl-PgDn (delete to end of cell).

Caution

Unlike most WordPerfect editing functions in a table, the Del and Backspace keys perform destructive deletions that can span the entire table if pressed and held. Del removes text from the cursor to the end of the table; Backspace moves the cursor to the left and deletes all text from the cursor to the beginning of the table. Only the text deleted from the cell in which the cursor is located when you release the key can be restored using Undelete. Text removed across cells with Del or Backspace **cannot** be restored using Undelete.

See Chapter 3 for more information about Delete and Undelete.

Editing a Table with the Table Editor

You can change the structure or format of a cell, row, column, or the entire table at any time. If you preplanned the table definition as suggested in "Planning a Table Definition" earlier in this chapter, you can define the table's format before you place any text in the table. You also can edit the table's structure after text has been added. Regardless of whether the table contains text, the steps for editing the structure and format of the table are the same.

Caution

Never edit a table's structure without first saving the table as a file on your disk.

The table editor lets you define or modify the structure or format of a table. Remember that the table *structure* is the physical layout of the rows and columns and the size and type of the graphical grid lines. The table *format* is the appearance of the text in the rows, columns, and cells. You can use the table editor any time you edit a document containing a table.

Reminder:
You access the table editor whenever you finish creating a table structure, or when you press Columns/Table.

WordPerfect automatically starts the table editor in these situations:

- You finish creating a new table's basic structure
- You press Columns/Table (Alt-F7) when the cursor is located in a cell

If a document contains one or more tables and the cursor is *not* located within a table, you can invoke the table editor by pressing Columns/Table (Alt-F7), selecting **T**ables (**2**), and selecting **E**dit (**2**). If you use a mouse, access the **L**ayout pull-down menu, select **T**able, and select **E**dit.

If a document contains only one table, WordPerfect automatically moves the cursor to cell A1 in that table when the table editor starts. If a document contains two or more tables, WordPerfect searches for a table from the cursor's location towards the top of the document. If no table is found WordPerfect searches down the document from the cursor's location.

WordPerfect moves the cursor to cell A1 in the first table it finds. If you start the table editor from within a table, WordPerfect assumes that you want to edit the cell in which the cursor is located and does not move it.

Tip

In a long document with a single table, invoke the table editor to locate the table. In a document containing multiple tables, start the table editor to locate the first table *above* the cursor.

With two exceptions, you can alter the table structure only by using the table editor. These exceptions are as follows:

- Deleting the table-definition code as explained in "Deleting the Table Structure" earlier in this chapter

- Using an Enhanced Keyboard to add or remove rows with Ctrl-Ins (insert row) and Ctrl-Del (delete row) (see table 19.4)

The margins and tab settings used by a table are the same as those used by the section of the document in which the table is created. The remainder of the table's structure and format are defined by defaults you can change. WordPerfect assigns priorities to formatting codes:

- Codes inserted with the function keys supersede the table's default format as well as formatting codes inserted with the table editor
- Codes inserted for cells with the table editor supersede the table's default format as well as formatting codes for columns inserted with the table editor
- The table's default formatting codes are in effect unless overridden by formatting codes inserted by either the function keys or table editor

WordPerfect makes one exception to these priorities. When a cell, row, or column is inserted or split within a table, the additional cells, rows, or columns do not assume formatting characteristics inserted with the function keys.

You can use two methods to change a table's format:

- Use the function keys to insert size, attribute, font, and tab codes into a cell or blocked group of cells while entering or editing text
- Use the table editor (which also can change the table's structure)

Defining and Changing Cell, Column, Row, and Table Formats

The table editor's **F**ormat (**2**) option lets you define or change the formatting characteristics of a single cell or column. If you use Block to highlight a section of the table, you can define or change the formatting characteristics of the cells in the area highlighted. The only way to change the formatting characteristics of a row in a single formatting action is to highlight the row before choosing the format option.

Reminder:
To change the format of a row, highlight the row before choosing a format option.

Table 19.4 lists each option accessible from the table-editor menu. Also listed are features not shown on the menu.

Note: The options for font size, font appearance, justification, and math operators work the same within a table as they do in the main WordPerfect document. Refer to Chapter 5 for information on font sizes and appearances and justification. Refer to Chapter 18 for information on math operators.

In the table, a hyphen between keys means to press both keys simultaneously. A comma between keys means to release one key before pressing the next. Some options require that cells be highlighted before you can use the option.

Tip
If a key sequence requires you to press Ctrl more than once, you can hold the Ctrl key while pressing the other key more than once. For example, instead of pressing Ctrl-Home, Ctrl-Home, hold Ctrl and press Home twice.

Table 19.4
Table-Editor Menu Options and Unlisted Features

Option	Function Performed
Ctrl-→	Expands the column containing the cursor one character width to the right each time the key combination is pressed. If you hold these keys, the column continues to expand until it occupies the maximum space available across the page. Depending on the table structure, the cells within the column may expand downward.
Ctrl-←	Contracts the column containing the cursor one character width to the left each time the key combination is pressed. If you hold these keys, the column continues to contract until it occupies the width of a single character. Depending on the table structure, the cells within the column may contract upward.
Ins	Inserts one or more columns or rows. If you use Block to highlight more than one column or row before invoking this feature, WordPerfect adds the same number of columns or rows as are highlighted.
Ctrl-Ins	Automatically inserts one row above the cursor's location. This feature is not listed on the table-editor menu and is available only on the Enhanced Keyboard if you have enhanced ROM BIOS.
Del	Deletes one or more columns or rows.
Ctrl-Home, <cell name>	Moves the cursor to the specified cell location. This feature is not listed on the table-editor menu.
Ctrl-Home, Ctrl-Home	Moves the cursor to the position it occupied before pressing the following keys or features: Ctrl-Home, <cell name>, PgUp, PgDn, numeric keypad –, or numeric keypad +.
Ctrl-F4	Moves, copies, deletes, or retrieves a block, cell, column, or row. ***Note:*** Text copied or moved with the table editor can be accessed only while using the table editor.
Size (**1**)	Adds or deletes one or more columns or rows to a table. The structure of the columns or rows added is that of the last column at the right edge of the table or that of the bottom row. ***Caution:*** Columns or rows deleted from the end of the table with this option cannot be restored using the Undelete feature.

Table 19.4 (continued)

Option	Function Performed
Format (**2**), Cell (**2**)	Displays a submenu that lets you select additional submenus in order to format the cell: **T**ype (**1**): **N**umeric (**1**); **T**ext (**2**) **A**ttribute (**2**), **S**ize (**1**): Su**p**rscpt (**1**); Su**b**scpt (**2**); **F**ine (**3**); **S**mall (**4**); **L**arge (**5**); **V**ry Large (**6**); **E**xt Large (**7**) **A**ttribute (**2**), **A**ppearance (**2**): **B**old (**1**); **U**ndln (**2**); **D**bl Under (**3**); **I**talc (**4**); **O**utln (**5**); Sh**a**dw (**6**); Sm **C**ap (**7**); **R**edln (**8**); S**t**kout (**9**) **A**ttribute (**2**), **N**ormal (**3**) **A**ttribute (**2**), **R**eset (**4**) **J**ustification (**3**): **L**eft (**1**); **C**enter (**2**); **R**ight (**3**); **F**ull (**4**); **D**ecimal Align (**5**); Re**s**et (**6**) **V**ertical Alignment (**4**): **T**op (**1**); **B**ottom (**2**); **C**enter (**3**) **L**ock (**5**): **O**n (**1**); Off (**2**)
Format (**2**), Co**l**umn (**3**)	Displays a submenu that lets you select additional submenus in order to format the column: **W**idth (**1**) **A**ttribute (**2**), **S**ize (**1**): Su**p**rscpt (**1**); Su**b**scpt (**2**); **F**ine (**3**); **S**mall (**4**); **L**arge (**5**); **V**ry Large (**6**); **E**xt Large (**7**) **A**ttribute (**2**), **A**ppearance (**2**): **B**old (**1**); **U**ndln (**2**); **D**bl Under (**3**); **I**talc (**4**); **O**utln (**5**); Sh**a**dw (**6**); Sm **C**ap (**7**); **R**edln (**8**); S**t**kout (**9**) **A**ttribute (**2**), **N**ormal (**3**) **A**ttribute (**2**), **R**eset (**4**) **J**ustification (**3**): **L**eft (**1**); **C**enter (**2**); **R**ight (**3**); **F**ull (**4**); **D**ecimal Align (**5**); Re**s**et (**6**) # **D**igits (**4**): Number of decimal places to the right of the decimal point (default is 2)
Format (**2**), **R**ow Height (**3**)	Displays a submenu that lets you designate the row height as Single Line **F**ixed (**1**); Single Line Au**t**o (**2**); Multi-Line Fi**x**ed (**3**); or Multi-Line **A**uto (**4**).
Lines (**3**)	Displays a submenu that lets you designate the grid-line styles for the cell's **L**eft (**1**); **R**ight (**2**); **T**op (**3**); or **B**ottom (**4**) lines. You also can set the table's **I**nside (**1**); **O**utside (**2**); or **A**ll (**3**) lines. For both the table's and the cell's lines, you can select the following types of lines:

5.1

Table 19.4 (continued)

Option	Function Performed
Lines (**3**) (continued)	**N**one (**1**); **S**ingle (**2**); **D**ouble (**3**); **D**ashed (**4**); **D**otted (**5**); **T**hick (**6**); or **E**xtra Thick (**7**). The original Lines menu also lets you designate the cell's **S**hade (**8**) as **O**n (**1**) or **Of**f (**2**).
Header (**4**)	Displays a submenu that lets you designate the number of rows in the header.
Math (**5**)	Displays a submenu that lets you designate the math operation to be performed in the cell: **C**alculate (**1**); **F**ormula (**2**); **C**opy Formula (**3**); – (**4**); = (**5**); * (**6**).
Options (**6**)	Displays a submenu that lets you designate the following: **S**pacing Between Text and Lines (**1**): **L**eft (**1**); **R**ight (**2**); **T**op (**3**); **B**ottom (**4**) **D**isplay for Negative Results (**2**): (minus sign or parentheses) **P**osition of Table (**3**): **L**eft (**1**); **R**ight (**2**); **C**enter (**3**); **F**ull (**4**); **S**et Position (**5**) **G**ray shading (% of black) (**4**)
Join (**7**)	Displays the following submenu that lets you combine two or more cells into a single cell, provided that the cells to be merged are highlighted with Block: Join Cells? No (Yes)
Split (**8**)	Displays the following submenu that lets you create new columns or rows in the space occupied by a column or row. If you use Block to highlight more than one column or row before invoking this feature, the columns or rows are all split. **Table Size: 1 R**ows; **2 C**olumns: **0**
Cancel (F1)	Restores the last block, column, or row deleted in the table editor. This feature is not listed on the table-editor menu.
Ctrl-Enter	Splits the table over a page break at the row on which the cursor is located. Inserts a hard-row code (**[Hrd Row]**) that cannot be deleted directly with the table editor. This feature is not listed on the table-editor menu.
Shift-F10	Retrieves the last text deleted from the table with Del. Although this feature works with other table-editor options, the results are unpredictable. This feature is not listed on the table-editor menu.

Using the Table Editor To Delete and Undelete Columns or Rows

To delete a column or a row from the TABLE.TST file and then undelete the row using the table editor, follow these steps:

1. Retrieve TABLE.TST. Move the cursor to the top of the document, *above* the table.

2. Press Columns/Table (Alt-F7), select **T**ables (**2**), and select **E**dit (**2**).

   ⌨ Access the **L**ayout pull-down menu, select **T**able, and select **E**dit.

   WordPerfect automatically moves the cursor to cell A1 and displays the table-editor menu shown in figure 19.14.

Black Acre	$50,000.00	50		Smith, T.
White Acre	$20,000.00	10		Jones, J.
Red Acre	$35,000.00	20		Hermanson
Green Acre	$60,000.00	12		Haney
Blue Acre	$50,000.00	17		Smith, H.
Yellow Acre	$25,000.00	22		Jones, S.
Brown Acre	$15,000.00	5.5		Hermanson
Orange Acre	$2,000.00	5.0		Smith, H.

Table Edit: Press Exit when done   Cell A1 Doc 1 Pg 1 Ln 1.47" Pos 1.12"

Ctrl-Arrows Column Widths; Ins Insert; Del Delete; Move Move/Copy;
1 Size; 2 Format; 3 Lines; 4 Header; 5 Math; 6 Options; 7 Join; 8 Split: 0

Fig. 19.14.
TABLE.TST with the table-editor menu.

3. Press GoTo (Ctrl-Home), type *D1*, and press Enter.

4. Press Del. WordPerfect displays this menu:

   Delete: 1 Rows; **2 C**olumns: **0**

5. Select **C**olumns (**2**). WordPerfect displays this prompt:

   Number of Columns: 1

   Press Enter to accept the default value of 1. Column D, including cells D1 through D9, is deleted (see fig. 19.15). The former column E is renamed column D.

6. Save the table as TABLE.TST.

Reminder:
When you delete rows or columns, WordPerfect renumbers the remaining rows and columns.

To delete a row, use the preceding steps and substitute **R**ow (**1**) for **C**olumn (**2**) in step 5.

To restore a deleted column or row from within the table editor, press Cancel (F1). WordPerfect displays a prompt asking whether you want to restore the column or row deleted. Select **Y**. The last deleted column or row is restored with its format and text intact.

Fig. 19.15.
TABLE.TST with column D deleted.

Black Acre	$50,000.00	50	Smith, T.
White Acre	$20,000.00	10	Jones, J.
Red Acre	$35,000.00	28	Hermanson
Green Acre	$60,000.00	12	Haney
Blue Acre	$50,000.00	17	Smith, H.
Yellow Acre	$25,000.00	22	Jones, S.
Brown Acre	$15,000.00	5.5	Hermanson
Orange Acre	$2,000.00	5.0	Smith, H.

```
Table Edit:  Press Exit when done        Cell D1 Doc 1 Pg 1 Ln 1.47" Pos 5"

Ctrl-Arrows Column Widths; Ins Insert; Del Delete; Move Move/Copy;
1 Size; 2 Format; 3 Lines; 4 Header; 5 Math; 6 Options; 7 Join; 8 Split; 0
```

Note: Move/Copy (Ctrl-F4) offers alternative deletion options from within the table editor. When you activate Move/Copy (Ctrl-F4), the submenu that appears includes options for deleting text within a cell or a group of cells (you can select the block, row, or column option). When you use the table editor, pressing Move/Copy (Ctrl-F4) is the only way you can alter the textual content of an individual cell without affecting the text in the rest of the row or column.

Inserting and Joining Cells, Columns, and Rows

You can use the table editor to insert cells, columns, and rows. In addition, you can join, or combine, cells into a larger cell. to experiment with these options, follow these steps:

1. Press Columns/Table (Alt-F7) and move the cursor to cell A1.

2. Press Ins. WordPerfect displays this menu:

    Insert: 1 Rows; **2 C**olumns: **0**

3. Select **R**ow (**1**). WordPerfect displays this prompt:

    Number of Rows: 1

    Press Enter to accept the default value of one row. WordPerfect adds a row of cells at the top of the table, above the cursor (see fig. 19.16). The new row is named A1-D1; the rows beneath it are renumbered by one.

Tip

If you have an Enhanced Keyboard and enhanced ROM BIOS, you can use Insert Row (Ctrl-Ins) to insert a single row above the cursor, regardless of whether you are using the table editor.

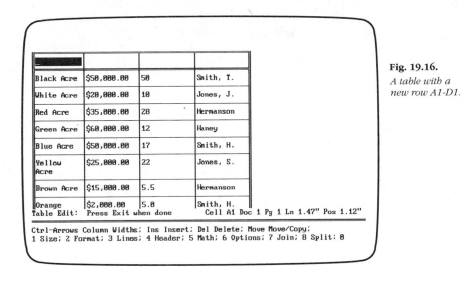

Fig. 19.16.

A table with a new row A1-D1.

4. Use Block to highlight cells A1 through D1. Select **J**oin (**7**) from the table-editor menu. WordPerfect displays the `Join cells? No (Yes)` prompt.

5. Select **Y**. Row A1-D1 becomes a single cell named A1 (see fig. 19.17).

Fig. 19.17.

Joined cells converting row A1-D1 into row A1.

Formatting Cells

You can format cells in a table in several different ways. You can affect the display of a cell, a column, or the height of a row; you can change the font-size and appearance attributes of the text in the cells (make it bold or underlined, for example); and you can select the justification of the text in the cell.

You access the formatting features of the table editor by selecting **F**ormat (**2**) from the table-editor menu. When you make this selection, WordPerfect displays the two-line menu shown at the bottom of figure 19.17. The top line shows format information for the cell and column in which the cursor is located:

```
Cell: Top;Left;Normal              Col:5.2";Left;Normal
```

Reading from the left, the information for the cell is its vertical alignment (`Top`), justification type (`Left`), and print/font attributes (`Normal`). The information for the column is its width (`5.2"`), justification type (`Left`), and print/font attributes (`Normal`).

Note: Except for the cell's width, the cell and column information shown in figure 19,17 are the default values for all tables created using Table (Alt-F7). Tables created with the Retrieve and Import features use the defaults of the original spreadsheets whenever possible.

The second line of the Format menu lists the format options:

> **Format: 1 C**ell; **2 C**olumn; **3 R**ow Height: **0**

Specifying Row Height

If you select **R**ow Height (**3**) from the Format menu, WordPerfect displays this menu:

> **Row Height—Single line: 1 F**ixed; **2 A**uto; **Multi-line: 3 F**ixed; **4 A**uto: **3**

If you select Single-Line: **F**ixed (**1**), WordPerfect displays the `Enter fixed height for row: 0.307"` prompt. If you enter any value for the row height, WordPerfect disables the automatic cell-expansion feature. As long as the cell is formatted with this option, you cannot enter more text than fits on a single line. When you enter a new row-height value such as 0.75", the cell appears to remain unchanged on-screen, however it prints as a 0.75-inch-high cell.

If you select Single-Line: **A**uto (**2**), WordPerfect returns you to the table-editor menu and disables the automatic cell-expansion feature. As long as the cell is formatted with this option, you cannot enter more text than fits on a single line. Even though the cell appears to remain unchanged on-screen, it automatically adjusts the vertical height to accommodate the font size used in the cell.

If you select Multi-Line: **Fi**xed (**3**), WordPerfect displays the `Enter fixed height for row: 0.307"` prompt. Regardless of the value you enter for row height (for example, 0.75"), WordPerfect does *not* disable the automatic cell-expansion feature. As long as the cell is formatted with this option, it continues to expand as you enter text. However, when you print the table, only the text that fits into the cell's designated height prints with the document.

The Multi-Line: **A**uto (**4**) option is the default setting. If you select this option, WordPerfect returns you to the table-editor menu. The cell automatically expands as you enter text, and all text you enter in the cell prints with the document.

Using the TABLE.TST example being developed by this chapter, do the following steps:

1. Select Single Line: **F**ixed (**1**). For the row height, type 3/4 and press Enter. WordPerfect translates this value to a decimal 0.75.

2. Save the table as TABLE.TST.

Specifying Cell Characteristics

This section applies some formats to the TABLE.TST example. Follow these steps to continue developing the example:

1. Retrieve TABLE.TST. Move the cursor to cell A1. Activate the table editor by pressing Columns/Table (Alt-F7).

2. Select **F**ormat (**2**). Select **C**ell (**1**), **A**ttributes (**2**), **A**ppearance (**2**), and then select **B**old (**1**). The Pos indicator at the lower right corner of the screen changes to the bold attribute.

3. Select **F**ormat (**2**) again. Then select **C**ell (**1**), **J**ustify (**2**), and **C**enter (**2**). The blinking cursor moves to the middle of the cell.

4. Select **F**ormat (**2**) yet again. Then select **C**ell (**1**) and **V**ertical Alignment (**4**). WordPerfect displays the following menu:

    Vertical Alignment: 1 Top; **2 B**ottom; **3 C**enter: **1**

5. Select **C**enter (**3**) so that the single line will print in the vertical middle of the cell.

Creating a Table Header

Table headers spruce up your table and let the reader know what information can be found in the table. One or more consecutive rows at the top of the table can be designated as the header. If the table extends beyond one page when you print, the header rows print as the top rows on the second and subsequent pages of the table.

Reminder:
If you specify a header for a table, the header prints at the top of all subsequent pages onto which the table may extend.

To create a table header for TABLE.TST, follow these instructions:

1. Retrieve TABLE.TST. Move to cell A1. Activate the table editor by pressing Columns/Table (Alt-F7).

2. Select **H**eader (**4**) from the table-editor menu. WordPerfect displays the Number of header rows: 0 prompt. Type the number of rows you want for the header (the header can be as long as the page). For this example, enter *1*.

3. Press Exit (F7) to leave the table-editor menu. Now type the text of the header: *1989 SALES FIGURES*. Press Enter. The text is bolded and centered in the cell (see fig. 19.18).

1989 SALES FIGURES _			
Black Acre	$50,000.00	50	Smith, T.
White Acre	$20,000.00	10	Jones, J.
Red Acre	$35,000.00	20	Hermanson

Fig. 19.18.
A table with a header.

You can use View Document to see how the document will look when printed (see fig. 19.19). The header row (cell A1) is printed in a bold font with the text evenly spaced between the top, bottom, left, and right margins.

Fig. 19.19.

Using View Document to display a table and header.

Formatting a Block of Cells with the Table Editor

Reminder:

You can highlight a block of text and then apply formatting codes to that block.

You can use the Block feature to highlight a specific group of cells and then apply formatting codes to the cells. To practice some of the techniques you use when working with blocks of text in a table, add column heads to the TABLE.TST file as described in the following steps:

1. Retrieve TABLE.TST and activate the table editor by pressing Columns/ Table (Alt-F7).

2. Move the cursor to cell A2. Press Ins to insert a new row above the second row. WordPerfect displays this menu:

    Insert: 1 Rows; **2 C**olumns: **0**

3. Select **R**ows (**1**). The Number of Rows: 1 prompt appears.

4. Press Enter to accept the default value of 1. WordPerfect inserts a new row A2-D2 at the cursor's location, moving the remainder of the table downward. (If you select **C**olumns, the specified number of columns is inserted to the right of the cursor.)

    Note: If you have an Enhanced Keyboard and enhanced ROM BIOS, you can press Insert Row (Ctrl-Ins) to insert a row above the cursor's location, regardless of whether you are in the table editor.

Tip

If you use Block to highlight one or more rows or columns and then press Ins, WordPerfect inserts the same number of rows above the cursor or the same number of columns to the left of the cursor as were highlighted.

5. You can define or alter the formatting characteristics of a group of cells in one operation. First highlight the group of cells, and then give the formatting commands. For this example, highlight row A2-D2. Select **F**ormat (**2**) from the table-editor menu, then select **C**ell (**1**), choose **A**ttributes (**2**), select **A**ppearance (**2**), and choose **B**old (**1**). The empty cells have been formatted for bold text; any text you enter is made bold automatically.

6. Continue applying formatting codes to the empty cells. Press Block, GoTo, GoTo. Select **F**ormat (**2**) from the table-editor menu, select **C**ell (**1**), choose **J**ustify (**2**), and select **C**enter (**2**).

7. Press Block, GoTo, GoTo. Select **F**ormat (**2**) from the table-editor menu, select **C**ell (**1**), select **V**ertical Alignment (**4**), and choose **C**enter (**3**). These actions align the text you type in the middle of the cells.

8. Type text in the formatted cells. Type the indicated text in the specified cells:

Cell	What You Type
A2	Parcel
B2	Sales Price
C2	No. of Acres
D2	Seller

Row A2-D2 should look like the one in figure 19.20.

1989 SALES FIGURES			
Parcel	Sales Price	No. of Acres	Seller_
Black Acre	$50,000.00	50	Smith, T.
White Acre	$20,000.00	10	Jones, J.

Fig. 19.20.
A table with column labels.

Note: If you can apply a formatting command to a single cell, you can apply it to a block of cells that you have highlighted.

Creating Columns or Rows with Split

The Split option on the table-editor menu lets you add one or more columns or rows to a table in a single operation. You can use S**p**lit (**8**) to insert rows *below* or columns to the *right* of the cursor's location. (Pressing Ins inserts rows above the cursor and columns to the left of the cursor.) With the TABLE.TST file on-screen (see fig. 19.20), and the table editor activated, perform the following steps to familiarize yourself with the Split option:

1. Move the cursor to cell C2. Use Block to highlight column C2-C11.

2. Select S**p**lit (**8**) from the table-editor menu. WordPerfect displays this menu:

   Split: 1 Rows; **2 C**olumns: **0**

Reminder:
Use Split instead of Ins if you want to insert rows below or columns to the right of the cursor.

3. Select **C**olumns (**2**). WordPerfect displays the `Number of Columns: 1` prompt.

For this example, enter *2*. WordPerfect adds a new column D2-D11 to the *right* of column C2-C11 (see fig. 19.21). The former column D2-D11 is moved to the right and becomes column E2-E11.

Fig. 19.21.

Inserting a column with Split.

Black Acre	$50,000.00	50		Smith, T.
White Acre	$20,000.00	10		Jones, J.
Red Acre	$35,000.00	20		Hermanson
Green Acre	$60,000.00	12		Haney
Blue Acre	$50,000.00	17		Smith, H.
Yellow Acre	$25,000.00	22		Jones, S.
Brown Acre	$15,000.00	5.5		Hermanson
Orange Acre	$2,000.00	5.0		Smith, H.
Purple Acre	$11,500.00	4.3	_	Jones, J.

C:\WP51\TABLE.TST   Cell D11 Doc 1 Pg 1 Ln 5.6" Pos 4.35"

Note: WordPerfect uses the column structure and format characteristics of the original column as a pattern for the new column or columns it creates with Split. Because of the limitations imposed by the document's side margins, you may have to alter the height and width of the existing and new columns to fit the available space. You can edit the table structure, format, or text (or a combination of these items) to fit the columns within space limitations.

4. Turn on Block and press GoTo, GoTo to rehighlight column C2-C11. Press → to include column D2-D11 in the highlighted area.

5. Select **F**ormat (**2**) from the table-editor menu, choose **C**olumn (**2**), and select **W**idth (**1**). WordPerfect displays the `Column width: 0.65"` prompt.

6. Type *1.3* and press Enter to expand the cells in columns C and D to 1.3 inches.

7. Exit the table editor by pressing Exit (F7). Move the cursor to cell D2 and type *Price per Acre*. This action places a label in the new column.

Aligning Letters or Numbers within Cells, Columns, or Rows

You can align text in columns in one of five ways: right, left, center, full, and on the decimal character. The default decimal character is defined in Setup and can be any character you want. If you specify the decimal character as a comma, for example,

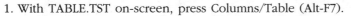

you can have addresses in a table column line up on the comma between city and state. This section explains how to format columns B, C, and D for decimal alignment. This section also explains how to set the number of decimal places to the right of the decimal character. To specify these preferences, follow these steps:

1. With TABLE.TST on-screen, press Columns/Table (Alt-F7).

2. Move the cursor to cell D3. Turn on Block, press GoTo (Ctrl-Home), type *D11*, and press Enter to highlight column D.

3. Select **F**ormat (**2**) from the table-editor menu, select Co**l**umn (**2**), and choose **J**ustify (**3**). WordPerfect displays the Justification menu:

    Justification: 1 Left; **2 C**enter; **3 R**ight; **4 F**ull; **5 D**ecimal Align: **1**

4. Select **D**ecimal Align (**5**) to specify that any numbers in the column are to be aligned on the decimal point.

5. Turn on Block and highlight column D3-D11 again. Select **F**ormat (**2**) from the table-editor menu, select Co**l**umn (**2**), and choose # of **D**igits (**4**). WordPerfect displays the `Number of decimal places (0-15): 2` prompt.

6. Type the number of decimal places you want to display in the column. Accept the default value of 2 by pressing Enter.

7. Move the cursor to cell B3. Turn on Block, press GoTo, type *C11*, and press Enter. Repeat steps 3 through 6 to change the format characteristics of the highlighted cells to decimal alignment with two decimal places.

8. Exit the table editor. The table appears as shown in figure 19.22.

9. To make the numbers in column C consistent as far as decimal places go, type *.0* at the end of the numbers in cells C3 through C8.

1989 SALES FIGURES				
Parcel	Sales Price	No. of Acres	Price per Acre	Seller
Black Acre	$50,000.00	50		Smith, T.
White Acre	$20,000.00	10		Jones, J.
Red Acre	$35,000.00	28		Hermanson
Green Acre	$60,000.00	12		Haney
Blue Acre	$50,000.00	17		Smith, H.
Yellow Acre	$25,000.00	22		Jones, S.
Brown Acre	$15,000.00	5.5		Hermanson
Orange Acre	$2,000.00	5.0		Smith, H.

Align char = .   Cell B3 Doc 1 Pg 1 Ln 2.7" Pos 2.52"

Fig. 19.22.

Aligning text in cells B3 through D11 on decimals.

Changing the Graphical Line Grid

A table is visually defined by a grid of graphical lines. Graphical lines are not ASCII characters and therefore are not highlighted when you block portions of the table.

5.1

Reminder:

Double lines surround the outside edge of a table and single lines surround individual cells; you can change how these lines appear.

Graphical lines print with a document only if your printer can print graphical images. The default line settings are as follows:

- Double lines surround the table's outside edges
- Single lines define the edges of each cell

The **Lines** (**3**) option on the table-editor menu allows you to edit the type of lines and the shading that define the table. To change the graphical lines that define TABLE.TST, follow these steps:

1. Activate the table editor.

2. Use Block to highlight row A11-E11. Select S**p**lit (**8**) from the table-editor menu and divide row A into three rows.

3. Use Block to highlight the new row A12-E12. Select **L**ines (**3**) from the table-editor screen. WordPerfect displays the menu shown in figure 19.23.

Fig. 19.23.

The table-editor Lines menu.

The first line of the two-line menu gives information about the type of lines composing the current cell. The top line of the menu shown in figure 19.24 explains that cell A12 is composed of single top line and a double left line. The bottom and right lines are not defined because—with two exceptions—unedited cells are defined by their top and left lines. What appears to be a cell's right and bottom lines are really the top and left lines of other cells. The exceptions are cells located on the right or bottom outside edges of the table.

Note: If you highlight a group of cells and select **L**ines (**3**), the first line of the Lines menu shows information about the last cell you highlighted.

The second line of the two-line menu lists the editing options. The first four options (**L**eft, **R**ight, **T**op, and **B**ottom) allow you to edit the lines defining the limits of an individual cell. If you select **R**ight or **B**ottom, you are really adding lines between the cell and the left or top lines of adjacent cells. If the cell is on the right or bottom edges of the table, selecting **R**ight or **B**ottom lets you change the line on the outside edge of the cell edited.

Inside (**5**) and **O**utside (**6**) let you edit all the inner or outer lines in one operation. **A**ll (**7**) lets you edit every line in the table—regardless of location—in one operation when the table is blocked. **S**hade (**8**) displays a menu that lets you designate whether the interior of a cell is shaded with gray for emphasis. The default percentage of gray shading is 10%, but you can changed this percentage using **O**ptions (**6**) from the table-editor menu.

4. Select **B**ottom (**4**) from the Lines menu. WordPerfect displays this menu:

   1 None; **2 S**ingle; **3 D**ouble; **4 D**ashed; **5 D**otted; **6 T**hick; **7 E**xtra Thick: **0**

   None (**1**) removes all lines from the table. Even though the lines are removed, the table's structure and formatting is unchanged. Cursor-movement and editing and formatting features perform unaltered.

   Single (**2**), **D**ouble (**3**), **D**ashed (**4**), **D**otted (**5**), **T**hick (**6**), and **E**xtra Thick (**7**) control the physical appearance of the selected cell line.

5. Select **D**ouble (**3**) as the type of line you want to use. Because you selected **T**op (**3**) as the line to edit, the line between rows A11-E11 and A12-E12 changes (see fig. 19.24).

```
┌──────────┬────────────┬──────┬──────┬───────────┐
│ Purple   │ $11,500.00 │ 4.3  │      │ Jones, J. │
│ Acre     │            │      │      │           │
├━━━━━━━━━━┿━━━━━━━━━━━━┿━━━━━━┿━━━━━━┿━━━━━━━━━━━┤
│ ████████ │            │      │      │           │
├──────────┼────────────┼──────┼──────┼───────────┤
│          │            │      │      │           │
└──────────┴────────────┴──────┴──────┴───────────┘


 Table Edit:  Press Exit when done        Cell A12 Doc 1 Pg 1 Ln 5.76" Pos 1.12"

 Top=Single; Left=Double; Bottom=None; Right=None
 Lines: 1 Left; 2 Right; 3 Top; 4 Bottom; 5 Inside; 6 Outside; 7 All; 8 Shade; 0
```

Fig. 19.24.

A double line between rows A11-E11 and A12-E12.

Copying/Moving Columns and Rows

The Copy and Move features work in the table editor in a manner almost identical to the way they function in the main document. The difference is that in the table editor these features primarily copy or move columns, rows, and blocks of cells instead of sentences, paragraphs, and pages. Columns, rows, and blocks of cells cannot be copied or moved outside the table editor.

Reminder:

To move or copy columns, rows, and blocks of cells, you must be in the table editor.

To move a row of text in TABLE.TST, follow these steps:

1. Move the cursor to cell A11. Press Move (Ctrl-F4). The following menu appears:

   Move: 1 Block; **2 R**ow; **3 C**olumn; **4 R**etrieve: **0**

2. Select **R**ow (**2**). The following option menu appears:

   1 Move; **2 C**opy; **3 D**elete: **0**

   Select **C**opy (**2**). WordPerfect displays the `Move cursor; press Enter to retrieve` prompt.

3. Move the cursor to cell A12. Press Enter. A duplicate of row A11-E11 is inserted as row A12-E12. The rows below the cursor's original location move down.

4. Press Exit (F7) to leave the table editor. Edit the text in row A12-E12 to read as shown in figure 19.25. Add the text in rows A13-E13 and A14-E14 as shown in figure 19.25.

Fig. 19.25.

*A table with
a new row
A12-E12.*

Blue Acre	$50,000.00	17.0		Smith, H.
Yellow Acre	$25,000.00	22.0		Jones, S.
Brown Acre	$15,000.00	5.5		Hermanson
Orange Acre	$2,000.00	5.0		Smith, H.
Purple Acre	$11,500.00	4.3		Jones, J.
Gray Acre	$22,300.20	80.0		Haney
Average:				Top Seller Gross Amt: Haney
TOTALS:_				

C:\WP51\TABLE.TST   Cell A14 Doc 1 Pg 1 Ln 6.66" Pos 1.82"

Combining Formatting Codes in a Table

You can use most of the function-key formatting features together with the table editor's formatting options. The function-key formatting codes are not transferred to new columns or rows created with the table editor's Insert or Split options. All the table editor's formatting characteristics transfer to new columns or rows created by the Insert or Split options.

Follow these instructions to use both the function-key and table-editor formatting options in the TABLE.TST file:

1. If it is not already on-screen, retrieve TABLE.TST and activate the table editor.

2. Select **F**ormat (**2**), **C**ell (**1**), **J**ustify (**3**), and then select **C**enter (**2**) to change the format in cells A14, E13, and E14 to center justification.

3. Select **F**ormat (**2**), **C**ell (**1**), **A**ttributes (**2**), **A**ppearance (**2**), and then select **B**old (**1**) to change the format in cells A13 and A14 to bold.

4. Exit from the table editor.

5. Move the cursor to the *A* in *Average* in cell A13. Change the relative tab settings to 0.27" and 1". Insert a hard tab (press Home, Tab). A hard tab is the easiest method to create a tab within a table. Press Ctrl-V followed by Tab or Shift-Tab to insert the regular **[Tab]** or **[Mar Rel]** codes. As a practical matter, you gain nothing by changing **[TAB]** or any other character within a table into a functioning **[Tab]** code.

   Note: A table uses the tab settings in effect for the document area in which the table is located. To change the tab settings for the entire table, move the cursor immediately before the table-definition code and change the tab settings. Use relative tabs to create tab settings that are the same distance from the left margin in each cell. Use absolute tabs to define tab settings that vary with each column. See Chapter 5 for information about tabs.

6. Move the cursor to cell E13. Use Block to highlight the words *Top Seller Gross Amt:* and press Bold (F6).

7. Use Block to highlight cells E13 and E14.

8. Select **J**oin (**7**) and select **Y** in response to the confirmation prompt to combine cells E13 and E14.

9. Press **Exit** (F7) and save the table as TABLE.TST.

10. Use Reveal Codes to look at the bottom section of the table (see fig. 19.26).

```
 Orange     │$2,000.00│    5.0  │         │Smith, H.
 Acre       │         │         │         │

 Purple     │$11,500.00│   4.3  │         │Jones, J.
 Acre       │          │        │         │

 Gray Acre  │$22,300.20│  80.0  │         │Haney

   Average: │          │        │         │Top Seller
            │          │        │         │Gross Amt:_
   TOTALS:  │          │        │         │    Haney
C:\WP51\TABLE.TST                 Cell E13 Doc 1 Pg 1 Ln 6.22" Pos 7.34"
[ ▲      ▲][ ▲     ▲][ ▲    ▲][ ▲     ▲][ ▲      ▲]
Acre[Cell]$11,500.00[Cell]4.3[Cell][Cell]Jones, J.
[Row][Cell]Gray Acre[Cell]$22,300.20[Cell]80.0[Cell][Cell]Haney
[Row][Cell][Tab Set:Rel: +0.27",+1"][TAB]Average:[Cell][Cell][Cell][Cell][BOLD]T
op Seller[SRt]
Gross Amt:[bold][SRt]
Haney
[Row][Cell]TOTALS:[Cell][Cell][Cell][Cell][Tbl Off]



Press Reveal Codes to restore screen
```

Fig. 19.26.
Formatting codes displayed by Reveal Codes.

Notice that the text formatted with the table editor is displayed without any formatting codes. The text in cells A13 and E13, however, shows the formatting codes inserted with the function keys outside the table editor.

Reminder:
Table text formatted with the table editor has no formatting codes; table text formatted with function keys does.

Tip

Use the function keys to insert formatting codes only when you want to change the formatting characteristics of a portion of a single cell. Use the table editor's formatting features to define the characteristics of the entire cell, a group of cells, and the table.

Adjusting the Width of Columns

The table editor can be used to adjust the width of one or more columns within the table. To adjust the column width in TABLE.TST, follow these steps:

1. If it is not already on-screen, retrieve TABLE.TST and activate the table editor.

2. Move the cursor to cell A3. Press Columns/Table (Alt-F7). Use Block to highlight cells A3 and B3.

3. Select **F**ormat (**2**), **C**olumn (**2**), **W**idth (**1**). WordPerfect displays the Column width: 1.3" prompt.

4. Enter *1.4"* in response to the prompt. Columns A2-A14 and B2-B14 expand (see fig. 19.27). Column C2-C14 automatically contracts.

5. Use the Column Width feature to contract column C2-C14 to 0.8". Save the table as TABLE.TST.

Fig. 19.27.

A table with expanded columns A2-A14 and B2-B14.

1989 SALES FIGURES				
Parcel	Sales Price	No. of Acres	Price per Acre	Seller
Black Acre	$50,000.00	50.0		Smith, T.
White Acre	$20,000.00	10.0		Jones, J.
Red Acre	$35,000.00	20.0		Hermanson
Green Acre	$60,000.00	12.0		Haney
Blue Acre	$50,000.00	17.0		Smith, H.
Yellow Acre	$25,000.00	22.0		Jones, S.
Brown Acre	$15,000.00	5.5		Hermanson
Orange Acre	$2,000.00	5.0		Smith, H.

```
Table Edit:  Press Exit when done          Cell A2 Doc 1 Pg 1 Ln 2.22" Pos 1.42"

Ctrl-Arrows Column Widths; Ins Insert; Del Delete; Move Move/Copy;
1 Size; 2 Format; 3 Lines; 4 Header; 5 Math; 6 Options; 7 Join; 8 Split; 0
```

Tip

You can use an alternative method for expanding or contracting the width of a column. Hold the Ctrl key and press → (expand) or ← (contract) to alter the column's size one character at a time. Hold the Ctrl and → keys, and the column continues to expand to fill all the available column space in the table. All columns to the right of the expanding column automatically compress until they are one-character wide. Hold the Ctrl and ← keys, and the column continues to contract until it is one-character wide.

Tip

You can use the Hyphenation feature in a table. Activate hyphenation if the text on a line in a cell is more than five characters from the cell's right margin. See Chapter 5 for a discussion of this feature. Even when Hyphenation feature is inactive, WordPerfect automatically splits a compound word containing a hyphen or any word containing a soft hyphen (Ctrl-hyphen).

Changing the Table's Location Relative to the Left Margin

When a table is created, WordPerfect moves the cursor to the left margin of the page. You can use **O**ption (**6**) from the table-editor menu to adjust an existing table's location relative to the left margin. To adjust the location, follow these steps:

1. Select **O**ption (**6**) from the table-editor menu. The Table Options menu appears (see fig. 19.28).

```
Table Options

   1 - Spacing Between Text and Lines
         Left                         0.083"
         Right                        0.083"
         Top                          0.1"
         Bottom                       0"

   2 - Display Negative Results        1
         1 = with minus signs
         2 = with parentheses

   3 - Position of Table              Left

   4 - Gray Shading (% of black)      10%
```

Fig. 19.28.

The Table Options menu.

2. Select **P**osition of Table (**3**). The following menu appears:

   Table Position: 1 Left; **2 R**ight; **3 C**enter; **4 F**ull; **5 S**et Position: **0**

3. Select **S**et Position (**5**). The prompt `Enter offset from left edge: 0"` appears. Enter *1.8"* for the offset value.

4. Press **Exit** (F7) and use View Document to see the table's new location on the sheet (see fig. 19.29).

Fig. 19.29.

The table's new position on the sheet.

5. Clear TABLE.TST from the screen without saving it.

Caution

Position of Table (**3**) overrides the margin settings for your document. A position setting of `0"` places the table's left edge flush with the left edge of the paper. A position setting greater than `8.5"` places the table completely off an 8.5-inch wide sheet.

Changing the Spacing between Text in Cells

Each cell has a nonprinting area called *gutter space* between the text and the grid lines. This area is similar to the margins surrounding the text of the main document. You can use the **S**pacing Between Text and Lines (**1**) option on the Table Options menu to adjust the spacing on the left, right, top, and bottom edges of the cell.

Importing Text and Numerical Data into a Table

WordPerfect offers several methods for importing text and numerical data in table format. The options include:

- Retrieving a spreadsheet using Retrieve (Shift-F10) or the List (F5) **R**etrieve (**1**) option

- Importing an ASCII, or DOS text, file using Text In/Out, highlighting the text with Block, and creating the table

- Retrieving a file into a cell using Retrieve (Shift-F10) or List (F5) (this method requires extensive editing)

- Retrieving text using the Undelete (F1), Copy (Ctrl-F4), or Move (Ctrl-F4) features as described earlier in this chapter

Cue:

*The easiest way to import a spreadsheet into table format is to press Text In/Out, select **S**preadsheet, and select **I**mport.*

The easiest method to create a table for existing data is to import a spreadsheet in table format. The Import feature works with spreadsheets created by PlanPerfect 3.0 and 5.0, Lotus 1-2-3 (Releases 1.0 through 2.2), Lotus 1-2-3 Release 3 (if the spreadsheet is in WK1 format), and Microsoft Excel (version 2.x). To import a spreadsheet, follow these steps:

1. Press Text In/Out (Ctrl-F5), select **S**preadsheet (**5**), and select **I**mport (**1**). WordPerfect displays the Spreadsheet: Import menu (see fig. 19.30).

Fig. 19.30.

The Spreadsheet: Import menu.

```
Spreadsheet: Import

     1 - Filename

     2 - Range

     3 - Type                    Table

     4 - Perform Import
```

2. Select **F**ilename (**1**) and enter the name of the file you want to import.

3. Select **P**erform Import (**4**).

The spreadsheet is imported with its cells converted to table cells. You can edit the spreadsheet in the same way that you edit a table created with the Table feature. See Chapter 16 for more information about importing and converting files.

The **R**ange (**2**) option allows you to define a portion of the spreadsheet for import as a table. The Undelete (F1), Copy (Ctrl-F4), and Move (Ctrl-F4) features have been discussed earlier in this chapter.

Using the Math Features with a Table

Although not as powerful as the math functions in a dedicated spreadsheet program, the Table math features are more powerful than those in most other word processors. Basic math operations such as addition (+), subtraction (–), multiplication (*), and division (/), which are entered from the keyboard; and functions such as subtotal (+), total (=), and grand total (*), which are selected from the Math submenu, are available. See Chapter 18 for information about the Math feature.

In addition, Table math allows creation of formulas that use values in specific cells, regardless of where the cells are located in the table. Math operator symbols typed outside the Math submenu are ignored by the Math feature. If a cell contains more than one number, the number closest to the bottom of the cell is used in the formula.

Reminder:

If a cell has more than one number in it, the number closest to the bottom is used by an equation that references that cell.

The subtotal, total, and grand total operators work only with the number values in the row *above* the operator. Formulas are calculated from left to right unless the calculation order is changed with parentheses. Each cell included in a formula must contain either a positive or negative integer or decimal (for example, 1, –1, 1.5, –1.5) to be recognized and used by the Math feature.

After creating a formula, you can copy it down the column, across the row, or to a specific cell. When a formula is copied, it uses relative cell references to update itself as appropriate. Inserting or deleting columns or rows does not automatically update a formula. Copying a formula does not transfer either the original cell's number value or format characteristics.

You can edit a formula at any time. The formulas are recalculated each time you return to the table-editor main menu from the Math menu. If you enter the formula before you enter the values it is to calculate, or if the formula contains an erroneous statement, the formula's cell displays ??. After calculating a formula, WordPerfect inserts a number value into the formula cell; you can alter or delete this value outside the table editor.

Using Combined Addition-Division Formulas

The Table's math operations can be combined to create mathematical formulas that perform several calculations in one cell. The following steps show you how to create an averaging formula that adds numbers in the column above a cell and then divides the result to give an average.

1. Retrieve TABLE.TST and move the cursor to cell B13. Press Columns/ Table (Alt-F7) and select **M**ath (**5**). WordPerfect displays the Math menu:

   Math: 1 Calculate; **2 F**ormula; **3 Co**py Formula; **4 +**; **5 =**; **6 *: 0**

2. Select **F**ormula (**2**) and enter the following as a formula:

   B3+B4+B5+B6+B7+B8+B9+B10+B11+B12/10

   When you press Enter, WordPerfect adds cells B3 through B12, divides the total by 10, and displays the answer in cell B13 (see fig. 19.31).

5.1

Fig. 19.31.

A math formula in cell B13.

Yellow Acre	$25,000.00	22.0		Jones, S.
Brown Acre	$15,000.00	5.5		Hermanson
Orange Acre	$2,000.00	5.0		Smith, H.
Purple Acre	$11,500.00	4.3		Jones, J.
Gray Acre	$22,300.20	80.0		Haney
Average:	29,000.02			Top Seller Gross Amt: Haney
TOTALS:				

```
=B3+B4+B5+B6+B7+B8+B9+B10+B11+B12/10    Cell B13 Doc 1 Pg 1 Ln 5.55" Pos 4.52"
Ctrl-Arrows Column Widths; Ins Insert; Del Delete; Move Move/Copy;
1 Size; 2 Format; 3 Lines; 4 Header; 5 Math; 6 Options; 7 Join; 8 Split; 0
```

3. Select **M**ath (**5**). Select Co**p**y (**3**). The following menu appears:

   Copy Formula To: 1 Cell; **2 D**own; **3 R**ight: **0**

4. Select **R**ight (**3**). The `Number of times to copy formula: 1` prompt appears. Press Enter to accept the default value of 1.

5. Repeat steps 3 and 4, selecting **D**own (**2**) instead of **R**ight (**3**).

6. Move the cursor to cell B14. Select **M**ath (**5**). Select **F**ormula (**2**) and press End. Press Backspace to delete the text *+B13/10* and press Enter. The formula automatically recalculates.

7. Select **M**ath (**5**), select Co**p**y Formula (**3**), and choose **C**ell (**1**). The message `Move cursor; press Enter to retrieve` appears.

8. Move the cursor to cell C14 and press Enter. WordPerfect calculates the formula (see fig. 19.32).

Fig. 19.32.

A math formula in cell C14.

White Acre	$20,000.00	10.0		Jones, J.
Red Acre	$35,000.00	20.0		Hermanson
Green Acre	$60,000.00	12.0		Haney
Blue Acre	$50,000.00	17.0		Smith, H.
Yellow Acre	$25,000.00	22.0		Jones, S.
Brown Acre	$15,000.00	5.5		Hermanson
Orange Acre	$2,000.00	5.0		Smith, H.
Purple Acre	$11,500.00	4.3		Jones, J.
Gray Acre	$22,300.20	80.0		Haney
Average:	29,088.02	23.38		Top Seller Gross Amt: Haney
TOTALS:	240,800.20	183.80		

```
=C4+C5+C6+C7+C8+C9+C10+C11+C12    Cell C14 Doc 1 Pg 1 Ln 5.84" Pos 4.52"
```

5.1

Note: When the cursor is in the cell, the formula displays at the lower left corner of the screen, regardless of whether the table editor is activated.

8. Press Exit (F7) and save the table as TABLE.TST.

Using Averaging Formulas with Cell References

The Table's math operations can refer to numbers in cells located in columns other than the column containing the formula. The following steps show you how to create an averaging formula that divides numbers in other columns.

1. Retrieve TABLE.TST and press Columns/Table (Alt-F7) to activate the table editor. Move the cursor to cell D3 and use Block to highlight column D3-D13.

2. Select **F**ormat (**2**), **C**ell (**1**); select **T**ype (**1**), and choose **N**umeric (**1**).

3. Move the cursor to cell D3, select **M**ath (**5**), and select **F**ormula (**2**). Type *(B3/C3)* and press Enter. This formula divides the value of cell B3 by the value of cell C3 and displays the result in cell D3.

4. Select **M**ath (**5**); select **C**opy Formula (**3**), choose **D**own (**2**), and type *10* to copy the formula down the column through cell D13. Press Exit (F7) to exit from the table editor.

5. Move the cursor to cell D14 and type *N/A.*

6. Press Exit (F7) and save the table as TABLE.TST.

Changing the Display of Negative Numbers

You can display a negative number using either a minus sign or parentheses. The default is the minus sign. Select **D**isplay Negative Results (**2**) on the Table Options menu to select the symbol you prefer. If you change the display method after a calculation has placed a negative number into a table, you must manually delete the original negative-number symbol. If you don't delete the original symbol, subsequent calculations result in a negative number displayed with both negative-number symbols.

Reminder:
If you change the negative-number symbol after a calculation places a negative number in a cell, recalculations show the negative number with both symbols.

Creating Newspaper Columns with Tables

A minor limitation of the Table feature is that it does not directly permit the creation of automatic, snaking, newspaper columns. Technically, all adjacent cells within a row function in a manner similar to parallel columns. You can overcome this limitation by following these steps:

1. Create a table with a single row of two or more adjacent columns of equal height and width.

2. Enter text into the first cell.

3. Manually move the cursor into the second and subsequent columns and enter remaining text into those columns.

Shading Cells, Columns, and Rows

If your printer has graphics capabilities, you can emphasize the contents of a cell with the table editor's Shade feature. When the Shade and Block features are used together, you can shade a row or column in a single operation. You can make the table easier to read by using the Shade feature on alternating rows or columns. You also can adjust the density of the shading. To shade a row in TABLE.TST, follow these steps:

1. Retrieve TABLE.TST and move the cursor to cell A4.

2. Activate the table editor and use the Block feature to highlight row A4-E4.

3. Press **L**ines (3) and select **S**hade (8). WordPerfect displays a menu at the lower left corner of the screen:

   Shading: 1 On; Off: **0**

4. Press **O**n (1). Although the screen does not change, the cells in row A4-E4 have been shaded.

5. Press Exit (F7) to leave the table editor, and then use View Document to see the shading (see fig. 19.33).

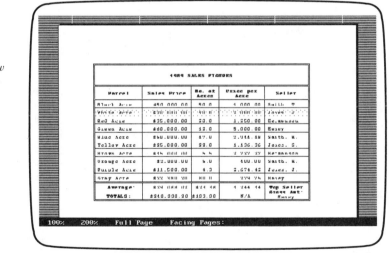

Fig. 19.33.

Table with Row A4-E4 shaded.

6. Repeat steps 2 through 5 to shade rows 6, 8, 10, and 12.

7. Move the cursor to cell E13 and shade it.

8. The default setting for gray shading is 10%. You can change the density setting by using the table editor. Select **O**ption (**6**). WordPerfect displays the Table Options menu (see fig. 19.28) which includes:

   4—Gray Shading (% of black) 10%

9. Select **G**ray Shading (**4**). Type *25* and press Enter. Press Exit (F7) to leave the table editor and then use View Document to see the shading (see fig. 19.34).

   Note: The setting for gray shading affects every shaded cell in the table. You cannot adjust the shading density for individual cells. When you change the amount of gray shading, the numbers in cells with decimal alignment may appear changed. The changes are illusory and disappear when you exit the table editor.

9. Clear the screen without saving TABLE.TST.

Fig. 19.34.
Table with shading set to 25%.

Using Tables with Other WordPerfect Features

You can use the Table feature in combination with many of WordPerfect's other features. The following list is intended to suggest the convenience and time-saving possibilities of the Table feature when used in tandem with other features.

- Use a macro to create the table structure; format one or more cells, columns, rows, or the entire table; and format or edit the text in the table. See Chapters 11 and 12 for more information about macros.

- Create a fill-in form by using a table that contains merge codes. See Chapter 13 for more about merge codes.

- Create or insert a table into a graphics box. Use this capability when you want the text of a document to wrap around a table or you want to place a table into newspaper columns. Place multiple tables into separate graphics boxes and arrange the graphics boxes how you want them. Tables created in a graphics box can be edited only through the graphics editor.

- Insert a graphic image into a table to enhance the appearance of the table.

- Create or insert a table into a header, footer, footnote, or endnote. Invoke the desired feature and press Columns/Table (Alt-F7) to place the table in the note, footer, or header. See Chapter 23 for more information about footnotes and endnotes.

- Use style codes to format one or more cells. You also can insert a table into a style code (when a table is inserted into a style code, you can edit the table only through the Style feature). Chapter 15 details the Style feature.

- Use document-reference features in a table. Chapter 25 describes the document-reference features.
- Sort data in a table using the Sort feature, described in Chapter 14.

Summary

In this chapter you have learned about WordPerfect's new Table feature—an option many users consider the most important addition since the introduction of the Macro Programming Language and expanded printer support in WordPerfect 5. Despite its power, the Table feature is easy to learn. It simplifies the use of columns and math through a cell grid similar in appearance to a spreadsheet. You can use the Table feature to do the following:

- ❏ Create automatic parallel columns and semi-automatic newspaper columns
- ❏ Perform all math functions available in the Math feature as well as some basic spreadsheet formula functions
- ❏ Create merge templates for use as fill-in forms that accept only the variable information inserted through the Merge feature
- ❏ Import spreadsheets as tables that can be edited as usual in WordPerfect
- ❏ Present data in logical sequences that can be changed easily to show different relationships

20

Customizing
WordPerfect

Judy Housman
wrote this chapter for
Using WordPerfect 5.

Stuart Bloom
extensively revised
the chapter for *Using
WordPerfect 5.1*,
Special Edition. Mr.
Bloom has
customized his copy
of WordPerfect so
completely that he
doubts anyone else
would recognize it as
WordPerfect.

E very office has different needs. As earlier chapters have demonstrated, you can adjust WordPerfect's features to your work habits. You can change the style of outlines, for example, to reflect the style you use in your documents. If your office customarily uses legal-size paper rather than letter-size, you can change WordPerfect's paper-size setting. If your office stamps documents with the time as well as the date, you can change the format in which WordPerfect displays dates.

> ### Reminder
> If you use a mouse with WordPerfect 5.1, you can click the right button to display the pull-down menus, and then select the desired option. You also can press Alt-= to access the pull-down menus, and then press the appropriate letter of the desired option. For all instructions, assume that if a block is required to activate a pull-down menu option, the text has been blocked before the pull-down menu is accessed. Instructions for pull-down menus and the mouse are marked with the mouse icon. For more information about the mouse, see Chapter 1. ▭⃞

Understanding the Setup Options

WordPerfect has many options you can use to make formatting changes as you create documents. Because everyone has preferred ways of working, WordPerfect accommodates these individual differences by enabling you to make changes that affect all future documents.

651

In addition to changing formatting features, you can change the way WordPerfect functions. For instance, you can change the location of special files, such as the dictionary files or macro files. You can change the action performed when you press a particular key or key combination. You even can change the "liveliness" of your mouse.

Several dozen options are available for customizing WordPerfect. This chapter explains how to customize WordPerfect using the options available through Setup (Shift-F1). You also can customize WordPerfect in several other places; changes you make other than through Setup are discussed elsewhere in this book.

Introducing the Setup Menu

Reminder:
Display the Setup menu by pressing Setup or accessing the File pull-down menu and selecting Setup.

When you press Setup (Shift-F1), the Setup menu shown in figure 20.1 appears. Each of the menu's options is described in the text that follows.

You can display the same Setup options with the mouse by accessing the **F**ile pull-down menu, selecting Se**t**up, and then selecting the desired option from the Setup pop-out menu (see fig. 20.2).

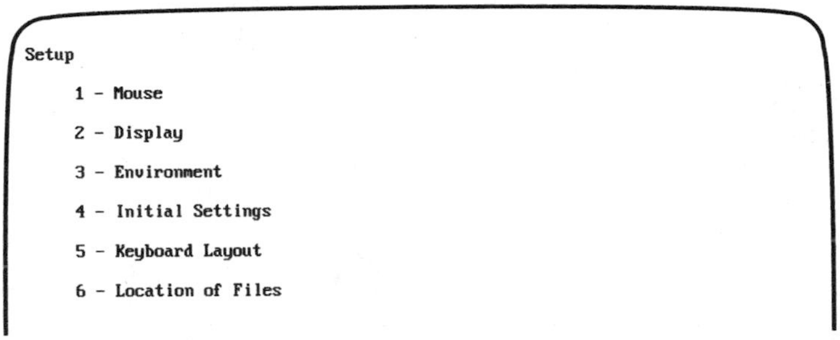

Fig. 20.1.
The Setup menu.

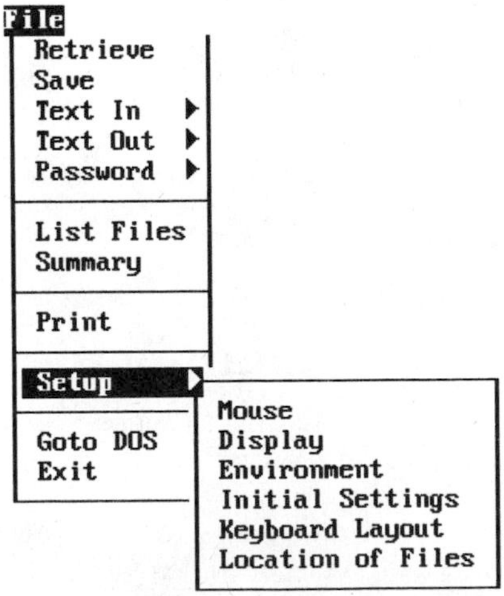

```
Setup

     1 - Mouse

     2 - Display

     3 - Environment

     4 - Initial Settings

     5 - Keyboard Layout

     6 - Location of Files
```

Fig. 20.2.
The F ile pull-down menu and the Set up pop-out menu.

```
File
    Retrieve
    Save
    Text In      ▶
    Text Out     ▶
    Password     ▶

    List Files
    Summary

    Print

    Setup        ▶    Mouse
                      Display
    Goto DOS          Environment
    Exit              Initial Settings
                      Keyboard Layout
                      Location of Files
```

Use the **M**ouse (**1**) option to tell WordPerfect what kind of mouse you use. You also can change some of the defaults WordPerfect uses to interact with your mouse.

Use the **D**isplay (**2**) option to change aspects of WordPerfect's on-screen display. You can specify whether comments are displayed or hidden and whether the file name is shown on the status line. You also can change the graphic or text driver you want WordPerfect to use, the colors or attributes WordPerfect uses to display different types of text, and many other aspects of the display. (See Chapter 5 for more information on display attributes.)

Environment (**3**) lets you specify which automatic backup options you want to use. You can specify when WordPerfect beeps, and you can control the speed of cursor movements. You can indicate whether you want to be prompted to enter document-summary information when saving a document, set certain default values for document summaries, and designate whether WordPerfect displays long or short file names with the List Files feature. You also can set hyphenation options and designate the default units of measurement that WordPerfect uses to display position values.

Use **I**nitial Settings (**4**) to customize the following options:

- The delimiters WordPerfect uses when you use a DOS text file as a secondary-merge file
- The format in which dates are displayed
- Equation-editing and equation-printing options
- Whether you want WordPerfect to format documents for the currently selected printer or for the printer in use when WordPerfect last saved the document
- The Initial Codes contained in all new documents
- The number of times the repeat key (usually the Esc key) causes the next character or WordPerfect feature to repeat
- The formatting of the Table of Authorities
- Default settings that concern printing

Use **K**eyboard Layout (**5**) to specify the effect of pressing any key or key combination used in WordPerfect.

WordPerfect uses a variety of auxiliary files in its operation. Because these files do not have to be in the same directory as the main WordPerfect program files, you can use **L**ocation of Files (**6**) to specify where these files are stored.

Some decisions you make under Setup affect the way WordPerfect works and acts, but they do so without embedding codes in individual documents. For example, you can specify where WordPerfect finds the auxiliary files vital to its operation. You can request automatic backups, change the cursor speed, control aspects of the screen display, and specify the conditions under which the pull-down menu system is activated.

Other changes *do* embed codes in documents. These changes affect only the documents you create after you make the change. For example, if you change the default tab setting, every subsequent document you create uses the new tab setting.

Reminder:

You can select Setup options that affect a document without embedding codes in the document.

If you retrieve a document created before you made the change, however, the tabs in that document are not affected.

Customizing the Mouse

Unlike previous versions of WordPerfect for the IBM PC, WordPerfect 5.1 includes support for a mouse. Many different types of mouse devices are available, and WordPerfect can work with most of them. However, you must specify what type of mouse you are using and how it is connected to your computer. In addition, you can change the way WordPerfect responds to some mouse operations. All these options are changed with the Setup: Mouse menu shown in figure 20.3.

Fig. 20.3.

The Setup: Mouse menu.

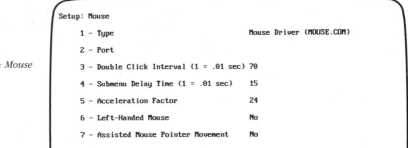

```
Setup: Mouse

     1 - Type                                    Mouse Driver (MOUSE.COM)

     2 - Port

     3 - Double Click Interval (1 = .01 sec) 70

     4 - Submenu Delay Time (1 = .01 sec)    15

     5 - Acceleration Factor                 24

     6 - Left-Handed Mouse                    No

     7 - Assisted Mouse Pointer Movement      No
```

Specifying the Mouse Type and Port

To recognize and interpret signals from a mouse, your computer needs information provided by a small program known as a *mouse driver*. Mouse manufacturers supply programs that you run to install the necessary mouse driver in the computer's memory.

The most popular mouse is the Microsoft Mouse; the driver program used with the mouse is called MOUSE.COM. The Microsoft Mouse has become a standard; many programs only support the Microsoft Mouse. Most other mouse manufacturers supply programs that emulate MOUSE.COM, so that a non-Microsoft mouse can operate with programs as if it were a Microsoft mouse.

Cue:

You can use the WordPerfect-supplied mouse driver or the driver supplied with your mouse; the driver supplied with your mouse usually provides better performance.

Unlike programs that support only the Microsoft Mouse, WordPerfect supports many different mouse drivers. With most mouse devices, you can use the MOUSE.COM driver usually supplied with the mouse or the special mouse driver supplied by WordPerfect. In most cases, if a special driver has been provided for the mouse, you get the best performance by using that driver. If WordPerfect does not supply a driver for the mouse, use the MOUSE.COM driver supplied with the mouse.

To use the MOUSE.COM driver with WordPerfect, you must run the MOUSE.COM program (or the mouse driver provided by the manufacturer of your mouse) before you start WordPerfect. You may want to enter the necessary command in your AUTOEXEC.BAT file to run the driver automatically whenever you boot the computer. See your mouse documentation for instructions.

If, in the steps that follow, you choose one of the mouse-specific options—anything other than the MOUSE.COM—you do not have to install an external driver before starting WordPerfect.

To specify the type of mouse you use with WordPerfect, follow these steps:

1. Press Setup (Shift-F1).

   ⌨ Access the **F**ile pull-down menu and select Se**t**up.

2. Choose **M**ouse (**1**). The Setup: Mouse menu appears.

3. Choose **T**ype (**1**). The Setup: Mouse Type menu appears, showing the mouse devices supported (See fig. 20.4).

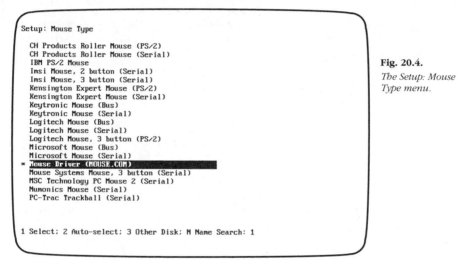

Fig. 20.4.
The Setup: Mouse Type menu.

4. Use the cursor keys to highlight the mouse you use and choose **S**elect (**1**).

   ⌨ Double-click the mouse you use.

   The Setup: Mouse menu reappears.

5. If you specified a serial mouse, continue by specifying a mouse port as described in the following instructions. Otherwise, press Exit (F7) to return to the editing screen.

If you selected a serial mouse from the Setup: Mouse Type menu (or if you use MOUSE.COM with a serial mouse) and your mouse is connected to COM2, COM3, or COM4, you must specify the port. You do not have to specify a port if you use a bus mouse (a mouse connected to your computer through a dedicated card).

To specify the port to which the mouse is connected, follow these steps:

1. Make sure that the Setup: Mouse menu is on the display.

2. Choose **P**ort (**2**). The following menu appears:

   Port: 1 COM1; **2** COM2; **3** COM3; **4** COM4: **0**

3. Press the number corresponding to the port you use for your mouse. The Setup: Mouse menu reappears.

4. Press Exit (F7) to return to the editing screen.

Setting Mouse-Performance Options

You can customize the way WordPerfect responds to your mouse in a number of ways. You can increase or decrease the distance the mouse pointer moves on-screen for a given amount of physical movement of the mouse, change the time it takes for a pop-out menu to "pop," and change the click interval WordPerfect uses to interpret when you press the mouse button. Experiment with different settings until you find those that feel most comfortable to you.

Setting the Double-Click Interval

Reminder:

You can set the time interval WordPerfect uses to distinguish between single clicks and double clicks.

The *double-click interval* is the time WordPerfect uses to distinguish a double click from two single clicks. If you press the left mouse button twice in succession, and both clicks occur within the specified time interval, WordPerfect considers the action a double click; if you do not press the button again until after the time interval has elapsed, WordPerfect considers the action two single clicks. If you find that WordPerfect treats what you intend to be double clicks as single clicks, increase the double-click interval.

To set the double-click interval, follow these steps:

1. Display the Setup menu and choose **M**ouse (**1**). The Setup: Mouse menu appears.

2. Choose **D**ouble Click Interval (**3**).

3. Type the desired interval in hundredths of a second. For example, to set the double-click interval to 0.50 seconds, type *50*. Then press Enter.

4. Press Exit (F7) to return to the editing screen.

Setting the Pop-Out Menu Delay Time

The WordPerfect pull-down menus incorporate a number of pop-out menus (or submenus), such as the Setup pop-out menu shown in figure 20.2. By default, WordPerfect displays the pop-out menu if the pointer rests on the main menu selection for 0.15 seconds. If menus "pop out" when you don't want them to, increase the delay time. If you find yourself waiting for the menu to appear, decrease the delay time.

To set the pop-out menu delay time, follow these steps:

1. Display the Setup menu and choose **M**ouse (**1**). The Setup: Mouse menu appears.

2. Choose **S**ubmenu Delay Time (**4**).

3. Type the desired delay time in hundredths of a second. For example, to set a delay time of 0.25 seconds, type *25*. Then press Enter.

4. Press Exit (F7) to return to the editing screen.

Setting the Acceleration Factor

The *acceleration factor* determines how sensitive the mouse pointer is to physical movements of the mouse. Setting a higher number means that for a given amount of mouse movement, the pointer moves farther; the mouse is "livelier." Setting a lower number decreases how far the pointer moves for the same movement of the mouse; the mouse is more sluggish.

To set the acceleration factor, follow these steps:

1. Display the Setup menu and choose **M**ouse (**1**). The Setup: Mouse menu appears.

2. Choose **A**cceleration Factor (**5**).

3. Set the desired acceleration factor by typing a number between 1 and 1200.

4. Press Exit (F7) to return to the editing screen.

Designating Left-Hand Operation

The mouse is designed to be placed on the right side of the keyboard for right-handed people. If you are left-handed, or if you prefer to place the mouse on the left side of the keyboard, clicking the left mouse button may feel clumsy. If you want, you can reverse the effect of the mouse buttons so that the button under your index finger is the one you use to click and drag.

Reminder:
You can change the mouse from right-handed to left-handed operation.

To designate left-hand operation for the mouse, follow these steps:

1. Display the Setup menu and choose **M**ouse (**1**). The Setup: Mouse menu appears.

2. Choose **L**eft-Handed Mouse (**6**).

3. At the **N**o (**Y**es) prompt, select **Y**.

4. Press Exit (F7) to return to the editing screen.

Choosing Assisted Mouse-Pointer Movement

By default, when you activate the pull-down menus with the mouse, the mouse pointer remains at its current location on the text screen (that is, it does not automatically move to the menu bar). Similarly, when WordPerfect displays a menu at the bottom of the screen, the mouse pointer does not automatically move to the menu. You can instruct WordPerfect to position the mouse pointer on the menu; you may find that this makes the mouse easier to use.

To change the setting for assisted mouse-pointer movement, do the following:

1. Display the Setup menu and choose **M**ouse (**1**). The Setup: Mouse menu appears.

2. Choose Assisted Mouse Pointer **M**ovement (**7**).

3. At the **N**o (**Y**es) prompt, select **Y** if you want WordPerfect to automatically position the mouse pointer on menus. If you do not want WordPerfect to move the mouse pointer to menus for you, select **N**.

4. Press Exit (F7) to return to the editing screen.

Customizing the Display

The **D**isplay (**2**) selection on the Setup menu controls many aspects of WordPerfect's screen display—for instance, how the text appears on the screen and how menu letters are displayed. All display options are customized from the Setup: Display menu (see fig. 20.5).

Fig. 20.5.
The Setup: Display menu.

```
Setup: Display

     1 - Colors/Fonts/Attributes

     2 - Graphics Screen Type        None Selected

     3 - Text Screen Type            Auto Selected

     4 - Menu Options

     5 - View Document Options

     6 - Edit-Screen Options
```

Setting Colors, Fonts, and Attributes

The many video systems available for the IBM PC and compatible computers differ in the way they display fonts and attributes. For example: monochrome graphics cards, such as the Hercules cards, can show "true" underlining on-screen; systems with the Color Graphics Adapter (CGA) cannot show underlining.

Reminder:
Depending on the type of display you use, you may see different submenus when you select Colors/Fonts/ Attributes (1).

The **C**olors/Fonts/Attributes (**1**) option on the Setup: Display menu controls the colors and fonts you can select to represent the text attributes you use (Chapter 5 describes the various text attributes). When you select this option, you may see a Setup: Fonts/Attributes submenu (see fig. 20.6) or a Setup: Colors/Fonts submenu (see fig. 20.7), depending on the kind of display you have. The Setup: Colors/Fonts submenu in figure 20.7 is used to select text display options and to access the Screen Colors menu; the Setup: Colors/Fonts submenu should not be confused with the Setup: Colors submenu, which appears when you choose colors for text attributes (see fig. 20.8).

Fig. 20.6.
The Setup: Fonts/Attributes submenu (figure shown uses a monochrome adaptor).

```
Setup: Fonts/Attributes

     1 - Screen Attributes

     2 - 12 Fonts, 256 Characters

     3 - 6  Fonts, 512 Characters

   *4 - Normal Font Only
```

```
Setup: Colors/Fonts

    1 - Screen Colors

    2 - Italics Font, 8 Foreground Colors

    3 - Underline Font, 8 Foreground Colors

    4 - Small Caps Font, 8 Foreground Colors

    5 - 512 Characters, 8 Foreground Colors

   *6 - Normal Font Only, 16 Foreground Colors
```

Fig. 20.7.

The Setup: Colors/Fonts submenu used to select text display options (figure shown uses a VGA/EGA adaptor).

```
Setup: Colors        A B C D E F G H I J K L M N O P
                     A B C D E F G H I J K L M N O P
Attribute            Foreground Background  Sample
Normal                   H          B       Sample
Blocked                  B          H       Sample
Underline                B          D       Sample
Strikeout                A          C       Sample
Bold                     P          B       Sample
Double Underline         B          C       Sample
Redline                  E          D       Sample
Shadow                   B          D       Sample
Italics                  D          B       Sample
Small Caps               E          C       Sample
Outline                  F          C       Sample
Subscript                E          H       Sample
Superscript              F          H       Sample
Fine Print               C          H       Sample
Small Print              I          H       Sample
Large Print              D          A       Sample
Very Large Print         E          A       Sample
Extra Large Print        F          A       Sample
Bold & Underline         J          D       Sample
Other Combinations       A          G       Sample

Switch documents; Move to copy settings     Doc 1
```

Fig. 20.8.

The Setup: Colors submenu used to choose colors for text attributes.

The colors available depend on the kind of video display your system has. Different video displays have different properties, and WordPerfect needs different information for each type of display. Because this is so, WordPerfect displays different menus for the Colors/Fonts/Attributes (**1**) option, depending on your video display. Normally, WordPerfect can determine the type of display you have; you can specify the display type explicitly using the techniques discussed under "Selecting Screen Types" later in this chapter.

Setting Colors on a Color Monitor

If you have a color monitor, WordPerfect displays font attributes such as bold, underline, and the like, in color. You may not like the colors WordPerfect uses to display one or more of these attributes. You can, if you want, use a different set of colors for Doc 1 and Doc 2, or you can set colors in one document and have WordPerfect copy those settings to the other document.

If you want to change some of the attribute colors, do the following:

1. Display the Setup menu and choose **D**isplay (**2**). The Setup: Display menu appears.

2. Select **C**olors/Fonts/Attributes (**1**). WordPerfect displays the Setup: Colors/ Fonts submenu or the Setup: Fonts/Attributes submenu, depending on the kind of display you use.

3. If you see the Setup: Fonts/Attributes submenu, follow these steps:

   a. Select the option whose colors you want to modify. For example, select **S**creen Attributes (**1**) if you want to modify the text attributes, such as normal, block, underline, strikeout, bold, and the like.

   b. When you are satisfied with any modifications and are ready to return to the editing screen, press Exit (F7). The Setup: Colors/Fonts submenu reappears.

   c. Press Enter to return to the Setup: Display menu (press Enter again to return to the Setup menu) or press Exit (F7) to return to the editing screen.

4. If you see a Setup: Colors/Fonts submenu like the one shown in figure 20.7, follow these steps:

   a. Select **S**creen Colors (**1**) if you want to modify the foreground and background colors of text attributes, such as normal, block, underline, strikeout, bold, and the like. A Setup: Colors submenu like the one in figure 20.8 appears. Each row corresponds to an attribute. For example, use the first row to specify how normal text is displayed; use the second row to specify how blocked text is displayed; and so on. For each attribute, you can specify a foreground color (for the text itself) and a background color.

   b. Use the ↓ and ↑ keys to select a row. Use the → and ← keys to select foreground or background. If you want to modify both foreground and background colors, you can alter either first.

      The first row of letters at the top of the screen specifies the key to press to choose a color in the corresponding row of letters below the first row. Sixteen foreground color options (black and seven normal-intensity colors; dark gray and seven bright colors) are available and are displayed against the background currently selected for the attribute. (In figure 20.8, the letter *A* is printed white against a black background so that you can see in the figure what you can't see on-screen: a black letter against a black background.)

      Eight background color options (black and seven normal-intensity colors) are available. Press the letter corresponding to the background color you want to use.

   c. When you are done modifying attribute colors, press Exit (F7) to return to the Setup: Colors/Fonts submenu.

5. Press Exit (F7) again to return to the editing screen.

Setting Text Display Speed

Certain display systems based on older CGA video cards are susceptible to *snow*. To eliminate this condition, you must slow down the display rate. If you have a CGA card that does not have snow problems, specify the faster display rate.

To enable or disable fast text display, do the following steps:

1. Display the Setup menu and choose **D**isplay (**2**).

2. Select **C**olors/Fonts/Attributes (**1**). A Setup: Colors submenu for a CGA monitor appears.

3. Select **F**ast Text (**2**); at the **Y**es (**No**) prompt, select **Y** to enable fast text or **N** to disable fast text.

Reminder:
If you have an older CGA display, slow down the display rate to eliminate snow; otherwise, speed up the display rate.

Customizing Display Attributes for a Hercules Graphics Card Plus

The Hercules Graphics Card Plus can use up to 12 different fonts to represent text attributes. If you have such a card, you can select the fonts used to represent the attributes through Setup.

You use the Setup: Fonts/Attributes menu (shown in fig. 20.6) to specify how many Hercules fonts WordPerfect is to use. You can use also the menu to specify the font to be used for any attribute. To access the Setup: Fonts/Attributes menu, display the Setup menu, choose **D**isplay (**2**), and select **C**olors/Fonts/Attributes (**1**).

You have three options related to the number of fonts you can choose. To make your choice, select option 2, 3, or 4 from the Setup: Fonts/Attributes menu. Option 1 is used to apply the selected fonts to specific attributes (for example, to specify that blocked text appear on-screen in reverse video).

The 12 Fonts, 256 Characters (**2**) option provides 12 fonts. If you choose this option, you can display on the editing screen 256 of the most common characters in the WordPerfect character sets. Other characters display as a "slug" character (■). Choose this option for the widest variety of attributes.

Following are some of the special characters that you can see on-screen if you have a Hercules Graphics Card Plus:

¶ § ¡ ¿ « » £ ¥ ℞ ƒ ª º ½ ¼ ¢ ² ñ ± ≤ ≥ ∝ ÷

You insert these characters into your text using Compose (Ctrl-2 or Ctrl-V). See Chapter 21 for more information on Compose.

The 6 Fonts, 512 Characters (**3**) option provides only 6 fonts, but displays 512 of the most common characters. Choose this option for the largest number of character-display options.

Normal Font Only (**4**) disables the special font characteristics of the Hercules Graphics Card Plus. The editing screen is used like a regular monochrome display: underlines and bold appear, but other fonts and attributes do not. Certain screen-capture programs have difficulty coexisting with the special Hercules fonts; use this option when you need to use one of those programs.

Once you select the number of fonts WordPerfect is to use with the Hercules Graphics Card Plus (by choosing option 2, 3, or 4 from the Setup: Fonts/Attributes menu), you can specify which fonts you want to apply to the WordPerfect attributes. To assign fonts to the various attributes, follow these steps:

1. Select **S**creen Attributes (**1**) from the Setup: Font/Attributes menu. The Setup: Font/Attributes submenu appears (see fig. 20.9).

   For each row of attributes, the Font column shows the number or letter WordPerfect uses to identify the font for that attribute. An example of the font is shown in the right column. In addition to the font, you can specify that an attribute be enhanced by reverse video, bold, underline, or strikeout characteristics. The word Sample in the far right column shows how text with the specified characteristics appears on-screen.

Fig. 20.9.

The Setup: Font/ Attributes submenu (figure shown uses a Hercules Graphics Card Plus).

```
Setup: Fonts/Attributes

Attribute            Font  Reverse  Bold  Underline  Strikeout  Sample
Normal                1      N       N       N          N       Sample
Blocked               1      Y       N       N          N       Sample
Underline             1      N       N       Y          N       Sample
Strikeout             1      N       N       N          Y       Sample
Bold                  1      N       Y       N          N       Sample
Double Underline      2      N       N       N          N       Sample
Redline               1      N       Y       N          N       Sample
Shadow                1      N       N       N          N       Sample
Italics               3      N       N       N          N       Sample
Small Caps            4      N       N       N          N       Sample
Outline               5      N       N       N          N       Sample
Subscript             6      N       N       N          N       Sample
Superscript           7      N       N       N          N       Sample
Fine Print            8      N       N       N          N       Sample
Small Print           9      N       N       N          N       Sample
Large Print           A      N       N       N          N       Sample
Very Large Print      B      N       N       N          N       Sample
Extra Large Print     C      N       N       N          N       Sample
Bold & Underline      1      N       Y       Y          N       Sample
Other Combinations    1      Y       N       N          N       Sample

Switch documents; Move to copy settings      Doc 1
```

2. Use the ↑ and ↓ keys to move the cursor to the row with the attribute you want to change. Press the space bar to cycle through the font choices (if you know which font you want to use, you can type the number or letter of the font). Watch the text in the Sample column change in appearance.

   The attributes for normal, blocked, underline, strikeout, bold, and bold & underline are linked by WordPerfect. The way these attributes are distinguished from each other on the screen has been preset. You cannot set these attributes separately; changing one of them changes all of them.

3. Once you select the desired font, use the → and ← keys to position the cursor in another column in the row to change the reverse, bold, underline, or strike-out characteristics of the attribute. Select **Y** to turn a characteristic on; select **N** to turn it off.

4. After you make all the desired changes, you can apply the same changes to Doc 1 and Doc 2. To do so, press Switch (Shift-F3), press Move (Ctrl-F4), and at the **N**o (**Y**es) prompt, select **Y**.

5. When you finish making changes, press Exit (F7) twice to return to the editing screen.

Selecting Screen Types

WordPerfect usually can detect the general type of display system you use. If you have certain types of displays, however, you must provide WordPerfect with some additional information, as described in the following sections.

Setting the Graphics Screen Type

The *graphics screen type* controls what graphics driver WordPerfect uses to display screens that use graphics. WordPerfect has three such screens: the View Document screen, the graphics editor screen, and the equation editor screen.

To specify the type of graphics screen you want to use, follow these steps:

1. Display the Setup menu and choose **D**isplay (**2**). The Setup: Display menu appears.

2. Select **G**raphics Screen Type (**2**). A list of graphics screen types appears (see fig. 20.10). The list that appears on your screen depends on the display you use and on the video resource files (files with the extension VRS) in the WordPerfect directory. If the VRS file you need is in a different directory, choose **O**ther Disk (**3**) from the menu bar at the bottom of the screen and type the drive and path name where the files are located.

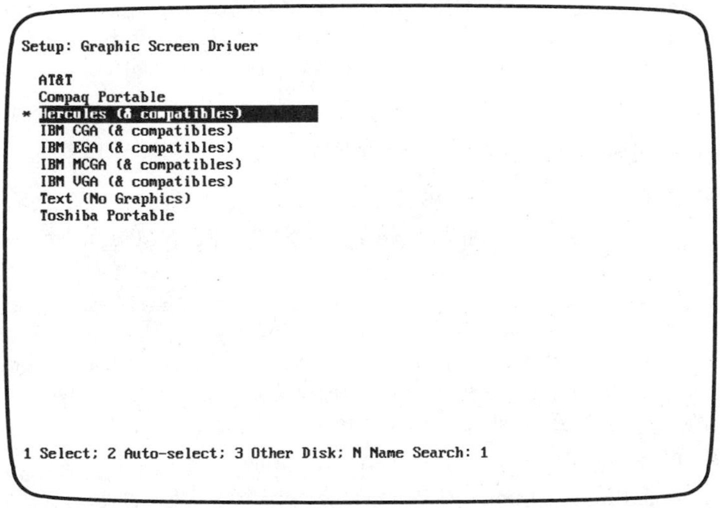

Reminder:
To control how WordPerfect displays graphics screens, set the graphics screen type.

```
Setup: Graphic Screen Driver

    AT&T
    Compaq Portable
  * Hercules (& compatibles)
    IBM CGA (& compatibles)
    IBM EGA (& compatibles)
    IBM MCGA (& compatibles)
    IBM VGA (& compatibles)
    Text (No Graphics)
    Toshiba Portable

















1 Select; 2 Auto-select; 3 Other Disk; N Name Search: 1
```

Fig. 20.10.
The Setup: Graphic Screen Driver menu.

3. Select the screen type that corresponds to your configuration by highlighting the appropriate option and choosing **S**elect (**1**). If none of the options apply, choose **A**uto-Select (**2**).

4. A second list of drivers appears that you use to refine the choice just made. Repeat step 3; the Setup menu reappears.

5. Press Exit (F7) to return to the editing screen.

Setting the Text Screen Type

The *text screen type* controls how WordPerfect handles text screens. If you have a monitor with special fonts or that can display more than the standard number of columns or rows of text, you can use this feature to select the appropriate driver. Text screens include the main editing screen, subsidiary editing screens (such as the footnote editor or style editor), help screens, and menus.

To specify the type of text screen you want to use, follow these steps:

1. Display the Setup menu and choose **D**isplay (**2**). The Setup: Display menu appears.

2. Select **T**ext Screen Type (**3**). A list of text screen types appears. The list that appears on your screen depends on the display you use and on the video resource files (files with the extension VRS) in the WordPerfect directory. If the VRS file you need is in a different directory, choose **O**ther Disk (**3**) from the menu at the bottom of the screen and type the drive and path name where the files are located.

3. Repeat steps 3 through 5 of the preceding section, "Setting the Graphics Screen Type."

Customizing WordPerfect Menus

With WordPerfect, you can customize the appearance of menus, including the new pull-down menus and the "old-style" full-screen and bottom-of-screen menus. You also can determine the circumstances under which the menu bar is displayed.

Changing the Appearance of the Menus

Reminder:

You can specify how the pull-down menus and full-screen menus appear.

To customize the appearance of the menus, follow these steps:

1. Display the Setup menu and choose **D**isplay (**2**). The Setup: Display menu appears.

2. Choose **M**enu Options (**4**). The Setup: Menu Options menu appears (see fig. 20.11). Options **4** and **8** are used to specify when the menu bar appears on-screen and are discussed under "Specifying when To Display the Menu Bar" later in this chapter. The other options control the attributes WordPerfect uses when displaying menus.

3. Select the menu characteristics you want to change:

   • To change the way the mnemonic letter appears in "old-style" menus, select **M**enu Letter Display (**1**).

   • To change the way the mnemonic letter appears in pull-down menus, select **P**ull-Down Letter Display (**2**).

   • To change the way the mnemonic letter appears in menu-bar selections, select Menu Bar **L**etter Display (**5**).

   • To change the way text appears in pull-down menus, select Pull-**D**own Text (**3**).

   • To change the way text appears in menu-bar selections, select Menu **B**ar Text (**6**).

```
Setup: Menu Options

      1 - Menu Letter Display          BOLD

Pull-Down Menu

      2 - Pull-Down Letter Display     REDLN

      3 - Pull-Down Text               SHADW

      4 - Alt Key Selects Pull-Down Menu No

Menu Bar

      5 - Menu Bar Letter Display      REDLN

      6 - Menu Bar Text                SHADW

      7 - Menu Bar Separator Line      No

      8 - Menu Bar Remains Visible     No
```

Fig. 20.11.

The Setup: Menu Options menu.

The following menu appears:

> **1 S**ize; **2 A**ppearance; **3 N**ormal: **0**

4. If you want to distinguish the selected characteristic with the colors or display attributes that otherwise indicate a size attribute, select **S**ize (**1**). If you want to use the display attribute normally reserved for an appearance attribute, select **A**ppearance (**2**). If you want the characteristic to appear as normal text, select **N**ormal (**3**).

    If you choose **S**ize (**1**), this menu appears:

    > **1** Su**p**rscpt; **2** Su**b**scpt; **3** Fine; **4 S**mall; **5 L**arge; **6 V**ry Large; **7 E**xt Large: **0**

    If you choose **A**ppearance (**2**), this menu appears:

    > **1 B**old **2 U**ndln **3 D**bl Und **4 I**talc **5 O**utln **6** Sh**a**dw **7** Sm **C**ap **8 R**edln **9 S**tkout: **0**

5. Select the size or appearance attribute you want to use from the menu at the bottom of the screen.

6. Repeat steps 3 through 5 for other menu characteristics.

7. To place a line under the menu bar (see fig. 20.12), select Menu Bar **S**eparator Line (**7**); at the **N**o (**Y**es) prompt, select **Y**. Select **N** to turn the line off.

    Note: If you use a monochrome monitor, the line under the menu bar is a double line. If you use an EGA or VGA monitor, the line is wide.

8. When you have made all your changes, press Exit (F7) to return to the editing screen.

```
File Edit Search Layout Mark Tools Font Graphics Help
─────────────────────────────────────────────────────────
```

Fig. 20.12.

The menu bar showing a separator line.

Specifying when To Display the Menu Bar

By default, WordPerfect displays the menu bar when you press the right mouse button or Alt-= (see Chapter 1). You can change this default through Setup.

Caution

The Alt-= key does not operate correctly if you select a keyboard definition originally created with WordPerfect 5, even if the keyboard definition does not define Alt-=. To overcome this problem, press Setup (Shift-F1), select **K**eyboard Layout, and do one of the following:

- Select **M**ap, move the cursor to Alt-=, and select **O**riginal.
- Select **E**dit (7), create a dummy key macro definition for Alt-=, and then delete it.
- If you previously defined Alt-=, select **E**dit (7), place the cursor on the Alt-= definition, and move it to another key.

Any of these three actions enables Alt-= to display the pull-down menus.

To change the conditions under which WordPerfect displays the menu bar, follow these steps:

1. Access the Setup menu and choose **D**isplay (**2**). The Setup: Display menu appears.

2. Select **M**enu Options (**4**). The Setup: Menu Options menu appears.

3. To display the menu bar on all editing screens, choose Menu Bar Remains **V**isible (**8**); at the **N**o (**Y**es) prompt, select **Y**. To disable this option, select **N**.

4. You can configure WordPerfect so that tapping the Alt key—pressing and releasing it without pressing another key—activates the menu bar. To enable the Alt-key menu-bar display, choose **A**lt Key Selects Pull-Down Menu (**4**); at the **N**o (**Y**es) prompt, select **Y**. To disable this option, select **N**. (Pressing Alt-= displays the menu bar whether or not the Alt-key method is enabled.)

5. Press Exit (F7) to return to the editing screen.

Setting View Document Options on EGA and VGA Monitors

If you have a high-resolution (EGA or VGA) color monitor, text (and bold characters) in View Document appears in the colors used in the text-editing screen, and graphic images are displayed in color. You can change these defaults. These options have no effect on monochrome or CGA color monitors.

To set the options for the View Document screen, follow these steps:

1. Display the Setup menu and choose **D**isplay (**2**). The Setup: Display menu appears.

2. Select **V**iew Document Options (**5**). The Setup: View Document Options menu appears (see fig. 20.13).

```
Setup: View Document Options

    1 - Text in Black & White      No

    2 - Graphics in Black & White  No

    3 - Bold Displayed with Color  Yes
```

Fig. 20.13.
The Setup: View Document Options menu.

3. To display View Document text in the colors in which it actually will print, select **T**ext in Black & White (**1**). At the **N**o (**Y**es) prompt, select **Y**. To return to the default, select **N**.

4. To view graphic images in black and white, select **G**raphics in Black & White (**2**). At the **N**o (**Y**es) prompt, select **Y**. To return to the default, select **N**.

5. To cause bold text to appear as slightly wider letters, select **B**old Displayed with Color. At the **Y**es (**N**o) prompt, select **N**. To display bold text in the same color as it appears on the main editing screen, select **Y**.

Note: The bold-text option also affects bold menu letters in other graphic screens such as the graphics editor and equation editor.

6. Press Exit (F7) to return to the editing screen.

Setting Edit-Screen Options

With WordPerfect, you can customize the display of the editing screens in a number of ways. You customize the screens by selecting **E**dit-Screen Options (**6**) from the Setup: Display menu.

Automatically Formatting and Rewriting the Screen

By default, WordPerfect reformats text and rewrites the screen as you edit. You can turn off this feature so that text is reformatted line-by-line as you move the cursor down. Most users probably want this feature turned on for convenience.

To specify whether the editing screen is automatically reformatted, do the following steps:

Reminder:
You can turn off the automatic reformatting and rewriting of the editing screen.

1. Display the Setup menu and select **D**isplay (**2**). The Setup: Display menu appears.

2. Select **E**dit-Screen Options (**6**). The Setup: Edit-Screen Options menu appears (see fig. 20.14).

3. Select **A**utomatically Format and Rewrite (**1**); at the **Y**es (**N**o) prompt, select **N** to turn off automatic rewrite or **Y** to turn it on.

4. Press Exit (F7) to return to the editing screen.

```
Setup: Edit-Screen Options
        1 - Automatically Format and Rewrite    Yes
        2 - Comments Display                     Yes
        3 - Filename on the Status Line          Yes
        4 - Hard Return Display Character
        5 - Merge Codes Display                  Yes
        6 - Reveal Codes Window Size             10
        7 - Side-by-side Columns Display         Yes
```

Fig. 20.14.
The Setup: Edit-Screen Options menu.

Displaying Comments

By default, WordPerfect displays document comments in most editing situations (comments cannot be displayed in columns). Document comments are notes you write to yourself in a document that are not printed; comments appear on the Reveal Codes screen as **[Comment]** (see Chapter 3). If you want to turn off comment display, you can do so by following this procedure:

1. Select **C**omments Display (**2**) from the Setup: Edit-Screen Options menu; at the **Y**es (**N**o) prompt, select **N** to turn off comment display or **Y** to restore comment display.

2. Press Exit (F7) to return to the editing screen.

With comment display turned off, a **[Comment]** code (but not the actual text of the comment) is visible in Reveal Codes.

Displaying the File Name on the Status Line

By default, WordPerfect displays the name of the current document on the status line at the bottom of the screen (unless, of course, you have not yet named the document). You can turn off the display of the file name if you want.

To turn off the file name display, follow these steps:

1. Choose **F**ilename on the Status Line (**3**) from the Setup: Edit-Screen Options menu; at the **Y**es (**N**o) prompt, select **N** to remove the file name display or **Y** to restore it.

2. Press Exit (F7) to return to the editing screen.

Choosing the Hard-Return Display Character

Reminder:
Although WordPerfect is designed with a clean screen, you can display hard returns to assist you in editing.

WordPerfect is based on a "clean screen" concept: control characters do not appear on the editing screen. To see control characters, you press Reveal Codes (Alt-F3 or F11).

Because you may want to have a visual indication of hard-return codes (that appear as **[HRt]** in Reveal Codes) on the editing screen, however, WordPerfect provides an option to show hard returns. You can tell WordPerfect to display **[HRt]** codes, and you can designate any character that WordPerfect can display as the hard-return character.

To display hard returns, follow these steps:

1. Choose **H**ard Return Display Character (**4**) from the Setup: Edit-Screen Options menu.

2. Type the character you want to use to represent **[HRt]** codes. You can enter special characters using the Compose feature (see Chapter 21). If the character you want to use is in the standard 256-character IBM character set, you can enter the character using the using the Alt key and the numeric keypad.

   For example, to enter the left-facing arrow (which has an ASCII code of 27) with the numeric keypad, hold the Alt key and type *27* on the numeric keypad (the number keys on the top row of the keyboard do not work). Release the Alt key. The character appears on the Setup: Edit-Screen Options menu.

3. Press Exit (F7) to return to the editing screen.

Displaying Merge Codes

Normally, when you work with a document that contains merge codes, the merge codes are visible on the editing screen. You may find these codes distracting. You can turn off the codes if you want. Even if you turn off the codes, you always can see merge codes in Reveal Codes.

To specify whether merge codes are displayed on-screen, follow these steps:

1. Select **M**erge Codes Display (**5**) from the Setup: Edit-Screen Options menu; at the **Y**es (**N**o) prompt, select **N** to turn off the display of codes. To turn on the display of merge codes, select **Y**.

2. Press Exit (F7) to return to the editing screen.

Changing the Window Size of Reveal Codes

One of the new features in WordPerfect 5.1 is the capability to change the size of the Reveal Codes window. The default setting, 10 lines, may be too large for some people and too small for others.

You can set the size of the Reveal Codes window anywhere between 1 and 19 lines on a standard 25-line editing screen (if you enter a number larger than 19, WordPerfect displays only 19 lines). If you have a screen that displays more than 25 lines, you can enter a number larger than 19 for the Reveal Codes window size.

If you choose a one-line Reveal Codes window, WordPerfect displays only the character or code on which the cursor is currently resting instead of the normal Reveal Codes display (see fig. 20.15).

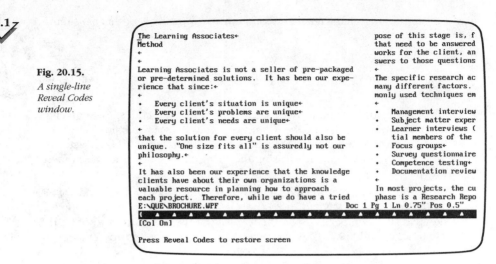

5.1

Fig. 20.15.
A single-line Reveal Codes window.

To change the size of the Reveal Codes screen, follow these steps:

5.1

1. Choose **R**eveal Codes Window Size (**6**) from the Setup: Edit-Screen Options menu, type the number of lines you want to appear in the Reveal Codes window, and press Enter.

2. Press Exit (F7) to return to the editing screen.

Turning Off Side-by-Side Columns Display

Reminder:
You can display columns consecutively down the screen or in side-by-side fashion.

By default, WordPerfect displays text columns side-by-side on-screen. Although this arrangement is convenient for some purposes, it sometimes can make editing difficult. If you want, you can display columns consecutively down the screen, with a page break between columns. Columns print side by side and appear side by side in View Document regardless of the setting of this option.

To specify whether side-by-side columns are displayed on-screen, follow these steps:

1. Choose **S**ide-by-side Columns Display (**7**) from the Setup: Edit-Screen Options menu; at the **Y**es (**N**o) prompt, select **N** to turn off the display of side-by-side columns. To reactivate side-by-side column display, select **Y**.

2. Press Exit (F7) to return to the editing screen.

Customizing the Environment

WordPerfect groups a number of setup options under the classification *environment*. In the following sections, you learn how to do the following:

- Set backup options
- Turn beeps on and off
- Vary the cursor speed
- Set document-summary options

- Customize the List Files display
- Turn Fast Save on and off
- Set hyphenation options
- Set unit-of-measure options

Each of these options is accessed from the Setup: Environment menu (see fig. 20.16). Access this menu by selecting **E**nvironment (**3**) from the Setup menu.

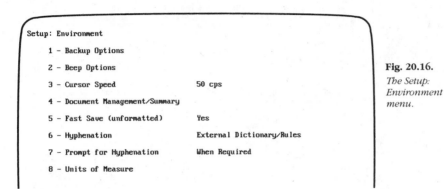

```
Setup: Environment

    1 - Backup Options

    2 - Beep Options

    3 - Cursor Speed              50 cps

    4 - Document Management/Summary

    5 - Fast Save (unformatted)   Yes

    6 - Hyphenation               External Dictionary/Rules

    7 - Prompt for Hyphenation    When Required

    8 - Units of Measure
```

Fig. 20.16.
The Setup: Environment menu.

Setting Backup Options

The **B**ackup Options (**1**) selection on the Setup: Environment menu lets you request one or both of two types of backups: **T**imed Document Backups and **O**riginal Document Backups.

You can have WordPerfect make *timed backup copies*. When you fail to exit "normally"—for example, when the power fails or your computer crashes—the timed backup is available when you restart WordPerfect. In many such situations, the timed backup is more recent than your last save. You are missing only what was added since the backup was made. If you're editing two documents simultaneously, WordPerfect makes backup copies of both documents. The backup file is named WP{WP}.BK1 for Doc 1, and WP{WP}.BK2 for Doc 2. WordPerfect maintains a timed backup by default.

Reminder:
WordPerfect automatically makes timed-backup copies of your files; you can specify the number of minutes between backups.

> **Caution**
>
> When you exit normally, WordPerfect erases the timed backup files. **Always** save your file before exiting with the F7 key. The timed-backup file is only for emergencies.

You also can instruct WordPerfect to make a backup of the old version of a document whenever you save a new version. When WordPerfect does this, the two most recent versions are maintained on-disk. If you select the **O**riginal Document Backup option, the backup copy has the same file name as the original file but with a BK! extension. WordPerfect does not make an original document backup unless you specify this option through Setup.

You can choose either or both of these backup options by completing the following steps:

1. Select **B**ackup Options (**1**) from the Setup: Environment menu. The Setup: Backup menu appears (see fig. 20.17).

Fig. 20.17.

The Setup: Backup menu.

```
Setup: Backup

        Timed backup files are deleted when you exit WP normally.  If you
        have a power or machine failure, you will find the backup file in the
        backup directory indicated in Setup: Location of Files.

        Backup Directory

    1 - Timed Document Backup              Yes
        Minutes Between Backups            30


    Original backup will save the original document with a .BK! extension
    whenever you replace it during a Save or Exit.

    2 - Original Document Backup           No
```

2. To disable timed backup, select **T**imed Document Backup (**1**). At the **Y**es (**N**o) prompt, select **N**.

   To reenable timed backup or to change the number of minutes between backups, select **T**imed Document Backup (**1**). At the **Y**es (**N**o) prompt, select **Y**. Then type the number of minutes you want WordPerfect to wait between timed backups and press Enter. You can specify a number between 1 and 38527.

3. To instruct WordPerfect to make a backup copy of the old version of a document, select **O**riginal Document Backup (**2**). At the **N**o (**Y**es) prompt, select **Y** to enable original document backup or **N** to disable the feature. You can set up a separate directory for both types of backup files (see "Changing the Location of Auxiliary Files," later in this chapter).

4. Press Exit (F7) to return to the editing screen.

Customizing the Beep

You can control the circumstances under which WordPerfect beeps. To change the beep settings, follow these steps:

1. Select B**e**ep Options (**2**) from the Setup: Environment menu. The Setup: Beep Options menu appears (see fig. 20.18).

```
Setup: Beep Options

    1 - Beep on Error              No

    2 - Beep on Hyphenation        Yes

    3 - Beep on Search Failure     No
```

Fig. 20.18.

The Setup: Beep Options menu.

2. To specify whether WordPerfect beeps on certain error conditions, select Beep on **E**rror (**1**); at the **N**o (**Y**es) prompt, select **Y** to enable the beep or **N** to disable it.

3. To specify whether WordPerfect beeps to confirm the proposed hyphenation of a word, select Beep on **H**yphenation (**2**); at the **Y**es (**N**o) prompt, select **Y** to enable the beep or **N** to disable it.

4. To specify whether WordPerfect beeps when a search fails, select Beep on **S**earch Failure (**3**); at the **N**o (**Y**es) prompt, select **Y** to enable the beep or **N** to disable it.

5. Press Exit (F7) to return to the editing screen.

Setting the Cursor Speed

If you hold down a key rather than press and release it, the key repeats its character as long as you hold the key. The repeat rate is usually very slow; you may want to increase it. You can change the rate easily, so experiment with different speeds until you find the one you like best.

Reminder:
You can change the repeat rate of the keys.

To change the cursor speed, follow these steps:

1. Select **C**ursor Speed (**3**) from the Setup: Environment menu. The following menu appears:

   Characters Per Second: 1 15; **2** 20; **3** 30; **4** 40; **5** 50; **6** Normal: **0**

2. Set the cursor speed by choosing a rate from the menu. For example, select **3** if you want a rate of 30 characters per second.

3. Press Exit (F7) to return to the editing screen.

Configuring Document-Summary Options

With WordPerfect, you can save a document summary with each document. You can enter important information about the document and the people who work on it in the document summary. See Chapter 6 for details on document summaries.

You can set several options related to document summaries. To set these options, follow these steps:

1. Choose **D**ocument Management/Summary (**4**) from the Setup: Environment menu. The Setup: Document Management/Summary menu appears (see fig. 20.19).

```
Setup: Document Management/Summary

    1 - Create Summary on Save/Exit    No

    2 - Subject Search Text            RE:

    3 - Long Document Names            No

    4 - Default Document Type
```

Fig. 20.19.
The Setup: Document Management/ Summary menu.

2. WordPerfect can prompt you to enter summary information the first time you save a document (and every subsequent time until you enter some information). Select **C**reate Summary on Save/Exit (**1**). At the **N**o (**Y**es) prompt, select **Y** to have WordPerfect automatically prompt you or **N** to disable the automatic prompt.

3. To establish the character or characters that WordPerfect uses to define the subject of a document, select **S**ubject Search Text (**2**) and type the characters you want WordPerfect to use. Then press Enter.

   For example, if you want WordPerfect to look for the subject of a document after the word TO:, type *TO:* and press Enter.

4. To establish the default extension that WordPerfect uses when displaying suggested file names, select Default Document **T**ype (**4**) and type one to three characters. Then press Enter.

   For example, if you want WordPerfect to suggest the file extension DOC, type *DOC* and press Enter.

   Note: **L**ong Document Names (**3**) is discussed in the following section, "Customizing List Files."

5. Press Exit (F7) to return to the editing screen.

Customizing List Files

WordPerfect provides you with the option to use long or short file names in the List Files display. You can change the display at any time from the List Files screen and the selection remains in effect for the rest of the session. You also can specify a default display through Setup. (See Chapter 10 for a discussion of the List Files feature.)

To designate a default of long or short file names for the List Files screen, follow these steps:

1. Choose **D**ocument Management/Summary (**4**) from the Setup: Environment menu. The Setup: Document Management/Summary menu appears.

2. Select **L**ong Document Names (**3**). At the **N**o (**Y**es) prompt, select **Y** if you want the default to be long document names; select **N** if you want the default to be short document names.

3. Press Exit (F7) to return to the editing screen.

Specifying a Fast Save

To save time, WordPerfect 5.1 does not format a document before saving it. This feature is called *Fast Save*. Although saving a document this way saves time, a disadvantage is that WordPerfect must take the time to format the document when you print the document.

To turn Fast Save on or off, follow these steps:

1. Select **F**ast Save (unformatted) (**5**) from the Setup: Environment menu. At the **Y**es (**N**o) prompt, select **N** to disable Fast Save or **Y** to enable it.

2. Press Exit (F7) to return to the editing screen.

Note: The operation of this feature has changed. In WordPerfect 5, Fast Save was off by default, and WordPerfect did not automatically format a Fast-Save document at print time; you had to retrieve the document, cursor through the document by pressing Home, Home, ↓, and then save the document again.

Customizing Hyphenation

Hyphenation has changed significantly with the last few versions of WordPerfect. WordPerfect 4.2 hyphenated by using a set of internal rules. WordPerfect 5 provided a separate optional hyphenation dictionary. With WordPerfect 5.1, the way hyphenation works has changed again. (Chapter 5 provides details about how to hyphenate with WordPerfect.)

With WordPerfect 5.1, you can choose hyphenation based on a dictionary, supplemented with internal rules when the word to be hyphenated is not in the dictionary; or you can choose hyphenation based strictly on the rules. The main dictionary file (the United States version is called WP{WP}US.LEX) contains hyphenation instructions for each word.

In addition to these two methods of hyphenation, you can tell WordPerfect what to do when a word must be hyphenated:

- Prompt you to confirm every hyphenation
- Let you make the choice when more than one correct hyphenation can be made or when a correct hyphenation cannot be determined
- Never prompt you for hyphenation instructions (if WordPerfect cannot hyphenate a word according to the hyphenation method you choose, the entire word is wrapped to the next line)

To specify hyphenation options, follow these steps:

1. To choose between dictionary-based and rule-based hyphenation, select **Hy**phenation (**6**) from the Setup: Environment menu. Make your selection from the following menu:

   Hyphenation: 1 External Dictionary/Rules; **2 I**nternal Rules: **1**

2. To tell WordPerfect when you want to be consulted about hyphenation, select **P**rompt for Hyphenation (**7**) from the Setup: Environment menu. Make your selection from the following menu:

   Prompt for Hyphenation: 1 Never; **2 W**hen Required; **3 A**lways: **2**

3. Press Exit (F7) to return to the editing screen.

Another hyphenation option, the size of the hyphenation zone, determines how much hyphenation occurs in a document. The hyphenation zone is established in Initial Codes. WordPerfect implements the hyphenation instructions only when hyphenation is turned on. Refer to "Changing the Default Initial Codes" later in this chapter to learn how to turn hyphenation on and how to set the hyphenation-zone default.

Setting Units of Measure

The **U**nits of Measure (**8**) option on the Setup: Environment menu specifies whether measurement units are displayed in inches, centimeters, points, WordPerfect 4.2 units (that is, lines and columns), or 1200ths of an inch. You can change the way the status line in your document appears, and you can change the measurements used for margins, tabs, and other settings with this option.

To set the default units of measure, follow these steps:

1. Select **U**nits of Measure (**8**) from the Setup: Environment menu. The Setup: Units of Measure menu appears (see fig. 20.20).

Fig. 20.20.

The Setup: Units of Measure menu.

```
Setup: Units of Measure

        1 - Display and Entry of Numbers          "
                for Margins, Tabs, etc.

        2 - Status Line Display                   "

Legend:

        " = inches
        i = inches
        c = centimeters
        p = points
        w = 1200ths of an inch
        u = WordPerfect 4.2 Units (Lines/Columns)
```

2. Select **D**isplay and Entry of Numbers (**1**) and type the letter of the unit you want to use for the display of margins, tabs, and other settings (refer to the legend on-screen for valid options). Press Enter.

3. Select **S**tatus Line Display (**2**) and type the letter of the unit you want to display on the status line. Press Enter.

4. Press Exit (F7) to return to the editing screen.

Customizing Initial Settings

By default, WordPerfect establishes a number of formatting rules and decisions that you can change in Setup. The Setup: Initial Settings menu shown in figure 20.21 is the route you use to accomplish many of these changes.

Fig. 20.21.

The Setup: Initial Settings menu.

```
Setup: Initial Settings

        1 - Merge

        2 - Date Format          3 1, 4
                                 November 1, 1989
        3 - Equations

        4 - Format Retrieved Documents    No
                for Default Printer

        5 - Initial Codes

        6 - Repeat Value         8

        7 - Table of Authorities

        8 - Print Options
```

Setting DOS Text-Merge Delimiters

You can use WordPerfect files or DOS text files as secondary files during a merge operation. (See Chapter 13 for information about merging files.) If you use DOS text files, you must specify what ASCII characters serve as the field and record delimiters in the text files.

To specify the delimiters used in a DOS text file, follow these steps:

1. Display the Setup menu and select **I**nitial Settings (**4**). The Setup: Initial Settings menu appears.

2. Choose **M**erge. The Setup: Merge DOS Text File menu appears (see fig. 20.22).

```
Setup: Merge DOS Text File

  1 - Field Delimiters  - Begin
                          End    ,

  2 - Record Delimiters - Begin
                          End    [CR]
```

Fig. 20.22.
The Setup: Merge DOS Text File menu.

3. Choose **F**ield Delimiters (**1**) and enter the character or characters that mark the beginning and end of each field. Either the beginning or end code may be blank. (Many database programs use commas to separate fields.)

4. Choose **R**ecord Delimiters (**1**) and enter the character or characters that mark the beginning and end of each record. Either the beginning or end code may be blank. (Many database programs use hard returns to separate records.)

5. Press Exit (F7) to return to the editing screen.

Customizing the Date Format

You can specify how to display dates that you create with the Date Text and Date Code selections on the Date/Outline (Shift-F5) screen. The date formats you select from are identical to those used by Date Format on the Date/Outline screen. When you set the formats in Setup, however, the formats are used as the defaults the next time you run WordPerfect.

To specify the date format by using the Initial Settings screen, follow these steps:

1. Display the Setup menu and select **I**nitial Settings (**4**). The Setup: Initial Settings menu appears.

2. Select **D**ate Format (**2**). The Date Format menu appears (see fig. 20.23).

3. Type the characters necessary to create the date format you want (the screen shows examples of how to enter a date format). Press Enter.

   The Setup: Initial Settings menu reappears with the current date shown in the chosen format.

4. Press Exit (F7) to return to the editing screen.

```
Date Format

     Character    Meaning
        1         Day of the Month
        2         Month (number)
        3         Month (word)
        4         Year (all four digits)
        5         Year (last two digits)
        6         Day of the Week (word)
        7         Hour (24-hour clock)
        8         Hour (12-hour clock)
        9         Minute
        0         am / pm
        %,$       Used before a number, will:
                     Pad numbers less than 10 with a leading zero or space
                     Abbreviate the month or day of the week

     Examples:  3 1, 4      = December 25, 1984
                %6 %3 1, 4  = Tue Dec 25, 1984
                %2/%1/5 (6) = 01/01/85 (Tuesday)
                $2/$1/5 ($6) = 1/ 1/85 (Tue)
                8:90        = 10:55am


Date format: 3 1, 4
```

Fig. 20.23.

The Date Format menu.

Customizing Equations

You have a number of options for customizing WordPerfect 5.1's new equation feature. You can specify how equations are printed, how equations are aligned in equation boxes, and what keyboard definition is activated when you enter the equation editor.

To customize any of these three options for the equation feature, start with these steps:

1. Display the Setup menu and select **I**nitial Settings (**4**). The Setup: Initial Settings menu appears.

2. Select **E**quations (**3**). The Setup: Equation Options menu appears (see fig. 20.24).

```
Setup: Equation Options

   1 - Print as Graphics      Yes

   2 - Graphical Font Size    Default

   3 - Horizontal Alignment   Center

   4 - Vertical Alignment     Center

   5 - Keyboard for Editing
```

Fig. 20.24.

The Setup: Equation Options menu.

3. Select one of the five options displayed. Each option is described in the following paragraphs.

To tell WordPerfect whether to print equations in text or graphics mode, select **P**rint as Graphics (**1**) from the Setup: Equation Options menu. If you want all characters in equations to print as graphics, select **Y** at the **Y**es (**N**o) prompt. If you want characters to print as text characters using your printer's fonts (when they are available), select **N**. The option you choose depends on the capabilities of your printer.

To designate the font size in which equations are printed as graphics, select **G**raphical Font Size (**2**). The following menu appears:

    1 Default Font; **2 S**et Point Size: **0**

WordPerfect normally prints equations in the current base-font size. If you want WordPerfect to do this, select **D**efault Font (**1**) from the Setup: Equation Options menu. To specify another point size, select **S**et Point Size (**2**) and type a point size at the `Point Size:` 0 prompt.

By default, WordPerfect centers an equation horizontally and vertically in an equation box. To change this alignment, select **H**orizontal Alignment (**3**) or **V**ertical Alignment (**4**) from the Setup: Equation Options menu.

If you chose **H**orizontal Alignment (**3**), this menu appears:

    Horizontal Alignment: 1 Left; **2 C**enter; **3 R**ight: **0**

If you chose **V**ertical Alignment (**4**), this menu appears:

    Vertical Alignment: 1 Top; **2 C**enter; **3 B**ottom: **0**

Select the desired alignment option from either or both of the menus.

Normally, if you select a custom keyboard definition, that keyboard definition is active at all times in WordPerfect. You have the option, however, of designating a keyboard definition to be activated automatically whenever you enter the equation editor. The specified keyboard definition is in effect only in the equation editor, superseding any other active keyboard definition while you are in the equation editor.

To select an equation-editor keyboard definition, choose **K**eyboard for Editing (**5**) from the Setup: Equation Options menu. The Setup: Keyboard Layout menu appears (shown later in this chapter as fig. 20.28). Choose a keyboard definition from the list (see "Selecting a Keyboard Definition" later in this chapter). WordPerfect 5.1 includes the EQUATION keyboard definition, which may be your best initial choice.

When you are finished specifying options for the equation feature, press Exit (F7) to return to the editing screen.

Reminder:
Although equations are usually centered in an equation box, you can specify the vertical and horizontal alignment of the equation in the box.

Formatting Documents for the Default Printer

When WordPerfect retrieves a file, it normally formats the document for the printer in effect at the time the document was saved. If you want, you can specify that WordPerfect format all retrieved documents for the currently selected printer.

To format retrieved documents for the currently selected printer or the printer at the time the document·was last saved, follow these steps:

    1. Display the Setup menu and select **I**nitial Settings (**4**). The Setup: Initial Settings menu appears.

2. Select **F**ormat Retrieved Documents for Default Printer (**4**); at the **N**o (**Y**es) prompt, select **Y** to format documents for the default printer; select **N** to format documents for the printer in effect at the time the document was saved.

3. Press Exit (F7) to return to the editing screen.

Changing the Default Initial Codes

WordPerfect makes certain assumptions concerning the paper size, left and right margin settings, justification of text, and many other formatting specifications that affect how a document looks on-screen and when printed. When you initially install WordPerfect, the program defaults to letter-size paper with left and right margins of one inch. For many people, the default settings match their preferences; WordPerfect sets the defaults for the most commonly used paper size, margins, date formats, and other specifications.

You may want to change the default format and style for a single document or for all subsequent documents. Initial Codes is a powerful option that enables you to decide which codes appear in the Initial Codes of subsequent documents. Initial Codes can be entered for a document in two ways: from Setup (Shift-F1) and from Format (Shift-F8). Both methods display a screen that looks like a document with Reveal Codes (see fig. 20.25). However, the Setup: Initial Codes screen affects every subsequent document; it does not affect the current document. The Format: Initial Codes screen affects only the current document. In both situations, you can enter any number of codes at this screen.

Fig. 20.25.

The Setup: Initial Codes screen with representative entries.

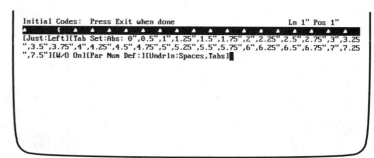

Table 20.2 lists WordPerfect's default document settings. You can change these defaults by selecting **I**nitial Codes (**5**) from the Setup: Initial Settings menu (as described later in this section).

Perhaps the default settings listed in table 20.2 don't suit your needs. Chapter 6 explains how to change the paper size and other initial settings for an individual document with Format (Shift-F8). If you only occasionally produce a document with different format options, change the settings for the individual documents. If you habitually use legal-size paper and always prefer 3/4-inch margins on each side, for example, you save time by using Setup (Shift-F1) to change the defaults permanently. When you change the defaults, all future documents have the newly specified Initial Codes.

Table 20.2
Default Document Settings for WordPerfect 5.1

Option	Setting
Baseline Placement for Typesetters	No
Center Page (top to bottom)	No (off)
Decimal/Align Character	.
Display Pitch	Automatic Yes
Initial Base Font	Printer Dependent
Hyphenation	No (off)
Hyphenation Zone —Left	10%
—Right	4%
Justification	Full
Language	US
Letter Spacing	Optimal
Leading Adjustment	
Primary—**[SRt]**	0"
Secondary—**[HRt]**	0"
Line Height	Automatic
Line Numbering	No (off)
Line Spacing	1
Margins —Left	1"
—Right	1"
—Top	1"
—Bottom	1"
Page Number Position	No page numbering
Page Number Style	^B
Paper Size	8.5" × 11"
Paper Type	Standard
Paragraph Number	
Definition	Outline
Enter Inserts Paragraph Number	Yes
Automatically Adjust to Current Level	Yes
Redline Method	Printer Dependent
Tab Settings	Relative from −1", every 0.5"
Thousands' Separator	,
Underline—Spaces	Yes
—Tabs	No
Widow/Orphan Protection	No (off)
Kerning	No (off)
Word Spacing	Optimal
Word Spacing Justification Limits	
Compressed to	60%
Expanded to	400%

You can change any of the default Initial Codes to suit your preference. If you use paper with a fancy border on the left side and bottom of the page, for example, you may want larger left and bottom margins.

To change the default settings, complete the following steps:

1. Display the Setup menu and select Initial Settings (4). The Setup: Initial Settings menu appears.

2. Choose Initial Codes (5). You see a split screen that looks like a document displaying Reveal Codes (see fig. 20.25). Notice that the status line does not contain a document number. If you have no existing initial codes, both halves of the screen are empty.

3. Enter the formatting defaults you want to establish. To enter default settings, press Format (Shift-F8) to enter format codes; press Graphics (Alt-F9) to enter box options; press Mark Text (Shift-F5) to enter paragraph-number definitions; press Footnote (Ctrl-F7) to enter footnote and endnote options; press Columns/Table (Alt-F7) to enter column definitions. Refer to the appropriate chapters in this book for information about entering specific options after pressing each of these keys.

4. Press Exit (F7) twice to return to the editing screen.

From now on, whenever you create a new document, the document has as its Initial Codes the options you just specified. To see this for yourself, create a new document. Look at the initial settings by pressing Format (Shift-F8), choosing Document (3), and then selecting Initial Codes (2).

> ### Caution
> Although WordPerfect enables you to change many Initial Codes through Setup, some formatting codes cannot be changed permanently in this way. These formatting codes include text formats, indents, tabs, comments, list definitions, fonts, attributes, styles, center page top to bottom, headers, footers, form size and type, and advance functions. Although you can enter these code changes on the Initial Codes screen, they are not retained: when you press Exit (F7), they disappear from the Initial Codes screen. To verify that the codes you specify are accepted, reexamine the Initial Codes screen. Place any codes missing from the Initial Codes screen at the very beginning of the document.

Setting the Repeat Value

The Repeat (Esc) key can be used in combination with other commands and cursor-movement instructions. By default, WordPerfect uses a repeat value of 8 when you press Repeat (Esc). You can change this default in Setup.

To change the default repeat value, follow these steps:

1. Display the Setup menu and select Initial Settings (4). The Setup: Initial Settings menu appears.

2. Select **R**epeat Value (**6**), type the desired repeat value, and press Enter.

3. Press Exit (F7) to return to the editing screen.

Customizing the Table of Authorities

Through Setup, you can change the default settings WordPerfect uses to create a Table of Authorities (ToA).

To change the ToA defaults, follow these steps:

1. Display the Setup menu and select **I**nitial Settings (**4**). The Setup: Initial Settings menu appears.

2. Choose Table of **A**uthorities (**7**). The Setup: Table of Authorities menu appears (see fig. 20.26).

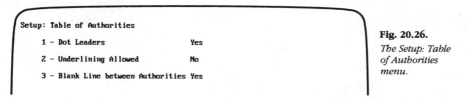

```
Setup: Table of Authorities

   1 - Dot Leaders                        Yes

   2 - Underlining Allowed                No

   3 - Blank Line between Authorities Yes
```

Fig. 20.26.

The Setup: Table of Authorities menu.

3. To include in the ToA a dot leader with page numbers aligned at the right margin, select **D**ot Leaders (**1**); at the **Y**es (**N**o) prompt, select **Y**. Select **N** to eliminate dot leaders altogether.

4. To retain in the ToA any underlining from the text of the entries, select **U**nderlining Allowed (**2**); at the **N**o (**Y**es) prompt, select **Y**. Select **N** to remove underlining from text entries.

5. To double-space the authorities in the ToA, select **B**lank Line between Authorities (**3**); at the **Y**es (**N**o) prompt, select **Y**. Select **N** to single-space the entries.

6. Press Exit (F7) to return to the editing screen.

Setting Print Options

WordPerfect establishes a number of defaults for printed documents. You can change some of these options at print time through the Print (F7) menu. You can change in Setup the *defaults* for some of these options so that the options affect all documents printed subsequently (you can override these defaults with the Print menu at print time). Setup also provides the opportunity to change several options not available on the Print menu.

To change the defaults for print options, follow these steps:

1. Display the Setup menu and select **I**nitial Settings (**4**). The Setup: Initial Settings menu appears.

2. Select **P**rint Options (**8**). The Setup: Print Options menu appears (see fig. 20.27).

Fig. 20.27.

The Setup: Print Options menu.

```
Setup: Print Options

     1 - Binding Offset                  0"

     2 - Number of Copies                1
         Multiple Copies Generated by    WordPerfect

     3 - Graphics Quality                Medium

     4 - Text Quality                    High

     5 - Redline Method                  Printer Dependent

     6 - Size Attribute Ratios - Fine    60%
         (% of Normal)          Small    80%
                                Large    120%
                           Very Large    150%
                          Extra Large    200%
                     Super/Subscript     60%
```

3. To change the binding width, select **B**inding Offset (**1**) and enter the desired offset. See Chapter 8 for information on binding offset.

4. To change the number of copies printed by each print command, select **N**umber of Copies (**2**), type the number of copies you want to print, and press Enter. The following menu appears:

    Multiple Copies Generated by: 1 WordPerfect; **2 P**rinter: **1**

    If your printer has enough memory and is "smart" enough to print multiple copies, you can select **P**rinter (**2**). Otherwise, accept the default of **W**ordPerfect (**1**). In most cases, if your printer can print multiple copies, you improve WordPerfect's performance by selecting **P**rinter (**2**) (but you have to collate the copies yourself). Chapter 9 defines how to use laser printers with WordPerfect.

5. To set the quality of printed graphics images, select **G**raphics Quality (**3**) and choose the desired quality. See Chapter 8 for information on graphics quality.

6. To set the quality of printed text, select **T**ext Quality (**4**) and choose the desired quality. See Chapter 8 for information on text quality.

7. To designate the method used to print redlined text, select **R**edline Method (**5**). The following menu appears:

    Redline Method: 1 Printer Dependent; **2 L**eft; **3 A**lternating: **1**

    If you want the redlining method to be determined by the characteristics of the printer, select **P**rinter Dependent (**1**). If you want redlining to be indicated by horizontal-bar characters in the left margin, select **L**eft (**2**). If you want redlining to appear in the left margin on even-numbered pages and in the right margin on odd-numbered pages, choose **A**lternating (**3**).

Reminder:

If your printer has the required font sizes, you can specify different sizes for seven types of text, based on the base-font size.

8. To select the percentage of the base-font size WordPerfect uses for fine, small, large, very large, extra large, superscript, and subscript text, choose **S**ize Attribute Ratios (**6**). Type the desired percentages for each font size, pressing Enter after each percentage.

    If the base font is 10 points, for example, and you accept the default values shown in figure 20.27, fine text print in 6 points, small text in 8 points, large text in 12 points, very-large text in 15 points, extra-large text in 20 points, and superscripts and subscripts in 6 points. To support these specification, however, your printer must have the necessary font sizes.

9. Press Exit (F7) to return to the editing screen.

Customizing Keyboards

An exciting and useful feature of WordPerfect is the capability to define the keyboard; that is, to change the actions performed by keys and key combinations. You can create several *keyboard definitions* for different purposes.

With the Keyboard Layout feature, you can do the following:

- Learn WordPerfect more easily by making the keyboard emulate programs with which you are already familiar
- Assign frequently performed commands or combinations of commands to easy-to-reach keys
- Redefine Alt-*keys*, Ctrl-*keys*, or regular *keys* for foreign or statistical typing (*key* can be a letter, numeral, or other key)
- Make the keyboard function as a macro library for specialized tasks

With WordPerfect, you can define nearly every key and key combination on the keyboard, including the following:

- Key combinations such as Alt-*key*, Ctrl-*key*, and Shift-*key*
- All the function keys, including F11 and F12 on the IBM Enhanced Keyboard, as well as function keys in combination with Alt, Ctrl, or Shift
- Any key that performs a function in WordPerfect, such as Del, Ins, or Esc
- Any key on the keyboard, such as R, r, 1, the Tab key, the question mark (?), and so on (you cannot assign actions to keys for which DOS does not return anything—such as pressing Ctrl-1, Ctrl-3 through Ctrl-5, or Ctrl-7 through Ctrl-0, using the top row of number keys)

Selecting a Keyboard Definition

You can use WordPerfect's standard keyboard definition, or you can select another keyboard definition, create a keyboard definition from scratch, or alter an existing keyboard definition. For instance, you may choose to use the ALTRNAT keyboard. That keyboard definition makes the actions of the WordPerfect keyboard work like many popular applications such as 1-2-3. With this keyboard definition, you use F1 to get help and Esc to cancel an action.

WordPerfect includes five useful alternative keyboard definitions. If you plan to use an alternative keyboard definition, be sure to instruct the Install program to copy the keyboard files to the directory you indicated for Keyboard/Macro Files on the Setup: Location of Files screen. If you do not specify a Keyboard/Macro directory, WordPerfect looks for keyboard definitions in the WordPerfect system directory.

Reminder:
WordPerfect supplies several keyboard-definition files; selecting one for use is easy.

The keyboards supplied with WordPerfect are as follows:

ALTRNAT — Remaps the F1, F3, and Esc keys to be more consistent with industry-standard uses for these keys.

ENHANCED — Supplies definitions for keys available only on the enhanced (101-key) keyboard, such as Shift-F11 and Ctrl-F12.

EQUATION — Remaps the keyboard for use in the equation editor.

MACROS — Assigns a group of useful macros to Alt-key and Ctrl-key combinations.

SHORTCUT — Assigns some common multikeystroke combinations to Alt-key and Ctrl-key combinations. The Alt-E macro on this keyboard is a useful way to edit many of WordPerfect's hidden codes.

The Keyboard Layout menu, accessed from the Setup menu, works in a manner similar to the List Files screen. Suppose that you want to perform a menu action such as deleting or editing a keyboard definition. You use the cursor keys to highlight the desired keyboard definition, and then you choose the desired action from the menu displayed at the bottom of the screen.

To select a keyboard definition, complete the following steps:

1. Display the Setup menu and select **K**eyboard Layout (**5**). The Setup: Keyboard Layout Menu appears (see fig. 20.28).

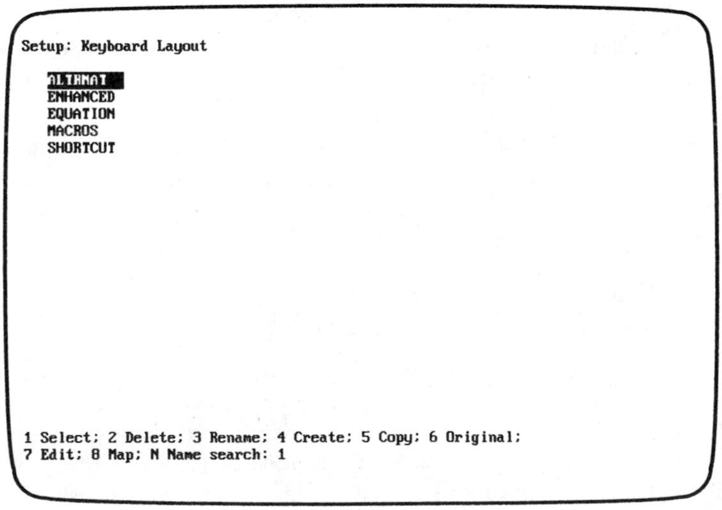

Fig. 20.28.

The Setup: Keyboard Layout menu.

```
Setup: Keyboard Layout

  ALTRNAT
  ENHANCED
  EQUATION
  MACROS
  SHORTCUT

















1 Select; 2 Delete; 3 Rename; 4 Create; 5 Copy; 6 Original;
7 Edit; 8 Map; N Name search: 1
```

2. Use the cursor keys to highlight the keyboard definition you want to select. For example, highlight ENHANCED.

3. Choose **S**elect (**1**) from the menu at the bottom of the screen.

4. Press Exit (F7) to return to the editing screen. Now the keyboard definition defined by the ENHANCED file is in effect.

Using Other Keyboard-Definition Options

You can perform other actions with a keyboard-definition file after you select it by choosing one of the other options from the Setup: Keyboard Layout menu at the bottom of the screen.

Select **D**elete (**2**) to delete a keyboard definition. Use **R**ename (**3**) to change the name of a keyboard definition. Select **C**reate (**4**) to design your own keyboard definition from scratch (see "Editing a Keyboard Definition" later in this chapter for instructions). Choose Cop**y** (**5**) to make a copy of an existing keyboard definition.

Choose **O**riginal (**6**) to restore the keyboard to the WordPerfect default. For instance, if you create and select a keyboard definition that causes you problems, use this option. You also can restore the original keyboard, for the current session only, from anywhere within WordPerfect by pressing Ctrl-6 (use the 6 key in the row across the top of the typewriter keys; pressing the numeric keypad 6 key has no effect).

Use **E**dit (**7**) to change an existing keyboard definition. See "Editing a Keyboard Definition" later in this chapter.

Use **M**ap (**8**) to display a map showing which keys are assigned and which are free for the keyboard definition. This feature is useful if you are searching for a "free key" on a crowded keyboard. Near the bottom of the screen are displayed the Description and Action for the key selected by the cursor. You can create and modify key definitions from the Map screen just as you do with the Keyboard: Edit menu, described in the next section.

Name Search (**N**) works just as it does in List Files. Select **N**ame Search and type the first letter (or first few letters) of the keyboard you want to select, edit, or perform some other action on.

Each keyboard definition is stored in a file with its given name and the extension WPK; for example, ALTRNAT.WPK. You can delete, rename, or copy keyboard definitions from WordPerfect's List Files (F5) screen or from DOS. You can access keyboard definitions altered in this way from the Setup: Keyboard Layout menu, provided that they have the extension WPK.

Reminder:
You can restore the keyboard to its original definition at any time by pressing Ctrl-6.

Editing a Keyboard Definition

To edit a keyboard definition, display the Setup: Keyboard Layout menu and highlight the keyboard definition you want to edit. Then follow these steps:

1. Select **E**dit (**7**) from the Setup: Keyboard Layout menu. The Keyboard: Edit menu appears (see fig. 20.29).

2. To change the action of an existing key definition, highlight the key and select **A**ction (**1**). The Key: Edit screen appears, which is identical to the Macro: Editing screen. You can use all the features available in WordPerfect macros, including advanced macro commands. See Chapters 11 and 12 for information about WordPerfect macros and the macro editor.

3. To change a description displayed on the Keyboard: Edit screen, highlight the desired key definition and select **D**scrptn (**2**). At the `Description:` prompt, enter a new description or edit the old one.

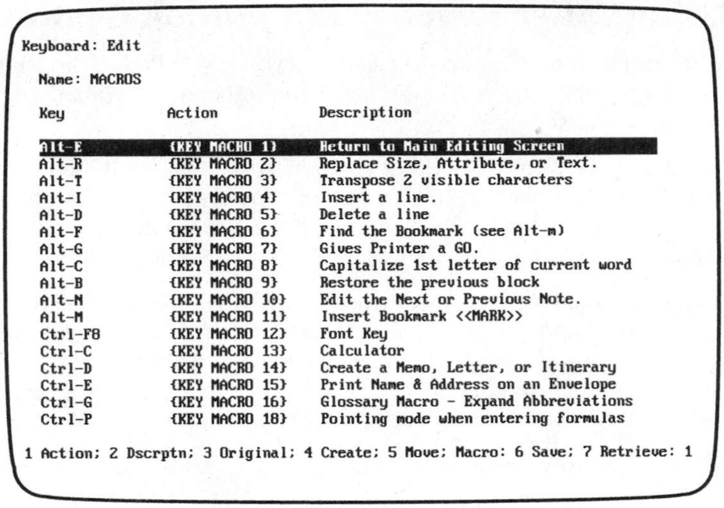

Fig. 20.29.

The Keyboard:
Edit menu for the
MACROS
keyboard.

```
Keyboard: Edit

   Name: MACROS

   Key          Action           Description

   Alt-E        {KEY MACRO 1}     Return to Main Editing Screen
   Alt-R        {KEY MACRO 2}     Replace Size, Attribute, or Text.
   Alt-T        {KEY MACRO 3}     Transpose 2 visible characters
   Alt-I        {KEY MACRO 4}     Insert a line.
   Alt-D        {KEY MACRO 5}     Delete a line
   Alt-F        {KEY MACRO 6}     Find the Bookmark (see Alt-m)
   Alt-G        {KEY MACRO 7}     Gives Printer a GO.
   Alt-C        {KEY MACRO 8}     Capitalize 1st letter of current word
   Alt-B        {KEY MACRO 9}     Restore the previous block
   Alt-N        {KEY MACRO 10}    Edit the Next or Previous Note.
   Alt-M        {KEY MACRO 11}    Insert Bookmark <<MARK>>
   Ctrl-F8      {KEY MACRO 12}    Font Key
   Ctrl-C       {KEY MACRO 13}    Calculator
   Ctrl-D       {KEY MACRO 14}    Create a Memo, Letter, or Itinerary
   Ctrl-E       {KEY MACRO 15}    Print Name & Address on an Envelope
   Ctrl-G       {KEY MACRO 16}    Glossary Macro - Expand Abbreviations
   Ctrl-P       {KEY MACRO 18}    Pointing mode when entering formulas

   1 Action; 2 Dscrptn; 3 Original; 4 Create; 5 Move; Macro: 6 Save; 7 Retrieve: 1
```

4. To delete a key definition from the keyboard, highlight the key definition and select **O**riginal (**3**). WordPerfect asks for confirmation; select **Y** to delete the key definition. The key will have its original (unmodified) definition when this keyboard is active.

5. To create a new key definition, select **C**reate (**4**). WordPerfect prompts for the key to be assigned; press the key you want to define. WordPerfect then prompts for a description; enter a description. WordPerfect then displays the Key: Edit screen. Delete any existing definition and enter a new definition (see step 2).

6. To reassign an existing definition to a different key, highlight the key you want to reassign and select **M**ove (**5**). WordPerfect prompts for the new key; press the key to which you want to reassign the definition.

7. To save a key definition as a macro (WPM) file, highlight the key definition and select **S**ave (**6**). WordPerfect prompts for the macro file name to be used. Type the file name (with or without the WPM extension) and press Enter.

8. To retrieve an existing macro (WPM) file into a key definition, select **R**etrieve (**7**). WordPerfect prompts for the key you want to assign; press the key. WordPerfect then prompts for the macro file to be used. Type the file name (the WPM extension is optional) and press Enter.

9. When you have finished editing the keyboard definition, press Exit (F7) to return to the Setup: Keyboard Layout menu.

10. You can select a new keyboard definition or press Exit (F7) to retain the currently selected keyboard. Either action returns you to the editing screen.

Changing the Location of Auxiliary Files

Structuring your hard disk into directories is similar to organizing your papers into categories with folders. Most people agree that both activities are important, but some disagreement exists concerning the best way to go about these tasks. Within limits, you can customize WordPerfect to fit the organization you choose.

You can choose where you keep backup files, keyboard and macro files, thesaurus and spelling/hyphenation files, printer files, style library files, graphic files, and document files.

Note: Before you can assign your files to directories, you first must create those directories.

To specify the directory location of specific kinds of files, follow these steps:

Reminder:
You can specify default directories where all types of WordPerfect files are stored.

1. Display the Setup menu and select **L**ocation of Files (**6**). The Setup: Location of Files menu appears (see fig. 20.30). The menu on your screen may show different file locations than those shown in figure 20.30.

```
Setup: Location of Files

    1 - Backup Files              C:\WP51

    2 - Keyboard/Macro Files      C:\WP51

    3 - Thesaurus/Spell/Hyphenation
                    Main          C:\WP51
                    Supplementary C:\WP51

    4 - Printer Files             C:\WP51

    5 - Style Files               C:\WP51
          Library Filename        LIBRARY.STY

    6 - Graphic Files             C:\WP51

    7 - Documents
```

Fig. 20.30.

The Setup: Location of Files menu.

2. To change the directory where timed backup files are stored, select **B**ackup Files (**1**), type a full path name, and press Enter. This selection does not affect the location of backups of original files, which are always stored in the same directory as the original file.

3. To change the directory where keyboard and macro files are stored, select **K**eyboard/Macro Files (**2**), type a full path name, and press Enter. If you do not enter a path for these files, WordPerfect looks in the WordPerfect system directory first, and then in the current directory for keyboards and macros.

4. To change the directory where main or supplemental dictionary, hyphenation, and thesaurus files are stored, select **T**hesaurus/Spell/ Hyphenation (**3**), type the full path name or names, and press Enter.

5. To change the directory where printer files are stored, select **P**rinter Files (**4**), type the full path name, and press Enter.

6. To change the directory where style files are stored, select **S**tyle Files (**5**), type the full path name, and press Enter. If you want WordPerfect to use a default style library when you first access the Style (Alt-F8) menu from within a document, type the name of that library file on the following line and press Enter. If you do not want to designate a default library file, leave the Library Filename line blank.

7. To change the directory where graphic files are stored, select **G**raphic Files (**6**), type the full path name, and press Enter. If you do not enter a path for these files, WordPerfect looks for graphics files in the current directory.

8. If you want to designate a default directory for WordPerfect documents, select **D**ocuments (**7**), type the full path name, and press Enter. If you do not enter a path for these files, WordPerfect looks in the current directory for documents.

9. Press Exit (F7) to return to the editing screen.

Once you have specified the directories where WordPerfect is to look for the various types of files, make sure that you move the files to the appropriate directories.

Summary

In this chapter, you have learned how to customize WordPerfect for your way of working. Specifically, you have learned the following:

❑ How to access the Setup menu

❑ How to customize WordPerfect to work with your mouse device

❑ How to customize your display, including fonts, color, display speed, menu appearance, Reveal Codes window size, and column display

❑ How to change the environment, including backup options, beeps, cursor speed, hyphenation and units-of-measure options, and document-summary options

❑ How to customize Initial Settings, including merge-file delimiters, date format, equation options, and Initial Codes

❑ How to customize the keyboard using keyboard-definition files

❑ How to customize the directory location where WordPerfect files are stored

21

Working with Special Characters and Foreign Languages

As an independent computer consultant and WordPerfect Certified Instructor in the Boston area, **Marilyn Horn Claff** has exceptional knowledge of WordPerfect Corporation software and experience in teaching advanced applications.

This chapter examines some of the features that enable you to print special characters and to work with foreign languages in WordPerfect. You will learn how to do the following:

- Enter over 1700 special characters in your documents
- Use the two key sequences that access the Compose feature (Ctrl-2 and Ctrl-V)
- Use mnemonic key combinations for the Compose feature
- Use the language codes to simplify working with foreign languages

Reminder

If you use a mouse with WordPerfect 5.1, you can click the right button to display the pull-down menu, and then select the desired option. You also can press Alt-= to access the pull-down menus, and then press the appropriate letter of the desired option. For all instructions, assume that if a block is required to activate a pull-down menu option, the text has been blocked before the pull-down menu is accessed. Instructions for pull-down menus and the mouse are marked with the mouse icon. For more information about the mouse, see Chapter 1. ⌨

Using Special Characters

WordPerfect offers several ways to enter the special characters that are not available on a standard PC keyboard. Special characters include nonkeyboard characters in the IBM Extended Character Set and characters in the WordPerfect character set. All special characters are represented internally as WordPerfect character set codes, regardless of which method you use to enter them.

Reminder:

Although you can use WordPerfect characters anywhere in WordPerfect, remember that they take up more space than regular characters.

You can use WordPerfect characters anywhere in the WordPerfect program. You should be warned, however, that they take up more space than regular characters. For this reason, you may find that you cannot type as many WordPerfect characters as regular characters. This can become a problem when the number of characters allowed in a user response is limited, such as when you are creating style names.

If you use regular characters for a style name, you can use up to 20 characters. If you use WordPerfect characters, however, you can use a maximum of 5 characters. You can, for example, name a style *àèìòù*, but not *äëïöü* or even *àèìòùy*.

The Control-Alt key mapping used in version 4.2 was replaced in WordPerfect version 5 by the Keyboard Layout and Compose features. The Compose feature is discussed in this chapter. See Chapter 20 for a discussion of keyboard definitions; see Chapter 22 for more information on entering scientific characters in equations.

Using the IBM Extended Character Set

Every character you see on-screen is represented internally (inside the computer) by a number, called its *ASCII code*. The uppercase letter *A*, for example, is ASCII 65; uppercase *B* is ASCII 66; and lowercase *a* is ASCII 97.

The term *ASCII* is an acronym for the *American Standard Code for Information Interchange*. The original ASCII code, which consisted of 128 characters (0 through 127), was extended to 256 (128 through 255) characters when IBM introduced the IBM PC. The IBM PC's 256-character set is therefore referred to as the *IBM Extended Character Set* or the *Extended ASCII Character Set* (see table 21.1). Characters 128 through 255 are sometimes called the *upper ASCII characters*.

Table 21.1
The IBM Extended Character Set

Dec	Hex	Screen	Key	Ctrl	Dec	Hex	Screen	Key	Ctrl
0	0		^@	NUL	11	B	♂	^K	VT
1	1	☺	^A	SOH	12	C	♀	^L	FF
2	2	●	^B	STX	13	D	♪	^M	CR
3	3	♥	^C	ETX	14	E	♫	^N	SO
4	4	♦	^D	EOT	15	F	☼	^O	SI
5	5	♣	^E	ENQ	16	10	►	^P	DLE
6	6	♠	^F	ACK	17	11	◄	^Q	DC1
7	7	•	^G	BEL	18	12	↕	^R	DC2
8	8	◘	^H	BS	19	13	‼	^S	DC3
9	9	○	^I	HT	20	14	¶	^T	DC4
10	A	◙	^J	LF	21	15	§	^U	NAK

Table 21.1 (continued)

Dec	Hex	Screen	Key	Ctrl	Dec	Hex	Screen
22	16	▬	^V	SYN	73	49	I
23	17	↕	^W	ETB	74	4A	J
24	18	↑	^X	CAN	75	4B	K
25	19	↓	^Y	EM	76	4C	L
26	1A	→	^Z	SUB	77	4D	M
27	1B	←	^[	ESC	78	4E	N
28	1C	∟	^\	FS	79	4F	O
29	1D	↔	^]	GS	80	50	P
30	1E	▲	^^	RS	81	51	Q
31	1F	▼	^_	US	82	52	R
32	20	Space			83	53	S
33	21	!			84	54	T
34	22	"			85	55	U
35	23	#			86	56	V
36	24	$			87	57	W
37	25	%			88	58	X
38	26	&			89	59	Y
39	27	'			90	5A	Z
40	28	(			91	5B	[
41	29	)			92	5C	\
42	2A	*			93	5D	]
43	2B	+			94	5E	^
44	2C	,			95	5F	_
45	2D	–			96	60	`
46	2E	.			97	61	a
47	2F	/			98	62	b
48	30	0			99	63	c
49	31	1			100	64	d
50	32	2			101	65	e
51	33	3			102	66	f
52	34	4			103	67	g
53	35	5			104	68	h
54	36	6			105	69	i
55	37	7			106	6A	j
56	38	8			107	6B	k
57	39	9			108	6C	l
58	3A	:			109	6D	m
59	3B	;			110	6E	n
60	3C	<			111	6F	o
61	3D	=			112	70	p
62	3E	>			113	71	q
63	3F	?			114	72	r
64	40	@			115	73	s
65	41	A			116	74	t
66	42	B			117	75	u
67	43	C			118	76	v
68	44	D			119	77	w
69	45	E			120	78	x
70	46	F			121	79	y
71	47	G			122	7A	z
72	48	H			123	7B	{

Table 21.1 (continued)

Dec	Hex	Screen	Dec	Hex	Screen	Dec	Hex	Screen
124	7C	|	168	A8	¿	212	D4	╘
125	7D	}	169	A9	⌐	213	D5	╒
126	7E	~	170	AA	¬	214	D6	╓
127	7F	Δ	171	AB	½	215	D7	╫
128	80	Ç	172	AC	¼	216	D8	╪
129	81	ü	173	AD	¡	217	D9	╛
130	82	é	174	AE	«	218	DA	╓
131	83	â	175	AF	»	219	DB	█
132	84	ä	176	B0	░	220	DC	▄
133	85	à	177	B1	▒	221	DD	▌
134	86	å	178	B2	▓	222	DE	▐
135	87	ç	179	B3	│	223	DF	▀
136	88	ê	180	B4	┤	224	E0	∝
137	89	ë	181	B5	╡	225	E1	β
138	8A	è	182	B6	╢	226	E2	Γ
139	8B	ï	183	B7	╖	227	E3	π
140	8C	î	184	B8	╕	228	E4	Σ
141	8D	ì	185	B9	╣	229	E5	σ
142	8E	Ä	186	BA	║	230	E6	µ
143	8F	Å	187	BB	╗	231	E7	τ
144	90	É	188	BC	╝	232	E8	Φ
145	91	æ	189	BD	╜	233	E9	Θ
146	92	Æ	190	BE	╛	234	EA	Ω
147	93	ô	191	BF	┐	235	EB	δ
148	94	ö	192	C0	└	236	EC	∞
149	95	ò	193	C1	┴	237	ED	φ
150	96	û	194	C2	┬	238	EE	∈
151	97	ù	195	C3	├	239	EF	∩
152	98	ÿ	196	C4	─	240	F0	≡
153	99	Ö	197	C5	┼	241	F1	±
154	9A	Ü	198	C6	╞	242	F2	≥
155	9B	¢	199	C7	╟	243	F3	≤
156	9C	£	200	C8	╚	244	F4	⌠
157	9D	¥	201	C9	╔	245	F5	⌡
158	9E	Pt	202	CA	╩	246	F6	÷
159	9F	ƒ	203	CB	╦	247	F7	≈
160	A0	á	204	CC	╠	248	F8	°
161	A1	í	205	CD	═	249	F9	∙
162	A2	ó	206	CE	╬	250	FA	·
163	A3	ú	207	CF	╧	251	FB	√
164	A4	ñ	208	D0	╨	252	FC	ⁿ
165	A5	Ñ	209	D1	╤	253	FD	²
166	A6	ª	210	D2	╥	254	FE	▮
167	A7	º	211	D3	╙	255	FF	

The original ASCII character set includes the characters found on an English-language typewriter: upper- and lowercase letters, digits, and punctuation. The term *ASCII file* refers to a file consisting exclusively of characters from the original ASCII character set. The IBM Extended Character Set added many foreign language characters, mathematical symbols, and line-drawing characters.

Cue:
An ASCII file is a file consisting exclusively of characters from the original ASCII character set.

If you are familiar with the IBM Extended Character Set, you may prefer to enter the character by using the numeric keypad rather than map it to a key or use the Compose feature described in another section of this chapter.

Note: When you enter a special character by using its ASCII code, WordPerfect converts it to the corresponding character in the WordPerfect character set.

Reminder:
You must enter special characters by typing on the numeric keypad; you cannot use the numbers on the top row of the keyboard.

To enter a special character, first look up the number of the character you want in a chart of the IBM Extended Character Set (see table 21.1). To enter the character, hold down the Alt key, and then type the ASCII number on the numeric keypad. The corresponding character appears on-screen when you release the Alt key. You must type the numbers on the numeric keypad; you cannot use the numbers on the top row of the keyboard.

For example, to insert the character *ê*, press and hold the Alt key and type *136*. For the mathematical intersection symbol ∩, hold Alt and type *239*.

Using WordPerfect's Character Sets

To facilitate foreign language and scientific word processing, WordPerfect Corporation designed its own character sets, consisting of 1,729 characters. The characters are grouped by subject into thirteen groups numbered 0 through 12 (see table 21.2). Each WordPerfect character is identified by a two-part numeric code. The first part is the number of the character set in which the character is contained. The second part is the number of the character within that character set. As an example, the section symbol (§, or ASCII 21) is located in Character Set 4 (Typographic Symbols), and is the sixth character in the set. The WordPerfect code for the section symbol is 4,6.

Table 21.2
WordPerfect Character Sets

Name	Number	Number of Characters	Description
ASCII	0	126	ASCII space through tilde
Multinational 1	1	233	Common capitalizable multinational characters, diacriticals, and noncapitalizable multinational characters
Multinational 2	2	27	Rarely used noncapitalizable multinational characters and diacriticals

Table 21.2 (continued)

Name	Number	Number of Characters	Description
Box-drawing Characters	3	87	All 81 double/single box-drawing characters
Typographic Symbols	4	78	Common typographic symbols not found in ASCII
Iconic Symbols	5	34	Rarely used "picture" (icon) symbols
Math/Scientific	6	218	Nonextensible, nonoversized math/scientific characters not found in ASCII
Math/Scientific Extension	7	222	Extensible and oversized math/scientific characters
Greek	8	206	Full Greek character set for ancient and modern applications
Hebrew	9	43	Hebrew characters
Cyrillic	10	101	Full Cyrillic character set for ancient and modern applications
Japanese Kana	11	99	Characters for Hiragana or Katakana (the type is determined by the typeface)
User Defined	12	255	255 user-definable characters (often used for Zapf dingbats with PostScript printers)

Displaying Special Characters On-screen

Cue:

By using special display adapters, you can display up to 512 different characters.

Most video-card and monitor combinations are limited to the 256 characters available with the IBM Extended Character set. If you have a special display adapter, such as the Hercules Graphics Card Plus, you can display up to 512 different characters (the IBM Extended Character set plus 256 other characters). The additional 256 characters, taken from various WordPerfect character sets, are hard-coded into WordPerfect. You cannot choose a different set of display characters without using an add-on product.

Whenever you use a character your monitor cannot display, WordPerfect represents the character on-screen as a small solid box (■). If your printer has graphics capability and can print that character, you will be able to see the character by accessing the Print menu (Shift-F7), and then selecting **V**iew

Document (**6**). Remember that **V**iew Document shows you exactly how the document will be printed on the currently selected printer. If your printer does not have graphics capability or does not have a font that contains that character, the character will not be displayed by **V**iew Document, and a blank space will be left when you print the document.

To determine the value of a nondisplayable-character box without leaving the main editing screen, press Reveal Codes (Alt-F3 or F11) and move the cursor to the character. When the cursor is directly on a special character, its WordPerfect code is visible in brackets. Figure 21.1 illustrates how the marked ballot box character ⊠ (5,25) appears on-screen and in Reveal Codes when the cursor is positioned on the character. When the cursor is not directly over a special character, the character appears the same in Reveal Codes as it does in the normal editing screen.

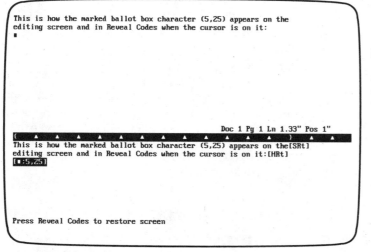

Fig. 21.1

The marked ballot box symbol displayed in Reveal Codes.

Because the characters in the WordPerfect character sets are grouped by subject, you easily can locate the character you need. Simply refer to the appropriate character chart in the Appendix of the WordPerfect manual.

Printing Special Characters

With WordPerfect 5.1, you can now print graphically any character in the WordPerfect set if your printer has graphics capability. WordPerfect will first look for the character in the current font. If the character is not found, WordPerfect looks for it in one of the substitute fonts for the current font. If the character is still not found, WordPerfect analyzes the character to see whether it can be printed as a regular character with a diacritical mark; WordPerfect will print the diacritical mark graphically if necessary. If the special character cannot be broken down this way, WordPerfect prints the entire character graphically.

Reminder:

If several characters are printed graphically, print speed will decrease.

Tip

If you need to print graphics characters, make sure that the WP.DRS file is in either your printer directory or in your WordPerfect program directory.

Setting Print Quality

The print quality for special characters created graphically is determined by the print quality setting for both text and graphics:

- If **T**ext Quality is set to **H**igh (**4**), the special characters will be printed at the high-quality setting.

- If **T**ext Quality is set to **M**edium (**2**) or **D**raft (**3**), WordPerfect uses the print-quality setting established for **G**raphics.

- If either **T**ext Quality or **G**raphics Quality is set to Do **N**ot Print, the special characters will not print.

Reminder:

CHARMAP.TST and CHARACTR.DOC provide additional information about the WordPerfect character sets.

The WordPerfect Conversion disk contains two files—CHARMAP.TST and CHARACTR.DOC—which provide additional information about the WordPerfect character sets. You can print CHARMAP.TST in each of your base fonts to see which characters your printer can print and determine which characters must be drawn graphically. You can print CHARACTR.DOC on any printer with graphics capability to obtain a complete list of each character as well as its descriptive name (see fig. 21.2 for a sample printout). CHARACTR.DOC is useful because it provides a description of each character in addition to the character number.

Entering WordPerfect Special Characters with Compose

Reminder:

The Compose feature provides two ways to enter special characters: the numeric *method and the* mnemonic *method.*

WordPerfect's Compose feature provides two ways to enter special characters: a *numeric* method and a *mnemonic* method. With the numeric method, you press Compose (Ctrl-2 or Ctrl-V), followed by a two-part character number. With the mnemonic method, you simply press Compose followed by the two component characters.

Using Ctrl-2 or Ctrl-V

Two key sequences can be used to access the Compose feature: Ctrl-2 and Ctrl-V. Ctrl-2, the primary Compose key sequence, works everywhere in the program, including the submenus and the macro editor. The alternative Compose key sequence—Ctrl-V—works in the main editing screen, but does not work in all submenus.

Sample Printout of CHARACTR.DOC

Multinational 2
Charset: 2
Contains: Rarely-used non-capitalizable multinational characters and
diacriticals.

2,0 Dot Below
2,1 Double Dot Below
2,2 Centered Ring
2,3 Ring Below
2,4 Apostrophe Accent Above Off Center
2,5 Circumflex Below
2,6 Double Underline
2,7 Macron Below (Underline)
2,8 Lowercase Greenlandic k
2,9 Half Circle Below
2,10 Vertical Tilde
2,11 Inverted Apostrophe Accent Above
2,12 Inverted Mirrored Apostrophe Accent Above
2,13 Mirrored Apostrophe Accent Below
2,14 Right Cedilla
2,15 Non-connecting Cedilla (Mirrored Ogonek)
2,16 Hook (Tail) to the Left
2,17 Hook (Tail) to the Right
2,18 Vertical Mark
2,19 Horn
2,20 Low Rising Tone Mark
2,21 Rude
2,22 Ayn
2,23 Alif/Hamzah
2,24 Upadhmaniya
2,25 Candrabindu
2,26 Mjagkij Znak
2,27 Tverdyj Znak

Fig. 21.2

A printout of the CHARACTR.DOC file.

Many users prefer Ctrl-V because it displays a prompt (Key =) on-screen to remind you that WordPerfect is waiting for you to enter a character number or mnemonic combination. If you prefer to see this prompt, use Ctrl-V rather than Ctrl-2. When the prompt Key = appears in the lower left corner of the screen, type the two characters, or enter the numeric code of a character from the WordPerfect character set.

Unlike the standard Compose key sequence (Ctrl-2), Ctrl-V is not accessible in all parts of the WordPerfect program. For example, Ctrl-V does not work in the macro editor, equation editor, or in the Document Summary screen. If Ctrl-V does not seem to work, use Ctrl-2.

Reminder:
Ctrl-V displays the prompt Key = ; Ctrl-2 does not display a prompt.

Using the Numeric Method

To enter special characters with Compose, press Compose (Ctrl-2 or Ctrl-V). Then enter the number of the WordPerfect character set, a comma (,), and the number of the character itself. No prompt is displayed on-screen, but if you enter a valid WordPerfect character code, the corresponding character (or a small box ■) will appear when you press Enter. Remember that you access Compose with the sequence Ctrl-2—not Ctrl-F2.

For example, to use the numeric method to enter the copyright © symbol (WordPerfect character set 4,23), follow these steps:

1. Press Compose (Ctrl-2).

    Access the F**o**nt menu and select **C**haracters.

2. Type *4,23* and press Enter.

Note: Not all characters will display on-screen. The mouse cannot be used to access the Compose feature in all parts of the program.

Using the Mnemonic Method

To make it easier to use special characters, WordPerfect 5.1 has built in several mnemonic shortcuts for the Compose feature. Compose enables you to enter certain characters if you can remember what they look like. If the character is a digraph (a combination of two characters) or a diacritical (a character plus a diacritical mark such as a circumflex ^), you probably can enter it with a Compose mnemonic character, without knowing its WordPerfect numeric code.

In WordPerfect 5, you would have to use the following steps to enter a special character:

1. Select Compose (Ctrl-2).
2. Enter *n1,n2.*
3. Press Enter.

   Note: n1 is the number of the WordPerfect Character Set, and *n2* is the number of the character within that set.

With WordPerfect 5.1's mnemonic method, you can press Compose and then enter the two keyboard characters that represent the character you want. WordPerfect's mnemonic combinations are often very ingenious. For example, to enter the ½ character, you press Compose, and then type */2.*

Only certain predefined pairs of characters work with Compose. The order in which you enter the characters is unimportant, but the case of the letters is sometimes important. For example, to enter the ç (cedilla c) character, you can select Compose, and then type either *c,* or *,c.*

> **Tip**
>
> When using the Compose mnemonic method, you do not need to use a comma between the two characters or press Enter afterward. This procedure *is* necessary when you use the numeric method, however.

To enter a character with a diacritical mark, press Compose (Ctrl-2 or Ctrl-V) followed by a letter and one of the characters listed in table 21.3. For example, selecting Compose and then typing *a'* produces à; selecting Compose and then typing *a'* produces á.

Table 21.3 lists the mnemonic characters for entering diacritical marks; table 21.4 lists the mnemonic characters for entering other special characters. Refer to these lists when using the Compose mnemonic method.

Table 21.3
WordPerfect Mnemonic Characters for Diacritical Marks

Mnemonic Character	Description	Examples
´	Acute accent	á Á é É í Í ó Ó ú Ú ŕ Ŕ
`	Grave accent	à À è È ì Ì ò Ò ù Ù Ỳ ỳ ř Ř
v	Caron (hachek)	č Č ď Ď ě Ě ǧ Ǧ Ǐ Ľ ň Ň ř Ř š Š ť Ť
,	Cedilla	ç Ç ş Ş ţ Ţ ķ Ķ
;	Ogonek (Polish hook)	ą Ą ę Ę į Į ų Ų
:	Centered dot	ŀ Ŀ
^	Circumflex	â ê î ô ŷ
-	Crossbar	đ Đ ŧ Ŧ ħ Ħ
.	Dot above	ė Ė ı İ
_	Macron (overbar)	ā Ā ē Ē ī Ī ō Ō ū Ū
/	Slash	ø Ø
\	Stroke	ł Ł
~	Tilde	ñ Ñ ã Ã ĩ Ĩ õ Õ ũ Ũ
"	Umlaut or diaeresis	ä Ä ë Ë ï Ï ö Ö ü Ü ÿ Ÿ
@	Circle above	å Å ů Ů
o	Circle above	å

Table 21.4
Other WordPerfect Mnemonic Characters

Mnemonic Character	Displayed Result	Description	Numeric Codes
Bullets			
*.	•	Small filled bullet	[4,3]
**	●	Medium filled bullet	[4,0]
*o	∘	Small hollow bullet	[4,45]
*O	○	Large hollow bullet	[4,1]
Fractions			
/2	½	One-half symbol	[4,17]
/4	¼	One-quarter symbol	[4,18]

Table 21.4 (continued)

Digraphs

Mnemonic Character	Displayed Result	Description	Numeric Codes
ss	ß	German double s	[1,23] (lowercase only)
AE	Æ	AE Digraph	[1,36]
ae	æ	ae Digraph	[1,37]
IJ	IJ	IJ Digraph	[1,138]
ij	ij	ij Digraph	[1,139] (Displays on-screen as y diaeresis [1,75] but is in fact a different character)
OE	Œ	OE Digraph	[1,166]
oe	œ	oe Digraph	[1,167]

Typographic Characters

Mnemonic Character	Displayed Result	Description	Numeric Codes
!!	¡	Inverted exclamation mark	[4,7]
??	¿	Inverted question mark	[4,8]
<<	«	Left double guillemet	[4,9]
>>	»	Right double guillemet	[4,10]
a=	ª	Feminine Spanish ordinal	[4,15]
o=	º	Masculine Spanish ordinal	[4,16]
n-	–	En dash	[4,33] (lowercase)
m-	—	Em dash	[4,34] (lowercase)
--	—	Em dash	[4,34]

Currency

Mnemonic Character	Displayed Result	Description	Numeric Codes	
L-	£	Pound/Sterling	[4,11]	(uppercase L)
Y=	¥	Yen	[4,12]	(uppercase Y)
Pt	₧	Pesetas	[4,13]	(uppercase P, lowercase t)
f-	ƒ	Florin/Guilders	[4,14]	(lowercase f)
c/	¢	Cents symbol	[4,19]	(lowercase c)
xo	¤	Currency symbol	[4,24]	(lowercase)

Table 21.4 (continued)

Mnemonic Character	Displayed Result	Description	Numeric Codes	
Legal Characters				
P|	¶	Paragraph symbol	[4,5]	(uppercase)
RO	®	Registered mark	[4,22]	(upper- or lowercase)
CO	©	Copyright symbol	[4,23]	(upper- or lowercase)
TM	™	Trademark symbol	[4,41]	(upper- or lowercase)
SM	℠	Servicemark symbol	[4,42]	(uppercase only)
Rx	℞	Prescription	[4,43]	(RX or Rx, but *not* rx)

Math/Scientific Characters

Mnemonic Character	Displayed Result	Description	Numeric Codes
+-	±	Plus or minus symbol	[6,1]
<=	≤	Less than or equal to	[6,2]
>=	≥	Greater than or equal to	[6,3]
~~	≈	Approximately equal	[6,13]
==	≡	Equivalent	[6,14]
/=	≠	Not equal symbol	[6,99]

Caution

The mnemonic characters are built into WordPerfect 5.1; you cannot use just any pair of letters, even if they look like they *should* work.

Creating Special Characters with Overstrike

Overstrike is another technique for creating special characters. You can overstrike up to 30 different characters. Overstrike sequences are treated as one indivisible character.

Attributes on the Font (Ctrl-F8) **S**ize and **A**ppearance menus, such as superscript and subscript characters, as well as bold and underline, can be included in the overstrike sequence.

As with previous versions of WordPerfect, the last character of the overstrike sequence is the one displayed on-screen. All the overstruck characters are visible

Reminder:

Only the last character of the overstrike sequence is displayed on-screen, but all overstruck characters are visible in Reveal Codes (Alt-F3 or F11).

in Reveal Codes (Alt-F3 or F11). In the example that follows, Reveal Codes shows that the WP "dot below" diacritical (2,0) is overstruck with the letter *n* to create the ṇ.

The "dot below" character is subscripted and boldfaced to make it more pronounced:

[Ovrstk:[SUBSCPT][BOLD]█[bold][subscpt]n]

Tip

Whenever possible, use the code from the WordPerfect character set rather than creating the code with the overstrike method. The character-set codes are more portable between printer drivers and do not interfere with spell checking (as do the overstrike characters). With a choice of over 1700 special characters and the strikeout attribute on the Font (Ctrl-F8) **A**ppearance menu, you probably will not need to use overstrike very often.

To create an overstrike sequence, you access the Format menu (Shift-F8), select **O**ther (**4**), select **O**verstrike (**5**), and then type the characters.

For example, to overstrike the letter *r* with a macron (overbar), follow these steps:

1. Press Format (Shift-F8), select **O**ther (**4**), and then select **O**verstrike (**5**).

   ⌨ Access the **L**ayout menu, select **O**ther, and then select **O**verstrike.

2. Select **C**reate (**1**).

   The prompt [Ovrstk] appears.

3. At the prompt [Ovrstk], press Compose (Ctrl-2), type *1,8* and press Enter; type *r* and press Enter. Then press Exit (F7) to return to the document.

   The overstrike character will appear on-screen as r because r is the last character in the overstrike sequence.

WordPerfect 5.1's Overstrike feature is powerful and well-designed. Overstruck characters act like a single character in every respect. You cannot inadvertently delete part of an overstrike sequence (as you could in WordPerfect 4.2). Separate menu choices for creating and editing overstrike characters and the 30-character limit make Overstrike convenient and flexible.

Tip

To save keystrokes, create a macro for special characters and overstrike combinations that you use frequently, or assign them to a keyboard layout. See Chapter 11 for more information on macros; see Chapter 20 for more information on the keyboard definitions.

Changing Fonts

With many word processing programs, you need to change fonts to access special characters. In WordPerfect, font changes are intended to change typeface or font size. Changing to another font to access a particular character should not be necessary if your printer is defined correctly.

When you use a character that is not available in your current font, WordPerfect's printer drivers look for that character in your other fonts. If the character is not available in another font, WordPerfect prints it graphically if your printer has graphics capability.

Working with Foreign Languages

WordPerfect's support for foreign languages and multilingual documents is surprisingly good for a mainstream word processor. If you work primarily in a language other than English, consider purchasing WordPerfect in that language version so that the on-screen prompts and documentation are in the language you are using.

Using Foreign Language Dictionaries and Thesauri

If you write primarily in English but often work with multilingual documents, you can purchase foreign language dictionaries, thesauri, and hyphenation files that work with the English version of WordPerfect. The Canadian versions, for example, are shipped with a United Kingdom English dictionary and a Canadian French dictionary. The documentation and screen prompts are in English or French, depending on the version.

For more information on the foreign language versions of WordPerfect and their available features, call WordPerfect Corporation's International Division for pricing and availability (801-222-4222).

> **Tip**
>
> If you have prepared a word list in WordPerfect or ASCII format, you can make your own foreign language dictionary by using the SPELL.EXE utility shipped with WordPerfect. For more information, see Chapter 7.

To use multiple dictionaries and thesauri with WordPerfect, you first copy all files on the distribution Speller and Thesaurus disks to the Thesaurus/Spell/Hyphenation (Main) directory. You must tell WordPerfect the name of this directory in Setup (see Chapter 20 and Chapter 7).

> **Tip**
>
> Although you can store the dictionary and thesaurus files in the WordPerfect program directory, keeping them in a separate directory is recommended, especially if you are working with more than one language. To make backing up easier, you also can keep supplementary dictionary files in a separate directory.

Each dictionary and thesaurus file name contains a two-letter language code for the corresponding language. For example, the U.S. English dictionary is named WP{WP}*US*.LEX, and the Spanish dictionary is named WP{WP}*ES*.LEX. Similarly, the U.S. English thesaurus is named WP{WP}*US*.THS, and the Spanish thesaurus is named WP{WP}*ES*.THS (see fig. 21.3). Some languages also have a hyphenation file, such as WP{WP}*US*.HYC for U.S. English.

Fig. 21.3

WordPerfect's Spanish thesaurus.

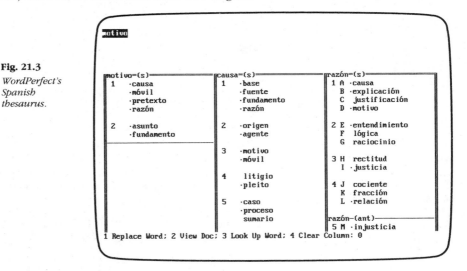

In addition to dictionary, thesaurus, and hyphenation files for specific languages, you should have a file called WP{WP}.SPW or WP{WP}.SPR. Which file you have depends on the specific language version of WordPerfect. SPW stands for "Spell By Word" (lookup), and SPR stands for "Spell By Rule" (algorithm). The U.S English version ships with the WP{WP}.SPW file.

Entering WordPerfect Language Codes

The key to WordPerfect's excellent foreign language support is the Language (4) code, tucked away on the Format (Shift-F8) Other menu. The language code determines which dictionary, thesaurus, and hyphenation files WordPerfect uses, how the date is formatted, what order WordPerfect uses for sorting, and what message WordPerfect prints if footnotes continue on another page. All these features are controlled automatically.

WordPerfect refers to the built-in language as the *package language*. If you have the U.S. version of WordPerfect, your package language is *US*; if you have the Italian version of WordPerfect, your package language is *IT*.

You can change languages by inserting language codes in the document as many times as you want. Each time you insert a language code, it stays in effect until WordPerfect encounters another language code.

Using language codes make it possible to switch languages in the middle of a document. When you spell-check a document that is part German and part Swedish, for example, WordPerfect will automatically use the German dictionary to spell-check the German sections and the Swedish dictionary to spell-check the Swedish sections, if you have the corresponding dictionaries. If you do not have the correct dictionary, WordPerfect displays the following message at the bottom of the screen:

WP{WP}SV.LEX not found: 1 Enter **P**ath; **2 S**kip Language; **3 E**xit Spell: **3**

Select **1** to enter the DOS **P**ath for the missing dictionary; select **2** to **S**kip that language (WordPerfect resumes the spell check at the next language code); or select **3** to stop the spell check and **E**xit the spell feature.

If you add words to the dictionary during the spell check, WordPerfect adds them to the appropriate supplementary dictionary, creating it if it does not already exist.

You can enter language codes anywhere in the document. If you enter a language code in Setup Initial Codes, that language will be the default language for all new documents. You also can enter language codes in Document Initial Codes, at any point in the document itself, or in Style definitions.

To enter a Language code, follow these steps (see fig. 21.4):

1. Press **F**ormat (Shift-F8). Select **O**ther (**4**) and then select **L**anguage (**4**).

   ▭ Access the **L**ayout menu, select **O**ther, and then select **L**anguage.

   WordPerfect displays the language code currently in effect (in fig. 21.4, the language is French [FR]).

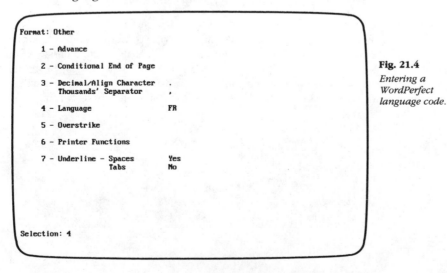

```
Format: Other

    1 - Advance

    2 - Conditional End of Page

    3 - Decimal/Align Character    .
        Thousands' Separator       ,

    4 - Language                   FR

    5 - Overstrike

    6 - Printer Functions

    7 - Underline - Spaces         Yes
                     Tabs          No




Selection: 4
```

Fig. 21.4

Entering a WordPerfect language code.

2. Type the two-letter code for the language you want, press Enter, and then press Exit (F7) to return to the document.

In Reveal Codes, the language code for French appears as **[Lang:FR]**.

Table 21.5 lists the language codes officially supported by WordPerfect.

Table 21.5
WordPerfect Language Codes

Language	Code	Language	Code
Catalan	CA	German (Switzerland)	GR
Czechoslovakian	CZ	Greek	GK
Danish	DK	Icelandic	IS
Dutch	NL	Italian	IT
English (Australia)	OZ	Norwegian	NO
English (U.K.)	UK	Portugese (Brazil)	PB
English (U.S.)	US	Portugese (Portugal)	PO
Finnish	SU	Russian	RU
French (Canada)	CF	Spanish	ES
French (France)	FR	Swedish	SV
German (Germany)	DE		

Using the Language Resource File (WP.LRS)

WordPerfect includes a special file, WP.LRS, that contains information about foreign language support in WordPerfect. The WP.LRS file is in WordPerfect *notebook* format. Notebook files are simply WordPerfect secondary-merge files that have a special record containing information used by the Notebook program. Notebook is available as part of WP Office or WP Office PC (formerly called WP Library).

If you work with a language for which no language code or definition is available, you can edit the WP.LRS file in either Notebook or in WordPerfect to create your own settings. Just add a new record to the WP.LRS file with the appropriate information (names and abbreviations for the months and the days of the week, how you want the date to be formatted, and the text for the footnote continuation messages).

> **Tip**
>
> WordPerfect always uses the message Footnote continued for the package language, unless a different language code is established in Document Initial Codes. All Footnote continued messages in a document are printed in the same language.

Summary

WordPerfect's support for special characters and foreign languages is truly exceptional for a mainstream word processor. Because WordPerfect has the capability to print any of the characters in its 1700-character WordPerfect character set on printers with graphics capability, documents with special characters print correctly on a wide variety of printers. By using WordPerfect instead of a special-purpose program for foreign language word processing, you can take advantage of WordPerfect's strong word processing features (often missing in special foreign language programs) and avoid the problems of file incompatibility (the bane of special-purpose programs). If you work with special characters and foreign languages, the features described in this chapter should make your work easier.

In this chapter, you learned how to do the following:

- ❏ Enter special characters into a document
- ❏ Print special characters on printers with graphics capability
- ❏ Use the Overstrike feature
- ❏ Work with multilingual documents

You also learned many mnemonic shortcuts for commonly used characters, the difference between the two Compose key sequences (Ctrl-2 and Ctrl-V), and the purpose of the Language Resource File (WP{WP}.LRS).

22

Creating Equations

Professor William J. Palm, Department of Mechanical Engineering, The University of Rhode Island, is the author of two engineering textbooks. Professor Palm has been using WordPerfect to create technical documents since 1984.

The equation editor, a feature new with WordPerfect 5.1, promises to make WordPerfect a major contender in the technical word processing market. The equation editor is easy to use, yet powerful enough to create mathematical expressions with very complex structures using a large variety of symbols.

The equation editor automatically positions, sizes, and aligns the elements in mathematical expressions, such as complex ratios, built-up fractions, and multilevel subscripts and/or superscripts. As a result, the equation editor is most useful for documents that contain such expressions.

The equation editor has its own screen, editing features, and command syntax. Each equation occupies its own graphics box, which can be aligned, sized, and placed in the document just as any other graphics box. The equation editor creates the equation file that forms the contents of the box. With the equation editor, managing equations in a document is similar to managing figures.

In this chapter, you will learn how to use the equation editor to create mathematical expressions. Equations can be printed as graphics characters that are automatically generated by WordPerfect or by using the printer's fonts. A major feature new with WordPerfect 5.1 is that it can print as graphics any characters missing from the printer's font, if the printer is capable of printing graphics. With WordPerfect 5.1, you can create equations that use virtually any character or mathematical symbol.

Using the Equation Editor

You can create equations in WordPerfect in two ways: you can use the equation editor, or you can use WordPerfect's normal text editor. In the text editor, you can use WordPerfect's formatting and positioning features and WordPerfect's character set. This can be a tedious process, however, especially if your document contains complicated mathematical expressions.

Using the equation editor to create equations has several advantages. You can, for example, print characters and symbols that are not included in the printer's font. Also, you can easily create complex equations like the ones described in this chapter.

> ### Reminder
>
> While using the equation editor, the pull-down menu is disabled, but the mouse remains active. You can use the mouse to select any of the equation editor's options by moving the mouse pointer to the option and clicking once.

Starting the Equation Editor

To start the equation editor, perform the following steps:

1. Press Graphics (Alt-F9), select **E**quation (**6**), and then select **C**reate (**1**).

   Access the **G**raphics pull-down menu, select **E**quation, and then select **C**reate (see fig. 22.1).

   WordPerfect displays the Definition: Equation menu (see fig. 22.2).

2. Select **E**dit (**9**). WordPerfect then displays the equation editor (see fig. 22.3).

Fig. 22.1

Accessing the Equation Editor from the Graphics pull-down menu.

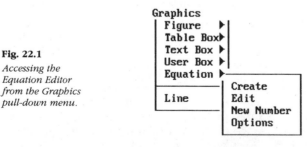

```
Graphics
   Figure      ►
   Table Box►
   Text Box  ►
   User Box  ►
   Equation  ►
                  Create
   Line           Edit
                  New Number
                  Options
```

The equation editor is displayed any time you select **E**dit for a graphics box whose contents are listed as `Equation`. (For more information on creating and using graphics boxes, see the section "Positioning and Sizing Equations," and Chapter 27.)

The equation editor screen consists of the following three windows (see fig. 22.3):

- The Editing Window
- The Equation Palette
- The Display Window

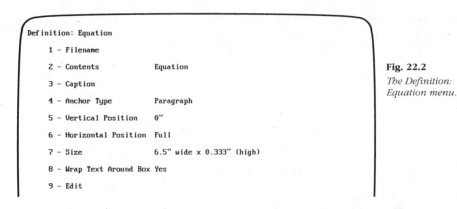

Definition: Equation

1 - Filename

2 - Contents   Equation

3 - Caption

4 - Anchor Type   Paragraph

5 - Vertical Position 0"

6 - Horizontal Position Full

7 - Size   6.5" wide x 0.333" (high)

8 - Wrap Text Around Box Yes

9 - Edit

Fig. 22.2
The Definition: Equation menu.

Examining the Editing and Display Windows

Figure 22.3 shows the screen presented by the equation editor when first accessed. The Editing Window and the Display Window are blank when first displayed. The Equation Palette, to the right of the screen, displays the default Commands menu. At the bottom of the screen is a line of prompts for using the Screen key (Ctrl-F3), the List key (F5), the Switch key (Shift-F3), and the Setup key (Shift-F1). ⌨ You can also select the functions by moving the mouse pointer to the option and clicking the mouse button. The functions of these keys will be treated in another section of this chapter.

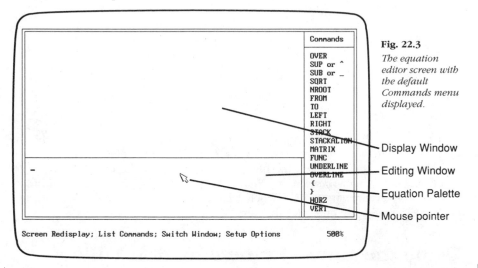

Fig. 22.3
The equation editor screen with the default Commands menu displayed.

Commands

OVER
SUP or ^
SUB or _
SQRT
NROOT
FROM
TO
LEFT
RIGHT
STACK
STACKALIGN
MATRIX — Display Window
FUNC
UNDERLINE — Editing Window
OVERLINE
{ — Equation Palette
}
HORZ
VERT — Mouse pointer

Screen Redisplay; List Commands; Switch Window; Setup Options   500%

You can create entries by typing from the keyboard. Your entries appear in the Editing Window, which is used to develop the equation with WordPerfect's equation commands and symbols. You can also enter commands and symbols into the Editing Window by selecting them from the Equation Palette. The resulting equation appears in the Display Window (the top window) when you press Screen (Ctrl-F3). You must have a graphics card to display the equation in the Display Window.

Reminder:
You must have a graphics card to display the equation in the Display Window.

You cannot edit the equation in the Display Window; you must perform all editing in the Editing Window. The Editing Window is active when a double bar appears at its right side (see fig. 22.3).

The Editing Window becomes active when you are in any of the following situations:

- You start the equation editor.
- You select an item from the Equation Palette.
- You use the Switch key (Shift-F3) to leave the Display Window.

These options are explained in later sections.

Examining the Equation Palette

Reminder:

Press List (F5) to access the Equation Palette.

You access the Equation Palette by pressing List (F5). The name of the menu appears at the top of the Palette, and a reverse-video highlighted bar appears. (The default menu is Commands.) You can move the bar up or down by using the arrow keys. Not all items on the Commands and Functions menu are always visible; you can scroll to the bottom of the list by using the down-arrow key.

The Palette contains eight menus; the default Commands menu is shown in figure 22.3. The following menus are available with the Palette:

- Commands (the default menu)
- Large
- Symbols
- Greek
- Arrows
- Sets
- Other
- Functions

Reminder:

Use the arrow keys to select individual items in the Equation Palette. Use PgUp and PgDn to select the menus.

You can scroll these menus up or down by pressing PgUp or PgDn while the Equation Palette is active. If the first menu is on-screen, the eighth menu appears when you press PgUp. When the highlighted bar is over the desired item, press Enter. The item then appears in the Editing Window at the current cursor position. When you select an item from the Palettes menus, the equation editor automatically inserts a space before and after the item.

Using the Mouse in the Equation Editor

You can use the mouse in the equation editor to select items from the equation editor's menus and the Equation Palette. For example, instead of pressing the Screen key (Ctrl-F3) to display an equation, you can move the mouse pointer to Screen in the menu at the bottom of the equation editor screen, and then click the left mouse button.

To access the Equation Palette with the mouse, click `List` at the menu at the bottom of the equation editor. To scroll through the Palette's menus, click `PgUp` or `PgDn` at the bottom right of the screen.

When you are in the Equation Palette, you can select an item by placing the mouse cursor over the item and double-clicking the left button. This sequence is equivalent to moving the normal cursor to the desired item with the arrow keys and then pressing Enter.

Reminder:

To access the Equation Palette with the mouse, click `List` *on the menu found at the bottom of the equation editor.*

Creating an Equation in the Editing Window

The following examples illustrate the use of the equation editor. To create the simple equation ax + b = y, follow these steps:

1. Access the equation editor by pressing Graphics (Alt-F9), selecting **E**quation (**6**), and then selecting **C**reate (**1**).

   Access the **G**raphics pull-down menu, select **E**quation, and then select **C**reate.

   The Definition: Equation menu is displayed.

2. Press **E**dit (**9**) to start the equation editor. The Editing Window will be active, and the Commands menu will be displayed in the Equation Palette.

3. Type the following:

   ax~+~b~=~y

3. Press Screen (Ctrl-F3) to see the equation in the Display Window (see fig. 22.4, but note that it includes variations on this equation, explained later).

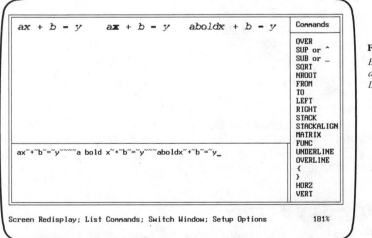

Fig. 22.4

Equations displayed in the Display Window.

Note: Pressing the space bar in the Editing Window does *not* insert a space into the equation. The space only enhances the readability of the text in the Editing Window or separates the equation-attribute commands from other elements.

The ~ (tilde) is the equation editor's symbol for a space that will appear in the printed equation. The ~ symbol will not be printed.

In the next example, which uses the BOLD command, the space bar is used to create nonprinting spaces before and after the BOLD command. These spaces are used to separate the BOLD command from the other elements in the line.

You can make the *x* in the preceding equation bold by typing the following:

a bold x~+~b~=~y

If you omit the spaces, however, and type *aboldx~+~b~=~y*, the equation editor will interpret the string *aboldx* as a six-letter variable with no bolding implied (see fig. 22.4).

Reminder:

Typing the tilde (~) in the Editing Window inserts a space into the printed equation; pressing the space bar inserts a nonprinting space in the Editing Window for readability and syntax purposes only.

The equation editor uses two types of normal-width spaces. To include in the printed equation a required space of normal width, you must create the space in the equation editor by typing the tilde (~) from the keyboard, or by selecting ~ from the Commands menu in the Equation Palette. The space created by the tilde will also appear in the equation in the Display Window.

The second type of normal-width space does not affect the printed equation or the equation in the Display Window. You create this type of space by pressing the space bar. You press the space bar in the Editing Window for readability and syntax purposes only.

The BOLD command tells WordPerfect to print in bold the variable that follows the command. If you prefer not to type the BOLD command, you can insert it into the equation by using the arrow keys to select BOLD on the Commands menu and then pressing Enter. When you do this, the equation editor automatically inserts a nonprinting space before and after the BOLD command.

Cue:

WordPerfect expands the equation in the Display Window, using characters as large as will fit in the window.

WordPerfect expands the equation in the Display Window using characters as large as will fit in the window. The percentage of increase is shown at the lower right corner of the screen (181% in fig. 22.4). The default percentage is 500%. See the section, "Altering the Equation Display," for more information.

Just as pressing the space bar inserts a nonprinting space, pressing Enter while in the Editing Window inserts a nonprinting hard return. The hard return moves the cursor to the next line in the Editing Window but does not affect the printed equation. You cannot create equations that consist of multiple lines by pressing Enter in the Editing Window, but you can use the STACK or STACKALIGN commands to create multiline expressions. See the section, "Creating Multiline Expressions with STACK and STACKALIGN," for more information.

Reviewing Key Terms

Reminder:

WordPerfect's Bold (F6) and Underline (F8) keys have no effect in the Equation Editor.

To help you understand the process of creating equations in the equation editor, the following is a review of special terms.

A *keyword* is an alphabetic description of a command, a symbol, or a Greek letter. For example, *bold* is the keyword for the BOLD command, *underline* is the keyword for the UNDERLINE command, and *beta* is the keyword for the lowercase

Greek letter beta (ß). WordPerfect's Bold (F6) and Underline (F8) keys have no effect in the equation editor.

A *symbol* is any item that is neither a number nor a character from the Latin alphabet. Examples of symbols include arrows, brackets, and Greek letters. Symbols are found on the keyboard, in the WordPerfect character set, and in six of the Palette's eight menus: Arrows, Greek, Large, Other, Sets, and Symbols.

A *variable* refers to any group of alphabetic characters or numbers that begins with an alphabetic character, and that the equation editor does not recognize as a reserved keyword. A variable must be followed by a nonalphabetic character (such as a symbol, a space, or Enter). Examples of variables include *a*, *x*, *x1*, and *A2a*.

Reminder:
A variable must be followed by a nonalphabetic character.

A *number* is any nonnegative integer (such as 0, 1, 2, or 4369) that is followed by a noninteger (such as a symbol, a space, a period, or an alphabetic character). *Real* numbers (negative numbers or numbers that have decimal parts) are treated as separate alphabetic, numeral, or operator parts by the equation editor. See the section, "Creating Subscripts and Superscripts," for an example of how real numbers can be handled in equations.

A *command* is a word with a reserved meaning to the equation editor. A command has some formatting function, such as printing a symbol in bold, underlining a symbol, or enclosing an expression with a square root symbol. Each command also has a specific syntax which governs its use. In this chapter, any specific command syntax is discussed when the individual command is explained.

A *function* is a set of alphabetic characters recognized by the equation editor as a standard mathematical function name such as *sin*, *cos*, *tan*, and *log*.

Later sections of this chapter will treat these terms in more detail.

Using Commands in the Editing Window

Table 22.1 lists the commands available with the Commands menu. Several of these commands will be described in more detail in later sections of the chapter.

Table 22.1
The Commands Menu

Command Keyword	Description	Command Keyword	Description
OVER	Fraction	RIGHT	Right delimiter
SUP or ^	Superscript	STACK	Vertical stack
SUB or _	Subscript	STACKALIGN	Vertical stack with character alignment
SQRT	Square Root		
NROOT	Nth root		
FROM	Limits	MATRIX	Matrix
TO	Limits	FUNC	User-defined function
LEFT	Left delimiter		

Table 22.1 (continued)

Command Keyword	Description	Command Keyword	Description
UNDERLINE	Underline	#	Row separator
OVERLINE	Overline	MATFORM	Matrix column format
{	Start group	ALIGNL	Align left
}	End group	ALIGNR	Align right
HORZ	Horizontal move	ALIGNC	Align center
VERT	Vertical move	PHANTOM	Place holder
~	Normal space	.	No delimiter
`	Thin space (1/4 of normal space)	\	Literal
		BOLD	Bold attribute
BINOM	Binomial	ITAL	Italic attribute
&	Column separator	OVERSM	Fraction small
		BINOMSM	Binomial small

Several rules govern the use of commands:

- All commands can be typed in uppercase or lowercase letters, or any combination of cases.
- A command must be separated from any variable that comes before and after the command. You can separate a command from a variable by typing a space, pressing Enter, or entering a symbol.
- When you select a command from the Equation Palette and press Enter, the equation editor automatically puts a space before and after the command, and then displays the command in uppercase letters.
- Commands act only on the single item following the command, unless braces { } are used to group an expression as discussed in the next section, "Understanding Precedence in the equation editor."

Understanding Precedence in the Equation Editor

The equation editor does not perform mathematical calculations. Rather, it uses a set of rules to format your entries for printing. These rules include commands such as BOLD and ITAL, as well as rules for positioning, sizing, alignment, and grouping.

To perform formatting operations on your entries, the equation editor uses its own priority list—the *order of precedence*. The equation editor performs operations on your entries in the following order:

1. Groups denoted by braces { }
2. Diacritical marks

3. Primes (', "), SUB, SUP, FROM, and TO

4. Roots

5. OVER and BINOM

6. Other elements in order from left to right

When the equation editor formats your entries, it first looks at the group within the innermost pair of braces, and then performs the commands specified within those braces. The equation editor then looks at the second innermost pair of braces and performs the commands contained within them, and so on. Within each group, the equation editor first attaches any diacritical marks (precedence level 2). Then it attaches primes and performs the SUB, SUP, FROM, and TO commands (precedence level 3), and so on for precedence levels 3 through 6.

You can override this priority list by creating groups using braces { }. The equation editor treats a + b, for example, as three elements, but treats {a + b} as a single group. Any commands that appear within braces are evaluated before commands that appear outside braces. When inner and outer braces are used, priority is given to the group within the inner braces. The generous use of braces prevents syntax errors. Remember to use braces in pairs when forming groups.

Reminder:
Use braces generously and in pairs to prevent syntax errors.

Altering the Equation Display

As you type more characters in the Editing Window and then display the equation, the equation editor normally displays the entire equation in the Display Window. To do this, WordPerfect must reduce the size of the screen font. As a result, the equation can become difficult to read. To avoid this problem, the equation editor enables you to change the way the equation is displayed in the Display Window.

To alter the displayed equation, press Switch (Shift-F3) while in the Editing Window. This displays the equation and moves you to the Display Window. You cannot use the cursor in the Editing Window while you are in the Display Window. You can tell that you are in the Display Window if a double line appears at the right of the window.

When you are in the Display Window, you can use the arrow keys to reposition the equation: left, right, up, or down. You also can use the PgUp and PgDn keys to enlarge or reduce the view of the equation. The editor normally displays the equation in a size five times larger than the equation's printed size. This is indicated by the 500% displayed in the lower right corner of the screen. When you use the PgUp or PgDn keys, this percentage indicator changes accordingly. To eliminate any changes made with the arrow, PgUp, or PgDn keys, press GoTo (Ctrl-Home) before leaving the Display Window.

Reminder:
Moving or resizing the equation in the Display Window by using the PgUp, PgDn, or arrow keys affects only the view of the equation in the Display Window— not the printed output.

Moving or resizing the equation in the Display Window with the PgUp, PgDn, or arrow keys do not affect the appearance of the equation when printed. Moving and resizing operations only affect the view of the equation in the Display Window.

To leave the Display Window and return to the Equation Editor, press Switch (Shift-F3) again, or press Exit (F7).

Entering Keyboard Characters

You can enter numbers, letters, and certain characters in the Editing Window by pressing the appropriate keys. The following characters, which are not available in the Equation Palette, must be entered directly from the keyboard:

    + – * / = < > ! . | @ , ; :

You also can enter certain other keyboard characters, as well as pairs of keyboard characters. These characters, however, have special meanings to the equation editor. Individual characters with special meanings to the equation editor include the following:

    ' " { } ( )

Pairs of characters with special meanings to the equation editor include the following:

    +– –+ –> <= >=

The meanings of these special characters and pairs of characters are described in later sections.

You also can enter characters by using the Equation keyboard, which is discussed in the next section, or by using the Equation Palette.

Tip

While in the equation editor, you can access any character in the WordPerfect character set by using the Compose feature. Press Ctrl-2, enter the number of the WordPerfect character set, a comma, the character number, and then press Enter. (For more information on Compose and the WordPerfect character set, see Chapter 21.)

Using the Equation Keyboard

Reminder:

The Equation keyboard provides the easiest way to enter symbols.

WordPerfect includes a special keyboard definition—the Equation keyboard—that is useful for typing some of the more common mathematical symbols, Greek letters, and formatting commands while you are in the equation editor.

The layout of the Equation keyboard assigns commonly used mathematical and scientific characters to keys on your keyboard. These key assignments are given in Appendix H of the WordPerfect Reference Manual.

To select the WordPerfect Equation keyboard, you must be in the normal text editor. Then follow these steps:

1. Press Setup (Shift-F1), select **I**nitial Settings (**4**), select **E**quations (**3**), and then select **K**eyboard for Editing (**5**.)

2. Select Equation from the list of choices.

   The WordPerfect Equation keyboard will then automatically be the active keyboard whenever you are in the equation editor.

When the WordPerfect Equation keyboard is the active keyboard, you use the Alt and Ctrl keys to enter commands and symbols. For example, pressing Alt-a inserts the lowercase Greek letter alpha (α) into the equation. Pressing Ctrl-z inserts the subscript command. If you frequently use characters or commands that are not found on the default Equation keyboard, you can edit the keyboard definition to create your own equation keyboard (see Chapter 20).

Using the Editing Keys

The equation will not display in the Display Window if there is a syntax error in the text in the Editing Window. When WordPerfect detects a syntax error, the message `Incorrect Format` appears, and the cursor returns to the place where the error occurs.

To correct typing errors, a subset of WordPerfect's editing features is available in the equation editor. The Backspace and Delete keys can be used to delete a character; Ctrl-End deletes from the cursor to the end of the line; and Ctrl-PgDn deletes in the Editing Window all the remaining text that follows the cursor position. You can use the arrow, End, and Home keys to move the cursor in the Editing Window just as in the normal WordPerfect text editor. WordPerfect's Block (Alt-F4) and Move (Ctrl-F4) features, however, are not available in the equation editor.

After making changes in the Editing Window, you can see the effects on the equation by pressing Screen (Ctrl-F3) to refresh the Display Window. When the equation is satisfactory, press Exit (F7) when in the Editing Window to terminate the editing process and return to the normal text editor. Pressing Cancel (F1) and then selecting **Y** (for Yes) while in the equation editor cancels any changes made to the equation and returns you to the Definition: Equation screen.

Using Functions in the Equation Editor

Table 22.2 describes the functions available from the Functions menu on the Equation Palette.

Table 22.2
Functions Menu

Keyword	Description	Keyword	Description
cos	Cosine	tanh	Hyperbolic tangent
sin	Sine		
tan	Tangent	cot	Cotangent
arccos	Arc cosine	coth	Hyperbolic cotangent
arcsin	Arc sine		
arctan	Arc tangent	sec	Secant
cosh	Hyberbolic cosine	cosec	Cosecant
sinh	Hyperbolic sine	exp	Exponent

Table 22.2 (continued)			
Keyword	*Description*	*Keyword*	*Description*
log	Logarithm	max	Maximum
ln	Natural logarithm	gcd	Greatest common denominator
lim	Limit		
liminf	Limit inferior	arc	Arc function
limsup	Limit superior	det	Determinant
min	Minimum	mod	Modulo

Several rules apply to the use of functions in the equation editor:

Reminder:

When you use braces before or after a command, you do not need to use spaces before or after the command to separate the command from variables.

- A function must be separated from any variable that comes before and after the function. You can separate the function from the variable by entering a space, pressing Enter, or entering a symbol such as a brace.
- When you enter a function from the Equation Palette, the equation editor automatically puts a space before and after the function, and then displays the function in lowercase. Functions retain the case you type them in, but normal mathematical practice is to type functions in lowercase.

Caution

In this book's conventions, italic type signifies material that you are to type. Do not confuse this use of italic type with the method in which the equation editor italicizes all alphabetic characters and treats them as variables.

The equation editor automatically treats all alphabetic characters (except Greek letters) as variables and italicizes them. The exceptions to this rule are the reserved commands such as BOLD and the functions contained in the Equation Palette. Functions are automatically formatted in the base (nonitalic) font.

Reminder:

Include the reverse-accent key (`) to insert the thin space before and after functions.

In mathematical typesetting, functions are often separated from variables by a thin space. In the equation editor, you can insert a thin space by pressing the reverse-accent key (`). A thin space is 1/4 of a normal space. The normal space is represented by the tilde (~).

The Display Window in figure 22.5, which shows the Functions menu as the active menu in the Equation Palette, shows three expressions that use functions. To produce the first expression in figure 22.5, you type the following:

A `tan `theta~+~B

The equation editor recognizes *tan* as a function and *theta* as the keyword for the Greek letter. Several variations will produce the same expression. You can use the space bar to separate characters in the Editing Window. You can include the Greek letter theta by selecting it from the Greek menu in the Palette, by using the Compose feature, or by using the Equation keyboard (see the section, "Using the Equation Keyboard").

```
┌──────────────────────────────────────────────────────┐
│ Atanθ + B   sin sin   slope slope │ Functions │
│                                   │ cos       │
│                                   │ sin       │
│                                   │ tan       │
│                                   │ arccos    │
│                                   │ arcsin    │
│                                   │ arctan    │
│                                   │ cosh      │
│                                   │ sinh      │
│                                   │ tanh      │
│                                   │ cot       │
│                                   │ coth      │
│                                   │ sec       │
│ A'tan'theta~+~B~~~                │ cosec     │
│ sin~ital{sin}~~~                  │ exp       │
│ func{slope}~slope_                │ log       │
│                                   │ ln        │
│                                   │ lin       │
│                                   │ lininf    │
│                                   │ linsup    │
│                                   │           │
│ Tangent                    PgUp/PgDn for more       │
└──────────────────────────────────────────────────────┘
```

Fig. 22.5

Expressions created using functions selected from the Functions menu on the Equation Palette.

The function and command names also can be treated as variables and italicized by the ITAL command. For example, to italicize the function name *sin*, you type *ital{sin}* (see fig. 22.5). Remember that you can type commands in either uppercase or lowercase.

Reminder:

You can type commands in either uppercase or lowercase.

Similarly, the FUNC command forces the equation editor to treat a group of characters as a function name. For example, if *slope* is a function that appears in your equation, and you do not wish to have it italicized, type *func{slope}* (see fig. 22.5).

To improve readability, you can place a space between the expression in braces and the ITAL or FUNC command.

Note from figure 22.5 that when the function *tan* is highlighted on the Functions menu on the Equation Palette, its description (Tangent) appears in the lower left corner of the screen.

Reminder:

When the Equation Palette is active, a description of the highlighted item appears in the lower left corner of the screen.

Using Commands To Create Equations

The equation editor provides some of the formatting commands available in the normal text editor, such as bold, italic, and underline. However, you need much more to create equations, which can contain such elements as multilevel subscripts and superscripts, symbols for integration and summation, complicated fractions, and many sizes of vertical lines, parentheses, brackets, and braces. This section shows how to use the equation editor's commands to create these expressions.

Creating Subscripts and Superscripts

Subscripts and superscripts are created with the SUB and SUP commands. Like all commands, you can type the SUB and SUP commands in any mixture of uppercase or lowercase letters; you can type *sub*, *Sub*, *sup*, or *Sup*. In addition, you can use the underscore (_) as an abbreviation for the SUB command, and the caret (^) as the abbreviation for the SUP command.

To produce the simple expression $y_2\ y^2$, type the following:

y sub 2~~~y sup 2

You can achieve the same results by selecting SUB and SUP from the Commands menu in the Equation Palette, or by typing the following:

y_2~~~y^2

Note that you must include a space before and after SUB and SUP so that the equation editor can distinguish them as commands. When you select a command like SUB by pressing Enter in the Palette, the equation editor automatically inserts a space before and after the command. Spaces, however, are not required with the abbreviations _ or ^ because they cannot be confused with variable names.

Tip
Note that typing *sup −0.5* will not place the real number −0.5 in the superscript. Only the minus sign − will be superscripted. You use braces to produce the desired result. You type *sup{−0.5}*.

The Display Window in figure 22.6, which shows the Arrows menu active in the Equation Palette, shows some of the more complicated expressions that you can produce with the equation editor. You can produce, for example, simultaneous subscripts and superscripts (one directly over the other) if the subscript is typed before the superscript. To place both a prime ' and a subscript on the same symbol, you must type the subscript command first.

Fig. 22.6
Examples of subscripts and superscripts produced with the equation editor.

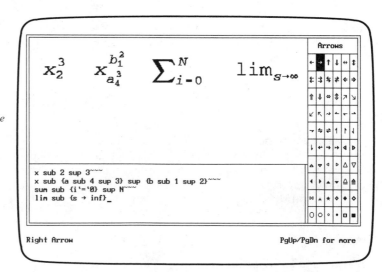

5.1

You produce the first expression in figure 22.6 by typing the following:

> *x sub 2 sup 3*

or

> *x_2^3*

To produce the second expression, you type the following:

> *x sub {a sub 4 sup 3} sup {b sub 1 sup 2}*

or

> *x_{a_4^3}^{b_1^2}*

The second expression contains multilevel subscripts and superscripts. Second-level subscripts and superscripts (normal subscripts and superscripts) are set in the superscript font, which is two-thirds the height of the base font if the characters are printed as graphics. Subscripts and superscripts that are third-level or greater are printed in the superscript font for the superscript font, and are printed at one-half the height of the base font if printed as graphics (see fig. 22.7).

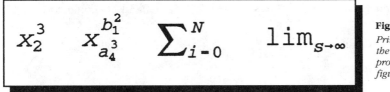

Fig. 22.7
Printed output of the expressions produced in figure 22.6.

If you need to conserve space in a document, you can use SUB and SUP in place of FROM and TO (see the section, "Using the INT and SUB Commands"). Using the SUB command in this way enables you to use the summation and limit expressions within an *inline* equation (one that appears with text).

To produce the third expression in figure 22.6, type the following:

> *sum sub {i`=`0} sup N~~~*

You can produce the fourth expression in figure 22.6 by typing the following:

> *lim sub {s → inf}*

The infinity symbol (∞) is found on the Symbols menu. Note that there is no keyword for the right-arrow symbol ($\rightarrow$), or for any other symbol on the Arrows menu. The symbol must be entered into the equation by using either the Palette, the equation keyboard, the Compose feature, or by typing ->.

Using the INT, SUM, FROM, and TO Commands

You can produce integrals and summations by using the keywords INT and SUM or by selecting the appropriate symbols from the Large menu in the Palette (see fig. 22.8). You can insert the symbols, rather than the keywords, into the Editing Window by pressing Ctrl-Enter instead of Enter. The symbol is shown in the Palette, but the corresponding keyword and description are shown in the lower left corner of the screen. If you prefer, you can type the keyword in the Editing Window.

Reminder:
You can insert symbols—rather than the keywords—into the Editing Window by pressing Ctrl-Enter instead of Enter.

5.1

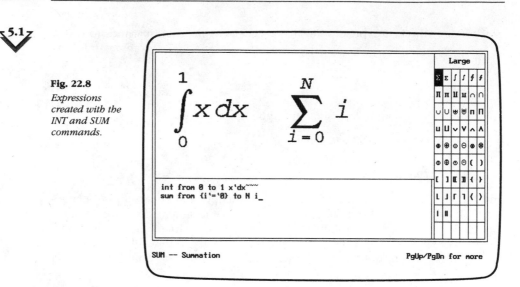

Fig. 22.8

Expressions created with the INT and SUM commands.

You can automatically position limits by using the FROM and TO commands in the Commands menu.

To produce the first expression in figure 22.8, you type the following:

int from 0 to 1 x`dx~~~

To produce the second expression in figure 22.8, you type the following:

sum from {i`=`0} to N i

Note the use of braces to indicate that the group $i`=`0$ is positioned below the summation sign. In the preceding expression, all spaces that were entered with the space bar are required except for the spaces before and after the braces.

The FROM command can be used with the *lim* function to position items below the *lim* function. Expressions acted on by the FROM and TO commands are printed in the superscript font. For example, to position $s \to \infty$ below the *lim* function, type the following:

lim from {s → inf}`Y(s)

Forming Fractions with the LEFT, RIGHT, and OVER Commands

Equations often contain complicated fractions that must be enclosed with *delimiters*, such as parentheses, brackets, braces, or vertical lines. The LEFT and RIGHT commands insert a delimiter that expands according to the size of the expression to be enclosed. The syntax of these commands is as follows:

LEFT *delimiter expression* RIGHT *delimiter*

You can use the OVER command with the LEFT and RIGHT commands to create fractions of considerable complexity. The syntax of the OVER command is as follows. To place x over y, you type the following:

x OVER y

Figure 22.9, which displays the Symbols menu on the Equation Palette, shows how you can use the OVER command to form complicated fractions. You produce the notation for absolute value with the LEFT and RIGHT commands applied to the vertical-line delimiter contained in the Symbols menu (its keyword is LINE).

You can produce the first expression in figure 22.9 by typing the following:

left line {alpha^2`+− `4} over {6 beta} right line ~~~

Note that the equation editor automatically expands the height of the delimiter to match the expression's height.

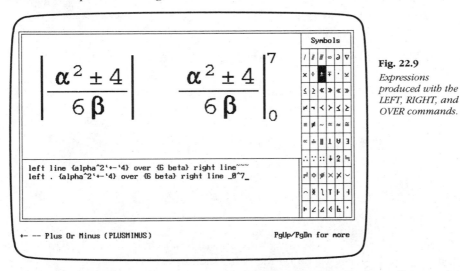

Fig. 22.9

Expressions produced with the LEFT, RIGHT, and OVER commands.

The second expression in figure 22.9 shows an expression that has a line on the right side only, with a subscript and a superscript. The LEFT and RIGHT commands are used to bracket the expression whose height determines the delimiter's height. When only one delimiter is required, a dummy LEFT or RIGHT command is needed. You create this dummy command by using a period (.) after the LEFT or RIGHT command. You must always use the LEFT and RIGHT commands as a pair.

Reminder:

The LEFT and RIGHT commands must always be used as a pair.

To produce the second expression in figure 22.9, you type the following:

left . {alpha^2`+− `4} over {6 beta} right line_0^7

Tip

The Greek alphabet is a class of keywords that is case sensitive. Typing *alpha* produces the lowercase letter (α) while typing ALPHA produces the uppercase letter (A).

Figure 22.10 shows three additional applications of the OVER command. To produce the first and second expressions in figure 22.10, type the following:

{a`b} over c~~~{17} over {315} y sup 7

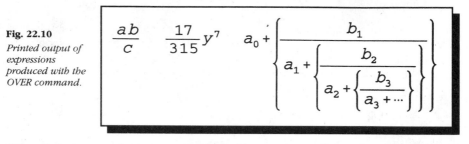

Fig. 22.10

Printed output of expressions produced with the OVER command.

Other delimiters on the Large menu include parentheses ( ), brackets [ ], and braces { }. When a brace is used as a delimiter, remember to precede the brace with the backslash symbol \ so that the brace will not be interpreted as a grouping command.

To produce the third expression in figure 22.10, type the following:

*a sub 0 `+` left \{ {b sub 1} over {a sub 1 `+`left \{ {b sub 2}
over { a sub 2 `+`left \{ {b sub 3} over {a sub 3 `+` DOTSAXIS }
right \} } right \} } right \}*

Caution

In this chapter, when text to be typed in the equation editor is displayed, line breaks are inserted only where the space (inserted when you press the space bar) is optional.

Note how the equation editor automatically positions and sizes braces. You include the centered ellipsis (...) by using the keyword DOTSAXIS (see fig. 22.10). The ellipsis symbol can be found on the Other menu.

The backslash symbol \ can also be used with the following symbols:

. ` ~ & #

Using the backslash character with these symbols forces the equation editor to treat them as characters rather than as commands. Use the backslash to force the equation editor to treat a command keyword literally. For example, if you type *bold*, the word *bold* is treated literally, and not as a command. The backslash can also force the equation editor to print the character in the normal rather than italic font. For example, typing *and* forces the word "and" to be printed in the normal font.

Creating Complex Integral Expressions

Integration symbols are often found in calculus applications. They can appear as line integrals or multiple integrals with complicated algebraic expressions. You can easily create these symbols with the equation editor.

Figure 22.11 shows the printed output of expressions created with the INT command when combined with the SUB, SUP, and OVER commands.

You produce the first expression in figure 22.11 by typing the following:

> *int from 0 to 5 e sup {– { 1 over 2 }*
> *left ({x `– `mu} over sigma right) sup 2} `dx*

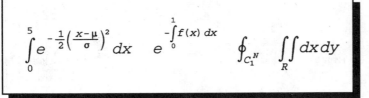

Fig. 22.11
The printed output of complex integral expressions.

The INT command can be used with the SUP command. You produce the second expression in figure 22.11 by typing the following:

> *e sup {– int from 0 to 1 f(x) `dx}*

The SUB command is useful in combination with the contour integral command OINT, which can be found on the Large menu. You produce the third expression in figure 22.11 by typing the following:

> *oint sub {C sub 1 sup N}*

You can produce double integrals easily. You produce the fourth expression in figure 22.11 by typing the following:

> *int from{`R} int dx`dy*

Using Roots

The square root SQRT and the *n*th root NROOT commands also expand automatically—in both height and width—to include the entire expression denoted by the grouping symbols—the left and right braces { }. The root commands can also be *nested*—used one inside the other.

Reminder:
The root commands can be nested.

Figure 22.12 shows the Sets menu as the active menu in the Equation Palette. To produce the first equation in figure 22.12, you type the following:

> *PARALLEL g PARALLEL` ≠ `SQRT {INT FROM a TO b p(x) `dx}*

The double line—whose keyword is DLINE—is on the Large menu. The Not Approximately Equal sign, which does not have a keyword, can be found on the Sets menu (see fig. 22.13). Note how the square root expands to include the integral sign.

Tip
Not all symbols have a keyword. Some must be entered using either the Equation Palette, the Compose method (Ctrl-2), or the Equation keyboard.

5.1

Fig. 22.12
Roots created using the equation editor.

$$\|g\| \neq \sqrt{\int_a^b p(x)\,dx} \qquad \sqrt[3]{1 + \sqrt{2 + \sqrt{3}}}$$

```
Sets

PARALLEL g PARALLEL` # `SQRT{INT FROM a TO b p(x)`dx}~~~
NROOT 3 {1`+`SQRT {2`+`SQRT 3}}_

Not Approximately Equal                    PgUp/PgDn for more
```

The syntax for NROOT is as follows:

NROOT *n*

n denotes the root number. These root symbols can be nested, as in the following example, which produces the second expression in figure 22.12:

NROOT 3 {1`+`SQRT {2`+`SQRT 3}}

Using Diacritical Marks

Reminder:
Diacritical marks—
*marks placed directly
above a character—
are found on the
Other menu.*

Diacritical marks, marks placed directly above a character, are available from the Other menu in the Equation Palette. When in the equation editor, use the space bar to create a space after the variable, and then type the command for the diacritical mark. Table 22.3 shows the available diacritical marks.

Table 22.3
Diacritical Marks

Keyword	Typed Input	Printed Output
Acute	*x acute*	$\acute{x}$
Bar	*x bar*	$\bar{x}$
Breve	*x breve*	$\breve{x}$
Check	*x check*	$\check{x}$
Circle	*x circle*	$\mathring{x}$
Dot	*x dot*	$\dot{x}$
DDot	*x ddot*	$\ddot{x}$
DDDot	*x dddot*	$\dddot{x}$
DYad	*x dyad*	$\ddot{x}$
Grave	*x grave*	$\grave{x}$
Hat	*x hat*	$\hat{x}$
Tilde	*x tilde*	$\tilde{x}$
Vec	*x vec*	$\vec{x}$

5.1

Figure 22.13 is an example of the use of the DOTSLOW keyword, which is also on the Other menu (see fig. 22.13).

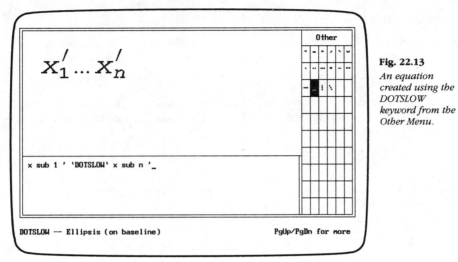

Fig. 22.13
An equation created using the DOTSLOW keyword from the Other Menu.

Using the Matrix Commands

Matrices and determinants contain elements that must be properly aligned. The structure of a matrix consists of elements or subgroups arranged in rows and columns. You align the elements by using a combination of the following commands:

Command	Function
MATRIX	Creates a matrix structure in the equation editor by specifying the row and column location of every subgroup
MATFORM	Specifies the horizontal alignment format to be applied to each subgroup (left, right, or centered within the column) using the commands ALIGNC, ALIGNL, and ALIGNR
ALIGNC	Aligns its accompanying variable in the center of the current subgroup or matrix column
ALIGNL	Aligns its accompanying variable on the left margin of the current subgroup or matrix column
ALIGNR	Aligns its accompanying variable on the right margin of the current subgroup or matrix column

Reminder:
ALIGNC—centered alignment—is the default alignment command.

To produce a matrix with two rows and three columns, you type the following:

MATRIX{a11 & a12 & a13 # a21 & a22 & a23}

The ampersand (&) serves as a column separator; the pound sign (#) serves as a row separator. The elements in the first row are a11, a12, and a13. The elements in the second row are a21, a22, and a23. The syntax for a matrix having *n* rows and *m* columns is a straightforward extension of the preceding example.

You must specify the type of brackets to surround your matrix. You use the LEFT and RIGHT commands for this purpose, along with the appropriate choice of delimiters, such as the square brackets [ ], the line (LINE), or braces \{ \}. (Remember that you must use the backslash \ with braces.)

For example, to produce the determinant whose first row consists of the numbers 213, 25, 8, and whose second row consists of 17, 219, 46, you type the following:

left line matrix{213& 25& 8#17& 219& 46}right line

The default alignment centers each element with respect to the element above it. To override this default, use the MATFORM command. The syntax of the MATFORM is as follows:

MATFORM{*alignment1 & alignment2 & alignment3 ...*}

alignment1 is either ALIGNL, ALIGNR, or ALIGNC. *alignment1* specifies whether the elements in column 1 are aligned left or right, or centered within the column. Similarly, *alignment2* specifies the alignment for column 2, and so on. The syntax for using MATFORM with MATRIX is as follows:

MATRIX{MATFORM{*alignment1&alignment2& ...*}a11&a12 ... #a21&a22 ... # ...}

You can produce the first matrix shown in figure 22.14 by typing the following:

left [matrix{matform{alignl& alignr}aaa& bbb#ii& jj#x& y}right]

Fig. 22.14
Matrixes produced with the MATRIX and MATFORM commands.

$$\begin{bmatrix} aaa & bbb \\ ii & jj \\ x & y \end{bmatrix} \begin{bmatrix} aaa & bbb \\ ii & jj \\ x & y \end{bmatrix} \begin{bmatrix} a_{11}^2 & \cdots & a_{1n}^2 \\ \vdots & \ddots & \vdots \\ a_{n1}^2 & \cdots & a_{nn}^2 \end{bmatrix}$$

Note the resulting alignment in the first expression—to the left in the first column and to the right in the second column. To center every element, producing the second matrix in figure 22.14, type the following:

left [matrix {matform {alignc & alignc}aaa& bbb # ii& jj # x& y} right]

Complicated expressions can be used in matrix subgroups. For example, to produce the third matrix in figure 22.14, you type the following:

left line matrix {{a sub {11} sup 2}& dotsaxis& {a sub {1n} sup 2}#
dotsvert& dotsdiag& dotsvert # {a sub {n1} sup 2}& dotsaxis& {a
sub {nn} sup 2}} right line

You do not need to specify MATFORM{ALIGNC&ALIGNC&ALIGNC} to produce this expression because the default is a centered alignment. You do not need to use the MATFORM command if the default centered alignment is acceptable.

Note: The commands DOTSVERT and DOTSDIAG are located on the Other menu.

The ALIGN commands can also be used with the OVER, FROM, and TO commands. For example, the default alignment for the OVER command is centered alignment. This alignment can be overridden using ALIGNL or ALIGNR.

Creating Multiline Expressions with STACK and STACKALIGN

The equation editor limits you to a one single-line expression per box. As elements are added to the expression, they expand the length of the equation line. Remember that pressing Enter in the Editing Window does not insert a hard return **[HRt]** in the printed equation. The # sign creates a hard return in the printed equation, but does not provide for alignment of multiline expressions. It is possible to create and control the alignment of multiline equations by using the STACK and STACKALIGN commands.

Reminder:
Use STACK and STACKALIGN to create multiline expressions.

The STACK command can be used to form a vertical stack of expressions. The ALIGN commands can be used to specify whether the expressions in the stack should be aligned to the left, right, or centered. The default alignment is centered.

Figure 22.15 shows the printed output of equations produced using the STACK and STACKALIGN commands. For example, suppose that you wanted to stack the following two equations in the same equation box:

$$-4x + y = 6132$$
$$x + 3y = 14$$

To stack these equations and produce the first expression in figure 22.15, you type the following:

stack{{-4x~+~y~=~6132} # {x~+~3y~=~14}}

$$-4x + y - 6132 \qquad -4x + y - 6132 \qquad -4x + y \quad 6132$$
$$x + 3y - 14 \qquad\quad x + 3y - 14 \qquad\quad x + 3y - \quad 14$$

Fig. 22.15
Printed output of equations aligned with STACK and STACKALIGN.

To override the default centered alignment of the STACK command, use ALIGNL or ALIGNR. For example, to align the second equation to the right, type the following:

stack{{-4x~+~y~=~6132} # alignr{x~+~3y~=~14}}

A more powerful way of creating stacks is provided by the STACKALIGN command, which enables you to align on an arbitrary character or symbol. The STACKALIGN command gives you more alignment control than the STACK command.

Reminder:
The STACKALIGN command provides more alignment control than the STACK command.

The syntax of STACKALIGN is as follows:

STACKALIGN{x alignchar& y # a alignchar& b}

alignchar is the character on which you want to align the column. The ampersand (&) terminates the alignment character, and thereby denotes it to the equation editor (&, however, is *not* part of the alignment character). The pound sign # creates a line break.

To align the second expression on the equal (=) sign, and thus produce the third expression in figure 22.15, type the following:

stackalign{-4x~+~y~=&~6132 # x~+~3y~=&~14}

Note the different alignments in figure 22.15: centered, aligned right, and aligned over the = sign.

Figure 22.16, which shows the Greek menu active on the Equation Palette, demonstrates another use of STACKALIGN. You can produce this expression by typing the following:

alpha`=`left \{ stackalign {x&~,~x` >= `0 # - x& ~,~x`<`0} right .

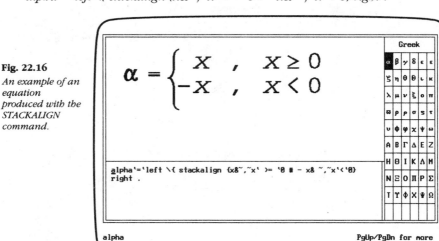

Fig. 22.16

An example of an equation produced with the STACKALIGN command.

Using Varying Symbol Sizes

As you have seen, the equation editor enables you to scale certain symbols, such as braces and brackets, to whatever size is necessary. Not all symbols, however, can be sized. For example, only two sizes are available for the symbols contained in the Large menu. These symbols include the integral, summation, product, and a variety of other symbols.

Examples of these symbols—both in small and large sizes—are shown in figure 22.17. You can produce the symbols shown in the figure by typing the following;

sum~smallsum~~int~smallint~~oint~smalloint~~
prod~smallprod~~bigcap~cap

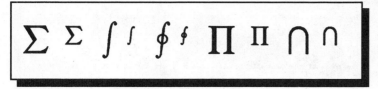

5.1

Fig. 22.17
Examples of symbol sizes found on the Large menu of the Equation Palette.

The keywords for symbols on the Large menu are not case-sensitive, so you can type them in either uppercase or lowercase letters.

Another example of a symbol that is limited to two sizes is the binomial symbol, which is used in probability and statistics applications. Two sizes of binomials are available. The syntax is as follows:

BINOM *x y*

or

BINOMSM *x y*

Either *x* or *y* can be expressions in braces. For example, to create the symbols shown in figure 22.18, type the following:

binom N {N~`1}~~~binomsm N {N~`1}

$$\binom{N}{N-1} \quad \binom{N}{N-1}$$

Fig. 22.18
Sizes of binomial symbols.

Using Miscellaneous Commands and Symbols

The examples in this chapter provide only a small sample of the many characters and symbols available in the Equation Palette. Virtually any mathematical character or symbol is available. For more information on these commands and symbols, see the *WordPerfect Reference Manual*.

Positioning and Sizing Equations

WordPerfect provides several options for modifying the view of the equation in the Display Window and for adjusting the position and size of the printed equation.

The standard type of equation box has an initial appearance that is commonly used for equations. This type of box has no box lines and is positioned from margin to margin. You can, however, use any type of graphics box to create an equation. Important equations in a document, for example, are sometimes displayed with surrounding box lines (see fig. 22.19).

Reminder:
The standard equation box is a graphics box with no border that extends from margin to margin.

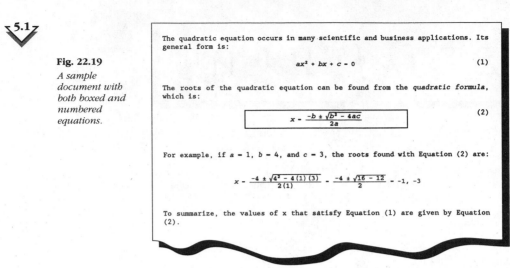

Fig. 22.19

A sample document with both boxed and numbered equations.

The quadratic equation occurs in many scientific and business applications. Its general form is:

$$ax^2 + bx + c = 0 \qquad (1)$$

The roots of the quadratic equation can be found from the *quadratic formula*, which is:

$$x = \frac{-b \pm \sqrt{b^2 - 4ac}}{2a} \qquad (2)$$

For example, if $a = 1$, $b = 4$, and $c = 3$, the roots found with Equation (2) are:

$$x = \frac{-4 \pm \sqrt{4^2 - 4(1)(3)}}{2(1)} = \frac{-4 \pm \sqrt{16 - 12}}{2} = -1, -3$$

To summarize, the values of x that satisfy Equation (1) are given by Equation (2).

You also may want to leave space for an equation number near the right margin so that you can use WordPerfect's search-and-replace features to renumber equations. The alternative is to change the equation number in the equation editor. This can be a time-consuming process if many equations are involved. Box types and their alignment and sizing options are discussed in Chapter 27.

All three equations in figure 22.19 were created with the equation editor. Equations (1) and (2) are contained in special equation boxes. Equation (1) is contained in a borderless box which is centered between the left and right margins. The equation number was created in the normal text editor by using the Flush Right (Alt-F6) key. Equation (2) was created in a similar way except that its box was specified to have a border. The third equation is contained in the default equation box of the equation editor. If, for some reason, equations (1) and (2) must be renumbered, such as when the text is to be included in another document, you can use the search-and-replace functions of the normal text editor to easily change the numbers.

Creating a Special Equation Box

To create a special box that does not have the default equation editor box characteristics, follow these steps:

1. Press Graphics (Alt-F9), select **F**igure (**1**), and then select **C**reate (**1**).

   ⌨ Access the Graphics pull-down menu, select **F**igure (**1**), and then select **C**reate (**1**).

   WordPerfect displays the Definition: Figure menu (see fig. 22.20).

2. Specify the box contents to be an equation by selecting **C**ontents (**2**) and then **E**quation (**4**).

3. Select **E**dit (**9**) to load the equation editor.

```
Definition: Figure

    1 - Filename

    2 - Contents              Empty

    3 - Caption

    4 - Anchor Type           Paragraph

    5 - Vertical Position     0"

    6 - Horizontal Position   Right

    7 - Size                  3.25" wide x 3.25" (high)

    8 - Wrap Text Around Box  Yes

    9 - Edit




Contents: 1 Graphic; 2 Graphic on Disk; 3 Text; 4 Equation: 0
```

Fig. 22.20

The Definition: Figure menu after selecting contents.

Figure 22.20 shows the Figure: Definition menu after the **C**ontents (**2**) selection has been made. After selecting **E**quation (**4**) for the contents of the box, select **H**orizontal Position (**6**) to change the position from the default setting of Right. Figure 22.21 shows the menu after this selection is made. To center the box, select **C**enter (**3**). You can change the other parameters of the box on this menu as well, just as with any graphics box. (See Chapter 27 for more information.)

To create a special equation box without a border, press Graphics (Alt-F9), select **F**igure (**1**), and then select **O**ptions (**4**). The Options: Figure menu is displayed. Then press **B**order Style (**1**) and select **N**one for the Left, Right, Top, and Bottom borders.

```
Definition: Figure

    1 - Filename

    2 - Contents              Equation

    3 - Caption

    4 - Anchor Type           Paragraph

    5 - Vertical Position     0"

    6 - Horizontal Position   Right

    7 - Size                  3.25" wide x 3.28" (high)

    8 - Wrap Text Around Box  Yes

    9 - Edit




Horizontal Position: 1 Left; 2 Right; 3 Center; 4 Full: 0
```

Fig. 22.21

The Definition: Figure menu after selecting Horizontal Position.

5.1

Using the HORZ and VERT Commands

Reminder:
Use the HORZ and VERT commands in the Editing Window to adjust the position of elements in the equation.

To adjust the position of elements in the equation, you can use the HORZ and VERT commands in the Editing Window.

The syntax of HORZ is as follows:

HORZ *n*

The syntax of VERT is as follows:

VERT *n*

n is the number of 0.012" (1200ths of an inch) to move in a relative direction to the *right* for HORZ and *up* for VERT. To move to the left or down, you must make *n* a negative number.

To move the equation 1.2 inches to the right, you type the following:

HORZ 100 x~=~y~+~5

Using the HORZ command is more convenient than typing many spaces using the ~ symbol. The VERT command can be used with the STACK and STACKALIGN commands to produce line spacing different than the normal line spacing.

The size of the characters and symbols in the printed equation can be changed by changing the size of the font in which the equation is printed. See the section, "Printing Equations."

Managing Equation Files

Reminder:
The equation file can be saved as a separate file.

Because an equation box is a type of graphics box, an equation is saved or retrieved when the document containing it is saved or retrieved using the normal WordPerfect Save (F10) and Retrieve (Shift-F10) features. However, you also can save and retrieve an equation as a separate file, independent of the document containing the equation.

Saving an Equation as a Separate File

To save an equation as a separate file, press Save (F10) while in the equation editor. WordPerfect then prompts you for a file name. Unless you enter a complete path name, the equation will be saved to the default directory. When an equation is saved as a separate file in this way, no alignment or printing options are saved with the equation.

If you want to use an equation as part of another equation, save the equation as a separate file.

Retrieving an Equation File

There are three ways to retrieve an equation previously saved as a separate file. The first way is to press Retrieve (Shift-F10) while in the equation editor. WordPerfect then prompts you for the name of the file. WordPerfect first searches the graphics

5.1

directory for the equation file, and then searches the default directory. The retrieved equation is merged at the current cursor position with whatever is present in the Editing Window.

The second way is to press Retrieve (Shift-F10) while in the equation editor, and then press List (F5). Then type a directory name or press Enter to display the files in the default directory. Select the desired file just as you do in the normal text editor by pressing **R**etrieve (**1**) when the highlighted bar is over the file name.

The third way to retrieve an equation file is to enter the file name under the **F**ilename (**1**) heading on the Definition: Equation menu. This is the only way to retrieve an equation file while not in the equation editor.

You can retrieve a WordPerfect file into the equation editor even if that file was not created by the equation editor. If you do, however, all codes will be removed except for the hard returns and the WordPerfect characters. The equation editor will format the file as an equation, so hard returns and spaces entered with the space bar will not separate text in the equation. This method of retrieving an equation file is useful for large equations whose files are more easily created and edited in the normal WordPerfect text editor.

Saving Equation Files in a Graphics Directory

It is convenient to save equation files in a separate directory. Press Files (Shift-F1) and select **L**ocation (**6**). You then can enter a path name for a graphics directory. WordPerfect will then prompt you to save your equation file in that directory.

Cue:
For convenience, save equation files in a separate graphics directory.

If you retrieve a file into the equation editor from *any* directory and then save it, WordPerfect displays the path name to the graphics directory, along with the equation file name. To save it in the graphics directory under the same file name, press Enter, and then press Y (for Yes). To change the path or file name, make the changes and then press Enter.

Printing Equations

WordPerfect is initially set to print all equations as graphics (without using the printer's fonts). When WordPerfect prints equations as graphics, it tries to emulate one of three fonts: Helvetica, Times Roman, or Courier. WordPerfect will use the one that is closest to the base font. (See Chapter 5 for a discussion of fonts and how to select the base font.)

Equations created in the equation editor are printed in the initial base font for the document unless there is a font-change code preceding the equation. If there is a font-change code, all subsequent equations are printed in that font.

Printing equations as graphics has at least three advantages:

- Symbols such as brackets, parentheses, and braces can be arbitrarily sized.
- Third-level superscripts and subscripts can be printed in a font that is smaller than that used for second-level characters. This smaller font is not available with many printers unless it is created as graphics.

Reminder:

Printing equations as graphics increases the printing time.

- Symbols and font attributes, like italics, can be printed even though they are not found in many printer fonts.

A disadvantage of printing equations as graphics is that the printing process is slower. A compromise is made possible by instructing WordPerfect to print as graphics only those characters not available in the printer's font.

You can specify whether or not equations should be printed as graphics in three different ways. You can use any one of the following three menus:

1. The Setup Initial Settings menu: press Setup (Shift-F1), select **I**nitial Settings (**4**), and then select **E**quations (**3**).

2. The Print menu: press Graphics Quality (Shift-F7), and then select Do **N**ot Print (**1**).

3. The Equation Editor Setup menu: press Setup (Shift-F1), select **P**rint as Graphics (**1**), and then answer **Y**es or **N**o.

Each method requires you to answer Y or N (for Yes or No) to the `Print As Graphics?` prompt.

The first method sets the default for all documents on startup. The second method overrides the default setting for a particular document, and the third method overrides the first two for a particular equation.

Summary

This chapter introduced a feature new with WordPerfect 5.1: the equation editor. You use the equation editor to create equations. The equation editor does not perform mathematical calculations, but formats your entries for printing equations according to an established set of rules and an order of precedence.

You learned how to do the following with the equation editor:

❑ Type entries and commands in the Editing Window

❑ View the equation in the Display Window

❑ Use the Equation Palette to enter symbols, functions, and commands

❑ Enter characters from the normal keyboard

❑ Enter symbols from the Equation keyboard

❑ Enter commands and symbols from the Equation Palette

❑ Make corrections using the editing keys

The equation editor is very easy to use after a little practice. It is an excellent tool for creating complex mathematical expressions.

Using Footnotes
and Endnotes

Susan Hafer combines her knowledge of WordPerfect with her degree in Language Studies from Wellesley College to write this chapter on using footnotes and endnotes in WordPerfect 5.1

People who write scholarly papers must include footnotes, endnotes, or a combination of the two in their documents. These notes provide a simple, standard way of referencing quotations as well as showing a reader additional parenthetical information. But writers must be wary of including in notes vital information necessary to the reader's understanding of the overall text, because many readers skim or ignore notes.

Footnotes are inserted at the foot of the page, and endnotes are grouped together at the end of the document or wherever you want them. Both types of notes are marked in the text by numbers, letters, or special characters such as asterisks. If you use both types of notes in one document, WordPerfect gives you the option of assigning the notes different numbering systems.

WordPerfect makes using footnotes and endnotes easy. If you ever have typed footnotes with a manual typewriter, the advantages of controlling them with the word processor are obvious. For example, figuring out how much space to leave for footnotes at the bottom of a page is *not* fun, nor is renumbering footnotes that have been relocated in the document. However, these tasks are simple for a computer. WordPerfect is designed to calculate automatically how much room you need at the bottom of each page for the footnotes, no matter how long (a note can be as long as 16,000 lines), and to renumber the notes automatically any time you add to, delete, or move them.

Creating and editing both types of notes are made even easier with 5.1's SHORTCUT keyboard layout (explained in Chapter 20). SHORTCUT also allows you to edit a note option code, a feature not available in previous versions of WordPerfect. Check the tips later in this chapter for more information about these note shortcuts.

You also can use WordPerfect's Cross Referencing feature (explained in Chapter 25) if you are referring to notes by their number in the context of paragraphs. For example, you can include the following reference in the paragraph: *(see explanation in endnote 6)*. You can type the note number; however, if the number changes in the final draft, you must review the entire text to check all embedded references. Although notes are automatically renumbered for you, references to those notes are not renumbered if you manually type the numbers. Using Cross Referencing rather than manually typing a note number being referenced takes care of this updating for you.

You can include WordPerfect equations (explained in Chapter 22) and graphics boxes (character type only) within the body of a note.

Because WordPerfect footnotes and endnotes are similar, this chapter concentrates on footnotes, with differences for endnotes highlighted. Also, some of the basics of endnotes are discussed so that you can see the similarity between the two types of notes. The menus (except for the Options menu) are identical for each type of note. For example, when you select **C**reate or **E**dit from the Footnote menu, a footnote is created or edited; and if you do the same from the Endnote menu, an endnote is created or edited.

This chapter also discusses how to create notes, look at them, change existing ones, delete them, move them from one place to another in the text, and change their styles. You also learn how to put endnotes someplace other than at the end of the document, and change footnotes to endnotes (and vice versa).

Reminder

If you use a mouse with WordPerfect 5.1, you can click the right button to display the pull-down menus, and then select the desired option. You also can press Alt-= to access the pull-down menus, and then press the appropriate letter of the desired option. For all instructions, assume that if a block is required to activate a pull-down menu option, the text has been blocked before the pull-down menu is accessed. Instructions for pull-down menus and the mouse are marked with the mouse icon. For more information about the mouse, see Chapter 1.

Using Footnotes

A *footnote* is a reference or some other parenthetical text that appears at the bottom of a page. Creating and then editing footnotes in WordPerfect are easy to do.

Creating Footnotes

Before creating a footnote, you naturally start with text that needs a note. For this example, type the text in italics—and don't forget to indent the long quotation by using Indent (F4):

In Charles Dickens's story of Nicholas Nickleby, one of the villains is Mr. Wackford Squeers:

> *Mr. Squeers's appearance was not prepossessing. He had but one eye, and the popular prejudice runs in favour of two.... The blank side of his face was much wrinkled and puckered up, which gave him a very sinister appearance, especially when he smiled, at which times his expression bordered closely on the villanous[sic].... He wore...a suit of scholastic black, but his coat sleeves being a great deal too long, and his trousers a great deal too short, he appeared ill at ease in his clothes, and as if he were in a perpetual state of astonishment at finding himself so respectable.*

Compare this description with one of the hero, Nicholas himself, whose face was "open, handsome, and ingenuous," and whose eyes were "bright with the light of intelligence and spirit. His figure was somewhat slight, but manly and well-formed; and apart from all the grace of youth and comeliness, there was an emanation from the warm young heart in his look and bearing...."

Once you have the text that needs footnoting, create the note by completing the following steps:

1. Place the cursor in the text where you want a footnote number to appear. For this example, place the cursor after the period following *so respectable* at the end of the indented quotation.

2. Press Footnote (Ctrl-F7).

   ▢▤ Access the **L**ayout pull-down menu and choose **F**ootnote.

   You see the Footnote/Endnote menu:

   1 **F**ootnote; **2** **E**ndnote; **3** Endnote **P**lacement

   Note: ▢▤ The pull-down menus do not show the Endnote **P**lacement option unless you select **E**ndnote from the **L**ayout menu.

   Choose **F**ootnote (**1**) to create, edit, change the style, and so on, for footnotes. Choose **E**ndnote (**2**) to perform the same operations for endnotes. Choose Endnote **P**lacement (**3**) to tell WordPerfect to place endnotes where the cursor is located in the document (more on this option later).

3. Select **F**ootnote (**1**). The Footnote menu appears:

   Footnote: 1 **C**reate; **2** **E**dit; **3** **N**ew Number; **4** **O**ptions

   Create (**1**) lets you create a new footnote; **E**dit (**2**) lets you make changes to an existing footnote; **N**ew Number (**3**) starts numbering any footnotes after the cursor at whatever number you specify; and **O**ptions (**4**) lets you change how footnotes appear in the document.

4. Select **C**reate (**1**) to create a footnote.

   The screen goes blank for a moment and then returns a footnote-entry screen, which closely resembles the normal WordPerfect workspace. In addition to typing text normally, you can use the function keys (Move, Underline, Font, Equation Box, and the like) to edit and enhance text. You even can use the spell-checker from within a footnote.

Reminder:
Place the cursor in the text where you want the footnote number to appear.

> **Tip**
>
> If you have selected the SHORTCUT keyboard layout that comes with WordPerfect 5.1 (explained in Chapter 20), you can combine all four of these steps into one by pressing (Ctrl-F) for Footnote Create.

Notice that a footnote number has already been typed for you and is displayed in whatever way WordPerfect is set up to display superscripts. The program places the footnote number just before the cursor so that you can begin typing the text of the footnote to be placed at the bottom of the page.

> **Tip**
>
> You can use List Files from within a note to retrieve text into the note.

5. Type the text of the footnote. For the first footnote, type the following:

   Charles Dickens, The Life and Adventures of Nicholas Nickleby (Philadelphia: University of Pennsylvania Press, 1982), vol.1, p. 24.

   When you finish typing, the screen should resemble the one in figure 23.1.

Fig. 23.1.

The footnote-entry screen with a footnote.

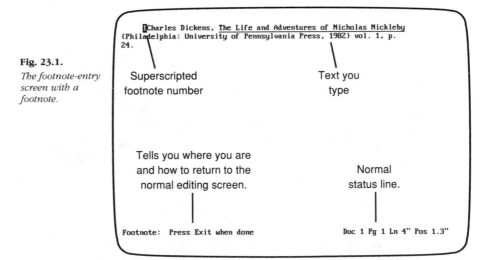

6. Press Exit (F7), as instructed at the bottom of the screen, when you finish typing the text of the footnote.

   The note is saved, and you return to the document where you were when you began the footnote. Now, however, you see a superscripted or highlighted number representing the location of the footnote you just entered. Notice that you do not see the text of the footnote, just the number (shown in fig. 23.2), even if you move the cursor to the bottom of the page.

Reminder:

Use Exit (F7) rather than Enter to end a note; Enter leaves a blank line at the end of the note text and adds a line to the bottom margin of that page.

```
In Charles Dickens's story of Nicholas Nickleby, one of the
villains is Mr. Wackford Squeers:

    Mr. Squeers's appearance was not prepossessing. He had
    but one eye, and the popular prejudice runs in favour of
    two.... The blank side of his face was much wrinkled and
    puckered up, which gave him a very sinister appearance,
    especially when he smiled, at which times his expression
    bordered closely on the villanous [sic].... He wore...a
    suit of scholastic black, but his coat sleeves being a
    great deal too long, and his trousers a great deal too
    short, he appeared ill at ease in his clothes, and as if
    he were in a perpetual state of astonishment at finding
    himself so respectable.▮

Compare this description with one of the hero, Nicholas himself,
whose face was "open, handsome, and ingenuous," and whose eyes were
"bright with the light of intelligence and spirit. His figure was
somewhat slight, but manly and well-formed; and apart from all the
grace of youth and comeliness, there was an emanation from the warm
young heart in his look and bearing...."

                                     Doc 1 Pg 1 Ln 3.17" Pos 3.86"
```

Fig. 23.2.

A footnote in the text.

Superscripted footnote number

Sometimes people forget to press Exit and end up typing the rest of the normal text in the footnote-entry screen. If you make this mistake, block the text that does not belong in the note, delete the block, press Exit to get back to the normal text, and undelete the block.

7. Repeat steps 1 through 6 to enter any other footnotes. For this example, you have two more footnotes to enter. Put footnote 2 after the quotation mark following *"ingenuous"* and type *Dickens, p. 19.* as the text of the footnote. Put footnote 3 after the quotation mark following *"bearing"* and again type *Dickens, p. 19.*

Tip

To avoid separating the page number (*24*, for example) from the page reference (*p.*), as happens in figure 23.1, insert a hard space (Home, space bar) instead of a normal space between the *p.* and the number that follows. Then the page number and the page reference (*p. 24*, for example) appear on the next line.

Looking at Footnotes

Now that you have made a footnote, how do you examine it? When you created the footnote and returned to the normal document, you saw only the superscripted or highlighted number on-screen. With WordPerfect, you can use a variety of ways to view footnotes: Reveal Codes, Print Document or View Document, or Footnote Edit.

Using Reveal Codes

Reveal Codes shows you the footnote code created earlier with the Footnote function key. You see the text surrounding the footnote and the information in the note itself; however, you cannot make changes to the note.

The Reveal Codes method is useful if you want to see the beginning of the footnote in the context of the normal text, because only the first few words of the footnote appear. If the note is long, it ends with an ellipsis (...), but do not think that the rest of the note is gone. The entire note is there, but cannot be seen in Reveal Codes. You can see an entire footnote by using other methods.

To view a footnote by using Reveal Codes, do the following steps:

1. Place the cursor under a footnote number (the first one, for this example) and press Reveal Codes (Alt-F3 or F11).

   The screen should look similar to the one in figure 23.3 and should have the following code blocked in the text:

   [Footnote:1;[Note Num]Charles Dickens, **[UND]**The Life and . . . **]**

2. Press Reveal Codes (Alt-F3 or F11) again to exit back to the normal document.

Fig. 23.3.

Reveal Codes of a footnote in the text.

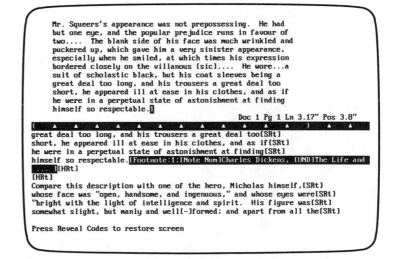

The blocked text is the footnote code you created earlier in this chapter. The part of the footnote you see in the normal screen is represented by the word *Footnote*, which tells WordPerfect to superscript the number that follows, in this case a *1*. Following the semicolon is the part of the note that appears at the bottom of the printed page, represented by the *Note Num* notation followed by the beginning of the text of the footnote.

Using Reveal Codes to see the notes is a quick solution; however, because you see only part of the note, you may prefer to check the notes by using one of the methods covered in the next two sections.

Using Print Document

If you do not have a printer set up to print, skim through this section for future reference but do not follow the instructions.

To view the footnotes by using a printer, follow the normal procedures to print the document. You can print the entire document or only the part that contains the note(s) you want to view.

To print a document, make sure that the printer is ready and on-line before pressing Print (Shift-F7) and selecting **F**ull Document (**1**) or **P**age (**2**). Conserve paper by printing only that part of a document you need; block the section of text and press Print (Shift-F7).

Cue:

Save paper by printing only the part of the document you need.

Compare the footnotes on the printout with those on-screen. The printout should look something like the one in figure 23.4.

```
In Charles Dickens's story of Nicholas Nickleby, one of the
villains is Mr. Wackford Squeers:

  Mr. Squeers's appearance was not prepossessing. He had
  but one eye, and the popular prejudice runs in favour of
  two.... The blank side of his face was much wrinkled and
  puckered up, which gave him a very sinister appearance,
  especially when he smiled, at which times his expression
  bordered closely on the villanous [sic].... He wore...a
  suit of scholastic black, but his coat sleeves being a
  great deal too long, and his trousers a great deal too
  short, he appeared ill at ease in his clothes, and as if
  he were in a perpetual state of astonishment at finding
  himself so respectable.[1]

Compare this description with one of the hero, Nicholas
himself, whose face was "open, handsome, and ingenuous,"[2]
and whose eyes were "bright with the light of intelligence
and spirit. His figure was somewhat slight, but manly and
well-formed; and apart from all the grace of youth and
comeliness, there was an emanation from the warm young
heart in his look and bearing...."[3]



  ‾‾‾‾‾‾‾‾‾‾‾‾‾‾‾‾
  [1]Charles Dickens, The Life and Adventures of Nicholas
Nickleby (Philadelphia: University of Pennsylvania Press,
1982), vol. 1, p. 24.
  [2]Dickens, p. 19
  [3]Dickens, p. 19
```

Fig. 23.4.

Sample document with footnotes.

Notice that you can see the numbers in the text and the complete footnotes at the bottom of the printed page. On the normal screen, you see only the footnote numbers. If the printer is capable of doing so, the numbers in the text are superscripted.

Using View Document

If you do not have a graphics card in your computer, you can't see superscripts, or the entire page, or zoom in to a particular point on the page. You can, however, see the footnotes in context.

Reminder:

Use View Document to see how the document looks when printed.

If you think printing the document just to see the footnotes is a waste of paper, you may want to use View Document. As you learned in Chapter 6, this WordPerfect feature allows you to see how the document looks when printed—with page numbers, spacing, headers and footers, footnotes, and so on.

To view the footnotes by using View Document, do the following steps:

1. Put the cursor on the same page as the footnote(s) to be viewed. In this example, the cursor still should be on a footnote and need not be moved.

Reminder:

Make sure that the selected printer setting is correct so that the View Document screen is accurate.

2. Press Print (Shift-F7) and select **V**iew Document (**6**) from the Print menu. After pressing Print, check to make sure the selected printer is correct if you want the view to be accurate.

3. If you do not see the entire page on-screen, select **F**ull Page (**3**) and look at the bottom of the page to be sure that the footnote is there (see fig. 23.5).

4. Select 100% (**1**) to zoom in more closely on the text (see fig 23.6).

5. If the footnote does not appear on-screen, move the cursor to the footnote number in the text to see what the number looks like. (The number should be superscripted.)

   For this example, all three footnote numbers do appear on-screen, so no movement is necessary.

6. Move the cursor to the bottom of the page with GoTo, ↓ (Ctrl-Home, ↓) to see the footnote at the bottom of the page.

7. Press Exit (F7) to return to the normal document.

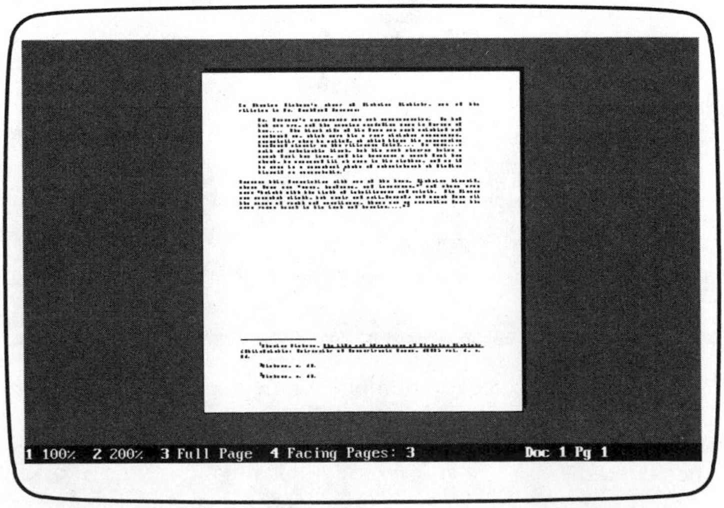

Fig. 23.5.

A Full Page View Document of text and footnotes.

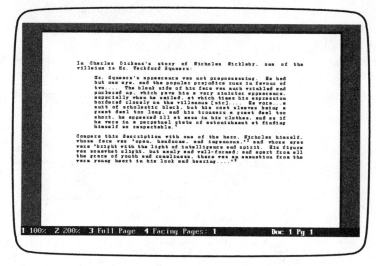

Fig. 23.6.

A 100% View Document of text with footnote numbers.

The Print Document and View Document methods of looking at the notes are helpful because you can see the complete footnotes as the readers see them—in context.

Using Footnote Edit

In the "Editing Footnotes" section later in this chapter, you see how to use the Footnote Edit feature to make changes to a note. You also can use Footnote Edit to examine the note without making changes. Although this method does not permit you to view both the note and the text surrounding the note at the same time, Footnote Edit is the only method that allows you to make changes in the note if you see something you do not like.

Adding Footnotes

Suppose that after entering several footnotes, you need one more somewhere in the midst of the others. WordPerfect automatically renumbers all the footnotes after you enter the new note.

Reminder:
WordPerfect automatically renumbers footnotes if you add one.

Suppose that you want to add an explanation of who Mr. Wackford Squeers is. The information is parenthetical, not vital, so you put the information in a footnote.

To add a new footnote to text previously containing footnotes, do the following:

1. Move the cursor to the place where you want to insert the footnote. For this example, move the cursor to the end of the first sentence, after *Mr. Wackford Squeers.*

2. Press Footnote (Ctrl-F7), select **F**ootnote (**1**), and then select **C**reate (**1**).

   ⌨ Access the **L**ayout pull-down menu, choose **F**ootnote, and then choose **C**reate.

3. Type the text of the footnote. For this footnote example, type the following sentence:

   Mr. Squeers was the schoolmaster of Dotheboy's Hall in this story.

4. Press Exit (F7). Notice that two footnotes appear to be numbered 1 (see fig. 23.7).

5. Press Screen (Ctrl-F3) and select **R**ewrite (**3**) to rewrite the screen. The numbers now have been corrected, and you have four footnotes in the proper order (shown in fig. 23.8).

Fig. 23.7.

A new note added before WordPerfect renumbers the footnotes.

```
In Charles Dickens's story of Nicholas Nickleby, one of the
villains is Mr. Wackford Squeers▌:

   Mr. Squeers's appearance was not prepossessing.  He had
   but one eye, and the popular prejudice runs in favour of
   two....  The blank side of his face was much wrinkled and
   puckered up, which gave him a very sinister appearance,
   especially when he smiled, at which times his expression
   bordered closely on the villanous [sic]....  He wore...a
   suit of scholastic black, but his coat sleeves being a
   great deal too long, and his trousers a great deal too
   short, he appeared ill at ease in his clothes, and as if
   he were in a perpetual state of astonishment at finding
   himself so respectable.▌
```

Fig. 23.8.

After rewriting the screen, WordPerfect renumbers the footnotes.

```
In Charles Dickens's story of Nicholas Nickleby, one of the
villains is Mr. Wackford Squeers▌:

   Mr. Squeers's appearance was not prepossessing.  He had
   but one eye, and the popular prejudice runs in favour of
   two....  The blank side of his face was much wrinkled and
   puckered up, which gave him a very sinister appearance,
   especially when he smiled, at which times his expression
   bordered closely on the villanous [sic]....  He wore...a
   suit of scholastic black, but his coat sleeves being a
   great deal too long, and his trousers a great deal too
   short, he appeared ill at ease in his clothes, and as if
   he were in a perpetual state of astonishment at finding
   himself so respectable.▌

Compare this description with one of the hero, Nicholas himself,
whose face was "open, handsome, and ingenuous,"▌ and whose eyes
were "bright with the light of intelligence and spirit.  His figure
was somewhat slight, but manly and well-formed; and apart from all
the grace of youth and comeliness, there was an emanation from the
warm young heart in his look and bearing...."▌

                              Doc 1 Pg 1 Ln 1.17" Pos 4.26"
```

Deleting Footnotes

Reminder:

To delete a footnote, just delete the footnote code.

As you read earlier, the entire footnote (the number and the text) is in one code; therefore, you can delete the footnote in the same way you delete any other code in WordPerfect. For example, you may decide that a note explaining part of the text is not necessary because the note interrupts the flow of text.

To delete a footnote, do the following steps:

1. Put the cursor under the footnote to be deleted. In this example, put the cursor under the first footnote, the one you just added.

2. Press Del and select **Y** when prompted whether you want to delete the footnote.

   If you have Reveal Codes on, WordPerfect does not ask you whether you're sure you want to delete a code, so be careful.

The footnote numbers following the deleted footnote are rewritten automatically when you delete a note.

Moving Footnotes

When editing a paper, you may want to move or copy a footnote, with or without the normal text surrounding the note. To move just the footnote, delete the code then undelete the code elsewhere. (Keep in mind that when you use Undelete or Cancel (F1), you can undelete up to the past three deletions, cycling through them by selecting **P**revious Deletion (**2**) from the Undelete menu.)

If you want to copy the note, delete the code as explained in the preceding section, then undelete the note in the original location, leaving the note untouched, and immediately move the cursor to the position where you want another copy of the same footnote to appear, and undelete the code again.

Cue:

Move or copy a footnote by first deleting and then undeleting the code whenever the need arises.

Moving the Footnote and Its Normal Text

When you move a footnote, usually you are more interested in moving the text that contains the note. For example, you may move a block of text in the document and not realize that the block contains a footnote. If you move the text, the footnotes become out of sequence; however, WordPerfect automatically corrects the sequence for you.

For example, you decide that the effect would be more striking to the reader to present the hero before the villain in the discussion of Nicholas Nickleby. Accordingly, you need to move the first two paragraphs to the end of the discussion.

To move a footnote and surrounding text, do the following steps:

1. Place the cursor at the beginning of the block of text to be deleted (moved). For this example, place the cursor at the beginning of the document.

2. Press Block (Alt-F4 or F12) to turn on Block, then move the cursor to the end of the block of text to be deleted (moved).

   🖱 Press and hold the left button, then drag the mouse to the end of the block of text to be deleted (moved) and release the button.

   Note: Move the cursor to the end of the indented quotation. Make sure that you include the footnote number in the block.

3. Press Del.

   🖱 Access the **E**dit pull-down menu and choose **D**elete (see fig. 23.9).

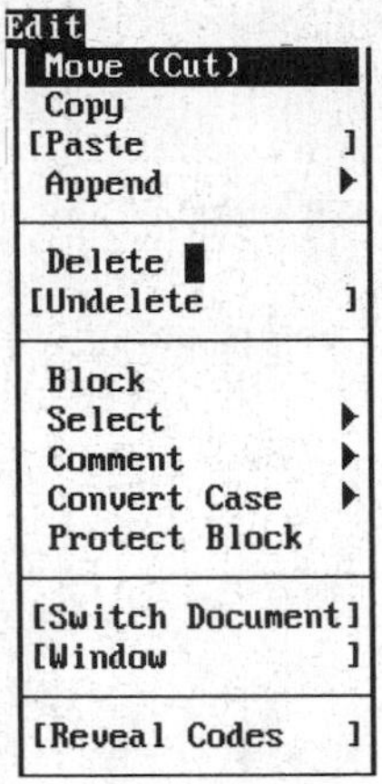

Fig. 23.9.

The Edit pull-down menu.

```
┌─Edit──────────────────┐
│ ███████████████████████│
│  Move (Cut)           │
│  Copy                 │
│ [Paste              ] │
│  Append             ▶ │
│                       │
│  Delete  █            │
│ [Undelete           ] │
│                       │
│  Block                │
│  Select             ▶ │
│  Comment            ▶ │
│  Convert Case       ▶ │
│  Protect Block        │
│                       │
│ [Switch Document]     │
│ [Window             ] │
│                       │
│ [Reveal Codes       ] │
└───────────────────────┘
```

4. Select **Y** when prompted whether you want to delete the block.

5. Move the cursor to the point where you want the deleted text to reappear. For this example, move the cursor to the end of the document.

6. Press Cancel (F1) to display the Undelete menu and select **R**estore (**1**) to undelete what was last deleted. WordPerfect automatically renumbers the footnotes.

If this were a real document, you now would go in and change the text by inserting and deleting blank lines and rewording the first paragraph to be the introductory text (see fig. 23.10).

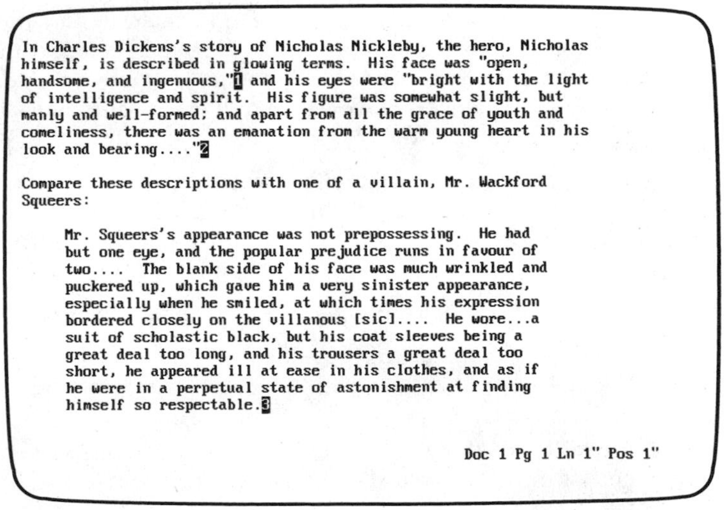

Fig. 23.10.

Edited text after moving the first two paragraphs.

```
In Charles Dickens's story of Nicholas Nickleby, the hero, Nicholas
himself, is described in glowing terms.  His face was "open,
handsome, and ingenuous,"█ and his eyes were "bright with the light
of intelligence and spirit.  His figure was somewhat slight, but
manly and well-formed; and apart from all the grace of youth and
comeliness, there was an emanation from the warm young heart in his
look and bearing...."█

Compare these descriptions with one of a villain, Mr. Wackford
Squeers:

     Mr. Squeers's appearance was not prepossessing.  He had
     but one eye, and the popular prejudice runs in favour of
     two....  The blank side of his face was much wrinkled and
     puckered up, which gave him a very sinister appearance,
     especially when he smiled, at which times his expression
     bordered closely on the villanous [sic]....  He wore...a
     suit of scholastic black, but his coat sleeves being a
     great deal too long, and his trousers a great deal too
     short, he appeared ill at ease in his clothes, and as if
     he were in a perpetual state of astonishment at finding
     himself so respectable.█

                              Doc 1 Pg 1 Ln 1" Pos 1"
```

Moving Just the Footnote

Moving only the footnote code (the superscripted number with the text of the note) is just a matter of locating, deleting, and undeleting the code wherever you want the code to reappear.

In the previous example, you changed the order of the footnotes, and now the first footnote no longer contains the complete reference information. You can delete and retype the footnote, or you can move footnotes 1 and 3 and then correct the page-number references.

To move a footnote number and the contents of the note to a different position in the text, do the following steps:

1. Position the cursor under the number of the footnote you want to move. In this case, you want to move the third note to the first footnote position, so place the cursor under footnote 3.

2. Press Del and select **Y** when asked whether you want to delete the footnote.

3. Move the cursor to the new position for the footnote. In this example, place the cursor under the first footnote so that the undeleted note appears just in front of the current footnote number 1.

4. Press Cancel (F1) to display the Undelete menu. As usual, the last thing deleted is highlighted on-screen. Only the note number appears for footnotes, however, because the note number is all you normally see. If you want to see the text of the deleted note as well as the number, go into Reveal Codes before pressing the Cancel key.

5. Select **R**estore (**1**) to undelete what was last deleted.

6. Press Reveal Codes (Alt-F3 or F11) to verify that the footnote is in the new location (see fig. 23.11).

   Notice that you now have two adjacent footnotes that appear as though you have a footnote *12* in the normal screen.

7. Press Reveal Codes (Alt-F3 or F11) again to return to the normal screen.

Repeat the instructions, moving the footnote now numbered *2* to the end of the document after the word *respectable*. You successfully have switched footnotes 1 and 3. To complete the process, you need to correct the page-number references.

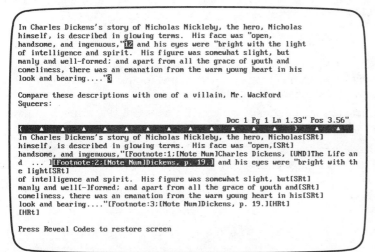

Fig. 23.11.
The Reveal Codes of the footnote in its new location.

Editing Footnotes

You have seen how to create, view, delete, and move notes; but, what do you do if you want to change a note you already have created? Suppose that you remembered only the title of a book and nothing else when you originally typed a footnote; now you want to enter the complete reference. Or perhaps the style of a footnote does not fit the person or journal to which you are sending the text, and you have to change the style. You already have seen that the entire note is a single code, so you know you cannot get into the note to make changes when you are in the normal text screen. Fortunately, WordPerfect provides an easy way to edit a footnote from the Footnote menu.

To edit a footnote from anywhere in the document, do the following:

1. Press the Footnote key (Ctrl-F7), select **F**ootnote (**1**), and then select **E**dit (**2**).

   ⌨ Access the **L**ayout pull-down menu, choose **F**ootnote, and then choose **E**dit.

Cue:

Always double-check the note number you are prompted with when you ask to edit a note.

   WordPerfect displays the `Footnote number?` prompt at the bottom of the screen followed by the number of the first footnote that follows the cursor. If the cursor follows the last footnote in the document, however, WordPerfect prompts you with a number for a footnote that does not exist! If you then press Enter to accept the number, WordPerfect displays the message `* Not found *`, and you must begin again. To avoid this waste of time, always verify the number with which WordPerfect prompts you.

2. Press Enter if the footnote number WordPerfect gives you matches the one you wish to edit, or type the correct number and then press Enter. For this example, type *3* and press Enter.

> ### Tip
>
> If you are using the SHORTCUT keyboard definition that comes with WordPerfect 5.1, you can use the Edit key on a footnote or endnote. Place the cursor on the note number code in the text and press Edit (Alt-E) rather than following steps 1 and 2.

3. Because you are now in a footnote edit screen, use normal cursor-movement and editing keys to change the footnote. In the example, change the page number from 19 to 24 (see fig. 23.12).

4. As instructed at the bottom of the screen, press Exit (F7) when you have finished editing the footnote.

Fig. 23.12.
An edited footnote.

```
 Dickens, p. 24.
```

Repeat these instructions for footnote 1 and change the page number from 24 to 19.

Tip

When you finish editing the footnote, the cursor is positioned just after the footnote in question. If you want to return the cursor to the original location, use the GoTo, GoTo (Ctrl-Home, Ctrl-Home) command.

Continuing Footnote Numbers across Documents

If you have a large document to create, you may want to break it into smaller documents to speed up the editing. If so, and you have notes scattered throughout the text, make sure that the notes are consecutively numbered from one document to the next. You can have consecutive numbering by using Master Document (explained in Chapter 26) or by using the **N**ew Number option from the appropriate Note menu.

Cue:
Use the Master Document feature to number notes continuously from one file to another.

Suppose that you have six footnotes in the first document, five in the second, and seven in the third. In the second document, which is a continuation of the first, you can insert a Footnote Number code at the beginning that tells WordPerfect to begin numbering at 7 instead of 1 (Footnote (Ctrl-F7), **N**ew Number (**3**), 7, Enter; the code looks like this: **[New Ftn Num:7]**). In the third document, you can start the footnote numbering at 12 instead of 1. However, using Master Document is more efficient. Master Document automates this and other processes; you don't have to worry about the number of notes changing in an earlier document and throwing off the count in the rest of the documents.

Changing Footnote Options

If you want to use footnotes, but don't like the way WordPerfect formats them, you can use the Footnote Options menu to change the style. Just press Footnote (Ctrl-F7), select **F**ootnote (**1**), and choose **O**ptions (**4**) to bring up the Footnote Options menu, as shown in figure 23.13. ▭ If you use a mouse, you can access the **L**ayout pull-down menu, select **F**ootnote, and then select **O**ptions.

Before you work on an example, look at the options available on the Footnote Options menu.

Tip

A note option code appears in Reveal Codes as **[Ftn Opt]** or **[End Opt]** with no indication of what, if anything, was changed. (Just looking at the menu and then pressing Exit (F7) rather than Cancel (F1) to return to the document leaves a code in the text.) To discover what a note option code does, place the cursor just *before* the code, look at the menu selections, and then press Cancel (F1) to return to the document. Next, move the cursor to a point just *after* the code and compare the menu selections with the previous ones; any changes you see were brought about by the note option code in question. If there were no changes, delete the code to clean up the document.

If you are using the SHORTCUT keyboard definition, you can edit the note option code by placing the cursor on the code and pressing Edit (Alt-E).

```
┌──────────────────────────────────────────────────────────────────┐
│  Footnote Options                                                  │
│                                                                    │
│      1 - Spacing Within Footnotes              1                   │
│             Between Footnotes                  0.167"              │
│                                                                    │
│      2 - Amount of Note to Keep Together       0.5"                │
│                                                                    │
│      3 - Style for Number in Text              [SUPRSCPT][Note Num][suprscpt]  │
│                                                                    │
│      4 - Style for Number in Note                    [SUPRSCPT][Note Num][suprscpt  │
│                                                                    │
│      5 - Footnote Numbering Method             Numbers             │
│                                                                    │
│      6 - Start Footnote Numbers each Page      No                  │
│                                                                    │
│      7 - Line Separating Text and Footnotes    2-inch Line         │
│                                                                    │
│      8 - Print Continued Message               No                  │
│                                                                    │
│      9 - Footnotes at Bottom of Page           Yes                 │
└──────────────────────────────────────────────────────────────────┘
```

Fig. 23.13.

The Footnote Options menu.

Reminder:

You can change the spacing between the lines of footnotes and between individual footnotes.

The first option, **S**pacing Within Footnotes and Between Footnotes (**1**), allows you to change the spacing within the footnotes (the text of the notes is single-spaced by default) as well as between the notes (the space between one note and the next, if more than one note is on the page). **S**pacing Within Footnotes is shown in lines; **S**pacing Between Footnotes is shown in inches (0.167" being one line if you are using a standard font at six lines per inch).

The most common change in the default setting of **S**pacing Within Footnotes is from 1 to 2. This change accommodates people who want to print drafts or print an article for a publisher who wants all text double-spaced. You can change the setting to 3 or some other spacing as well.

> ### Tip
>
> To change the spacing in a single footnote, you can use the Format function key (Shift-F8) from within the footnote-entry screen. Do not forget to change it back to the original spacing at the end of the note.

You also can change the amount of blank space between footnotes that appear on the same page. This feature is helpful if you need to squeeze more text on a page (reducing the space between footnotes) or spread text out (increasing the space between footnotes). If you prefer, you can enter the value in a unit other than inches (1 cm, for example), and WordPerfect converts the value for you.

The second option, **A**mount of Note to Keep Together (**2**), is used when you have a long footnote that may not fit at the bottom of the page. This option allows you to decide how much of a given footnote WordPerfect should keep together on one page before continuing the rest of the note on the bottom of the next page. You can change the default 0.5" setting (one-half inch, or three lines at the normal six lines per inch) to 1", for example, if you want more than just 0.5 inch of a footnote to stay together.

Choosing this footnote option does not mean that every footnote longer than 0.5 inch is split across pages. Instead, the option means that if the footnote is more than 0.5-inch long and the entire footnote does not fit at the bottom of the page because the reference is close to the bottom, then the footnote becomes split. If less than 0.5 inch of the note fits at the bottom of the page, however, WordPerfect moves both the text containing the footnote number and the entire footnote to the next page. If the footnote is long enough to split across pages, a page break appears in the footnote as you type.

Choose Style for Number in **T**ext (**3**) to change the appearance of the footnotes if you don't like the footnote numbers superscripted in the text or if the printer doesn't handle superscripts well. For example, you can have the note numbers appear in brackets. Or, if the printer has the capability, you can use a different font attribute.

Note: If the printer has the capability to print in different font sizes, WordPerfect automatically formats footnote numbers as a Fine font size.

Cue:
If the printer doesn't handle superscripting well, change note numbering from superscripts to numbers inside brackets [].

If you want to change the style of the superscripted number in the footnote itself, choose Style for Number in **N**ote (**4**). You can change the footnote to be just the number followed by a period, and a Tab or five spaces. The instructions for including the **[Note Num]** code are the same as for the third option.

Suppose that you want to change the footnote numbering style to a legal style where the footnote number is underlined and followed by a slash (/). For reasons described later, you change the style in the Document Initial Codes:

1. Press Format (Shift-F8), select **D**ocument (**3**), and then select **I**nitial Codes (**2**).

   ⌨ Access the **L**ayout pull-down menu, select **D**ocument, and then select **I**nitial Codes (**2**).

2. Press **F**ootnote (Ctrl-F7), select **F**ootnote, and then select **O**ptions.

   ⌨ Access the **L**ayout pull-down menu, select **F**ootnote, and then select **O**ptions.

3. Select Style for Number in **T**ext (**3**).

4. Move the cursor past the **[SUPRSCPT]** code to the beginning of the **[Note Num]** code.

5. Press Underline (F8).

6. Move the cursor past the **[Note Num]** code and press Underline (F8) again.

7. Type a slash (/). The codes now look like this:

   [SUPRSCPT][UND][Note Num][und]/[suprscpt]

   If you wanted to use this style, you would probably want to change the codes for the Style for Number in **N**ote (**4**) as well.

8. Press Exit (F7) three times to return to the document.

Choose Footnote Numbering **M**ethod (**5**) if you do not want to use numbers for the footnotes. You can set up the notes with letters (a, b, c instead of 1, 2, 3) by choosing **L**etters (**2**), or with different characters (*, **, *** instead of 1, 2, 3) by selecting **C**haracters (**3**). You even can have more than one type of character by

Reminder:
You can change footnote numbers to letters or characters.

entering something like *#, for example, so that the order is *, #, **, ##, and so on. By using multiple characters, you avoid long references (footnote 6, for example, would be ### instead of ******).

Occasionally, you may need to use footnotes and endnotes in the same document. To help the reader in such cases, you should use different numbering systems for the footnotes and endnotes. However, the numbering system you use depends on why you are using both types of notes.

For example, you may want to collect the source references at the end of the document, yet still make parenthetical comments about the text at the bottom of the page. In this case, use numbers for the endnotes, and characters for the footnotes. However, if you are using footnotes for the source references, but also need to provide notes for tables or figures, you probably want to use numbers for the footnotes and letters for the notes in the tables or figures. In addition, by using endnotes in the tables, you easily can gather all the table notes at the bottom of the table using the Endnote Placement feature discussed in the next section.

If you change the default numbers setting, remember that when you edit a footnote, you must enter the number of the note in the new style (for example, ** instead of 2).

The default setting for Start Footnote Numbers each **P**age (**6**) is **N**o; therefore, WordPerfect numbers the footnotes consecutively throughout the document. However, if you have all the footnote numbers marked with asterisks instead of numbers, for example, the footnotes start to take up space after just a few notes (footnote 6 is ******). One way to avoid the long references is to start the footnotes at 1 on each page by setting this option to **Y**es.

Figure 23.4 shows an example of the default setting for the separator—a 2-inch line printed at the left margin—between text and footnotes. You can change the separator by selecting **L**ine Separating Text and **F**ootnotes (**7**). To have a line that stretches all the way across the page, choose **M**argin to Margin (**3**); to have no line at all, choose **N**o Line (**1**).

Cue:

If you have long footnotes, have a (...continued) message appear to help the reader follow the notes.

If you have long footnotes that WordPerfect breaks up from one page to the next, you may want the program to signal this break to the reader. If you set Print **C**ontinued Message (**8**) to **Y**es, WordPerfect prints a (...continued) message on both the last line of the footnote on the first page and on the first line of the footnote on the next page.

> ### Tip
>
> Put a language code (explained in Chapter 21) in the Initial Codes of a document to have the (...continued) message print in a language other than English.

The last option on the Footnote Options menu, Footnotes at **B**ottom of Page (**9**), allows you to alter the location on the page where the footnotes are printed. In figure 23.4, the footnotes are printed at the very bottom of the page, leaving several inches of blank space between the text and the footnotes. If you would rather have the notes printed just below the text, leaving the blank space after the footnotes instead, set this option to **N**o.

You may have noticed that options do not exist for left and right margins for notes in the Options menu. Margins are determined by the following:

1. The individual margin settings within each note.
2. The margins set in the Document Initial Codes.
3. Whatever margin settings are in effect when you add a footnote option code.

If you want the notes to have the same margins (1.5 inches, for example), with different margins for the normal document text, change the margins to 1.5" in the Format: Document Initial Codes menu, then change the normal text margins for the document within the body of the text.

Tip

If you add a footnote option code within a document, all footnotes from that point take on the current formatting in the document, including margins, tab settings, font sizes, and so on.

If you want different formatting for the footnotes, but *must* change the footnote options within the document, change all formatting immediately before the footnote option code, then return the formatting to the document settings immediately after the code.

Assume that you are printing footnotes with 1.5-inch margins, but are printing the document with 1-inch margins. Before you add a footnote option code within the document, change the margins to 1.5 inch, add the option code, then change the margins back to 1 inch. Because this can be confusing, a better strategy is to set the footnote options in Document Initial codes and not change them within the document.

Using Endnotes

An *endnote* is a reference or some other parenthetical text that appears at the end of a document (or wherever you specify). Unless you say otherwise, WordPerfect puts the endnotes at the end of the text without a page break. You may want to place a hard page return at the very end of the document and add a title (NOTES, centered on the line, for example) at the top of the last page.

Tip

By default, WordPerfect puts endnotes at the end of the document. This means that the endnotes appear after any indexes or lists you prepare using WordPerfect's automatic index or list feature. If you want the endnotes to appear before indexes and lists, you must use the **E**ndnote **P**lacement option.

Working with Endnotes

Reminder:

Work with endnotes the same way you do with footnotes.

Working with endnotes is essentially the same as working with footnotes. You can create, view, edit, delete, and move endnotes just as you do footnotes.

When you are ready to enter an endnote, do the following steps:

1. Place the cursor where you want the endnote number to appear.

2. Press Footnote (Ctrl-F7) and select **E**ndnote (**2**).

    ⌨ Access the **L**ayout pull-down menu and select **E**ndnote.

    The following menu appears:

    Endnote: 1 Create; **2 E**dit; **3 N**ew Number; **4 O**ptions

    Note: If you are using the pull-down menus, you also see the **E**ndnote **P**lacement option.

3. Select **C**reate (**1**) to create an endnote. The cursor appears in an endnote-entry screen, similar to the footnote-entry screen except that the number is at the left margin, is not superscripted, and is followed by a period.

> **Tip**
>
> If you are using the SHORTCUT keyboard definition, you can reach this point by pressing Ctrl-E for Endnote Create.

4. Tab once or press the space bar once or twice to separate the period after the number from the text you are about to enter.

5. Type the text of the note. As with footnotes, you can use most of WordPerfect's features here (for example, underline, bold, italics, and equation boxes).

6. When you have finished, press Exit (F7) to get back to the normal document.

This procedure, using the default endnote settings, produces an endnote that appears as follows at the end of a document:

1. Charles Dickens, <u>The Life and Adventures of Nicholas Nickleby</u> (Philadelphia: University of Pennsylvania Press, 1982), vol. 1, p. 24.

Notice how the number is neither superscripted nor indented. Unfortunately, most style guides require endnotes to be in the same format as footnotes. The next section describes how to change the endnote style.

You can delete and undelete the endnote code (which looks the same as a footnote, but begins with the word **[Endnote:...]**) in exactly the same way you do a footnote code.

Look at the text of an endnote by pressing Print (Shift-F7) and selecting **V**iew Document (**6**). Remember to go to the end of the entire document to find the notes.

> **Tip**
>
> WordPerfect allows you to see *all* endnotes in View Document instead of just the first page of notes. Pressing Home, Home, ↓ in View Document takes you to the last page of normal text; press PgDn to go past that point. Continue using PgDn until all endnotes have been viewed.

Changing Endnote Options

The Endnote Options menu is very much like the Footnote Options menu except that the Endnote menu has fewer options (see fig. 23.14). In addition, the Style for Numbers in **N**ote (**4**) option on the Endnote Options menu simply has **[Note Num]** followed by a period instead of being surrounded by superscript notations.

```
Endnote Options

    1 - Spacing Within Endnotes          1
              Between Endnotes           0.167"

    2 - Amount of Endnote to Keep Together  0.5"

    3 - Style for Numbers in Text        [SUPRSCPT][Note Num][suprscpt]

    4 - Style for Numbers in Note        [Note Num].

    5 - Endnote Numbering Method         Numbers
```

Fig. 23.14.

The Endnote Options menu.

As previously noted, the default style for endnotes is different from the default style for footnotes. With a few simple changes in the Endnote Options menu, however, you can adjust the style so that endnote style is the same as footnote style

Reminder:

The default endnote style differs from the default footnote style.

Note: Because you will be matching the endnotes style with the footnotes style in the following example, before you do the following steps, you may want to change the footnote style back to the default. To do this, return to Document Initial Codes and delete the **[Ftn Opt]** code.

To achieve the proper style for the endnotes, do the following steps:

1. Position the cursor before the point where the first endnote appears in the document.

2. Press Format (Shift-F8), select **D**ocument (**3**), and select Initial **C**odes (**2**).

   ▭ Access the **L**ayout pull-down menu, select **D**ocument, and select Initial **C**odes (**2**).

   Note: Putting the endnote style code into the document's Initial Codes is more efficient if you want *all* endnotes in the document to be affected.

2. Press Footnote (Ctrl-F7), select **E**ndnote (**2**), and select **O**ptions (**4**) to display the Endnote Options menu.

   ▭ Access the **L**ayout pull-down menu, select **E**ndnote, and select **O**ptions.

3. Select Style for Numbers in **N**ote (**4**) to change the way the endnote numbers appear at the end of the document. The prompt `Replace with:` appears at the bottom of the screen.

4. Press the space bar five times so that each endnote is indented five spaces from the left margin.

5. Insert a superscript code by pressing Font (Ctrl-F8), selecting **S**ize (**1**), and then selecting **S**uperscript (**1**).

6. Insert a note number code by pressing Footnote (Ctrl-F7), selecting **E**ndnote (**2**), and then selecting **N**umber Code (**2**).

7. Press Enter to save the new endnote style. Notice that WordPerfect automatically inserts an end superscript code (**[suprscpt]**).

8. Press Exit (F7) (three times if you inserted the code into the document's Initial Codes) to save the new endnote options and return to the document.

You then enter the endnotes following the steps outlined at the beginning of this section, but without tabbing or spacing after the endnote number. The endnote numbers are superscripted, and you can begin typing the text of a note immediately after the note number without the intervening tab or spaces. The new style takes care of the spaces for you.

Positioning Endnotes

Reminder:

You can specify where in the document you want the endnotes to appear.

The one remaining difference between footnotes and endnotes is that you can tell WordPerfect to put endnotes anywhere in the document. If you don't select Endnote **P**lacement (**3**), however, the program automatically places the endnotes at the end of the document.

To insert a code that puts the endnotes at some place other than the end of the document, do the following steps:

1. Place the cursor where you want the program to place the endnotes.

2. Press Footnote (Ctrl-F7) and select Endnote **P**lacement (**3**).

   ⌨ Access the **L**ayout pull-down menu, choose **E**ndnote, and choose **P**lacement.

   The prompt `Restart endnote numbering? Yes(No)` appears.

3. Select **Y** if you want the endnotes that follow to begin at 1 (or whatever number you specify); select **N** if you want the endnotes to continue with the same numbering as any previous endnotes.

   After making the choice, the following message appears on-screen:

   ```
   Endnote Placement
    It is not known how much space endnotes requires here.
    Generate to determine.
   ```

   This message shows in Reveal Codes as **[Endnote Placement][HPg]**. If you selected **Y** to restart endnote numbering, you also see a **[New End Num:1]** code.

WordPerfect does not keep track of the space the endnotes occupy because you may be deleting, adding, or moving notes throughout the document. Because people usually work with page limitations for their writing, however, WordPerfect provides a way to see how many lines the endnotes use.

Cue:

Generate the document to calculate the endnote placement space.

If you want to see how many pages the endnotes occupy, do the following steps:

1. Press Mark Text (Alt-F5) and select **G**enerate (**6**).

    ⌨ Access the **M**ark pull-down menu and select **G**enerate.

2. Select **G**enerate Tables, Indexes, Cross-References (**5**).

3. Select **Y** when prompted whether you want to continue.

After the generation process, you might expect to see the endnotes appear. Instead, the boxed message changes to `Endnote Placement`, and you see the line count, in the status line at the bottom of the screen, that reflects how many lines the endnotes use.

Note: You may find that even after generating the endnotes, the notes at the Endnote Placement code are chopped off in View Document if they continue past the end of the current page.

If you want to add text after endnotes on the same page, be careful; you must type a hard return after the Endnote Placement code, as in the following example:

[Endnote Placement][HRt]

[HRt]

text[HPg]

If you do not add the hard return, the text prints before the endnotes even if the text follows the Endnote Placement code in Reveal Codes. If you choose View Document, you see that the following example produces text that prints before the endnotes:

[Endnote Placement]text[HPg]

You also can delete the **[HPg]** code WordPerfect automatically inserts after the **[Endnote Placement]** code if you do not want a page break in this location.

Using Macros

If you want to change footnotes to endnotes (or vice versa), WordPerfect provides macros to accomplish the task. To change a footnote to an endnote, for example, edit the footnote, move or cut the text, delete the footnote, create an endnote, and retrieve the cut block of text into the new endnote. The macros provided with WordPerfect 5.1 (FOOTEND.WPM for converting footnotes to endnotes, and ENDFOOT.WPM for the opposite conversion) do all this for you.

Reminder:

Use the FOOTEND and ENDFOOT macros to turn footnotes into endnotes and endnotes into footnotes.

If you convert one type of note to the other, you can confirm the procedure with View Document. You may want to go back to the beginning of the document to change the note options if the newly converted notes don't look the way you want them to look.

Summary

In this chapter, you have learned how to do the following tasks:

❑ Create a footnote or endnote

❑ Look at notes by using Reveal Codes, Print Document, View Document, or Footnote Edit

❑ Delete and move notes, as you do any other WordPerfect code

❑ Edit existing notes

❑ Continue note numbering across several documents

❑ Change note options

❑ Specify endnote placement

❑ Change footnotes to endnotes, or vice versa, by using a macro

24

Outlining, Paragraph Numbering, and Line Numbering

Susan Hafer, the Microcomputer Specialist for Academic Computing at Wellesley College, contributes to this chapter her knowledge of the various numbering methods in WordPerfect 5.l.

In this chapter you learn various numbering methods in WordPerfect: outlining, paragraph numbering, and line numbering. All provide automatic numbering.

Why bother with automatic numbering when you can type these numbers yourself? Automatic numbering helps you create outlines without having to remember what number you should enter. Automatic numbering also helps you make changes easily. For example, after you number paragraphs, you then can delete, add, or change the order of the paragraphs, and WordPerfect automatically renumbers them. Without this feature, you have to renumber paragraphs by hand. With version 5.1's new approach to outlining, you also can delete and move groups or "families" within an outline more easily.

Line numbering, the simplest form of automatic numbering, numbers each line along the left edge of the text. You begin and end the numbering at any place you choose, and you can specify the interval for numbers to appear (for example, every line or every five lines). The numbers do not appear on-screen as you edit the document, but you can see them when you print the document or when you use View Document.

With the Outline and Paragraph Numbering options, paragraphs are numbered using one of several numbering styles. Do not let the option names mislead you. The differences between these two features are in the way the numbers are created and how easily they can be changed rather than how they appear on paper. Outline is more automated and more restrictive than Paragraph Numbering. With Paragraph

765

Numbering, the program inserts a paragraph number only when you ask for one, and all keystrokes work normally. With Outline, some keystrokes have special meanings, and WordPerfect can automatically generate a new paragraph number or style every time you press Enter.

In this chapter, you explore the following automatic numbering features:

- Outline—to create an outline and generate paragraph numbers automatically
- Paragraph Numbering—to generate paragraph numbers when you choose
- Line Numbering—to number lines automatically

In addition, you learn how to do the following:

- Make editing changes to the outline
- Change the numbering style used for Outline and Paragraph Numbering
- Change the defaults for Line Numbering

Reminder

If you use a mouse with WordPerfect 5.1, you can click the right button to display the pull-down menus, and then select the desired option. You also can press Alt-= to access the pull-down menus, and then press the appropriate letter of the desired option. For all instructions, assume that if a block is required to activate a pull-down menu option, the text has been blocked before the pull-down menu is accessed. Instructions for pull-down menus and the mouse are marked with the mouse icon. For more information about the mouse, see Chapter 1. ⌨

Outlining a Document

Outlines in WordPerfect essentially are normal text with **[Par Num]** codes where paragraph numbers appear. When using Outline, an **[Outline On]** code precedes the outline, and all text between that code and the end of the document or an **[Outline Off]** code is treated in a special way. The Outline feature automatically generates and inserts these codes.

Turning On Outline

Reminder:

Use Outline to automatically number paragraphs as you type them and press Enter.

Use Outline when you want to generate paragraph numbers automatically. With Outline on, each time you press Enter, you create a new paragraph number or style. The style you select determines the characters used for different levels (I., A., 1., a., and so on). The default paragraph-numbering style is Outline.

Note: You may have selected a style using characters, such as bullets, or even a set of codes with no numbering using the new Outline Style feature; if so, then pressing Enter will create a new paragraph with a bullet, specified codes, or whatever you have defined. In this chapter, for clarity's sake, *paragraph numbers* refers to any of those possibilities.

Refer to figure 24.1 to create a sample outline.

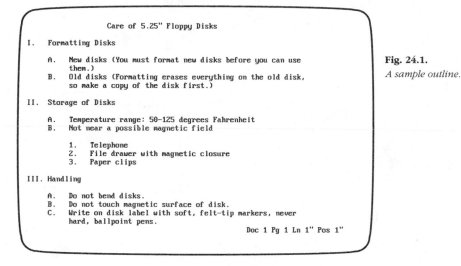

Care of 5.25" Floppy Disks

I.   Formatting Disks

     A.   New disks (You must format new disks before you can use
          them.)
     B.   Old disks (Formatting erases everything on the old disk,
          so make a copy of the disk first.)

II. Storage of Disks

     A.   Temperature range: 50-125 degrees Fahrenheit
     B.   Not near a possible magnetic field

          1.   Telephone
          2.   File drawer with magnetic closure
          3.   Paper clips

III. Handling

     A.   Do not bend disks.
     B.   Do not touch magnetic surface of disk.
     C.   Write on disk label with soft, felt-tip markers, never
          hard, ballpoint pens.
                                           Doc 1 Pg 1 Ln 1" Pos 1"

Fig. 24.1.

A sample outline.

You may want to type a title before turning on Outline. For this example, do the following steps:

1. Press Center (Shift-F6) if you want to center a title.

2. Type a title for the outline and press Enter. Because the title is not part of the outline, you type the title before turning on Outline.

   For this example, type *Care of 5.25" Floppy Disks* and press Enter.

3. Place the cursor where you want to begin the outline. For this example, press Enter to leave a blank line; start the outline on the next line.

To turn on Outline, complete the following steps:

1. Press Date/Outline (Shift-F5).

   ⌨ Access the **T**ools pull-down menu and choose **O**utline.

   The following menu appears:

   1 Date **T**ext; **2** Date **C**ode; **3** Date **F**ormat; **4** Outline; **5** **P**ara Num; **6** **D**efine: **0**

2. From the Date/Outline menu, select **O**utline (**4**). The following menu appears:

   Outline: 1 **O**n; **2** **O**ff; **3** **M**ove Family; **4** **C**opy Family; **5** **D**elete Family: **0**

3. Select **O**n (**1**) to turn on the automatic outlining feature. The word Outline appears at the bottom of the screen, replacing the name of the file if one was displayed. Turning on Outline inserts a code in the document; when Outline appears on-screen, the Enter, Tab, and Margin Release keys perform specific functions (explained in the next section).

You may want to press Reveal Codes (Alt-F3 or F11) to see the **[Outline On]** code and the succeeding paragraph-numbering codes (see fig. 24.2). Although the figures shown in this chapter have Reveal Codes on so that you can see what is happening, you do not need to use Reveal Codes to use Outline.

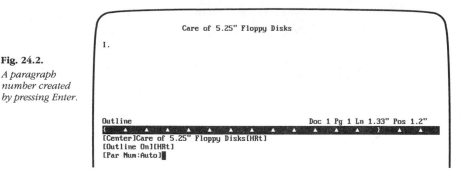

Fig. 24.2.

A paragraph number created by pressing Enter.

Creating Level Numbers

For Outline style, levels are determined by tab stops in the following manner: numbers at the left margin (first level) are uppercase Roman numerals (I, II, III); numbers at the first tab stop (second level) are capital letters (A, B, C); numbers at the second tab stop (third level) are digits or Arabic numerals (1, 2, 3), and so on. Other styles have different level numbers. See "Defining the Numbering Style" later in this chapter.

When Outline is on, the Enter, Tab, and Margin Release keys have special functions. The Enter key, in addition to inserting a carriage return in the text, creates a new paragraph number **[Par Num:Auto]** on the new line. When the cursor is positioned just after this new code, the Tab key has another function. In addition to inserting a **[Tab]** code and moving the cursor over one tab stop, pressing Tab pulls the paragraph number over with the cursor and changes the number's level to the right. Alternatively, Margin Release pulls the number over and changes the number's level in the opposite direction. For example, if pressing Enter created *I*, and you pressed Tab, the number would change to *A*; pressing Indent would move the number back and change it to *I* again.

Once Outline is on, you can create numbered paragraphs in the following manner:

1. Press Enter to create a paragraph number. Because Outline is on, WordPerfect generates a paragraph number and places the cursor after the number. The default style determines the number (a Roman numeral one or *I.* in the example in fig. 24.2) for the levels.

   If you press Enter again, you may expect the number to remain in place and the cursor to move down a line. Because Outline is on, the number moves down with the cursor and leaves a blank line behind.

   With WordPerfect 5.1, the new paragraph number created when you press Enter is created *at the same level as the previous number.*

2. To move the cursor after setting the paragraph number with Enter, Tab, or Margin Release (Shift-Tab) as required, press Indent (F4) or the space bar.

   Alternatively, you can press Home and Tab for a hard tab code. You must press Home before pressing Tab, or the number moves with the cursor. If you use Indent (F4), the text wraps so that any second line is aligned underneath the first character of the first line, creating a hanging indent and making a more appealing and readable outline.

3. Type the text for this level. (Remember that another paragraph number is created as soon as you press Enter again.) The text may be a short heading or a paragraph. For this example, type *Formatting Disks*.

4. Press Enter. WordPerfect generates the next paragraph number. In the default style, this number is *II*.

5. Press Enter again to leave a blank line between paragraphs. Note that the number moves with the cursor.

6. Press Tab to move in one level. The number follows and changes, in this case to *A*. (see fig. 24.3).

   Notice that pressing Tab in this step does not affect the outline's hanging indents, because you press →Indent (F4) in the next step.

   If you press Tab too many times, press Margin Release (Shift-Tab) to move back one tab stop. No code is inserted, but the number moves back a tab stop and changes back one level.

   With Outline on, the Tab key operates similar to the Enter key: the number stays with the cursor as the cursor moves. Unlike the Enter key, however, the Tab key determines the level number, changing the number and moving the number forward.

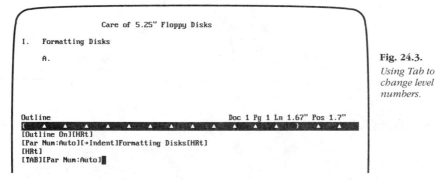

Fig. 24.3.

Using Tab to change level numbers.

7. Press →Indent (F4) to leave the number, or press Home followed by Tab, or press the space bar to position the cursor for text entry after the paragraph number.

8. Type the text for this level. For this example, type the following:

   New disks (You must format new disks before you can use them.)

9. Repeat these steps to complete the outline shown in fig. 24.1.

If you use an older version of WordPerfect, remember that with 5.1, pressing Enter creates a paragraph number on the same level as the previous-numbered paragraph rather than a top-level number at the left margin. If you prefer the old way, refer to "Investigating Numbering Styles."

> **Tip**
>
> You can create outlines within headers, footers, endnotes, footnotes, and text boxes; they will be completely independent of any outlines within the main body of the document.

Turning Off Outline

When you complete the outline and want to return to creating normal paragraphs, turn off Outline in the following manner:

1. Place the cursor after the outline in the text.
2. Press Date/Outline (Shift-F5).
3. Select **O**utline (**4**) and then O**ff** (**2**) to turn off Outline.

   ⌨ Access the **T**ools pull-down menu, select **O**utline, and then select O**ff**.

   An **[Outline Off]** code is inserted.

If you aren't certain whether Outline is on or off, look at the bottom left corner of the screen: if Outline appears, the Outline feature is on.

Reminder:

Even after you exit from Outline mode, moving the cursor between the outline codes makes Enter and Tab work as they do in Outline mode.

When you turn off Outline, the Enter and Tab keys revert back to their normal functions. You now can enter normal paragraphs after the outline. Moving the cursor back into the text between the **[Outline On]** and **[Outline Off]** codes automatically causes the Enter and Tab keys to once again perform special functions.

Defining Numbering Styles

Outline, the default numbering style, uses standard Roman numerals. You can choose another numbering style if you want. For example, you can change the outline you just created to a paragraph-numbering style.

To change the numbering style, complete the following steps:

1. Place the cursor at the beginning of the outline. For this example, the outline is at the beginning of the document, so press Home, Home, ↑.
2. Press Date/Outline (Shift-F5) and select **D**efine (**6**).

   ⌨ Access the **T**ools pull-down menu and choose **D**efine.

   The Paragraph Number Definition menu appears (see fig. 24.4). The current definition appears in the center of the screen. Notice that the numbering levels match those for Outline style, the default. Options 2 through 6 are the other numbering choices. New with 5.1 are options 7 through 9, discussed later in this chapter.

3. Select the new numbering style you want (see "Investigating Numbering Styles" later in this chapter for a description of each option.)

   For this example, select **P**aragraph (**2**). Notice that the current definition in the center of the screen changes to reflect the new style.

```
Paragraph Number Definition

    1 - Starting Paragraph Number          1
        (in legal style)
                                        Levels
                          1     2     3     4     5     6     7     8
    2 - Paragraph         1.    a.    i.    (1)   (a)   (i)   1)    a)
    3 - Outline           I.    A.    1.    a.    (1)   (a)   i)    a)
    4 - Legal (1.1.1)     1     .1    .1    .1    .1    .1    .1    .1
    5 - Bullets           •     o     -     ▪     *     +     ·     x
    6 - User-defined

    Current Definition    I.    A.    1.    a.    (1)   (a)   i)    a)
    Attach Previous Level       No    No    No    No    No    No    No

    7 - Enter Inserts Paragraph Number     Yes

    8 - Automatically Adjust to Current Level   Yes

    9 - Outline Style Name
```

Fig. 24.4.

The Paragraph Number Definition menu.

4. Press Exit (F7) or Enter to enter the new current definition into the document and return to the Date/Outline menu.

   Whenever you press Exit (F7) from the Paragraph Number Definition menu, WordPerfect inserts a paragraph-number definition code into the document and begins numbering the subsequent paragraph with 1. If you notice that the paragraphs are numbered *1, 2, 3, 1, 2* rather than *1, 2, 3, 4, 5*, press Reveal Codes (Alt-F3 or F11) to find the **[Par Num Def]** code embedded in the middle of the outline and delete the code. If you do not want to save the settings in the Paragraph Number Definition menu, press Cancel (F1) instead of Exit (F7) or Enter. No code is inserted in the document.

5. Press Exit (F7) or Enter to return to the document from the Date/Outline menu.

6. Press Screen (Ctrl-F3) and select **R**ewrite (**3**) to display the document again so that you can make sure that the entire outline has been renumbered to match the new numbering style definition (see fig. 24.5).

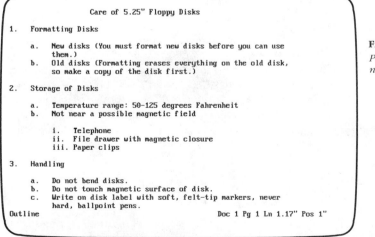

```
               Care of 5.25" Floppy Disks

    1.   Formatting Disks

         a.   New disks (You must format new disks before you can use
              them.)
         b.   Old disks (Formatting erases everything on the old disk,
              so make a copy of the disk first.)

    2.   Storage of Disks

         a.   Temperature range: 50-125 degrees Fahrenheit
         b.   Not near a possible magnetic field

              i.    Telephone
              ii.   File drawer with magnetic closure
              iii.  Paper clips

    3.   Handling

         a.   Do not bend disks.
         b.   Do not touch magnetic surface of disk.
         c.   Write on disk label with soft, felt-tip markers, never
              hard, ballpoint pens.
    Outline                        Doc 1 Pg 1 Ln 1.17" Pos 1"
```

Fig. 24.5.

Paragraph numbering style.

If the numbering did not change, check the procedure by doing the following:

1. If Reveal Codes is off, turn it on by pressing Reveal Codes (Alt-F3 or F11).

2. Be sure that the **[Par Num Def]** code is at the beginning of the outline, not at the end.

3. Check to be sure that the document has no other **[Par Num Def]** code canceling out the one you just entered. If you pressed Enter or Exit (F7) instead of Cancel (F1) from the Paragraph Number Definition menu, you may have inserted an additional code without intending to do so.

4. Turn off Reveal Codes by pressing Reveal Codes (Alt-F3 or F11) if you prefer typing on an uncluttered screen.

Cue:

Create a macro to make the change in numbering style for you.

If you change frequently to one particular outline style, you can create a macro to speed up the process by following these steps:

1. Press Macro Def (Ctrl-F10).

   ⌨ Access the **T**ools pull-down menu and choose **M**acro, then **D**efine.

2. Give the macro a name (for example, *PN-DEF* for *Paragraph Numbering Definition*).

3. Type a brief description (such as *Paragraph Numbering Def*) and press Enter.

4. Follow steps 2 through 6 in the procedure for selecting a new style.

5. Press Macro Def (Ctrl-F10) to end the definition.

   ⌨ Access the **T**ools pull-down menu and choose **M**acro, then **D**efine.

To use the macro, do the following:

1. Place the cursor above the outline to be defined.

2. Press Macro (Alt-F10).

   ⌨ Access the **T**ools pull-down menu and choose **M**acro, then **E**xecute.

3. Type the macro name (*PN-DEF*, for example) and press Enter.

> **Tip**
>
> If you use the same definition throughout a document, put the definition code into the Initial Codes from the Document Format menu. Then, wherever you want to begin a new outline with that style, just access the Paragraph Number Definition menu and press Exit (F7) to insert a new code that restarts numbering in the desired style. Or, if Outline was turned off, just turning it on again restarts numbering using the same style. You also can put the definition code into the Initial Settings from Setup, but the document then does not have the correct style if you use the document on another computer.

Investigating Numbering Styles

To view the Paragraph Number Definition menu shown in figure 24.4, press Date/ Outline (Shift-F5) and select **D**efine (**6**). The first selection in the menu restarts paragraph numbering; options 2 through 6 are numbering styles; options 7 through 9 are new with version 5.1 and are discussed in detail in this section.

With **S**tarting Paragraph Number (**1**), you begin a new paragraph number by accepting the default 1, or you can choose another number. You may choose another number when you want to embed one outline in another, for example. Then you can continue the first outline's numbering scheme after you finish the embedded outline.

To enter another number, specify the number in legal style, as shown in option **4** of the menu. Enter the exact number of the paragraph you want to begin with, not the level of the paragraph in the outline hierarchy. For example, if the paragraph is at level 1, but is the third paragraph in the text, enter *3* rather than *1* for the paragraph's position in the text. If a paragraph is three paragraphs into the first level, four into the second level, and two into the third level (3.d.ii), you enter *3.4.2* in legal style.

Paragraph (**2**) is the generic paragraph-numbering style (see fig. 24.5). To the right of the menu choice in figure 24.4 are eight defined levels for this style.

Outline (**3**) is the default numbering style (see fig. 24.1). WordPerfect uses the default unless you specify another style. Again, notice the eight defined levels for this style to the right of the menu choice.

Legal (**4**) is the style used most often by law offices. Figure 24.6 shows an example of this numbering style.

```
                    Care of 5.25" Floppy Disks
  1    Formatting Disks

       1.1  New disks (You must format new disks before you can use
            them.)
       1.2  Old disks (Formatting erases everything on the old disk,
            so make a copy of the disk first.)

  2    Storage of Disks

       2.1  Temperature range: 50-125 degrees Fahrenheit
       2.2  Not near a possible magnetic field

            2.2.1     Telephone
            2.2.2     File drawer with magnetic closure
            2.2.3     Paper clips

  3    Handling

       3.1  Do not bend disks.
       3.2  Do not touch magnetic surface of disk.
       3.3  Write on disk label with soft, felt-tip markers, never
            hard, ballpoint pens.
  Outline                              Doc 1 Pg 1 Ln 1.17" Pos 1"
```

Fig. 24.6.

Legal numbering style.

Bullets (**5**) uses different characters to set off levels (see fig. 24.7). You should test on your printer a sample outline that uses this style, however, because not all printers can print all the characters.

Cue:

If you choose the Bullets numbering style, print a sample of the document to make sure that your printer supports the characters.

```
                        Care of 5.25" Floppy Disks

   •    Formatting Disks

        o    New disks (You must format new disks before you can use
             them.)
        o    Old disks (Formatting erases everything on the old disk,
             so make a copy of the disk first.)

   •    Storage of Disks

        o    Temperature range: 50-125 degrees Fahrenheit
        o    Not near a possible magnetic field

             -    Telephone
             -    File drawer with magnetic closure
             -    Paper clips

   •    Handling

        o    Do not bend disks.
        o    Do not touch magnetic surface of disk.
        o    Write on disk label with soft, felt-tip markers, never
             hard, ballpoint pens.
 Outline                                  Doc 1 Pg 1 Ln 1.17" Pos 1"
```

Fig. 24.7.

Bullet numbering style.

If not all the bullet-style characters print, you may want to create a numbering style by using similar characters that the printer can print. **U**ser-defined (**6**) allows you to create a numbering style. For example, if you define the first level as *(1)*, all top level numbers are surrounded by parentheses without a period. Figure 24.8 shows a user-defined numbering style.

```
                        Care of 5.25" Floppy Disks

 (1)  Formatting Disks

        A.   New disks (You must format new disks before you can use
             them.)
        B.   Old disks (Formatting erases everything on the old disk,
             so make a copy of the disk first.)

 (2)  Storage of Disks

        A.   Temperature range: 50-125 degrees Fahrenheit
        B.   Not near a possible magnetic field

             1.   Telephone
             2.   File drawer with magnetic closure
             3.   Paper clips

 (3)  Handling

        A.   Do not bend disks.
        B.   Do not touch magnetic surface of disk.
        C.   Write on disk label with soft, felt-tip markers, never
             hard, ballpoint pens.
 Outline                                  Doc 1 Pg 1 Ln 1.17" Pos 1"
```

Fig. 24.8.

User-defined numbering style.

To define a customized numbering style, complete the following steps:

1. Press Date/Outline (Shift-F5), and choose **D**efine (**6**).

   ⌨ Access the **T**ools pull-down menu and chose **D**efine.

2. Select **U**ser-defined (**6**).

   You move to the `Current Definition` line in the center of the screen. The tools you use to build a paragraph number appear at the bottom of the screen.

2. Type the character(s) you want for the first level. For this example, type *(1)* to have digits enclosed in parentheses. You can use the Compose (Ctrl-2) feature to insert special characters such as bullets.

3. Press Enter to move to the next level to the right, or press ↓ to attach the previous level to the current level.

   If you select **Y**es in response to the `Attach Previous Level` prompt for any individual level definition, whenever that level number appears in the text, that number and the number from the previous level are stuck together with a **.** between them. For example, paragraph A., B., and C. under number I, could be shown as I.A., I.B., and I.C. Legal is the only numbering style already defined that uses this feature (refer to fig. 24.6).

4. After defining all the levels you want to change, press Exit (F7) three times to return to the document (once to exit the Current Definition level, once to exit the Paragraph Number Definition menu, and once to exit the Date/Outline menu).

Enter Inserts Paragraph Number (**7**) in the Paragraph Number Definition menu is new with 5.1. This option blurs the distinction between the automatic Outline function and the Paragraph Numbering function discussed later in this chapter. Option 7 is normally set to `Yes`, so that if the cursor is between **[Outline On]** and **[Outline Off]** codes and you press Enter, you automatically get a paragraph number. Setting this option to `No` means that you can press Enter without automatically inserting a paragraph number. When you use this option, you must manually insert paragraph numbers where you want them to appear.

When you retrieve a version 5 document that contains a **[Par Num Def]** code into 5.1, option 7 is set to `Yes` because that is how version 5 worked.

Automatically Adjust to Current Level (**8**) is a new feature with 5.1 that determines the level of a number when you press Enter. When set to `Yes`, the default, the level of the number generated is the same as the previous number; when set to `No`, the number generated is always a first-level number at the left margin.

When you retrieve a WordPerfect 5 document that contains a **[Par Num Def]** code into 5.1, option 8 is set to `No` because version 5 did not have this feature.

Outline Style **N**ame (**9**) is discussed later in this chapter in the "Using Outline Styles" section.

Editing an Outline

Once you create an outline, you may want to go back to make structural changes such as deleting, adding, or moving numbered paragraphs. The real advantage of using automatic numbering is the ease of editing and renumbering.

Tip

You can move quickly from one level to another if you have an Extended Keyboard. Press Alt-↓ or Alt-↑ to move the cursor forward or backward to the next paragraph number of the same (or preceding) level. Press Alt-← or Alt-→ to move the cursor backward or forward to the next paragraph number, regardless of the level.

Cue:
You can use Compose to insert bullets or other characters not on the normal keyboard.

Deleting a Paragraph Number

Paragraph numbers are just another WordPerfect code in the document; therefore, you can delete the **[Par Num]** code the same way you delete any other code.

To delete a paragraph number, complete the following steps:

1. Press Reveal Codes (Alt-F3 or F11) and move the cursor to the **[Par Num]** code that represents the number you want to delete.

   ⌨ Access the **E**dit pull-down menu and choose **R**eveal Codes.

2. Press Del to delete the code, then press Reveal Codes (Alt-F3 or F11) to return to the normal screen.

Adding a Paragraph Number

If you accidentally delete a paragraph number or if you create an unnumbered paragraph and later decide to add a number, you easily can add a paragraph number.

To add a paragraph number with the Outline feature on and with **E**nter Inserts Paragraph Number (**7**) set to Yes in the Paragraph Number Definition menu, do the following steps:

1. Place the cursor at the end of the paragraph preceding the one you want to number.

2. Press Enter to create a new number.

3. Press Tab or Margin Release (if necessary) to set the appropriate level and place the number.

4. Press →Indent (F4), the space bar, or Home, Tab to move the text over, if necessary.

5. Delete any extra hard returns to space the outline correctly.

To create another numbered paragraph immediately after this one, be sure to put the cursor at the end of the last line of this paragraph before continuing.

To add a paragraph number with the Outline feature off or with **E**nter Inserts Paragraph Number (**7**) set to No, follow the steps under "Creating Numbered Paragraphs" later in this chapter.

Changing a Paragraph Number

When reorganizing an outline, you may decide to change the level of a number (*1* to *a* for example) for a numbered paragraph. Remember that the position on the line determines the level of a number.

To change the level of a single paragraph number, complete the following steps:

1. Place the cursor under the number you want to change.

2. Press Tab to move the line to the right; the paragraph number changes to a lower level. Press Margin Release (Shift-Tab) to move the line to the left; the paragraph number changes to a higher level.

Note: If Outline is on, no [**←Mar Rel**] code is inserted; if Outline is off, a code is inserted. Instead of using Margin Release if Outline is off, just delete an unnecessary **[Tab]** code.

3. Press Screen (Ctrl-F3) and choose **R**ewrite (**3**) to redisplay and renumber the text.

If you have changed levels using previous versions of WordPerfect, you may appreciate one of 5.1's new features: Sections of an outline are grouped into "families" that can be moved, copied, or deleted easily. To change the level of a family of numbered paragraphs (one paragraph and all the following sublevels of numbered paragraphs), refer to "Moving a Numbered Paragraph" later in this chapter.

Deleting a Numbered Paragraph

When editing the outline, you may want to delete an entire section. For example, in the outline you created earlier in this chapter, you may decide to delete the "Storage of Disks" section.

The text to be deleted is what version 5.1 calls a family within an outline. A *family* is a set of numbered paragraphs grouped under higher-level numbers. In figure 24.9, the *i* through *iii* numbers are part of the *b.* family; the *a.* and *b.* numbers are part of the *2.* family. You easily can delete, move, or copy a family within an outline.

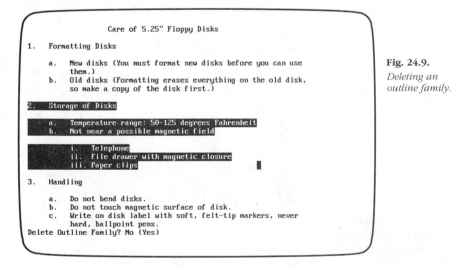

Fig. 24.9.

Deleting an outline family.

To delete a numbered paragraph family with Outline on, complete the following steps:

1. Place the cursor under the number of the top level of the family you want to delete. For this example, place the cursor under the *2.* at the beginning of the "Storage of Disks" section.

2. Press Date/Outline (Shift-F5), select **O**utline (**4**), and then select **D**elete Family (**5**).

   ⌨ Access the **T**ools pull-down menu, choose **O**utline, and select **D**elete Family.

   The prompt `Delete Outline Family? No (Yes)` appears. If Outline is not on, you instead see the message `ERROR: Not in an outline` and you are returned to the document.

3. Select **Y** if the highlighted family is the one you want to delete.

4. If you decide that you deleted the wrong text, you can press Undelete (F1) to bring back the paragraphs. For this example, undelete the paragraph in preparation for the next section.

If the paragraphs you want to delete are not considered a family, or if Outline is off, use Block to delete the text. Using Block to delete paragraphs is not as straightforward as deleting a family, so you may need to tidy up the outline by adding or deleting additional hard returns so that the spacing of the outline is correct.

Reminder:

WordPerfect renumbers the outline after you delete paragraphs.

After you delete a paragraph or a family, WordPerfect renumbers the subsequent paragraphs (see fig. 24.10).

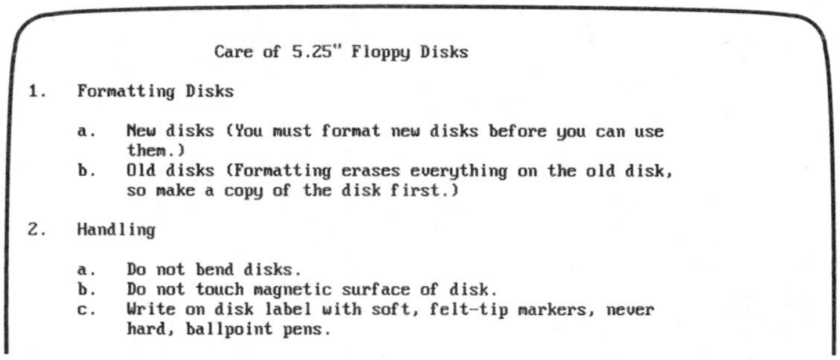

Fig. 24.10.

Paragraphs renumbered after deleting a family.

```
                    Care of 5.25" Floppy Disks

1.   Formatting Disks

     a.   New disks (You must format new disks before you can use
          them.)
     b.   Old disks (Formatting erases everything on the old disk,
          so make a copy of the disk first.)

2.   Handling

     a.   Do not bend disks.
     b.   Do not touch magnetic surface of disk.
     c.   Write on disk label with soft, felt-tip markers, never
          hard, ballpoint pens.
```

Moving a Numbered Paragraph

In addition to deleting numbered paragraphs, you can move a paragraph or an entire family to another vertical location within an outline, or you can move a family horizontally, changing *all levels within the family* at the same time without adding or deleting tabs at each numbered paragraph within the family.

For example, instead of deleting the storage information, you can move the section and make it follow the section on handling disks.

Tip

To move a numbered paragraph, you can delete the text by following the directions in "Deleting a Numbered Paragraph" and then undelete the text elsewhere.

To move a family of paragraphs, do the following:

1. Place the cursor under the number at the top level of the family you want to move. For this example, place the cursor under the *2.* of "Storage of Disks."

2. Press Date/Outline (Shift-F5), select **O**utline (**4**), and then select **M**ove Family (**3**).

   ▭ Access the **T**ools pull-down menu, choose **O**utline, and select **M**ove Family.

Caution

If you use the 11/9/89 release of 5.1, be aware that once you select **M**ove Family (**3**), you cannot Cancel (F1) out of the item. Pressing Cancel (F1) leaves the family wherever the cursor is positioned when Cancel is pressed.

If Outline is not on, you see the ERROR: Not in an outline message, and you are returned to the document.

3. Press → or ← to move the family right or left within the outline. For this example, see what happens to the outline when you press → (refer to fig. 24.11). Return the family to its previous position by pressing ←.

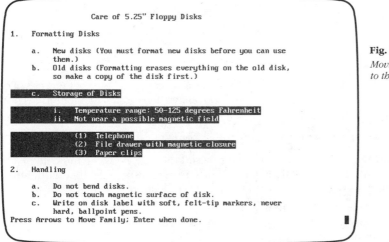

```
                 Care of 5.25" Floppy Disks
 1.   Formatting Disks

        a.   New disks (You must format new disks before you can use
             them.)
        b.   Old disks (Formatting erases everything on the old disk,
             so make a copy of the disk first.)

        c.   Storage of Disks

             i.   Temperature range: 50-125 degrees Fahrenheit
             ii.  Not near a possible magnetic field

                  (1)  Telephone
                  (2)  File drawer with magnetic closure
                  (3)  Paper clips

 2.   Handling

        a.   Do not bend disks.
        b.   Do not touch magnetic surface of disk.
        c.   Write on disk label with soft, felt-tip markers, never
             hard, ballpoint pens.
 Press Arrows to Move Family; Enter when done.
```

Fig. 24.11.

Moving the family to the right.

Reminder:

Press ↑ and ↓ to move the selected family up or down in the outline.

4. Press ↑ or ↓ to move the family up or down within the hierarchy of the outline. For this example, press ↓ to move the family to the end of the sample outline.

5. When you have positioned the family where you want it, press Enter to fix the family in place.

6. If you want a blank line above the newly moved family—as you do in this example—press Enter to create a new line and an unwanted paragraph number, then press Backspace to delete the extra number; press Backspace again if the paragraph was indented a level too far, as is the case in this example.

The paragraph numbers change again as soon as you move this numbered paragraph (see fig. 24.12).

Fig. 24.12.

Paragraphs renumbered after moving the family.

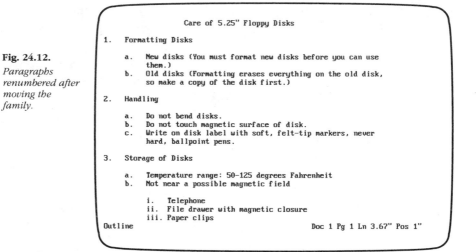

Adding a Numbered Paragraph

Besides deleting and moving paragraphs, you also can add new paragraphs. For example, in the outline you created, you may decide to include a section explaining how to help prevent a disaster to the disks.

To add a paragraph or group of paragraphs, complete the following steps:

1. Place the cursor where you want to insert the text, between the Outline On and Off codes. In this example, place the cursor after the "Formatting Disks" section and before the "Handling" section.

2. Press Enter to create new numbered paragraphs; press Tab, if necessary, to change the correct level for each paragraph. For this example, insert the paragraphs shown in figure 24.13.

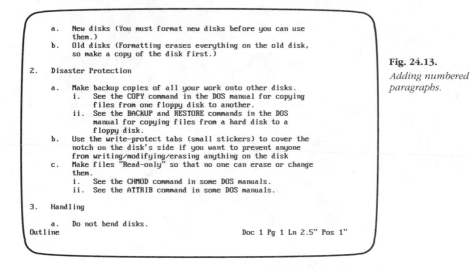

```
         a.   New disks (You must format new disks before you can use
              them.)
         b.   Old disks (Formatting erases everything on the old disk,
              so make a copy of the disk first.)
    2.   Disaster Protection

         a.   Make backup copies of all your work onto other disks.
              i.   See the COPY command in the DOS manual for copying
                   files from one floppy disk to another.
              ii.  See the BACKUP and RESTORE commands in the DOS
                   manual for copying files from a hard disk to a
                   floppy disk.
         b.   Use the write-protect tabs (small stickers) to cover the
              notch on the disk's side if you want to prevent anyone
              from writing/modifying/erasing anything on the disk
         c.   Make files "Read-only" so that no one can erase or change
              them.
              i.   See the CHMOD command in some DOS manuals.
              ii.  See the ATTRIB command in some DOS manuals.

    3.   Handling

         a.   Do not bend disks.
Outline                                    Doc 1 Pg 1 Ln 2.5" Pos 1"
```

Fig. 24.13.

Adding numbered paragraphs.

Adding a Paragraph without a Number

In an outline, you may want to add paragraphs, such as explanations under headings, that are not numbered. You can add unnumbered paragraphs by completing the following steps:

1. Place the cursor where you want the new paragraph to begin. For this example, place the cursor at the end of the paragraph that begins *Old disks* (see fig. 24.14).

```
              Care of 5.25" Floppy Disks

    1.   Formatting Disks

         a.   New disks (You must format new disks before you can use
              them.)
         b.   Old disks (Formatting erases everything on the old disk,
              so make a copy of the disk first.)

              It's a good idea to format old disks (after copying
              everything to another disk) because the format program
              marks off any physically damaged parts ("bad sectors")
              of a disk, and you can replace any damaged disks.
```

Fig. 24.14.

Adding an unnumbered paragraph.

2. Press Enter twice to insert a blank line. A number appears because Outline is on and the **E**nter Inserts Paragraph Number (**7**) option is set to Yes.

3. Press Backspace to get rid of the number.

4. Press →Indent (F4) to line up the new paragraphs underneath preceding levels. In this example, press →Indent (F4) twice so that the paragraph lines up with the text beginning *Old disks*.

5. Type the new paragraph. For this example, type the text shown in figure 24.14.

6. Press Enter to end the paragraph. Another paragraph number is created.

7. Press Backspace to delete the new paragraph number.

Tip

If you want to add many paragraphs without numbers, you can insert a new **[Par Num Def]** code before and after each section of unnumbered paragraphs. At the beginning of the section, change **E**nter Inserts Paragraph Number (**7**) to No; at the end of the section of unnumbered paragraphs, set the option back to Yes. If you also set the **S**tarting Paragraph Number (**1**) option to ?.?.?.?.?.?.?.? at each end of the section, *the outline continues with the same numbering*. Because these keystrokes do not change, regardless of the type of outline you are using, create two macros to enter these settings for you.

Using Outline Styles

New with 5.1 is a combination of Styles (explained in Chapter 15) and the Outline feature. Outline styles allow you to organize up to eight layers of styles, which may include paragraph numbers within them. You can create an outline style that automatically inserts a right indent after the paragraph number for each of the eight levels, or you can create an outline style that does not use paragraph numbers, but that formats different sections of text in different ways (one level in italics, indented; one in a large font, centered; another without any formatting changes) for a hierarchical document that does not need paragraph numbers.

Although outline styles can be created from the normal Styles menu or from the Paragraph Number Definition menu, they can be accessed only from the latter. See Chapter 15 for more information about creating outline styles "from scratch" or by combining several layers of existing normal styles into one outline style.

Reminder:

You can use the three outline styles that come with WordPerfect 5.1.

Three outline styles are shipped with WordPerfect 5.1 in the file LIBRARY.STY. All are described in Chapter 15.

If you installed LIBRARY.STY when you set up WordPerfect, and you have selected it as the default style library, you can use one of these outline styles by doing the following steps:

1. Place the cursor where you want the outline style to take affect. For this example, place the cursor at the beginning of the outline already typed in, but after any **[Par Num Def]** codes.

2. Press Date/Outline (Shift-F5), select **D**efine (**6**), and then select Outline Style **N**ame (**9**).

   ⌨ Access the **T**ools pull-down menu and choose **D**efine.

   A list of available outline styles appears (see fig. 24.15).

3. Use ↓ and ↑ to highlight the style you want to use, then choose **S**elect (**1**) from the menu at the bottom of the screen. For this example, choose Right Par (right-aligned paragraph numbers).

4. Press Exit (F7) twice to return to the document.

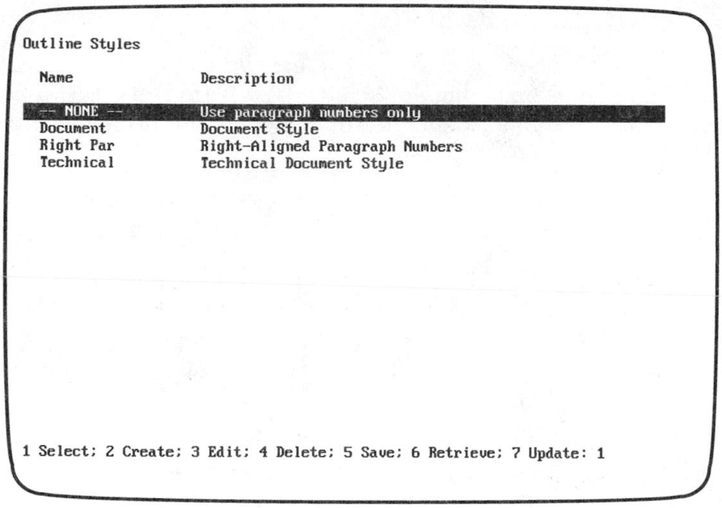

```
  Outline Styles

     Name           Description

     -- NONE --      Use paragraph numbers only
     Document        Document Style
     Right Par       Right-Aligned Paragraph Numbers
     Technical       Technical Document Style










  1 Select; 2 Create; 3 Edit; 4 Delete; 5 Save; 6 Retrieve; 7 Update: 1
```

Fig. 24.15.

Predefined outline styles in LIBRARY.STY.

If paragraph-numbering codes are included within the style you choose, the codes use whatever numbering style is selected in the Paragraph Number Definition menu.

Notice that the outline on the screen is spaced oddly now, as explained in the next paragraph.

If you chose an outline style for existing outline text, you may have to clean up the codes. For example, right indents within the outline style and within the main body of the outline text cause the text to indent too far to the right. Reposition the text by blocking the outline text (if you have normal document text around the outline text that should not be changed) and using Replace (Alt-F2) to replace all right indents with nothing (press F2 when prompted `Replace with:`). Only the right indents within the normal text are erased; those within the outline style are left untouched.

Numbering a Paragraph

You have seen that using Outline automatically creates numbered paragraphs. You also can use the Paragraph Numbering option to create numbered paragraphs. Although both techniques use the same style of numbering, the options differ in the way the numbers are created and in how easily they are moved and edited.

If you use Outline to number paragraphs, but you also want to include unnumbered paragraphs, you must complete several steps (as described earlier in this chapter). If you have many unnumbered paragraphs mixed in with numbered ones, these extra steps are cumbersome. If you use Paragraph Numbering instead, you must explicitly request the numbers; they are not generated automatically.

Reminder:

Outline numbers every paragraph; including unnumbered paragraphs requires additional work. Paragraph Numbering numbers and "unnumbers" text easily.

Defining the Numbering Style

Just as you can define a numbering style for Outline, you also can select a numbering style for Paragraph Numbering. In fact, the **[Par Num Def]** code used by Outline is the same code used by Paragraph Numbering. If you do not change the numbering style, the default style is Outline.

If you have changed the numbering style, do the following steps to change the style back to Outline:

1. Place the cursor where you want the new paragraph numbering style to begin (at the beginning of the outline if you've already typed the outline, or at the place you start typing).

   For this example, you type a new outline (refer to fig. 24.16) at the end of the document, so press Home, Home, ↓.

2. Press Date/Outline (Shift-F5) and select **D**efine (**6**).

   ▭ Access the **T**ools pull-down menu and choose **D**efine.

   The Paragraph Number Definition menu appears.

3. Select the style you want. For this example, select **O**utline (**3**) to choose the Roman-numeral outline style.

4. Press Exit (F7) or Enter twice to select the current definition and return to the document.

See "Investigating Numbering Styles" earlier in this chapter for more information on available styles.

Creating Numbered Paragraphs

After selecting or defining the style, you begin typing the outline and specifying paragraph numbers by doing the following steps:

1. Press Enter. If a paragraph number is generated, Outline is on. Turn Outline off and delete the number. Otherwise, you can continue.

2. You may want to type a centered title for your numbered paragraphs, as in the example. If so, press Center (Shift-F6), type a title, and press Enter. For this example, type *Paragraph Numbering and Outlining in WordPerfect* and press Enter, then press Enter again to insert a blank line.

2. Be sure that the cursor is at the left margin.

3. Press Date/Outline (Shift-F5) and select **P**ara Num (**5**).

   ▭ Access the **T**ools pull-down menu and choose **P**aragraph Number.

4. When prompted with Paragraph Level, press Enter for automatic numbering.

   WordPerfect chooses the appropriate number according to the cursor's position on the line. Because you are at the left margin, WordPerfect assigns *I.* as the first level number. Remember that the style you select determines the level numbers the program uses.

5. Press Indent (F4), Tab, or space; type the text for this numbered paragraph. For this example, press Indent (F4) and type *Defining the Style*.

   If you use Indent (F4), text automatically wraps underneath the tab stop. Unlike using Outline, pressing Tab does not pull the number with the cursor and change the number level; the move is just a normal Tab.

6. Press Enter twice to insert a blank line and begin a new paragraph.

7. Press Tab to place the cursor for the next paragraph.

8. Follow steps 3 through 6 to complete the outline from figure 24.16.

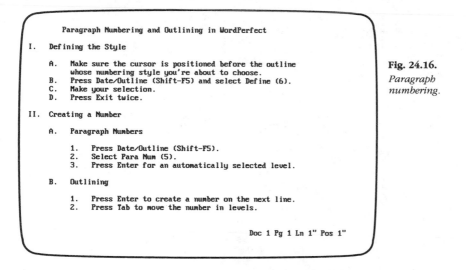

Fig. 24.16.

Paragraph numbering.

Once you position the cursor (at the left margin or in one or more tab stops), you use the same keystrokes (steps 3 through 6) to create a number. You can create a macro, especially if you give the macro a short name such as *PN* for paragraph number.

To create a macro that uses this style, follow these steps:

1. Press Macro Def (Ctrl-F10) and name the macro by typing *PN* (for paragraph number). Press Enter.

   ▢⊞ Access the **T**ools pull-down menu and choose **M**acro, then **D**efine.

2. Type *paragraph number* for the description and press Enter.

3. Press Date/Outline (Shift-F5), select **P**ara Num (**5**), and press Enter.

4. Press Indent (F4), then end the macro by pressing Macro Def (Ctrl-F10).

   ▢⊞ Access the **T**ools pull-down menu and choose **M**acro, then **D**efine.

Using Fixed Paragraph Levels

Normally, WordPerfect automatically chooses what level a paragraph number should be by the position on a line: first-level numbers are used when the cursor is at the left margin, second-level numbers at the first tab stop, third-level numbers at the second tab stop, and so on. This numbering system makes reorganizing the material much easier: you just add or delete tabs before the number, and the level number is automatically adjusted.

You may, however, want all the numbers, regardless of level, to line up at the left margin or in the first tab stop. If so, you can force the level numbers to be whatever you request.

1. Position the cursor under the level number you want to make static. For example, place the cursor under the *I.* in the sample outline.

2. Press Tab to line the number up with the second-level numbers.

3. Press Screen (Ctrl-F3) and select **R**ewrite (**3**). The number changes to *A.* and subsequent paragraph numbers change as well (see fig. 24.17).

Fig. 24.17.

Moving the first paragraph number.

```
┌──────────────────────────────────────────────────────────────┐
│                                                              │
│          Paragraph Numbering and Outlining in WordPerfect     │
│                                                              │
│       A.   Defining the Style                                │
│                                                              │
│       B.   Make sure the cursor is positioned before the outline │
│            whose numbering style you're about to choose.      │
│       C.   Press Date/Outline (Shift-F5) and select Define (6).│
│       D.   Make your selection.                              │
│       E.   Press Exit twice.                                 │
│                                                              │
│    I.   Creating a Number                                    │
│                                                              │
│       A.   Paragraph Numbers                                 │
│                                                              │
│            1.   Press Date/Outline (Shift-F5).               │
│            2.   Select Para Num (5).                         │
│            3.   Press Enter for an automatically selected level.│
│                                                              │
│       B.   Outlining                                         │
│                                                              │
│            1.   Press Enter to create a number on the next line.│
│            2.   Press Tab to move the number in levels.      │
│                                                              │
│                                    Doc 1 Pg 1 Ln 1.33" Pos 1.5" │
└──────────────────────────────────────────────────────────────┘
```

4. Move the cursor back under the level number you want to force. For example, place the cursor under the first *A.* in the outline

5. Press Del to delete the **[Par Num:Auto]** code. You may want to do this step in Reveal Codes (Alt-F3 or F11). The number disappears and the other second-level numbers revert to their original order (see fig. 24.18).

6. Press Date/Outline (Shift-F5), select **P**ara Num (**5**), but **do not** press Enter.

   ⌨ Access the **T**ools pull-down menu and choose **P**aragraph Number

7. Type the level number you want to assign and press Enter. For example, type *1* and press Enter.

   WordPerfect ignores the cursor position and assigns *I.* instead of *A.* to this paragraph number (see fig. 24.19).

8. Press Screen (Ctrl-F3) and select **R**ewrite (**3**) to redisplay text.

9. Repeat this process for any other paragraph number levels you want to change. For example, you can change the *II.* in the outline. Remember to type *1* for the level number rather than *2* for the actual number.

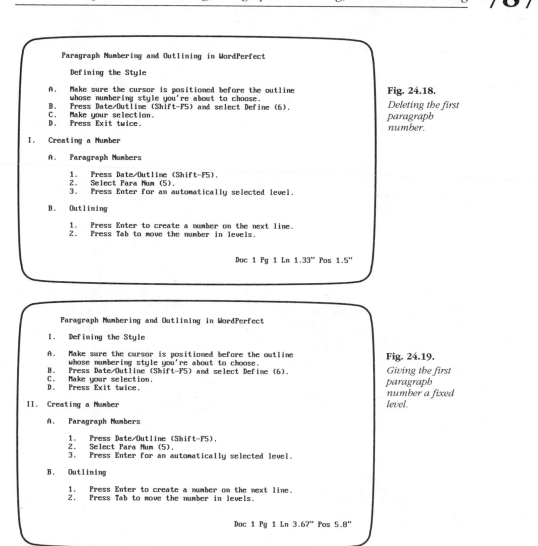

```
        Paragraph Numbering and Outlining in WordPerfect

        Defining the Style

    A.  Make sure the cursor is positioned before the outline
        whose numbering style you're about to choose.
    B.  Press Date/Outline (Shift-F5) and select Define (6).
    C.  Make your selection.
    D.  Press Exit twice.

I.  Creating a Number

    A.  Paragraph Numbers

        1.  Press Date/Outline (Shift-F5).
        2.  Select Para Num (5).
        3.  Press Enter for an automatically selected level.

    B.  Outlining

        1.  Press Enter to create a number on the next line.
        2.  Press Tab to move the number in levels.


                          Doc 1 Pg 1 Ln 1.33" Pos 1.5"
```

Fig. 24.18.

Deleting the first paragraph number.

```
        Paragraph Numbering and Outlining in WordPerfect

    I.  Defining the Style

    A.  Make sure the cursor is positioned before the outline
        whose numbering style you're about to choose.
    B.  Press Date/Outline (Shift-F5) and select Define (6).
    C.  Make your selection.
    D.  Press Exit twice.

II. Creating a Number

    A.  Paragraph Numbers

        1.  Press Date/Outline (Shift-F5).
        2.  Select Para Num (5).
        3.  Press Enter for an automatically selected level.

    B.  Outlining

        1.  Press Enter to create a number on the next line.
        2.  Press Tab to move the number in levels.


                          Doc 1 Pg 1 Ln 3.67" Pos 5.8"
```

Fig. 24.19.

Giving the first paragraph number a fixed level.

If you know that you want a number at a fixed level as you type the outline, enter the fixed level then. Type the level number instead of just pressing Enter at the `Paragraph Level` prompt.

The last point you should know about numbering paragraphs is how to edit them. You edit numbered paragraphs the same way you edit paragraphs created using Outline. The only exception is that you cannot use with Paragraph Numbering the family instruction available with Outline. See "Editing an Outline" earlier in this chapter.

Numbering a Line

In addition to numbering paragraphs, you also can number lines. You can use Line Numbering for legal documents, for example, or for any document where referencing a particular passage in the text is made easier with numbered lines. You can use Line Numbering also when several people edit the same document. In a group, you can discuss the work easily by referring, for example, to the word *cheap* on page 10, line 32.

When you use Line Numbering, the program inserts a **[Ln Num:On]** code into the document and begins numbering that line (or the next line if **[Ln Num:On]** is not inserted at the beginning of the current line) at 1. Remember to put the cursor at the point where you want the line numbering to begin (normally, the beginning of the text). The numbers are not displayed on-screen as you enter text, but you can check the numbers before printing by pressing Print (Shift-F7) and selecting **V**iew Document (**6**).

Tip

Line numbers are printed in whatever base font is selected where the **[Ln Num:On]** code appears in the text. If you want the line numbers to be less conspicuous, select a small font, turn on line numbering, and then select the normal font for the text. The only text that appears in the small font is the line numbers.

Ensure that the font you select for line numbering is the same size or smaller than the font selected for the normal document, because line height is determined by the font used in the text and *not* by the line numbers. Using a large font for line numbers results in those numbers appearing "squished."

Turning On Line Numbering

To use Line Numbering, complete the following steps:

1. Place the cursor where you want line numbering to begin. For this example, press Home, Home, ↑ to place the cursor at the beginning of the document.

2. Press Format (Shift-F8) and select **L**ine (**1**).

   Access the **L**ayout pull-down menu and choose **L**ine.

3. Select Line **N**umbering (**5**) and select **Y** to turn on Line Numbering. The Line Numbering menu appears. (See "Changing Line Numbering Settings" later in this chapter for details about each of the options.)

4. Press Enter to accept the default settings.

5. Press Exit (F7) to return to the document.

Checking Line Numbering

Remember that line numbers do not appear on-screen. You can use Reveal Codes to see the **[Ln Num:On]** code. To see the line numbers, you can either print the document or use View Document.

Reminder:
Print the document or use View Document to see line numbers.

To view the document, complete the following steps:

1. Press Print (Shift-F7) and select **V**iew Document (**6**).

   ▭ Access the **F**ile pull-down menu and choose **P**rint.

2. Select 100% (**1**) to see the numbers more clearly. Notice that the line numbers appear down the left margin (see fig. 24.20).

3. Press Exit (F7) to return to the editing screen.

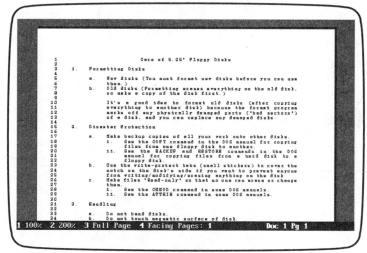

Fig. 24.20.

100% View Document with Line Numbering.

Turning Off Line Numbering

If you want to remove all line numbering from the document, delete the code inserted when you turned on Line Numbering.

To delete the line-numbering code, do the following steps:

1. Press Reveal Codes (Alt-F3 or F11) and move the cursor to the **[Ln Num:On]** code.

2. Press Del.

3. Press Reveal Codes (Alt-F3 or F11) to return to the normal screen.

> **Tip**
>
> If you entered more than one line-numbering code, use Forward Search (F2) or Replace (Alt-F2) from the beginning of the document to make sure that you delete all the codes.

If you want only part of a document to contain line numbers, turn off Line Numbering at the end of the numbered section.

To turn off Line Numbering, do the following steps:

1. Place the cursor where you want line numbers to stop.

2. Press Format (Shift-F8) and select **L**ine (**1**).

   ▭▤ Access the **L**ayout pull-down menu and choose **L**ine.

3. Select Line **N**umbering (**5**) and select **N** to turn off Line Numbering.

4. Press Exit (F7) to return to the document.

You may want to use View Document to be sure that you turned off Line Numbering in the correct place.

Changing Line Numbering Settings

Reminder:

You can set line numbers so that they appears at specified intervals (every five lines, for example).

Because the default settings for Line Numbering may not suit your preferences, you can change the defaults. For example, you may prefer to number only every fifth line instead of every line.

To change the default settings, complete the following steps:

1. Press Format (Shift-F8) and select **L**ine (**1**).

   ▭▤ Access the **L**ayout pull-down menu and choose **L**ine.

2. Select Line **N**umbering (**5**) and select **Y** to turn on Line Numbering. The Format: Line Numbering menu appears (see fig. 24.21).

Fig. 24.21.

The Format: Line Numbering menu.

```
Format: Line Numbering

   1 - Count Blank Lines                       Yes

   2 - Number Every n Lines, where n is        1

   3 - Position of Number from Left Edge       0.6"

   4 - Starting Number                         1

   5 - Restart Numbering on Each Page          Yes
```

3. Select the item you want to change. For example, select **N**umber Every n Lines (**2**).

4. Enter the change. For this example, type *5* to number only every fifth line; press Enter.

5. Press Exit (F7) to return to the document.

6. Use View Document to see the difference this selection has made.

The Format: Line Numbering menu has five options from which you can select. The following paragraphs describe these options more fully.

If you want to specify whether blank lines are numbered, select **C**ount Blank Lines (**1**). The default setting is Yes, which means that blank lines *are* numbered. If you want the program to skip blank lines so that they are not counted, select **N**.

Note: Full-width graphics boxes, including equation boxes, are not included in line numbering.

Choose **N**umber Every n Lines (**2**) when you want to change the interval used to number lines. When you change the value of *n*, WordPerfect still counts every line, but prints the line number only at the interval you specify. For example, if you type 5 and press Enter, the program prints numbers every fifth line.

By default, line numbers are printed six-tenths of an inch from the left edge of the paper. To change this measurement, select **P**osition of Number from Left Edge (**3**), type a new measurement, and press Enter. For example, you may prefer to have numbers at the left edge of each page or closer to the text.

If you have a document with a left margin of only six-tenths of an inch, you *must* change this setting to something smaller than the margin, or WordPerfect prints the line numbers on top of the text. For example, if you have a left margin of one-half inch, set **P**osition of Number from Left Edge (**3**) to three-tenths of an inch.

Reminder:
Make sure that line numbers are not printed on top of text by printing them within the left margin.

By default, lines are numbered starting with number 1, regardless of the actual line number in the text. Use **S**tarting Number (**4**) to specify a new starting number—for example, line 25. The first line of the document after the **[Ln Num: On]** code is then numbered 25. This numbering feature is useful if you do not want the first part of a page to be numbered, but you want WordPerfect to number line 25 as line 25 and not as line 1.

Normally, line numbering begins over again at 1 on each page so that you can refer to something on page 12, line 22. If you don't have page numbers, however, you may want line numbering to continue unbroken from one page to the next so that you can refer to something on line 334 without using a page number. To print continuous numbers, select **R**estart Numbering on Each Page (**5**) and select **N**.

Regardless of the choice you make for **R**estart Numbering on Each Page (**5**), however, View Document shows line numbers starting at 1 on every page. If you specified No for this option, numbers print correctly at the printer.

Summary

You have explored three of WordPerfect's automatic numbering systems: Outlining, Paragraph Numbering, and Line Numbering. With these options you can do the following tasks:

❏ Turn on Outline to number paragraphs automatically

❏ Use Paragraph Numbering to number paragraphs only when you request a number

❏ Edit (delete, add, or move) both types of paragraph numbering and watch WordPerfect automatically renumber the paragraphs

❏ Change the numbering style used to number paragraphs

❏ Use Line Numbering to number each line on the page

❏ Change the default settings for line numbering to specify when and how WordPerfect numbers lines

❏ Check line numbering with View Document

Assembling Document References

Anders R. Sterner is a partner of Tanner Propp Fersko & Sterner, a Manhattan law firm. He is a WordPerfect beta tester, having been addicted since version 3. He wrote this chapter for *Using WordPerfect 5*.

C. Brian Scott is a partner in the Portland, Oregon law firm of Danner, Scott & Martin. Installation of his firm's PC network plunged him into the world of computers and WordPerfect's network version 4. He revised this chapter for *Using WordPerfect 5.1, Special Edition*.

For many writing tasks, the main text is just the tip of the iceberg. Often you need tables of contents, indexes, and other document references to help a reader navigate through what you have written.

In the old days, writers had to stop days before a document was due and start combing through the main text to prepare the document references. One of WordPerfect 5.1's handiest features is that it speeds up that process. With a little foresight and planning, you can work on a document to within a few hours before a deadline, confident that as the main text changes, the document references can keep up.

This chapter shows you how to create lists, tables of contents, tables of authorities, and indexes. You also learn to use automatic cross-referencing, which allows you to change the structure of your document and automatically maintain accurate references to footnotes, pages, and sections. Finally, you learn to use the Document Compare feature so that you can show someone else what was omitted from, or added to, a document without having to mark all those changes yourself.

If you use a mouse or the pull-down menus, you can find all the tools discussed in this chapter on the Mark pull-down menu (see fig. 25.1).

The central example in this chapter is a sample legal brief and an accompanying affidavit. Both are used to explain the principles for marking and generating document references. Indexing is explained with a partial index from a book chapter, and the Document Compare feature is demonstrated with successive versions of two paragraphs from this chapter.

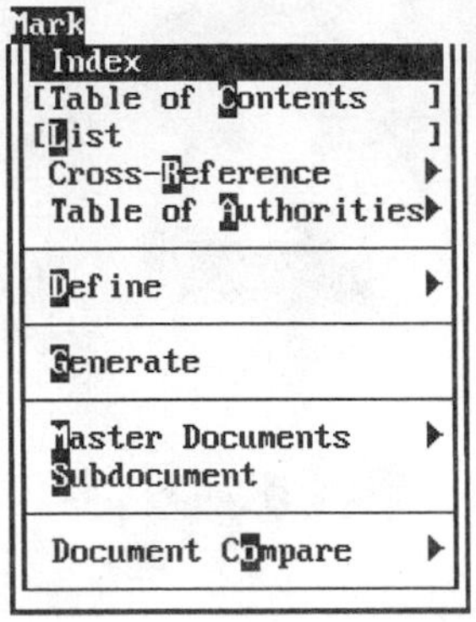

Fig. 25.1.

The Mark pull-down menu.

```
Mark
 Index
[Table of Contents    ]
[List                 ]
 Cross-Reference     ▶
 Table of Authorities▶

 Define              ▶

 Generate

 Master Documents    ▶
 Subdocument

 Document Compare    ▶
```

Before you read about each type of document reference, keep in mind that these techniques require you to *plan ahead*. The techniques work better if you know at the outset which document references you want and can provide for them as you go along. Planning ahead is especially important for a function like Document Compare, which compares an edited version of a document with the original.

When you know you need document references, you cannot afford the attitude, "Right now I just want to get it on paper; I'll do the fancy stuff later." Later will come, and you'll pay in the form of anxious, high-pressure, catch-up work against an inexorable deadline.

You should *start* work on a document by creating first the preliminary pages, or front matter. In each major section of this chapter, you find instructions to set up pages for the tables and lists described. Before you write the first word, then, you should do the following:

- Create a cover page with the caption and title, complete with a paragraph-numbering scheme. End the cover page with a hard page break (Ctrl-Enter).

- Restart page numbering with Roman numerals, place the Table of Contents title, and put in the ToC definition. End this page with a hard page break (Ctrl-Enter).

- On the next page, place the Table of Authorities title and the subheadings you want for the Table of Authorities. End this page with a hard page break (Ctrl-Enter).

- On the next page, restart page numbering in Arabic numerals. Save the document (F10) and start writing.

If doing all this seems overwhelming, don't despair. Read on to learn to create all these reference aids, beginning with lists.

> **Reminder**
>
> If you use a mouse with WordPerfect 5.1, you can click the right button to display the pull-down menus, and then select the desired option. You also can press Alt-= to access the pull-down menus, and then press the appropriate letter of the desired option. Both pull-down menu and mouse instructions are marked with the mouse icon. For all instructions, assume that if a block is required to activate a pull-down menu option, the text has been blocked before the pull-down menu is accessed. See Chapter 1 for more information on using the mouse and the pull-down menus.

Creating Lists

WordPerfect's List function is the simplest reference feature. If you're creating a legal document, you may want a list of exhibits; a scientific paper may need a list of tables; a book chapter may need a list of figures. The List feature enables you to mark specific items in the text as you create a document. When you finish editing the document, WordPerfect generates a list of the marked items, followed by page numbers or other identifying features. On the final list, items appear in the order in which they occur in the document.

Reminder:
Mark items as you create a document so that you can obtain a list of those items.

Starting with the model affidavit, you are introduced to a number of basic techniques for making lists. Although the suggestions for automating list-marking do not save much time, these techniques save a great deal of sweat and error with Table of Contents and the other document-reference functions.

You can create as many as 10 lists per document. Each item must be marked for the list in which it is to be included, as well as for features (such as boldfacing) that you want to include with the items on that list. List references contain only what you mark. Because you cannot specify separate text to be reported in the list (as you can with a Table of Authorities), your writing style has to be consistent. You must say *The lease is Exhibit B, and the notice is Exhibit C* instead of *The lease and notice are Exhibits B and C, respectively.* Writing in this manner enables you to mark *Exhibit B* and *Exhibit C* separately.

Suppose that an affidavit mentions several leases, referred to as Exhibit A, Exhibit B, and so forth. As you write the affidavit, you mark each Exhibit reference (at the point each Exhibit is introduced) for inclusion in the list. Then, no matter how many times you edit the document, WordPerfect can find the item and generate a list of all marked items, in the proper order, with correct page numbers.

Marking Text for Lists

When you mark text for lists, you mark an item to include any codes for features you want to appear with that item on the list. You can choose one of two approaches to mark text for lists.

Remember to mark text for lists *as you write*. You can always go back and delete items you don't want, but it's time-consuming and risky to search for things to mark after you finish writing the document.

Marking Text the Hard Way (Manually)

The method in this section is called the "hard way" because you use several keystrokes, which are enough to disrupt the creative process. Furthermore, placing the keystrokes in a macro that marks text for you doesn't work because material to be included varies from case to case. (If you're not familiar with macros, see Chapters 11 and 12.)

Suppose that you want a list of all exhibits referred to in an affidavit, along with the page numbers on which the exhibits first appear. Also suppose that you just typed the first item, *Exhibit A*, on your screen.

Reminder:

*To include text in a list, block the text, choose **List** from the Mark menu, and type the list number.*

To mark *Exhibit A* for inclusion in a list, follow these steps:

1. Block, or highlight, the word or phrase you want to include in the list (for example, *Exhibit A*). Chapter 4 explains the Block command.

2. Mark the blocked text for a particular list. Press Mark Text (Alt-F5) and select **L**ist (**2**) from the menu at the bottom of the screen:

    Mark for: 1 To**C**; **2 L**ist; **3 I**ndex; **4** To**A**: **0**.

    ⌨ Access the **M**ark pull-down menu and select **L**ist.

3. The List Number: prompt appears, asking for the number of the list (from 1 through 10) in which you want to include the marked block. Type *1* for List 1 and press Enter. The highlighted block disappears, and you return to the document.

If you want to see the hidden codes marking this phrase for List 1, press Reveal Codes (Alt-F3 or F11). The codes should resemble those shown in figure 25.2.

Repeat steps 1 through 3 for any other words or phrases you want to include in List 1.

> ### Tip
> If you have several lists in your document and want to avoid confusion, keep a written record of them. The best method is to define your lists before you start writing. That way, you can allocate marked text to different lists as you write.

WordPerfect offers specialized lists with dedicated functions. The following are dedicated lists, shown with the features that appear automatically without using feature codes:

```
    3.    Defendant had theretofore, daily and hourly,

harangued, pestered, screamed at, vilified, and subjected to

shrill contempt and contumely all her neighbors, including

me.  Indeed, more than 40 people testified against her at

trial.  See People v. Therblig, unreported, decision annexed

hereto as Exhibit A.  She was fined the sum of $50, which
C:\BOOK\CHAP25\AFF.51                    Doc 2 Pg 1 Ln 9.25" Pos 2.2"
[▮ ▲  ▲  ▲  ▲  ▲  ▲  ▲  ▲  ▲  ▲  ]
shrill contempt and contumely all her neighbors, including[SRt]
me.  Indeed, more than 40 people testified against her at[SRt]
trial.  [UND]See[und] [Target(CONVICT)][UND]People v. Therblig[und], unreported,
 decision annexed[SRt]
hereto as [Mark:List,1][BOLD]Exhibit A[bold][End Mark:List,1].  She was fined th
e sum of $50, which[SPg]
was paid to the State, whereupon she was released to return[SRt]
to her charac-teristic scolding ways.[HRt]
[Ln Spacing:1][HRt]
[Ln Spacing:2][TAB][Par Num:1].[TAB]Of all those subjected to her scolding, I su

Press Reveal Codes to restore screen
```

Fig. 25.2.

The Reveal Codes of text marked for inclusion in List 1.

List	Features
6	Includes captions (if any) in figure boxes
7	Includes captions of table boxes
8	Includes captions of text boxes
9	Includes captions of user-defined boxes
10	Includes captions of equation boxes (new with 5.1)

If you define List 10, for example, a list of equation boxes appears at the List 10 definition code when you generate. With WordPerfect 5.1, you cannot assign a list number to a graphics box; to obtain a list of these boxes, you must insert into the document the definition code for the appropriate list; WordPerfect then generates the list without further input from you.

Marking Text the Easy Way (Using Styles)

Styles give you a way to automate document formatting. The following sections discuss the use of styles for marking text. (For an in-depth exploration of styles, see Chapter 15.)

Creating a Style

Before you write a document, you can create a style for marking text. You don't have to use a style to mark text, but a style speeds up the process of marking text for a list. More important, the principles that follow are vital to the generation of a Table of Contents. To create a style, perform the following steps:

Cue:
Create a style to mark text.

1. Press Style (Alt-F8). The Style screen appears. If you have already defined some styles and indicated the style library file in Setup, the styles are listed on this screen.

   ⌨ Access the **L**ayout pull-down menu and select **S**tyle.

2. Select **C**reate (**3**). The Styles: Edit menu appears.

3. Select **N**ame (**1**), type *List 1* as the name for the list in this example, and press Enter.

4. Leave **P**aired for **T**ype (**2**); select **D**escription (**3**), type a descriptive phrase such as *Includes in Exhibit List*, and press Enter. Your screen should look like the one in figure 25.3.

Fig. 25.3.

*The Styles: Edit menu with **N**ame and **D**escription defined.*

```
Styles: Edit

   1 - Name            List 1

   2 - Type            Paired

   3 - Description     Includes in Exhibit List

   4 - Codes

   5 - Enter           HRt
```

5. Select **C**odes (**4**). You see what looks like a Reveal Codes screen with the cursor at the left edge highlighting **[Comment]**. **[Comment]** stands for the text you will insert when the style is used.

6. Use the keyboard or the mouse to highlight the **[Comment]** code.

7. Mark the **[Comment]** code for inclusion in the list. Press Mark Text (Alt-F5) and select **L**ist (**2**).

   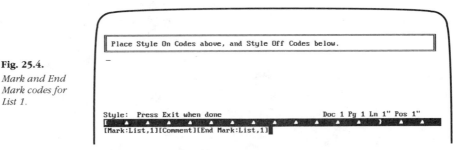 Access the **M**ark pull-down menu and select **L**ist.

8. Type the desired list number at the List Number: prompt (*1* for this example). The comment is surrounded by list codes (see fig. 25.4).

Fig. 25.4.

Mark and End Mark codes for List 1.

```
Place Style On Codes above, and Style Off Codes below.
 _




Style:  Press Exit when done                      Doc 1 Pg 1 Ln 1" Pos 1"
[ ▲  ▲  ▲  ▲  ▲  ▲  ▲  ▲  ▲  ▲  ]  ▲  ▲
[Mark:List,1][Comment][End Mark:List,1]
```

9. Press Exit (F7) twice to return to the Style screen and menu. List 1 and the brief description of it are now visible in the list of styles.

10. Select **S**ave (**6**) from the menu at the bottom of the screen to save the style. At the prompt Filename:, type the name of your style library file (if you're adding to existing styles) or a new file name (if you're creating a new style library). You must specify the full path of the style library if you have not designated a styles directory in Setup (Shift-F1), **L**ocation of Files (**6**), **S**tyle Files (**5**).

If you're adding to an existing library, select **Y** to respond to the question whether to replace that file. Press Enter and end the procedure by pressing Exit (F7).

Using a Created Style

Once you define a style for marking text, use the following procedure to mark existing text—for example, text already written that you decide to mark.

To mark existing text, follow these steps:

Reminder:
Use an existing style to mark text for inclusion in a list. Highlight the text, press Style, and turn the desired list selection on.

1. Use the keyboard (Alt-F4 or F12) or the mouse to block the text you want to include in the list. Make sure that you include any formatting codes, such as bold or underline, that you want in the list.

2. Press Style (Alt-F8).

   ⌨ Access the **L**ayout pull-down menu and select **S**tyle.

3. Move the cursor to List 1 and turn the style **O**n (**1**).

If you press Reveal Codes (Alt-F3 or F11) for this example, the screen displays the following codes surrounding the first list entry. As you can see, the bold formatting codes are part of the text format:

[Style On:List 1][BOLD]Exhibit A**[bold].[Style Off:List 1]**

To mark text as you write it, follow these steps instead:

1. Press Style (Alt-F8).

   ⌨ Access the **L**ayout pull-down menu and select **S**tyle.

2. Select List 1.

3. Type the item to be included in the list.

4. Press → to close the style.

Creating Macros for a Style To Mark Text

You can simplify even more the process of marking text as you write if you create a macro that turns the style on. You then type the item and press → to end the style. The macro reduces the process of marking text to just a few extra keystrokes.

Note: If you aren't familiar with WordPerfect 5.1's macro feature, see Chapters 11 and 12.

To create a macro to mark text with a style, follow these steps:

Cue:
Create a macro that turns on the desired style and pauses for you to type the text you want to mark.

1. Press Macro Define (Ctrl-F10).

   ⌨ Access the **T**ools pull-down menu and select **M**acro **D**efine.

2. At the Define Macro: prompt, type a name for the macro (something like *L1* for List 1) and press Enter. Use this name to invoke the macro when you want to run it.

3. At the Description: prompt, type a descriptive title for the macro (such as *First List*) and press Enter.

4. At the `Macro Def` prompt, press Style (Alt-F8). Then press Search (F2 or **N**), type the exact name of the first-list style (*List 1* in this example—the style created in the preceding section), and press Enter. Turn the style **On** (**1**) and return to the document.

5. Insert a {PAUSE} in the macro by pressing Ctrl-PgUp, **P** or **1**, and Enter. ({PAUSE} gives the user time to enter the text to be marked.) Press → to get outside the style code.

6. Press Macro Define (Ctrl-F10).

   ⌷ Access the **T**ools pull-down menu and select **M**acro **D**efine.

To use the L1 macro to mark text as you type it, press Macro (Alt-F10). ⌷ If you use a mouse, access the **T**ools pull-down menu and select **M**acro E**x**ecute. At the Macro: prompt, enter *L1* to invoke the macro. Type the text you want to mark. Press Enter to get outside the style and end the macro.

Defining a List

Defining means telling WordPerfect where you want to place the list of marked items and how you want the list to look. If you marked all exhibits in the affidavit, you are ready to set up a page in the affidavit where you want the list to print. Usually, you place the list on a page by itself. To illustrate defining a list, set up the page in the affidavit as described in the following procedures.

To create a List of Exhibits page, press Home, Home, ↓ to move the cursor to the end of the document. Press Ctrl-Enter for a hard page break. Set up appropriate page numbering. For instance, you may want to number the page in Roman numerals because the list follows the main text. You may want to turn off numbering entirely.

Reminder:

Before you generate a list, define it by selecting the style of page numbering you want the list to use.

Type *List of Exhibits* for a title. To define the list of exhibits, place the cursor where you want the list to start and follow these steps:

1. Press Mark Text (Alt-F5) and select **D**efine (**5**) from the menu at the bottom of the screen. Select **D**efine List (**2**) from the Mark Text: Define menu (see fig. 25.5).

   ⌷ Access the **M**ark pull-down menu, select **D**efine, and then select **L**ist.

Fig. 25.5.
The Mark Text: Define menu.

```
Mark Text: Define

    1 - Define Table of Contents

    2 - Define List

    3 - Define Index

    4 - Define Table of Authorities

    5 - Edit Table of Authorities Full Form
```

2. Type the number of the list you want to define (in this example, type *1*). A List Definition menu appears with the list number you just typed (see fig. 25.6). This menu offers five ways to handle the page numbers included in the list.

```
List 1  Definition

     1 - No Page Numbers

     2 - Page Numbers Follow Entries

     3 - (Page Numbers) Follow Entries

     4 - Flush Right Page Numbers

     5 - Flush Right Page Numbers with Leaders
```

Fig. 25.6.
*The List
Definition menu.*

3. Select the page-numbering format you want. If you select **N**o Page Numbers (**1**), the list is pointless (the list usually is used to refer to the page in the document on which the reference occurs). For most work, select Flush Right Page Numbers with **L**eaders (**5**), which is easiest to read. If you use Reveal Codes to see what you have just done, you see **[Def Mark:List,1:5]** under the heading for the first list.

4. End the page with a hard page break (Ctrl-Enter) and save the document (F10) before generating the list. If you use a mouse, access the **F**ile pull-down menu and select **S**ave.

Generating Document References

All lists, as well as the Table of Contents, Table of Authorities, and cross-references, are generated in a single sweep, usually just before printing. As with all other functions in this chapter, you should plan to generate lists well ahead of the deadline for the document. Beware of long documents with several document references; the generating process can be quite slow. In addition, you should plan to generate lists twice. The first time, you find your mistakes; the second time, you get it right.

Caution

Before you generate document references, save the document and save an additional copy of it elsewhere (on a floppy disk). This advice is especially important when you generate references for large documents. Long operations are more vulnerable to power disruptions, "bad spots" on a disk, and other calamities. If you carefully save your document and save a second copy elsewhere, your precious text is safe.

Tip

Except when generating the simplest, smallest lists, clear the second screen to free up as much RAM as possible before you start generating document references. If you need still more RAM to generate references, use Setup to deactivate any keyboard definitions you may be using (Setup is described in Chapter 20).

Reminder:

To generate a list, select Generate from the Mark Text: Generate menu and select the type of table you want to create.

To generate a list, save the file and follow these steps:

1. Press Mark Text (Alt-F5) and select **G**enerate (**6**) from the menu at the bottom of the screen to display the Mark Text: Generate menu (see fig. 25.7).

   ⌨ Access the **M**ark pull-down menu and select **G**enerate.

Fig. 25.7.

The Mark Text: Generate menu.

```
Mark Text: Generate

      1 - Remove Redline Markings and Strikeout Text from Document

      2 - Compare Screen and Disk Documents and Add Redline and Strikeout

      3 - Expand Master Document

      4 - Condense Master Document

      5 - Generate Tables, Indexes, Cross References, etc.
```

2. Select **G**enerate Tables, Indexes, Cross References, etc. (**5**). WordPerfect issues the message Existing tables, lists, and indexes will be replaced. Continue? Yes (No). If you're sure that you want to go ahead, select **Y**. WordPerfect begins generating, passing through the document several times to compile document references, and reporting any irregularities it finds. When generating is done, your document appears on-screen with all tables and lists updated.

3. Press Save (F10) to preserve the generated document.

   ⌨ Access the **F**ile pull-down menu and select **S**ave.

The list of exhibits marked in the affidavit appears on-screen as shown in figure 25.8.

Fig. 25.8.

The list of exhibits.

```
                      LIST OF EXHIBITS

                Page numbers record first mention of
                   each exhibit in this affidavit

      Exhibit A. . . . . . . . . . . . . . . . . . . . . . 1
      Exhibit B. . . . . . . . . . . . . . . . . . . . . . 2
      Exhibit C. . . . . . . . . . . . . . . . . . . . . . 2
      Exhibit D. . . . . . . . . . . . . . . . . . . . . . 3
      Exhibit E. . . . . . . . . . . . . . . . . . . . . . 3
```

Caution

When you generate lists for the first time, WordPerfect inserts an **[EndDef]** code after each completed document reference. WordPerfect uses this code to determine what to delete when you generate again. **Don't move or delete this code under any circumstances.** Although WordPerfect will not delete anything, it will report that it can't find the **[EndDef]** code and produce two tables, one after the other.

Tip

Some lists are better ordered alphabetically than by order of appearance. You can use an index to organize your list this way, but you can have only one index in a document (or in a collection of master and subdocuments). You can use a list to accomplish the same thing: generate the list (to get the **[EndDef]** code), and then block and sort the list between the **[DefMark:List,1:5]** and **[EndDef]** codes. Although this sounds easy, you may have some complications. Because each entry in a list begins with **[→Indent←][Mar Rel]**, the sorter reads the text as being in field 3. Also, unless you do something to prevent it, the **[DefMark:List,1:5]** code is included in the sort and may end up in the middle of the list, producing weird results the next time you generate. If you use Line Sort, but have some multiline entries in the list, the sort produces hash. If you try to solve the problem with a Paragraph Sort, you find that single-spaced paragraphs are defined by two **[HRt]** codes, and a list has only a single **[HRt]** at the end of each item. Finally, if you have multiline entries in the list, you may want to separate them with an extra blank line.

LSTSRT.ARC, in Data Library 0 (zero) of CompuServe's WordPerfect Support Group forum—GO WPSG—contains a macro that deals with all these problems for WordPerfect 5. Because of differences between versions 5 and 5.1 (primarily in the location of the menu numbers for Setup), however, the macro must be modified before you can use it with 5.1. The macro provides a useful starting place for anyone prepared to tackle the modifications using the macro editor. Teaching you to develop the macro yourself is beyond the scope of this chapter because it requires the use of the WordPerfect Programming Language.

◆ 5.1

Considering Other Uses for Lists

As you learn in the next chapter, WordPerfect enables you to generate tables, lists, and cross-references involving several separate but related documents. You may, for instance, have a brief that refers to an affidavit, which you want to generate together. You may have a dissertation or book spread out among any number of files. And what if the affidavit is so long that it has its own table of contents?

WordPerfect can handle only one table of contents for a set of related documents. The solution is to create a list in the affidavit and let the list masquerade as a table of contents. This list cannot have the number of any other list in the set of related documents. Although lists don't have different heading levels, you can create artificial hierarchies within lists. Do this by enclosing within the list the formatting codes (left and right indents, tabs, underlining, and the like) used by the document itself to distinguish the level of headings. If you want the headings separated by a blank line, enclose a final hard return after each heading.

Cue:

Because WordPerfect can generate only one table of contents for related documents, use a list as a "subtable of contents."

Creating a Table of Contents

This section assumes that you read and understood the preceding discussion of lists. Many of the procedures are identical or similar enough to be described by their differences.

Setting Up Automatic Paragraph Numbering

Cue:
Use automatic paragraph numbering if you want to create cross-references; the numbers are updated if you delete or move paragraphs.

You can use automatic paragraph numbering to number paragraphs or headings and subheads in hierarchical material. Do this for two reasons: paragraph and outline numbers are necessary for cross-references, and the numbers adjust automatically if you move or delete paragraphs or headings during editing.

Before you mark text for paragraph numbering, you should define your paragraph-numbering scheme. If you haven't already defined the system in Setup, or if you want to use a system different from the one you specified, use the procedures in this section.

To view the current paragraph numbering scheme, follow these steps:

1. Press Date/Outline (Shift-F5) and select **D**efine (**6**) from the menu at the bottom of the screen to see the Paragraph Number Definition menu with default settings (see fig. 25.9).

   Access the **T**ools pull-down menu and select **D**efine.

2. Select **P**aragraph (**2**). The current definition of paragraph levels is displayed.

```
Paragraph Number Definition

     1 - Starting Paragraph Number                1
           (in legal style)
                                                Levels
                                  1    2    3    4    5    6    7    8
     2 - Paragraph                1.   a.   i.   (1)  (a)  (i)  1)   a)
     3 - Outline                  I.   A.   1.   a.   (1)  (a)  i)   a)
     4 - Legal (1.1.1)            1    .1   .1   .1   .1   .1   .1   .1
     5 - Bullets                  •    o    -    ■    *    +    ·    x
     6 - User-defined

     Current Definition           I.   A.   1.   a.   (1)  (a)  i)   a)
     Attach Previous Level             No   No   No   No   No   No   No

     7 - Enter Inserts Paragraph Number           Yes

     8 - Automatically Adjust to Current Level    Yes

     9 - Outline Style Name
```

Fig. 25.9.
The Paragraph Number Definition menu.

Suppose that you want to use the following scheme to number paragraphs:

		Levels		
1	2	3	4	5
1	(a)	(1)	(A)	(i)

To change the current definition to incorporate this scheme, follow these steps:

1. Select **U**ser-defined (**6**) from the Paragraph Number Definition menu. The cursor moves to the first column so that you can define the number style and punctuation for Level-1 paragraphs.

2. Type *1* and press Enter. (If *1* already exists, just press Enter.) The cursor moves to the second column so that you can define styles for Level-2 paragraphs.

3. Type *(a)* and press Enter. The cursor jumps to the third column. Type *(1)* and press Enter. At the fourth column, type *(A)* and press Enter. At the fifth column, type *(i)* and press Enter.

4. To delete the default styles for heading levels 6, 7, and 8, press space bar, Enter, space bar, Enter, space bar, Enter. Unless you also want to adjust the attachment of outline levels (see Chapter 24), press Cancel (F1) or Escape to end paragraph-number definition. Your screen should look like the one in figure 25.10.

Tip

You can use the remaining three paragraph-numbering definitions for anything you like. For example, you may want to use different kinds of bullets, inserted with the Compose function (Ctrl-2). See the discussion of Compose in Chapter 21.

Tip

You should not define paragraph-numbering definitions to include trailing periods, because such definitions show up in automatic cross-referencing like this:

```
See section 1.(a).(1).(B).(ii). above.
```

Instead, include trailing periods in the macro or style that invokes automatic numbering.

```
Paragraph Number Definition

  1 - Starting Paragraph Number            1
       (in legal style)
                                     Levels
                          1    2    3    4    5    6    7    8
  2 - Paragraph           1.   a.   i.   (1)  (a)  (i)  1)   a)
  3 - Outline             I.   A.   1.   a.   (1)  (a)  i)   a)
  4 - Legal (1.1.1)       1    .1   .1   .1   .1   .1   .1   .1
  5 - Bullets             •    o    -    ■    *    +    ·    x
  6 - User-defined

  Current Definition      1    (a)  (1)  (A)  (i)
  Attach Previous Level        No   No   No   No   No   No   No

  7 - Enter Inserts Paragraph Number       Yes

  8 - Automatically Adjust to Current Level Yes

  9 - Outline Style Name
```

Fig. 25.10.

The Paragraph Number Definition menu after changing the numbering scheme.

If you are writing a document with numbered paragraphs, you can create a macro to end one paragraph and begin the next by putting in the appropriate number. If you ordinarily write in double-space and want three blank lines between paragraphs, you can define the macro to do this as well.

Use these steps to create a macro that inserts paragraph numbers, double spaces the text, and inserts three blank lines between paragraphs:

Note: These instructions assume that you have custom-defined the paragraph-numbering scheme as just described. If this is not true, make appropriate adjustments in the macro. Adding the period manually after the number, instead of including it in the paragraph-numbering definition, has advantages when you want to automatically cross-reference the document.

1. Press Macro Define (Ctrl-F10).

    ▭ Access the **T**ools pull-down menu and select **M**acro **D**efine.

2. At the prompt `Define Macro:`, press Alt-Z. At the prompt `Description:`, type *Paragraph Change.*

3. Record the following keystrokes to put two blank lines between paragraphs:

    Format (Shift-F8), **L**ine (**1**), Line **S**pacing (**6**), 1

4. Press Exit (F7) to exit from the Line Format menu.

5. Press Enter to create a third line between paragraphs.

6. Press the following keys to change the line spacing back to double-space and return to the screen:

    Format (Shift-F8), **L**ine (**1**), Line **S**pacing (**6**), 2, Enter, Exit (F7)

7. Tab to the position for the paragraph number.

8. Press Date/Outline (Shift-F5), select **P**ara Num (**5**), type *1* (for the paragraph level), and press Enter.

    ▭ Access the **T**ools pull-down menu, select **P**aragraph Number, type *1*, and press Enter.

    The paragraph number appears on-screen.

9. Type a period after the number and press Tab to return to the start of the text.

10. End macro definition by pressing Macro Define (Ctrl-F10).

    ▭ Access the **T**ools pull-down menu and select **M**acro **D**efine.

For guidelines on storing and managing macro files, see Chapters 11 and 12.

Marking Text for a Table of Contents

In general, you mark text for the Table of Contents (ToC) by blocking the text and any desired codes and specifying the level of that heading.

When you mark chapter or section headings for inclusion in the ToC, you must make an initial decision about how you want the result to look. WordPerfect puts a blank line before all first-level ToC entries, but subheads are not separated by blank lines.

With section titles (as opposed to headings of logical argument in legal statements) you can choose how you want the titles to print—centered or flush left, for example—in the ToC.

Marking ToC Entries the Hard Way

Suppose that you want to center the "Argument" title for the legal brief used as an example in this chapter, with the first-level headings flush left and the second-level subheads indented.

To mark this title for the ToC so that it is centered, follow these steps:

1. Press Reveal Codes (Alt-F3 or F11).

   ⌨ Access the **E**dit pull-down menu and select **R**eveal Codes.

2. Place the cursor to the left of the center code, turn on Block (press Alt-F4 or F12 or press and hold the left mouse button), and move the cursor to the right of the centered text.

3. Press Mark Text (Alt-F5) and select To**C** (**1**).

   ⌨ Access the **M**ark pull-down menu and select Table of **C**ontents.

4. At the prompt for ToC level, type *1*.

To mark the first-level heading, follow these steps:

1. Press Reveal Codes (Alt-F3 or F11).

   ⌨ Access the **E**dit pull-down menu and select **R**eveal Codes.

2. Position the cursor on the **[Par Num:1]** code, turn on Block (press Alt-F4 or F12 or press and hold the left mouse button), and move the cursor to the right of the centered text.

3. Press Mark Text (Alt-F5) and select To**C** (**1**).

   ⌨ Access the **M**ark pull-down menu and select Table of **C**ontents.

4. At the prompt for ToC level, type *1*. The text appears as shown in figure 25.11.

To mark a second-level subhead, repeat the procedure, but in the last step specify the ToC level as *2*. Go through the entire document, marking each level of heading.

Figure 25.12 shows what a partial ToC looks like after generating. Notice that no line separates first-level headings from second-level subheads.

In the next section, you see how to mark text so that a blank line appears between all headings and subheads.

Reminder:
WordPerfect inserts blank lines in the ToC between first-level heads; subheads are not separated by blank lines.

Reminder:
To mark a title for the ToC, press Reveal Codes, highlight the text, press Mark Text, and type the number of the ToC level.

Fig. 25.11.

Marking text for a first-level heading in the Table of Contents.

```
                    more appropriate method of fact-finding in this unusual
                    case.

                                        Argument

                    1.    HISTORICALLY, TRIAL BY JURY AS WE KNOW IT IS A
                          RECENT UPSTART, BY NO MEANS UNIVERSAL. _

C:\BOOK\CHAP25\BRIEF.TXT                          Doc 1 Pg 2 Ln 2.67" Pos 5.8"
        {      ▲   ▲    ▲    ▲    ▲    ▲    ▲    ▲    ▲    ▲  ]  ▲    ▲   ▲
[HRt]
[HRt]
[Mark:ToC,1][Par Num:1].[→Indent]HISTORICALLY, TRIAL BY JURY AS WE KNOW IT IS A[
SRt]
RECENT UPSTART, BY NO MEANS UNIVERSAL.[End Mark:ToC,1][HRt]
[HRt]
[HRt]
[Mark:ToC,2][Tab][Par Num:2][→Indent][UND]The Founding Fathers, When They Guaran
teed The[SRt]
Right to Trial By Jury, Did Not Mean To Exclude[SRt]

Press Reveal Codes to restore screen
```

Fig. 25.12.

Generated Table of Contents with no blank line between headings and subheads (partial ToC shown).

```
                            TABLE OF CONTENTS


Introduction  . . . . . . . . . . . . . . . . . . . . . .  1

                            Argument  . . . . . . . . . .  2

1.    HISTORICALLY, TRIAL BY JURY AS WE KNOW IT IS A RECENT
      UPSTART, BY NO MEANS UNIVERSAL. . . . . . . . . . . .  2
            (a)   The Founding Fathers, When They Guaranteed The
                  Right to Trial By Jury, Did Not Mean To Exclude
                  Older Forms of Trial. . . . . . . . . . .  2
            (b)   The Laws of This State Do Not Expressly Forbid
                  Trial by Alternative Means. . . . . . . .  3

2.    TRIAL BY FIRE IS MORE APPROPRIATE THAN TRIAL BY JURY IN
      THIS CASE. . . . . . . . . . . . . . . . . . . . . .  4
            (a)   The Offense Charged is Ancient, Venerable, and
                  Ineluctably Associated with Trial by
                  Alternative Means. . . . . . . . . . . . .  4

C:\BOOK\CHAP25\TOC.50                         Doc 1 Pg 1 Ln 1.17" Pos 1"
```

Marking All ToC Entries as Level-1 Headings

Cue:

Mark each ToC entry as a first-level heading to insert blank lines between each entry.

WordPerfect always places a blank line before first-level headings. If the subheads tend to be long, however, the ToC may end up looking crowded. You can go back through the ToC after you generate it and manually place a blank line before each subhead, but this method is tedious. On the other hand, you can mark each entry as first-level to separate each entry by a blank line, and then differentiate the lower-level headings by some other means. What you want to end up with is a Table of Contents like the one shown in figure 25.13.

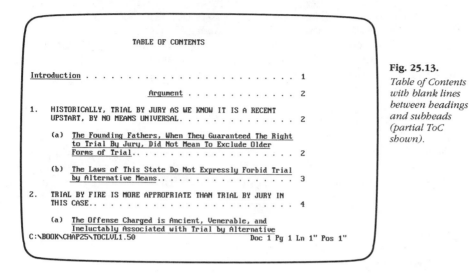

Fig. 25.13.

Table of Contents with blank lines between headings and subheads (partial ToC shown).

If you mark text to include the codes for indentation, underlining, and other format factors, the ToC appears with these features. The next example uses the same legal brief to explain how to mark text to include format features:

1. Block each subhead separately, starting at the left margin and continuing until you capture all the codes for that level. Be sure to capture the codes for underlining and indentation at second and subsequent levels, or the headings do not appear subordinate to first-level headings at the left margin.

2. Mark all entries as ToC level *1*. Figure 25.14 shows a second-level subhead marked as a first-level heading. Notice that the **[Mark:ToC,1]** code precedes the codes for **[→Indent]** and **[Par Num:2]**.

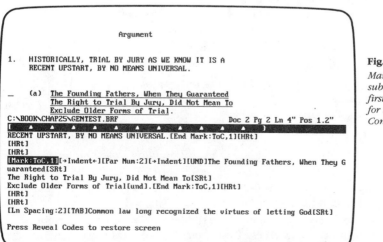

Fig. 25.14.

Marking a subhead as a first-level heading for the Table of Contents.

If the ToC is several pages long, you may be disappointed to find that headings and subheads are split between succeeding pages. You cannot avoid this split automatically, but you can correct it by going back through the ToC after you generate it and using block protect to rejoin any split headings. (Block-protect codes within ToC codes are removed in the generation process.)

Marking ToC Entries the Easy Way

Cue:

Use styles to mark ToC entries easily; change the style to change the way all headings appear.

So far, you have seen how to mark headings for inclusion in the ToC using a method equivalent to that shown for lists. As with lists, you also can define a paired style for every level of the ToC. Each style should contain all the formatting codes (including the automatic paragraph-numbering code manually set for the correct level) that you use for the level of heading in question. (If you need a basic understanding of WordPerfect styles, see Chapter 15.)

With the style method of marking ToC entries, you can not only save keystrokes but also change the way a particular heading level is handled by using a single command. For example, you can put a second indent in front of second-level subheads throughout the document by editing the heading-2 style. This section explains how to prepare a style for a second-level subhead like the following:

(a) <u>The Offense Charged is Ancient, Venerable, and Ineluctably Associated with Trial by Alternative Means</u>............4

To prepare a style to use for marking ToC text, follow these steps:

1. Press Style (Alt-F8).

   ▭▤ Access the **L**ayout pull-down menu and select **S**tyle.

   If you have designated a style-library file name in Setup, the styles from that library file appear.

2. Select **C**reate (**3**). From the resulting menu, select **N**ame (**1**), type an appropriate name (such as *Heading 2*, and press Enter. Leave the **T**ype (**2**) option as `Paired`, select **D**escription (**3**), and enter something like *Marks Heading for Level 2 ToC*.

3. Select **C**odes (**4**) to bring up the Codes screen with its comment section.

4. Press Format (Shift-F8) and select **L**ine (**1**).

   ▭▤ Access the **L**ayout pull-down menu and select **L**ine.

5. Select Line **S**pacing (**6**), type *1*, and press Enter. Press Exit (F7) to return to the Style screen.

6. Press Left/Right indent (Shift-F4).

7. Put in the automatic paragraph code by pressing Date/Outline (Shift-F5). Choose **P**ara Num (**5**), type *2* (or the level you chose), and press Enter.

   ▭▤ Access the **T**ools pull-down menu, select **P**aragraph Number, type the number of the desired level, and press Enter.

8. Press Indent (F4) and Underline (F8). Move the cursor to the right side of the **[Comment]** code. Press Underline (F8) to turn underlining off. Type a period to include the period in the ToC subhead but to prevent its being underlined.

9. Press Enter two or more times for blank lines to separate the subhead from the text that follows.

10. If the ToC is to be separately formatted for single-space, position the cursor *after* the **[Ln Spacing:1]** but immediately *before* the first **[→Indent←]** code. To ensure single-spacing for each ToC entry—regardless of the formatting the ToC uses—include the **[Ln Spacing:1]** code within the marked block.

11. Turn on Block (press Alt-F4 or F12 or hold the left mouse button) and move the cursor to a point immediately to the *left* of the first **[HRt]** code.

12. Mark the highlighted block for inclusion in the ToC by pressing Mark Text (Alt-F5). Select To**C** (**1**), type *2*, and press Enter.

    ⌦ Access the **M**ark pull-down menu, select Table of **C**ontents, type *2*, and press Enter.

    The **[Comment]** and its associated codes to be transferred to the ToC are now surrounded by the ToC codes (see fig. 25.15).

13. Press Exit (F7) twice and select **S**ave (**6**). End by pressing Exit (F7) again.

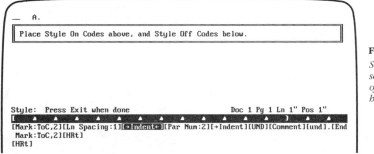

Fig. 25.15.
Style codes for a second-level Table of Contents heading.

When you are ready to type a second-level heading, use the style you just created. Press Style (Alt-F8) access the **L**ayout pull-down menu and select **S**tyle. Move the cursor to Heading 2 and turn the style **O**n (**1**). Type the text for the heading and press →.

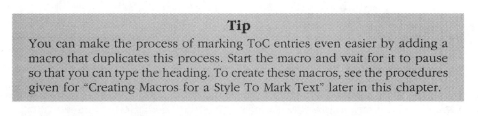

Tip
You can make the process of marking ToC entries even easier by adding a macro that duplicates this process. Start the macro and wait for it to pause so that you can type the heading. To create these macros, see the procedures given for "Creating Macros for a Style To Mark Text" later in this chapter.

Defining the Table of Contents

Plan the ToC as part of the front matter before you start writing. The ToC is generally placed just after the cover or title page.

First, start the ToC page on a new page by moving the cursor to the bottom of the cover or title page and pressing Ctrl-Enter to insert a hard page break. The cursor is now at the top of what will be the ToC page.

To create the Table of Contents page, follow these steps:

1. To start page numbering with lowercase Roman numerals, press Format (Shift-F8) and select **P**age (**2**). Then select Page **N**umbering (**6**), **N**ew Page Number (**1**), type *i*, and press Enter. Press Exit (F7) to return to the editing screen.

   ⌨ Access the **L**ayout pull-down menu, select **P**age, and follow the remaining procedures in step 1.

2. Press Center (Shift-F6) and type *Table of Contents*. With the cursor two or three lines below the title of the Table of Contents, press Mark Text (Alt-F5) and select **D**efine (**5**) (see fig. 25.5). When you select Define Table of **C**ontents (**1**), the menu in figure 25.16 appears.

   Unless you want to wrap the last level, don't select **D**isplay Last Level in Wrapped Format (**2**).

3. Select **N**umber of Levels (**1**) and type *5*. The Flush Rt with **L**eader (5) style option is automatically applied to all five levels. To see the other style options for the ToC, select **P**age Numbering (**3**). The following menu displays along the bottom of the screen:

   1 None; **2 P**g # Follows; **3 (**Pg # Follows); **4 F**lush Rt; **5** Flush Rt with **L**eader

Fig. 25.16.

The Table of Contents Definition menu.

```
Table of Contents Definition

1 - Number of Levels           1

2 - Display Last Level in      No
      Wrapped Format

3 - Page Numbering - Level 1   Flush right with leader
                     Level 2
                     Level 3
                     Level 4
                     Level 5
```

4. Press Reveal Codes (Alt-F3 or F11) to display the following:

   [Def Mark:ToC,5:5,5,5,5]

5. End the ToC with a hard page break (Ctrl-Enter).

Generating the Table of Contents

As you remember, all document references are generated together. To generate a Table of Contents, follow the steps presented under "Generating Document References" earlier in this chapter.

Using Multiple Tables of Contents

For help with problems associated with generating Tables of Contents for two related documents, see the earlier discussion, "Considering Other Uses for Lists."

Creating a Table of Authorities

The Table of Authorities (ToA) in a document provides long-form references to any authorities cited in the text. In the brief used as an example in this chapter, a ToA includes the exact sources of cases cited in the argument. Once the long-form citation for a particular authority is established, the writer can later refer to that authority by a short-form abbreviation of the citation. In the following sections, you see how to mark the text temporarily as you write and how to go back into the edited document and use those marks and a macro to mark all items for the ToA.

Reminder:

A Table of Authorities lists any authorities cited in the text.

Adjusting Setup for the ToA

Before starting your document, you should first enter Setup to specify some features of the ToA. Decide whether you want underlining in text marked for a ToA to be included in the actual table. If you don't want underlining to appear in the table, skip the following procedure. (Ordinarily, you want underlining to carry through; as it comes from the factory, WordPerfect 5.1 is set to exclude it from the ToA. This procedure changes that default—you should need to do it only one time.)

Reminder:

Change Setup if you want the ToA to include underlining.

To maintain underlining on items included in a ToA, follow these steps:

1. Press Setup (Shift-F1) and select **I**nitial Settings (**4**).

    ⌨ Access the **F**ile pull-down menu, select Se**t**up, and then select **I**nitial Settings.

2. Select Table of **A**uthorities (**7**). The menu in figure 25.17 appears.

3. Select **U**nderlining Allowed (**2**) and select **Y** to change the default setting to Yes. Press Exit (F7) twice to return to the editing screen.

```
Setup: Table of Authorities

    1 - Dot Leaders                    Yes

    2 - Underlining Allowed            No

    3 - Blank Line between Authorities Yes
```

Fig. 25.17.

The Setup: Table of Authorities menu.

Marking Text for the ToA

Before you begin marking citations for the Table of Authorities, decide how many sections you want the ToA to have. WordPerfect allows up to 16 separate sections in a Table of Authorities. Normally, you create a separate section for each type of authority, such as Federal Cases, State Cases, Federal Statutes, State Statutes, Miscellaneous Authorities, and the like. Keep a list of all the sections you plan to use so that you can easily assign a particular citation to the correct section as you mark the citation.

Cue:

Mark ToA entries after you finish the document.

Unlike marking items for Tables of Contents and Lists, marking cases for inclusion in a Table of Authorities is best done not as you go along, but when the document is nearly ready for final printing—when you finish editing. Nothing is worse than going through the completed document and trying to find the cases you added during editing.

If an authority is cited several times, you may want to use the MARK macro (described later in this chapter) after you edit. On the other hand, you should fully mark treatises, statutes, and other authorities besides cases that are clearly going to be cited only once—this action saves finding them later, and the macro does not work well with them.

Marking a brief for a ToA is virtually impossible if you are not the author; if you are the author, such a task is still hard if someone else does the typing for you. The person marking really has to know what to look for, such as the kinds of citations that may not fit the general rules outlined here.

> ### Tip
>
> As you mark cases, keep a handwritten list (or a list in WordPerfect's second window) of the authorities you have already marked. Some authorities appear more than once in long document, and putting in a second long-form ToA code by mistake is easy.

When you refer to a case in the text, use either the long form of citation (the complete, official title of the case) or a short form of citation not only unique to that case but also not duplicated elsewhere in the text. For instance, the short form for *United Airlines, Inc. v. AFL-CIO* is *United Airlines*, not *United*, because the word *united* can appear elsewhere in text not referring to the case.

If you refer to different decisions in the same case, use designations like *Tavoulareas (I)* and *Tavoulareas (II)*. Notice that the parentheses are needed to differentiate between the two. If you search for *Tavoulareas I*, WordPerfect picks up *Tavoulareas II* as well. The parentheses make each case unique.

If at all possible, make the short form of reference to an item duplicate part of the long form so that a search for the short form finds the long-form citations as well. Cite each case the same way every time, and be absolutely consistent in your use of short references.

Marking Temporarily while You Write

To mark authorities efficiently, you must observe a few rules in the course of creating the document. The process of creating a ToA for case citations works best when you mark temporarily as you write, and then search for the marks when you are ready to mark the cases for the ToA.

The best way to mark cases temporarily as you write is to place a character not otherwise used in the text, such as a backslash (\), immediately before the long-form citation. In Reveal Codes, a citation looks like the following:

\[**UND**]U.S. v. Royall[**und**], 57 U.S. 427 (1837)

Don't bother marking short-form citations temporarily.

Leave the backslashes in the document as you edit. After you settle on a version of the text, do the cite check and make all corrections to citations. At this point you should not have marked any case citations (that is, citations other than books, statutes, and the like) with anything other than the backslash.

After all the citations have been corrected, you can use the macro system described later in this chapter to mark text for the ToA in one sweep.

Marking the Finished Document

To mark case citations for inclusion in the ToA, follow these steps:

1. Find the first citation (which should be in long form). Find the citation by doing an Extended Search (Home, F2) for the backslash. If you didn't use the backslash, search for the underline code.

2. Press Backspace to delete the backslash or use the left arrow to position the cursor to left of the underline code. Use the keyboard (Alt-F4 or F12) or the mouse to highlight the entire citation (including any parentheses).

3. Press Mark Text (Alt-F5) and select To**A** (**4**).

    🖱 Access the **M**ark pull-down menu, select Table of **A**uthorities, and then select Mark **F**ull.

4. Enter the number of the ToA section (WordPerfect allows from 1 to 16 sections) where you want to place the citation. A screen appears showing the blocked text; edit the text to look as you want it in the ToA. (In particular, remove any reference to a specific page—other than the first page—of the reference.) Lines do not wrap in a ToA, so press Enter at the end of the first line of a multiple-line citation about two inches from the right margin; tab once for the second and subsequent lines, which also end two inches from the right margin (see fig. 25.18).

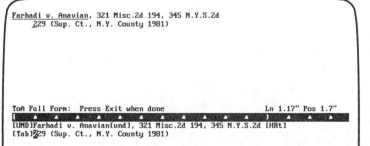

Fig. 25.18.

Editing screen for the full form of the authority.

5. When you finish editing the citation, WordPerfect asks you for the unique short form you want to use to refer to that authority. Type exactly the form you want to use (or edit the suggested string on the prompt line).

For the example shown in figure 25.18, the prompt line displays the following:

> Short Form: Farhadi v. Anavian, 321 Misc.2d 194, 345

Using cursor and delete keys, edit this line to read as follows:

> Short Form: Farhadi

6. To check that the short form also captures the long form in a search—and to prepare for using the MARK macro—search for the short-form reference after you finish defining the long form. WordPerfect should display the first long-form reference to the case, which you just marked.

7. To mark all the other long-form and short-form references to the same case, use the MARK macro described in the next section.

Creating the MARK Macro To Mark Text for ToA

Once you create the MARK macro, you can let WordPerfect find authorities for you. This macro is the easiest way to go about marking cases for a ToA.

Note: Creating the MARK macro requires you to use the WordPerfect Programming Language. If you haven't read Chapters 11 and 12 on macros and the Programming Language, do so before proceeding. At the very least, you should be familiar with the basics of macro creation. You can download the MARK macro, with complete documentation, from the CompuServe WordPerfect Support Group forum. At the CompuServe prompt, enter *GO WPSG*. MARK.WPM is in CASES.ARC in Data Library 0 (zero).

To create the MARK macro yourself, follow these steps:

1. Press Macro Define (Ctrl-F10); at the Define Macro: prompt, enter *MARK*.

   ▣ Access the **T**ools pull-down menu, select M**a**cro **D**efine, and enter *MARK*.

2. For a description, type *Marks Cases for ToA*. At the flashing Define macro: prompt, hold the Alt key and type *023* on the numeric keypad (not the number keys across the top of the keyboard). A funny-looking ASCII symbol (↕) appears on-screen when you release the Alt key. The symbol marks your starting point so that WordPerfect can return after marking the other references to the case.

3. Press Macro Define (Ctrl-F10) to end the macro.

   ▣ Access the **T**ools, pull down menu and select M**a**cro **D**efine.

Cue:

Use the macro editor to access an existing macro and make changes to it.

These steps created the first part of the MARK macro. Now you must access the macro editor and modify MARK. Chapter 11 explained that you cannot use the editor to create a macro from scratch. You can get to the editor only from the menu that appears when you try to create a macro with the same name as an existing macro. To modify the MARK macro to include the other steps of the macro, do the following:

1. Press Macro Define (Ctrl-F10) again. At the `Define macro:` prompt, enter *MARK*.

   ⌨ Access the **T**ools pull-down menu, select M**a**cro **D**efine, and enter *MARK*.

   Because this is the name of an existing macro, a menu appears that enables you to edit existing macros.

2. Select **E**dit (**2**). The macro edit screen for MARK displays, showing {DISPLAY OFF} (the default) and the ASCII 023 code. Move the cursor to the left of the ASCII 023 code and enter the following macro commands:

   {ON NOT FOUND}{GO}b~~

   After entering these commands, move the cursor to the right of the ASCII 023 code and enter the rest of the commands. See Chapters 11 and 12 if you have any questions about how to enter these commands.

   {LABEL}a~
   {Home}{Search}{Search}
   {Mark Text}4{Enter}
   {GO}a~

   {LABEL}b~
   {Home}{Search Left}{Search}↕{Backspace}

   When you have completed entering these commands, the macro editing screen for your MARK macro should match the screen shown in figure 25.19.

```
Macro: Action

    File            MARK.WPM

    Description     Mark cases for ToA

    ┌─────────────────────────────────────────────────────────┐
    │ {DISPLAY OFF}                                            │
    │ {ON NOT FOUND}{GO}b~~                                    │
    │ ‡                                                        │
    │                                                         │
    │ {LABEL}a~                                               │
    │  {Home}{Search}{Search}                                  │
    │  {Mark Text}4{Enter}                                     │
    │  {GO}a~                                                  │
    │                                                         │
    │ {LABEL}b~                                               │
    │  {Home}{Search Left}‡{Search}{Backspace}                │
    │                                                         │
    │                                                         │
    │                                                         │
    │                                                         │
    └─────────────────────────────────────────────────────────┘

Ctrl-PgUp for macro commands;  Press Exit when done
```

Fig. 25.19.
The MARK macro in the macro editor.

After you exit the macro editor and return to the document, you use the MARK macro by pressing Macro (Alt-F10) and entering *MARK*. Once WordPerfect finds all occurrences of the first authority, you are ready to search for the next authority, mark it, search for the short form, and invoke the MARK macro again. The macro assumes that the search finds the proper citation and marks it; if the search does not find the proper citation, you must change the short form. **Do not run the**

MARK macro until you have searched for and found the first occurrence of the short-form reference of the authority for which you are presently marking all other occurrences.

Correcting Mistaken References

Inevitably, you find mistakes or necessary changes after you mark citations. If you have to change the way a citation is reported in the ToA, follow these steps:

1. From the first page of the main text (to avoid an already-generated ToA) do an Extended Search (Home, F2) for the short-form citation; the first reference you come to should contain the long-form code. Using this chapter's example, press Extended Search (Home, F2), type *Farhadi*, and press Extended Search again.

2. Move the cursor a little below the reference WordPerfect found, press Mark Text (Alt-F5), and select **D**efine (**5**).

3. Select **E**dit Table of Authorities Full Form (**5**) and make changes on the editing screen.

   ⌨ Access the **M**ark pull-down menu, select Table of **A**uthorities, select **E**dit Full, and make changes.

4. When the corrections are made, press Exit (F7). WordPerfect prompts you for the section number; change it if you marked it wrong in the first place.

> **Tip**
> Remember that if you have a mistake in the original citation, you must edit both the citation and the full-form ToA code.

Marking a large brief can take a couple of hours, especially if you allow for a few dry runs. Generating the ToA takes a long time; leave yourself plenty of time for this process.

Defining a Table of Authorities

You should define the ToA when you start to write the document. Although you can amend it if necessary, you should try to get it right at the start.

Cue:

Number the Table of Authorities separately from the rest of the document.

As with all other tables, the Table of Authorities should be contained in a separately numbered part of the document. Specifically, you must have a hard page break and a new page-number code after the last Table of Authorities section definition and before the first citation marked for inclusion.

The first page of the ToA usually follows the last page of the Table of Contents in a legal brief. Front matter for a brief usually consists of the following (in this order): cover page, Table of Contents, and Table of Authorities.

Make certain that you put a hard page break (Ctrl-Enter) at the bottom of the ToC page. Follow these steps to set up the Table of Authorities page:

1. Type *Table of Authorities*, center it on the page, and mark the title for inclusion in the Table of Contents.

2. Press Enter three times. Press Center (Shift-F6), press Underline (F8), and type the name of first section heading. In a legal brief, for instance, you may have separate sections labeled "Decisions," "Statutes," and "Other Authorities." In the example used in this chapter, the first section is entitled "Decisions—State." The subsequent sections are entitled "Decisions—Federal," "Statutes," and "Other Authorities."

3. After the first section head, enter the Table of Authorities definition (see the next procedure for defining a Table of Authorities).

4. If you have more than one type of authority, repeat steps 1 through 3 until you create a section for each. You may have up to 16 different sections in a ToA. If you want, create a "Table of Authorities Continued" header for subsequent pages.

5. Press Ctrl-Enter to insert a hard page break to end the ToA page.

To define each section for the Table of Authorities, follow these steps:

1. Move the cursor to a point below the corresponding section title where you want the first citation when you generate.

2. Press Mark Text (Alt-F5) and select **D**efine (**5**). Choose Define Table of **A**uthorities (**4**).

   ⌨ Access the **M**ark pull-down menu, select **D**efine, and select Table of **A**uthorities.

3. Type the section number where WordPerfect requests it. For the example shown in this chapter, type *1* to specify the first section. A menu for defining the format of the first section of the ToA is displayed (see fig. 25.20).

4. Change the default to include underlining, if you haven't done so already. (If you followed the steps for changing this default through Setup, you don't need to change the menu now.) In most cases you select dot leaders, underlining, and a blank line, as shown in figure 25.20.

5. Exit the menu by pressing Enter. You return to the editing screen.

6. Repeat steps 1 through 5 for each section of the Table of Authorities.

```
Definition for Table of Authorities 1

    1 - Dot Leaders                         Yes

    2 - Underlining Allowed                 Yes

    3 - Blank Line Between Authorities       Yes
```

Fig. 25.20.

Format definitions defined for the first section of the Table of Authorities.

Generating the Table of Authorities

To generate a Table of Authorities, follow the steps outlined under "Generating Document References" earlier in this chapter. Figure 25.21 shows the first page of a printed ToA.

Fig. 25.21.
A printed Table of Authorities.

TABLE OF AUTHORITIES

Decisions--State

Farhadi v. Anavian, 321 Misc.2d 194, 345 N.Y.S.2d 229 (Sup. Ct., N.Y. County 1981) 4

Goodbody v. Ingalls, 198 N.Y. 307, 114 N.E. 124 (1908) 3

Jumbville v. Soc. of Elysian Masters, 114 Misc.2d 245, 127 N.Y.S.2d 125 (Sup. Ct., N.Y. County 1984) 3

Thimsley v. Blankwort, 329 A.D.2d 157, 157 N.Y.S.2d 115 (1st Dept. 1983) 3

Decisions--Federal

Marshall v. Taney, 37 U.S. 146 (1807) 3

U.S. v. Royall, 57 U.S. 427 (1837) 1, 2

Statutes

New York Penal Law, §2106(c) 4

Other Authorities

Blackstone, Commentaries, p. 98 4

Savonarola, Report on Medieval Survivals in Those Areas of the United States Formerly Under the Dominion of Great Britain (1805), p. 1,317 5

ii

Creating an Index

Reminder:
You either can mark text to be included in the index or create entries manually.

A good index anticipates the "search procedures" that readers use to find information in a document. WordPerfect's index feature creates an alphabetized list of index entries and subentries for a document. You can mark preexisting text in your document for inclusion in an index, or you can create entries manually.

Because an index is the least-common reader aid in a legal document, indexes almost never show up in legal work. In this section you see how the index feature can be used to index part of a book.

Creating an index is similar to, although not quite the same as, creating a List or a Table of Contents. You mark each index entry, define the index format, and generate the index. You can omit page numbers or display them in any of several formats. The procedure for marking index entries is somewhat different from that for marking entries for a list or a table of contents. Moreover, an index must be defined and generated at the *end* of the document.

WordPerfect has tried to make the monumental job of preparing an index a little less daunting by providing the concordance feature. A *concordance* file is a regular WordPerfect file into which you place a list of words or phrases repeated throughout the document. Somewhat like the MARK macro described earlier in this chapter, the concordance then searches the document and notes each instance of words or phrases in the concordance file. Still, marking text for an index often is done painstakingly by hand to ensure accuracy. WordPerfect offers two levels of classification for items in an index: headings and subheadings. Proper use of these levels requires some planning and knowledge of your subject matter.

Marking Text for the Index

Marking text for lists and tables of contents involves blocking or highlighting the text. Marking text for indexes is a bit different. When the index entry is a single word, you don't need to block the text first. When the index entry is two words or more, you do need to mark the text as a block first.

Marking Text the Hard Way

To mark a one-word index entry, place the cursor anywhere in the word, press Mark Text (Alt-F5), and select **I**ndex (**3**). ⌨ If you use a mouse, access the **M**ark pull-down menu and select **I**ndex. The prompt Index heading: appears on the status line, followed by the word selected for the index. To have WordPerfect mark the word for the index, press Enter. WordPerfect enters the word as a major heading, then prompts you for a subheading. Type a subheading and press Enter. If you do not want a subheading, press Enter.

To mark an index entry longer than one word, move the cursor to the beginning of the phrase and block the text you want to mark. Press Mark Text (Alt-F5) and select **I**ndex (**3**). ⌨ If you use a mouse, access the **M**ark pull-down menu and select **I**ndex. To accept the marked text as an index entry, press Enter. At the prompt for a subheading entry, either enter a subheading or press Enter.

Reminder:
To mark a phrase for an index, highlight the text, press Mark Text, select Index, press Enter, and type a subheading if you want.

Suppose, for example, that you are indexing a book of database applications. One of the applications can be used to keep track of product sales. You mark the first mention of *Sales-tracking system* as a major head. At the Subheading: prompt, you type *functions* and press Enter. If you press Reveal Codes (Alt-F3 or F11), you see the following hidden code embedded in the text:

[**Index:** Sales-tracking system; functions]

Sales-tracking system is a major head. The word *functions*, which follows that head, is listed as a subhead when the index is generated.

WordPerfect automatically includes in the index the word or phrase in the document that has been marked for the index; the program also can create custom headings and subheadings. At the Index heading: prompt, type the heading you want to include in the index and press Enter. Then type a subheading, if you want one, and press Enter.

You can repeat this procedure hundreds of times throughout the document, or you can construct a macro for each word or phrase to be indexed. To mark for indexing, a macro should go to the top of the document, do a recursive Extended Search for the phrase in question, and mark it for the index each time the phrase is found. To do this, you need many, many macros. If you are fluent with macros, you can construct a macro that prompts you for the phrase to mark and how to mark it, does the marking, goes to page 1 of the main text (using the GoTo command instead of Home, Home, ↑) and prompts you for the next word or phrase. When you are finished with the macro, press Cancel (F1).

Marking Text Using a Concordance

A concordance file is a regular WordPerfect file. In this file, you put any words and phrases to be included in the index. Be sure that you put each index entry on a separate line (press Enter after each entry to insert a hard return). To create a concordance file for the entries under *Sales-tracking system*, for example, enter these items in a file:

> block diagram
> file structures
> functions
> master files
> opening data files
> printing sales reports
> procedure files
> program development
> purging sales transactions
> system memory file
> transaction file

Cue:

Sort the concordance alphabetically to save time when you generate the index.

The list does not have to be typed in alphabetical order; WordPerfect alphabetizes the items when it builds the index. You can, however, speed up the generation of the index substantially, depending on the size of the concordance file, by alphabetizing the concordance before generating the index. See Chapter 14 for more information on sorting files.

Press Save (F10) to save this file to the same subdirectory or disk where you store the document you are indexing. ▢ If you use a mouse, access the **F**ile pull-down menu and select **S**ave.

When you instruct the program to generate the index, WordPerfect asks for the name of the concordance file. WordPerfect matches the entries in the concordance file to the identical phrases in the main document, and, treating each occurrence of the entires in the main document as though it is marked, includes the items in the index.

Cue:

The concordance treats each entry as a main heading; if you want an entry to be a subheading, code the entry as a subheading.

One problem with concordance files is that, unless the concordance entries are otherwise marked, WordPerfect treats all entries in the concordance as main headings. If you want entries to appear as subheadings, you must mark them as such. As many users have discovered, the concordance feature is a blunt instrument. If you use it, be sure you really want every instance of a word or phrase reported in the same place in the index.

Suppose that you want the entries in the concordance-file example shown earlier to be subheads under the main heading *Sales-tracking system*. With the concordance file on-screen, follow these steps:

1. Move the cursor to the first line of the file and highlight the *block diagram* entry. (You don't have to highlight one-word entries.)

2. Press Mark Text (Alt-F5) and select Index (**3**).

   ▭ Access the **M**ark pull-down menu and select **I**ndex.

   The following prompt appears:

   ```
   Index heading: Block diagram
   ```

   WordPerfect assumes that you want *block diagram* to appear as a main heading. Instead, type *Sales-tracking system* for the main heading and press Enter.

3. Press Enter at the `Subheading: block diagram` prompt to make that entry a subheading. Repeat this procedure for each item that you want as a subheading for *Sales-tracking system*.

If you want some entries in the concordance as subheadings for different main headings, type the appropriate headings at the `Index heading:` prompt. If you want an entry to be a main heading, you don't have to mark it at all. When WordPerfect generates the index, it treats an unmarked concordance entry as a main heading.

Marking Text Manually and with the Concordance

You can mark text for the index using the manual method in combination with a concordance file. If a word or phrase in the concordance has also been marked manually in the main text, the word appears in the index twice: once with the associated code in the concordance and once with the code in the main text.

Cue:
A word included in a concordance file and marked manually in text appears twice in the index.

Be careful not to index the same word or phrase in too many ways. If you put the word *exhibit* in the concordance, and mark one occurrence of *exhibit* in the text as *Briefs, Exhibits in* and another as *Affidavits, Exhibits in*, the concordance cannot tell which way to sort unmarked occurrences of the word *exhibit*. The only solution is to leave *exhibit* out of the concordance entirely and mark each occurrence appropriately by hand.

Defining the Index Format

WordPerfect has the same options for formatting page numbers in an index as are available for lists and tables of contents. The index usually follows the text it analyzes, although an index can be defined anywhere within a document. Defining the index places a **[Def Mark:Index,#]** code at the cursor location. When the index is generated, it is placed at that code. Text marked manually for inclusion in the index that appears before the **[Def Mark:Index,#]** code is included in the index, but text marked after the code is excluded. A concordance, however, picks up matching entries that occur after the **[Def Mark:Index,#]** code.

To create an index page, follow these steps:

1. Press Home, Home, ↓ to move the cursor to the end of the document. Press Ctrl-Enter to place a hard page break after the main text.

2. Type a title, such as *Index*. Press Enter two or more times to leave blank lines between the title and body of the index.

3. Press Mark Text (Alt-F5), select **D**efine (**5**), and select Define **I**ndex (**3**).

   ◻▤ Access the **M**ark pull-down menu, select **D**efine, and select **I**ndex.

4. Enter the name of the concordance file you want to use (if any), and select the numbering style for the index. The numbering-style choices are the same five as for Table of Contents, Table of Authorities, and lists. Select the one that best suits the format of the index (see fig. 25.22).

   Option **2** is the most popular format for index entries; in this format, a comma comes after each entry, followed by the page reference.

Fig. 25.22.
*The Index
Definition menu.*

```
Index Definition

  1 - No Page Numbers

  2 - Page Numbers Follow Entries

  3 - (Page Numbers) Follow Entries

  4 - Flush Right Page Numbers

  5 - Flush Right Page Numbers with Leaders
```

Generating the Index

Generate the index using the steps in "Generating Document References" earlier in this chapter. You can issue the command to generate an index from any spot in a document. Before you generate the index, however, be sure that all entries are marked. Also, be sure that the index format is defined.

Remember that placing a word or phrase in a concordance and manually marking the same text in the document results in two entries in the index for the single occurrence of the marked text in the document. When the index is printed, all index entries are alphabetized. Main index entries are printed at the left margin, with subheads indented one tab stop.

Caution

If the concordance file is large, you may not have enough RAM to use it when you generate an index. If you run out of memory, WordPerfect displays the following prompt:

`Not enough memory to use entire concordance file. Continue? No (Yes)`

Select **Y** to instruct WordPerfect to use as much of the file as possible. If you select **Y**, WordPerfect generates as much of the index as it can and drops the rest, a dangerous result if you don't realize that the index is incomplete. Select **N** to abort index generation. If you have limited RAM, don't let the concordance file get too large.

The entries under *Sales-tracking system* from the example given earlier look like this when generated:

Sales-tracking system, 133-227
      block diagram, 136-139
      file structures, 134
      functions, 133-134
      master files, 135-136
      opening data files, 141
      printing sales reports, 179-186
      procedure files, 199
      program development, 140
      purging sales transactions, 194-195
      system memory file, 142
      transaction file, 142

Preparing Indexes for Multiple Related Documents

If you must include separate documents in the same file for cross-referencing purposes, you may have a problem with indexing. Assume that you have main text, which you want indexed, and three related documents, which you want cross-referenced. If you want to generate an index for only the main text, you must mark index items manually and place the **[DefMark:Index,2]** code at the end of the main text and in front of the subdocuments. If you use a concordance, the entire expanded document is searched; phrases matching concordance entries, no matter where they are located, are included in the index when you generate later to obtain the cross-references. Because the index must come after the manually marked material to which it refers, the index picks up only the words and phrases preceding it.

Cue:
If you have subdocuments that you do not want to index, place them after the text to be indexed.

Using Automatic Cross-Referencing

The Automatic Cross-Referencing (ACR) feature is essential for lawyers, academics, and anyone who writes using references to text located elsewhere in a document. ACR helps writers keep track of where a topic is first discussed.

Until now, a phrase like *see discussion on page 25* could cause problems during editing. The writer had to be careful about reorganizing and maintaining proper references. Writers had three unsatisfactory choices for handling the problem of cross-referencing:

- Avoid cross-references containing a specific location.
- Find all references before printing to see whether the page numbers are still accurate.
- Leave locations blank during writing and try to find page numbers after editing. (By this time, most writers forget to what they were referring.)

With WordPerfect 5.1, cross-referencing encompasses page numbers, footnote numbers, and section numbers (if sections are numbered with outlining or automatic paragraph numbering). Cross-referencing also includes endnotes and graphics-box numbers. WordPerfect even handles cross-references made across document boundaries with the Master Document feature (discussed in Chapter 26).

Nevertheless, true WordPerfect aficionados are demanding cross-references to line numbers, if line numbering is on, and some kind of directional sensor so that, if the reference moves, *above* becomes *below* (or *supra* becomes *infra*) automatically.

Marking Text for Automatic Cross-Referencing

Cue:

Cross-references need a target *(the text referred to) and a* reference *(the text doing the referring).*

Cross-referencing is easy; the only potential pitfall is in the terminology you use to refer to text. If you refer on page 50 to a discussion on page 21, you mark the text on page 50 as a *reference* and the text on page 21 as a *target*. A *target* (the discussion referred to) can have any number of *references* in the document. For each target, you need a unique name or identifier that links the target and reference.

When WordPerfect performs automatic cross-referencing, target and reference marks find each other using a unique short-form name. In a document with several targets and references, keeping a list of the names is a good idea. A list helps you remember the names of the different references and prevents accidental duplication of names.

Depending on your preferred method, you can mark a target when you first write about it, knowing you will mark references to it later, or you can mark both target and reference at the same time. These marks identify references to footnotes and to sections of main text. You can even use the marks to set up page numbering in footers.

Marking References to Footnotes

Automatic referencing is particularly handy when you need to refer to a footnote. You can refer to a footnote even before you create the target footnote. You also can have one footnote refer to another. The following sections tell you how to mark footnote text as a target or a reference.

Marking Footnote References when the Footnote Doesn't Yet Exist

Use these steps to make a footnote reference before you create the footnote:

1. Type the phrase you usually use to introduce a reference, such as *see discussion, fn. , supra*. In this phrase, *fn.* is followed by the footnote-reference code. (WordPerfect's manual says to type up to the point of the reference, but this example includes the phrase in which the footnote will be placed. Typing the whole phrase and returning to type the reference is easier.)

2. Move the cursor back to the comma (or where you want the footnote number to appear). Press Mark Text (Alt-F5) and select Cross **R**ef (**1**). The menu in figure 25.23 appears. Select Mark **R**eference (**1**).

⌨ If you use a mouse, access the **M**ark pull-down menu, select **C**ross Reference, and select **R**eference.

The menu in figure 25.24 appears.

```
Mark Text: Cross Reference

    1 - Mark Reference

    2 - Mark Target

    3 - Mark Both Reference and Target
```

Fig. 25.23.
The Mark Text: Cross Reference menu.

```
Tie Reference to:

    1 - Page Number

    2 - Paragraph/Outline Number

    3 - Footnote Number

    4 - Endnote Number

    5 - Graphics Box Number
```

Fig. 25.24.
The automatic reference submenu used to identify the target.

3. Select **F**ootnote Number (**3**). At the `Target Name:` prompt, type a unique code name for this reference. Write down the code so that you remember to use it for the target footnote when you create that footnote.

4. Press Enter. The marked reference appears as `See discussion, fn. ?, supra`. The question mark changes to the correct footnote number when you identify the target footnote and generate.

Always make the target code the first thing in the target footnote itself. Don't put the target code in the main text after the superscripted footnote number. Although a code placed after the superscript correctly records the preceding footnote, leaving the code behind is easy if you move the footnote. If this happens, the orphaned code in the text reports the next preceding footnote and throws off numbering. If you form the habit of putting the code in the footnote itself, even before the **[Note Num]** code, you'll always know where to find it.

Cue:
Put the target code at the beginning of the target footnote so that you know where it is.

Marking Footnote References when the Footnote Already Exists

To generate a footnote reference, follow the first two steps of the procedure for marking text when the footnote doesn't yet exist. Continue by following these steps:

1. Select Mark **B**oth Reference and Target (**3**) from the Mark Text: Cross Reference menu.

⌨ Access the **M**ark pull-down menu, select Cross **R**eference, and select **B**oth.

The following message appears:

After selecting a reference type, go to the location
of the item you want to reference in your document and
press Enter to mark it as the "target".

2. Select **F**ootnote Number (**3**) from the automatic reference submenu.

3. Press Footnote (Ctrl-F7), select **F**ootnote (**1**), and choose **E**dit (**2**).

   ⌨ Access the **L**ayout pull-down menu, select **F**ootnote, and then select **E**dit.

4. Enter the number of the footnote to which you are referring (the target). The target footnote appears. Press Enter. At the prompt, type a unique code for the target (write the code down in case you want to refer to that footnote again).

5. Press Enter to accept the target name you typed and return to the reference. The reference now correctly reports the number of the footnote to which you referred.

Referring from One Footnote to Another

To refer from one footnote to another, follow these steps:

1. Select Mark **B**oth Reference and Target (**3**) from the Mark Text: Cross Reference menu.

   ⌨ Access the **M**ark pull-down menu, select Cross **R**eference, and select **B**oth.

   The following message appears:

   After selecting a reference type, go to the location
   of the item you want to reference in your document and
   press Enter to mark it as the "target".

2. Select **F**ootnote Number (**3**) and press Exit (F7) to return to the main text.

3. Select **F**ootnote (**1**) and **E**dit (2).

   ⌨ Access the **L**ayout pull-down menu, select **F**ootnote, and then select **E**dit.

4. Enter the number of the footnote to which you are referring (the target). The target footnote appears. Press Enter. At the prompt, type a unique code for the target (write the code down in case you need to refer to that footnote again).

5. Press Enter to accept the target name you typed and return to the reference. The reference now correctly reports the footnote to which you referred.

Marking Endnotes

Mark endnotes the same way you do footnotes, but be sure to place the target codes for page references to endnotes in the endnotes themselves.

Marking a Reference to a Page

The procedure for marking a reference to a page is essentially the same as the one for referring to a footnote. Follow these steps:

1. Press Mark Text (Alt-F5) and select Cross **R**ef (**1**). Select Mark **B**oth Reference and Target (**3**); then select **P**age Number (**1**).

   ⌨ Access the **M**ark pull-down menu, select Cross **R**eference, select **B**oth, and then select **P**age Number.

2. To move to the target-reference page, press GoTo (Ctrl-Home), type the page number, and press Enter. You see the message `Press Enter to select page.` The Enter you pressed after GoTo just gets you to the page but does not plant the target code.

3. Move the cursor to the first text on that page to which you are actually referring and press Enter to mark. Putting the code in a key word is a good idea so that if the text is moved, the code moves with it.

4. At the `Target Name:` prompt, type a unique code and press Enter. Make a note of the code and its reference.

Marking a Reference to a Paragraph or Section

With automatic cross-referencing, you can give a precise address for a particular target using the subordination of paragraphs. Earlier in this chapter, you read about the importance of redefining the paragraph numbering scheme. Here is one place where it pays off.

Reminder:
Use automatic cross-referencing to give a precise address for a target.

You read that you could supply any periods needed after paragraph or outline section numbers; doing so means that periods aren't carried into automatic cross-referencing where trailing periods are not wanted. Consider the following heading organization:

1. Primary Heading.
   (a) Secondary Heading the First.
   (b) Secondary Heading the Second.
      (1) Last Level Heading.

Suppose that you want to refer to the material under the Last Level Heading. The cross-reference should appear as follows: *see section 1(b)(1), supra.* You don't want the period after the main heading number (1.) to appear in the cross-reference.

Mark section references exactly as you mark page references (see the preceding section). The best place for the code is probably right after the heading itself or even inside it (the code isn't incorporated in the Table of Contents).

Marking Boxes

Place target codes for references to graphics boxes in the captions, inside the boxes themselves. (See Chapter 27 for an explanation of how to create graphics boxes in WordPerfect 5.1.)

Creating "Page 2 of 20" Footers

Cue:

You can make a header or footer give the present page and update the last page.

The reference-and-target marking system can be used in headers and footers, making it possible for a footer to give the present page and update the last page automatically. For this type of page numbering, follow these steps:

1. Press Format (Shift-F8) and Select **P**age (**2**).

   ⌨ Access the **L**ayout pull-down menu and select **P**age.

2. Select Page **N**umbering (**6**), select **P**age Number Position (**4**), and select **N**o Page Numbers (**9**) to turn off ordinary page numbering.

3. Press Esc and select **F**ooters (**4**). Then select Footer **A** (**1**) and Every **P**age (**2**).

4. Issue the desired formatting commands; for example, press Center (Shift-F6), type *Page*, and press Ctrl-B (the screen reads Page ^B). Type *of*.

5. Press Mark Text (Alt-F5) and select Cross **R**ef (**1**) and Mark **R**eference (**1**).

   ⌨ Access the **M**ark pull-down menu, select **C**ross Reference, and then select **R**eference.

6. Select **P**age Number (**1**). WordPerfect requests a target name; type a unique code, such as *lastpage*. Press Enter to return to the Footer screen, which now reads Page ^B of ?.

7. Press Exit (F7) twice to return to the text.

After you finish the first draft of the document, when you are sure what the last page is, put the target code on that page (the target code matches the reference code *lastpage*). Do this by moving to the bottom of the last page of your document (Home, Home, ↓), and pressing Mark Text (Alt-F5), **1**, **2**. ⌨ If you use a mouse, access the **M**ark pull-down menu, select **C**ross Reference, and then select **T**arget. At the Enter Target Name: prompt, type *lastpage* and press Enter. The number of pages adjusts to subsequent editing as long as this code remains in the last page.

Unless the target has been identified, references appear as ? in the text. Once the target is identified, WordPerfect updates all cross-references every time you generate.

Generating Cross-References

Cross-references are generated in the same manner as Lists, Tables of Contents, Indexes, and Tables of Authority. See "Generating Document References" earlier in this chapter.

Using Automatic Document Comparison

Cue:

You can compare different versions of documents if you save the original document under a different file name.

Document Compare is extremely convenient to run. But in Document Compare, more than any other area, foresight is necessary. Always keep a copy of the original document so that you have something with which to compare the new version of a document. You can compare documents only when the new version is on-screen and the old version is saved under another name.

When you start editing an old draft, ask yourself where someone may want to see exactly what changes were made. The following sections explain the process used to compare two versions of a document.

Saving an Old-Version Document for Comparison

To allow for automatic document comparisons, follow these steps:

1. Press List (F5).

    ⌨ Access the **F**ile pull-down menu and select List **F**iles.

2. Press Enter, move the cursor to the document you want to edit, and select **R**etrieve (**1**).

3. Press List (F5) again and put the cursor on the same file name. Select **M**ove/Rename (**3**) and change the file name to something else, such as MYDOC.OLD.

4. Make changes to the on-screen file and save the file using Save (F10).

    ⌨ Access the **F**ile pull-down menu and select **S**ave.

Don't forget to save your edits before you do the automatic comparison. You may find that some editing is necessary before you print a comparison document, particularly where text affected involves codes for automatic paragraph numbering and indents.

Tip

If you use DOS 4.01 or a network with the DOS SHARE.EXE program active, you may want to use these procedures:

1. Highlight the file name on the List Files screen and select **C**opy (**8**).

2. Enter a new file name.

3. Move the cursor to the top of the file list to `Current` and press Enter twice to see the new file name.

4. Select **R**etrieve (**1**) and edit the file.

Comparing a New Version to an Old Version

To compare the new version on-screen with the old version on-disk, follow these steps:

1. Press Mark Text (Alt-F5), select **G**enerate (**6**), and then select **C**ompare (**2**).

    ⌨ Access the **M**ark pull-down menu, select **D**ocument Compare, and then select **A**dd Markings.

2. WordPerfect asks for a file to compare to, giving the name of the screen file as a default. Type the name of the old version of the file and press Enter.

The new version of the document is redlined automatically, showing new material in redline and deleted material in strikeout. However, neither redlining nor strikeout shows up much different than ordinary text on most monitors. If you have a graphics card and monitor, you can see a "reasonable" representation of the results by viewing the document. For a really clear look at the results, *print* the compared file. Press Print (Shift-F7) and select **F**ull Document (**1**) to see the printed results (see fig. 25.25). ⌨ If you have a mouse, access the **F**ile pull-down menu and select **P**rint.

Fig. 25.25.

*An edited
document
compared to its
original version.*

```
Creating "Page 2 of 20" Footers

The reference and target marking system can be used in headers
and footers, finally making it possible to have a footer that
automatically gives the present page and updates the last page.
For this type of page numbering, follow these steps. Press Format
(Shift-F8). Select Page (2)***, then ***select Page Number***ing
(6).

***>>Mouse note: Select Page from the Layout menu.***

***Now type 9 to turn off ordinary page numbering. Select Page
(2) and select Page Number Position (7). Now type 9 to turn off
ordinary page numbering. Select Footers (4). Then select Footer A
(1) and then Every Page (2). Depending on the format you want,
press Center (Shift F6), type Page, and press Ctrl-***B***-in
which case your screen then reads Page ***^B***, and press
Ctrl-N$mdin which case your screen then reads Page $afN. Type of
and press Mark Text (Alt-F5). Select ***Cross Ref***(1). ***

***>>Mouse note: Select Reference under Cross Reference on the
Mark menu.***

***Select Mark Reference (1) and specify ******Page Number (1).
Select AutoRef (1). Select Mark Reference (1) and specify Tie
Reference to Page Number (1). Where WordPerfect requests a target
name, type a unique code, such as LASTPAGE. You then return to
the Footer Screen, which now reads Page ***^B*** of ?-which now
reads Page $afN of ?. Press Exit (F7) twice to return to the
text.

After you finish the first draft of the document, when you are
sure what the last page is (for example, at the bottom of a
signature page), put the target code on that page with the unique
code (LASTPAGE) that identifies it. You do this by moving to the
bottom of the last page of your document (Home, Home, ↓) $da), and
pressing Mark Text (Alt-F5), 1, 2. ***

***>>Mouse note: Select Target under Cross Reference on the Mark
menu.***

***At the Enter Target Name: At the Enter Target Name: prompt,
type lastpage and press Enter. The number of pages adjusts  to
subsequent editing as long as that code in fact remains in the
last page.

Unless the target has been identified, references appear as ? in
the text. Once the target is identified, WordPerfect updates all
cross-references every time you generate.

Generating Cross-References

Cross-references are generated in the same manner as lists,
tables of contents, indexes, and tables of authority. See the
section on "Generating Document References" that appears earlier
in this chapter.
```

In figure 25.25, text shaded in gray represents redlined text; text marked for strikeout has a line running through it. These formats are the factory defaults for laser printers (the actual appearance of your document depends on your printer). You can use PTR.EXE to modify the PRS file for your printer to change the way the printer indicates redline and strikeout.

The appearance of redline can be modified to show a vertical bar in the left margin of all pages, or a vertical bar in the left margin of even pages and in the right margin of odd pages. This feature can be set permanently through Setup (see Chapter 20) or temporarily for the current document. To change the appearance of redline temporarily, follow these steps:

1. Press Format (Shift-F8) and select **D**ocument (**3**).

   ⌨ Access the **L**ayout pull-down menu and select **D**ocument.

2. Select **R**edline Method (**4**). This menu appears at the bottom of the screen:

   Redline Method: 1 Printer Dependent; **2 L**eft; **3 A**lternating: **1**

3. Select **P**rinter Dependent (**1**) to have the redline appearance determined by the printer driver. Select **L**eft (**2**) to print a vertical bar in the left margin of every page next to redlined text. Select **A**lternating (**3**) to print the vertical bar in the left margin of even-numbered pages and in the right margin of odd-numbered pages.

WordPerfect's Document Compare function works in phrases. *Phrases* are strings of words bounded by punctuation marks, hard-return codes **[HRt]**, hard-page codes **[HPg]**, footnote codes **[Footnote:#;[Note Num] text]**, endnote codes **[Endnote:#;[Note Num] text]**, and the end of the document. If you change a single word in a phrase two lines long, Document Compare reports that change by printing in redline the entire phrase with the changed word, followed by the entire phrase as originally written, struck-through. If you move a chunk of material from one place to another, Document Compare brackets that material in its new location with an explanatory message in strikeout.

Purging Redlining from a Saved Document

If you accidentally save the on-screen document with redlining over the edited file, you can retrieve the file and get rid of the redlining and strikeout. To purge a file of redlining, follow these steps:

1. Press Mark Text (Alt-F5), select **G**enerate (**6**), and select **R**emove (**1**).

   ⌨ Access the **M**ark pull-down menu, select **D**ocument Compare, and then select **R**emove Markings.

   All redlined text reverts to its normal state, and the strikeout marks disappear.

2. Save (F10) the document.

Unfortunately, Document Compare is one of the least successful innovations introduced in WordPerfect 5. These problems become apparent with use:

- The user lacks control over the degree of resolution for redlining.
- No option exists to indicate that something was taken out without saying what it was. Often, just indicating that something has been omitted is clearer.
- The user lacks substantial control of how redlining is indicated.

- Redlining is as broad as the phrase in which the changed text is contained. This practice redlines more than the actual change, in many cases obscuring rather than highlighting the change.

Tip

Use a macro to replace selected text marked for strikeout with a special symbol to indicate that something was deleted. The STRIKE.ARC file in Data Library 0 (zero) in the CompuServe WordPerfect Support Group forum contains the STRIKE.WPM macro and accompanying documentation.

If you invoke the STRIKE macro, the program goes to the top of the document and sequentially blocks and presents each bit of text marked for strikeout. It then asks whether you want to replace the text with the strikeout code. If you select **Y**, the text is replaced, and the program goes on. If you select **N**, the block is turned off, and the program goes on. The question is necessary because the messages indicating that a section was moved appear in strikeout, and you probably don't want to delete them. If you select anything but **Y** or **N**, a prompt appears telling you to press Y or N. A symbol you may want to use to show that something was deleted is a bold underlined bullet with a caret over it in braces ([•]). This symbol may be specific to certain printers (it appears on a LaserJet 2686A running the A and F cartridges). Identify the spot in the macro where the symbol is inserted and change the symbol to anything that suits your fancy.

Summary

In this chapter, you learned the following:

- ❑ How to set up a List, a Table of Contents, and a Table of Authorities.
- ❑ How to mark text for a List, a Table of Contents, a Table of Authorities, and an Index.
- ❑ How to make an index using a concordance file coupled with markings in the main text.
- ❑ How to use styles to mark titles and headings for inclusion in the Table of Contents.
- ❑ How to set up automatic paragraph numbering to get the most from WordPerfect's generating capabilities.
- ❑ How to make automatic cross-references.
- ❑ How to compare a document with one of its ancestors and print a document showing the differences between them.

The next chapter examines the ways in which some of these techniques can (or cannot) be used across document boundaries through WordPerfect's Master Document feature.

26

Using the Master Document Feature for Large Projects

Joel Shore, Senior Editor of LANWEEK for *Computer Reseller News* and president of the private consulting firm Documentation Systems, contributed this chapter to *Using WordPerfect 5*.

Charles O. Stewart III revised this chapter to reflect the changes with WordPerfect 5.1. A product specialist and staff writer for Que Corporation, Stewart coauthored *WordPerfect Tips, Tricks, and Traps* and contributed to *Using WordPerfect 5*.

This chapter examines the techniques used to create subdocuments and master documents and shows how to take advantage of the power of other WordPerfect features with master documents.

With the Master Document feature you can employ the following cycle to manage large projects:

- Maintain and store the sections of a long document as individual files called subdocuments

- Build a skeleton or master document that includes the name of each subdocument

- Temporarily expand the master document and link the individual files to work with all the individual files simultaneously (generating a table of contents or printing the entire document, for example)

- Separate, or condense, the expanded document into its component subdocument files

A master document consists of two kinds of files: master document files and subdocument files. The master document is an ordinary WordPerfect file, which contains codes that reference the subdocument files. In addition to these codes, the master document can contain anything else you would put in a document, such as definition codes for a table of contents, styles, or text.

Reminder:
A master document consists of two kinds of files: master document files and subdocument files.

The second kind of file, the subdocument, contains the text for each section of the total document. You can use as many subdocuments as you need. Advantages to using subdocument

835

files include saving memory and time retrieving and saving files. Remember that instead of one large file, you have several smaller files.

Before you begin working with master documents, you should be familiar with defining and generating tables of contents, lists, indexes, automatic cross-references, and tables of authorities. These topics are covered in Chapter 25.

Reminder

If you use a mouse with WordPerfect 5.1, you can click the right button to display the pull-down menus and then select the desired option. You also can press Alt-= to access the pull-down menus and then press the appropriate letter of the desired option. For all instructions, assume that if a block is required to activate a pull-down menu option, the text has been blocked before the pull-down menu is accessed. Instructions for pull-down menus and the mouse are marked with the mouse icon. For more information about the mouse, see Chapter 1. ⌨

Creating Master and Subdocuments

To illustrate the techniques of creating and working with a master document, assume that you are working on a doctoral dissertation. Because the dissertation will be long and complex, you've developed a plan of attack that consists of two phases: first, you write the dissertation and save each section as a separate file; second, after you finish writing, you create a master document. Within the master document, you identify and place all the subdocuments in the order they should appear in the printed version.

Adopting this approach to managing large projects is desirable for several reasons. First, creating each chapter as a separate file is natural: you can save each section of writing in its own file, you can work on the section of the document you want without having to worry about the order within a larger document, and you can concentrate on your writing. Second, you create the subdocuments before the master document because you must enter actual file names to build a master document. You can enter file names for nonexistent subdocuments, but unless you actually create these later, WordPerfect won't include them in the master document when it is expanded. Third, building a master document allows you to perform efficiently such operations as spell-checking.

Working with Subdocuments

You do not use a special feature to create a subdocument; any WordPerfect file can be used as a subdocument. WordPerfect imposes no limits on the number of subdocuments you can specify in a master document, so you can create as many individual files as you need to keep a project organized. These files can be as large or small as needed.

For instance, if you're writing a book, you'll probably want to maintain each chapter and appendix as a separate file. The dissertation used as an example in this chapter is divided into 12 sections, each saved as a separate file. Some of the dissertation's subdocuments are less than a page long; others are much longer.

> ### Caution
>
> Codes contained in a subdocument file override codes in the master document. You won't encounter a problem for codes to bold or underline specific blocks of text, but you should be careful about codes that affect document formatting, such as margins and base font. You should insert these codes near the beginning of the master document and omit them from the subdocuments. Inserting codes in only the master document ensures that all subdocuments are formatted with the same initial codes.

When you finish composing all the subdocuments, you can begin to build the master file. The subdocuments of the dissertation consist of 12 files (see fig. 26.1).

```
12-07-89  10:40p              Directory C:\WP51\DISSERTA\*.*
Document size:       0  Free: 1,744,896 Used:    318,995      Files:      12

.    Current   <Dir>                     ..    Parent    <Dir>
ABSTRACT.        1,086  11-19-89 06:59p │ ACKNOWL .        1,411  11-19-89 07:00p
APPENDIX.        4,862  11-19-89 07:01p │ BIBLIOG .        3,182  11-19-89 07:02p
CHAPTER .1      40,643  07-16-89 12:39a │ CHAPTER .2      92,069  11-19-89 06:55p
CHAPTER .3      51,259  11-19-89 07:02p │ CHAPTER .4      84,254  11-19-89 07:04p
CHAPTER .5      38,643  11-19-89 07:05p │ COPYRITE.          414  11-19-89 06:45p
DEDICATE.          429  11-19-89 06:50p │ TITLE   .PG        743  11-19-89 06:48p
```

Fig. 26.1.

A List Files display showing the dissertation's individual files.

As you build the master document, you include the subdocuments in the order you choose. For the dissertation, the order is determined by guidelines published by the educational institution. For example, dissertations submitted to the University of Illinois at Urbana-Champaign must be assembled in the order shown in table 26.1.

Table 26.1
Order of Documents in Dissertation

Section Name	Page Numbering Requirements
Notice of Copyright	No page number
Title page	No page number
Abstract	Page iii, if included
Dedication	Roman numerals
Acknowledgments	Roman numerals
Table of Contents	Roman numerals
List of Tables	Roman numerals
Text	Page 1
Endnotes	Arabic numerals
Appendixes	Arabic numerals
Works Cited	Arabic numerals
Vita	Arabic numerals

Remember that you won't have files for the table of contents, list of tables, and endnotes because you will, of course, use WordPerfect to generate these for you.

Building the Master Document

Reminder:

When you create the master document, start with a clear screen.

After you determine the order of the subdocuments, you can begin building the master document, adding the subdocuments in the order you want them. Clear the screen before beginning this procedure; remember that you are creating a new document.

For the example, the guidelines indicate that the copyright page must be the first page in the dissertation. The file COPYRITE contains the text for this page, so you want to include this file first in the master document.

To include a subdocument in a master document, complete the following steps:

1. Use the keyboard or the mouse to move the cursor to where you want the subdocument to appear.
2. Press Mark Text (Alt-F5) and choose **S**ubdoc (**2**).

   Access the **M**ark menu and select **S**ubdocument.

   WordPerfect displays the prompt `Subdoc Filename:`
3. Type the file name (including drive letter and path if necessary) of the subdocument and press Enter. For the example, type *COPYRITE* and press Enter.

   WordPerfect inserts a hidden code for the COPYRITE subdocument just to the left of the cursor. When you place the cursor on the hidden code, a box appears on-screen labeled `Subdoc:` followed by the file name (see fig. 26.2).

   Note that because you cannot use List (F5), you must know the name of the subdocument file before starting this procedure. Also, you are not prompted if a file does not exist.

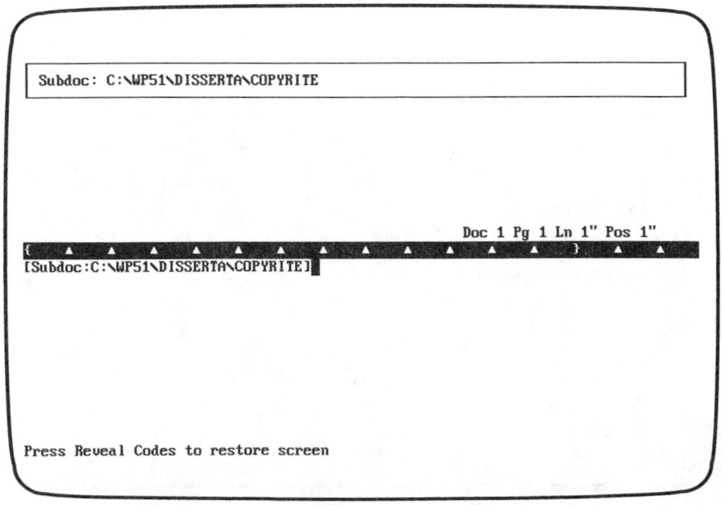

Fig. 26.2.
A subdocument box and its associated code.

4. Press Hard Page (Ctrl-Enter) to force the text following the subdocument to start on a new page, or omit the hard page break to make subsequent text continue immediately following the end of the subdocument.

5. Use the same procedure to include additional subdocuments.

6. After selecting all the subdocuments, name and save the master document. For this example, use the name MASTER.DOC. For instructions, see "Saving the Master Document" in this chapter.

Figure 26.3 shows the COPYRITE, TITLE.PG, and ABSTRACT files as subdocuments in a master document. The hard page breaks cause each subdocument to print on a new sheet of paper. Figure 26.4 shows the same information in Reveal Codes.

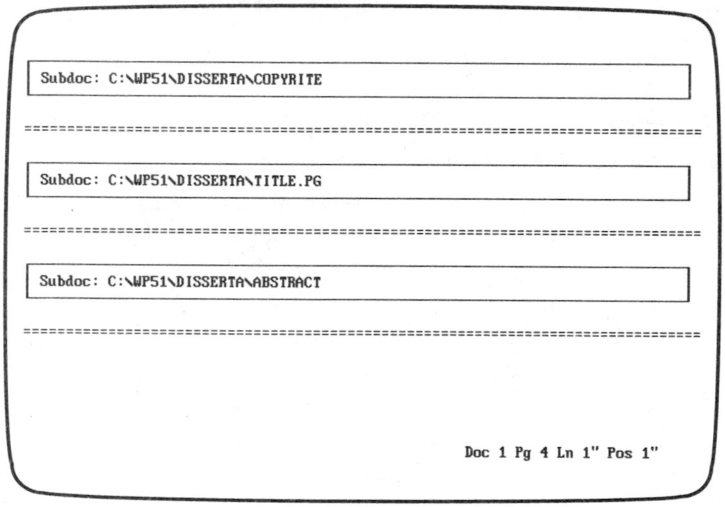

```
Subdoc: C:\WP51\DISSERTA\COPYRITE

==============================================================

Subdoc: C:\WP51\DISSERTA\TITLE.PG

==============================================================

Subdoc: C:\WP51\DISSERTA\ABSTRACT

==============================================================




                              Doc 1 Pg 4 Ln 1" Pos 1"
```

Fig. 26.3.
Three subdocuments separated by hard page breaks.

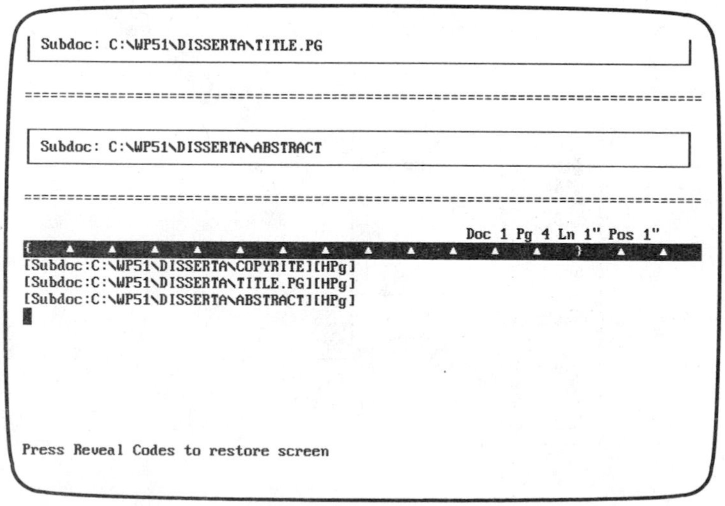

```
Subdoc: C:\WP51\DISSERTA\TITLE.PG

==============================================================

Subdoc: C:\WP51\DISSERTA\ABSTRACT

==============================================================
                              Doc 1 Pg 4 Ln 1" Pos 1"
[  ▲    ▲    ▲    ▲    ▲    ▲   ▲    ▲    ▲    ▲   }   ▲    ▲ ]
[Subdoc:C:\WP51\DISSERTA\COPYRITE][HPg]
[Subdoc:C:\WP51\DISSERTA\TITLE.PG][HPg]
[Subdoc:C:\WP51\DISSERTA\ABSTRACT][HPg]




Press Reveal Codes to restore screen
```

Fig. 26.4.
The same three documents shown in Reveal Codes.

Deleting a Subdocument

As you can see from figure 26.4, subdocuments are simply WordPerfect codes—no different than a margin setting or an indent. To delete a subdocument, simply delete its corresponding code; subdocument codes include **[Subdoc:]** followed by the file name.

Expanding the Master Document

Expanding the master document lets you work with all the subdocuments at the same time to perform such WordPerfect operations as printing or spell-checking and generating tables of contents that affect the entire project. Working with all the files saves you time.

Complete the following steps to expand the master document:

1. Make sure the master document is displayed on-screen.

2. Press Mark Text (Alt-F5) and select **G**enerate (**6**).

   ⌨ Access the **M**ark menu and select **G**enerate.

   WordPerfect displays the Mark Text: Generate menu (see fig. 26.5).

Fig. 26.5.
The Mark Text: Generate menu.

```
Mark Text: Generate

    1 - Remove Redline Markings and Strikeout Text from Document

    2 - Compare Screen and Disk Documents and Add Redline and Strikeout

    3 - Expand Master Document

    4 - Condense Master Document

    5 - Generate Tables, Indexes, Cross-References, etc.
```

3. Select **E**xpand Master Document (**3**).

   ⌨ Access the **M**ark menu, select **M**aster Documents, and choose **E**xpand (see fig. 26.6).

Fig. 26.6.
The Expand Master Documents pop-out menu.

```
Mark
   Index
  [Table of Contents    ]
  [List                 ]
   Cross-Reference      ▶
   Table of Authorities▶

   Define               ▶

   Generate

   Master Documents     ▶    ┌─────────┐
   Subdocument               │ Expand  │
                             │ Condense│
   Document Compare          └─────────┘
```

WordPerfect begins combining all the specified subdocuments into the master document skeleton. If WordPerfect can't locate a specified subdocument, you see the prompt Subdoc not found (Press Enter to skip): followed by the file name. You can press Enter to skip this subdocument and go on to the next, or you can edit the file name.

When WordPerfect expands the master document, each subdocument box is replaced by a pair of boxes: one to mark the beginning of that subdocument's text and another to mark the end. WordPerfect then inserts the entire subdocument between the beginning and ending codes. Figure 26.7 shows the copyright page in an expanded master document.

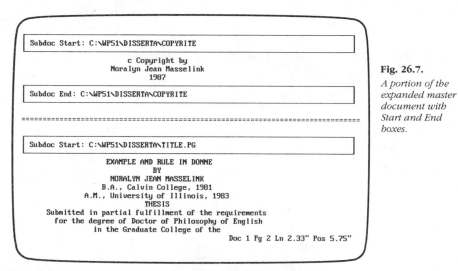

Fig. 26.7.

A portion of the expanded master document with Start and End boxes.

> **Caution**
>
> Never delete the **[Subdoc Start]** or **[Subdoc End]** codes. These codes are a matched set, and if you delete them, WordPerfect cannot keep track of individual subdocuments.
>
> If you want to delete a subdocument, delete the subdocument code from the nonexpanded master document (see "Deleting a Subdocument" in this chapter).

When all subdocuments have been included, WordPerfect returns you to the expanded master document. You can edit the text of any of the subdocuments or perform any other WordPerfect operation—for example, a spell-check. Remember that an expanded document is slightly larger than the sum of its parts because of the subdocument codes.

Creating a Table of Contents, List, Index, or Table of Authorities

The Master Document feature lets you generate tables of contents, lists, indexes, and tables of authorities that span all the subdocuments. (Chapter 25 discusses

Reminder:
In the expanded master document you can edit the text of a subdocument or perform any other WordPerfect operation.

Reminder:
The Master Document feature lets you generate tables of contents, lists, indexes, and tables of authorities that span all the subdocuments.

these features in detail.) The master document pulls in each subdocument file one at a time during generation.

This chapter illustrates how to generate a table of contents for a master document; to generate lists, indexes, and tables of authorities for master documents, follow the same procedure.

You create a table of contents in a master document and associated subdocuments almost exactly as you create a table of contents for an ordinary document. You follow three separate procedures: marking text for inclusion in the table of contents, defining the table of contents, and generating the table of contents.

Marking Text for the Table of Contents

Marking text tells WordPerfect what to include in the table of contents. The material you include in the table of contents is contained in the subdocuments, not in the master document. Before text can be marked, it must be blocked.

Note: You block text in one of three ways: by pressing Block (Alt-F4 or F12) and moving the cursor, by selecting **B**lock from the **E**dit menu and moving the cursor, or by dragging the mouse pointer from the beginning to the end of the text to be marked and releasing the mouse button. Blocking text is covered in detail in Chapter 4.

To mark blocked text for inclusion in the table of contents, complete the following steps:

1. Press Mark Text (Alt-F5) and select To**C**.

   ⌨ Access the **M**ark menu and select Table of Contents.

   WordPerfect displays the prompt ToC Level:

2. Type the appropriate level number for each table of contents entry.

Repeat this procedure for all the subdocuments and the master document if you typed text that you want included in the table of contents.

Defining the Table of Contents

After marking the text for the table of contents, you next define the style for the table of contents. Defining a table of contents specifies where the table is to appear and how the table should be formatted.

Complete the following steps to define the table of contents in the master document:

1. Make sure that the master document is displayed on-screen. If you are working with a subdocument, save it and clear the screen before retrieving the master document.

2. Move the cursor to the location in the master document where you want the table of contents to appear. You may want to insert a hard page break (Ctrl-Enter) so that the table of contents prints on a new page.

3. If you want, type and center the title of the table of contents. For this example, press Center (Shift-F6).

⌨ Access the **L**ayout menu, select **A**lign, and select **C**enter.

4. Type *Table of Contents* and press Enter.

5. Press Enter several times to insert blank lines between the title and the actual table of contents.

6. Press Mark Text (Alt-F5), select **D**efine (**5**), and select Define Table of **C**ontents (**1**).

⌨ Access the **M**ark menu, select **D**efine, and choose Table of **C**ontents from the pop-out menu.

The Table of Contents Definition menu appears.

7. Define the number of levels you want to appear in the table of contents, the wrap option, and the numbering style. Even if you mark text for five levels, only the number of levels you enter here prints in the generated table of contents.

8. Press Enter to return to document.

Figure 26.8 shows a table of contents definition in a master document in Reveal Codes.

Caution

Don't define the table of contents in the subdocuments of a master document; if you do, you will generate multiple copies of the table.

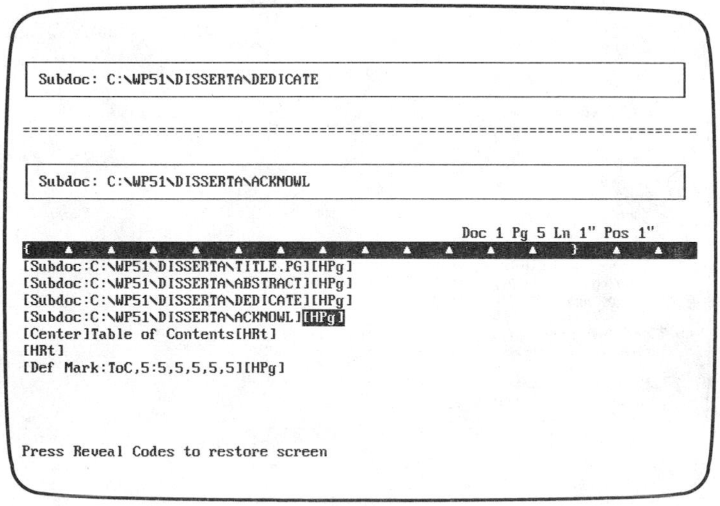

```
Subdoc: C:\WP51\DISSERTA\DEDICATE

==================================================================

Subdoc: C:\WP51\DISSERTA\ACKNOWL

                                        Doc 1 Pg 5 Ln 1" Pos 1"
[    ▲    ▲    ▲    ▲    ▲    ▲    ▲    ▲    ▲    }    ▲    ▲   ]
[Subdoc:C:\WP51\DISSERTA\TITLE.PG][HPg]
[Subdoc:C:\WP51\DISSERTA\ABSTRACT][HPg]
[Subdoc:C:\WP51\DISSERTA\DEDICATE][HPg]
[Subdoc:C:\WP51\DISSERTA\ACKNOWL][HPg]
[Center]Table of Contents[HRt]
[HRt]
[Def Mark:ToC,5:5,5,5,5,5][HPg]



Press Reveal Codes to restore screen
```

Fig. 26.8.
The table of contents definition code in the master document.

Generating the Table of Contents

After marking the entries you want to include in the table of contents and defining the location and style of the table in the master document, you're ready to generate the actual table.

Complete the following steps to generate the table of contents:

1. Make sure that the master document is displayed on-screen. If a subdocument is displayed, save it and clear the screen before retrieving the master document.

2. Press Mark Text (Alt-F5), select **G**enerate (**6**), and select **G**enerate Tables, Indexes, Cross-References, etc. (**5**).

   ⌨ Access the **M**ark menu, select **G**enerate, and choose **G**enerate Tables, Indexes, Cross-References, etc. (**5**)

   You are prompted Existing tables, lists, and indexes will be replaced. Continue? Yes (No)

3. Select **Y**es or press Enter to continue; select **N**o to stop. When you answer yes, WordPerfect generates and displays on-screen the table of contents.

If the master file is not already expanded, WordPerfect expands it before generating the table of contents and displays the prompt Update Subdocs? Yes (No). Select **Y**es to direct WordPerfect to save each subdocument. Select **N**o and the files are not saved. Remember that the subdocuments are already on the disk. You need answer yes only if the subdocument was changed (hyphenation prompts or document conversion, for example).

Figure 26.9 shows part of the generated table of contents.

Fig. 26.9.

A part of the master document's generated table of contents.

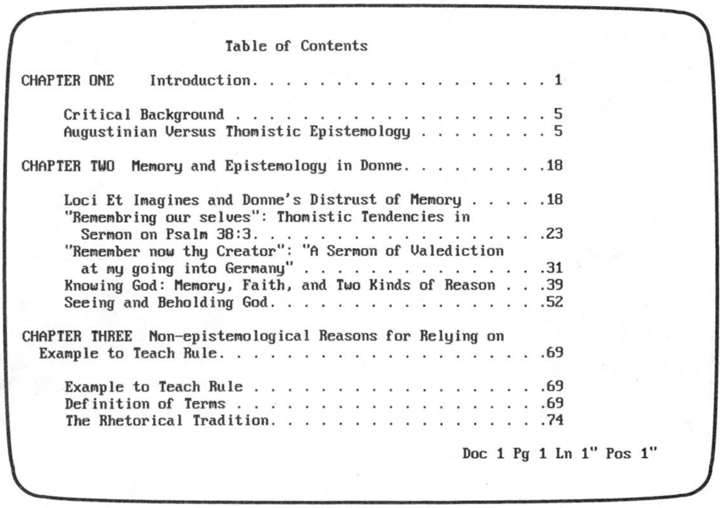

```
                       Table of Contents

CHAPTER ONE      Introduction. . . . . . . . . . . . . . . . .1

        Critical Background . . . . . . . . . . . . . . . . .5
        Augustinian Versus Thomistic Epistemology . . . . . . . .5

CHAPTER TWO  Memory and Epistemology in Donne. . . . . . . . .18

        Loci Et Imagines and Donne's Distrust of Memory . . . .18
        "Remembring our selves": Thomistic Tendencies in
          Sermon on Psalm 38:3. . . . . . . . . . . . . . . . .23
        "Remember now thy Creator": "A Sermon of Valediction
          at my going into Germany" . . . . . . . . . . . . .31
        Knowing God: Memory, Faith, and Two Kinds of Reason . . .39
        Seeing and Beholding God. . . . . . . . . . . . . . . .52

CHAPTER THREE  Non-epistemological Reasons for Relying on
        Example to Teach Rule. . . . . . . . . . . . . . . . .69

        Example to Teach Rule . . . . . . . . . . . . . . . . .69
        Definition of Terms . . . . . . . . . . . . . . . . . .69
        The Rhetorical Tradition. . . . . . . . . . . . . . . .74

                                        Doc 1 Pg 1 Ln 1" Pos 1"
```

Printing the Master Document

You can print either the complete expanded master document or the condensed skeleton master document. If you print the expanded master document, all text from the subdocuments and any text contained in the master document print. If you print the condensed document, only text contained in the master document prints; text from the subdocument does not print.

To print the entire master document, first expand it and then print. To print just the condensed master document, print the document without first expanding it, or condense the master document if it is already expanded.

Condensing the Master Document

When you finish working with the expanded master document, you can condense it into its individual subdocument files. To condense an expanded master document, complete the following steps:

1. Press Mark Text (Alt-F5), select **G**enerate (6), and select **Co**ndense Master Document (**4**).

   ⌨ Access the **M**ark menu, select **M**aster Document, and choose **C**ondense from the pop-out menu.

   WordPerfect displays the prompt Save Subdocs? Yes (No).

2. Select **Y**es to save the individual subdocuments to disk or select **N**o to condense without saving the subdocuments. If you modified the subdocuments, you should select **Y**es.

   If you choose to save the subdocuments, WordPerfect checks for duplicate file names. If you have already created and named the files, WordPerfect displays the prompt Replace: followed by the file name and the following menu:

   1 Yes; **2 N**o; **3 R**eplace all remaining.

3. Select **Y**es (**1**) to replace just the current subdocument; select **N**o (**2**) if you want to edit the file name before continuing; or select **R**eplace All Remaining (**3**) to replace all the subdocuments without being prompted.

Saving the Master Document

When you finish working with the master document, save it. You can save the master document in condensed or expanded form (although you don't gain anything and you waste disk space by saving an expanded master document). Condense the master document before saving unless you have special reasons for doing otherwise.

Complete the following steps to save the master document:

1. Press Exit (F7). WordPerfect prompts Save document? Yes (No).

2. Press Enter or select **Y**es to save the document. WordPerfect prompts `Document is expanded, condense it? Yes (No)`.

3. Press Enter or select **Y**es to condense the master document. If you select **N**o, WordPerfect no longer displays this prompt when saving the master document. If, in the future, you want to save a condensed version, you must first condense the master document (see the section "Condensing the Master Document" in this chapter) and then save it.

   WordPerfect prompts `Save Subdocs? Yes (No)`.

4. Select **N**o if you saved the subdocuments when you condensed the master document or if you did not make any changes. Press Enter or select **Y**es if you made any changes; the updated subdocument files are saved.

   If you press Enter or select **Y**es, you are prompted `Replace:` for each subdocument. See the instructions in "Condensing the Master Document" to review the options. Once you have selected an option, WordPerfect prompts: `Document to be saved:`

5. For a new file, type a document name and press Enter. For an existing file, confirm the name by pressing Enter, or edit the file name and then press Enter.

Using Other Features in a Master Document

Many of WordPerfect's features can be used with master documents—for instance, page numbering, searching and replacing, spell-checking, and cross-references with master documents.

Inserting a New Page Number

You can insert new page-number codes in a master document so that all pages from that point forward for all subdocuments are sequentially numbered. For example, in the dissertation, the numbering begins with the abstract on page iii in Roman numerals, and the text itself on page 1 (see table 26.1). To control page numbering in the dissertation, insert two new page number codes in the master document: one at the beginning of the abstract file to start numbering with Roman numeral iii and another at the top of the first text page to start numbering with Arabic numeral 1.

To set a new page number, complete the following steps:

1. Move the cursor to where you want the new page-number code to appear by pressing GoTo (Ctrl-Home).

   ▭ Access the **S**earch menu and select **G**oTo.

   Type *3* and press Enter to move to the abstract page.

2. Turn on Reveal Codes to make sure that you position the cursor before the subdocument code.

3. Press Format (Shift-F8) and select **P**age (**2**).

   ▭ Access the **L**ayout menu and select **P**age.

4. From the Format: Page menu, select Page **N**umbering (**6**).

5. From the Format: Page Numbering menu, select **N**ew Page Number (**1**). Type the new page number and press Enter.

For the dissertation in the example, you would type *iii* for Roman numeral page three and press Enter.

6. Press Exit (F7) to return to the document.

To force the text section to start with page 1, repeat the preceding steps, but move the cursor so that it is immediately before the subdocument code for the first chapter and type *1* for the new page number.

Using Search and Replace

You can use the Search and Replace features in a master document to perform the operation across all the subdocument files simultaneously. (See Chapter 3 for more information about Search and Replace.)

Suppose that the dissertation in the example has a name misspelled throughout the entire document. You could retrieve the individual files one by one and perform a Replace on each to correct the mistake, but this method would be time-consuming and tedious. Fortunately, by first expanding the master document, you can perform the Replace operation just once.

To search and replace across all the subdocument files at once, complete the following:

1. Make sure that the master document file is displayed on-screen.

   Note: If you are working with a subdocument, save it and clear the screen before retrieving the master document.

2. Expand the master document.

3. Perform the Replace.

4. Condense the master document.

5. Select **Y**es in response to the Save Subdocs? prompt.

Spell-Checking

Spell-checking is similar to Replace. You can spell-check an individual subdocument in the normal way, or you can spell-check all subdocuments at once. (See Chapter 7 for complete instructions on using the Speller.)

To spell-check all the subdocument files at once, complete the following steps:

1. Make sure the master document is displayed on-screen.

   Note: If you are working with a subdocument, save it and clear the screen before retrieving the master document.

2. Expand the master document.

3. Spell-check the expanded master document.

4. Condense the master document.

5. Select **Y**es in response to the Save Subdocs? prompt if you corrected any misspellings.

Adding Footnotes and Endnotes

You can use footnotes and endnotes with the master document. When you use these features, you need to consider the footnote and endnote options and footnote numbering. (Chapter 23 discusses footnote and endnotes in detail.)

If you use a footnote option code or an endnote option code, be sure that you have no more than one of each, and be sure to place these codes in the master document only. Remember that codes in the master document apply to all subdocuments unless overridden by codes placed in a subdocument. If you place in the subdocuments footnote option codes that are slightly different, you end up with a different style of footnote in each chapter.

Tip

The best method for adding footnotes and endnotes is to place one footnote option code and one endnote option code at the beginning of the master document. Don't place any option codes in any of the subdocuments.

Numbering Footnotes

You can number footnotes consecutively throughout the dissertation, or you can begin footnotes for each chapter with 1.

To number footnotes consecutively throughout, create the footnotes in each subdocument in the usual manner. You don't need to follow any special procedures.

When you work with an individual subdocument, the footnotes always begin with 1. When you expand the master document, all the dissertation's footnotes are numbered sequentially.

Instead of consecutively numbered footnotes, however, you might want each chapter's footnotes to start with number 1. To force this numbering, you must place a Footnote: New Number code at the beginning of every subdocument. Restarting footnote numbering is one of the rare occasions when you want to override the codes in a master document.

To begin each chapter's footnotes with number 1, complete the following steps:

1. Make sure a subdocument is displayed on-screen.

   Note: If the master document appears on-screen, save it and clear the screen before retrieving a subdocument file.

2. Press Home, Home, ↑ to go to the beginning of the subdocument.

3. Press Footnote (Ctrl-F7), select **F**ootnote (**1**), and select **N**ew Number (**3**).

  ⌨ Access the **L**ayout menu, select **F**ootnote, and choose **N**ew Number from the pop-out menu.

  WordPerfect prompts `Footnote number?`

4. Type *1* and press Enter.

Repeat this procedure for every subdocument file. When you expand the master document, the footnotes for each chapter begin with number 1.

Placing Endnotes

Although you do not need to follow any special procedures for creating endnotes in a subdocument, you should consider carefully the endnote placement. If you want all endnotes gathered in one place, then insert a single endnote-placement code at that point in the master document. In the dissertation example, the endnotes occur just before the appendix.

If you want the endnotes for each chapter to print at the end of the chapter, insert an endnote-placement code at the appropriate location in each subdocument file and override any option codes in the master document.

To place an endnote-placement code in the master document, complete the following steps:

1. Make sure the master document is displayed on-screen.

  Note: If you are working with a subdocument, be sure to save it and clear the screen before retrieving the master document.

2. Move the cursor to the desired location for the endnotes.

3. Press Footnote (Ctrl-F7) and select Endnote **P**lacement (**3**).

  ⌨ Access the **L**ayout menu, select **F**ootnote, and select **P**lacement from the pop-out menu.

  WordPerfect prompts `Restart endnote numbering? Yes (No)`

4. Press Enter or select **Y**es to restart endnote numbering.

Tip

Place hard page breaks before and after the endnote-placement code to make sure that the endnotes start on a new page and to keep text following the endnotes on its own page.

Using Cross-References

Master documents and automatic cross-references work well together. You can create cross-references with the reference in one document and the target in another document. For example, in the dissertation you can mark references in several chapters that refer to a target contained in the appendix subdocument.

Reminder:

Master documents and automatic cross-references work well together.

Normally WordPerfect would not be able to match references and targets contained in different files; but by expanding the master document, all references and targets are combined into one file.

When you choose **G**enerate (**5**) to generate a table of contents, list, index, or table of authorities, WordPerfect updates any cross-references in the master or subdocuments also. When you condense the master document, be sure to save the updated subdocuments.

Creating Subdocuments within Subdocuments

Reminder:

You can make any document (including a subdocument file) into a master document by simply inserting a subdocument code.

You can make any document (including a subdocument file) into a master document simply by inserting a subdocument code. Imagine that Chapter 2 of the dissertation requires a table listing all the characters that appeared in a particular literary work. You can build this table right into the body of the chapter, or you can create the table as a separate file (called TABLE-2.1 for example) and, at the appropriate place, insert a subdocument code into the CHAPTER.2 file. By creating the files this way, CHAPTER.2 is both a subdocument (to the dissertation as a whole) and a master document (to the TABLE-2.1 file).

Finding Other Uses for Master Documents

Using master documents to manage a large dissertation or a book is a natural application. You can use this feature in other ways to improve the appearance of the document and to make your work easier.

Building Legal Contracts

Cue:

If you create legal contracts, save sections in subdocuments and use a master document to assemble just what you need.

If you have ever rented an apartment or bought a house, you know how complicated a contract can be. Preprinted contracts, because they must be all things to all people, frequently include many sections and subsections that don't apply to a particular transaction. These sections are sometimes crossed out by hand or stamped with the word delete.

Imagine now that you work in a law office preparing contracts of this type. With master documents, you can save each section of a contract as individual files. Then, when you need to create a printed contract, you simply use the Master Document feature to pull together only those sections that you need. Every contract is a now a custom job!

Managing Group Writing

Cue:

Master documents are useful for collaborative writing projects.

Many writers, for instance technical writers, frequently work in groups; each writer is assigned a specific set of tasks. Combining all these individual efforts into a single cohesive document is a time-consuming chore that can take away from the time available for researching and writing. Creating a master document saves time because you no longer have to combine manually the individual files for generating a table of contents or printing the final product.

Summary

This chapter illustrates how the Master Document feature helps you work more efficiently by separating a large document into small, easy-to-handle pieces. You can cut large jobs down to size with the Master Document feature, which allows you to:

❑ Work with individual subdocument files, creating as many you need

❑ Build a master document, placing the subdocuments in the order you want them to appear

❑ Simplify editing tasks, such as spell-checking and replacing, by performing these options on all the files at once

❑ Generate a table of contents, an index, lists, and a table of authorities for an entire project

❑ Print the complete, edited master document

Part IV

Using WordPerfect for Desktop Publishing

Integrating Text and Graphics

Producing Publications

5.1

Integrating Text
and Graphics

Karen Rose, author of this chapter for *Using WordPerfect 5*, teaches desktop publishing courses at Sonoma State University; she is also a desktop publishing trainer for businesses through Ron Person & Co.

Stuart Bloom has been incorporating graphics into technical documents for nearly 20 years and was overjoyed when he was able to replace the glue pot and scissors with WordPerfect. He revised this chapter for *Using WordPerfect 5.1*, Special Edition.

Desktop publishing means being able to create a publication-quality document using the computer on your desk. Because of WordPerfect 5.1's advanced formatting capabilities—such as working with columns and tables, including different font sizes and styles, and creating and importing graphics—you no longer need a special desktop publishing program to produce an attractive document.

What distinguishes an ordinary document from a publication-quality document? For the most part, the document's graphical appearance makes a document publication-quality. In addition to presenting text in columns and varying the size and style of text, you can improve the appearance of a document by including graphics.

With WordPerfect 5, you can include two types of graphics in your document. First, you can create graphic elements, such as lines, boxes, and shades. Second, you can import graphics created in graphics programs.

One major difference between a dedicated desktop publishing program and a word processing program is the appearance of the document on the computer screen. In a desktop publishing program like PageMaker, what you see on-screen closely resembles what you see on the printed page. When editing with WordPerfect, graphics on-screen represent—but don't look like—what you see when you print the document. Figure 27.1 shows text as it appears on the WordPerfect screen; figure 27.2 shows the same text when it is printed.

Fig. 27.1.

Text on-screen.

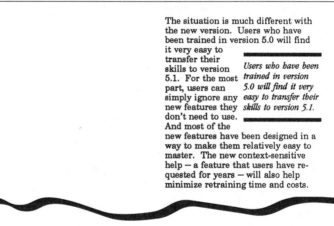

```
  released a        was a major change from what had
d by far the        gone before; for many users, upgrad-
essor in the        ing was as difficult as starting over
h to top, the       with a new software package.
some pleasant
                    The situation is much different with
                    the new version.  Users who have
                    been trained in version 5.0 will find
                    it very easy to    ┌TBL I────────┐
 new features       transfer their     │             │
re.  Some of the    skills to version  │             │
 :                  5.1.  For the most │             │
                    part, users can    │             │
                    simply ignore any  │             │
dsheet import       new features they  │             │
 merge capa-        don't need to use. └─────────────┘
                    And most of the
                    new features have been designed in a
                    way to make them relatively easy to
                    master.  The new context-sensitive
 features, Word-    help — a feature that users have re-
ed a number of      quested for years — will also help
ques into the       minimize retraining time and costs.
the confusing
E:\QUE\NEWSEXAM.WPF        Col 3 Doc 1 Pg 1 Ln 8.22" Pos 5.3"
```

Fig. 27.2.

Printed text.

The situation is much different with the new version. Users who have been trained in version 5.0 will find it very easy to transfer their skills to version 5.1. For the most part, users can simply ignore any new features they don't need to use. And most of the new features have been designed in a way to make them relatively easy to master. The new context-sensitive help — a feature that users have requested for years — will also help minimize retraining time and costs.

Users who have been trained in version 5.0 will find it very easy to transfer their skills to version 5.1.

In this chapter, you learn how to do the following to enhance a document:

- Create figures, tables, text boxes, user-defined boxes, and equation boxes
- Select the options for each type of box: for instance, the borders of the box, the caption, and the spacing within the text
- Import graphics into boxes
- Edit the graphic image, making it smaller or larger, rotating it, or inverting it
- Draw lines

> ### Reminder
> If you use a mouse with WordPerfect 5.1, you can click the right button to display the pull-down menus, and then select the desired option. You also can press Alt-= to access the pull-down menus, and then press the appropriate letter of the desired option. For all instructions you can assume that if a block is required to activate a pull-down menu option, the text has been blocked before the pull-down menu is accessed. Both pull-down menu and mouse instructions are marked with the mouse icon. For more information about the mouse, refer to Chapter 1.

Choosing the Type of Box

You can include boxes in a publication to highlight important text, such as a memorable quote; to separate a special type of text (a table of contents, for example) from the rest of the document; to frame a graphic; or to leave space for an illustration to be added later.

To create a box, you complete three basic steps: first, you choose the type of box you want; second, you define the appearance of the box; and third, you create the box and define its contents.

WordPerfect offers you five different types of boxes: figure, table box, text box, user-defined box, and equation. You follow the same steps to create each box, and you can include text, graphics, or equations in any type of box. The distinction exists primarily for design convenience—you define each type of box as having specific design elements.

Reminder:
You can select one of five types of boxes to hold special text or graphics.

Figure 27.3 shows the default design for a figure box; figure 27.4 shows the default design for a table box. The default design for a text box is shown in figure 27.5, and figure 27.6 shows the default design for a user-defined box. Figure 27.7 shows the default design for an equation box. You can change the default design, the borders of the box, the caption, the spacing within the text, and other options for each type of box as necessary.

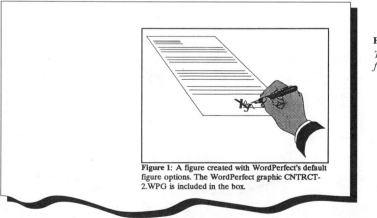

Fig. 27.3.
The default box for a figure.

Figure 1: A figure created with WordPerfect's default figure options. The WordPerfect graphic CNTRCT-2.WPG is included in the box.

Fig. 27.4.

The default box for a table.

Table I: A WordPerfect table box, using default options. The table inside the table box was created with WordPerfect's table feature.

STAFF MEETING TIMES
July 1989

	Dept. A	Dept. B	Dept. C
Week 1	9:00	10:00	1:30
Week 2	10:00	3:00	1:30
Week 3	9:00	10:00	1:30
Week 4	3:00	1:30	10:00

Fig. 27.5.

The default box for text.

The new features of WordPerfect 5.1 make life easier for the user, while minimizing retraining costs for the organization.

1: This is WordPerfect's default text box, with a file retrieved.

Fig. 27.6.

The default box for a user-defined box.

1: A WordPerfect user-defined box, using default options for style. The WordPerfect graphic MAILBAG.WPG is included.

$$s = \sqrt{\frac{\sum_{i=1}^{n} (y_i - \bar{y})^2}{n-1}}$$

(1) A WordPerfect equation box, using the default styling options. The equation was created with the equation editor.

Fig. 27.7.
The default box for an equation.

If you publish a newsletter such as the one shown in figure 27.8, you may want to include several types of items in boxes: nameplate, headlines, quotes, and graphics. To manage the appearance of each, you can define the elements that make up each type of box and then assign each item to a type of box. Some of the elements you can define are the kinds of borders, the amount of gray shading, the typefaces, and the caption style.

Reminder:
You can define the elements that make up each type of box and then assign items to the box.

Fig. 27.8.
A sample newsletter.

In addition to design convenience, assigning types of boxes also enables WordPerfect to keep track of each different type of box. For example, you can create a list of all the figure boxes and another list of all the table boxes. (See Chapter 25 for information on defining and using lists.)

To choose the type of box you want to create, complete the following steps:

1. Press Graphics (Alt-F9) and select the desired type of box.

   Access the **G**raphics pull-down menu and choose the desired type of box. Figure 27.9 shows the **G**raphics pull-down menu with the **F**igure pop-out menu active.

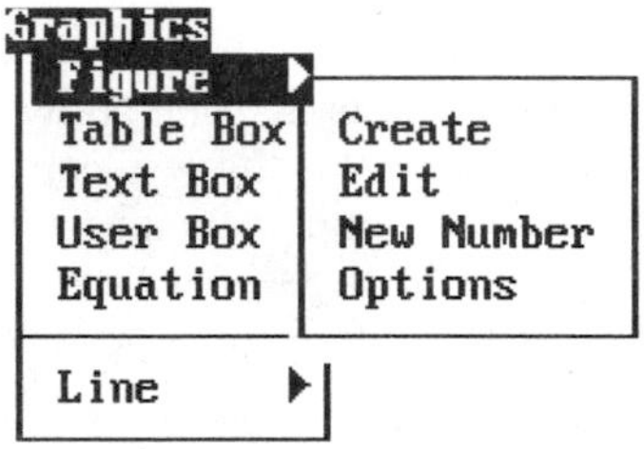

Fig. 27.9.

*The G raphics
pull-down menu
with the F igure
pop-out menu.*

```
Graphics
  Figure        ▶
  Table Box │ Create
  Text Box  │ Edit
  User Box  │ New Number
  Equation  │ Options

  Line          ▶
```

2. Select the appropriate option from the Figure menu, depending on the stage of publication:

Option	When To Use
Options (**4**)	In planning stage to design the box
Create (**1**)	After designing the box
Edit (**2**)	In later stage to edit contents or design
New Number (**3**)	In later stage to renumber

Choosing Box Options

As you plan your document, decide in advance the use of each of the different types of boxes and how each is to look. For example, if you are designing a newsletter such as the one shown in figure 27.8, you may decide to use figure boxes to hold graphics created in another program. In this case, define the figure box with single borders. You may decide to use table boxes to call out important text in your document. In this case, define the table box with thick top and bottom borders and no side borders. You may want to put the nameplate in a text box defined with thick top and bottom borders and 10% gray shading. You may decide to use user-defined boxes for major headlines, defined with no borders or shading.

Reminder:

*When you define
options for a box,
those options are in
effect whenever you
draw another box of
that type.*

When you define box options, those options remain in effect from that point forward in your document. Make sure that you define options before you draw the box. If you want the options to be in effect for the entire document, select **F**ormat **D**ocument **I**nitial Codes and put the options into the Initial Codes area (see Chapter 6). If you want to change the options after you draw a box, position the cursor in front of the box, using Reveal Codes (Alt-F3 or F11) to check the cursor's position, select **E**dit (**4**) and change the options.

To define the options for a box, complete the following steps:

1. Select **O**ptions (**4**) from the **G**raphics **F**igure pop-out menu. The Options: Figure menu appears (see fig. 27.10). (The name of the menu varies depending on the type of box you are defining.)

2. You can change the border style, the space between the border and the text, the space between the border and the contents of the box, the caption (numbering and placement), and the shading. The following sections explain each option. If you decide to keep the predefined options, press Exit (F7) from the Options: Figure menu.

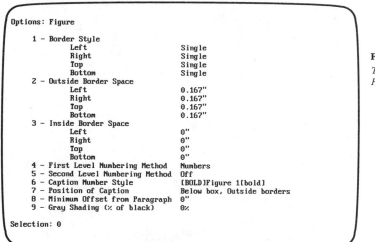

```
Options: Figure

    1 - Border Style
           Left                           Single
           Right                          Single
           Top                            Single
           Bottom                         Single
    2 - Outside Border Space
           Left                           0.167"
           Right                          0.167"
           Top                            0.167"
           Bottom                         0.167"
    3 - Inside Border Space
           Left                           0"
           Right                          0"
           Top                            0"
           Bottom                         0"
    4 - First Level Numbering Method      Numbers
    5 - Second Level Numbering Method     Off
    6 - Caption Number Style              [BOLD]Figure 1[bold]
    7 - Position of Caption               Below box, Outside borders
    8 - Minimum Offset from Paragraph     0"
    9 - Gray Shading (% of black)         0%

Selection: 0
```

Fig. 27.10.

The Options: Figure menu.

Choosing the Border Style

A box has four sides. You can define each side to appear the way you choose. The sides can all look the same, or they can all be different.

Reminder:
You can specify a different style for each side of the box.

To choose a border style for a box, complete the following steps:

1. Select **B**order Style (**1**) from the Options menu shown in figure 27.10. The following menu appears:

   1 None; **2 S**ingle; **3 D**ouble; **4 D**ashed; **5 D**otted; **6 T**hick; **7 E**xtra Thick: **0**

2. Select a border style for the left border. You can simply press Enter to leave the style unchanged and move to the next choice.

3. Select border styles for the right, top, and bottom borders in the same way. Figure 27.11 shows some sample borders.

Fig. 27.11.

Different types of borders.

WordPerfect®
Training Newsletter

This is a box with thick top and bottom borders and single left and right borders.

Users who have been trained in version 5.0 will find it very easy to transfer their skills to version 5.1.

Here's a box with double borders on all sides.

This box has no side borders and extra thick top and bottom borders.

Name:_____

Address: _____

Phone Number: _____

This box with a dotted border would make a good coupon.

Setting Space between Border and Text

Because you don't want the text of your publication to run into the box, use **O**utside Border Space to specify how much space is to be left between the box and the text that surrounds the box.

Reminder:

Units of measure are specified by Initial Setup values; you can enter measurements in inches, picas, centimeters, or units.

The measurements you enter for border space and other options depend on the Initial Setup values. WordPerfect's default unit of measurement is inches; for the examples in this chapter, inches are used. You can change the measurement to picas, centimeters, or units (columns and rows) in Setup, and then enter measurements in these units (see Chapter 20 for information on Setup).

To choose an outside border space, complete the following steps:

1. Select **O**utside Border Space (**2**) from the Options menu (see fig. 27.10).

2. Type a distance for the left outside border and press Enter. If you're working in inches, type the distance as a decimal. (You can press Enter to leave the measurement unchanged and move to the next border.)

3. Type distances for each of the three remaining outside border spaces, pressing Enter after each choice.

Setting Space between Border and Contents

In addition to space between the text and the box, you probably want some distance between what's inside the box and the border of the box. The **I**nside Border Space selection on the Options menu measures the distance between the contents of the box and the border.

Reminder:
You can specify inside and outside border spaces independently.

To specify the space between the contents of the box and the border, complete the following steps:

1. Select **I**nside Border Space (**3**) from the Options menu (see fig. 27.10).

2. Type a distance for the left inside border and press Enter. If you're working in inches, type the distance as a decimal. (You can press Enter to leave the measurement unchanged and move to the next border.)

3. Type distances for each of the three remaining inside border spaces, pressing Enter after each choice.

Choosing the Caption-Numbering Style

As you create individual boxes, you specify whether to include a caption. If you do include captions, WordPerfect can number them automatically. With the Options menu, you select the style of caption numbering to be used for the caption.

If you choose automatic numbering, WordPerfect numbers each of the four box types consecutively by type. For example, if you include three figure and two table boxes in your document, the boxes are numbered Figure 1, Figure 2, Figure 3, Table I, and Table II (depending on the style of numbering you choose). You can create lists of these figures and tables automatically.

Reminder:
You can number boxes in numbers, letters, or Roman numerals.

You can select two levels of numbering. If your document is divided into chapters, you can number the boxes by chapter. If you have three figure boxes in Chapter 1, for example, the boxes are numbered Figure 1.1, Figure 1.2, and Figure 1.3. Chapter 2 initializes the numbering; boxes are numbered Figure 2.1, Figure 2.2, and so on. You tell WordPerfect to start a new level with the **N**ew Number option, described under "Editing a Box" later in this chapter. The highest number WordPerfect can use for either chapter or consecutive figure number is 2,047.

You can specify numbers, letters, or Roman numerals for each level. Letters and Roman numerals for first-level box numbering print in uppercase. Letters and Roman numerals for second-level box numbering print in lowercase. For example, if you number equation boxes with Roman numerals for the first level and letters for the second level, the boxes are numbered Equation I.a, Equation I.b, Equation II.a, and so on.

To choose the numbering style, complete the following steps:

1. Select **F**irst Level Numbering Method (**4**) from the Options menu. A menu appears; select the numbering style you want.

2. Select **S**econd Level Numbering Method (**5**) from the Options menu if you want to include a second number in the caption. A menu appears; select the numbering style you want.

Specifying Caption Style

In addition to defining caption-numbering style, you also define the caption appearance and the text contained in the caption. Captions can include any text, formatted in any way. For example, WordPerfect's default caption-number style for figures is **[BOLD]**Figure 1**[bold]**; the number *1* indicates first-level numbering. The caption appears as **Figure 1** when printed.

You can change the default to suit your preferences. For instance, you may want the figure captions to read Fig. 1.2 and to be underlined. The instructions in this section explain how to set the *style* for the caption; the text of the caption itself is entered when you actually create the box.

To specify the caption-number style, complete the following steps:

1. Select **C**aption Number Style (**6**) from the Options menu (see fig. 27.10).

2. In response to the Replace with prompt, enter any text-formatting codes (bold, underline, or font size and appearance) you want included in the captions. For example, to underline the caption, press Underline (F8).

3. Type the text of the caption. Type *1* to include first-level caption numbering; type *2* for second-level numbering. Also, include any punctuation between levels; for example, type *Fig. 1.2* to specify a two-level numbering style with the levels separated by a period.

4. Enter any ending formatting codes. For example, press Underline (F8).

5. Press Enter.

Setting the Position for Captions

Captions can appear either below or above boxes, and either inside or outside the border. For equation boxes, you have another option: you can specify that the caption appear on the left or right side of the equation.

To choose the caption position, complete the following steps:

1. Select **P**osition of Caption (**7**) from the Options menu. For all box types except equation, the following menu appears:

   Caption Position: 1 Below Box; **2 A**bove Box: **2**

   For equation boxes, this menu appears:

   Caption Position: 1 Below Box; **2 A**bove Box; **3 L**eft Side; **4 R**ight Side: **4**

2. With WordPerfect 5.1, you then select the position where you want the caption to appear. If you are setting options for any box type except equation, the following menu appears:

   Caption: 1 Outside of Border; **2 I**nside of Border: **1**

3. Select **O**utside of Border (**1**) to position the caption outside the border of the box; select **I**nside of Border (**2**) to position the caption inside the border of the box.

Determining Offset from Paragraph

When you define a box as a paragraph (see "Anchoring a Box to the Text" later in this chapter), you attach the box to the paragraph, and the box stays with the paragraph.

If the box cannot fit on the same page as the paragraph, WordPerfect first tries to fit the box on the page by reducing the distance between the top of the paragraph and the start of the box. With the **M**inimum Offset from Paragraph option, you specify the distance this space can be reduced.

For example, when you create the box, you can specify that the box should be two inches from the top of the paragraph. With the Options menu, you specify that this two-inch space can be reduced to one inch if necessary. If the box doesn't fit two inches from the top of the paragraph, WordPerfect pushes the box up to within one inch of the top of the paragraph. If the box still doesn't fit, WordPerfect moves the box to the next page.

To set the minimum paragraph offset, complete the following steps:

1. Select **M**inimum Offset from Paragraph (**8**) from the Options menu (see fig. 27.10).

2. Type the minimum offset distance and press Enter.

Determining Percent of Gray Shading

If your printer supports gray shading, you can add shading to boxes. A light gray shading, for example, is like a screen or tint on a printed publication. Use shading to highlight text or add graphic interest to a page.

Gray shading is measured as a percent of black. Zero percent shading is no shading; 100 percent shading is black. Ten percent shading makes a good background for text. The nameplate in figure 27.8 contains 10% shading.

To specify percent of gray shading, complete the following steps:

1. Select **G**ray Shading (% of black) (**9**) from the Options menu (see fig. 27.10).

2. Type a number from 1 to 100 and press Enter.

Aligning Equations within Boxes

By default, WordPerfect centers an equation in a box. You may not find this alignment good for every purpose. If you want to move the equation to the left side of the box, for example, you can change the default alignment. Change the alignment through Setup, as explained in Chapter 20.

Creating the Box

After you define the types of boxes by selecting options for each type of box, you're ready to create boxes. (If you create boxes without first choosing options, WordPerfect uses default box settings.)

To create a box, complete the following steps:

1. Position the cursor at the place in your document where you want the box to appear. If you want the box to appear at a specific point within text, position the cursor where you want the box to appear. If you want the box to stay with a paragraph, put the cursor at the beginning of that paragraph. If you want to locate the box at a designated point on a page, put the cursor at the top of that page. See "Anchoring a Box to the Text" later in this chapter for more details on locating boxes.

2. Press Graphics (Alt-F9) and select a box type (figure, table, text box, user-defined box, or equation).

   ⌨ Access the **G**raphics pull-down menu and choose the box type you want to create. For instance, select **F**igure (**1**) to create a figure box.

3. Select **C**reate (**1**). The Definition: Figure menu appears (see fig. 27.12). The name of the menu varies depending on the type of box you select.

4. Press Enter to accept the defaults for the definitions or select the definitions you want to change.

You can enter a file name to import a graphics or text file, specify the contents of the box, add a caption, select the anchor type, position the box on the page, specify the size of the box, and edit the contents of the box using the Definition menu. Each of these options is explained in the following sections.

Fig. 27.12.

The Definition: Figure menu.

```
Definition: Figure

    1 - Filename

    2 - Contents              Empty

    3 - Caption

    4 - Anchor Type           Paragraph

    5 - Vertical Position     0"

    6 - Horizontal Position   Right

    7 - Size                  3.25" wide x 3.25" (high)

    8 - Wrap Text Around Box  Yes

    9 - Edit
```

Entering a File Name

Reminder:

Type a file name in the Definition menu to retrieve that file into the box you are creating.

When you create a box, it can be empty, filled with text, or filled with a graphic. If you want to retrieve a text or graphics file, enter the file name, and the file is inserted in the box. If you don't specify a file name, you create an empty box. You can type the text to be included in the box as you create the box. (Including text in the box is discussed in "Entering Text in a Box" later in this chapter.)

To retrieve a file into the box, complete the following steps:

1. Select **F**ilename (**1**) from the Definition menu shown in figure 27.12.

2. At the prompt `Enter filename:`, type the name of the file to retrieve and press Enter. If you do not remember the name of the file, press List (F5) and retrieve the file from the List Files display. See Chapter 10 for information on using List Files.

Determining the Type of Contents

You can use a WordPerfect box for one of three distinct types of material: a graphic image, a block of text, or an equation. Use the **C**ontents option to tell WordPerfect which type of material the box is to contain.

You do not have to use the **C**ontents option. If you designate a graphic file through the **F**ilename option of the Definition menu, WordPerfect defaults to `Graphics` contents. If you designate a WordPerfect text file or start typing in an empty box, WordPerfect defaults to `Text` contents. The **C**ontents option is mandatory only if you use the `Graphics on Disk` or `Equations` features.

Reminder:
You have to specify the contents of the box only if the box contains an equation or a piece of clip art stored separately on disk.

Deciding How Graphics Are Stored

If the box is to contain a graphic image, you have two choices. You can store the graphic image right in the WordPerfect document file, or you can instruct WordPerfect to use a graphic file stored separately on disk. The same image is printed in your document no matter which option you choose, and you have the same editing capabilities with either choice (see "Editing a Graphic Image" later in this chapter).

The advantage of storing the graphic image in your document is portability; to print the document on another computer, you need only transfer the document file. On the other hand, instructing WordPerfect to use a graphic stored on disk has three advantages:

- You can dynamically update the graphic. If you edit the graphic file with a paint or drawing program, the change is reflected in the document the next time you print.
- The document file is smaller because it does not include the graphic. This is a particular advantage if you use the same image more than once—for example, as a logo or an icon.
- You can use a graphic stored in a disk file in a style.

Specifying the Contents

To specify the box contents, complete the following steps:

1. Select **C**ontents (**2**) from the Definition menu. The following menu appears:

   Contents: 1 Graphic; **2** Graphic on **D**isk; **3 T**ext; **4 E**quation: **0**

2. Select the type of contents for the box. If you choose **E**quation (**4**) and then select **E**dit (**9**) from the Definition menu, you are placed into the equation editor. See Chapter 22 for information on using the equation editor.

Entering a Caption

With the **C**aption option, you choose whether to include a caption for each box and whether to add text to the caption. Remember that when you defined the options for this type of box, you specified the caption-numbering style and the caption.

To enter a caption for a box, complete the following steps:

1. Select **C**aption (**3**) from the Definition menu. A screen appears with the default caption number you have assigned.
2. Type any additional text to appear in the caption. You can delete the existing caption by pressing Backspace.

If you change your mind about the replacement, press Graphics (Alt-F9) to restore the default caption.

You can use any character-formatting commands to enhance the appearance of the text in the caption. Captions conform to the width of the box with which they're associated.

Anchoring a Box to the Text

You can define a box with one of three anchor types: paragraph, page, or character. The box type determines the relationship between the box and the surrounding text.

A *paragraph box* stays with its paragraph: if the paragraph moves, so does the box. The box can be offset from the top of the paragraph. Use this type of box when the box explains the text of the paragraph. In the sample newsletter in figure 27.8, the pull quote is in a paragraph-type box.

A *page box* is anchored to a specific page and stays on that page regardless of changes to surrounding text. Use this type box for headlines, for instance. In the sample newsletter, the nameplate is in a page-type box so that the nameplate always stays at the top of the page.

A *character box* is treated as a character, no matter how big the box is. If a character-type box is included in a line of text that wraps to the next line, the wrapped text appears below the box. (Only character-type boxes can be used in footnotes and endnotes.)

In the next section, "Aligning a Box," you learn how to position a box in relation to the paragraph, page, or character.

To determine the box type, complete the following steps:

1. Select **A**nchor Type (**4**) from the Definition menu (see fig. 27.12).

2. Select the way you want the box to be anchored. If you use WordPerfect 5.1 and select **P**age (**2**), you see this prompt:

   ```
   Number of pages to skip: 0
   ```

   If you want the box to appear on the current page, just press Enter to accept the default of 0. If you want the box to appear on the following page, type 1 and press Enter. If you are on page 1 and you want the box to appear on page 10, type *9* (to skip 9 pages) and press Enter.

If the document contains fewer pages than you designate to be skipped, WordPerfect prints the box on the page following the last page in the document.

Aligning a Box

The box type determines how you align the box. Box alignment defines where the box appears on the page. You specify two types of box alignment: vertical and horizontal.

Aligning a Paragraph Box

The vertical (top-to-bottom) alignment for a paragraph-type box is measured from the top of the paragraph. The horizontal (left-to-right) alignment for a paragraph-type box is measured from the margins of the paragraph.

Reminder:
You set alignment of paragraph boxes based on the top and bottom lines and left and right margins of the paragraph.

To align a paragraph-type box, complete the following steps:

1. Select **V**ertical Position (**5**) from the Definition menu (see fig. 27.12). The following message appears:

   ```
   Offset from top of paragraph: 0"
   ```

   The number following the prompt represents the current distance of the cursor from the top of the paragraph. If the number is 0 (zero), the cursor is in the top line of the paragraph.

2. To place the box where the cursor is currently located in the paragraph, press Enter. Alternatively, type the distance the box should be offset from the top of the paragraph and press Enter.

   To line up the box with the top of the paragraph, type *0* and press Enter. To place the box one-half inch below the top of the paragraph, type *0.5* and press Enter.

   If the paragraph starts close to the bottom of the page, the box may move up in the paragraph in order to fit on the page (see "Determining Offset from Paragraph" earlier in this chapter). If the box still doesn't fit, the box moves to the next page or column.

3. Select **H**orizontal Position (**6**) from the Definition menu. The following menu appears:

   Horizontal Position: 1 Left; **2 R**ight; **3 C**enter; **4 F**ull: **0**

4. Select **L**eft (**1**) to align the box with the left margin, **R**ight (**2**) to align the box with the right margin, **C**enter (**3**) to center the box between the two margins, or **F**ull (**4**) to extend the box from margin to margin (in versions before 5.1, **F**ull was labeled **B**oth Left & Right).

Aligning a Page Box

You can position a page-type box anywhere on the current page or on any following page. For example, you can specify that a nameplate box appear at the top of the page.

To align a page-type box, complete the following steps:

1. Select **V**ertical Position (**5**) from the Definition menu shown in figure 27.12. The following menu appears:

Vertical Position: 1 Full Page; **2 T**op; **3 C**enter; **4 B**ottom; **5 S**et Position: **0**

2. Select **F**ull Page (**1**) to expand the box to fill the entire page, **T**op (**2**) to align the box with the top margin, **C**enter (**3**) to center the box between the top and bottom margin, or **B**ottom (**4**) to align the box with the bottom margin (above any footers or footnotes).

To specify an exact position on the page, select **S**et Position (**5**). When prompted `Offset from top of page:`, type the distance the box should be offset from the top of the page and press Enter.

The measurement that appears for **S**et Position (**5**) reflects the current distance of the cursor from the top of the page; if you want the box to be anchored at that point, don't change this distance.

3. Select **H**orizontal Position (**6**) from the Definition menu to specify the horizontal position of the box. The following menu appears:

Horizontal Position: 1 Margins; **2 C**olumns; **3 S**et Position: **0**

4. Select the placement you want, as described in the following paragraphs.

To align the box with the margins of the page, complete the following steps:

1. Select **M**argins (**1**) from the Horizontal Position menu. The following menu appears:

Horizontal Position: 1 Left; **2 R**ight; **3 C**enter; **4 F**ull: **0**

2. Select **L**eft (**1**) to align the box with the left margin, **R**ight (**2**) to align the box with the right margin, **C**enter (**3**) to center the box between the two margins, or **F**ull (**4**) to extend the box from margin to margin.

If the document includes columns, you can align a page-type box inside a specific column, or you can make the page-type box span several columns. To align the box within a column, do the following steps:

1. Select **C**olumns (**2**) from the original Horizontal Position menu.

2. When prompted `Enter column(s):1`, specify the column or columns in which you want the box aligned and press Enter. If you want the box

to span multiple columns, separate the column numbers by a dash (to span columns 2 and 3, for example, type *2-3*). The following menu appears:

Horizontal Position: 1 Left; **2** Right; **3** Center; **4** Full: **0**

3. Select **L**eft (**1**) to align the box with the left margin of the designated column or columns, **R**ight (**2**) to align the box with the right margin, **C**enter (**3**) to center the box between the left and right column margins, or **F**ull (**4**) to extend the box the complete width of the column or columns.

To specify an exact horizontal position on the page, complete the following steps:

1. Select **S**et Position (**3**) from the original Horizontal Position menu. You see the prompt `Offset from left of page: 0"`

2. Type the distance for the box to be offset from the left margin and press Enter.

Aligning a Character Box

The character-type box always aligns horizontally to the right of the character before the box. You can specify the vertical alignment of the text relative to the box (rather than choosing the alignment of the box relative to a margin or column).

To align a character box, complete the following steps:

1. Select **V**ertical Position (**5**) from the Definition menu (see fig. 27.12). The following menu appears:

Character Box Alignment: 1 Top; **2** Center; **3** Bottom; **4** Baseline: **0**

2. Select **T**op (**1**) to align the text with the top of the box, **C**enter (**2**) to align the text with the center of the box, **B**ottom (**3**) to align text with bottom of the box, or **B**aseline (**4**) to align the last line of text in the box with the line of text where the character box is located. (The **B**aseline option is new with WordPerfect 5.1.)

Reminder:

Character boxes always align horizontally with the character in front of the box; you specify vertical alignment of the text relative to the box.

Selecting the Box Size

After you specify the alignment of the box, you then select the size of the box. Boxes are measured in decimal inches (unless you change the units of measurement in Setup, as described in Chapter 20).

You can set the box width and let WordPerfect calculate the height based on the size of the graphic or the amount of text the box contains. For instance, you may want a text box to be three inches wide. Because you are not sure how much height the text will take when it is inserted in a three-inch box, let WordPerfect calculate the height. As an alternative, you can set the box height and let WordPerfect calculate the width. Or, you can set both width and height.

Reminder:

You can specify both the height and width of a box, or you can set one and let WordPerfect calculate the other.

To select the size of the box, complete the following steps:

1. Select **S**ize (**7**) from the Definition menu. The following menu appears:

   1 Set **W**idth/Auto Height; **2** Set **H**eight/Auto Width; **3** Set **B**oth; **4** **A**uto Both: **0**

2. Select **W**idth/Auto Height (**1**) to specify the width of the box and let WordPerfect calculate the height based on the contents of the box. Select **H**eight/Auto Width (**2**) to specify the height of the box and let WordPerfect calculate the width based on the contents of the box. Select Set **B**oth (**3**) to specify both the width and height. Select **A**uto Both (**4**) to instruct WordPerfect to calculate both the height and width. **A**uto Both is the default.

3. Type the width, height, or both measurements (depending on your selection in step 2) and press Enter.

Wrapping Text around the Box

If you want to wrap text around the boxes you create, WordPerfect notes the position of the box. Any text you type goes around the box without touching its edges (see fig. 27.13). The **O**utside Border Space specified when you defined the box determines how close the text comes to the box.

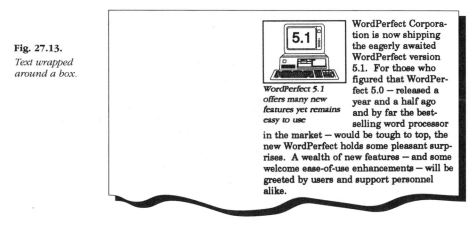

Fig. 27.13.

Text wrapped around a box.

By default, WordPerfect wraps text. You can wrap text around 20 boxes on a page; if you include more than 20 boxes, text prints through them. Text wraps only to the left of a box created in the center of a page; if you want text to the right of the box as well, use columns.

To change the text-wrap feature, complete the following steps:

1. Select **W**rap Text Around Box (**8**) from the Definition menu (see fig. 27.12).

2. Select **Y** to wrap text around the box or **N** if you want text to print through the box.

> **Tip**
>
> To superimpose one graphics image over another, or to print text on top of a graphics image, set **W**rap Text Around Box to **N**o. Define the first box, then define the second box. Use Advance to position the second box over the first. (See Chapter 6 for information on using Advance.) The *5.1* on the computer screen in figure 27.13 was created by superimposing text on one of the graphic images supplied with WordPerfect 5.1.

Entering Text in a Box

You can include text in a box by retrieving an existing text file; you also can include text directly in a box by using **E**dit (**9**). You can format the text while you type or use the Block command to make formatting changes after you type the text. Formatting options include bold, underline, and font attributes such as size and appearance. You also can define and use columns (see Chapter 17), create or import tables (see Chapter 19), enter merge codes (see Chapter 13), or import spreadsheets (see Chapter 16).

Reminder:
You can import a text file into a box, or you can type text directly into the box.

To enter text in a box, complete the following steps:

1. Select **E**dit (**9**) from the Definition menu (see fig. 27.12). A special screen for entering text appears.

2. Type the text, using any of WordPerfect's text-formatting capabilities.

3. Press Graphics (Alt-F9) if you want to rotate the text. (Text can be rotated counterclockwise if your printer supports rotated text.) If you press Alt-F9, the following menu appears:

    Rotate: 1 0°; **2** 90°; **3** 180°; **4** 270°: **1**

    Select a degree of rotation.

4. When you have finished, press Exit (F7) to return to the Definition menu.

The Edit command can be used to modify the appearance of a graphic (see "Editing a Graphic Image" later in this chapter) or to enter or edit an equation (see Chapter 22).

Remember that text in a box doesn't appear on-screen; you can see only the outline of the box. Use View Document to see the contents of a box.

Note: Any time you select **C**reate (**1**) to create a figure, table, text box, user-defined box, or equation box, and then press Exit (F7) to leave the Definition menu, you create a box. To exit without creating a box, press Cancel (F1).

Reminder:
To leave the Definition menu without creating a box, press Cancel (F1).

Editing a Box

Once you create a box, you can edit the box, whether the box is a figure, a table, a text box, a user-defined box, or an equation box, and whether the box is empty or contains text, a graphic, or an equation.

Reminder:

To edit an existing box, you must identify the box by type and number.

Boxes are labeled and numbered on-screen. The first figure you create is shown on-screen as FIG 1; the first table is TAB 1, the first text box is TXT 1, the first user-defined box is USR 1, and the first equation box is EQU 1. (The label for a figure box is displayed as *FIG 1*; the default caption is *Figure 1*.) To edit a box, you must identify the box by type and number.

Follow these steps to edit a box:

1. Press Graphics (Alt-F9) and select the type of box.

   ▭ Access the **G**raphics pull-down menu and select the type of box.

2. Select **E**dit (**2**).

3. Type the number of the box you want to edit and press Enter. The Definition menu appears as shown in figure 27.12.

4. Make the desired changes. To change the type of an existing box, press Graphics (Alt-F9) from the Definition menu.

5. Press Exit (F7) to return to the document.

Reminder:

You can change the numbering scheme for boxes.

Box numbering begins with 1 (or I or A) at the beginning of the document and continues consecutively through the document. You can change the numbering at any time. The new numbering remains in effect until you change it again. For example, if you include four figures in your document, they are numbered by default as Figure 1, Figure 2, Figure 3, and Figure 4. Suppose that you want to skip number 3 and continue with 4 and 5.

To change a box number, complete the following steps:

1. Move the cursor to the place in the document where you want numbering to change.

2. Press Graphics (Alt-F9) and select the type of box.

   ▭ Access the **G**raphics pull-down menu and select the type of box.

3. Select **N**ew Number (**3**), type the new number, and press Enter.

4. Press Exit (F7) to return to the document.

Move the cursor past the newly numbered box to see the change.

You can enter the new number in any format—numeric, Roman, or letter—and the number translates into the format being used for the selected box type. For example, if your figures are numbered 1, 2, 3, 4, and you enter the new number as *D*, the number automatically translates to *4*.

Importing Graphics

Importing graphics is an integral part of creating a box. WordPerfect supports many types of graphics files, either directly or indirectly. See Chapter 28 for a complete list of graphics files you can import.

Cue:

WordPerfect comes with clip-art you can use in your documents.

On one of the WordPerfect distribution diskettes is a limited selection of clip-art graphics you can use. Some of these images are shown in figure 27.14. All the supplied graphic files have the extension WPG.

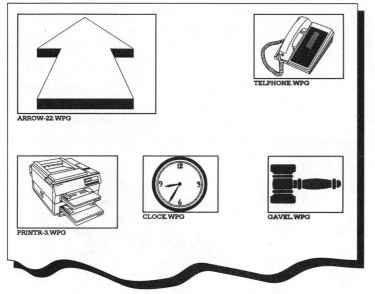

Fig. 27.14.
A sampling of the graphic images supplied on the distribution diskettes.

To import a graphic into a box, complete the following steps:

1. Press Graphics (Alt-F9) and select the type of box into which you want to import the graphic.

   ⌨ Access the **G**raphics pull-down menu and select the type of box.

2. Select **C**reate (**1**).

3. Select **F**ilename (**1**) from the Definition menu.

4. Type the name of the graphics file and press Enter. For example, to use the butterfly shown in figure 27.15, type *BUTTRFLY.WPG* and press Enter.

5. By default, WordPerfect 5.1 selects the Graphics content type when you retrieve a graphics file. If you prefer to use the Graphics on Disk type, change the Contents line on the Definition menu (see "Deciding How Graphics Are Stored" earlier in this chapter).

6. Press Exit (F7) to return to the document.

If you do not specify the box size, WordPerfect calculates an initial box size based on the space remaining on the page. When you import a graphic image, WordPerfect adjusts the proportions of the box to suit the image. You can modify the size of the box at any time.

Editing a Graphic Image

Once you import a graphic, you can manipulate it to suit your preferences.

To edit a graphic, complete the following steps:

1. Press Graphics (Alt-F9) and select the type of box in which the graphic resides.

   ⌨ Access the **G**raphics pull-down menu and select the type of box .

2. Select **E**dit (**2**).

3. Type the box number and press Enter.

4. Select **E**dit (**9**) from the Definition menu.

The graphic appears on-screen (see fig. 27.15). The menu bar at the bottom of the screen shows the editing changes you can make, including keys you can use as shortcuts.

Fig. 27.15.

Editing a graphics image.

Moving an Image

When you move a graphic image, the graphic moves, but the box stays where it is. You can move or *crop* an image so that only part of the image is visible in the box (see fig. 27.16).

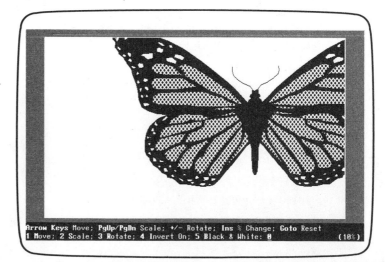

Fig. 27.16.

A cropped image.

To move an image inside the box using the shortcut method, press ↑ to move the image up, ↓ to move the image down, → to move the image to the right, or ← to move the image to the left. The image is moved the percent amount shown in the bottom right of the screen. (You can change this percentage by pressing Ins until the amount you want appears: 1%, 5%, 10%, or 25%.)

To move an image a specified distance, complete the following steps:

1. Select **M**ove (**1**) from the menu bar at the bottom of the graphics screen.

2. Type the horizontal distance to move and press Enter. Enter a positive number to move the image to the right; enter a negative number to move the image to the left. For instance, type *1* and press Enter to move the butterfly to the right 1 inch.

3. Type the vertical distance to move and press Enter. Enter a positive number to move the image up; enter a negative number to move the image down. For instance, type *1* and press Enter to move the image up 1 inch.

Reminder:
Use the arrow keys to move the image; check the percentage in the bottom right corner to see how much each keystroke moves the image.

Scaling an Image

Scaling an image means changing its size—making it larger or smaller. Only the graphic changes; the box size stays the same.

To scale an image using the shortcut method, press PgUp to make the image larger; press PgDn to make the image smaller. The image is scaled on both axes by the percentage shown at the bottom right of the screen. Press Ins to change the amount that each keypress scales the image.

To scale an image up or down by a specified percent, complete the following steps:

1. Select **S**cale (**2**) from the menu bar at the bottom of the graphics screen.

2. For Scale X:, type the percent to scale the image horizontally (from side to side) and press Enter. For example, type *150* and press Enter.

3. For Scale Y:, type the percent to scale the image vertically (from top to bottom) and press Enter. For example, type *150* and press Enter.

Reminder:
You can scale the size of an image both horizontally and vertically; you can stretch or condense an image in one dimension or in both dimensions.

To make an image smaller, enter amounts less than 100 for steps 2 and 3; to make an image larger, enter amounts larger than 100 for steps 2 and 3. Figure 27.17 shows the butterfly scaled 150 percent both horizontally and vertically. You can scale the image nonproportionally, using different percentages for horizontal and vertical scales.

Rotating and Mirroring an Image

In addition to moving or scaling an image, you also can rotate or mirror the image. *Rotating* an image turns it clockwise or counterclockwise inside the box; *mirroring* an image flips the image over so that it faces in the opposite direction.

Fig. 27.17.
An image scaled up.

To rotate the image using a shortcut, press Screen Up (– on the numeric keypad) to rotate the image clockwise; press Screen Down (+ on the numeric keypad) to rotate the image counterclockwise. Press Ins to change the amount that each keypress rotates the image.

To rotate an image by a specified amount, complete the following steps:

1. Select **R**otate (**3**) from the menu bar at the bottom of the graphics screen.

2. Type the number of degrees to rotate the image and press Enter. For example, type *90* and press Enter (see fig. 27.18).

   A full circle is 360 degrees. You can rotate an image counterclockwise (to the left) only with this method; to rotate clockwise (to the right), use the keyboard shortcut.

   If you don't want to rotate the image, but want only to mirror the image, type *0* (zero) and press Enter.

3. In response to the `Mirror Image?` prompt, select **Y** if you want to mirror the image; select **N** otherwise. If you select **Y**, a mirrored image appears on the page. The butterfly from figure 27.18 is shown mirrored in figure 27.19.

Reminder:

WordPerfect does not add rotation values (it starts from 0 each time).

Rotation and mirroring values are always absolute; they start from the image's *original* orientation. In other words, if you rotate an image 90 degrees, and you attempt to rotate it another 90 degrees, the image is not rotated 180 degrees. The rotation remains 90.

If you mirror an image by selecting **Y** in step 3, the only way to restore the image to its original orientation is to select **N**.

Fig. 27.18.
An image rotated 90 degrees.

Fig. 27.19.
A mirrored image.

Inverting an Image

You can use two distinct types of images in WordPerfect documents: *vector images* (also called *object-oriented images*), and *bit-mapped images*. These types of images are discussed in more detail in Chapter 28.

To invert an image, select **I**nvert (**4**) from the menu bar at the bottom of the graphics screen. The graphics editor shows the effect of inverting the image. The following sections explain what happens with vector and bit-mapped images when they are inverted.

Inverting Vector Images

Several different elements make up a vector image: black lines, white space, and colored areas. When the colors in a vector image are viewed on a monochrome monitor or printed on a black-and-white printer, they are converted by WordPerfect to a series of gray scales.

When you invert a vector image, black lines and white space are reversed. Put another way, the black lines become white lines and the white space becomes "black space." The colors—and, correspondingly, the gray scales—are not affected in any way.

The butterfly image shown in this chapter is a vector image. Figure 27.20 shows the butterfly inverted. Notice that the body of the butterfly—which is colored in the original image, and thus a gray scale in the figure—is not affected by the change.

Fig. 27.20.
An inverted vector image

Inverting Bit-Mapped Images

A bit-mapped image consists of dots. In a monochrome image, each dot is either "on" or "off." In a colored image, each dot has a color value. When WordPerfect inverts a monochrome bit-mapped image, it changes the black dots to white and the white areas to black. Inverting a color bit-mapped image has no effect on the image.

> **Caution**
>
> If you have a monitor that displays color graphics but a printer that only prints in black and white, inverting a bit-mapped image has no effect on the way the image appears on-screen. Inverting the image does, however, affect the appearance of the printed copy. If you want to ensure that you see exactly what is printed, use Setup (F1) to have the WordPerfect graphics screens display images in black and white. See Chapter 20 for details.

Printing an Image in Black and White

When you print an image in black and white, the colored or gray-scaled areas of vector images convert to solid black. With bit-mapped images, some colors are affected and others are not. Printing a color image in black and white is chiefly useful for special effects.

To print an image in black and white, complete the following steps:

1. Select **B**lack & White (**5**) from the menu bar at the bottom of the screen.

2. In response to `Print/Display image in black & white?`, select **Y**. The image prints with the shaded areas in solid black (see fig. 27.21). To change back to a shaded image, select **N**.

Fig. 27.21.
A black-and-white image.

Restoring an Image to its Original State

You can restore, at any time, an image to its original, unedited state. To do so, press GoTo (Ctrl-Home). Restoring an image to its *original state* means that **all** editing changes are canceled. You cannot recover the editing changes unless you redo them all manually.

Reminder:

*Pressing GoTo cancels **all** editing changes.*

Creating Graphics Lines

You can draw lines and boxes by using Line Draw or Graphics. (Line Draw is described later in this chapter.) When you use Graphics to create lines and boxes, the lines and boxes are objects separate from, yet attached to, the text. Drawing graphics in this manner has several advantages, the most important of which is that the line or box stays intact when you make changes to the text. A paragraph wraps around a figure, for example, and a column goes up to, but not over, a line. You cannot see a graphics line on the normal editing screen. (Use the View Document command to see the lines you create.)

You create graphics lines in much the same way you create graphics boxes. For example, you can create lines in different widths and different shades, and you can position lines anywhere on the page.

You can draw two types of lines in WordPerfect: horizontal (from side to side on the page), and vertical (up and down on the page). Actually, you don't draw the lines; rather you describe how they look and then define where they appear on the page.

Creating Horizontal Lines

Use horizontal lines to set off text on the page. The sample newsletter in figure 27.8 contains a horizontal line below the nameplate to separate it from the text.

To draw a horizontal line, complete the following steps:

1. Press Graphics (Alt-F9) and select **L**ine (**5**) from the menu.

   ⌨ Access the **G**raphics pull-down menu and select **L**ine (fig. 27.22 shows the **G**raphics pull-down menu with the **L**ine pop-out menu displayed).

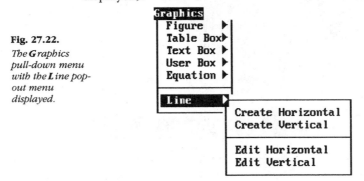

Fig. 27.22.

The G raphics pull-down menu with the L ine pop- out menu displayed.

2. Select Create Line: **H**orizontal (**1**).

   ⌨ Select Create **H**orizontal from the **L**ine pop-out menu.

   The Graphics: Horizontal Line menu appears (see fig. 27.23).

Fig. 27.23.

The Graphics: Horizontal Line menu.

```
Graphics: Horizontal Line

    1 - Horizontal Position      Full

    2 - Vertical Position        Baseline

    3 - Length of Line

    4 - Width of Line            0.013"

    5 - Gray Shading (% of black) 100%
```

You can accept the default horizontal line and return to the editing screen by pressing Exit (F7). The default produces a solid black horizontal line, from left margin to right margin, vertically positioned at the current cursor position, and 0.013" (approximately 1 point) thick. The line "floats" vertically if the hidden code specifying the line is moved.

Reminder:
The default horizontal line is solid black, 1 point thick, as wide as the margins allow it to be, and moves vertically if its hidden code is moved.

Changing the Horizontal Position

To change the horizontal position of the line, follow these steps:

1. Select **H**orizontal Position (**1**) from the Graphics: Horizontal Line menu. The following menu appears:

   Horizontal Pos: 1 **L**eft; **2** **R**ight; **3** **C**enter; **4** **F**ull; **5** **S**et Position: **0**

2. Select **L**eft (**1**) to start the line at the left margin, **R**ight (**2**) to start the line at the right margin, **C**enter (**3**) to center the line between the margins, or **F**ull (**4**) to extend the line from the left to the right margin.

   Select **S**et Position (**5**) to specify an exact location for the line. In response to the `Offset from left of page:` prompt, type the distance from the left edge of the paper at which the line should begin and press Enter.

Changing the Vertical Position

With WordPerfect 5.1, you can change the vertical position of the line. With WordPerfect 5, you could not set the vertical position for a horizontal line; the line was automatically positioned at the current cursor position. If the hidden line code was later moved—intentionally or unintentionally—the position of the line changed.

In WordPerfect 5.1, you can duplicate the behavior of version 5 by accepting the default `Baseline` vertical positioning. As an alternative, you can designate a specific vertical position; if you do so, WordPerfect always prints the line at the specified position, even if the hidden code is moved.

To set the vertical position, complete these steps:

1. Select **V**ertical Position (**2**) from the Graphics: Horizontal Line menu. The following menu appears:

   Vertical Position: 1 **B**aseline; **2** **S**et Position: **0**

2. Select **B**aseline (**1**) to establish the line at the current cursor position and to cause the line to "float" as the horizontal line code moves.

   Select **S**et Position (**2**) to specify an exact location. Then type the distance from the top of the page where the line should appear (the default presented by WordPerfect is the current cursor position).

▽ **5.1** ▽

Reminder:
WordPerfect's default is to vertically position a horizontal line at the current cursor location, but you can specify a location for the line.

Changing the Line Length

Unless you have specified a horizontal position of `Full` (the length of the line is equal to the distance between the left and right margins), you can specify the length of the horizontal line with the **L**ength of Line option. Depending on the placement of the line, WordPerfect may have calculated the line length for you. The length of the line is calculated as the distance between the cursor and the left margin.

To change the line length, complete these procedures:

1. Select **L**ength of Line (**3**) from the Graphics: Horizontal Line menu.

2. Enter the length of the line.

You can specify a line length as precise as three decimal places (although WordPerfect only displays the length to two decimal places), and you can specify a line of up to 54 inches in length. Most printers don't accommodate paper that wide, however. In any case, the line can be no wider than the distance between the two margins.

Creating Vertical Lines

As with horizontal lines, you define a vertical line by its position on the page, its length, its width, and its shading. In addition, you can position a vertical line between two text columns. In the sample newsletter in figure 27.8, vertical lines separate the columns of text.

To create a vertical line, follow these steps:

1. Press Graphics (Alt-F9) and select **L**ine (**5**) from the menu.

   ⌨ Access the **G**raphics pull-down menu and select **L**ine.

2. Select Create Line: **V**ertical (**2**).

   ⌨ Select Create **V**ertical from the **L**ine pop-out menu.

   The Graphics: Vertical Line menu appears (see fig. 27.24).

Reminder:

The default vertical line is solid black, 1 point thick, and the length of the page.

You can accept the default vertical line and return to the editing screen by pressing Exit (F7). The default produces a solid black vertical line at the left margin, extending from the top margin to the bottom margin, and 0.013" (approximately 1 point) thick.

Fig. 27.24.

The Graphics: Vertical Line menu.

```
Graphics: Vertical Line

    1 - Horizontal Position      Left Margin

    2 - Vertical Position        Full Page

    3 - Length of Line

    4 - Width of Line            0.013"

    5 - Gray Shading (% of black) 100%
```

Changing the Horizontal Position

By default, a vertical line is created at the left margin. You can change the position with the **H**orizontal Position option.

To change the horizontal position, follow these procedures:

1. Select **H**orizontal Position (**1**) from the Graphics: Vertical Line menu. The following menu appears:

   Horizontal Position: 1 Left; **2 R**ight; **3** Between Columns; **4 S**et Position: **0**

2. Select **L**eft (**1**) to place the line on the left margin or **R**ight (**2**) to place the line on the right margin.

   Select **B**etween Columns (**3**) to place the line between any two text columns. In response to the Place line to right of column: 1 prompt, specify the column the line should appear to the *right* of and press Enter. This option must be specified after the column-definition code.

   Select **S**et Position (**4**) to place the line at a specific distance from the left edge of the paper. Type the distance from the left edge of the paper at which the line should appear and press Enter.

An easy way to set the line's horizontal position is to move the cursor where you want the line to begin before you select **S**et Position (**4**). WordPerfect automatically calculates the cursor's horizontal position (how far it is from the left edge of the page) and enters that number for you.

Changing the Vertical Position

By default, WordPerfect creates a vertical line spanning the full page (from top to bottom margin). You can change the start point of the line and the length of the line with the **V**ertical Position and **L**ength of Line options.

To change vertical position, follow these procedures:

1. Select **V**ertical Position (**2**) from the Graphics: Vertical Line menu. The following menu appears:

   Vertical Position: 1 Full Page; **2** Top; **3** Center; **4 B**ottom; **5 S**et Position: **0**

2. Select **F**ull Page (**1**) to extend the line from the top margin to the bottom margin, **T**op (**2**) to start the line at the top margin, Center (**3**) to center the line between the top and bottom margins, or Bottom (**4**) to start the line at the bottom margin.

   Select **S**et Position (**5**), type the distance from the top edge of the paper at which you want the line to begin, and press Enter.

An easy way to set the line's vertical position is to move the cursor where you want the line to begin before you select **S**et Position (**5**). WordPerfect automatically calculates the cursor's vertical position (how far it is from the top edge of the page) and enters that number.

Changing the Line Length

WordPerfect automatically calculates the length of the vertical line based on the Vertical Position setting. For any setting other than Full Page, you can change the calculated length with the **L**ength of Line option.

To change the line length, follow these procedures:

1. Select **L**ength of Line (**3**) from the Graphics: Vertical Line menu.

2. Type the line length and press Enter.

Changing the Appearance of Lines

You can change the appearance of a horizontal or vertical line by changing its width or the degree of gray shading. The *width* of a line is its thickness. You can choose a width up to three decimal points in precision, creating a line as narrow as 0.001" or as wide as 54 inches. Keep in mind that the precision of the printed line depends on your printer. A laser printer can produce a very fine line, while the thinnest line a dot-matrix printer can print may be much coarser.

To change line width, complete these procedures:

1. Select **W**idth of Line (**4**) from either the Graphics: Horizontal or Graphics: Vertical Line menu.

2. Enter the width of the line. By default, WordPerfect uses inches as the unit of measure. You can change the unit of measure through Setup, as described in Chapter 20.

Gray shading is calculated as a percentage of black. A 100% shade is black; 0% is white. Any value in between is a gray shade or a *screen*.

To change gray shading for lines, complete these procedures:

1. Select **G**ray Shading (% of black) (**5**) from either the Graphics: Horizontal or Graphics: Vertical Line menu.

2. Enter a value describing the shade of gray you want.

Returning to the Editing Screen

When you have finished changing the lines in the document, press Exit (F7) to return to the main editing screen. Because the lines created with the Graphics menu cannot be seen on the normal editing screen, use Reveal Codes (Alt-F3 or F11) or View Document to see the line codes you created. (Chapter 8 describes the use of View Document.)

Editing Graphics Lines

You can edit a graphic line after you have created it. To select the graphic line you want to edit, follow these procedures:

1. Press Graphics (Alt-F9) and select **L**ine (**5**) from the menu.

   ⌨ Access the **G**raphics pull-down menu and select **L**ine.

2. Select Edit Line: **H**orizontal (**3**) to edit a horizontal line or Edit Line: **V**ertical (**4**) to edit a vertical line.

   ⌨ Select Edit **H**orizontal or Edit **V**ertical from the **L**ine pop-out menu.

   WordPerfect searches for an existing horizontal or vertical line. WordPerfect first searches backwards from the current cursor position to the beginning of the document; the first line WordPerfect finds that matches the specified line is selected for editing. If no line is found, WordPerfect then searches forward to the end of the document. If no line is found on the forward search, WordPerfect displays * Not Found *.

   Depending on the type of line you specified to edit, WordPerfect displays the Graphics: Horizontal Line menu or the Graphics: Vertical Line menu.

3. Edit the desired options. Refer to "Creating Horizontal Lines," "Creating Vertical Lines," and "Changing the Appearance of Lines" earlier in this chapter.

Using Line Draw

If you plan to edit your document, use Graphics to draw lines and boxes so that the images don't change inadvertently as you edit. If you want, you can use Line Draw to draw a line or box by just moving the cursor. Line Draw is quick and easy.

Lines and boxes drawn with Line Draw are actually composed of characters and are part of the text. You cannot type over them or around them without disturbing them. Be sure to experiment with line drawing before you plan a document using this tool.

Cue:
Use Line Draw instead of the Graphics Line options to draw a quick and easy line or box.

To draw a line or box, complete the following steps:

1. Press Screen (Ctrl-F3) and select **L**ine Draw (**2**).

   ⌨ Access the **T**ools pull-down menu and select **L**ine Draw.

   The following menu appears:

   1 |; **2** ||; **3** *; **4** Change; **5** Erase; **6** Move: **1**

2. Select **1** for a single line, **2** for a double line, or **3** to draw a line of asterisks (like this: ****).

4. Use the cursor keys to draw the line or box.

5. Press Exit (F7) to quit Line Draw.

Changing the Line Style

You can change the style of the line to something other than single, double, or asterisk lines by selecting **C**hange (**4**) from the Line Draw menu.

To change the line style, complete the following steps:

1. Select **C**hange (**4**) from the Line Draw menu. The following menu appears:

   1 ▌; **2** ▌; **3** ▌; **4** ▌; **5** ▬; **6** ▎; **7** ▎; **8** ▪; **9** Other: **0**

2. Select any of the eight line styles shown or press 9 and type the character you want to use for the lines. You return to the Line Draw menu; the new style replaces the asterisk as selection 3.

3. Use the cursor keys to draw the line.

4. Press Exit (F7) to quit Line Draw.

Erasing the Line

You can erase the line drawn with Line Draw in the same way you drew it:

1. Choose **E**rase (**5**) from the Line Draw menu.

2. Use the cursor keys to trace over the line you want to erase.

   To start drawing again after you erase a line, select one of the line-drawing tools (1, 2, or 3).

3. Press Exit (F7) to quit Line Draw.

To move the cursor without drawing, select **M**ove (**6**) from the Line Draw menu and use the cursor keys.

Note: If you use proportionally spaced type, lines and boxes drawn with Line Draw don't print correctly. If you use a laser printer with fonts like Times, Helvetica, or any of the Bitstream fonts, for example, you must switch to a nonproportional font, such as Courier, to make the Line Draw characters line up correctly. If you're doing laser-printed desktop publishing, you should avoid the Line Draw command altogether.

Summary

WordPerfect has powerful graphics capabilities. In this chapter, you learned how to integrate text with graphics such as lines, boxes, screens, and imported graphics images. In addition, you experimented with the following options:

❑ Creating any of five types of boxes: figure, table box, text box, user-defined box, or equation box

❑ Defining the appearance of each type of box and specifying line style (single, double, dashed, dotted, thick, or thicker line), amount of space around the box, shading inside the box, and captions (numbering, position, and style)

❑ Inserting a file (text or graphic) in a box

❑ Positioning the box on the page and specifying how the box is anchored to the text

❑ Creating graphics lines and defining each line's appearance (line style and width) and location on the page (on a margin, near a margin, between margins, between columns)

28

Producing Publications

As owner of a newsletter production and management company, **Karen Rose** uses desktop publishing extensively in her work. Her company, Write on Target, produces seven newsletters and an international quarterly. She originally wrote this chapter for *Using WordPerfect 5*.

As a principal in Learning Associates, a training development company, **Stuart Bloom** has used the desktop publishing features of WordPerfect on projects for clients and for literature promoting Learning Associates. He revised this chapter for *Using WordPerfect 5.1*, Special Edition.

Over the past few years, a new wave of technology has swept the computer industry like a giant tsunami. Called *desktop publishing*, it has made major changes in the way people produce and think about publications. Modern business people save time and money producing their own newsletters, magazines, reports, brochures, and ads. More than that, the way people think about the appearance of documents has changed. With desktop publishing, you can create attractive and professional-looking pages, no matter what the subject. People have come to expect forms, flyers, press releases, resumes, reports, business presentations, and even letters and memos to look attractive.

Desktop publishing programs—like PageMaker and Ventura Publisher—are powerful tools. In the hands of a skilled user, these dedicated programs can produce beautifully formatted publications. But they achieve much of their power through specialization; the programs excel at dressing up existing text; they have limited text creation and editing capabilities. The programs are also very complex.

Traditional word processors, on the other hand, can do little more than replicate typed output—with a few simple enhancements like boldface and full justification.

Where does WordPerfect fit into this picture? WordPerfect does not have the formatting capabilities of a dedicated desktop publishing program, but it does have features like graphics, styles, fonts, tables, equations, and columns that most word processors lack. WordPerfect's desktop publishing features enable you to produce a surprising variety of attractive publications. WordPerfect also beats dedicated desktop publishing programs hands down when it comes to sophisticated and easy-to-use text creation and editing. WordPerfect's built-in data manipulation capabilities far surpass anything desktop publishing programs or most other word processors even attempt.

WordPerfect, then, is a superb tool for those who want to produce attractive, professional-looking documents efficiently; who want a single tool that integrates text creation, text editing, data manipulation, and high-quality printing; and who need "publication quality" output but can live with a few limitations.

Chapter 27 provided some hands-on experience integrating text and graphics. This chapter moves to creating entire publications, combining several WordPerfect features: columns, font changes, graphics boxes and lines, and others. Use this chapter as a primer on desktop publishing:

- Start by reading about some general desktop publishing principles and design guidelines. Use these pointers on document appearance to help plan your publication.

- Consider the desktop publishing features WordPerfect offers. Decide which elements you want to incorporate in your publication design.

- Look at the list of graphics programs you can use with WordPerfect.

- Review a list of tips that help you get the best results from WordPerfect's desktop publishing features.

- Study a series of specification sheets for sample publications: a newsletter, a brochure, a form, and an annual report. You can modify any of these specifications to meet your own needs.

> ### Reminder
>
> If you use a mouse with WordPerfect 5.1, you can click the right button to display the pull-down menus, and then select the desired option. You also can press Alt-= to access the pull-down menus, and then press the appropriate letter of the desired option. For all instructions, assume that if a block is required to activate a pull-down menu option, the text has been blocked before the pull-down menu is accessed. Instructions for pull-down menus and the mouse are marked with the mouse icon. For more information about the mouse, see Chapter 1. ⌨

Realizing the Potential of Desktop Publishing

The difference between a plain document and a carefully laid out document can be subtle. Both contain the same information, maybe even in the same order. Both contain the same title, subtitles, and paragraphs of text. One document is, however, more inviting to the reader, more visually appealing, and perhaps even easier to read.

Plain documents are usually prepared by a word processing program using traditional typewriter-like techniques. Text enhancements are limited to tricks like underlining or bolding text, typing words in all uppercase letters, and centering lines. Text is printed margin to margin, and sections of the document are presented one after the other, with no indication of relative importance.

Documents like the ones you see in this chapter are prepared using desktop publishing techniques. The text can be presented in easier-to-read columns. The desktop-published document can use different type for headlines, subheads, and captions, as well as graphics.

With WordPerfect 5.1, you step past word processing into desktop publishing. However, you may not need to take that step. Does a simple memo benefit from large headlines, graphics, and fancy fonts? Probably not. Can an ad be improved with those attention-getting techniques? Yes! Does a three-page technical report intended for a small and highly interested audience merit the time it takes to arrange the text in columns and boxes? Maybe not. Will a promotional newsletter meant for customers and prospects be better received if it is spiced up with columns and graphics? Definitely!

Cue:

Although WordPerfect 5.1 offers desktop publishing features, these features may not be appropriate for your document.

Designing Publications That Work

"Form follows function" is a cliche, but it's a cliche that has guided successful designers for years. The function of a publication is to *communicate*, and by communicating, to *inform* or *persuade*. If the format of a document is too cute, uses too many fonts, or lets visual gimmickry get in the way of effective communication, then function is being sacrificed to form, and your efforts are for nought.

The guidelines that follow help you use form to enhance function to help your publication communicate. But there's one guideline that's more important than any of the others: *keep it simple*. Even experienced professional designers—who can, when they have to, use complex formats successfully—often choose the simple path. Why? Because they know that the simple solution is often the best solution, that less is often really more.

Reminder:

The surest route to a publication that communicates effectively is often the simplest one.

Consistency—Establish a format for your publication and stick with it! Decide on the features and formats: the margins; number of columns; headers and footers; graphics boxes, lines, and captions; size and style typefaces for text elements (headlines, subheads, and body copy); and colors for ink and paper. Design a strong and appropriate nameplate (masthead) for the publication.

Clarity—A page should not be confusing. Can you look at the page and immediately know where to begin reading? Do you immediately know what the publication is about? Do you know from whom it comes? Is the message clear, obvious, and foremost?

Emphasis—Put important ideas first. Most designers agree that every page has four areas of importance. Top left is the most important and first to be read. Bottom right is least important and last to be read. Your publication should have only one title. If you need to say more than a single title permits, use a subtitle. Similarly, each article should have only one headline, and articles of equal importance should have headlines of equal size, type, and weight. Use type size to signal importance.

Unity—Keep text together. Remember that readers expect to read from left to right, top to bottom. Text itself is a graphic element, and scattering it over the page is confusing—the eye doesn't know where to go.

White space—Learn to love white space, the space on the page where nothing appears. White space is an important part of any design; make it work by including it deliberately in the design.

Balance—Surprisingly, a carefully imbalanced page can be more interesting than a perfectly balanced page. If you have two photos to use with a story, for example, make the more important one larger.

Proportion—Be sure that the elements on a page are proportioned appropriately. An unimportant illustration is inappropriate if made too large; a major headline gets lost if made too small.

Drama—You can achieve a feeling of drama if one visual element dominates the page. It may be a graphic, a headline, or a block of copy.

Dimension—A page may be flat, but a publication usually isn't. A two-page spread (the two pages you see when you hold a magazine open, for example) isn't perceived as two separate pages, but rather as one double-wide page. A book or magazine held in the hand has zones that are easily and quickly seen (the outside edges of the pages, for example) and zones that remain more hidden (the inside edges).

Cue:
Experiment with the design of your publication.

Experimentation—Be willing to experiment. Planning is imperative, and consistency is necessary, but plan some flexibility into your publication. Leave room for some experimentation. Have fun with it!

Enhancing a Publication

Now that you have reviewed some general guidelines for page layout, think about the effects you can achieve with WordPerfect features. Using WordPerfect 5.1 as a publishing tool, you can enhance your document with the features described in the following sections.

Using Columns

Cue:
Use columns to improve the appearance and readability of your document; vary the width and start and end points of the columns.

Columns make text easier to read, add graphic interest to a page, and create areas of white space. When you plan your publication, decide how many columns you want. Remember that columns don't have to start and end at the same place. Also, you can vary column width to add interest. Chapter 17 explains how to define newspaper-type columns.

When you work with columns, remember a few rules to keep pages neat. First, avoid widows and orphans. A *widow* is the first line of a paragraph left alone at the bottom of a column. An *orphan* is the last line of a paragraph left alone at the top of a column. If possible, keep two lines of a paragraph together at the top or bottom of a column. Second, you can leave the bottoms of columns widely uneven for graphic interest. If columns are almost even, however, make them exactly even at the bottom. The document looks unfinished if column lengths differ by only half a line.

One way you can balance columns is with WordPerfect's Advance feature. You can make small adjustments in the spacing between paragraphs by putting Advance Up or Advance Down codes at the beginning of each paragraph. If the individual adjustments are relatively small, the reader won't notice that adjacent columns have different interparagraph spacing. Look closely at the newsletter in figure 28.14 that appears later in this chapter and notice that the paragraph spacing in the right column differs from that of the middle column; but the average reader would never notice this difference.

Tip

If you want to insert several identical Advance codes, put them into an open style. If you decide to change the Advance settings, you can change them all simultaneously by editing the style definition. See Chapter 15 for more information on Styles.

Another balancing technique is to change the default leading in a column. *Leading* (pronounced led´ding) is the spacing between individual lines; by default, WordPerfect uses two points of leading. Leading adjustments should be very small— a fraction of a point—to avoid notice. However, because the leading adjustment affects the spacing between each line, its effect is cumulative, and you often can balance your paragraphs this way. Chapter 17 explains how to change the leading in columns.

Varying Paragraphs

The paragraph is the basic building block of the document. You can find many ways to vary paragraphs to create an interesting texture. You can design paragraphs flush left; you can justify them, center them, or align them flush right for special effects. Creative indenting and paragraph spacing also can add interest to a page. Figure 28.1 shows various paragraph alignments.

J o h a n n e s Gutenberg, the fifteenth-century i n v e n t o r o f m o v a b l e t y p e, b r o u g h t t h e written word to the public, and thus is responsible for publishing as it has been known for f i v e h u n d r e d years.	Johannes Gutenberg, the fifteenth-century inventor of movable type, brought the written word to the public, and thus is responsible for publishing as it has been known for five hundred years.	Johannes Gutenberg, the fifteenth-century inventor of movable type, brought the written word to the public, and thus is responsible for publishing as it has been known for five hundred years.	Johannes Gutenberg, the fifteenth-century inventor of movable type, brought the written word to the public, and thus is responsible for publishing as it has been known for five hundred years.
JUSTIFIED	**FLUSH LEFT**	**FLUSH RIGHT**	**CENTERED**

Fig. 28.1.

Varying paragraph styles.

Choosing Fonts

A *font* is a set of characters with a specific typeface, size, and weight. You can use different fonts (though not too many different fonts!) in your publication, and you can vary their size and appearance. The printer you use dictates which fonts are available. (See Chapters 8 and 9 on printing.)

Use regular-sized fonts (9 through 12 points) for text. Large font sizes are perfect for headlines, for the nameplate of a publication, for subtitles, and for subheadings. Use small font sizes (8 points and less) only for the "fine print" that isn't crucial; don't ever use large blocks of small text. Many designers find that a series of font sizes are useful for representing relative importance (see fig. 28.2).

Fig. 28.2.
A series of stepped font sizes to show relative levels of importance.

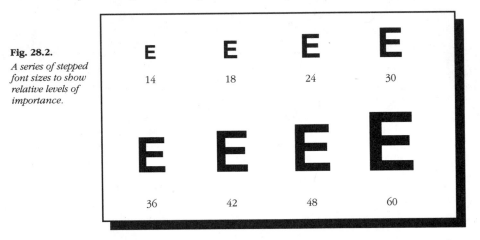

You can use different fonts in addition to font size. Figure 28.3 shows some popular fonts, all in 12-point size. Remember that you should not use too many fonts in a publication, or the publication looks cluttered.

Fig. 28.3.
A variety of 12-point fonts.

This is Baskerville.
This is Century Schoolbook.
This is Garamond Condensed.
This is Garamond Condensed Italic.
This is regular width Helvetica.
This is Helvetica Condensed.
This is Helvetica Condensed Italic.
This is Helvetica Condensed Bold.
This is Helvetica Condensed Black.
This is Palatino.
This is Times Roman.
This is Times Roman Italic.

In addition to varying font size, you can change the appearance of a font. Use variations in font weight to enhance titles and subtitles, adding weight and emphasis. Figure 28.3 shows the difference between regular Helvetica Condensed, Helvetica Condensed Italic, Helvetica Condensed Bold, and Helvetica Condensed Black. Limit the use of font weights within the text to avoid distracting the eye. Italics often can replace both bold and underlined text for emphasis.

Use uppercase and lowercase characters for text and headlines for reading ease. Rely on font size and font weight to indicate relative levels of importance. Reserve uppercase characters and shadow and outline fonts for special effects.

Don't overuse font effects. Sometimes less is more. Your pages look better when you use a few compatible effects than when you try to squeeze in every font in your collection.

Adding Lines and Boxes

With a little extra labor, you can add a lot of graphic impact to a publication by including lines, boxes, and shades.

A common use for vertical lines or rules is to separate columns of text. Use horizontal lines to mark the top and bottom edges of the page, to separate articles, or to border a special area of text. Chapter 27 explains how to create and incorporate lines in a publication.

Boxes add visual variety to a page and usually frame text or graphics. Use a box to set apart the contents of a box from the rest of the text, to emphasize important points (for instance, to highlight quotations or important messages), and to enclose certain types of text. A table of contents, for example, stands out as a separate block of text that's quickly recognized if it's inside a box.

Cue:
Use boxes to visually set off blocks of text or graphics from the rest of the publication.

Creating Special Effects

You can add graphic interest to text subtly but effectively with WordPerfect's built-in text enhancement, line, and box features. For instance, you can turn text into graphics several ways. A commonly used special effect is the pull quote; a *pull quote* is an excerpt from text, set apart for visual interest and emphasis (see fig. 28.4). You can call attention to a pull quote in a variety of ways: make it bold or italicized, stretch it across two or more columns, or put it in a box or between bars.

Large initial caps (sometimes called *drop caps*) are fun and graphical. You can put a single giant letter at the beginning of an article or the start of a pull quote. Separated from the text, enlarged, bold, maybe shadowed, outlined, or italicized, the letter becomes a picture.

Fig. 28.4.

A pull quote.

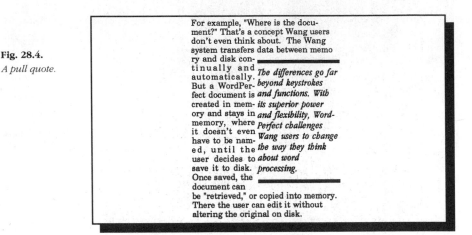

For example, "Where is the document?" That's a concept Wang users don't even think about. The Wang system transfers data between memory and disk continually and automatically. But a WordPerfect document is created in memory and stays in memory, where it doesn't even have to be named, until the user decides to save it to disk. Once saved, the document can be "retrieved," or copied into memory. There the user can edit it without altering the original on disk.

The differences go far beyond keystrokes and functions. With its superior power and flexibility, WordPerfect challenges Wang users to change the way they think about word processing.

Creating and Using "Two-Up" Pages

WordPerfect's Labels feature can be used for more than mailing labels. By using a landscape form and defining two full-page "labels," you can print two pages side-by-side on a single sheet of paper (see fig. 28.5). This format is called a "two-up" page.

WordPerfect treats each page on the physical sheet of paper as a "logical" page. Handle a logical page as you would any other page in WordPerfect. If you include a header or footer, the header or footer appears twice on each physical page: once at the top of each logical page. If you specify a page-number position, the page number appears at the designated location on each logical page.

Cue:

Use two-up pages instead of columns if you want separate page numbers for each logical page printed on the paper.

Because WordPerfect's newspaper-style columns feature has some limitations, you may want to use a two-up definition instead of columns. With columns, for example, you cannot place a separate page number in each column; you *can* with two-up pages.

Fig. 28.5.

A two-up document.

Fall 1989

The Learning Associates Method

Learning Associates is not a seller of pre-packaged or pre-determined solutions. It has been our experience that since:

- Every client's *situation* is unique
- Every client's *problems* are unique
- Every client's *needs* are unique

that the *solution* for every client should also be unique. "One size fits all" is assuredly *not* our philosophy.

It has also been our experience that the knowledge clients have about their own organizations is a valuable resource in planning how to approach each project. Therefore, while we do have a tried and proven *methodology*, we do not try to apply a *formula* to each client's situation. We modify our approach based on the client's perceptions of what is right for the organization.

Project Plan

Learning Associates begins each project with a Project Plan. The Project Plan outlines the activities we propose to undertake to solve the client's problem. It also specifies who needs to be involved from the client in each activity and provides a suggested time line for each activity.

The initial Project Plan is developed from information we have gathered during the process of proposal development. The Project Plan is presented to and reviewed thoroughly with the client. Learning Associates revises the Project Plan in accordance with the client's wishes.

Research

In most projects, the next step after the approval of the revised Project Plan is research. The purpose of this stage is, first, to identify the questions that need to be answered to ensure that the solution works for the client, and second, to find the answers to those questions.

Fall 1989

The specific research activities will vary based on many different factors. Some of the more commonly used techniques employ:

- Management interviews
- Subject matter expert interviews
- Learner interviews (i.e., interviews with potential members of the identified target audience)
- Focus groups
- Survey questionnaires
- Competence testing
- Documentation review

In most projects, the culmination of the research phase is a Research Report, prepared by Learning Associates and presented to the client. The Research Report summarizes our findings, presents our conclusions, and projects implications of the findings for the conclusions.

Program Design

The next stage is the design of the program. This is the most critical phase. A well-thought-out program design leads to a successful solution for the client.

Because of the critical nature of this stage, two or more Learning Associates principals collaborate on each program design. We analyze the research in the light of the client's expressed needs and apply our many years of experience in the design of effective training programs. The result is a document which specifies:

- The overall organization of the recommended training program, including recommended instructional media, major modules, who among the learner population should take each module, and relative size of each module.
- The specific objectives each learner is to achieve in each module, arranged in the order in which they will be mastered.

Creating a Two-Up Paper Definition

This section explains how to create a two-up paper definition with the margins shown in figure 28.5. Change the settings in the procedures if you want pages with different margins. To create a two-up paper definition, follow these steps:

1. Press Format (Shift-F8) and select **P**age (**2**).

   ⌨ Access the **L**ayout menu and select **P**age.

2. Select Paper **S**ize (**7**). The Format: Paper Size/Type menu appears (see fig. 28.6).

```
Format: Paper Size/Type

                                              Font  Double
Paper type and Orientation    Paper Size   Prompt Loc    Type  Sided  Labels

Envelope - Wide               9.5" x 4"    Yes  Manual   Land  No
Labels                        8.5" x 11"   No   Contin   Port  No      3 x 10
Standard                      8.5" x 11"   No   Contin   Port  No
Standard - Wide               11" x 8.5"   No   Contin   Land  No
[ALL OTHERS]                  Width ≤ 8.5" Yes  Manual         No






1 Select; 2 Add; 3 Copy; 4 Delete; 5 Edit; N Name Search: 1
```

Fig. 28.6.

The Format: Paper Size/Type menu.

3. Select **A**dd (**2**). The Format: Paper Type menu appears, listing options like **S**tandard (**1**), **B**ond (**2**), **L**etterhead (**3**), **L**abels (**4**), **E**nvelope (**5**), **T**ransparency (**6**), **C**ardstock (**7**), and **O**ther (**9**). The paper type you select from this menu determines how the two-up definition is identified on the Format: Paper Size/Type menu.

4. Press **O**ther (**9**) from the Format: Paper Type menu. At the `Other form type:` prompt, type *Two-Up Landscape* and press Enter. The Format: Edit Paper Definition menu appears (see fig. 28.7).

```
Format: Edit Paper Definition

       Filename                OKLAS6.PRS

1 - Paper Size                 8.5" x 11"

2 - Paper Type                 Two-Up Landscape

3 - Font Type                  Portrait

4 - Prompt to Load             No

5 - Location                   Continuous

6 - Double Sided Printing      No

7 - Binding Edge               Left

8 - Labels                     No

9 - Text Adjustment - Top      0"
                     Side      0"
```

Fig. 28.7.

The Format: Edit Paper Definition menu.

5. Choose Paper **S**ize (**1**). The Format: Paper Size menu appears (see fig. 28.8).

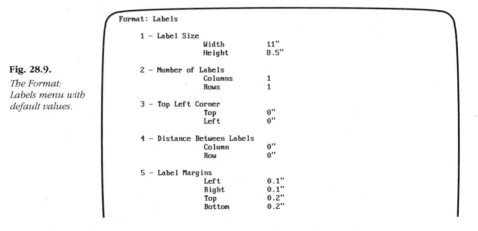

Fig. 28.8.

The Format: Paper Size menu.

```
Format: Paper Size              Width  Height

      1 - Standard              (8.5" x 11")

      2 - Standard Landscape    (11" x 8.5")

      3 - Legal                 (8.5" x 14")

      4 - Legal Landscape       (14" x 8.5")

      5 - Envelope              (9.5" x 4")

      6 - Half Sheet            (5.5" x 8.5")

      7 - US Government         (8" x 11")

      8 - A4                    (210mm x 297mm)

      9 - A4 Landscape          (297mm x 210mm)

      o - Other
```

6. Choose **S**tandard Landscape (**2**). The Format: Edit Paper Definition menu reappears.

7. Choose **F**ont Type (**3**). Select **L**andscape (**2**) from the following menu:

   Orientation: 1 Portrait; **2 L**andscape: **0**

8. Choose La**b**els (**8**) and select **Y**es.

9. The Format: Labels menu appears as shown in figure 28.9. The defaults on this menu vary depending on your printer.

Fig. 28.9.

The Format: Labels menu with default values.

```
Format: Labels

      1 - Label Size
                    Width       11"
                    Height      8.5"

      2 - Number of Labels
                    Columns     1
                    Rows        1

      3 - Top Left Corner
                    Top         0"
                    Left        0"

      4 - Distance Between Labels
                    Column      0"
                    Row         0"

      5 - Label Margins
                    Left        0.1"
                    Right       0.1"
                    Top         0.2"
                    Bottom      0.2"
```

10. Select Label **S**ize (**1**). Type *5* (for Width) and press Enter; type *8.5* (for Height) and press Enter.

11. Select **N**umber of Labels (**2**). Type *2* (for Columns) and press Enter; type *1* (for Rows) and press Enter.

12. Select Top Left **C**orner (**3**). Type *0* (for Top) and press Enter; type *1* (for Left) and press Enter. These settings provide a 1-inch margin on the left side of the paper. Use a decimal (such as *0.75*) for the Left setting if you want a smaller margin.

13. Select **D**istance Between Labels (**4**). Type *0* (for Column) and press Enter; type *0* (for Row) and press Enter.

14. Select Label **M**argins (**5**). Type *0* (for Left) and press Enter; type *1* (for Right) and press Enter; type *0.75* (for Top) and press Enter; type *0.75* (for Bottom) and press Enter.

15. Press Exit (F7). The Format: Edit Paper Definition menu reappears.

    If the paper you intend to use for the logical forms is arranged other than in the standard `Continuous` manner (form-fed paper), or if you want WordPerfect to prompt you to load the paper, you may need to change some settings on this menu. See Chapter 6 for information about the options on this menu.

16. When you finish making changes to the Format: Edit Paper Definition menu, press Exit (F7) three times to return to the document.

The following section explains how to use the new two-up paper definition.

Using Two-Up Pages

To use a two-up page definition, follow these procedures:

1. Place the cursor at the point in the document where you want to start using logical pages. In most cases, this is the beginning of the document. As an alternative, you can put the code to begin two-up pages into Document Initial Codes. See Chapter 6 for information about Document Initial Codes.

2. Press Format (Shift-F8) and select **P**age (**2**).

    ▭ Access the **L**ayout pull-down menu and select **P**age.

3. Select Paper **S**ize (**7**). The Format: Paper Size/Type menu appears (see fig. 28.10).

4. Choose **S**elect (**1**) and press Exit (F7) to return to the editing screen.

```
Format: Paper Size/Type
                                           Font Double
Paper type and Orientation    Paper Size  Prompt Loc  Type Sided Labels

Envelope - Wide               9.5" x 4"    Yes  Manual Land No
Labels                        8.5" x 11"   No   Contin Port No     3 x 10
Standard                      8.5" x 11"   No   Contin Port No
Standard                      8.5" x 11"   No   Contin Port No
Standard - Wide               11" x 8.5"   No   Contin Land No
Two-Up Landscape - Wide       11" x 8.5"   No   Contin Land No     2 x 1
[ALL OTHERS]                  Width ≤ 8.5" Yes  Manual      No




1 Select; 2 Add; 3 Copy; 4 Delete; 5 Edit; N Name Search: 1
```

Fig. 28.10.

The Format: Paper Size/Type menu.

Including Illustrations

In addition to using WordPerfect's text enhancements for graphic interest, you can add illustrations. Chapter 27 explains how to import and manipulate graphics files created in other software packages or included with WordPerfect as clip-art files.

You can include illustrations (graphics and photographs, typically lumped together as "artwork" by designers and printers) in documents in two ways. You can include computer-based charts, graphic elements, illustrations, and even photographs (if the photo has been scanned into the computer) directly into the computer-generated pages from which the copies are made. For unscanned photographs or artwork that is not computer based, you can include defined space (using an empty graphics box, for example) into which you paste the artwork. If the publication is being copied by a printer, ask whether you should paste artwork directly onto the "master" pages or whether you should just identify each piece of artwork and the space into which it goes so that the printer can "strip in" the art for you.

Reminder:

You can get graphics for your publications from drawing programs, spreadsheet programs, or clip-art packages.

Computer art can come from a variety of sources. Many graphics programs, such as Windows Draw, PC Paint, and GEM Paint, can be used to create drawings. Other programs, like the spreadsheet programs 1-2-3, Microsoft Excel, and PlanPerfect, can generate graphs based on data. You can use these drawings and graphs in your publications.

Computer clip-art is another source of graphic images (see fig. 28.11). You can buy packages of computer clip-art from companies like Micrografx, Inc. or DeskTop Art. These images, like the clip-art images supplied by WordPerfect on the PTR Program/ Graphics diskettes, are ready-to-use pictures of various subjects. Many graphics programs, like Lotus Freelance Plus or DrawPerfect, include an extensive library of clip-art.

Fig. 28.11.
Computer clip-art.

Figure 1: This Encapsulated PostScript clip art graphic is from a collection by T/Maker Company.

Figure 2: This Encapsulated PostScript clip art image is from T/Maker Company in Mountain View, California

Another source of graphics is a scanner or digitizer. This equipment "reads" a picture and converts it into a digital format that can be used by WordPerfect.

Understanding Types of Graphics

If you include graphics in your computer-generated pages, you work with one of four file formats: two formats relate to graphics programs, one is for scanned images, and one is used with the page-description language PostScript. Each is described in the following sections.

Vector and Bit-Mapped Images

Graphics programs create two types of images: vector (sometimes called *object-oriented*) images and bit-mapped images. A *vector* graphic is built from lines and shapes (see fig. 28.12); a *bit-mapped* image is composed of dots (see fig. 28.13).

This graphic from the WordPerfect Fonts/Graphics disk is an object-oriented image.

Fig. 28.12.
A vector graphic.

This graphic from the DeskTop Art Collection by Dynamic Graphics, Inc., is a bit-mapped image.

Fig. 28.13.
A bit-mapped graphic.

Vector graphics are composed of straight lines, curves, boxes, polygons, and other shapes that can be either empty or filled. Once drawn, a box is forever a box, made up of sides, corners, and sometimes a fill. You can change the box's size or shape, you can change the style of its lines, and you can change its fill. You cannot cut away

Reminder:
You can change the size and shape of vector graphics.

the box's corner because the corner is part of the box's identity. The graphics supplied on the WordPerfect PTR Program/Graphics diskette are vector images.

Graphics files from 1-2-3, MGI PicturePak, Symphony, DrawPerfect, and Freelance Plus are vector files and can be imported directly into WordPerfect. Table 28.1 lists other programs and the format into which the file must be exported if you want to use the files with WordPerfect.

Table 28.1
Graphics Programs

Program	Exported Format
1-2-3 1A, 2.0, 2.2	PIC (Lotus 1-2-3 PIC Format)
1-2-3 3.0	PCX (PC Paintbrush PCX Format), CGM (Computer Graphics Metafile)
Adobe Illustrator	EPS (Encapsulated PostScript)
Anvil-5000	HPGL (Hewlett-Packard Graphics Language Plotter File)
Arts & Letters	CGM
AutoCAD 9.0, 10.0	HPGL, DXF*
AutoSketch 1.03	HPGL, DXF*
Boeing Graph 4.0	IMG (GEM Paint IMG Format)
CCS Designer	HPGL
ChartMaster 6.21	HPGL
Chemfile 11	HPGL
Chemtext	EPS
CIES (Compuscan)	TIFF (Tagged Image File Format)
DesignCAD	HPGL, DXF*
DesignCAD 3D	HPGL, DXF*
Designer 1.2 (Micrografx)	HPGL
Designer 2.0 (Micrografx)	CGM, EPS, PCX, TIFF
DFI Handy Scanner	IMG, TIFF
DIAGRAM MASTER 5.02	HPGL
Diagraph	HPGL
Dr. HALO II, III	DHP
DrawPerfect	CGM, HPGL, WPG (WordPerfect Graphics)
Easyflow 4.4	HPGL
Energraphics 2.1	IMG, TIFF
Freelance Plus 2.0, 3.0	CGM
GEM Draw	GEM
GEM Paint 2.0	IMG, TIFF
GEM Scan	IMG, TIFF
Generic CAD	HPGL
GeniScan	TIFF
Graph-in-the-Box 2.0	HPGL
Graph Plus 1.3 (Micrografx)	CGM, EPS, HPGL, PCX, TIFF

Table 28.1 (continued)

Program	Exported Format
Graphics Editor 200	HPGL
GraphWriter	CGM
Harvard Graphics 2.1	HPGL, CGM, EPS
HIJAAK	WPG
HOTSHOT Graphics 1.5	WPG
HP Graphics Gallery	TIFF, PCX
HP Scanning Gallery A.01	TIFF, PCX
IBM CADAM	HPGL
IBM CATIA	HPGL
IBM CBDS	HPGL
IBM GDDM	HPGL
IBM GPG	HPGL
MacPaint	PNTG
Microsoft Chart	HPGL
Mirage	HPGL
Paradox	PIC
PC Paint + 1.5, 2.0	PIC
PC Paintbrush	PCX
PicturePak	CGM, PCX, WPG
Pixie	CGM
Pizazz 1.01	PCX, TIFF
PlanPerfect 3.0, 5.0	CGM
PFS: First Publisher	PCX
Reflex 2.0	PIC
Quattro	PIC, EPS
SAS/Graph	HPGL
ScanMan	TIFF
Schema	HPGL
SIGN-MASTER 5.11	HPGL
SlideWrite Plus	HPGL, TIFF, PCX
SuperCalc 4	PIC
Symphony	PIC
Versacad	HPGL
VGA Paint	WPG, PCX, TIFF
VP Graphics	HPGL
VP Planner	PIC
Windows Draw	HPGL
Windows Paint	MSP
Words & Figures	PIC

* DXF files must be processed by the GRAPHCNV program supplied with WordPerfect
  before they can be used in WordPerfect.

Reminder:

You cannot change the size and shape of bit-mapped graphics.

Bit-mapped graphics are composed of dots. Although a bit-mapped box is drawn the same way and looks the same as a vector box, it behaves differently. The bit-mapped box is not a whole object; rather, it is a series of dots arranged in the shape of a box. You cannot change the size, shape, or border style of the box. If you want to change the box, you must erase it and draw a new box.

Reminder:

Once imported into WordPerfect, bit-mapped and vector graphics can be scaled and moved.

Once part of a WordPerfect file, both vector and bit-mapped graphics can be edited. They can be scaled larger or smaller, and they can be moved around inside a box. Both types of images can be rotated or mirrored; bit-mapped graphics can be inverted. Chapter 27 explains how to edit a graphics file.

TIFF Files

TIFF (Tagged Image File Format) is used by most scanning equipment. TIFF is a special format that enables scanners to register gray scales on a photograph. TIFF files are usually extremely large; they can be slow and awkward to work with and extremely slow to print. For these reasons, many desktop publishers prefer to treat photographs conventionally, leaving a space in the publication for the printer to add (or strip in) a prepared photograph.

WordPerfect can accept TIFF files directly without any special conversion process.

> **Tip**
>
> If you want to include a scanned image for the proofing and approval stages of a document but avoid the size and speed crunches, scan the photograph with reduced gray scaling (most scanners let you set the gray scale to level 2 or 4). Use the scanned image for review stages and have the printer strip in the photo for the final copies.

EPS Files

EPS (Encapsulated PostScript) files are produced by some advanced graphics programs like Adobe Illustrator. PostScript is a page-description language used by some laser printers and typesetting machines. You can print an EPS graphic at very high resolution (up to 2400 dots per inch) on typesetting equipment that supports PostScript. You cannot print an EPS graphic if you do not have a PostScript printer.

Converting Graphics Files with GRAPHCNV.EXE

WordPerfect supplies a program for converting graphic files in other formats to WordPerfect's WPG file. The GRAPHCNV.EXE (GRAPHics CoNVersion) program is installed from the Install/Learn/Utility diskette using the Install program (see Appendix A).

GRAPHCNV.EXE is the only way that you can use files in certain formats, such as the AutoCAD DXF format. Processing any graphics file through GRAPHCNV.EXE, however, results in a smaller file that WordPerfect can load faster than the original file.

To use GRAPHCNV.EXE, exit from WordPerfect to the DOS command line. To convert a file using GRAPHCNV.EXE, follow these steps:

1. Change to the directory where GRAPHCNV.EXE is located or make sure that the directory in which GRAPHCNV.EXE is located is in your DOS path.

2. Type *GRAPHCNV* and press Enter.

3. When prompted for the name of the file to be converted, type the file name—including the path (if the file isn't in the current directory) and the extension—and press Enter.

4. If a file with that name and a WPG extension already exists in the current directory, GRAPHCNV.EXE asks whether it can replace the existing file. Press Y to confirm.

GRAPHCNV.EXE processes the specified file and reports when finished. The converted file has the same name as the original file with a WPG extension.

You can use several options with GRAPHCNV.EXE. These options are executed by typing a *switch*—a slash (/) and some additional text—after you type *GRAPHCNV* in step 2 (for example, type *GRAPHCNV /b=2*). Following are some of the switches you can use:

Cue:
Use GRAPHCNV.EXE to make smaller any graphics files already compatible with WordPerfect.

Switch	Description
Note: You can type the switches in either uppercase or lowercase letters.	
/b=#	Sets background color for a WPG file. # can be any of the following values: 0 = Black 1 = Blue 2 = Green 3 = Cyan 4 = Red 5 = Magenta 6 = Brown 7 = White If you do not specify a color, the default background color is intense white.
/c=w	Converts all color values to white. This option can be used with vector files only.
/c=b	Converts all color values to black. This option can be used with vector files only.
/c=2	Converts color values to monochrome (black & white).
/c=16	Converts color values to the WordPerfect standard 16-color palette.
/c=256	Converts color values to the WordPerfect standard 256-color palette. Use this option if you have a graphics adapter capable of displaying 256 colors.
/g=16	Converts color values to the WordPerfect standard 16-shades-of-gray palette.
/g=256	Converts color values to the 16-shades-of-gray palette present in the WordPerfect standard 256-color palette. Use this option if you have a graphics adapter capable of displaying 256 colors.

Using WordPerfect as a Desktop Publisher

The most important guideline to remember when you use WordPerfect as a desktop publishing program is *simplicity.* You can use WordPerfect to create columns of text, different text sizes, and special text effects, and you can create a great variety of shaded figures, framed graphics, horizontal bars, and vertical rules. Although all these features are available, use discretion when selecting the features you use.

Some operations are more difficult in WordPerfect than in dedicated desktop publishing programs such as PageMaker or Ventura Publisher. The process of creating graphics, for example, is not visual: you cannot arbitrarily draw a line from one point on the page to another. You need to know beforehand exactly where the line is to appear, and how long and wide the line should be. For this reason, you must plan your publication carefully. With WordPerfect, experimentation is sometimes difficult.

Once you decide on the placement of a graphic, you begin the three-part creation process. As explained in Chapter 27, to draw a box, you access the Graphics Definition menu and go through several steps to define the size, shape, location, and contents of the box. You return to the document, and finally, you use View Document to see the box as it will appear when printed.

Another area of potential difficulty is in the way WordPerfect presents graphics on-screen. When you work on a document, you don't see the page as it appears when you print the page. Instead, you see a *representation* of the page. A graphic, for example, appears on-screen as an outline (even the outline doesn't appear until you move the cursor beyond the place on the page where you placed the graphic). You *can* preview the page by using Print View, however.

A final area of difficulty is in editing. Once you lay out a page, some changes can be difficult to make. To change a line, for example, you must use Reveal Codes, find the code for the line—not an easy process if you have a lot of lines on the page—press Graphics (Alt-F9), and edit the line. Finally, you should return to the document and use View Document to check the appearance of the line. If the line still isn't right, you must repeat the process.

Getting the Most from WordPerfect as a Desktop Publisher

Because of the difficulties described in the preceding section, desktop publishing with WordPerfect can be a very slow process. Yet WordPerfect has desktop publishing power, and you can use WordPerfect to produce successful documents. If you understand WordPerfect well, know how codes work, and are pretty good at troubleshooting, give desktop publishing with WordPerfect a try. Keep in mind two guiding principles: simplicity and preplanning.

The following tips show how to get the most from WordPerfect as a desktop publishing tool:

- Practice using graphics, columns, and fonts before you begin a serious publishing project.

- Familiarize yourself with all the codes you plan to use. Understand how to apply codes and what codes look like. Use Reveal Codes to ferret out areas of trouble.

- Before you begin the design, look carefully at publications similar to the one you are planning. See what looks best and evaluate why the publication works. Make a sketch of the page layout before you start.

- Keep the layout simple. Decide in advance how many pages your publication will contain, what regular features you will include, and what types of graphics (photos, clip-art, graphs) you will use.

- Design columns of text to extend the full length of the page. This layout is easier to create and edit than creating a three-column article on the top of the page and another three-column article on the bottom of the page.

- Because WordPerfect is a linear program, think about working through your document step-by-step. Be careful to keep codes and graphics in the correct position on the page. When you insert a code to turn on a feature, for example, the feature affects only the text following the code. Look for out-of-place codes when you run into difficulties.

- Plan graphics (lines and boxes) to line up with a margin or column or to be centered on the page. Placing graphics this way is easier than placing them a specific distance from some element on the page.

- Place the graphics first when you lay out a page and let text wrap around them.

- Use relative tabs if you use tabbed paragraphs in a multicolumn layout.

- Use View Document frequently to check your progress. Don't assume that your page will look the way you think it will.

Developing a Template

Because some publications are published periodically and have a consistent design, you can save time by developing a template to use with each issue. A *template* is like a publication stripped bare of its contents. For instance, a template for a newsletter can include the nameplate on page 1, the columns for the text, headers and footers, box definitions, and anything else that repeats from issue to issue. A template saves you the time of reconstructing each of these elements whenever you produce an issue.

Give your template an obvious name, like NLTEMP. When you're ready to develop the summer issue, for example, retrieve the file NLTEMP and resave it as NLSUMMER. That way, your template remains intact for use with the next issue.

Cue:

Create a template if you use the same formats for periodically published documents.

Placing Graphics

You should place *page-type* boxes, which are anchored to a margin or column and must stay in position on the page, on the page before you type (or retrieve) text. You can create the graphics in the appropriate size and location on the page and let text wrap around them. If you have too much material on the page, you can delete some text or reduce the box size. If you don't have enough material, you can enlarge a box or create a pull quote in a separate box.

You should not place *paragraph-type* boxes, which are anchored to specific paragraphs, on the page first. Instead, create this type of box when you type (or retrieve) the paragraph to which it belongs. This type of box can move on the page (to a different column or even a different page) if you add or delete text later.

Adding Text

You can add text to your publication in two ways: type text directly or retrieve a previously created file. You may find it easier to create the text files independently so that you can make most editing changes before you place text. The final step in the production process is then the assembly of the text files. Remember that extensive editing can throw off formatting.

Cue:
Do all character formatting before you import a text file into a publication, or use a style to format text.

If you choose to retrieve text files you have already created, do all character formatting before you retrieve the files. You can even set up a style (containing font and formatting choices) to create the individual files (styles are explained in Chapter 15). If you decide to type the text, simply position the cursor and begin typing.

Creating a Newsletter

A newsletter is a publication issued monthly, bimonthly, quarterly, or at other intervals. A newsletter has an underlying theme or purpose and usually contains timely information. Many clubs and associations publish newsletters to make their members aware of past and upcoming events. Businesses use newsletters to keep in touch with clients or employees. Subscription newsletters often provide high-value information to subscribers who are willing to pay for the service.

Most newsletters are formatted with a large nameplate (sometimes known as the *masthead* or *banner*) at the top of page 1; have text arranged in at least two columns; and have graphic enhancements such as lines, boxes, illustrations, photographs, and special text treatments. Newsletters commonly use a consistent design for every issue, and most include repetitive text elements such as a table of contents, an editorial from the club president, a new-product-announcement section, or a monthly calendar. Most newsletters are printed on regular letter-size paper.

Figure 28.14 is an example of a newsletter. Notice that the following special graphic techniques are used to give the *WordPerfect Training Newsletter* greater visual appeal:

- Title of the newsletter in large print across the top of page
- The date of the issue and the publisher's name enclosed between horizontal rules

- Narrow rules between columns
- Asymmetrical column layout
- Pull quote in a Text box
- Three-column format
- Text in Century Schoolbook; pull quotes in Garamond Condensed Italic; headlines in Helvetica Condensed Black
- One or two articles on page 1 (articles can continue on subsequent pages)

Fig. 28.14.
A sample newsletter.

A template was created for the *WordPerfect Training Newsletter* that includes the format settings (margin, base font, binding offset), a nameplate, a subtitle, a title placeholder, newspaper-style text columns, and box definitions. Defining the boxes in a template provides a consistent set of graphic-box styles to use in your publication.

Table 28.2 shows the specifications for the sample newsletter.

Table 28.2
Newsletter

Element	Option	Setting		
Format: Line	Hyphenation		Auto	
	Justification		No	
	Margins	Left	0.625"	
		Right	0.625"	
	Line Spacing		1	
Format: Other	Printer	Leading Primary	-1 pt.	
		Leading Secondary	-1 pt.	
Printer: Options	Binding		0.125"	
Columns	Type		Newspaper	
	Number		3	
	Margins	Column	Left	Right
		1	0.75"	2.1"
		2	2.4"	5.1"
		3	5.3"	8"
Fonts	Text		Century Schoolbook, 11 pt.	
	Nameplate		Century Schoolbook, 36 pt.	
	Nameplate		Century Schoolbook Ital., 36 pt.	
	Trademark®		Century Schoolbook, 22 pt.	
	Footer		Century Schoolbook, 9 pt.	
	Headline		Helvetica Cond. Black, 24 pt.	
	Lead Paragraph		Garamond Cond. Ital., 13 pt.	
	Lead Paragraph		Garamond Cond. Bold Ital., 13 pt.	
	"Continued" Paragraph		Garamond Cond. Bold Ital., 13 pt.	
	Table of Contents		Garamond Cond. Ital., 12 pt.	
	Pull Quote		Garamond Cond. Ital., 13 pt.	
	Pointing Finger		Glyphix Zingbats, 14 pt.	

Lines

Element	Option	Setting
Horizontal Line	Horizontal Position	Full
	Length of Line	WP calculates
	Width of Line	0.013"
Vertical Line	Horizontal Position	Column 1
	Vertical Position	2.12"
	Length of Line	WP calculates
	Width of Line	0.013"

Table 28.2 (continued)

Element	Option	Setting	
Text Box 1: Nameplate			
Text Box Options	Border Style	Left	Single
		Right	Single
		Top	Thick
		Bottom	Thick
	Outside Border Space	Left	0"
		Right	0.167"
		Top	0.167"
		Bottom	0.05"
	Inside Border Space	Left	0.167"
		Right	0.167"
		Top	0.167"
		Bottom	0"
	Gray Shading		10%
Creation Options	Contents		Text
	Anchor Type		Page
	Vertical Position		Top
	Horizontal Position		Margin, Full
	Size		WP calculates
User Box 1: Headline			
User Box Options	Border Style		None (all sides)
	Outside Border Space		0.167" (all sides)
	Inside Border Space		0" (all sides)
	Gray Shading		0%
Creation Options	Contents		Text
	Anchor Type		Page
	Vertical Position		2.12"
	Horizontal Position		Column(s) 2-3, Full
	Size		WP calculates
Table Box 1: Pull Quote			
Table Box Options	Border Style	Left	None
		Right	None
		Top	Thick
		Bottom	Thick
	Outside Border Space	Left	0.05"
		Right	0.167"
		Top	0.05"
		Bottom	0.05"
	Inside Border Space	Left	0"
		Right	0"
		Top	01"
		Bottom	0.05"
	Gray Shading		0%

Table 28.2 (continued)

Element	Option	Setting
Creation Options	Contents	Text
	Anchor Type	Paragraph
	Vertical Position	0.7"
	Horizontal Position	Right
	Size	WP calculates

Creating a Two-Fold Brochure

Like a newsletter, a brochure is designed to inform readers about a business, product, service, organization, program, or event. Unlike a newsletter, a brochure is short—usually not more than a single piece of paper printed on both sides. Because a brochure is brief, its message is concise and direct. A brochure is less time-sensitive than a periodical; typically it contains information, but not news. A brochure, usually a one-time-only publication, is intended to promote one idea one time.

Most often, a brochure is smaller than a single sheet of letter-size paper, and very often, the format of a brochure is a variation on that single sheet of paper. A common format is the two-fold brochure: a letter-size piece of paper printed horizontally and folded twice to form a three-panel piece that fits neatly into a standard business envelope.

You can use WordPerfect's desktop publishing tools to produce a two-fold brochure such as the one shown in figures 28.15A and figure 28.15B.

Fig. 28.15A.

A brochure created on a standard letter-size piece of paper.

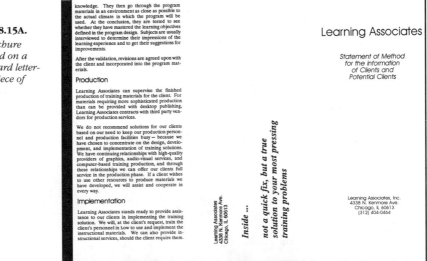

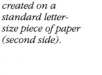

The Learning Associates Method

Learning Associates is not a seller of prepackaged or predetermined solutions. It has been our experience that because ...

- Every client's *situation* is unique
- Every client's *problems* are unique
- Every client's *needs* are unique

... the *solution* for every client should also be unique. "One size fits all" is assuredly *not* our philosophy.

It has also been our experience that the knowledge clients have about their own organizations is a valuable resource in planning how to approach each project. Therefore, although we do have a tried and proven *methodology*, we do not try to apply a *formula* to each client's situation. We modify our approach based on the client's perceptions of what is right for the organization.

Project Plan

Learning Associates begins each project with a Project Plan. The Project Plan outlines the activities we propose to undertake to solve the client's problem. It also specifies who needs to be involved from the client in each activity and provides a suggested time line for each activity.

The initial Project Plan is developed from information we have gathered during the process of proposal development. The Project Plan is presented to and reviewed thoroughly with the client. Learning Associates revises the Project Plan in accordance with the client's wishes.

Research

In most projects, the next step after the approval of the revised Project Plan is research. The pur-

pose of this stage is, first, to identify the questions that need to be answered to ensure that the solution works for the client, and second, to find the answers to those questions.

The specific research activities will vary based on many different factors. Some of the more commonly used techniques employ:

- Management interviews
- Subject matter expert interviews
- Learner interviews (i.e., interviews with potential members of the identified target audience)
- Focus groups
- Survey questionnaires
- Competence testing
- Documentation review

In most projects, the culmination of the research phase is a Research Report, prepared by Learning Associates and presented to the client. The Research Report summarizes our findings, presents our conclusions, and projects implications of the findings for the conclusions.

Program Design

The next stage is the design of the program. This is the most critical phase. A well-thought-out program design leads to a successful solution for the client.

Because of the critical nature of this stage, two or more Learning Associates principals collaborate on each program design. We analyze the research in the light of the client's expressed needs and apply our many years of experience in the design of effective training programs. The result is a document which specifies:

- The overall organization of the recommended training program, including recommended instructional media, major modules, who among the learner population should take each module, and relative size of each module.

- The specific objectives each learner is to achieve in each module, arranged in the order in which they will be mastered.
- A detailed description of the instructional events that will take place to enable the learner to achieve each objective.
- A detailed list of the instructional materials that will be supplied to enable each instructional event to occur.
- An outline of the content that the learner must master to achieve each objective.

In projects for which the research and design phase has been budgeted and proposed separately, the program design is accompanied by a proposal for the development, validation, production, and implementation of the recommended instructional materials.

The program design (and the proposal, if appropriate) is presented to the client and exhaustively reviewed. Changes are made in accordance with the client's wishes.

Development

In the development phase, the instructional materials specified in the Project Plan are developed in draft form. The materials can include instructor guides, learner materials, audio or video scripts, overhead transparencies, job aids, reference materials, and many other types of documents.

All materials are submitted to the client for review. For all but the smallest projects, materials are developed and submitted in stages, to give the client the opportunity to see how the work is progressing. Revisions are incorporated at the client's direction.

Validation

The process of validation involves "trying out" the draft materials on typical members of the target learner group. In most validations, subjects are pre-tested to determine their entry-level skill and

Fig. 28.15B.

A brochure created on a standard letter-size piece of paper (second side).

Because you fold the paper to create the brochure, notice the layout. Use landscape mode to print the document sideways on the paper. (To print in landscape, your printer must support rotated text or have a landscape font.)

Each page of the brochure has three columns, and each column makes up one panel of the brochure. You can use newspaper-style columns to create the columns, or you can create a three-up form using the techniques described in "Creating and Using Two-Up Pages" earlier in this chapter. If you're creating a brochure as a one-time project, you can save time by using newspaper-style columns. If you plan to produce a number of two-fold brochures, you may save time by working with a three-up form.

When you fold the paper on which the brochure is printed, the following occurs:

Column 1 becomes the inside panel.

Column 2 becomes the back panel.

Column 3 becomes the front panel.

Columns 4, 5, and 6 on the second side become inside panels.

When you create a brochure, make a sketch to check the layout. If you create many brochures, you can, as with the newsletter, create a template you can use again.

Table 28.3 shows the specifications for the brochure shown in figures 28.15A and 28.15B.

Reminder:

Print a brochure in landscape mode if your printer supports rotated text or has a landscape font.

Table 28.3
Brochure

Element	Option		Setting
Format: Line	Margins	Left	0.5"
		Right	0.5"
	Justification		Full
	Hyphenation		On
	Hyphenation Zone	Left	5%
		Right	4%
	Tab Set		Relative, 0", 0.25"
Format: Page	Paper Size/Type		11" x 8.5", Standard
	Margins	Top	0.75"
		Bottom	0.5"
Format: Other	Leading	Primary	-1 pt.
		Secondary	-2 pt.
Columns	Type		Newspaper
	Number		3
	Distance Between Columns		0.5"
Fonts	Text		Times Roman, 10 pt.
			Times Roman Ital., 10 pt
	Brochure Title		Avant Garde, 24 pt.
	Brochure Subtitle		Avant Garde Ital., 14 pt.
	Main Title		Avant Garde Bold, 18 pt.
	Subtitles		Avant Garde Bold, 14 pt.

Panel 2: User-Defined Box 1

Note: This panel was created as a graphic image because the printer cannot print portrait and landscape fonts on the same page.

User-defined	Border Style	None
	Outside Border Space	0.167" on all sides
	Inside Border Space	0"
Creation Options	Type	Page
	Vertical Position	Center
	Horizontal Position	Column 2, Center
	Size	0.75" wide x 6.42" high

Creating a Form

Using a combination of WordPerfect's lines, boxes, and text, you can create useful forms for many business applications. Make forms such as membership applications, order forms, invoices, account statements, registration forms, and many more. For instance, you can create the order form in figure 28.16 using WordPerfect. .

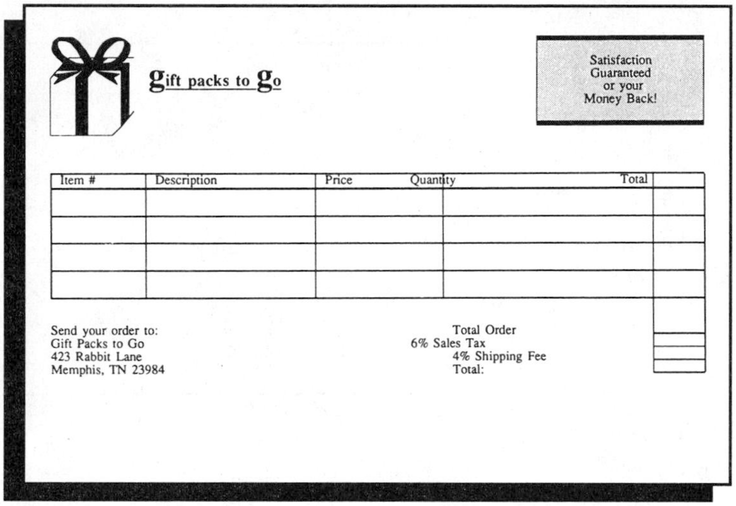

Gift packs to Go

Satisfaction Guaranteed or your Money Back!

Item #	Description	Price	Quantity	Total

Send your order to:
Gift Packs to Go
423 Rabbit Lane
Memphis, TN 23984

Total Order
6% Sales Tax
4% Shipping Fee
Total:

Fig. 28.16.
An order form.

To save copying costs, print a half-page form twice on the same page; the print shop then can cut between the forms. If your form is an invoice or a statement, you may want to take the form to a commercial printer and duplicate it on multipart paper or pin-feed perforated paper that rolls through an impact printer.

Cue:
Save printing costs by printing a half-page form twice on one page.

You create the form with intersecting lines, rather than graphic boxes, because you cannot create a line inside a box. To match the lines exactly, you must measure the lengths of some of the lines and create the lines to that precise length.

To create your own form, review the specifications in table 28.4 used to create the form in figure 28.16.

Table 28.4
Order Form

Element	*Option*		*Setting*
Format: Line	Margins	Left	0.37"
		Right	0.37"
Format: Page	Margins	Top	0.37"
		Bottom	0.37"
Text	Type, use tabs to space column headings		
Title	Font	Size	*G*s: Extra Large
		Size	Other text: Large
		Appearance	Underlined (except *G*s)

Table 28.4 (continued)

Element	Option	Setting
Figure 1: Logo		
Figure Options	Border Style	None
	Outside Border Space	0"
	Inside Border Space	0"
Creation Options	Filename	PRESENT.WPG
	Type	Page
	Vertical Position	Top
	Horizontal Position	Margin, Left
	Size	Width 1"
Text Box 1: Satisfaction Guaranteed Box		
Text Box Options	Border	Left Single
		Right Single
		Top Thick
		Bottom Thick
	Gray Shading	10%
Creation Options	Type	Page
	Horizontal Position	Margin, Right
	Size	Width 2"
	Edit	Type text
Lines		
Horizontal Lines	Horizontal Position	Place cursor Left & Right
	Width of line	0.01"
Vertical Lines	Horizontal Position	Place cursor, Set position
	Vertical Position	Place cursor, Set position
	Length	Place cursor, Set position
Short Lines	Horizontal Position	Place cursor, Right

Creating an Annual Report

To create an annual report, a manual, or any other document that contains many pages divided into several sections, you can use a number of WordPerfect features to make your job easier.

Figures 28.17A and 28.17B show the first two pages of an annual report created with WordPerfect. The specifications for this report are shown in table 28.5. Page 1 includes the company logo and the title of the report; the report includes figure boxes used for photographs (pasted in later) and table boxes used for charts (imported from a graphics program).

Fig. 28.17A.
Page 1 of an annual report.

Table 28.5
Annual Report

Element	Option		Setting
Format: Line	Hyphenation		No
	Justification		Yes
	Margins	Left	1.25"
		Right	1.25"
	Widow/Orphan		Yes
Format: Page	Margins	Top	1.5"
		Bottom	1.5"
Print: Options	Binding		0.25"
Text	Text file		
*G*s in Title	Font	Size	Extra Large
		Appearance	Bold

Fig. 28.17B.

Page 2 of an annual report.

Gift baskets from Gift Packs to Go come in several varieties. One of our simplest baskets includes a bottle of fine wine from Napa Valley's famed Domaine Chandon vineyards. Along with the wine, the basket includes two flute glasses, a package of rich butter cookies, and a jar of delicious Kozlowski farms raspberry preserves. Like all our baskets, this one also includes napkins and a butter knife for spreading the preserves. In fact, all our baskets include everything you need for a picnic or a snack. Other baskets include delicacies such as fine cheeses, cookies, crackers, wines, fruit preserves, and tinned foods such as caviar and kippered herring.

We ship our gift packs anywhere in the world. For continental deliveries, we guarantee three-day service, so you can be sure your gift pack arrives fresh and on time. Overseas deliveries are made within a week. Of course, if you like, we'll include a card from you.

A Successful New Idea

Gift Packs to Go is a new idea, and it's an idea that's been very successful in our first three years of operation--as you'll see when you open our third annual report and look at our sales charts. Growth has been steady and well-paced, allowing us to continue offering dependable products and service.

We thank you for your support, and look forward to sharing our success with you long into the future.

Gift Packs to Go is a new way to shop for gifts. It saves you time, because you shop by mail or by telephone. It saves you money, because all our gift baskets are very reasonably priced. And, when you choose any of our tantalizing gift baskets, you can be sure you're purchasing a gift that your special someone will truly appreciate.

Sales Have Increased Steadily in Our First Three Years

Gift Packs to Go is a new idea, and it's an idea that's been very successful in our first three years of operation--as you'll see when you open our third annual report and look at our sales charts. Growth has been steady and well-paced, allowing us to continue offering dependable products and service.

We thank you for your support, and look forward to sharing our success with you long into the future.

Gift baskets from Gift Packs to Go come in several varieties. One of our simplest baskets includes a bottle of fine wine from Napa Valley's famed Domaine Chandon vineyards. Along with the wine, the basket includes two flute glasses, a package of rich butter cookies, and a jar of delicious Kozlowski farms raspberry preserves. Like all our baskets, this one also includes napkins and a butter knife for spreading the preserves. In fact, all our baskets include everything you need for a picnic or a snack. Other baskets include delicacies such as fine cheeses, cookies, crackers, wines, fruit preserves, and tinned foods such as caviar and kippered herring.

Page 2   *Gift Packs to Go*

Table 28.5 (continued)

Element	Option		Setting
Rest of Title	Font	Size	Large
		Appearance	Underlined
New sections	Start on odd-numbered page		
	Copy title		
Footnotes	Font	Appearance	Italic
	Even		Page, Flush Right, Logo
	Odd		Title, Flush Right, Page
Figure Options	Border Style		Single
	Outside Border Space		0.16"
	Inside Border Space		0.16"
	Caption		Italic, no numbering

Table 28.5 (continued)

Element	Option	Setting
Table Options	Border Style	Single
	Outside Border Space	0.16"
	Inside Border Space	0.16"
	Caption	Chart 1, numbering

User-defined Box 1: Logo

Element	Option	Setting
User-defined Options	Border Style	None
	Outside Border Space	0"
	Inside Border Space	0"
Creation Options	Filename	PRESENT.WPG
	Type	Page
	Vertical Position	Top
	Horizontal Position	Margin, Center
	Size	Width 2"

Summary

Not long ago, desktop publishing—the ability to create publications using a desktop computer—revolutionized two major industries: the computer industry and the publishing industry. In its early days, desktop publishing stood alone. Word processing was a separate, but related, part of the publishing process. With WordPerfect 5.1, word processing and desktop publishing join hands. Although dedicated desktop publishing programs have their place, in this chapter you have seen some examples of what you can do with WordPerfect.

This chapter has provided the following information that you can use to develop your publications:

❑ Design guidelines you should review before planning and designing a publication

❑ Techniques to enhance your publication, including how to use two-up pages, columns, paragraphs, fonts, and special effects

❑ Information about the four types of graphic files you may encounter and which formats are compatible with WordPerfect 5.1

❑ Instructions for using the GRAPHCNV.EXE program to convert incompatible graphics files to WordPerfect graphics files

❑ Guidelines you can follow to create a newsletter, a two-fold brochure, a form, and an annual report

A

WordPerfect 5.1 Installation and Startup

This appendix introduces you to WordPerfect's installation program and explains the various start-up options you can choose to add to the basic command for starting the program. For additional information, see your WordPerfect manual.

Installing WordPerfect

WordPerfect Corporation has designed the installation program, INSTALL.EXE, to simplify—and demystify—your preparation for running WordPerfect 5.1. The procedure is self-explanatory; follow the prompts and menus and you should not experience any problems. You *must* use INSTALL.EXE to install WordPerfect 5.1 to diskettes or a hard disk. The following list of steps summarizes the installation procedure:

1. Insert the Install/Learn/Utilities 1 diskette in drive A.
2. Change to drive A, type *INSTALL* and press Enter.
3. Answer Yes to continue installation.
4. Answer Yes to install to a hard disk or No to install to floppy diskettes. (**Note:** It is strongly recommended that you use a hard disk to run WordPerfect 5.1.)
5. From the main installation menu, select the type of installation you want to perform. Table A.1 describes each of the six available choices.

   Most WordPerfect 5.1 users can choose the Basic installation, which is the most straightforward. Install makes sure that all files are copied to your diskettes or hard disk. If you are an experienced WordPerfect user, you may want to choose the Custom installation. Network managers will want to choose the Network installation.

6. Follow the screen prompts, placing the appropriate disk in drive A as directed.

Table A.1
Installation Options for WordPerfect 5.1

Choice	Description
Basic	Install WordPerfect in a standard manner to either floppy diskettes or a hard disk. If you install to a hard disk, all files are copied to the \WP51 subdirectory the installation program creates on the hard disk. Learn files, which WordPerfect Corporation provides as a tutorial, are copied to a new directory called \WP51\LEARN.
Custom	Install WordPerfect to directories you specify. The installation program creates the directories. You are presented with a menu from which to install individual sections of WordPerfect.
Network	Similar to Custom installation; in addition, Network installation allows creation of an environment file in the \WP51 subdirectory for specifying type of network and location of setup files.
Printer	Installs a new printer for use by WordPerfect.
Update	Copies files from new or updated WordPerfect disks.
Copy Disks	Copies all files from any WordPerfect 5.1 disk. Use this option if you want to copy ALL printer files to hard disk.

7. Note that Install modifies the CONFIG.SYS and AUTOEXEC.BAT files.

   For WordPerfect 5.1 to operate correctly, the CONFIG.SYS file must contain the directive FILES=20, which enables DOS to have up to 20 files open at one time. If the CONFIG.SYS file does not contain this directive, Install adds it. If the root directory of your hard disk does not contain a CONFIG.SYS file, the program creates the file and adds the FILES=20 directive.

   If your AUTOEXEC.BAT file does not contain the PATH statement PATH=C:\WP51, Install adds it. If this file already contains a PATH statement, Install adds ;C:\WP51\; to it. If the AUTOEXEC.BAT file does not exist, Install creates it and adds the PATH statement.

8. Install a printer for WordPerfect 5.1.

9. Enter your registration number (see the registration card in your WordPerfect binder).

After installation is complete, remove the installation disk from drive A and reboot the computer by pressing Ctrl-Alt-Del. You must reboot the computer to activate the changes in CONFIG.SYS and AUTOEXEC.BAT. To start WordPerfect, type *wp* at the DOS prompt and press Enter.

Considering Startup Options

When you start WordPerfect, you can add to the WP command information to alter WordPerfect's operation with various *startup options*. Most of these options begin with the slash character (/) and consist of one or more letters. For some options, you must provide extra information, such as a name. In these cases, the option is followed by a hyphen or equal sign and the extra data. You can type this information in either uppercase or lowercase letters, and you can combine some options.

Table A.2 describes WordPerfect's startup options.

Table A.2
Startup Options for WordPerfect 5.1

Option	Description
/cp=codepage	Lets you automatically set your keyboard and ASCII character set to a foreign language. For example, WP /CP=863 starts WordPerfect and specifies the keyboard and ASCII character set for Canadian French.
/d-drive\directory	Puts WordPerfect temporary files in the drive and directory you specify.
filename	Retrieves a document (*filename*) upon startup. For example, the command WP LETTER.TXT starts WordPerfect and immediately retrieves the file LETTER.TXT.
/f2	Used to correct problems with the screen display for video adapters that display more than 25 rows and 80 columns of text. If the /ss startup option does not enable WordPerfect to display the correct number of rows and columns of text, use /f2.
/m-name	Executes a macro upon startup.
/mono	Use this option if your video adapter emulates both monochrome and color/graphics adapters. Frequently used with COMPAQ portable and desktop computers that can switch between high-resolution text and graphics displays.
/nb	Turns off the Original Backup feature. Use this option if you are short on disk space.
/nc	Disables keyboard speed-up. Use this option if WordPerfect's keyboard speed-up conflicts with your hardware or memory-resident software.
/ne	Disallows the use of LIM-type expanded memory.

Table A.2
Startup Options for WordPerfect 5.1

Option	Description
/nf	With some Color/Graphics Adapters (CGA), the monitor may "flash" or show "snow" when it changes from screen to screen. Or, if you use WordPerfect with a windowing environment program—such as DESQView or Windows—characters may appear outside their assigned windows. The /nf (nonfast) option should eliminate these problems.
/nk	Eliminates some problems with the keyboard and some not-quite-compatible computers or terminate-and-stay-resident (TSR) programs.
/no	Keeps the Keyboard Reset key (Ctrl-6) from returning the keyboard layout to its original mapping.
/ps=path	Specifies where WordPerfect can find the setup file (SET). Allows users on a network to have their own customized setup for WordPerfect.
/r	Loads most of WordPerfect 5.1 into expanded memory, if it is available, thereby speeding up the program.
/ss=rows,columns	Allows you to adjust the screen size if WordPerfect cannot automatically detect the screen size of your video adapter and monitor. Example: WP /SS=80,150.
/w=conventional memory,expanded memory	Enables you to alter how WordPerfect uses memory for its workspace. When you use this option, the value for conventional memory is a mandatory entry, but expanded memory is optional. For example, the command WP /W=100,256 would start WordPerfect with 100K of conventional memory and 256K of expanded memory.
/x	Restores the default setup values.

B

WordPerfect 5.1
for 5 Users

Michael McCoy is a microcomputer trainer and consultant in the Washington, D.C. area and has been teaching and supporting WordPerfect and other software packages since 1983. He works for WORDPRO, Inc., a computer training and consulting organization in Rockville, MD.

If you are using WordPerfect 5, you may be thinking about upgrading to WordPerfect 5.1 and how you can make the transition easily. Also, you may want a quick guide to features that have been changed in or added to version 5.1. This appendix discusses upgrading and summarizes the changes and additions to WordPerfect 5.1.

Making 5 Compatible with 5.1

Although much of version 5 is compatible with 5.1, you may need to make minor adjustments in version 5 documents, macros, keyboard layouts and printer drivers before you can use them in 5.1. The following sections provide additional information.

Formatting Documents

You can use most version 5 documents in 5.1 without converting them. However, 5.1 changed the way WordPerfect calculates the automatic line height, leading, and space sizes to improve printing consistency from one printer to another. Consequently, some documents may not format in WordPerfect 5.1 exactly as they did in 5.

If you want 5.1 documents to format exactly as they did in 5, follow the instructions in "Retaining WordPerfect 5 Formatting" at the end of this chapter.

Editing Macros

You can use WordPerfect 5 macros in version 5.1. However, some menu selections were changed, so you may find that

925

some of the macros do not work properly. When version 5 macros fail, use the macro editor to modify them so that they run properly. Currently, the macro editor in WordPerfect Library or WordPerfect Office does not edit 5.1 macros. However, WordPerfect Corporation has scheduled an upgrade of these packages for early 1990. The macro editor in the upgrades will work with 5.1 macros.

Adapting Keyboard Layouts

Generally, keyboard definitions made with version 5 work with WordPerfect 5.1. However, the Alt-= combination, which activates the pull-down menu bar, and certain other key combinations on Enhanced Keyboards (101 or more keys) may not work as they did in version 5. Also, as with version 5 macros, some key reassignments do not work properly because some features were reorganized. The only way to ensure that the keyboard definitions and key assignments work properly is to create new definitions using WordPerfect 5.1.

Converting Printer Drivers

Although you can convert WordPerfect 5 printer drivers to 5.1., you should use the new 5.1 drivers to make full use of 5.1's printing capabilities. If you use fonts created by a third-party program (such as Bitstream), you must convert version 5's printer driver to use the fonts in 5.1. Use the converted printer driver until the third-party program upgrades its fonts for use in 5.1.

To convert a version 5 printer driver to 5.1 format, do the following steps from the DOS prompt:

1. Copy the ALL file you want to convert to the subdirectory that contains the 5.1 printer files.
2. Change to the 5.1 printer subdirectory.
3. Type *PTR/CONVERT filename* and press Enter. (Replace *filename* with the name of the ALL or PRS file.)

The Printer program converts the version 5 ALL to a version 5.1 ALL format and ends the program. You may now select the printer the way you normally select a printer. See Chapter 8, "Printing and Print Options," for more information.

Understanding Changes to Existing Features

WordPerfect 5.1 changed many version 5 features to make them easier to use, or to give them greater capabilities. Table B.1 summarized these changes.

Table B.1
Changes to Existing Features

Feature	Chapter	Summary
Flush Right and Center	5	Easily add dot leaders.
Help	1	Now context-sensitive.
Hyphenation	7	Dictionary-based, with internal and external dictionaries.
Installation	A	Must be done using Install program.
Justification	5	Four types: Left, Right, Center, Full.
Keyboard Layout	20	Keyboard map shows key reassignments for each keyboard.
Location of Files	20	Can designate location of graphics, documents and style library.
Macros	11, 12	New commands added.
Merge	13	Codes changed, programming language added.
Outlines	21	Can move, copy, delete entire subsections or "families." Can define individual outline styles.
Page Numbering and Numbering Style	6	Three styles: Arabic, uppercase Roman, lowercase Roman. Can define numbering style to include text.
Paper Type/Size	6	All definitions of paper forms done with Format: Page menu. Do not need to define forms within printer definitions.
Reveal Codes	3	Can change size of Reveal Codes window.
Speller	7	Finds incorrect capitalizations such as *tHe*.
Tabs	5	Can be *absolute* from edge of paper or *relative* from margin. Special tab codes change with changes in tab setting, or remain unchanged using hard tabs.
Units of Measure	5	Can enter measurements as fractions (7/16); WordPerfect converts to decimal.

Using the New Features in WordPerfect 5.1

Version 5.1 offers nearly a dozen new features, which are summarized in table B.2.

Table B.2
New Features with WordPerfect 5.1

Feature	Chapter	Summary
Dormant Hard Returns	6	The first Hard Return code after a soft-page code is made dormant; the blank line that normally results is suppressed.
Equations	22	Complex equations can be entered using common terms and symbols.
Labels	13	Can define labels as a paper type and easily enter information for continuous-feed or sheet labels.
Long Document Names	10	Document names can be up to 68 characters or spaces. List Files can show short or long names.
Printing	8	Can print document summaries or selected pages of a document on-screen. Multiple pages can be generated by WordPerfect or the printer. Added support for double-sided printing.
Pull-Down Menus and Mouse Support	1, 20	Version 5.1 makes pull-down menus available and supports use of mouse.
Special Keyboard Layouts	20	Version 5.1 comes with several keyboards that use macros for quick cursor movement, code editing, and equation entry.
Special Characters	21	WordPerfect supports more than 1,500 characters. Users with graphics printers can print all characters.
Spreadsheet Import and Linking	16	Brings spreadsheets directly into 5.1. Links spreadsheets to documents so that changes in spreadsheets also update documents.
Tables	19	Simple definition and formatting of tables, including use of simple math calculations.
Text Drivers		Support added for monitors that support extended text modes.

Retaining WordPerfect 5 Formatting

WordPerfect 5.1 has a new way to calculate line height, leading, and space sizes. The result may be that documents created in WordPerfect 5 may not format exactly the same in 5.1. To retain the version 5 formatting, try the instructions in the following sections.

Changing Automatic Font

If automatic font-changes (fine, small, large, very large, extra large) applied to your document in WordPerfect 5 do not work correctly in version 5.1, you can change the way 5.1 calculates the proper size for the font-changes by doing the following steps:

1. Press Setup (Shift-F1) and select **I**nitial Settings (**4**).

   ⌨ Access the **F**ile pull-down menu, select Se**t**up, and then choose **I**nitial Settings.

2. Select **P**rint Options (**8**).

3. Select **S**ize Attribute Ratios and change them to one of the following settings:

Fine	55%
Small	73%
Large	127%
Very Large	182%
Extra Large	255%
Super/Subscript	55%

4. Select the printer. See Chapter 8 for detailed instructions.

Maintaining Number of Lines per Page

If the number of lines on a page changes in the 5.1 document, and you must retain version 5 lines-per-page format, you must, *while in WordPerfect 5*, add codes to fix the line height at every size-change or base-font change. To add these codes, do the following steps:

1. Start WordPerfect 5 and retrieve the document.

2. Go to the bottom of the document.

3. Move backward in the document until you reach a size-change or base-font change. Place the cursor immediately after the size-code or base-font code.

4. Enter the fixed line height for the font by pressing Format (Shift-F8), selecting **L**ine (**1**), Line **H**eight (**4**), **F**ixed (**2**), and then pressing Enter.

5. Repeat steps 3 and 4 for every size-code or base-font code in the document.

6. Save the document and then retrieve it into WordPerfect 5.1.

Changing Word-Spacing

At any point within the document, you can change the way WordPerfect 5.1 spaces words by doing the following steps:

1. Position the cursor in the document where you want to change the word-spacing.

2. Press Format (Shift-F8) and select **O**ther (**4**).

   ⌨ Access the **L**ayout pull-down menu and select **O**ther.

3. Select **P**rinter Functions (**6**) and **W**ord Spacing (**3**).

4. If the font size is between 10-point and 14-point, change the Word-Spacing value to between 124 percent and 130 percent. Remember, the larger the font, the smaller the word-spacing value.

Index

1-2-3 see Lotus 1-2-3, 535

— A —

acceleration factor (mouse), 657
aligning
  characters within cells, 636-637
  tabs, 124
alignment
  horizontal, 679
  vertical, 679
alphanumeric keys, 24-25
Alt-D (Delete Line) key, 68
anchor types, 868
  character aligning, 871
  page aligning, 870
  paragraph aligning, 869
annual reports, 916-919
antonyms, 184, 209
appending blocks of text, 93, 105
ascending order, 487-488
ASCII
  character set, 692-695
  file format, 544
  sort order, 487
AT&T 6300, 14
attribute characters, 365-367
attributes
  color display, 660
  graphics display, 661-662
authorities table, 683
AUTOEXEC.BAT file, 15-17, 922
auxiliary files location, 688-690

— B —

backup document option, 671-672
Backward Search (Shift-F2)
  command, 79-81
base font, 41, 97
  changing, 137-138
  setting, 248-249
beep options, 672-673
binding offset selection, 236
bit-mapped images, 901-904
Bitstream Fontware, installing, 257,
265
Block (Alt-F4 or F12) command,
89-107, 197, 226-227
Block Protect selection, 572-574
blocks, 87-107
  appending, 93, 105
  boldfacing, 95
  case, 99
  centering, 100-101
  changing type fonts, 96-98
  copying, 91-92, 102-105
  deleting, 92, 105

  enhancing, 95-102
  highlighting, 89
  moving, 91, 102-105
  pasting see copying, 92
  printing, 94, 226-227
  redlining, 101
  rehighlighting, 90-91
  restoring, 92
  saving, 93-94
  sorting, 499-500
  strikeout, 101
  styles, creating, 106
  underlining, 95
boilerplate text, 440
Bold (F6) command, 78
boldfacing text, 78, 95
boxes, 895
  anchors
    characters, 868, 871
    page, 868, 870
    paragraph, 868-869
  border space, 862-863
  border style, 861
  caption numbering
    automatic, 863
    positioning, 864-865
    style, 864
  contents, 867-868, 873
  creating, 857-860, 866, 867
  default alignment, 865
  editing, 873-874
  entering text, 866-867, 873
  gray shading, 865
  marking for cross-references, 829
  paragraph offset, 865
  size, 871-872
  surrounding with text, 872
  types, 857-860
bullets, mnemonic characters list,
701
BULLETS.WPM macro, 428-430

— C —

calculation, columns, 589, 594-599
calling macros with macros, 319-
323
Cancel (F1) command, 51, 70, 90,
310
carriage returns
  see also returns
  display on screen, 668
  hard and soft, 42
cartridge fonts, 253-263
  installing, 256-257
  setting up, 257-259
  troubleshooting, 263

case
  blocks of text, 99
  correcting, 190-191
cells, 497-499, 603
  characteristics, 633
  formatting, 625-628, 631-632
    blocks, 634-635
  printing with shading, 648-649
Center (Shift-F6) command, 100,
126-127, 564
centering
  blocks of text, 100-101
  text, 126-12
  top to bottom, 150-151
chained macros, 320-323
citation styles, 530
clipboard feature, 299-301
codes
  column-definition, 562-563
  formatting in table, 640-641
  hidden, 19, 32, 71, 111-112
    editing, 76-77
    list of, 72-75
  initial, 757-759, 761-762
    document, 111-112
    setup, 679-682
    table, 606
  initial setup, 111-112
  key-command, 418-419
  language, 180, 706-708
  macro command, 417-418
  merge, 442-443
  printer escape, 180-181
  style
    changing, 516-517
    deleting, 517
  subdocument override, 837
  table structure, 609-610
  text-enhancement, 102
  WordPerfect keys, 392-393
Color Graphics Adapter (CGA), 14
colors
  fonts-attributes, 658-660
  printing, 238-239
  setting monitor display, 659-660
column leading, 577-578
columns, 559-578
  calculation, 589, 594-599
    operators, 595-597
  changing
    column leading, 577-578
    line spacing, 576-578
  combining with regular text, 564-
565, 574-575
  copying, 639
  creating tables, 604

creating with split function, 635-636
cursor movement, 563-567
defining, 560-562, 571-572
  code, 562-563
deleting, 629-630
  canceling, 629-630
editing, 566, 567-575
format, 625-628
headings, centering, 564
inserting, 630-631
joining, 630-631
math, 592-602
  default settings, 590-591
moving, 575-576, 639
newspaper style, 559-570
  combining with regular text, 564-565
  macros, 569-570
numeric, 582
  default settings, 583
  displaying results, 588
  entering data, 584-587
  math operators, 585-587
parallel, 559, 570-575
  combining with regular text, 574-575
  macros, 579
previewing, 567-569
printing with shading, 648-649
side-by-side display option, 670
text, 589, 892-893
total, 589, 591-594
typing, 563-564, 572-574
width (tables), 641-642
Columns/Tables (Alt-F7) command, 561-575, 606-609, 624-645, 647
COM (parallel) port, 221
combining files during retrieval, 65
command keys, 21, 23-24
COMMAND.COM file, 15
commands
  Backward Search (Shift-F2), 79-81
  Block (Alt-F4 or F12), 87, 89-107
  Bold (F6), 78
  Cancel (F1), 51, 70, 310
  Center (Shift-F6), 126-127, 564
  Columns/Tables (Alt-F7), 561-575, 606-609, 624-647
  Compose (Ctrl-2 or Ctrl-V), 698-703
  Date/Outline (Shift-F5), 767-787
  End Field (F9), 450-451
  Exit (F7), 38, 54-55
  Flush Right (Alt-F6), 128
  Font (Ctrl-F8), 138-144, 223, 238-239, 250-251
  Footnote (Ctrl-F7), 743-745, 749-752, 754-763

Format (Shift-F8), 110, 112, 115, 126, 136-137, 148-149, 151-181, 249-250, 583, 788-791, 897-899
Forward Search (F2), 79-81, 154
GoTo (Ctrl-Home), 46-47
Graphics (Alt-F9), 155, 712-715, 736-738, 860, 866, 874-888
Help (F3), 32-34
Indent (F4), 117, 119
Left-Right Indent (Shift-F4), 118
List (F5), 62-64, 200, 227-228, 276-302
Macro (Alt-F10), 310, 312-313, 318-319, 321
Macro Commands (Ctrl-PgUp), 314-318
Macro Define (Ctrl-F10), 307-309, 311-330, 335-342, 503-504, 570, 579, 601-602
Margin Release (Shift-Tab), 116, 119
Mark Text (Alt-F5), 838-845
Math/Columns (Alt-F7), 584-600
Merge (Shift-F9), 445, 446, 448-451, 455-459
Merge Codes (Shift-F9), 455-459
Merge/Sort (Ctrl-F9), 451-453, 490-504, 542
Move (Ctrl-F4), 91, 103-105, 566-567
Print (Shift-F7), 216, 218-237, 248, 252-254, 257-261, 265-267, 568-569, 747-748
Replace (Alt-F2), 80-82, 154
Retrieve (Shift-F10), 65, 279
Reveal Codes (Alt-F3 or F11), 32, 71-77, 101-102, 104
Save (F10), 53-55
Screen (Ctrl-F3), 50-51, 123, 887-888
Setup (Shift-F1), 111-112, 114, 129-130, 175, 652-690
Spell (Ctrl-F2), 187-189, 195, 197, 201
Style (Alt-F8), 106, 505, 509-523, 797-800
Switch (Shift-F3), 49-51
Tab (Ctrl-F6), 124, 584-586
Text In/Out (Ctrl-F5), 83-84, 537-540, 545-546
Thesaurus (Alt-F1), 210
Underline (F8), 79
Comment, macro command, 421
COMPAQ Portable III/386, 14
comparing
  document versions, 830-834
  macros, 352-354
Compose (Ctrl-2 or Ctrl-V) command, 698-703
concordance file, 822-823

condensing master documents, 845
CONFIG.SYS file, 922
control characters
  attribute, 365-367
  cursor-positioning, 365, 367-369
Control Printer screen, 229-232
conversion strategies, 533-535
CONVERT program, 548-556
converting
  databases, 540-544, 551-552, 554
  dictionaries, 184, 203
  document comments to text, 84-85
  documents, 62
  DOS text files, 544-546
  files, 547-556
  graphics, 904-905
  lowercase letters to capitals, 423-427
  spreadsheets, 535-540, 551, 554
  text to document comments, 85
  WordPerfect 5 to 5.1, 925-930
copy files
  List (F5) command, 287
  clipboard feature, 299-301
COPY.WPM macro, 427-428
copying
  blocks of text, 91-92, 102-105
  columns, 639
  macro, 427-428
  rows, 639
cross-references
  creating, 826-830
  generating, 830
  master documents, 849-850
Ctrl-2 (Compose) key, 698-700
Ctrl-Del (Move) key, 91, 103-105
Ctrl-Home (GoTo) key, 46-47, 90
Ctrl-Ins (Copy) key, 91, 103-105
Ctrl-PgUp (Macro Commands) key, 314-315, 318
Ctrl-V (Compose) key, 698-700
currency, mnemonic characters list, 702
current date, 455-456
cursor, 18
  movement
    columnar text, 563-564, 566-567
    keys, 26-27, 42-47
    List Files screen, 279
    mouse, 47-48
    tables, 610-613
    positioning characters, 365, 367-369
    speed, 673
customizing
  attributes, 661-662
  date format, 677
  equations, 678-679
  graphics screen, 663

hyphenation, 675
keyboards, 685-690
menus, 664-666
text screen, 664
mouse, 654-657
screen displays 658, 661-666,
    669-670
    automatic formatting, 667-668
    colors, 659-660
    rewriting, 667-668
WordPerfect, 651-690

— D —

database, 486, 489-504, 540, 544
date fields, 543
delimiting files, 541-543
files
    converting, 551-554
    merging, 541-542
date
display, 278
format customizing, 677
Date/Outline (Shift-F5) command,
767-787
decimal tab, 179
defaults, 19, 41, 111-123
document settings, 175, 681
hyphenation, 129-130
math columns, 590-591
numeric columns, 583
printer settings, 679-684
underlining, 141-142
defining
columns
    newspaper style, 560-562
    parallel, 571-572
fonts, 222-223
index format, 823-824
label forms (Labels) macro, 169-
    170
lists, 800-801
printers, 217-219
pull-down menu display, 666
table of authorities, 818-819
table of contents, 811-812, 842-
    843
tables, 605
two-up pages, 897-898
units of measure, 676
Definition: Figure menu, 866
deleting
blocks of text, 92, 105
columns, 629-630
    canceling, 629-630
files, 280
footnotes, 750-751
lines of text, 68
paragraph numbers, 776-777

rows, 629-630
    canceling, 629-630
style definitions, 518-519
styles, 517-518
    style library, 523-524
subdocuments, 840
table structure, 617-618
tables, 621
text, 67-68
text within a table, 621-623
words from dictionary, 206
delimiting database files, 541-542
descending order, 487-488
desktop publishing, 889-919
diacritical marks, mnemonic
    characters list, 701
dictionaries
see also speller, 183
algorithmic, 203-204
conversion
    versions 4.2 to 5.1, 184, 203
expanding, 203
foreign language, 183, 705-708
hyphenation, 184, 203
supplemental
    adding words, 204-206
    compressing dictionary, 207-209
    deleting words, 206
    expanding, 207-209
    functions, 185, 198-203
    passwords, 188
digraphs, mnemonic characters list,
    702
disks
speller/thesaurus installation, 185
storing macros, 333
supplemental dictionary, 198-199,
    202
WordPerfect start up, 15-17
display
customizing, 658-660, 663-666,
    669-670
    automatic formatting, 667
    document comments, 668
    file name on status line, 668
    screen rewriting, 667
    text speed, 661-662
pitch, 176
displaying
document comments, 668
equations, 719-720
footnotes, 745-748
hard carriage returns, 668-669
math results, 588
merge codes, 669
special characters on-screen, 696-
    697
tab ruler, 123

dissertation styles, 526-528
document
backup option, 671-672
comments, 83
    converting, 84-85
    displaying, 668
    hiding, 85-86
comparison, 830-834
conversion, 62
format defaults, 175
initial codes, 111-112
references, 793, 795-800, 804-818,
    820-834
    cross-references, 826-830
    document comparison, 830-834
    generating, 801-803, 812, 819,
        824-825, 830
    indexes, 820-825
    lists, 795-802
    table of authorities, 813-819
    table of contents, 804-812
retrieving, 62-63
    changing paths, 64
    combining files, 65
setting defaults, 681
summaries, 177-178
Document Preview, 144-145
Document-Summary options, 673-
674
documents
creating, 39-42
editing, 61-86
    comments, 84-86
    inserting comments, 83
formatting, 147, 174-181
    WordPerfect 5 to 5.1, 925
master, 835-851
outlining, 766-772, 774-775
    editing, 773
previewing, 253
saving, 53-55
subdocuments, 835-840, 850
summaries, 177-178
dormant hard returns, 162
DOS text files
converting to WordPerfect, 544-
    546
creating, 546
importing, 544-546
merge delimiters
    setting, 677
print files
    creating, 547
    retrieving, 544-545
secondary files, 452-453
double-click interval (mouse), 656
downloadable fonts, 223, 236, 264-
267

installing, 265
printer command files, 236
setting up, 265-267
drawing lines, 887-888
duplicating text *see* copying blocks,
91

— E —

editing
boxes, 873-874
comments
in document, 84-85
columns
newspaper style, 566-567
parallel, 575
documents, 61-86
comments, 84-86
inserting comments, 83
equations, 721-723
footnotes, 754-755
graphic
images, 875-882
lines, 887
keyboard definition, 687-688
macros, 335-342
WordPerfect 5 to 5.1, 925-926
math definitions, 599-600
outlines, 775
styles, 516
tables, 624-643
text
deleting, 67-70
inserting, 71
tables, 615-616
words, 192-193
End Field (F9) command, 450-451
endnotes, 741-742, 759-763
macros, 763
marking for cross-references, 828
master documents, 849
options, 761-762
Enhanced Graphics Adapter (EGA),
14
enhancing
blocks of text, 95-102
codes, 102
text, 109, 137-145
boldfacing, 78
underlining, 78-79
entering
fields, 450-451
records, 450-451
special characters, 698
equations, 720-722
mnemonic method, 700-703
numeric method, 699-700
text, 42
box, 866-873
tables, 613-615

EPS (Encapsulated PostScript) files,
904
equation editor, 711-740
boxes, 857-860
display windows, 713, 715-717
equation palette, 714
file managing, 739-740
retrieving, 738-740
saving, 738-740
functions menu, 721-722
keyboard, 720-722
list of commands, 717-718
matrix commands, 731-733
order of precedence, 718-719
positioning equations, 735-738
printing, 739-740
sizing equations, 735-738
starting, 712
equations
creating, 711-718
diacritical marks, 730-731
integral expressions, 728-729
keyword commands, 725-727
matrix commands, 731-732
roots, 729-730
subscripts/superscripts, 723-725
symbol sizes, 734-735
customizing, 679
displaying, 719-720
editing, 721-723
entering characters, 720-722
erasing lines, 888
Excel, spreadsheet conversion, 535
executing macros, 309-310
Exit (F7) command, 38, 54-55
exiting WordPerfect, 38, 54-55
expanding master documents, 840-
844
expressions
macros, 352-353
list, 353

— F —

fast save
defining, 674-675
enable/disable, 674-675
fields, 441, 486
adding, 455
entering, 450-451
naming, 445-450
skipping, 453-455
figure
boxes, 857-860
numbers, 863-865
file name, 53-54
files
AUTOEXEC.BAT, 15-17, 922
auxiliary location, 688-690
combining, 65

COMMAND.COM, 15
concordance, 822-823
CONFIG.SYS, 922
converting, 548-556
copying, 287
deleting, 280
finding, 287-288, 294
restricting the search, 289-293
search patterns, 292-293
input, 486-487, 490, 493
LIBRARY.STY (sample Style
library), 525-526
list customizing, 674
Look feature, 282-286, 299-302
marking, 297-299
moving/renaming, 280-281
name search, 294-296
other directory, 285-286
output, 487, 490, 493
password protecting, 301-302
primary merge, 440, 442-449,
451-455, 469-471
printing, 281
PRS (printer), 163-164
retrieving, 62-63, 279-280
changing paths, 64
combining files, 65
secondary merge, 440-444, 450-
455, 469-470
short/long display, 281-282
WHHELP.FIL, 32-34
WP.LRS (Language Resource),
278, 708
WP{WP}US.LEX, 184-185
WP{WP}US.SPW, 185
WP{WP}US.SUP, 185, 200-201
fixed information, 440, 444-446
floppy disks
speller/thesaurus
installation, 185
start up, 186
storing macros, 333
supplemental dictionary, 198-199,
202
Flush Right (Alt-F6) command, 128
Font (Ctrl-F8) command, 97-98,
101, 138-144, 223, 238-239,
250-251
fonts
appearance, 140-142
attributes 139-142
base, 41, 97
setting, 248-249
cartridge, 253-259, 263
changed with 5.1, 929
changing, 249, 705
base, 97-98, 137-138
block of text, 96-98
choosing, 894-895

converting version 5 to 5.1, 269-271
defining, 222-223
downloading, 223, 236, 264-267
initial base, 223
internal, 253-254, 256
laser printers, 244
libraries, 223
pitch, 246
printer command files, 236
selecting
  by name, 250-251
  by size, 249-251
size, 139-140, 244
soft, 253, 255-257, 260, 261, 263-264
spacing
  fixed, 245
  proportional, 245
specifying, 222-223
style, 244
weight, 245
footers
  creating, 152
  designing, 151-152
  editing, 153
  including graphics, 154-155
  margin allowance, 150
  page numbering, 152
  search and replace, 154
  suppressing, 153
  viewing, 152
Footnote (Ctrl-F7) command, 743-745, 749-750, 754-763
footnotes, 741-759
  adding, 749-750
  creating, 742-745
  deleting, 750-751
  displaying, 745-748
  editing, 754-755
  macros, 763
  marking for cross-references, 826-828
  master documents, 848-849
  moving, 751-753
  options, 755-759
  shortcut, 744
foreign language
  dictionaries, 183, 705-708
  thesaurus, 705-708
  versions of WordPerfect, 705-708
Format (Shift-F8) command, 110, 112, 115, 126, 136-137, 148-149, 151-181, 249-250, 583, 788-791, 897-899
formatting
  cells, 625-628, 631-632, 634-635
  codes, 640-641
  columns, 625-628

documents, 147, 174-181
  WordPerfect 5 to 5.1, 925
letters
  with macros, 316-319
lines, 110
pages, 148-174
paragraphs, 110
rows, 625-628
tables, 625-628
text, 109-137
forms
  creating, 914-916
  specifications, 915-916
Forward Search (F2) command, 79-81, 154
fractions, mnemonic characters list, 701
French styles, 530
FROM command, equation editor, 725
function keys, 21-24

— G —

generic word processing files, 546
GoTo (Ctrl-Home) command, 46-47, 90
GRAPHCNV.EXE program, 904
  switches, 905
graphics, 901-905
  converting files, 904-905
  customizing, 661, 662
    screen type, 663
  editing images, 875-882
  importing, 874-875
  headers/footers, 154-155
  images
    black and white, 881
    mirroring, 877-878
    moving, 876-877
    rotating, 877-878
  integrating with text, 855-888
  inverting images, 879-880
  lines
    appearance, 886
    creating, 881-886
    editing, 887
    length, 883-884, 886
    positions, 883, 885-886
  positioning, 908
  programs list, 902-903
  scaling, 877
  storing, 867
Graphics (Alt-F9) command, 155, 712-715, 736-737, 860, 866, 874-887
grids, 603, 637-639

— H —

hanging paragraphs, 118
hard carriage return, 669
hard disk
  speller/thesaurus installation, 185
  supplemental dictionary, 198-199, 202
hard fonts *see* cartridge fonts, 254
hard page breaks, 158-159, 161-162
hardware requirements 5.1, 13-15
headers
  creating, 152
  designing, 151-152
  editing, 153
  including graphics, 154-155
  margin allowance, 150
  page numbering, 152
  search and replace, 154
  suppressing, 153
  viewing, 152
headings, 315-316
headwords, 184, 21-212
height of rows, 632
Help (F3) command, 32-34
Hercules Graphics Card, 14, 661-662
hidden codes, 19, 32, 71, 111-112
  editing, 76-77
  list of, 72-75
  search and replace, 82-83
highlighting text, 87, 89, 107
horizontal alignment, 679
horizontal orientation *see* orientation, landscape
hyphenation
  customizing, 675
  defaults, 129-130
  interrupting, 131
  text, 128-135
  types, 132-135
  zones, 131-132, 562-563, 571
hyphens, 133-135

— I —

IBM 8514/A, 14
illustrations, 900
images
  bit-mapped, 901-904
  vector, 901-904
importing
  DOS text files, 544-546
  graphics, 874-875
  numerical data into tables, 644
  spreadsheets, 537
    linking with documents, 538-540
  text into tables, 644
Indent (F4) command, 117-119

indexes
  creating, 820-825, 841-842
  defining format, 823-824
  generating, 824-825
initial
  base font, 223
  codes, 111-112, 606, 757-759,
    761-762
  setup, 679-682
initializing printer, 236
input file, 486-487, 490, 493
Insert mode, 70-71
inserting
  blank lines, 42
  columns, 630-631
  comments
    in document, 83
  current date, 455-456
  page numbers, 846-847
  rows, 630-631
  text, 48, 70-71
INSTALL.EXE program, 921-922
installation support WordPerfect
  Corporation, 7
installing
  downloadable fonts, 265
  printer fonts, 256-261
  WordPerfect, 921-922
INT command, equation editor, 725
integer variables, 350-352
internal fonts, 253-254, 256
inverting graphic images, 879-880
INVOICE.WPM macro, 432-437
  loops, 431
  structure, 431
invoices, creating with macros,
  431-437

— J —

job list, printing, 216, 225, 229,
  231-232
joining cells, 630-631
justification
  changing, 126
  text, 125-126

— K —

kerning letters, 142-144
key
  codes, 392-393
  command codes, 418-419
keyboards, 19-20
  alphanumeric keys, 24-25
  canceling blocks, 90
  command keys, 21, 23-24
  cursor movement keys, 26-27, 42-
    47
  customizing, 685-690
  definition, 687-688
  function keys, 21-24
  highlighting text (blocks), 89, 107
  input during merge, 458-459
  layout, 686, 926
  numeric keypad, 25-26
keys
  Alt-= (pull-down menu), 41, 62,
    88, 110, 147, 184, 216, 243, 276,
    306, 439, 485, 506, 534, 559,
    582, 603, 651, 666, 691, 742,
    766, 795, 836, 857, 890
  Alt-F1 (Thesaurus), 210
  Alt-F2 (Replace), 80-82
  Alt-F3 (Reveal Codes), 32, 71,
    562, 575-576, 746
  Alt-F4 (Block), 89, 90, 197, 226,
    497, 499, 564, 567, 576, 751
  Alt-F5 (Mark Text), 838, 841-845
  Alt-F6 (Flush Right), 128
  Alt-F7 (Columns/Tables), 561-
    562, 564-565, 571, 584, 588-589,
    599, 606, 624, 645
  Alt-F8 (Style), 505, 509, 511-518,
    521, 523, 797
  Alt-F9 (Graphics), 155, 712, 860,
    866, 874-875, 882-884, 887
  Alt-F10 (Macro), 169-170, 310,
    312-313, 318-319, 321
  Cancel (F1), 90
  Ctrl-2 (Compose), 698-700
  Ctrl-Del (Move), 91, 103-105, 335,
    338-342, 503-504, 570, 579, 601-
    602
  Ctrl-F2 (Spell), 187-189, 195, 197,
    201
  Ctrl-F3 (Screen), 50-51, 123, 887-
    888
  Ctrl-F3 (Switch), 99, 103-105
  Ctrl-F4 (Move), 91, 103-105, 566,
    567
  Ctrl-F5 (Text In/Out), 83-84, 537-
    540, 545-546
  Ctrl-F6 (Tab), 124, 584
  Ctrl-F7 (Footnote), 743-745, 749-
    750, 754-755, 760-761, 763
  Ctrl-F8 (Fonts), 97-98, 101, 138,
    140-144, 223, 238-239, 250-251
  Ctrl-F9 (Merge/Sort), 451, 490,
    493, 498, 500, 503-504, 542
  Ctrl-F10 (Macro Define), 307-309,
    311-315, 317-321, 324-330,
  Ctrl-Home (GoTo), 46-47
  Ctrl-Ins (Copy), 91, 103-105
  Ctrl-PgUp (Macro Commands),
    314-315, 318
  Ctrl-V (Compose), 698-700
  cursor movement, 610-613
  F1 (Cancel), 51, 70, 310
  F2 (Forward Search), 79-81, 154
  F3 (Help), 32-34
  F4 (Indent), 117, 119
  F5 (List), 62, 200, 228, 276-277,
    289-290, 297, 299-302
  F6 (Bold), 78
  F7 (Exit), 38, 54-55
  F8 (Underline), 79
  F9 (End Field), 450-451
  F10 (Save), 53-54
  F11 (Reveal Codes), 32, 71, 562,
    575-576, 746
  F12 (Block), 89-90, 197, 226, 497,
    499, 564, 567, 576, 751
  GoTo (Ctrl-Home), 90
  Print (Shift-F7), 94
  Shift-F1 (Setup), 111-112, 114,
    129-130, 175, 652, 655
  Shift-F10 (Retrieve), 65
  Shift-F2 (Backward Search), 79
  Shift-F3 (Switch), 49, 51
  Shift-F4 (Left-Right Indent), 118
  Shift-F5 (Date/Outline), 767, 770,
    772, 774, 778-779, 782, 784-785,
    786-787
  Shift-F6 (Center), 100, 126-127,
    564
  Shift-F7 (Print), 216, 218, 220-221,
    224-227, 229, 248, 252-254,
    257, 260, 265, 568, 747-748
  Shift-F8 (Format), 110, 112, 115,
    126, 136-137, 148-149, 151-154,
    156-160, 163, 173, 175-178, 180-
    181, 249, 583, 788-790, 897
  Shift-F9 (Merge), 445, 448-451,
    455-456, 458-459
  Shift-Tab (Margin Release), 116,
    119
keywords, equation editor, 716-718

— L —

labels
  defining, 168-170, 172-173, 463-
    465
  mailing, 462-466
language codes, 180, 706-708
Language Resource file (WP.LRS),
  708
laser printers, 243-273
  configuring, 247, 252-253
  downloadable fonts, 264-267
  fonts, 244-245, 250-251, 253-261
    installing, 256-257
    setting up, 257-261
  forms, 261-262, 267
  paper sizes, 262

pitch, 246
troubleshooting, 262-264, 272-273
LaserJet printers, 246
memory boards, 264
Layout menu, 148-149
leading *see* line height
LEFT command, equation editor,
726-727
left-hand operation (mouse), 657
Left-Right Indent (Shift-F4)
command, 118
legal characters, mnemonic
characters list, 703
letterhead styles, 528-529
letters, formatting, 316-319
LIBRARY.STY (sample Style library)
file, 525-526
line
feed/carriage return, converting
to WordPerfect, 544-546
height, 135-136
spacing, 136-137
within columns, 576-578
publications, 893
lines
drawing, 887-888
erasing, 888
formatting, 110
graphic
appearance, 886
creating, 881-886
editing, 887
length, 883-884, 886
positions, 883, 885-886
in publications, 895
numbering, 765-766, 788-791
linking spreadsheets and
documents, 538-540
List (F5) command, 62-64, 200,
227-228, 276-302
copying files, 287
deleting files, 280
finding files, 287-288, 294
restricting the search, 289-293
search patterns, 292-293
look feature, 282-286, 299-302
marking files, 297-299
moving/renaming files, 280-281
name search, 294-296
other directory, 285-286
printing files, 281
retrieving files, 279-280
short/long display, 281-282
List Files display screen
file listing, 277-279
heading, 277
menu, 277, 279-288
internal fonts, 254

lists
creating, 795-800, 841-842
defining, 800-801
generating, 801-803
locking files, 301-302
logical operators, 353-354
Look feature, 282-286, 299-302
loops
in macro commands, 381-387
merge, 478
writing, 387
{FOR EACH}, 383-385
{FOR}, 381-383
{WHILE}, 385-387
Lotus 1-2-3, converting
spreadsheets, 535
LPT (serial) port, 221

— **M** —

Macro (Alt-F10) command, 310,
312-313, 318-319, 321
macro command codes, 417-418
macro commands
{ASSIGN}, 356
{BELL}, 354, 364
{Block Append}, 422
{Block Copy}, 422
{Block Move}, 422
{BREAK}, 382, 384-385, 389, 391
{CALL}, 372-373
{CANCEL OFF}, 412-413
{CANCEL ON}, 412-413
{CASE CALL}, 376
{CASE}, 374-375
{CHAIN}, 377
{CHAR}, 355, 360-361
Comment, 421
{DISPLAY OFF}, 420, 431-432
{DISPLAY ON}, 420, 431-432
{ELSE}, 375, 389-390
{END FOR}, 382, 384
{END IF}, 389-390
{END WHILE}, 385
{FOR EACH}, 383-384
{FOR}, 381, 382
{GO}, 355, 377-378
{IF EXISTS}, 390
{IF}, 388
{INPUT}, 362
{Item Down}, 423
{Item Left}, 423
{Item Right}, 423
{Item Up}, 423
{KTON}, 391-394
{LABEL}, 378
{LEN}, 359-360
{LOOK}, 361
{MENU OFF}, 420-421

{MENU ON}, 420-421
{MID}, 360
{NEST}, 379
{NEXT}, 382, 384, 386-387
{NTOK}, 391, 394
{ON CANCEL}, 355, 413
{ON ERROR}, 414
{ON NOT FOUND}, 414-415
{ORIGINAL KEY}, 421-422
{Para Down}, 423
{Para Up}, 423
{PAUSE KEY}, 363
{PAUSE}, 362
{PROMPT}, 354-355, 363
{QUIT}, 415
{RESTART}, 415
{RETURN CANCEL}, 379-380
{RETURN ERROR}, 379-380
{RETURN NOT FOUND}, 379-380
{RETURN}, 379-380
{SHELL MACRO}, 422
{SPEED}, 416
{STATE}, 391, 394-395
{STATUS PROMPT}, 364
{STEP OFF}, 416
{STEP ON}, 416
{SYSTEM}, 391, 396-412
{TEXT}, 361
{VAR n}, 358-359
{VARIABLE}, 357-358
{WAIT}, 416
{WHILE}, 385
Macro Commands (Ctrl-PgUp)
command, 314-318
Macro Define (Ctrl-F10) command,
307-309, 311-330, 335-342, 503-
504, 570, 579, 601-602
macro editor, 335-342
macros, 305-342
advanced, 345-437
check system status, 391-412
controlling display, 420-421
controlling execution, 415-419
decimal arithmetic, 432
error handling, 412-415
keystroke emulation, 422-423
loops, 381-387
miscellaneous commands, 421-
422
program control, 369-370
subroutines, 370-371
nesting, 372
Alt-D (delete line), 68
BULLETS.WPM, 428-430
calling macros, 319-323
controlling, 313-323
COPY.WPM, 427-428
creating, 307-309, 324-332

editing, 335-342, 925-926
executing, 309-310
expressions, 352-353
footnotes and endnotes, 763
INVOICE.WPM, 431-437
logical operators, 353-354
passing variables, 372
pausing, 315-319
relational operators, 386
repeating, 314
replacing, 310-312
running, 309-310
stopping, 310
storing on floppy disks, 333
syntax, 354-364, 372-396, 412-416, 420-421
TOUPPER.WPM, 423-427
types, 307-309
using to sort, 503-504
with a mouse, 29
mailing labels using merge, 462-466
Margin Release (Shift-Tab) command, 116, 119
margins
changing, 115-116, 119, 149-150
headers/footers allowance, 150
paper feeding, 150
Mark Text (Alt-F5) command, 838-845
master documents, 835-851
condensing, 845
creating, 836-839
cross-references, 849-850
endnotes, 849
expanding, 840-844
footnotes, 848-849
page numbers, 846-847
printing, 845
saving, 845-846
search and replace, 847
spell checking, 847-848
math columns, 592-602
default settings, 590-591
macro, 600-602
Math Definition screen, 590-600
math operators, 585
displaying results, 588
functions, 586-587
math/scientific characters, mnemonic characters list, 703
mathematical operators, 351-352
menu numbers
{SYSTEM} command, 404-411
menus
creating, 346
macros, 428-430
customizing, 664-666
Definition: Figure, 866

Layout, 148-149
List Files display screen, 279-302
Paper Size/Type, 163-164, 171-173
pop-out, 28-29
Print, 227-229, 233-237
Pull-Down, defining, 666
Setup, 652-690
Sort, 487-488
Thesaurus, 210-212
merge, 439-484
codes, 442-443
{END RECORD}, 451
{FIELD}, 445-446
directly to printer, 457-458
fixed information, 440, 444-446
including keyboard input, 458-459
loops, 478
special documents, 460-466
subroutines, 476-478
variable information, 440, 444-445, 447-451
Merge (Shift-F9) command, 445-451, 455-459
merge code display option, 669
merge commands
{ASSIGN}, 471
{BELL}, 474
{CALL}, 476
{CANCEL OFF}, 482
{CANCEL ON}, 483
{CASE CALL}, 477
{CASE}, 477
{CHAIN MACRO}, 477
{CHAIN PRIMARY}, 478
{CHAIN SECONDARY}, 479
{CHAR}, 474
{COMMENT}, 466-469
{CTON}, 482
{DATE}, 484
{DOCUMENT}, 480
{END FIELD}, 469
{END RECORD}, 469-470
{FIELD NAMES}, 469
{FIELD}, 469-470
{GO}, 477
{IF BLANK}, 481-482
{IF EXISTS}, 481
{IF NOT BLANK}, 481-482
{IF}, 481
{INPUT}, 475
{KEYBOARD}, 475
{LABEL}, 477
{LEN}, 472
{LOCAL}, 472
{LOOK}, 474
{MID}, 473
{MRG CMND}, 484

{NEST MACRO}, 477-478
{NEST PRIMARY}, 480
{NEST SECONDARY}, 480
{NEXT RECORD}, 469-470
{NTOC}, 482
{ON CANCEL}, 483
{ON ERROR}, 483
{PAGE OFF}, 484
{PAGE ON}, 484
{PRINT}, 484
{PROCESS}, 477
{PROMPT}, 474
{QUIT}, 483
{RETURN CANCEL}, 477
{RETURN ERROR}, 477
{RETURN}, 477
{REWRITE}, 484
{STATUS PROMPT}, 475
{STEP OFF}, 483
{STEP ON}, 483
{STOP}, 483
{SUBST PRIMARY}, 480
{SUBST SECONDARY}, 480
{SYSTEM}, 482
{TEXT}, 475
{VARIABLE}, 472
{WAIT}, 484
merge delimiters, 677
Merge/Sort (Ctrl-F9) command, 451-453, 490-504, 542
merging database files, 541-542
mirroring graphic images, 877-878
mnemonic method, special character entry, 700-703
mode
Insert, 48
typeover, 48-49
mouse, 14-15, 29-31
acceleration factor, 657
canceling blocks, 90
cursor movement, 47-48
customizing, 654-657
deleting text, 69
double-click interval, 656
driver, 654-655
equation editor, 714
highlighting blocks of text, 89, 107
icon, 2, 41
left-hand operation, 657
pop-out menu delay time, 656
port, 654-655
pull-down menu, 27-28, 41
type, 654-655
MOUSE.COM program, 654-655
Move (Ctrl-F4) command, 91, 103-105, 566-567
moving
between windows, 49-51

blocks, 91, 102-105
columns, 639
  parallel, 575-576
files, 280-281
footnotes, 751-753
graphic images, 876-877
numbered paragraphs, 778-780
rows, 639
multiple files, selecting, 297-299

— N —

name search, 294-296
named variables, 349
nested macros, 322-323
newsletters
  creating, 908-912
  specifications, 910-912
newspaper style columns, 559
  combining with regular text, 564-565
  defining, 560-562
  editing, 566-567
  previewing, 567-569
  typing, 563-564
numbered variables, 349
numbering
  lines, 765-766, 788-791
  pages, 155-158
  paragraphs, 765-766, 768-770, 783
    adding, 776, 780
    changing, 776-778
    creating, 784-785
    defining numbering styles, 784-785
    deleting, 776-777
    moving, 778-780
    tab override, 785-787
  styles
    defining, 784-785
    macro, 772
    outlining, 770-775
numeric
  columns
    default settings, 583
    displaying results, 588
    entering data, 584-587
    math operators, 585-587
  keypad, 25-2
  method, special character entry, 699-700
  sorting, 500-501

— O —

open style, 507, 509-510
operators
  logical, 353-354
  mathmatical, 351-352
  relational, 386

order of precedence, equation editor, 718-719
orientation
  landscape, 162, 166, 246
  portrait, 162, 166, 246
orphan line, 160
outline style, 507-508, 513
outlining, 765-775
  defining numbering styles, 770-772
  documents, 766-775
  editing, 775
  numbering styles, 772-775
  turning off, 770
  Styles, 782-783
output file, 487, 490, 493
OVER command, equation editor, 726-727
overstrike, 108
  creating special characters, 703-704
overwriting text, 48-49, 71

— P —

page
  breaks
    controlling, 158-162
    hard, 158-162
    soft, 158-159, 161-162
  formatting, 148-174
  lines, 929
  numbers, 150, 155-158
    automatic, 152
    inserting, 846-847
    margin allowance, 150
    master documents, 846-847
    positioning, 155-156
    suppressing, 157
    two-up, 896-899
    viewing, 155
  template, 163-174
PageMaker, 889
paired style, 507
  applying to existing text, 515
  creating, 510-512
  inserting with block, 513
  turning off, 512
paper
  orientation
    landscape, 162, 166, 246
    portrait, 162, 166, 246
  size, 162, 166, 246
Paper Size/Type menu, 163-164, 171-173
paragraphs
  adding, 781-783
  formatting, 110
  hanging, 118

numbering, 765-766, 768-770, 783, 804-806
  adding, 776, 780
  changing, 776-778
  creating, 784-785
  defining numbering styles, 784-785
  deleting, 776-777
  moving, 778-780
  tab override, 785-787
records, 486, 489
  sorting, 491-493
  varying for interest, 893
parallel columns, 559, 570
  combining with regular text, 574-575
  defining, 571-572
  editing, 575
  moving, 575-576
  typing, 572-574
password protecting files, 301-302
paths, changing, 64
pausing macros, 315-319
pitch display, 176
PlanPerfect, 535
pop-out menu, 28-29
  delay time (mouse), 656
ports
  parallel (LPT), 221
  serial (COM), 221
positioning graphics, 908
PostScript printer, 246
primary merge file, 440, 442-449, 451-455, 469-471
Print (Shift-F7) command, 216, 218-237, 248, 252-254, 257-261, 265-267, 568-569, 747-748
print (Shift-F7) key, 94
Print menu, 227-229, 233-237
printers
  Advance function, 178-179
  binding offset selection, 236
  common problems, 240-241
  Control screen, 229-232
  defining, 163-174, 217-219
  drivers, 926
  escape code, 180-181
  fonts, 222-223
  initializing, 236
  kerning letters, 142-144
  laser printers, 243-273
    configuring, 247, 252-253
  options, 215
  selecting, 217-219
  setting, 220-223, 679-684
  sheet feeders, 221
  viewing document before printing, 236

printing, 52-53, 142-144, 215-241
  blocks of text, 94, 226-227
  color, 238-239
  documents created before 5.1,
    239-240
  equations, 739-740
  files, 281
  forms, 221-222, 261-262, 267
  graphic images in black and
    white, 881
  job list, 216, 225, 229, 231-232
  master documents, 845
  merging files, 457-458
  multiple copies, 233-237
  selected pages, 228-229
  setting print quality, 698
  special characters, 697-698
  unsaved documents, 52-53
program control macro commands,
  369-370
programs
  CONVERT, 548-556
  GRAPHCNV.EXE, 904-905
  INSTALL.EXE, 921-922
  MOUSE.COM, 654-655
  PTR (Printer), 269-271
  SPELL.EXE, 201, 705-708
proportional spacing, 139, 245
protecting blocks of text, 572-574
pull-down menu, 27-28
  defining, 666

— R —

records, 441, 486
  entering, 450-451
  line, 486, 489
    sorting, 490-491
  paragraph, 486, 489
    sorting, 491-493
  secondary-merge file, 486, 489,
    493-496
  table, 486, 489
    sorting, 496-499
redlining
  text, 101, 176-177
  purging from a saved document,
    833-834
rehighlighting blocks, 90
relational operators, 386
  list of, 386
Replace (Alt-F2) command, 79-82,
  154
replacing
  macros, 310-312
  text, 80-82
  words (thesaurus) 211
restarting WordPerfect, 16-17
restoring
  deleted text, 70, 92

table structure, 619-621
Retrieve (Shift-F10) command, 65,
  279
retrieving
  blocks of text, 94
  document, 62-63
    changing paths, 64
    combining files, 65
  DOS text files, 544-545
  equation files, 738-740
  files, 62-65, 279-280
  spreadsheets, 535-537
  style definitions, 521-523
returns
  dormant hard, 162
  hard, 42
  soft, 42, 132-135
Reveal Codes (Alt-F3 or F11)
  command, 32, 71-77, 101-102,
  104, 562-563, 575-576, 746
revising text, 66
RIGHT command, equation editor,
  726-727
rotating graphic images, 877-878
rows, 497
  copying, 639
  creating tables, 604
  deleting, 629-630
    canceling, 629-630
  format changing, 625-628
  height, 632
  inserting, 630-631
  joining, 630-631
  moving, 639
  printing with shading, 648-649

— S —

Save (F10) command, 53-54
saving
  blocks of text, 93-94
  documents on disk, 53-55
  equation files, 738-740
  master documents, 845-846
  styles, 518
    definitions, 521
scaling graphic images, 877
Screen (Ctrl-F3) command, 50-51,
  123, 887-888
screen
  prints, 52-53
  splitting, 49-51
  type graphics, 663
  text, 664
Search and Replace, 79-82
  headers and footers, 154
  hidden codes, 82-83
  master documents, 847
search patterns, 292-293

secondary-merge file, 440-444, 450-
  455, 469-470
  adding fields, 455
  DOS text file, 452-453
  records, 486, 489, 493-496
selecting
  fonts
    by name, 250-251
    by size, 249-251
  pages to print, 228-229
  printers, 217-219
  records with sort, 501-504
  styles, 514-515
  words (thesaurus), 211-212
setting
  defaults, 111-123
  tab stops, 119-122
    for math, 583
    hard, 122
Setup (Shift-F1) command, 111-112,
  114, 129-130, 175, 652-690
Setup menu, 652-690
sheet feeders, 221-222
Shift-Tab (Margin Release) key,
  116, 119
size, font, 139-140
snaking columns see newspaper
  style columns, 559
soft
  fonts, 253, 255-257, 260-261, 263-
    264
    installing, 257
    setting up, 260-261
    troubleshooting, 263-264
  hyphens, 133-135
  page breaks, 158-159, 161-162
  returns, 132-135
sorting
  blocks, 499-500
  data, 485-489
  lines, 490-491
  numerics, 500-501
  paragraphs, 491-493
  secondary merge file records,
    493-496
  selecting records, 501-504
  tables, 496-499
  types of, 489-504
  with macros, 503-504
Sort menu, 487-488
sort order
  ascending, 487-488
  descending, 487-488
special characters, 691-704
  ASCII extended characters, 692-
    695
  creating with overstrike, 703-704
  entering, 698
    mnemonic method, 700-703

numeric method, 699-700
on-screen display, 696-697
printing, 697-698
setting print quality, 698
WordPerfect character sets, 695-696
special documents using merge, 460-466
specifications
annual reports, 917-919
forms, 915-916
newsletters, 910-912
two-fold brochure, 914
Spell (Ctrl-F2) command, 187-189, 195, 197, 201
spell checking master documents, 847-848
SPELL.EXE program, 201, 705-708
speller, 183-209
adding words, 191-192, 204-206
block of text, 197
compressing dictionary, 207-209
correcting case, 190-191
deleting words, 206
document comments, 197-198
editing words, 192-193, 194
eliminating double words, 193
ending command, 194-196
expanding dictionary, 207-209
looking up words, 195-196
main dictionary (WP{WP}US.LEX) file, 185
selecting correct spelling, 189-190
skipping words, 191
start up, 186-189
supplemental dictionary (WP{WP}US.SUP), 185, 198-203
unchecked text, 197
wildcards, 195-196
words with numbers, 197
Speller Utility
adding words, 204-206
compressing dictionary, 207-209
deleting words, 206
expanding dictionary, 207-209
file, 185, 201
supplemental dictionary functions, 185, 198, 201-203
passwords, 188
speller/thesaurus
copy files to RAM, 186
installation
floppy disk system, 185
hard disk system, 185
location of files, 186
start up, 186
supplemental dictionary
floppy disk system, 198-199, 202
hard disk system, 198-199, 202

splitting the screen, 49-51
spreadsheets
converting with CONVERT, 551, 554
importing, 537-540
linking with documents, 538-540
retrieving, 537
STACK/STACKALIGN commands, equation editor, 733-734
startup—WordPerfect
floppy system, 15
hard disk system, 15-17
status line displaying file name, 668
storing
graphics, 867
macros, floppy disks, 333
strikeout blocks of text, 101
string variables, 350-352
Style (Alt-F8) command, 106, 505, 509, 510-523, 797-800
style codes
changing, 516-517
deleting, 517
Style Off code, 577
Style On code, 577
styles, 111, 113, 505-513
changing, 516-517
citation, 530
creating, 106, 797-798, 515
macros, 799-800
definitions
deleting, 518-519
retrieving, 521-523
saving, 521
deleting, 517-518
dissertation, 526-528
editing, 516
French, 530
letterhead, 528-529
library
creating, 519-524
deleting styles, 523-524
sample, 525-527
open, 507, 509-510
outline, 507-508, 513
outlining, 782-783
paired, 507, 510-513, 515
saving, 518
selecting, 514-515
updating, 522-523
viewing with reveal codes, 515
windows, 106
subdocuments, 835-840, 850
code override, 837
creating, 836-839
deleting, 840
subroutines
call commands, 371
macro, 370-372

merge, 476, 477, 478
subscripts, 723-725
suffix *see* file extension, 53-54
SUM command, equation editor, 725
superscripts, 723-725
Switch (Shift-F3) command, 49, 51
symbol, 717
synonyms, 184, 209
syntax, macros, 354-364, 372-394, 396, 412-416, 420-421

— T —

Tab (Ctrl-F6) command, 124, 584-586
tab ruler, 49, 51, 123
tab stops, 118-122
table boxes, 857-860
table editor, 624-649
menu options list, 626-628
table position, 642-643
table of authorities, 683
creating, 813-815, 819, 841-842
macros, 816-818
defining, 818-819
generating, 819
table of contents
creating, 804-812, 841-842
defining, 811-812, 842-843
generating, 812, 844
marking text, 842
paragraph numbering, 804-812
tables, 486
creating, 603-649
headers, 633-634
defining, 605
deleting, 621
text within a table, 621-623
table structure, 617-618
editing, 615-616, 624-631, 633-643
entering text, 613-615
format, 625-628
importing
numerial data, 644
text, 644
math features, 645-647
records, 486, 489
sorting, 496-499
restoring table structure, 619-621
structure codes, 609-610
tabs, 119-123
aligning, 124
decimal, 179
setting
for math, 583
hard, 122
templates
developing, 907
page, 163-174
publications, 907

text
boxes, 857-860
boilerplate, 440
centering, 126-127
top to bottom, 150-151
columns, 589, 892-893
customizing screen type, 664
deleting, 67-68, 621-623
editing, 67-71, 615-616
enhancing, 109, 137-145
boldfacing, 78
underlining, 78-79
entering, 42, 613-615, 866-867, 873
flush right, 128
formatting, 109-137
hyphenation, 128-135
indenting, 117-119
inserting, 48, 70-71
integrating with graphics, 855-888
justification, 125-126
marking
for cross-references, 826-829
for indexes, 821
concordance file, 822-823
for lists, 795-800
for table of authorities, 813-815
for table of contents, 806-812
macros, 816-818
overwriting, 48-49, 71
redlining, 176-177
replacing, 80-82
restoring, 70
revising, 66
searching, 79-81
surrounding boxes, 872
Text In/Out (Ctrl-F5) command, 83-84, 537-540, 545-546
thesaurus, 183-186, 209-214
cursor movements, 212-214
foreign language, 705-708
replacing words, 211
selecting words, 211-212
words in context, 213-214
Thesaurus (Alt-F1) command, 210
TIFF (Tagged Image File Format) files, 904
tilde (~), 445, 449, 450, 716
TO command, equation editor, 725
total columns, 589, 591-594
TOUPPER.WPM macro, 423-427
troubleshooting
cartridge fonts, 263
laser printers, 262-264, 272-273
restarting, 16-17
soft fonts, 263-264
start up problems, 16-17
two-fold brochure
creating, 912-914

specifications, 914
two-up pages
creating, 896
defining, 897-898
using, 899
typeface, 244
appearance, 251
PostScript printers, 268-269
Typeover mode *see* overwriting, 71
types of hyphenation, 132-135
typing columns
newspaper style, 563-565
parallel, 572-574
typographic characters, mnemonic characters list, 702

— U —

undelete, 51, 70
Underline (F8) command, 79
underlining
blocks of text, 95
text, 78-79
units of measure
changing, 113-114
defining, 676
upgrading to 5.1, 925-930

— V —

variable information, 440, 444-445, 447-451
variables, 348-354
equation editor, 717
integer, 350-352
manipulating, 356-360
named, 349
numbered, 349
passing, 372
string, 350-352
{SYSTEM} command, 396-403
varying paragraphs for interest, 893
vector images, 901-904
Ventura Publisher, 889
vertical alignment, 679
vertical orientation *see* orientation, portrait
Video Graphics Aray (VGA), 14
View Document, 181
footnotes, 746, 748
options
EGA/VGA monitors, 666-668
selection, 233-235, 567-569
special characters, 697
viewing
before printing
documents, 233-236
newspaper style columns, 567-569

styles with Reveal Codes, 515

— W —

widow line, 160
Widow/Orphan Protection, 158-161
width, columns, 641-642
wildcards with speller, 195-196
windows, 49-51
moving between, 49, 51
screen splitting, 50
styles, 106
word processing files, creating, generic, 546
word spacing, changing with 5.1, 930
WordPerfect
5.1 features, 13, 924-930
character sets, 695-696
conversion program (CONVERT), 548-556
converting
databases, 540-544
DOS text files, 544-546
spreadsheets, 535-540
customizing, 651-690
date and time display, 278
exiting, 38, 54, 55
foreign language versions, 705-708
graphics cards, 14
hardware requirements, 13
help feature, 32-34
key codes, 392-393
keyboards, 19-20, 22-27
language codes, 706-708
menus, 27-29
monitors, 14
mouse, 14-15, 29-31
printers, 14
restarting, 16-17
startup
floppy system, 15
hard disk system, 15-17
options, 928-929
tutorial, 34-37
writing tips, 55-60
WordPerfect Corporation telephone support, 7
WordPerfect Support Group (WPSG), 7
WordPerfectionist Newsletter, 7]
word-wrap, 42
WP.LRS (Language Resource) file, 278, 708
WPHELP.FIL files, 32-34
WP{WP}US.LEX file, 184-185
WP{WP}US.SPW file, 185
WP{WP}US.SUP file, 185, 200-201

More Computer Knowledge from Que

Free Catalog!

Mail us this registration form today, and we'll send you a free catalog featuring Que's complete line of best-selling books.

Name of Book _____

Name _____

Title _____

Phone (   ) _____

Company _____

Address _____

City _____

State _____ ZIP _____

Please check the appropriate answers:

1. Where did you buy your Que book?
   - ☐ Bookstore (name: _____)
   - ☐ Computer store (name: _____)
   - ☐ Catalog (name: _____)
   - ☐ Direct from Que
   - ☐ Other: _____

2. How many computer books do you buy a year?
   - ☐ 1 or less
   - ☐ 2-5
   - ☐ 6-10
   - ☐ More than 10

3. How many Que books do you own?
   - ☐ 1
   - ☐ 2-5
   - ☐ 6-10
   - ☐ More than 10

4. How long have you been using this software?
   - ☐ Less than 6 months
   - ☐ 6 months to 1 year
   - ☐ 1-3 years
   - ☐ More than 3 years

5. What influenced your purchase of this Que book?
   - ☐ Personal recommendation
   - ☐ Advertisement
   - ☐ In-store display
   - ☐ Price
   - ☐ Que catalog
   - ☐ Que mailing
   - ☐ Que's reputation
   - ☐ Other: _____

6. How would you rate the overall content of the book?
   - ☐ Very good
   - ☐ Good
   - ☐ Satisfactory
   - ☐ Poor

7. What do you like *best* about this Que book?
   _____
   _____

8. What do you like *least* about this Que book?
   _____
   _____

9. Did you buy this book with your personal funds?
   - ☐ Yes   ☐ No

10. Please feel free to list any other comments you may have about this Que book.
    _____
    _____
    _____

que

Order Your Que Books Today!

Name _____

Title _____

Company _____

City _____

State _____ ZIP _____

Phone No. (   ) _____

Method of Payment:

Check ☐ (Please enclose in envelope.)

Charge My: VISA ☐   MasterCard ☐

American Express ☐

Charge # _____

Expiration Date _____

Order No.	Title	Qty.	Price	Total

You can **FAX** your order to **1-317-573-2583**. Or call **1-800-428-5331, ext. ORDR** to order direct. Please add $2.50 per title for shipping and handling.

Subtotal _____

Shipping & Handling _____

Total _____

que

BUSINESS REPLY MAIL
First Class Permit No. 9918   Indianapolis, IN

Postage will be paid by addressee

11711 N. College
Carmel, IN 46032

BUSINESS REPLY MAIL
First Class Permit No. 9918   Indianapolis, IN

Postage will be paid by addressee

11711 N. College
Carmel, IN 46032